THE COMPLETE GREEK DRAMA

THE RANDOM HOUSE

Lifetime Library

The Theatre at Epidaurus

THE
Complete Greek Drama

ALL THE EXTANT TRAGEDIES OF AESCHYLUS,
SOPHOCLES AND EURIPIDES, AND THE
COMEDIES OF ARISTOPHANES AND
MENANDER, IN A VARIETY OF
TRANSLATIONS

EDITED BY

WHITNEY J. OATES

AND

EUGENE O'NEILL, JR.

IN TWO VOLUMES

VOLUME TWO

RANDOM HOUSE · NEW YORK

Fifteenth Printing

MANUFACTURED IN THE UNITED STATES OF AMERICA

CONTENTS · VOLUME I

PREFACE   vii
GENERAL INTRODUCTION   xiii

TRAGEDIES

Aeschylus

Translated by

THE SUPPLIANTS	E. D. A. Morshead	7
THE PERSIANS	Robert Potter	51
THE SEVEN AGAINST THEBES	E. D. A. Morshead	89
PROMETHEUS BOUND	Paul Elmer More	127
AGAMEMNON	E. D. A. Morshead	167
THE CHOEPHORI	E. D. A. Morshead	229
THE EUMENIDES	E. D. A. Morshead	271

Sophocles

AJAX	R. C. Trevelyan	315
OEDIPUS THE KING	R. C. Jebb	369
ANTIGONE	R. C. Jebb	423
THE TRACHINIAE	R. C. Jebb	465
ELECTRA	R. C. Jebb	505
PHILOCTETES	Thomas Francklin	555
OEDIPUS AT COLONUS	R. C. Jebb	613

Euripides

ALCESTIS	Richard Aldington	677
MEDEA	E. P. Coleridge	723
HIPPOLYTUS	E. P. Coleridge	763
HECUBA	E. P. Coleridge	807
ANDROMACHE	E. P. Coleridge	847
THE HERACLEIDAE	E. P. Coleridge	885
THE SUPPLIANTS	E. P. Coleridge	919
THE TROJAN WOMEN	Gilbert Murray	959
HERACLES	E. P. Coleridge	1017
IPHIGENIA IN TAURIS	Robert Potter	1059
ION	Robert Potter	1121

CONTENTS · VOLUME II

TRAGEDIES

Euripides (continued) *Translated by*

HELEN	E. P. Coleridge	7
ELECTRA	E. P. Coleridge	67
ORESTES	E. P. Coleridge	111
THE PHOENISSAE	E. P. Coleridge	171
THE BACCHAE	Gilbert Murray	227
IPHIGENIA IN AULIS	F. M. Stawell	289
RHESUS	Gilbert Murray	351
THE CYCLOPS	E. P. Coleridge	395

COMEDIES

Aristophanes

THE ACHARNIANS	Translator Anonymous	429
THE KNIGHTS	” ”	481
THE CLOUDS	” ”	541
THE WASPS	” ”	609
PEACE	” ”	671
THE BIRDS	” ”	733
LYSISTRATA	” ”	809
THE THESMOPHORIAZUSAE	” ”	867
THE FROGS	Gilbert Murray	919
THE ECCLESIAZUSAE	Translator Anonymous	1007
PLUTUS	” ”	1063

Menander

THE GIRL FROM SAMOS	L. A. Post	1125
THE ARBITRATION	L. A. Post	1147
THE SHEARING OF GLYCERA	L. A. Post	1179
GLOSSARY		1201

THE PLAYS
OF EURIPIDES (Continued)

XII
HELEN

Characters in the Play

HELEN, *wife of* MENELAUS
TEUCER, *a Greek warrior, who fought at Troy*
CHORUS OF CAPTIVE GREEK WOMEN, *attending* HELEN
MENELAUS, *King of Sparta*
PORTRESS *of* THEOCLYMENUS
FIRST MESSENGER
SECOND MESSENGER
THEONOE, *sister of* THEOCLYMENUS
THEOCLYMENUS, *King of Egypt*
SERVANT *of* THEOCLYMENUS
THE DIOSCURI
Guards, attendants, etc.

INTRODUCTION

THE *Helen*, which can be dated with some accuracy in 412 B.C., has been interpreted variously by scholars and critics. Some have taken it as a serious play, while others, notably A. W. Verrall in his *Essays on Four Plays of Euripides*, have seen in it a piece which Euripides composed as a parody of his own works. Two aspects of the *Helen* largely account for the disagreement. In the first place it is strikingly similar in many respects to the *Iphigenia in Tauris*, and secondly, it presents a version of the legend of Helen which departs from the more generally received tradition.

Helen seems to have been worshipped as a heroine in several communities of the ancient world in the earlier historical epoch. Her position as a demi-goddess perhaps accounts for the fact that a variant story of her Trojan adventures came into existence. The usual account made Helen guilty in large measure for all the woe and misery of the Trojan War. It is natural therefore to suppose that her devotees would endeavour to evolve some myth which would relieve her of the blame which tradition had placed upon her. Hence we are not surprised to find that there was a story current which held that Helen never went to Troy. Whether ultimately responsible for the theory or not, Stesichorus, a Greek poet of the early sixth century B.C., developed this theme in his verse in such a way as to attract wide attention. In fact, a story about Stesichorus grew up in this connection. He is said to have composed a poem on Helen in which he treated her with traditional animus, whereupon immediately he was struck blind. Rightly understanding the reason for his blindness, so the story goes, he hastened to write his famous *Palinode* or *Recantation*, in which he maintained that not Helen, but only a phantom went with Paris to Troy. The Greeks and Trojans in their delusion for ten years fought for the possession of this wraith. Meanwhile the real Helen had been transported by the gods to Egypt, where she had remained under the protection of Proteus, then King of Egypt. Menelaus at last came to Egypt and the couple were reunited.[1] Stesichorus retracted his disparagement of Helen in these terms, and his eyesight was forthwith restored.

[1] Herodotus in his *History*, Book II, 112–120, records a version of the story of Helen in Egypt which was told him by the Egyptian priests.

5

Euripides in his play relies heavily upon the Stesichorean version of the legend. Helen herself speaks at the beginning of the prologue and relates how Paris judged the beauty of the three goddesses, Hera, Aphrodite, and Athena, and how he gave the award to Aphrodite on condition that he himself might have Helen for his bride. At this point the untraditional features are introduced into the story, for Helen says that Hera, in anger at Paris' decision, contrived that he should never enjoy Aphrodite's bride. Hera therefore fashioned a phantom Helen whom Paris carried off to Troy, and commanded that the real Helen be conveyed to Egypt. We are then informed that all went well in Egypt, so long as Helen's protector, Proteus, was alive, but that now, after his death, his son and heir, Theoclymenus, desires to marry her. Euripides completes the prologue by introducing Teucer as a protatic character, from whom Helen learns all that has taken place at Troy during the war that has recently ended.

Out of this dramatic situation Euripides develops a play of romantic adventure in which he seems clearly to be reinvoking the dramatic formula of the *Iphigenia in Tauris*. Here again the hero and heroine find themselves in a predicament out of which they work their way by the use of clever resourcefulness. Such a play could not fail to have an appeal to the Greek audience, not only because it was in itself exciting, but also because it exhibited this quality of resourcefulness in operation, a phenomenon which always captured the attention of the Greek, as is witnessed, for example, by the high position as a popular hero consistently held by the Homeric Odysseus. If the poet's purpose was to present an exciting, romantic melodrama and to employ relatively novel subject-matter, any criticism must be regarded as captious which insists on judging the play according to the criteria applicable only to true tragedy. For example, the rôle of the prophetess, Theonoe, would be unconvincing were the play truly tragic, but in the *Helen* as it now stands, it seems to perform a perfectly legitimate function in a melodramatic plot. If the play be taken for what it patently is, there will arise no need to look for some tragic significance which is not there, and furthermore there will be no occasion to adopt the untenable theory that Euripides is engaged in parody of himself.

HELEN

(SCENE:—*Before the palace of* THEOCLYMENUS *in Egypt. It is near the mouth of the Nile. The tomb of Proteus, the father of* THEOCLYMENUS, *is visible.* HELEN *is discovered alone before the tomb.*)

HELEN

Lo! THESE are the fair virgin streams of Nile, the river that waters Egypt's tilth, fed by pure melting snow instead of rain from heaven. Proteus during his life-time was king of this land, dwelling in the isle of Pharos, and ruling o'er Egypt; and he took to wife one of the daughters of the sea, Psamathe, after she left the embraces of Aeacus. Two children she bare in this his palace, a son Theoclymenus, who hath passed his life in duteous service to the gods, and likewise a noble daughter, her mother's pride, called Eido in her infancy, but when she reached her youthful prime, the age for wedded joys, renamed Theonoe; for well she knew whate'er the gods design, both present and to come, for she had won this guerdon from her grandsire Nereus. Nor is my fatherland unknown to fame, e'en Sparta, or my sire Tyndareus; for a legend tells how Zeus winged his way to my mother Leda's breast, in the semblance of a bird, even a swan, and thus as he fled from an eagle's pursuit, achieved by guile his amorous purpose, if this tale be true. My name is Helen, and I will now recount the sorrows I have suffered. To a hollow vale on Ida came three goddesses to Paris, for beauty's prize contending, Hera and Cypris, and the virgin child of Zeus, eager to secure his verdict on their loveliness. Now Cypris held out my beauty,—if aught so wretched deserves that name,—as a bride before the eyes of Paris, saying he should marry me; and so she won the day; wherefore the shepherd of Ida left his steading, and came to Sparta, thinking to win me for his bride. But Hera, indignant at not defeating the goddesses, brought to naught my marriage with Paris, and gave to Priam's princely son not Helen, but a phantom endowed with life, that she made in my image out of the breath of heaven; and Paris thought that I was his, although I never was,—an idle fancy! Moreover, the counsels of Zeus added further troubles unto these; for

7

upon the land of Hellas and the hapless Phrygians he brought a war, that he might lighten mother-earth of her myriad hosts of men, and to the bravest of the sons of Hellas bring renown. So I was set up as a prize for all the chivalry of Hellas, to test the might of Phrygia, yet not I, but my name alone; for Hermes caught me up in the embracing air, and veiled me in a cloud; for Zeus was not unmindful of me; and he set me down here in the house of Proteus, judging him to be the most virtuous of all mankind; that so I might preserve my marriage with Menelaus free from taint. Here then I abide, while my hapless lord has gathered an army, and is setting out for the towers of Ilium to track and recover me. And there by Scamander's streams hath many a life breathed out its last, and all for me; and I, that have endured all this, am accursed, and seem to have embroiled all Hellas in a mighty war by proving a traitress to my husband. Why, then, do I prolong my life? Because I heard Hermes declare, that I should yet again make my home on Sparta's glorious soil, with my lord,—for Hermes knew I never went to Ilium,—that so I might never submit to any other's wooing. Now as long as Proteus gazed upon yon glorious sun, I was safe from marriage; but when o'er him the dark grave closed, the dead man's son was eager for my hand. But I, from regard to my former husband, am throwing myself down in suppliant wise before this tomb of Proteus, praying him to guard my husband's honour, that, though through Hellas I bear a name dishonoured, at least my body here may not incur disgrace.

(TEUCER *enters.*)

TEUCER
Who is lord and master of this fenced palace? The house is one I may compare to the halls of Plutus, with its royal bulwarks and towering buildings. Ha! great gods! what sight is here? I see the counterfeit of that fell murderous dame, who ruined me and all the Achaeans. May Heaven show its loathing for thee, so much dost thou resemble Helen! Were I not standing on a foreign soil, with this well-aimed shaft had I worked thy death, thy reward for resembling the daughter of Zeus.

HELEN
Oh! why, poor man, whoe'er thou art, dost thou turn from me, loathing me for those troubles Helen caused?

TEUCER
I was wrong; I yielded to my anger more than I ought; my reason was, the hate all Hellas bears to that daughter of Zeus. Pardon me, lady, for the words I uttered.

HELEN

Who art thou? whence comest thou to visit this land?

TEUCER

One of those hapless Achaeans am I, lady.

HELEN

No wonder then that thou dost hate Helen. But say, who art thou?
Whence comest? By what name am I to call thee?

TEUCER

My name is Teucer; my sire was Telamon, and Salamis is the land that
nurtured me.

HELEN

Then why art thou visiting these meadows by the Nile?

TEUCER

A wanderer I, an exile from my native land.

HELEN

Thine must be a piteous lot; who from thy country drives thee out?

TEUCER

My father Telamon. Couldst find a nearer and a dearer?

HELEN

But why? This case is surely fraught with woe.

TEUCER

The death of Ajax my brother at Troy was my ruin.

HELEN

How so? surely 'twas not thy sword that stole his life away?

TEUCER

He threw himself on his own blade and died.

HELEN

Was he mad? for who with sense endowed would bring himself to this?

TEUCER

Dost thou know aught of Achilles, son of Peleus?

HELEN

He came, so I have heard, to woo Helen once.

TEUCER

When he died, he left his arms for his comrades to contest.

HELEN

Well, if he did, what harm herein to Ajax?

TEUCER

When another won these arms, to himself he put an end.

HELEN

Art thou then a sufferer by woes that he inflicted?

TEUCER

Yes, because I did not join him in his death.

HELEN

So thou camest, sir stranger, to Ilium's famous town?

TEUCER

Aye, and, after helping to sack it, myself did learn what ruin meant.

HELEN

Is Troy already fired and utterly by flames consumed?

TEUCER

Yea, so that not so much as one vestige of her walls is now to be seen.

HELEN

Woe is thee, poor Helen! thou art the cause of Phrygia's ruin.

TEUCER

And of Achaea's too. Ah! 'tis a tale of grievous misery!

HELEN

How long is it since the city was sacked?

TEUCER

Nigh seven fruitful seasons have come and gone.

HELEN

And how much longer did ye abide in Troy?

TEUCER

Many a weary month, till through ten full years the moon had held her course.

HELEN

And did ye capture that Spartan dame?

TEUCER

Menelaus caught her by the hair, and was for dragging her away.

HELEN

Didst thou thyself behold that unhappy one? or art thou speaking from hearsay?

TEUCER

As plain as I now see thee, I then saw her.

HELEN

Consider whether ye were but indulging an idle fancy sent by heaven.

TEUCER

Bethink thee of some other topic; no more of her!

HELEN

Are you so sure this fancy was reliable?

TEUCER

With these eyes I saw her face to face, if so be I see thee now.

HELEN

Hath Menelaus reached his home by this time with his wife?

TEUCER

No; he is neither in Argos, nor yet by the streams of Eurotas.

HELEN

Ah me! here is evil news for those to whom thou art telling it.

TEUCER

'Tis said he disappeared with his wife.

HELEN

Did not all the Argives make the passage together?

TEUCER

Yes; but a tempest scattered them in every direction.

HELEN

In what quarter of the broad ocean?

TEUCER

They were crossing the Aegean in mid channel.

HELEN

And after that, doth no man know of Menelaus' arrival?

TEUCER

No, none; but through Hellas is he reported to be dead.

HELEN

Then am I lost. Is the daughter of Thestius alive?

TEUCER

Dost speak of Leda? She is dead; aye, dead and gone.

HELEN

Was it Helen's shame that caused her death?

TEUCER

Aye, 'tis said she tied the noose about her noble neck.

HELEN

Are the sons of Tyndareus still alive or not?

TEUCER

Dead, and yet alive: 'tis a double story.

HELEN

Which is the more credible report? Woe is me for my sorrows!

TEUCER

Men say that they are gods in the likeness of stars.

HELEN

That is happy news; but what is the other rumour?

TEUCER

That they by self-inflicted wounds gave up the ghost because of their sister's shame. But enough of such talk! I have no wish to multiply my griefs. The reason of my coming to this royal palace was a wish to see that famous prophetess Theonoe. Do thou the means afford, that I from her may obtain an oracle how I shall steer a favourable course to the sea-girt shores of Cyprus; for there Apollo hath declared my home shall be, giving to it the name of Salamis, my island home, in honour of that fatherland across the main.

HELEN

That shall the voyage itself explain, sir stranger; but do thou leave these shores and fly, ere the son of Proteus, the ruler of this land, catch sight of thee. Now is he away with his trusty hounds tracking his savage quarry to the death; for every stranger that he catcheth from the land of Hellas doth he slay. His reason never ask to know; my lips are sealed; for what could word of mine avail thee?

TEUCER

Lady, thy words are fair. Heaven grant thee a fair requital for this kindness! For though in form thou dost resemble Helen, thy soul is not like hers, nay, very different. Perdition seize her! May she never reach the streams of Eurotas! But thine be joy for evermore, lady!

(TEUCER *departs. The* CHORUS OF CAPTIVE GREEK WOMEN *enter. They sing responsively with* HELEN.)

HELEN

Ah me! what piteous dirge shall I strive to utter, now that I am beginning my strain of bitter lamentation? What Muse shall I approach with tears or songs of death or woe? Ah me! ye Sirens, Earth's virgin daughters, wingèd maids, come, oh! come to aid my mourning, bringing with you the Libyan flute or pipe, to waft to Persephone's ear a tearful plaint, the echo of my sorrow, with grief for grief, and mournful chant for chant, with songs of death and doom to match my lamentation, that in return she may receive from me, besides my tears, dirges for the departed dead beneath her gloomy roof!

CHORUS

Beside the deep-blue water I chanced to be hanging purple robes along the tendrils green and on the sprouting reeds, to dry them in the sun-god's golden blaze, when lo! I heard a sound of woe, a mournful wail, the voice of one crying aloud in her anguish; yea, such a cry of woe as Naiad nymph might send ringing o'er the hills, while to her cry the depths of rocky grots re-echo her screams at the violence of Pan.

HELEN

Woe! woe! ye maids of Hellas, booty of barbarian sailors! one hath come, an Achaean mariner, bringing fresh tears to me, the news of Ilium's overthrow, how that it is left to the mercy of the foeman's flame, and all for me the murderess, or for my name with sorrow fraught. While for anguish at my deed of shame, hath Leda sought her death by hanging; and on the deep, to weary wandering doomed my lord hath met his end; and Castor and his brother, twin glory of their native land, are vanished from men's sight, leaving the plains that shook to their galloping steeds, and the course beside reed-fringed Eurotas, where those youthful athletes strove.

CHORUS

Ah, misery! Alas! for thy grievous destiny! Woe for thy sad lot, lady! Ah! 'twas a day of sorrow meted out for thee when Zeus came glancing through the sky on snowy pinions like a swan and won thy

mother's heart. What evil is not thine? Is there a grief in life that
thou hast not endured? Thy mother is dead; the two dear sons of
Zeus have perished miserably, and thou art severed from thy country's sight, while through the towns of men a rumour runs, consign-
ing thee, my honoured mistress, to a barbarian's bed; and 'mid the
ocean waves thy lord hath lost his life, and never, never more shalt
thou fill with joy thy father's halls or Athena's temple of the "Brazen
House."

HELEN

Ah! who was that Phrygian, who was he, that felled that pine with
sorrow fraught for Ilium, and for those that came from Hellas?
Hence it was that Priam's son his cursed barque did build, and sped
by barbarian oars sailed unto my home, in quest of beauty, woman's
curse, to win me for his bride; and with him sailed the treacherous
queen of Love, on slaughter bent, with death alike for Priam's sons,
and Danai too. Ah me! for my hard lot! Next, Hera, stately bride of
Zeus, seated on her golden throne, sent the son of Maia, swift of foot,
who caught me up as I was gathering fresh rose-buds in the folds of
my robe, that I might go to the "Brazen House," and bore me through
the air to this loveless land, making me an object of unhappy strife
'twixt Hellas and the race of Priam. And my name is but a sound
without reality beside the streams of Simois.

LEADER OF THE CHORUS

Well I know thou hast a bitter lot to bear; still 'tis best to bear as
lightly as we may the ills that life is heir to.

HELEN

Good friends, to what a fate am I united? Did not my mother bear me
to be a monster to the world? For no woman, Hellene or barbarian, gives
birth to babes in eggs inclosed, as they say Leda bare me to Zeus. My life
and all I do is one miracle, partly owing to Hera, and partly is my beauty
to blame. Would God I could rub my beauty out like a picture, and assume hereafter in its stead a form less comely, and oh! that Hellas had
forgotten the evil fate that now I bear, and were now remembering my
career of honour as surely as they do my deeds of shame. Now, if a man
doth turn his eyes to a single phase of fortune, and meets ill-usage at
heaven's hands, 'tis hard no doubt; but still it can be borne; but I in
countless troubles am involved. First, although I never sinned, my good
name is gone. And this is a grief beyond the reality, if a man incurs blame
for sins that are not his. Next, have the gods removed me from my native
land, to dwell with men of barbarous ways, and reft of every friend, I am
become a slave though free by birth; for amongst barbarians all are slaves

but one. And the last anchor that held my fortunes, the hope that my husband would return one day, and rid me of my woes, is now no more, lost since the day he died. My mother too is dead, and I am called her murderess, unjustly it is true, but still that injustice is mine to bear; and she that was the glory of my house, my darling child, is growing old and grey, unwedded still; and those twin brethren, called the sons of Zeus, are now no more. But 'tis fortune, not my own doing, that hath crushed me with sorrow and slain me. And this is the last evil of all; if ever I come to my native land, they will shut me up in prison, thinking me that Helen of Ilium, in quest of whom Menelaus came thither. Were my husband still alive, we might have recognized each other, by having recourse to tokens which ourselves alone would know. But now this may not be, nor is there any chance of his escape. Why then do I prolong my life? What fortune have I still in store? Shall I choose marriage as an alternative of evils, and dwell with a barbarian lord, seated at his sumptuous board? No! when a husband she loathes is mated with a woman, even life is loathly to her. Best for her to die; but how shall I die a noble death? The dangling noose is an uncomely end; even slaves consider it disgrace; to stab oneself hath something fair and noble in it; 'tis a small thing that moment of ridding the flesh of life. Yes, it must be; I am plunged so deep in misery; for that beauty, which to other women is a boon, to me hath been a very bane.

LEADER

Helen, never believe that the stranger, whoe'er he was that came, has spoken naught but truth.

HELEN

Yet he said so clearly that my lord was dead.

LEADER

There is much that falsehood seems to make quite clear.

HELEN

The word of truth hath a very different sound to falsehood.

LEADER

Thou art inclined to misfortune, rather than to luck.

HELEN

Fear girds me with terrors as with a garment, and takes me in her train.

LEADER

What friends hast thou within the palace?

HELEN

All are my friends here save him who seeks to wed me.

LEADER

Thy action then is clear; leave thy seat at the tomb.

HELEN

To what words or advice art thou leading up?

LEADER

Go in and question the daughter of the ocean Nereid, who knoweth all things, even Theonoe, whether thy husband is still alive, or whether he hath left the light of day; and when thou knowest for certain, be glad or sorrowful, as fits thy fortune. But before thou hast right knowledge, what shall sorrow avail thee? Nay, hearken to me; leave this tomb and seek the maiden's company, that she may tell thee the truth, for from her shalt thou learn all. If thou abide here in this seat, what prospect hast thou? And I will myself go in with thee, and with thee inquire of the maiden's oracles; for 'tis a woman's bounden duty to share a sister's trouble.

(*The following lines are chanted responsively by* HELEN *and the* CHORUS.)

HELEN

Kind friends, I welcome your advice. Come in, come in, that ye may learn the result of my struggle within the palace .

CHORUS

Thy invitation comes to very willing ears.

HELEN

Woe for this heavy day! Ah me! what mournful tidings shall I hear?

CHORUS

Dear mistress mine, be not a prophetess of sorrow, forestalling lamentation.

HELEN

What is the fate of my poor husband? Doth he still behold the light turning towards the sun-god's chariot and the stars in their courses? Or among the dead, beneath the earth, is he to death consigned?

CHORUS

Of the future take a brighter view, whatever shall betide.

HELEN

On thee I call, and thee adjure, Eurotas green with river-reeds, to
tell me if this rumour of my husband's death be true.

CHORUS

What boots this meaningless appeal?

HELEN

About my neck will I fasten the deadly noose from above, or drive
the murderous knife with self-aimed thrust deep into my throat to
sever it, striving to cut my flesh, a sacrifice to those goddesses three
and to that son of Priam, who in days gone by would wake the music
of his pipe around his steading.

CHORUS

Oh may sorrow be averted otherwhither, and thou be blest!

HELEN

Woe is thee, unhappy Troy! Thou through deeds not done by thee
art ruined, and hast suffered direst woe; for the gift that Cypris gave
to me, hath caused a sea of blood to flow, and many an eye to weep,
with grief on grief and tear on tear. All this hath Ilium suffered and
mothers have lost their children; and virgin sisters of the slain have
cut off their tresses by the swollen tide of Phrygian Scamander. And
the land of Hellas hath lifted her voice of woe and broken forth in
wailing, smiting on her head, and making tender cheeks to stream
with gore beneath the rending nail. Ah blest maid Callisto, who long
ago in Arcady didst find favour with Zeus, in the semblance of a
beast four-footed, how much happier was thy lot than my mother's,
for thou hast changed the burden of thy grief and now with savage
eye art weeping o'er thy shaggy monster-shape; aye, and hers was
a happier lot, whom on a day Artemis drove from her choir, changed
to a hind with horns of gold, the fair Titanian maid, daughter of
Merops, because of her beauty; but my fair form hath proved the
curse of Dardan Troy and doomed Achaea's sons.

(HELEN *and the* CHORUS *go into the palace. After the doors have
closed upon them,* MENELAUS *enters. He is alone and clad in
rags.*)

MENELAUS

Ah! Pelops, easy victor long ago o'er thy rival Oenomaus in the chariot-
race on Pisa's plain, would thou hadst ended thy career amongst the gods
that day thou wert beguiled into making a banquet for them, or ever
thou hadst begotten my father Atreus, to whom were born by Aerope his

wife, Agamemnon and myself Menelaus, an illustrious pair; and herein I make no idle boast, for 'twas a mighty host, I trow, that I their leader carried o'er the sea to Troy, using no violence to make them follow me, but leading all the chivalry of Hellas by voluntary consent. And some of these must we number 'mid the slain, and some to their joy have 'scaped the sea, bearing to their homes again names long reckoned dead. But I, poor wretch, go wandering o'er grey Ocean's swell a weary space, long as that which saw me sack the towers of Ilium; and for all my longing to reach my country I am not counted worthy of this boon by heaven, but to Libya's desert cheerless roadsteads have I sailed, to each and all of them; and whensoe'er I draw me near my native land, the storm-wind drives me back again, and never yet have favouring breezes filled my sails, to let me reach my fatherland. And now a wretched, shipwrecked mariner, my friends all lost, am I cast up upon this shore; and my ship is shattered in a thousand pieces against the rocks; and its keel was wrested from its cunning fastenings; thereon did I with difficulty escape, most unexpectedly, and Helen also, for her had I rescued from Troy and had with me. But the name of this country and its people I know not; for I blushed to mingle with the crowd to question them, anxious for very shame to hide my misfortunes which reduce me to these sorry rags. For when a man of high degree meets with adversity, he feels the strangeness of his fallen state more keenly than a sufferer of long standing. Dire want is wasting me; for I have neither food, nor raiment to gird myself withal; behold the facts before you to judge from—I am clad in tatters cast up from the ship; while all the robes I once did wear, glorious attire and ornaments, hath the sea swallowed; and in a cavern's deep recesses have I hidden my wife, the cause of all my trouble, and have come hither, after straitly charging the survivors of my friends to watch her. Alone am I come, seeking for those there left some help, if haply I may find it after careful search. So when I saw this palace girt with towering walls and stately gates of some prosperous lord, I drew nigh; for I have hope to obtain somewhat for my sailors from this wealthy house, whereas from houses which have no store, the inmates for all their goodwill could furnish naught. Ho! there, who keeps the gate and will come forth to bear my tale of woe into the house?

(*A* PORTRESS *comes out of the palace in answer to his call.*)

PORTRESS

Who stands before the door? Begone from the house! stand not at the court-yard gate, annoying my masters! otherwise shalt thou die, for thou art a Hellene born. and with them have we no dealings.

MENELAUS

Mother, herein sayest thou rightly on all points. 'Tis well; I will obey;
but moderate thy words.

PORTRESS

Away! stranger, my orders are to admit no Hellene to this palace.

MENELAUS

Ha! do not seek to push me hence, or thrust me away by violence.

PORTRESS

Thou dost not heed my words, and therefore hast thyself to blame.

MENELAUS

Carry my message to thy master in the palace.

PORTRESS

Some one would rue it, methinks, were I to take thy message.

MENELAUS

I come as a shipwrecked man and a stranger, whom heaven protects.

PORTRESS

Well, get thee to some other house than this.

MENELAUS

Nay, but I will pass into the house; so listen to me.

PORTRESS

Let me tell thee thou art unwelcome, and soon wilt be forcibly ejected.

MENELAUS

Ah me! where are now those famous troops of mine?

PORTRESS

Elsewhere maybe thou wert a mighty man; thou art not here.

MENELAUS

O fortune! I have not deserved such insult.

PORTRESS

Why are thy eyes with tear-drops wet? Why so sad?

MENELAUS

'Tis the contrast with my fortunes erst so blest.

PORTRESS

Hence! then, and give thy friends those tears.

MENELAUS

What land is this? whose is the palace?

PORTRESS

Proteus lives here. It is the land of Egypt.

MENELAUS

Egypt? Woe is me! to think that hither I have sailed!

PORTRESS

Pray, what fault hast thou to find with the race of Nile?

MENELAUS

'Twas no fault I found; my own disasters I lament.

PORTRESS

There be plenty in evil case; thou art not the only one.

MENELAUS

Is the king, of whom thou speakest, here within?

PORTRESS

There is his tomb; his son rules in his stead.

MENELAUS

And where may he be? abroad, or in the house?

PORTRESS

He is not within. To Hellas is he a bitter foe.

MENELAUS

His reason, pray, for this enmity? the results whereof I have experienced.

PORTRESS

Beneath this roof dwells the daughter of Zeus, Helen.

MENELAUS

What mean'st thou? what is it thou hast said? Repeat, I pray, thy words.

PORTRESS

The daughter of Tyndareus is here, who erst in Sparta dwelt.

MENELAUS

Whence came she? What means this business?

PORTRESS
She came from Lacedaemon hither.

MENELAUS
When? Surely I have never been robbed of my wife from the cave!

PORTRESS
Before the Achaeans went to Troy, sir stranger. But get thee hence; for somewhat hath chanced within, whereat the whole palace is in an uproar. Thou comest most unseasonably; and if my master catch thee, death will be thy stranger's gift. This say I, because to Hellas I am well disposed, albeit I gave thee harsh answers for fear of my master.
(*The* PORTRESS *goes back into the palace.*)

MENELAUS
What can I think or say? For after my previous troubles, this is a fresh piece of ill-luck I hear, if, indeed, after recovering my wife from Troy and bringing her hither, and putting her for safety in the cave, I am then to find another woman living here with the same name as my wife. She called her the begotten child of Zeus. Can there be a man that hath the name of Zeus by the banks of Nile? The Zeus of heaven is only one, at any rate. Where is there a Sparta in the world save where Eurotas glides between his reedy banks? The name of Tyndareus is the name of one alone. Is there any land of the same name as Lacedaemon or Troy? I know not what to say; for naturally there are many in the wide world that have the same names, cities and women too; there is nothing, then, to marvel at. Nor yet again will I fly from the alarm a servant raises; for there is none so cruel of heart as to refuse me food when once he hears my name. All have heard of Ilium's burning, and I, that set it ablaze, am famous now throughout the world, I, Menelaus. I therefore wait the master of this house. There are two issues I must watch; if he prove somewhat stern of heart, I will to my wreck and there conceal myself; but if he show any sign of pity, I will ask for help in this my present strait. This is the crowning woe in all my misery, to beg the means of life from other princes, prince though I be myself; still needs must I. Yea, this is no saying of mine, but a word of wisdom, "Naught in might exceedeth dread necessity."
(HELEN *and the* CHORUS *enter from the palace. They do not notice* MENELAUS.)

CHORUS (*singing*)
I have heard the voice of the maiden inspired. Clear is the answer she hath vouchsafed within yon palace, declaring that Menelaus is not yet dead and buried, passed to the land of shades, where darkness

takes the place of light; but on the stormy main is wearing out his
life, nor yet hath reached the haven of his country, a wanderer dragging out a piteous existence, reft of every friend, setting foot in every
corner of the world, as he voyageth home from Troy.

HELEN

Lo! once again I seek the shelter of this tomb, with Theonoe's sweet
tidings in my ears; she that knoweth all things of a truth; for she saith
my lord is yet alive and in the light of day, albeit he is roaming to and fro
after many a weary voyage, and hither shall he come whenso he reach the
limit of his toils, no novice in the wanderer's life. But one thing did she
leave unsaid. Is he to escape when he hath come? And I refrained from
asking that question clearly, so glad was I when she told me he was safe.
For she said that he was somewhere nigh this shore, cast up by shipwreck
with a handful of friends. Ah! when shall I see thee come? How welcome
will thy advent be! (*She catches sight of* MENELAUS.) Ha! who is this?
Am I being snared by some trick of Proteus' impious son? Oh! let me, like
a courser at its speed, or a votary of Bacchus, approach the tomb! for
there is something wild about this fellow's looks, who is eager to o'ertake
me.

MENELAUS

Ho there! thou that with fearful effort seekest to reach the basement
of the tomb and the pillars of burnt sacrifice, stay thee. Wherefore art
flying? Ah! with what speechless amaze the sight of thee affects me!

HELEN

O friends! I am being ill-treated. This man is keeping me from the
tomb, and is eager to take and give me to his master, whose wooing I was
seeking to avoid.

MENELAUS

No robber I, or minister of evil.

HELEN

At any rate the garb wherein thou art clad is unseemly.

MENELAUS

Stay thy hasty flight; put fear aside.

HELEN

I do so, now that I have reached this spot.

MENELAUS

Who art thou? whom do I behold in thee, lady?

HELEN
Nay, who art thou? The self-same reason prompts us both.

MENELAUS
I never saw a closer resemblance.

HELEN
Great God! Yea, for to recognize our friends is of God.

MENELAUS
Art thou from Hellas, or a native of this land?

HELEN
From Hellas; but I would learn thy story too.

MENELAUS
Lady, in thee I see a wondrous likeness to Helen.

HELEN
And I in thee to Menelaus; I know not what to say.

MENELAUS
Well, thou hast recognized aright a man of many sorrows.

HELEN
Hail! to thy wife's arms restored at last!

MENELAUS
Wife indeed! Lay not a finger on my robe.

HELEN
Th wife that Tyndareus, my father, gave thee.

MENELAUS
O Hecate, giver of light, send thy visions favourably!

HELEN
In me thou beholdest no spectre of the night, attendant on the queen of phantoms.

MENELAUS
Nor yet am I in my single person the husband of two wives.

HELEN
What other woman calls thee lord?

MENELAUS
The inmate of yonder cave, whom I from Troy convey.

HELEN

Thou hast none other wife but me.

MENELAUS

Can it be my mind is wandering, my sight failing?

HELEN

Dost not believe thou seest in me thy wife?

MENELAUS

Thy form resembles her, but the real truth robs me of this belief.

HELEN

Observe me well; what need hast thou of clearer proof?

MENELAUS

Thou art like her; that will I never deny.

HELEN

Who then shall teach thee, unless it be thine own eyes?

MENELAUS

Herein is my dilemma; I have another wife.

HELEN

To Troy I never went; that was a phantom.

MENELAUS

Pray, who fashions living bodies?

HELEN

The air, whence thou hast a wife of heaven's workmanship.

MENELAUS

What god's handiwork? Strange is the tale thou tellest.

HELEN

Hera made it as a substitute, to keep me from Paris.

MENELAUS

How then couldst thou have been here, and in Troy, at the same time?

HELEN

The name may be in many a place at once, though not the body.

MENELAUS

Unhand me! the sorrows I brought with me suffice.

HELEN
What! wilt leave me, and take that phantom bride away?

MENELAUS
For thy likeness unto Helen, fare thee well.

HELEN
Ruined! in thee I found my lord only to lose thee.

MENELAUS
The greatness of my troubles at Troy convinces me; thou dost not.

HELEN
Ah, woe is me! who was ever more unfortunate than I? Those whom I love best are leaving me, nor shall I ever reach Hellas, my own dear native land.

(*The* FIRST MESSENGER *enters in haste.*)

MESSENGER
At last I find thee, Menelaus, after an anxious search, not till I have wandered through the length and breadth of this foreign strand; I am sent by thy comrades, whom thou didst leave behind.

MENELAUS
What news? surely you are not being spoiled by the barbarians?

MESSENGER
A miracle hath happened; my words are too weak for the reality.

MENELAUS
Speak; for judging by this haste, thou hast stirring news.

MESSENGER
My message is: thy countless toils have all been toiled in vain.

MENELAUS
That is an old tale of woe to mourn! come, thy news?

MESSENGER
Thy wife hath disappeared, soaring away into the embracing air; in heaven she now is hidden, and as she left the hollowed cave where we were guarding her, she hailed us thus, "Ye hapless Phrygians, and all Achaea's race! for me upon Scamander's strand by Hera's arts ye died from day to day, in the false belief that Helen was in the hands of Paris. But I, since I have stayed my appointed time, and kept the laws of fate, will now depart unto the sky that gave me birth; but the unhappy daughter cf Tyndareus, through no fault of hers, hath borne an evil name with-

out reason." (*Catching sight of* HELEN) Daughter of Leda, hail to thee, so thou art here after all! I was just announcing thy departure to the hidden starry realms, little knowing that thou couldst fly at will. I will not a second time let thee flout us thus, for thou didst cause thy lord and his comrades trouble all for naught in Ilium.

MENELAUS

This is even what she said; her words are proved true; O longed-for day, how hath it restored thee to my arms!

HELEN

O Menelaus, dearest husband, the time of sorrow has been long, but joy is now ours at last. Ah, friends, what joy for me to hold my husband in a fond embrace after many a weary cycle of yon blazing lamp of day!

MENELAUS

What joy for me to hold my wife! but with all that I would ask about these years, I now know not where I may first begin.

HELEN

O rapture! the very hair upon my head starts up for joy! my tears run down! Around thy neck I fling my arms, dear husband, to hug my joy to me.

MENELAUS

O happy, happy sight! I have no fault to find; my wife, the daughter of Zeus and Leda, is mine again, she whom her brothers on their snow-white steeds, whilst torches blazed, made my happy bride, but gods removed her from my home. Now is the deity guiding us to a new destiny, happier than of yore.

HELEN

Evil into good transformed hath brought us twain together at last, dear husband; but late though it be, God grant me joy of my good luck!

MENELAUS

God grant thee joy! I join thee in the self-same prayer; for of us twain one cannot suffer without the other.

HELEN

No more, my friends, I mourn the past; no longer now I grieve. My own dear husband is restored to me, whose coming from Troy I have waited many a long year.

MENELAUS

I to thee, and thou to me. And after these long, long years I have at
last discovered the fraud of the goddess. But these tears, in gladness shed,
are tears of thankfulness rather than of sorrow.

HELEN

What can I say? What mortal heart could e'er have had such hope?
To my bosom I press thee, little as I ever thought to.

MENELAUS

And I to mine press thee, who all men thought hadst gone to Ida's town
and the hapless towers of Ilium.

HELEN

Ah me! ah me! that is a bitter subject to begin on.

MENELAUS

Tell me, I adjure thee, how wert thou from my home conveyed?

HELEN

Alas! alas! 'tis a bitter tale thou askest to hear.

MENELAUS

Speak, for 1 must hear it; all that comes is Heaven's gift.

HELEN

I loathe the story I am now to tell.

MENELAUS

Tell it for all that. 'Tis sweet to hear of trouble past.

HELEN

I ne'er set forth to be the young barbarian's bride, with oars and wings
of lawless love to speed me on my way.

MENELAUS

What deity or fate tore thee from thy country, then?

HELEN

Ah, my lord! 'twas Hermes, the son of Zeus, that brought and placed
me by the banks of Nile.

MENELAUS

A miracle! Who sent thee thither? O monstrous story!

HELEN

I wept, and still my eyes are wet with tears. 'Twas the wife of Zeus
that ruined me.

MENELAUS

Hera? wherefore should she afflict us twain?

HELEN

Woe is me for my awful fate! Woe for those founts and baths where the goddesses made brighter still that beauty, which evoked the fatal verdict!

MENELAUS

Why did Hera visit thee with evil regarding this verdict?

HELEN

To wrest the promise of Cypris—

MENELAUS

How now? Say on.

HELEN

From Paris, to whom that goddess pledged me.

MENELAUS

Woe for thee!

HELEN

And so she brought me hither to Egypt to my sorrow.

MENELAUS

Then she gave him a phantom in thy stead, as thou tellest me?

HELEN

And then began those woes of thine, ah, mother! woe is me!

MENELAUS

What meanest thou?

HELEN

My mother is no more; my shameful marriage made her fix the noose about her neck.

MENELAUS

Ah me! is our daughter Hermione yet alive?

HELEN

Still unwed, childless still, she mourns my fatal marriage.

MENELAUS

O Paris, who didst utterly o'erthrow my home, here was thy ruin too and theirs, those countless mail-clad Danai.

HELEN

From my country, city, and from thee heaven cast me forth unhappy and accursed, because I left,—and yet not I,—home and husband for a union of foul shame.

LEADER OF THE CHORUS

If haply ye find happiness in the future, it will suffice when to the past ye look.

MESSENGER

Menelaus, grant me too a portion of that joy which, though mine own eyes see, I scarcely comprehend.

MENELAUS

Come then, old friend, and share with us our talk.

MESSENGER

Was it not then in her power to decide all the trouble in Troy?

MENELAUS

It was not; I was tricked by the gods into taking to my arms a misty phantom-form, to my sorrow.

MESSENGER

How so? was it then for this we vainly toiled?

MENELAUS

'Twas Hera's handiwork, and the jealousy of three goddesses.

MESSENGER

Is this real woman, then, thy wife?

MENELAUS

This is she; trust my word for that.

MESSENGER

Daughter, how changeful and inscrutable is the nature of God! With some good end doth he vary men's fortune—now up, now down; one suffers; another who ne'er knew suffering, is in his turn to awful ruin brought, having no assurance in his lot from day to day. Thou and thy husband have had your share of trouble—thou in what the world has said, he in battle's heat. For all the striving that he strove, he got him naught; while now, without an effort made, every blessing fortune boasts is his. And thou, in spite of all, hast brought no shame upon thy aged sire, or those twin sons of Zeus, nor art thou guilty of those rumoured crimes. Now again do I recall thy wedding rites, remembering the blazing torch

I bore beside thee in a four-horsed chariot at full gallop; while thou with this thy lord, a new-made bride, wert driving forth from thy happy home. A sorry servant he, whoso regardeth not his master's interest, sympathizing with his sorrows and his joys. Slave though I was born, yet may I be numbered amongst honest servants; for in heart, though not in name, I am free. For this is better far than in my single person to suffer these two evils, to feel my heart corrupt, and as the slave of others to be at my neighbour's beck and call.

MENELAUS

Come, old friend, oft hast thou stood side by side with me and taken thy full share of toil; so now be partner in my happiness. Go, tell my comrades, whom I left behind, the state of matters here, as thou hast found them, and the issue of my fortunes; and bid them wait upon the beach and abide the result of the struggle, which I trow awaits me; and if mayhap we find a way to take this lady from the land by stealth, tell them to keep good watch that we may share the luck and escape, if possible, from the barbarian's clutch.

MESSENGER

It shall be done, O king. Now I see how worthless are the seers' tricks, how full of falsehood; nor is there after all aught trustworthy in the blaze of sacrifice or in the cry of feathered fowls; 'tis folly, the very notion that birds can help mankind. Calchas never by word or sign showed the host the truth, when he saw his friends dying on behalf of a phantom, nor yet did Helenus; but the city was stormed in vain. Perhaps thou wilt say, 'twas not heaven's will that they should do so. Then why do we employ these prophets? Better were it to sacrifice to the gods, and crave a blessing, leaving prophecy alone; for this was but devised as a bait to catch a livelihood, and no man grows rich by divination if he is idle. No! sound judgment and discernment are the best of seers.

(*The* MESSENGER *departs.*)

LEADER

My views about seers agree exactly with this old man's: whoso hath the gods upon his side will have the best seer in his house.

HELEN

Good! so far all is well. But how camest thou, poor husband, safe from Troy? though 'tis no gain to know, yet friends feel a longing to learn all that their friends have suffered.

MENELAUS

That one short sentence of thine contains a host of questions. Why should I tell thee of our losses in the Aegean, or of the beacon Nauplius lighted on Euboea? or of my visits to Crete and the cities of Libya, or of the peaks of Perseus? For I should never satisfy thee with the tale, and by telling thee should add to my own pain, though I suffered enough at the time; and so would my grief be doubled.

HELEN

Thy answer shows more wisdom than my question. Omit the rest, and tell me only this; how long wert thou a weary wanderer o'er the wide sea's face?

MENELAUS

Seven long years did I see come and go, besides those ten in Troy.

HELEN

Alas, poor sufferer! 'twas a weary while. And thou hast thence escaped only to bleed here.

MENELAUS

How so? what wilt thou tell? Ah wife, thou hast ruined me.

HELEN

Escape and fly with all thy speed from this land. Thou wilt be slain by him whose house this is.

MENELAUS

What have I done to merit such a fate?

HELEN

Thou hast arrived unexpectedly to thwart my marriage.

MENELAUS

What! is some man bent on wedding my wife?

HELEN

Aye, and on heaping those insults on me, which I have hitherto endured.

MENELAUS

Is he some private prince, or a ruler of this land?

HELEN

The son of Proteus, king of the country.

MENELAUS

This was that dark saying I heard the servant tell.

HELEN

At which of the barbarian's gates wert thou standing?

MENELAUS

Here, whence like a beggar I was like to be driven.

HELEN

Surely thou wert not begging food? Ah, woe is me!

MENELAUS

That was what I was doing, though I had not the name of beggar.

HELEN

Of course thou knowest, then, all about my marriage.

MENELAUS

I do. But whether thou hast escaped thy lover, I know not.

HELEN

Be well assured I have kept my body chaste.

MENELAUS

How wilt thou convince me of this? If true, thy words are sweet.

HELEN

Dost see the wretched station I have kept at this tomb?

MENELAUS

I see, alas! a bed of straw; but what hast thou to do with it?

HELEN

There I crave escape from this marriage as a suppliant.

MENELAUS

For want of an altar, or because it is the barbarians' way?

HELEN

This was as good a protection to me as the gods' temples.

MENELAUS

May I not then even bear thee homeward on my ship?

HELEN

The sword far sooner than thy wife's embrace is waiting thee.

MENELAUS

So should I be of all men the most miserable.

HELEN

Put shame aside, and fly from this land.

MENELAUS

Leaving thee behind? 'twas for thy sake I sacked Troy.

HELEN

Better so, than that our union should cause thy death.

MENELAUS

Oh! these are coward words, unworthy of those days at Troy!

HELEN

Thou canst not slay the prince, thy possible intent.

MENELAUS

Hath he, then, a body which steel cannot wound?

HELEN

Thou shalt hear. But to attempt impossibilities is no mark of wisdom.

MENELAUS

Am I to let them bind my hands, and say nothing?

HELEN

Thou art in a dilemma; some scheme must be devised.

MENELAUS

I had liefer die in action than sitting still.

HELEN

There is one hope, and only one, of our safety.

MENELAUS

Will gold, or daring deeds, or winning words procure it?

HELEN

We are safe if the prince learn not of thy coming.

MENELAUS

Will any one tell him it is I? He certainly will not know who I am.

HELEN

He hath within his palace an ally equal to the gods.

MENELAUS

Some voice divine within the secret chambers of his house?

HELEN

No; his sister; Theonoe men call her.

MENELAUS

Her name hath a prophetic sound; tell me what she doth.

HELEN

She knoweth everything, and she will tell her brother thou art come.

MENELAUS

Then must we die; for I cannot escape her ken.

HELEN

Perchance we might by suppliant prayers win her over.

MENELAUS

To what end? To what vain hope art thou leading me?

HELEN

That she should not tell her brother thou art here.

MENELAUS

Suppose we persuade her, can we get away?

HELEN

Easily, if she connive thereat; without her knowledge, no.

MENELAUS

Be that thy task; women deal best with women.

HELEN

I will not fail, be sure, to clasp her knees.

MENELAUS

Come, then; only, suppose she reject our proposals?

HELEN

Thou wilt be slain, and I, alas! wedded by force.

MENELAUS

Thou wilt betray me; that "force" of thine is but an excuse.

HELEN

Nay, by thy life I swear a sacred oath.

MENELAUS

What meanest thou? dost swear to die and never to another husband yield?

HELEN

Yes, by the self-same sword; I will fall by thy side.

MENELAUS

On these conditions touch my right hand.

HELEN

I do so, swearing I will quit the light of day if thou art slain.

MENELAUS

I, too, will end my life if I lose thee.

HELEN

How shall we die so as to gain fame?

MENELAUS

I will slay thee and then myself upon the summit of the tomb. But first will I in doughty fight contest another's claim to thee; and let who will draw nigh! for I will not sully the lustre of my Trojan fame, nor will I, on my return to Hellas, incur a storm of taunts, as one who robbed Thetis of Achilles; saw Ajax, son of Telamon, fall a weltering corpse; and the son of Neleus of his child bereft; shall I then flinch myself from death for my own wife? No, no! For if the gods are wise, o'er a brave man by his foes laid low they lightly sprinkle the earth that is his tomb, while cowards they cast forth on barren rocky soil.

LEADER

Grant, heaven, that the race of Tantalus may at last be blest, and pass from sorrow unto joy!

HELEN

Ah, woe is me! Yea, all my lot is woe; O Menelaus, we are utterly undone! Behold! from forth the house comes Theonoe, the prophetess. The palace echoes as the bolts are unfastened; fly! yet what use to fly? For whether absent or present she knows of thy arrival here. Ah me! how lost am I! Saved from Troy and from a barbarian land, thou hast come only to fall a prey to barbarian swords.

(THEONOE *enters, attended by hand-maidens carrying torches.*)

THEONOE

Lead on, bearing before me blazing brands, and, as sacred rites ordain, purge with incense every cranny of the air, that I may breathe heaven's breath free from taint; meanwhile do thou, in case the tread of unclean feet have soiled the path, wave the cleansing flame above it, and brandish the torch in front, that I may pass upon my way. And when to heaven ye have paid the customs I exact, bear back into the house the brand from

off the hearth. What of my prophecy, Helen? how stands it now? Thou
hast seen thy husband Menelaus arrive without disguise, reft of his ships,
and of thy counterfeit. Ah, hapless man! what troubles hast thou escaped,
and art come hither, and yet knowest not whether thou art to return or
to abide here; for there is strife in heaven, and Zeus this very day will sit
in solemn conclave on thee. Hera, who erst was thy bitter foe, is now
grown kind, and is willing to bring thee and thy wife safe home, that
Hellas may learn that the marriage of Paris was all a sham, assigned to
him by Cypris; but Cypris fain would mar thy homeward course, that she
may not be convicted, or proved to have bought the palm of beauty at
the price of Helen in a futile marriage. Now the decision rests with me,
whether to ruin thee, as Cypris wishes, by telling my brother of thy
presence here, or to save thy life by taking Hera's side, concealing thy
coming from my brother, for his orders are that I should tell him, whensoe'er thou shouldst reach these shores. Ho! one of you, go show my
brother this man is here, that I may secure my safety.

HELEN

Maiden, at thy knees I fall a suppliant, and seat myself in this sad
posture on behalf of myself and him, whom I am in danger of seeing slain,
after I have so hardly found him. Oh! tell not thy brother that my husband is returned to these loving arms; save us, I beseech thee; never for
thy brother's sake sacrifice thy character for uprightness, by evil and
unjust means bidding for his favour. For the deity hates violence, and
biddeth all men get lawful gains without plundering others. Wealth unjustly gotten, though it bring some power, is to be eschewed. The breath
of heaven and the earth are man's common heritage, wherein to store his
home, without taking the goods of others, or wresting them away by
force. Me did Hermes at a critical time, to my sorrow, intrust to thy
father's safe keeping for this my lord, who now is here and wishes to re-
claim me. But how can he recover me if he be slain? How could thy sire
restore the living to the dead? Oh! consider ere that the will of heaven
and thy father's too; would the deity or would thy dead sire restore their
neighbour's goods, or would they forbear? restore them, I feel sure. It is
not, therefore, right that thou shouldst more esteem thy wanton brother
than thy righteous father. Yet if thou, prophetess as thou art and believer
in divine providence, shalt pervert the just intention of thy father and
gratify thy unrighteous brother, 'tis shameful thou shouldst have full
knowledge of the heavenly will, both what is and what is not, and yet be
ignorant of justice. Oh! save my wretched life from the troubles which
beset it, granting this as an accession to our good fortune; for every living
soul loathes Helen, seeing that there is gone a rumour throughout Hellas
that I was false unto my lord, and took up my abode in Phrygia's sumptu-

ous halls. Now, if I come to Hellas, and set foot once more in Sparta, they will hear and see how they were ruined by the wiles of goddesses, while I was no traitress to my friends after all; and so will they restore to me my virtuous name again, and I shall give my daughter in marriage, whom no man now will wed; and, leaving this vagrant life in Egypt, shall enjoy the treasures in my home. Had Menelaus met his doom at some funeral pyre, with tears should I be cherishing his memory in a far-off land, but must I lose him now when he is alive and safe? Ah! maiden, I beseech thee, say not so; grant me this boon, I pray, and reflect thy father's justice; for this is the fairest ornament of children, when the child of a virtuous sire resembles its parents in character.

LEADER

Piteous thy pleading, and a piteous object thou! But I fain would hear what Menelaus will say to save his life.

MENELAUS

I will not deign to throw myself at thy knees, or wet mine eyes with tears; for were I to play the coward, I should most foully blur my Trojan fame. And yet men say it shows a noble soul to let the tear-drop fall in misfortune. But that will not be the honourable course that I will choose in preference to bravery, if what I shall say is honourable. Art thou disposed to save a stranger seeking in mere justice to regain his wife, why then restore her and save us likewise; if not, this will not be the first by many a time that I have suffered, though thou wilt get an evil name. All that I deem worthy of me and honest, all that will touch thy heart most nearly, will I utter at the tomb of thy sire with regret for his loss. Old king beneath this tomb of stone reposing, pay back thy trust! I ask of thee my wife whom Zeus sent hither unto thee to keep for me. I know thou canst never restore her to me thyself, for thou art dead; but this thy daughter will never allow her father once so glorious, whom I invoke in his grave, to bear a tarnished name; for the decision rests with her now. Thee, too, great god of death, I call to my assistance, who hast received full many a corpse, slain by me for Helen, and art keeping thy wage; either restore those dead now to life again, or compel the daughter to show herself a worthy equal of her virtuous sire, and give me back my wife. But if ye will rob me of her, I will tell you that which she omitted in her speech. Know then, maiden, I by an oath am bound, first, to meet thy brother sword to sword, when he or I must die; there is no alternative. But if he refuse to meet me fairly front to front, and seek by famine to chase away us suppliants twain at this tomb, I am resolved to slay Helen, and then to plunge this two-edged sword through my own heart, upon the top of the sepulchre, that our streaming blood may trickle down the tomb; and our two corpses will be lying side by side upon this polished slab, a source of deathless grief to thee, and to thy sire reproach. Never shall thy brother wed Helen, nor shall any other; I will bear her hence myself, if not to my house, at any rate to death. And why this stern resolve? Were I to resort to women's ways and weep, I should be a pitiful creature, not a man of action. Slay me, if it seems thee good; I will not die ingloriously; but better yield to what I say, that thou mayst act with justice, and I regain my wife.

LEADER

On thee, maiden, it rests to judge between these arguments. Decide in such a way as to please one and all.

THEONOE

My nature and my inclination lean towards piety; myself, too, I respect, and I will never sully my father's fair name, or gratify my brother at the cost of bringing myself into open dishonour. For justice hath her temple firmly founded in my nature, and since I have this heritage from Nereus I will strive to save Menelaus; wherefore, seeing it is Hera's will to stand thy friend, I will give my vote with her. May Cypris be favourable to me! though in me she hath no part, and I will try to remain a maid alway. As for thy reproaches against my father at this tomb; lo! I have the same words to utter; I should be wronging thee, did I not restore thy wife; for my sire, were he living, would have given her back into thy keeping, and thee to her. Yea, for there is recompense for these things as well amongst the dead as amongst all those who breathe the breath of life. The soul indeed of the dead lives no more, yet hath it a consciousness that lasts for ever, eternal as the ether into which it takes the final plunge. Briefly then to end the matter, I will observe strict silence on all that ye prayed I should, and never with my counsel will I aid my brother's wanton will. For I am doing him good service, though he little thinks it, if I turn him from his godless life to holiness. Wherefore devise yourselves some way of escape; my lips are sealed; I will not cross your path. First with the goddesses begin, and of the one,—and that one Cypris,—crave permission to return unto thy country; and of Hera, that her goodwill may abide in the same quarter, even her scheme to save thee and thy husband. And thou, my own dead sire, shalt never, in so far as rests with me, lose thy holy name to rank with evil-doers.

(THEONOE *and her attendants enter the palace.*)

LEADER

No man ever prospered by unjust practices, but in a righteous cause there is hope of safety.

HELEN

Menelaus, on the maiden's side are we quite safe. Thou must from that point start, and by contributing thy advice, devise with me a scheme to save ourselves.

MENELAUS

Hearken then; thou hast been a long while in the palace, and art intimate with the king's attendants.

HELEN

What dost thou mean thereby? for thou art suggesting hopes, as if resolved on some plan for our mutual help.

MENELAUS

Couldst thou persuade one of those who have charge of cars and steeds to furnish us with a chariot?

HELEN

I might; but what escape is there for us who know nothing of the country and the barbarian's kingdom?

MENELAUS

True; 'tis impossible. Well, supposing I conceal myself in the palace and slay the king with this two-edged sword?

HELEN

His sister would never refrain from telling her brother that thou wert meditating his death.

MENELAUS

We have not so much as a ship to make our escape in; for the sea hath swallowed the one we had.

HELEN

Hear me, if haply even a woman can utter words of wisdom. Dost thou consent to be dead in word, though not really so?

MENELAUS

'Tis a bad omen; still, if by saying so I shall gain aught, I am ready to be dead in word, though not in deed.

HELEN

I, too, will mourn thee with hair cut short and dirges, as is women's way, before this impious wretch.

MENELAUS

What saving remedy doth this afford us twain? There is deception in thy scheme.

HELEN

I will beg the king of this country leave to bury thee in a cenotaph, as if thou hadst really died at sea.

MENELAUS

Suppose he grant it; how, e'en then, are we to escape without a ship, after having committed me to my empty tomb?

HELEN

I will bid him give me a vessel, from which to let drop into the sea's embrace thy funeral offerings.

MENELAUS

A clever plan in truth, save in one particular; suppose he bid thee rear the tomb upon the strand, thy pretext comes to naught.

HELEN

But I shall say it is not the custom in Hellas to bury those who die at sea upon the shore.

MENELAUS

Thou removest this obstacle too; I then will sail with thee and help stow the funeral garniture in the same ship.

HELEN

Above all, it is necessary that thou and all thy sailors who escaped from the wreck should be at hand.

MENELAUS

Be sure if once I find a ship at her moorings, they shall be there man for man, each with his sword.

HELEN

Thou must direct everything; only let there be winds to waft our sails and a good ship to speed before them!

MENELAUS

So shall it be; for the deities will cause my troubles to cease. But from whom wilt thou say thou hadst tidings of my death?

HELEN

From thee; declare thyself the one and only survivor, telling how thou wert sailing with the son of Atreus, and didst see him perish.

MENELAUS

Of a truth the garments I have thrown about me, will bear out my tale that they were rags collected from the wreckage.

HELEN

They come in most opportunely, but they were near being lost just at the wrong time. Maybe that misfortune will turn to fortune.

MENELAUS

Am I to enter the palace with thee, or are we to sit here at the tomb quietly?

HELEN

Abide here; for if the king attempts to do thee any mischief, this tomb and thy good sword will protect thee. But I will go within and cut off my hair, and exchange my white robe for sable weeds, and rend my cheek with this hand's blood-thirsty nail. For 'tis a mighty struggle, and I see two possible issues; either I must die if detected in my plot, or else to my country shall I come and save thy soul alive. O Hera! awful queen, who sharest the couch of Zeus, grant some respite from their toil to two unhappy wretches; to thee I pray, tossing my arms upward to heaven, where thou hast thy home in the star-spangled firmament. Thou, too, that didst win the prize of beauty at the price of my marriage; O Cypris! daughter of Dione, destroy me not utterly. Thou hast injured me enough aforetime, delivering up my name, though not my person, to live amongst barbarians. Oh! suffer me to die, if death is thy desire, in my native land. Why art thou so insatiate in mischief, employing every art of love, of fraud, and guileful schemes, and spells that bring bloodshed on families? Wert thou but moderate, only that!—in all else thou art by nature man's most welcome deity; and I have reason so to say.

(HELEN *enters the palace and* MENELAUS *withdraws into the background.*)

CHORUS (*singing*)

strophe 1

Thee let me invoke, tearful Philomel, lurking 'neath the leafy covert in thy place of song, most tuneful of all feathered songsters, oh! come to aid me in my dirge, trilling through thy tawny throat, as I sing the piteous woes of Helen, and the tearful fate of Trojan dames made subject to Achaea's spear, on the day that there came to their plains one who sped with foreign oar across the dashing billows, bringing to Priam's race from Lacedaemon thee his hapless bride, O Helen,—even Paris, luckless bridegroom, by the guidance of Aphrodite.

antistrophe 1

And many an Achaean hath breathed his last amid the spearmen's thrusts and hurtling hail of stones, and gone to his sad end; for these their wives cut off their hair in sorrow, and their houses are left without a bride; and one [1] of the Achaeans, that had but a single ship, did light a blazing beacon on sea-girt Euboea, and destroy full many of them, wrecking them on the rocks of Caphareus and the shores that front the Aegean main, by the treacherous gleam he kindled; when thou, O Menelaus, from the very day of thy start, didst drift to harbourless hills, far from thy country before the breath of the storm, bearing on thy ship a prize that was no prize, but a phantom made by Hera out of cloud for the Danai to struggle over.

strophe 2

What mortal claims, by searching to the utmost limit, to have found out the nature of God, or of his opposite, or of that which comes between, seeing as he doth this world of man tossed to and fro by waves of contradiction and strange vicissitudes? Thou, Helen, art the daughter of Zeus; for thy sire was the bird that nestled in Leda's bosom; and yet for all that art thou become a by-word for wickedness, through the length and breadth of Hellas, as faithless, treacherous wife and godless woman; nor can I tell what certainty is, whatever may pass for it amongst men. That which gods pronounce have I found true.

antistrophe 2

O fools! all ye who try to win the meed of valour through war and serried ranks of chivalry, seeking thus to still this mortal coil, in senselessness; for if bloody contests are to decide, there will never be any lack of strife in the towns of men; the maidens of the land of Priam left their bridal bowers, though arbitration might have put thy quarrel right, O Helen. And now Troy's sons are in Hades' keeping in the world below, and fire hath darted on her walls, as darts the flame of Zeus, and thou art bringing woe on woe to hapless sufferers in their misery.

(THEOCLYMENUS *and his hunting attendants enter.*)

THEOCLYMENUS

All hail, my father's tomb! I buried thee, Proteus, at the place where men go out, that I might often greet thee; and so, ever as I go out and in, I, thy son Theoclymenus, call on thee, father. Ho! servants, to the palace take my hounds and hunting nets! How often have I blamed myself for never punishing those miscreants with death! I have just heard that a son of Hellas has come openly to my land, escaping the notice of the guard, a spy maybe or a would-be thief of Helen; death shall be his lot if only I can catch him. Ha! I find all my plans apparently frustrated, the daughter of Tyndareus has deserted her seat at the tomb and sailed away from my shores. Ho! there, undo the bars, loose the horses from their stalls, bring forth my chariot, servants, that the wife, on whom my heart is set, may not get away from these shores unseen, for want of any trouble I can take. Yet stay; for I see the object of my pursuit is still in the palace, and has not fled. (HELEN *enters from the palace, clad in the garb of mourning.*) How now, lady, why hast thou arrayed thee in sable weeds instead of white raiment, and from thy fair head hast shorn thy tresses with the steel, bedewing thy cheeks the while with tears but lately shed? Is it in response to visions of the night that thou art mourning, or, because thou hast heard some warning voice within, art thus distraught with grief?

HELEN

My lord,—for already I have learnt to say that name,—I am undone; my luck is gone; I cease to be.

THEOCLYMENUS

In what misfortune art thou plunged? What hath happened?

HELEN

Menelaus, ah me! how can I say it? is dead, my husband.

THEOCLYMENUS

How knowest thou? Did Theonoe tell thee this?

HELEN

Both she, and one who was there when he perished.

THEOCLYMENUS

What! hath one arrived who actually announces this for certain?

HELEN

One hath; oh may he come e'en as I wish him to!

THEOCLYMENUS

Who and where is he? that I may learn this more surely.

HELEN

There he is, sitting crouched beneath the shelter of this tomb.

THEOCLYMENUS

Great Apollo! how clad in unseemly rags!

HELEN

Ah me! methinks my own husband too is in like plight.

THEOCLYMENUS

From what country is this fellow? whence landed he here?

HELEN

From Hellas, one of the Achaeans who sailed with my husband.

THEOCLYMENUS

What kind of death doth he declare that Menelaus died?

HELEN

The most piteous of all; amid the watery waves at sea.

THEOCLYMENUS

On what part of the savage ocean was he sailing?

HELEN

Cast up on the harbourless rocks of Libya.

THEOCLYMENUS

How was it this man did not perish if he was with him aboard?

HELEN

There are times when churls have more luck than their betters.

THEOCLYMENUS

Where left he the wreck, on coming hither?

HELEN

There, where perdition catch it, but not Menelaus!

THEOCLYMENUS

He is lost; but on what vessel came this man?

HELEN

According to his story sailors fell in with him and picked him up.

THEOCLYMENUS

Where then is that ill thing that was sent to Troy in thy stead?

HELEN

Dost mean the phantom-form of cloud? It hath passed into the air.

THEOCLYMENUS

O Priam, and thou land of Troy, how fruitless thy ruin!

HELEN

I too have shared with Priam's race their misfortunes.

THEOCLYMENUS

Did this fellow leave thy husband unburied, or consign him to the grave?

HELEN

Unburied; woe is me for my sad lot!

THEOCLYMENUS

Wherefore hast thou shorn the tresses of thy golden hair?

HELEN

His memory lingers fondly in this heart, whate'er his fate.

THEOCLYMENUS

Are thy tears in genuine sorrow for this calamity?

HELEN

An easy task no doubt to escape thy sister's detection!

THEOCLYMENUS

No, surely; impossible. Wilt thou still make this tomb thy abode?

HELEN

Why jeer at me? canst thou not let the dead man be?

THEOCLYMENUS

No, thy loyalty to thy husband's memory makes thee fly from me.

HELEN

I will do so no more; prepare at once for my marriage.

THEOCLYMENUS

Thou hast been long in bringing thyself to it; still I do commend thee now.

HELEN

Dost know thy part? Let us forget the past.

THEOCLYMENUS

On what terms? One good turn deserves another.

HELEN

Let us make peace; be reconciled to me.

THEOCLYMENUS
I relinquish my quarrel with thee; let it take wings and fly away.

HELEN
Then by thy knees, since thou art my friend indeed,—

THEOCLYMENUS
What art so bent on winning, that to me thou stretchest out a suppliant hand?

HELEN
My dead husband would I fain bury.

THEOCLYMENUS
What tomb can be bestowed on lost bodies? Wilt thou bury a shade?

HELEN
In Hellas we have a custom, whene'er one is drowned at sea—

THEOCLYMENUS
What is your custom? The race of Pelops truly hath some skill in matters such as this.

HELEN
To hold a burial with woven robes that wrap no corpse.

THEOCLYMENUS
Perform the ceremony; rear the tomb where'er thou wilt.

HELEN
'Tis not thus we give drowned sailors burial.

THEOCLYMENUS
How then? I know nothing of your customs in Hellas.

HELEN
We unmoor, and carry out to sea all that is the dead man's due.

THEOCLYMENUS
What am I to give thee then for thy dead husband?

HELEN
Myself I cannot say; I had no such experience in my previous happy life.

THEOCLYMENUS
Stranger, thou art the bearer of tidings I welcome.

MENELAUS
Well, I do not, nor yet doth the dead man.

THEOCLYMENUS
How do ye bury those who have been drowned at sea?

MENELAUS
Each according to his means.

THEOCLYMENUS
As far as wealth goes, name thy wishes for this lady's sake.

MENELAUS
There must be a blood-offering first to the dead.

THEOCLYMENUS
Blood of what? Do thou show me and I will comply.

MENELAUS
Decide that thyself; whate'er thou givest will suffice.

THEOCLYMENUS
Amongst barbarians 'tis customary to sacrifice a horse or bull.

MENELAUS
If thou givest at all, let there be nothing mean in thy gift.

THEOCLYMENUS
I have no lack of such in my rich herds

MENELAUS
Next an empty bier is decked and carried in procession.

THEOCLYMENUS
It shall be so; what else is it customary to add?

MENELAUS
Bronze arms; for war was his delight.

THEOCLYMENUS
These will be worthy of the race of Pelops, and these will we give

MENELAUS
And with them all the fair increase of productive earth.

THEOCLYMENUS
And next, how do ye pour these offerings into the billows?

MENELAUS
There must be a ship ready and rowers.

THEOCLYMENUS
How far from the shore does the ship put out?

MENELAUS
So far that the foam in her wake can scarce be seen from the strand.

THEOCLYMENUS
Why so? wherefore doth Hellas observe this custom?

MENELAUS
That the billow may not cast up again our expiatory offerings.

THEOCLYMENUS
Phoenician rowers will soon cover the distance.

MENELAUS
'Twill be well done, and gratifying to Menelaus, too.

THEOCLYMENUS
Canst thou not perform these rites well enough without Helen?

MENELAUS
This task belongs to mother, wife, or children.

THEOCLYMENUS
'Tis her task then, according to thee, to bury her husband.

MENELAUS
To be sure; piety demands that the dead be not robbed of their due.

THEOCLYMENUS
Well, let her go; 'tis my interest to foster piety in a wife. And thou, enter the house and choose adornment for the dead. Thyself, too, will I not send empty-handed away, since thou hast done her a service. And for the good news thou hast brought me, thou shalt receive raiment instead of going bare, and food, too, that thou mayst reach thy country; for as it is, I see thou art in sorry plight. As for thee, poor lady, waste not thyself in a hopeless case; Menelaus has met his doom, and thy dead husband cannot come to life.

MENELAUS
This then is thy duty, fair young wife; be content with thy present husband, and forget him who has no existence; for this is thy best course in face of what is happening. And if ever I come to Hellas and secure my

safety, I will clear thee of thy former ill-repute, if thou prove a dutiful wife to thy true husband.

HELEN

I will; never shall my husband have cause to blame me; thou shalt thyself attend us and be witness thereto. Now go within, poor wanderer, and seek the bath, and change thy raiment. I will show my kindness to thee, and that without delay. For thou wilt perform all service due with kindlier feeling for my dear lord Menelaus, if at my hands thou meet with thy deserts.

(THEOCLYMENUS, HELEN, MENELAUS *enter the palace.*)

CHORUS (*singing*)

strophe 1

Through wooded glen, o'er torrent's flood, and ocean's booming waves rushed the mountain-goddess, mother of the gods,² in frantic haste, once long ago, yearning for her daughter lost, whose name men dare not utter; loudly rattled the Bacchic castanets in shrill accord, what time those maidens, swift as whirlwinds, sped forth with the goddess on her chariot yoked to wild creatures, in quest of her that was ravished from the circling choir of virgins; here was Artemis with her bow, and there the grim-eyed goddess, sheathed in mail, and spear in hand. But Zeus looked down from his throne in heaven, and turned the issue otherwhither.

antistrophe 1

Soon as the mother ceased from her wild wandering toil, in seeking her daughter stolen so subtly as to baffle all pursuit, she crossed the snow-capped heights of Ida's nymphs; and in anguish cast her down amongst the rocks and brushwood deep in snow; and, denying to man all increase to his tillage from those barren fields, she wasted the human race; nor would she let the leafy tendrils yield luxuriant fodder for the cattle, wherefore many a beast lay dying; no sacrifice was offered to the gods, and on the altars were no cakes to burn; yea, and she made the dew-fed founts of crystal water to cease their flow, in her insatiate sorrow for her child.

strophe 2

But when for gods and tribes of men alike she made an end to festal cheer, Zeus spoke out, seeking to soothe the mother's moody soul, "Ye stately Graces, go banish from Demeter's angry heart the grief her wanderings bring upon her for her child, and go, ye Muses too, with tuneful choir." Thereon did Cypris, fairest of the blessed gods, first catch up the crashing cymbals, native to that land, and the drum with tight-stretched skin, and then Demeter smiled, and in her hand did take the deep-toned flute, well pleased with its loud note.

antistrophe 2
Thou hast wedded as thou never shouldst have done in defiance of all right, and thou hast incurred, my daughter, the wrath of the great mother by disregarding her sacrifices. Oh! mighty is the virtue in a dress of dappled fawn-skin, in ivy green that twineth round a sacred thyrsus, in whirling tambourines struck as they revolve in air, in tresses wildly streaming for the revelry of Bromius, and likewise in the sleepless vigils of the goddess, when the moon looks down and sheds her radiance o'er the scene. Thou wert confident in thy charms alone.

(HELEN *comes out of the palace alone.*)

HELEN
My friends, within the palace all goes well for us; for the daughter of Proteus, who is privy to our stealthy scheme, told her brother nothing when questioned as to my husband's coming, but for my sake declared him dead and buried. Most fortunate it is my lord hath had the luck to get these weapons; for he is now himself clad in the harness he was to plunge into the sea, his stalwart arm thrust through the buckler's strap, and in his right hand a spear, on pretence of joining in homage to the dead. He hath girded himself most serviceably for the fray, as if to triumph o'er a host of barbarian foes when once we are aboard yon oarèd ship; instead of his rags from the wreck hath he donned the robes I gave for his attire, and I have bathed his limbs in water from the stream, a bath he long hath wanted. But I must be silent, for from the house comes forth the man who thinks he has me in his power, prepared to be his bride; and thy goodwill I also claim and thy strict silence, if haply, when we save ourselves, we may save thee too some day.
(THEOCLYMENUS *and* MENELAUS *enter, with a train of attendants bearing the offerings for the funeral rites.*)

THEOCLYMENUS
Advance in order, servants, as the stranger hath directed, bearing the funeral gifts the sea demands. But thou, Helen, if thou wilt not misconstrue my words, be persuaded and here abide; for thou wilt do thy husband equal service whether thou art present or not. For I am afraid that some sudden shock of fond regret may prompt thee to plunge into the swollen tide, in an ecstasy of gratitude toward thy former husband; for thy grief for him, though he is lost, is running to excess.

HELEN

O my new lord, needs must I honour him with whom I first shared married joys; for I could even die with my husband, so well I loved him; yet how could he thank me, were I to share death's doom with him? Still, let me go and pay his funeral rites unto the dead in person. The gods grant thee the boon I wish and this stranger too, for the assistance he is lending here! And thou shalt find in me a wife fit to share thy house, since thou art rendering kindness to Menelaus and to me; for surely these events are to some good fortune tending. But now appoint someone to give us a ship wherein to convey these gifts, that I may find thy kindness made complete.

THEOCLYMENUS (*to an attendant*)

Go thou, and furnish them with a Sidonian galley of fifty oars and rowers also.

HELEN

Shall not he command the ship who is ordering the funeral?

THEOCLYMENUS

Most certainly; my sailors are to obey him.

HELEN

Repeat the order, that they may clearly understand thee.

THEOCLYMENUS

I repeat it, and will do so yet again if that is thy pleasure.

HELEN

Good luck to thee and to me in my designs!

THEOCLYMENUS

Oh! waste not thy fair complexion with excessive weeping.

HELEN

This day shall show my gratitude to thee.

THEOCLYMENUS

The state of the dead is nothingness; to toil for them is vain.

HELEN

In what I say, this world, as well as that, hath share.

THEOCLYMENUS

Thou shalt not find in me a husband at all inferior to Menelaus.

HELEN

With thee have I no fault to find; good luck is all I need.

THEOCLYMENUS

That rests with thyself, if thou show thyself a loving wife to me.

HELEN

This is not a lesson I shall have to learn now, to love my friends.

THEOCLYMENUS

Is it thy wish that I should escort thee in person with active aid?

HELEN

God forbid! become not thy servant's servant, O king!

THEOCLYMENUS

Up and away! I am not concerned with customs which the race of Pelops holds. My house is pure, for Menelaus did not die here; go some one now and bid my vassal chiefs bring marriage-offerings to my palace; for the whole earth must re-echo in glad accord the hymn of my wedding with Helen, to make men envious. Go, stranger, and pour into the sea's embrace these offerings to Helen's former lord, and then speed back again with my bride, that after sharing with me her marriage-feast thou mayst set out for home, or here abide in happiness.

(THEOCLYMENUS *and his retinue enter the palace.*)

MENELAUS

O Zeus, who art called the father of all and god of wisdom, look down on us and change our woe to joy! Lend us thy ready help, as we seek to drag our fortunes up the rugged hill; if with but thy finger-tip thou touch us, we shall reach our longed-for goal. Sufficient are the troubles we ere this have undergone. Full oft have I invoked you gods to near my joys and sorrows; I do not deserve to be for ever unhappy, but to advance and prosper. Grant me but this one boon, and so will ye crown my future with blessing.

(MENELAUS, HELEN *and their train of attendants depart.*)

CHORUS (*singing*)

strophe 1

Hail! thou swift Phoenician ship of Sidon! dear to the rowers, mother to the foam, leader of fair dolphins' gambols, what time the deep is hushed and still, and Ocean's azure child, the queen of calm, takes up her parable and says: "Away! and spread your canvas to the ocean-breeze. Ho! sailors, ho! come grip your oars of pine, speeding Helen on her way to the sheltered beach where Perseus dwelt of yore." [3]

antistrophe 1

It may be thou wilt find the daughters of Leucippus beside the brimming river or before the temple of Pallas, when at last with dance and revelry thou joinest in the merry midnight festival of Hyacinthus, him whom Phoebus slew in the lists by a quoit hurled o'er the mark; wherefore did the son of Zeus ordain that Laconia's land should set apart that day for sacrifice; there too shalt thou find the tender maid, whom ye left in your house, for as yet no nuptial torch has shed its light for her.

strophe 2

Oh! for wings to cleave the air in the track of Libyan cranes, whose serried ranks leave far behind the wintry storm at the shrill summons of some veteran leader, who raises his exultant cry as he wings his way o'er plains that know no rain and yet bear fruitful increase. Ye feathered birds with necks outstretched, comrades of the racing clouds, on! on! till ye reach the Pleiads in their central station and Orion, lord of the night; and as ye settle on Eurotas' banks proclaim the glad tidings that Menelaus hath sacked the city of Dardanus, and will soon be home.

antistrophe 2

Ye sons of Tyndareus at length appear, speeding in your chariot through the sky, denizens of heaven's courts beneath the radiant whirling stars, guide this lady Helen safely o'er the azure main, across the foam-flecked billows of the deep-blue sea, sending the mariners a favouring gale from Zeus; and from your sister snatch the ill-repute of wedding with a barbarian, even the punishment bequeathed to her from that strife on Ida's mount, albeit she never went to the land of Ilium, to the battlements of Phoebus.

(*The* SECOND MESSENGER *enters in haste, as* THEOCLYMENUS *comes out of the palace.*)

SECOND MESSENGER

O king, at last have I found thee in the palace; for new tidings of woe art thou soon to hear from me.

THEOCLYMENUS

How now?

MESSENGER

Make haste to woo a new wife; for Helen hath escaped.

THEOCLYMENUS

Borne aloft on soaring wings, or treading still the earth?

MESSENGER

Menelaus has succeeded in bearing her hence; 'twas he that brought the news of his own death.

THEOCLYMENUS

O monstrous story! what ship conveyed her from these shores? Thy tale is past belief.

MESSENGER

The very ship thou didst thyself give the stranger; and that thou may-est briefly know all, he is gone, taking thy sailors with him.

THEOCLYMENUS

How was it? I long to know, for I never thought that a single arm could master all those sailors with whom thou wert despatched.

MESSENGER

Soon as the daughter of Zeus had left this royal mansion and come unto the sea, daintily picking her way, most craftily she set to mourn her husband, though he was not dead but at her side. Now when we reached thy docks well walled, we began to launch the fastest of Sidonian ships, with her full complement of fifty rowers, and each task in due succession followed; some set up the mast, others ranged the oars with their blades ready, and stored the white sails within the hold, and the rudder was let down astern and fastened securely. While we were thus employed, those Hellenes, who had been fellow-voyagers with Menelaus, were watching us, it seems, and they drew nigh the beach, clad in the rags of shipwrecked men,—well built enough, but squalid to look upon. And the son of Atreus, directly he saw them approach, bespoke them, craftily introducing the reason for his mourning: "Ye hapless mariners, how have ye come hither? your Achaean ship where wrecked? Are ye here to help bury dead Atreus' son, whose missing body this lady, daughter of Tyndareus, is honouring with a cenotaph?" Then they with feigned tears proceeded to the ship, bearing aboard the offerings to be thrown into the deep for Menelaus. Thereat were we suspicious, and communed amongst ourselves regarding the number of extra voyagers; but still we kept silence out of respect for thy orders, for by intrusting the command of the vessel to the stranger thou didst thus spoil all. Now the other victims gave no trouble, and we easily put them aboard; only the bull refused to go forward along the gangway, but rolled his eyes around and kept bellowing, and, arching his back and glaring askance towards his horns, he would not let us touch him. But Helen's lord cried out: "O! ye who laid waste the town of Ilium, come pick up yon bull, the dead man's offering, on your stout shoulders, as is the way in Hellas, and cast him into the hold;" and as he spoke he drew his sword in readiness. Then they at his command came and caught up the bull and carried him bodily on to the deck. And Menelaus stroked the horse on neck and brow, coaxing it to go aboard. At length, when the ship was fully freighted, Helen climbed the ladder with graceful step and took her seat midway betwixt the rowers' benches, and he sat by her side, even Menelaus who was called dead; and the rest, equally divided on the right and left side of the ship, sat them down, each beside his man, with swords concealed beneath their cloaks, and the billows soon were echoing to the rowers' song, as we heard the boatswain's note. Now when we were put out a space, not very far nor very near, the helmsman asked, "Shall we, sir stranger, sail yet further on our course, or will this serve? For thine it is to command the ship." And he answered: " 'Tis far enough for me," while in his right hand he gripped his sword and stepped on to the prow; then standing o'er the bull to slay it, never a word said he of any dead man, but cut its throat and thus made prayer: "Poseidon, lord of the sea, whose home is in the deep, and ye holy daughters of Nereus, bring me and my wife safe and sound to Nauplia's strand from hence!" Anon a gush of blood, fair omen for the stranger, spouted into the tide. One cried, "There is treachery in this voyage; why should we now sail to Nauplia? Give the order, helmsman, turn thy rudder." But the son of Atreus, standing where he slew the bull, called to his comrades, "Why do ye, the pick of Hellas, delay to smite and slay the barbarians and fling them from the ship into the waves?" While to thy crew the boatswain cried the opposite command: "Ho! some of you catch up chance spars, break up the benches, or snatch the oar-blade from the thole, and beat out the brains of these our foreign foes." Forthwith up sprang each man, the one part armed with poles that sailors use, the other with swords. And the ship ran down with blood; while Helen from her seat upon the stern thus cheered them on: "Where is the fame ye won in Troy? show it against these barbarians." Then as they hasted to the fray, some would fall and some rise up again, while others hadst thou seen laid low in death. But Menelaus in full armour, made his way, sword in hand, to any point where his watchful eye perceived his comrades in distress; so we leapt from the ship and swam, and he cleared the benches of thy rowers. Then did the prince set himself to steer, and bade them make a straight course to Hellas. So they set up the mast, and favouring breezes blew; and they are clear away, while I, from death escaped, let myself down by the anchor chain into the sea; and, just as I was spent, one threw me a rope and rescued me, and drew me to land to bring to thee this message. Ah! there is naught more serviceable to mankind than a prudent distrust.

LEADER OF THE CHORUS
I would never have believed that Menelaus could have eluded us and
thee, O king, in the way he did on his coming.

THEOCLYMENUS
Woe is me! cozened by a woman's tricks! My bride hath escaped me.
If the ship could have been pursued and overtaken, I would have used
every means forthwith to catch the strangers; as it is, I will avenge myself
upon my treacherous sister, in that she saw Menelaus in my palace and
did not tell me. Wherefore shall she nevermore deceive another by her
prophetic art.

(*A* SERVANT *comes out of the palace.*)

SERVANT
Ho, there! whither away so fast, my lord? on what bloody thought
intent?

THEOCLYMENUS
Whither Justice calls me. Out of my path!

SERVANT
I will not loose thy robe, for on grievous mischief art thou bent.

THEOCLYMENUS
Shalt thou, a slave, control thy master?

SERVANT
Yea, for I am in my senses.

THEOCLYMENUS
I should not say so, if thou wilt not let me—

SERVANT
Nay, but that I never will.

THEOCLYMENUS
Slay my sister most accursed.

SERVANT
Say rather, most righteous.

THEOCLYMENUS
"Righteous?" She who betrayed me?

SERVANT
There is an honourable treachery, which 'tis right to commit.

THEOCLYMENUS
By giving my bride to another?

SERVANT
Only to those who had a better right.

THEOCLYMENUS
Who hath any rights o'er mine?

SERVANT
He that received her from her father.

THEOCLYMENUS
Nay, but fortune gave her to me.

SERVANT
And destiny took her away.

THEOCLYMENUS
'Tis not for thee to decide my affairs.

SERVANT
Only supposing mine be the better counsel.

THEOCLYMENUS
So I am thy subject, not thy ruler.

SERVANT
Aye, a subject bound to do the right, and eschew the wrong.

THEOCLYMENUS
It seems thou art eager to be slain.

SERVANT
Slay me; thy sister shalt thou never slay with my consent, but me perchance; for to die for their masters is the fairest death that noble slaves
can find.

(THE DIOSCURI *appear from above.*)

DIOSCURI
Restrain those bursts of rage that hurry thee to undue lengths, O
Theoclymenus, king of this country. We are the twin sons of Zeus that call
to thee by name, whom Leda bore one day, with Helen too who hath fled
from thy palace. For thou art wroth for a marriage never destined for thee;
nor is thy sister Theonoe, daughter of a Nereid goddess, wronging thee
because she honours the word of God and her father's just behests. For
it was ordained that Helen should abide within thy halls up till the present

time, but since Troy is razed to the ground and she hath lent her name to
the goddesses, no longer need she stay, now must she be united in the
self-same wedlock as before, and reach her home and share it with her
husband. Withhold then thy malignant blade from thy sister, and believe
that she herein is acting with discretion. Long, long ago had we our sister
saved, seeing that Zeus has made us gods, but we were too weak for
destiny as well as the deities, who willed these things to be. This is my
bidding to thee; while to my sister I say, "Sail on with thy husband; and
ye shall have a prosperous breeze; for we, thy brethren twain, will course
along the deep and bring you safely to your fatherland. And when at last
thy goal is reached and thy life ended, thou shalt be famous as a goddess,
and with thy twin brethren share the drink-offering, and like us receive
gifts from men, for such is the will of Zeus. Yea, and that spot where the
son of Maia first appointed thee a home when from Sparta he removed
thee, after stealing an image of thee from Heaven's mansions to prevent
thy marriage with Paris, even the isle that lies like a sentinel along the
Attic coast, shall henceforth be called by thy name amongst men, for that
it welcomed thee when stolen from thy home. Moreover, Heaven ordains
that the wanderer Menelaus shall find a home within an island of the
blest; for to noble souls hath the deity no dislike, albeit these oft suffer
more than those of no account."

THEOCLYMENUS
Ye sons of Leda and of Zeus, I will forego my former quarrel about your
sister, nor no longer seek to slay mine own. Let Helen to her home repair,
if such is Heaven's pleasure. Ye know that ye are sprung of the same stock
as your sister, best of women, chastest too; hail then for the true nobility
of Helen's soul, a quality too seldom found amongst her sex!

CHORUS (*chanting*)
Many are the forms the heavenly will assumes; and many a thing
God brings to pass contrary to expectation: that which was looked
for is not accomplished, while Heaven finds out a way for what we
never hoped; e'en such has been the issue here.[4]

COLERIDGE's translation has been slightly modified in the following lines: 228, 274, 322, 326, 455, 551, 554, 630–631, 664, 689, 758, 786, 791, 809, 834, 841, 890, 893, 918, 955, 956, 995, 1001, 1043, 1056, 1106, 1165, 1204, 1218, 1523, 1550, 1682.

1. *i.e.,* Nauplius.

2. *i.e.,* Demeter.

3. The reference is to Mycenae which Perseus is said to have founded.

4. These lines are found likewise at the conclusion of the *Alcestis, Andromache, The Bacchae,* and, with a slight addition, the *Medea.*

XIII
ELECTRA

CHARACTERS IN THE PLAY

A PEASANT OF MYCENAE, *husband of* ELECTRA
ELECTRA, *daughter of Agamemnon*
ORESTES, *son of Agamemnon*
PYLADES, *friend of* ORESTES
CHORUS OF ARGIVE COUNTRY-WOMEN
CLYTEMNESTRA, *widow of Agamemnon*
OLD MAN, *formerly servant of Agamemnon*
MESSENGER
THE DIOSCURI
Attendants

INTRODUCTION

In the *Electra*, which was produced probably in 413 B.C.,[1] Euripides offers his interpretation of the famous legend of the House of Atreus. The play deals with exactly those episodes of the story which Aeschylus presents in his *Choephori*, and Sophocles in his *Electra*. As in the Sophoclean version Euripides opens his tragedy some years after the murder of Agamemnon by Clytemnestra and Aegisthus. In its main features, *viz.*, the return of Orestes, the killing of Aegisthus, and the final matricide, the Euripidean play corresponds with its counterparts by Aeschylus and Sophocles, but in detail there have been injected several innovations which alter the general significance and the major emphases of the tragedy.

Aeschylus' *Choephori* is integrated into the larger unit of the trilogy, the *Oresteia*, whose central orientation is towards the problem of evil and the nature of the Supreme Being behind the universe. Sophocles in his *Electra* seems to be primarily interested in the psychological study of his main character while she is in the process of bringing about her revenge. He does not explore the religious or theological implications of his problem, nor does he attempt to analyze the psychological or emotional states of his protagonists after the crimes of revenge have been accomplished. Euripides, however, has plumbed more deeply than Sophocles the psychological and emotional states of his characters, and in addition focuses his attention sharply upon them after they have committed their crimes. In this latter respect Euripides' play resembles the *Oresteia*, though of course it does not have the profound religious significance of the Aeschylean tragedy. In effect, Euripides is answering in his play some such questions as these: What happens to people in their inner being who have lived for years with a single overpowering thought,—to exact revenge? What happens to them when once that desire has been realized?

The prologue of the *Electra* gives us immediately a clue with regard to Euripides' purpose. Here we meet with the first of the playwright's innovations, for we discover that Electra has been cruelly compelled by Aegisthus to marry a poor peasant, in order that if she ever bore any progeny, they would be of such inferior quality as never to constitute a

[1] The date is fixed by a fairly certain allusion to the Sicilian expedition in lines 1347 ff.

63

serious threat to her step-father's royal authority. Electra is living in the peasant's lowly hut, is clad in rags, and is forced to perform menial tasks unsuited to her lofty birth. This opening scene perhaps is an instance of Euripides' illegitimate use of certain dubious means in order to produce pathos. At all events, Electra is placed in a milieu which lends itself to the emotional and psychological analysis to which the poet subjects her.

As the play progresses, Orestes and his trusty Pylades enter, and brother and sister duly recognize one another. And here, by the way, Euripides apparently indulges in criticism of the corresponding recognition scene in Aeschylus' *Choephori*, for the devices which the older poet had used to discover Orestes to Electra are scornfully rejected, and the final recognition is brought about when Electra identifies her brother by means of a scar. From this point on, Euripides works out the remainder of the play in such a fashion as to delineate fully the characters of Clytemnestra, Orestes, and Electra. The Queen, who as a person does not possess the power and force of Aeschylus' Clytemnestra, has often been compared with Hamlet's mother. She relies upon her regular defences, namely that Agamemnon slew her daughter, and brought home from Troy as his concubine the princess, Cassandra. At the same time she gives no evidence that she has any deep convictions, but merely accepts and does not scrutinize too closely the situations in which she has successively found herself. Orestes is presented as a not very strong-willed character who feels that it is his duty to avenge his father, yet who shrinks from the act of matricide. Electra dominates him, and nerves him to commit the murders. She from the outset is portrayed as a woman who long since has given up any hope of achieving happiness. As Gilbert Murray has pointed out,[2] she has been consumed simultaneously by love and hate, and both these passions have remained unsatisfied. For years she has hated her mother and step-father, and has loved her long-exiled brother and murdered father. On the whole neither Orestes nor Electra entirely commands our sympathy, yet their sudden reaction into a state of abject remorse after Clytemnestra has been killed, helps to give them stature. As they face their lives at the end of the play, they seem to have attained to the level of tragic characters.

Euripides closes his drama by employing the device of the *deus ex machina*. The Dioscuri appear, and, after a more than tacit criticism of Apollo for directing Orestes to kill his mother, command the youth to go to Athens where finally in the court of the Areopagus he will be cleared of his guilt. This final scene brings the play in general line with the Aeschylean version, but how much can be inferred from the scene to throw light on Euripides' religious views remains a question. It may be that here Euripides is leveling an attack against the superstitious belief in a god

[2] Cf. the introduction to his translation of the *Electra*, p. viii.

like Apollo who wreaks such havoc with human lives as he has in the case of Orestes. On the other hand the Dioscuri may simply be the playwright's mechanical device of bringing the play to an end, after he has completed the psychological study of his main characters. Or finally, the scene may reflect a central doubt in Euripides' mind as to whether man may ever know anything about the divine nature, and it may further reveal the poet's conviction that man lives under some kind of divine control, and that it is his obligation to face that life, and endure it courageously, no matter what may be its terms.

ELECTRA

(SCENE:—*Before the hut of the* PEASANT, *in the country on the borders of Argolis. It is just before sunrise. The* PEASANT *is discovered alone.*)

PEASANT

O ARGOS, ancient land, and streams of Inachus, whence on a day king Agamemnon sailed to the realm of Troy, carrying his warriors aboard a thousand ships; and after he had slain Priam who was reigning in Ilium and captured the famous city of Dardanus, he came hither to Argos and has set up high on the temple-walls many a trophy, spoil of the barbarians. Though all went well with him in Troy, yet was he slain in his own palace by the guile of his wife Clytemnestra and the hand of Aegisthus, son of Thyestes. So he died and left behind him the ancient sceptre of Tantalus, and Aegisthus reigns in his stead, with the daughter of Tyndareus, Agamemnon's queen, to wife. Now as for those whom he left in his halls, when he sailed to Troy, his son Orestes and his tender daughter Electra,—the boy Orestes, as he was like to be slain by Aegisthus, his sire's old foster-father secretly removed to the land of Phocis and gave to Strophius to bring up, but the maid Electra abode in her father's house, and soon as she had budded into maidenhood, came all the princes of Hellas asking her hand in marriage. But Aegisthus kept her at home for fear she might bear a son to some chieftain who would avenge Agamemnon, nor would he betroth her unto any. But when e'en thus there seemed some room for fear that she might bear some noble lord a child by stealth and Aegisthus was minded to slay her, her mother, though she had a cruel heart, yet rescued the maiden from his hand. For she could find excuses for having slain her husband, but she feared the hatred she would incur for her children's murder. Wherefore Aegisthus devised this scheme; on Agamemnon's son who had escaped his realm by flight he set a price to be paid to any who should slay him, while he gave Electra to me in marriage, whose ancestors were citizens of Mycenae. It is not *that* I blame myself for; my family was noble enough, though certainly impoverished, and so

my good birth suffers. By making for her this weak alliance he thought
he would have little to fear. For if some man of high position had married her, he might have revived the vengeance for Agamemnon's murder,
which now is sleeping; in which case Aegisthus would have paid the
penalty. But Cypris is my witness that I have ever respected her maidenhood; she is still as though unwed. Unworthy as I am, honour forbids that
I should so affront the daughter of a better man. Yea, and I am sorry for
Orestes, hapless youth, who is called my kinsman, to think that he should
ever return to Argos and behold his sister's wretched marriage. And whoso
counts me but a fool for leaving a tender maid untouched when I have her
in my house, to him I say, he measures purity by the vicious standard of
his own soul, a standard like himself.

(ELECTRA *enters from the hut, carrying a water pitcher on her head. She
is meanly clad.*)

ELECTRA

O sable night, nurse of the golden stars! beneath thy pall I go to fetch
water from the brook with my pitcher poised upon my head, not indeed
because I am forced to this necessity, but that to the gods I may display
the affronts Aegisthus puts upon me, and to the wide firmament pour out
my lamentation for my sire. For my own mother, the baleful daughter
of Tyndareus, hath cast me forth from her house to gratify her lord; for
since she hath borne other children to Aegisthus she puts me and Orestes
on one side at home.

PEASANT

Oh! why, poor maiden, dost thou toil so hard on my behalf, thou that
aforetime wert reared so daintily? why canst thou not forego thy labour,
as I bid thee?

ELECTRA

As a god's I count thy kindness to me, for in my distress thou hast
never made a mock at me. 'Tis rare fortune when mortals find such healing balm for their cruel wounds as 'tis my lot to find in thee. Wherefore
I ought, though thou forbid me, to lighten thy labours, as far as my
strength allows, and share all burdens with thee to ease thy load. Thou
hast enough to do abroad; 'tis only right that I should keep thy house in
order. For when the toiler cometh to his home from the field, it is pleasant
to find all comfortable in the house.

PEASANT

If such thy pleasure, go thy way; for, after all, the spring is no great
distance from my house. And at break of day I will drive my steers to my
glebe and sow my crop. For no idler, though he has the gods' names ever
on his lips, can gather a livelihood without hard work.

(ELECTRA *and the* PEASANT *go out. A moment later* ORESTES *and* PYLADES
   enter.)

ORESTES

Ah! Pylades, I put thee first 'mongst men for thy love, thy loyalty and
friendliness to me; for thou alone of all my friends wouldst still honour
poor Orestes, in spite of the grievous plight whereto I am reduced by
Aegisthus, who with my accursed mother's aid slew my sire. I am come
from Apollo's mystic shrine to the soil of Argos, without the knowledge
of any, to avenge my father's death upon his murderers. Last night I
went unto his tomb and wept thereon, cutting off my hair as an offering
and pouring o'er the grave the blood of a sheep for sacrifice, unmarked by
those who lord it o'er this land. And now though I enter not the walled
town, yet by coming to the borders of the land I combine two objects; I
can escape to another country if any spy me out and recognize me, and at
the same time seek my sister, for I am told she is a maid no longer but is
married and living here, that I may meet her, and, after enlisting her aid
in the deed of blood, learn for certain what is happening in the town.
Let us now, since dawn is uplifting her radiant eye, step aside from this
path. For maybe some labouring man or serving maid will come in sight,
of whom we may inquire whether it is here that my sister hath her home.
Lo! yonder I see a servant bearing a full pitcher of water on her shaven
head; let us sit down and make inquiry of this bond-maid, if haply we
may glean some tidings of the matter which brought us hither, Pylades.
   (*They retire a little, as* ELECTRA *returns from the spring.*)

ELECTRA (*chanting*)

strophe 1

Bestir thy lagging feet, 'tis high time; on, on o'er thy path of
tears! ah misery! I am Agamemnon's daughter, she whom Clytemnestra, hateful child of Tyndareus, bare; hapless Electra is the name
my countrymen call me. Ah me! for my cruel lot, my hateful existence! O my father Agamemnon! in Hades art thou laid, butchered
by thy wife and Aegisthus. Come, raise with me that dirge once more;
uplift the woful strain that brings relief.

antistrophe 1

On, on o'er thy path of tears! ah misery! And thou, poor brother,
in what city and house art thou a slave, leaving thy suffering sister
behind in the halls of our fathers to drain the cup of bitterness?
Oh! come, great Zeus, to set me free from this life of sorrow, and to
avenge my sire in the blood of his foes, bringing the wanderer home
to Argos.

strophe 2

Take this pitcher from my head, put it down, that I may wake
betimes, while it is yet night, my lamentation for my sire, my doleful
chant, my dirge of death, for thee, my father in thy grave, which
day by day I do rehearse, rending my skin with my nails, and smiting on my shaven head in mourning for thy death. Woe, woe! rend
the cheek; like a swan with clear loud note beside the brimming
river calling to its parent dear that lies a-dying in the meshes of the
crafty net, so I bewail thee, my hapless sire,

antistrophe 2

After that last fatal bath of thine laid out most piteously in death.
Oh! the horror of that axe which hacked thee so cruelly, my sire! oh!
the bitter thought that prompted thy return from Troy! With no garlands or victor's crowns did thy wife welcome thee, but with his two-
edged sword she made thee the sad sport of Aegisthus and kept her
treacherous paramour.

(*The* CHORUS OF ARGIVE COUNTRY-WOMEN *enter. The following
lines between* ELECTRA *and the* CHORUS *are sung responsively.*)

CHORUS

strophe

O Electra, daughter of Agamemnon, to thy rustic cot I come, for
a messenger hath arrived, a highlander from Mycenae, one who lives
on milk, announcing that the Argives are proclaiming a sacrifice for
the third day from now, and all our maidens are to go to Hera's
temple.

ELECTRA

Kind friends, my heart is not set on festivity, nor do necklaces of
gold cause any flutter in my sorrowing bosom, nor will I stand up
with the maidens of Argos to beat my foot in the mazy dance. Tears
have been my meat day and night; ah misery! See my unkempt hair,
my tattered dress; are they fit for a princess, a daughter of Agamemnon, or for Troy which once thought of my father as its captor?

CHORUS

antistrophe

Mighty is the goddess; so come, and borrow of me broidered robes
for apparel and jewels of gold that add a further grace to beauty's
charms. Dost think to triumph o'er thy foes by tears, if thou honour
not the gods? 'Tis not by lamentation but by pious prayers to heaven
that thou, my daughter, wilt make fortune smile on thee.

ELECTRA

No god hearkens to the voice of lost Electra, or heeds the sacrifices offered by my father long ago. Ah woe for the dead! woe for the living wanderer, who dwelleth in some foreign land, an outcast and a vagabond at a menial board, sprung though he is of a famous sire! Myself, too, in a poor man's hut do dwell, wasting my soul with grief, an exile from my father's halls, here by the scarred hill-side; while my mother is wedded to a new husband in a marriage stained by blood.

LEADER OF THE CHORUS

Many a woe to Hellas and thy house did Helen, thy mother's sister, cause.

ELECTRA (*catching sight of* ORESTES *and* PYLADES)

Ha! Friends, I break off my lament; yonder are strangers just leaving the place of ambush where they were couching, and making for the house. We must seek to escape the villains by flying, thou along the path and I into my cottage.

ORESTES

Stay, poor maid; fear no violence from me.

ELECTRA

O Phoebus Apollo! I beseech thee spare my life.

ORESTES

Give me the lives of others more my foes than thou!

ELECTRA

Begone! touch me not! thou hast no right to.

ORESTES

There is none I have a better right to touch.

ELECTRA

How is it then thou waylayest me, sword in hand, near my house?

ORESTES

Wait and hear, and thou wilt soon agree with me

ELECTRA

Here I stand; I am in thy power in any case, since thou art the stronger

ORESTES

I am come to thee with news of thy brother.

ELECTRA

O best of friends! is he alive or dead?

ORESTES

Alive; I would fain give thee my good news first.

ELECTRA

God bless thee! in return for thy welcome tidings.

ORESTES

I am prepared to share that blessing between us.

ELECTRA

In what land is my poor brother spending his dreary exile?

ORESTES

His ruined life does not conform to the customs of any one city.

ELECTRA

Surely he does not want for daily bread?

ORESTES

Bread he has, but an exile is a helpless man at best.

ELECTRA

What is this message thou hast brought from him?

ORESTES

He asks, "Art thou alive? and if so, How art thou faring?"

ELECTRA

Well, first thou seest how haggard I am grown.

ORESTES

So wasted with sorrow that I weep for thee.

ELECTRA

Next mark my head, shorn and shaven like a Scythian's.

ORESTES

Thy brother's fate and father's death no doubt disturb thee.

ELECTRA

Yes, alas! for what have I more dear than these?

ORESTES

Ah! and what dost thou suppose is dearer to thy brother?

ELECTRA

He is far away, not here to show his love to me.

ORESTES

Wherefore art thou living here far from the city?

ELECTRA

I am wedded, sir; a fatal match!

ORESTES

Alas! for thy brother; I pity him. Is thy husband of Mycenae?

ELECTRA

He is not the man to whom my father ever thought of betrothing me.

ORESTES

Tell me all, that I may report it to thy brother.

ELECTRA

I live apart from my husband in this house.

ORESTES

The only fit inmate would be a hind or herd.

ELECTRA

Poor he is, yet he displays a generous consideration for me.

ORESTES

Why, what is this consideration that attaches to thy husband?

ELECTRA

He has never presumed to claim from me a husband's rights.

ORESTES

Is he under a vow of chastity? or does he disdain thee?

ELECTRA

He thought he had no right to flout my ancestry.

ORESTES

How was it he was not overjoyed at winning such a bride?

ELECTRA

He does not recognize the right of him who disposed of my hand.

ORESTES

I understand; he was afraid of the vengeance of Orestes hereafter.

ELECTRA

There was that fear, but he was a virtuous man as well.

ORESTES

Ah! a noble nature this! He deserves kind treatment.

ELECTRA

Yes, if ever the wanderer return.

ORESTES

But did thy own mother give in to this?

ELECTRA

'Tis her husband, not her children that a woman loves, sir stranger.

ORESTES

Wherefore did Aegisthus put this affront on thee?

ELECTRA

His design in giving me to such a husband was to weaken my offspring

ORESTES

To prevent thee bearing sons, I suppose, who should punish him?

ELECTRA

That was his plan; God grant I may avenge me on him for it!

ORESTES

Does thy mother's husband know that thou art yet a maid?

ELECTRA

He does not; our silence robs him of that knowledge.

ORESTES

Are these women friends of thine, who overhear our talk?

ELECTRA

They are, and they will keep our conversation perfectly secret.

ORESTES

What could Orestes do in this matter, if he *did* return?

ELECTRA

Canst thou ask? Shame on thee for that! Is not this the time for action?

ORESTES

But suppose he comes, how could he slay his father's murderers?

ELECTRA

By boldly meting out the same fate that his father had meted out to him by his foes.

ORESTES

Wouldst thou be brave enough to help him slay his mother?

ELECTRA

Aye, with the self-same axe that drank my father's blood.

ORESTES

Am I to tell him this, and that thy purpose firmly holds?

ELECTRA

Once I have shed my mother's blood o'er his, then welcome death!

ORESTES

Ah! would Orestes were standing near to hear that!

ELECTRA

I should not know him, sir, if I saw him.

ORESTES

No wonder; you were both children when you parted.

ELECTRA

There is only one of my friends would recognize him.

ORESTES

The man maybe who is said to have snatched him away from being murdered?

ELECTRA

Yes, the old servant who tended my father's childhood long ago.

ORESTES

Did thy father's corpse obtain burial?

ELECTRA

Such burial as it was, after his body had been flung forth from the palace.

ORESTES

O God! how awful is thy story! Yes, there *is* a feeling, arising even from another's distress, that wrings the human heart. Say on, that when I know the loveless tale, which yet I needs must hear, I may carry it to thy brother. For pity, though it has no place in ignorant natures, is inborn in

the wise; still it may cause trouble to find excessive cleverness amongst
the wise.

LEADER

I too am stirred by the same desire as the stranger. For dwelling so
far from the city I know nothing of its ills, and I should like to hear
about them now myself.

ELECTRA

I will tell you, if I may; and surely I may tell a friend about my own
and my father's grievous misfortunes. Now since thou movest me to
speak, I entreat thee, sir, tell Orestes of our sorrows; first, describe the
dress I wear, the load of squalor that oppresses me, the hovel I inhabit
after my royal home; tell him how hard I have to work at weaving
clothes myself or else go barely clad and do without; how I carry home
on my head water from the brook; no part have I in holy festival, no
place amid the dance; a maiden still I turn from married dames and
from Castor too, to whom they betrothed me before he joined the heavenly host, for I was his kinswoman. Meantime my mother, 'mid the spoils
of Troy, is seated on her throne, and at her foot-stool slaves from Asia
stand and wait, captives of my father's spear, whose Trojan robes are
fastened with brooches of gold. And there on the wall my father's blood
still leaves a deep dark stain, while his murderer mounts the dead man's
car and fareth forth, proudly grasping in his blood-stained hands the
sceptre with which Agamemnon would marshal the sons of Hellas. Dishonoured lies his grave; naught as yet hath it received of drink out-
poured or myrtle-spray, but bare of ornament his tomb is left. Yea, and
'tis said that noble hero who is wedded to my mother, in his drunken
fits, doth leap upon the grave, and pelt with stones my father's monument, boldly gibing at us on this wise, "Where is thy son Orestes? Is he
ever coming in his glory to defend thy tomb?" Thus is Orestes flouted
behind his back. Oh! tell him this, kind sir, I pray thee. And there be
many calling him to come,—I am but their mouthpiece,—these suppliant
hands, this tongue, my broken heart, my shaven head, and his own father
too. For 'tis shameful that the sire should have destroyed Troy's race and
the son yet prove too weak to pit himself against one foe unto the death,
albeit he has youth and better blood as well.

LEADER

Lo! here is thy husband hurrying homeward, his labour done.

PEASANT

(*entering and catching sight of strangers talking to* ELECTRA)
Ha! who are these strangers I see at my door? And why are they come

hither to my rustic gate? can they want my help? for 'tis unseemly for a woman to stand talking with young men.

ELECTRA

Dear husband, be not suspicious of me. For thou shalt hear the truth; these strangers have come to bring me news of Orestes. Good sirs, pardon him those words.

PEASANT

What say they? is that hero yet alive and in the light of day?

ELECTRA

He is; at least they say so, and I believe them.

PEASANT

Surely then he hath some memory of his father and thy wrongs?

ELECTRA

These are things to hope for; a man in exile is helpless.

PEASANT

What message have they brought from Orestes?

ELECTRA

He sent them to spy out my evil case.

PEASANT

Well, they only see a part of it, though maybe thou art telling them the rest.

ELECTRA

They know all; there is nothing further they need ask.

PEASANT

Long ere this then shouldst thou have thrown open our doors to them. Enter, sirs; for in return for your good tidings, shall ye find such cheer as my house affords. Ho! servants, take their baggage within; make no excuses, for ye are friends sent by one I love; and poor though I am, yet will I never show meanness in my habits.

ORESTES

'Fore heaven! is this the man who is helping thee to frustrate thy marriage, because he will not shame Orestes?

ELECTRA

This is he whom they call my husband, woe is me!

ORESTES

Ah! there is no sure mark to recognize a man's worth; for human nature
hath in it an element of confusion. For I have seen ere now the son of a
noble sire prove himself a worthless knave, and virtuous children sprung
from evil parents; likewise dearth in a rich man's spirit, and in a poor
man's frame a mighty soul. By what standard then shall we rightly judge
these things? By wealth? An evil test to use. By poverty then? Nay,
poverty suffers from this, that it teaches a man to play the villain from
necessity. To martial prowess must I turn? But who could pronounce who
is the valiant man merely from the look of his spear? Better is it to leave
these matters to themselves without troubling. For here is a man of no
account in Argos, with no family reputation to boast, one of the common
herd, proved a very hero. A truce to your folly! ye self-deceivers, swollen with idle fancies; learn to judge men by their converse, and by their
habits decide who are noble. Such are they who rule aright both states
and families; while those forms of flesh, devoid of intellect, are but figure-
heads in the market-place. The strong arm, again, no more than the weak
awaits the battle-shock, for this depends on natural courage. Well! absent
or present, Agamemnon's son, whose business brings us here, deserves
this of us, so let us accept a lodging in this house. (*Calling to his servants*)
Ho! sirrahs, go within. A humble host, who does his best, in preference
to a wealthy man for me! And so I thankfully accept this peasant's prof-
fered welcome, though I could have preferred that thy brother were conducting me to share his fortune in his halls. Maybe he yet will come; for
the oracles of Loxias are sure, but to man's divining "Farewell" say I.
    (ORESTES, PYLADES *and their attendants go into the hut.*)

LEADER

Electra, I feel a warmer glow of joy suffuse my heart than ever heretofore; perchance our fortune, moving on at last, will find a happy resting-place.

ELECTRA

O reckless man, why didst thou welcome strangers like these, so far
beyond thy station, knowing the poverty of thy house?

PEASANT

Why? if they are really as noble as they seem, surely they will be
equally content with rich or humble fare.

ELECTRA

Well, since thou hast made this error, poor man as thou art, go to my
father's kind old foster-sire; on the bank of the river Tanaus, the bound-
ary 'twixt Argos and the land of Sparta, he tends his flocks, an outcast

from the city; bid him come hither to our house and make some provision for the strangers' entertainment. Glad will he be, and will offer thanks to heaven to hear that the child, whom once he saved, is yet alive. I shall get nothing from my mother from my ancestral halls; for we should rue our message, were she to learn, unnatural wretch! that Orestes liveth.

PEASANT

I will take this message to the old man, if it seem good to thee; but get thee in at once and there make ready. A woman, when she chooses, can find dainties in plenty to garnish a feast. Besides, there is quite enough in the house to satisfy them with food for one day at least. 'Tis in such cases, when I come to muse thereon, that I discern the mighty power of wealth, whether to give to strangers, or to expend in curing the body when it falls sick; but our daily food is a small matter; for all of us, rich as well as poor, are in like case, as soon as we are satisfied.

(*The* PEASANT *departs as* ELECTRA *enters the hut.*)

CHORUS (*singing*)

strophe 1

Ye famous ships, that on a day were brought to land at Troy by those countless oars, what time ye led the Nereids' dance, where the dolphin music-loving rolled and gambolled round your dusky prows, escorting Achilles, nimble son of Thetis, when he went with Agamemnon to the banks of Trojan Simois:

antistrophe 1

When Nereids left Euboea's strand, bringing from Hephaestus' golden forge the harness he had fashioned for that warrior's use; him long they sought o'er Pelion and Ossa's spurs, ranging the sacred glens and the peaks of Nymphaea, where his knightly sire was training up a light for Hellas, even the sea-born son of Thetis, a warrior swift to help the sons of Atreus.

strophe 2

One that came from Ilium, and set foot in the haven of Nauplia, told me that on the circle of thy far-famed targe, O son of Thetis, was wrought this blazon, a terror to the Phrygians; on the rim of the buckler Perseus with winged sandals, was bearing in his hand across the main the Gorgon's head, just severed by the aid of Hermes, the messenger of Zeus, that rural god whom Maia bore;

antistrophe 2

While in the centre of the shield the sun's bright orb flashed light on the backs of his winged coursers; there too was the heavenly choir

of stars, Pleiades and Hyades, to dazzle Hector's eyes and make him
flee; and upon his gold-forged helm were sphinxes, bearing in their
talons the prey of which the minstrels sing; on his breast-plate was a
lioness breathing flame, her eye upon Peirene's steed,[1] in eagerness to
rend it.

There too in murderous fray four-footed steeds were prancing,
while o'er their backs uprose dark clouds of dust. But he who led
these warriors stout, was slain by wedding thee, malignant child of
Tyndareus! Wherefore shall the gods of heaven one day send thee to
thy doom, and I shall yet live to see the sword at thy throat, drinking
its crimson tide.

(*The* OLD MAN, *the former servant of Agamemnon, enters.* ELECTRA
presently appears at the door of the hut.)

OLD MAN

Where is the young princess, my mistress, Agamemnon's daughter,
whom I nursed in days gone by? Oh! how steep is the approach to this
house, a hard climb for these old wasted feet of mine! Still, to reach such
friends as these, I must drag my bent old back and tottering knees up it.
Ah, daughter!—for I see thee now at thy door,—lo! I have brought thee
this tender lamb from my own flock, having taken it from its dam, with
garlands too and cheese straight from the press, and this flask of choice
old wine with fragrant bouquet; 'tis small perhaps, but pour a cup thereof
into some weaker drink, and it is a luscious draught. Let some one carry
these gifts into the house for the guests; for I would fain wipe from my
eyes the rising tears on this tattered cloak.

ELECTRA

Why stands the tear-drop in thine eye, old friend? Is it that my sorrows have been recalled to thee after an interval? or art thou bewailing
the sad exile of Orestes, and my father's fate, whom thou didst once
fondle in thy arms, in vain, alas! for thee and for thy friends?

OLD MAN

Ah yes! in vain; but still I could not bear to leave him thus; and so
I added this to my journey that I sought his grave, and, falling thereupon,
wept o'er its desolation; then did I open the wine-skin, my gift to thy
guests, and poured a libation, and set myrtle-sprigs round the tomb. And
lo! upon the grave itself I saw a black ram had been offered, and there
was blood, not long poured forth, and severed locks of auburn hair. Much
I wondered, my daughter, who had dared approach the tomb; certainly
'twas no Argive. Nay, thy brother may perchance have come by stealth,

and going thither have done honour to his father's wretched grave. Look at the hair, compare it with thy own, to see if the colour of these cut locks is the same; for children in whose veins runs the same father's blood have a close resemblance in many features.

ELECTRA

Old sir, thy words are unworthy of a wise man, if thou thinkest my own brave brother would have come to this land by stealth for fear of Aegisthus. In the next place, how should our hair correspond? His is the hair of a gallant youth trained up in manly sports, mine a woman's curled and combed; nay, that is a hopeless clue. Besides, thou couldst find many, whose hair is of the same colour, albeit not sprung from the same blood. No, maybe 'twas some stranger cut off his hair in pity at his tomb, or one that came to spy this land privily.

OLD MAN

Put thy foot in the print of his shoe and mark whether it correspond with thine, my child.

ELECTRA

How should the foot make any impression on stony ground? and if it did, the foot of brother and sister would not be the same in size, for a man's is the larger.

OLD MAN

Hast thou no mark, in case thy brother *should* come, whereby to recognize the weaving of thy loom, the robe wherein I snatched him from death that day?

ELECTRA

Dost thou forget I was still a babe when Orestes left the country? and even if I had woven him a robe, how should he, a mere child then, be wearing the same now, unless our clothes and bodies grow together?

OLD MAN

Where are these guests? I fain would question them face to face about thy brother.
(*As he speaks,* ORESTES *and* PYLADES *come out of the hut.*)

ELECTRA

There they are, in haste to leave the house.

OLD MAN

Well born, it seems, but that may be a sham; for there be plenty such prove knaves. Still I give them greeting.

ORESTES

All hail, father! To which of thy friends, Electra, does this old relic of mortality belong?

ELECTRA

This is he who nursed my sire, sir stranger.

ORESTES

What! do I behold him who removed thy brother out of harm's way?

ELECTRA

Behold the man who saved his life; if, that is, he liveth still.

ORESTES

Ha! why does he look so hard at me, as if he were examining the bright device on silver coin? Is he finding in me a likeness to some other?

ELECTRA

Maybe he is glad to see in thee a companion of Orestes.

ORESTES

A man I love full well. But why is he walking round me?

ELECTRA

I, too, am watching his movements with amaze, sir stranger.

OLD MAN

My honoured mistress, my daughter Electra, return thanks to heaven,—

ELECTRA

For past or present favours? which?

OLD MAN

That thou hast found a treasured prize, which God is now revealing.

ELECTRA

Hear me invoke the gods. But what dost thou mean, old man?

OLD MAN

Behold before thee, my child, thy nearest and dearest.

ELECTRA

I have long feared thou wert not in thy sound senses

OLD MAN

Not in my sound senses, because I see thy brother?

ELECTRA

What mean'st thou, aged friend, by these astounding words?

OLD MAN

That I see Orestes, Agamemnon's son, before me.

ELECTRA

What mark dost see that I can trust?

OLD MAN

A scar along his brow, where he fell and cut himself one day in his father's home when chasing a fawn with thee.

ELECTRA

Is it possible? True; I see the mark of the fall.

OLD MAN

Dost hesitate then to embrace thy own dear brother?

ELECTRA

No! not any longer, old friend; for my soul is convinced by the tokens thou showest. O my brother, thou art come at last, and I embrace thee, little as I ever thought to.

ORESTES

And thee to my bosom at last I press.

ELECTRA

I never thought that it would happen.

ORESTES

All hope in me was also dead.

ELECTRA

Art thou really he?

ORESTES

Aye, thy one and only champion, if I can but safely draw to shore the cast I mean to throw; and I feel sure I shall; else must we cease to believe in gods, if wrong is to triumph o'er right.

CHORUS (*singing*)

At last, at last appears thy radiant dawn, O happy day! and as a beacon to the city hast thou revealed the wanderer, who, long ago, poor boy! was exiled from his father's halls. Now, lady, comes our turn for victory, ushered in by some god. Raise hand and voice in prayer, beseech the gods that good fortune may attend thy brother's entry to the city.

ORESTES

Enough! sweet though the rapture of this greeting be, I must wait and return it hereafter. Do thou, old friend so timely met, tell me how I am to avenge me on my father's murderer, and on my mother, the partner in his guilty marriage. Have I still in Argos any band of kindly friends? or am I, like my fortunes, bankrupt altogether? With whom am I to league myself? by night or day shall I advance? point out a road for me to take against these foes of mine.

OLD MAN

My son, thou hast no friend now in thy hour of adversity. No! that is a piece of rare good luck, to find another share thy fortunes alike for better and for worse. Thou art of every friend completely reft, all hope is gone from thee; be sure of what I tell thee; on thy own arm and fortune art thou wholly thrown to win thy father's home and thy city.

ORESTES

What must I do to compass this result?

OLD MAN

Slay Thyestes' son and thy mother.

ORESTES

I came to win that victor's crown, but how can I attain it?

OLD MAN

Thou wouldst never achieve it if thou didst enter the walls.

ORESTES

Are they manned with guards and armed sentinels?

OLD MAN

Aye truly; for he is afraid of thee, and cannot sleep secure.

ORESTES

Well then, do thou next propose a scheme, old friend.

OLD MAN

Hear me a moment; an idea has just occurred to me.

ORESTES

May thy counsel prove good, and my perception keen!

OLD MAN

I saw Aegisthus, as I was slowly pacing hither—

ORESTES

I welcome thy words. Where was he?

OLD MAN

Not far from these fields, at his stables.

ORESTES

What was he doing? I see a gleam of hope after our helplessness.

OLD MAN

I thought he was preparing a feast for the Nymphs.

ORESTES

In return for the bringing up of children or in anticipation of a birth?

OLD MAN

All I know is this, he was preparing to sacrifice oxen.

ORESTES

How many were with him? or was he alone with his servants?

OLD MAN

There was no Argive there; only a band of his own followers.

ORESTES

Is it possible that any of them will recognize me, old man?

OLD MAN

They are only servants, and they have never even seen thee.

ORESTES

Will they support me, if I prevail?

OLD MAN

Yes, that is the way of slaves, luckily for thee.

ORESTES

On what pretext can I approach him?

OLD MAN

Go to some place where he will see thee as he sacrifices.

ORESTES

His estate is close to the road then, I suppose.

OLD MAN

Yes, and when he sees thee there, he will invite thee to the feast.

ORESTES

So help me God! He shall rue his invitation.

OLD MAN

After that, form thy own plan according to circumstances.

ORESTES

Good advice! But my mother, where is she?

OLD MAN

At Argos; but she will yet join her husband for the feast.

ORESTES

Why did she not come forth with him?

OLD MAN

From fear of the citizens' reproach she stayed behind.

ORESTES

I understand; she knows that the city suspects her.

OLD MAN

Just so; her wickedness makes her hated.

ORESTES

How shall I slay her and him together?

ELECTRA

Mine be the preparation of my mother's slaying!

ORESTES

Well, as for the other, fortune will favour us.

ELECTRA

Our old friend here must help us both.

OLD MAN

Aye, that will I; but wnat is thy scheme for slaying thy mother?

ELECTRA

Go, old man, and tell Clytemnestra from me that I have given birth to a son.

OLD MAN

Some time ago, or quite recently?

ELECTRA

Ten days ago, which are the davs of my purification.

OLD MAN
Suppose it done; but how doth this help towards slaying thy mother?

ELECTRA
She will come, when she hears of my confinement.

OLD MAN
What! dost think she cares aught for thee, my child?

ELECTRA
Oh yes! she will weep no doubt over my child's low rank.

OLD MAN
Perhaps she may; but go back again to the point.

ELECTRA
Her death is certain, if she comes.

OLD MAN
In that case, let her come right up to the door of the house.

ELECTRA
Why then it were a little thing to turn her steps into the road to Hades' halls.

OLD MAN
Oh! to see this one day, then die!

ELECTRA
First of all, old friend, act as my brother's guide.

OLD MAN
To the place where Aegisthus is now sacrificing to the gods?

ELECTRA
Then go, find my mother and give her my message.

OLD MAN
Aye, that I will, so that she shall think the very words are thine.

ELECTRA (*to* ORESTES)
Thy work begins at once; thou hast drawn the first lot in the tragedy.

ORESTES
I will go, if some one will show me the way.

OLD MAN
I will myself conduct thee nothing loth.

ORESTES

O Zeus, god of my fathers, vanquisher of my foes, have pity on us, for a piteous lot has ours been.

ELECTRA

Oh! have pity on thy own descendants.

ORESTES

O Hera, mistress of Mycenae's altars, grant us the victory, if we are asking what is right.

ELECTRA

Yes, grant us vengeance on them for our father's death.

ORESTES

Thou too, my father, sent to the land of shades by wicked hands, and Earth, the queen of all, to whom I spread my suppliant palms, up and champion thy dear children. Come with all the dead to aid, all they who helped thee break the Phrygians' power, and all who hate ungodly crime. Dost hear me, father, victim of my mother's rage?

ELECTRA

Sure am I he heareth all; but 'tis time to part. For this cause too I bid thee strike Aegisthus down, because, if thou fall in the struggle and perish, I also die; no longer number me amongst the living; for I will stab myself with a two-edged sword. And now will I go indoors and make all ready there, for, if there come good news from thee, my house shall ring with women's cries of joy; but, if thou art slain, a different scene must then ensue. These are my instructions to thee.

ORESTES

I know my lesson well.

> (ORESTES, PYLADES, *the* OLD MAN, *and attendants, depart.*)

ELECTRA

Then show thyself a man. And you, my friends, signal to me by cries the certain issue of this fray. Myself will keep the sword ready in my grasp, for I will never accept defeat, and yield my body to my enemies to insult.

> (ELECTRA *goes into the hut.*)

CHORUS (*singing*)

strophe 1

Still the story [2] finds a place in time-honoured legends, how on a day Pan, the steward of husbandry, came breathing dulcet music on his jointed pipe, and brought with him from its tender dam on Argive hills, a beauteous lamb with fleece of gold; then stood a herald high upon the rock and cried aloud, "Away to the place of assembly, ye folk of Mycenae! to behold the strange and awful sight vouchsafed to our blest rulers." Anon the dancers did obeisance to the family of Atreus;

antistrophe 1

The altar-steps of beaten gold were draped; and through that Argive town the altars blazed with fire; sweetly rose the lute's clear note, the handmaid of the Muse's song; and ballads fair were written on the golden lamb, saying that Thyestes had the luck; for he won the guilty love of the wife of Atreus, and carried off to his house the strange creature, and then coming before the assembled folk he declared to them that he had in his house that hornèd beast with fleece of gold.

strophe 2

In the self-same hour it was that Zeus changed the radiant courses of the stars, the light of the sun, and the joyous face of dawn, and drave his car athwart the western sky with fervent heat from heaven's fires, while northward fled the rain-clouds, and Ammon's strand grew parched and faint and void of dew, when it was robbed of heaven's genial showers.

antistrophe 2

'Tis said, though I can scarce believe it, the sun turned round his glowing throne of gold, to vex the sons of men by this change because of the quarrel amongst them. Still, tales of horror have their use in making men regard the gods; of whom thou hadst no thought, when thou slewest thy husband, thou mother of this noble pair.

LEADER OF THE CHORUS

Hark! my friends, did ye hear that noise, like to the rumbling of an earthquake, or am I the dupe of idle fancy? Hark! hark! once more that wind-borne sound swells loudly on mine ear. Electra! mistress mine! come forth from the house!

ELECTRA (*rushing out*)

What is it, good friends? how goes the day with us?

LEADER

I hear the cries of dying men; no more I know.

ELECTRA

I heard them too, far off, but still distinct.

LEADER

Yes, the sound came stealing from afar, but yet 'twas clear.

ELECTRA

Was it the groan of an Argive, or of my friends?

LEADER

I know not; for the cries are all confused.

ELECTRA

That word of thine is my death-warrant; why do I delay?

LEADER

Stay, till thou learn thy fate for certain.

ELECTRA

No, no; we are vanquished; where are our messengers?

LEADER

They will come in time; to slay a king is no light task.

(*A* MESSENGER *enters in haste.*)

MESSENGER

All hail! ye victors, maidens of Mycenae, to all Orestes' friends his triumph I announce; Aegisthus, the murderer of Agamemnon, lies weltering where he fell; return thanks to heaven.

ELECTRA

Who art thou? What proof dost thou give of this?

MESSENGER

Look at me, dost thou not recognize thy brother's servant?

ELECTRA

O best of friends! 'twas fear that prevented me from recognizing thee; now I know thee well. What sayst thou? Is my father's hateful murderer slain?

MESSENGER

He is; I repeat it since it is thy wish.

LEADER

Ye gods, and Justice, whose eye is on all, at last art thou come.

ELECTRA

I fain would learn the way and means my brother took to slay Thyestes'
son.

MESSENGER

After we had set out from this house, we struck into the broad high-
road, and came to the place where was the far-famed King of Mycenae.
Now he was walking in a garden well-watered, culling a wreath of tender
myrtle-sprays for his head, and when he saw us, he called out, "All hail!
strangers; who are ye? whence come ye? from what country?" To him
Orestes answered, "We are from Thessaly, on our way to Alpheus' banks
to sacrifice to Olympian Zeus." When Aegisthus heard that, he said, "Ye
must be my guests to-day, and share the feast, for I am even now sacrificing to the Nymphs; and by rising with tomorrow's light ye will be just
as far upon your journey; now let us go within." Therewith he caught us
by the hand and led us by the way; refuse we could not; and when we
were come to the house, he gave command: "Bring water for my guests
to wash forthwith, that they may stand around the altar near the laver."
But Orestes answered, " 'Twas but now we purified ourselves and washed
us clean in water from the river. So if we strangers are to join your citizens
in sacrifice, we are ready, King Aegisthus, and will not refuse." So ended
they their private conference. Meantime the servants, that composed
their master's bodyguard, laid aside their weapons, and one and all were
busied at their tasks. Some brought the bowl to catch the blood, others
took up baskets, while others kindled fire and set cauldrons round about
the altars, and the whole house rang. Then did thy mother's husband take
the barley for sprinkling, and began casting it upon the hearth with these
words, "Ye Nymphs, who dwell among the rocks, grant that I may often
sacrifice with my wife, the daughter of Tyndareus, within my halls, as
happily as now, and ruin seize my foes!" (whereby he meant Orestes and
thyself). But my master, lowering his voice, offered a different prayer,
that he might regain his father's house. Next Aegisthus took from a
basket a long straight knife, and cutting off some of the calf's hair, laid
it with his right hand on the sacred fire, and then cut its throat when the
servants had lifted it upon their shoulders, and thus addressed thy
brother; "Men declare that amongst the Thessalians this is counted honourable, to cut up a bull neatly and to manage steeds. So take the knife,
sir stranger, and show us if rumour speaks true about the Thessalians."
Thereon Orestes seized the Dorian knife of tempered steel and cast from
his shoulders his graceful buckled robe; then choosing Pylades to help
him in his task, he made the servants withdraw, and catching the calf
by the hoof, proceeded to lay bare its white flesh, with arm outstretched,
and he flayed the hide quicker than a runner ever finishes the two laps

of the horses' race-course; next he laid the belly open, and Aegisthus took the entrails in his hands and carefully examined them. Now the liver had no lobe, while the portal vein leading to the gall-bladder portended a dangerous attack on him who was observing it. Dark grows Aegisthus' brow, but my master asks, "Why so despondent, good sir?" Said he, "I fear treachery from a stranger. Agamemnon's son of all men most I hate, and he hates my house." But Orestes cried, "What! fear treachery from an exile! thou the ruler of the city? Ho! take this Dorian knife away and bring me a Thessalian cleaver, that we by sacrificial feast may learn the will of heaven; let me cleave the breast-bone." And he took the axe and cut it through. Now Aegisthus was examining the entrails, separating them in his hands, and as he was bending down, thy brother rose on tiptoe and smote him on the spine, severing the bones of his back; and his body gave one convulsive shudder from head to foot and writhed in the death-agony. No sooner did his servants see it, than they rushed to arms, a host to fight with two; yet did Pylades and Orestes of their valiancy meet them with brandished spears. Then cried Orestes, "I am no foe that come against this city and my own servants, but I have avenged me on the murderer of my sire, I, ill-starred Orestes. Slay me not, my father's former thralls!" They, when they heard him speak, restrained their spears, and an old man, who had been in the family many a long year, recognized him. Forthwith they crown thy brother with a wreath, and utter shouts of joy. And lo! he is coming to show thee the head, not the Gorgon's, but the head of thy hated foe Aegisthus; his death to-day has paid in blood a bitter debt of blood.

CHORUS (*singing*)
  Dear mistress, now with step as light as fawn join in the dance;
lift high the nimble foot and be glad. Victory crowns thy brother;
he hath won a fairer wreath than ever victor gained beside the
streams of Alpheus; so raise a fair hymn to victory, the while I dance.

ELECTRA
O light of day! O bright careering sun! O earth! and night erewhile
my only day; now may I open my eyes in freedom, for Aegisthus is dead,
my father's murderer. Come friends, let me bring out whate'er my house
contains to deck his head and wreath with crowns my conquering brother's
brow.

CHORUS (*singing*)
  Bring forth thy garlands for his head, and we will lead the dance
the Muses love. Now shall the royal line, dear to us in days gone by,
resume its sway o'er the realm, having laid low the usurper as he deserves. So let the shout go up, whose notes are those of joy.

(ORESTES *and* PYLADES *enter, followed by attendants who are bearing the body of Aegisthus.*)

ELECTRA

Hail! glorious victor, Orestes, son of a sire who won the day 'neath
Ilium's walls, accept this wreath to bind about the tresses of thy hair.
Not in vain hast thou run thy course unto the goal and reached thy home
again; no! but thou hast slain thy foe, Aegisthus, the murderer of our
father. Thou too, O Pylades, trusty squire, whose training shows thy
father's sterling worth, receive a garland from my hand, for thou no less
than he hast a share in this emprise; and so I pray, good luck be thine for
ever!

ORESTES

First recognize the gods, Electra, as being the authors of our fortune,
and then praise me their minister and fate's. Yea, I come from having
slain Aegisthus in very deed, no mere pretence; and to make thee the
more certain of this, I am bringing thee his corpse, which, if thou wilt,
expose for beasts to rend, or set it upon a stake for birds, the children of
the air, to prey upon; for now is he thy slave, once called thy lord and
master.

ELECTRA

I am ashamed to utter my wishes.

ORESTES

What is it? speak out, for thou art through the gates of fear.

ELECTRA

I am ashamed to flout the dead. for fear some spite assail me.

ORESTES

No one would blame thee for this.

ELECTRA

Our folk are hard to please, and love to blame.

ORESTES

Speak all thy mind, sister; for we entered on this feud with him on
terms admitting not of truce.

ELECTRA

Enough! (*Turning to the corpse of Aegisthus*) With which of thy iniquities shall I begin my recital? With which shall I end it? To which allot
a middle place? And yet I never ceased, as each day dawned, to rehearse
the story I would tell thee to thy face, if ever I were freed from my old

terrors; and now I am; so I will pay thee back with the abuse I fain had uttered to thee when alive. Thou wert my ruin, making me and my brother orphans, though we had never injured thee, and thou didst make a shameful marriage with my mother, having slain her lord who led the host of Hellas, though thyself didst never go to Troy. Such was thy folly, thou didst never dream that my mother would prove thy curse when thou didst marry her, though thou wert wronging my father's honour. Know this; whoso defiles his neighbour's wife, and afterward is forced to take her to himself, is a wretched wight, if he supposes she will be chaste as his wife, though she sinned against her former lord. Thine was a life most miserable, though thou didst pretend 'twas otherwise; well thou knewest how guilty thy marriage was, and my mother knew she had a villain for husband. Sinners both ye took each other's lot, she thy fortune, thou her curse. While everywhere in Argos thou wouldst hear such phrases as, "that woman's husband," never "that man's wife." Yet 'tis shameful for the wife and not the man to rule the house; wherefore I loathe those children, who are called in the city not the sons of the man, their father, but of their mother. For if a man makes a great match above his rank, there is no talk of the husband but only of the wife. Herein lay thy grievous error, due to ignorance; thou thoughtest thyself some one, relying on thy wealth, but this is naught save to stay with us a space. 'Tis nature that stands fast, not wealth. For it, if it abide unchanged, exalts man's horn; but riches dishonestly acquired and in the hands of fools, soon take their flight, their blossom quickly shed. As for thy sins with women, I pass them by, 'tis not for maiden's lips to mention them, but I will shrewdly hint thereat. And then thy arrogance! because forsooth thou hadst a palace and some looks to boast. May I never have a husband with a girl's face, but one that bears him like a man! For the children of these latter cling to a life of arms, while those, who are so fair to see, do only serve to grace the dance. Away from me! (*Spurning the corpse with her foot*) Time has shown thy villainy, little as thou reckest of the forfeit thou hast paid for it. Let none suppose, though he have run the first stage of his course with joy, that he will get the better of Justice, till he have reached the goal and ended his career.

LEADER OF THE CHORUS
Terrible alike his crime and your revenge; for mighty is the power of justice.

ORESTES
'Tis well. Carry his body within the house and hide it, sirrahs, that, when my mother comes, she may not see his corpse before she is smitten herself.

(PYLADES *and the attendants take the body into the hut.*)

ELECTRA

Hold! let us strike out another scheme.

ORESTES

How now? Are those allies from Mycenae whom I see?

ELECTRA

No, 'tis my mother, that bare me.

ORESTES

Full into the net she is rushing, oh, bravely!

ELECTRA

See how proudly she rides in her chariot and fine robes!

ORESTES

What must we do to our mother? Slay her?

ELECTRA

What! has pity seized thee at sight of her?

ORESTES

O God! how can I slay her that bare and suckled me?

ELECTRA

Slay her as she slew thy father and mine.

ORESTES

O Phoebus, how foolish was thy oracle—

ELECTRA

Where Apollo errs, who shall be wise?

ORESTES

In bidding me commit this crime—my mother's murder!

ELECTRA

How canst thou be hurt by avenging thy father?

ORESTES

Though pure before, I now shall carry into exile the stain of a mother's blood.

ELECTRA

Still, if thou avenge not thy father, thou wilt fail in thy duty.

ORESTES

And if I slay my mother, I must pay the penalty to her.

ELECTRA

And so must thou to him, if thou resign the avenging of our father.

ORESTES

Surely it was a fiend in the likeness of the god that ordered this!

ELECTRA

Seated on the holy tripod? I think not so.

ORESTES

I cannot believe this oracle was meant.

ELECTRA

Turn not coward! Cast not thy manliness away!

ORESTES

Am I to devise the same crafty scheme for her?

ELECTRA

The self-same death thou didst mete out to her lord Aegisthus.

ORESTES

I will go in; 'tis an awful task I undertake; an awful deed I have to do;
still if it is Heaven's will, be it so; I loathe and yet I love the enterprise.

(*As* ORESTES *withdraws into the hut,* CLYTEMNESTRA *enters in a chariot.
Her attendants are hand-maidens attired in gorgeous apparel.*)

CHORUS (*singing*)

Hail! Queen of Argos, daughter of Tyndareus, sister of those two
noble sons of Zeus,[3] who dwell in the flame-lit firmament amid the
stars, whose guerdon high it is to save the sailor tossing on the sea.
All hail! because of thy wealth and high prosperity, I do thee homage
as I do the blessed gods. Now is the time, great queen, for us to pay
our court unto thy fortunes.

CLYTEMNESTRA

Alight from the car, ye Trojan maids, and take my hand that I may
step down from the chariot. With Trojan spoils the temples of the gods
are decked, but I have obtained these maidens as a special gift from Troy,
in return for my lost daughter, a trifling boon no doubt, but still an ornament to my house.

ELECTRA

And may not I, mother, take that highly-favoured hand of thine? I am
a slave like them, an exile from my father's halls in this miserable abode.

CLYTEMNESTRA

See, my servants are here; trouble not on my account.

ELECTRA

Why, thou didst make me thy prisoner by robbing me of my home; like
these I became a captive when my home was taken, an orphan all forlorn

CLYTEMNESTRA

True; but thy father plotted so wickedly against those of his own kin
whom least of all he should have treated so. Speak I must; albeit, when a
woman gets an evil reputation, there is a feeling of bitterness against all
she says; unfairly indeed in my case, for it were only fair to hate after
learning the circumstances, and seeing if the object deserves it; otherwise,
why hate at all? Now Tyndareus bestowed me on thy father not that I or
any children I might bear should be slain. Yet he went and took my
daughter from our house to the fleet at Aulis, persuading me that Achilles
was to wed her; and there he held her o'er the pyre, and cut Iphigenia's
snowy throat. Had he slain her to save his city from capture, or to benefit
his house, or to preserve his other children, a sacrifice of one for many, I
could have pardoned him. But, as it was, his reasons for murdering my
child were these: the wantonness of Helen and her husband's folly in not
punishing the traitress. Still, wronged as I was, my rage had not burst
forth for this, nor would I have slain my lord, had he not returned to me
with that frenzied maiden and made her his mistress, keeping at once two
brides beneath the same roof. Women maybe are given to folly, I do not
deny it; this granted, when a husband goes astray and sets aside his own
true wife, she fain will follow his example and find another love; and then
in our case hot abuse is heard, while the men, who are to blame for this,
escape without a word. Again, suppose Menelaus had been secretly
snatched from his home, should I have had to kill Orestes to save Menelaus, my sister's husband? How would thy father have endured this?
Was he then to escape death for slaying what was mine, while I was to
suffer at his hands? I slew him, turning, as my only course, to his enemies.
For which of all thy father's friends would have joined me in his murder?
Speak all that is in thy heart, and prove against me with all free speech,
that thy father's death was not deserved.

ELECTRA

Justly urged! but thy justice is not free from shame; for in all things
should every woman of sense yield to her husband. Whoso thinketh otherwise comes not within the scope of what I say. Remember, mother, those
last words of thine, allowing me free utterance before thee.

CLYTEMNESTRA

Daughter, far from refusing it, I grant it again.

ELECTRA

Thou wilt not, when thou hearest, wreak thy vengeance on me?

CLYTEMNESTRA

No, indeed; I shall welcome thy opinion.

ELECTRA

Then will I speak, and this shall be the prelude of my speech: Ah, mother mine! would thou hadst had a better heart; for though thy beauty and Helen's win you praises well deserved, yet are ye akin in nature, a pair of wantons, unworthy of Castor. She was carried off, 'tis true, but her fall was voluntary: and thou hast slain the bravest soul in Hellas, excusing thyself on the ground that thou didst kill a husband to avenge a daughter; the world does not know thee so well as I do, thou who before ever thy daughter's death was decided, yea, soon as thy lord had started from his home, wert combing thy golden tresses at thy mirror. That wife who, when her lord is gone from home, sets to beautifying herself, strike off from virtue's list; for she has no need to carry her beauty abroad, save she is seeking some mischief. Of all the wives in Hellas thou wert the only one I know who wert overjoyed when Troy's star was in the ascendant, while, if it set, thy brow was clouded, since thou hadst no wish that Agamemnon should return from Troy. And yet thou couldst have played a virtuous part to thy own glory. The husband thou hadst was no whit inferior to Aegisthus, for he it was whom Hellas chose to be her captain. And when thy sister Helen wrought that deed of shame, thou couldst have won thyself great glory, for vice is a warning and calls attention to virtue. If, as thou allegest, my father slew thy daughter, what is the wrong I and my brother have done thee? How was it thou didst not bestow on us our father's halls after thy husband's death, instead of bartering them to buy a paramour? Again, thy husband is not exiled for thy son's sake, nor is he slain to avenge my death, although by him this life is quenched twice as much as e'er my sister's was; so if murder is to succeed murder in requital, I and thy son Orestes must slay thee to avenge our father; if that was just, why so is this. Whoso fixes his gaze on wealth or noble birth and weds a wicked woman, is a fool; better is a humble partner in his home, if she be virtuous, than a proud one.

LEADER OF THE CHORUS

Chance rules the marriages of women; some I see turn out well, others ill, amongst mankind.

CLYTEMNESTRA

Daughter, 'twas ever thy nature to love thy father. This too one finds; some sons cling to their father, others have a deeper affection for their mother. I will forgive thee, for myself am not so exceeding glad at the deed that I have done, my child.

But thou,—why thus unwashed and clad in foul attire, now that the days of thy lying-in are accomplished? Ah me, for my sorry schemes! I have goaded my husband into anger more than e'er I should have done.

ELECTRA

Thy sorrow comes too late; the hour of remedy has gone from thee; my father is dead. Yet why not recall that exile, thy own wandering son?

CLYTEMNESTRA

I am afraid; 'tis my interest, not his that I regard. For they say he is wroth for his father's murder.

ELECTRA

Why, then, dost thou encourage thy husband's bitterness against us?

CLYTEMNESTRA

'Tis his way; thou too hast a stubborn nature.

ELECTRA

Because I am grieved; yet will I check my spirit.

CLYTEMNESTRA

I promise then he shall no longer oppress thee.

ELECTRA

From living in my home he grows too proud.

CLYTEMNESTRA

Now there! 'tis thou that art fanning the quarrel into new life.

ELECTRA

I say no more; my dread of him is even what it is.

CLYTEMNESTRA

Peace! Enough of this. Why didst thou summon me, my child?

ELECTRA

Thou hast heard, I suppose, of my confinement; for this I pray thee, since I know not how, offer the customary sacrifice on the tenth day after birth, for I am a novice herein, never having had a child before.

CLYTEMNESTRA

This is work for another, even for her who delivered thee.

ELECTRA

I was all alone in my travail and at the babe's birth.

CLYTEMNESTRA

Dost live so far from neighbours?

ELECTRA

No one cares to make the poor his friends.

CLYTEMNESTRA

Well, I will go to offer to the gods a sacrifice for the child's completion of the days; and when I have done thee this service, I will seek the field where my husband is sacrificing to the Nymphs. Take this chariot hence, my servants, and tie the horses to the stalls; and when ye think that I have finished my offering to the gods, attend me, for I must likewise pleasure my lord.

(She goes into the hut.)

ELECTRA

Enter our humble cottage; but, prithee, take care that my smoke-grimed walls soil not thy robes; now wilt thou offer to the gods a fitting sacrifice. There stands the basket ready, and the knife is sharpened, the same that slew the bull, by whose side thou soon wilt lie a corpse; and thou shalt be his bride in Hades' halls whose wife thou wast on earth. This is the boon I will grant thee, while thou shalt pay me for my father's blood.

(ELECTRA follows her into the hut.)

CHORUS *(chanting)*

strophe

Misery is changing sides; the breeze veers round, and now blows fair upon my house. The day is past when my chief fell murdered in his bath, and the roof and the very stones of the walls rang with this his cry: "O cruel wife, why art thou murdering me on my return to my dear country after ten long years?"

antistrophe

The tide is turning, and justice that pursues the faithless wife is drawing within its grasp the murderess, who slew her hapless lord, when he came home at last to these towering Cyclopean walls,—aye, with her own hand she smote him with the sharpened steel, herself the axe uplifting. Unhappy husband! whate'er the curse that possessed that wretched woman. Like a lioness of the hills that rangeth through the woodland for her prey, she wrought the deed.

CLYTEMNESTRA (*within*)
O my children, by Heaven I pray ye spare your mother.

CHORUS (*chanting*)
Dost hear her cries within the house?

CLYTEMNESTRA
O God! ah me!

CHORUS (*chanting*)
I too bewail thee, dying by thy children's hands. God deals out
His justice in His good time. A cruel fate is thine, unhappy one; yet
didst thou sin in murdering thy lord.
(ORESTES *and* ELECTRA *come out of the hut, followed by attendants
    who are carrying the two corpses. The following lines between*
    ELECTRA, ORESTES *and the* CHORUS *are chanted.*)
But lo! from the house they come, dabbled in their mother's fresh-
spilt gore, their triumph proving the piteous butchery. There is not
nor ever has been a race more wretched than the line of Tantalus.

ORESTES
O Earth, and Zeus whose eye is over all! behold this foul deed of
blood, these two corpses lying here that I have slain in vengeance
for my sufferings.

ELECTRA
Tears are all too weak for this, brother; and I am the guilty cause.
Ah, woe is me! How hot my fury burned against the mother that
bare me!

ORESTES
Alas! for thy lot, O mother mine! A piteous, piteous doom, aye,
worse than that, hast thou incurred at children's hands! Yet justly
hast thou paid forfeit for our father's blood. Ah, Phoebus! thine was
the voice that praised this vengeance; thou it is that hast brought
these hideous scenes to light, and caused this deed of blood. To what
city can I go henceforth? what friend, what man of any piety will
bear the sight of a mother's murderer like me?

ELECTRA
Ah me! alas! and whither can I go? What share have I henceforth
in dance or marriage rite? What husband will accept me as his bride?

ORESTES
Again thy fancy changes with the wind; for now thou thinkest
aright, though not so formerly; an awful deed didst thou urge thy

brother against his will to commit, dear sister. Oh! didst thou see how the poor victim threw open her robe and showed her bosom as I smote her, sinking on her knees, poor wretch? And her hair I—

ELECTRA

Full well I know the agony through which thou didst pass at hearing thy own mother's bitter cry.

ORESTES

Ah yes! she laid her hand upon my chin, and cried aloud, "My child, I entreat thee!" and she clung about my neck, so that I let fall the sword.

ELECTRA

O my poor mother! How didst thou endure to see her breathe her last before thy eyes?

ORESTES

I threw my mantle o'er them and began the sacrifice by plunging the sword into my mother's throat.

ELECTRA

Yet 'twas I that urged thee on, yea, and likewise grasped the steel. Oh! I have done an awful deed.

ORESTES

Oh! take and hide our mother's corpse beneath a pall, and close her gaping wound. (*Turning to the corpse*) Ah! thy murderers were thine own children.

ELECTRA (*covering the corpse*)

There! thou corpse both loved and loathed; still o'er thee I cast a robe, to end the grievous troubles of our house.

CHORUS

See! where o'er the roof-top spirits are appearing, or gods maybe from heaven, for this is not a road that mortals tread. Why come they thus where mortal eyes can see them clearly?

(THE DIOSCURI *appear from above*.)

DIOSCURI

Hearken, son of Agamemnon. We, the twin sons of Zeus, thy mother's sisters, call thee, even Castor and his brother Polydeuces. 'Tis but now we have reached Argos after stilling the fury of the sea for mariners, having seen the slaying of our sister, thy mother. She hath received her

just reward, but thine is no righteous act, and Phoebus—but no! he is
my king, my lips are sealed—is Phoebus still, albeit the oracle he gave
thee was no great proof of his wisdom. But we must acquiesce herein.
Henceforth must thou follow what Zeus and destiny ordain for thee. On
Pylades bestow Electra for his wife to take unto his home; do thou leave
Argos, for after thy mother's murder thou mayst not set foot in the city.
And those grim goddesses of doom, that glare like savage hounds, will
drive thee mad and chase thee to and fro; but go thou to Athens and
make thy prayer to the holy image of Pallas, for she will close their fierce
serpents' mouths, so that they touch thee not, holding o'er thy head her
aegis with the Gorgon's head. A hill there is, to Ares sacred, where first the
gods in conclave sat to decide the law of blood, in the day that savage
Ares slew Halirrothius, son of the ocean-king, in anger for the violence
he offered to his daughter's honour; from that time all decisions given
there are most holy and have heaven's sanction. There must thou have
this murder tried; and if equal votes are given, they shall save thee from
death in the decision, for Loxias will take the blame upon himself, since
it was his oracle that advised thy mother's murder. And this shall be the
law for all posterity; in every trial the accused shall win his case if the
votes are equal. Then shall those dread goddesses, stricken with grief at
this, vanish into a cleft of the earth close to the hill, revered by men
henceforth as a place for holy oracles; whilst thou must settle in a city of
Arcadia on the banks of the river Alpheus near the shrine of Lycaean
Apollo, and the city shall be called after thy name. To thee I say this. As
for the corpse of Aegisthus, the citizens of Argos must give it burial; but
Menelaus, who has just arrived at Nauplia from the sack of Troy, shall
bury thy mother, Helen helping him; for she hath come from her sojourn
in Egypt in the halls of Proteus, and hath never been to Troy; but Zeus,
to stir up strife and bloodshed in the world, sent forth a phantom of Helen
to Ilium.[4] Now let Pylades take his maiden wife and bear her to his home
in Achaea; also he must conduct thy so-called kinsman [5] to the land of
Phocis, and there reward him well. But go thyself along the narrow
Isthmus, and seek Cecropia's happy home. For once thou hast fulfilled
the doom appointed for this murder, thou shalt be blest and free from all
thy troubles.

(The remaining lines of the play are chanted.)

CHORUS
Ye sons of Zeus, may we draw near to speak with you?

DIOSCURI
Ye may, since ye are not polluted by this murder.

ORESTES

May I too share your converse, sons of Tyndareus?

DIOSCURI

Thou too! for to Phoebus will I ascribe this deed of blood.

CHORUS

How was it that ye, the brothers of the murdered woman, gods too, did not ward the doom-goddesses from her roof?

DIOSCURI

'Twas fate that brought resistless doom to her, and that thoughtless oracle that Phoebus gave.

ELECTRA

But why did the god, and wherefore did his oracles make me my mother's murderer?

DIOSCURI

A share in the deed, a share in its doom; one ancestral curse hath ruined both of you.

ORESTES

Ah, sister mine! at last I see thee again only to be robbed in a moment of thy dear love; I must leave thee, and by thee be left.

DIOSCURI

Hers are a husband and a home; her only suffering this, that she is quitting Argos.

ORESTES

Yet what could call forth deeper grief than exile from one's fatherland? I must leave my father's house, and at a stranger's bar be sentenced for my mother's blood.

DIOSCURI

Be of good cheer; go to the holy town of Pallas; keep a stout heart only.

ELECTRA

O my brother, best and dearest! clasp me to thy breast; for now is the curse of our mother's blood cutting us off from the home of our fathers.

ORESTES

Throw thy arms in close embrace about me. Oh! weep as o'er my grave when I am dead.

DIOSCURI

Ah me! that bitter cry makes even gods shudder to hear. Yea, for in my breast and in every heavenly being's dwells pity for the sorrows of mankind.

ORESTES

Never to see thee more!

ELECTRA

Never again to stand within thy sight!

ORESTES

This is my last good-bye to thee.

ELECTRA

Farewell, farewell, my city! and ye my fellow-countrywomen, a long farewell to you!

ORESTES

Art thou going already, truest of thy sex?

ELECTRA

I go, the tear-drop dimming my tender eyes.

ORESTES

Go, Pylades, and be happy; take and wed Electra.

DIOSCURI

Their only thoughts will be their marriage; but haste thee to Athens, seeking to escape these hounds of hell, for they are on thy track in fearful wise, swart monsters, with snakes for hands, who reap a harvest of man's agony. But we twain must haste away o'er the Sicilian main to save the seaman's ship. Yet as we fly through heaven's expanse we help not the wicked; but whoso in his life loves piety and justice, all such we free from troublous toils and save. Wherefore let no man be minded to act unjustly, or with men foresworn set sail; such the warning I, a god, to mortals give.

(THE DIOSCURI *vanish.*)

CHORUS

Farewell! truly that mortal's is a happy lot, who can thus fare, unafflicted by any woe.

COLERIDGE's translation has been slightly modified in the following lines: 16, 57, 294, 295, 297, 298, 336, 338, 340, 369, 425, 523, 624, 648, 842, 904, 936, 1209, 1349, 1359.

1. *i.e.*, Pegasus.

2. Coleridge's note here, which explains in some measure the allusions in this choral ode, runs as follows: "The story was that Atreus and Thyestes, the sons of Pelops, being rival claimants to the throne of Mycenae, agreed that whichever should be able to exhibit some portent should be king. Now Atreus found a golden lamb among his flocks, and would have exhibited it, but Thyestes, by guilty collusion with his brother's wife Aerope, cheated him and produced the lamb as his. Accordingly he received the kingdom; but Atreus avenged himself by drowning his wife, and by killing the children of Thyestes and serving them up as food to their father, whom he then slew. Whereat Zeus reversed the whole order of nature, to make men suffer for these crimes."

3. *i.e.*, the Dioscuri.

4. It is interesting to note that Euripides adopts here the "Stesichorean" version of the story of Helen, which he treated at length in the *Helen*.

5. The reference is to the Peasant to whom Electra had been married.

XIV
ORESTES

Characters in the Play

ELECTRA, *daughter of Agamemnon and Clytemnestra*
HELEN, *wife of* MENELAUS
CHORUS OF ARGIVE MAIDENS
ORESTES, *brother of* ELECTRA
MENELAUS, *brother of Agamemnon; King of Argos*
PYLADES, *friend of* ORESTES
MESSENGER, *formerly servant of Agamemnon*
HERMIONE, *daughter of* MENELAUS *and* HELEN
A PHRYGIAN EUNUCH, *in* HELEN'S *retinue*
APOLLO
TYNDAREUS, *father of Clytemnestra*
Attendants

INTRODUCTION

In 408 B.C., approximately five years after the composition of the *Electra*, Euripides returned to the same subject-matter and produced his *Orestes*. The play was apparently very popular in antiquity, in all probability because it contains a number of brilliant and exciting individual scenes. In its entirety it embodies a far different interpretation of the legendary material from the one submitted in the *Electra*. In the prologue we discover that the time of the action is on the sixth day after the murder of Clytemnestra and Aegisthus. Orestes has lost his sanity and is being carefully nursed by his sister Electra. The scene itself is most effective, and Euripides in his portrayal of the half-crazed Orestes has produced the most notable study of abnormal psychological states which has come down to us from antiquity.

After this opening there follows a most amazing play, shot through with dramatic anachronism, sizzling melodrama, cold, formal debate, and palpable topical allusions. This agglomeration of relatively disparate elements is brought to an end in an extraordinary fashion. Orestes, Pylades, and Electra have been sentenced to death for the crime of matricide. In order to get revenge before they die, they attempt to kill Helen, who mysteriously vanishes, and so they turn to Helen's blameless daughter, Hermione. Orestes appears on the palace roof, holding a sword at Hermione's throat while Menelaus from below pleads with him to spare her life. In the meantime the palace has been set on fire by Pylades and Electra. In this hair-raising situation Apollo appears as a very timely *deus ex machina*, and forthwith puts all to rights. He directs Orestes to go to Athens that he may be purged of his guilt, and then to return and marry Hermione. Electra is to become the wife of Pylades, and peace is evidently in store for everyone.

Because of this happy ending, and because of other elements in the play which have been interpreted as comic (for example, the report given by the Phrygian Eunuch of Helen's mysterious disappearance), the *Orestes* has been considered by some critics to have been a substitute for a satyr-play. If this theory be accepted, it would have to be regarded as in the same general class of plays as the *Alcestis*. Other scholars have

109

urged that the drama throughout keeps its emphasis upon the mental instability of Orestes, and paints on the whole a repelling picture of all these characters who have become tainted by the curse upon the House of Atreus. Furthermore, they would maintain that there is implicit in the play more than a veiled attack on contemporary social and political evils. For example, Orestes' everlasting desire to discuss each issue as though it were a subject for a formal debate is seen as Euripides' indictment of the newer educational tendencies of the time. Likewise, such critics would argue that the playwright is protesting vigorously against the dangers of demagoguery when he describes the assembly which condemned Orestes. Those who hold this general view of the play are somewhat embarrassed by Apollo's appearance at the conclusion, and they have been compelled therefore to maintain that the final portion of the play is not genuine.

The very fact that critics have reached no general agreement in their interpretations inevitably forces us to conclude that Euripides has failed to fuse organically the various ingredients of his drama. What we seem to have in the *Orestes* is a vivid example of Euripides' characteristic strength and weakness. There can be no doubt that he possesses an uncanny sense of the dramatic potentialities of any particular scene, as many of the episodes of this play clearly testify, but on the other hand he is sadly wanting, at least here and in several other plays, in the ability to synthesize the individual scenes into a coherent dramatic whole. Perhaps in the *Orestes,* Euripides was satisfied to construct out of this old traditional material a series of thrilling and melodramatic episodes, and at the same time to make the old material his vehicle for expressing his strictures on the Athens of his day. If these constituted his major purposes, and if he desired also to have his play meet with popular success, he may not have been so deeply concerned with the problem of its total integration.

ORESTES

(SCENE:—*Before the royal palace at Argos. It is the sixth day after the murder of Clytemnestra and Aegisthus.* ELECTRA *is discovered alone.* ORESTES *lies sleeping on a couch in the background.*)

ELECTRA

THERE is naught so terrible to describe, be it physical pain or heaven-sent affliction,[1] that man's nature may not have to bear the burden of it. Tantalus, they say, once so prosperous,—and I am not now taunting him with his misfortunes,—Tantalus, the reputed son of Zeus, hangs suspended in mid air, quailing at the crag which looms above his head; paying this penalty, they say, for the shameful weakness he displayed in failing to keep a bridle on his lips, when admitted by gods, though he was but a mortal, to share the honours of their feasts like one of them.

He it was that begat Pelops, the father of Atreus, for whom the goddess, when she had carded her wool, spun a web of strife, even to the making of war with his own brother Thyestes. But why need I repeat that hideous tale?

Well, Atreus slew Thyestes' children and feasted him on them; but,—passing over intermediate events,—from Atreus and Aerope of Crete sprang Agamemnon, that famous chief,—if his was really fame,—and Menelaus. Now it was this Menelaus who married Helen, Heaven's abhorrence; while his brother, King Agamemnon, took Clytemnestra to wife, name of note in Hellas, and we three daughters were his issue, Chrysothemis, Iphigenia, and myself Electra; also a son Orestes; all of that one accursed mother, who slew her lord, after snaring him in a robe that had no outlet. Her reason a maiden's lips may not declare, and so I leave that unexplained for the world to guess at. What need for me to charge Phoebus with wrong-doing, though he instigated Orestes to slay his own mother, a deed that few approved; still it was his obedience to the god that made him slay her; I, too, feebly as a woman would, shared in the deed of blood, as did Pylades who helped us to bring it about.

After this my poor Orestes fell sick of a cruel wasting disease; upon his

III

couch he lies prostrated, and it is his mother's blood that goads him into frenzied fits; this I say, from dread of naming those goddesses, whose terrors are chasing him before them,—even the Eumenides. 'Tis now the sixth day since the body of his murdered mother was committed to the cleansing fire; since then no food has passed his lips, nor hath he washed his skin; but wrapped in his cloak he weeps in his lucid moments, whenever the fever leaves him; otherwhiles he bounds headlong from his couch, as a colt when it is loosed from the yoke. Moreover, this city of Argos has decreed that no man give us shelter at his fireside or speak to matricides like us; yea, and this is the fateful day on which Argos will decide our sentence, whether we are both to die by stoning, or to whet the steel and plunge it in our necks. There is, 'tis true, one hope of escape still left us; Menelaus has landed from Troy; his fleet now crowds the haven of Nauplia where he is come to anchor, returned at last from Troy after ceaseless wanderings; but Helen, that "lady of sorrows," as she styles herself, hath he sent on to our palace, carefully waiting for the night, lest any of those parents whose sons were slain beneath the walls of Troy, might see her if she went by day, and set to stoning her. Within she sits, weeping for her sister and the calamities of her family, and yet *she* hath still some solace in her woe; for Hermione, the child she left at home in the hour she sailed for Troy,—the maid whom Menelaus brought from Sparta and entrusted to my mother's keeping,—is still a cause of joy to her and a reason to forget her sorrows.

I, meantime, am watching each approach, against the moment I see Menelaus arriving; for unless we find some safety there, we have but a feeble anchor to ride on otherwise.

A helpless thing, an unlucky house!

(HELEN *enters from the palace.*)

HELEN

Daughter of Clytemnestra and Agamemnon, hapless Electra, too long now left a maid unwed! how is it with thee and thy brother, this ill-starred Orestes who slew his mother! Speak; for referring the sin as I do to Phoebus, I incur no pollution by letting thee accost me; and yet I am truly sorry for the fate of my sister Clytemnestra, on whom I ne'er set eyes after I was driven by heaven-sent frenzy to sail on my disastrous voyage to Ilium; but now that I am parted from her I bewail our misfortunes.[2]

ELECTRA

Prithee, Helen, why should I speak of that which thine own eyes can see the son of Agamemnon in his misery?

Beside his wretched corpse I sit, a sleepless sentinel; for corpse he is, so faint his breath; not that I reproach him with his sufferings; but thou art highly blest and thy husband too, and ye are come upon us in the hour of adversity.

HELEN

How long hath he been laid thus upon his couch?

ELECTRA

Ever since he spilt his mother's blood—.

HELEN

Unhappy wretch! unhappy mother! what a death she died!

ELECTRA

Unhappy enough to succumb to his misery.

HELEN

Prithee, maiden, wilt hear me a moment?

ELECTRA

Aye, with such small leisure as this watching o'er a brother leaves.

HELEN

Wilt go for me to my sister's tomb?

ELECTRA

Wouldst have me seek my mother's tomb? And why?

HELEN

To carry an offering of hair and a libation from me.

ELECTRA

Art forbidden then to go to the tombs of those thou lovest?

HELEN

Nay, but I am ashamed to show myself in Argos.

ELECTRA

A late repentance surely for one who left her home so shamefully then.

HELEN

Thou hast told the truth, but thy telling is not kind to me.

ELECTRA

What is this supposed modesty before the eyes of Mycenae that possesses thee?

HELEN

I am afraid of the fathers of those who lie dead beneath the walls of Ilium.

ELECTRA

Good cause for fear; thy name is on every tongue in Argos.

HELEN

Then free me of my fear and grant me this boon.

ELECTRA

I could not bear to face my mother's grave.

HELEN

And yet 'twere shame indeed to send these offerings by a servant's hand.

ELECTRA

Then why not send thy daughter Hermione?

HELEN

'Tis not seemly for a tender maid to make her way amongst a crowd.

ELECTRA

And yet she would thus be repaying her dead foster-mother's care.

HELEN

True; thou hast convinced me, maiden. Yes, I will send my daughter; for thou art right. (*Calling*) Hermione, my child, come forth before the palace; (HERMIONE *and attendants come out of the palace.*) take these libations and these tresses of mine in thy hands, and go pour round Cly-temnestra's tomb a mingled cup of honey, milk, and frothing wine; then stand upon the heaped-up grave, and proclaim therefrom, "Helen, thy sister, sends thee these libations as her gift, fearing herself to approach thy tomb from terror of the Argive mob"; and bid her harbour kindly thoughts towards me and thee and my husband; towards these two wretched sufferers, too, whom Heaven hath afflicted. Likewise promise that I will pay in full whatever funeral gifts are due from me to a sister. Now go, my child, and tarry not; and soon as thou hast made the offer-ing at the tomb, bethink thee of thy return.

(HELEN *goes into the palace as* HERMIONE *and her attendants depart with the offerings.*)

ELECTRA

O human nature, what a grievous curse thou art in this world! and what salvation, too, to those who have a goodly heritage therein!

Did ye mark how she cut off her hair only at the ends, careful to pre-serve its beauty? 'Tis the same woman as of old. May Heaven's hate pursue thee! for thou hast proved the ruin of me and my poor brother and all Hellas.

Alack! here are my friends once more, coming to unite their plaintive
dirge with mine; they will soon put an end to my brother's peaceful sleep
and cause my tears to flow when I see his frenzied fit.

(*The* CHORUS OF ARGIVE MAIDENS *enters quietly. The following lines
between* ELECTRA *and the* CHORUS *are chanted responsively.*)

Good friends, step softly; not a sound; not a whisper! for though
this kindness is well-meant, rouse him and I shall rue it.

CHORUS

Hush! hush! let your footsteps fall lightly! not a sound! not a
whisper!

ELECTRA

Further, further from his couch! I beseech ye.

CHORUS

There! there! I obey.

ELECTRA

Hush! hush! good friend, I pray. Soft as the breath of slender
reedy pipe be thy every accent!

CHORUS

Hark, how soft and low I drop my voice!

ELECTRA

Yes, lower thy voice e'en thus; approach now, softly, softly! Tell
me what reason ye had for coming at all. 'Tis so long since he laid
him down to sleep.

CHORUS

How is it with him? Impart thy news, dear lady. Is it weal or woe
I am to tell?

ELECTRA

He is still alive, but his moans grow feeble.

CHORUS

What sayest thou? (*Turning to* ORESTES) Poor wretch!

ELECTRA

Awake him from the deep sweet slumber he is now enjoying and
thou wilt cause his death.

CHORUS

Ah, poor sufferer! victim of Heaven's vengeful hate!

ELECTRA

Ah, misery! It seems it was a wicked utterance by a wicked god delivered, the day that Loxias from his seat upon the tripod of Themis decreed my mother's most unnatural murder.

CHORUS

He stirs beneath his robe! Dost see?

ELECTRA

Alas! I do; thy noisy words have roused him from his sleep.

CHORUS

Nay, methinks he slumbers still.

ELECTRA

Begone! quit the house! retrace thy footsteps! a truce to this din!

CHORUS

He sleeps. Thou art right.

ELECTRA

O Night, majestic queen, giver of sleep to toiling men, rise from the abyss of Erebus and wing thy way to the palace of Agamemnon! For beneath our load of misery and woe we sink, aye, sink oppressed.

There! (*To the* CHORUS) that noise again! Be still and keep that high-pitched voice of thine away from his couch; suffer him to enjoy his sleep in peace!

CHORUS

Tell me, what end awaits his troubles?

ELECTRA

Death, death; what else? for he does not even miss his food.

CHORUS

Why, then his doom is full in view.

ELECTRA

Phoebus marked us out as his victims by imposing a foul unnatural task, even the shedding of the blood of our mother, who slew our sire.

CHORUS

'Twas just, but 'twas not well.

ELECTRA

Dead, dead, O mother mine! and thou hast slain a father and these the children of thy womb; for we are dead or as the dead. Yes, thou art in thy grave, and more than half my life is spent in weeping and wailing and midnight lamentations; oh, look on me! a maid unwed, unblest with babes, I drag out a joyless existence as if for ever.

LEADER OF THE CHORUS

My daughter Electra, from thy near station there see whether thy brother hath not passed away without thy knowing it; for I like not his utter prostration.

ORESTES (*awaking refreshed*)

Sweet charm of sleep! saviour in sickness! how dear to me thy coming was! how needed! All hail, majestic power, oblivion of woe! How wise this goddess is, how earnestly invoked by every suffering soul! (*Addressing* ELECTRA) Whence came I hither? How is it I am here? for I have lost all previous recollection and remember nothing.

ELECTRA

Dearest brother, how glad I was to see thee fall asleep! Wouldst have me take thee in my arms and lift thy body?

ORESTES

Take, oh! take me in thy arms, and from this sufferer's mouth and eyes wipe off the flakes of foam.

ELECTRA

Ah! 'tis a service I love; nor do I scorn with sister's hand to tend a brother's limbs.

ORESTES

Prop me up, thy side to mine; brush the matted hair from off my face, for I see but dimly.

ELECTRA

Ah, poor head! how squalid are thy locks become! How wild thy look from remaining so long uncleansed!

ORESTES

Lay me once more upon the couch; when my fit leaves me, I am all unnerved, unstrung.

ELECTRA (*as she lays him down*)

Welcome to the sick man is his couch, for painful though it be to take thereto, yet is it necessary.

ORESTES

Set me upright once again, turn me round; it is their helplessness makes the sick so hard to please.

ELECTRA

Wilt put thy feet upon the ground and take a step at last? Change is always pleasant.

ORESTES

That will I; for that has a semblance of health; and that seeming, though it be far from the reality, is preferable to this.

ELECTRA

Hear me then, O brother mine, while yet the avenging fiends permit thee to use thy senses.

ORESTES

Hast news to tell? so it be good, thou dost me a kindness; but if it tend to my hurt, lo! I have sorrow enough.

ELECTRA

Menelaus, thy father's brother, is arrived; in Nauplia his fleet lies at anchor.

ORESTES

Ha! is he come to cast a ray of light upon our gloom, a man of our own kin who owes our sire a debt of gratitude?

ELECTRA

Yes, he is come, and is bringing Helen with him from the walls of Troy; accept this as a sure proof of what I say.

ORESTES

Had he returned alone in safety, he were more to be envied; for if he is bringing his wife with him, he is bringing a load of evil.

ELECTRA

Tyndareus begat a race of daughters notorious for the shame they earned, infamous throughout Hellas.

ORESTES

Be thou then different from that evil brood, for well thou mayest, and that not only in profession, but also in heart.

ELECTRA

Ah! brother, thine eye is growing wild, and in a moment art thou passing from thy recent saneness back to frenzy.

ORESTES (*starting up wildly*)

Mother, I implore thee! let not loose on me those maidens with their bloodshot eyes and snaky hair. Ha! see, see where they approach to leap upon me!

ELECTRA

Lie still, poor sufferer, on thy couch; thine eye sees none of the things which thy fancy paints so clear.

ORESTES

O Phoebus! they will kill me, yon hounds of hell, death's priestesses with glaring eyes, terrific goddesses.

ELECTRA

I will not let thee go; but with arms twined round thee will prevenɩ thy piteous tossing to and fro.

ORESTES

Loose me! thou art one of those fiends that plague me, and art gripping me by the waist to hurl my body into Tartarus.

ELECTRA

Woe is me! what succour can I find, seeing that we have Heaven's forces set against us?

ORESTES

Give me my horn-tipped bow, Apollo's gift, wherewith that god declared that I should defend myself against these goddesses, if ever they sought to scare me with wild transports of madness.

A mortal hand will wound one of these goddesses, unless she vanish from my sight. Do ye not heed me, or mark the feathered shaft of my far-shooting bow ready to wing its flight? What! do ye linger still? Spread your pinions, skim the sky, and blame those oracles of Phoebus.

Ah! why am I raving, panting, gasping? Whither, oh! whither have I leapt from off my couch? Once more the storm is past; I see a calm.

Sister, why weepest thou, thy head wrapped in thy robe? I am ashamed that I should make thee a partner in my sufferings and distress a maid like thee through sickness of mine. Cease to fret for my troubles; for though thou didst consent to it, yet 'twas I that spilt our mother's blood. 'Tis Loxias I blame, for urging me on to do a deed most damned, encouraging me with words but no real help; for I am sure that, had I asked my father to his face whether I was to slay my mother, he would have implored me oft and earnestly by this beard never to plunge a murderer's sword into my mother's breast, since he would not thereby regain his life, whilst I, poor wretch, should be doomed to drain this cup of sorrow.

E'en as it is, dear sister, unveil thy face and cease to weep, despite our abject misery; and whensoe'er thou seest me give way to despair, be it thine to calm and soothe the terrors and distorted fancies of my brain; likewise when sorrow comes to thee, I must be at thy side and give thee words of comfort; for to help our friends like this is a gracious task.

Seek thy chamber now, poor sister; lie down and close awhile thy sleepless eyes; take food and bathe thy body; for if thou leave me or fall sick from nursing me, my doom is sealed; for thou art the only champion I now have, by all the rest deserted, as thou seest.

ELECTRA

I leave thee! never! With thee I am resolved to live and die; for 'tis the same; if thou diest, what can I, a woman, do? How shall I escape alone, reft of brother, sire, and friends?

Still if it be thy pleasure, I must do thy bidding. But lay thee down upon thy couch, and pay not too great heed to the terrors and alarms that scare thee from thy rest; lie still upon thy pallet bed; for e'en though one be not sick but only fancy it, this is a source of weariness and perplexity to mortals.

(ELECTRA *enters the palace, as* ORESTES *lies back upon his couch.*)

CHORUS (*singing*)

strophe

Ah! ye goddesses terrific, swiftly careering on outspread pinions, whose lot it is 'mid tears and groans to hold revel not with Bacchic rites; ye avenging spirits swarthy-hued, that dart along the spacious firmament, exacting a penalty for blood, a penalty for murder, to you I make my suppliant prayer: suffer the son of Agamemnon to forget his wild whirling frenzy!

Ah, woe for the troublous task! which thou, poor wretch, didst strive to compass to thy ruin, listening to the voice prophetic, proclaimed aloud by Phoebus from the tripod throughout his sanctuary, where is a secret spot they call "the navel of the earth."

antistrophe

O Zeus! What pity will be shown? what deadly struggle is here at hand, hurrying thee on o'er thy path of woe, a victim on whom some fiend is heaping tribulation, by bringing on thy house thy mother's bloodshed which drives thee raving mad? I weep for thee, for thee I weep.

Great prosperity abideth not amongst mankind; but some power divine, shaking it to and fro like the sail of a swift galley, plunges it deep in the waves of grievous affliction, boisterous and deadly as the waves of the sea. For what new family am I henceforth to honour by preference other than that which sprung from a marriage divine, even from Tantalus?

Behold a king draws near, prince Menelaus! From his magnificence 'tis plain to see that he is a scion of the race of Tantalus.

All hail! thou that didst sail with a thousand ships to Asia's strand, and by Heaven's help accomplish all thy heart's desire, making good-fortune a friend to thyself.

(MENELAUS *and his retinue enter.*)

MENELAUS

All hail, my home! Some joy I feel on seeing thee again on my return from Troy, some sorrow too the sight recalls; for never yet have I beheld a house more closely encircled by the net of dire affliction.

Concerning Agamemnon's fate and the awful death he died at his wife's hands I learnt as I was trying to put in at Malea, when the sailors' seer from out the waves, unerring Glaucus, Nereus' spokesman, brought the news to me; for he stationed himself in full view by our ship and thus addressed me, "Yonder, Menelaus, lies thy brother slain, plunged in a fatal bath, the last his wife will ever give him"; filling high the cup of tears for me and my brave crew. Arrived at Nauplia, my wife already on the point of starting hither, I was dreaming of folding Orestes, Aga-memnon's son, and his mother in a fond embrace, as if 'twere well with them, when I heard a mariner relate the murder of the daughter of Tyn-dareus. Tell me then, good girls, where to find the son of Agamemnon, the daring author of that fearful crime; for he was but a babe in Clytem-nestra's arms that day I left my home to go to Troy, so that I should not recognize him, e'en were I to see him.

ORESTES (*staggering towards him from the couch*)

Behold the object of thy inquiry, Menelaus; this is Orestes. To thee will I of mine own accord relate my sufferings. But as the prelude to my speech I clasp thy knees in suppliant wise, seeking thus to tie to thee the prayer of lips that lack the suppliant's bough; save me, for thou art ar-rived at the very crisis of my trouble.

MENELAUS

Ye gods! what do I see? what death's-head greets my sight?

ORESTES

Thou art right; I *am* dead through misery, though I still gaze upon the sun.

MENELAUS

How wild the look thy unkempt hair gives thee, poor wretch!

ORESTES

'Tis not my looks, but my deeds that torture me.

MENELAUS
How terribly thy tearless eyeballs glare!

ORESTES
My body is vanished and gone, though my name hath not yet deserted me.

MENELAUS
Unsightly apparition, so different from what I expected!

ORESTES
In me behold a man that hath slain his hapless mother.

MENELAUS
I have heard all; be chary of thy tale of woe.

ORESTES
I will; but the deity is lavish of woe to me.

MENELAUS
What ails thee? what is thy deadly sickness?

ORESTES
My conscience; I know that I am guilty of an awful crime.

MENELAUS
Explain thyself; wisdom is shown in clearness, not in obscurity.

ORESTES
'Tis grief that is my chief complaint.

MENELAUS
True; she is a goddess dire; yet are there cures for her.

ORESTES
Mad transports too, and the vengeance due to a mother's blood.

MENELAUS
When did thy fit begin? which day was it?

ORESTES
On the day I was heaping the mound o'er my poor mother's grave.

MENELAUS
When thou wast in the house, or watching by the pyre?

ORESTES
As I was waiting by night to gather up her bones.

MENELAUS
Was any one else there to help thee rise?

ORESTES
Yes, Pylades who shared with me the bloody deed, my mother's murder.

MENELAUS
What phantom forms afflict thee thus?

ORESTES
Three maidens black as night I seem to see.

MENELAUS
I know of whom thou speakest, but I will not name them.

ORESTES
Do not; they are too dread; thou wert wise to avoid naming them.

MENELAUS
Are these the fiends that persecute thee with the curse of kindred blood?

ORESTES
Oh! the torment I endure from their hot pursuit!

MENELAUS
That they who have done an awful deed should be so done by is not strange.

ORESTES
Ah, well! I must have recourse in these troubles—

MENELAUS
Speak not of dying; that were folly.

ORESTES
To Phoebus, by whose command I shed my mother's blood.

MENELAUS
Showing a strange ignorance of what is fair and right.

ORESTES
We must obey the gods, whatever those gods are.

MENELAUS
Spite of all this doth not Loxias help thy affliction?

ORESTES

He will in time; to wait like this is the way with gods.

MENELAUS

How long is it since thy mother breathed her last?

ORESTES

This is now the sixth day; her funeral pyre is still warm.

MENELAUS

How soon the goddesses arrived to require thy mother's blood of thee!

ORESTES

To cleverness I lay no claim, but I was a true friend to friends.

MENELAUS

Does thy father afford thee any help at all?

ORESTES

Not as yet; and delaying to do so is, methinks, equivalent to not doing it.

MENELAUS

How dost thou stand towards the city after that deed of thine?

ORESTES

So hated am I that I cannot speak to any man.

MENELAUS

Have not thy hands been even cleansed of their blood-guiltiness, as the law requires?

ORESTES

No; for where'er I go, the door is shut against me.

MENELAUS

Which of the citizens drive thee from the land?

ORESTES

Oeax, who refers to my father his reason for hating Troy.

MENELAUS

I understand; he is visiting on thee the blood of Palamedes.

ORESTES

I at least had naught to do with that; yet am I utterly o'erthrown.

MENELAUS

Who else? some of the friends of Aegisthus perhaps?

ORESTES

Yes, they insult me, and the city listens to them now.

MENELAUS

Will it not suffer thee to keep the sceptre of Agamemnon?

ORESTES

How should it? seeing that they will not suffer me to remain alive.

MENELAUS

What is their method? canst thou tell me plainly?

ORESTES

To-day is sentence to be passed upon me.

MENELAUS

Exile, or death, or something else?

ORESTES

Death by stoning at the hands of the citizens.

MENELAUS

Then why not cross the frontier and fly?

ORESTES

Why not? because I am hemmed in by a ring of armed men.

MENELAUS

Private foes or Argive troops?

ORESTES

By all the citizens, to the end that I may die; 'tis shortly told.

MENELAUS

Poor wretch! thou hast arrived at the extremity of woe.

ORESTES

In thee I still have hopes of escape from my troubles. Yea, since fortune smiles upon thy coming, impart to thy less favoured friends some of thy prosperity, not reserving that luck exclusively for thyself; no! take thy turn too at suffering, and so pay back my father's kindness to those who have a claim on thee. For such friends as desert us in the hour of adversity, are friends in name but not in reality.

LEADER OF THE CHORUS

Lo! Tyndareus, the Spartan, is making his way hither with the step
of age, clad in black raiment, with his hair shorn short in mourning for
his daughter.

ORESTES

Menelaus, I am ruined. See! Tyndareus approaches, the man of all
others I most shrink from facing, because of the deed I have done; for
he it was that nursed me when a babe, and lavished on me many a fond
caress, carrying me about in his arms as the son of Agamemnon, and so
did Leda; for they both regarded me as much as the Dioscuri.

Ah me! my wretched heart and soul! 'twas a sorry return I made
them. What darkness can I find to veil my head? what cloud can I spread
before me in my efforts to escape the old man's eye?

(TYNDAREUS *and his attendants enter.*)

TYNDAREUS

Where, where may I find Menelaus, my daughter's husband? for as
I was pouring libations on Clytemnestra's grave I heard that he was come
to Nauplia with his wife, safe home again after many a long year. Lead
me to him; for I would fain stand at his right hand and give him greeting as a friend whom at last I see again.

MENELAUS

Hail, reverend father! rival of Zeus for a bride!

TYNDAREUS

All hail to thee! Menelaus, kinsman mine! Ha! (*Catching sight of*
ORESTES) What an evil it is to be ignorant of the future! There lies that
matricide before the house, a viper darting venom from his eyes, whom
my soul abhors. What! Menelaus, speaking to a godless wretch like him?

MENELAUS

And why not? He is the son of one whom I loved well.

TYNDAREUS

This his son? this creature here?

MENELAUS

Yes, his son; and therefore worthy of respect, albeit in distress.

TYNDAREUS

Thou hast been so long amongst barbarians that thou art one of them.

MENELAUS

Always to respect one's kith and kin is a custom in Hellas.

TYNDAREUS

Aye, another custom is to yield a willing deference to the laws.

MENELAUS

The wise hold that everything which depends on necessity, is its slave.

TYNDAREUS

Keep that wisdom for thyself; I will not admit it.

MENELAUS

No, for thou art angry, and old age is not wise.

TYNDAREUS

What could a dispute about wisdom have to do with him? If right and wrong are clear to all, who was ever more senseless than this man, seeing that he never weighed the justice of the case, nor yet appealed to the universal law of Hellas? For when Agamemnon breathed his last beneath the blow my daughter dealt upon his head,—a deed most foul, which I will never defend,—he should have brought a charge against his mother and inflicted the penalty allowed by law for bloodshed, banishing her from his house; thus would he have gained the credit of forbearance from the calamity, keeping strictly to the law and showing his piety as well. As it is, he is come into the same misfortune as his mother; for though he had just cause for thinking her a wicked woman, he has surpassed her himself by murdering her. I will ask thee, Menelaus, just one question. Take this case: the wife of his bosom has slain him; *his* son follows suit and kills his mother in revenge; next the avenger's son to expiate this murder commits another; where, pray, will the chain of horrors end?

Our forefathers settled these matters the right way. They forbade any one with blood upon his hands to appear in their sight or cross their path; "purify him by exile," said they, "but no retaliation!" Otherwise there must always have been one who, by taking the pollution last upon his hands, would be liable to have his own blood shed.

For my part I abhor wicked women, especially my daughter who slew her husband; Helen, too, thy own wife, will I ne'er commend; no! I would not even speak to her, and little I envy thee a voyage to Troy for so worthless a woman. But the law will I defend with all my might, seeking to check this brutal spirit of murder, which is always the ruin of countries and cities alike. Wretch! (*Turning to* ORESTES) Hadst thou no heart when thy mother was baring her breast in her appeal to thee? True; I did not witness that awful deed, yet do my poor old eyes run down with tears. One thing at least attests the truth of what I say: thou art abhorred by Heaven, and this aimless wandering, these transports of

madness and terror are thy atonement for a mother's blood. What need
have I of others to testify where I can see for myself? Take warning therefore, Menelaus; seek not to oppose the gods from any wish to help this
wretch, but leave him to be stoned to death by his fellow-citizens; else
set not foot on Sparta's soil. My daughter is dead, and she deserved her
fate; but it should not have been his hand that slew her. In all except my
daughters have I been a happy man; there my fortune stopped.

LEADER

His is an enviable lot, who is blest in his children, and does not find
himself brought into evil notoriety.

ORESTES

I am afraid to speak before thee, aged prince in a matter where I am
sure to grieve thee to the heart. Only let thy years, which frighten me
from speaking, set no barrier in the path of my words, and I will go forward; but, as it is, I fear thy grey hairs. My crime is, I slew my mother;
yet on another count this is no crime, being vengeance for my father.
What ought I to have done? Set one thing against another. My father
begat me; thy daughter gave me birth, being the field that received the
seed from another; for without a sire no child would ever be born. So I
reasoned thus: I ought to stand by the author of my being rather than
the woman who undertook to rear me. Now thy daughter—*mother* I blush
to call her—was engaged in secret intrigues with a lover (reviling her I
shall revile myself; yet speak I will); Aegisthus was that stealthy paramour who lived with her; him I slew, and after him I sacrificed my
mother,—a crime, no doubt, but done to avenge my father. Now, as regards the reasons for which I deserve to be stoned as thou threatenest,
hear the service I am conferring on all Hellas. If women become so bold
as to murder their husbands, taking refuge in their children, with the
mother's breast to catch their pity, they would think naught of destroying
their husbands on any plea whatsoever. But I, by a horrible crime—such
is thy exaggerated phrase—have put an end to this custom. I hated my
mother and had good cause to slay her. She was false to her husband
when he was gone from his home to fight for all Hellas at the head of its
armies, neither did she keep his honour undefiled; and when her sin
had found her out, she wreaked no punishment upon herself, but, to
avoid the vengeance of her lord, visited her sins on my father and slew
him. By Heaven! ill time as it is for me to mention Heaven, when defending the cause of murder; still, suppose I had by my silence consented to
my mother's conduct, what would the murdered man have done to me?
Would he not now for very hate be tormenting me with avenging fiends?
or are there goddesses to help my mother, and are there none to aid him

in his deeper wrong? Thou, yes! thou, old man, hast been my ruin by begetting a daughter so abandoned; for it was owing to her audacious deed that I lost my father and became my mother's murderer.

Attend, I say. Telemachus did not kill the wife of Odysseus; why? because she wedded not a second husband, but the marriage-bed remained untainted in her halls. Once more; Apollo, who makes the navel of the earth his home, vouchsafing unerring prophecies to man, the god whom we obey in all he saith,—'twas he to whom I hearkened when I slew my mother. Find him guilty of the crime, slay him; his was the sin, not mine. What ought I to have done? or is not the god competent to expiate the pollution when I refer it to him? Whither should one fly henceforth, if he will not rescue me from death after giving his commands? Say not then that the deed was badly done, but unfortunately for me who did it.

A blessed life those mortals lead who make wise marriages; but those who wed unhappily are alike unfortunate without and within their homes.

LEADER

'Tis ever woman's way to thwart men's fortunes to the increase of their sorrow.

TYNDAREUS

Since thou adoptest so bold a tone, suppressing naught, but answering me back in such wise that my heart is vexed within me, thou wilt incense me to go to greater lengths in procuring thy execution; and I shall regard this as a fine addition to my purpose in coming hither to deck my daughter's grave. Yes; I will go to the chosen council of Argos and set the citizens, whether they will or not, on thee and thy sister, that ye may suffer stoning. She deserves to die even more than thou, for it was she who embittered thee against thy mother by carrying tales to thine ear from time to time to whet thy hate the more announcing dreams from Agamemnon, and speaking of the amour with Aegisthus as an abomination to the gods in Hades, for even here on earth it was hateful, till she set the house ablaze with fires never kindled by Hephaestus. This I tell thee, Menelaus; and more,—I will perform it. If then thou makest my hatred or our connection of any account, seek not to avert this miscreant's doom in direct defiance of the gods, but leave him to be stoned to death by the citizens; else never set foot on Spartan soil. Remember thou hast been told all this, and choose not for friends the ungodly, excluding more righteous folk.

Ho! servants, lead me hence.

(TYNDAREUS *and his attendants depart.*)

ORESTES

Get thee gone! that the remainder of my speech may be addressed
to Menelaus without interruption, free from the restrictions thy old age
exerts.

Wherefore, Menelaus, art thou pacing round and round to think the
matter over, up and down in thought perplexed?

MENELAUS

Let me alone! I am at a loss, as I turn it over in my mind, towards
which side I am to lean.

ORESTES

Do not then decide finally, but after first hearing what I have to say,
then make up thy mind.

MENELAUS

Good advice! say on. There are occasions when silence would be better
than speech; there are others when the reverse holds good.

ORESTES

I will begin forthwith. A long statement has advantages over a short
one and is more intelligible to hear. Give me nothing of thine own, Menelaus, but repay what thou didst thyself receive from my father. (*As*
MENELAUS *makes a deprecating gesture*) 'Tis not goods I mean; save
my life, and that is goods, the dearest I possess.

Say I am doing wrong. Well, I have a right to a little wrong-doing at
thy hands to requite that wrong, for my father Agamemnon also did
wrong in gathering the host of Hellas and going up against Ilium, not that
he had sinned himself, but he was trying to find a cure for the sin and
wrong-doing of thy wife. So this is one thing thou art bound to pay me
back. For he had really sold his life to thee, a duty owed by friend to
friend, toiling hard in the press of battle that so thou mightest win thy
wife again. This is what thou didst receive at Troy; make me the same
return. For one brief day exert thyself, not ten full years, on my behalf,
standing up in my defence.

As for the loan paid to Aulis in the blood of my sister, I leave that to
thy credit, not saying "Slay Hermione"; for in my present plight thou
must needs have an advantage over me and I must let that pass. But
grant my hapless sire this boon, my life and the life of her who has pined
so long in maidenhood, my sister; for by my death I shall leave my
father's house without an heir.

"Impossible!" thou'lt say. Why, there's the point of that old adage,
"Friends are bound to succour friends in trouble." But when fortune
giveth of her best, what need of friends? for God's help is enough of itself when he chooses to give it.

All Hellas credits thee with deep affection for thy wife—and I am not saying this with any subtle attempt at wheedling thee—by her I implore thee. (*As* MENELAUS *turns away*) Ah me, my misery! at what a pass have I arrived! what avails my wretched effort? Still, (*preparing to make a final appeal*) 'tis my whole family on whose behalf I am making this appeal! O my uncle, my father's own brother! imagine that the dead man in his grave is listening, that his spirit is hovering o'er thy head and speaking through my lips. I have said my say with reference to tears and groans and misfortunes, and I have begged my life—the aim of every man's endeavour, not of mine alone.

LEADER

I, too, weak woman though I am, beseech thee, as thou hast the power, succour those in need.

MENELAUS

Orestes, thou art a man for whom I have a deep regard, and I would fain help thee bear thy load of woe; yea, for it is a duty, too, to lend a kinsman such assistance by dying or slaying his enemies, provided Heaven grants the means. I only wish I had that power granted me by the gods; as it is, I have arrived destitute of allies, after my long weary wanderings, with such feeble succour as my surviving friends afford. As then we should never get the better of Pelasgian Argos by fighting, our hopes now rest on this, the chance of prevailing by persuasion; and we must try that, for how can you win a great cause by small efforts? it were senseless even to wish it. For when the people fall into a fury and their rage is still fresh, they are as hard to appease as a fierce fire is to quench; but if you gently slacken your hold and yield a little to their tension, cautiously watching your opportunity, they may possibly exhaust their power; and then as soon as they have spent their rage, thou mayest obtain whatever thou wilt from them without any trouble; for they have a natural sense of pity, and a hot temper too, an invaluable quality if you watch it closely. So I will go and try to persuade Tyndareus and the citizens to moderate their excessive anger against thee; for it is with them as with a ship; she dips if her sheet is hauled too taut, but rights herself again if it is let go.

Attempts to do too much are as keenly resented by the citizens as they are by the gods; and so it must be by cleverness, not by the force of superior numbers, I frankly tell thee, that I must try to save thee. No prowess of mine as perhaps thou fanciest, could do it; for, had it been so easy to triumph single-handed over the troubles that beset thee, I should never have tried to bring Argives over to the side of mercy; but, as it is, the wise find themselves forced to bow to fortune.

(MENELAUS *and his retinue depart.*)

ORESTES

O thou that hast no use, save to head a host in a woman's cause! thou
traitor in thy friends' defence! dost turn thy back on me? What Agamemnon did is all forgotten.

Ah, my father! thy friends, it seems, desert thee in adversity. Alas! I
am betrayed; no longer have I any hope of finding a refuge where I may
escape the death-sentence of Argos; for this man was my haven of safety.

Ha! a welcome sight, there comes Pylades, my best of friends, running
hither from Phocis. A trusty comrade is a more cheering sight in trouble
than a calm is to sailors.

(PYLADES *enters alone.*)

PYLADES

On my way hither I traversed the town with more haste than I need
have used, to find thee and thy sister, having heard or rather myself
seen the citizens assembling, under the belief that they intend your immediate execution. What is happening here? how is it with thee? how farest
thou, my best of comrades, friends, and kin? for thou art all these to me.

ORESTES

Let one brief word declare to thee my evil case—it is "Ruin."

PYLADES

Include me then in it; for friends have all in common.

ORESTES

Menelaus is a traitor to me and my sister.

PYLADES

'Tis only natural that the husband of a traitress should prove a traitor.

ORESTES

He no more repaid me when he came than if he had never come.

PYLADES

Has he really arrived then in this land?

ORESTES

He was a long time coming, but very soon detected for all that in
treachery to his friends.

PYLADES

And did he bring his wife, that queen of traitresses, with him on his
ship?

ORESTES

It was not he who brought her, but she him.

PYLADES

Where is she who proved the ruin of so many Achaeans, though she was only a woman?

ORESTES

In my house; if, that is, I ought to call it mine.

PYLADES

And thou—what didst thou say to thy father's brother?

ORESTES

I besought him not to look on, while I and my sister were slain by the citizens.

PYLADES

By heaven! what said he to this? I fain would know.

ORESTES

Caution was the line he took—the usual policy of traitorous friends.

PYLADES

What excuse does he allege? when I have heard that, I know all.

ORESTES

The worthy sire arrived, who begat those peerless daughters.

PYLADES

Thou meanest Tyndareus; he was angry with thee, perhaps, for his daughter's sake.

ORESTES

Thou hast it; and Menelaus preferred his relationship to my father's.

PYLADES

Had he not courage enough to share thy troubles, when he *did* come?

ORESTES

Not he; he never was a warrior, though a doughty knight amongst women.

PYLADES

Thy case is desperate, it seems, and thou must die.

ORESTES

The citizens are to give their vote about us on the question of the murder.

PYLADES

And what is that to decide? tell me, for I am alarmed.

ORESTES

Our life or death; so short the words that tell of things so long!

PYLADES

Leave the palace, then, with thy sister and fly.

ORESTES

Look! we are being watched by guards on every side.

PYLADES

I saw that the streets of the city were secured with armed men.

ORESTES

We are as closely beleaguered as a city by its foes.

PYLADES

Ask me also of my state; for I too am ruined.

ORESTES

By whom? this would be a further sorrow to add to mine.

PYLADES

Strophius, my father, in a fit of anger, hath banished me his halls.

ORESTES

On some private charge, or one in which the citizens share?

PYLADES

He says it is a crime to have helped thee slay thy mother.

ORESTES

Woe is me! it seems my troubles will cause thee grief as well.

PYLADES

I am not like Menelaus; this must be endured.

ORESTES

Art thou not afraid that Argos will desire thy death as well as mine?

PYLADES

I am not theirs to punish; I belong to Phocis.

ORESTES

A terrible thing is the mob, when it has villains to lead it.

PYLADES

Aye, but with honest leaders its counsels are honest.

ORESTES

Go to; we must consult together.

PYLADES

What is it we must consider?

ORESTES

Suppose I go and tell the citizens—

PYLADES

That thy action was just—

ORESTES

In avenging my father?

PYLADES

I am afraid they will be glad enough to catch thee.

ORESTES

Well, am I to crouch in fear and die without a word?

PYLADES

That were cowardly.

ORESTES

How then shall I act?

PYLADES

Suppose thou stay here, what means of safety hast thou?

ORESTES

None.

PYLADES

And if thou go away, is there any hope of escaping thy troubles?

ORESTES

There might be possibly.

PYLADES

Well, is not that better than staying?

ORESTES

Am I to go, then?

PYLADES
Yes; if thou *art* slain, there will be some honour in dying thus.

ORESTES
True; thus I escape cowardice.

PYLADES
Better than by staying.

ORESTES
After all, I can justify my action.

PYLADES
Pray that this may be the only view they take.

ORESTES
Some one or two maybe will pity me—

PYLADES
Yes, thy noble birth is a great point.

ORESTES
Resenting my father's death.

PYLADES
That is all quite clear.

ORESTES
I must go, for to die ignobly is a coward's part.

PYLADES
Well said!

ORESTES
Shall we tell my sister?

PYLADES
God forbid!

ORESTES
True, there might be tears.

PYLADES
Would not that be a grave omen?

ORESTES
Yes, silence is manifestly the better course.

PYLADES

Thou wilt thus gain time.

ORESTES

There is only one obstacle in my way,—

PYLADES

What fresh objection now?

ORESTES

I am afraid the goddesses will prevent me by madness.

PYLADES

Nay, but I will take care of thee.

ORESTES

A wretched task, to come in contact with a sick man.

PYLADES

That is not my view in thy case.

ORESTES

Beware of becoming a partner in my madness.

PYLADES

Let that pass!

ORESTES

Thou wilt not hesitate?

PYLADES

Not I; hesitation is a grave ill amongst friends.

ORESTES

On then, pilot of my course!

PYLADES

A service I am glad to render.

ORESTES

And guide me to my father's tomb.

PYLADES

For what purpose?

ORESTES

That I may appeal to him to save me.

PYLADES

No doubt that is the proper way

ORESTES

May I not even see my mother's grave!

PYLADES

No; she was an enemy. But hasten, supporting those limbs, so slow from sickness, on mine, that the decision of Argos may not catch thee first; for I will carry thee through the town, careless of the mob and unabashed. For how shall I prove my friendship if not by helping thee in sore distress?

ORESTES

Ah! the old saying again, "Get friends, not relations only." For a man whose soul is knit with thine, though he is not of thy kin, is better worth owning as a friend than a whole host of relations.

(ORESTES *and* PYLADES *go out.*)

CHORUS (*singing*)

strophe

Long, long ago, by reason of an old misfortune to their house, the sons of Atreus saw the tide roll back from weal to woe, carrying with it their great prosperity and that prowess proudly vaunted through the length of Hellas and by the streams of Simois, on the day that strife found its way to the sons of Tantalus—that strife for a golden ram,[3] to end in bitter banqueting and the slaughter of high-born babes; and this is why a succession of murders committed by kinsmen never fails the twin Atreidae.

antistrophe

What seemed so right became so wrong, to cut a mother's skin with ruthless hand and show the bloodstained sword to the sun's bright beams; and yet her guilty deed was a piece of frantic wickedness and the folly of beings demented. Hapless daughter of Tyndareus! in terror of death she screamed to him, "My son, this is a crime, thy bold attempt upon thy mother's life; do not, whilst honouring thy father, fasten on thyself an eternity of shame." To stain the hand in a mother's blood!

epode

What affliction on earth surpasseth this? what calls for keener grief or pity? Oh! what an awful crime Agamemnon's son committed, ending in his raving madness, so that he is become a prey to the avenging fiends for the murder, darting distracted glances round him! O the wretch! to have seen a mother's bosom o'er her robe of golden woof, and yet make her his victim, in recompense for his father's sufferings!

(ELECTRA *comes out of the palace.*)

ELECTRA

Surely, friends, my poor Orestes hath never left the house, mastered by the heaven-sent madness?

LEADER OF THE CHORUS

No; but he is gone to stand the trial appointed concerning his life before the Argive populace, in which it will be decided whether he and thou are to live or die.

ELECTRA

Oh! why did he do it? who persuaded him?

LEADER

Pylades; but this messenger, now close at hand, will no doubt tell us thy brother's fate at the trial.
(*A* MESSENGER, *formerly a servant of Agamemnon, enters.*)

MESSENGER

Woe is thee, unhappy daughter of our captain Agamemnon, my lady Electra! hearken to the sad tidings I bring thee.

ELECTRA

Alas! our fate is sealed; thy words show it; thou art clearly come with tidings of woe.

MESSENGER

To-day have the folk decided by vote that thou and thy brother are to die, poor lady.

ELECTRA

Alas! my expectation has come to pass; I have long feared this, and been wasting away in mourning for what was sure to happen. But come, old friend, describe the trial, and tell me what was said in the Argive assembly to condemn us and confirm our doom; is it stoning or the sword that is to cut short my existence? for I share my brother's misfortunes.

MESSENGER

I had just come from the country and was entering the gates, anxious to learn what was decided about thee and Orestes—for I was ever well-disposed to thy father, and it was thy house that fed and reared me, poor,

'tis true, yet loyal in the service of friends—when lo! I saw a crowd
streaming to their seats on yonder height, where 'tis said Danaus first
gathered his people and settled them in new homes, when he was paying the penalty to Aegyptus. So, when I saw them thronging together, I
asked a citizen, "What news in Argos? Have tidings of hostilities ruffled
the city of Danaus?" But he replied, "Dost thou not see the man Orestes
on his way to be tried for his life?" Then I beheld an unexpected sight,
which I would I ne'er had seen—Pylades and thy brother approaching
together; the one with his head sunken on his breast, weakened by sickness; the other like a brother in the way he shared his friend's sorrow,
tending his complaint with constant care.

Now when the Argives were fully gathered, a herald rose and asked,
"Who wishes to give his opinion whether Orestes is to be slain or not for
the murder of his mother?" Then up stood Talthybius, who helped thy
father sack the Phrygians' city. He adopted a trimming tone, a mere tool
of those in power as he always is, expressing high admiration for thy
father, but saying not a word for thy brother, urging his crooked sentiments in specious words, to this effect: "it is not a good precedent he is
establishing as regards parents," and all the while he had a pleasant look
for the friends of Aegisthus. That is like the tribe of heralds; they always
trip across to the lucky side; whoso hath influence in the city or a post
in the government, he is the friend for them. After him prince Diomedes
made harangue; not death but exile was the punishment he would have
had them inflict on thee and thy brother, and so keep clear of guilt. Some
murmured their assent, saying his words were good, but others disap-
proved.

Next stood up a fellow, who cannot close his lips; one whose impudence
is his strength; an Argive, but not of Argos; [4] an alien forced on us; confident in bluster and licensed ignorance, and plausible enough to involve
his hearers in some mischief sooner or later; for when a man with a pleasing trick of speech, but of unsound principles, persuades the mob, it is a
serious evil to the state; whereas all who give sound and sensible advice
on all occasions, if not immediately useful to the state, yet prove so afterwards. And this is the light in which to regard a party leader; for the
position is much the same in the case of an orator and a man in office. This
fellow was for stoning thee and Orestes to death, but it was Tyndareus
who kept suggesting arguments of this kind to him as he urged the death
of both of you.

Another then stood up, not fair to outward view perhaps but a brave
man, rarely coming in contact with the town or the gatherings in the
market-place; a yeoman, one of a class who form the only real support of
our country; shrewd enough, and eager to grapple with the arguments;
his character without a blemish, his walk in life beyond reproach. He

moved that they should crown Orestes, the son of Agamemnon, for showing his willingness to avenge a father in the blood of a wicked profligate
who was preventing men from taking up arms and going on foreign
service; "since," said he, "those, who remain behind, corrupt and seduce
our wives left as keepers of our homes." To the better sort his words carried conviction; and no one rose to speak after him. So thy brother advanced and spoke. "Ye dwellers in the land of Inachus! Pelasgians in ancient times, and later Danai, I helped you no less than my father when I
slew my mother; for if the murder of men by women is to be sanctioned,
then the sooner you die, the better for you; otherwise you must needs
become the slaves of women; and that will be doing the very reverse of
what ye should. As it is, she who betrayed my father's honour has met her
death, but if ye take my life, as is proposed, the strictness of the law
becomes relaxed, and the sooner every one of you is dead, the better; for
it will never be daring at any rate that they will lack." Yet, for all he
seemed to speak so fair, he could not persuade the assembly; but that
villain who spoke in favour of slaying thee and thy brother, gained his
point by appealing to the mob.

Orestes, poor wretch, scarce prevailed on them to spare him death by
stoning, promising to die by his own hand, and thou by thine, within the
space of to-day; and Pylades is now bringing him from the conclave,
weeping the while, and his friends bear him company, with tears and
lamentation; so he cometh, a sad and piteous sight for thee to see. Make
ready the sword, prepare the noose for thy neck, for thou must die; thy
noble birth availed thee naught, nor Phoebus either from his seat on the
tripod at Delphi; no! he was thy undoing.

(The MESSENGER *withdraws.)*

LEADER

Ah, hapless maid! How dumb thou art, thy face veiled and bent upon
the ground, as if ere long to start on a course of lamentation and wailing!

ELECTRA (*chanting*)

Land of Argos! I take up the dirge, doing bloody outrage on my
cheek with pearly nail, and beating on my head, the meed of Persephone that fair young goddess of the nether world. Let the land of the
Cyclops break forth into wailing for the sorrows of our house, laying
the steel upon the head to crop it close. This is the piteous strain that
goeth up for those who are doomed to perish, the chieftains once of
Hellas.

Gone, gone and brought to naught is all the race of Pelops' sons!
and with them the blessedness that crowned their happy home of
yore; the wrath of God gat hold on them and that cruel murdering
vote which prevails among the citizens.

Woe to you! ye tribes of short-lived men, full of tears and born to suffering, see how fate runs counter to your hopes! All in time's long march receive in turn their several troubles; and man throughout his life can never rest.

Oh! to reach that rock which hangs suspended midway 'twixt earth and heaven, that fragment from Olympus torn, which swings on chains of gold in ceaseless revolution, that I may utter my lament to Tantalus my forefather, who begat the ancestors of my house; these were witnesses of infatuate deeds when Pelops in four-horsed car drove winged steeds in hot pursuit along the sea, hurling the corpse of murdered Myrtilus into the heaving deep, after his race near the foam-flecked strand of Geraestus. From this came a woful curse upon my house, in the day that there appeared among the flocks of Atreus, breeder of horses, that baleful portent of a lamb with golden fleece, the creation of the son of Maia; for from it sprang a quarrel, which made the sun's winged steeds swerve from their course, turning them by a westward track along the sky towards the single horse of Dawn; and Zeus diverted the career of the seven Pleiads into a new path; yea, and it is that banquet to which Thyestes gave his name, and the guilty love of Cretan Aerope, the treacherous wife, that is requiting those murders with others; but the crowning woe is come on me and on my sire by reason of the bitter destinies of our house.

CHORUS (*chanting*)

See where thy brother comes, condemned to die, and with him Pylades, most loyal of friends, true as a brother, guiding the feeble steps of Orestes, as he paces carefully at his side.

(ORESTES *and* PYLADES *enter.*)

ELECTRA

Ah! brother mine, I weep to see thee stand before the tomb, face to face with the funeral pyre. Again that sigh escapes me; my senses leave me as I take my last fond look at thee.

ORESTES

Peace! an end to womanish lamenting! resign thyself to thy fate. True, 'tis a piteous end, but yet we needs must bear the present.

ELECTRA

How can I hold my peace, when we poor sufferers are no more to gaze upon the sun-god's light?

ORESTES

Oh! spare me *that* death! Enough that this unhappy wretch is already slain by Argives; forego our present sufferings.

ELECTRA

Alas for thy young life, Orestes! alas for the untimely death o'ertaking it! Thou shouldst have begun to live just as thou art dying.

ORESTES

Unman me not, I do adjure thee! bringing me to tears by the recollection of my sorrows.

ELECTRA

We are to die, and I cannot but bemoan our fate; for all men grieve to lose dear life.

ORESTES

This is the day appointed us; and we must fit the dangling noose about our necks or whet the sword for use.

ELECTRA

Be thou my executioner, brother, that no Argive may insult the child of Agamemnon and slay her.

ORESTES

Enough that I have a mother's blood upon me; thee I will not slay; but die by any self-inflicted death thou wilt.

ELECTRA

Agreed; I will not be behind thee in using the sword; only I long to throw my arms about thy neck.

ORESTES

Enjoy that idle satisfaction, if embraces have any joy for those who are come so nigh to death.

ELECTRA

Dear brother mine! bearer of a name that sounds most sweet in thy sister's ear, partner in one soul with her!

ORESTES

Oh! thou wilt melt my heart. I long to give thee back a fond embrace; and why should such a wretch as I feel any shame henceforth? (*Embracing* ELECTRA) Heart to heart, O sister mine! how sweet to me this close embrace! In place of wedded joys, in place of babes, this greeting is all that is possible to us in our misery.

ELECTRA

Ah, would the self-same sword, if only it might be, could slay us both, and one coffin of cedar-wood receive us!

ORESTES

That would be an end most sweet; but surely thou seest we are too destitute of friends to be allowed to share one tomb.

ELECTRA

Did not that coward Menelaus, that traitor to my father's memory, even speak for thee, making an effort to save thy life?

ORESTES

He did not so much as show himself, but having his hopes centred on the throne he was more cautious than to attempt the rescue of relatives. Ah! well, let us take care to quit ourselves gallantly and die as most befits the children of Agamemnon. I, for my part, will let this city see my noble spirit when I plunge the sword to my heart, and thou, for thine, must imitate my brave example. Do thou, Pylades, stand umpire to our bloody feat, and, when we both are dead, lay out our bodies decently; then carry them to our father's grave and bury us there with him. Farewell now; I go to do the deed, as thou seest.

PYLADES

Stay a moment; there is first one point I have to blame thee for, if thou thinkest I care to live when thou art dead.

ORESTES

But why art thou called on to die with me?

PYLADES

Canst ask? What is life to me with thee my comrade gone?

ORESTES

Thou didst not slay thy mother, as I did to my sorrow.

PYLADES

At least I helped thee; and so I ought to suffer alike.

ORESTES

Surrender to thy father; and seek not to die with me. Thou hast still a city, while I no longer have; thou hast still thy father's home, and mighty stores of wealth; and though thou art disappointed in thy marriage with my poor sister, whom I betrothed to thee from a deep regard for thy fellowship, yet choose thee another bride and rear a family; for the tie which bound us binds no more. Fare thee well, my comrade fondly called; for us such faring cannot be, for thee perhaps; for we that are as dead are robbed of joy henceforth.

PYLADES

How far thou art from grasping what I mean! Oh! may the fruitful earth, the radiant sky refuse to hold my blood, if ever I turn traitor and desert thee when I have cleared myself; for I not only shared in the murder, which I will not disown, but also schemed the whole plot for which thou art now paying the penalty; wherefore I ought also to die as much as thou or she; for I consider her, whose hand thou didst promise me, as my wife. What specious tale shall I ever tell, when I reach Delphi, the citadel of Phocis? I who, before your misfortunes came, was so close a friend, but ceased to be, when thou wert unlucky. That must not be; no! this is my business too. But since we are to die, let us take counsel together that Menelaus may share our misfortune.

ORESTES

Best of friends! if only I could see this ere I die!

PYLADES

Hearken then, and defer awhile the fatal stroke.

ORESTES

I will wait in the hope of avenging me of my foe.

PYLADES

Hush! I have small confidence in women.

ORESTES

Have no fear of these; for they are our friends who are here.

PYLADES

Let us kill Helen, a bitter grief to Menelaus.

ORESTES

How? I am ready enough, if there is any chance of success.

PYLADES

With our swords; she is hiding in thy house.

ORESTES

Aye, that she is, and already she is putting her seal on everything.

PYLADES

She shall do so no more, after she is wedded to Hades.

ORESTES

Impossible! she has her barbarian attendants.

PYLADES

Barbarians indeed! I am not the man to fear any Phrygian.

ORESTES

Creatures only fit to look after mirrors and unguents!

PYLADES

What! has she brought Trojan effeminacy with her here?

ORESTES

So much so that Hellas is become too small for her to live in.

PYLADES

The race of slaves is no match for free-born men.

ORESTES

Well, if I can do this deed, I fear not death twice over.

PYLADES

No, nor I either, if it is thee I am avenging.

ORESTES

Declare the matter and tell me what thou proposest.

PYLADES

We will enter the house on the pretence of going to our death.

ORESTES

So far I follow thee, but not beyond.

PYLADES

We will begin bewailing our sufferings to her.

ORESTES

Aye, so that she will shed tears, although her heart is glad.

PYLADES

And we shall then be in the same predicament as she.

ORESTES

How shall we proceed next in the enterprise?

PYLADES

We shall have swords concealed in our cloaks.

ORESTES

But, before attacking her, how are we to kill her attendants?

PYLADES

We will shut them up in different parts of the house.

ORESTES

And whoever refuses to be quiet, we must kill.

PYLADES

That done, our very deed shows us to what we must direct our efforts.

ORESTES

To Helen's slaughter; I understand that watchword.

PYLADES

Thou hast it; now hear how sound my scheme is; if we had drawn the sword upon a woman of greater chastity,[5] it would have been foul murder; but, as it is, she will be punished for the sake of all Hellas, whose sires she slew; while those whose children she destroyed, whose wives she widowed, will shout aloud for joy and kindle the altars of the gods, invoking on our heads a thousand blessings, because we shed this wicked woman's blood; for after killing her, thy name shall no more be "the matricide," but, resigning that title, thou shalt succeed to a better and be called "the slayer of Helen the murderess." It can never, never be right that Menelaus should prosper, and thy father, thy sister and thou be put to death, and thy mother too—(but I pass that by, for it is not seemly to mention it); —while he possesses thy home, though it was by Agamemnon's prowess that he regained his wife. May I perish then, if I draw not my sword upon her! But if after all we fail to compass Helen's death, we will fire the palace and die; for we will not fail to achieve one distinction, be it an honourable death or an honourable escape therefrom.

LEADER OF THE CHORUS

The daughter of Tyndareus, who has brought shame on her sex, has justly earned the hate of every woman.

ORESTES

Ah! there is nothing better than a trusty friend, neither wealth nor princely power; mere number is a senseless thing to set off against a noble friend. Such art thou, for thou didst not only devise the vengeance we took on Aegisthus, but didst stand by me at the gates of danger, and now again thou art offering me a means to punish my foes and dost not stand aloof thyself; but I will cease praising thee, for there is something wearisome even in being praised to excess. Now since in any case I must breathe my last, I would fain my death should do my foes some hurt, that I may requite with ruin those who betrayed me, and that they too who made me suffer may taste of sorrow. Lo! I am the son of that Agamemnon, who was counted worthy to rule Hellas, exerting no tyrant's power but yet possessed of almost god-like might; him will I not disgrace by submitting to die like a slave; no! my last breath shall be free and I will avenge me on Menelaus. For could we but secure one object we should be lucky, if from some unexpected quarter a means of safety should arise and we be the slayers, not the slain; this is what I pray for; for this wish of mine is a pleasant dream to cheer the heart, without cost, by means of the tongue's winged utterances.

ELECTRA

Why, brother, I have it! a means of safety, first for thee, then for him, and thirdly for myself.

ORESTES

Divine providence, I suppose. But what use in suggesting that? seeing that I know the natural shrewdness of thy heart.

ELECTRA

Hearken a moment; (*to* PYLADES) do thou likewise attend.

ORESTES

Say on; the prospect of hearing good news affords a certain pleasure.

ELECTRA

Thou knowest Helen's daughter? of course thou must.

ORESTES

Hermione, whom my own mother reared,—know her? yes.

ELECTRA

She hath gone to Clytemnestra's grave.

ORESTES

With what intent? What hope art thou hinting at?

ELECTRA

Her purpose was to pour a libation over the tomb of our mother.

ORESTES

Well, granting that, how does this which thou hast mentioned conduce to our safety?

ELECTRA

Seize her as a hostage on her way back.

ORESTES

What good can thy suggested remedy do us three friends?

ELECTRA

If, after Helen's slaughter, Menelaus does anything to thee or to Pylades and me,—for we three friends are wholly one,—say thou wilt slay Hermione; then draw thy sword and keep it at the maiden's throat. If Menelaus, when he sees Helen weltering in her blood, tries to save thee to insure his daughter's life, allow him to take his child to his father's arms; but if he makes no effort to curb the angry outburst and leaves thee to die, then do thou plunge thy sword in his daughter's throat. Methinks, though he show himself violent at first, he will gradually grow milder; for he is not naturally bold or brave. That is the tower of defence I have for us, and now my tale is told.

ORESTES

O thou that hast the spirit of a man, though thy body clearly shows thee a tender woman, how far more worthy thou to live than die! This, Pylades, is the peerless woman thou wilt lose to thy sorrow, or, shouldst thou live, wilt marry to thy joy!

PYLADES

Then may I live and may she be brought to the capital of Phocis with, all the honours of a happy marriage!

ORESTES

How soon will Hermione return to the palace? All else thou saidst was well, if only we are lucky in catching the villain's child.

ELECTRA

I expect she is near the house already, for the time agrees exactly.

ORESTES

'Tis well. Plant thyself before the palace, Electra my sister, and await the maid's approach; keep watch in case any one, an ally maybe or my father's brother, forestall us by his entry, ere the bloody deed is completed; and then make a signal to be heard inside the house, either by beating on a panel of the door or calling to us within.

Let us enter now, Pylades, and arm ourselves for the final struggle, for thou art the comrade that sharest the enterprise with me. Hearken! father, in thy home of darkest gloom! it is thy son Orestes who is calling thee to come to the rescue of the destitute; it is on thy account I am unjustly suffering woe, and it is by thy brother that I have been betrayed for practising justice; wherefore I would fain take and slay his wife; and do thou help us compass this.

ELECTRA

Oh! come, my father, come! if within the ground thou hearest the cry of thy children, who for thy sake are dying.

PYLADES

Hear my prayer too, Agamemnon, kinsman of my father, and save thy children.

ORESTES

I slew my mother,—

PYLADES

I held the sword—

ELECTRA

'Twas I that urged them on and set them free from fear—

ORESTES

All to succour thee, my sire.

ELECTRA

I proved no traitress either.

PYLADES

Wilt thou not hearken then to these reproaches and save thy children?

ORESTES

With tears I pour thee a libation.

ELECTRA

And I with notes of woe.

PYLADES

Cease, and let us about our business. If prayers do really penetrate the ground, he hears. O Zeus, god of my fathers, O Justice, queen revered, vouchsafe us three success; three friends are we, but one the struggle, one the forfeit all must pay, to live or die.

(ORESTES *and* PYLADES *enter the palace. The following lines between* ELECTRA *and the* CHORUS *are chanted.*)

ELECTRA

My own townswomen, of foremost rank in Argos, the home of the Pelasgi!

CHORUS

Mistress, why dost thou address us? for still this honoured name is left thee in the Danaid town.

ELECTRA

Station yourselves, some here along the high road, others yonder
on some other path, to watch the house.

CHORUS

But why dost thou summon me to this service? tell me, dear mistress.

ELECTRA

I am afraid that some one, who is stationed at the house for a
bloody purpose, may cause troubles, only to find them himself.

FIRST SEMI-CHORUS

Lead on; let us hasten; I will keep careful watch upon this track
towards the east.

SECOND SEMI-CHORUS

And I on this, that leadeth westward. Throw a glance sideways,
letting the eye range from point to point; then look back again.

FIRST SEMI-CHORUS

We are directing them as thou biddest.

ELECTRA

Cast your eyes around, let them peer in every direction through
your tresses.

SECOND SEMI-CHORUS

Who is that on the road? Who is yonder countryman I see wandering round thy house?

ELECTRA

Ah! friends, we are undone; he will at once reveal to our enemies
the armed ambush of that lion-like pair.

FIRST SEMI-CHORUS (*reconnoitring*)

Calm thy fears; the road is not occupied, as thou thinkest, dear
mistress.

ELECTRA (*turning to the other watchers*)

And can I count thy side safe still? reassure me; is yonder space
before the court-yard still deserted?

SECOND SEMI-CHORUS

All goes well here; look to thy own watch, for no Argive is approaching us.

FIRST SEMI-CHORUS
Thy report agrees with mine; there is no noise here either.

ELECTRA
Well then, let me make myself heard in the gateway. (*Calling through the door*) Why are ye within the house delaying to spill your victim's blood, now that all is quiet? They do not hear; ah, woe is me! Can it be that their swords have lost their edge at the sight of her beauty? Soon will some mail-clad Argive, hurrying to her rescue, attack the palace. Keep a better look-out; 'tis no time for sitting still; bestir yourselves, some here, some there.

CHORUS
My eye is ranging to and fro all along the road.

HELEN (*within*)
Help, Pelasgian Argos! I am being foully murdered.

FIRST SEMI-CHORUS
Heard ye that? Those men are now about the bloody deed.

SECOND SEMI-CHORUS
'Tis Helen screaming, so it seems.

ELECTRA
Come, eternal might of Zeus, oh, come to help my friends!

HELEN (*within*)
Menelaus, I am being murdered, but thou, though near, affordest me no aid.

ELECTRA
Cut, stab, and kill; all eager for the fray dart out your swords, double-handed, double-edged, against the woman who left her father's home and husband's side, and did to death so many of the men of Hellas, slain beside the river-bank, where tears rained down beneath the iron darts all round Scamander's eddying tides.

LEADER OF THE CHORUS
Hush! hush! I caught the sound of a foot-fall on the road near the house.

ELECTRA
Ladies, my dearest friends, it is Hermione advancing into the midst of the bloodshed. Let our clamour cease; on she comes headlong into the meshes of the net. Fair will the quarry prove if caught. Resume your

station, looks composed and faces not betraying what has happened; and I too will wear a look of melancholy, as if forsooth I knew nothing of that desperate deed. (HERMIONE *enters.*) Ah! maiden, hast thou come from wreathing Clytemnestra's grave and from pouring libations to the dead?

HERMIONE

Yes, I have returned after securing a gracious recognition; but I was filled with some alarm as to the import of a cry I heard in the palace as I was still at a distance.

ELECTRA

But why? Our present lot gives cause for groans.

HERMIONE

Hush! What is thy news?

ELECTRA

Argos has sentenced Orestes and myself to death.

HERMIONE

Kinsfolk of my own! God forbid!

ELECTRA

It is decreed; the yoke of necessity is on our necks.

HERMIONE

Was this the reason then of the cry within?

ELECTRA

Yes, 'twas the cry of the suppliant as he fell at Helen's knees.

HERMIONE

Who is he? I am none the wiser, if thou tell me not.

ELECTRA

Orestes the hapless, entreating mercy for himself and me.

HERMIONE

Good reason then has the house to cry out.

ELECTRA

What else would make a man entreat more earnestly? Come, throw thyself before thy mother in her proud prosperity, and join thy friends in beseeching Menelaus not to look on and see us die. O thou that wert nursed in the same mother's arms as I, have pity on us and relieve our pain. Come hither to the struggle, and I myself will be thy guide; for thou and thou alone, hast the issue of our safety in thy hands.

HERMIONE

Behold me hastening to the house; as far as rests with me, regard yourselves as safe.

(HERMIONE *enters the palace.*)

ELECTRA

Now, friends, secure the prey in your armed ambush in the house.

HERMIONE (*calling from within*)

Ah! who are these I see?

ORESTES (*within*)

Silence! 'tis our safety, not thine, thou art here to insure.

ELECTRA

Hold her hard and fast; point a sword at her throat; then wait in
silence, that Menelaus may learn that they are men, not Phrygian
cowards, whom he has found and treated as only cowards deserve.

(*She enters the palace.*)

CHORUS (*chanting*)

What ho! my comrades, raise a din, a din and shouting before the
house, that the murder done may not inspire the Argives with wild
alarm, to make them bring aid to the royal palace, before I see for
certain whether Helen's corpse lies weltering in the house or hear
the news from one of her attendants; for I know but a part of the
tragedy, of the rest I am not sure. Thanks to Justice the wrath of
God has come on Helen; for she filled all Hellas with tears because
of her accursed paramour, Paris of Ida, who took our countrymen
to Troy.

But the bolts of the palace-doors rattle; be silent; for one of her
Phrygians is coming out, from whom we will inquire how it is within.

(*The* PHRYGIAN EUNUCH *enters from the palace. The following lines
between the* CHORUS *and the* PHRYGIAN *are sung or chanted.*)

PHRYGIAN (*expressing the most abject terror*)

From death escaped, in my barbaric slippers have I fled away, away
from the Argive sword, escaping as best a barbarian might by clam-
bering over the cedar beams that roof the porch and through the
Doric triglyphs. (O my country, my country!) Alack, alack! oh!
whither can I fly, ye foreign dames, winging my way through the
clear bright sky or over the sea, whose circle hornèd Ocean draws,
as he girdles the world in his embrace?

CHORUS

What news, slave of Helen, creature from Ida?

PHRYGIAN

Ah me for Ilium, for Ilium, the city of Phrygia, and for Ida's holy
hill with fruitful soil! in foreign accents hear me raise a plaintive
strain over thee, whose ruin luckless Helen caused,—that lovely child
whom Leda bore to a feathered swan, to be a curse to Apollo's towers
of polished stone. Ah! well-a-day! woe to Dardania for the wailings
wrung from it by the steeds that bought his minion Ganymede for
Zeus.

CHORUS

Tell us plainly exactly what happened in the house, for till now I
have been guessing at what I do not clearly understand.

PHRYGIAN

"Ah, for Linus! woe is him!" That is what barbarians say in their
eastern tongue as a prelude to the dirge of death, whene'er royal
blood is spilt upon the ground by deadly iron blades.

To tell thee exactly what happened: there came into the palace
two lion-like men of Hellas, twins in nature; your famous chief was
sire of one, 'twas said; the other was the son of Strophius; a crafty
knave was he, like to Odysseus, subtle, silent, but staunch to his
friends, daring enough for any valiant deed, versed in war and blood-
thirsty as a serpent. Ruin seize him for his quiet plotting, the villain!

In they came, their eyes bedimmed with tears, and took their seats
in all humility near the chair of the lady whom Paris the archer once
wedded, one on this side, one on that, to right and left, with weapons
on them; and both threw their suppliant arms round the knees of
Helen; whereon her Phrygian servants started to their feet in wild
alarm, each in his terror calling to his fellow, "Beware of treachery!"
To some there seemed no cause, but others thought that the viper
who had slain his mother, was entangling the daughter of Tyndareus
in the toils of his snare.

CHORUS

And where wert thou the while? fled long before in terror?

PHRYGIAN

It happened that I, in Phrygian style, was wafting the breeze past
Helen's curls with a round feather-fan, stationed before her face; and
she the while, as eastern ladies use, was twisting flax on her distaff
with her fingers, but letting her yarn fall on the floor, for she was

minded to embroider purple raiment as an offering from the Trojan spoils, a gift for Clytemnestra at her tomb.

Then to the Spartan maid Orestes spake, "Daughter of Zeus, quit thy chair and cross the floor to a seat at the old altar of Pelops, our ancestor, to hear something I have to say." Therewith he led the way and she followed, little guessing his designs. Meantime his accomplice, the Phocian miscreant, was off on other business. "Out of my way! Well, Phrygians always were cowards." So he shut them up in different parts of the house, some in the stables, others in private chambers, one here, one there, disposing of them severally at a distance from their mistress.

CHORUS

What happened next?

PHRYGIAN

Mother of Ida, mighty parent! Oh! the murderous scenes and lawless wickedness that I witnessed in the royal palace! They drew forth swords from under their purple cloaks, each darting his eye all round him in either direction to see that none was near, and then, like boars that range the hills, they stood at bay before her, crying, "Thou must die; it is thy craven husband that will slay thee, because he betrayed his brother's son to death in Argos." But she with piercing screams brought down her snow-white arm upon her bosom and loudly smote on her poor head; then turned her steps in flight, shod in her golden shoon; but Orestes, outstripping her slippered feet, clutched his fingers in her hair and bending back her neck on to her left shoulder was on the point of driving the grim steel into her throat.

CHORUS

Where were those Phrygians in the house to help her then?

PHRYGIAN

With a loud cry we battered down the doors and doorposts of the rooms we had been penned in, by means of bars, and ran to her assistance from every direction, one arming himself with stones, another with javelins, a third having a drawn sword; but Pylades came to meet us, all undaunted, like Hector of Troy or Ajax triple-plumed, as I saw him on the threshold of Priam's palace; and we met point to point. But then it became most manifest how inferior we Phrygians were to the warriors of Hellas in martial prowess. There was one man flying, another slain, a third wounded, yet another craving mercy to stave off death; but we escaped under cover of the darkness: while some were falling, others staggering, and some laid low in death. And just as her unhappy mother sunk to the ground to die, came luckless Hermione to the palace; whereon those twain, like Bacchanals when they drop their wands and seize a mountain-cub, rushed and seized her; then turned again to the daughter of Zeus to slay her; but lo! she had vanished from the room, passing right through the house by magic spells or wizards' arts or heavenly fraud; O Zeus and earth, O day and night!

What happened afterwards I know not, for I stole out of the palace and ran away. So Menelaus went through all his toil and trouble to recover his wife Helen from Troy to no purpose.

(ORESTES *comes out of the palace.*)

LEADER OF THE CHORUS
Behold another strange sight succeeding its predecessors; I see Orestes sword in hand before the palace, advancing with excited steps.

ORESTES
Where is he who fled from the palace to escape my sword?

PHRYGIAN (*falling at the feet of* ORESTES)
Before thee I prostrate myself, O prince, and do obeisance in my foreign way.

ORESTES
'Tis not Ilium that is now the scene, but the land of Argos.

PHRYGIAN
No matter where, the wise love life more than death.

ORESTES
I suppose that shouting of thine was not for Menelaus to come to the rescue?

PHRYGIAN
Oh no! it was to help thee I called out, for thou art more deserving.

ORESTES
Was it a just fate that overtook the daughter of Tyndareus?

PHRYGIAN
Most just, though she had had three throats to die with.

ORESTES
Thy cowardice makes thee glib; these are not thy real sentiments.

PHRYGIAN

Why, surely she deserved it for the havoc she made of Hellas as well as Troy?

ORESTES

Swear thou art not saying this to humour me, or I will slay thee.

PHRYGIAN

By my life I swear,—an oath likely to be true in my case.

ORESTES

Did every Phrygian in Troy show the same terror of steel as thou dost?

PHRYGIAN

Oh, take thy sword away! held so near it throws a horrid gleam of blood.

ORESTES

Art thou afraid of being turned to a stone, as if it were a Gorgon thou seest?

PHRYGIAN

To a stone, no! but to a corpse; that Gorgon's head is not within my ken.

ORESTES

A slave, and so fearful of death, which will release thee from trouble!

PHRYGIAN

Bond or free, every one is glad to gaze upon the light.

ORESTES

Well said! thy shrewdness saves thee; go within.

PHRYGIAN

Thou wilt not kill me after all?

ORESTES

Thou art spared!

PHRYGIAN

O gracious words!

ORESTES

Come, I shall change my mind—

PHRYGIAN

Ill-omened utterance!

ORESTES

Thou fool! dost think I could endure to plunge my sword in throat of thine, thou that neither art woman nor amongst men hast any place? The reason I left the palace was to gag thy noisy tongue; for Argos is quickly roused, once it hears a cry to the rescue. As for Menelaus, we are not afraid of measuring swords with him; no! he may go upon his way proud of the golden ringlets on his shoulders; for if, to avenge the slaying of Helen, he gathers the Argives and leads them against the palace, refusing to attempt the rescue of me, my sister, and Pylades my fellow-conspirator, he shall have two corpses to behold, his daughter's as well as his wife's.

(*The* PHRYGIAN *departs as* ORESTES *re-enters the palace.*)

CHORUS (*singing*)

Ah! fortune, fortune! again and yet again the house is entering on a fearful contest for the race of Atreus.

FIRST SEMI-CHORUS (*chanting*)

What are we to do? carry tidings to the town, or hold our peace?

SECOND SEMI-CHORUS (*chanting*)

It is safer to keep silence, friends.

FIRST SEMI-CHORUS (*chanting*)

Look, look at that sudden rush of smoke to the sky in front of the palace, telling its tale in advance!

SECOND SEMI-CHORUS (*chanting*)

They are kindling torches to fire the halls of Tantalus; they do not shrink even from murder.

CHORUS (*singing*)

God holds the issue in his hand, to give to mortal men what end he will. Some mighty power is his; it was through a vengeful fiend that this family started on its career of murder, by hurling Myrtilus from the chariot.

But lo! I see Menelaus approaching the palace in hot haste; no doubt he has heard what is happening here. What ho! within, descendants of Atreus, make haste and secure the doors with bars. A man in luck is a dangerous adversary for luckless wretches like thyself, Orestes.

(ORESTES *and* PYLADES *appear on the roof, holding* HERMIONE. MENELAUS *and his attendants enter.*)

MENELAUS

Strange news of violent deeds done by a pair of savages,—men I do not
call them,—has brought me hither. What I heard was that my wife was
not killed after all, but had vanished out of sight,—an idle rumour doubtless, brought to me by some dupe of his own terror; a ruse perhaps of the
matricide to turn the laugh against me.

Throw wide the palace doors! My orders to my servants are that they
force the doors, that I may rescue my child at any rate from the hands
of the murderers and recover my poor wife's corpse, that dear partner
whose slayers must die with her by my arm.

ORESTES (*from the roof*)

Ho, fellow! Keep thy fingers off those bolts, thou Menelaus, who
vauntest thyself so high; else will I tear off the ancient parapet, the work
of masons, and shatter thy skull with this coping-stone. The doors are
bolted and barred, which will prevent thy entrance to the palace and thy
eagerness to bring aid.

MENELAUS

Ha! what now? I see a blaze of torches and men standing at bay on
the house-top yonder, with a sword held at my daughter's throat.

ORESTES

Wouldst question me or hear me speak?

MENELAUS

Neither; but I suppose I *must* hear thee.

ORESTES

Well, if thou art anxious to know, I intend to slay thy daughter.

MENELAUS

After slaying Helen, art thou bent on adding another murder?

ORESTES

I would I had compassed that, instead of being duped by the gods!

MENELAUS

Dost thou deny having slain her, saying this out of wanton insult?

ORESTES

Yes, I do deny it to my sorrow. Would God—

MENELAUS

Would God—what? Thou provokest my fears.

ORESTES

I had hurled to Hades the pollution of Hellas!

MENELAUS

Surrender my wife's dead body, that I may bury her.

ORESTES

Ask the gods for her; but thy daughter I will slay.

MENELAUS

This matricide is bent on adding murder to murder.

ORESTES

This champion of his sire, betrayed by thee to death.

MENELAUS

Art thou not content with the stain of the mother's blood which is on thee?

ORESTES

I should not grow tired if I had these wicked women to slay for ever.

MENELAUS

Art thou too, Pylades, a partner in this bloody work?

ORESTES

His silence says he is; so my saying it will suffice.

MENELAUS

Not without thy ruing it, unless thou take wings and fly.

ORESTES

Fly we never will, but will fire the palace.

MENELAUS

What! wilt thou destroy the home of thy ancestors?

ORESTES

To prevent thee getting it I will, offering this maid in sacrifice upon its flames.

MENELAUS

Kill her, for thou wilt be punished by me for such a murder.

ORESTES

Agreed.

MENELAUS

No, no! refrain!

ORESTES

Silence! thy sufferings are just; endure them.

MENELAUS

Pray, is it just that thou shouldst live?

ORESTES

And rule a kingdom, yes.

MENELAUS

A kingdom—where?

ORESTES

Here in Pelasgian Argos.

MENELAUS

Thou art so well qualified to handle sacred water!

ORESTES

And, pray, why not?

MENELAUS

And to slay victims before battle!

ORESTES

Well, art thou?

MENELAUS

Yes, my hands are clean.

ORESTES

But not thy heart.

MENELAUS

Who would speak to thee?

ORESTES

Every man that loves his father.

MENELAUS

And the man who honours his mother?

ORESTES

He's a happy man.

MENELAUS

Thou didst not honour thine, at any rate.

ORESTES

No, for I delight not in your wicked women.

MENELAUS

Remove that sword from my daughter's throat.

ORESTES

Thou art wrong.

MENELAUS

What! wilt slay her?

ORESTES

Right once more.

MENELAUS

Ah me! what can I do?

ORESTES

Go to the Argives and persuade them—

MENELAUS

To what?

ORESTES

Entreat the city that we may not die.

MENELAUS

Otherwise, will ye slay my child?

ORESTES

That is the alternative.

MENELAUS

Alas for thee, Helen!

ORESTES

And is it not "alas!" for me?

MENELAUS

I brought her back from Troy only for thee to butcher.

ORESTES

Would I had!

MENELAUS

After troubles innumerable.

ORESTES

Except where I was concerned.

MENELAUS

Dread treatment mine!

ORESTES

The reason being thy refusal to help me then?

MENELAUS

Thou hast me.

ORESTES

Thy own cowardice has. (*Calling from the roof to* ELECTRA) Ho there!
fire the palace from beneath, Electra; and, Pylades, my trusty friend,
kindle the parapet of yonder walls. (*The palace is seen to be ablaze.*)

MENELAUS

Help, help, ye Danai! gird on your harness and come, ye dwellers in
knightly Argos! for here is a fellow trying to wrest his life from your
whole city, though he has caused pollution by shedding his mother's blood.
                    (APOLLO *appears from above with* HELEN.)

APOLLO

Menelaus, calm thy excited mood; I am Phoebus, the son of Latona,
who draw nigh to call thee by name, and thou no less, Orestes, who, sword
in hand, art keeping guard on yonder maid, that thou mayst hear what I
have come to say. Helen, whom all thy eagerness failed to destroy, when
thou wert seeking to anger Menelaus, is here as ye see in the enfolding air,
rescued from death instead of slain by thee. 'Twas I that saved her and
snatched her from beneath thy sword at the bidding of her father Zeus;
for she his child must put on immortality, and take her place with Castor
and Polydeuces in the bosom of the sky, a saviour to mariners. Choose
thee then another bride and take her to thy home, for the gods by means
of Helen's loveliness embroiled Troy and Hellas, causing death thereby,
that they might lighten mother Earth of the outrage done her by the
increase of man's number. Such is Helen's end.

But as for thee, Orestes, thou must cross the frontier of this land and
dwell for one whole year on Parrhasian soil, which from thy flight thither
shall be called the land of Orestes by Azanians and Arcadians; and when
thou returnest thence to the city of Athens, submit to be brought to trial
by "the Avenging Three" for thy mother's murder, for the gods will be
umpires between you and will pass a most righteous sentence on thee upon
the hill of Ares, where thou art to win thy case. Likewise, it is ordained,
Orestes, that thou shalt wed Hermione, at whose neck thou art pointing
thy sword; Neoptolemus shall never marry her, though he thinks he will;

for his death is fated to o'ertake him by a Delphian sword, when he claims satisfaction of me for the death of his father Achilles. Bestow thy sister's hand on Pylades, to whom thou didst formerly promise her; the life awaiting him henceforth is one of bliss.

Menelaus, leave Orestes to rule Argos; go thou and reign o'er Sparta, keeping it as the dowry of a wife, who till this day ne'er ceased exposing thee to toils innumerable. Between Orestes and the citizens, I, who forced his mother's murder on him, will bring about a reconciliation.

ORESTES

Hail to thee, prophetic Loxias, for these thy utterances! Thou art not a lying prophet after all, but a true seer; and yet there came a dreadful thought into my heart that it was some fiend I had listened to, when I seemed to hear thy voice; but all is ending well, and I obey thy word. There! I release Hermione from a violent death and agree to make her my wife whenever her father gives consent.

MENELAUS

All hail, Helen, daughter of Zeus! I wish thee joy of thy home in heaven's happy courts. To thee, Orestes, I betroth my daughter according to the word of Phoebus, and good luck attend thee, a noble wooer nobly wived, and me the parent of thy bride!

APOLLO

Repair each one to the place appointed by me; reconcile all strife.

MENELAUS

Obedience is a duty.

ORESTES

I think thus also, Menelaus; so here I make a truce with sorrow and with thy oracles, O Loxias.

APOLLO (*chanting*)

Go your ways, and honour Peace, most fair of goddesses; I, meantime, will escort Helen to the mansions of Zeus, soon as I reach the star-lit firmament. There, seated side by side with Hera and Hebe, the bride of Heracles, she shall be honoured by men with drink-offerings as a goddess for ever, sharing with those Zeus-born sons of Tyndareus their empire o'er the sea, for the good of mariners.

(APOLLO *and* HELEN *vanish.*)

CHORUS (*chanting*)

Hail! majestic Victory, still in thy keeping hold my life and ne'er withhold the crown! [6]

COLERIDGE's translation has been slightly modified in the following lines: 5, 168, 181, 226, 248, 394, 496, 564, 569, 604, 635, 641, 688, 700, 794, 859, 928–929, 1051, 1055, 1147, 1298, 1368, 1549, 1554, 1616, 1617, 1642, 1680.

1. *i.e.,* madness.

2. It is interesting to note that Euripides in this play follows the traditional legend of Helen.

3. Cf. Euripides, *Electra,* note 2.

4. This is usually taken to be a reference to Cleophon, the demagogue of Athens, who was of Thracian extraction.

5. The Greek word here is the adjectival form of *sophrosyne.* Cf. Euripides, *Hippolytus,* note 1.

6. Cf. the *Iphigenia in Tauris,* note 3.

XV
THE PHOENISSAE

CHARACTERS IN THE PLAY

JOCASTA, *wife of* OEDIPUS
OLD SERVANT, *an attendant of* ANTIGONE
ANTIGONE, *daughter of* OEDIPUS
CHORUS OF PHOENICIAN MAIDENS
POLYNEICES, *exiled son of* OEDIPUS
ETEOCLES, *now King of Thebes; son of* OEDIPUS
CREON, *brother of* JOCASTA
TEIRESIAS, *a blind prophet*
MENOECEUS, *son of* CREON
FIRST MESSENGER
SECOND MESSENGER
OEDIPUS, *formerly King of Thebes*
Daughter of TEIRESIAS, *guards, attendants*

INTRODUCTION

LIKE the *Orestes*, *The Phoenissae* enjoyed great popularity in antiquity. It was first presented probably about 409 B.C. and it evidently was in demand for revival as is indicated by the fact that the present text contains lines and passages which seem clearly to have come from the hand of a redactor. The most striking characteristic of the play is its great range and sweep of incidents. Euripides has taken the famous Theban story of Oedipus and of the curse upon the House of the Labdacidae, altered certain elements in it, and has presented within the limits of a single play a dramatic version of almost the entire legend. It must be remembered, however, that the original play probably was not so great in extent as it is in its present form.

One unique feature of *The Phoenissae* is the Chorus from which the play takes its name. The group is composed of Phoenician Maidens who have been dedicated by their native city to the service of Apollo. On their way to Delphi they have stopped for a time at Thebes, a city with which they have certain traditional ties. They are therefore able to serve in the play as relatively objective yet essentially sympathetic commentators upon the action as it develops.

The particular episodes of the legend which Euripides presents in his tragedy take place on the day when the Argive host under the leadership of Polyneices attacks Thebes. The dramatic date therefore is precisely the same as that of Aeschylus' *The Seven Against Thebes*. Euripides, however, has departed somewhat from the traditional version of the legend, for in his play both the aged blind Oedipus and his wife, Jocasta, are still living. In other respects the poet follows in general the received account which records the quarrel between Eteocles and Polyneices over the throne, the latter's exile, his attack upon the city, and the last fatal combat between the brothers when each fell by the other's hand.

The fact that both Oedipus and Jocasta are still alive in this revised version of the story enables Euripides to introduce into his play a number of effective dramatic scenes. The most striking of all occurs when Polyneices enters the city under the protection of a truce to see his mother, Jocasta. She in turn brings her two sons face to face and makes a final and

160

futile effort to bring about their reconciliation. This episode gives Euripides the opportunity to develop the contrasting characters of the brothers.
Eteocles is portrayed as an individual consumed with ambition and who
vigorously defends his attitude on virtually Nietzschean grounds. Polyneices on the other hand shrinks from and detests the criminal character
of the acts which he is about to commit, yet is inevitably driven to them
by the unbearable injustice which he has been made to suffer by Eteocles.

Not only is *The Phoenissae* interesting because of its relationship with
Aeschylus' *The Seven Against Thebes,* but also because it reflects to some
extent Sophocles' *Oedipus the King* and *Antigone.* For example, Antigone's betrothal to Haemon figures in the play, as well as the question
whether or not the body of Polyneices shall receive ritual burial. Likewise
the perennial seer Teiresias appears and is handled by Euripides in a manner clearly reminiscent of the prophet's appearance in *Oedipus the King.*
The final scene of *The Phoenissae* obviously suggests the *Oedipus at
Colonus,* for here we see the old king as he bitterly departs into exile, attended by his faithful daughter, Antigone, yet at the same time we are
made aware that he looks forward to the peace which he will find at
Colonus. Since Sophocles' play is generally supposed to have been written
after *The Phoenissae,* critics have been disposed to conclude that this
last scene is not genuine, but has been added to the play, in order that it
might conform more closely with the Sophoclean tradition.[1]

Any careful criticism of *The Phoenissae* would have to contend that
Euripides has here wrought an absorbing and fascinating drama. Many
of the individual scenes are brilliantly done, and likewise in Jocasta and
Polyneices, to take the most notable examples, the poet has created great
tragic characters. The play as a whole has been well unified, and the
dramatist by pulling together all the varied episodes of the legend has
been able to produce a total effect which has undeniable power. Perhaps
Euripides has not developed the larger religious or moral implications of
his play, but he has presented in his protagonists human individuals who
possess basic human dignity as they face manfully the complex and bitter
stuff of human life.

[1] This argument cannot be regarded as absolutely final. For a complete discussion of
those passages of the play whose genuineness has been suspected, cf. the introduction
to J. U. Powell's edition of *The Phoenissae* (London, 1911).

THE PHOENISSAE

(SCENE:—*Before the royal palace of Thebes.* JOCASTA *enters from the palace alone.*)

JOCASTA

O SUN-GOD, who cleavest thy way along the starry sky, mounted on golden-studded car, rolling on thy path of flame behind fleet coursers, how curst the beam thou didst shed on Thebes, the day that Cadmus left Phoenicia's realm beside the sea and reached this land! He it was that in days long gone wedded Harmonia, the daughter of Cypris, and begat Polydorus from whom they say sprung Labdacus, and Laius from him. I am known as the daughter of Menoeceus, and Creon is my brother by the same mother. Men called me Jocasta, for so my father named me, and I am married to Laius. Now when he was still childless after being wedded to me a long time, he went and questioned Phoebus, craving moreover that our love might be crowned with sons born to his house. But the god said, "King of Thebes for horses famed! seek not to beget children against the will of heaven; for if thou beget a son, that child shall slay thee, and all thy house shall wade through blood." But he, yielding to his lust in a drunken fit, begat a son of me, and when his babe was born, conscious of his sin and of the god's warning, he gave the child to shepherds to expose in Hera's meadow on mount Cithaeron, after piercing his ankles with iron spikes; whence it was that Hellas named him Oedipus. But the keepers of the horses of Polybus finding him took him home and laid him in the arms of their mistress. So she suckled the child that I had borne and persuaded her husband she was its mother. Soon as my son was grown to man's estate, the tawny beard upon his cheek, either because he had guessed the fraud or learnt it from another, he set out for the shrine of Phoebus, eager to know for certain who his parents were; and likewise Laius, my husband, was on his way thither, anxious to find out if the child he had exposed was dead. And they twain met where the branching roads to Phocis unite; and the charioteer of Laius called to him, "Out of the way, stranger, room for my lord!" But he, with never a word, strode on in his pride; and the horses with their hoofs drew blood

from the tendons of his feet. Then—but why need I tell aught beyond the
sad issue?—son slew father, and taking his chariot gave it to Polybus his
foster-father. Now when the Sphinx was grievously harrying our city
after my husband's death, my brother Creon proclaimed that he would
wed me to any who should guess the riddle of that crafty maiden. By some
strange chance, my own son, Oedipus, guessed the Sphinx's riddle, and
so he became king of this land and received its sceptre as his prize, and
married his mother, all unwitting, luckless wretch! nor did I his mother
know that I was wedded to my son; and I bore him two sons, Eteocles
and the hero Polyneices, and two daughters as well; the one her father
called Ismene, the other, which was the elder, I named Antigone. Now
when Oedipus, that awful sufferer, learnt that I his wedded wife was his
mother too, he inflicted a ghastly outrage upon his eyes, tearing the bleeding orbs with a golden brooch. But since my sons have grown to bearded
men, they have confined their father closely, that his misfortune, needing
as it did full many a shift to hide it, might be forgotten. He is still living
in the palace, but his misfortunes have so unhinged him that he imprecates
the most unholy curses on his sons, praying that they may have to draw
the sword before they share this house between them. So they, fearful that
heaven may accomplish his prayer if they dwell together, have made an
agreement, arranging that Polyneices, the younger, should first leave the
land in voluntary exile, while Eteocles should stay and hold the sceptre for
a year and then change places. But as soon as Eteocles was seated high in
power, he refused to give up the throne, and drove Polyneices into exile
from the kingdom; so Polyneices went to Argos and married into the
family of Adrastus, and having collected a numerous force of Argives is
leading them hither; and he is come up against our seven-gated walls,
demanding the sceptre of his father and his share in the kingdom. Wherefore I, to end their strife, have prevailed on one son to meet the other
under truce, before appealing to arms; and the messenger I sent tells
me that he will come. O Zeus, whose home is heaven's radiant vault, save
us, and grant that my sons may be reconciled! For thou, if thou art really
wise, must not suffer the same poor mortal to be for ever wretched.

(JOCASTA *re-enters the palace, as the* OLD SERVANT *appears on the roof.*)

OLD SERVANT

Antigone, choice blossom in a father's house, although thy mother
allowed thee at thy earnest treaty to leave thy maiden chamber for the
topmost story of the house, thence to behold the Argive host, yet stay a
moment that I may first reconnoitre the path, whether there be any of
the citizens visible on the road, lest reproach, little as it matters to a slave
like me, fasten on thee, my royal mistress; and when I am quite sure I
will tell thee everything that I saw and heard from the Argives, when I

carried the terms of the truce to and fro between this city and Polyneices. (*After a slight pause*) No, there is no citizen approaching the palace; so mount the ancient cedar steps, and view the plains that skirt Ismenus and the fount of Dirce to see the mighty host of foemen.

(ANTIGONE *appears beside him. She chants her replies to him.*)

ANTIGONE

Stretch out thy hand to me from the stairs, the hand of age to youth, helping me to mount.

OLD SERVANT

There! clasp it, my young mistress; thou art come at a lucky moment; for Pelasgia's host is just upon the move, and their several contingents are separating.

ANTIGONE

O Hecate, dread child of Latona! the plain is one blaze of bronze.

OLD SERVANT

Ah! this is no ordinary home-coming of Polyneices; with many a knight and clash of countless arms he comes.

ANTIGONE

Are the gates fast barred, and the brazen bolts shot home into Amphion's walls of stone?

OLD SERVANT

Never fear! all is safe within the town. But mark him who cometh first, if thou wouldst learn his name.

ANTIGONE

Who is that with the white crest, who marches in the van, lightly bearing on his arm a buckler all of bronze?

OLD SERVANT

A chieftain, lady—

ANTIGONE

Who is he? whose son? his name? tell me, old man.

OLD SERVANT

Mycenae claims him for her son; in Lerna's glens he dwells, the prince Hippomedon.

ANTIGONE

Ah! how proud and terrible his mien! like to an earth-born giant
he moves, with stars engraved upon his targe, resembling not a child
of earth.

OLD SERVANT

Dost see yon chieftain crossing Dirce's stream?

ANTIGONE

His harness is quite different. Who is that?

OLD SERVANT

Tydeus, the son of Oeneus; true Aetolian spirit fires his breast.

ANTIGONE

Is this he, old man, who wedded a sister of the wife of Polyneices?
What a foreign look his armour has! a half-barbarian he!

OLD SERVANT

Yes, my child; all Aetolians carry shields, and are most unerring marks-
men with their darts.

ANTIGONE

How art thou so sure of these descriptions, old man?

OLD SERVANT

I carefully noted the blazons on their shields before when I went with
the terms of the truce to thy brother; so when I see them now I know
who carry them.

ANTIGONE

Who is that youth passing close to the tomb of Zethus, with long
flowing hair, but a look of fury in his eye? is he a captain? for crowds
of warriors follow at his heels.

OLD SERVANT

That is Parthenopaeus, Atalanta's son.

ANTIGONE

May Artemis, who hies o'er the hills with his mother, lay him low
with an arrow, for coming against my city to sack it!

OLD SERVANT

May it be so, my daughter; but with justice are they come hither, and
my fear is that the gods will take the rightful view.

ANTIGONE

Where is he who was born of the same mother as I was by a cruel
destiny? Oh! tell me, old friend, where Polyneices is.

OLD SERVANT

He is yonder, ranged next to Adrastus near the tomb of Niobe's seven
unwed daughters. Dost see him?

ANTIGONE

I see him, yes! but not distinctly; 'tis but the outline of his form,
the semblance of his stalwart limbs I see. Would I could speed
through the sky, swift as a cloud before the wind, towards my own
dear brother, and throw my arms about my darling's neck, so long,
poor boy! an exile. How bright his golden weapons flash like the
sun-god's morning rays!

OLD SERVANT

He will soon be here, to fill thy heart with joy, according to the truce.

ANTIGONE

Who is that, old man, on yonder car driving snow-white steeds?

OLD SERVANT

That, lady, is the prophet Amphiaraus; with him are the victims, whose
streaming blood the thirsty earth will drink.

ANTIGONE

Daughter of Latona with the dazzling zone, O moon, thou orb of
golden light! how quietly, with what restraint he drives, goading first
one horse, then the other! But where is Capaneus who utters those
dreadful threats against this city?

OLD SERVANT

Yonder he is, calculating how he may scale the towers, taking the
measure of our walls from base to summit.

ANTIGONE

O Nemesis, with booming thunder-peals of Zeus and blazing levin-
light, thine it is to silence such presumptuous boasting. Is this the
man, who says he will give the maids of Thebes as captives of his
spear to Mycenae's dames, to Lerna's Trident,[1] and the waters of
Amymone, dear to Poseidon, when he has thrown the toils of slavery
round them? Never, never, Artemis, my queen revered, child of Zeus
with locks of gold, may I endure the yoke of slavery!

OLD SERVANT

My daughter, go within, and abide beneath the shelter of thy maiden chamber, now that thou hast had thy wish and seen all that thy heart desired; for I see a crowd of women moving toward the royal palace, confusion reigning in the city. Now the race of women by nature loves to find fault; and if they get some slight handle for their talk they exaggerate it, for they seem to take a pleasure in saying everything bad of one another.

(ANTIGONE *and the* OLD SERVANT *descend into the palace, as the* CHORUS OF PHOENICIAN MAIDENS *enters.*)

CHORUS (*singing*)

strophe 1

From the Tyrian main I come, an offering choice for Loxias from a Phoenician isle, to minister to Phoebus in his halls, where his fane lies nestling 'neath the snow-swept peaks of Parnassus; over the Ionian sea I rowed my course, for above the plains unharvested, that fringe the coast of Sicily, the boisterous west-wind coursed, piping sweetest music in the sky.

antistrophe 1

Chosen from my city as beauty's gift for Loxias, to the land of Cadmus I came, sent thither to the towers of Laius, the home of my kin, the famous sons of Agenor; and there I became the handmaid of Phoebus, dedicated like his offerings of wrought gold. But as yet the water of Castaly is waiting for me to bedew the maiden glory of my tresses for the service of Phoebus.

epode

Hail! thou rock that kindlest bright fire above the twin-peaked heights of Dionysus. Hail! thou vine, that, day by day, makest the lush bunches of thy grapes to drip. Hail! awful cavern of the serpent, and the god's outlook on the hills, and sacred mount by snow-storms lashed! would I were now circling in the dance of the death-less god, free from wild alarms, having left Dirce ere this for the vales of Phoebus at the centre of the world!

strophe 2

But now I find the impetuous god of war is come to battle before these walls, and hath kindled murder's torch in this city. God grant he fail! for a friend's sorrows are also mine; and if this land with its seven towers suffer any mischance, Phoenicia's realm must share it. Ah me! our stock is one; all children we of Io, that hornèd maid, whose sorrows I partake.

antistrophe 2

Around the city a dense array of serried shields is rousing the spectre of bloody strife, whose issue Ares shall soon learn to his cost, if he brings upon the sons of Oedipus the horrors of the curse. O Argos, city of Pelasgia! I dread thy prowess and the vengeance Heaven sends; for he who cometh against our home in full panoply is entering the lists with justice on his side.

(POLYNEICES *enters alone.*)

POLYNEICES

Those who kept watch and ward at the gate admitted me so readily within the walls that my only fear is, that now they have caught me in their toils, they will not let me out unscathed; so I must turn my eye in every direction, hither and thither, to guard against all treachery. Armed with this sword, I shall inspire myself with the trust that is born of boldness. (*Starting*) What ho! who goes there? or is it an idle sound I fear? Everything seems a danger to venturous spirits, when their feet begin to tread an enemy's country. Still I trust my mother, and at the same time mistrust her for persuading me to come hither under truce. Well, there is help at hand, for the altar's hearth is close and there are people in the palace. Come, let me sheath my sword in its dark scabbard and ask these maidens standing near the house, who they are.

Ladies of another land, tell me from what country ye come to the halls of Hellas.

LEADER OF THE CHORUS

Phoenicia is my native land where I was born and bred; and Agenor's children's children sent me hither as a first-fruits of the spoils of war for Phoebus; but when the noble son of Oedipus was about to escort me to the hallowed oracle and the altars of Loxias, came Argives meantime against his city. Now tell me in return who *thou* art that comes to this fortress of the Theban realm with its seven gates.

POLYNEICES

My father was Oedipus, the son of Laius; my mother Jocasta, daughter of Menoeceus; and I am called Polyneices by the folk of Thebes.

CHORUS (*chanting*)

O kinsman of Agenor's race, my royal masters who sent me hither, at thy feet, prince, I throw myself, according to the custom of my home. At last art thou come to thy native land; at last! Hail to thee! all hail! Come forth, my honoured mistress, open wide the doors. Dost hear, O mother of this chief? Why art thou delaying to leave the sheltering roof to fold thy son in thy embrace?

(JOCASTA *enters from the palace.*)

JOCASTA (*chanting*)

Maidens, I hear you call in your Phoenician tongue, and my old
feet drag their tottering steps to meet my son. O my son, my son,
at last after many a long day I see thee face to face; throw thy arms
about thy mother's bosom; reach hither thy cheek to me and thy
dark locks of clustering hair, o'ershadowing my neck therewith. Hail
to thee! all hail! scarce now restored to thy mother's arms, when
hope and expectation both were dead. What can I say to thee? how
recall in every way, by word, by deed, the bliss of days long past,
expressing my joy in the mazy measures of the dance? Ah! my son,
thou didst leave thy father's halls desolate, when thy brother's despite drove thee thence in exile. Truly thou wert missed alike by thy
friends and Thebes. This was why I cut off my silvered locks and
let them fall for grief with many a tear, not clad in robes of white,
my son, but instead thereof taking for my wear these sorry sable
tatters; while within the palace that aged one with sightless orbs,
ever nursing the sorrow of a double regret for the pair of brethren
estranged from their home, rushed to lay hands upon himself with
the sword or by the noose suspended o'er his chamber-roof, moaning
his curses on his sons; and now he buries himself in darkness, weeping ever and lamenting. And thou, my child,—I hear thou hast taken
an alien to wife and art begetting children to thy joy in thy home;
they tell me thou art courting a foreign alliance, a ceaseless woe to
me thy mother and to Laius thy ancestor, to have this woeful marriage foisted on us. 'Twas no hand of mine that lit for thee the
marriage-torch, as custom ordains and as a happy mother ought; no
part had Ismenus at thy wedding in supplying the luxurious bath;
and there was silence through the streets of Thebes, what time thy
young bride entered her home. Curses on them! whether it be the
sword or strife or thy sire that is to blame, or heaven's visitation that
hath burst so riotously upon the house of Oedipus; for on me is come
all the anguish of these troubles.

LEADER OF THE CHORUS

Wondrous dear to woman is the child of her travail, and all her race
hath some affection for its babes.

POLYNEICES

Mother, I have come amongst enemies wisely or foolishly; but all men
needs must love their native land; whoso saith otherwise is pleased to say
so but his thoughts are turned elsewhere. So fearful was I and in such
terror, lest my brother might slay me by treachery that I made my way
through the city sword in hand, casting my eyes all round me. My only
hope is the truce and thy plighted word which induced me to enter my

paternal walls; and many a tear I shed by the way, seeing after a weary while my home and the altars of the gods, the training ground, scene of my childhood, and Dirce's founts from which I was unjustly driven to sojourn in a strange city, with tears ever gushing from mine eyes. Yea, and to add to my grief I see thee with hair cut short and clad in sable robe; woe is me for my sorrows!

How terrible, dear mother, is hatred 'twixt those once near and dear; how hard it makes all reconciliation! What doth my aged sire within the house, his light all darkness now? what of my sisters twain? Ah! they, I know, bewail my bitter exile.

JOCASTA

Some god with fell intent is plaguing the race of Oedipus. Thus it all began; I broke God's law and bore a son, and in an evil hour married thy father and thou wert born. But why repeat these horrors? what Heaven sends we have to bear. I am afraid to ask thee what I fain would, for fear of wounding thy feelings; yet I long to.

POLYNEICES

Nay, question me, leave naught unsaid; for thy will, mother, is my pleasure too.

JOCASTA

Well then, first I ask thee what I long to have answered. What means exile from one's country? is it a great evil?

POLYNEICES

The greatest; harder to bear than tell.

JOCASTA

What is it like? what is it galls the exile?

POLYNEICES

One thing most of all; he cannot speak his mind.

JOCASTA

This is a slave's lot thou describest, to refrain from uttering what one thinks.

POLYNEICES

The follies of his rulers must he bear.

JOCASTA

That too is bitter, to join in the folly of fools.

POLYNEICES

Yet to gain our ends we must submit against our nature.

JOCASTA
Hope, they say, is the exile's food.

POLYNEICES
Aye, hope that looks so fair; but she is ever in the future.

JOCASTA
But doth not time expose her futility?

POLYNEICES
She hath a certain winsome charm in misfortune.

JOCASTA
Whence hadst thou means to live, ere thy marriage found it for thee?

POLYNEICES
One while I had enough for the day, and then maybe I had it not.

JOCASTA
Did not thy father's friends and whilom guests assist thee?

POLYNEICES
Seek to be prosperous; once let fortune lour, and the aid supplied by friends is naught.

JOCASTA
Did not thy noble breeding exalt thy horn for thee?

POLYNEICES
Poverty is a curse; breeding would not find me food.

JOCASTA
Man's dearest treasure then, it seems, is his country.

POLYNEICES
No words of thine could tell how dear.

JOCASTA
How was it thou didst go to Argos? what was thy scheme?

POLYNEICES
I know not; the deity summoned me thither in accordance with my destiny.

JOCASTA
He doubtless had some wise design; but how didst thou win thy wife?

POLYNEICES

Loxias had given Adrastus an oracle.

JOCASTA

What was it? what meanest thou? I cannot guess.

POLYNEICES

That he should wed his daughters to a boar and a lion.

JOCASTA

What hadst thou, my son, to do with the name of beasts?

POLYNEICES

It was night when I reached the porch of Adrastus.

JOCASTA

In search of a resting-place, or wandering thither in thy exile?

POLYNEICES

Yes, I wandered thither; and so did another like me.

JOCASTA

Who was he? he too it seems was in evil plight.

POLYNEICES

Tydeus, son of Oeneus, was his name.

JOCASTA

But why did Adrastus liken you to wild beasts?

POLYNEICES

Because we came to blows about our bed.

JOCASTA

Was it then that the son of Talaus understood the oracle?

POLYNEICES

Yes, and he gave to us his daughters twain.

JOCASTA

Art thou blest or curst in thy marriage?

POLYNEICES

As yet I have no fault to find with it.

JOCASTA

How didst thou persuade an army to follow thee hither?

POLYNEICES

To me and to Tydeus who is my kinsman by marriage, Adrastus sware an oath, even to the husbands of his daughters twain, that he would restore us both to our country, but me the first. So many a chief from Argos and Mycenae has joined me, doing me a bitter though needful service, for 'tis against my own city I am marching. Now I call heaven to witness, that it is not willingly I have raised my arm against parents whom I love full well. But to thee, mother, it belongs to dissolve this unhappy feud, and, by reconciling brothers in love, to end my troubles and thine and this whole city's. 'Tis an old-world maxim, but I will cite it for all that: "Men set most store by wealth, and of all things in this world it hath the greatest power." This am I come to secure at the head of my countless host; for good birth is naught if poverty go with it.

LEADER

Lo! Eteocles comes hither to discuss the truce. Thine the task, O mother Jocasta, to speak such words as may reconcile thy sons.

(ETEOCLES *and his retinue enter.*)

ETEOCLES

Mother, I am here; but it was only to pleasure thee I came. What am I to do? Let some one begin the conference; for I stopped marshalling the citizens in double lines around the walls, that I might hear thy arbitration between us; for it is under this truce that thou hast persuaded me to admit this fellow within the walls.

JOCASTA

Stay a moment; haste never carries justice with it; but slow deliberation oft attains a wise result. Restrain the fierceness of thy look, that panting rage; for this is not the Gorgon's severed head but thy own brother whom thou seest here. Thou too, Polyneices, turn and face thy brother; for if thou and he stand face to face, thou wilt adopt a kindlier tone and lend a readier ear to him. I fain would give you both one piece of wholesome counsel; when a man that is angered with his friend confronts him face to face, he ought only to keep in view the object of his coming, forgetting all previous quarrels. Polyneices my son, speak first, for thou art come at the head of a Danaid host, alleging wrongful treatment; and may some god judge betwixt us and reconcile the trouble.

POLYNEICES

The words of truth are simple, and justice needs no subtle interpretations, for it hath a fitness in itself; but the words of injustice, being rotten in themselves, require clever treatment. I provided for his interests and mine in our father's palace, being anxious to avoid the curse which Oedipus once uttered against us; of my own free-will I left the land, allowing him to rule our country for one full year, on condition that I should then take the sceptre in turn, instead of plunging into deadly enmity and thereby doing others hurt or suffering it myself, as is now the case. But he, after consenting to this and calling the gods to witness his oath, has performed none of his promises, but is still keeping the sovereignty in his own hands together with my share of our heritage. Even now am I ready to take my own and dismiss my army from this land, receiving my house in turn to dwell therein, and once more restore it to him for a like period instead of ravaging our country and planting scaling-ladders against the towers, as I shall attempt to do if I do not get my rights. Wherefore I call the gods to witness that spite of my just dealing in everything I am being unjustly robbed of my country by most godless fraud. Here, mother, have I stated the several points on their own merits, without collecting words to fence them in, but urging a fair case, I think, alike in the judgment of skilled or simple folk.

LEADER

To me at least, albeit I was not born and bred in Hellas, thy words seem full of sense.

ETEOCLES

If all were at one in their ideas of honour and wisdom, there would have been no strife to make men disagree; but, as it is, fairness and equality have no existence in this world beyond the name; there is really no such thing. For instance, mother, I will tell thee this without any concealment; I would ascend to the rising of the stars and the sun or dive beneath the earth, were I able so to do, to win a monarch's power, the chief of things divine. Therefore, mother, I will never yield this blessing to another, but keep it for myself; for it were a coward's act to lose the greater and to win the less. Besides, I blush to think that he should gain his object by coming with arms in his hand and ravaging the land; for this were foul disgrace to glorious Thebes, if I should yield my sceptre up to him for fear of Argive might. He ought not, mother, to have attempted reconcilement by armed force, for words compass everything that even the sword of an enemy might effect. Still, if on any other terms he cares to dwell here, he may; but the sceptre will I never willingly let go. Shall I become his slave, when I can be his master? Never! Wherefore come fire, come sword! harness your steeds, fill the plains with chariots, for I will not forego my throne for him. For if we must do wrong, to do so for a kingdom were the fairest cause, but in all else virtue should be our aim.

LEADER

Fair words are only called for when the deeds they crown are fair; otherwise they lose their charm and offend justice.

JOCASTA

Eteocles, my child, it is not all evil that attends old age; sometimes its experience can offer sager counsel than can youth. Oh! why, my son, art thou so set upon Ambition, that worst of deities? Forbear; that goddess knows not justice; many are the homes and cities once prosperous that she hath entered and left after the ruin of her votaries; she it is thou madly followest. Better far, my son, prize Equality that ever linketh friend to friend, city to city, and allies to each other; for Equality is man's natural law; but the less is always in opposition to the greater, ushering in the dayspring of dislike. For it is Equality that hath set up for man measures and divisions of weights and hath distinguished numbers; night's sightless orb, and radiant sun proceed upon their yearly course on equal terms, and neither of them is envious when it has to yield. Though sun and gloom then both are servants in man's interests, wilt not thou be content with thy fair share of thy heritage and give the same to him? if not, why where is justice? Why prize beyond its worth the monarch's power, injustice in prosperity? why think so much of the admiring glances turned on rank? Nay, 'tis vanity. Or wouldst thou by heaping riches in thy halls, heap up toil therewith? what advantage is it? 'tis but a name; for the wise find that enough which suffices for their wants. Man indeed hath no possessions of his own; we do but hold a stewardship of the gods' property; and when they will, they take it back again. Riches make no settled home, but are as transient as the day. Come, suppose I put before thee two alternatives, whether thou wilt rule or save thy city? Wilt thou say "Rule"?

Again, if Polyneices win the day and his Argive warriors rout the ranks of Thebes, thou wilt see this city conquered and many a captive maid brutally dishonoured by the foe; so will that wealth thou art so bent on getting become a grievous bane to Thebes; but still ambition fills thee. This I say to thee; and this to thee, Polyneices; Adrastus hath conferred a foolish favour on thee; and thou too hast shown little sense in coming to lay thy city waste. Suppose thou conquer this land (which Heaven forefend!) tell me, I conjure thee, how wilt thou rear a trophy to Zeus? how wilt thou begin the sacrifice after thy country's conquest or inscribe the spoils at the streams of Inachus with "Polyneices gave Thebes to the flames and dedicated these shields to the gods"? Oh! never, my son, be it thine to win such fame from Hellas! If, on the other hand, thou art worsted and thy brother's cause prevail, how shalt thou return to Argos, leaving countless dead behind? Some one will be sure to say, "Out on thee! Adrastus. for the evil bridegroom thou hast brought unto thy house; thanks to one maid's marriage, ruin is come on us."

Towards two evils, my son, art thou hasting,—loss of influence there and ruin in the midst of thy efforts here. Oh! my children, lay aside your violence; two men's follies, once they meet, result in very deadly evil.

LEADER

O heaven, avert these troubles and reconcile the sons of Oedipus in some way!

ETEOCLES

Mother, the season for parley is past; the time we still delay is idle waste; thy good wishes are of no avail, for we shall never be reconciled except upon the terms already named, namely, that I should keep the sceptre and be king of this land: wherefore cease these tedious warnings and let me be. (*Turning to* POLYNEICES) And as for thee, outside the walls, or die!

POLYNEICES

Who will slay me? who is so invulnerable as to plunge his sword in my body without reaping the self-same fate?

ETEOCLES

Thou art near him, aye, very near; dost see my arm?

POLYNEICES

I see it; but wealth is cowardly, a craven too fond of life.

ETEOCLES

Was it then to meet a dastard thou camest with all that host to war?

POLYNEICES

In a general caution is better than foolhardiness.

ETEOCLES

Relying on the truce, which saves thy life, thou turnest boaster.

POLYNEICES

Once more I ask thee to restore my sceptre and share in the kingdom.

ETEOCLES

I have naught to restore; 'tis my own house, and I will dwell therein.

POLYNEICES

What! and keep more than thy share?

ETEOCLES

Yes, I will. Begone!

POLYNEICES

O altars of my fathers' gods!—

ETEOCLES

Which thou art here to raze.

POLYNEICES

Hear me.

ETEOCLES

Who would hear thee after thou hast marched against thy fatherland?

POLYNEICES

O temples of those gods that ride on snow-white steeds! [2]

ETEOCLES

They hate thee.

POLYNEICES

I am being driven from my country.

ETEOCLES

Because thou camest to drive others thence.

POLYNEICES

Unjustly, O ye gods!

ETEOCLES

Call on the gods at Mycenae, not here.

POLYNEICES

Thou hast outraged right—

ETEOCLES

But I have not like thee become my country's foe.

POLYNEICES

By driving me forth without my portion.

ETEOCLES

And further I will slay thee.

POLYNEICES

O father, dost thou hear what I am suffering?

ETEOCLES

Yea, and he hears what thou art doing.

POLYNEICES

Thou too, mother mine?

ETEOCLES

Thou hast no right to mention thy mother.

POLYNEICES

O my city!

ETEOCLES

Get thee to Argos, and invoke the waters of Lerna.

POLYNEICES

I will; trouble not thyself; all thanks to thee though, mother mine.

ETEOCLES

Forth from the land!

POLYNEICES

I go, yet grant me to behold my father.

ETEOCLES

Thou shalt not have thy wish.

POLYNEICES

At least then my tender sisters.

ETEOCLES

No! them too thou shalt never see.

POLYNEICES

Ah, sisters mine!

ETEOCLES

Why dost thou, their bitterest foe, call on them?

POLYNEICES

Mother dear, to thee at least farewell!

JOCASTA

A joyous faring mine in sooth, my son!

POLYNEICES

Thy son no more!

JOCASTA

Born to sorrow, endless sorrow, I!

POLYNEICES

'Tis because my brother treats me despitefully.

ETEOCLES

I am treated just the same.

POLYNEICES

Where wilt thou be stationed before the towers?

ETEOCLES

Why ask me this?

POLYNEICES

I will array myself against thee for thy death.

ETEOCLES

I too have the same desire.

JOCASTA

Woe is me! what will ye do, my sons?

POLYNEICES

The event will show.

JOCASTA

Oh, fly your father's curse!

(JOCASTA *enters the palace.*)

ETEOCLES

Destruction seize our whole house!

POLYNEICES

Soon shall my sword be busy, plunged in gore. But I call my native land and heaven too to witness, with what contumely and bitter treatment I am being driven forth, as though I were a slave, not a son of Oedipus as much as he. If aught happen to thee, my city, blame him, not me; for I came not willingly, and all unwillingly am I driven hence. Farewell, king Phoebus, lord of highways; farewell palace and comrades; farewell ye statues of the gods, at which men offer sheep; for I know not if I shall ever again address you, though hope is still awake, which makes me confident that with heaven's help I shall slay this fellow and rule my native Thebes.

(POLYNEICES *departs.*)

ETEOCLES

Forth from the land! 'twas a true name our father gave thee, when, prompted by some god, he called thee Polyneices, a name denoting strife.

CHORUS (*singing*)

strophe

To this land came Cadmus of Tyre, at whose feet an unyoked heifer threw itself down, giving effect to an oracle on the spot where the god's response bade him take up his abode in Aonia's rich corn-lands, where gushing Dirce's fair rivers of water pour o'er verdant fruitful fields; here was born the Bromian god by her whom Zeus made a mother, round whom the ivy twined its wreaths while he was yet a babe, swathing him amid the covert of its green foliage as a child of happy destiny, to be a theme for Bacchic revelry among the maids and wives inspired in Thebes.

antistrophe

There lay Ares' murderous dragon, a savage warder, watching with roving eye the watered glens and quickening streams; him did Cadmus slay with a jagged stone, when he came thither to draw him lustral water, smiting that fell head with a blow of his death-dealing arm; but by the counsel of Pallas, motherless goddess, he cast the teeth upon the earth into deep furrows, whence sprang to sight a mail-clad host above the surface of the soil; but grim slaughter once again united them to the earth they loved, bedewing with blood the ground that had disclosed them to the sunlit breath of heaven.

epode

Thee too, Epaphus, child of Zeus, sprung from Io our ancestress, I call on in my foreign tongue; all hail to thee! hear my prayer uttered in accents strange, and visit this land; 'twas in thy honour thy descendants settled here, and those goddesses of twofold name, Persephone and kindly Demeter or Earth the queen of all, that feedeth every mouth, won it for themselves; send to the help of this land those torch-bearing queens; for to gods all things are easy.

ETEOCLES (*to an attendant*)

Go, fetch Creon son of Menoeceus, the brother of Jocasta my mother; tell him I fain would confer with him on matters affecting our public and private weal, before we set out to battle and the arraying of our host. But lo! he comes and saves thee the trouble of going; I see him on his way to my palace.

(CREON *enters*.)

CREON

To and fro have I been, king Eteocles, in my desire to see thee, and have gone all round the gates and sentinels of Thebes in quest of thee.

ETEOCLES

Why, and I was anxious to see thee, Creon; for I found the terms of peace far from satisfactory, when I came to confer with Polyneices.

CREON

I hear that he has wider aims than Thebes, relying on his alliance with the daughter of Adrastus and his army. Well, we must leave this dependent on the gods; meantime I am come to tell thee our chief obstacle.

ETEOCLES

What is that? I do not understand what thou sayest.

CREON

There is come one that was captured by the Argives.

ETEOCLES

What news does he bring from their camp?

CREON

He says the Argive army intend at once to draw a ring of troops round the city of Thebes, about its towers.

ETEOCLES

In that case the city of Cadmus must lead out its troops.

CREON

Whither? art thou so young that thine eyes see not what they should?

ETEOCLES

Across yon trenches for immediate action.

CREON

Our Theban forces are small, while theirs are numberless.

ETEOCLES

I well know they are reputed brave.

CREON

No mean repute have those Argives among Hellenes.

ETEOCLES

Never fear! I will soon fill the plain with their dead.

CREON

I could wish it so; but I see great difficulties in this.

ETEOCLES

Trust me, I will not keep my host within the walls.

CREON

Still victory is entirely a matter of good counsel.

ETEOCLES

Art anxious then that I should have recourse to any other scheme?

CREON

Aye to every scheme, before running the risk once for all.

ETEOCLES

Suppose we fall on them by night from ambuscade?

CREON

Good! provided in the event of defeat thou canst secure thy return hither.

ETEOCLES

Night equalizes risks, though it rather favours daring.

CREON

The darkness of night is a terrible time to suffer disaster.

ETEOCLES

Well, shall I fall upon them as they sit at meat?

CREON

That might cause them fright, but victory is what we want.

ETEOCLES

Dirce's ford is deep enough to prevent their retreat.

CREON

No plan so good as to keep well guarded.

ETEOCLES

What if our cavalry make a sortie against the host of Argos?

CREON

Their troops too are fenced all round with chariots.

ETEOCLES

What then can I do? am I to surrender the city to the foe?

CREON

Nay, nay! but of thy wisdom form some plan.

ETEOCLES

Pray, what scheme is wiser than mine?

CREON

They have seven chiefs, I hear.

ETEOCLES

What is their appointed task? their might can be but feeble.

CREON

To lead the several companies and storm our seven gates.

ETEOCLES

What are we to do? I will not wait till every chance is gone.

CREON

Choose seven chiefs thyself to set against them at the gates.

ETEOCLES

To lead our companies, or to fight single-handed?

CREON

Choose our very bravest men to lead the troops.

ETEOCLES

I understand; to repel attempts at scaling our walls.

CREON

With others to share the command, for one man sees not everything.

ETEOCLES

Selecting them for courage or thoughtful prudence?

CREON

For both; for one is naught without the other.

ETEOCLES

It shall be done; I will away to our seven towers and post captains at the gates, as thou advisest, pitting them man for man against the foe. To tell thee each one's name were grievous waste of time, when the foe is camped beneath our very walls.³ But I will go, that my hands may no longer hang idle. May I meet my brother face to face, and encounter him hand to hand, e'en to the death, for coming to waste my country! But if I suffer any mischance, thou must see to the marriage 'twixt Antigone my sister and Haemon, thy son; and now, as I go forth to battle, I ratify their previous espousal. Thou art my mother's brother, so why need I say more? take care of her, as she deserves, both for thy own sake and mine. As for my sire he hath been guilty of folly against himself in putting out his eyes; small praise have I for him; by his curses maybe he will slay us too. One thing only have we still to do, to ask Teiresias, the seer, if he has aught to tell of heaven's will. Thy son Menoeceus, who bears thy father's name, will I send to fetch Teiresias hither, Creon; for with thee

he will readily converse, though I have ere now so scorned his art prophetic to his face, that he has reasons to reproach me. This command-
ment, Creon, I lay upon the city and thee; should my cause prevail, never
give Polyneices' corpse a grave in Theban soil, and if so be some friend
should bury him, let death reward the man. Thus far to thee; and to
my servants thus, bring forth my arms and coat of mail, that I may start
at once for the appointed combat, with right to lead to victory. To save
our city we will pray to Caution, the best goddess to serve our end.

(ETEOCLES *and his retinue go out.*)

CHORUS (*singing*)

strophe

O Ares, god of toil and trouble! why, why art thou possessed by a
love of blood and death, out of harmony with the festivals of
Bromius? 'Tis for no crowns of dancers fair that thou dost toss thy
youthful curls to the breeze, singing the while to the lute's soft breath
a strain to charm the dancers' feet; but with warriors clad in mail
thou dost lead thy sombre revelry, breathing into Argive breasts a
lust for Theban blood; with no wild waving of the thyrsus, clad in
fawnskin thou dancest, but with chariots and bitted steeds wheelest
thy charger strong of hoof. O'er the waters of Ismenus in wild career
thou art urging thy horses, inspiring Argive breasts with hate of the
earth-born race, arraying in brazen harness against these stone-built
walls a host of warriors armed with shields. Truly Strife is a goddess to fear, who devised these troubles for the princes of this land,
for the much-enduring sons of Labdacus.

antistrophe

O Cithaeron, apple of the eye of Artemis, holy vale of leaves, amid
whose snows full many a beast lies couched, would thou hadst never
reared the child exposed to die, Oedipus the fruit of Jocasta's womb,
when as a babe he was cast forth from his home, marked with a
golden brooch; and would the Sphinx, that wingèd maid, fell monster
from the hills, had never come to curse our land with inharmonious
strains; she that erst drew nigh our walls and snatched the sons of
Cadmus away in her taloned feet to the pathless fields of light, a fiend
sent by Hades from hell to plague the men of Thebes; once more
unhappy strife is bursting out between the sons of Oedipus in city
and home. For never can wrong be right, nor children of unnatural
parentage come as a glory to the mother that bears them, but as a
stain on the marriage of him who is father and brother at once.

epode

O earth, thou once didst bear,—so long ago I heard the story told
by foreigners in my own home,—a race which sprang of the teeth
of a snake with blood-red crest, that fed on beasts, to be the glory
and reproach of Thebes. In days gone by the sons of heaven came to
the wedding of Harmonia, and the walls of Thebes arose to the
sound of the lyre and her towers stood up as Amphion played, in
the midst between the double streams of Dirce, that watereth the
green meadows fronting the Ismenus; and Io, our hornèd ancestress
was mother of the kings of Thebes; thus our city through an endless
succession of divers blessings has set herself upon the highest pin-
nacle of martial glory.

(TEIRESIAS *enters, led by his daughter. They are accompanied by*
MENOECEUS.)

TEIRESIAS

Lead on, my daughter; for thou art as an eye to my blind feet, as
certain as a star to mariners; lead my steps on to level ground; then go
before, that we stumble not, for thy father has no strength; keep safe for
me in thy maiden hand the auguries I took in the days I observed the
flight and cries of birds seated in my holy prophet's chair. Tell me, young
Menoeceus, son of Creon, how much further toward the city is it ere I
reach thy father? for my knees grow weary, and I can scarce keep up
this hurried pace.

CREON

Take heart, Teiresias, for thou hast reached thy moorings and art near
thy friends; take him by the hand, my child; for just as every carriage
has to wait for outside help to steady it, so too hath the step of age.

TEIRESIAS

Enough; I have arrived; why, Creon, dost thou summon me so urgently?

CREON

I have not forgotten that; but first collect thyself and regain breath,
shaking off the fatigue of thy journey.

TEIRESIAS

I am indeed worn out, having arrived here only yesterday from the
court of the Erechtheidae; for they too were at war, fighting with Eumolpus, in which contest I insured the victory of Cecrops' sons; and I received the golden crown, which thou seest me wearing, as first-fruits of
the enemy's spoil.

CREON

I take thy crown of victory as an omen. We, as thou knowest, are exposed to the billows of an Argive war, and great is the struggle for Thebes. Eteocles, our king, is already gone in full harness to meet Mycenae's champions, and hath bidden me inquire of thee our best course to save the city.

TEIRESIAS

For Eteocles I would have closed my lips and refrained from all response, but to thee I will speak, since 'tis thy wish to learn. This country, Creon, has been long afflicted, ever since Laius became a father in heaven's despite, begetting hapless Oedipus to be his own mother's husband. That bloody outrage on his eyes was planned by heaven as an ensample to Hellas; and the sons of Oedipus made a gross mistake in wishing to throw over it the veil of time, as if forsooth they could outrun the gods' decree; for by robbing their father of his due honour and allowing him no freedom, they enraged their luckless sire; so he, stung by suffering and disgrace as well, vented awful curses against them; and I, because I left nothing undone or unsaid to prevent this, incurred the hatred of the sons of Oedipus. But death inflicted by each other's hands awaits them, Creon; and the many heaps of slain, some from Argive, some from Theban missiles, shall cause bitter lamentation in the land of Thebes. Alas! for thee, poor city, thou art being involved in their ruin, unless I can persuade one man. The best course was to prevent any child of Oedipus becoming either citizen or king in this land, since they were under a ban and would overthrow the city. But as evil has the mastery of good, there is still one other way of safety; but this it were unsafe for me to tell, and painful too for those whose high fortune it is to supply their city with the saving cure. Farewell! I will away; amongst the rest must I endure my doom, if need be; for what will become of me?

CREON

Stay here, old man.

TEIRESIAS

Hold me not.

CREON

Abide, why dost thou seek to fly?

TEIRESIAS

'Tis thy fortune that flies thee, not I.

CREON

Tell me what can save Thebes and her citizens.

TEIRESIAS

Though this be now thy wish, it will soon cease to be.

CREON

Not wish to save my country? how can that be?

TEIRESIAS

Art thou still eager to be told?

CREON

Yea; for wherein should I show greater zeal?

TEIRESIAS

Then straightway shalt thou hear my words prophetic. But first I would fain know for certain where Menoeceus is, who led me hither.

CREON

Here, not far away, but at thy side.

TEIRESIAS

Let him retire far from my prophetic voice.

CREON

He is my own son and will preserve due silence.

TEIRESIAS

Wilt thou then that I tell thee in his presence?

CREON

Yea, for he will rejoice to hear the means of safety.

TEIRESIAS

Then hear the purport of my oracle, the which if ye observe ye shall save the city of Cadmus.

Thou must sacrifice Menoeceus thy son here for thy country, since thine own lips demand the voice of fate.[4]

CREON

What mean'st thou? what is this thou hast said, old man?

TEIRESIAS

To that which is to be thou also must conform.

CREON

O the eternity of woe thy minute's tale proclaims!

TEIRESIAS

Yes to thee, but to thy country great salvation.

CREON

I shut my ears; I never listened; to city now farewell!

TEIRESIAS

Ha! the man is changed; he is drawing back.

CREON

Go in peace; it is not thy prophecy I need.

TEIRESIAS

Is truth dead, because thou art curst with woe?

CREON

By thy knees and honoured locks I implore thee!

TEIRESIAS

Why implore me? thou art craving a calamity hard to guard against.

CREON

Keep silence; tell not the city thy news.

TEIRESIAS

Thou biddest me act unjustly; I will not hold my peace.

CREON

What wilt thou then do to me? slay my child?

TEIRESIAS

That is for others to decide; I have but to speak.

CREON

Whence came this curse on me and my son?

TEIRESIAS

Thou dost right to ask me and to test what I have said. In yonder lair, where the earth-born dragon kept watch and ward o'er Dirce's springs, must this youth be offered and shed his life-blood on the ground by reason of Ares' ancient grudge against Cadmus, who thus avenges the slaughter of his earth-born snake. If ye do this, ye shall win Ares as an ally; and if the earth receive crop for crop and human blood for blood, ye shall find her kind again, that erst to your sorrow reared from that dragon's seed a crop of warriors with golden casques; for needs must one sprung from the dragon's teeth be slain. Now thou art our only survivor of the seed of that sown race, whose lineage is pure alike on mother's and on father's side, thou and these thy sons. Haemon's marriage debars him from being the victim, for he is no longer single; for even if he have not consummated his marriage, yet is he betrothed; but this tender youth, consecrated to the city's service, might by dying rescue his country; and bitter will he make the return of Adrastus and his Argives, flinging o'er their eyes death's dark pall, and will glorify Thebes. Choose thee one of these alternatives; either save the city or thy son.

Now hast thou all I have to say. Daughter, lead me home. A fool, the man who practises the diviner's art; for if he should announce an adverse answer, he makes himself disliked by those who seek to him; while, if from pity he deceives those who are consulting him, he sins against Heaven. Phoebus should have been man's only prophet, for he fears no man.

(*His daughter leads* TEIRESIAS *out.*)

LEADER OF THE CHORUS

Why so silent, Creon, why are thy lips hushed and dumb? I too am no less stricken with dismay.

CREON

Why, what could one say? 'Tis clear what my words must be. For I will never plunge myself so deeply into misfortune as to devote my son to death for the city; for love of children binds all men to life, and none would resign his own son to die. Let no man praise me into slaying my children. I am ready to die myself—for I am ripe in years—to set my country free. But thou, my son, ere the whole city learn this, up and fly with all haste away from this land, regardless of these prophets' unbridled utterances; for he will go to the seven gates and the captains there and tell all this to our governors and leaders; now if we can forestall him, thou mayst be saved, but if thou art too late, we are undone and thou wilt die.

MENOECEUS

Whither can I fly? to what city? to which of our guest-friends?

CREON

Fly where thou wilt be furthest removed from this land.

MENOECEUS

'Tis for thee to name a place, for me to carry out thy bidding.

CREON

After passing Delphi—

MENOECEUS

Whither must I go, father?

CREON

To Aetolia.

MENOECEUS

Whither thence?

CREON

To the land of Thesprotia.

MENOECEUS

To Dodona's hallowed threshold?

CREON

Thou followest me.

MENOECEUS

What protection shall I find me there?

CREON

The god will send thee on thy way.

MENOECEUS

How shall I find the means?

CREON

I will supply thee with money.

MENOECEUS

A good plan of thine, father. So go; for I will to thy sister, Jocasta,
at whose breast I was suckled as a babe when reft of my mother and
left a lonely orphan, to give her kindly greeting and then will I seek my
safety. Come, come! be going, that there be no hindrance on thy part.

(CREON *departs.*)

How cleverly, ladies, I banished my father's fears by crafty words to
gain my end; for he is trying to convey me hence, depriving the city of
its chance and surrendering me to cowardice. Though an old man may be
pardoned, yet in my case there is no excuse for betraying the country that
gave me birth. So I will go and save the city, be assured thereof, and give
my life up for this land. For this were shame, that they whom no oracles
bind and who have not come under Fate's iron law, should stand there,
shoulder to shoulder, with never a fear of death, and fight for their country before her towers, while I escape the kingdom like a coward, a traitor
to my father and brother and city; and wheresoe'er I live, I shall appear
a dastard. Nay, by Zeus and all his stars, by Ares, god of blood, who
'stablished the warrior-crop that sprung one day from earth as princes
of this land, that shall not be! but go I will, and standing on the topmost
battlements, will deal my own death-blow over the dragon's deep dark
den, the spot the seer described, and will set my country free. I have
spoken. Now I go to make the city a present of my life, no mean offering,

to rid this kingdom of its affliction. For if each were to take and expend all
the good within his power, contributing it to his country's weal, our
states would experience fewer troubles and would for the future prosper.

(MENOECEUS *goes out.*)

CHORUS (*singing*)

strophe

Thou cam'st, O winged fiend, spawn of earth and hellish viper-
brood, to prey upon the sons of Cadmus, rife with death and fraught
with sorrow, half a monster, half a maid, a murderous prodigy, with
roving wings and ravening claws, that in days gone by didst catch
up youthful victims from the haunts of Dirce, with discordant note,
bringing a deadly curse, a woe of bloodshed to our native land. A
murderous god he was who brought all this to pass. In every house
was heard a cry of mothers wailing and of wailing maids, lamentation
and the voice of weeping, as each took up the chant of death from
street to street in turn. Loud rang the mourners' wail, and one great
cry went up, whene'er that winged maiden bore some victim out of
sight from the city.

antistrophe

At last came Oedipus, the man of sorrow, on his mission from
Delphi to this land of Thebes, a joy to them then but afterwards a
cause of grief; for, when he had read the riddle triumphantly, he
formed with his mother an unhallowed union, woe to him! polluting
the city; and by his curses, luckless wight, he plunged his sons into
a guilty strife, causing them to wade through seas of blood. All reverence do we feel for him, who is gone to his death in his country's
cause, bequeathing to Creon a legacy of tears, but destined to crown
with victory our seven fenced towers. May our motherhood be
blessed with such noble sons, O Pallas, kindly queen, who with well-
aimed stone didst spill the serpent's blood, rousing Cadmus as thou
didst to brood upon the task, whereof the issue was a demon's curse
that swooped upon this land and harried it.

(*The* FIRST MESSENGER *enters.*)

MESSENGER

Ho there! who is at the palace-gates? Open the door, summon Jocasta
forth. Ho there! once again I call; spite of this long delay come forth;
hearken, noble wife of Oedipus; cease thy lamentation and thy tears of
woe.

(JOCASTA *enters from the palace in answer to his call.*)

JOCASTA

Surely thou art not come, my friend, with the sad news of Eteocles'
death, beside whose shield thou hast ever marched, warding from him
the foeman's darts? What tidings art thou here to bring me? Is my son
alive or dead? Declare that to me.

MESSENGER

To rid thee of thy fear at once, he lives; that terror banish.

JOCASTA

Next, how is it with the seven towers that wall us in?

MESSENGER

They stand unshattered still; the city is not yet a prey.

JOCASTA

Have they been in jeopardy of the Argive spear?

MESSENGER

Aye, on the very brink; but our Theban warriors proved too strong for
Mycenae's might.

JOCASTA

One thing tell me, I implore; knowest thou aught of Polyneices, is he
yet alive? for this too I long to learn.

MESSENGER

As yet thy sons are living, the pair of them.

JOCASTA

God bless thee! How did you succeed in beating off from our gates the
Argive hosts, when thus beleaguered? Tell me, that I may go within and
cheer the old blind man, since our city is still safe.

MESSENGER

After Creon's son, who gave up life for country, had taken his stand on
the turret's top and plunged a sword dark-hilted through his throat to
save this land, thy son told off seven companies with their captains to
the seven gates to keep watch on the Argive warriors, and stationed
cavalry to cover cavalry, and infantry to support infantry, that assistance
might be close at hand for any weak point in the walls. Then from our
lofty towers we saw the Argive host with their white shields leaving
Teumessus, and, when near the trench, they charged up to our Theban
city at the double. In one loud burst from their ranks and from our
battlements rang out the battle-cry and trumpet-call. First to the Neistian
gate, Parthenopaeus, son of the huntress maid, led a company bristling

with serried shields, himself with his own peculiar badge in the centre of his targe, Atalanta slaying the Aetolian boar with an arrow shot from far. To the gates of Proetus came the prophet Amphiaraus, bringing the victims on a chariot; no vaunting blazon he carried, but weapons chastely plain. Next prince Hippomedon came marching to the Ogygian port with this device upon his boss, Argus the all-seeing with his spangled eyes upon the watch whereof some open with the rising stars, while others he closes when they set, as one could see after he was slain. At the Homoloian gates Tydeus was posting himself, a lion's skin with shaggy mane upon his buckler, while in his right hand he bore a torch, like Titan Prometheus, to fire the town. Thy own son Polyneices led the battle 'gainst the Fountain gate; upon his shield for blazon were the steeds of Potniae galloping at frantic speed, revolving by some clever contrivance on pivots inside the buckler close to the handle, so as to appear distraught. At Electra's gate famed Capaneus brought up his company, bold as Ares for the fray; this device his buckler bore upon its iron back, an earth-born giant carrying on his shoulders a whole city which he had wrenched from its base, a hint to us of the fate in store for Thebes. Adrastus was stationed at the seventh gate; a hundred vipers filled his shield with graven work, as he bore on his left arm that proud Argive badge, the hydra, and serpents were carrying off in their jaws the sons of Thebes from within their very walls. Now I was enabled to see each of them, as I carried the watch-word along the line to the leaders of our companies. To begin with, we fought with bows and thonged javelins, with slings that shoot from far and showers of crashing stones; and as we were conquering, Tydeus and thy son on a sudden cried aloud, "Ye sons of Argos, before being riddled by their fire, why delay to fall upon the gates with might and main, the whole of you, light-armed and horse and charioteers?" No loitering then, soon as they heard that call; and many a warrior fell with bloody crown, and not a few of us thou couldst have seen thrown to the earth like tumblers before the walls, after they had given up the ghost, bedewing the thirsty ground with streams of gore. Then Atalanta's son, who was not an Argive but an Arcadian, hurling himself like a hurricane at the gates, called for fire and picks to raze the town; but Periclymenus, son of the ocean-god, stayed his wild career, heaving on his head a waggon-load of stone, even the coping torn from the battlements; and it shattered his head with the hair and crashed through the sutures of the skull, dabbling with blood his cheek just showing manhood's flush; and never shall he go back alive to his fair archer-mother, the maid of Maenalus.

Thy son then, seeing these gates secure, went on to the next, and I with him. There I saw Tydeus and his serried ranks of targeteers hurling their Aetolian spears into the opening at the top of the turrets, with such good aim that our men fled and left the beetling battlements: but thy son rallied them once more, as a huntsman cheers his hounds, and made them man the towers again. And then away we hastened to other gates, after stopping the panic there. As for the madness of Capaneus, how am I to describe it? There was he, carrying with him a long scaling-ladder and loudly boasting that even the awful lightning of Zeus would not stay him from giving the city to utter destruction; and even as he spoke, he crept up beneath the hail of stones, gathered under the shelter of his shield, mounting from rung to rung on the smooth ladder; but, just as he was scaling the parapet of the wall, Zeus smote him with a thunderbolt; loud the earth re-echoed, and fear seized every heart; for his limbs were hurled from the ladder far apart as from a sling, his head toward the sky, his blood toward earth, while his legs and arms went spinning round like Ixion's wheel, till his charred corpse fell to the ground. But when Adrastus saw that Zeus was leagued against his army, he drew the Argive troops outside the trench and halted them. Meantime our horse, marking the lucky omen of Zeus, began driving forth their chariots, and our men-at-arms charged into the thick of the Argives, and everything combined to their discomfiture; men were falling and hurled headlong from chariots, wheels flew off, axles crashed together, while ever higher grew the heaps of slain; so for to-day at least have we prevented the destruction of our country's bulwarks; but whether fortune will hereafter smile upon this land, that rests with Heaven; for, even as it is, it owes its safety to some deity.

Victory is fair; and if the gods are growing kinder, it would be well with me.

JOCASTA
Heaven and fortune smile; for my sons are yet alive and my country hath escaped ruin. But Creon seems to have reaped the bitter fruit of my marriage with Oedipus, by losing his son to his sorrow, a piece of luck for Thebes, but bitter grief to him. Prithee to thy tale again and say what my two sons next intend.

MESSENGER
Forbear to question further; all is well with thee so far.

JOCASTA
Thy words but rouse my suspicions; I cannot leave it thus.

MESSENGER
Hast thou any further wish than thy sons' safety?

JOCASTA
Yea, I would learn whether in the sequel I am also blest.

MESSENGER

Let me go; thy son is left without his squire.

JOCASTA

There is some evil thou art hiding, veiling it in darkness.

MESSENGER

Maybe; I would not add ill news to the good thou hast heard.

JOCASTA

Thou must, unless thou take wings and fly away.

MESSENGER

Ah! why didst thou not let me go after announcing my good news, in- stead of forcing me to disclose evil? Those two sons of thine are resolved on deeds of shameful recklessness, a single combat apart from the host, addressing to Argives and Thebans alike words I would they had never uttered. Eteocles, taking his stand on a lofty tower, after ordering silence to be proclaimed to the army, began on this wise, "Ye captains of Hellas, chieftains of Argos here assembled, and ye folk of Cadmus, barter not your lives for Polyneices or for me! For I myself excuse you from this risk, and will engage my brother in single combat; and if I slay him, I will possess my palace without rival, but if I am worsted I will bequeath the city to him. Ye men of Argos, give up the struggle and return to your land, nor lose your lives here; of the earth-sown folk as well there are dead enough in those already slain."

So he; then thy son Polyneices rushed from the array and assented to his proposal; and all the Argives and the people of Cadmus shouted their approval, as though they deemed it just. On these terms the armies made a truce, and in the space betwixt them took an oath of each other for their leaders to abide by. Forthwith in brazen mail those two sons of aged Oedipus were casing themselves; and lords of Thebes with friendly care equipped the captain of this land, while Argive chieftains armed the other. There they stood in dazzling sheen, neither blenching, all eagerness to hurl their lances each at the other. Then came their friends to their side, first one, then another, with words of encouragement, to wit:

"Polyneices, it rests with thee to set up an image of Zeus as a trophy, and crown Argos with fair renown."

Others hailed Eteocles: "Now art thou fighting for thy city; now, if victorious, thou hast the sceptre in thy power."

So spake they, cheering them to the fray.

Meantime the seers were sacrificing sheep and noting the tongues and forks of fire, the damp reek which is a bad omen, and the tapering flame, which gives decisions on two points, being both a sign of victory and defeat. But, if thou hast any power or subtle speech or charmèd spell, go, stay thy children from this fell affray, for great is the risk they run. The issue thereof will be grievous sorrow for thee, if to-day thou art reft of both thy sons.

(*The* MESSENGER *departs in haste as* ANTIGONE *comes out of the palace.*)

JOCASTA
Antigone, my daughter, come forth before the palace; this heaven-sent crisis is no time for thee to be dancing or amusing thyself with girlish pursuits. But thou and thy mother must prevent two gallant youths, thy own brothers, from plunging into death and falling by each other's hand.

ANTIGONE
Mother mine, what new terror art thou proclaiming to thy dear ones before the palace?

JOCASTA
Daughter, thy brothers are in danger of their life.

ANTIGONE
What mean'st thou?

JOCASTA
They have resolved on single combat.

ANTIGONE
O horror! what hast thou to tell, mother?

JOCASTA
No welcome news; follow me.

ANTIGONE
Whither away from my maiden-bower?

JOCASTA
To the army.

ANTIGONE
I cannot face the crowd.

JOCASTA
Modesty is not for thee now.

ANTIGONE
But what can I do?

JOCASTA
Thou shalt end thy brothers' strife.

ANTIGONE

By what means, mother mine?

JOCASTA

By falling at their knees with me.

ANTIGONE

Lead on till we are 'twixt the armies; no time for lingering now.

JOCASTA

Haste, my daughter, haste! For, if I can forestall the onset of my sons,
I may yet live; but if they be dead, I will lay me down and die with them.
(JOCASTA *and* ANTIGONE *hurriedly depart.*)

CHORUS (*singing*)

strophe

Ah me! my bosom thrills with terror; and through my flesh there
passes a throb of pity for the hapless mother. Which of her two sons
will send the other to a bloody grave? ah, woe is me! O Zeus, O earth,
alas! brother severing brother's throat and robbing him of life, cleaving through his shield to spill his blood? Ah me! ah me! which of
them will claim my dirge of death?

antistrophe

Woe unto thee, thou land of Thebes! two savage beasts, two murderous souls, with brandished spears will soon be draining each his
fallen foeman's gore. Woe is them, that they ever thought of single
combat! in foreign accent will I chant a dirge of tears and wailing in
mourning for the dead. Close to murder stands their fortune; the
coming day will decide it. Fatal, ah! fatal will this slaughter be, because of the avenging fiends.

But I see Creon on his way hither to the palace with brow o'ercast;
I will check my present lamentations.

(CREON *enters. He is followed by attendants carrying the body of*
MENOECEUS.)

CREON

Ah me! what shall I do? Am I to mourn with bitter tears myself or my
city, round which is settling a swarm thick enough to send us to Acheron?
My own son hath died for his country, bringing glory to his name but
grievous woe to me. His body I rescued but now from the dragon's rocky
lair and sadly carried the self-slain victim hither in my arms; and my
house is filled with weeping; but now I come to fetch my sister Jocasta,

age seeking age, that she may bathe my child's corpse and lay it out. For the living must reverence the nether god by paying honour to the dead.

LEADER OF THE CHORUS

Thy sister, Creon, hath gone forth and her daughter Antigone went with her.

CREON

Whither went she? and wherefore? tell me.

LEADER

She heard that her sons were about to engage in single combat for the royal house.

CREON

What is this? I was paying the last honours to my dead son, and so am late in learning this fresh sorrow.

LEADER

'Tis some time, Creon, since thy sister's departure, and I expect the struggle for life and death is already decided by the sons of Oedipus.

CREON

Alas! I see an omen there, the gloomy look and clouded brow of yonder messenger coming to tell us the whole matter.

(*The* SECOND MESSENGER *enters.*)

MESSENGER

Ah, woe is me! what language can I find to tell my tale?

CREON

Our fate is sealed; thy opening words do naught to reassure us.

MESSENGER

Ah, woe is me! I do repeat; for beside the scenes of woe already enacted I bring tidings of new horror.

CREON

What is thy tale?

MESSENGER

Thy sister's sons are now no more, Creon.

CREON

Alas! thou hast a heavy tale of woe for me and Thebes

LEADER

O house of Oedipus, hast thou heard these tidings?

CREON

Of sons slain by the self-same fate.

LEADER

A tale to make it weep, were it endowed with sense.

CREON

Oh! most grievous stroke of fate! woe is me for my sorrows! woe!

MESSENGER

Woe indeed! didst thou but know the sorrows still to tell.

CREON

How can they be more hard to bear than these?

MESSENGER

With her two sons thy sister has sought her death.

CHORUS (*chanting*)

Loudly, loudly raise the wail, and with white hands smite upon your heads!

CREON

Ah! woe is thee, Jocasta! what an end to life and marriage hast thou found the riddling of the Sphinx! But tell me how her two sons wrought the bloody deed, the struggle caused by the curse of Oedipus.

MESSENGER

Of our successes before the towers thou knowest, for the walls are not so far away as to prevent thy learning each event as it occurred. Now when they, the sons of aged Oedipus, had donned their brazen mail, they went and took their stand betwixt the hosts, chieftains both and generals too, to decide the day by single combat. Then Polyneices, turning his eyes towards Argos, lifted up a prayer; "O Hera, awful queen,—for thy servant I am, since I have wedded the daughter of Adrastus and dwell in his land,—grant that I may slay my brother, and stain my lifted hand with the blood of my conquered foe. A shameful prize it is I ask, my own brother's blood." And to many an eye the tear would rise at their sad fate, and men looked at one another, casting their glances round.

But Eteocles, looking towards the temple of Pallas with the golden shield, prayed thus, "Daughter of Zeus, grant that this right arm may launch the spear of victory against my brother's breast and slay him who hath come to sack my country." Soon as the Tuscan trumpet blew, the signal for the bloody fray, like the torch that falls,[5] they darted wildly at one another and, like boars whetting their savage tusks, began the fray, their beards wet with foam; and they kept shooting out their spears, but each crouched beneath his shield to let the steel glance idly off; but if either saw the other's face above the rim, he would aim his lance thereat, eager to outwit him.

But both kept such careful outlook through the spy-holes in their shields, that their weapons found naught to do; while from the on-lookers far more than the combatants trickled the sweat caused by terror for their friends. Suddenly Eteocles, in kicking aside a stone that rolled beneath his tread, exposed a limb outside his shield, and Polyneices seeing a chance of dealing him a blow, aimed a dart at it, and the Argive shaft went through his leg; whereat the Danai, one and all, cried out for joy. But the wounded man, seeing a shoulder unguarded in this effort, plunged his spear with all his might into the breast of Polyneices, restoring gladness to the citizens of Thebes, though he brake off the spear-head; and so, at a loss for a weapon, he retreated foot by foot, till catching up a splintered rock he let it fly and shivered the other's spear; and now was the combat equal, for each had lost his lance. Then clutching their sword-hilts they closed, and round and round, with shields close-locked, they waged their wild warfare. Anon Eteocles introduced that crafty Thessalian trick, having some knowledge thereof from his intercourse with that country; disengaging himself from the immediate contest, he drew back his left foot but kept his eye closely on the pit of the other's stomach from a distance; then advancing his right foot he plunged his weapon through his navel and fixed it in his spine. Down falls Polyneices, blood-bespattered, ribs and belly contracting in his agony. But that other, thinking his victory now complete, threw down his sword and set to spoiling him, wholly intent thereon, without a thought for himself. And this indeed was his ruin; for Polyneices, who had fallen first, was still faintly breathing, and having in his grievous fall retained his sword, he made a last effort and drove it through the heart of Eteocles. There they lie, fallen side by side, biting the dust with their teeth, without having decided the mastery.

LEADER OF THE CHORUS

Ah, woe is thee! Oedipus, for thy sorrows! how I pity thee! Heaven, it seems, has fulfilled those curses of thine.

MESSENGER

Now hear what further woes succeeded. Just as her two sons had fallen and lay dying, comes their wretched mother on the scene, her daughter with her, in hot haste; and when she saw their mortal wounds, "Too late," she moaned, "my sons, the help I bring"; and throwing herself on each in turn she wept and wailed, sorrowing o'er all her toil in suckling them; and so too their sister, who was with her, "Supporters of your mother's age! dear brothers, leaving me forlorn, unwed!" Then prince Eteocles

with one deep dying gasp, hearing his mother's cry, laid on her his moist
hand, and though he could not say a word, his tear-filled eyes were eloquent to prove his love. But Polyneices was still alive, and seeing his sister
and his aged mother he said, "Mother mine, our end is come; I pity thee
and my sister Antigone and my dead brother. For I loved him though he
turned my foe, I loved him, yes! in spite of all. Bury me, mother mine,
and thou, my sister dear, in my native soil; pacify the city's wrath that I
may get at least that much of my own fatherland, although I lost my
home. With thy hand, mother, close mine eyes (therewith he himself
places her fingers on the lids); and fare ye well; for already the darkness
wraps me round."

So both at once breathed out their life of sorrow. But when their
mother saw this sad mischance, in her o'ermastering grief she snatched
from a corpse its sword and wrought an awful deed, driving the steel right
through her throat; and there she lies, dead with the dead she loved so
well, her arms thrown round them both.

Thereon the host sprang to their feet and fell to wrangling, we main-
taining that victory rested with my master, they with theirs; and amid
our leaders the contention raged, some holding that Polyneices gave the
first wound with his spear, others that, as both were dead, victory rested
with neither. Meantime Antigone crept away from the host; and those
others rushed to their weapons, but by some lucky forethought the folk of
Cadmus had sat down under arms; and by a sudden attack we surprised
the Argive host before it was fully equipped. Not one withstood our onset,
and they filled the plain with fugitives, while blood was streaming from
the countless dead our spears had slain. Soon as victory crowned our warfare, some began to rear an image to Zeus for the foe's defeat, others were
stripping the Argive dead of their shields and sending their spoils inside
the battlements; and others with Antigone are bringing her dead brothers
hither for their friends to mourn. So the result of this struggle to our city
hovers between the two extremes of good and evil fortune.

(*The* MESSENGER *goes out.*)

CHORUS (*chanting*)
No longer do the misfortunes of this house extend to hearsay only;
three corpses of the slain lie here at the palace for all to see, who by
one common death have passed to their life of gloom.

(*During the lament,* ANTIGONE *enters, followed by servants who
bear the bodies of* JOCASTA, ETEOCLES, *and* POLYNEICES.)

ANTIGONE (*chanting*)
No veil I draw o'er my tender cheek shaded with its clustering
curls; no shame I feel from maiden modesty at the hot blood man-

tling 'neath my eyes, the blush upon my face, as I hurry wildly on in death's train, casting from my hair its tire and letting my delicate robe of saffron hue fly loose, a tearful escort to the dead. Ah me!

Woe to thee, Polyneices! rightly named, I trow; woe to thee, Thebes! no mere strife to end in strife was thine; but murder completed by murder hath brought the house of Oedipus to ruin with bloodshed dire and grim. O my home, my home! what minstrel can I summon from the dead to chant a fitting dirge o'er my tearful fate, as I bear these three corpses of my kin, my mother and her sons, a welcome sight to the avenging fiend that destroyed the house of Oedipus, root and branch, in the hour that his shrewdness solved the Sphinx's riddling rhyme and slew that savage songstress. Woe is me! my father! what other Hellene or barbarian, what noble soul among the bygone tribes of man's poor mortal race ever endured the anguish of such visible afflictions?

Ah! poor maid, how piteous is thy plaint! What bird from its covert 'mid the leafy oak or soaring pine-tree's branch will come to mourn with me, the maid left motherless, with cries of woe, lamenting, ere it comes, the piteous lonely life, that henceforth must be always mine with tears that ever stream? On which of these corpses shall I throw my offerings first, plucking the hair from my head? on the breast of the mother that suckled me, or beside the ghastly death-wounds of my brothers' corpses? Woe to thee, Oedipus, my aged sire with sightless orbs, leave thy roof, disclose the misery of thy life, thou that draggest out a weary existence within the house, having cast a mist of darkness o'er thine eyes. Dost hear, thou whose aged step now gropes its way across the court, now seeks repose on wretched pallet couch?

(OEDIPUS *enters from the palace. He chants the following lines responsively with* ANTIGONE.)

OEDIPUS

Why, daughter, hast thou dragged me to the light, supporting my blind footsteps from the gloom of my chamber, where I lie upon my bed and make piteous moan, a hoary sufferer, invisible as a phantom of the air, or as a spirit from the pit, or as a dream that flies?

ANTIGONE

Father, there are tidings of sorrow for thee to bear; no more thy sons behold the light, or thy wife who ever would toil to tend thy blind footsteps as with a staff. Alas for thee, my sire!

OEDIPUS

Ah me, the sorrows I endure! I may well say that. Tell me, child,
what fate o'ertook those three, and how they left the light.

ANTIGONE

Not to reproach or mock thee say I this, but in all sadness; 'tis
thy own avenging curse, with all its load of slaughter, fire, and
ruthless war, that is fallen on thy sons. Alas for thee, my sire!

OEDIPUS

Ah me!

ANTIGONE

Why dost thou groan?

OEDIPUS

'Tis for my sons.

ANTIGONE

Couldst thou have looked towards yon sun-god's four-horsed car
and turned the light of thine eyes on these corpses, it would have
been agony to thee.

OEDIPUS

'Tis clear enough how their evil fate o'ertook my sons; but she,
my poor wife—oh! tell me, daughter, how she came to die.

ANTIGONE

All saw her weep and heard her moan, as she rushed forth to carry
to her sons her last appeal, a mother's breast. But the mother found
her sons at the Electran gate, in a meadow where the lotus blooms,
fighting out their duel like lions in their lair, eager to wound each
other with spears, their blood already congealed, a murderous libation to the Death-god poured out by Ares. Then, snatching from a
corpse a sword of hammered bronze, she plunged it in her flesh, and
in sorrow for her sons fell with her arms around them. So to-day,
father, the god, whose'er this issue is, has gathered to a head the
sum of suffering for our house.

LEADER OF THE CHORUS

To-day is the beginning of many troubles to the house of Oedipus;
may he live to be more fortunate!

CREON

Cease now your lamentations; 'tis time we bethought us of their burial.
Hear what I have to say, Oedipus. Eteocles, thy son, left me to rule this

land, by assigning it as a marriage portion to Haemon with the hand of thy daughter Antigone. Wherefore I will no longer permit thee to dwell therein, for Teiresias plainly declared that the city would never prosper so long as thou wert in the land. So begone! And this I say not to flout thee, nor because I bear thee any grudge, but from fear that some calamity will come upon the realm by reason of those fiends that dog thy steps.

OEDIPUS

O destiny! to what a life of pain and sorrow didst thou bear me beyond all men that ever were, e'en from the very first; yea for when I was yet unborn, or ever I had left my mother's womb and seen the light, Apollo foretold to Laius that I should become my father's murderer; woe is me! So, as soon as I was born, my father tried to end again the hapless life he had given, deeming me his foe, for it was fated he should die at my hand; so he sent me still unweaned to make a pitiful meal for beasts, but I escaped from that. Ah! would that Cithaeron had sunk into hell's yawning abyss, in that it slew me not! Instead thereof Fate made me a slave in the service of Polybus; and I, poor wretch, after slaying my own father came to wed my mother to her sorrow, and begat sons that were my brothers, whom also I have destroyed, by bequeathing unto them the legacy of curses I received from Laius. For nature did not make me so void of understanding, that I should have devised these horrors against my own eyes and my children's life without the intervention of some god. Let that pass. What am I, poor wretch, to do? Who now will be my guide and tend the blind man's step? Shall she, that is dead? Were she alive, I know right well she would. My pair of gallant sons, then? But they are gone from me. Am I still so young myself that I can find a livelihood? Whence could I? O Creon, why seek thus to slay me utterly? For so thou wilt, if thou banish me from the land. Yet will I never twine my arms about thy knees and betray cowardice, for I will not belie my former gallant soul, no! not for all my evil case.

CREON

Thy words are brave in refusing to touch my knees, and I am equally resolved not to let thee abide in the land. For these dead, bear one forthwith to the palace; but the other, who came with stranger folk to sack his native town, the dead Polyneices, cast forth unburied beyond our frontiers. To all the race of Cadmus shall this be proclaimed, that whosoe'er is caught decking his corpse with wreaths or giving it burial, shall be requited with death; unwept, unburied let him lie, a prey to birds. As for thee, Antigone, leave thy mourning for these lifeless three and betake thyself indoors to abide there in maiden state until to-morrow, when Haemon waits to wed thee.

ANTIGONE

O father, in what cruel misery are we plunged! For thee I mourn more than for the dead; for in thy woes there is no opposite to trouble, but universal sorrow is thy lot. As for thee, thou new-made king, why, I ask, dost thou mock my father thus with banishment? Why start making laws over a helpless corpse?

CREON

This was what Eteocles, not I, resolved.

ANTIGONE

A foolish thought, and foolish art thou for entertaining it!

CREON

What! ought I not to carry out his behests?

ANTIGONE

No; not if they are wrong and ill-advised.

CREON

Why, is it not just for that other to be given to the dogs?

ANTIGONE

Nay, the vengeance ye are exacting is no lawful one.

CREON

It is; for he was his country's foe, though not a foeman born.

ANTIGONE

Well, to fate he rendered up his destinies.

CREON

Let him now pay forfeit in his burial too.

ANTIGONE

What crime did he commit in coming to claim his heritage?

CREON

Be very sure of this, yon man shall have no burial.

ANTIGONE

I will bury him, although the state forbids.

CREON

Do so, and thou wilt be making thy own grave by his.

ANTIGONE

A noble end, for two so near and dear to be laid side by side!

CREON (*to his servants*)
Ho! seize and bear her within the palace.

ANTIGONE
Never! for I will not loose my hold upon this corpse.

CREON
Heaven's decrees, girl, fit not thy fancies.

ANTIGONE
Decrees! here is another, "No insult to the dead."

CREON
Be sure that none shall sprinkle over the corpse the moistened dust.

ANTIGONE
O Creon, by my mother's corpse, by Jocasta, I implore thee!

CREON
'Tis but lost labour; thou wilt not gain thy prayer.

ANTIGONE
Let me but bathe the dead body—

CREON
Nay, that would be part of what the city is forbidden.

ANTIGONE
At least let me bandage the gaping wounds.

CREON
No; thou shalt never pay honour to this corpse.

ANTIGONE
O my darling! one kiss at least will I print upon thy lips.

CREON
Do not let this mourning bring disaster on thy marriage.

ANTIGONE
Marriage! dost think I will live to wed thy son?

CREON
Most certainly thou must; how wilt thou escape his bed?

ANTIGONE
Then if I must, our wedding-night will find another Danaid bride in me.

CREON (*turning to* OEDIPUS)
Dost witness how boldly she reproached me?

ANTIGONE
Witness this steel, the sword by which I swear!

CREON
Why art so bent on being released from this marriage?

ANTIGONE
I mean to share my hapless father's exile.

CREON
A noble spirit thine but somewhat touched with folly.

ANTIGONE
Likewise will I share his death, I tell thee further.

CREON
Go, leave the land; thou shalt not murder son of mine.
(CREON *goes out, followed by his attendants who carry with them the
body of* MENOECEUS.)

OEDIPUS
Daughter, for this loyal spirit I thank thee.

ANTIGONE
Were I to wed, then thou, my father, wouldst be alone in thy exile.

OEDIPUS
Abide here and be happy; I will bear my own load of sorrow.

ANTIGONE
And who shall tend thee in thy blindness, father?

OEDIPUS
Where fate appoints, there will I lay me down upon the ground.

ANTIGONE
Where is now the famous Oedipus, where that famous riddle?

OEDIPUS
Lost for ever! one day made, and one day marred my fortune.

ANTIGONE
May not I too share thy sorrows?

OEDIPUS

To wander with her blinded sire were shame unto his child.

ANTIGONE

Not so, father, but glory rather, if she be a maid discreet.

OEDIPUS

Lead me nigh that I may touch thy mother's corpse.

ANTIGONE

So! embrace the aged form so dear to thee.

OEDIPUS

Woe is thee, thy motherhood, thy marriage most unblest!

ANTIGONE

A piteous corpse, a prey to every ill at once!

OEDIPUS

Where lies the corpse of Eteocles, and of Polyneices, where?

ANTIGONE

Both lie stretched before thee, side by side.

OEDIPUS

Lay the blind man's hand upon his poor sons' brows.

ANTIGONE

There then! touch the dead, thy children.

OEDIPUS

Woe for you! dear fallen sons, sad offspring of a sire as sad!

ANTIGONE

O my brother Polyneices, name most dear to me!

OEDIPUS

Now is the oracle of Loxias being fulfilled, my child.

ANTIGONE

What oracle was that? canst thou have further woes to tell?

OEDIPUS

That I should die in glorious Athens after a life of wandering.

ANTIGONE

Where? what fenced town in Attica will take thee in?

OEDIPUS

Hallowed Colonus, home of the god of steeds. Come then, attend on thy blind father, since thou art minded to share his exile.

(OEDIPUS *and* ANTIGONE *chant their remaining lines as they slowly depart.*)

ANTIGONE

To wretched exile go thy way; stretch forth thy hand, my aged sire, taking me to guide thee, like a breeze that speedeth barques.

OEDIPUS

See, daughter, I am advancing; be thou my guide, poor child.

ANTIGONE

Ah, poor indeed! the saddest maid of all in Thebes.

OEDIPUS

Where am I planting my aged step? Bring my staff, child.

ANTIGONE

This way, this way, father mine! plant thy footsteps here, like a dream for all the strength thou hast.

OEDIPUS

Woe unto thee that art driving my aged limbs in grievous exile from their land! Ah me! the sorrows I endure!

ANTIGONE

"Endure"! why speak of enduring? Justice regardeth not the sinner and requiteth not men's follies.

OEDIPUS

I am he whose name passed into high songs of victory because I guessed the maiden's baffling riddle.

ANTIGONE

Thou art bringing up again the reproach of the Sphinx. Talk no more of past success. This misery was in store for thee all the while, to become an exile from thy country and die thou knowest not where; while I, bequeathing to my girlish friends tears of sad regret, must go forth from my native land, roaming as no maiden ought.

Ah! this dutiful resolve will crown me with glory in respect of my father's sufferings. Woe is me for the insults heaped on thee and on my brother whose dead body is cast forth from the palace unburied; poor boy! I will yet bury him secretly, though I have to die for it, father.

OEDIPUS

To thy companions show thyself.

ANTIGONE

My own laments suffice.

OEDIPUS

Go pray then at the altars.

ANTIGONE

They are weary of my piteous tale.

OEDIPUS

At least go seek the Bromian god in his hallowed haunt amongst the Maenads' hills.

ANTIGONE

Offering homage that is no homage in Heaven's eyes to him in whose honour I once fringed my dress with the Theban fawn-skin and led the dance upon the hills for the holy choir of Semele?

OEDIPUS

My noble fellow-countrymen, behold me; I am Oedipus, who solved the famous riddle, and once was first of men, I who alone cut short the murderous Sphinx's tyranny am now myself expelled the land in shame and misery. Go to; why make this moan and bootless lamentation? Weak mortal as I am, I must endure the fate that God decrees.

CHORUS (*chanting*)

Hail! majestic Victory! keep thou my life nor ever cease to crown my song! [6]

COLERIDGE's translation has been slightly altered in the following lines: 198, 199, 268, 341, 429, 499, 585, 610, 729, 875, 888, 889, 1208, 1276, 1307, 1328, 1439, 1440–1441, 1560, 1674.

1. The reference is to a spot in Argolis where Poseidon struck the ground with his trident and caused a fountain to appear. He did so because he had become enamoured of Amymone, one of the Danaids, who at the time was searching for water to take to Argos during a drought.

2. Polyneices is alluding to Amphion and Zethus, the Theban Dioscuri.

3. This seems to be an obvious criticism of the corresponding passage in Aeschylus' *The Seven Against Thebes*.

4. The following passages may be compared with the sacrifice of Polyxena in the *Hecuba* and of Macaria in *The Heracleidae*. Also cf. the closing scene of the *Iphigenia in Aulis*.

5. Coleridge's note here runs as follows: "This was the signal for the start at the Lampadephoria, an Athenian ceremony at the festivals of the fire-gods Prometheus, Hephaestus, and Athena."

6. Cf. the *Iphigenia in Tauris*, note 3.

XVI
THE BACCHAE

CHARACTERS IN THE PLAY

DIONYSUS, THE GOD; *son of Zeus and of the Theban princess Semele*
CADMUS, *formerly King of Thebes, father of Semele*
PENTHEUS, *King of Thebes, grandson of Cadmus*
AGAVE, *daughter of Cadmus, mother of Pentheus*
TEIRESIAS, *an aged Theban prophet*
A SOLDIER OF PENTHEUS' GUARD
TWO MESSENGERS
A CHORUS OF INSPIRED DAMSELS, *following Dionysus from the East*

INTRODUCTION

SOMETIME between the production of the *Orestes* in 408 B.C. and Euripides' death in 407–406 B.C., the poet left Athens to go to Macedonia, on the invitation of King Archelaus. There seems to be little doubt that he departed from his once beloved city in a spirit of disillusionment and despair. The great Athens to which he had been so devoted and of which he had been so proud in earlier days, had crumbled sadly in the later stages of the Peloponnesian War. Euripides had implicitly expressed in *The Trojan Women* his bitter feeling that the integrity of Athens had somehow become tainted. The same feeling of disillusionment manifests itself in the last play he wrote, *The Bacchae,* composed during his self-imposed exile, and probably not quite finished at his death. It seems not to have been produced in Athens before 405 B.C.

In *The Bacchae* Euripides turns his attention directly to the question of religion. It is generally supposed that in Macedonia he had an opportunity to witness first hand the wild and orgiastic worship of the god, Dionysus, and all its attendant ritual mysticism. It was a religion of enthusiasm and intoxication, containing elements of the fertility cult as well as the idea that through participation in the rites the devotee became cleansed of his sins and became mystically one with the god. Likewise a curious kind of animal symbolism pervaded the worship, one important part of which was the sacrifice of a bull, who was in a mystic sense also the god, through whose blood came purification. It is this type of religion which Euripides studies in his play and hence for his material he turns to the myths which explain the origin of the Dionysiac worship.

The myth of Dionysus' birth which Euripides follows in *The Bacchae* recorded that Semele, daughter of the Theban Cadmus, was once loved by Zeus, and asked that the god come to her in his complete majesty. Zeus was bound to grant her wish, appeared to her in a great flash of lightning by which she was consumed. Before she died, however, she gave birth prematurely to Zeus' child whom she was carrying. Zeus saved the life of the child, who was to be the god Dionysus, by opening his own flesh, enclosing and fostering the infant. In due course he brought forth the god, by a mysterious second birth. This second birth was an important

223

factor in the worship of Dionysus as many allusions to it in *The Bacchae* more than adequately attest.

The god himself speaks the prologue of the play. We learn that Thebes, the native city of the god's mother, Semele, has slighted his worship, and that he has arrived to establish himself as a deity and his religion among the Thebans. We also are informed that Cadmus, the old king, has turned over the royal power to his grandson, Pentheus, who is the son of Agave, a sister of Semele. The dramatic action which follows is rich, strange, and in places horrifying. The Chorus, composed of maidens who are inspired followers of Dionysus, has a more integral connection with the central structure of the play than is apparent in the majority of Euripides' compositions. Not only does the Chorus contribute to the action, but also it sings lyric odes of rare beauty which rank among the greatest to be found in Greek. It is noteworthy as well that these odes are "romantic" in tone, in the sense that they display a delight in and a sensitive awareness of wild nature, qualities which are usually and falsely denied to the Greeks by critics in general.

In *The Bacchae* also are many finished characterizations. The poet portrays almost comically the two old men, Cadmus and Teiresias, who at the outset decide to do reverence to the god, largely on the grounds of wishing to remain on the safe side. Then there is the supremely tragic presentation of Pentheus, who out of the purest motives, brutally attempts to stamp out this new religion as something which is subversive of the best interests of his country. In many ways Pentheus is not unlike Creon in Sophocles' *Antigone*. And finally there is the delineation of the god Dionysus, who at the beginning of the play seems to be a great and good divinity but who at the end exhibits what is apparently unmitigated cruelty, his only defence for which is his assertion that all these happenings were decreed by the will of Zeus.

The most notable individual scene of the play occurs when Agave enters, carrying the head of her slain son. No episode in all Greek tragedy has so much stark horror packed into it. Agave is still in the grips of religious transport and in sheer ecstasy of triumph bears her ghastly burden which she believes to be the head of a lion that she and her fellow orgiasts have slain with their bare hands. She regards it as vivid proof of the power of the god that is within them. Gradually her horrified father, Cadmus, brings her to her senses. The dramatic impact is tremendous when at length she fully realizes what she has done. The scene is saved from being completely repelling by the courageous way in which both Cadmus and Agave meet the punishment which the god has put upon them.

The Bacchae is the most difficult of all the Greek tragedies to interpret. For example, the long scene between Pentheus and Dionysus, when the king finally surrenders to the god, is most puzzling. Murray, in his translation, has presented a most convincing interpretation, when he supposes that Pentheus is gradually being hypnotized by Dionysus. Also there is the extraordinary scene in which the palace is destroyed by an earthquake, or so the text would lead us to believe. Some critics maintain that the destruction is only the reflection of a subjective state in the minds of Dionysus and the Chorus, while others hold that only a part of the palace crashed in ruins, since no character at the end of the play notices anything unusual about the condition of the building. No adequate answer has ever been given to this problem. Again, there are scholars who believe that the "Lydian Stranger" is not Dionysus. This theory seems to be untenable on the ground that much of the magnificent dramatic effect of the first scene between Pentheus and the so-called "Lydian Stranger" would be lost, were the latter not Dionysus in disguise. As Murray has interpreted it, the scene contains dramatic irony which definitely rivals that to be found in Sophocles' *Oedipus the King*. Lastly, to add to all these other problems, at the end of the play a crucial page or more has unfortunately been lost from the manuscript. This missing section may very well have contained vital information relevant to the drama's central interpretation.

One cannot fail to be impressed by the difference which obtains between Euripides' study of religion in *The Bacchae* and that to be found in the plays of Aeschylus. Euripides has focussed his attention upon man in a religious milieu, and examines him as he is swept by surging emotion and violent religious frenzy. What the poet actually believes or means to communicate must probably remain an enigma. At one moment we feel that he regards religion as the most valuable and important element in man's life, while at another he seems to present it as a curse and an abomination. Perhaps he is asserting that religion is supremely important but that nothing is more terrible than its excesses. Whatever may be its precise interpretation, in this last play critics are right in seeing one of Euripides' greatest artistic creations.

THE BACCHAE

(SCENE:—*The background represents the front of the Castle of* PEN-
THEUS, *King of Thebes. At one side is visible the sacred Tomb of Semele,
a little enclosure overgrown with wild vines, with a cleft in the rocky floor
of it from which there issues at times steam or smoke. The God* DIONYSUS
is discovered alone.)

DIONYSUS
Behold, God's Son is come unto this land
Of Thebes, even I, Dionysus, whom the brand
Of heaven's hot splendour lit to life, when she
Who bore me, Cadmus' daughter Semele,
Died here. So, changed in shape from God to man,
I walk again by Dirce's streams and scan
Ismenus' shore. There by the castle side
I see her place, the Tomb of the Lightning's Bride,
The wreck of smouldering chambers, and the great
Faint wreaths of fire undying—as the hate
Dies not, that Hera held for Semele.
    Aye, Cadmus hath done well; in purity
He keeps this place apart, inviolate,
His daughter's sanctuary; and I have set
My green and clustered vines to robe it round.
    Far now behind me lies the golden ground
Of Lydian and of Phrygian; far away
The wide hot plains where Persian sunbeams play,
The Bactrian war-holds, and the storm-oppressed
Clime of the Mede, and Araby the Blest,
And Asia all, that by the salt sea lies
In proud embattled cities, motley-wise
Of Hellene and Barbarian interwrought;
And now I come to Hellas—having taught
All the world else my dances and my rite

227

Of mysteries, to show me in men's sight
Manifest God.
         And first of Hellene lands
I cry this Thebes to waken; set her hands
To clasp my wand, mine ivied javelin,
And round her shoulders hang my wild fawn-skin.
For they have scorned me whom it least beseemed,
Semele's sisters; mocked my birth, nor deemed
That Dionysus sprang from Dian [1] seed.
My mother sinned, said they; and in her need,
With Cadmus plotting, cloaked her human shame
With the dread name of Zeus; for that the flame
From heaven consumed her, seeing she lied to God.
    Thus must they vaunt; and therefore hath my rod
On them first fallen, and stung them forth wild-eyed
From empty chambers; the bare mountain side
Is made their home, and all their hearts are flame.
Yea, I have bound upon the necks of them
The harness of my rites. And with them all
The seed of womankind from hut and hall
Of Thebes, hath this my magic goaded out.
And there, with the old King's daughters, in a rout
Confused, they make their dwelling-place between
The roofless rocks and shadowy pine trees green.
Thus shall this Thebes, how sore soe'er it smart,
Learn and forget not, till she crave her part
In mine adoring; thus must I speak clear
To save my mother's fame, and crown me here
As true God, born by Semele to Zeus.

    Now Cadmus yieldeth up his throne and use
Of royal honour to his daughter's son
Pentheus; who on my body hath begun
A war with God. He thrusteth me away
From due drink-offering, and, when men pray,
My name entreats not. Therefore on his own
Head and his people's shall my power be shown.
Then to another land, when all things here
Are well, must I fare onward, making clear
My godhead's might. But should this Theban town
Essay with wrath and battle to drag down
My maids, lo, in their path myself shall be,
And maniac armies battled after me!

For this I veil my godhead with the wan
Form of the things that die, and walk as Man.

   O Brood of Tmolus o'er the wide world flown,
O Lydian band, my chosen and mine own,
Damsels uplifted o'er the orient deep
To wander where I wander, and to sleep
Where I sleep; up, and wake the old sweet sound,
The clang that I and mystic Rhea found,
The Timbrel of the Mountain! Gather all
Thebes to your song round Pentheus' royal hall.
I seek my new-made worshippers, to guide
Their dances up Cithaeron's pine-clad side.

*(As he departs, there comes stealing in from the left a band
of fifteen Eastern Women, the light of the sunrise
streaming upon their long white robes and ivy-bound
hair. They wear fawn-skins over the robes, and carry
some of them timbrels, some pipes and other instruments. Many bear the thyrsus, or sacred Wand, made
of reed ringed with ivy. They enter stealthily till they
see that the place is empty, and then begin their mystic
song of worship.)*

CHORUS (*singing*)

A Maiden
From Asia, from the dayspring that uprises,
   To Bromios ever glorying we came.
We laboured for our Lord in many guises;
   We toiled, but the toil is as the prize is;
    Thou Mystery, we hail thee by thy name!

Another
Who lingers in the road? Who espies us?
   He shall hide him in his house nor be bold.
Let the heart keep silence that defies us;
For I sing this day to Dionysus
   The song that is appointed from of old.

All the Maidens
Oh, blessèd he in all wise,
  Who hath drunk the Living Fountain,
   Whose life no folly staineth,
    And his soul is near to God;

Whose sins are lifted, pall-wise,
　As he worships on the Mountain,
　And where Cybele ordaineth,
　　Our Mother, he has trod:

　His head with ivy laden
　　And his thyrsus tossing high,
　　　For our God he lifts his cry;
　"Up, O Bacchae, wife and maiden,
　　　Come, O ye Bacchae, come;
　Oh, bring the Joy-bestower,
　God-seed of God the Sower,
　Bring Bromios in his power
　　　From Phrygia's mountain dome;
　To street and town and tower,
　　　Oh, bring ye Bromios home!"

Whom erst in anguish lying
　For an unborn life's desire,
　　As a dead thing in the Thunder
　　His mother cast to earth;
For her heart was dying, dying,
　In the white heart of the fire;
　　Till Zeus, the Lord of Wonder,
　　Devised new lairs of birth;

　　Yea, his own flesh tore to hide him,
　　　And with clasps of bitter gold
　　　Did a secret son enfold,
　　And the Queen knew not beside him,
　　　Till the perfect hour was there;
　　Then a hornèd God was found,
　　And a God with serpents crowned;
　　And for that are serpents wound
　　　In the wands his maidens bear,
　　And the songs of serpents sound
　　　In the mazes of their hair.

Some Maidens
All hail, O Thebes, thou nurse of Semele!
　With Semele's wild ivy crown thy towers;
Oh, burst in bloom of wreathing bryony,
　　Berries and leaves and flowers:

Uplift the dark divine wand,
The oak-wand and the pine-wand,
And don thy fawn-skin, fringed in purity
With fleecy white, like ours.

Oh, cleanse thee in the wands' waving pride!
Yea, all men shall dance with us and pray,
When Bromios his companies shall guide
Hillward, ever hillward, where they stay,
The flock of the Believing,
The maids from loom and weaving
By the magic of his breath borne away.

Others
Hail thou, O Nurse of Zeus, O Caverned Haunt
Where fierce arms clanged to guard God's cradle rare,
For thee of old some crested Corybant
First woke in Cretan air
The wild orb of our orgies,
Our Timbrel; and thy gorges
Rang with this strain; and blended Phrygian chant
And sweet keen pipes were there.

But the Timbrel, the Timbrel was another's,
And away to Mother Rhea it must wend;
And to our holy singing from the Mother's
The mad Satyrs carried it, to blend
In the dancing and the cheer
Of our third and perfect Year;
And it serves Dionysus in the end!

A Maiden
O glad, glad on the mountains
To swoon in the race outworn,
When the holy fawn-skin clings,
And all else sweeps away,
To the joy of the red quick fountains,
The blood of the hill-goat torn,
The glory of wild-beast ravenings,
Where the hill-tops catch the day;
To the Phrygian, Lydian, mountains!
'Tis Bromios leads the way.

Another Maiden

Then streams the earth with milk, yea, streams
With wines and nectar of the bee,
And through the air dim perfume steams
Of Syrian frankincense; and He,
Our leader, from his thyrsus spray
A torchlight tosses high and higher,
A torchlight like a beacon-fire,
To waken all that faint and stray;
And sets them leaping as he sings.
His tresses rippling to the sky,
And deep beneath the Maenad cry
  His proud voice rings:
   "Come, O ye Bacchae, come!"

All the Maidens

Hither, O fragrant of Tmolus the Golden,
 Come with the voice of timbrel and drum;
Let the cry of your joyance uplift and embolden
 The God of the joy-cry; O Bacchanals, come!
With pealing of pipes and with Phrygian clamour,
 On, where the vision of holiness thrills,
And the music climbs and the maddening glamour,
 With the wild White Maids, to the hills, to the hills!
Oh, then, like a colt as he runs by a river,
 A colt by his dam, when the heart of him sings,
With the keen limbs drawn and the fleet foot a-quiver,
  Away the Bacchanal springs!

(*Enter* Teiresias. *He is an old man and blind, leaning
 upon a staff and moving with slow stateliness,
 though wearing the Ivy and the Bacchic fawn-skin.*)

Teiresias

Ho, there, who keeps the gate?—Go, summon me
Cadmus, Agenor's son, who crossed the sea
From Sidon and upreared this Theban hold.
Go, whosoe'er thou art. See he be told
Teiresias seeketh him. Himself will gauge
Mine errand, and the compact, age with age,
I vowed with him, grey hair with snow-white hair,
To deck the new God's thyrsus, and to wear
His fawn-skin, and with ivy crown our brows.
(*Enter* Cadmus *from the Castle. He is even older than*
 Teiresias, *and wears the same attire.*)

CADMUS

True friend! I knew that voice of thine, that flows
Like mellow wisdom from a fountain wise.
And, lo, I come prepared, in all the guise
And harness of this God. Are we not told
His is the soul of that dead life of old
That sprang from mine own daughter? Surely then
Must thou and I with all the strength of men
Exalt him.
        Where then shall I stand, where tread
The dance and toss this bowed and hoary head?
O friend, in thee is wisdom; guide my grey
And eld-worn steps, eld-worn Teiresias.—Nay;
I am not weak.
*(At the first movement of worship his manner begins to
   change; a mysterious strength and exaltation enter
   into him.)*
        Surely this arm could smite
The wild earth with its thyrsus, day and night,
And faint not! Sweetly and forgetfully
The dim years fall from off me!

TEIRESIAS
        As with thee,
With me 'tis likewise. Light am I and young,
And will essay the dancing and the song.

CADMUS

Quick, then, our chariots to the mountain road.

TEIRESIAS

Nay; to take steeds were to mistrust the God.

CADMUS

So be it. Mine old arms shall guide thee there.

TEIRESIAS

The God himself shall guide! Have thou no care.

CADMUS

And in all Thebes shall no man dance but we?

TEIRESIAS

Aye, Thebes is blinded. Thou and I can see.

CADMUS

'Tis weary waiting; hold my hand, friend; so.

TEIRESIAS

Lo, there is mine. So linkèd let us go.

CADMUS

Shall things of dust the Gods' dark ways despise?

TEIRESIAS

Or prove our wit on Heaven's high mysteries?
Not thou and I! That heritage sublime
Our sires have left us, wisdom old as time,
No word of man, how deep soe'er his thought
And won of subtlest toil, may bring to naught.
   Aye, men will rail that I forget my years,
To dance and wreathe with ivy these white hairs;
What recks it? Seeing the God no line hath told
To mark what man shall dance, or young or old;
But craves his honours from mortality
All, no man marked apart; and great shall be!

CADMUS

(*after looking away toward the Mountain*)
Teiresias, since this light thou canst not read,
I must be seer for thee. Here comes in speed
Pentheus, Echion's son, whom I have raised
To rule my people in my stead.—Amazed
He seems. Stand close, and mark what we shall hear.
(*The two stand back, partially concealed, while there enters
   in hot haste* PENTHEUS, *followed by a bodyguard. He
   is speaking to the* SOLDIER *in command.*)

PENTHEUS

Scarce had I crossed our borders, when mine ear
Was caught by this strange rumour, that our own
Wives, our own sisters, from their hearths are flown
To wild and secret rites; and cluster there
High on the shadowy hills, with dance and prayer
To adore this new-made God, this Dionyse,
Whate'er he be!—And in their companies
Deep wine-jars stand, and ever and anon
Away into the loneliness now one
Steals forth, and now a second, maid or dame,
Where love lies waiting, not of God! The flame,
They say, of Bacchios wraps them. Bacchios! Nay,

'Tis more to Aphrodite that they pray.
   Howbeit, all that I have found, my men
Hold bound and shackled in our dungeon den;
The rest, I will go hunt them! Aye, and snare
My birds with nets of iron, to quell their prayer
And mountain song and rites of rascaldom!
   They tell me, too, there is a stranger come,
A man of charm and spell, from Lydian seas,
A head all gold and cloudy fragrancies,
A wine-red cheek, and eyes that hold the light
Of the very Cyprian. Day and livelong night
He haunts amid the damsels, o'er each lip
Dangling his cup of joyance!—Let me grip
Him once, but once, within these walls, right swift
That wand shall cease its music, and that drift
Of tossing curls lie still—when my rude sword
Falls between neck and trunk! 'Tis all his word,
This tale of Dionysus; how that same
Babe that was blasted by the lightning flame
With his dead mother, for that mother's lie,
Was re-conceived, born perfect from the thigh
Of Zeus, and now is God! What call ye these?
Dreams? Gibes of the unknown wanderer? Blasphemies
That crave the very gibbet?
                          Stay! God wot,
Here is another marvel! See I not
In motley fawn-skins robed the vision-seer
Teiresias? And my mother's father here—
O depth of scorn!—adoring with the wand
Of Bacchios?—Father!—Nay, mine eyes are fond;
It is not your white heads so fancy-flown!
It cannot be! Cast off that ivy crown,
O mine own mother's sire! Set free that hand
That cowers about its staff.
                          'Tis thou hast planned
This work, Teiresias! 'Tis thou must set
Another altar and another yet
Amongst us, watch new birds, and win more hire
Of gold, interpreting new signs of fire!
But for thy silver hairs, I tell thee true,
Thou now wert sitting chained amid thy crew
Of raving damsels, for this evil dream
Thou hast brought us, of new Gods! When once the gleam

Of grapes hath lit a Woman's Festival,
In all their prayers is no more health at all!

LEADER OF THE CHORUS
(*the words are not heard by* PENTHEUS)
Injurious King, hast thou no care for God,
Nor Cadmus, sower of the Giants' Sod,[2]
Life-spring to great Echion and to thee?

TEIRESIAS
Good words, my son, come easily, when he
That speaks is wise, and speaks but for the right.
Else come they never! Swift are thine, and bright
As though with thought, yet have no thought at all.
    Lo, this new God, whom thou dost flout withal,
I cannot speak the greatness wherewith He
In Hellas shall be great! Two spirits there be,
Young Prince, that in man's world are first of worth.
Demeter one is named; she is the Earth—
Call her which name thou will!—who feeds man's frame
With sustenance of things dry. And that which came
Her work to perfect, second, is the Power
From Semele born. He found the liquid shower
Hid in the grape. He rests man's spirit dim
From grieving, when the vine exalteth him.
He giveth sleep to sink the fretful day
In cool forgetting. Is there any way
With man's sore heart, save only to forget?
    Yea, being God, the blood of him is set
Before the Gods in sacrifice, that we
For his sake may be blest.—And so, to thee,
That fable shames him, how this God was knit
Into God's flesh? Nay, learn the truth of it,
Cleared from the false.—When from that deadly light
Zeus saved the babe, and up to Olympus' height
Raised him, and Hera's wrath would cast him thence,
Then Zeus devised him a divine defence.
A fragment of the world-encircling fire [3]
He rent apart, and wrought to his desire
Of shape and hue, in the image of the child,
And gave to Hera's rage. And so, beguiled
By change and passing time, this tale was born,
How the babe-god was hidden in the torn

Flesh of his sire. He hath no shame thereby.
    A prophet is he likewise. Prophecy
Cleaves to all frenzy, but beyond all else
To frenzy of prayer. Then in us verily dwells
The God himself, and speaks the thing to be.
Yea, and of Ares' realm a part hath he.
When mortal armies, mailèd and arrayed,
Have in strange fear, or ever blade met blade,
Fled maddened, 'tis this God hath palsied them.
Aye, over Delphi's rock-built diadem
Thou yet shalt see him leaping with his train
Of fire across the twin-peaked mountain-plain,
Flaming the darkness with his mystic wand,
And great in Hellas.—List and understand,
King Pentheus! Dream not thou that force is power;
Nor, if thou hast a thought, and that thought sour
And sick, oh, dream not thought is wisdom!—Up,
Receive this God to Thebes; pour forth the cup
Of sacrifice, and pray, and wreathe thy brow.
    Thou fearest for the damsels? Think thee now;
How toucheth this the part of Dionyse
To hold maids pure perforce? In them it lies,
And their own hearts; and in the wildest rite
Cometh no stain to her whose heart is white.
    Nay, mark me! Thou hast thy joy, when the Gate
Stands thronged, and Pentheus' name is lifted great
And high by Thebes in clamour; shall not He
Rejoice in his due meed of majesty?
    Howbeit, this Cadmus whom thou scorn'st and I
Will wear His crown, and tread His dances! Aye,
Our hairs are white, yet shall that dance be trod!
I will not lift mine arm to war with God
For thee nor all thy words. Madness most fell
Is on thee, madness wrought by some dread spell,
But not by spell nor leechcraft to be cured!

CHORUS

Grey prophet, worthy of Phoebus is thy word,
And wise in honouring Bromios, our great God.

CADMUS

My son, right well Teiresias points thy road.
Oh, make thine habitation here with us,
Not lonely, against men's uses. Hazardous

Is this quick bird-like beating of thy thought
Where no thought dwells.—Grant that this God be naught,
Yet let that Naught be Somewhat in thy mouth;
Lie boldly, and say He Is! So north and south
Shall marvel, how there sprang a thing divine
From Semele's flesh, and honour all our line.

(Drawing nearer to PENTHEUS*)*

Is there not blood before thine eyes even now?
Our lost Actaeon's blood, whom long ago
His own red hounds through yonder forest dim
Tore unto death, because he vaunted him
Against most holy Artemis? Oh, beware,
And let me wreathe thy temples. Make thy prayer
With us, and walk thee humbly in God's sight.

(He makes as if to set the wreath on PENTHEUS' *head.)*

PENTHEUS

Down with that hand! Aroint thee to thy rite,
Nor smear on me thy foul contagion!

(Turning upon TEIRESIAS*)*

This
Thy folly's head and prompter shall not miss
The justice that he needs!—Go, half my guard,
Forth to the rock-seat where he dwells in ward
O'er birds and wonders; rend the stone with crow
And trident; make one wreck of high and low,
And toss his bands to all the winds of air!
Ha, have I found the way to sting thee, there?
The rest, forth through the town! And seek amain
This girl-faced stranger, that hath wrought such bane
To all Thebes, preying on our maids and wives.
Seek till ye find; and lead him here in gyves,
Till he be judged and stoned, and weep in blood
The day he troubled Pentheus with his God!

(The guards set forth in two bodies; PENTHEUS *goes into the Castle.)*

TEIRESIAS

Hard heart, how little dost thou know what seed
Thou sowest! Blind before, and now indeed
Most mad!—Come, Cadmus, let us go our way,
And pray for this our persecutor, pray
For this poor city, that the righteous God

Move not in anger.—Take thine ivy rod
And help my steps, as I help thine. 'Twere ill,
If two old men should fall by the roadway. Still,
Come what come may, our service shall be done
To Bacchios, the All-Father's mystic son.

O Pentheus, named of sorrow! [4] Shall he claim
From all thy house fulfilment of his name,
Old Cadmus?—Nay, I speak not from mine art,
But as I see—blind words and a blind heart!

(*The two Old Men go off towards the Mountain.*)

CHORUS (*singing*)

Some Maidens
Thou Immaculate on high;
Thou Recording Purity;
Thou that stoopest, Golden Wing,
Earthward, manward, pitying,
Hearest thou this angry King?
Hearest thou the rage and scorn
   'Gainst the Lord of Many Voices,
Him of mortal mother born,
   Him in whom man's heart rejoices,
Girt with garlands and with glee,
First in Heaven's sovranty?
   For his kingdom, it is there,
   In the dancing and the prayer,
In the music and the laughter,
   In the vanishing of care,
And of all before and after;
In the Gods' high banquet, when
   Gleams the grape-blood, flashed to heaven:
Yea, and in the feasts of men
Comes his crownèd slumber; then
   Pain is dead and hate forgiven!

Others
Loose thy lips from out the rein;
Lift thy wisdom to disdain;
Whatso law thou canst not see,
Scorning; so the end shall be
Uttermost calamity!
'Tis the life of quiet breath,
   'Tis the simple and the true,

Storm nor earthquake shattereth,
    Nor shall aught the house undo
Where they dwell. For, far away,
Hidden from the eyes of day,
    Watchers are there in the skies,
    That can see man's life, and prize
Deeds well done by things of clay.
    But the world's Wise are not wise,
Claiming more than mortal may.
Life is such a little thing;
    Lo, their present is departed,
And the dreams to which they cling
Come not. Mad imagining
    Theirs, I ween, and empty-hearted!

Divers Maidens
Where is the Home for me?
O Cyprus, set in the sea,
Aphrodite's home in the soft sea-foam,
    Would I could wend to thee;
Where the wings of the Loves are furled,
And faint the heart of the world.

Aye, unto Paphos' isle,
    Where the rainless meadows smile
With riches rolled from the hundred-fold
    Mouths of the far-off Nile,
Streaming beneath the waves
To the roots of the seaward caves.

But a better land is there
    Where Olympus cleaves the air,
The high still dell where the Muses dwell,
    Fairest of all things fair!
O there is Grace, and there is the Heart's Desire,
And peace to adore thee, thou Spirit of Guiding Fire!
    A God of Heaven is he,
    And born in majesty;
Yet hath he mirth in the joy of the Earth,
    And he loveth constantly
Her who brings increase,
The Feeder of Children, Peace.
    No grudge hath he of the great:

No scorn of the mean estate;
But to all that liveth His wine he giveth,
    Griefless, immaculate;
Only on them that spurn
Joy, may his anger burn.

Love thou the Day and the Night;
Be glad of the Dark and the Light;
And avert thine eyes from the lore of the wise,
    That have honour in proud men's sight.
The simple nameless herd of Humanity
Hath deeds and faith that art truth enough for me!

(*As the Chorus ceases, a party of the guards return, leading in
the midst of them* DIONYSUS, *bound. The* SOLDIER *in command stands forth, as* PENTHEUS, *hearing the tramp of
feet, comes out from the Castle.*)

SOLDIER

Our quest is finished, and thy prey, O King,
Caught; for the chase was swift, and this wild thing
Most tame; yet never flinched, nor thought to flee,
But held both hands out unresistingly—
No change, no blanching of the wine-red cheek.
He waited while we came, and bade us wreak
All thy decree; yea, laughed, and made my hest
Easy, till I for very shame confessed
And said: 'O stranger, not of mine own will
I bind thee, but his bidding to fulfil
Who sent me.'
            And those prisoned Maids withal
Whom thou didst seize and bind within the wall
Of thy great dungeon, they are fled, O King,
Free in the woods, a-dance and glorying
To Bromios. Of their own impulse fell
To earth, men say, fetter and manacle,
And bars slid back untouched of mortal hand.
Yea, full of many wonders to thy land
Is this man come. . . . Howbeit, it lies with thee!

PENTHEUS

Ye are mad!—Unhand him. Howso swift he be,
My toils are round him and he shall not fly.
(*The guards loose the arms of* DIONYSUS; PENTHEUS *studies him*

for a while in silence, then speaks jeeringly. DIONYSUS *remains gentle and unafraid.*)
Marry, a fair shape for a woman's eye,
Sir stranger! And thou seek'st no more, I ween!
Long curls, withal! That shows thou ne'er hast been
A wrestler!—down both cheeks so softly tossed
And winsome! And a white skin! It hath cost
Thee pains, to please thy damsels with this white
And red of cheeks that never face the light!
                           (DIONYSUS *is silent.*)
Speak, sirrah; tell me first thy name and race.

DIONYSUS
No glory is therein, nor yet disgrace.
Thou hast heard of Tmolus, the bright hill of flowers?

PENTHEUS
Surely; the ridge that winds by Sardis' towers.

DIONYSUS
Thence am I; Lydia was my fatherland.

PENTHEUS
And whence these revelations, that thy band
Spreadeth in Hellas?

DIONYSUS
                           Their intent and use
Dionysus oped to me, the Child of Zeus.

PENTHEUS (*brutally*)
Is there a Zeus there, that can still beget
Young Gods?

DIONYSUS
                           Nay, only He whose seal was set
Here in thy Thebes on Semele.

PENTHEUS
                           What way
Descended he upon thee? In full day
Or vision of night?

DIONYSUS
                           Most clear he stood, and scanned
My soul, and gave his emblems to mine hand.

PENTHEUS
What like be they, these emblems?

DIONYSUS
That may none
Reveal, nor know, save his Elect alone.

PENTHEUS
And what good bring they to the worshipper?

DIONYSUS
Good beyond price, but not for thee to hear.

PENTHEUS
Thou trickster! Thou wouldst prick me on the more
To seek them out!

DIONYSUS
His mysteries abhor
The touch of sin-lovers.

PENTHEUS
And so thine eyes
Saw this God plain; what guise had he?

DIONYSUS
What guise
It liked him. 'Twas not I ordained his shape.

PENTHEUS
Aye, deftly turned again. An idle jape,
And nothing answered!

DIONYSUS
Wise words being brought
To blinded eyes will seem as things of nought.

PENTHEUS
And comest thou first to Thebes, to have thy God
Established?

DIONYSUS
Nay; all Barbary hath trod
His dance ere this.

PENTHEUS
A low blind folk, I ween,
Beside our Hellenes!

DIONYSUS
Higher and more keen
In this thing, though their ways are not thy way.

PENTHEUS
How is thy worship held, by night or day?

DIONYSUS
Most oft by night; 'tis a majestic thing,
The darkness.

PENTHEUS
Ha! with women worshipping?
'Tis craft and rottenness!

DIONYSUS
By day no less,
Whoso will seek may find unholiness.

PENTHEUS
Enough! Thy doom is fixed, for false pretence
Corrupting Thebes.

DIONYSUS
Not mine; but thine, for dense
Blindness of heart, and for blaspheming God!

PENTHEUS
A ready knave it is, and brazen-browed.
This mystery-priest!

DIONYSUS
Come, say what it shall be,
My doom; what dire thing wilt thou do to me?

PENTHEUS
First, shear that delicate curl that dangles there.
(*He beckons to the soldiers, who approach* DIONYSUS.)

DIONYSUS
I have vowed it to my God; 'tis holy hair.
(*The soldiers cut off the tress.*)

PENTHEUS
Next, yield me up thy staff!

DIONYSUS
                    Raise thine own hand
To take it. This is Dionysus' wand.
                    (PENTHEUS *takes the staff.*)

PENTHEUS
Last, I will hold thee prisoned here.

DIONYSUS
                    My Lord
God will unloose me, when I speak the word.

PENTHEUS
He may, if e'er again amid his bands
Of saints he hears thy voice!

DIONYSUS
                    Even now he stands
Close here, and sees all that I suffer.

PENTHEUS
                    What?
Where is he? For mine eyes discern him not.

DIONYSUS
Where I am! 'Tis thine own impurity
That veils him from thee.

PENTHEUS
                    The dog jeers at me!
At me and Thebes! Bind him!
                    (*The soldiers begin to bind him.*)

DIONYSUS
                    I charge ye, bind
Me not! I having vision and ye blind!

PENTHEUS
And I, with better right, say bind the more!
                    (*The soldiers obey.*)

DIONYSUS
Thou knowest not what end thou seekest, nor
What deed thou doest, nor what man thou art!

PENTHEUS (*mocking*)
Agave's son, and on the father's part
Echion's, hight Pentheus!

DIONYSUS
                  So let it be,
A name fore-written to calamity!

PENTHEUS
Away, and tie him where the steeds are tied;
Aye, let him lie in the manger!—There abide
And stare into the darkness!—And this rout
Of womankind that clusters thee about,
Thy ministers of worship, are my slaves!
It may be I will sell them o'er the waves,
Hither and thither; else they shall be set
To labour at my distaffs, and forget
Their timbrel and their songs of dawning day!

DIONYSUS
I go; for that which may not be, I may
Not suffer! Yet for this thy sin, lo, He
Whom thou deniest cometh after thee
For recompense. Yea, in thy wrong to us,
Thou hast cast Him into thy prison-house!
(DIONYSUS, *without his wand, his hair shorn, and his arms tightly
    bound, is led off by the guards to his dungeon.* PENTHEUS
    returns into the Palace.)

CHORUS (*singing*)

Some Maidens
Achelous' roaming daughter,
Holy Dirce, virgin water,
Bathed he not of old in thee,
The Babe of God, the Mystery?
When from out the fire immortal
    To himself his God did take him,
    To his own flesh, and bespake him:
"Enter now life's second portal,
Motherless Mystery; lo, I break
Mine own body for thy sake,
    Thou of the Twofold Door, and seal thee
Mine, O Bromios,"—thus he spake—
    "And to this thy land reveal thee."

All

Still my prayer towards thee quivers,
　Dirce, still to thee I hie me;
Why, O Blessèd among Rivers,
　Wilt thou fly me and deny me?
　　By his own joy I vow,
　　By the grape upon the bough,
Thou shalt seek Him in the midnight, thou shalt love
Him, even now!

Other Maidens

Dark and of the dark impassioned
Is this Pentheus' blood; yea, fashioned
　Of the Dragon, and his birth
　From Echion, child of Earth.
He is no man, but a wonder;
　Did the Earth-Child not beget him,
　As a red Giant, to set him
Against God, against the Thunder?
He will bind me for his prize,
Me, the Bride of Dionyse;
　And my priest, my friend, is taken
Even now, and buried lies;
　In the dark he lies forsaken!

All

Lo, we race with death, we perish,
　Dionysus, here before thee!
Dost thou mark us not, nor cherish,
　Who implore thee, and adore thee?
　　Hither down Olympus' side,
　　Come, O Holy One defied,
Be thy golden wand uplifted o'er the tyrant in his pride!

A Maiden

Oh, where art thou? In thine own
Nysa, thou our help alone?
O'er fierce beasts in orient lands
　Doth thy thronging thyrsus wave,
　By the high Corycian Cave,
Or where stern Olympus stands;
In the elm-woods and the oaken,
　There where Orpheus harped of old,
　And the trees awoke and knew him,

And the wild things gathered to him,
As he sang amid the broken
   Glens his music manifold?
Blessed Land of Pierie,
Dionysus loveth thee;
   He will come to thee with dancing,
Come with joy and mystery;
With the Maenads at his hest
Winding, winding to the West;
   Cross the flood of swiftly glancing
Axios in majesty;
Cross the Lydias, the giver
   Of good gifts and waving green;
Cross that Father-Stream of story,
Through a land of steeds and glory
Rolling, bravest, fairest River
   E'er of mortals seen!

A VOICE WITHIN

Io! Io!
Awake, ye damsels; hear my cry,
   Calling my Chosen; hearken ye!

A MAIDEN

Who speaketh? Oh, what echoes thus?

ANOTHER

A Voice, a Voice, that calleth us!

THE VOICE

Be of good cheer! Lo, it is I,
   The Child of Zeus and Semele.

A MAIDEN

O Master, Master, it is Thou!

ANOTHER

O Holy Voice, be with us now!

THE VOICE

Spirit of the Chained Earthquake,
Hear my word; awake, awake!
(*An Earthquake suddenly shakes the pillars of the Castle.*)

A MAIDEN
Ha! what is coming? Shall the hall
Of Pentheus racked in ruin fall?

LEADER
Our God is in the house! Ye maids adore Him!

CHORUS
We adore Him all!

THE VOICE
Unveil the Lightning's eye; arouse
The fire that sleeps, against this house!
(*Fire leaps up on the Tomb of Semele.*)

A MAIDEN
Ah, saw ye, marked ye there the flame
From Semele's enhallowed sod
Awakened? Yea, the Death that came
Ablaze from heaven of old, the same
Hot splendour of the shaft of God?

LEADER
Oh, cast ye, cast ye, to the earth! The Lord
Cometh against this house! Oh, cast ye down,
Ye trembling damsels; He, our own adored,
God's Child hath come, and all is overthrown!
(*The Maidens cast themselves upon the ground, their eyes
earthward.* DIONYSUS, *alone and unbound, enters from the
Castle.*)

DIONYSUS
Ye Damsels of the Morning Hills,[5] why lie ye thus dismayed?
Ye marked him, then, our Master, and the mighty hand he laid
On tower and rock, shaking the house of Pentheus?—But arise,
And cast the trembling from your flesh, and lift untroubled eyes.

LEADER
O Light in Darkness, is it thou? O Priest, is this thy face?
My heart leaps out to greet thee from the deep of loneliness.

DIONYSUS
Fell ye so quick despairing, when beneath the Gate I passed?
Should the gates of Pentheus quell me, or his darkness make me fast?

LEADER

Oh, what was left if thou wert gone? What could I but despair?
How hast thou 'scaped the man of sin? Who freed thee from the snare?

DIONYSUS

I had no pain nor peril; 'twas mine own hand set me free.

LEADER

Thine arms were gyvèd!

DIONYSUS

                Nay, no gyve, no touch, was laid on me!
'Twas there I mocked him, in his gyves, and gave him dreams for food.
For when he led me down, behold, before the stall there stood
A Bull of Offering. And this King, he bit his lips, and straight
Fell on and bound it, hoof and limb, with gasping wrath and sweat.
And I sat watching!—Then a Voice; and lo, our Lord was come,
And the house shook, and a great flame stood o'er his mother's tomb.
And Pentheus hied this way and that, and called his thralls amain
For water, lest his roof-tree burn; and all toiled, all in vain.
Then deemed a-sudden I was gone; and left his fire, and sped
Back to the prison portals, and his lifted sword shone red.
But there, methinks, the God had wrought—I speak but as I guess—
Some dream-shape in mine image; for he smote at emptiness,
Stabbed in the air, and strove in wrath, as though 'twere me he slew.
Then 'mid his dreams God smote him yet again! He overthrew
All that high house. And there in wreck for evermore it lies,
That the day of this my bondage may be sore in Pentheus' eyes!
    And now his sword is fallen, and he lies outworn and wan
Who dared to rise against his God in wrath, being but man.
And I uprose and left him, and in all peace took my path
Forth to my Chosen, recking light of Pentheus and his wrath.
    But soft, methinks a footstep sounds even now within the hall;
'Tis he; how think ye he will stand, and what words speak withal?
I will endure him gently, though he come in fury hot.
For still are the ways of Wisdom, and her temper trembleth not!

(*Enter* PENTHEUS *in fury*)

PENTHEUS

It is too much! This Eastern knave hath slipped
His prison, whom I held but now, hard gripped
In bondage.—Ha! 'Tis he!—What, sirrah, how
Show'st thou before my portals?

(*He advances furiously upon him.*)

DIONYSUS
                    Softly thou!
And set a quiet carriage to thy rage.

PENTHEUS
How comest thou here? How didst thou break thy cage?
Speak!

DIONYSUS
            Said I not, or didst thou mark not me,
There was One living that should set me free?

PENTHEUS
Who? Ever wilder are these tales of thine.

DIONYSUS
He who first made for man the clustered vine.

PENTHEUS
I scorn him and his vines!

DIONYSUS
                    For Dionyse
'Tis well; for in thy scorn his glory lies.

PENTHEUS (*to his guard*)
Go swift to all the towers, and bar withal
Each gate!

DIONYSUS
            What, cannot God o'erleap a wall?

PENTHEUS
Oh, wit thou hast, save where thou needest it!

DIONYSUS
Whereso it most imports, there is my wit!—
Nay, peace! Abide till he who hasteth from
The mountain side with news for thee, be come.
We will not fly, but wait on thy command.
(*Enter suddenly and in haste a Messenger from the Mountain*)

MESSENGER
Great Pentheus, Lord of all this Theban land,
I come from high Cithaeron, where the frore
Snow spangles gleam and cease not evermore. . . .

PENTHEUS

And what of import may thy coming bring?

MESSENGER

I have seen the Wild White Women there, O King,
Whose fleet limbs darted arrow-like but now
From Thebes away, and come to tell thee how
They work strange deeds and passing marvel. Yet
I first would learn thy pleasure. Shall I set
My whole tale forth, or veil the stranger part?
Yea, Lord, I fear the swiftness of thy heart,
Thine edgèd wrath and more than royal soul.

PENTHEUS

Thy tale shall nothing scathe thee.—Tell the whole.
It skills not to be wroth with honesty.
Nay, if thy news of them be dark, 'tis he
Shall pay it, who bewitched and led them on.

MESSENGER

Our herded kine were moving in the dawn
Up to the peaks, the greyest, coldest time,
When the first rays steal earthward, and the rime
Yields, when I saw three bands of them. The one
Autonoe led, one Ino, one thine own
Mother, Agave. There beneath the trees
Sleeping they lay, like wild things flung at ease
In the forest; one half sinking on a bed
Of deep pine greenery; one with careless head
Amid the fallen oak leaves; all most cold
In purity—not as thy tale was told
Of wine-cups and wild music and the chase
For love amid the forest's loneliness.
Then rose the Queen Agave suddenly
Amid her band, and gave the God's wild cry,
"Awake, ye Bacchanals! I hear the sound
Of hornèd kine. Awake ye!"—Then, all round,
Alert, the warm sleep fallen from their eyes,
A marvel of swift ranks I saw them rise,
Dames young and old, and gentle maids unwed
Among them. O'er their shoulders first they shed
Their tresses, and caught up the fallen fold
Of mantles where some clasp had loosened hold,
And girt the dappled fawn-skins in with long

Quick snakes that hissed and writhed with quivering tongue
And one a young fawn held, and one a wild
Wolf cub, and fed them with white milk, and smiled
In love, young mothers with a mother's breast
And babes at home forgotten! Then they pressed
Wreathed ivy round their brows, and oaken sprays
And flowering bryony. And one would raise
Her wand and smite the rock, and straight a jet
Of quick bright water came. Another set
Her thyrsus in the bosomed earth, and there
Was red wine that the God sent up to her,
A darkling fountain. And if any lips
Sought whiter draughts, with dipping finger-tips
They pressed the sod, and gushing from the ground
Came springs of milk. And reed-wands ivy-crowned
Ran with sweet honey, drop by drop.—O King,
Hadst thou been there, as I, and seen this thing,
With prayer and most high wonder hadst thou gone
To adore this God whom now thou rail'st upon!

   Howbeit, the kine-wardens and shepherds straight
Came to one place, amazed, and held debate;
And one being there who walked the streets and scanned
The ways of speech, took lead of them whose hand
Knew but the slow soil and the solemn hill,
And flattering spoke, and asked: "Is it your will,
Masters, we stay the mother of the King,
Agave, from her lawless worshipping,
And win us royal thanks?"—And this seemed good
To all; and through the branching underwood
We hid us, cowering in the leaves. And there
Through the appointed hour they made their prayer
And worship of the Wand, with one accord
Of heart and cry—"Iacchos, Bromios, Lord,
God of God born!"—And all the mountain felt,
And worshipped with them; and the wild things knelt
And ramped and gloried, and the wilderness
Was filled with moving voices and dim stress.

   Soon, as it chanced, beside my thicket-close
The Queen herself passed dancing, and I rose
And sprang to seize her. But she turned her face
Upon me: "Ho, my rovers of the chase,
My wild White Hounds, we are hunted! Up, each rod
And follow, follow, for our Lord and God!"

Thereat, for fear they tear us, all we fled
Amazed; and on, with hand unweaponèd
They swept towards our herds that browsed the green
Hill grass. Great uddered kine then hadst thou seen
Bellowing in sword-like hands that cleave and tear,
A live steer riven asunder, and the air
Tossed with rent ribs or limbs of cloven tread,
And flesh upon the branches, and a red
Rain from the deep green pines. Yea, bulls of pride,
Horns swift to rage, were fronted and aside
Flung stumbling, by those multitudinous hands
Dragged pitilessly. And swifter were the bands
Of garbèd flesh and bone unbound withal
Than on thy royal eyes the lids may fall.

  Then on like birds, by their own speed upborne,
They swept towards the plains of waving corn
That lie beside Asopus' banks, and bring
To Thebes the rich fruit of her harvesting.
On Hysiae and Erythrae that lie nursed
Amid Cithaeron's bowering rocks, they burst
Destroying, as a foeman's army comes.
They caught up little children from their homes,
High on their shoulders, babes unheld, that swayed
And laughed and fell not; all a wreck they made;
Yea, bronze and iron did shatter, and in play
Struck hither and thither, yet no wound had they;
Caught fire from out the hearths, yea, carried hot
Flames in their tresses and were scorchèd not!

  The village folk in wrath took spear and sword,
And turned upon the Bacchae. Then, dread Lord,
The wonder was. For spear nor barbèd brand
Could scathe nor touch the damsels; but the Wand,
The soft and wreathèd wand their white hands sped,
Blasted those men and quelled them, and they fled
Dizzily. Sure some God was in these things!

  And the holy women back to those strange springs
Returned, that God had sent them when the day
Dawned, on the upper heights; and washed away
The stain of battle. And those girdling snakes
Hissed out to lap the waterdrops from cheeks
And hair and breast.
                        Therefore I counsel thee,
O King, receive this Spirit, whoe'er he be,

To Thebes in glory. Greatness manifold
Is all about him; and the tale is told
That this is he who first to man did give
The grief-assuaging vine. Oh, let him live;
For if he die, then Love herself is slain,
And nothing joyous in the world again!

LEADER

Albeit I tremble, and scarce may speak my thought
To a king's face, yet will I hide it not.
Dionyse is God, no God more true nor higher!

PENTHEUS

It bursts hard by us, like a smothered fire,
This frenzy of Bacchic women! All my land
Is made their mock.—This needs an iron hand!
   Ho, Captain! Quick to the Electran Gate;
Bid gather all my men-at-arms thereat;
Call all that spur the charger, all who know
To wield the orbèd targe or bend the bow;
We march to war!—'Fore God, shall women dare
Such deeds against us? 'Tis too much to bear!

DIONYSUS

Thou mark'st me not, O King, and holdest light
My solemn words; yet, in thine own despite,
I warn thee still. Lift thou not up thy spear
Against a God, but hold thy peace, and fear
His wrath! He will not brook it, if thou fright
His Chosen from the hills of their delight.

PENTHEUS

Peace, thou! And if for once thou hast slipped thy chain,
Give thanks!—Or shall I knot thine arms again?

DIONYSUS

Better to yield him prayer and sacrifice
Than kick against the pricks, since Dionyse
Is God, and thou but mortal.

PENTHEUS

          That will I!
Yea, sacrifice of women's blood, to cry
His name through all Cithaeron!

DIONYSUS
                    Ye shall fly,
All, and abase your shields of bronzen rim
Before their wands.

PENTHEUS
                    There is no way with him,
This stranger that so dogs us! Well or ill
I may entreat him, he must babble still!

DIONYSUS
Wait, good my friend! These crooked matters may
Even yet be straightened.
(PENTHEUS *has started as though to seek his army at the gate.*)

PENTHEUS
                    Aye, if I obey
Mine own slaves' will; how else?

DIONYSUS
                            Myself will lead
The damsels hither, without sword or steed.

PENTHEUS
How now?—This is some plot against me!

DIONYSUS
                                    What
Dost fear? Only to save thee do I plot.

PENTHEUS
It is some compact ye have made, whereby
To dance these hills for ever!

DIONYSUS
                    Verily,
That is my compact, plighted with my Lord!

PENTHEUS (*turning from him*)
Ho, armourers! Bring forth my shield and sword!—
And thou, be silent!

DIONYSUS
(*after regarding him fixedly, speaks with resignation*)
                    Ah!—Have then thy will!
(*He fixes his eyes upon* PENTHEUS *again, while the armourers
bring out his armour; then speaks in a tone of command.*)

Man, thou wouldst fain behold them on the hill
Praying!

PENTHEUS

(*who during the rest of this scene, with a few exceptions,
simply speaks the thoughts that* DIONYSUS *puts into him,
losing power over his own mind*)
That would I, though it cost me all
The gold of Thebes!

DIONYSUS
So much? Thou art quick to fall
To such great longing.

PENTHEUS

(*somewhat bewildered at what he has said*)
Aye; 'twould grieve me much
To see them flown with wine.

DIONYSUS
Yet cravest thou such
A sight as would much grieve thee?

PENTHEUS
Yes; I fain
Would watch, ambushed among the pines.

DIONYSUS
'Twere vain
To hide. They soon will track thee out.

PENTHEUS
Well said!
'Twere best done openly.

DIONYSUS
Wilt thou be led
By me, and try the venture?

PENTHEUS
Aye, indeed!
Lead on. Why should we tarry?

DIONYSUS
First we need
A rich and trailing robe of fine linen
To gird thee.

PENTHEUS

Nay; am I a woman, then,
And no man more?

DIONYSUS

Wouldst have them slay thee dead?
No man may see their mysteries.

PENTHEUS

Well said!—
I marked thy subtle temper long ere now.

DIONYSUS

'Tis Dionyse that prompteth me.

PENTHEUS

And how
Mean'st thou the further plan?

DIONYSUS

First take thy way
Within. I will array thee.

PENTHEUS

What array?
The woman's? Nay, I will not.

DIONYSUS

Doth it change
So soon, all thy desire to see this strange
Adoring?

PENTHEUS

Wait! What garb wilt thou bestow
About me?

DIONYSUS

First a long tress dangling low
Beneath thy shoulders.

PENTHEUS

Aye, and next?

DIONYSUS

The said
Robe, falling to thy feet; and on thine head
A snood.

PENTHEUS
And after? Hast thou aught beyond?

DIONYSUS
Surely; the dappled fawn-skin and the wand.

PENTHEUS (*after a struggle with himself*)
Enough! I cannot wear a robe and snood.

DIONYSUS
Wouldst liefer draw the sword and spill men's blood?

PENTHEUS (*again doubting*)
True, that were evil.—Aye; 'tis best to go
First to some place of watch.

DIONYSUS
Far wiser so,
Than seek by wrath wrath's bitter recompense.

PENTHEUS
What of the city streets? Canst lead me hence
Unseen of any?

DIONYSUS
Lonely and untried
Thy path from hence shall be, and I thy guide!

PENTHEUS
I care for nothing, so these Bacchanals
Triumph not against me! . . . Forward to my halls
Within!—I will ordain what seemeth best.

DIONYSUS
So be it, O King! 'Tis mine to obey thine hest,
Whate'er it be.

PENTHEUS
(*after hesitating once more and waiting*)
Well, I will go—perchance
To march and scatter them with serried lance,
Perchance to take thy plan. . . . I know not yet.
(*Exit* PENTHEUS *into the Castle*)

DIONYSUS
Damsels, the lion walketh to the net!
He finds his Bacchae now, and sees and dies.

And pays for all his sin!—O Dionyse,
This is thine hour and thou not far away.
Grant us our vengeance!—First, O Master, stay
The course of reason in him, and instil
A foam of madness. Let his seeing will,
Which ne'er had stooped to put thy vesture on,
Be darkened, till the deed is lightly done.
Grant likewise that he find through all his streets
Loud scorn, this man of wrath and bitter threats
That made Thebes tremble, led in woman's guise.

    I go to fold that robe of sacrifice
On Pentheus, that shall deck him to the dark,
His mother's gift!—So shall he learn and mark
God's true Son, Dionyse, in fulness God,
Most fearful, yet to man most soft of mood.

(*Exit* DIONYSUS, *following* PENTHEUS *into the Castle*)

CHORUS (*singing*)

Some Maidens

Will they ever come to me, ever again,
    The long long dances,
On through the dark till the dim stars wane?
Shall I feel the dew on my throat, and the stream
Of wind in my hair? Shall our white feet gleam
    In the dim expanses?
Oh, feet of a fawn to the greenwood fled,
    Alone in the grass and the loveliness;
Leap of the hunted, no more in dread,
    Beyond the snares and the deadly press:
Yet a voice still in the distance sounds,
A voice and a fear and a haste of hounds;
O wildly labouring, fiercely fleet,
    Onward yet by river and glen . . .
Is it joy or terror, ye storm-swift feet? . . .
    To the dear lone lands untroubled of men,
Where no voice sounds, and amid the shadowy green
The little things of the woodland live unseen.

What else is Wisdom? [6] What of man's endeavour
    Or God's high grace, so lovely and so great?
To stand from fear set free, to breathe and wait;
To hold a hand uplifted over Hate;
And shall not Loveliness be loved for ever?

Others

O Strength of God, slow art thou and still,
    Yet failest never!
On them that worship the Ruthless Will,
On them that dream, doth His judgment wait.
Dreams of the proud man, making great
    And greater ever,
Things which are not of God. In wide
    And devious coverts, hunter-wise,
He coucheth Time's unhasting stride,
    Following, following, him whose eyes
Look not to Heaven. For all is vain,
The pulse of the heart, the plot of the brain,
That striveth beyond the laws that live.
And is thy Faith so much to give,
Is it so hard a thing to see,
That the Spirit of God, whate'er it be,
The Law that abides and changes not, ages long,
The Eternal and Nature-born—these things be strong?

What else is Wisdom? What of man's endeavour
    Or God's high grace so lovely and so great?
To stand from fear set free, to breathe and wait;
    To hold a hand uplifted over Hate;
And shall not Loveliness be loved for ever?

LEADER

    Happy he, on the weary sea
Who hath fled the tempest and won the haven.
    Happy whoso hath risen, free,
Above his striving. For strangely graven
    Is the orb of life, that one and another
    In gold and power may outpass his brother.
    And men in their millions float and flow
And seethe with a million hopes as leaven;
    And they win their Will, or they miss their Will,
    And the hopes are dead or are pined for still;
        But whoe'er can know,
        As the long days go,
That To Live is happy, hath found his Heaven!

(*Re-enter* DIONYSUS *from the Castle*)

DIONYSUS

O eye that cravest sights thou must not see,
O heart athirst for that which slakes not! Thee,
Pentheus, I call; forth and be seen, in guise
Of woman, Maenad, saint of Dionyse,
To spy upon His Chosen and thine own
Mother!

(*Enter* PENTHEUS, *clad like a Bacchanal, and strangely excited,
a spirit of Bacchic madness overshadowing him*)

             Thy shape, methinks, is like to one
Of Cadmus' royal maids!

PENTHEUS

             Yea; and mine eye
Is bright! Yon sun shines twofold in the sky,
Thebes twofold and the Wall of Seven Gates. . . .
And is it a Wild Bull this, that walks and waits
Before me? There are horns upon thy brow!
What art thou, man or beast? For surely now
The Bull is on thee!

DIONYSUS

             He who erst was wrath,
Goes with us now in gentleness. He hath
Unsealed thine eyes to see what thou shouldst see.

PENTHEUS

Say; stand I not as Ino stands, or she
Who bore me?

DIONYSUS

             When I look on thee, it seems
I see their very selves!—But stay; why streams
That lock abroad, not where I laid it, crossed
Under the coif?

PENTHEUS

             I did it, as I tossed
My head in dancing, to and fro, and cried
His holy music!

DIONYSUS (*tending him*)

             It shall soon be tied
Aright. 'Tis mine to tend thee. . . . Nay, but stand
With head straight.

PENTHEUS
In the hollow of thy hand
I lay me. Deck me as thou wilt.

DIONYSUS
Thy zone
Is loosened likewise; and the folded gown
Not evenly falling to the feet.

PENTHEUS
'Tis so,
By the right foot. But here, methinks, they flow
In one straight line to the heel.

DIONYSUS (*while tending him*)
And if thou prove
Their madness true, aye, more than true, what love
And thanks hast thou for me?

PENTHEUS (*not listening to him*)
In my right hand
Is it, or thus, that I should bear the wand,
To be most like to them?

DIONYSUS
Up let it swing
In the right hand, timed with the right foot's spring. . . .
'Tis well thy heart is changed!

PENTHEUS (*more wildly*)
What strength is this!
Cithaeron's steeps and all that in them is—
How say'st thou?—Could my shoulders lift the whole?

DIONYSUS
Surely thou canst, and if thou wilt! Thy soul,
Being once so sick, now stands as it should stand.

PENTHEUS
Shall it be bars of iron? Or this bare hand
And shoulder to the crags, to wrench them down?

DIONYSUS
Wouldst wreck the Nymphs' wild temples, and the brown
Rocks, where Pan pipes at noonday?

PENTHEUS

Nay; not I!
Force is not well with women. I will lie
Hid in the pine-brake.

DIONYSUS

Even as fits a spy
On holy and fearful things, so shalt thou lie!

PENTHEUS (*with a laugh*)
They lie there now, methinks—the wild birds, caught
By love among the leaves, and fluttering not!

DIONYSUS
It may be. That is what thou goest to see,
Aye, and to trap them—so they trap not thee!

PENTHEUS
Forth through the Thebans' town! I am their king,
Aye, their one Man, seeing I dare this thing!

DIONYSUS
Yea, thou shalt bear their burden, thou alone;
Therefore thy trial awaiteth thee!—But on;
With me into thine ambush shalt thou come
Unscathed; then let another bear thee home!

PENTHEUS
The Queen, my mother.

DIONYSUS
Marked of every eye.

PENTHEUS
For that I go!

DIONYSUS
Thou shalt be borne on high!

PENTHEUS
That were like pride!

DIONYSUS
Thy mother's hands shall share
Thy carrying.

PENTHEUS
Nay; I need not such soft care!

DIONYSUS
So soft?

PENTHEUS
Whate'ei it be, I have earned it well!
(*Exit* PENTHEUS *towards the Mountain*)

DIONYSUS
Fell, fell art thou; and to a doom so fell
Thou walkest, that thy name from South to North
Shall shine, a sign for ever!—Reach thou forth
Thine arms, Agave, now, and ye dark-browed
Cadmeian sisters! Greet this prince so proud
To the high ordeal, where save God and me,
None walks unscathed!—The rest this day shall see.
(*Exit* DIONYSUS *following* PENTHEUS)

CHORUS (*singing*)

Some Maidens
O hounds raging and blind,
    Up by the mountain road,
Sprites of the maddened mind,
    To the wild Maids of God;
Fill with your rage their eyes,
    Rage at the rage unblest,
Watching in woman's guise,
    The spy upon God's Possessed.

A Bacchanal
Who shall be first, to mark
    Eyes in the rock that spy,
Eyes in the pine-tree dark—
    Is it his mother?—and cry:
"Lo, what is this that comes,
    Haunting, troubling still,
Even in our heights, our homes,
    The wild Maids of the Hill?
What flesh bare this child?
    Never on woman's breast
Changeling so evil smiled;
    Man is he not, but Beast!

Lion-shape of the wild,
Gorgon-breed of the waste!"

All the Chorus

Hither, for doom and deed!
Hither with lifted sword,
Justice, Wrath of the Lord,
Come in our visible need!
Smite till the throat shall bleed,
Smite till the heart shall bleed,
Him the tyrannous, lawless, Godless, Echion's earth-born seed!

Other Maidens

Tyrannously hath he trod;
Marched him, in Law's despite,
Against thy Light, O God,
Yea, and thy Mother's Light;
Girded him, falsely bold,
Blinded in craft, to quell
And by man's violence hold
Things unconquerable.

A Bacchanal

A strait pitiless mind
Is death unto godliness;
And to feel in human kind
Life, and a pain the less.
Knowledge, we are not foes!
I seek thee diligently;
But the world with a great wind blows,
Shining, and not from thee;
Blowing to beautiful things,
On, amid dark and light,
Till Life, through the trammellings
Of Laws that are not the Right,
Breaks, clean and pure, and sings
Glorying to God in the height!

All the Chorus

Hither for doom and deed!
Hither with lifted sword,
Justice, Wrath of the Lord,
Come in our visible need!
Smite till the throat shall bleed,

Smite till the heart shall bleed,
Him the tyrannous, lawless, Godless, Echion's earth-born seed!

LEADER

Appear, appear, whatso thy shape or name
　O Mountain Bull, Snake of the Hundred Heads,
　　Lion of Burning Flame!
O God, Beast, Mystery, come! Thy mystic maids
Are hunted!—Blast their hunter with thy breath,
　　Cast o'er his head thy snare;
And laugh aloud and drag him to his death,
　Who stalks thy herded madness in its lair!

(*Enter hastily a* MESSENGER *from the Mountain, pale and dis-*
traught)

MESSENGER

Woe to the house once blest in Hellas! Woe
To thee, old King Sidonian, who didst sow
The dragon-seed on Ares' bloody lea!
Alas, even thy slaves must weep for thee!

LEADER

News from the mountain?—Speak! How hath it sped?

MESSENGER

Pentheus, my king, Echion's son, is dead!

LEADER

　All hail, God of the Voice,
　　Manifest ever more!

MESSENGER

What say'st thou?—And how strange thy tone, as though
In joy at this my master's overthrow!

LEADER

　With fierce joy I rejoice,
　　Child of a savage shore;
For the chains of my prison are broken, and the dread where I
　cowered of yore!

MESSENGER

And deem'st thou Thebes so beggared,[7] so forlorn
Of manhood, as to sit beneath thy scorn?

LEADER

Thebes hath o'er me no sway!
None save Him I obey,
Dionysus, Child of the Highest, Him I obey and adore!

MESSENGER

One can forgive thee!—Yet 'tis no fair thing,
Maids, to rejoice in a man's suffering.

LEADER

Speak of the mountain side!
Tell us the doom he died,
The sinner smitten to death, even where sin was sore!

MESSENGER

We climbed beyond the utmost habitings
Of Theban shepherds, passed Asopus' springs,
And struck into the land of rock on dim
Cithaeron—Pentheus, and, attending him,
I, and the Stranger who should guide our way.
Then first in a green dell we stopped, and lay,
Lips dumb and feet unmoving, warily
Watching, to be unseen and yet to see.
   A narrow glen it was, by crags o'ertowered,
Torn through by tossing waters, and there lowered
A shadow of great pines over it. And there
The Maenad maidens sate; in toil they were,
Busily glad. Some with an ivy chain
Tricked a worn wand to toss its locks again;
Some, wild in joyance, like young steeds set free,
Made answering songs of mystic melody.
   But my poor master saw not the great band
Before him. "Stranger," cried he, "where we stand
Mine eyes can reach not these false saints of thine.
Mount we the bank, or some high-shouldered pine,
And I shall see their follies clear!" At that
There came a marvel. For the Stranger straight
Touched a great pine-tree's high and heavenward crown,
And lower, lower, lower, urged it down
To the herbless floor. Round like a bending bow,
Or slow wheel's rim a joiner forces to,
So in those hands that tough and mountain stem
Bowed slow—oh, strength not mortal dwelt in them!—
To the very earth. And there he sat the King,

And slowly, lest it cast him in its spring,
Let back the young and straining tree, till high
It towered again amid the towering sky;
And Pentheus in the branches! Well, I ween,
He saw the Maenads then, and well was seen!
For scarce was he aloft, when suddenly
There was no Stranger any more with me,
But out of Heaven a Voice—oh, what voice else?—
'Twas He that called! "Behold, O damosels,
I bring ye him who turneth to despite
Both me and ye, and darkeneth my great Light.
'Tis yours to avenge!" So spake he, and there came
'Twixt earth and sky a pillar of high flame.
And silence took the air, and no leaf stirred
In all the forest dell. Thou hadst not heard
In that vast silence any wild thing's cry.
And up they sprang; but with bewildered eye,
Agaze and listening, scarce yet hearing true.
Then came the Voice again. And when they knew
Their God's clear call, old Cadmus' royal brood,
Up, like wild pigeons startled in a wood,
On flying feet they came, his mother blind,
Agave, and her sisters, and behind
All the wild crowd, more deeply maddened then,
Through the angry rocks and torrent-tossing glen,
Until they spied him in the dark pine-tree:
Then climbed a crag hard by and furiously
Some sought to stone him, some their wands would fling
Lance-wise aloft, in cruel targeting.
But none could strike. The height o'ertopped their rage,
And there he clung, unscathed, as in a cage
Caught. And of all their strife no end was found.
Then, "Hither," cried Agave; "stand we round
And grip the stem, my Wild Ones, till we take
This climbing cat-o'-the-mount! He shall not make
A tale of God's high dances!" Out then shone
Arm upon arm, past count, and closed upon
The pine, and gripped; and the ground gave, and down
It reeled. And that high sitter from the crown
Of the green pine-top, with a shrieking cry
Fell, as his mind grew clear, and there hard by
Was horror visible. 'Twas his mother stood
O'er him, first priestess of those rites of blood.

He tore the coif, and from his head away
Flung it, that she might know him, and not slay
To her own misery. He touched the wild
Cheek, crying: "Mother, it is I, thy child,
Thy Pentheus, born thee in Echion's hall!
Have mercy, Mother! Let it not befall
Through sin of mine, that thou shouldst slay thy son!"
    But she, with lips a-foam and eyes that run
Like leaping fire, with thoughts that ne'er should be
On earth, possessed by Bacchios utterly,
Stays not nor hears. Round his left arm she put
Both hands, set hard against his side her foot,
Drew . . . and the shoulder severed!—Not by might
Of arm, but easily, as the God made light
Her hand's essay. And at the other side
Was Ino rending; and the torn flesh cried,
And on Autonoe pressed, and all the crowd
Of ravening arms. Yea, all the air was loud
With groans that faded into sobbing breath,
Dim shrieks, and joy, and triumph-cries of death.
And here was borne a severed arm, and there
A hunter's booted foot; white bones lay bare
With rending; and swift hands ensanguinèd
Tossed as in sport the flesh of Pentheus dead.
    His body lies afar. The precipice
Hath part, and parts in many an interstice
Lurk of the tangled woodland—no light quest
To find. And, ah, the head! Of all the rest,
His mother hath it, pierced upon a wand,
As one might pierce a lion's, and through the land,
Leaving her sisters in their dancing place,
Bears it on high! Yea, to these walls her face
Was set, exulting in her deed of blood,
Calling upon her Bromios, her God,
Her Comrade, Fellow-Render of the Prey,
Her All-Victorious, to whom this day
She bears in triumph . . . her own broken heart!
    For me, after that sight, I will depart
Before Agave comes.—Oh, to fulfil
God's laws, and have no thought beyond His will,
Is man's best treasure. Aye, and wisdom true,
Methinks, for things of dust to cleave unto!
                    (*The* MESSENGER *departs into the Castle.*)

CHORUS (*singing*)

Some Maidens
Weave ye the dance, and call
        Praise to God!
        Bless ye the Tyrant's fall!
        Down is trod
Pentheus, the Dragon's Seed!
Wore he the woman's weed?
Clasped he his death indeed,
        Clasped the rod?

A Bacchanal
Yea, the wild ivy lapt him, and the doomed
Wild Bull of Sacrifice before him loomed!

Others
Ye who did Bromios scorn,
        Praise Him the more,
Bacchanals, Cadmus-born;
        Praise with sore
Agony, yea, with tears!
Great are the gifts he bears!
Hands that a mother rears
        Red with gore!

LEADER
But stay, Agave cometh! And her eyes
Make fire around her, reeling! Ho, the prize
Cometh! All hail, O Rout of Dionyse!
(*Enter from the Mountain* AGAVE, *mad, and to all seeming
        wondrously happy, bearing the head of* PENTHEUS *in
        her hand. The* CHORUS MAIDENS *stand horror-struck at
        the sight; the* LEADER, *also horror-struck, strives to ac-
        cept it and rejoice in it as the God's deed.*)

AGAVE
Ye from the lands of Morn!

LEADER
Call me not; I give praise!

AGAVE
Lo, from the trunk new-shorn
Hither a Mountain Thorn

Bear we! O Asia-born
Bacchanals, bless this chase!

LEADER

I see. Yea; I see.
Have I not welcomed thee?

AGAVE
(*very calmly and peacefully*)
He was young in the wildwood:
Without nets I caught him!
Nay; look without fear on
    The Lion; I have ta'en him!

LEADER

Where in the wildwood?
Whence have ye brought him?

AGAVE
Cithaeron. . . .

LEADER
                Cithaeron?

AGAVE
The Mountain hath slain him!

LEADER
Who first came nigh him?

AGAVE
I, I, 'tis confessèd!
And they named me there by him
Agave the Blessèd!

LEADER
Who was next in the band on him?

AGAVE
The daughters. . . .

LEADER
                The daughters?

AGAVE
Of Cadmus laid hand on him.
But the swift hand that slaughters

Is mine; mine is the praise!
Bless ye this day of days!
(*The* LEADER *tries to speak, but is not able;* AGAVE
begins gently stroking the head.)

AGAVE

Gather ye now to the feast!

LEADER

Feast!—O miserable!

AGAVE

See, it falls to his breast,
Curling and gently tressed,
The hair of the Wild Bull's crest—
The young steer of the fell!

LEADER

Most like a beast of the wild
That head, those locks defiled.

AGAVE
(*lifting up the head, more excitedly*)
He wakened his Mad Ones,
A Chase-God, a wise God!
He sprang them to seize this!
He preys where his band preys.

LEADER (*brooding, with horror*)
In the trail of thy Mad Ones
Thou tearest thy prize, God!

AGAVE

Dost praise it?

LEADER

I praise this?

AGAVE

Ah, soon shall the land praise!

LEADER

And Pentheus, O Mother,
Thy child?

AGAVE

He shall cry on
My name as none other,
Bless the spoils of the Lion!

LEADER

Aye, strange is thy treasure!

AGAVE

And strange was the taking!

LEADER

Thou art glad?

AGAVE

Beyond measure;
Yea, glad in the breaking
Of dawn upon all this land,
By the prize, the prize of my hand!

LEADER

Show then to all the land, unhappy one,
The trophy of this deed that thou hast done!

AGAVE

Ho, all ye men that round the citadel
And shining towers of ancient Thebe dwell,
Come! Look upon this prize, this lion's spoil,
That we have taken—yea, with our own toil,
We, Cadmus' daughters! Not with leathern-set
Thessalian javelins, not with hunter's net,
Only white arms and swift hands' bladed fall.
Why make ye much ado, and boast withal
Your armourers' engines? See, these palms were bare
That caught the angry beast, and held, and tare
The limbs of him! . . . Father! . . . Go, bring to me
My father! . . . Aye, and Pentheus, where is he,
My son? He shall set up a ladder-stair
Against this house, and in the triglyphs there
Nail me this lion's head, that gloriously
I bring ye, having slain him—I, even I!
(*She goes through the crowd towards the Castle, showing the
head and looking for a place to hang it. Enter from the
Mountain* CADMUS, *with attendants, bearing the body
of* PENTHEUS *on a bier.*)

CADMUS

On, with your awful burden. Follow me,
Thralls, to his house, whose body grievously
With many a weary search at last in dim
Cithaeron's glens I found, torn limb from limb,
And through the interweaving forest weed
Scattered.—Men told me of my daughter's deed,
When I was just returned within these walls,
With grey Teiresias, from the Bacchanals.
And back I hied me to the hills again
To seek my murdered son. There saw I plain
Actaeon's mother, ranging where he died,
Autonoe; and Ino by her side,
Wandering ghastly in the pine-copses.
   Agave was not there. The rumour is
She cometh fleet-foot hither.—Ah! 'Tis true;
A sight I scarce can bend mine eyes unto.

AGAVE

(*turning from the Palace and seeing him*)
My father, a great boast is thine this hour.
Thou hast begotten daughters, high in power
And valiant above all mankind—yea, all
Valiant, though none like me! I have let fall
The shuttle by the loom, and raised my hand
For higher things, to slay from out thy land
Wild beasts! See, in mine arms I bear the prize,
That nailed above these portals it may rise
To show what things thy daughters did! Do thou
Take it, and call a feast. Proud art thou now
And highly favoured in our valiancy!

CADMUS

O depth of grief, how can I fathom thee
Or look upon thee!—Poor, poor, bloodstained hand!
Poor sisters!—A fair sacrifice to stand
Before God's altars, daughter; yea, and call
Me and my citizens to feast withal!
   Nay, let me weep—for thine affliction most,
Then for mine own. All, all of us are lost,
Not wrongfully, yet is it hard, from one
Who might have loved—our Bromios our own!

AGAVE

How crabbèd and how scowling in the eyes
Is man's old age!—Would that my son likewise
Were happy of his hunting, in my way,
When with his warrior bands he will essay
The wild beast!—Nay, his violence is to fight
With God's will! Father, thou shouldst set him right. . . .
Will no one bring him hither, that mine eyes
May look on his, and show him this my prize!

CADMUS

Alas, if ever ye can know again
The truth of what ye did, what pain of pain
That truth shall bring! Or were it best to wait
Darkened for evermore, and deem your state
Not misery, though ye know no happiness?

AGAVE

What seest thou here to chide, or not to bless?

CADMUS
(*after hesitation, resolving himself*)
Raise me thine eyes to yon blue dome of air!

AGAVE

'Tis done. What dost thou bid me seek for there?

CADMUS

Is it the same, or changèd in thy sight?

AGAVE

More shining than before, more heavenly bright!

CADMUS

And that wild tremor, is it with thee still?

AGAVE (*troubled*)
I know not what thou sayest; but my will
Clears, and some change cometh, I know not how.

CADMUS

Canst hearken then, being changed, and answer, now?

AGAVE

I have forgotten something; else I could.

CADMUS
What husband led thee of old from mine abode?

AGAVE
Echion, whom men named the Child of Earth.

CADMUS
And what child in Echion's house had birth?

AGAVE
Pentheus, of my love and his father's bred.

CADMUS
Thou bearest in thine arms an head—what head?

AGAVE
(*beginning to tremble, and not looking at what she carries*)
A lion's—so they all said in the chase.

CADMUS
Turn to it now—'tis no long toil—and gaze.

AGAVE
Ah! But what is it? What am I carrying here?

CADMUS
Look once upon it full. till all be clear!

AGAVE
I see . . . most deadly pain! Oh, woe is me!

CADMUS
Wears it the likeness of a lion to thee?

AGAVE
No; 'tis the head—O God!—of Pentheus, this!

CADMUS
Blood-drenched ere thou wouldst know him! Aye, 'tis his.

AGAVE
Who slew him?—How came I to hold this thing?

CADMUS
O cruel Truth, is this thine home-coming?

AGAVE
Answer! My heart is hanging on thy breath!

CADMUS

'Twas thou.—Thou and thy sisters wrought his death.

AGAVE

In what place was it? His own house, or where?

CADMUS

Where the dogs tore Actaeon, even there.

AGAVE

Why went he to Cithaeron? What sought he?

CADMUS

To mock the God and thine own ecstasy.

AGAVE

But how should we be on the hills this day?

CADMUS

Being mad! A spirit drove all the land that way.

AGAVE

'Tis Dionyse hath done it! Now I see.

CADMUS (*earnestly*)

Ye wronged Him! Ye denied his deity!

AGAVE (*turning from him*)

Show me the body of the son I love!

CADMUS (*leading her to the bier*)

'Tis here, my child. Hard was the quest thereof.

AGAVE

Laid in due state?
(*As there is no answer, she lifts the veil of the bier, and sees.*)
Oh, if I wrought a sin,
'Twas mine! What portion had my child therein?

CADMUS

He made him like to you, adoring not
The God; who therefore to one bane hath brought
You and his body, wrecking all our line,
And me. Aye, no man-child was ever mine;
And now this first-fruit of the flesh of thee,
Sad woman, foully here and frightfully
Lies murdered! Whom the house looked up unto,
(*kneeling by the body*)

O Child, my daughter's child! who heldest true
My castle walls; and to the folk a name
Of fear thou wast; and no man sought to shame
My grey beard, when they knew that thou wast there,
Else had they swift reward!—And now I fare
Forth in dishonour, outcast, I, the great
Cadmus, who sowed the seed-rows of this state
Of Thebes, and reaped the harvest wonderful.
O my belovèd, though thy heart is dull
In death, O still belovèd, and alway
Belovèd! Never more, then, shalt thou lay
Thine hand to this white beard, and speak to me
Thy "Mother's Father"; ask "Who wrongeth thee?
Who stints thine honour, or with malice stirs
Thine heart? Speak, and I smite thine injurers!"
But now—woe, woe, to me and thee also,
Woe to thy mother and her sisters, woe
Alway! Oh, whoso walketh not in dread
Of Gods, let him but look on this man dead!

LEADER

Lo, I weep with thee. 'Twas but due reward
God sent on Pentheus; but for thee . . . 'Tis hard.

AGAVE

My father, thou canst see the change in me,
 *   *   *   *   *
 *   *   *   *   *

[*A page or more has here been torn out of the MS. from which
all our copies of "The Bacchae" are derived. It evidently contained
a speech of Agave (followed presumably by some words of the*
CHORUS), *and an appearance of* DIONYSUS *upon a cloud. He must
have pronounced judgment upon the Thebans in general, and
especially upon the daughters of* CADMUS, *have justified his own
action, and declared his determination to establish his godhead.
Where the MS. begins again, we find him addressing* CADMUS.]
 *   *   *   *   *

DIONYSUS

 *   *   *   *   *
 *   *   *   *   *

And tell of Time, what gifts for thee he bears,
What griefs and wonders in the winding years.
For thou must change and be a Serpent Thing [8]

Strange, and beside thee she whom thou didst bring
Of old to be thy bride from Heaven afar,
Harmonia, daughter of the Lord of War.
Yea, and a chariot of kine—so spake
The word of Zeus—thee and thy Queen shall take
Through many lands, Lord of a wild array
Of orient spears. And many towns shall they
Destroy beneath thee, that vast horde, until
They touch Apollo's dwelling, and fulfil
Their doom, back driven on stormy ways and steep.
Thee only and thy spouse shall Ares keep,
And save alive to the Islands of the Blest.
    Thus speaketh Dionysus, Son confessed
Of no man but of Zeus!—Ah, had ye seen
Truth in the hour ye would not, all had been
Well with ye, and the Child of God your friend!

AGAVE

Dionysus, we beseech thee! We have sinned!

DIONYSUS

Too late! When there was time, ye knew me not!

AGAVE

We have confessed. Yet is thine hand too hot

DIONYSUS

Ye mocked me, being God; this is your wage.

AGAVE

Should God be like a proud man in his rage?

DIONYSUS

'Tis as my sire, Zeus, willed it long ago.

AGAVE

(turning from him almost with disdain)
Old Man, the word is spoken; we must go.

DIONYSUS

And seeing ye must, what is it that ye wait?

CADMUS

Child, we are come into a deadly strait,
All; thou, poor sufferer, and thy sisters twain,
And my sad self. Far off to barbarous men,

A grey-haired wanderer, I must take my road.
And then the oracle, the doom of God,
That I must lead a raging horde far-flown
To prey on Hellas; lead my spouse, mine own
Harmonia, Ares' child, discorporate
And haunting forms, dragon and dragon-mate,
Against the tombs and altar-stones of Greece,
Lance upon lance behind us; and not cease
From toils, like other men, nor dream, nor past
The foam of Acheron find my peace at last.

AGAVE

Father! And I must wander far from thee!

CADMUS

O Child, why wilt thou reach thine arms to me,
As yearns the milk-white swan, when old swans die?

AGAVE

Where shall I turn me else? No home have I.

CADMUS

I know not; I can help thee not.

AGAVE

Farewell, O home, O ancient tower!
Lo, I am outcast from my bower,
And leave ye for a worser lot.

CADMUS

Go forth, go forth to misery,
The way Actaeon's father went!

AGAVE

Father, for thee my tears are spent.

CADMUS

Nay, Child, 'tis I must weep for thee;
For thee and for thy sisters twain!

AGAVE

On all this house, in bitter wise,
Our Lord and Master, Dionyse,
Hath poured the utter dregs of pain!

DIONYSUS

In bitter wise, for bitter was the shame
Yet did me, when Thebes honoured not my name.

AGAVE

Then lead me where my sisters be;
    Together let our tears be shed,
    Our ways be wandered; where no red
Cithaeron waits to gaze on me;
Nor I gaze back; no thyrsus stem,
    Nor song, nor memory in the air.
    Oh, other Bacchanals be there,
Not I, not I, to dream of them!

(AGAVE *with her group of attendants goes out on the side away
from the Mountain.* DIONYSUS *rises upon the Cloud and
disappears.*)

CHORUS (*singing*)

There be many shapes of mystery.
And many things God makes to be,
    Past hope or fear.
And the end men looked for cometh not,
And a path is there where no man thought.
    So hath it fallen here.[9]

(*Exeunt*)

1. *i.e.,* belonging to Zeus.

2. Murray's note here runs: "Cadmus, by divine guidance, slew a dragon and sowed the teeth of it like seed in the 'Field of Ares.' From the teeth rose a harvest of Earth-born, or 'Giant' warriors, of whom Echion was one."

3. *i.e.,* the ether out of which phantoms or apparitions were made.

4. *i.e.,* the name, Pentheus, suggests *penthos,* sorrow or mourning.

5. Murray, in a note to this passage, remarks that the following scene in longer metre seems to him to be somewhat unlike Euripides in style, and also inferior. He adds that it may mark one of the unfinished parts of the play.

6. Murray's note here runs: "The refrain of this chorus about the fawn is difficult to interpret. I have practically interpolated the third line ('To stand from fear set free, to breathe and wait'), in order (1) to show the connection of ideas; (2) to make clearer the meaning (as I understand it) of the two Orphic formulae, 'What is beautiful is beloved forever', and 'A hand uplifted over the head of Hate.' If I am wrong, the refrain is probably a mere cry for revenge, in the tone of the refrain, 'Hither for doom and deed,' on p. 266. It is one of the many passages where there is a sharp antagonism between the two spirits of the Chorus, first, as furious Bacchanals, and, secondly, as exponents of the idealized Bacchic religion of Euripides, which is so strongly expressed in the rest of this wonderful lyric."

7. Murray points out that this couplet is incomplete in the manuscript, but that the sense needed is obvious.

8. Murray remarks in his note to the passage that a prophecy like this is a very common occurrence in the last scene of Euripides' tragedies. He adds: "The prophecy was that Cadmus and Harmonia should be changed into serpents and should lead a host of barbarian invaders—identified with an Illyrian tribe, the Encheleis—against Hellas; they should prosper until they laid hands on the treasures of Delphi, and then be destroyed. Herodotus says that the Persians were influenced by this prophecy when they refrained from attacking Delphi (Book IX, 42)."

9. These lines are found likewise at the conclusion of the *Alcestis, Helen, Andromache,* and, with a slight addition, the *Medea.*

XVII
IPHIGENIA IN AULIS

CHARACTERS IN THE PLAY

AGAMEMNON, *Commander-in-Chief of the Greek Army*
MENELAUS, *his brother*
CLYTEMNESTRA, *his queen*
IPHIGENIA, *his daughter*
ORESTES, *his little son*
ACHILLES
AN OLD SERVANT
A MESSENGER
CHORUS OF WOMEN FROM CHALCIS
In the Epilogue, ANOTHER MESSENGER

INTRODUCTION

THE exact date of the *Iphigenia in Aulis* is not known, though scholars usually maintain that it was composed at the very end of Euripides' life, the period in which he wrote *The Bacchae*. We do know that the play remained unfinished at the poet's death, and that his son, the younger Euripides, completed it and subsequently produced it in 406 B.C. The spirit of the play is in sharp contrast to that of *The Bacchae,* and seems clearly to identify it closely with the dramatic creations of the fourth century B.C. The text as we now have it contains a number of passages which are apparently not genuine. For example, there seem to be two prologues, one a scene in dialogue, the other a conventional narrative passage, which have been worked together. The translator, F. M. Stawell, has relegated to an appendix all those lines and passages which she believes were not in the original version.

In his play Euripides has chosen to dramatize a crucial episode in the saga of the Trojan War. Prior to the opening of the action, Paris has taken away Helen, Menelaus has appealed to his powerful brother Agamemnon for assistance, and the latter has brought together the great Greek host at Aulis, where they are awaiting embarkation for Troy. However, the fleet have long been becalmed and the army has been growing increasingly restless and impatient of the delay. Agamemnon has just been told by Calchas that favourable winds will blow and the expedition will be able to sail if he sacrifices his daughter Iphigenia to Artemis. At first he refused, but then he yielded to the persuasions of Menelaus, the claims of his own ambition, and his fear of the army which he felt would deal violently with him if he abandoned his plan to go against Troy. Agamemnon therefore has written to his wife, Clytemnestra, telling her to bring Iphigenia to Aulis on the pretext that she is to be married to Achilles before the army departs. As the plays opens, Agamemnon's decision has weakened, and he has composed a letter to his wife, destined never to reach her, which bade the mother not to come with their daughter to the camp.

In the dramatic action which follows Euripides presents several excellent characterizations. Agamemnon is revealed as a weak-willed, ambitious, yet by no means unkindly man, who is caught in a situation which is really too great for him to overcome. He is spiritually torn by the conflicting claims which press upon him, but does not possess enough strength to conquer his vanity and his lust for power. Achilles is not the great heroic figure of the *Iliad*, but a soldier who is eager to fight for the life of Iphigenia, and yet does not seem willing to do anything to stop her from giving up her life for her country, when once she has determined upon that course of action. Clytemnestra is first presented as a matron excited by the prospect of having her daughter married so successfully to the famous Achilles, but her real masterful and overpowering nature emerges after she learns the truth. Her plea to Agamemnon to spare their daughter's life begins by her furious declaration that she has always hated him and her speech continues relentlessly in a withering vituperation of her husband. Iphigenia is beautifully delineated. Her excitement at her coming wedding and her devotion to her father whom she so obviously loves deeply make her a most appealing figure. She takes on more reality when she shrinks in horror on realizing the fate in store for her, and finally she commands our whole-souled admiration when she regains her self-control, and decides to sacrifice herself in a spirit of true martyrdom to a greater cause. If we look at all these characterizations, we can immediately see that Euripides has taken conventional epic figures, brought them down from the epic level, and with great dexterity has "humanized" or personalized them to such an extent that the play as a whole becomes almost a social or domestic tragedy.

Three more points remain to be mentioned. Most noteworthy is Euripides' effective exploitation of dramatic irony in the scene immediately after Clytemnestra and Iphigenia have arrived at the camp. Every word of happiness uttered by the mother and daughter assails Agamemnon and the audience, who know the truth, with overwhelming force. Secondly, attention should be called to the fact that the Chorus has very little or nothing to do with the action of the play. Here Euripides is following his usual practice, from which he deviated most notably in *The Bacchae*. And finally, we should note the translator's treatment of the end of the play. In her opinion, Euripides concluded his piece with the departure of Iphigenia to the sacrificial altar. The epilogue, which records how the maiden was miraculously saved, hence is regarded as a later addition, written to make the play conform with the version of the legend upon which Euripides relied in the *Iphigenia in Tauris*.[1]

---

[1] Acknowledgment of indebtedness should be made to the introduction and appendices of the separate edition of Stawell's translation of the play, where several points mentioned above receive full and excellent treatment.

IPHIGENIA IN AULIS

(SCENE:—*The quarters of the Greek army at Aulis. Before the King's
tent. Between midnight and dawn.* AGAMEMNON *enters from the tent.*)

AGAMEMNON

COME out, old man, out from the tent to me!

OLD SERVANT (*entering*)

Coming, my lord!
What new plan is afoot,
King Agamemnon?

AGAMEMNON

O, make haste, make haste!

OLD SERVANT

All that you will, my lord.
I'm a light sleeper yet.

AGAMEMNON

What star is yonder, travelling in the sky?

OLD SERVANT

                                 Sirius;
Close to the sevenfold voyaging Pleiades,
Still high overhead.

AGAMEMNON

No sound from the birds;
No sound from the sea.
The hush of the winds
Broods over Euripus.

OLD SERVANT

Why did you hasten out of the tent,
Lord Agamemnon?

No one is stirring in Aulis yet:
Nothing has roused
The guards on the ramparts.
Let us go in.

AGAMEMNON

O, you are fortunate,
Fortunate, all of you humble men,
Unknown, unhonoured, and free from fear!
Leaders may envy your lot.

OLD SERVANT

Ay, but glory is theirs.

AGAMEMNON

And in that glory lies their grief.
Suddenly, full in their pride of place
The wrath of the high gods shatters their life,
Or the quarrels of men
Mock them and thwart them.

OLD SERVANT

Are those the words of a chief? For shame!
You were not born for a life of ease,
Lord Agamemnon!
Joy and grief are a mortal's lot,
And the will of the high gods stronger than we.
But what has troubled you
All through the night? You kindled a torch,
Wrote on that tablet you hold in your hand,
Wrote and rewrote, sealed it, unsealed,
Dashed out the torch and burst into tears,
As though you were crazed.
Tell me, trust me, a faithful man,
Who came with your queen from her father's home,
One of the guard for the bride.†

AGAMEMNON

Here lie our men, all banded against Troy
To win back Helen for her rightful lord,
My brother Menelaus. I lead the host—
Doubtless they chose me for my brother's sake—
This glorious host of men and steeds and ships.

† Omitted Passage I, translated in the appendix, page 337, follows this speech.

Would I had not been chosen! Here we lie,
Becalmed at Aulis, helpless! In our need
We asked the prophet Calchas, and he said
That I must sacrifice my own dear child,
Iphigenia, to soften Artemis,
The Goddess of this plain. Then, only then,
The fleet could sail, and we should conquer Troy.
When I heard that,
I told my herald to dismiss the host:—
I could not be my daughter's murderer.
But then my brother came and plied me hard,
And I, I yielded. A letter went from me
To the queen my wife, bidding her send our girl
To wed Achilles, for he was too proud,—
Or so I said,—to sail with me to Troy
Unless he had a child of ours to wife.
I thought this tale would work upon the queen
To send the girl. None knew of it but four,
Menelaus, Calchas, Odysseus, and myself.
But I have changed, I have repented me.
I wrote this other letter in the night,
The one you see here. Take it.—
Go with it straight to Argos. Stay. I'll read
What I have written. You're my faithful man.

OLD SERVANT
Do so: I'll speak the better to the queen.

AGAMEMNON
"Daughter of Leda, do not send our girl,
As I wrote first, unto this wide-winged gulf,
Where no waves dash on the deep-bosomed shore,
The marriage-feast
We must hold later."

OLD SERVANT
But, Achilles, sire,—
What of his anger if he lose his bride?
Will it not flame against you and your lady?

AGAMEMNON
O, that was dreadful too!

OLD SERVANT
                    What can you mean?

AGAMEMNON

I only used his name. He has not heard
Aught of our plans nor any word of marriage.†

OLD SERVANT

Ill done, O king, using him for a lure
To make your child the victim for the army.

AGAMEMNON

Alas, some madness seized me, I was lost!
But hasten now, old man! Forget your age!

OLD SERVANT

Trust me, my lord.

AGAMEMNON

                    Let nothing make you loiter:
No cool spring in the shade, no drowsiness.

OLD SERVANT

O, do not say such things!

AGAMEMNON

Scan all the crossways on your road, for fear
The chariot pass you bringing the maid to us.
And if you meet her, quick, turn back the steeds,
Drive with loose rein to Argos!

OLD SERVANT

So I will.

AGAMEMNON

          Undo the barriers, go.

OLD SERVANT

What sign is there to show I come from you?

AGAMEMNON

The seal upon this tablet. Guard it! Quick!
The dawn is whitening in the sky, the sun's bright car
Will soon be here.—

                    (*The* OLD SERVANT *hurries out.*)
Woe's me for mortal men!
None have been happy yet.
(AGAMEMNON *goes into the tent. Enter the* CHORUS; *Greek
women from Chalcis in the island opposite Aulis.*)

† Omitted Passage II follows here.

CHORUS (*singing*)

To the sands of the bay
Where the salt waves run
Over the narrows
We come, we come,
From Chalcis our harbour-town,—
Nurse of the Naiad
Whose waters neighbour the sea,
Arethusa of all renown,—
To gaze on our chivalry.

Ten thousand sail
Across the sea to Troy,—
Our husbands have told us the tale,—
They follow their far-famed, fair-haired kings
For the sake of that queen
Whom the Herdsman [1] beguiled
By the reedy Spartan springs,
Whom the Cyprian gave,
When Hera and Pallas and she
Met by the dews of the mountain-lake,
Met in their rivalry.

Up through the grove,—
The victim-place
That Artemis hallows,—
We sped apace;
Blushed at our boldness,
A new shy red in our cheeks
For all that we longed to see,
Aflame to see
Bulwark and buckler and cavalry,
Camp of our fighters,
Armed host of our horses and men.†

(*Enter* MENELAUS *and the* OLD SERVANT, *struggling together*)

OLD SERVANT
Shame on you, Menelaus! You have no right.

MENELAUS
Off! You are far too faithful to your lord.

† Omitted Passage III follows here.

OLD SERVANT

That sneer's my boast.

MENELAUS
You'll soon repent your zeal.

OLD SERVANT
You had no right to read the words I bore.

MENELAUS
Nor you to bear what would destroy the Greeks.

OLD SERVANT
Argue that out with others! Give me the letter.

MENELAUS
I will not.

OLD SERVANT
Then I will not let you go.

MENELAUS
You'll bleed for that! Your head shall feel my sceptre.

OLD SERVANT
Fair fame is his who dies to serve his lord.

MENELAUS
Let go! How the slave chatters!

OLD SERVANT
Master, help!
Help, Agamemnon! Thieves!—This man has stolen
The letter that you gave me.
(*Enter* AGAMEMNON)

AGAMEMNON
Ha! What's this?
What means this brawling at my very gate?

MENELAUS
Hear me! I am the one to speak, not he.

AGAMEMNON
Menelaus struggling with my man? How's this?

MENELAUS
First look me in the face and then I'll speak.

AGAMEMNON
You think 1 dare not? I, King Atreus' son?

MENELAUS
You see this tablet, you know its shameful words?

AGAMEMNON
It's mine. Give it to me.

MENELAUS
                    No, not until
I show the army what you've written there.

AGAMEMNON
You broke the seal, then, read what was not yours?

MENELAUS
Yes, to lay bare your guilt.

AGAMEMNON
                    Have you no shame?
Where did you get it?

MENELAUS
                    On the road to Argos,
Watching to see if they would send your girl.

AGAMEMNON
And who set you to watch and spy on me?

MENELAUS
My own will set me. I'm no slave of yours.

AGAMEMNON
You dare? Can I not rule my house myself?

MENELAUS
No, for you change and veer with every wind.

AGAMEMNON
Well argued! But the wit of cruel men
Is hateful.

MENELAUS
                    And the purpose of weak men
Contemptible, and treacherous to boot.
O, you're the same man still! I'll show you that.
Hush, no more raging! I'll be fair enough.

Do you remember when your heart was set,
Though you concealed it, on this high command?
How suave you were, how friendly to each clown,
Doors open to the world, so affable,
Ready to talk with all, even when they would not!
And so you bought your power. But power won,
My lord was changed. He scarcely could be seen,
His old friends friends no more. Yet a true man
Will use his power most to help his friends.
So much for that. We sailed to Aulis then,
And lay becalmed, until the other lords
Bade you dismiss the fleet, nor linger here.
You came to me; you cried, "What can I do?
How keep the army, my command, my fame?"
Then Calchas bade you sacrifice your child
To Artemis, and she would send the wind.
And you were glad; you promised all he asked.
You wrote for her yourself,—you cannot say
Any man forced you,—bidding the queen your wife
Send her, to wed Achilles, so you feigned;
The eternal heavens hearkened to your words.
Now you betray us, writing fine new things;
You cannot be your daughter's murderer!
O, the trick's not uncommon! Many a chief
Endures at first, then fails; some through the fault
Of foolish citizens, but some because
They have not wit to keep their own land safe.
Alas for Hellas! I mourn most for her.
Equipped for glory, she must leave her foes,
Barbarians, to mock her,—through your girl and you.
Choose no man leader for his name, say I,
In peace or war. A general should have brains,
And it's the man of sense who rules the land.

LEADER OF THE CHORUS
Bitter are brothers when they fall to strife.

AGAMEMNON
Now I'll speak in my turn and show your faults
Frankly and plainly, yes, but soberly,
More like a brother. A good man should not rail.
Why are you fierce and your eyes full of blood?
How have I wronged you? What is it you want?

A lovely wife? I cannot help you there.
You could not rule the one you had. Must I
Suffer for you? Is my ambition blamed?
No, no, it's that fair woman you desire,
Careless of honour or of righteousness.
If I repent the evil thought I had,
Do you call me mad? Why, you are mad yourself,
Seeking a wicked wife, once rid of her.†
Enough! I will not slay my child to win
Unjust success for you, and for myself
Long nights and days of weeping bitter tears
For monstrous crime against my own dear children.
Do as you like; I will not do this deed.
There is my answer, short and clear enough.

LEADER OF THE CHORUS

Ah, he has changed, repented! It is well.

MENELAUS

Woe's me! I have no friends.

AGAMEMNON
Not if you slay them.

MENELAUS

Are you my brother?

AGAMEMNON
In good deeds, not in vile.

MENELAUS

Brothers should share their griefs.

AGAMEMNON
Exhort me not

To death and ruin.

MENELAUS
Will you not help Greece?

AGAMEMNON

Some god has sent Greece mad and you with her.

MENELAUS

Guard your king's sceptre, traitor to your kin!
I'll turn to other means and other friends.
(*Enter* MESSENGER)

† Omitted Passage IV follows here.

MESSENGER

Leader of Hellas, Agamemnon, Lord!
I come to tell you I have brought your child,
Iphigenia, and her mother too,
The queen herself, your lady Clytemnestra,
And young Orestes, that you should have joy
Seeing them now, so far away from home.
Even while I speak they are resting by the stream
In a smooth, grassy meadow, taking food
While I come to prepare you. But already
The army knows they are here. Rumour runs quick.
And all the people throng to see your daughter,
For all men worship splendour. And they ask,
"Is it a marriage, or her father's love
That brings the maiden?" Or I hear some say,
"They mean to give the girl to Artemis,
Lady of Aulis." Who's to lead her here?
Tell me, prepare the rites, and crown yourselves,
You and lord Menelaus. The marriage-song,
The sound of flutes and dancing feet should fill
King's tent and camp.—
It is a day of glory for the girl.

AGAMEMNON

I thank you. Get you in. All shall go well.
                    (*The* MESSENGER *goes into the tent.*)
Woe, woe is me, unhappy, caught by fate,
Outwitted by the cunning of the gods!
O that I were base-born! Then I could weep.
What can I do, a king? Our dignity
Still rules our lives, and still we serve the mob.
I shame to weep, and yet I shame to weep not,
In this sore strait. What shall I tell my wife?
How can I greet her, look her in the face?
She has undone me, coming now, uncalled,
Coming to wed her daughter, full of love,
To find me thus, a murderer. And she,
Poor hapless maiden, now the bride of Death!
The pity of it! I hear her call to me,
"Father, O father, would you slay your child?
A bitter bridal have you made for me:
I would you had the like!" And he, the boy,
Little Orestes, he will cry with her,

Knowing and knowing not. Accursed Paris,
Thy rape of Helen hath destroyed me!

LEADER OF THE CHORUS
I am a stranger to these lords, and yet
My heart is sick to feel the sorrow here.

MENELAUS
Brother, give me your hand.

AGAMEMNON
There.—You have won,
And I must suffer.

MENELAUS
No, it shall not be!
I swear by Pelops, grandsire of us both,
And by our father Atreus, I will speak
The very truth, out of my heart of hearts.
I saw you weep, I pitied you, and now
Unsay my words. I cannot torture you.
I cannot bid you slay your child for me.
Why should you mourn and I have joy thereby?
Your dear ones fall and mine have light and life?
There are more women if I lost this one.
Why should I slay my brother, my own flesh,
And take back Helen, an ill gift for a good?
I was mad, blinded, till I looked and saw
What this thing meant. Yes, and I pity her,
Poor maid, my brother's child, if she should die
To win my wife. What's Helen to your daughter,
Disband the army: send the host away.
Dry your eyes, brother; do not make me weep.
That prophecy you heard about your child,
I'll none of it: I leave it all to you.
My cruel thoughts have gone, and it is well
That love and pity for my own have changed me.

LEADER OF THE CHORUS
Gallantly spoken! You do not shame your sires.

AGAMEMNON
I thank you, Menelaus, for this change,
Sudden and worthy of yourself.† But I,
I am compelled to that dread slaughter now.

† Omitted Passage V follows here.

MENELAUS
How so? Who'll force you now to kill your child?

AGAMEMNON
The army: this great concourse of the Greeks.

MENELAUS
Not if you send her back again to Argos.

AGAMEMNON
That we could hide: there's more cannot be hid.

MENELAUS
And what? We should not shrink before the mob.

AGAMEMNON
Calchas will tell them all the prophecy.

MENELAUS
Not if we stop his mouth, and that's soon done.

AGAMEMNON
He's base, ambitious, like every prophet born.

MENELAUS
They do no good: they are never any use.

AGAMEMNON
But there's another danger, is there not?

MENELAUS
How can I say? What danger do you mean?

AGAMEMNON
The son of Sisyphus [2] knows everything.

MENELAUS
Odysseus? He's no match for you and me.

AGAMEMNON
He's full of cunning, and he rules the mob.

MENELAUS
Yes,—he's ambitious.—Curse on that curse of men!

AGAMEMNON
Can you not hear him, risen in his place,
Telling the army all that Calchas said

And how I promised I would give my child
And then drew back?—Thus he'll goad on the men
To kill us, and then sacrifice the girl.
Or if we fled to Argos they would follow,
Conquer the land, and lay the great walls low.
See how the gods have compassed us about
With suffering,—no escape now! O, my brother,
Do this one thing for me! Go to the army
And see that Clytemnestra shall not learn
What must be, till I give my child to Death.
Let my tears be enough. And you, my friends,
Strangers, yet friends too,—keep the secret safe.
(MENELAUS *goes to the camp,* AGAMEMNON *and the* OLD
    SERVANT *into the king's tent.*)

CHORUS (*singing*)

Thrice blest the calmer natures, the stronger hearts of passion,
Peace-possessed, though the god,
Gold-haired, twin-souled, should smite them.
Keen are his darts for rapture, and keen, keen for ruin!
O Cyprian, grant us rest,
Come not for our undoing!
But send us holy love,
Thou dearest, loveliest,
All madness far above.

The ways of man are many, and changeful all their fashion;
The true Good still shines fair,
And souls that are schooled
Shall still draw nigh to her.
Reverence shall sit in Wisdom's place,
Hers is the high, compelling grace
To find, thought-led, the right,
Whence glories flow,
Failing not in this life.
Seek virtue, for the search is great,
Where woman's hidden love may grow,
A splendour in the soul of man,
Strengthening thousand-fold the State.

The king's son [1] herded cattle,
A lad alone on Ida,
Playing tunes on his pipe, strange melodies,

Like the airs Olympus sang,
Suddenly called from sleek white herds at pasture
To judge the goddesses
And sent forthwith to Hellas.
Beneath pearl-carven portals
His eyes looked deep in Helen's,
A long and answered look.
Love he gave, love he took,
Paris, athrob and trembling. But from that joy rose war,
 war that will not yield,
All Hellas sailing for Troy
With sword and spear and shield.

(*The royal car appears with* CLYTEMNESTRA, IPHIGENIA,
 ORESTES, *and their attendants.*)

LEADER OF THE CHORUS

See, O see!
Iphigenia the young princess,
Clytemnestra the queen!
Great are the joys of the great,
Born from kings and for long renown!
Like gods in their splendour they seem
To us, weak mortals and poor.
Gather round, daughters of Chalcis,
Help the queen from her car
Courteously, gently! Disturb not the child
Nor startle the stranger princesses.

CLYTEMNESTRA

I thank you, women, for your kindly words,
Words of good omen, for I come, I hope,
To a good marriage, bringing the young bride.
Take out the dowries I have brought for her.
Carry them in, right carefully. And now,
My darling child, here we must leave the car.
Lift her down, maidens, take her in your arms;
She's a frail flower. Give me a hand too, some one,
The chariot-step is high. Carry the child,
Orestes: he's a babe. What, fast asleep
With all the driving? Wake up, little lad,
Wake for your sister's wedding! Chieftain's child,
Brother-in-law to Thetis' godlike son!
Put him here, Iphigenia, at my feet,

And stand beside me there yourself. The strangers
Will envy me for my rich motherhood.

(*Enter* AGAMEMNON)

CLYTEMNESTRA

There comes your father! Let us greet him, girl!
Most honoured lord, King Agamemnon, hail!
We come at your behest.

IPHIGENIA

O mother, blame me not! Let me go first
And put my arms about my father's neck.†

CLYTEMNESTRA

Go, go, my girl. You always loved your father
More than the other children.

IPHIGENIA

Father, how glad it makes my heart to see you!
It is so long since you have been away!

AGAMEMNON

Yes, and mine too; your words are for us both!

IPHIGENIA

How good it was of you to send for me!

AGAMEMNON

No, child, not good; and yet there's good in it.

IPHIGENIA

Why, what is it? There's trouble in your face,
Your eyes are sad. You are not glad to see me!

AGAMEMNON

A general and a king has many cares.

IPHIGENIA

O, stay with me now; send your cares away!

AGAMEMNON

Why, all my cares are only for your sake.

IPHIGENIA

Then smooth your face, unknit your brows, and smile!

† Omitted Passage VI follows here.

AGAMEMNON
I am as glad as I can be, my child.

IPHIGENIA
And all the while the tears are in your eyes!

AGAMEMNON
The parting that must come will be for long.

IPHIGENIA
O, father dear, I do not understand.

AGAMEMNON
Had you the sense I should but suffer more.

IPHIGENIA
Then I'll talk nonsense, if that pleases you.

AGAMEMNON
I cannot bear this. But I thank you, child.

IPHIGENIA
Stay with your children, father, stay at home.

AGAMEMNON
I would I could; I cannot have my will.

IPHIGENIA
Ruin take the army and my uncle's wrongs!

AGAMEMNON
They will ruin others. They have ruined me.

IPHIGENIA
How long you have been here in Aulis Bay!

AGAMEMNON
And something holds me still from setting out.

IPHIGENIA
Father, where is it that the Phrygians live?

AGAMEMNON
Where Paris never should have found a home.

IPHIGENIA
Will it be long till you return to me?

AGAMEMNON

As long for me as you, my darling child.

IPHIGENIA

If you could take me on the journey too!

AGAMEMNON

There is another journey you must take—
And you will not forget your father there.

IPHIGENIA

Shall I go with my mother, or alone?

AGAMEMNON

Alone, alone, severed from both of us.

IPHIGENIA

Father, it is not to another home?

AGAMEMNON

Hush, hush! A maiden must not know such things.

IPHIGENIA

Well, conquer Troy and come back soon to me.

AGAMEMNON

I have a sacrifice to offer first.

IPHIGENIA

We ask God's will, I know, in solemn rites.

AGAMEMNON

Yes. You will stand beside the bowl and learn.

IPHIGENIA

And lead the dances round the altar too?

AGAMEMNON

O, you are happy, for you do not know!
Go to the tent, my child. It is not fit
For maidens to be seen—
Give me the bitter sweetness of your kiss,
Give me your hand,—you will be long away.

O face, dear face, O breast, O golden hair!
A heavy burden has been laid on you
By Troy and Helen! I must speak no more,

I must not touch you: the tears fill my eyes.
Now go within.

(IPHIGENIA *goes into the tent.*)
Forgive me, O my queen,
If I seem too much moved, wedding our child
To young Achilles. 'Tis a goodly match,
But fathers feel it when they lose their girls.

CLYTEMNESTRA
I have my feelings too. I shall shed tears,
I know, like you. But all such things must be,
And time will help us. Tell me of the groom:
His name I know, but tell me of his race.

AGAMEMNON
Aegina was the daughter of Asopus.

CLYTEMNESTRA
Who was her husband? A mortal or a god?

AGAMEMNON
Zeus. Aeacus their child, Oenone's lord.

CLYTEMNESTRA
What son of Aeacus succeeded him?

AGAMEMNON
Peleus, and Peleus won the Nereid.

CLYTEMNESTRA
By the gods' grace, or in the gods' despite?

AGAMEMNON
Zeus gave her, Zeus, the best of guarantors.

CLYTEMNESTRA
Where was the bridal? Not in the ocean-surge?

AGAMEMNON
Where Cheiron dwelt among the solemn hills.

CLYTEMNESTRA
Ah, where they say the Centaurs had their haunts?

AGAMEMNON
Ay, there the high gods held the marriage-feast.

CLYTEMNESTRA
Did Thetis rear Achilles or his sire?

AGAMEMNON
Neither of them. They sent him unto Cheiron
To train him up far from the sins of men.

CLYTEMNESTRA
Wise teacher, wiser parents.

AGAMEMNON
                    And a fine son-in-law.

CLYTEMNESTRA
He's not unworthy. Where has he his home?

AGAMEMNON
In Phthia, by the river.

CLYTEMNESTRA
                    Will you take her there?

AGAMEMNON
That we must leave to him.

CLYTEMNESTRA
                    Well, good go with them!—
When is the bridal?

AGAMEMNON
When the moon is full.

CLYTEMNESTRA
And have you slain the victim for the goddess?

AGAMEMNON
I shall do so: I must.

CLYTEMNESTRA
                    The marriage-feast,
You hold it later?

AGAMEMNON
                    When I have sacrificed
What the gods call for.

CLYTEMNESTRA
And we women, where
Hold we our banquet?

AGAMEMNON
There, beside the ships.

CLYTEMNESTRA
Among the ropes and anchors? Well, so be it.

AGAMEMNON
Listen to me, wife: bear with me in this.

CLYTEMNESTRA
Do I not do so always? What's your wish?

AGAMEMNON
To give the bride myself.

CLYTEMNESTRA
Without her mother?
And where will you send me?

AGAMEMNON
Why, home to Argos
To guard our unwed daughters.

CLYTEMNESTRA
Leaving her?
My eldest child? Who'll hold the marriage-torch?

AGAMEMNON
I will.

CLYTEMNESTRA
Unheard-of! You think naught of that?

AGAMEMNON
A naval camp is no fit place for you.

CLYTEMNESTRA
But fitting, and most fitting, I should be
At my own daughter's bridal.

AGAMEMNON
Nor should our girls
Be left alone at Argos.

CLYTEMNESTRA
Oh, for that,
They are well cared for in their maiden-halls.

AGAMEMNON
Good wife, be counselled.

CLYTEMNESTRA
Now, by Hera, husband,
Do your man's work and leave the home to me.†

(CLYTEMNESTRA *goes into the tent with her escort.*)

AGAMEMNON
All's vain! I cannot rid myself of her.
Ah! how I twist and turn, how fruitlessly,
Plotting against my dearest every way!
It is for Hellas. I go to Calchas now
And plan with him what best will please the goddess
Although it crush me. Ah, the prudent man
Will choose for wife a helpmeet, or choose none
　　　　　(*He goes out towards the camp.*)

CHORUS (*singing*)
They shall come to the streams
Silver-swift on Apollo's shores,
Our host of Greeks, our ships, our warriors.
There the wild Cassandra
Will loose her laurelled hair,
Bright hair tossed wide on a wind of dreams,
And cry aloud when God
Cries to men through her.

Right well must Troy be manned
When our war, ocean-borne, full in flood
Sweeps their land.
Lords of the air are Helen's brothers,
Twins enskied,
But Greeks bring home the bride,
Home with shield and spear.

Towered Troy shall be ta'en
In a closed ring of blood,

† Omitted Passage VII follows here.

Red whelming waters;
Her women wail for horror,
The queen and all her train
Of weeping daughters,
When our stroke smites their city,
Spares not, has no pity.

All Lydia's golden dames reproach the bride,
The bride of error,
Weaving their webs, lamenting, terrified:—
(O far from me or mine that terror!)
One to another they say,—
Whispering, shaken:—
"Which of the foemen will drag me away,
Making grim spoil of the long bright hair,
When our city is taken?"

Through thee, through thee, thou fair-faced child of the Swan! [3]
Of the Swan, if it be
That the tale is sooth,
Not only the idle song
Of a singer laughing at truth.

(Enter ACHILLES*)*

ACHILLES
Where is the captain of the hosts of Greece?
Tell him Achilles stands without the door,
The son of Peleus, asking speech of him.†
I have left my home Pharsalus and my sire
To linger here along Euripus' beach
And wait upon these winds that will not blow.
My Myrmidons grow restless: day by day
Their murmur swells: "More waiting! How much more
Before we launch upon our voyage for Troy?
Act, son of Peleus, if to act at all
Be your intent: else take us home, and leave
The sons of Atreus to their own delays."

(Enter CLYTEMNESTRA *from the tent)*

CLYTEMNESTRA
Son of the Nereid, we were in the tent
And heard your voice, and now come forth to greet you.

† Omitted Passage VIII follows here.

ACHILLES

How's this? A woman? So stately and so fair!

CLYTEMNESTRA

You are amazed because you know us not,
Never have seen us yet.

ACHILLES

Who are you, lady?
How have you come, a woman, to the camp?

CLYTEMNESTRA

My name is Clytemnestra, Leda's daughter
And Agamemnon's wife.

ACHILLES

All thanks, great queen,
For your high courtesy. But I must go:
I should not talk with women.

CLYTEMNESTRA

Why should you go?
Stay here: give me your hand, and may the clasp
Be pledge of happy married days to come!

ACHILLES

I? Clasp your hand? Agamemnon would be wroth!
I have no right.

CLYTEMNESTRA

Surely the best of rights,
Wedding my daughter.

ACHILLES

Wedding your daughter? How?
Lady, I cannot speak. What dream is this?

CLYTEMNESTRA

I know it must be strange to meet new friends
Speaking of marriage on your wedding-eve.

ACHILLES

I was no suitor for your daughter, lady;
The sons of Atreus never spoke of her.

CLYTEMNESTRA

What can this mean? My words are strange to you,
But even so strange to me is all you say.

ACHILLES

We both must wonder: both have cause for wonder,
For surely both speak truth.

CLYTEMNESTRA

              Am I deceived, then?
Have I been made to woo you for my daughter
Against your will? O, I am all abashed.

ACHILLES

Someone, it seems, has played upon us both.
But let it pass, and care not overmuch.

CLYTEMNESTRA

Farewell. I cannot look you in the face,
Thus put to shame and made to speak a lie.

ACHILLES

I am shamed too, O queen! But I will go
Into the tent and ask your husband all.
    (*The* OLD SERVANT *appears at the tent-door.*)

OLD SERVANT

Wait, son of Aeacus! Wait, Leda's daughter!

ACHILLES

Who calls? Some frightened man, opening the door!

OLD SERVANT

A slave: I'll own that now.

ACHILLES

              Whose? None of mine:
My men and Agamemnon's keep apart.

OLD SERVANT

I am the queen's: her sire gave me to her.

ACHILLES

Speak, we are waiting: tell us what you want.

OLD SERVANT

Are you alone? Is no one near the gates?

CLYTEMNESTRA
We are alone. Come out and speak with us.

OLD SERVANT
O luck and wits of mine! Save those I love!

ACHILLES
He'll not speak till to-morrow. He's afraid.

CLYTEMNESTRA
Surely you trust me? Tell me: have no fear.

OLD SERVANT
You know that I have served you faithfully.

CLYTEMNESTRA
Long years, I know, you have served my house and me.

OLD SERVANT
Agamemnon only got me with your dower.

CLYTEMNESTRA
Yes, yes.
You came with me to Argos on my marriage.

OLD SERVANT
So I am yours, and Agamemnon's less.

CLYTEMNESTRA
Come, come, your secret! Out with it at last!

OLD SERVANT
He means to kill your child, his child!

CLYTEMNESTRA
What? Are your wits turning, man?

OLD SERVANT
                              I say the steel
Is sharpening now for that white neck of hers.

CLYTEMNESTRA
What horror's here? Or is my husband mad?

OLD SERVANT
O, sane enough, except for you and her.

CLYTEMNESTRA
But what's his purpose? What devil drives him on?

OLD SERVANT
The prophet Calchas, that the fleet may sail.

CLYTEMNESTRA
And whither?—O, my child, my child!—

OLD SERVANT
To Troy,
So Menelaus get his wife again.

CLYTEMNESTRA
And so for Helen's sake my girl is doomed?

OLD SERVANT
Even as you say. He'll sacrifice the maid
To Artemis.

CLYTEMNESTRA
Then it was all a lie,
That marriage?

OLD SERVANT
Yes; to lure you from your home.

CLYTEMNESTRA
O, we are lost, my child and I! Lost, lost!

OLD SERVANT
Most piteously, and Agamemnon damned.

CLYTEMNESTRA
Utterly lost! I cannot stop my tears.

OLD SERVANT
What mother could? Let your tears have their way.

CLYTEMNESTRA
You say it's true, old man,—how do you know?

OLD SERVANT
He sent me to you with another letter.

CLYTEMNESTRA
Bidding us come, that he might murder her?

OLD SERVANT
No, stopping you. He had relented then.

CLYTEMNESTRA
But how was it you did not give it me?

OLD SERVANT
Menelaus seized it. He's the cause of all.

CLYTEMNESTRA
Son of the Nereid, do you hear these words?

ACHILLES
Dread words for you, and grim enough for me.

CLYTEMNESTRA
They used your name to lure my child to death.

ACHILLES
Ill done, by Heaven, ill done!

CLYTEMNESTRA
                    O goddess-born!
You see a wretched woman at your knees!
All pride has left me. What should I care for now
Except my daughter? Help me, Thetis' son!
Pity my need, and pity your poor bride,
Bride but in name, I know, yet none the less
I decked her for you, dreamt she would be yours,
Brought her to you,—and brought her to her death.
You will be shamed if you desert her now,
Poor hapless maid, not yours, and yet called yours!
Now by your right hand and your mother's soul
Your name destroyed us,—save it and save us!
This is my only altar, at your knees!
I have no friend here else: you heard yourself
Lord Agamemnon's cruelty—I stand
Alone, a helpless woman, as you see,
Among a crowd of sailors, lawless men,
Fierce men, if goaded, yet much good in them,
When they're so minded. If you champion me,
You save us: if you stand aside, we die.

LEADER OF THE CHORUS
There speaks a mother's heart, the thrall of love;
She will dare all things for her children's sake.

ACHILLES

My blood's on fire. All tyrants I detest,
Though I yield gladly to a tempered rule.†
Noble old Cheiron taught me to love truth,
And I'll obey our chiefs when they lead well,
Not when they counsel crimes. Here and in Troy
I'll keep my spirit free, my sword unstained.
Lady, indeed you have been foully used,
Even at the hands where you should look for love;
And all the pity that a soldier can
I give you freely. Fear not for your child,
Mine she was called, and to the sacrifice
I will not yield her. I'll not play decoy
To lure the victim to the net of death.
My name it was, though I touched not the steel,
Mine which should slay your daughter. True, the cause
Is Agamemnon: yet I needs must bear
The stain of murder if she perish thus,
Betrayed and cheated through her trust in me,
Outraged, dishonoured. I must count myself
The meanest man in all the host of Greece,
Viler than Menelaus, child of hell,
Not son of Peleus, should I lend my name
To be the accomplice of your husband's deed.
Now by the sea-born founder of my line,
Nereus, the sire of Thetis, who gave me birth,
Never shall Agamemnon touch your child—
No, not the merest fringes of her robe.‡
The steel shall answer, red with clots of gore,
Long before Troy is reached, if any man
Should drag your daughter from me. Be at rest:
I seem a god to you and I am none,
Yet will I play this part you choose for me.

LEADER OF THE CHORUS

Fit words, O son of Peleus, for yourself
And for your mother, the sea-pure Nereid!

CLYTEMNESTRA

I have no words—my words would seem too wild
And yet too poor where so great thanks are due.
A generous heart, I know, will turn from praise—

† Omitted Passage IX follows here.
‡ Omitted Passage X follows here.

How dare I praise you, sick with my own griefs
And you a stranger with no part in them?
Yet a true man will help a stranger's need.
O pity us, for pitiable we are!
I took you for my son, an empty hope,
Yes, and an evil omen for yourself
If she must die who once was called your bride,
My daughter. Never let that omen be!
But you have answered nobly, first and last,
And through your help my daughter will be saved.
Or should I bring her here to clasp your knees?
No maiden's part, yet if you will she'll come,
Her eyes still brave and free in her shy face.
But, would you grant us all without her coming,
I'd keep her back. I know the girl is proud,
Too proud,—though modesty becomes a maid.

ACHILLES

I would not have you bring her to me thus,
For we must shun the gossip of the crowd:
Scandal's the joy of an idle army.
Nor do I need more prayers to help you now;
It is my pride to save you and my joy.
And of one thing be sure: I keep my pledge.
If I play false and make but idle boast,
Death be my lot: but if I save her, life.

CLYTEMNESTRA

Heaven help you for your help in our distress!

ACHILLES

Now hear my plan, and all may yet be well.

CLYTEMNESTRA

Say what you wish: in all I will obey.

ACHILLES

Let us persuade your lord to better thoughts.

CLYTEMNESTRA

He is a coward, and he fears the army.

ACHILLES

Yet reasons good may conquer reasons bad.

CLYTEMNESTRA

Small hope of that! Yet say what I should do.

ACHILLES

Plead with the father for the daughter's life:
If he should still refuse you, turn to me.
But should he listen, good; I need not act.
You are safe without it. And I'd treat a friend
More fairly thus, nor could the army blame me
If I had won by reason, not by force,
While you yourself would have more peace at home
If all seemed done without me and done well.

CLYTEMNESTRA

Wise are your words. I will do all you say.
Yet if we not accomplish what we hope,
Where shall I find you, whither turn to reach
Your hand, your succour, in our desperate need?

ACHILLES

I will keep watch myself, and wait for you,
That none may see you hurrying through the host
Alone in all your grief, a great man's daughter.

CLYTEMNESTRA

So let it be! Surely one day the gods
Will bless you for your generous help to me,—
If gods there are: if not, what use our toil? [4]
(CLYTEMNESTRA *goes into the tent,* ACHILLES *towards the camp.*)

CHORUS (*singing*)

Who knows the marriage-song that once so proudly rang
To the flute and the pipe and the dancer's lyre,
The song the Muses sang?
Up Pelion's glades they danced,
The bright Pierian choir:
Their golden sandals glanced,
Their tresses gleamed as they made their way,
Chanting the names, the names of bride and bridegroom,
Through woods where Centaurs lay
To the god-given feast
For Thetis and her lover.
Page Ganymede, the Phrygian boy,
Darling of Zeus, his luxury's toy,
Poured wine in golden beakers.

Far down on white-lit sand
Beside Aegaean waters
Danced, circling hand-in-hand,
The Nereid maids,
The Sea-king's fifty daughters.

With green grass crowned and pine
Did the revelling Centaurs race
To the bowl of the Bacchanal wine,
Their horse-hoofs thudding apace,
And one, the prophet, Apollo's friend,
Cheiron, shouted and sang of what should be in the end:—
"Hearken, child of the sea!
Thou shalt bear a son, a son to be
Light and glory for Thessaly.
Shield and spear shall he send to destroy
The land of Priam, sack
The far-famed town of Troy,
Gold-helmed, gold harness on his back,
Harness a god had wrought,
Harness his mother brought."
High rose that revelry
When gods made cheer for bride and groom,
For Peleus and the Nereid,
The first-born of the sea.

Ah, but thou! Thou shalt be crowned for thy doom,
Thy fair hair garlanded,
Like a dappled heifer ensnared
On lone hills in a cavern's gloom.
Blood will the Argives draw from thy throat,
Though no pipe drew thee, no herdsman's cord;
Nay, but thy mother to be the bride
Of a Grecian lord.

Honour hath vanished and faithfulness fled,
Their faces faint as the face of the dead.
Sin grows strong, crime bears rule,
Lost is the loyal endeavour, the school
Of holy dread.

(CLYTEMNESTRA *hurries out from the tent.*)

CLYTEMNESTRA

Where is my lord? I come to look for him.
He has been long away, and my poor child
Is all in tears, learning the cruel death
Her father means for her. Ah, there he comes,
His children's murderer!—as I shall prove.

(*Enter* AGAMEMNON *from the camp*)

AGAMEMNON

Well met, my wife, alone! I have things to say
Not fit for brides to hear.

CLYTEMNESTRA

And what is it
For which you seize the chance?

AGAMEMNON

Send out the girl
Here to her father. All is ready now,
The lustral water, the flour, the cleansing fire,
The heifers that must fall to please the goddess
Before the marriage.†

CLYTEMNESTRA

Truly, your words are fair;
Your deeds, how shall I name them?

(*She goes to the tent-door.*)
Come, my girl;
You know your father's will. Come, bring with you
The child, Orestes.

(IPHIGENIA *and* ORESTES *come from the tent.*)
Here is your daughter, sire,
At your command. Now will I speak for her.

AGAMEMNON

Why do you weep, my girl? No smile for me?
Your eyes fixed on the ground? Your sweet face hid?

CLYTEMNESTRA

O, which of all my wrongs shall I take first?
For first and last and midmost, all are first.

AGAMEMNON

What is it? What has happened to you all?
Sad, drooping faces, trouble-darkened eyes?

† Omitted Passage XI follows here.

CLYTEMNESTRA
Speak truth, my husband, in what I ask you now.

AGAMEMNON
No need to bid me: ask me what you will.

CLYTEMNESTRA
Your daughter, yours and mine, you mean to kill her?

AGAMEMNON
Hold!
You dare ask that? There's something you suspect?

CLYTEMNESTRA
Rage not, my lord:
Answer my question.

AGAMEMNON
Such questions are not fit.

CLYTEMNESTRA
I have no others.

AGAMEMNON
O, my wretched fate!

CLYTEMNESTRA
And mine and hers, all three thrice miserable.

AGAMEMNON
Whom have I injured?

CLYTEMNESTRA
You ask that of me? †

AGAMEMNON
Betrayed, betrayed! My secret has been sold.

CLYTEMNESTRA
I know, I have learnt, all that you mean to do.
Your silence and your groanings,—they confess,
They speak for you. O, weary not yourself!

AGAMEMNON
See, I am silent: I'll not add lies to grief.

† Omitted Passage XII follows here.

CLYTEMNESTRA

Then hear me now. I'll speak the naked truth,
No dark hints now! By force you wedded me,
I never loved you! Tantalus you slew,
My first dear husband; and my little son,
You tore him from my breast. And when my brothers,
The sons of God, flashed to me on their steeds,
My father pitied you, his suppliant,
Gave me to you for wife. And a true wife I was,
Yes, chaste and true, and cared well for your home.
Such wives are not so common!—
Three girls I bore you and a son, and now
You rob me of the first! Your reason, pray,
If men should ask it? O, I'll answer that.—
To win back Helen! Your own child for a wanton,
Your dearest for a foe! A proper bargain!
If you do this, if you are long at Troy,
What will my heart be like, think you, at home,
When I look on my daughter's empty chair,
And empty room, sitting there all alone,
Companied by my tears, still muttering,
"Your father killed you, child, killed you himself!"
What will your wages be when you come back?
We who are left, we shall not want much urging
To greet you with the welcome you deserve! ⁵
O, by the gods, drive me not thus to sin,
Nor sin yourself!
If once you killed your child, how could you pray?
What good thing ask for? Rather for defeat,
Disgrace, and exile! Nor could I pray for you:
We make fools of the gods if we suppose
They can love murderers. If you come home,
Will you dare kiss your girls? Or they dare come,
That you may choose another for the knife?
Have you once thought of this? Are you a man?
Or nothing but a sceptre and a sword?
You should have gone among the Greeks and said,
"You wish to sail for Troy? Good, then draw lots,
And see whose child must die." That had been fair;
Or Menelaus should have slain his own,—
Hermione for Helen. But I, the chaste,
I must be robbed, and she come home in triumph
To find her daughter! Answer, if I am wrong!
If not, give up this murder! Sin no more!

LEADER OF THE CHORUS

O listen, listen! Help to save your child!
Yield, Agamemnon! Not a man will blame you.

IPHIGENIA

Had I the voice of Orpheus, O my father,
If I could sing so that the rocks would move,
If I had words to win the hearts of all,
I would have used them. I have only tears.
See, I have brought them! They are all my power.
I clasp your knees, I am your suppliant now,
I, your own child; my mother bore me to you.
O, kill me not untimely! The sun is sweet!
Why will you send me into the dark grave?
I was the first to sit upon your knee,
The first to call you father, first to give
Dear gifts and take them. And you used to say,
"My darling, shall I see you safely wed,
In some good husband's home, a happy wife,
As I would have you?" Then I'd answer you,
Stroking your beard, the beard that I touch now,
"What shall I do for you, O father mine?
Welcome you, a loved guest, in my own house,
Pay you for all your nursing-care of me?
Oh, I remember every word we said,
But you forget them, and you wish my death.
Have pity, for your father Atreus' sake
And for my mother's; she has suffered once
When I was born, and she must suffer now.
What can I have to do with Helen's love?
How is it she has come to ruin me?
My father, look at me, and kiss me once,
That I may take this memory at least
Unto the grave with me, if I must die.
(*She turns to the child* ORESTES.)
O, brother, you are young to help your friends,
Yet come and cry with me, kneel down and pray
For your poor sister's life. O father, see!
Even children understand when sorrow comes!
He asks for mercy though he cannot speak;
Yes, we two children touch your beard and pray,
We, your grown daughter and your little son.
Now will I gather all prayers into one,

And that must conquer. Life is sweet, is sweet!
The dead have nothing. Those who wish to die
Are out of reason. Life, the worst of lives,
Is better than the proudest death can be!

LEADER OF THE CHORUS
Accursed Helen! Through your love and you
Torture has come upon this royal house!

AGAMEMNON
I know the touch of pity, know it well:
I love my children,—I am no madman, wife.
It is a fearful thing to do this deed,
Yet fearful not to do it: I am bound.

(*He turns to* IPHIGENIA.)
You see this host of ships and mail-clad men,—
They cannot reach the towers of Iliun,
They cannot take the far-famed steep of Troy,
Unless I sacrifice you as he bids,
Calchas, the prophet. And our Greeks are hot
To smite the foe, nor let them steal our wives.
If I refuse the Goddess, they will come
To Argos, kill your sisters, you and me!
I am no slave of Menelaus, child;
I do not bow to him, I bow to Hellas,
As bow I must, whether I will or no.
She is the greater. For her we live, my child,
To guard her freedom. Foreigners must not rule
Our land, nor tear our women from their homes.

(*He goes out to the camp.*)

CLYTEMNESTRA
O, my child! O, my friends!
You must die! You must die!
Your father has fled,
He has flung you to death!

IPHIGENIA
Mother, mother! O, mourn with me!
The daylight has died,
I have lost the light of the sun!

(*She flings herself in her mother's arms.*)

CHORUS (*singing*)

Far snow-bound glens of Phrygia's lonely mountains,
Where Priam's babe was left, left by his father,
Cast out to die, hapless unmothered boy,
Paris the shepherd-lad, born prince of Troy!

Would he had died there, left lone by his father,
Lone by the lake-side, the nymph-haunted fountains,
Meadows of hyacinth, starry with roses
The goddesses gather!

Pallas came, Hera came, came Beauty's queen,—
Hermes the messenger led,—
Pallas, proud of her lance,
Hera, vaunting the royal bed,
Beauty, guile-hearted, waked love with her glance.
Ah, the prize, fraught with hate,
For Beauty's lovely head!

IPHIGENIA

Fraught with my fate, for the glory of Greece.

LEADER OF THE CHORUS

Artemis orders your sacrifice,
Maiden, for Ilium.

IPHIGENIA (*chanting*)

Mother, my father has gone,
Left me, betrayed and alone!
I have seen Helen, her face was death.
And I am hunted to my doom,
A cruel doom, by a cruel father.

O that they never had come,
The bronze-beaked, pine-oared ships,
To the shores of Aulis Bay!
O that God had not sent
Contrary winds on the sea,
Gentle breezes for some,
Sailing and harbour for some,
Sorrow and doom for us!
Yes, we are children of sorrow, of sorrow, who live for the
space of a day:
Trouble must rise up afresh for the race of man evermore

Helen, O Helen, the woe thou hast wrought, the grief and
the suffering!

LEADER OF THE CHORUS
I pity you and your unhappy fate.
Alas, it never should have come on you!
(ACHILLES *enters with a small band of armed men.*)

IPHIGENIA
O mother, mother! Armed men are coming here!

CLYTEMNESTRA
Our friend the hero, child, for whom you came.

IPHIGENIA
Open the door! Quick! Let me hide myself.

CLYTEMNESTRA
Why so?

IPHIGENIA
I cannot meet Achilles now.

CLYTEMNESTRA
Why not, I pray you?

IPHIGENIA
My marriage—I am shamed.

CLYTEMNESTRA
No time this for such whimsies! Stay here, girl!
Let all pride go, if only—

ACHILLES
Leda's child!
Daughter of sorrow.

CLYTEMNESTRA
Sorrow? True enough!

ACHILLES
A cry goes through the army, a dread cry.

CLYTEMNESTRA
What for?

ACHILLES
Your daughter—

CLYTEMNESTRA
O, that means worst!

ACHILLES
It means her murder.

CLYTEMNESTRA
No man took her part?

ACHILLES
I did: I faced their mob.

CLYTEMNESTRA
What did they do?

ACHILLES
Do? Tried to stone me.

CLYTEMNESTRA
Because you'd save my girl?

ACHILLES
Even so.

CLYTEMNESTRA
Who'd dare to lay a hand on you?

ACHILLES
Who? All the army.

CLYTFMNESTRA
You had your Myrmidons?

ACHILLES
The first to turn against me.

CLYTEMNESTRA
Child, we are lost!

ACHILLES
They called me lovesick, sneered—

CLYTEMNESTRA
You answered them?

ACHILLES
No slaughter for my bride!

CLYTEMNESTRA
You answered well.

ACHILLES
Her father promised me—

CLYTEMNESTRA
Brought her from Argos.

ACHILLES
But I was shouted down—

CLYTEMNESTRA
The cursed mob!

ACHILLES
Yet I will save you.

CLYTEMNESTRA
One man against a host?

ACHILLES
You see these men-at-arms behind me?

CLYTEMNESTRA
Ay!
Now bless you for your thought!

ACHILLES
And blest we shall be.

CLYTEMNESTRA
There's hope then, and my girl need not be slain?

ACHILLES
Not while I live.

CLYTEMNESTRA
They come to seize her here?

ACHILLES
Ten thousand strong: Odysseus leads them.

CLYTEMNESTRA
He?
That son of Sisyphus?

ACHILLES
The very man.

CLYTEMNESTRA
Self-chosen was he, or elected? Which?

ACHILLES
Why, both at once.

CLYTEMNESTRA
Elected murderers!

ACHILLES
I'll keep him off.

CLYTEMNESTRA
Ah, would he drag the girl
Against her will?

ACHILLES
What else can you expect?
Seizing those long fair tresses.

CLYTEMNESTRA
O, and I?
What can I do?

ACHILLES
Hold her, and hold her fast.

CLYTEMNESTRA
O God, if that can save her, she is safe!

ACHILLES
It's come to that now.

IPHIGENIA
Mother, let me speak! [6]
This anger with my father is in vain,
Vain to use force for what we cannot win.
Thank our brave friend for all his generous zeal,
But never let us broil him with the host,
No gain to us, and ruin for himself.
I have been thinking, mother,—hear me now!—
I have chosen death: it is my own free choice.
I have put cowardice away from me.
Honour is mine now. O, mother, say I am right!

Our country—think, our Hellas—looks to me,
On me the fleet hangs now, the doom of Troy,
Our women's honour all the years to come.
My death will save them, and my name be blest,
She who freed Hellas! Life is not so sweet
I should be craven. You who bore your child,
It was for Greece you bore her, not yourself.
Think! Thousands of our soldiers stand to arms,
Ten thousand man the ships, and all on fire
To serve their outraged country, die for Greece:
And is my one poor life to hinder all?
Could we defend that? Could we call it just?
And, mother, think! How could we let our friend
Die for a woman, fighting all his folk?
A thousand women are not worth one man!
The goddess needs my blood: can I refuse?
No: take it, conquer Troy! This shall be
My husband, and my children, and my fame.
Victory, mother, victory for the Greeks!
The foreigner must never rule this land,
Our own land! They are slaves and we are free.

LEADER OF THE CHORUS

O maiden, all is generous in your heart,
But fortune and the goddess are to blame.

ACHILLES

Agamemnon's daughter, I had been thrice blest
If you could be my bride. Hellas and you,
Ye are happy in each other! All your words
Are grandly spoken, worthy of your land.†
I see your nature now, see what you are,
And thirst to win you, soul of nobleness!
Come, I would help you, serve you all I can,
And take you to my home. I count it ill,
By Thetis! if I may not fight the Greeks
And save you. Think; death is a fearful thing.

IPHIGENIA

I will say one word, without fear of shame.
The face of Helen has roused war enough,
Battles of men and murders. O my friend,

† Omitted Passage XIII follows here.

Die not because of me, slay none for me.
Let me save Hellas if I have the power.

ACHILLES

O glorious heart! What is there I can say
Against your purpose? O, your soul is great!
Why should I not speak truth? Yet, none the less,
For it may be this thought of yours will change,
Hear what I have resolved. I will go hence,
And set my men about the altar's side,
That I may save you, and not let you die.
Even you may find a meaning in my words
When the sharp steel is close upon your neck.
Your rashness must not bring you to your death.
These men of mine shall take their stand with me
Hard by the temple, and await you there.

(ACHILLES *goes out.*)

IPHIGENIA

Mother, why are you weeping silently?

CLYTEMNESTRA

Have I not cause enough to be heart-sick?

IPHIGENIA

Hush! Do not weaken me; grant what I ask.

CLYTEMNESTRA

Ask on, my child; I cannot do you wrong.

IPHIGENIA

I would not have you cut your hair for me
Nor wear black raiment—

CLYTEMNESTRA

          What is it you say?
When you are lost—

IPHIGENIA

          O, never speak like that!
I am saved, saved! You will be proud of me.

CLYTEMNESTRA

I must not mourn?

IPHIGENIA
No place for mourning here,
No tomb.

CLYTEMNESTRA
Surely the slain have burial?

IPHIGENIA
The holy altar is my monument.

CLYTEMNESTRA
I will obey you, child; your words are good.

IPHIGENIA
My lot is good, and I do good to Greece.

CLYTEMNESTRA
What shall I tell your sisters of all this?

IPHIGENIA
Ah, do not dress them, either, in black robes!

CLYTEMNESTRA
Shall I not take some message to the girls,
Some loving word from you?

IPHIGENIA
Yes, my farewell.
And Orestes—O, take care of him for me,
And bring him up to manhood.

CLYTEMNESTRA
Hold him now,
Draw him to you, look your last look on him.

IPHIGENIA (*to* ORESTES)
Darling, you gave me all the help you could.

CLYTEMNESTRA
Is there no more that I can do to please you?

IPHIGENIA
O, hate him not,—my father, and your husband!

CLYTEMNESTRA
He has an evil course to run for you.

IPHIGENIA

He offers me to Greece against his will.

CLYTEMNESTRA

By treachery, unworthy of his house.

IPHIGENIA

Who will go with me, lead me to the place,
Before they drag me thither by the hair?

CLYTEMNESTRA

I will, beside you.

IPHIGENIA

No . . . it is not fit.

CLYTEMNESTRA

Clutching your garments.

IPHIGENIA

Listen, mother dear.
Stay here; that is far better for us both.
One of my father's men will go with me
To the field of Artemis, where I must die.

CLYTEMNESTRA

Child, are you going?

IPHIGENIA

Yes, I will not come back.

CLYTEMNESTRA

You leave your mother?

IPHIGENIA

Yes, not as I would.

CLYTEMNESTRA

O, leave me not!
(CLYTEMNESTRA *falls fainting and is carried into the tent.*)

IPHIGENIA

I will not shed a tear.
(*She turns to the women.*)
Now sing the paean for my destiny!
Sing to the child of Zeus, to Artemis;
Let the glad sound be heard by all the Greeks.

Let them lift up the baskets, light the fire,
And fling the barley; bid my father come
And touch the altar. I will bring this day
Victory and salvation unto Greece.

Follow me now, the victor,
Follow the taker of Troy!
Crown my head with a garland,
Wash my hands for the rite.
Dance!
On to the shrine of the Maiden,
Artemis the blest!
She calls me, and I,
I come as the victim, I give my blood,
Fulfil the seer's command.

LEADER OF THE CHORUS
O sovereign Lady, O Queen and Mother,
Now we may give you our tears.
No tears must be shed at the rite.

IPHIGENIA
Sing, O sing unto Artemis,
Queen of the Aulis-land
And the harbour-mouth,
Where the swords are athirst for me.
Farewell Pelasgia, motherland of mine!
Farewell my nurse, Mycenae!

LEADER OF THE CHORUS
You call on the city where Perseus dwelt,
Where the Cyclops built the walls?

IPHIGENIA
You bare me for a light to Greece.
In death I will remember you.

LEADER OF THE CHORUS
Ah, your glory will not die!

IPHIGENIA
Hail! All hail!
Torch-bearer! Giver of brightness! Day!
O flame of God! I leave you, I go
To another life, to another world!
Dear sunlight, farewell, farewell!

(IPHIGENIA *goes out, with one attendant, followed by the*
   CHORUS *chanting solemnly.*)

CHORUS

Behold!
Behold the conqueror of Troy!
She is crowned and made pure for a goddess's joy.
She goes to the dead,
Her white neck pierced, her blood running red.

The lustral waters wait,
Her father and the army wait
For the wind that shall waft them to high-towered Troy.
Come, let us call on Artemis,
Goddess of all gods great,
Virgin, huntress and queen,
That she bless them in this!

O Maiden, glad of maiden's blood,
Send our Greeks like a flood on the treacherous town!
Let their leader be crowned by his warriors' spears
For the glory of Greece
With undying renown,
Unforgotten throughout the years.†

† Omitted Passage XIV follows here.

APPENDIX

Omitted Passages

I. Lines 49–88.

AGAMEMNON

Leda, the child of Thespius, had three daughters,
Phoebe, then Clytemnestra, my own queen,
Last Helen, whom the flower of Grecian youth
Sought for in marriage. Dire the rivalry,
Breathing out slaughter against the chosen man.
Then Tyndarus her father, at a loss
Whether to give or not to give his girl
And pondering how best to meet this hap,
Bound all the suitors by a solemn oath,
Striking right hand in hand before the gods,
To help the bridegroom whom his daughter chose
Against the man, if such should ever come,
Foreign or Greek, to lure away the bride
From her true lord, fighting that man till death,
Sacking his town. And so they took the oath,—
The old man's cunning won its way with them,—
And then he bade his daughter choose herself
Where Aphrodite's dearest zephyrs blew.
And she chose one she never should have chosen,
Menelaus. Then the Phrygian came to Sparta
Who judged the goddesses, so runs the tale.
Flower-like he shone in soft embroidered raiment
Gleaming with gold and foreign luxury.
Helen and he were lovers from the first
And, Menelaus being far from home,
He fled with her to Ida's lonely steadings.
Then rushed the bridegroom to the men of Greece
Calling to mind the oath that they had sworn

337

To right the wronged. Straightway they flew to arms,
And came unto this narrow-mouthed deep harbour
With ship and shield and horse and chariot.
Then I was chosen leader for his sake,
My brother's. But the glory should have gone
To someone else. O would it had been so!
For now, the host assembled, here we lie
Becalmed at Aulis, helpless!

II. Lines 130–132.

                       Nor that I promised
To bring my daughter to his bridal-bed.

III. Lines 192–302.

And there we spied
Ajax of Salamis,
Bulwark and crown of his land,
Side by side with Ajax the Less:
Protesilaus and Prince Palamede
Of the Sea-god's line,
Playing at chess,
Mirthfully plotting their play:
And lord Diomede
Who hurled the big quoits
And laughed as he hurled,
With Meriones, the War-god's squire,
The wonder of all the world:
Odysseus the wise
From his island-hills,
And Nireus, goodliest man!
Swift as the wind
When it swiftliest flies,
Achilles the racer ran,—
Thetis bore him and Cheiron trained,—
We watched him race in his battle-gear
Pace for pace with the four-horse car
Along by the inshore sand.
We heard the shouts of the charioteer,
Eumelus, Pheres' son,
We marked the splendid horses,

The gold-wrought bridles,
The thrusting goad,
Two of them, dappled, bearing the yoke,
And two with the traces, red roan,
Wheeling the car at the turns,
Their flanks agleam in the light.
Achilles raced them, armoured, bright,
Breasting the chariot-rim,
As we gazed at the horses and him.

Then we counted the ships,
A marvellous sight,
Filling our womanish eyes with delight
Sweet as honey is sweet to the lips.
The right wing held by the Myrmidons' war,
Fifty sail of the line
With golden Nereids set for a sign
To mark Achilles' might.

Hard by as many from Argos sailed
Beneath the son of Talaos, with Sthenelus to aid.
Sixty keels from Attica the child of Theseus brought;
His sign was Pallas Athena, wrought
Driving her four-horsed, swift-winged car
To carry his mariners high and far.

Then followed the battle-ships of Thebes,
Fifty farers over the seas.
Each with its blazon set on the stern,—
Golden the snake and Cadmus burn—
And earth-born Leitus led them.
From Phocis and Locris as many were manned
By Ajax the Less, lord of the Thronian land.

Next from Mycenae, the fortress of old,
A hundred ships all told
Did the son of Atreus send,
Adrastus their admiral, friend by friend
Playing his part that Greece might take
Requital for one who fled from her home
For a foreigner's sake.
And there did the sign of Nestor blaze,—
Nestor of Pylos, the ancient of days,—

Alpheus bull-foot over the foam,
Alpheus the river that runs by his home.

And twelve from Aenia under their lord
Gouneus, and beside them moored
The princes of Elis, whom men call
Epeians, Eurytus ruling all.
Near by on the waters the white oars shone
Of the Taphians with Meges, Phylus' son,
From the jagged islands that sailors dread.

Last Ajax of Salamis closed the ring,
Facing the right on the far left wing
With twelve trim vessels close-set.
All this we learnt as we scanned the fleet,
Too great for the foreigner's rafts to meet.
None could escape it if once they met!
So mighty the armament we eyed
Ourselves, and then we remember beside
All we have heard of the men.

IV. Lines 391–395.

That oath to Tyndarus was sworn by men
Mad with desire. Hope is their goddess now,
Stronger than you and all your strength. So take them,
Lead them to war. The fools will follow you,
Fools, for the gods discern what oaths are wicked
Forced upon men through their own foolishness.

V. Lines 508–510.

Lust and ambition mar a brother's bond.
Bitter the kinship grows and ill to bear.

VI. Lines 635–637.

O, let me put my arms about your neck,
Let me run first and look into your eyes,
My father! Blame me not!

VII. Line 741.

All that a maid should have when she is wed.

VIII. Lines 804–809.

Things go not even here beside the strait.
Some of our host are bachelors and leave
Their houses empty: some have wife and child,
So fierce a lust hath seized men for this war
Through some strange spirit. I must claim my rights,
Let others speak for what concerns themselves.

IX. Lines 922–925.

Such men are wise and keep their judgment straight
All their lives long. For if at times 'tis sweet
To let thought go, judgment is still our need.

X. Lines 952–969.

Else savage Sipylos shall be the land
Whence we must choose the generals for our wars
And Phthia's name no more be heard by men.
Bitter shall be the water and the barley
For prophet Calchas. What's a prophet worth?
His lies are many: should he once speak truth,
It is by chance, and, should he fail, he flies.
I speak not of my marriage: maids enough
Woo me, pursue me, but Agamemnon's deed
Is insult here. He should have asked my leave
Before he took my name to lure the girl.
'Twas that above all else wrought on the queen
To bring her daughter. I would have yielded her
Unto all Hellas, if in truth there were
No other way to Troy, nor withstood
My comrades' need and their great enterprise.
But I am flouted by our leaders now.
Valour and slackness are all one to them.

XI. Line 1114.

For Artemis, dark founts of spirting blood.

XII. Line 1139.

Mindless the man's mind as he shows it here.

XIII. Lines 1409, 1410.

Fighting the gods no more, who master you,
You have learnt to see the right and what must be.

XIV. Lines 1532–1629. Epilogue.

(*Enter a* MESSENGER)

MESSENGER
Daughter of Tyndarus, Clytemnestra, Queen,
Come from the tent and listen to my tidings.

CLYTEMNESTRA
I hear your voice and come, but come in dread,
Trembling and shattered, fearful of more woe
And I have woes enough.

MESSENGER
My tidings, queen,
Are of your daughter, strange and marvellous.

CLYTEMNESTRA
O, tell me, tell me! Make no more delay!

MESSENGER
Dear mistress. I will tell you everything
From first to last, unless my tongue should stumble
Through my heart's haste. Soon as we reached the grove
And flowered fields of Artemis the blest
Where lay the host, bringing the maid with us,
Straightway they flocked about us. And the king,
Seeing his daughter coming for her death,
Groaned bitterly and turned his head away
Holding his cloak to hide the falling tears.
But she came up and stood beside him, saying,
"My father, I am here, to give my life
Willingly for my country, for our Greece.
Now lead me to the altar of the goddess
And sacrifice me as the seer bids.
For me, I pray now for your victory
And safe return unto our native land.
Therefore let no man lay a hand on me.
I will stand quietly; I will not flinch."
Such were her words and all the army wondered

At her great heart. And then the herald rose,
Stood in the midst, calling aloud for silence
And Calchas took the golden basket up,
Laying the sharp sword naked in the barley,
And crowned the maiden. Then Achilles came,
Lifted the basket, sprinkling all the shrine,
And made libation, crying, "Artemis,
Daughter of Zeus and huntress, queen of shades,
Guiding the light in darkness, now receive
The victim that we soldiers bring to thee,
The Achaean army and their lord and king,
This unstained body of a perfect maid.
And may there be no failing of the fleet:
Send us to Troy and let us take the town."
He spoke and all the host stood motionless,
Their eyes fixed on the ground. And the priest prayed,
Lifting the knife and gazing at her neck
To see where he should strike. Then my heart failed me,
I dropped my eyes, when lo, a sudden wonder!
All might have heard the thud, but no man saw
Where the maid vanished. Calchas cried aloud
And all the army, marking a miracle,
Unhoped-for, not to be believed, though seen.
A panting hind lay in the victim's place,
Most beautiful, and deer's blood stained the altar.
Think of the joy for Calchas! He turned and cried,
"Lords of the Argives and this gathered host,
Behold the victim that the goddess chose
For her own altar, a wild doe of the hills.
She will not stain her shrine with generous blood,
Gladly she takes the substitute and grants
Passage to you and swift attack on Troy.
Now let all sailors' hearts be high and now
Go to the ships. For on this very day
We leave the Aulis hollows for the sea
And cross the open waters." Then they burned
The sacrifice to ashes and all prayed
For safe return. The king has sent me here
To tell you of the lot the gods have given
Unto your daughter and her deathless fame.
And I who saw it tell you. She has risen
Straight to the gods. So shall you lay aside
Your grief and all your anger with your lord.

The ways of the gods no mortal can foresee:
They save the souls they love. And this one day
Has known your daughter's death, your daughter's life.

LEADER OF THE CHORUS
O, joy has filled us now we hear these tidings!
Your daughter lives, he tells us, with the gods.

CLYTEMNESTRA
Stolen, my child, by the gods?
What gods?
Where shall I call you?
What shall I say?
An idle story to cheat my sorrow!

LEADER OF THE CHORUS
And here Lord Agamemnon comes himself
To tell you the same tale.
(Enter AGAMEMNON *from the camp)*

AGAMEMNON
Glad may we be,
Wife, for our daughter, she is with the gods.
Now take this youngling steer, and home again.
The army looks to sea. Farewell. From Troy
I will send word. May all go well with you.

CHORUS
Rejoice, O king, go forth in joy,
In joy return to us, bringing rich booty,
Home again from captured Troy.

1. *i.e.*, Paris.
2. A later tradition made Odysseus the son of Sisyphus. Allusion to this origin is always for the purpose of disparaging him.
3. Leda, to whom, according to the legend, Zeus came in the form of a swan, gave birth to Helen and the Dioscuri.
4. Euripides frequently has his characters express such sentiments as this concerning the gods.
5. These lines foreshadow the fate which ultimately awaits Agamemnon, according to the tradition.
6. This whole scene may be compared with those parts of the *Hecuba* which are concerned with Polyxena.

XVIII
RHESUS

CHARACTERS IN THE PLAY

HECTOR, *Prince of Ilion and General of the Trojan Armies*
AENEAS, *a Trojan Prince*
DOLON, *a Trojan*
PARIS, *also called* ALEXANDER, *brother of* HECTOR
RHESUS, *King of Thrace, son of the River Strymon and the* MUSE OF
    THE MOUNTAINS
A THRACIAN, *the King's Charioteer*
ODYSSEUS, *a Greek chieftain, famous for craft and daring*
DIOMEDES, *a Greek chieftain, famous for valour*
A SHEPHERD

The Goddess ATHENA
The MUSE OF THE MOUNTAINS

CHORUS *of Trojan Guards with their* LEADER
Some THRACIANS *with their* CAPTAIN, *Attendants, etc.*

INTRODUCTION

As GILBERT MURRAY has remarked,[1] the *Rhesus* has had the misfortune to become a literary problem. Neither its date nor its authorship is certain, and opinions on these questions among scholars are widely divergent. Some believe it to be a consciously archaistic work of an unknown poet of the fourth century B.C., while others would place its date somewhere in the middle of the fifth century, while still others declare that it is a genuine but early work of Euripides. Murray, the present translator, espouses this latter view, on the basis of several rather compelling arguments. On the whole, Murray's theory seems sound, though it must be said that the great majority of critics have not held the play to be genuine.

The *Rhesus* is a dramatization of the so-called *Doloneia*, that is, the tenth book of the *Iliad*. As such it presupposes a certain acquaintance with the epic as a whole, and in a sense a reading of the *Iliad* would constitute the best introduction to this play. In fact, it proves to be a very absorbing task to compare the *Doloneia* point for point with the *Rhesus*, in order to discover those features in the former which the dramatist has altered because of the exigencies of his form. It is profitable to note likewise the additions which he has made with the result that the play has become a self-sufficient dramatic entity, with more than a merely episodic significance.

In the *Iliad*, before the tenth book, the Trojans under the leadership of Hector have gained a definite advantage. Because of his quarrel with Agamemnon, Achilles has withdrawn from the fight, and the Greeks are consequently hard-pressed. They have built a wall and ditch before their ships, which are drawn up on the shore, in order the better to resist the Trojans who are now definitely on the offensive. At the end of the eighth book, the Trojans have bivouacked on the field of battle, ready to renew the attack on the following morning. In the ninth book, the Greeks send an embassy to Achilles which attempts unsuccessfully to persuade him to rejoin the fighting. The tenth book records how Odysseus and Diomedes

[1] Murray makes this point in the introduction to the separate edition of his translation. This introduction is particularly valuable because it contains an admirable summary of the whole "*Rhesus* question."

349

set out during this night to spy on the Trojan camp, how Dolon was sent out simultaneously by Hector to spy on the Greeks, how the two Greek heroes captured and slew Dolon, went on to kill the recently arrived Thracian king, Rhesus, and successfully raided his camp.

The *Rhesus* presents dramatically these episodes, and as a result the play is filled with swift action and tense excitement. The Chorus does not figure largely in the play, and the odes are not particularly noteworthy, except in one or two instances, such as the lovely short lyric on the nightingale. Most critics complain that the character-drawing in the play is faulty. In some respects, this may be true, but one cannot fail to be impressed by the portrait of Hector, the conscientious, over-anxious leader, whose "wit" Aeneas does not scruple to impugn, who is eager to press the military advantage which his troops now hold. The tension of the moment makes him upbraid Rhesus upon the latter's arrival for not having brought aid sooner, and at the same time betrays him into a lack of caution which is in some ways responsible for the catastrophe to the Thracian king. At the very end of the play we are strongly drawn towards Hector, for though he says confidently that victory is in store for him, we feel he believes in his heart that, no matter what he does, defeat alone is ahead. Our attention is likewise held by the presentation of Rhesus' fate, which comes into sharp dramatic focus in the extraordinary scene when his mother, the Muse, appears and laments the death of her warrior son whose body she holds in her arms. Both this scene and the full characterization of Hector make the play more than a mere drama of war and action. Hence it seems far better to conclude that the *Rhesus* contains within it the essence of tragedy.

RHESUS

(SCENE:—*It is a cloudy but moonlight night on the plain before Troy.
The Trojans and their allies have won a decisive victory and are camping
on the open field close to the Greek outposts. The scene is in front of a rude
tent or hut that has been set up for* HECTOR, *the Trojan leader. A watch-
fire burns low in front. Far off at the back can be seen rows of watch-fires
in the Greek camp. The road to Troy is in front to the left; the road to
Mount Ida leads far away to the right.*

*All is silence; then a noise outside. Enter tumultuously a band of
Trojan Pickets.*)

VARIOUS VOICES
[*The dash — in these passages indicates a new speaker.*]

On to the Prince's quarters!—Ho!
Who is awake? What man-at-arms,
Or squire or groom?—Let Hector know
    New rumour of alarms
From sentinels who stand at mark
The four long watches of the dark,
While others sleep.—Uplift thine head,
O Hector! On thine elbow rise,
Unhood the eagle of thine eyes,
    Up from thy leaf-strewn bed!—

Lord Hector!

HECTOR (*coming out from the tent*)
    Who goes there? Who cries?
A friend? The watchword! . . . By what right
Do men come prowling in the night
Across my quarters? Come! Speak out.

LEADER
A picket, Lord.

351

HECTOR
In such a rout?

LEADER
Be not afraid, Lord.

HECTOR
I am not.
Is there an ambush? No? Then what,
In God's name, brings you from your post
    With no clear tale to speak,
To spread this turmoil through a host
That lies in harness—do ye all
Know nothing?—out against the wall
    And gateways of the Greek?

CHORUS (*various voices confusedly chanting*)

strophe

To arms! To arms, Lord Hector!—Send
    First where the allied armies lie,
Bid them draw sword and make an end
    Of sleep.—Let someone fly
And get the horses' armour on!—
Who goes with me to Panthoos' son?—
Who's for Sarpedon and the Lycians?—None
    Hath seen the priest go by?—
Ho, Captain of the Runners, ho!—
Ho, Trojans of the hornèd bow!
    String, string! For need is nigh.

HECTOR
Ha, silence there! . . .
                        First words of fear,
    Then comfort. All an empty swell!
It seems the lash of trembling Pan
Hath caught you. Speak, if speak ye can.
What tidings? Not a word is clear
    Of the whole tale ye tell.

(*The turmoil subsides, the* LEADER *comes forward.*)

LEADER

antistrophe

Great beacons in the Argive line
    Have burned, my chief, through half the night.

The shipyard timbers seemed to shine.
　Then, clear against the light,
Toward Agamemnon's tent the whole
Army in tumult seemed to roll,
As stirred by some strange voice, shoal after shoal.
　A night of such discord
Was never seen. And we, in dread
Watch such things boded, turned and sped
　Hither; dost blame us, Lord?

　　　HECTOR (*after a moment of thought*)
No! Welcome, friend, with all thy tale of fear!
It shows they mean to fly: they mean to clear
Decks in the dark and so delude my sight . . .
I like that beacon-burning in the night.

　O Zeus above, who checked my conquering way,
Who baulked the hungry lion of his prey
Or ever I could sweep my country clear
Of these despoilers, dost thou hate my spear?
Had but the sun's bright arrows failed me not,
I ne'er had rested till the ships were hot
With fire, and through the tents upon the plain
This bloody hand had passed and passed again!
Myself, I longed to try the battle-cast
By night, and use God's vantage to the last,
But sage and prophet, learned in the way
Of seercraft, bade me wait for dawn of day,
And then—leave no Greek living in the land.
They wait not, they, for what my prophets planned
So sagely. In the dark a runaway
Beats a pursuer.
　　　　　Through our whole array
Send runners! Bid them shake off sleep and wait
Ready with shield and spear. 'Tis not too late
To catch them as they climb on board, and slash
Their crouching shoulders till the gangways splash
With blood, or teach them, fettered leg and arm,
To dig the stiff clods of some Trojan farm.

　　　　　　LEADER
My Prince, thy words run fast. Nor thou nor I
Have knowledge yet that the Greeks mean to fly.

HECTOR

Whaι makes them light their beacons? Tell me, what?

LEADER

God knows! And, for my part, I like it not.

HECTOR

What, feared? Thou wouldst be feared of everything!

LEADER

They never lit such light before, O King.

HECTOR

They never fled, man, in such wild dismay.

LEADER (*yielding*)

'Twas all thy work.—Judge thou, and we obey.

HECTOR

My word is simple. Arm and face the foe.
(*A sound of marching without*)

LEADER

Who comes? Aeneas, and in haste, as though
Fraught with some sudden tiding of the night.
(*Enter* AENEAS)

AENEAS

Hector, what means it? Watchers in affright
Who gather shouting at thy doors, and then
Hold midnight council, shaking all our men?

HECTOR

To arms, Aeneas! Arm from head to heel!

AENEAS

What is it? Tidings? Doth the Argive steal
Some march, some ambush in the day's eclipse?

HECTOR

'Tis flight, man! They are marching to the ships.

AENEAS

How know'st thou?—Have we proof that it is flight?

HECTOR

They aι e burning beacon-fires the livelong night.
They never mean to wait till dawn. Behind

That screen of light they are climbing in the blind
Dark to their ships—unmooring from our coast.

AENEAS
(*looking towards the distant fires: after a pause*)
God guide them!—Why then do you arm the host?

HECTOR
I mean to lame them in their climbing, I
And my good spear, and break them as they fly.
Black shame it were, and folly worse than shame,
To let these spoilers go the road they came
Unpunished, when God gives them to us here.

AENEAS
Brother, I would thy wit were like thy spear!
But Nature wills not one man should be wise
In all things; each must seek his separate prize.
And thine is battle pure. There comes this word
Of beacons, on the touch thy soul is stirred:
"They fly! Out horse and chariots!"—Out withal
Past stake and trench, while night hangs like a pall!
Say, when we cross that coiling depth of dyke,
We find the foe not fled, but turned to strike;
One check there, and all hope of good return
Is gone. How can our men, returning, learn
The tricks of the palisade? The chariots how
Keep to the bridges on the trenches' brow,
Save with jammed wheels and broken axles? Aye,
And say thou conquer: other wars yet lie
Before thee. Peleus' son, for all his ire,
Will never let thee touch the ships with fire
Or pounce on his Greek lambs. The man will bide
No wrong and standeth on a tower of pride.
    Nay, brother, let the army, head on shield,
Sleep off its long day's labour in the field:
Then, send a spy; find someone who will dare
Creep to yon Argive camp. Then, if 'tis clear
They mean flight, on and smite them as they fly.
Else, if the beacons hide some strategy,
The spy will read it out, and we can call
A council.—Thus speak I, my general.

CHORUS (*singing*)

strophe

'Tis good! 'Tis wisdom! Prince, give heed
And change the word thy passion gave.
No soldier loveth, in his need,
The glory of a chief too brave.
A spy is best: a spy, to learn
For what strange work those beacons burn
All night beside the guarded wave.

HECTOR

Ye all so wish it?—Well, ye conquer me.
(*to* AENEAS)
Go thou and calm the allies. There will be
Some stir among them, hearing of these high
And midnight councils.—I will seek the spy
To send to the Greek camp. If there we learn
Of some plot hatching, on the man's return
I straight will call thee and share counsels. So.
But wait attentive. If he says they go
Shipward and plan to escape, one trumpet call
Shall warn thee, and I wait no more, but fall
On camp and hulls, or ever dawn can rise.

AENEAS

Aye, haste and send him. Now thy plans are wise,
And when need comes I am with thee, sword by sword.
(*Exit* AENEAS)

HECTOR

(*turning to the Guards and other Soldiers*)
Ye gathered Trojans, sharers of my word,
Who dares to creep through the Greek lines alone?
Who will so help his fatherland?
Doth none
Offer? Must I do everything, one hand
Alone, to save our allies and our land?
(*A lean dark man pushes forward from the back.*)

DOLON

I, Prince!—I offer for our City's sake
To go disguised to the Greek ships, to make
Their counsels mine, and here bring word to thee.
If that be thy full service, I agree.

HECTOR

Dolon the Wolf! A wise wolf and a true!
Thy father's house was praised when first I knew
Troy: this shall raise it twofold in our eyes.

DOLON

'Tis wise to do good work, but also wise
To pay the worker. Aye, and fair reward
Makes twofold pleasure, though the work be hard.

HECTOR

So be it: an honest rule. Do thou lay down
What guerdon likes thee best—short of my crown.

DOLON

I care not for thy crowned and care-fraught life.

HECTOR

Wouldst have a daughter of the King to wife?

DOLON

I seek no mate that might look down on me.

HECTOR

Good gold is ready, if that tempteth thee.

DOLON

We live at ease and have no care for gold.

HECTOR

Well, Troy hath other treasures manifold.

DOLON

Pay me not now, but when the Greeks are ta'en.

HECTOR

The Greeks! . . . Choose any save the Atreidae twain.

DOLON

Kill both, an it please thee. I make prayer for none.

HECTOR

Thou wilt not ask for Ajax, Ileus' son?

DOLON

A princely hand is skill-less at the plough.

HECTOR

'Tis ransom, then? . . . What prisoner cravest thou?

DOLON

I said before, of gold we have our fill.

HECTOR

For spoils and armour . . . thou shalt chose at will.

DOLON

Nail them for trophies on some temple wall.

HECTOR

What seeks the man? What prize more rich than all?

DOLON

Achilles' horses! [1]

(*Murmurs of surprise*)

Yes, I need a great
Prize. I am dicing for my life with Fate.

HECTOR

'Fore God, I am thy rival, if thy love
Lies there. Undying was the breed thereof,
And these shall never die, who bear to war
Great Peleus' son, swift gleaming like a star.
Poseidon, rider of the wild sea-drift,
Tamed them, men say, and gave them for his gift
To Peleus.—None the less, since I have stirred
Hopes, I will baulk them not. I pledge my word,
Achilles' steeds, a rare prize, shall be thine.

DOLON

I thank thee.—'Tis indeed a prize more fine
Than all in Troy.—Grudge me not that; there be
Guerdons abundant for a Prince like thee.

(*Exit* HECTOR)

CHORUS (*singing*)

antistrophe

O peril strange, O fearful prize!
Yet win it and thy life hath wings:
A deed of glory in men's eyes,
A greatness, to be wooed of kings.
If God but hearken to the right,

Thou drinkest to the full this night
The cup of man's imaginings.

DOLON

(*He stands waiting a moment looking out into the dark.*)
There lies the way.—But first I must go find
At home some body-shelter to my mind;
Then, forward to the ships of Argolis!

LEADER

What other raiment wilt thou need than this?

DOLON

A garb for work, for night; a thieving guise.

LEADER

'Tis good to learn the wisdoms of the wise.
What will thy wrapping be?

DOLON

A grey wolf's hide
Shall wrap my body close on either side;
My head shall be the mask of gleaming teeth,
My arms fit in the forepaws, like a sheath,
My thighs in the hinder parts. No Greek shall tell
'Tis not a wolf that walks, half visible,
On four feet by the trenches and around
The ship-screen. When it comes to empty groun
It stands on two.—That is the plan, my friend!

LEADER

Now Maian Hermes guide thee to thy end
And home safe! Well he loves all counterfeit . . .
Good work is there; may good luck go with it!

DOLON

(*to himself, gazing out towards the Greek camp*)
There, and then back! . . . And on this belt shall bleed
Odysseus' head—or why not Diomede?—
To prove my truth. Ere dawn can touch the land
I shall be here, and blood upon my hand.

(*Exit* DOLON)

CHORUS (*singing*)
Thymbraean, Delian, Birth divine,
That walkest Lycia's inmost shrine,

Come, strong to guard, to guide, to follow,
　　Come, bow in hand and girt with night,
To help thy Dardans as of old,
When stone by stone thy music rolled—
　　O conquering Strength, O Sire Apollo!—
　　Young Ilion into towers of light.[3]

Grant that he reach the shipyard, creep
Keen-eyed through all that host asleep,
　　Then back to home and hearth, yet living,
　　Where now his father prays alone:
Yea, grant that, when the Greeks are slain,
Our wolf shall mount with scourge and rein
　　Those coursers of the sea-god's giving,
　　　　Whom Peleus drove in days foregone.

Alone in those Greek ships to stake
His life, for home and country's sake:
　　'Tis wondrous! Few be hearts so true
When seas across the bulwark break,
　　And sunlight sickens o'er the crew.
Ah, Phrygia still hath hearts of rock!
The Phrygian spear flies fast and far!
Where shall ye find the fool to mock
　　　　Our works in war?

Whom will he stab a-sleeping, whom,
The quick grey wolf, the crawling doom?
　　Grant that he slay the Spartan! Nay,
Or Agamemnon's head and plume
　　To Helen bear at dawn of day!
A lightsome dawn to hear her wail
Her brother sworn, her King who came
　　To Ilion with his thousand sail,
　　　　And swords, and flame!

(*As the song ends* Dolon *reappears, in the disguise of a
wolf. The Guards gather round him, bidding him god-
speed as he crawls off in the dark towards the Greek
camp. Meantime from the direction of Mount Ida has
entered a* Shepherd *who goes to* Hector's *door and
calls. The Guards seeing him return to their places.*)

SHEPHERD

Ho, Master!

(*Enter* HECTOR *from tent*)

I would it ofttimes were my luck to share
As goodly news with thee as now I bear.

HECTOR

What dulness hangs about these shepherds! Block,
Com'st thou to us with tidings of thy flock
Here in the field in arms? Who wants thee here?
Thou know'st my house; thou know'st my father's. There
Tell all about thy lucky lambs.—Now go.

SHEPHERD

Dull wits, we shepherds! Ay, 'twas alway so.
Yet still, there is some good news to be told.

HECTOR

A truce there to thy gossip of the fold!
Our dealings are of war, of sword and spear.

(*He turns to go.*)

SHEPHERD

Aye; so were mine. That is what brought me here.

(HECTOR's *manner changes.*)

A chief comes yonder, leading a great band
Of spears, with help to thee and all the land.

HECTOR

From whence? How do his name and lineage run?

SHEPHERD

He comes from Thrace, the River Strymon's son.

HECTOR

Rhesus! Not Rhesus, here on Trojan soil?

SHEPHERD

Thou hast guessed. That eases me of half my toil.

HECTOR

What makes he there towards Ida? All astray
Thus from the plain and the broad waggon-way!

SHEPHERD

I know not rightly, though one well may guess.
'Tis hard to land at night, with such a press

Of spears, on a strange coast, where rumours tell
Of foes through all the plain-land. We that dwell
On Ida, in the rock, Troy's ancient root
And hearth-stone, were well frighted, through the mute
And wolfish thickets thus to hear him break.
A great and rushing noise those Thracians make,
Marching. We, all astonied, ran to drive
Our sheep to the upmost heights. 'Twas some Argive,
We thought, who came to sweep the mountain clear
And waste thy folds; till suddenly our ear
Caught at their speech, and knew 'twas nothing Greek.
Then all our terror fled. I ran to seek
Some scout or pioneer who led the van
And called in Thracian: "Ho, what child of man
Doth lead you? From what nation do ye bring
This host with aid to Ilion and her king?"
     He told me what I sought, and there I stood
Watching; and saw one gleaming like a God,
Tall in the darkness on a Thracian car.
A plate of red gold mated, like a bar,
His coursers' necks, white, white as fallen snow.
A carven targe, with golden shapes aglow,
Hung o'er his back. Before each courser's head
A Gorgon, to the frontlet riveted,
With bells set round—like stories that they tell
Of Pallas' shield—made music terrible.
The numbers of that host no pen could write
Nor reckon; 'tis a multitudinous sight,
Long lines of horsemen, lines of targeteers,
Archers abundant; and behind them veers
A wavering horde, light-armed, in Thracian weed.
     A friend is come to Ilion in her need
'Gainst whom no Argive, let him fly or stand,
Shall aught avail nor 'scape his conquering hand.

LEADER
Lo, when the Gods breathe gently o'er a town,
All runs to good, as water-streams run down.

HECTOR (*bitterly*)
Aye, when my spear hath fortune, when God sends
His favour, I shall find abundant friends.
I need them not; who never came of yore
To help us, when we rolled to death before

The war-swell, and the wind had ripped our sail.
Then Rhesus taught us Trojans what avail
His words are.—He comes early to the feast;
Where was he when the hunters met the beast?
Where, when we sank beneath the Argive spear?

LEADER

Well may'st thou mock and blame thy friend. Yet here
He comes with help for Troy. Accept him thou.

HECTOR

We are enough, who have held the wall till now.

LEADER

Master, dost think already that our foe
Is ta'en?

HECTOR

I do. To-morrow's light will show.

LEADER

Have care. Fate often flings a backward cast.

HECTOR

I hate the help that comes when need is past. . . .
Howbeit, once come, I bid him welcome here
As guest—not war-friend; guest to share our cheer.
The thanks are lost, he might have won from us.

LEADER

My general, to reject an ally thus
Must needs make hatred.

SHEPHERD
                    The mere sight of those
I saw would sure cast fear upon our foes.

HECTOR (*yielding reluctantly, with a laugh*)
Ah, well; thy words are prudent; and (*to* SHEPHERD) thine eyes
See glorious things. With all these panoplies
Of gold that filled our Shepherd's heart with joy,
Bid Rhesus welcome, as war-friend to Troy.
(*Exit* SHEPHERD; HECTOR *returns to his tent, amid the joy of
the soldiers.*)

CHORUS (*singing*)
Now Adrasteia be near and guard
Our lips from sin, lest the end be hard!
But he cometh, he cometh, the Child of the River!
The pride of my heart it shall roll unbarred.

We carved thy coming; yea, need was strong
In the Hall of thy lovers, O child of Song;
Thy mother the Muse and her fair-bridged River
They held thee from us so long, so long!

By Strymon's torrent alone she sang,
And Strymon shivered and coiled and sprang;
And her arms went wide to the wild sweet water,
And the love of the River around her rang.

We hail thee, Fruit of the River's seed,
Young Zeus of the Dawn, on thy starry steed!
O ancient City, O Ida's daughter,
Is God the Deliverer found indeed?

And men shall tell of thee, Ilion mine,
Once more a-harping at day's decline,
'Mid laughing of lovers and lays and dances
And challenge on challenge of circling wine?

When the Greek is smitten that day shall be,
And fled to Argolis over the sea:
O mighty of hand, O leader of lances,
Smite him, and heaven be good to thee!

Thou Rider golden and swift and sheer,
Achilles falters: appear! appear!
The car like flame where the red shield leapeth,
The fell white steeds and the burning spear!

No Greek shall boast he hath seen thy face
And danced again in the dancing place;
And the land shall laugh for the sheaves she reapeth,
Of spoilers dead by a sword from Thrace.

(*Enter* RHESUS *in dazzling white armour, followed by his
Charioteer and Attendants. The Charioteer carries his*

golden shield. The CHORUS *break into a shout of "All Hail!"*)

LEADER

All hail, great King! A whelp indeed
    Is born in Thracia's lion fold,
Whose leap shall make strong cities bleed.
    Behold his body girt with gold,
And hark the pride of bells along
    The frontlet of that targe's hold.

CHORUS

A God, O Troy, a God and more!
'Tis Ares' self, this issue strong
Of Strymon and the Muse of song,
    Whose breath is fragrant on thy shore!
                                        (*Re-enter* HECTOR)

RHESUS

Lord Hector, Prince of Ilion, noble son
Of noble sires, all hail! Long years have run
Since last we greeted, and 'tis joy this day
To see thy fortunes firm and thine array
Camped at the foe's gate. Here am I to tame
That foe for thee, and wrap his ships in flame.

HECTOR

Thou child of Music and the Thracian flood,
Strymonian Rhesus, truth is alway good
In Hector's eyes. I wear no double heart.
    Long, long ago thou shouldst have borne thy part
In Ilion's labours, not have left us here,
For all thy help, to sink beneath the spear.
Why didst thou—not for lack of need made plain!—
Not come, not send, not think of us again?
What grave ambassadors prayed not before
Thy throne, what herald knelt not at thy door?
What pride of gifts did Troy not send to thee?
And thou, a lord of Barbary even as we,
Thou, brother of our blood, like one at sup
Who quaffs his fill and flings away the cup,
Hast flung to the Greeks my city! Yet, long since,
'Twas I that found thee but a little prince
And made thee mighty, I and this right hand;

When round Pangaion and the Paion's land,
Front against front, I burst upon the brood
Of Thrace and broke their targes, and subdued
Their power to thine. The grace whereof, not small,
Thou hast spurned, and when thy kinsmen, drowning, call,
Comest too late. Thou! Others there have been
These long years, not by nature of our kin . . .
Some under yon rough barrows thou canst see
Lie buried; they were true to Troy and me;
And others, yet here in the shielded line
Or mid the chariots, parching in the shine
Of noonday, starving in the winds that bite
Through Ilion's winter, still endure and fight
On at my side. 'Twas not their way, to lie
On a soft couch and, while the cups go by,
Pledge my good health, like thee, in Thracian wine.

　　I speak as a free man. With thee and thine
Hector is wroth, and tells thee to thy face.

RHESUS

Thy way is mine, friend. Straight I run my race
In word and deed, and bear no double tongue.

　　I tell thee, more than thine my heart was wrung,
Yea, angered past all durance, thus to stay
Back from thy battles. 'Twas a folk that lay
Hard on my borders, Scythians of the north;
Just when my host for Troy had started forth,
They fell upon our homes. I had reached the coast
Of the Friendless Sea [4] and purposed to have crossed
My Thracians there. We turned; and all that plain
Is trampled in a mire of Scythian slain
Ploughed by our spears, and blood of Thrace withal
Not stinted. This it was that drowned thy call
For help and held me back from Ilion's need.
I broke their power; the princes of their breed
I took to hostage, made their elders swear
To bring my house due tribute, year by year,
Then, never lagging, crossed the Pontus mouth,
Marched by long stages through Bithynia south
And here am come . . . not drunken with the feast,
As thou wouldst have me be, not lulled to rest
In golden chambers. In this harness hard
I have borne my nights of winter storm that starred

The Euxine into ice and scared the strong
Paeonians.
    Long I have been, but not too long
To save thee yet. Friend, this is the tenth year
Thou labourest on unceasing, with no clear
Vantage; day creeps by day, and Ares throws
The same red dice for thee and for thy foes.
Now, hear my vow. Before one day's eclipse
I swear to break their wall, to burn their ships
And slay their princes. On the second day
I leave this soil and take my homeward way,
Thy pains relieved. No Trojan of the land
Need move, nor turn the buckler in his hand.
Alone my late-comers will turn the tide
And smite your Greeks, for all their bitter pride.

CHORUS (*singing*)
(*The Trojan soldiers, who have been listening with delight, here
  break out in irrepressible applause.*)
  All hail!
  Sweet words and faithful heart!
  Only may Zeus avert
From those proud lips the Wrath that none may bear!
  Never a galleon bore,
  Now, nor in days of yore,
Prince like to thee, so valiant and so fair.
  How shall Achilles, how
  Shall Ajax bear him now,
Or face thy lance? May I but stand that day
  Watching to see him reel
  Broken beneath thy steel,
And once in blood his many murders pay!

RHESUS
Yea, more atonement thou shalt take from me
For this slow help.—May Adrasteia see
My heart and pardon!—When we two have set
Troy free from these who compass her with hate,
Soon as the Gods have had their first-fruits, I
With thee will sail—so help me Zeus on high!—
And sack all Hellas with the sword, till these
Doers of deeds shall know what suffering is.

HECTOR

By heaven, could I once see this peril rolled
Past us, and live in Ilion as of old,
Untrembling, I would thank my gods! To seek
Argos and sack the cities of the Greek—
'Twere not such light work as thou fanciest.

RHESUS

These Greeks that face thee, are they not their best?

HECTOR

We seek not better. These do all we need.

RHESUS

When these are beaten, then, we have done the deed.

HECTOR

Lose not thy path watching a distant view.

RHESUS

Thou seem'st content to suffer, not to do?

HECTOR

I have a kingdom large by mine own right. . . .

What station will best please thee in this fight
To ground the targe and stablish thine array?
Right, left, or midmost in the allies? Say.

RHESUS

'Twould please me best to fight these Greeks alone.
Yet, if 'twould irk thine honour not to have thrown
One firebrand on the ships with me, why, then
Set us to face Achilles and his men.

HECTOR

Achilles? Nay, his spear ye cannot meet.

RHESUS

How so? Fame said he sailed here with the fleet.

HECTOR

He sailed, and he is here. But some despite
'Gainst the great King now keeps him from the fight.

RHESUS

Who next to him hath honour in their host?

HECTOR

Next, to my seeming, Ajax hath the most,
Or Diomede.—But Odysseus is a tough
And subtle fox, and brave; aye, brave enough.
No man of them hath harmed us more than he.
He climbed here to Athena's sanctuary
One night and stole her image clean away
To the Argive ships. Yes, and another day,
Guised as a wandering priest, in rags, he came
And walked straight through the Gates, made loud acclaim
Of curses on the Greek, spied out alone
All that he sought in Ilion, and was gone—
Gone, and the watch and helpers of the Gate
Dead! And in every ambush they have set
By the old Altar, close to Troy, we know
He sits—a murderous reptile of a foe! [5]

RHESUS

No brave man seeks so dastardly to harm
His battle-foes; he meets them arm to arm.
This Greek of thine, this sitter like a thief
In ambush, I will make of him my chief
Care. I will take him living, drive a straight
Stake through him, and so star him at the Gate
To feed your wide-winged vultures. 'Tis the death
Most meet for a lewd thief, who pillageth
God's sanctuary, or so we hold in Thrace.

HECTOR (*making no answer*)

Seek first some sleep. There still remains a space
Of darkness.—I will show the spot that best
May suit you, somewhat sundered from the rest.
Should need arise, the password of the night
Is Phoebus: see your Thracians have it right.
                    (*Turning to the Guards before he goes*)
Advance beyond your stations, men, at some
Distance, and stay on watch till Dolon come
With word of the Argives' counsel. If his vow
Prosper, he should be nearing us by now.
(*Exeunt* HECTOR *and* RHESUS *and Attendants. The Guards, who
    have been below, come forward sleepily from the camp fire,
    and sit watching by* HECTOR'S *tent.*)

CHORUS

Say, whose is the watch? Who exchanges
  With us? The first planets to rise
Are setting; the Pleiades seven
Move low on the margin of heaven,
And the Eagle is risen and ranges
  The mid-vault of the skies.

ANOTHER

No sleeping yet! Up from your couches
  And watch on, the sluggards ye are!
The moon-maiden's lamp is yet burning.

THIRD GUARD

Oh, the morning is near us, the morning!
Even now his fore-runner approaches,
  Yon dim-shining star.

DIVERS GUARDS (*talking*)

Who drew the first night-watch?

ANOTHER

                            'Twas one
Koroibos, called the Mygdon's Son.

THE GUARD

And after?

THE OTHER

            The Mount Taurus men
Had second watch: from them again
The Mysians took it. We came then.

A GUARD

'Tis surely time. Who will go tell
The fifth watch? 'Tis the Lycians' spell
By now; 'twas thus the portions fell.

ANOTHER

Nay, hearken! Again she is crying
  Where death-laden Simois falls,
Of the face of dead Itys that stunned her,
Of grief grown to music and wonder:
Most changeful and old and undying
  The nightingale calls.

ANOTHER

And on Ida the shepherds are waking
  Their flocks for the upland. I hear
The skirl of a pipe very distant.

ANOTHER

And sleep, it falls slow and insistent.
'Tis perilous sweet when the breaking
    Of dawn is so near.

DIVERS GUARDS (*talking*)

Why have we still no word nor sign
Of that scout in the Argive line?

ANOTHER

I know not; he is long delayed.

ANOTHER

God send he trip not on the blade
Of some Greek in an ambuscade!

ANOTHER

It may be. I am half afraid.

LEADER

Our time is past! Up, men, and tell
The fifth watch. 'Tis the Lycians' spell
Now, as the portions fairly fell.

(*The Guards pass out to waken the Lycians. The stage is
    empty and dark except for the firelight, when a whis-
    per is heard at the back. Presently enter* ODYSSEUS
    and DIOMEDE *in dull leather armour,* DIOMEDE *carry-·
    ing at his belt* DOLON'S *wolf-skin and mask.*) [6]

ODYSSEUS

Diomede, hist!—A little sound of arms
Clanking . . . or am I full of void alarms?

DIOMEDE

No. 'Tis some horse tied to the chariot rail
That clanks his chain.—My heart began to fail
A moment, till I heard the horse's champ.
(*They steal on further, keeping in the shadow.*)

ODYSSEUS

Mind—in that shade—the watchers of the camp.

DIOMEDE

I keep in shadow, but I am staring hard.

ODYSSEUS

Thou know'st the watchword, if we stir some guard?

DIOMEDE

Phoebus. 'Twas the last sign that Dolon gave.
(*They creep forward in silence to the entrance of* HECTOR'S *tent.*)

ODYSSEUS

Now, forward!
　　　　(*They dash into the tent, swords drawn; then return.*)
　　　　God! All empty as the grave!

DIOMEDE

Yet Dolon told us Hector's couch was made
Just here. For none but him I drew this blade.

ODYSSEUS

What means it? To some ambush is he gone?

DIOMEDE

Maybe, to work some craft on us at dawn.

ODYSSEUS

He is hot with courage when he is winning, hot.

DIOMEDE

What must we do, Odysseus?—He was not
Laid where we thought him, and our hopes are lost.

ODYSSEUS

Back to our own ship-rampart at all cost!
The God who gave him victory saves him still.
We cannot force Fortune against her will.

DIOMEDE

Could we not find Aeneas? Or the bed
Of Paris the accurst, and have his head?

ODYSSEUS

Go by night searching through these lines of men
For chiefs to kill? 'Twere death and death again.

DIOMEDE

But to go empty back—what shame 'twill be!—
And not one blow struck home at the enemy!

ODYSSEUS

How not one blow? Did we not baulk and kill
Dolon, their spy, and bear his tokens still?
Dost think the whole camp should be thine to quell?
(DIOMEDE *takes* DOLON's *wolf-mask off his belt and hangs it in*
HECTOR's *tent, then turns.*) [7]

DIOMEDE

Good. Now for home! And may the end be well!
(*As they turn there appears at the back a luminous and gigantic
shape, the Goddess* ATHENA.)

ATHENA

What make ye, from these sleepers thus to part
Desponding and with sorrow-wounded heart
If Hector be not granted you to slay
Nor Paris? Little know ye what great stay
Of help is found for Troy. This very night
Rhesus is come; who, if he see the light
Of morning, not Achilles nor the rack
Of Ajax' spear hath power to hold him back,
Ere wall and gate be shattered and inside
Your camp a spear-swept causeway builded wide
To where beached galleys flame above the dead.
Him slay, and all is won. Let Hector's head
Sleep where it lies and draw unvexèd breath;
Another's work, not thine, is Hector's death.

ODYSSEUS

Most high Athena, well I know the sound
Of that immortal voice. 'Tis ever found
My helper in great perils.—Where doth lie
Rhesus, mid all this host of Barbary?

ATHENA

Full near he lies, not mingled with the host
Of Troy, but here beyond the lines—a post
Of quiet till the dawn, that Hector found.
And near him, by his Thracian chariot bound,
Two snow-white coursers gleam against the wan
Moon, like the white wing of a river swan.

Their master slain, take these to thine own hearth,
A wondrous spoil; there hides not upon earth
A chariot-team of war so swift and fair.

ODYSSEUS
Say, Diomede, wilt make the men thy share,
Or catch the steeds and leave the fight to me?

DIOMEDE
I take the killing, thou the stablery:
It needs keen wit and a neat hand. The post
A man should take is where he helpeth most.

ATHENA
Behold, 'tis Paris, hasting there towards
This tent. Methinks he knoweth from the guard
Some noise of prowling Argives hither blown.

DIOMEDE
Comes he alone or with his guards?

ATHENA
                        Alone;
Toward Hector's quarters, as I deem, he plies
His message. He hath heard some tale of spies.

DIOMEDE
Then he shall be the first dead Trojan!

ATHENA
                        No;
Beyond the ordainèd end thou canst not go.
Fate hath not willed that Paris by thy deed
Shall die; it is another who must bleed
To-night. Therefore be swift!
                    (*Exeunt* ODYSSEUS *and* DIOMEDE)
                        For me, my guise
Shall melt and change in Alexander's eyes,
Yea, till he dream 'tis Cypris, his delight
And help in need, that meets him in the night,
And soft shall be my words to him I hate.
So speak I; but on whom my spell is set
He hears not, sees not, though so near I stand.
(*She becomes invisible where she stands. Enter* PARIS)

PARIS

Ho, Hector! Brother! General of the land!
Sleepest thou still? We need thy waking sight.
Our guards have marked some prowler of the night,
We know not if a mere thief or a spy.

(ATHENA *becomes visible again, but seems changed and her voice
    softer.*)

ATHENA

Have comfort thou! Doth not the Cyprian's eye
Mark all thy peril and keep watch above
Thy battles? How shall I forget the love
I owe thee, and thy faithful offices?
To crown this day and all its victories,
Lo, I have guided here to Troy a strong
Helper, the scion of the Muse of song
And Strymon's flood, the crownèd stream of Thrace.

PARIS (*standing like one in a dream*)

Indeed thy love is steadfast, and thy grace
Bounteous to Troy and me. Thou art the joy
And jewel of my days, which I to Troy
Have brought, and made thee hers.—O Cyprian,
I heard, not clearly,—'twas some talk that ran
Among the pickets—spies had passed some spot
Close by the camp. The men who saw them not
Talk much, and they who saw, or might have seen,
Can give no sign nor token. It had been
My purpose to find Hector where he lay.

ATHENA

Fear nothing. All is well in Troy's array.
Hector is gone to help those Thracians sleep.

PARIS

Thy word doth rule me, Goddess. Yea, so deep
My trust is, that all thought of fear is lost
In comfort, and I turn me to my post.

ATHENA

Go. And remember that thy fortunes still
Are watched by me, and they who do my will
Prosper in all their ways. Aye, thou shalt prove
Ere long, if I can care for those I love.

(*Exit* PARIS; *she raises her voice.*)

Back, back, ye twain! Are ye in love with death?
Laertes' son, thy sword into the sheath!
Our golden Thracian gaspeth in his blood;
The steeds are ours; the foe hath understood
And crowds against you. Haste ye! haste to fly,—
Ere yet the lightning falleth, and ye die!

(ATHENA *vanishes; a noise of tumult is heard. Enter a crowd of
Thracians running in confusion, in the midst of them* ODYS-
SEUS *and* DIOMEDE.)

VOICES (*amid the tumult*)
Ha! Ha!—At them! At them! After them! Down with them!—Where
are they?

CAPTAIN
Who is that fellow? Look! That yonder!

A MAN
Rascal thieves, the sort that crawl
And vex an army in the dark!

CAPTAIN
Ho, this way! Follow! This way all!
(*They pursue* ODYSSEUS *and* DIOMEDE; *catch them and bring them
back.*)

A MAN
I have them! I have caught them!

CAPTAIN (*to* ODYSSEUS)
Whence comest thou? What art thou? Say; what captain and what company?

ODYSSEUS (*indignantly*)
'Tis not for thee to know. This day thou diest for thy knavery!

CAPTAIN
Stop! Give the watchword quick, before I have thy body on my pike.

ODYSSEUS (*in a tone of authority*)
Halt every man and have no fear!

CAPTAIN
Come, gather round. Be quick to strike.

ODYSSEUS (*to* CAPTAIN)
Twas thou that killed King Rhesus'

CAPTAIN
No: 'tis I that kill the man that killed . . .
(*Flies at* ODYSSEUS, *but other men hold him back.*)

ODYSSEUS

Hold back all!

VOICES
No more holding back!

ODYSSEUS (*as they attack him*)
What, strike an ally in the field?

CAPTAIN

Then give the watchword!

ODYSSEUS
Phoebus.

CAPTAIN
Right. Ho, every man hold back his spear!—
Then know'st thou where the men are gone?

ODYSSEUS
We saw them running, somewhere here.
(*He makes off into the darkness.* DIOMEDE *follows, and some* THRACIANS.)

CAPTAIN

Off every one upon their track!

A MAN
Or should we rouse the army?

CAPTAIN
No;
To stir the allies in the night and make more panic! Let us go.
(*The* THRACIANS *go off in pursuit. Meantime the original Guards who
form the* CHORUS *have hastened back. The two Greeks are presently
seen crossing at the back in a different direction.*)

CHORUS (*chanting*)
Who was the man that passed?
Who, that, so madly bold,
Even as I held him fast,
Laughed, and I loosed my hold?
Where shall I find him now?
What shall I deem of him,

To steal thro' the guards a-row,
Quaking not, eye nor limb,
On thro' the starlight dim?
Is he of Thessaly,
Born by the Locrian sea,
Or harvester of some starved island's corn?
What man hath seen his face?
What was his name or race,
What the high God by whom his sires have sworn?

DIVERS GUARDS (*talking*)
This night must be Odysseus' work, or whose?—
Odysseus? Aye, to judge by ancient use.—
Odysseus surely!—That is thy belief?—
What else? It seems he hath no fear
Of such as we!—Whom praise ye there?
Whose prowess? Say!—Odysseus.—Nay,
Praise not the secret stabbing of a thief!

CHORUS (*chanting*)
He came once, of old,
Up thro' the city throng,
Foam on his lips, a-cold,
Huddled in rags that hung
Covering just the sword
Hid in his mantle's pleat;
His face grimed and scored,
A priest of wandering feet,
Who begged his bread in the street.
Many and evil things
He cast on the brother kings
Like one long hurt, who nurseth anger sore;
Would that a curse, yea, would
The uttermost wrath of God
Had held those feet from walking Ilion's shore!

DIVERS GUARDS (*talking*)
Odysseus or another, 'tis the guard
Will weep for this. Aye, Hector will be hard.—
What will he say?—He will suspect.—Suspect?
What evil? What should make you fear?—
'Twas we that left a passage clear.—
A passage?—Yea, for these men's way,
Who came by night into the lines unchecked.

(*A sound of moaning outside in the darkness, which has been heard during the last few lines, now grows into articulate words.*)

VOICE

Woe, woe!
The burden of the wrath of fate!

GUARDS

Ha, listen! Wait.
Crouch on the ground; it may be yet
Our man is drawing to the net.

VOICE

Woe, woe!
The burden of the hills of Thrace!

LEADER

An ally? None of Hellene race.

VOICE

Woe, woe!
Yea, woe to me and woe to thee,
My master! Once to set thine eye
On Ilion the accurst, and die!

LEADER (*calling aloud*)

Ho there! What ally passes? The dim night
Blurreth mine eyes; I cannot see thee right.

VOICE

Ho, some one of the Trojan name!
Where sleeps your king beneath his shield,
Hector? What marshal of the field
Will hear our tale . . . the men who came
And struck us and were gone; and we,
We woke and there was nought to see,
        But our own misery.

LEADER

I cannot hear him right; it sounds as if
The Thracians were surprised or in some grief.
(*There enters a wounded man, walking with difficulty; he is the* THRACIAN, *the Charioteer who came with* RHESUS.)

THRACIAN

The army lost and the king slain,
Stabbed in the dark! Ah, pain! pain!
This deep raw wound . . . Oh, let me die
By thy side, Master, by thy side!
In shame together let us lie
Who came to save, and failed and died.

LEADER

This needs no surmise: 'tis disaster plain
That comes. He speaketh of some ally slain.

THRACIAN

Disaster, yea: and with disaster shame,
Which lights Disaster to a twofold flame
Of evil. For to die in soldier's wise,
Since die we needs must . . . though the man who dies
Hath pain . . . to all his house 'tis praise and pride;
But we, like laggards and like fools we died!
    When Hector's hand had showed us where to rest
And told the watchword, down we lay, oppressed
With weariness of that long march, and slept
Just as we fell. No further watch was kept,
Our arms not laid beside us; by the horse
No yoke nor harness ordered. Hector's force
Had victory, so my master heard, and lay
Secure, just waiting for the dawn of day
To attack. So thought we all, and our lines broke
And slept. After a little time I woke,
Thinking about my horses, that the morn
Must see them yoked for war. I found the corn
And gave them plenteously. Then in the deep
Shadow I saw two men who seemed to creep
Close by our line, but swiftly, as I stirred,
Crouched and were seeking to make off unheard.
I shouted then, and bade them keep away:
Two thieves, I thought, from the great host that lay
Round us. They never answered, and, for me,
I said no more but turned and presently
Was sleeping. In my sleep there came a dream.
I seemed to see the horses—mine own team
I had trained long since and drove at Rhesus' side—
But wolves were on their backs, wolves, couched astride,

Who drove and scourged; I saw the horses rear
And stagger with wide nostrils, stiff with fear,
And, starting up to drive the beasts away,
I woke.—A terror of great darkness lay
About me, but I lifted up my head
And listened. There was moaning, like the dead
That moan at night, and over me there flowed,
So soft, so warm—it was my master's blood,
Who writhed beside me, dying! With a bound
I sprang up, empty-handed, groping round
For spear or sword, when, lo, a young strong man
Was close to me and slashed, and the sword ran
Deep through my flank. I felt its passage well,
So deep, so wide, so spreading . . . then I fell.
And they, they got the bridles in their hand
And fled . . . Ah! Ah! This pain. I cannot stand.
(*The Guards catch him as he reels, and lay him on the ground.*)
I know, I saw, thus much. But why or how
Those dead men went to death I cannot know,
Nor by whose work. But this I say; God send
'Tis not foul wrong wrought on us by a friend.

LEADER
Good charioteer of that ill-fortuned king,
Suspect us not. 'Tis Greeks have done this thing.
But yonder Hector comes. He hath been shown
The foul deed, and thy sorrows are his own.
(*Enter* HECTOR *in wrath, with a band of Guards*)

HECTOR
Ye workers of amazement! Have your eyes
No sight? Ye watch and let these Argive spies
Pass—and our friends are butchered in their sleep—
And then pass back unwounded, laughing deep
Amid the galleys at the news they bring
Of Trojan sluggards and the fool their king?
Great God, ye never baulked them as they came,
Nor smote them as they went!
                              (*His eye falls on the* CAPTAIN.)
                              Who bears the blame
Of this but thou? Thou wast the watcher set
To guard this host till morn. I tell thee yet
For this deed—I have sworn by Zeus our Lord!—
The scourge of torment or the headsman's sword

Awaits thee. Else, be Hector in your thought
Writ down a babbler and a man of nought.

LEADER (*grovelling before* HECTOR)
Woe, woe! It was for thee, only for thee,
I must have gone, O Help and Majesty,
That time with message that the fires were burning.
Mine eye was keen; I swear by Simois river,
It never drooped nor slumbered, never, never,
        From eve till morning!
My master, verily, I am innocent utterly,
Build not such wrath against me, Lord, nor harden
    Thy heart; let Time be judge; and if in deed
    Or word I have offended, let me bleed!
Bury me here alive! I ask no pardon.
(HECTOR *is standing over him ready to strike when the Chari-
    oteer speaks.*)

THRACIAN
Why threaten them? Art thou a Greek to blind
My barbarous wit so nimbly, in a wind
Of words? This work was thine. And no man's head
Is asked by us, the wounded and the dead,
Save thine. It needs more play, and better feigned,
To hide from me that thou hast slain thy friend
By craft, to steal his horses.—That is why
He stabs his friends. He prays them earnestly,
Prays them to come; they came and they are dead.
A cleaner man was Paris, when he fled
With his host's wife. He was no murderer.

    Profess not thou that any Greek was there
To fall on us. What Greek could pass the screen
Of Trojan posts in front of us, unseen?
Thyself was stationed there, and all thy men.
What man of yours was slain or wounded when
Your Greek spies came? Not one; 'tis we, behind,
Are wounded, and some worse than wounded, blind
Forever to the sunlight. When we seek
Our vengeance, we shall go not to the Greek.
What stranger in that darkness could have trod
Straight to where Rhesus lay—unless some God
Pointed his path? They knew not, whispered not,
Rhesus had ever come. . . . 'Tis all a plot.

HECTOR (*steadied and courteous again*)
Good allies I have had since first the Greek
Set foot in Troy, and never heard them speak
Complaint of Hector. Thou wilt be the first.
I have not, by God's mercy, such a thirst
For horses as to murder for their sake.

(*He turns to his own men.*)
Odysseus! Yet again Odysseus! Take
All the Greek armies, is there one but he
Could have devised, or dared, this devilry?
I fear him; yea, fear in mine own despite,
Lest Dolon may have crossed him in the night
And perished; 'tis so long he cometh not.

THRACIAN
I know not who Odysseus is, nor what.
I know it was no Greek that wounded us.

HECTOR
To think thus pleasures thee? Well, have it thus.

THRACIAN
Home, home! To die at home and rest my head!

HECTOR
Nay, die not, friend. We have enough of dead.

THRACIAN
How can I live? Lost, and my master slain.

HECTOR
My house will shelter thee and heal thy pain.

THRACIAN
Thy house? Will murderers' nursing give me peace?

HECTOR
Still the same tale! This man will never cease.

THRACIAN
My curse rest—not on Hector, but on those
Who stabbed us, as thou say'st.—Ah, Justice knows!

HECTOR
There, lift him.—Bear him to my house. Take pains,
If care can do it, that the man complains

No more of Troy.—Ye others, bear withal
To Priam and the Elders of the Wall
My charge, that, where the cart-road from the plain
Branches, they make due burial for our slain.

(*One party of Guards lifts carefully the wounded* THRACIAN *and
goes off bearing him: another departs with the message to
Troy.*)

CHORUS (*chanting*)
Back from the heights of happiness,
Back, back, to labour and distress
Some god that is not ours doth lead
Troy and her sons; He sows the seed,
    Who knows the reaping?

(*In the air at the back there appears a Vision of the* MUSE
    holding the body of her dead son RHESUS.)
            Ah! Ah!
My king, what cometh? There appears
Some Spirit, like a mist of tears;
And in her arms a man lieth,
So young, so wearied unto death;
To see such vision presageth
        Wrath and great weeping.

(*The Guards hide their heads in their mantles.*)

MUSE
Nay, look your fill, ye Trojans. It is I,
The many-sistered Muse, of worship high
In wise men's hearts, who come to mourn mine own
Most pitifully loved, most injured, son,
For whose shed blood Odysseus yet shall pay
Vengeance, who crawled and stabbed him where he lay.

With a dirge of the Thracian mountains,
    I mourn for thee, O my son.
For a mother's weeping, for a galley's launching, for the way to
    Troy;
A sad going, and watched by spirits of evil.
His mother chid him to stay, but he rose and went.
His father besought him to stay, but he went in anger.
    Ah, woe is me for thee, thou dear face,
        My belovèd and my son!

LEADER

Goddess, if tears for such as thee may run
In our low eyes, I weep for thy dead son.

MUSE

I say to thee: Curse Odysseus,
  And cursèd be Diomede!
For they made me childless, and forlorn for ever, of the flower of
  sons.
Yea, curse Helen, who left the houses of Hellas.
She knew her lover, she feared not the ships and sea.
She called thee, called thee, to die for the sake of Paris,
  Belovèd, and a thousand cities
    She made empty of good men.
O conquered Thamyris, is this thy bane
Returned from death to pierce my heart again?
Thy pride it was, and bitter challenge cast
'Gainst all the Muses, did my flesh abase
To bearing of this Child, what time I passed
Through the deep stream and looked on Strymon's face,
And felt his great arms clasp me, when to old
Pangaion and the earth of hoarded gold
We Sisters came with lutes and psalteries,
Provoked to meet in bitter strife of song
That mountain wizard, and made dark the eyes
Of Thamyris, who wrought sweet music wrong.
I bore thee, Child; and then, in shame before
My sisterhood, my dear virginity,
I stood again upon thy Father's shore
And cast thee to the deeps of him; and he
Received and to no mortal nursing gave
His child, but to the Maidens of the Wave.
And well they nursed thee, and a king thou wast
And first of Thrace in war; yea, far and near
Through thine own hills thy bloody chariot passed,
Thy battered helm flashed, and I had no fear;
Only to Troy I charged thee not to go:
I knew the fated end: but Hector's cry,
Borne overseas by embassies of woe,
Called thee to battle for thy friends and die.

And thou, Athena—nothing was the deed
Odysseus wrought this night nor Diomede—

'Tis thine, all thine; dream not thy cruel hand
Is hid from me! Yet ever on thy land
The Muse hath smiled; we gave it praise above
All cities, yea, fulfilled it with our love.
The light of thy great Mysteries was shed
By Orpheus, very cousin of this dead
Whom thou hast slain; and thine high citizen
Musaeus, wisest of the tribes of men,
We and Apollo guided all his way:
For which long love behold the gift ye pay!
I wreathe him in my arms; I wail his wrong
Alone, and ask no other mourner's song.

(*She weeps over* RHESUS.)

LEADER

Hector, thou hearest. We were guiltless here,
And falsely spake that Thracian charioteer.

HECTOR

Always I knew it. Had we any need
Of seers to tell this was Odysseus' deed?
   For me, what could I else, when I beheld
The hosts of Argos camped upon this field,
What but with prayers and heralds bid my friend
Come forth and fight for Ilion ere the end?
He owed me that.—Yet, now my friend is slain,
His sorrow is my sorrow. On this plain
I will uplift a wondrous sepulchre,
And burn about it gifts beyond compare
Of robes and frankincense. To Troy's relief
He came in love and parteth in great grief.

MUSE

My son shall not be laid in any grave
Of darkness; thus much guerdon will I crave
Of Death's eternal bride, the heavenly-born
Maid of Demeter, Life of fruits and corn,
To set this one soul free. She owes me yet,
For Orpheus widowed, an abiding debt.
   To me he still must be—that know I well—
As one in death, who sees not. Where I dwell
He must not come, nor see his mother's face.
Alone for ever, in a caverned place
Of silver-veinèd earth, hid from men's sight,

A Man yet Spirit, he shall live in light:
As under far Pangaion Orpheus lies,
Priest of great light and worshipped of the wise.
  Howbeit an easier anguish even to me
Falls than to Thetis in her azure sea;
For her son too shall die; and sorrowing,
First on the hills our band for thee shall sing,
Then for Achilles by the weeping wave.
Pallas could murder thee, but shall not save
Thy foe; too swift Apollo's bolt shall fly.
  O fleshly loves of sad mortality,
O bitter motherhood of these that die,
She that hath wisdom will endure her doom,
The days of emptiness, the fruitless womb;
Not love, not bear love's children to the tomb.
(*The* Vision *rises through the air and vanishes.*)

LEADER

The dead man sleepeth in his mother's care;
But we who battle still—behold, the glare
Of dawn that rises. Doth thy purpose hold,
Hector, our arms are ready as of old.

HECTOR

March on; and bid the allies with all speed
Be armed, bind fast the yoke upon the steed,
Then wait with torches burning, till we sound
The Tuscan trump.—This day we shall confound,
God tells me, their Greek phalanx, break their high
Rampart and fire the galleys where they lie.
               (*Pointing to the dawn*)
Yon first red arrow of the Sun, that brings
The dawn to Troy, hath freedom on his wings.

(*During the following lines* Hector *goes to his tent to get his
shield, and as he enters sees* Dolon's *bloody wolf-skin hanging. He takes it, looks at it, and throws it down without a
word.[8] Then he puts on his helmet, takes his shield and spear,
and follows the Guards as they march off.*)

CHORUS (*singing*)
The Chief hath spoken: let his will
  Be law, ye Trojans.—Raise the cry
To Arms! To Arms! and down the line

Of allies pass the battle-sign.
The God of Ilion liveth still;
And men may conquer ere they die.

(Exeunt)

1. These horses were particularly famous. Cf. especially the end of Book XVI of the *Iliad;* also the end of Book XIX.

2. This stage direction, as well as some others in the play, is conjectural, as Murray indicates in his notes. Hence they all should be regarded as means employed by the translator to sharpen his interpretation of the dramatic action.

3. The reference is to the part Apollo played according to the legend in building the walls of Troy.

4. *i.e.,* the Euxine or the Black Sea. Murray is evidently taking the etymological meaning of Euxine, which is friendly or hospitable, to be a euphemism.

5. Hector is alluding to various exploits performed by Odysseus earlier in the war. Cf., *e.g., Odyssey,* Book IV, lines 242 ff., and Book XIV, lines 468 ff.

6. Cf. note 2. Murray gives plausible reasons in his notes for supposing that Odysseus and Diomedes bring in the wolf-skin taken from Dolon, and leave it in Hector's tent.

7. Cf. notes 2 and 6.

8. Cf. notes 2 and 6.

XIX
THE CYCLOPS

Characters in the Play

Silenus, *old servant of the* Cyclops
Chorus of Satyrs
Odysseus
The Cyclops
Companions of Odysseus

INTRODUCTION

The Cyclops, for the date of which there is no available information, is very significant for the history of Greek drama because it is the only complete satyr-play which is now extant. From it therefore we can reasonably infer what was expected of the tragic poet in his fourth play, when he submitted a tetralogy in the dramatic competitions. The satyr-play apparently had to be considerably lighter in tone than the tragedy, and yet not be completely divorced from the tragic context. Hence it seems to occupy a kind of middle ground between tragedy and straight comedy. As such it served not only to test the creative virtuosity of the tragic poet, but also to provide in its presentation welcome relief to an audience which had just witnessed three tragedies in succession.

Like the *Rhesus, The Cyclops* is a dramatization of an episode from the epic. In this play, Euripides presents the familiar story of Odysseus' adventures with the Cyclops, Polyphemus, which is found in the ninth book of the *Odyssey*. The playwright has not departed from his epic source to any great extent. He has, to be sure, added a Chorus of Satyrs and the character Silenus, whom he presents as enslaved in the service of the Cyclops. From these additions Euripides is able to derive much of the humour in his play. Odysseus himself proves to be the butt of some very amusing satire, while the scene in which the Cyclops becomes drunk is excellent broad comedy. Polyphemus fortunately engages in his cannibal activity off-stage, and hence this phase of the play cannot be taken too seriously. The incident, however, illustrates nicely the difference between the satyr-play and comedy, for it is easy to see that the Cyclops story as subject-matter would be definitely inappropriate to the latter medium. If Euripides' piece is a typical satyr-play, we can readily understand the part which this form was expected to play in the Greek dramatic festivals.

393

THE CYCLOPS

(SCENE:—*Before the great cave of the* CYCLOPS *at the foot of Mount Aetna.* SILENUS *enters. He has a rake with him, with which he cleans up the ground in front of the cave as he soliloquizes.*)

SILENUS

O BROMIUS, unnumbered are the toils I bear because of thee, no less now than when I was young and hale; first, when thou wert driven mad by Hera and didst leave the mountain nymphs, thy nurses; next, when in battle with earth-born spearmen I stood beside thee on the right as squire, and slew Enceladus, smiting him full in the middle of his targe with my spear. Come, though, let me see; must I confess 'twas all a dream? No, by Zeus! since I really showed his spoils to the Bacchic god. And now am I enduring to the full a toil still worse than those. For when Hera sent forth a race of Tyrrhene pirates against thee, that thou mightest be smuggled far away, I, as soon as the news reached me, sailed in quest of thee with my children; and, taking the helm myself, I stood on the end of the stern and steered our trim craft; and my sons, sitting at the oars, made the grey billows froth and foam as they sought thee, my liege. But just as we had come nigh Malea in our course, an east wind blew upon the ship and drove us hither to the rock of Aetna, where in lonely caverns dwell the one-eyed children of ocean's god, the murdering Cyclopes. Captured by one of them we are slaves in his house; Polyphemus they call him whom we serve; and instead of Bacchic revelry we are herding a godless Cyclops's flocks; and so it is my children, striplings as they are, tend the young thereof on the edge of the downs; while my appointed task is to stay here and fill the troughs and sweep out the cave, or wait upon the ungodly Cyclops at his impious feasts. His orders now compel obedience; I have to scrape out his house with the rake you see, so as to receive the Cyclops, my absent master, and his sheep in clean caverns.

But already I see my children driving their browsing flocks towards me.

What means this? is the beat of feet in the Sicinnis dance the same to

395

you now as when ye attended the Bacchic god in his revelries and made
your way with dainty steps to the music of lyres to the halls of Althaea?

(*The* Chorus of Satyrs *enters, driving a flock of goats and sheep. Servants follow them.*)

Chorus (singing)

strophe

Offspring of well-bred sires and dams, pray whither wilt thou be
gone from me to the rocks? Hast thou not here a gentle breeze, and
grass to browse, and water from the eddying stream set near the cave
in troughs? and are not thy young ones bleating for thee? Pst! pst!
wilt thou not browse here, here on the dewy slope? Ho! ho! ere long
will I cast a stone at thee. Away, away! O horned one, to the fold-
keeper of the Cyclops, the country-ranging shepherd.

antistrophe

Loosen thy bursting udder; welcome to thy teats the kids, whom
thou leavest in the lambkins' pens. Those little bleating kids, asleep
the livelong day, miss thee; wilt then leave at last the rich grass pastures on the peaks of Aetna and enter the fold? . . .

epode

Here we have no Bromian god; no dances here, or Bacchantes
thyrsus-bearing; no roll of drums, or drops of sparkling wine by
gurgling founts; nor is it now with Nymphs in Nysa I sing a song of
Bacchus, Bacchus! to the queen of love, in quest of whom I once sped
on with Bacchantes, white of foot. Dear friend, dear Bacchic god,
whither art roaming alone, waving thy auburn locks, while I, thy
minister, do service to the one-eyed Cyclops, a slave and wanderer I,
clad in this wretched goat-skin dress, severed from thy love?

Silenus

Hush, children! and bid our servants fold the flocks in the rock-roofed
cavern.

Leader of the Chorus (to Servants)

Away! (*To* Silenus) But prithee, why such haste, father?

Silenus

I see the hull of a ship from Hellas at the shore, and men, that wield the
oar, on their way to this cave with some chieftain. About their necks they
carry empty vessels and pitchers for water; they are in want of food.
Luckless strangers! who can they be? They know not what manner of
man our master Polyphemus is, to have set foot here in his cheerless abode

and come to the jaws of the cannibal Cyclops in an evil hour. But hold ye your peace, that we may inquire whence they come to the peak of Sicilian Aetna.

(ODYSSEUS *and his companions enter. They carry baskets for provisions and water jars.*)

ODYSSEUS

Pray tell us, sirs, of some river-spring whence we might draw a draught to slake our thirst, or of someone willing to sell victuals to mariners in need.

Why, what is this? We seem to have chanced upon a city of the Bromian god; here by the caves I see a group of Satyrs. To the eldest first I bid "All hail!"

SILENUS

All hail, sir! tell me who thou art, and name thy country.

ODYSSEUS

Odysseus of Ithaca, king of the Cephallenians' land.

SILENUS

I know him for a prating knave, one of Sisyphus' shrewd offspring.[1]

ODYSSEUS

I am the man; abuse me not.

SILENUS

Whence hast thou sailed hither to Sicily?

ODYSSEUS

From Ilium and the toils of Troy.

SILENUS

How was that? didst thou not know the passage to thy native land?

ODYSSEUS

Tempestuous winds drove me hither against my will.

SILENUS

God wot! thou art in the same plight as I am.

ODYSSEUS

Why, wert thou too drifted hither against thy will?

SILENUS

I was, as I pursued the pirates who carried Bromius off.

ODYSSEUS
What land is this and who are its inhabitants?

SILENUS
This is mount Aetna, the highest point in Sicily.

ODYSSEUS
But where are the city-walls and ramparts?

SILENUS
There are none; the headlands, sir, are void of men.

ODYSSEUS
Who then possess the land? the race of wild creatures?

SILENUS
The Cyclopes, who have caves, not roofed houses.

ODYSSEUS
Obedient unto whom? or is the power in the people's hands?

SILENUS
They are rovers; no man obeys another in anything.

ODYSSEUS
Do they sow Demeter's grain, or on what do they live?

SILENUS
On milk and cheese and flesh of sheep.

ODYSSEUS
Have they the drink of Bromius, the juice of the vine?

SILENUS
No indeed! and thus it is a joyless land they dwell in.

ODYSSEUS
Are they hospitable and reverent towards strangers?

SILENUS
Strangers, they say, supply the daintiest meat.

ODYSSEUS
What, do they delight in killing men and eating them?

SILENUS
No one has ever arrived here without being butchered.

ODYSSEUS

Where is the Cyclops himself? inside his dwelling?

SILENUS

He is gone hunting wild beasts with hounds on Aetna.

ODYSSEUS

Dost know then what to do, that we may be gone from the land?

SILENUS

Not I, Odysseus; but I would do anything for thee.

ODYSSEUS

Sell us food, of which we are in need.

SILENUS

There is nothing but flesh, as I said.

ODYSSEUS

Well, even that is a pleasant preventive of hunger.

SILENUS

And there is cheese curdled with fig-juice, and the milk of kine.

ODYSSEUS

Bring them out; a man should see his purchases.

SILENUS

But tell me, how much gold wilt thou give me in exchange?

ODYSSEUS

No gold bring I, but Dionysus' drink.

SILENUS (*joyfully*)

Most welcome words! I have long been wanting that.

ODYSSEUS

Yes, it was Maron, the god's son, who gave me a draught.

SILENUS

What! Maron whom once I dandled in these arms?

ODYSSEUS

The son of the Bacchic god, that thou mayst learn more certainly.

SILENUS

Is it inside the ship, or hast thou it with thee?

ODYSSEUS

This, as thou seest, is the skin that holds it, old sir.

SILENUS

Why, that would not give me so much as a mouthful.

ODYSSEUS

This, and twice as much again as will run from the skin.

SILENUS

Fair the rill thou speakest of, delicious to me.

ODYSSEUS

Shall I let thee taste the wine unmixed, to start with?

SILENUS

A reasonable offer; for of a truth a taste invites the purchase.

ODYSSEUS

Well, I haul about a cup as well as the skin.

SILENUS

Come, let it gurgle in, that I may revive my memory by a pull at it.

ODYSSEUS (*pouring*)

There then!

SILENUS (*smelling it*)

Ye gods! what a delicious scent it has!

ODYSSEUS

What! didst thou see it?

SILENUS

No, i' faith, but I smell it.

ODYSSEUS

Taste it then, that thy approval may not stop at words.

SILENUS (*taking a drink*)

Zounds! Bacchus is inviting me to dance; ha! ha!

ODYSSEUS

Did it not gurgle finely down thy throttle?

SILENUS

Aye that it did, to the ends of my fingers.

ODYSSEUS

Well, we will give thee money besides.

SILENUS

Only undo the skin, and never mind the money.

ODYSSEUS

Bring out the cheeses then and lambs.

SILENUS

I will do so, with small thought of any master. For let me have a single cup of that and I would turn madman, giving in exchange for it the flocks of every Cyclops and then throwing myself into the sea from the Leucadian rock, once I have been well drunk and smoothed out my wrinkled brow. For if a man rejoice not in his drinking, he is mad; for in drinking it's possible for this to stand up straight, and then to fondle breasts, and to caress well tended locks, and there is dancing withal, and oblivion of woe. Shall not I then purchase so rare a drink, bidding the senseless Cyclops and his central eye go hang?

(SILENUS *goes into the cave.*)

LEADER

Hearken, Odysseus, let us hold some converse with thee.

ODYSSEUS

Well, do so; ours is a meeting of friends.

LEADER

Did you take Troy and capture the famous Helen?

ODYSSEUS

Aye, and we destroyed the whole family of Priam.

LEADER

After capturing your blooming prize, were all of you in turn her lovers? for she likes variety in husbands; the traitress! the sight of a man with embroidered breeches on his legs and a golden chain about his neck so fluttered her, that she left Menelaus, her excellent little husband. Would there had never been a race of women born into the world at all, unless it were for me alone!

SILENUS (*reappearing with food*)

Lo! I bring you fat food from the flocks, king Odysseus, the young of bleating sheep and cheeses of curdled milk without stint. Carry them away with you and begone from the cave at once, after giving me a drink of merry grape-juice in exchange.

LEADER

Alack! yonder comes the Cyclops; what shall we do?

ODYSSEUS

Then truly are we lost, old sir! whither must we fly?

SILENUS

Inside this rock, for there ye may conceal yourselves.

ODYSSEUS

Dangerous advice of thine, to run into the net!

SILENUS

No danger; there are ways of escape in plenty in the rock.

ODYSSEUS

No, never that; for surely Troy will groan and loudly too, if we flee
from a single man, when I have oft withstood with my shield a countless
host of Phrygians. Nay, if die we must, we will die a noble death; or, if
we live, we will maintain our old renown at least with credit.

(*The* CYCLOPS *enters as* SILENUS *goes into the cave. The* CYCLOPS, *not
noticing* ODYSSEUS *and his companions, addresses the* CHORUS *in
anger.*)

CYCLOPS

A light here! hold it up! what is this? what means this idleness, your
Bacchic revelry? Here have we no Dionysus, nor clash of brass, nor roll
of drums. Pray, how is it with my newly-born lambs in the caves? are
they at the teat, running close to the side of their dams? Is the full amount
of milk for cheeses milked out in baskets of rushes? How now? what say
you? One of ye will soon be shedding tears from the weight of my club;
look up, not down.

LEADER

There! my head is bent back till I see Zeus himself; I behold both the
stars and Orion.

CYCLOPS

Is my breakfast quite ready?

LEADER

'Tis laid; be thy throat only ready.

CYCLOPS

Are the bowls too full of milk?

LEADER

Aye, so that thou canst swill off a whole hogshead, so it please thee.

CYCLOPS

Sheep's milk or cows' milk or a mixture of both?

LEADER

Whichever thou wilt; don't swallow me, that's all.

CYCLOPS

Not I; for you would start kicking in the pit of my stomach and kill me by your antics. (*Catching sight of* ODYSSEUS *and his followers*) Ha! what is this crowd I see near the folds? Some pirates or robbers have put in here. (SILENUS *comes out of the cave. He has made himself appear as though he had just suffered a terrible beating.*) Yes, I really see the lambs from my caves tied up there with twisted osiers, cheese-presses scattered about, and old Silenus with his bald pate all swollen with blows.

SILENUS

Oh! oh! poor wretch that I am, pounded to a fever.

CYCLOPS

By whom? who has been pounding thy head, old sirrah?

SILENUS

These are the culprits, Cyclops, all because I refused to let them plunder thee.

CYCLOPS

Did they not know I was a god and sprung from gods?

SILENUS

That was what I told them, but they persisted in plundering thy goods, and, in spite of my efforts, they actually began to eat the cheese and carry off the lambs; and they said they would tie thee in a three-cubit pillory and tear out thy bowels by force at thy navel, and flay thy back thoroughly with the scourge; and then, after binding thee, fling thy carcase down among the benches of their ship to sell to someone for heaving up stones, or else throw thee into a mill.

CYCLOPS

Oh, indeed! Be off then and sharpen my cleavers at once; heap high the faggots and light them; for they shall be slain forthwith and fill this maw of mine, what time I pick my feast hot from the coals, waiting not for carvers, and fish up the rest from the cauldron boiled and sodden; for I have had my fill of mountain-fare and sated myself with banquets of lions and stags, but 'tis long I have been without human flesh.

SILENUS

Truly, master, a change like this is all the sweeter after everyday fare; for just of late there have been no fresh arrivals of strangers at these caves.

ODYSSEUS

Hear the strangers too in turn, Cyclops. We had come near the cave from our ship, wishing to procure provisions by purchase, when this fellow sold us the lambs and handed them over for a stoup of wine to drink himself,—a voluntary act on both sides,—there was no violence employed at all. No, there is not a particle of truth in the story he tells, now that he has been caught selling thy property behind thy back.

SILENUS

I? Perdition catch thee!

ODYSSEUS

If I am lying, yes.

SILENUS (*in agitation*)

O Cyclops, by thy sire Poseidon, by mighty Triton and Nereus, by Calypso and the daughters of Nereus, by the sacred billows and all the race of fishes! I swear to thee, most noble sir, dear little Cyclops, master mine, it is not I who sell thy goods to strangers, else may these children, dearly as I love them, come to an evil end.

LEADER

Keep that for thyself; with my own eyes I saw thee sell the goods to the strangers; and if I lie, perdition catch my sire! but injure not the strangers.

CYCLOPS

Ye lie; for my part I put more faith in him than Rhadamanthus, declaring him more just. But I have some questions to ask. Whence sailed ye, strangers? of what country are you? what city was it nursed your childhood?

ODYSSEUS

We are Ithacans by birth, and have been driven from our course by the winds of the sea on our way from Ilium, after sacking its citadel.

CYCLOPS

Are ye the men who visited on Ilium, that bordereth on Scamander's wave, the rape of Helen, worst of women?

ODYSSEUS

We are; that was the fearful labour we endured.

CYCLOPS

A sorry expedition yours, to have sailed to the land of Phrygia for the sake of one woman!

ODYSSEUS

It was a god's doing; blame not any son of man. But thee do we implore, most noble son of Ocean's god, speaking as free-born men; be not so cruel as to slay thy friends on their coming to thy cave, nor regard us as food for thy jaws, an impious meal; for we preserved thy sire, O king, in possession of his temple-seats deep in the nooks of Hellas; and the sacred port of Taenarus and Malea's furthest coves remain unharmed; and Sunium's rock, the silver-veined, sacred to Zeus-born Athena, still is safe, and Geraestus, the harbour of refuge; and we did not permit Phrygians to put such an intolerable reproach on Hellas. Now in these things thou too hast a share, for thou dwellest in a corner of the land of Hellas beneath Aetna's fire-streaming rock; and although thou turn from arguments, still it is a custom amongst mortal men to receive shipwrecked sailors as their suppliants and show them hospitality and help them with raiment; not that these should fill thy jaws and belly, their limbs transfixed with spits for piercing ox-flesh. The land of Priam hath emptied Hellas quite enough, drinking the blood of many whom the spear laid low, with the ruin it has brought on widowed wives, on aged childless dames, and hoary-headed sires; and if thou roast and consume the remnant,—a meal thou wilt rue,—why, where shall one turn? Nay, be persuaded by me, Cyclops; forego thy ravenous greed and choose piety rather than wickedness; for on many a man ere now unrighteous gains have brought down retribution.

SILENUS

I will give thee a word of advice! as for his flesh, leave not a morsel of it, and if thou eat his tongue, Cyclops, thou wilt become a monstrous clever talker.

CYCLOPS

Wealth, manikin, is the god for the wise; all else is mere vaunting and fine words. Plague take the headlands by the sea, on which my father seats himself! Why hast thou put forward these arguments? I shudder not at Zeus's thunder, nor know I wherein Zeus is a mightier god than I, stranger; what is more, I reck not of him; my reasons hear. When he pours down the rain from above, here in this rock in quarters snug, feasting on roast calf's flesh or some wild game and moistening well my upturned paunch with deep draughts from a tub of milk, I rival the thunder-claps of Zeus with my artillery; and when the north wind blows from Thrace and sheddeth snow, I wrap my carcase in the hides of beasts and light a fire, and what care I for snow? The earth perforce, whether she like it or not, produces grass and fattens my flocks, which I sacrifice to no one save myself and this belly, the greatest of deities; but to the gods, not I! For surely to eat and drink one's fill from day to day and give oneself no grief at all, this is the king of gods for your wise man, but lawgivers go hang, chequering, as they do, the life of man! And so I will not cease from indulging myself by devouring thee; and thou shalt receive this stranger's gift, that I may be free of blame,—fire and my father's element yonder, and a cauldron to hold thy flesh and boil it nicely in collops. So in with you, that ye may feast me well, standing round the altar to honour the cavern's god.

(*The* CYCLOPS *goes into his cave, driving* ODYSSEUS' *men before him.*)

ODYSSEUS

Alas! escaped from the troubles of Troy and the sea, my barque now strands upon the whim and forbidding heart of this savage.

O Pallas, mistress mine, goddess-daughter of Zeus, help me, help me now; for I am come to toils and depths of peril worse than all at Ilium; and thou, O Zeus, the stranger's god, who hast thy dwelling 'mid the radiant stars, behold these things; for, if thou regard them not, in vain art thou esteemed the great god Zeus, though but a thing of naught.

(*He follows the* CYCLOPS *reluctantly.* SILENUS *also goes in.*)

CHORUS (*singing*)

Ope wide the portal of thy gaping throat, Cyclops; for strangers' limbs, both boiled and grilled, are ready from off the coals for thee to gnaw and tear and mince up small, reclining in thy shaggy goat-skin coat.

Relinquish not thy meal for me; keep that boat for thyself alone. Avaunt this cave! avaunt the burnt-offerings, which the godless Cyclops offers on Aetna's altars, exulting in meals on strangers' flesh! Oh! the ruthless monster! to sacrifice his guests at his own hearth, the suppliants of his halls, cleaving and tearing and serving up to his loathsome teeth a feast of human flesh, hot from the coals.

ODYSSEUS (*reappearing with a look of horror*)

O Zeus! what can I say after the hideous sights I have seen inside the cave, things past belief, resembling more the tales men tell than aught they do?

LEADER OF THE CHORUS

What news, Odysseus? has the Cyclops, most godless monster, been feasting on thy dear comrades?

ODYSSEUS

Aye, he singled out a pair, on whom the flesh was fattest and in best condition, and took them up in his hand to weigh.

LEADER

How went it with you then, poor wretch?

ODYSSEUS

When we had entered yonder rocky abode, he lighted first a fire, throwing logs of towering oak upon his spacious hearth, enough for three wagons to carry as their load; next, close by the blazing flame, he placed his couch of pine-boughs laid upon the floor, and filled a bowl of some ten firkins, pouring white milk thereinto, after he had milked his kine; and by his side he put a can of ivy-wood, whose breadth was three cubits and its depth four maybe; next he set his brazen pot a-boiling on the fire, spits too he set beside him, fashioned of the branches of thorn, their points hardened in the fire and the rest of them trimmed with the hatchet, and the blood-bowls of Aetna for the axe's edge. Now when that hell-cook, god-detested, had everything quite ready, he caught up a pair of my companions and proceeded deliberately to cut the throat of one of them over the yawning brazen pot; but the other he clutched by the tendon of his heel, and, striking him against a sharp point of rocky stone, dashed out his brains; then, after hacking the fleshy parts with glutton cleaver, he set to grilling them, but the limbs he threw into his cauldron to seethe. And I, poor wretch, drew near with streaming eyes and waited on the Cyclops; but the others kept cowering like frightened birds in crannies of the rock, and the blood forsook their skin. Anon, when he had gorged himself upon my comrades' flesh and had fallen on his back, breathing heavily, there came a sudden inspiration to me. I filled a cup of this Maronian wine and offered him a draught, saying, "Cyclops, son of Ocean's god, see here what heavenly drink the grapes of Hellas yield, glad gift of Dionysus." He, glutted with his shameless meal, took and drained it at one draught, and, lifting up his hand, he thanked me thus, "Dearest to me of all my guests! fair the drink thou givest me to crown so fair a feast." Now when I saw his delight, I gave him another cup, knowing the wine would make him rue it, and he would soon be paying the penalty. Then he set to singing; but I kept filling bumper after bumper and heating him with drink. So there he is singing discordantly amid the weeping of my fellow-sailors, and the cave re-echoes; but I have made my way out quietly and would fain save thee and myself, if thou wilt. Tell me then, is it your wish, or is it not, to fly from this unsocial wretch and take up your abode with Naiad nymphs in the halls of the Bacchic god? Thy father within approves this scheme; but there! he is powerless, getting all he can out of his liquor; his wings are snared by the cup as if he had flown against bird-lime, and he is fuddled; but thou art young and lusty; so save thyself with my help and regain thy old friend Dionysus, so little like the Cyclops.

LEADER
Best of friends, would we might see that day, escaping the godless Cyclops!

ODYSSEUS
Hear then how I will requite this vile monster and rescue you from thraldom.

LEADER
Tell me how; no note of Asiatic lyre would sound more sweetly in our ears than news of the Cyclops' death.

ODYSSEUS
Delighted with this liquor of the Bacchic god, he fain would go a-revelling with his brethren.

LEADER
I understand; thy purpose is to seize and slay him in the thickets when alone, or push him down a precipice.

ODYSSEUS
Not at all; my plan is fraught with subtlety.

LEADER
What then? Truly we have long heard of thy cleverness.

ODYSSEUS
I mean to keep him from this revel, saying he must not give this drink to his brethren but keep it for himself alone and lead a happy life. Then when he falls asleep, o'ermastered by the Bacchic god, I will put a point with this sword of mine to an olive-branch I saw lying in the cave, and will set it on fire; and when I see it well alight, I will lift the heated brand, and, thrusting it full in the Cyclops' eye, melt out his sight with its blaze; and, as when a man in fitting the timbers of a ship makes his auger spin to and fro with a double strap, so will I make the brand revolve in the eye that gives the Cyclops light and will scorch up the pupil thereof.

LEADER

Ho! ho! how glad I feel! wild with joy at the contrivance!

ODYSSEUS

That done, I will embark thee and those thou lovest with old Silenus in the deep hold of my black ship, my ship with double banks of oars, and carry you away from this land.

LEADER

Well, can I too lay hold of the blinding brand, as though the god's libation had been poured? for I would fain have a share in this offering of blood.

ODYSSEUS

Indeed thou *must*, for the brand is large, and thou must help hold it.

LEADER

How lightly would I lift the load of e'en a hundred wains, if that will help us to grub out the eye of the doomed Cyclops, like a wasp's nest.

ODYSSEUS

Hush! for now thou knowest my plot in full, and when I bid you, obey the author of it; for I am not the man to desert my friends inside the cave and save myself alone. And yet I might escape; I am clear of the cavern's depths already; but no! to desert the friends with whom I journeyed hither and only save myself is not a righteous course.

(*He re-enters the cave.*)

FIRST SEMI-CHORUS (*singing*)

Come, who will be the first and who the next to him upon the list to grip the handle of the brand, and, thrusting it into the Cyclops' eye, gouge out the light thereof?

SECOND SEMI-CHORUS (*singing*)

Hush! hush! Behold the drunkard leaves his rocky home, trolling loud some hideous lay, a clumsy tuneless clown, whom tears await. Come, let us give this boor a lesson in revelry. Ere long will he be blind at any rate.

FIRST SEMI-CHORUS (*singing*)

Happy he who plays the Bacchanal amid the precious streams distilled from grapes, stretched at full length for a revel, his arm around the friend he loves, and some fair dainty damsel on his couch, his hair perfumed with nard and glossy, the while he calls, "Oh! who will ope the door for me?"

(*The* CYCLOPS *enters. He is obviously drunk.*)

CYCLOPS (*singing*)

Ha! ha! full of wine and merry with a feast's good cheer am I,
my hold freighted like a merchant-ship up to my belly's very top.
This turf graciously invites me to seek my brother Cyclopes for a
revel in the spring-tide.

Come, stranger, bring the wine-skin hither and hand it over to me.

SECOND SEMI-CHORUS (*singing*)

Forth from the house its fair lord comes, casting his fair glance
round him. We have someone to befriend us. A hostile brand is awaiting thee, no tender bride in dewy grot. No single colour will those
garlands have, that soon shall cling so close about thy brow.

ODYSSEUS

(*returning with the wine-skin. He is followed by* SILENUS, *who is also
drunk.*)

Hearken, Cyclops; for I am well versed in the ways of Bacchus, whom
I have given thee to drink.

CYCLOPS

And who is Bacchus? some reputed god?

ODYSSEUS

The greatest god men know to cheer their life.

CYCLOPS

I like his after-taste at any rate.

ODYSSEUS

This is the kind of god he is; he harmeth no man.

CYCLOPS

But how does a god like being housed in a wine-skin?

ODYSSEUS

Put him where one may, he is content there.

CYCLOPS

It is not right that gods should be clad in leather.

ODYSSEUS

What of that, provided he please thee? does the leather hurt thee?

CYCLOPS

I hate the wine-skin, but the liquor we have here I love.

ODYSSEUS

Stay, then, Cyclops; drink and be merry.

CYCLOPS

Must I not give my brethren a share in this liquor?

ODYSSEUS

No. keep it thyself and thou wilt appear of more honour.

CYCLOPS

Give it my friends and I shall appear of more use.

ODYSSEUS

Revelling is apt to end in blows, abuse, and strife.

CYCLOPS

I may be drunk, but no man will lay hands on me for all that.

ODYSSEUS

Better stay at home, my friend, after a carouse.

CYCLOPS

Who loves not revelling then is but a simpleton.

ODYSSEUS

But whoso stays at home, when drunk, is wise.

CYCLOPS

What shall we do, Silenus? art minded to stay?

SILENUS

That I am; for what need have we of others to share our drink, Cyclops?

CYCLOPS

Well, truly the turf is soft as down with its fresh flowering plants.

SILENUS (*seating himself*)

Aye, and 'tis pleasant drinking in the warm sunshine. Come, let me see thee stretch thy carcase on the ground.

CYCLOPS (*sitting down*)

There then! Why art thou putting the mixing-bowl behind me?

SILENUS

That no one passing by may upset it.

CYCLOPS

Nay, but thy purpose is to drink upon the sly; set it between us. (*To* ODYSSEUS) Now tell me, stranger, by what name to call thee.

(SILENUS *is drinking steadily and stealthily.*)

ODYSSEUS

Noman. What boon shall I receive of thee to earn my thanks?

CYCLOPS

I will feast on thee last, after all thy comrades.

ODYSSEUS

Fair indeed the honour thou bestowest on thy guest, sir Cyclops!

CYCLOPS (*turning suddenly to* SILENUS)

Ho, sirrah! what art thou about? taking a stealthy pull at the wine?

SILENUS

No, but it kissed me for my good looks.

CYCLOPS

Thou shalt smart, if thou kiss the wine when it kisses not thee.

SILENUS

Oh! but it did, for it says it is in love with my handsome face.

CYCLOPS (*holding out his cup*)

Pour in; only give me my cup full.

SILENUS

H'm! how is it mixed? just let me make sure.

(*Takes another pull.*)

CYCLOPS

Perdition! give it me at once.

SILENUS

Oh, no! I really cannot, till I see thee with a crown on, and have another taste myself.

CYCLOPS

My cup-bearer is a cheat.

SILENUS

No really, but the wine is so luscious. Thou must wipe thy lips, though, to get a draught.

CYCLOPS

There! my lips and beard are clean now.

SILENUS

Bend thine elbow gracefully, and then quaff thy cup, as thou seest me do, and as now thou seest me not. (*Burying his face in his cup*)

CYCLOPS

Aha! what next?

SILENUS

I drunk it off at a draught with much pleasure.

CYCLOPS

Stranger, take the skin thyself and be my cup-bearer.

ODYSSEUS

Well, at any rate the grape is no stranger to my hand.

CYCLOPS

Come, pour it in.

ODYSSEUS

In it goes! keep silence, that is all.

CYCLOPS

A difficult task when a man is deep in his cups.

ODYSSEUS

Here, take and drink it off; leave none. Thou must be silent and only give in when the liquor does.

CYCLOPS

God wot! it is a clever stock that bears the grape.

ODYSSEUS

Aye, and if thou but swallow plenty of it after a plentiful meal, moistening thy belly till its thirst is gone, it will throw thee into slumber; but if thou leave aught behind, the Bacchic god will parch thee for it.

CYCLOPS

Ha! ha! what a trouble it was getting out! This is pleasure unalloyed; earth and sky seem whirling round together; I see the throne of Zeus and all the godhead's majesty. Kiss *thee!* no! There are the Graces trying to tempt me. I shall rest well enough with my Ganymede here; yea, by the Graces, right fairly; for I like lads better than the wenches.

SILENUS

What! Cyclops, am I Ganymede, Zeus's minion?

CYCLOPS (*attempting to carry him into the cave*)
To be sure, Ganymede whom I am carrying off from the halls of Dardanus.

SILENUS

I am undone, my children; outrageous treatment waits me.

LEADER OF THE CHORUS

Dost find fault with thy lover? dost scorn him in his cups?

SILENUS

Woe is me! most bitter shall I find the wine ere long.
(SILENUS *is dragged into the cave by the* CYCLOPS.)

ODYSSEUS

Up now, children of Dionysus, sons of a noble sire, soon will yon creature in the cave, relaxed in slumber as ye see him, spew from his shameless maw the meat. Already the brand inside his lair is vomiting a cloud of smoke; and the only reason we prepared it was to burn the Cyclops' eye; so mind thou quit thee like a man.

LEADER

I will have a spirit as of rock or adamant; but go inside, before my father suffers any shameful treatment; for here thou hast things ready.

ODYSSEUS

O Hephaestus, lord of Aetna, rid thyself for once and all of a troublesome neighbour by burning his bright eye out. Come, Sleep, as well, offspring of sable Night, come with all thy power on the monster god-detested; and never after Troy's most glorious toils destroy Odysseus and his crew by the hands of one who recketh naught of God or man; else must we reckon Chance a goddess, and Heaven's will inferior to hers.
(ODYSSEUS *re-enters the cave.*)

CHORUS (*singing*)
Tightly the pincers shall grip the neck of him who feasts upon his guests; for soon will he lose the light of his eye by fire; already the brand, a tree's huge limb, lurks amid the embers charred.

Oh! come ye then and work his doom, pluck out the maddened Cyclops' eye, that he may rue his drinking. And I too fain would leave the Cyclops' lonely land and see king Bromius, ivy-crowned, the god I sorely miss. Ah! shall I ever come to that?

ODYSSEUS (*leaving the cave cautiously*)

Silence, ye cattle! I adjure you; close your lips; make not a sound! I'll not let a man of you so much as breathe or wink or clear his throat, that yon pest awake not, until the sight in the Cyclops' eye has passed through the fiery ordeal.

LEADER OF THE CHORUS

Silent we stand with bated breath.

ODYSSEUS

In then, and mind your fingers grip the brand, for it is splendidly red-hot.

LEADER

Thyself ordain who first must seize the blazing bar and burn the Cyclops' eye out, that we may share alike whate'er betides.

FIRST SEMI-CHORUS

Standing where I am before the door, I am too far off to thrust the fire into his eye.

SECOND SEMI-CHORUS

I have just gone lame.

FIRST SEMI-CHORUS

Why, then, thou art in the same plight as I; for somehow or other I sprained my ankle, standing still.

ODYSSEUS

Sprained thy ankle, standing still?

SECOND SEMI-CHORUS

Yes, and my eyes are full of dust or ashes from somewhere or other.

ODYSSEUS

These are sorry fellows, worthless as allies.

LEADER

Because I feel for my back and spine, and express no wish to have my teeth knocked out, I am a coward, am I? Well, but I know a spell of Orpheus, a most excellent one, to make the brand enter his skull of its own accord, and set alight the one-eyed son of Earth.

ODYSSEUS

Long since I knew thou wert by nature such an one, and now I know it better; I must employ my own friends; but, though thou bring no active aid, cheer us on at any rate, that I may find my friends emboldened by thy encouragement.

(ODYSSEUS *goes back into the cave.*)

LEADER

That will I do; the Carian ² shall run the risk for us; and as far as encouragement goes, let the Cyclops smoulder.

CHORUS (*singing*)

What ho! my gallants, thrust away, make haste and burn his eyebrow off, the monster's guest-devouring. Oh! singe and scorch the shepherd of Aetna; twirl the brand and drag it round and be careful lest in his agony he treat thee to some wantonness.

CYCLOPS (*bellowing in the cave*)

Oh! oh! my once bright eye is burnt to cinders now.

LEADER OF THE CHORUS

Sweet indeed the triumph-song; pray sing it to us, Cyclops.

CYCLOPS (*from within*)

Oh! oh! once more; what outrage on me and what ruin! But never shall ye escape this rocky cave unpunished, ye worthless creatures; for I will stand in the entrance of the cleft and fit my hands into it thus. (*Staggering to the entrance*)

LEADER

Why dost thou cry out, Cyclops?

CYCLOPS

I am undone.

LEADER

Thou art indeed a sorry sight.

CYCLOPS

Aye, and a sad one, too.

LEADER

Didst fall among the coals in a drunken fit?

CYCLOPS

Noman has undone me.

LEADER

Then there is no one hurting thee after all.

CYCLOPS

Noman is blinding me.

LEADER

Then art thou not blind.

CYCLOPS

As blind as thou, forsooth.

LEADER

How, pray, could no man have made thee blind?

CYCLOPS

Thou mockest me; but where is this Noman?

LEADER

Nowhere, Cyclops.

CYCLOPS

It was the stranger, vile wretch! who proved my ruin, that thou mayst understand rightly, by swilling me with the liquor he gave me.

LEADER

Ah! wine is a terrible foe, hard to wrestle with.

CYCLOPS

Tell me, I adjure thee, have they escaped or are they still within?

(*During the following lines,* ODYSSEUS *and his men slip by the* CYCLOPS, *despite his efforts to stop them.*)

LEADER

Here they are ranged in silence, taking the rock to screen them.

CYCLOPS

On which side?

LEADER

On thy right.

CYCLOPS

Where?

LEADER

Close against the rock. Hast caught them?

CYCLOPS

Trouble on trouble! I have run my skull against the rock and cracked it

LEADER

Aye, and they are escaping thee.

CYCLOPS

This way, was it not? 'Twas this way thou saidst.

LEADER

No, not this way.

CYCLOPS

Which then?

LEADER

They are getting round thee on the left.

CYCLOPS

Alas! I am being mocked; ye jeer me in my evil plight.

LEADER

They are no longer there; but facing thee that stranger stands.

CYCLOPS

Master of villainy, where, oh! where art thou?

ODYSSEUS

Some way from thee I am keeping careful guard over the person of Odysseus.

CYCLOPS

What, a new name! hast changed thine?

ODYSSEUS

Yes, Odysseus, the name my father gave me. But thou wert doomed to pay for thy unholy feast; for I should have seen Troy burned to but sorry purpose, unless I had avenged on thee the slaughter of my comrades.

CYCLOPS

Woe is me! 'tis an old oracle coming true; yes, it said I should have my eye put out by thee on thy way home from Troy; but it likewise foretold that thou wouldst surely pay for this, tossing on the sea for many a day.

ODYSSEUS

Go hang! E'en as I say, so have I done. And now will I get me to the beach and start my hollow ship across the sea of Sicily to the land of my fathers.

CYCLOPS

Thou shalt not; I will break a boulder off this rock and crush thee, crew and all, beneath my throw. Blind though I be, I will climb the hill, mounting through yonder tunnel.

LEADER

As for us, henceforth will we be the servants of Bacchus, sharing the voyage of this hero Odysseus.

COLERIDGE's translation has been modified in the following lines: 169–171, 546, and 584.

1. Reference to Odysseus as the son of Sisyphus is for the purpose of casting a slur upon him. Cf. the *Iphigenia in Aulis,* note 2.

2. Coleridge's note here in part runs: "*i.e.,* to let some one, whose life is less valuable, run the risk instead of doing so oneself. The Carians, being the earliest mercenaries, were commonly selected for any very dangerous enterprise, and so this proverb arose."

THE PLAYS OF
ARISTOPHANES

I

THE ACHARNIANS

Characters in the Play

Dicaeopolis
Herald
Amphitheus
Ambassadors
Pseudartabas
Theorus
Daughter of Dicaeopolis
Slave of Euripides
Euripides
Lamachus
A Megarian
Two Young Girls, *daughters of the Megarian*
An Informer
A Boeotian
Nicarchus
Slave of Lamachus
A Husbandman
A Wedding Guest
Chorus of Acharnian Charcoal Burners

INTRODUCTION

PRODUCED at the Lenaean festival in 425 under the pseudonym of Callis-
tratus, *The Acharnians* is the earliest comedy of Aristophanes that we
possess and the third which we know him to have written. In competition
with productions of the older and famous Eupolis and Cratinus the work
of the youngster was awarded the highest prize, and this was doubtless
the first victory of his career. The play is remarkable less for the skill
with which it is constructed or for the essential humour of the plot itself,
than for the variety of its incidents and the brilliance of their treatment.
Clearly political, rather than social or literary, in its theme, it constitutes,
with *Peace* and *Lysistrata*, a triad of political plays that have as their
underlying purpose the urging of a truce on the Athenian populace.

When the play opens, we are presented with Dicaeopolis, that model of
what Aristophanes thought a "good citizen" ought to be, sitting alone in
the Pnyx, waiting for the arrival of a characteristically belated Athenian
Assembly and musing on the many misfortunes and few joys which have
been his since the beginning of the war. The Assembly finally convenes,
with Dicaeopolis firmly resolved to let nothing stand in the way of concluding a truce with the Peloponnesians, but he is quickly and bitterly
disappointed when the wretched Amphitheus is silenced after proposing
just such a measure. Driven to desperation by the absurd reports and
spurious specimens of the wonders of Persia presented by the newly returned embassy, the "good citizen" commissions Amphitheus to negotiate
with Sparta a private truce for him and his family.

While he is impatiently awaiting the return of his envoy he is forced to
listen to another ambassadorial report, this time concerning the Thracian
Sitalces, and to witness the wretched samples of northern soldiery
proudly introduced as the "host of the Odomanti." Affecting to have felt
a drop of rain, he announces it as an omen, and on this preposterous pretext the magistrates adjourn the grateful Assembly. At this juncture
Amphitheus returns, hotly pursued by the Elders of Acharnae; his youthful vigour, however, has enabled him to outdistance his followers sufficiently to give Dicaeopolis an opportunity to taste and to test the sample

425

truces that Sparta is willing to offer, and furthermore to select and to ratify that of thirty years' duration as the most delectable and desirable.

As soon as he has entered his house to prepare for the celebration of the rural Dionysia and Amphitheus has fled, never to return, the Chorus of Acharnian Elders enters, fiercely searching for the man who has had the impudence and the temerity to conclude a truce with Sparta. Soon Dicaeopolis emerges from his dwelling, followed by his family, and the phallic procession is organized and commenced. The Acharnians, perceiving that this is the man they are looking for, set upon him and are on the point of stoning him, when he exhibits the characteristic resourcefulness of an Aristophanic hero, rushes into the house, and a moment later returns with a basket of charcoal. Using this "fellow-citizen" of the Acharnians as a hostage, he persuades or coerces them into letting him plead his case with his head on a block.

Realizing that it is pity above all that he must arouse, and distrustful of his own oratorical talents, he resolves to go to Euripides, whose house, with comic convenience, is juxtaposed to his, and to borrow the theatrical costume of the most miserable of the many wretched heroes which that eminently pathetic tragedian has introduced on the stage. Dicaeopolis succeeds in obtaining almost everything he needs from the exasperated poet, who feels that the foundations of his art are thus being undermined; "Miserable man! you are stealing a whole tragedy," he exclaims. Dicaeopolis, now garbed in the most pitiable manner possible, returns to the Acharnians, lays his head on the block, and delivers a sound and telling speech in favour of the Spartans.

The effect is to divide the Chorus; half of them are won over, half stubbornly unaffected, and a scuffle ensues. The leader of the die-hards calls for assistance on the belligerent Lamachus, whom the demands of the play have forced to dwell next to Euripides and but two doors from the pacificistic Dicaeopolis. The doughty general immediately sallies forth, fully and resplendently panoplied, but the subtle arguments of the "good citizen" are too much for him, and he returns to his house in evident discomfiture. Dicaeopolis now proclaims the cessation of all war-time boycotts so far as he is concerned, and enters his house, leaving the stage to the Chorus, which delivers the parabasis.

The anapests contain a recital of the services which the poet claims to have rendered to his native city, chief amongst them being the caution against the deceptive flattery of foreigners. The ode celebrates the Muse of Acharnae in lyric and fiery language whose metaphors, like so many others in this comedy, are derived from charcoal-burning. The epirrheme pleads the case of Acharnae and particularly that of the old against the young. The antode and the antepirrheme extend and elaborate this motif.

At the conclusion of the parabasis, Dicaeopolis comes out of his house and defines his market-place. Immediately a Megarian enters and vividly portrays, as much in his own wretched person as by the reports which he gives of conditions at home, the distress caused by Pericles' famous and fulminous decree. The Megarian is succeeded by a Boeotian, who is effectively contrasted with his predecessor; sleek and fat, possessing good victuals in abundance, he is perhaps meant to indicate what Megara might have had if the fatal boycott had not been applied. As soon as Dicaeopolis and the Boeotian have come to the conclusion that the only Athenian product not found in Boeotia is informers, Nicarchus, an eminent representative of that despicable profession, appears; he is forthwith seized and packed in hay, like a vase, and carried off by the Boeotian. A slave belonging to Lamachus approaches and seeks to purchase a Copaic eel, but Dicaeopolis refuses to sell him one, thus fulfilling to the last detail the proclamation made before the parabasis, to the effect that his market is to be open to the Megarians and to the Boeotians but closed to Lamachus.

A herald appears and announces the Anthesterian feast, and Dicaeopolis sets his slaves to work preparing the fine foods which he can now enjoy. While this pleasant exercise is occupying the "good citizen" another herald arrives and proclaims to Lamachus that the generals have ordered him to set forth on an expedition immediately. The ensuing scene, in which Dicaeopolis is gaily preparing for the feast and Lamachus gloomily getting ready for the campaign, is one of the best in the play, and the poet makes full use of the opportunities which this sharp and suggestive contrast offers. Finally both worthies depart in opposite directions amid the impartial felicitations of the Chorus. In the final scene both Lamachus and Dicaeopolis return almost simultaneously from their respective activities, the former having been badly wounded in a ridiculous adventure, the latter magnificently inebriated and amusing each hand with a different girl. The comedy ends with a varied lyric passage in which the pained and woeful groans of the general alternate with the triumphant and amorous shouts of the pacifist.

It has been sagely observed that if we had the misfortune to possess but a single comedy of Aristophanes, we should be least afflicted if the sole representative of his art were *The Acharnians,* and indeed this composition acquaints us with a comfortable majority of his talents and nearly all of the objects of his scorn. Many of the later comedies are more abundantly endowed with artistic unity and comic intensity, but there is little of importance in them which is not clearly, if briefly, foreshadowed in *The Acharnians.* Almost as if he were writing a dramatic introduction to all his works and a general analysis of his own heart, the son of Philippus dilates our eyes and delights our minds with a gaudy and compendious succession of scenes in which the tragic follies of the war-party, the lugubrious fopperies of Euripides, the proud gullibility of the Athenians, and the careless inhumanity of their foreign policy are equally and effectively lampooned.

A further uniqueness of *The Acharnians* is discernible in the fact that of all his heroes none is so dear to Aristophanes as Dicaeopolis, and nowhere else has the poet elected to fill the mouth of an individual with sentiments so clearly his own; the "good citizen" even speaks of himself as having written comedies! Amongst the eleven comedies that have come down to us, there are several which are evidently better than *The Acharnians;* there is none which is so comprehensively Aristophanic.

THE ACHARNIANS

(SCENE:—*The Orchestra represents the Pnyx at Athens; in the back-ground are the usual houses, this time three in number, belonging to Dicaeopolis, Euripides, and Lamachus respectively.*)

DICAEOPOLIS (*alone*)

WHAT cares have not gnawed at my heart and how few have been the pleasures in my life! Four, to be exact, while my troubles have been as countless as the grains of sand on the shore! Let me see! of what value to me have been these few pleasures? Ah! I remember that I was delighted in soul when Cleon had to cough up those five talents; I was in ecstasy and I love the Knights for this deed; "it is an honour to Greece." But the day when I was impatiently awaiting a piece by Æschylus,[1] what tragic despair it caused me when the herald called, "Theognis, introduce your Chorus!" Just imagine how this blow struck straight at my heart! On the other hand, what joy Dexitheus caused me at the musical competition, when right after Moschus he played a Boeotian melody on the lyre! But this year by contrast! Oh! what deadly torture to hear Chaeris perform the prelude in the Orthian mode!—Never, however, since I began to bathe, has the dust hurt my eyes as it does to-day. Still it is the day of assembly; all should be here at daybreak, and yet the Pnyx is still deserted. They are gossiping in the market-place, slipping hither and thither to avoid the vermilioned rope.[2] The Prytanes even do not come; they will be late, but when they come they will push and fight each other for a seat in the front row. They will never trouble themselves with the question of peace. Oh! Athens! Athens! As for myself, I do not fail to come here before all the rest, and now, finding myself alone, I groan, yawn, stretch, fart, and know not what to do; I make sketches in the dust, pull out my loose hairs, muse, think of my fields, long for peace, curse town life and regret my dear country home, which never told me to "buy fuel, vinegar or oil"; there the word "buy," which cuts me in two, was unknown; I harvested everything at will. Therefore I have come to the assembly fully prepared to bawl, interrupt and abuse the speakers, if they talk of anything but peace. (*The Orchestra begins to fill with people.*) But here come the Prytanes, and high time too, for it is midday! There, just as I said, they are pushing and fighting for the front seats.

HERALD (*officiously*)
Step forward, step forward; get within the consecrated area.

AMPHITHEUS (*rising*)
Has anyone spoken yet?

HERALD
Who asks to speak?

AMPHITHEUS
I do.

HERALD
Your name?

AMPHITHEUS
Amphitheus.

HERALD
Are you not a man?

AMPHITHEUS
No! I am an immortal! Amphitheus was the son of Ceres and Triptolemus; of him was born Celeus, Celeus wedded Phaenereté, my grandmother, whose son was Lycinus, and, being born of him I am an immortal; it is to me alone that the gods have entrusted the duty of treating with the Lacedaemonians. But, citizens, though I am immortal, I am dying of hunger; the Prytanes give me nothing.

HERALD (*calling*)
Officers!

AMPHITHEUS (*as the Scythian policemen seize him*)
Oh, Triptolemus and Celeus, do ye thus forsake your own blood?

DICAEOPOLIS (*rising*)
Prytanes, in expelling this citizen, you are offering an outrage to the Assembly. He only desired to secure peace for us and to sheathe the sword.
(*The Scythians release Amphitheus.*)

HERALD
Sit down! Silence!

DICAEOPOLIS

No, by Apollo, I will not, unless you are going to discuss the question of peace.

HERALD (*ignoring this; loudly*)

The ambassadors, who are returned from the Court of the King!

DICAEOPOLIS

Of what King? I am sick of all those fine birds, the peacock ambassa‑dors and their swagger.

HERALD

Silence!

DICAEOPOLIS (*as he perceives the entering ambassadors dressed in the Persian mode*)

Oh! oh! By Ecbatana, what a costume!

AMBASSADOR (*pompously*)

During the archonship of Euthymenes, you sent us to the Great King on a salary of two drachmae per diem.

DICAEOPOLIS (*aside*)

Ah! those poor drachmae!

AMBASSADOR

We suffered horribly on the plains of the Cayster, sleeping under a tent, stretched deliciously on fine chariots, half dead with weariness.

DICAEOPOLIS (*aside*)

And I was very much at ease, lying on the straw along the battlements!

AMBASSADOR

Everywhere we were well received and forced to drink delicious wine out of golden or crystal flagons. . . .

DICAEOPOLIS (*aside*)

Oh, city of Cranaus, thy ambassadors are laughing at thee!

AMBASSADOR

For great feeders and heavy drinkers are alone esteemed as men by the barbarians.

DICAEOPOLIS (*aside*)

Just as here in Athens, we only esteem the wenchers and pederasts.

AMBASSADOR

At the end of the fourth year we reached the King's Court, but he had left with his whole army to take a crap, and for the space of eight months he was thus sitting on the can in the midst of the golden mountains.

DICAEOPOLIS (*aside*)

And how long did it take him to close his arse? A month?

AMBASSADOR

After this he returned to his palace; then he entertained us and had us served with oxen roasted whole in an oven.

DICAEOPOLIS (*aside*)

Who ever saw an ox roasted in an oven? What a lie!

AMBASSADOR

And one day, by Zeus, he also had us served with a bird three times as large as Cleonymus, and called the Hoax.

DICAEOPOLIS (*aside*)

And do we give you two drachmæ, that you should hoax us thus?

AMBASSADOR

We are bringing to you Pseudartabas, the King's Eye.

DICAEOPOLIS

I would a crow might pluck out yours with his beak, you cursed am-bassador!

HERALD (*loudly*)

The King's Eye!

(*Enter* PSEUDARTABAS, *in Persian costume; his mask is one great eye; he is accompanied by two eunuchs.*)

DICAEOPOLIS (*as he sees him*)

Good God! Friend, with your great eye, round like the hole through which the oarsman passes his sweep, you have the air of a galley doubling a cape to gain port.

AMBASSADOR

Come, Pseudartabas, give forth the message for the Athenians with which you were charged by the Great King.

PSEUDARTABAS

I ártamáne Xárxas ápiaóna satrá.[3]

AMBASSADOR (*to* DICAEOPOLIS)
Do you understand what he says?

DICAEOPOLIS
God, no!

AMBASSADOR (*to the* PRYTANES)
He says that the Great King will send you gold. (*to* PSEUDARTABAS)
Come, utter the word 'gold' louder and more distinctly.

PSEUDARTABAS
Thou shalt not have gold, thou gaping-arsed Ionian.

DICAEOPOLIS
Ah! God help us, but *that's* clear enough!

AMBASSADOR
What does he say?

DICAEOPOLIS
That the Ionians are gaping-arsed, if they expect to receive gold from
the barbarians.

AMBASSADOR
Not so, he speaks of bushels of gold.

DICAEOPOLIS
What bushels? You're nothing but a wind-bag; get out of the way; I
will find out the truth by myself. (*to* PSEUDARTABAS) Come now, answer
me clearly, if you do not wish me to dye your skin red. Will the Great
King send us gold? (PSEUDARTABAS *makes a negative sign.*) Then our
ambassadors are seeking to deceive us? (PSEUDARTABAS *signs affirma-
tively.*) These fellows make signs like any Greek; I am sure that they
are nothing but Athenians. Oh! ho! I recognize one of these eunuchs; it
is Clisthenes, the son of Sibyrtius. Behold the effrontery of this shaven
and provocative arse! How, you big baboon, with such a beard do you
seek to play the eunuch to us? And this other one? Is it not Straton?

HERALD
Silence! Sit down! The Senate invites the King's Eye to the Prytaneum.
(*The* AMBASSADORS *and* PSEUDARTABAS *depart.*)

DICAEOPOLIS
Is this not sufficient to drive a man to hang himself? Here I stand
chilled to the bone, whilst the doors of the Prytaneum fly wide open to
lodge such rascals. But I will do something great and bold. Where is Amphitheus? Come and speak with me.

AMPHITHEUS

Here I am.

DICAEOPOLIS

Take these eight drachmae and go and conclude a truce with the Lacedæmonians for me, my wife and my children; I leave you free, my dear Prytanes, to send out embassies and to stand gaping in the air.

(AMPHITHEUS *rushes out.*)

HERALD

Bring in Theorus, who has returned from the Court of Sitalces.

THEORUS (*rising; he wears a Thracian costume.*)

I am here.

DICAEOPOLIS (*aside*)

Another humbug!

THEORUS

We should not have remained long in Thrace . . .

DICAEOPOLIS

. . . if you had not been well paid.

THEORUS

. . . if the country had not been covered with snow; the rivers were ice-bound . . .

DICAEOPOLIS (*aside*)

That was when Theognis produced his tragedy.

THEORUS

. . . during the whole of that time I was holding my own with Sitalces cup in hand; and, in truth, he adored you to such a degree that he wrote on the walls, "How beautiful are the Athenians!" His son, to whom we gave the freedom of the city, burned with desire to come here and eat sausages at the feast of the Apaturia; he prayed his father to come to the aid of his new country and Sitalces swore on his goblet that he would succour us with such a host that the Athenians would exclaim, "What a cloud of grasshoppers!"

DICAEOPOLIS (*aside*)

Damned if I believe a word of what you tell us! Excepting the grasshoppers, there is not a grain of truth in it all!

THEORUS

And he has sent you the most warlike soldiers of all Thrace.

DICAEOPOLIS (*aside*)

Now we shall begin to see clearly.

HERALD

Come hither, Thracians, whom Theorus brought.

(*A few Thracians are ushered in; they have a most unwarlike appearance; the most striking feature of their costume is the circumcised phallus.*)

DICAEOPOLIS

What plague have we here?

THEORUS

The host of the Odomanti.

DICAEOPOLIS

Of the Odomanti? Tell me what it means. Who sliced their tools like that?

THEORUS

If they are given a wage of two drachmae, they will put all Boeotia to fire and sword.

DICAEOPOLIS

Two drachmae to those circumcised hounds! Groan aloud, ye people of rowers, bulwark of Athens! (*The Odomanti steal his sack*) Ah! great gods! I am undone; these Odomanti are robbing me of my garlic! Give me back my garlic.

THEORUS

Oh! wretched man! do not go near them; they have eaten garlic.

DICAEOPOLIS

Prytanes, will you let me be treated in this manner, in my own country and by barbarians? But I oppose the discussion of paying a wage to the Thracians; I announce an omen; I have just felt a drop of rain.[4]

HERALD

Let the Thracians withdraw and return the day after tomorrow; the Prytanes declare the sitting at an end.

(*All leave except* DICAEOPOLIS.)

DICAEOPOLIS

Ye gods, what garlic I have lost! But here comes Amphitheus returned from Lacedaemon. Welcome, Amphitheus.

(AMPHITHEUS *enters, very much out of breath.*)

AMPHITHEUS

No, there is no welcome for me and I fly as fast as 1 can, for I am pursued by the Acharnians.

DICAEOPOLIS

Why, what has happened?

AMPHITHEUS

I was hurrying to bring your treaty of truce, but some old dotards from Acharnae got scent of the thing; they are veterans of Marathon, tough as oak or maple, of which they are made for sure—rough and ruthless. They all started shouting: "Wretch! you are the bearer of a treaty, and the enemy has only just cut our vines!" Meanwhile they were gathering stones in their cloaks, so I fled and they ran after me shouting.

DICAEOPOLIS

Let 'em shout as much as they please! But have you brought me a treaty?

AMPHITHEUS

Most certainly, here are three samples to select from, this one is five years old; taste it.

(*He hands* DICAEOPOLIS *a bottle.*)

DICAEOPOLIS

Faugh!

AMPHITHEUS

What's the matter?

DICAEOPOLIS

I don't like it; it smells of pitch and of the ships they are fitting out.

AMPHITHEUS (*handing him another bottle*)

Here is another, ten years old; taste it.

DICAEOPOLIS

It smells strongly of the delegates, who go around the towns to chide the allies for their slowness.[5]

AMPHITHEUS (*handing him a third bottle*)

This last is a truce of thirty years, both on sea and land.

DICAEOPOLIS

Oh! by Bacchus! what a bouquet! It has the aroma of nectar and ambrosia; this does not say to us, "Provision yourselves for three days." But it lisps the gentle numbers. "Go whither you will." I accept it, ratify it, drink it at one draught and consign the Acharnians to limbo. Freed from the war and its ills, I shall celebrate the rural Dionysia.

AMPHITHEUS
And I shall run away, for I'm mortally afraid of the Acharnians.
(AMPHITHEUS *runs off.* DICAEOPOLIS *goes into his house, carrying his truce. The* CHORUS OF ACHARNIAN CHARCOAL BURNERS *enters, in great haste and excitement.*)

LEADER OF THE CHORUS
This way all! Let us follow our man; we will demand him of everyone we meet; the public weal makes his seizure imperative. Ho, there! tell me which way the bearer of the truce has gone.

CHORUS (*singing*)
He has escaped us, he has disappeared. Damn old age! When I was young, in the days when I followed Phayllus, running with a sack of coals on my back, this wretch would not have eluded my pursuit, let him be as swift as he will.

LEADER OF THE CHORUS
But now my limbs are stiff; old Lacratides feels his legs are weighty and the traitor escapes me. No, no, let us follow him; old Acharnians like our selves shall not be set at naught by a scoundrel . . .

CHORUS (*singing*)
. . . who has dared, by Zeus, to conclude a truce when I wanted the war continued with double fury in order to avenge my ruined lands. No mercy for our foes until I have pierced their hearts like a sharp reed, so that they dare never again ravage my vineyards.

LEADER OF THE CHORUS
Come, let us seek the rascal; let us look everywhere, carrying our stones in our hands; let us hunt him from place to place until we trap him; I could never, never tire of the delight of stoning him.

DICAEOPOLIS (*from within*)
Peace! profane men!

LEADER OF THE CHORUS
Silence all! Friends, do you hear the sacred formula? Here is he, whom we seek! This way, all! Get out of his way, surely he comes to offer an oblation.
(*The* CHORUS *withdraws to one side.*)

DICAEOPOLIS (*comes out with a pot in his hand; he is followed by his wife, his daughter, who carries a basket, and two slaves, who carry the phallus.*)

Peace, profane men! Let the basket-bearer come forward, and thou, Xanthias, hold the phallus well upright. Daughter, set down the basket and let us begin the sacrifice.

DAUGHTER OF DICAEOPOLIS (*putting down the basket and taking out the sacred cake*)

Mother, hand me the ladle, that I may spread the sauce on the cake.

DICAEOPOLIS

It is well! Oh, mighty Bacchus, it is with joy that, freed from military duty, I and all mine perform this solemn rite and offer thee this sacrifice; grant that I may keep the rural Dionysia without hindrance and that this truce of thirty years may be propitious for me. Come, my child, carry the basket gracefully and with a grave, demure face. Happy he who shall be your possessor and embrace you so firmly at dawn, that you fart like a weasel. Go forward, and have a care they don't snatch your jewels in the crowd. Xanthias, walk behind the basket-bearer and hold the phallus well erect; I will follow, singing the Phallic hymn; thou, wife, look on from the top of the terrace. Forward!

(*He sings*)

Oh, Phalés, companion of the orgies of Bacchus, night reveller, god of adultery and of pederasty, these past six years I have not been able to invoke thee. With what joy I return to my farmstead, thanks to the truce I have concluded, freed from cares, from fighting and from Lamachuses! How much sweeter, oh Phalés, Phalés, is it to surprise Thratta, the pretty woodmaid, Strymodorus' slave, stealing wood from Mount Phelleus, to catch her under the arms, to throw her on the ground and lay her, Oh, Phalés, Phalés! If thou wilt drink and bemuse thyself with me, we shall to-morrow consume some good dish in honour of the peace, and I will hang up my buckler over the smoking hearth.

(*The procession reaches the place where the* CHORUS *is hiding.*)

LEADER OF THE CHORUS

That's the man himself. Stone him, stone him, stone him, strike the wretch. All, all of you, pelt him, pelt him!

DICAEOPOLIS (*using his pot for a shield*)

What is this? By Heracles, you will smash my pot.

(*The daughter and the two slaves retreat.*)

CHORUS (*singing excitedly*)

It is you that we are stoning, you miserable scoundrel.

DICAEOPOLIS

And for what sin, Acharnian elders, tell me that!

CHORUS (*singing, with greater excitement*)

You ask that, you impudent rascal, traitor to your country; you alone amongst us all have concluded a truce, and you dare to look us in the face!

DICAEOPOLIS

But you do not know *why* I have treated for peace. Listen!

CHORUS (*singing fiercely*)

Listen to you? No, no, you are about to die, we will annihilate you with our stones.

DICAEOPOLIS

But first of all, listen. Stop, my friends.

CHORUS (*singing; with intense hatred*)

I will hear nothing; do not address me; I hate you more than I do Cleon, whom one day I shall flay to make sandals for the Knights. Listen to your long speeches, after you have treated with the Laconians? No, I will punish you.

DICAEOPOLIS

Friends, leave the Laconians out of debate and consider only whether I have not done well to conclude my truce.

LEADER OF THE CHORUS

Done well! when you have treated with a people who know neither gods nor truth, nor faith.

DICAEOPOLIS

We attribute too much to the Laconians; as for myself, I know that they are not the cause of all our troubles.

LEADER OF THE CHORUS

Oh, indeed, rascal! You dare to use such language to me and then expect me to spare you!

DICAEOPOLIS

No, no, they are not the cause of all our troubles, and I who address you claim to be able to prove that they have much to complain of in us.

LEADER OF THE CHORUS

This passes endurance; my heart bounds with fury. Thus you dare to defend our enemies.

DICAEOPOLIS

Were my head on the block I would uphold what I say and rely on the approval of the people.

LEADER OF THE CHORUS

Comrades, let us hurl our stones and dye this fellow purple.

DICAEOPOLIS

What black fire-brand has inflamed your heart! You will not hear me? You really will not, Acharnians?

LEADER OF THE CHORUS

No, a thousand times, no.

DICAEOPOLIS

This is a hateful injustice.

LEADER OF THE CHORUS

May I die if I listen.

DICAEOPOLIS

Nay, nay! have mercy, have mercy, Acharnians.

LEADER OF THE CHORUS

You shall die.

DICAEOPOLIS

Well, blood for blood! I will kill your dearest friend. I have here the hostages of Acharnae; I shall disembowel them.

(*He goes into the house.*)

LEADER OF THE CHORUS

Acharnians, what means this threat? Has he got one of our children in his house? What gives him such audacity?

DICAEOPOLIS (*coming out again*)

Stone me, if it please you; I shall avenge myself on this. (*He shows them a basket.*) Let us see whether you have any love for your coals.

LEADER OF THE CHORUS

Great Gods! this basket is our fellow-citizen. Stop, stop, in heaven's name!

DICAEOPOLIS

I shall dismember it despite your cries; I will listen to nothing.

CHORUS (*singing; tragically*)
How, will you kill this coal-basket, my beloved comrade?

DICAEOPOLIS
Just now you would not listen to me.

CHORUS (*singing; plaintively*)
Well, speak now, if you will; tell us, tell us you have a weakness
for the Lacedaemonians. I consent to anything; never will I forsake
this dear little basket.

DICAEOPOLIS
First, throw down your stones.

CHORUS (*singing; meekly*)
There! it's done. And you put away your sword.

DICAEOPOLIS
Let me see that no stones remain concealed in your cloaks.

CHORUS (*singing; petulantly*)
They are all on the ground; see how we shake our garments. Come,
no haggling, lay down your sword; we threw away everything while
crossing from one side of the Orchestra to the other.

DICAEOPOLIS
What cries of anguish you would have uttered had these coals of Parnes
been dismembered, and yet it came very near it; had they perished, their
death would have been due to the folly of their fellow-citizens. The poor
basket was so frightened, look, it has shed a thick black dust over me, the
same as a cuttle-fish does. What an irritable temper! You shout and throw
stones, you will not hear my arguments—not even when I propose to
speak in favour of the Lacedaemonians with my head on the block; and
yet I cling to life.
(*He goes into the house.*)

CHORUS (*singing; belligerently again*)
Well then, bring out a block before your door, scoundrel, and let
us hear the good grounds you can give us; I am curious to know
them. Now mind, as you proposed yourself, place your head on the
block and speak.

DICAEOPOLIS (*coming out of his house, carrying a block*)
Here is the block; and, though I am but a very sorry speaker, I wish
nevertheless to talk freely of the Lacedaemonians and without the protection of my buckler. Yet I have many reasons for fear. I know our rus-

tics; they are delighted if some braggart comes, and rightly or wrongly, loads both them and their city with praise and flattery; they do not see that such toad-eaters are traitors, who sell them for gain. As for the old men, I know their weakness; they only seek to overwhelm the accused with their votes. Nor have I forgotten how Cleon treated me because of my comedy last year; he dragged me before the Senate and there he uttered endless slanders against me; it was a tempest of abuse, a deluge of lies. Through what a slough of mud he dragged me! I almost perished. Permit me, therefore, before I speak, to dress in the manner most likely to draw pity.

CHORUS (*singing; querulously*)

What evasions, subterfuges and delays! Wait! here is the sombre helmet of Pluto with its thick bristling plume; Hieronymus lends it to you; then open Sisyphus' bag of wiles; but hurry, hurry, for our discussion does not admit of delay.

DICAEOPOLIS

The time has come for me to manifest my courage, so I will go and seek Euripides. (*Knocking on* EURIPIDES' *door*) Ho! slave, slave!

SLAVE (*opening the door and poking his head out*)
Who's there?

DICAEOPOLIS

Is Euripides at home?

SLAVE

He is and he isn't; understand that, if you can.

DICAEOPOLIS

What's that? He is and he *isn't!*

SLAVE

Certainly, old man; busy gathering subtle fancies here and there, his mind is not in the house, but he himself is; perched aloft, he is composing a tragedy.

DICAEOPOLIS

Oh, Euripides, you are indeed happy to have a slave so quick at repar-tee! Now, fellow, call your master.

SLAVE

Impossible! (*He slams the door.*)

DICAEOPOLIS

Too bad. But I will not give up. Come, let us knock at the door again. Euripides, my little Euripides, my darling Euripides, listen; never had man greater right to your pity. It is Dicaeopolis of the Chollidan Deme who calls you. Do you hear?

EURIPIDES (*from within*)

I have no time to waste.

DICAEOPOLIS

Very well, have yourself wheeled out here.

EURIPIDES

Impossible.

DICAEOPOLIS

Nevertheless . . .

EURIPIDES

Well, let them roll me out; as to coming down, I have not the time.
(*The eccyclema turns and presents the interior of the house.* EURIPIDES *is lying on a bed, his slave beside him. On the back wall are hung up tragic costumes of every sort and a multitude of accessories is piled up on the floor.*)

DICAEOPOLIS

Euripides . . .

EURIPIDES

What words strike my ear?

DICAEOPOLIS

You perch aloft to compose tragedies, when you might just as well do them on the ground. No wonder you introduce cripples on the stage. And why do you dress in these miserable tragic rags? No wonder your heroes are beggars. But, Euripides, on my knees I beseech you, give me the tatters of some old piece; for I have to treat the Chorus to a long speech, and if I do it badly it is all over with me.

EURIPIDES

What rags do you prefer? Those in which I rigged out Oeneus on the stage, that unhappy, miserable old man?

DICAEOPOLIS

No, I want those of some hero still more unfortunate.

EURIPIDES

Of Phœnix, the blind man?

DICAEOPOLIS

No, not of Phœnix, you have another hero more unfortunate than him.

EURIPIDES (*to himself*)

Now, what tatters *does* he want? (*to* DICAEOPOLIS) Do you mean those of the beggar Philoctetes?

DICAEOPOLIS

No, of another far more beggarly.

EURIPIDES

Is it the filthy dress of the lame fellow, Bellerophon?

DICAEOPOLIS

No, not Bellerophon; the one I mean was not only lame and a beggar, but boastful and a fine speaker.

EURIPIDES

Ah! I know, it is Telephus, the Mysian.

DICAEOPOLIS

Yes, Telephus. Give me his rags, I beg of you.

EURIPIDES

Slave! give him Telephus' tatters; they are on top of the rags of Thyestes and mixed with those of Ino. There they are; take them.

DICAEOPOLIS (*holding up the costume for the audience to see*)

Oh! Zeus, whose eye pierces everywhere and embraces all, permit me to assume the most wretched dress on earth. Euripides, cap your kindness by giving me the little Mysian hat, that goes so well with these tatters. I must to-day have the look of a beggar; "be what I am, but not appear to be"; the audience will know well who I am, but the Chorus will be fools enough not to, and I shall dupe them with my subtle phrases.

EURIPIDES

I will give you the hat; I love the clever tricks of an ingenious brain like yours.

DICAEOPOLIS

Rest happy, and may it befall Telephus as I wish. Ah, I already feel myself filled with quibbles. But I must have a beggar's staff.

EURIPIDES (*handing him a staff*)

Here you are, and now get away from this porch.

DICAEOPOLIS

Oh, my soul! You see how you are driven from this house, when I still
need so many accessories. But let us be pressing, obstinate, importunate.
Euripides, give me a little basket with a lamp lighted inside.

EURIPIDES

Whatever do you want such a thing as that for?

DICAEOPOLIS

I do not need it, but I want it all the same.

EURIPIDES (*handing him a basket*)

You importune me; get out of here!

DICAEOPOLIS

Alas! may the gods grant you a destiny as brilliant as your mother's.[6]

EURIPIDES

Leave me in peace.

DICAEOPOLIS

Oh, just a little broken cup.

EURIPIDES (*handing him a cup*)

Take it and go and hang yourself. (*to himself*) What a tiresome fellow!

DICAEOPOLIS

Ah! you do not know all the pain you cause me. Dear, good Euripides,
just a little pot with a sponge for a stopper.

EURIPIDES

Miserable man! You are stealing a whole tragedy. Here, take it and be
off.

(*He hands* DICAEOPOLIS *a pot.*)

DICAEOPOLIS

I am going, but, great gods! I need one thing more; unless I have it, I
am a dead man. Hearken, my little Euripides, only give me this and I go,
never to return. For pity's sake, do give me a few small herbs for my
basket.

EURIPIDES

You wish to ruin me then. Here, take what you want; but it is all over
with my plays!

(*He hands him some herbs.*)

DICAEOPOLIS

I won't ask another thing; I'm going. I am too importunate and forget that I rouse against me the hate of kings. (*He starts to leave, then returns quickly*) Ah! wretch that I am! I am lost! I have forgotten one thing, without which all the rest is as nothing. Euripides, my excellent Euripides, my dear little Euripides, may I die if I ask you again for the smallest present; only one, the last, absolutely the last; give me some of the chervil your mother left you in her will.

EURIPIDES

Insolent hound! Slave, lock the door! (*The eccyclema turns back again.*)

DICAEOPOLIS

Oh, my soul! we must go away without the chervil. Art thou sensible of the dangerous battle we are about to engage upon in defending the Lacedaemonians? Courage, my soul, we must plunge into the midst of it. Dost thou hesitate and art thou fully steeped in Euripides? That's right! do not falter, my poor heart, and let us risk our head to say what we hold for truth. Courage and boldly to the front. I am astonished at my bravery.

(*He approaches the block.*)

CHORUS (*singing; excitedly*)

What do you purport doing? what are you going to say? What an impudent fellow! what a brazen heart! to dare to stake his head and uphold an opinion contrary to that of us all! And he does not tremble to face this peril! Come, it is you who desired it, speak!

DICAEOPOLIS

Spectators, be not angered if, although I am a beggar, I dare in a comedy to speak before the people of Athens of the public weal; even Comedy can sometimes discern what is right. I shall not please, but I shall say what is true. Besides, Cleon shall not be able to accuse me of attacking Athens before strangers; we are by ourselves at the festival of the Lenæa; the time when our allies send us their tribute and their soldiers is not yet here. There is only the pure wheat without the chaff; as to the resident aliens settled among us, they and the citizens are one, like the straw and the ear.

I detest the Lacedaemonians with all my heart, and may Posidon, the god of Taenarus, cause an earthquake and overturn their dwellings! My vines too have been cut. But come (there are only friends who hear me), why accuse the Laconians of all our woes? Some men (I do not say the city, note particularly that I do not say the city), some wretches, lost in vices, bereft of honour, who were not even citizens of good stamp, but strangers, have accused the Megarians of introducing their produce fraudulently, and not a cucumber, a leveret, a suckling pig, a clove of garlic, a lump of salt was seen without its being said, "Halloa! these come from Megara," and their being instantly confiscated. Thus far the evil was not serious and we were the only sufferers. But now some young drunkards go to Megara and carry off the harlot Simaetha; the Megarians, hurt to the quick, run off in turn with two harlots of the house of Aspasia; and so for three whores Greece is set ablaze. Then Pericles, aflame with ire on his Olympian height, let loose the lightning, caused the thunder to roll, upset Greece and passed an edict, which ran like the song, "That the Megarians be banished both from our land and from our markets and from the sea and from the continent." Meanwhile the Megarians, who were beginning to die of hunger, begged the Lacedaemonians to bring about the abolition of the decree, of which those harlots were the cause; several times we refused their demand; and from that time there was a horrible clatter of arms everywhere. You will say that Sparta was wrong, but what should she have done? Answer that. Suppose that a Lacedaemonian had seized a little Seriphian dog on any pretext and had sold it, would you have endured it quietly? Far from it, you would at once have sent three hundred vessels to sea, and what an uproar there would have been through all the city! there it's a band of noisy soldiery, here a brawl about the election of a Trierarch; elsewhere pay is being distributed, the Pallas figure-heads are being regilded, crowds are surging under the market porticos, encumbered with wheat that is being measured, wine-skins, oarleathers, garlic, olives, onions in nets; everywhere are chaplets, sprats, flute-girls, black eyes; in the arsenal bolts are being noisily driven home, sweeps are being made and fitted with leathers; we hear nothing but the sound of whistles, of flutes and fifes to encourage the workers. That is what you assuredly would have done, and would not Telephus have done the same? So I come to my general conclusion; we have no common sense.

LEADER OF FIRST SEMI-CHORUS

Oh! wretch! oh! infamous man! You are naught but a beggar and yet you dare to talk to us like this! you insult their worships the informers!

LEADER OF SECOND SEMI-CHORUS

By Posidon! he speaks the truth; he has not lied in a single detail.

LEADER OF FIRST SEMI-CHORUS

But though it be true, need he say it? But you'll have no great cause to be proud of your insolence!

LEADER OF SECOND SEMI-CHORUS

Where are you running to? Don't you move; if you strike this man, I shall be at you.

FIRST SEMI-CHORUS (*bursting into song*)
Oh! Lamachus, whose glance flashes lightning, whose plume petrifies thy foes, help! Oh! Lamachus, my friend, the hero of my tribe and all of you, both officers and soldiers, defenders of our walls, come to my aid; else is it all over with me!
(LAMACHUS *comes out of his house armed from head to foot.*)

LAMACHUS
Whence comes this cry of battle? where must I bring my aid? where must I sow dread? who wants me to uncase my dreadful Gorgon's head?

DICAEOPOLIS
Oh, Lamachus, great hero! Your plumes and your cohorts terrify me.

CHORUS-LEADER
This man, Lamachus, incessantly abuses Athens.

LAMACHUS
You are but a mendicant and you dare to use language of this sort?

DICAEOPOLIS
Oh, brave Lamachus, forgive a beggar who speaks at hazard.

LAMACHUS
But what have you said? Let us hear.

DICAEOPOLIS
I know nothing about it; the sight of weapons makes me dizzy. Oh! I adjure you, take that fearful Gorgon somewhat farther away.

LAMACHUS
There.

DICAEOPOLIS
Now place it face downwards on the ground.

LAMACHUS
It is done.

DICAEOPOLIS
Give me a plume out of your helmet.

LAMACHUS
Here is a feather.

DICAEOPOLIS
And hold my head while I vomit; the plumes have turned my stomach.

LAMACHUS

Hah! what are you proposing to do? do you want to make yourself vomit with this feather?

DICAEOPOLIS

Is it a feather? what bird's? a braggart's?

LAMACHUS

Hah! I will rip you open.

DICAEOPOLIS

No, no, Lamachus! Violence is out of place here! But as you are so strong, why did you not circumcise me? You have all the tools you need for the operation there.

LAMACHUS

A beggar dares thus address a general!

DICAEOPOLIS

How? Am I a beggar?

LAMACHUS

What are you then?

DICAEOPOLIS

Who am I? A good citizen, not ambitious; a soldier, who has fought well since the outbreak of the war, whereas you are but a vile mercenary.

LAMACHUS

They elected me . . .

DICAEOPOLIS

Yes, three cuckoos did! If I have concluded peace, it was disgust that drove me; for I see men with hoary heads in the ranks and young fellows of your age shirking service. Some are in Thrace getting an allowance of three drachmae, such fellows as Tisamenophaenippus and Panurgippar-chides. The others are with Chares or in Chaonia, men like Geretotheo-dorus and Diomialazon; there are some of the same kidney, too, at Cama-rina, at Gela, and at Catagela.

LAMACHUS

They were elected.

DICAEOPOLIS

And why do you always receive your pay, when none of these others ever gets any? Speak, Marilades, you have grey hair; well then, have you ever been entrusted with a mission? See! he shakes his head. Yet he is

an active as well as a prudent man. And you, Anthracyllus or Euphorides
or Prinides, have you knowledge of Ecbatana or Chaonia? You say no, do
you not? Such offices are good for the son of Coesyra and Lamachus, who,
but yesterday ruined with debt, never pay their shot, and whom all their
friends avoid as foot passengers dodge the folks who empty their slops out
of window.

LAMACHUS
Oh! in freedom's name! are such exaggerations to be borne?

DICAEOPOLIS
Not unless Lamachus gets paid for it.

LAMACHUS
But I propose always to war with the Peloponnesians, both at sea, on
land and everywhere to make them tremble, and trounce them soundly.
                                        (*He goes back into his house.*)

DICAEOPOLIS
For my own part, I make proclamation to all Peloponnesians, Me-
garians and Boeotians, that to them my markets are open; but I debar
Lamachus from entering them.
                                        (*He goes into his house.*)

LEADER OF THE CHORUS
Convinced by this man's speech, the folk have changed their view and
approve him for having concluded peace. But let us prepare for the recital
of the parabasis.
                (*The* CHORUS *moves forward and faces the audience.*)
Never since our poet presented comedies, has he praised himself upon
the stage; but, having been slandered by his enemies amongst the volatile
Athenians, accused of scoffing at his country and of insulting the people,
to-day he wishes to reply and regain for himself the inconstant Athenians.
He maintains that he has done much that is good for you; if you no longer
allow yourselves to be too much hoodwinked by strangers or seduced by
flattery, if in politics you are no longer the ninnies you once were, it is
thanks to him. Formerly, when delegates from other cities wanted to deceive you, they had but to style you, "the people crowned with violets,"
and at the word "violets" you at once sat erect on the tips of your bums.
Or if, to tickle your vanity, someone spoke of "rich and sleek Athens," in
return for that "sleekness" he would get anything he wanted, because he
spoke of you as he would have of anchovies in oil. In cautioning you
against such wiles, the poet has done you great service as well as in forcing you to understand what is really the democratic principle. Thus the
strangers, who came to pay their tributes, wanted to see this great poet,

who had dared to speak the truth to Athens. And so far has the fame of
his boldness reached that one day the Great King, when questioning the
Lacedæmonian delegates, first asked them which of the two rival cities
was the superior at sea, and then immediately demanded at which it was
that the comic poet directed his biting satire. "Happy that city," he
added, "if it listens to his counsel; it will grow in power, and its victory is
assured." This is why the Lacedaemonians offer you peace, if you will cede
them Aegina; not that they care for the isle, but they wish to rob you of
your poet. As for you, never lose him, who will always fight for the cause
of justice in his comedies; he promises you that his precepts will lead
you to happiness, though he uses neither flattery, nor bribery, nor intrigue,
nor deceit; instead of loading you with praise, he will point you to the
better way. I scoff at Cleon's tricks and plotting; honesty and justice
shall fight my cause; never will you find me a political poltroon, a prostitute to the highest bidder.

First Semi-Chorus (*singing*)

I invoke thee, Acharnian Muse, fierce and fell as the devouring
fire; sudden as the spark that bursts from the crackling oaken coal
when roused by the quickening fan to fry little fishes, while others
knead the dough or whip the sharp Thasian pickle with rapid hand,
so break forth, my Muse, and inspire thy tribesmen with rough, vigorous, stirring strains.

Leader of First Semi-Chorus

We others, now old men and heavy with years, we reproach the city;
so many are the victories we have gained for the Athenian fleets that we
well deserve to be cared for in our declining life; yet far from this, we are
ill-used, harassed with law-suits, delivered over to the scorn of stripling
orators. Our minds and bodies being ravaged with age, Posidon should
protect us, yet we have no other support than a staff. When standing before the judge, we can scarcely stammer forth the fewest words, and of
justice we see but its barest shadow, whereas the accuser, desirous of con-
ciliating the younger men, overwhelms us with his ready rhetoric; he
drags us before the judge, presses us with questions, lays traps for us;
the onslaught troubles, upsets and ruins poor old Tithonus, who, crushed
with age, stands tongue-tied; sentenced to a fine, he weeps, he sobs and
says to his friend, "This fine robs me of the last trifle that was to have
bought my coffin."

Second Semi-Chorus (*singing*)

Is this not a scandal? What! the clepsydra is to kill the white-
haired veteran, who, in fierce fighting, has so oft covered himself with
glorious sweat, whose valour at Marathon saved the country! We

were the ones who pursued on the field of Marathon, whereas now it is wretches who pursue us to the death and crush us. What would Marpsias reply to this?

LEADER OF SECOND SEMI-CHORUS
What an injustice that a man, bent with age like Thucydides, should be brow-beaten by this braggart advocate, Cephisodemus, who is as savage as the Scythian desert he was born in! I wept tears of pity when I saw a Scythian maltreat this old man, who, by Ceres, when he was young and the true Thucydides, would not have permitted an insult from Ceres herself! At that date he would have floored ten orators like Euathlus, he would have terrified three thousand Scythians with his shouts; he would have pierced the whole line of the enemy with his shafts. Ah! but if you will not leave the aged in peace, decree that the advocates be matched; thus the old man will only be confronted with a toothless greybeard, the young will fight with the braggart, the ignoble with the son of Clinias; make a law that in the future, the old man can only be summoned and convicted at the courts by the aged and the young man by the youth.

DICAEOPOLIS (*coming out of his house and marking out a square in front of it*)
These are the confines of my market-place. All Peloponnesians, Megarians, Boeotians, have the right to come and trade here, provided they sell their wares to me and not to Lamachus. As market-inspectors I appoint these three whips of Leprean leather, chosen by lot. Warned away are all informers and all men of Phasis. They are bringing me the pillar on which the treaty is inscribed and I shall erect it in the centre of the market, well in sight of all.
(*He goes back into the house just as a Megarian enters from the left, carrying a sack on his shoulder and followed by his two little daughters.*)

MEGARIAN
Hail! market of Athens, beloved of Megarians. Let Zeus, the patron of friendship, witness, I regretted you as a mother mourns her son. Come, poor little daughters of an unfortunate father, try to find something to eat; listen to me with the full heed of an empty belly. Which would you prefer? To be sold or to cry with hunger?

DAUGHTERS
To be sold, to be sold!

MEGARIAN
That is my opinion too. But who would make so sorry a deal as to buy you? Ah! I recall me a Megarian trick; I am going to disguise you as

little porkers, that I am offering for sale. Fit your hands with these hoofs and take care to appear the issue of a sow of good breed, for, if I am forced to take you back to the house, by Hermes! you will suffer cruelly of hunger! Then fix on these snouts and cram yourselves into this sack. Forget not to grunt and to say wee-wee like the little pigs that are sacrificed in the Mysteries. I must summon Dicaeopolis. Where is he? (*Loudly*) Dicaeopolis, do you want to buy some nice little porkers?

DICAEOPOLIS (*coming out of his house*)
Who are you? a Megarian?

MEGARIAN
I have come to your market.

DICAEOPOLIS
Well, how are things at Megara?

MEGARIAN
We are crying with hunger at our firesides.

DICAEOPOLIS
The fireside is jolly enough with a piper.[7] But what else is doing at Megara?

MEGARIAN
What else? When I left for the market, the authorities were taking steps to let us die in the quickest manner.

DICAEOPOLIS
That is the best way to get you out of all your troubles.

MEGARIAN
True.

DICAEOPOLIS
What other news of Megara? What is wheat selling at?

MEGARIAN
With us it is valued as highly as the very gods in heaven!

DICAEOPOLIS
Is it salt that you are bringing?

MEGARIAN
Aren't you the ones that are holding back the salt?[8]

DICAEOPOLIS
Is it garlic then?

MEGARIAN

What! garlic! do you not at every raid like mice grub up the ground with your pikes to pull out every single head?

DICAEOPOLIS

What *are* you bringing then?

MEGARIAN

Little sows, like those they immolate at the Mysteries.[9]

DICAEOPOLIS

Ah! very well, show me them.

MEGARIAN

They are very fine; feel their weight. See! how fat and fine.

DICAEOPOLIS (*feeling around in the sack*)
Hey! what's *this?*

MEGARIAN

A sow.

DICAEOPOLIS

A *sow,* you say? Where from, then?

MEGARIAN

From Megara. What! isn't it a sow then?

DICAEOPOLIS (*feeling around in the sack again*)
No, I don't believe it is.

MEGARIAN

This is too much! what an incredulous man! He says it's not a sow; but we will stake, if you will, a measure of salt ground up with thyme, that in good Greek this is called a sow and nothing else.

DICAEOPOLIS

But a sow of the human kind.

MEGARIAN

Without question, by Diocles! of my own breed! Well! What think you? would you like to hear them squeal?

DICAEOPOLIS

Yes, I would.

MEGARIAN

Cry quickly, wee sowlet; squeak up, hussy, or by Hermes! I take you back to the house.

DAUGHTERS

Wee-wee, wee-wee!

MEGARIAN

Is that a little sow, or not?

DICAEOPOLIS

Yes, it seems so; but let it grow up, and it will be a fine fat thing.

MEGARIAN

In five years it will be just like its mother.

DICAEOPOLIS

But it cannot be sacrificed.

MEGARIAN

And why not?

DICAEOPOLIS

It has no tail.

MEGARIAN

Because it is quite young, but in good time it will have a big one, thick and red. But if you are willing to bring it up you will have a very fine sow.

DICAEOPOLIS

The two are as like as two peas.

MEGARIAN

They are born of the same father and mother; let them be fattened, let them grow their bristles, and they will be the finest sows you can offer to Aphrodité.

DICAEOPOLIS

But sows are not immolated to Aphrodité.

MEGARIAN

Not sows to Aphrodité! Why, she's the only goddess to whom they are offered! the flesh of my sows will be excellent on your spit.

DICAEOPOLIS

Can they eat alone? They no longer need their mother?

MEGARIAN
Certainly not, nor their father.

DICAEOPOLIS
What do they like most?

MEGARIAN
Whatever is given them; but ask for yourself.

DICAEOPOLIS
Speak! little sow.

DAUGHTERS
Wee-wee, wee-wee!

DICAEOPOLIS
Can you eat chick-pease? [10]

DAUGHTERS
Wee-wee, wee-wee, wee-wee!

DICAEOPOLIS
And Attic figs?

DAUGHTERS
Wee-wee, wee-wee!

DICAEOPOLIS
What sharp squeaks at the name of figs. Come, let some figs be brought
for these little pigs. Will they eat them? Goodness! how they munch them,
what a grinding of teeth, mighty Heracles! I believe those pigs hail from
the land of the Voracians.

MEGARIAN (*aside*)
But they have not eaten all the figs; I took this one myself.

DICAEOPOLIS
Ah! what curious creatures! For what sum will you sell them?

MEGARIAN
I will give you one for a bunch of garlic, and the other, if you like, for a
quart measure of salt.

DICAEOPOLIS
I'll buy them. Wait for me here.

(*He goes into the house.*)

MEGARIAN

The deal is done. Hermes, god of good traders, grant I may sell both my wife and my mother in the same way!

(*An* INFORMER *enters.*)

INFORMER

Hi! fellow, what country are you from?

MEGARIAN

I am a pig-merchant from Megara.

INFORMER

I shall denounce both your pigs and yourself as public enemies.

MEGARIAN

Ah! here our troubles begin afresh!

INFORMER

Let go of that sack. I'll teach you to talk Megarian!

MEGARIAN (*loudly*)

Dicaeopolis, Dicaeopolis, they want to denounce me.

DICAEOPOLIS (*from within*)

Who dares do this thing? (*He comes out of his house.*) Inspectors, drive out the informers. Ah! you offer to enlighten us without a lamp! [11]

INFORMER

What! I may not denounce our enemies?

DICAEOPOLIS (*with a threatening gesture*)

Watch out for yourself, and go off pretty quick and denounce else-where.

(*The* INFORMER *runs away.*)

MEGARIAN

What a plague to Athens!

DICAEOPOLIS

Be reassured, Megarian. Here is the price for your two sowlets, the garlic and the salt. Farewell and much happiness!

MEGARIAN

Ah! we never have that amongst us.

DICAEOPOLIS

Oh, I'm sorry if I said the wrong thing.

MEGARIAN

Farewell, dear little sows, and seek, far from your father, to munch your bread with salt, if they give you any.

(*He departs and* DICAEOPOLIS *takes the "sows" into his house.*)

CHORUS (*singing*)

Here is a man truly happy. See how everything succeeds to his wish. Peacefully seated in his market, he will earn his living; woe to Ctesias, and all other informers who dare to enter there! You will not be cheated as to the value of wares, you will not again see Prepis wiping his big arse, nor will Cleonymus jostle you; you will take your walks, clothed in a fine tunic, without meeting Hyperbolus and his unceasing quibblings, without being accosted on the public place by any importunate fellow, neither by Cratinus, shaven in the fashion of the adulterers, nor by this musician, who plagues us with his silly improvisations, that hyper-rogue Artemo, with his arm-pits stinking as foul as a goat, like his father before him. You will not be the butt of the villainous Pauson's jeers, nor of Lysistratus, the disgrace of the Cholargian deme, who is the incarnation of all the vices, and endures cold and hunger more than thirty days in the month.

(*A* BOEOTIAN *enters, followed by his slave, who is carrying a large assortment of articles of food, and by a troop of flute players.*)

BOEOTIAN

By Heracles! my shoulder is quite black and blue. Ismenias, put the penny-royal down there very gently, and all of you, musicians from Thebes, strike up on your bone flutes "The Dog's Arse."

(*The Musicians immediately begin an atrocious rendition of a vulgar tune.*)

DICAEOPOLIS

Enough, damn you; get out of here! Rascally hornets, away with you! Whence has sprung this accursed swarm of Chaeris fellows which comes assailing my door?

(*The Musicians depart.*)

BOEOTIAN

Ah! by Iolas! Drive them off, my dear host, you will please me immensely; all the way from Thebes, they were there piping behind me and they have completely stripped my penny-royal of its blossom. But will you buy anything of me, some chickens or some locusts?

DICAEOPOLIS

Ah! good day, Boeotian, eater of good round loaves. What do *you* bring?

BOEOTIAN

All that is good in Boeotia, marjoram, penny-royal, rush-mats, lamp-wicks, ducks, jays, woodcocks, water-fowl, wrens, divers.

DICAEOPOLIS

A regular hail of birds is beating down on my market.

BOEOTIAN

I also bring geese, hares, foxes, moles, hedgehogs, cats, lyres, martins, otters and eels from the Copaic lake.

DICAEOPOLIS

Ah! my friend, you, who bring me the most delicious of fish, let me salute your eels.

BOEOTIAN (*in tragic style*)

Come, thou, the eldest of my fifty Copaic virgins, come and complete the joy of our host.

DICAEOPOLIS (*likewise*)

Oh! my well-beloved, thou object of my long regrets, thou art here at last then, thou, after whom the comic poets sigh, thou, who art dear to Morychus. Slaves, hither with the stove and the bellows. Look at this charming eel, that returns to us after six long years of absence. Salute it, my children; as for myself, I will supply coal to do honour to the stranger. Take it into my house; death itself could not separate me from her, if cooked with beet leaves.

BOEOTIAN

And what will you give me in return?

DICAEOPOLIS

It will pay for your market dues. And as to the rest, what do you wish to sell me?

BOEOTIAN

Why, everything.

DICAEOPOLIS

On what terms? For ready-money or in wares from these parts?

BOEOTIAN

I would take some Athenian produce, that we have not got in Boeotia.

DICAEOPOLIS

Phaleric anchovies, pottery?

BOEOTIAN

Anchovies, pottery? But these we have. I want produce that is wanting with us and that is plentiful here.

DICAEOPOLIS

Ah! I have the very thing; take away an informer, packed up carefully as crockery-ware.

BOEOTIAN

By the twin gods! I should earn big money, if I took one; I would exhibit him as an ape full of spite.

DICAEOPOLIS (*as an informer enters*)

Hah! here we have Nicarchus, who comes to denounce you。

BOEOTIAN

How small he is!

DICAEOPOLIS

But all pure evil.

NICARCHUS

Whose are these goods?

DICAEOPOLIS

Mine; they come from Boeotia, I call Zeus to witness.

NICARCHUS

I denounce them as coming from an enemy's country.

BOEOTIAN

What! you declare war against birds?

NICARCHUS

And I am going to denounce you too.

BOEOTIAN

What harm have I done you?

NICARCHUS

I will say it for the benefit of those that listen; you introduce lamp-wicks from an enemy's country.

DICAEOPOLIS

Then you even denounce a wick.

NICARCHUS

It needs but one to set an arsenal afire.

DICAEOPOLIS

A wick set an arsenal ablaze! But how, great gods?

NICARCHUS

Should a Boeotian attach it to an insect's wing, and, taking advantage
of a violent north wind, throw it by means of a tube into the arsenal and
the fire once get hold of the vessels, everything would soon be devoured
by the flames.

DICAEOPOLIS

Ah! wretch! an insect and a wick devour everything!

(*He strikes him.*)

NICARCHUS (*to the* CHORUS)

You will bear witness, that he mishandles me.

DICAEOPOLIS (*to the* BOEOTIAN)

Shut his mouth. Give me some hay; I am going to pack him up like a
vase, that he may not get broken on the road.

(*The* INFORMER *is bound and gagged and packed in hay.*)

LEADER OF THE CHORUS

Pack up your goods carefully, friend; that the stranger may not break
it when taking it away.

DICAEOPOLIS

I shall take great care with it. (*He hits the* INFORMER *on the head and
a stifled cry is heard.*) One would say he is cracked already; he rings with
a false note, which the gods abhor.

LEADER OF THE CHORUS

But what will be done with him?

DICAEOPOLIS

This is a vase good for all purposes; it will be used as a vessel for holding all foul things, a mortar for pounding together law-suits, a lamp for
spying upon accounts, and as a cup for the mixing up and poisoning of
everything.

LEADER OF THE CHORUS

None could ever trust a vessel for domestic use that has such a ring
about it.

DICAEOPOLIS

Oh! it is strong, my friend, and will never get broken, if care is taken
to hang it head downwards.

LEADER OF THE CHORUS (*to the* BOEOTIAN)
There! it is well packed now!

BOEOTIAN
Well then, I will proceed to carry off my bundle.

LEADER OF THE CHORUS
Farewell, worthiest of strangers, take this informer, good for anything, and fling him where you like.

DICAEOPOLIS
Bah! this rogue has given me enough trouble to pack! Here! Boeotian, pick up your pottery.

BOEOTIAN
Stoop, Ismenias, that I may put it on your shoulder, and be very care-- ful with it.

DICAEOPOLIS
You carry nothing worth having; however, take it, for you will profit by your bargain; the informers will bring you luck.
(*The* BOEOTIAN *and his slave depart;* DICAEOPOLIS *goes into his house; a slave comes out of* LAMACHUS' *house.*)

SLAVE
Dicaeopolis!

DICAEOPOLIS (*from within*)
What's the matter? Why are you calling me?

SLAVE
Lamachus wants to keep the Feast of Cups, and I come by his order to bid you one drachma for some thrushes and three more for a Copaic eel.

DICAEOPOLIS (*coming out*)
And who is this Lamachus, who demands an eel?

SLAVE (*in tragic style*)
He is the terrible, indefatigable Lamachus, who is always brandishing his fearful Gorgon's head and the three plumes which o'ershadow his helmet.

DICAEOPOLIS
No, no, he will get nothing, even though he gave me his buckler. Let him eat salt fish while he shakes his plumes, and, if he comes here mak- ing any din, I shall call the inspectors. As for myself, I shall take away all these goods; (*in tragic style*) I go home on thrushes' wings and black- birds' pinions. (*He goes into his house.*)

First Semi-Chorus (*singing*)

You see, citizens, you see the good fortune which this man owes
to his prudence, to his profound wisdom. You see how, since he has
concluded peace, he buys what is useful in the household and good
to eat hot. All good things flow towards him unsought. Never will I
welcome the god of war in *my* house; never shall *he* sing the "Harmodius" at my table; he is a sot, who comes feasting with those who
are overflowing with good things and brings all manner of mischief
in his train. He overthrows, ruins, rips open; it is vain to make him
a thousand offers, to say "be seated, pray, and drink this cup, prof-
fered in all friendship"; he burns our vine-stocks and brutally spills
on the ground the wine from our vineyards.

Second Semi-Chorus (*singing*)

This man, on the other hand, covers his table with a thousand
dishes; proud of his good fortunes, he has had these feathers cast
before his door to show us how he lives. (*A woman appears, bearing the attributes of Peace.*) Oh, Peace! companion of fair Aphrodité and of the sweet Graces, how charming are thy features and
yet I never knew it! Would that Eros might join me to thee, Eros
crowned with roses as Zeuxis shows him to us! Do I seem somewhat old to thee? I am yet able to make thee a threefold offering;
despite my age I could plant a long row of vines for you; then beside these some tender cuttings from the fig; finally a young vine-
stock, loaded with fruit, and all around the field olive trees, to furnish us with oil wherewith to anoint us both at the New Moons.

(*A Herald enters.*)

Herald

Oyez, oyez! As was the custom of your forebears, empty a full pitcher
of wine at the call of the trumpet; he who first sees the bottom shall
get a wine-skin as round and plump as Ctesiphon's belly.

Dicaeopolis (*coming out of the house; to his family within*)

Women, children, have you not heard? Faith! do you not heed the
herald? Quick! let the hares boil and roast merrily; keep them turning;
withdraw them from the flame; prepare the chaplets; reach me the
skewers that I may spit the thrushes.

Leader of First Semi-Chorus

I envy you your wisdom and even more your good cheer.

Dicaeopolis

What then will you say when you see the thrushes roasting?

LEADER OF FIRST SEMI-CHORUS
Ah! true indeed!

DICAEOPOLIS
Slave! stir up the fire.

LEADER OF FIRST SEMI-CHORUS
See, how he knows his business, what a perfect cook! How well he understands the way to prepare a good dinner!

(*A* HUSBANDMAN *enters in haste.*)

HUSBANDMAN
Ah! woe is me!

DICAEOPOLIS
Heracles! What have we here?

HUSBANDMAN
A most miserable man.

DICAEOPOLIS
Keep your misery for yourself.

HUSBANDMAN
Ah! friend! since you alone are enjoying peace, grant me a part of your truce, were it but five years.

DICAEOPOLIS
What has happened to you?

HUSBANDMAN
I am ruined; I have lost a pair of steers.

DICAEOPOLIS
How?

HUSBANDMAN
The Boeotians seized them at Phylé.

DICAEOPOLIS
Ah! poor wretch! and do you still wear white?

HUSBANDMAN
Their dung made my wealth.

DICAEOPOLIS
What can I do in the matter?

HUSBANDMAN

Crying for my beasts has lost me my eyesight. Ah! if you care for poor Dercetes of Phylé, anoint mine eyes quickly with your balm of peace.

DICAEOPOLIS

But, my poor fellow, I do not practise medicine.

HUSBANDMAN

Come, I adjure you; perhaps I shall recover my steers.

DICAEOPOLIS

Impossible; away, go and whine to the disciples of Pittalus.

HUSBANDMAN

Grant me but one drop of peace; pour it into this little reed.

DICAEOPOLIS

No, not a particle; go and weep somewhere else.

HUSBANDMAN (*as he departs*)

Oh! oh! oh! my poor beasts!

LEADER OF SECOND SEMI-CHORUS

This man has discovered the sweetest enjoyment in peace; he will share it with none.

DICAEOPOLIS (*to a slave*)

Pour honey over this tripe; set it before the fire to dry.

LEADER OF SECOND SEMI-CHORUS

What lofty tones he uses! Did you hear him?

DICAEOPOLIS (*to the slaves inside the house*)

Get the eels on the gridiron!

LEADER OF SECOND SEMI-CHORUS

You are killing me with hunger; your smoke is choking your neighbours, and you split our ears with your bawling.

DICAEOPOLIS

Have this fried and let it be nicely browned.
(*He goes back into the house. A* WEDDING GUEST *enters, carrying a package.*)

WEDDING GUEST

Dicaeopolis! Dicaeopolis!

DICAEOPOLIS

Who are you?

WEDDING GUEST

A young bridegroom sends you these viands from the marriage feast.

DICAEOPOLIS

Whoever he be, I thank him.

WEDDING GUEST

And in return, he prays you to pour a glass of peace into this vase, that he may not have to go to the front and may stay at home to make love to his young wife.

DICAEOPOLIS

Take back, take back your viands; for a thousand drachmae I would not give a drop of peace. (*A young woman enters*) But who is she?

WEDDING GUEST

She is the matron of honour; she wants to say something to you from the bride privately.

DICAEOPOLIS

Come, what do you wish to say? (*The* MATRON OF HONOUR *whispers in his ear.*) *Ah!* what a ridiculous demand! The bride burns with longing to keep her husband's tool at home. Come! bring hither my truce; to her alone will I give some of it, for she is a woman, and, as such, should not suffer under the war. Here, friend, hand me your vial. And as to the manner of applying this balm, tell the bride, when a levy of soldiers is made, to rub some in bed on her husband, where most needed. (*The* MATRON OF HONOUR *and the* WEDDING GUEST *depart.*) There, slave, take away my truce! Now, quick, bring me the wine-flagon, that I may fill up the drinking bowls!

(*The slave leaves. A* HERALD *enters.*)

LEADER OF THE CHORUS (*in tragic style*)

I see a man, "striding along apace, with knitted brows; he seems to us the bearer of terrible tidings."

HERALD (*in tragic style*)

Oh! toils and battles and Lamachuses!

(*He knocks on* LAMACHUS' *door.*)

LAMACHUS (*from within; in tragic style*)

What noise resounds around my dwelling, where shines the glint of arms.

(*He comes out of his house.*)

HERALD

The Generals order you forthwith to take your battalions and your plumes, and, despite the snow, to go and guard our borders. They have learnt that a band of Boeotians intend taking advantage of the Feast of Cups to invade our country.

LAMACHUS

Ah! the Generals! they are numerous, but not good for much! It's cruel, not to be able to enjoy the feast!

DICAEOPOLIS

Oh! warlike host of Lamachus!

LAMACHUS

Wretch! do you dare to jeer me?

DICAEOPOLIS

Do you want to fight this four-winged Geryon?

LAMACHUS

Oh! oh! what fearful tidings!

DICAEOPOLIS

Ah! ah! I see another herald running up; what news does he bring me?
(Another HERALD *enters.)*

HERALD

Dicaeopolis!

DICAEOPOLIS

What is the matter?

HERALD

Come quickly to the feast and bring your basket and your cup; it is the priest of Bacchus who invites you. But hasten, the guests have been waiting for you a long while. All is ready—couches, tables, cushions, chaplets, perfumes, dainties and whores to boot; biscuits, cakes, sesamé-bread, tarts, lovely dancing women, and the "Harmodius." But come with all speed.

LAMACHUS

Oh! hostile gods!

DICAEOPOLIS

This is not astounding; you have chosen this great ugly Gorgon's head for your patron. *(To a slave)* You, shut the door, and let someone get ready the meal.

LAMACHUS
Slave! slave! my knapsack!

DICAEOPOLIS
Slave! slave! a basket!

LAMACHUS
Take salt and thyme, slave, and don't forget the onions.

DICAEOPOLIS
Get some fish for me; I cannot bear onions.

LAMACHUS
Slave, wrap me up a little stale salt meat in a fig-leaf.

DICAEOPOLIS
And for me some nice fat tripe in a fig-leaf; I will have it cooked here.

LAMACHUS
Bring me the plumes for my helmet.

DICAEOPOLIS
Bring me wild pigeons and thrushes.

LAMACHUS
How white and beautiful are these ostrich feathers!

DICAEOPOLIS
How fat and well browned is the flesh of this wood-pigeon!

LAMACHUS (*to* DICAEOPOLIS)
My friend, stop scoffing at my armour.

DICAEOPOLIS (*to* LAMACHUS)
My friend, stop staring at my thrushes.

LAMACHUS (*to his slave*)
Bring me the case for my triple plume.

DICAEOPOLIS (*to his slave*)
Pass me over that dish of hare.

LAMACHUS
Alas! the moths have eaten the hair of my crest.

DICAEOPOLIS
Shall I eat my hare before dinner?

LAMACHUS

My friend, will you kindly not speak to me?

DICAEOPOLIS

I'm not speaking to you; I'm scolding my slave. (*To the slave*) Shall we
wager and submit the matter to Lamachus, which of the two is the best
to eat, a locust or a thrush?

LAMACHUS

Insolent hound!

DICAEOPOLIS

He much prefers the locusts.

LAMACHUS

Slave, unhook my spear and bring it to me.

DICAEOPOLIS

Slave, slave, take the sausage from the fire and bring it to me.

LAMACHUS

Come, let me draw my spear from its sheath. Hold it, slave, hold it
tight.

DICAEOPOLIS

And you, slave, grip well hold of the skewer.

LAMACHUS

Slave, the bracings for my shield.

DICAEOPOLIS

Pull the loaves out of the oven and bring me these bracings of my
stomach.

LAMACHUS

My round buckler with the Gorgon's head.

DICAEOPOLIS

My round cheese-cake.

LAMACHUS

What clumsy wit!

DICAEOPOLIS

What delicious cheese-cake!

LAMACHUS

Pour oil on the buckler. Hah! hah! I can see reflected there an old man who will be accused of cowardice.

DICAEOPOLIS

Pour honey on the cake. Hah! hah! I can see an old man who makes Lamachus of the Gorgon's head weep with rage.

LAMACHUS

Slave, full war armour.

DICAEOPOLIS

Slave, my beaker; that is *my* armour.

LAMACHUS

With this I hold my ground with any foe.

DICAEOPOLIS

And I with this in any drinking bout.

LAMACHUS

Fasten the strappings to the buckler.

DICAEOPOLIS

Pack the dinner well into the basket.

LAMACHUS

Personally I shall carry the knapsack.

DICAEOPOLIS

Personally I shall carry the cloak.

LAMACHUS

Slave, take up the buckler and let's be off. It is snowing! God help us! A wintry business!

DICAEOPOLIS

Take up the basket, mine's a festive business.

(*They depart in opposite directions.*)

LEADER OF THE CHORUS

We wish you both joy on your journeys, which differ so much. One goes to mount guard and freeze, while the other will drink, crowned with flowers, and then lie with a young beauty till he gets his tool all sore.

CHORUS (*singing*)

I say it freely; may Zeus confound Antimachus, the poet-his-torian, the son of Psacas! When Choregus at the Lenaea, alas! alas!

he dismissed me dinnerless. May I see him devouring with his eyes a cuttle-fish, just served, well cooked, hot and properly salted; and the moment that he stretches his hand to help himself, may a dog seize it and run off with it. Such is my first wish. I also hope for him a misfortune at night. That returning all-fevered from horse practice, he may meet an Orestes, mad with drink, who will crack him over the head; that wishing to seize a stone, he, in the dark, may pick up a fresh turd, hurl, miss him and hit Cratinus.

(*The slave of* LAMACHUS *enters.*)

SLAVE OF LAMACHUS (*knocking on the door of* LAMACHUS' *house, in tragic style*)
Captives present within the house of Lamachus, water, water in a little pot! Make it warm, get ready cloths, cerate, greasy wool and bandages for his ankle. In leaping a ditch, the master has hurt himself against a stake; he has dislocated and twisted his ankle, broken his head by falling on a stone, while his Gorgon shot far away from his buckler. His mighty braggadocio plume rolled on the ground; at this sight he uttered these doleful words, "Radiant star, I gaze on thee for the last time; my eyes close to all light, I die." Having said this, he falls into the water, gets out again, meets some runaways and pursues the robbers with his spear at their backsides. But here he comes, himself. Get the door open.

(*In this final scene all the lines are sung.*)

LAMACHUS (*limping in with the help of two soldiers and singing a song of woe*)
Oh! heavens! oh! heavens! What cruel pain! I faint, I tremble! Alas! I die! the foe's lance has struck me! But what would hurt me most would be for Dicaeopolis to see me wounded thus and laugh at my ill-fortune.

DICAEOPOLIS (*enters with two courtesans, singing gaily*)
Oh! my gods! what breasts! Swelling like quinces! Come, my treasures, give me voluptuous kisses! Glue your lips to mine. Haha! I was the first to empty my cup.

LAMACHUS
Oh! cruel fate! how I suffer! accursed wounds!

DICAEOPOLIS
Hah! hah! Hail! Lamachippus!

LAMACHUS

Woe is me!

DICAEOPOLIS (*to the one girl*)

Why do you kiss me?

LAMACHUS

Ah, wretched me!

DICAEOPOLIS (*to the other girl*)

And why do you bite me?

LAMACHUS

'Twas a cruel score I was paying back!

DICAEOPOLIS

Scores are not evened at the Feast of Cups!

LAMACHUS

Oh! Oh! Paean, Paean!

DICAEOPOLIS

But to-day is not the feast of Paean.

LAMACHUS (*to the soldiers*)

Oh! take hold of my leg, do; ah! hold it tenderly, my friends!

DICAEOPOLIS (*to the girls*)

And you, my darlings, take hold of my tool, both of you!

LAMACHUS

This blow with the stone makes me dizzy; my sight grows dim.

DICAEOPOLIS

For myself, I want to get to bed; I've got an erection and I want
to make love in the dark.

LAMACHUS

Carry me to the surgeon Pittalus. Put me in his healing hands!

DICAEOPOLIS

Take me to the judges. Where is the king of the feast? The wine-
skin is mine!

LAMACHUS (*as he is being carried away*)

That spear has pierced my bones; what torture I endure!

DICAEOPOLIS (*to the audience*)
You see this empty cup! I triumph! I triumph!

CHORUS
Old man, I come at your bidding! You triumph! you triumph!

DICAEOPOLIS
Again I have brimmed my cup with unmixed wine and drained it at a draught!

CHORUS
You triumph then, brave champion; thine is the wine-skin!

DICAEOPOLIS
Follow me, singing "Triumph! Triumph!"

CHORUS
Aye! we will sing of thee, thee and thy sacred wine-skin, and we all, as we follow thee, will repeat in thine honour, "Triumph, Triumph!"

1. Such was the esteem in which Aeschylus was held by his country-men that even after his death it was especially decreed that his plays might be produced at the dramatic festivals, which otherwise were devoted exclusively to new compositions, and he is reported to have won several posthumous victories on such occasions.

2. The Athenian democracy presupposed a maximum of popular participation in the business of government, just as the Socialist democracy of the Soviet Union does today, and it is interesting to discover that in ancient times also certain special efforts had to be made to overcome human indolence and apathy in political matters. So many Athenians preferred the bustle of the market-place to the solemnity of the Assembly that it was customary to round up the dilatory with a long and freshly reddened rope; fines for tardiness would then be imposed on all who exhibited the telltale vermilion stripe.

3. The ingenuity of scholarship has yet to extract a satisfactory or apposite meaning from this jargon. Such passages usually mean something in Aristophanes, and the second speech of Pseudartabas is, as Dicaeopolis remarks, clear enough, but this line may be nothing more than a sample of what Persian sounded like to a Greek. The accents indicate the metre.

4. Many Athenians seem to have been as ready to leave, as they were reluctant to attend, the Assembly, and adjournment must occasionally have been effected on somewhat flimsy grounds.

5. While carrying out the comparison between truce-tasting and wine sampling, Aristophanes manages to convey his views on what sort of peace ought to be made; one of five years' duration would be merely a breathing spell for an armaments race, and one of ten would only give additional time for the conclusion of military alliances.

6. Aristophanes never tires of twitting Euripides with the fact or fancy that his mother had sold vegetables.

7. Dicaeopolis has misunderstood the Megarian, taking *peinames*, "we starve" for *pinomes*, "we drink"; hence his apparently inappropriate reply.

474

8. At this time the Athenians had possession of the island of Minoa off the Megarian coast; they were thus able to intercept all her maritime commerce, and they incidentally controlled her salt-works also.

9. This brilliant scene is a riotous tissue of plays on the double meaning of the Greek word *choiros,* which signifies not only "sow" but also "female genitalia." The English word "pussy" has comparable senses, but is regrettably ill-adapted to the needs of this particular scene, which must thus remain the Hellenist's delight and the translator's despair.

10. Here we find a pun similar to that on *choiros,* for the word *erebiñthos* means both "chick-pea" and "penis"; the remark about figs in the next line seems also to contain such a *double entendre.*

11. This remark is a pun on the word *phainein,* which means both "to light" and "to inform against."

II
THE KNIGHTS

Characters in the Play

Demosthenes
Nicias
Agoracritus, *a Sausage-Seller*
Cleon
Demos
Chorus of Knights

INTRODUCTION

JUST a year after the success of *The Acharnians,* at the Lenaea of 424, Aristophanes, under his own name, produced *The Knights* and was again victorious, this time with what is very nearly the poorest of the eleven comedies that have come down to us. In sharp contrast with the gay variety of *The Acharnians, The Knights* is sadly deficient in amusing incidents and all too liberally endowed with political and uncomic hate. Primarily and essentially a vitriolic attack on the demagogue Cleon, who but a few months previously had returned in triumph from Sphacteria and was now at the height of his powers, the play is a greater tribute to its author's courage and sincerity than to his art and taste. As a work of literature rather than as an historical and biographical document, perhaps the best that can be said in its favour is that it contributes materially to our knowledge of the formal and metrical structure of the Agon.

The opening scene introduces us to the amorphous characters and harassed situation of Demosthenes and Nicias, two faithful servants of Demos, who personifies the Athenian people. In a long speech addressed to the spectators Demosthenes explains that the chief cause of his distress is a recent addition to Demos' household, "a Paphlagonian tanner, an arrant rogue, the incarnation of calumny." This domineering and dishonest slave has rendered life intolerable for the others, and it is imperative that he be got rid of immediately. An oracle filched from his great collection reveals that the tanner is to be succeeded by a sausage-seller, and no sooner is this prophecy disclosed than just such a merchant appears and is astonished to find himself hailed as the saviour of Athens.

In a little while the Paphlagonian emerges from the house and the still bewildered sausage-seller is about to beat a hasty retreat, but Demosthenes summons the Knights to his rescue and the Chorus is thus introduced. Their vigorous attack on Cleon rallies the sausage-seller's ebbing spirits and a loud contest of vulgar denigration ensues between him and the tanner. This culminates in the decision of both combatants to go to the Senate in order to test in practice their demagogic talents. Their departure leaves the stage to the Chorus and the parabasis is now delivered.

479

The anapests explain why Aristophanes had hitherto concealed his identity beneath pseudonyms, and in the course of this pronounce a number of interesting animadversions on the precariousness of the comic poet's profession. The ode invokes and celebrates the god Posidon. The epirrheme extolls the courage of the earlier Athens and proclaims the patriotic devotion of the Knights. In the antode the Chorus calls to its aid Athene, the patron goddess of the city. The antepirrheme praises the Knights in a discreet and indirect fashion by lauding the valour and the exploits of their steeds.

At the conclusion of the parabasis the sausage-seller returns in triumph to announce and to narrate his victory over the Senate. As soon as he has done this the Paphlagonian arrives, bursting with fury and not yet willing to admit that the other is clearly his master in the very game in which he specializes. In accord with normal Athenian legislative procedure the decision is now put to the sovereign people, and Demos is summoned from his home to the Pnyx, where he listens gladly and proudly to the extravagant protestations of devotion made by the Paphlagonian and the sausage-seller. At long last the latter emerges triumphant and the tanner retires in utter confusion. Agoracritus, for the sausage-seller's name is now finally revealed, goes with Demos into his house and the Chorus delivers a sort of second parabasis, a passage filled with singular obscenity and personal vituperation. After this Agoracritus comes out of the house followed by a rejuvenated Demos, who intends to reestablish the pristine discipline of Athens.

Thus ends a comedy at once brave and bad, in which, however, the braveness does not quite compensate for the badness; Aristophanes is so eager to attack the detested Cleon that he neglects to write a real comedy. From Euripides to Odets this is what has always happened when the playwright is so misguided as to become primarily the propagandist. Aristophanes allows his hatred of Cleon to betray him into a surprisingly large number of inconsistencies and lapses of artistic restraint, and the fact that the play was crowned with the first prize may be variously attributed to the inferior merit of the comedies with which it competed, to popular participation in the author's political views, or to the admiration with which his obvious courage may have inspired the spectators; in any case the victory of *The Knights*, like the failure of *The Birds* a decade later, clearly demonstrates the whimsical instability and the dubious value of the vulgar taste.

THE KNIGHTS

(SCENE:—*The Orchestra represents the Pnyx at Athens; in the back-ground is the house of* DEMOS.)

DEMOSTHENES

OH! alas! alas! Oh! woe! oh! woe! Miserable Paphlagonian! may the gods destroy both him and his cursed advice! Since that evil day when this new slave entered the house he has never ceased belabouring us with blows.

NICIAS

May the plague seize him, the arch-fiend—him and his lying tales!

DEMOSTHENES

Hah! my poor fellow, what is your condition?

NICIAS

Very wretched, just like your own.

DEMOSTHENES

Then come, let us sing a duet of groans in the style of Olympus.

DEMOSTHENES AND NICIAS

Boo, hoo! boo, hoo! boo, hoo! boo, hoo! boo, hoo! boo, hoo!!

DEMOSTHENES

Bah! it's lost labour to weep! Enough of groaning! Let us consider how to save our pelts.

NICIAS

But how to do it! Can you suggest anything?

DEMOSTHENES

No, you begin. I cede you the honour.

NICIAS

By Apollo! no, not I. Come, have courage! Speak, and then I will say what I think.

481

DEMOSTHENES (*in tragic style*)
"Ah! would you but tell me what I should tell you!"

NICIAS
I dare not. How could I express my thoughts with the pomp of Euripides?

DEMOSTHENES
Oh! please spare me! Do not pelt me with those vegetables,[1] but find some way of leaving our master.

NICIAS
Well, then! Say "Let-us-bolt," like this, in one breath.

DEMOSTHENES
I follow you—"Let-us-bolt."

NICIAS
Now after "Let-us-bolt" say "at-top-speed!"

DEMOSTHENES
"At-top-speed!"

NICIAS
Splendid! Just as if you were masturbating; first slowly, "Let-us-bolt"; then quick and firmly, "at-top-speed!"

DEMOSTHENES
Let-us-bolt, let-us-bolt-at-top-speed!

NICIAS
Hah! does that not please you?

DEMOSTHENES
Yes, indeed, yet I fear your omen bodes no good to my hide.

NICIAS
How so?

DEMOSTHENES
Because masturbation chafes the skin.

NICIAS
The best thing we can do for the moment is to throw ourselves at the feet of the statue of some god.

DEMOSTHENES
Of which statue? Any statue? Do you then believe there are gods?

NICIAS

Certainly.

DEMOSTHENES

What proof have you?

NICIAS

The proof that they have taken a grudge against me. Is that not enough?

DEMOSTHENES

I'm convinced it is. But to pass on. Do you consent to my telling the spectators of our troubles?

NICIAS

There's nothing wrong with that, and we might ask them to show us by their manner, whether our facts and actions are to their liking.

DEMOSTHENES

I will begin then. We have a very brutal master, a perfect glutton for beans, and most bad-tempered; it's Demos of the Pnyx, an intolerable old man and half deaf. The beginning of last month he bought a slave, a Paphlagonian tanner, an arrant rogue, the incarnation of calumny. This man of leather knows his old master thoroughly; he plays the fawning cur, flatters, cajoles, wheedles, and dupes him at will with little scraps of leavings, which he allows him to get. "Dear Demos," he will say, "try a single case and you will have done enough; then take your bath, eat, swallow and devour; here are three obols." Then the Paphlagonian filches from one of us what we have prepared and makes a present of it to our old man. The other day I had just kneaded a Spartan cake at Pylos, the cunning rogue came behind my back, sneaked it and offered the cake, which was my invention, in his own name. He keeps us at a distance and suffers none but himself to wait upon the master; when Demos is dining, he keeps close to his side with a thong in his hand and puts the orators to flight. He keeps singing oracles to him, so that the old man now thinks of nothing but the Sibyl. Then, when he sees him thoroughly obfuscated, he uses all his cunning and piles up lies and calumnies against the household; then we are scourged and the Paphlagonian runs about among the slaves to demand contributions with threats and gathers them in with both hands. He will say, "You see how I have had Hylas beaten! Either content me or die at once!" We are forced to give, for otherwise the old man tramples on us and makes us crap forth all our body contains. (*To* NICIAS) There must be an end to it, friend Let us see! what can be done? Who will get us out of this mess?

NICIAS

The best thing, friend, is our famous "Let-us-bolt!"

DEMOSTHENES

But none can escape the Paphlagonian, his eye is everywhere. And what a stride! He has one leg on Pylos and the other in the Assembly; his arse gapes exactly over the land of the Chaonians, his hands are with the Aetolians and his mind with the Clopidians.

NICIAS

It's best then to die; but let us seek the most heroic death.

DEMOSTHENES

Let me think, what *is* the most heroic?

NICIAS

Let us drink the blood of a bull; that's the death Themistocles chose.

DEMOSTHENES

No, not that, but a bumper of good unmixed wine in honour of the Good Genius; perchance we may stumble on a happy thought.

NICIAS

Look at him! "Unmixed wine!" Your mind is on drink intent? Can a man strike out a brilliant thought when drunk?

DEMOSTHENES

Without question. Go, ninny, blow yourself out with water; do you dare to accuse wine of clouding the reason? Quote me more marvellous effects than those of wine. Look! when a man drinks, he is rich, everything he touches succeeds, he gains lawsuits, is happy and helps his friends. Come, bring hither quick a flagon of wine, that I may soak my brain and get an ingenious idea.

NICIAS

My God! What can your drinking do to help us?

DEMOSTHENES

Much. But bring it to me, while I take my seat. Once drunk, I shall strew little ideas, little phrases, little reasonings everywhere.
(NICIAS *enters the house and returns almost immediately with a bottle.*)

NICIAS

It is lucky I was not caught in the house stealing the wine.

DEMOSTHENES

Tell me, what is the Paphlagonian doing now?

NICIAS

The wretch has just gobbled up some confiscated cakes; he is drunk and lies at full-length snoring on his hides.

DEMOSTHENES

Very well, come along, pour me out wine and plenty of it.

NICIAS

Take it and offer a libation to your Good Genius.

DEMOSTHENES (*to himself*)

Inhale, ah, inhale the spirit of the genius of Pramnium. (*He drinks. Inspiredly*) Ah! Good Genius, thine the plan, not mine!

NICIAS

Tell me, what is it?

DEMOSTHENES

Run indoors quick and steal the oracles of the Paphlagonian, while he is asleep.

NICIAS

Bless me! I fear this Good Genius will be but a very Bad Genius for me.
(*He goes into the house.*)

DEMOSTHENES

And I'll set the flagon near me, that I may moisten my wit to invent some brilliant notion.
(NICIAS *enters the house and returns at once.*)

NICIAS

How loudly the Paphlagonian farts and snores! I was able to seize the sacred oracle, which he was guarding with the greatest care, without his seeing me.

DEMOSTHENES

Oh! clever fellow! Hand it here, that I may read. Come, pour me out some drink, bestir yourself! Let me see what there is in it. Oh! prophecy! Some drink! some drink! Quick!

NICIAS

Well! what says the oracle?

DEMOSTHENES

Pour again.

NICIAS

Is "pour again" in the oracle?

DEMOSTHENES

Oh, Bacis!

NICIAS

But what is in it?

DEMOSTHENES

Quick! some drink!

NICIAS

Bacis is very dry!

DEMOSTHENES

Oh! miserable Paphlagonian! This then is why you have so long taken such precautions; your horoscope gave you qualms of terror.

NICIAS

What does it say?

DEMOSTHENES

It says here how he must end.

NICIAS

And how?

DEMOSTHENES

How? the oracle announces clearly that a dealer in oakum must first govern the city.²

NICIAS

That's one tradesman. And after him, who?

DEMOSTHENES

After him, a sheep-dealer.³

NICIAS

Two tradesmen, eh? And what is this one's fate?

DEMOSTHENES

To reign until a filthier scoundrel than he arises; then he perishes and in his place the leather-seller appears, the Paphlagonian robber, the bawler, who roars like a torrent.

NICIAS

And the leather-seller must destroy the sheep-seller?

DEMOSTHENES

Yes.

NICIAS

Oh! woe is me! Where can another seller be found, is there ever a one left?

DEMOSTHENES

There is yet one, who plies a first-rate trade.

NICIAS

Tell me, pray, what is that?

DEMOSTHENES

You really want to know?

NICIAS

Yes.

DEMOSTHENES

Well then! it's a sausage-seller who must overthrow him.

NICIAS

A sausage-seller! Ah! by Posidon! what a fine trade! But where can this man be found?

DEMOSTHENES

Let's seek him. But look! there he is, going towards the market-place; 'tis the gods, the gods who send him! (*Calling out*) This way, this way, oh, lucky sausage-seller, come forward, dear friend, our saviour, the saviour of our city.

(*Enter* AGORACRITUS, *a seller of sausages, carrying a basket of his wares.*)

SAUSAGE-SELLER

What is it? Why do you call me?

DEMOSTHENES

Come here, come and learn about your good luck, you who are Fortune's favourite!

NICIAS

Come! Relieve him of his basket-tray and tell him the oracle of the god; I will go and look after the Paphlagonian.

(*He goes into the house.*)

DEMOSTHENES

First put down all your gear, then worship the earth and the gods.

SAUSAGE-SELLER

Done. What is the matter?

DEMOSTHENES

Happiness, riches, power; to-day you have nothing, to-morrow you will have all, oh! chief of happy Athens.

SAUSAGE-SELLER

Why not leave me to wash my tripe and to sell my sausages instead of making game of me?

DEMOSTHENES

Oh! the fool! Your tripe! Do you see these tiers of people?

SAUSAGE-SELLER

Yes.

DEMOSTHENES

You shall be master to them all, governor of the market, of the harbours, of the Pnyx; you shall trample the Senate under foot, be able to cashier the generals, load them with fetters, throw them into gaol, and you will fornicate in the Prytaneum.

SAUSAGE-SELLER

What! I?

DEMOSTHENES

You, without a doubt. But you do not yet see all the glory awaiting you. Stand on your basket and look at all the islands that surround Athens.

SAUSAGE-SELLER

I see them. What then?

DEMOSTHENES

Look at the storehouses and the shipping.

SAUSAGE-SELLER

Yes, I am looking.

DEMOSTHENES

Exists there a mortal more blest than you? Furthermore, turn your right eye towards Caria and your left toward Carthage!

SAUSAGE-SELLER

Then it's a blessing to be cock-eyed!

DEMOSTHENES

No, but you are the one who is going to trade away all this. According to the oracle you must become the greatest of men.

SAUSAGE-SELLER

Just tell me how a sausage-seller can become a great man.

DEMOSTHENES

That is precisely why you will be great, because you are a sad rascal without shame, no better than a common market rogue.

SAUSAGE-SELLER

I do not hold myself worthy of wielding power.

DEMOSTHENES

Oh! by the gods! Why do you not hold yourself worthy? Have you then such a good opinion of yourself? Come, are you of honest parentage?

SAUSAGE-SELLER

By the gods! No! of very bad indeed.

DEMOSTHENES

Spoilt child of fortune, everything fits together to ensure your greatness.

SAUSAGE-SELLER

But I have not had the least education. I can only read, and that very badly.

DEMOSTHENES

That is what may stand in your way, almost knowing how to read. A demagogue must be neither an educated nor an honest man; he has to be an ignoramus and a rogue. But do not, do not let go this gift, which the oracle promises.

SAUSAGE-SELLER

But what does the oracle say?

DEMOSTHENES

Faith, it is put together in very fine enigmatical style, as elegant as it is clear: "When the eagle-tanner with the hooked claws shall seize a stupid dragon, a blood-sucker, it will be an end to the hot Paphlagonian pickled garlic. The god grants great glory to the sausage-sellers unless they prefer to sell their wares."

SAUSAGE-SELLER

In what way does this concern me? Please instruct my ignorance.

DEMOSTHENES

The eagle-tanner is the Paphlagonian.

SAUSAGE-SELLER

What do the hooked claws mean?

DEMOSTHENES

It means to say, that he robs and pillages us with his claw-like hands.

SAUSAGE-SELLER

And the dragon?

DEMOSTHENES

That is quite clear. The dragon is long and so also is the sausage; the sausage like the dragon is a drinker of blood. Therefore the oracle says, that the dragon will triumph over the eagle-tanner, if he does not let himself be cajoled with words.

SAUSAGE-SELLER

The oracles of the gods flatter me! Faith! I do not at all understand how I can be capable of governing the people.

DEMOSTHENES

Nothing simpler. Continue your trade. Mix and knead together all the state business as you do for your sausages. To win the people, always cook them some savoury that pleases them. Besides, you possess all the attributes of a demagogue; a screeching, horrible voice, a perverse, cross-grained nature and the language of the market-place. In you all is united which is needful for governing. The oracles are in your favour, even including that of Delphi. Come, take a chaplet, offer a libation to the god of Stupidity and take care to fight vigorously.

SAUSAGE-SELLER

Who will be my ally? for the rich fear the Paphlagonian and the poor shudder at the sight of him.

DEMOSTHENES

You will have a thousand brave Knights, who detest him, on your side; also the honest citizens amongst the spectators, those who are men of brave hearts, and finally myself and the god. Fear not, you will not see his features, for none have dared to make a mask resembling him. But the public have wit enough to recognize him.

NICIAS (*from within*)[4]

Oh! mercy! here comes the Paphlagonian!

(CLEON *rushes out of the house.*)

CLEON

By the twelve gods! Woe betide you, who have too long been conspir-
ing against Demos. What means this Chalcidian cup? No doubt you are
provoking the Chalcidians to revolt. You shall be killed and butchered,
you brace of rogues.

DEMOSTHENES (*to the* SAUSAGE-SELLER)

What! are you for running away? Come, come, stand firm, bold Sausage-seller, do not betray us. To the rescue, oh, Knights. Now is the time.
Simon, Panaetius, get you to the right wing; they are coming on; hold
tight and return to the charge. I can see the dust of their horses' hoofs;
they are galloping to our aid. (*To the* SAUSAGE-SELLER) Courage! Attack
him, put him to flight.

(*The* CHORUS OF KNIGHTS *enters at top speed.*)

LEADER OF THE CHORUS

Strike, strike the villain, who has spread confusion amongst the ranks
of the Knights, this public robber, this yawning gulf of plunder, this devouring Charybdis, this villain, this villain, this villain! I cannot say the
word too often, for he *is* a villain a thousand times a day. Come, strike,
drive, hurl him over and crush him to pieces; hate him as we hate him;
stun him with your blows and your shouts. And beware lest he escape
you; he knows the way Eucrates took straight to a bran sack for concealment.

CLEON

Oh! veteran Heliasts, brotherhood of the three obols, whom I fostered
by bawling at random, help me; I am being beaten to death by rebels.

LEADER OF THE CHORUS

And justly too; you devour the public funds that all should share in;
you treat the treasury officials like the fruit of the fig tree, squeezing them
to find which are still green or more or less ripe; and, when you find a
simple and timid one, you force him to come from the Chersonese, then
you seize him by the middle, throttle him by the neck, while you twist his
shoulder back; he falls and you devour him. Besides, you know very well
how to select from among the citizens those who are as meek as lambs,
rich, without guile and loathers of lawsuits.

CLEON

Eh! what! Knights, are you helping them? But, if I am beaten, it is in
your cause, for I was going to propose to erect a statue in the city in
memory of your bravery.[5]

LEADER OF THE CHORUS

Oh! the impostor! the dull varlet! See! he treats us like old dotards and crawls at our feet to deceive us; but the cunning wherein his power lies shall this time recoil on himself; he trips up himself by resorting to such artifices.

CLEON

Oh citizens! oh people! see how these brutes are bursting my belly.

LEADER OF THE CHORUS

What shouts! but it's this very bawling that incessantly upsets the city!

SAUSAGE-SELLER

I can shout too—and so loud that you will flee with fear.

LEADER OF THE CHORUS

If you shout louder than he does I will strike up the triumphal hymn; if you surpass him in impudence the cake is ours.

CLEON

I denounce this fellow; he has had tasty stews exported from Athens for the Spartan fleet.

SAUSAGE-SELLER

And I denounce *him;* he runs into the Prytaneum with an empty belly and comes out with it full.

DEMOSTHENES

And by Zeus! he carries off bread, meat, and fish, which is forbidden. Pericles himself never had this right.

(*A screaming match now ensues, each line more raucous than the last. The rapidity of the dialogue likewise increases.*)

CLEON

You are travelling the right road to get killed.

SAUSAGE-SELLER

I'll bawl three times as loud as you.

CLEON

I will deafen you with my yells.

SAUSAGE-SELLER

And I you with my bellowing.

CLEON

I shall calumniate you, if you become a Strategus.

SAUSAGE-SELLER

Dog, I will lay your back open with the lash.

CLEON

I will make you drop your arrogance.

SAUSAGE-SELLER

I will baffle your machinations.

CLEON

Dare to look me in the face!

SAUSAGE-SELLER

I too was brought up in the market-place.

CLEON

I will cut you to shreds if you whisper a word.

SAUSAGE-SELLER

If you open your mouth, I'll shut it with shit.

CLEON

I admit I'm a thief; that's more than you do.

SAUSAGE-SELLER

By our Hermes of the market-place, if caught in the act, why, I perjure myself before those who saw me.

CLEON

These are my own special tricks. I will denounce you to the Prytanes as the owner of sacred tripe, that has not paid tithe.

CHORUS (*singing*)

Oh! you scoundrel! you impudent bawler! everything is filled with your daring, all Attica, the Assembly, the Treasury, the decrees, the tribunals. As a furious torrent you have overthrown our city; your outcries have deafened Athens and, posted upon a high rock, you have lain in wait for the tribute moneys as the fisherman does for the tunny-fish.

CLEON (*somewhat less loudly*)

I know your tricks; it's an old plot resoled.

SAUSAGE-SELLER

If you know naught of soling, I understand nothing of sausages; you, who cut bad leather on the slant to make it look stout and deceive the country yokels. They had not worn it a day before it had stretched some two spans.

DEMOSTHENES
That's the very trick he played on me; both my neighbours and my friends laughed heartily at me, and before I reached Pergasae I was swimming in my shoes.

CHORUS (*singing*)
Have you not always shown that blatant impudence, which is the sole strength of our orators? You push it so far, that you, the head of the State, dare to milk the purses of the opulent aliens and, at sight of you, the son of Hippodamus melts into tears. But here is another man who gives me pleasure, for he is a much greater rascal than you; he will overthrow you; 'tis easy to see, that he will beat you in roguery, in brazenness and in clever turns. Come, you, who have been brought up among the class which to-day gives us all our great men, show us that a liberal education is mere tomfoolery.

SAUSAGE-SELLER
Just hear what sort of fellow that fine citizen is.

CLEON
Will you not let me speak?

SAUSAGE-SELLER
Assuredly not, for I too am an awful rascal.

DEMOSTHENES
If he does not give in at that, tell him your parents were awful rascals too.

CLEON
Once more, will you let me speak?

SAUSAGE-SELLER
No, by Zeus!

CLEON
Yes, by Zeus, you shall!

SAUSAGE-SELLER
No, by Posidon! We will fight first to see who shall speak first.

CLEON
I will die sooner.

SAUSAGE-SELLER

I will not let you . . .

DEMOSTHENES

Let him, in the name of the gods, let him die.

CLEON

What makes you so bold as to dare to speak to my face?

SAUSAGE-SELLER

Because I know both how to speak and how to cook.

CLEON

Hah! the fine speaker! Truly, if some business matter fell your way, you would know thoroughly well how to attack it, to carve it up alive! Shall I tell you what has happened to you? Like so many others, you have gained some petty lawsuit against some alien. Did you drink enough water to inspire you? Did you mutter over the thing sufficiently through the night, spout it along the street, recite it to all you met? Have you bored your friends enough with it? And for this you deem yourself an orator. You poor fool!

SAUSAGE-SELLER

And what do you drink yourself then, to be able all alone by yourself to dumbfound and stupefy the city so with your clamour?

CLEON

Can you match me with a rival? Me? When I have devoured a good hot tunny-fish and drunk on top of it a great jar of unmixed wine. I say "to Hell with the generals of Pylos!"

SAUSAGE-SELLER

And I, when I have bolted the tripe of an ox together with a sow's belly and swallowed the broth as well, I am fit, though slobbering with grease, to bellow louder than all orators and to terrify Nicias.

DEMOSTHENES

I admire your language so much; the only thing I do not approve is that you swallow all the broth yourself.

CLEON

Even though you gorged yourself on sea-dogs, you would not beat the Milesians.

SAUSAGE-SELLER

Give me a bullock's breast to devour, and I am a man to traffic in mines.

CLEON

I will rush into the Senate and set them all by the ears.

SAUSAGE-SELLER

And I will pull out your arse to stuff like a sausage.

CLEON

As for me, I will seize you by the rump and hurl you head foremost through the door.

DEMOSTHENES

By Posidon, only after you have thrown *me* there first.

CLEON

(Beginning another crescendo of competitive screeching)
Beware of the carcan!

SAUSAGE-SELLER

I denounce you for cowardice.

CLEON

I will tan your hide.

SAUSAGE-SELLER

I will flay you and make a thief's pouch with the skin.

CLEON

I will peg you out on the ground.

SAUSAGE-SELLER

I will slice you into mince-meat.

CLEON

I will tear out your eyelashes.

SAUSAGE-SELLER

I will slit your gullet.

DEMOSTHENES

We will set his mouth open with a wooden stick as the cooks do with pigs; we will tear out his tongue, and, looking down his gaping throat, will see whether his inside has any pimples.

CHORUS *(singing)*

Thus then at Athens we have something more fiery than fire, more impudent than impudence itself! 'Tis a grave matter; come, we will push and jostle him without mercy. There, you grip him tightly un-

der the arms; if he gives way at the onset, you will find him nothing
but a craven; I know my man.

DEMOSTHENES

That he has been all his life and he has only made himself a name by
reaping another's harvest; and now he has tied up the ears he gathered
over there, he lets them dry and seeks to sell them.

CLEON

I do not fear you as long as there is a Senate and a people which stands
like a fool, gaping in the air.

CHORUS (*singing*)

What unparalleled impudence! 'Tis ever the same brazen front. If
I don't hate you, why, I'm ready to take the place of the one blanket
Cratinus wets; I'll offer to play a tragedy by Morsimus. Oh! you
cheat! who turn all into money, who flutter from one extortion to another; may you disgorge as quickly as you have crammed yourself!
Then only would I sing, "Let us drink, let us drink to this happy
event!" Then even the son of Ulius, the old wheat-fairy, would
empty his cup with transports of joy, crying, "Io, Paean! Io, Bacchus!"

CLEON

By Posidon! You! would you beat me in impudence! If you succeed,
may I no longer have my share of the victims offered to Zeus on the city
altar.

SAUSAGE-SELLER

And I, I swear by the blows that have so oft rained upon my shoulders
since infancy, and by the knives that have cut me, that I will show more
effrontery than you; as sure as I have rounded this fine stomach by feeding on the pieces of bread that had cleansed other folk's greasy fingers.

CLEON

On pieces of bread, like a dog! Ah! wretch! you have the nature of a
dog and you dare to fight a dog-headed ape?

SAUSAGE-SELLER

I have many another trick in my sack, memories of my childhood's
days. I used to linger around the cooks and say to them, "Look, friends,
don't you see a swallow? It's the herald of springtime." And while they
stood, their noses in the air, I made off with a piece of meat.

LEADER OF THE CHORUS

Oh! most clever man! How well thought out! You did as the eaters of artichokes, you gathered them before the return of the swallows.[6]

SAUSAGE-SELLER

They could make nothing of it; or, if they suspected a trick, I hid the meat in my crotch and denied the thing by all the gods; so that an orator, seeing me at the game, cried, "This child will get on; he has the mettle that makes a statesman."

LEADER OF THE CHORUS

He argued rightly; to steal, perjure yourself and make your arse receptive are three essentials for climbing high.

CLEON

I will stop your insolence, or rather the insolence of both of you. I will throw myself upon you like a terrible hurricane ravaging both land and sea at the will of its fury.

SAUSAGE-SELLER

Then I will gather up my sausages and entrust myself to the kindly waves of fortune so as to make you all the more enraged.

DEMOSTHENES

And I will watch in the bilges in case the boat should make water.

CLEON

No, by Demeter! I swear, it will not be with impunity that you have thieved so many talents from the Athenians.

DEMOSTHENES (*to the* SAUSAGE-SELLER)

Oh! oh! reef your sail a bit! Here is a Northeaster blowing calumniously.

SAUSAGE-SELLER

I know that you got ten talents out of Potidaea.

CLEON

Wait! I will give you one; but keep it dark!

DEMOSTHENES (*aside*)

Hah! that will please him mightily; (*to the* SAUSAGE-SELLER) now you can travel under full sail. The wind has lost its violence.

CLEON

I will bring four suits against you, each of one hundred talents.

SAUSAGE-SELLER

And I twenty against you for shirking duty and more than a thousand for robbery.

CLEON

I maintain that your parents were guilty of sacrilege against the god-dess.

SAUSAGE-SELLER

And I, that one of your grandfathers was a satellite. . . .

CLEON

To whom? Explain!

SAUSAGE-SELLER

To Byrsina, the mother of Hippias.

CLEON

You are an impostor.

SAUSAGE-SELLER

And you are a rogue.

(*He strikes* CLEON *with a sausage.*)

DEMOSTHENES

Hit him hard.

CLEON

Alas! The conspirators are murdering me!

DEMOSTHENES (*to the* SAUSAGE-SELLER)

Hit him! Hit him with all your might! Bruise his belly and lash him with your guts and your tripe! Punish him with both hands!

(CLEON *sinks beneath the blows.*)

CHORUS-LEADER

Oh! vigorous assailant and intrepid heart! See how you have totally routed him in this duel of abuse, so that to us and to the citizens you seem the saviour of the city. How shall I give tongue to my joy and praise you sufficiently?

CLEON (*recovering his wits*)

Ah! by Demeter! I was not ignorant of this plot and these machinations that were being forged and nailed and put together against me.

DEMOSTHENES (*to the* SAUSAGE-SELLER)

Look out, look out! Come. outfence him with some wheelwright slang.[7]

SAUSAGE-SELLER

His tricks at Argos do not escape me. Under pretence of forming an alliance with the Argives, he is hatching a plot with the Lacedæmonians there; and I know why the bellows are blowing and the metal that is on the anvil; it's the question of the prisoners.

DEMOSTHENES

Well done! Forge on, if he be a wheelwright.

SAUSAGE-SELLER

And there are men at Sparta who are hammering the iron with you; but neither gold nor silver nor prayers nor anything else shall impede my denouncing your trickery to the Athenians.

CLEON

As for me, I hasten to the Senate to reveal your plotting, your nightly gatherings in the city, your trafficking with the Medes and with the Great King, and all you are foraging for in Boeotia.

SAUSAGE-SELLER

What price then is paid for forage by Boeotians?

CLEON

Oh! by Heracles! I will tan your hide.

(*He departs.*)

DEMOSTHENES

Come, if you have both wit and heart, now is the time to show it, as on the day when you hid the meat in your crotch, as you say. Hasten to the Senate, for he will rush there like a tornado to calumniate us all and give vent to his fearful bellowings.

SAUSAGE-SELLER

I am going, but first I must rid myself of my tripe and my knives; I will leave them here.

DEMOSTHENES

Stay! rub your neck with lard; in this way you will slip between the fingers of calumny.

SAUSAGE-SELLER

Spoken like a finished wrestling coach.

DEMOSTHENES

Now, bolt down these cloves of garlic.

SAUSAGE-SELLER

Pray, what for?

DEMOSTHENES

Well primed with garlic, you will have greater mettle for the fight. Bu
hurry, make haste rapidly!

SAUSAGE-SELLER

That's just what I'm doing.

(*He departs.*)

DEMOSTHENES

And, above all, bite your foe, rend him to atoms, tear off his comb and
do not return until you have devoured his wattles.

(*He goes into the house of* DEMOS.)

LEADER OF THE CHORUS

Go! make your attack with a light heart, avenge me and may Zeus
guard you! I burn to see you return the victor and laden with chaplets of
glory. And you, spectators, enlightened critics of all kind of poetry, lend
an ear to my anapests. (*The Chorus moves forward and faces the audience.*)

Had one of the old authors asked me to mount this stage to recite
his verses, he would not have found it hard to persuade me. But our poet
of to-day is likewise worthy of this favour; he shares our hatred, he dares
to tell the truth, he boldly braves both waterspouts and hurricanes. Many
among you, he tells us, have expressed wonder, that he has not long since
had a piece presented in his own name, and have asked the reason why.
This is what he bids us say in reply to your questions; it is not without
grounds that he has courted the shade, for, in his opinion, nothing is more
difficult than to cultivate the comic Muse; many court her, but very few
secure her favours. Moreover, he knows that you are fickle by nature and
betray your poets when they grow old. What fate befell Magnes, when his
hair went white? Often enough had he triumphed over his rivals; he had
sung in all keys, played the lyre and fluttered wings; he turned into a
Lydian and even into a gnat, daubed himself with green to become a frog.
All in vain! When young, you applauded him; in his old age you hooted
and mocked him, because his genius for raillery had gone. Cratinus again
was like a torrent of glory rushing across the plain, up-rooting oak, plane
tree and rivals and bearing them pell-mell in his wake. The only songs at
the banquet were, "Doro, shod with lying tales" and "Adepts of the Lyric
Muse," so great was his renown. Look at him now! he drivels, his lyre has
neither strings nor keys, his voice quivers, but you have no pity for him,
and you let him wander about as he can, like Connas, his temples circled

with a withered chaplet; the poor old fellow is dying of thirst; he who, in honour of his glorious past, should be in the Prytaneum drinking at his ease, and instead of trudging the country should be sitting amongst the first row of the spectators, close to the statue of Dionysus and loaded with perfumes. Crates, again, have you done hounding him with your rage and your hisses? True, it was but meagre fare that his sterile Muse could offer you; a few ingenious fancies formed the sole ingredients, but nevertheless he knew how to stand firm and to recover from his falls. It is such examples that frighten our poet; in addition, he would tell himself, that before being a pilot, he must first know how to row, then to keep watch at the prow, after that how to gauge the winds, and that only then would he be able to command his vessel. If then you approve this wise caution and his resolve that he would not bore you with foolish nonsense, raise loud waves of applause in his favour this day, so that, at this Lenaean feast, the breath of your favour may swell the sails of his triumphant galley and the poet may withdraw proud of his success, with head erect and his face beaming with delight.

First Semi-Chorus (*singing*)

Posidon, god of the racing steeds, I salute you, you who delight in their neighing and in the resounding clatter of their brass-shod hoofs, god of the swift galleys, which, loaded with mercenaries, cleave the seas with their azure beaks, god of the equestrian contests, in which young rivals, eager for glory, ruin themselves for the sake of distinction with their chariots in the arena, come and direct our chorus; Posidon with the trident of gold, you, who reign over the dolphins, who are worshipped at Sunium and at Geraestus beloved of Phormio, and dear to the whole city above all the immortals, I salute you!

Leader of First Semi-Chorus

Let us sing the glory of our forefathers; ever victors, both on land and sea, they merit that Athens, rendered famous by these, her worthy sons, should write their deeds upon the sacred peplus. As soon as they saw the enemy, they at once sprang at him without ever counting his strength. Should one of them fall in the conflict he would shake off the dust, deny his mishap and begin the struggle anew. Not one of these generals of old time would have asked Cleaenetus to be fed at the cost of the State; but our present men refuse to fight, unless they get the honours of the Prytaneum and precedence in their seats. As for us, we place our valour gratuitously at the service of Athens and of her gods; our only hope is that, should peace ever put a term to our toils, you will not grudge us our long, scented hair nor our delicate care for our toilet.

SECOND SEMI-CHORUS (*singing*)

Oh! Pallas, guardian of Athens, you, who reign over the most pious
city, the most powerful, the richest in warriors and in poets, hasten
to my call, bringing in your train our faithful ally in all our expedi-
tions and combats, Victory, who smiles on our choruses and fights
with us against our rivals. Oh! goddess! manifest yourself to our
sight; this day more than ever we deserve that you should ensure our
triumph.

LEADER OF SECOND SEMI-CHORUS

We will sing likewise the exploits of our steeds! they are worthy of our
praises; in what invasions, what fights have I not seen them helping us!
But especially admirable were they, when they bravely leapt upon the
galleys, taking nothing with them but a coarse wine, some cloves of garlic
and onions; despite this, they nevertheless seized the sweeps just like
men, curved their backs over the thwarts and shouted, "*Hippapai!* Give
way! Come, all pull together! Come, come! How! Samphoras! Are you
not rowing?" They rushed down upon the coast of Corinth, and the youngest hollowed out beds in the sand with their hoofs or went to fetch cover-
ings; instead of luzern, they had no food but crabs, which they caught on
the strand and even in the sea; so that Theorus causes a Corinthian crab
to say, " 'Tis a cruel fate, oh Posidon neither my deep hiding-places,
whether on land or at sea, can help me to escape the Knights."

(The SAUSAGE-SELLER *returns.)*

LEADER OF THE CHORUS

Welcome, oh, dearest and bravest of men! How distracted I have been
during your absence! But here you are back, safe and sound. Tell us about
the fight you have had.

SAUSAGE-SELLER

The important thing is that I have beaten the Senate.

CHORUS (*singing*)

All glory to you! Let us burst into shouts of joy! You speak well,
but your deeds are even better. Come, tell me everything in detail;
what a long journey would I not be ready to take to hear your tale!
Come, dear friend, speak with full confidence to your admirers.

SAUSAGE-SELLER

The story is worth hearing. Listen! From here I rushed straight to the
Senate, right in the track of this man; he was already letting loose the
storm, unchaining the lightning, crushing the Knights beneath huge
mountains of calumnies heaped together and having all the air of truth;
he called you conspirators and his lies caught root like weeds in every

mind; dark were the looks on every side and brows were knitted. When I saw that the Senate listened to him favourably and was being tricked by his imposture I said to myself, "Come, gods of rascals and braggarts, gods of all fools, and toad-eaters, and thou too, oh market-place, wherein I was bred from my earliest days, give me unbridled audacity, an untiring chatter and a shameless voice." No sooner had I ended this prayer than a pederast farted on my right.[8] "Hah! a good omen," said I, and prostrated myself; then I burst open the door by a vigorous push with my arse, and, opening my mouth to the utmost, shouted, "Senators, I wanted you to be the first to hear the good news; since the war broke out, I have never seen anchovies at a lower price!" All faces brightened at once and I was voted a chaplet[9] for my good tidings; and I added, "With a couple of words I will reveal to you how you can have quantities of anchovies for an obol; all you have to do is to seize on all the dishes the merchants have." With mouths gaping with admiration, they applauded me. However, the Paphlagonian winded the matter and, well knowing the sort of language which pleases the Senate best, said, "Friends, I am resolved to offer one hundred oxen to the goddess in recognition of this happy event." The Senate at once veered to his side. So when I saw myself defeated by this ox dung, I outbade the fellow, crying, "Two hundred!" And beyond this I moved that a vow be made to Diana of a thousand goats if the next day anchovies should only be worth an obol a hundred. And the Senate looked towards me again. The other, stunned with the blow, grew delirious in his speech, and at last the Prytanes and the Scythians dragged him out. The Senators then stood talking noisily about the anchovies. Cleon, however, begged them to listen to the Lacedaemonian envoy, who had come to make proposals of peace; but all with one accord cried "Certainly it's not the moment to think of peace now! If anchovies are so cheap, what need have we of peace? Let the war take its course!" And with loud shouts they demanded that the Prytanes should close the sitting and then they leapt over the rails in all directions. As for me, I slipped away to buy all the coriander seed and leeks there were on the market and gave it to them gratis as seasoning for their anchovies. It was marvellous! They loaded me with praises and caresses; thus I conquered the Senate with an obol's worth of leeks, and here I am.

CHORUS (*singing*)

Bravo! you are the spoilt child of Fortune. Ah! our knave has found his match in another, who has far better tricks in his sack, a thousand kinds of knaveries and of wily words. But the fight begins afresh; take care not to weaken; you know that I have long been your most faithful ally.

SAUSAGE-SELLER

Ah! ah! here comes the Paphlagonian! One would say it was a hurricane lashing the sea and rolling the waves before it in its fury. He looks as if he wanted to swallow me up alive! Ye gods! what an impudent knave!

CLEON (*as he rushes in*)

To my aid, my beloved lies! I am going to destroy you, or my name is lost.

SAUSAGE-SELLER

Oh! how he diverts me with his threats! His bluster makes me laugh! And I dance the *mothon* for joy, and sing at the top of my voice, cuckoo!

CLEON

Ah! by Demeter! if I do not kill and devour you, may I die!

SAUSAGE-SELLER

If you do not devour me? and I, if I do not drink your blood to the last drop, and then burst with indigestion.

CLEON

I, I will strangle you, I swear it by the front seat which Pylos gained me.

SAUSAGE-SELLER

By the front seat! Ah! might I see you fall into the hindmost seat!

CLEON

By heaven! I will put you to the torture.

SAUSAGE-SELLER

What a lively wit! Come, what's the best to give you to eat? What do you prefer? A purse?

CLEON

I will tear out your insides with my nails.

SAUSAGE-SELLER

And I will cut off your victuals at the Prytaneum.

CLEON

I will haul you before Demos, who will mete out justice to you.

SAUSAGE-SELLER

And I too will drag you before him and belch forth more calumnies than you.

CLEON

Why, poor fool, he does not believe you, whereas I play with him at will.

SAUSAGE-SELLER

Is then Demos your property, your contemptible creature?

CLEON

It's because I know the dishes that please him.

SAUSAGE-SELLER

And these are little mouthfuls, which you serve to him like a clever nurse. You chew the pieces and place some in small quantities in his mouth, while you swallow three parts yourself.

CLEON

Thanks to my skill, I know exactly how to enlarge or contract this gullet.

SAUSAGE-SELLER

My arse is just as clever.

CLEON

Well, my friend, you tricked me at the Senate, but take care! Let us go before Demos.

SAUSAGE-SELLER

That's easily done; come, let's do it right away.

CLEON (*loudly*)

Oh, Demos! Come, I adjure you to help me, my father!

SAUSAGE-SELLER (*more loudly*)

Come, oh, my dear little Demos; come and see how I am insulted.

DEMOS (*coming out of his house followed by* DEMOSTHENES)

What a hubhub! To the Devil with you, bawlers! Alas! my olive branch, which they have torn down! [10] Ah! it's you, Paphlagonian. And who, pray, has been maltreating you?

CLEON

You are the cause of this man and these young people having covered me with blows.

DEMOS

And why?

CLEON

Because you love me passionately, Demos.

DEMOS (*to the* SAUSAGE-SELLER)

And you, who are you?

SAUSAGE-SELLER

His rival. For many a long year have I loved you, have I wished to do you honour, I and a crowd of other men of means. But this rascal here has prevented us. You resemble those young men who do not know where to choose their lovers; you repulse honest folks; to earn your favours. one has to be a lamp-seller, a cobbler, a tanner or a currier.

CLEON

I am the benefactor of the people.

SAUSAGE-SELLER

In what way, please?

CLEON

In what way? I supplanted the Generals at Pylos, I hurried thither and I brought back the Laconian captives.

SAUSAGE-SELLER

And I, whilst simply loitering, cleared off with a pot from a shop, which another fellow had been boiling.

CLEON

Demos, convene the assembly at once to decide which of us two loves you best and most merits your favour.

SAUSAGE-SELLER

Yes, yes, provided it be not at the Pnyx.

DEMOS

I could not sit elsewhere; it is at the Pnyx that you must appear before me.

(*He sits down on a stone in the Orchestra.*)

SAUSAGE-SELLER

Ah! great gods! I am undone! At home this old fellow is the most sensible of men, but the instant he is seated on those cursed stone seats, he is there with mouth agape as if he were hanging up figs by their stems to dry.

FIRST SEMI-CHORUS (*singing*)

Come, loose all sail. Be bold, skilful in attack and entangle him in arguments which admit of no reply. It is difficult to beat him, for he is full of craft and pulls himself out of the worst corners. Collect all your forces to come forth from this fight covered with glory.

LEADER OF THE CHORUS
But take care! Let him not assume the attack, get ready your grapples and advance with your vessel to board him!

CLEON
Oh! guardian goddess of our city! oh! Athené if it be true that next to Lysicles, Cynna and Salabaccho none have done so much good for the Athenian people as I, suffer me to continue to be fed at the Prytaneum without working; but if I hate you, if I am not ready to fight in your defence alone and against all, may I perish, be sawn to bits alive and my skin cut up into thongs.

SAUSAGE-SELLER
And I, Demos, if it be not true, that I love and cherish you, may I be cooked in a stew; and if that is not saying enough, may I be grated on this table with some cheese and then hashed, may a hook be passed through my balls and let me be dragged thus to the Ceramicus!

CLEON
Is it possible, Demos, to love you more than I do? And firstly, as long as you have governed with my consent, have I not filled your treasury, putting pressure on some, torturing others or begging of them, indifferent to the opinion of private individuals, and solely anxious to please you?

SAUSAGE-SELLER
There is nothing so wonderful in all that, Demos; I will do as much; I will thieve the bread of others to serve up to you. No, he has neither love for you nor kindly feeling; his only care is to warm himself with your wood, and I will prove it. You, who, sword in hand, saved Attica from the Median yoke at Marathon; you, whose glorious triumphs we love to extol unceasingly, look, he cares little whether he sees you seated uncomfortably upon a stone; whereas I, I bring you this cushion, which I have sewn with my own hands. Rise and try this nice soft seat. Did you not put enough strain on your bottom at Salamis?
(*He gives* DEMOS *the cushion;* DEMOS *sits on it.*)

DEMOS
Who are you then? Can you be of the race of Harmodius? Upon my faith, that is nobly done and like a true friend of Demos.

CLEON
Petty flattery to prove him your goodwill!

SAUSAGE-SELLER

But you have caught him with even smaller baits!

CLEON

Never had Demos a defender or a friend more devoted than myself; on my head, on my life, I swear it!

SAUSAGE-SELLER

You pretend to love him and for eight years you have seen him housed in casks, in crevices and dovecots,[11] where he is blinded with the smoke, and you lock him in without pity; Archeptolemus brought peace and you tore it to ribbons; the envoys who come to propose a truce you drive from the city with kicks in their arses.

CLEON

The purpose of this is that Demos may rule over all the Greeks; for the oracles predict that, if he is patient, he must one day sit as judge in Arcadia at five obols per day. Meanwhile, I will nourish him, look after him and, above all, I will ensure to him his three obols.

SAUSAGE-SELLER

No, little you care for his reigning in Arcadia, it's to pillage and impose on the allies at will that you reckon; you wish the war to conceal your rogueries as in a mist, that Demos may see nothing of them, and harassed by cares, may only depend on yourself for his bread. But if ever peace is restored to him, if ever he returns to his lands to comfort himself once more with good cakes, to greet his cherished olives, he will know the blessings you have kept him out of, even though paying him a salary; and, filled with hatred and rage, he will rise, burning with desire to vote against you. You know this only too well; it is for this you rock him to sleep with your lies.

CLEON

Is it not shameful, that you should dare thus to calumniate me before Demos, me, to whom Athens, I swear it by Demeter, already owes more than it ever did to Themistocles?

SAUSAGE-SELLER (*declaiming*)

Oh! citizens of Argos, do you hear what he says? (*to* CLEON) You dare to compare yourself to Themistocles, who found our city half empty and left it full to overflowing, who one day gave us the Piraeus for dinner, and added fresh fish to all our usual meals. You, on the contrary, you, who compare yourself with Themistocles, have only sought to reduce our city in size, to shut it within its walls, to chant oracles to us. And Themistocles goes into exile, while you gorge yourself on the most excellent fare.

CLEON

Oh! Demos! Am I compelled to hear myself thus abused, and merely because I love you?

DEMOS

Silence! stop your abuse! All too long have I been your dupe.

SAUSAGE-SELLER

Ah! my dear little Demos, he is a rogue who has played you many a scurvy trick; when your back is turned, he taps at the root the lawsuits initiated by the peculators, swallows the proceeds wholesale and helps himself with both hands from the public funds.

CLEON

Tremble, knave; I will convict you of having stolen thirty thousand drachmae.

SAUSAGE-SELLER

For a rascal of your kidney, you shout rarely! Well! I am ready to die if I do not prove that you have accepted more than forty minae from the Mitylenaeans.

SECOND SEMI-CHORUS (*singing*)

This indeed may be termed talking. Oh, benefactor of the human race, proceed and you will be the most illustrious of the Greeks. You alone shall have sway in Athens, the allies will obey you, and, trident in hand, you will go about shaking and overturning everything to enrich yourself. But, stick to your man, let him not go; with lungs like yours you will soon have him finished.

CLEON

No, my brave friends, no, you are running too fast; I have done a sufficiently brilliant deed to shut the mouth of all enemies, so long as one of the bucklers of Pylos remains.

SAUSAGE-SELLER

Of the bucklers! Hold! I stop you there and I hold you fast. For if it be true that you love the people, you would not allow these to be hung up with their rings;[12] but it's with an intent you have done this. Demos, take knowledge of his guilty purpose; in this way you no longer can punish him at your pleasure. Note the swarm of young tanners, who really surround him, and close to them the sellers of honey and cheese; all these are at one with him. Very well! you have but to frown, to speak of ostracism and they will rush at night to these bucklers, take them down and seize our granaries.

DEMOS

Great gods! what! the bucklers retain their rings! Scoundrel! ah! too
long have you had me for your dupe, cheated and played with me!

CLEON

But, dear sir, never you believe all he tells you. Oh! never will you find
a more devoted friend than me; unaided, I have known how to put down
the conspiracies; nothing that is hatching in the city escapes me, and I
hasten to proclaim it loudly.

SAUSAGE-SELLER

You are like the fishers for eels; in still waters they catch nothing, but
if they thoroughly stir up the slime, their fishing is good; in the same way
it's only in troublous times that you line your pockets. But come, tell me,
you, who sell so many skins, have you ever made him a present of a pair
of soles for his slippers? and you pretend to love him!

DEMOS

No, he has never given me any.

SAUSAGE-SELLER

That alone shows up the man; but I, I have bought you this pair of
shoes; accept them.

(*He gives* DEMOS *the shoes;* DEMOS *puts them on.*)

DEMOS

None ever, to my knowledge, has merited so much from the people; you
are the most zealous of all men for your country and for my toes.

CLEON

Can a wretched pair of slippers make you forget all that you owe me?
Is it not I who curbed the pederasts by erasing Gryttus' name from the
lists of citizens?

SAUSAGE-SELLER

Ah! noble Inspector of Arses, let me congratulate you. Moreover, if
you set yourself against this form of lewdness, this pederasty, it was for
sheer jealousy, knowing it to be the school for orators. But you see this poor
Demos without a cloak and that at his age too! so little do you care for
him, that in mid-winter you have not given him a garment with sleeves.
Here, Demos, here is one, take it!

(*He gives* DEMOS *a cloak;* DEMOS *puts it on.*)

DEMOS

This even Themistocles never thought of; the Piraeus was no doubt a
happy idea, but I think this tunic is quite as fine an invention.

CLEON

Must you have recourse to such jackanapes' tricks to supplant me?

SAUSAGE-SELLER

No, it's your own tricks that I am borrowing, just as a drunken guest, when he has to take a crap, seizes some other man's shoes.

CLEON

Oh! you shall not outdo me in flattery! I am going to hand Demos this garment; all that remains to you, you rogue, is to go and hang yourself.

DEMOS (*as* CLEON *throws a cloak around his shoulders*)
Faugh! may the plague seize you! You stink of leather horribly.

SAUSAGE-SELLER

Why, it's to smother you that he has thrown this cloak around you on top of the other; and it is not the first plot he has planned against you. Do you remember the time when silphium was so cheap?

DEMOS

Aye, to be sure I do!

SAUSAGE-SELLER

Very well! it was Cleon who had caused the price to fall so low, that all might eat it, and the jurymen in the Courts were almost asphyxiated from farting in each others' faces.

DEMOS

Hah! why, indeed, a Dungtownite told me the same thing.

SAUSAGE-SELLER

Were you not yourself in those days quite red in the gills with farting?

DEMOS

Why, it was a trick worthy of Pyrrhandrus!

CLEON

With what other idle trash will you seek to ruin me, you wretch!

SAUSAGE-SELLER

Oh! I shall be more brazen than you, for it's the goddess who has commanded me.

CLEON

No, on my honour, you will not! Here, Demos, feast on this dish; it is your salary as a dicast, which you gain through me for doing naught.

SAUSAGE-SELLER

Wait! here is a little box of ointment to rub into the sores on your legs.

CLEON

I will pluck out your white hairs and make you young again.

SAUSAGE-SELLER

Take this hare's tail to wipe the rheum from your eyes.

CLEON

When you wipe your nose, clean your fingers on my head.

SAUSAGE-SELLER

No, on mine.

CLEON

On *mine*. (*To the* SAUSAGE-SELLER) I will have you made a trierarch and you will get ruined through it; I will arrange that you are given an old vessel with rotten sails, which you will have to repair constantly and at great cost.

SAUSAGE-SELLER

Our man is on the boil; enough, enough, he is boiling over; remove some of the embers from under him and skim off his threats.

CLEON

I will punish your self-importance; I will crush you with imposts; I will have you inscribed on the list of the rich.

SAUSAGE-SELLER

For me no threats—only one simple wish. That you may be having some cuttle-fish fried on the stove just as you are going to set forth to plead the cause of the Milesians, which, if you gain it, means a talent in your pocket; that you hurry over devouring the fish to rush off to the Assembly; suddenly you are called and run off with your mouth full so as not to lose the talent and choke yourself. There! that is my wish.

LEADER OF THE CHORUS

Splendid! by Zeus, Apollo and Demeter!

DEMOS

Faith! here is an excellent citizen indeed, such as has not been seen for a long time. He's truly a man of the lowest scum! As for you, Paphlagonian, who pretend to love me, you only feed me on garlic. Return me my ring, for you cease to be my steward.

CLEON

Here it is, but be assured, that if you bereave me of my power, my successor will be worse than I am.

DEMOS

This cannot be my ring; I see another device, unless I am going purblind.

SAUSAGE-SELLER

What was your device?

DEMOS

A fig-leaf, stuffed with bullock's fat.[13]

SAUSAGE-SELLER

No, that is not it.

DEMOS

What is it then?

SAUSAGE-SELLER

It's a gull with beak wide open, haranguing the people from the top of a stone.

DEMOS

Ah! great gods!

SAUSAGE-SELLER

What is the matter?

DEMOS

Away! away out of my sight! It's not my ring he had, it was that of Cleonymus. (*To the* SAUSAGE-SELLER) Wait, I'll give you this one; you shall be my steward.

CLEON

Master, I adjure you, decide nothing till you have heard my oracles.

SAUSAGE-SELLER

And mine.

CLEON

If you believe him, you will have to prostitute yourself for him.

SAUSAGE-SELLER

If you listen to him, you'll have to let him peel you to the very stump.

CLEON

My oracles say that you are to reign over the whole earth, crowned with chaplets.

SAUSAGE-SELLER

And mine say that, clothed in an embroidered purple robe, you shall pursue Smicythé and her spouse, standing in a chariot of gold and with a crown on your head.

DEMOS

Go, fetch me your oracles, that the Paphlagonian may hear them.

SAUSAGE-SELLER

Willingly.

DEMOS

And you yours.

CLEON

I'll run.

(*He rushes into the house of* DEMOS.)

SAUSAGE-SELLER

And I'll run too; nothing could suit me better!

(*He departs in haste.*)

CHORUS (*singing*)

Oh! happy day for us and for our children if Cleon perish. Yet just now I heard some old cross-grained pleaders on the market-place who hold not this opinion discoursing together. Said they, "If Cleon had not had the power, we should have lacked two most useful tools, the pestle and the soup-ladle." [14] You also know what a pig's education he has had; his school-fellows can recall that he only liked the Dorian style and would study no other; his music-master in displeasure sent him away, saying; "This youth, in matters of harmony, will only learn the Dorian style because it is akin to bribery." [15]

CLEON (*coming out of the house with a large package*)

There, look at this heap; and yet I'm not bringing them all.

SAUSAGE-SELLER (*entering with an even larger package*)

Ugh! The weight of them is squeezing the crap right out of me, and still I'm not bringing them all!

DEMOS

What are these?

CLEON

Oracles.

DEMOS

All these?

CLEON

Does that astonish you? Why, I have another whole boxful of them.

SAUSAGE-SELLER

And I the whole of my attic and two rooms besides.

DEMOS

Come, let us see, whose are these oracles?

CLEON

Mine are those of Bacis.

DEMOS (*to the* SAUSAGE-SELLER)

And whose are yours?

SAUSAGE-SELLER (*without hesitating*)

Glanis's, the elder brother of Bacis.

DEMOS

And of what do they speak?

CLEON

Of Athens and Pylos and you and me and everything.

DEMOS

And yours?

SAUSAGE-SELLER

Of Athens and lentils and Lacedæmonians and fresh mackerel and scoundrelly flour-sellers and you and me. Ah! ha! now watch him gnaw his own tool with chagrin!

DEMOS

Come, read them out to me and especially that one I like so much, which says that I shall become an eagle and soar among the clouds.

CLEON

Then listen and be attentive! "Son of Erechtheus, understand the meaning of the words, which the sacred tripods set resounding in the sanctuary of Apollc. Preserve the sacred dog with the jagged teeth, that barks and howls in your defence; he will ensure you a salary and, if he fails, will perish as the victim of the swarms of jays that hunt him down with their screams."

DEMOS

By Demeter! I do not understand a word of it. What connection is there between Erechtheus, the jays and the dog?

CLEON

I am the dog, since I bark in your defence. Well! Phoebus commands you to keep and cherish your dog.

SAUSAGE-SELLER

That is not what the god says; this dog seems to me to gnaw at the oracles as others gnaw at doorposts. Here is exactly what Apollo says of the dog.

DEMOS

Let us hear, but I must first pick up a stone; an oracle which speaks of a dog might bite my tool.

SAUSAGE-SELLER

"Son of Erechtheus, beware of this Cerberus that enslaves free men; he fawns upon you with his tail when you are dining, but he is lying in wait to devour your dishes should you turn your head an instant; at night he sneaks into the kitchen and, true dog that he is, licks up with one lap of his tongue both your dishes and . . . the islands."

DEMOS

By god, Glanis, you speak better than your brother.

CLEON

Condescend again to hear *me* and then judge: "A woman in sacred Athens will be delivered of a lion, who shall fight for the people against clouds of gnats with the same ferocity as if he were defending his whelps; care ye for him, erect wooden walls around him and towers of brass." Do you understand that?

DEMOS

Not the least bit in the world.

CLEON

The god tells you here to look after me, for I am your lion.

DEMOS

How! You have become a lion and I never knew a thing about it?

SAUSAGE-SELLER

There is only one thing which he purposely keeps from you; he does not say what this wall of wood and brass is in which Apollo warns you to keep and guard him.

DEMOS

What does the god mean, then?

SAUSAGE-SELLER

He advises you to fit him into a five-holed wooden collar.

DEMOS

Hah! I think that oracle is about to be fulfilled.

CLEON

Do not believe it; these are but jealous crows, that caw against me; but never cease to cherish your good hawk; never forget that he brought you those Lacedaemonian fish, loaded with chains.

SAUSAGE-SELLER

Ah! if the Paphlagonian ran any risk that day, it was because he was drunk. Oh, too credulous son of Cecrops, do you accept that as a glorious exploit? A woman would carry a heavy burden if only a man had put it on her shoulders. But to fight! Go to! he would empty his bowels before he would ever fight.

CLEON

Note this Pylos in front of Pylos, of which the oracle speaks, "Pylos is before Pylos."

DEMOS

How "in front of Pylos"? What does he mean by that?

SAUSAGE-SELLER

He says he will seize upon your bath-tubs.[16]

DEMOS

Then I shall not bathe to-day.

SAUSAGE-SELLER

No, as he has stolen our baths. But here is an oracle about the fleet, to which I beg your best attention.

DEMOS

Read on! I am listening; let us first see how we are to pay our sailors.

SAUSAGE-SELLER

"Son of Ægeus, beware of the tricks of the dog-fox, he bites from the rear and rushes off at full speed; he is nothing but cunning and perfidy." Do you know what the oracle intends to say?

DEMOS

The dog-fox is Philostratus.

SAUSAGE-SELLER

No, no, it's Cleon; he is incessantly asking you for light vessels to go and collect the tributes, and Apollo advises you not to grant them.

DEMOS

What connection is there between a galley and dog-fox?

SAUSAGE-SELLER

What connection? Why, it's quite plain—a galley travels as fast as a dog.

DEMOS

Why, then, does the oracle not say dog instead of dog-fox?

SAUSAGE-SELLER

Because he compares the soldiers to young foxes, who, like them, eat the grapes in the fields.

DEMOS

Good! Well then! how am I to pay the wages of my young foxes?

SAUSAGE-SELLER

I will undertake that, and in three days too! But listen to this further oracle, by which Apollo puts you on your guard against the snares of the greedy fist.

DEMOS

Of what greedy fist?

SAUSAGE-SELLER

The god in this oracle very clearly points to the hand of Cleon, who incessantly holds his out, saying, "Fill it."

CLEON

That's a lie! Phoebus means the hand of Diopithes. But here I have a winged oracle, which promises you shall become an eagle and rule over all the earth.

SAUSAGE-SELLER

I have one, which says that you shall be King of the Earth and of the Red Sea too, and that you shall administer justice in Ecbatana, eating fine rich stews the while.

CLEON

I have seen Athené in a dream, pouring out full vials of riches and health over the people.

SAUSAGE-SELLER

I too have seen the goddess, descending from the Acropolis with an owl perched upon her helmet; on your head she was pouring out ambrosia, on that of Cleon garlic pickle.

DEMOS

Truly Glanis is the wisest of men. I shall yield myself to you; guide me in my old age and educate me anew.

CLEON

Ah! I adjure you! not yet; wait a little; I will promise to distribute barley every day.

DEMOS

Ah! I will not hear another word about barley; you have cheated me too often already, both you and Theophanes.

CLEON

Well then! you shall have flour-cakes all piping hot.

SAUSAGE-SELLER

I will give you cakes too, and nice cooked fish; all you'll have to do is eat.

DEMOS

Very well, mind you keep your promises. To whichever of you shall treat me best I hand over the reins of state.

CLEON

I will be first.

(*He rushes into the house.*)

SAUSAGE-SELLER

No, no, *I* will.

(*He runs off.*)

CHORUS (*singing*)

Demos, you are our all-powerful sovereign lord; all tremble before you, yet you are led by the nose. You love to be flattered and fooled; you listen to the orators with gaping mouth and your mind is led astray.

DEMOS (*singing*)

It's rather you who have no brains, if you think me so foolish as all that; it is with a purpose that I play this idiot's rôle, for I love to drink the livelong day, and so it pleases me to keep a thief for my minister. When he has thoroughly gorged himself, then I overthrow and crush him.

CHORUS (*singing*)

What profound wisdom! If it be really so, why! all is for the best. Your ministers, then, are your victims, whom you nourish and feed up expressly in the Pnyx, so that, the day your dinner is ready, you may immolate the fattest and eat him.

DEMOS (*singing*)

Look, see how I play with them, while all the time they think themselves such adepts at cheating me. I have my eye on them when they thieve, but I do not appear to be seeing them; then I thrust a judgment down their throat as it were a feather, and force them to vomit up all they have robbed from me.

(*Cleon comes out of the house with a bench and a large basket; at the same moment the* SAUSAGE-SELLER *arrives with another basket; the two are placed beside one another.*)

CLEON

Get out of here!

SAUSAGE-SELLER

Get out yourself!

CLEON

Demos, all is ready these three hours; I await your orders and I burn with desire to load you with benefits.

SAUSAGE-SELLER

And I ten, twelve, a thousand hours, a long, long while, an infinitely long long, long while.

DEMOS

As for me, it's thirty thousand hours that I have been impatient; very long, infinitely long, long, long that I have cursed you.

SAUSAGE-SELLER

Do you know what you had best do?

DEMOS

I will, if you tell me.

SAUSAGE-SELLER

Declare the lists open and we will contend abreast to determine who shall treat you the best.

DEMOS

Splendid! Draw back in line!

CLEON

I am ready.

DEMOS

Off you go!

SAUSAGE-SELLER (*to* CLEON)

I shall not let you get to the tape.

DEMOS

What fervent lovers! If I am not to-day the happiest of men, it will be because I am the most disgusted.

CLEON (*putting down the bench for* DEMOS)

Look! I am the first to bring you a seat.

SAUSAGE-SELLER

And I a table.

(*He places his sausage-tray in front of* DEMOS.)

CLEON

Wait, here is a cake kneaded of Pylos barley.

SAUSAGE-SELLER

Here are crusts, which the ivory hand of the goddess has hallowed.

DEMOS

Oh! Mighty Athené! How large are your fingers!

CLEON

This is pea-soup, as exquisite as it is fine; Pallas the victorious goddess at Pylos is the one who crushed the peas herself.

SAUSAGE-SELLER

Oh, Demos! the goddess watches over you; she is stretching forth
over your head . . . a stew-pan full of broth.

DEMOS

And should we still be dwelling in this city without this protecting
stew-pan?

CLEON

Here are some fish, given to you by her who is the terror of our foes.

SAUSAGE-SELLER

The daughter of the mightiest of the gods sends you this meat cooked
in its own gravy, along with this dish of tripe and some paunch.

DEMOS

That's to thank me for the peplus I offered to her; good.

CLEON

The goddess with the terrible plume invites you to eat this long cake;
you will row the harder on it.

SAUSAGE-SELLER

Take this also.

DEMOS

And what shall I do with this tripe?

SAUSAGE-SELLER

She sends it you to belly out your galleys, for she is always showing
her kindly anxiety for our fleet. Now drink this drink composed of three
parts of water to two of wine.

DEMOS

Ah! what delicious wine, and how well it stands the water.[17]

SAUSAGE-SELLER

The goddess who came from the head of Zeus mixed this liquor with
her own hands.

CLEON

Hold, here is a piece of good rich cake.

SAUSAGE-SELLER

But I offer you an entire cake.

CLEON

But you cannot offer him stewed hare as I do.

SAUSAGE-SELLER (*aside*)

Ah! great gods! stewed hare! where shall I find it? Oh! brain of mine, devise some trick!

CLEON (*showing him the hare*)

Do you see this, you rogue?

SAUSAGE-SELLER (*pretending to look afar*)

A fig for that! Here are some people coming to seek me. They are envoys, bearing sacks bulging with money.

CLEON

(*Hearing money mentioned* CLEON *turns his head, and the* SAUSAGE-SELLER *seizes the opportunity to snatch away the stewed hare.*)
Where, where, I say?

SAUSAGE-SELLER

Bah! What's that to you? Will you not even now let the strangers alone? Dear Demos, do you see this stewed hare which I bring you?

CLEON

Ah! rascal! you have shamelessly robbed me.

SAUSAGE-SELLER

You have robbed too, you robbed the Laconians at Pylos.

DEMOS

Please tell me, how did you get the idea to filch it from him?

SAUSAGE-SELLER

The idea comes from the goddess; the theft is all my own.

CLEON

And I had taken such trouble to catch this hare and I was the one who had it cooked.

DEMOS (*to* CLEON)

Get you gone! My thanks are only for him who served it.

CLEON

Ah! wretch! you have beaten me in impudence!

SAUSAGE-SELLER

Well then, Demos, say now, who has treated you best, you and your stomach? Decide!

DEMOS

How shall I act here so that the spectators shall approve my judgment?

SAUSAGE-SELLER

I will tell you. Without saying anything, go and rummage through my basket, and then through the Paphlagonian's, and see what is in them; that's the best way to judge.

DEMOS

Let us see then, what is there in yours?

SAUSAGE-SELLER

Why, it's empty, dear little father; I have brought everything to you.

DEMOS

This is a basket devoted to the people.

SAUSAGE-SELLER

Now hunt through the Paphlagonian's. (*Pause, as Demos does so*) Well?

DEMOS

Oh! what a lot of good things! Why it's quite full! Oh! what a huge great part of this cake he kept for himself! He had only cut off the least little tiny piece for me.

SAUSAGE-SELLER

But this is what he has always done. Of everything he took, he only gave you the crumbs, and kept the bulk.

DEMOS (*to* CLEON)

Oh! rascal! was this the way you robbed me? And I was loading you with chaplets and gifts!

CLEON

I robbed for the public weal.

DEMOS (*to* CLEON)

Give me back that crown; I shall give it to him.

SAUSAGE-SELLER

Return it quick, quick, you gallows-bird.

CLEON

No, for the Pythian oracle has revealed to me the name of him who shall overthrow me.

SAUSAGE-SELLER

And that name was mine, nothing can be clearer.

CLEON

Reply and I shall soon see whether you are indeed the man whom the god intended. Firstly, what school did you attend when a child?

SAUSAGE-SELLER

It was in the kitchens, where I was taught with cuffs and blows.

CLEON

What's that you say? (*aside*) Ah! this is truly what the oracle said. (*To the* SAUSAGE-SELLER) And what did you learn from the master of exercises?

SAUSAGE-SELLER

I learnt to take a false oath without a smile, when I had stolen something.

CLEON (*frightened; aside*)

Oh! Phoebus Apollo, god of Lycia! I am undone! (*To the* SAUSAGE-SELLER) And when you had become a man, what trade did you follow?

SAUSAGE-SELLER

I sold sausages and did a bit of fornication.

CLEON (*in consternation; aside*)

Oh! my god! I am a lost man! Ah! still one slender hope remains. (*to the* SAUSAGE-SELLER) Tell me, was it on the market-place or near the gates that you sold your sausages?

SAUSAGE-SELLER

Near the gates, in the market for salted goods.

CLEON (*in tragic despair*)

Alas! I see the prophecy of the god is verily come true. Alas! roll me home. I am a miserable ruined man. Farewell, my chaplet. 'Tis death to me to part with you. So you are to belong to another; 'tis certain he cannot be a greater thief, but perhaps he may be a luckier one.

(*He gives the chaplet to the* SAUSAGE-SELLER.)

SAUSAGE-SELLER

Oh! Zeus, protector of Greece! 'tis to you I owe this victory!

DEMOSTHENES

Hail! illustrious conqueror, but forget not, that if you have become a great man, 'tis thanks to me; I ask but a little thing; appoint me secretary of the law-court in the room of Phanus.

DEMOS (*to the* SAUSAGE-SELLER)

But what is your name then? Tell me.

SAUSAGE-SELLER

My name is Agoracritus, because I have always lived on the market-
place in the midst of lawsuits.

DEMOS

Well then, Agoracritus, I stand by you; as for the Paphlagonian, 1
hand him over to your mercy.

AGORACRITUS

Demos, I will care for you to the best of my power, and all shall admit
that no citizen is more devoted than I to this city of simpletons.

(*They all enter the house of* DEMOS.)

CHORUS (*singing*)

What fitter theme for our Muse, at the close as at the beginning of
our work, than this, to sing the hero who drives his swift steeds down
the arena? Why afflict Lysistratus with our satires on his poverty,
and Thumantis, who has not so much as a lodging? He is dying of
hunger and can be seen at Delphi, his face bathed in tears, clinging
to your quiver, oh, Apollo! and supplicating you to take him out of
his misery.

LEADER OF THE CHORUS

An insult directed at the wicked is not to be censured; on the contrary, the honest man, if he has sense, can only applaud. Him, whom I
wish to brand with infamy, is little known himself; he's the brother of
Arignotus. I regret to quote this name which is so dear to me, but whoever can distinguish black from white, or the Orthian mode of music
from others, knows the virtues of Arignotus, whom his brother, Ariphrades, in no way resembles. He gloats in vice, is not merely a dissolute
man and utterly debauched—but he has actually invented a new form
of vice; for he pollutes his tongue with abominable pleasures in brothels,
befouling all of his body.[18] Whoever is not horrified at such a monster
shall never drink from the same cup with me.

CHORUS (*singing*)

At times a thought weighs on me at night; I wonder whence
comes this fearful voracity of Cleonymus. 'Tis said that when dining with a rich host, he springs at the dishes with the gluttony of a
wild beast and never leaves the bread-bin until his host seizes him
round the knees, exclaiming, "Go, go, good gentleman, in mercy go,
and spare my poor table!"

LEADER OF THE CHORUS

It is said that the triremes assembled in council and that the oldest
spoke in these terms, "Are you ignorant, my sisters, of what is plotting
in Athens? They say that a certain Hyperbolus, a bad citizen and an
infamous scoundrel, asks for a hundred of us to take them to sea against
Carthage." All were indignant, and one of them, as yet a virgin, cried,
"May god forbid that I should ever obey him! I would prefer to grow
old in the harbour and be gnawed by worms. No! by the gods I swear it,
Nauphanté, daughter of Nauson, shall never bend to his law; that's as
true as I am made of wood and pitch. If the Athenians vote for the proposal of Hyperbolus, let them! we will hoist full sail and seek refuge by
the temple of Theseus or the shrine of the Eumenides. No! he shall not
command us! No! he shall not play with the city to this extent! Let him
sail by himself for Tartarus, if such please him, launching the boats in
which he used to sell his lamps."

(*The* SAUSAGE-SELLER *comes out of the house of* DEMOS, *splendidly*
robed.)

AGORACRITUS (*solemnly*)

Maintain a holy silence! Keep your mouths from utterance! call no
more witnesses; close these tribunals, which are the delight of this city,
and gather at the theatre to chant the Paean of thanksgiving to the gods
for a fresh favour.

LEADER OF THE CHORUS

Oh! torch of sacred Athens, saviour of the Islands, what good tidings
are we to celebrate by letting the blood of the victims flow in our market-
places?

AGORACRITUS

I have freshened Demos up somewhat on the stove and have turned
his ugliness into beauty.

LEADER OF THE CHORUS

I admire your inventive genius; but, where is he?

AGORACRITUS

He is living in ancient Athens, the city of the garlands of violets.

LEADER OF THE CHORUS

How I should like to see him! What is his dress like, what his manner?

AGORACRITUS

He has once more become as he was in the days when he lived with
Aristides and Miltiades. But you will judge for yourselves, for I hear the

vestibule doors opening. Hail with your shouts of gladness the Athens of old, which now doth reappear to your gaze, admirable, worthy of the songs of the poets and the home of the illustrious Demos.

LEADER OF THE CHORUS

Oh! noble, brilliant Athens, whose brow is wreathed with violets, show us the sovereign master of this land and of all Greece.

(DEMOS *comes from his house, rejuvenated and joyous.*)

AGORACRITUS

Lo! here he is coming with his hair held in place with a golden band and in all the glory of his old-world dress; perfumed with myrrh, he spreads around him not the odour of lawsuits, but that of peace.

LEADER OF THE CHORUS

Hail! King of Greece, we congratulate you upon the happiness you enjoy; it is worthy of this city, worthy of the glory of Marathon.

DEMOS

Come, Agoracritus, come, my best friend; see the service you have done me by freshening me up on your stove.

AGORACRITUS

Ah! if you but remembered what you were formerly and what you did, you would for a certainty believe me to be a god.

DEMOS

But what did I do? and how was I then?

AGORACRITUS

Firstly, so soon as ever an orator declared in the Assembly, "Demos, I love you ardently; it is I alone who dream of you and watch over your interests"; at such an exordium you would look like a cock flapping his wings or a bull tossing his horns.

DEMOS

What, I?

AGORACRITUS

Then, after he had fooled you to the hilt, he would go.

DEMOS

What! they would treat me so, and I never saw it?

AGORACRITUS

You knew only how to open and close your ears like a sunshade.

DEMOS

Was I then so stupid and such a dotard?

AGORACRITUS

Worse than that; if one of two orators proposed to equip a fleet for
war and the other suggested the use of the same sum for paying out to
the citizens, it was the latter who always carried the day. Well! you
droop your head! Why do you turn away your face?

DEMOS

I am blushing at my past errors.

AGORACRITUS

Think no more of them; it's not you who are to blame, but those who
cheated you in this sorry fashion. But, come, if some impudent lawyer
dared to say, "Dicasts, you shall have no wheat unless you convict this
accused man!" what would you do? Tell me.

DEMOS

I would have him removed from the bar, I would bind Hyperbolus
about his neck like a stone and would fling him into the Barathrum.

AGORACRITUS

Well spoken! but what other measures do you wish to take?

DEMOS

First, as soon as ever a fleet returns to the harbour, I shall pay up the
rowers in full.

AGORACRITUS

That will soothe many a worn and chafed bottom.

DEMOS

Further, the hoplite enrolled for military service shall not get transferred to another service through favour, but shall stick to that given
him at the outset.

AGORACRITUS

This will strike the buckler of Cleonymus full in the centre.

DEMOS

None shall ascend the rostrum, unless his chin is bearded.

AGORACRITUS

What then will become of Clisthenes and of Strato?

DEMOS

I wish only to refer to those youths who loll about the perfume shops, babbling at random, "What a clever fellow is Phaeax! How cleverly he escaped death! how concise and convincing is his style! what phrases! how clear and to the point! how well he knows how to quell an interruption!"

AGORACRITUS

I thought you were the lover of those fairies.

DEMOS

The gods forefend it! and I will force all such fellows to go hunting instead of proposing decrees.

AGORACRITUS

In that case, accept this folding-stool, and, to carry it, this well-grown, big-balled slave lad. Besides, you may put him to any other purpose you please.

DEMOS

Oh! I am happy indeed to find myself as I was of old!

AGORACRITUS

Aye, you will deem yourself happy, when I have handed you the truce of thirty years. Truce! step forward!
(*Enter Truce, in the form of a beautiful young girl, magnificently attired.*)

DEMOS

Great gods! how charming she is! Can I do with her as I wish? where did you discover her, pray?

AGORACRITUS

That Paphlagonian had kept her locked up in his house, so that you might not enjoy her. As for myself, I give her to you; take her with you into the country.

DEMOS

And what punishment will you inflict upon this Paphlagonian, the cause of all my troubles?

AGORACRITUS

It will not be over-terrible. I condemn him to follow my old trade: posted near the gates, he must sell sausages of asses' and dogs' meat: perpetually drunk, he will exchange foul language with prostitutes and will drink nothing but the dirty water from the baths.

DEMOS

Well conceived! he is indeed fit to wrangle with harlots and bathmen; as for you, in return for so many blessings, I invite you to take the place at the Prytaneum which this rogue once occupied. Put on his frog-green mantle and follow me. As for the other, let them take him away; let him go sell his sausages in full view of the foreigners, whom he used formerly to insult so wantonly.

1. Aristophanes never tires of twitting Euripides with the fact or fancy that his mother had sold vegetables.

2. Eucrates: see the Glossary.

3. Lysicles: see the Glossary.

4. The same actor played the parts of both Nicias and Cleon; hence Nicias does not reappear in the comedy.

5. The cavalry had been responsible for an Athenian victory at Corinth in 425.

6. Artichokes were tenderest in early spring.

7. In order to endear themselves to the masses, the demagogues were wont to vulgarize their oratory with terms derived from various trades.

8. Thunder on the right was a favourable omen.

9. The Athenians had three ways of signifying their gratitude to persons who had served the state outstandingly well. They might grant: 1) The privilege of dining in the Prytaneum; 2) A chaplet or garland, the ancient equivalent of a medal of honour; 3) A front seat in the theatre.

10. In the Pyanepsian procession the children carried olive branches around which were wound strips of linen. After the festival these were hung up over the doors of the houses. Modern superstition exhibits analogous actions on Palm Sunday.

11. In the early years of the Peloponnesian War the Spartans invaded Attica almost every year, and the rural population was forced to move into the city, where they were very inadequately housed.

12. When bucklers were hung up as trophies it was usual to detach the ring or brace, in order to render them useless for military purposes.

13. There is a pun here on the Greek words *démos,* "people" and *demós,* "fat."

14. The implication of this remark is that Cleon is so adept at crushing and overturning the fortunes of Athens that he is to be credited with the invention of the utensils with which these operations are culinarily performed.

15. Aristophanes has here coined the word *Dorodokisti,* which is patterned after *Doristi,* "in the Dorian mode," with the added suggestion of

533

dorodokos, "taker of bribes." Following the lead of a French translator, we might speak of the "louis d'or-ian mode."

16. The Greek word for bath-tub was *pyelos.*

17. The ancients regularly diluted their wine with a more or less generous admixture of water.

18. The original here contains, and the translation omits, a number of details on the new form of vice. Only a pedant would demand their inclusion, for like many other parts of this play they are totally deficient in humour. Cunnilingual activities are not particularly new nowadays anyway, and our psychologists will inform the curious more thoroughly and more reliably than Aristophanes.

III
THE CLOUDS

Characters in the Play

Strepsiades
Phidippides
Servant of Strepsiades
Disciples of Socrates
Socrates
Just Discourse
Unjust Discourse
Pasias, *a Money-lender*
Amynias, *another Money-lender*
Chorus of Clouds

INTRODUCTION

THE consecutive successes of *The Acharnians* and *The Knights* in 425 and 424 had filled Aristophanes with pride and bereft him of judgment, and at the Great Dionysia of 423 he expectantly produced what he misguidedly considered his best comedy, *The Clouds*. The award of the third and lowest prize was a disappointment at once bitter and salutary; if the poet never quite forgave the Athenian populace for its eminently just verdict, he at least did not again endeavour to create comedy out of intellectual backwardness and none of his later plays is so lacking in levity or so fettered with message.

The piece opens with a soliloquy by Strepsiades, an old and stupid rustic for whom Aristophanes shows traces of an affection difficult to comprehend and impossible to share. Deeply in debt because of the extravagance of his horse-racing son Phidippides and sleepless with worry over what to do, he finally decides to call in the aid of the new science by which Sophists enable their pupils to confute their creditors and preserve their fortunes. When his request that Phidippides learn this useful art is summarily rejected Strepsiades resolves to study it himself and goes over to the Thoughtery, the house of Socrates, which is next door to his own. Here he finds the disciples of the Sophist engaged in a number of ridiculous travesties on scientific investigation and soon the Master himself appears, suspended in a basket and "contémplating the sun."

Strepsiades begs to be accepted as a pupil and swears to pay whatever sum Socrates may name. The mention of the gods leads Socrates to expound the truth about celestial matters, and the Clouds, the genii of his school, are invoked with prayers and praises. In this way the poet motivates the entrance of the Chorus and prepares for the scene that follows, in which the new learning is repeatedly and sharply lampooned. Finally Socrates accepts Strepsiades as a pupil and both of them enter the Thoughtery, leaving the stage to the Chorus, which now delivers the parabasis.

The anapests take the Athenians to task for their unappreciative reception of the play, and here for the first time we realize that we are reading a later version of *The Clouds* and not necessarily the one which Aris-

537

tophanes produced in 423. There is, however, no reason to believe that any essential or extensive changes were made; the poet was too stubbornly fond of the play for that, and we may therefore conclude that what we possess is the reading version published by the author after the production, and probably altered only in the parabasis. The ode is a prayer to Zeus, Posidon, and Apollo. The epirrheme recounts the services of the Clouds to Athens. The antode invokes Apollo, Artemis, Athené, and Dionysus. The antepirrheme reports the Moon's good wishes for Athens, but also her annoyance at the inadequacy of the Athenian calendar.

At the conclusion of the parabasis Socrates comes out of his Thoughtery infuriated at the stupidity of Strepsiades but gallantly resolved not to abandon his attempt to teach him. He decides to continue his efforts in the fresh air, and the spectators are given several samples of the old man's ineptitude. This finally exhausts even Socrates' patience and he leaves in disgust. The Chorus counsels Strepsiades to have his son educated in his stead, and Phidippides this time yields with unexpected and inconsistent readiness.

Socrates decides to have him instructed by none other than the Just and the Unjust Discourses themselves, and soon these worthies appear and engage in a lengthy argument in which the former nostalgically portrays the virtues of olden times and the latter expounds the utility of the modern science. The contest ends with the complete defeat of the Just Discourse, and his triumphant opponent takes over the education of Phidippides and leads him into the Thoughtery. The Chorus ominously voices the opinion that Strepsiades will regret this, and then sings a brief ode in which the power of the Clouds is extolled. At the conclusion of this Socrates appears and presents Strepsiades with his made-over son, now very pale and intellectual looking. The old man takes him home exultantly and is able, even without the scientific assistance of his son, to get rid of two creditors in short order. The Chorus sings a reflective ode, suggestive of those which precede the catastrophe in many tragedies, and immediately Strepsiades runs out of his house, hotly pursued by his ungrateful son, who has beaten his father and now proves that he has been morally quite justified in so doing; he is also willing to demonstrate that he would have a right to inflict the same treatment on his mother, but Strepsiades now perceives what the poet evidently regards as the light and realizing that it is the insidious science of Socrates that has brought him these troubles, he and a slave set fire to the little house in which these subversive studies are pursued.

Such is the plot of the comedy which Aristophanes thought worthy of the highest prize. Our judgment on this question is hampered by the fact that we do not possess the plays which were ranked above it, but we may safely assume that unless they were exceptionally poor, *The Clouds* received just what it deserved. It is not a good comedy for a number of reasons and a recital of these is hardly necessary here. Its chief defect, however, lies in its central character, the Aristophanic Socrates. To be amusing, a caricature must strongly resemble its original in all important essentials. These will be grossly exaggerated, to be sure, but to be funny they must be true. If Adolf Hitler were married it might be amusing to portray him as a hen-pecked husband, but no one in his senses would expect an audience to be entertained by such a picture now. Yet Socrates rejected the natural science of his day; refused to organize any school of philosophy; never took pay for his teaching, which he gave gratis to anyone who would discuss ethics or metaphysics with him; made no claims to omniscience, but affected rather to know nothing. In all these respects the character which Aristophanes put on the stage in *The Clouds* is an inept caricature, but it is more flagrantly so in the most important point of all, for no man in Athens was more devoted to truth, honesty, justice, and morality than was Socrates. The irritating dialectician of the market-place must have been a familiar figure to almost every member of the poet's audience, yet the fact that they rejected the Aristophanic Socrates testifies little to their love for the real one and a great deal to their love for good caricatures.

THE CLOUDS

(SCENE:—*In the background are two houses, that of Strepsiades and that of Socrates, the Thoughtery. The latter is small and dingy; the interior of the former is shown and two beds are seen, each occupied.*)

STREPSIADES (*sitting up*)

GREAT gods! will these nights never end? will daylight never come? I heard the cock crow long ago and my slaves are snoring still! Ah! it wasn't like this formerly. Curses on the war! has it not done me ills enough? Now I may not even chastise my own slaves.[1] Again there's this brave lad, who never wakes the whole long night, but, wrapped in his five coverlets, farts away to his heart's content. (*He lies down*) Come! let me nestle in well and snore too, if it be possible . . . oh! misery, it's vain to think of sleep with all these expenses, this stable, these debts, which are devouring me, thanks to this fine cavalier, who only knows how to look after his long locks, to show himself off in his chariot and to dream of horses! And I, I am nearly dead, when I see the moon bringing the third decade in her train and my liability falling due. . . . Slave! light the lamp and bring me my tablets. (*The slave obeys.*) Who are all my creditors? Let me see and reckon up the interest. What is it I owe? . . . Twelve minæ to Pasias. . . . What! twelve minæ to Pasias? . . . Why did I borrow these? Ah! I know! It was to buy that thoroughbred, which cost me so much. How I should have prized the stone that had blinded him!

PHIDIPPIDES (*in his sleep*)

That's not fair, Philo! Drive your chariot straight, I say.

STREPSIADES

This is what is destroying me. He raves about horses, even in his sleep.

PHIDIPPIDES (*still sleeping*)

How many times round the track is the race for the chariots of war?

STREPSIADES

It's your own father you are driving . . . to death . . . to ruin.
Come! what debt comes next, after that of Pasias? . . . Three minæ to
Amynias for a chariot and its two wheels.

PHIDIPPIDES (*still asleep*)

Give the horse a good roll in the dust and lead him home.

STREPSIADES

Ah! wretched boy! it's my money that you are making roll. My creditors have distrained on my goods, and here are others again, who demand
security for their interest.

PHIDIPPIDES (*awaking*)

What is the matter with you, father, that you groan and turn about the
whole night through?

STREPSIADES

I have a bum-bailiff in the bedclothes biting me.

PHIDIPPIDES

For pity's sake, let me have a little sleep. (*He turns over.*)

STREPSIADES

Very well, sleep on! but remember that all these debts will fall back on
your shoulders. Oh! curses on the go-between who made me marry your
mother! I lived so happily in the country, a commonplace, everyday life,
but a good and easy one—had not a trouble, not a care, was rich in bees,
in sheep and in olives. Then indeed I had to marry the niece of Megacles,
the son of Megacles; I belonged to the country, she was from the town;
she was a haughty, extravagant woman, a true Coesyra. On the nuptial
day, when I lay beside her, I was reeking of the dregs of the wine-cup, of
cheese and of wool; she was redolent with essences, saffron, voluptuous
kisses, the love of spending, of good cheer and of wanton delights. I will
not say she did nothing; no, she worked hard . . . to ruin me, and pretending all the while merely to be showing her the cloak she had woven
for me, I said, "Wife you go too fast about your work, your threads are
too closely woven and you use far too much wool."

(*A slave enters with a lamp.*)

SLAVE

There is no more oil in the lamp.

STREPSIADES

Why then did you light such a thirsty lamp? Come here, I am going to
beat you.

SLAVE

What for?

STREPSIADES

Because you have put in too thick a wick. . . . Later, when we had this boy, what was to be his name? It was the cause of much quarrelling with my loving wife. She insisted on having some reference to a horse in his name, that he should be called Xanthippus, Charippus or Callippides.[2] I wanted to name him Phidonides after his grandfather. We disputed long, and finally agreed to style him Phidippides. . . . She used to fondle and coax him, saying, "Oh! what a joy it will be to me when you have grown up, to see you, like my father, Megacles, clothed in purple and standing up straight in your chariot driving your steeds toward the town." And I would say to him, "When, like your father, you will go, dressed in a skin, to fetch back your goats from Phelleus." Alas! he never listened to me and his madness for horses has shattered my fortune. (*He gets out of bed.*) But by dint of thinking the livelong night, I have discovered a road to salvation, both miraculous and divine. If he will but follow it, I shall be out of my trouble! First, however, he must be awakened, but it must be done as gently as possible. How shall I manage it? Phidippides! my little Phidippides!

PHIDIPPIDES (*awaking again*)

What is it, father?

STREPSIADES

Kiss me and give me your hand.

PHIDIPPIDES (*getting up and doing as his father requests*)

There! What's it all about?

STREPSIADES

Tell me! do you love me?

PHIDIPPIDES

By Posidon, the equestrian Posidon! yes, I swear I do.

STREPSIADES

Oh, do not, I pray you, invoke this god of horses; he is the one who is the cause of all my cares. But if you really love me, and with your whole heart, my boy, believe me.

PHIDIPPIDES

Believe you? about what?

STREPSIADES

Alter your habits forthwith and go and learn what I tell you.

PHIDIPPIDES

Say on, what are your orders?

STREPSIADES

Will you obey me ever so little?

PHIDIPPIDES

By Bacchus, I will obey you.

STREPSIADES

Very well then! Look this way. Do you see that little door and that little house?

PHIDIPPIDES

Yes, father. But what are you driving at?

STREPSIADES

That is the Thoughtery of wise souls. There they prove that we are coals enclosed on all sides under a vast snuffer, which is the sky. If well paid, these men also teach one how to gain law-suits, whether they be just or not.

PHIDIPPIDES

What do they call themselves?

STREPSIADES

I do not know exactly, but they are deep thinkers and most admirable people.

PHIDIPPIDES

Bah! the wretches! I know them; you mean those quacks with pale faces, those barefoot fellows, such as that miserable Socrates and Chaerephon?

STREPSIADES

Silence! say nothing foolish! If you desire your father not to die of hunger, join their company and let your horses go.

PHIDIPPIDES

No, by Bacchus! even though you gave me the pheasants that Leogoras raises.

STREPSIADES

Oh! my beloved son, I beseech you, go and follow their teachings.

PHIDIPPIDES

And what is it I should learn?

STREPSIADES

It seems they have two courses of reasoning, the true and the false, and that, thanks to the false, the worst law-suits can be gained. If then you learn this science, which is false, I shall not have to pay an obolus of all the debts I have contracted on your account.

PHIDIPPIDES

No, I will not do it. I should no longer dare to look at our gallant horsemen, when I had so ruined my tan.

STREPSIADES

Well then, by Demeter! I will no longer support you, neither you, nor your team, nor your saddle-horse. Go and hang yourself, I turn you out of house and home.

PHIDIPPIDES

My uncle Megacles will not leave me without horses; I shall go to him and laugh at your anger.
                    (*He departs.* STREPSIADES *goes over to* SOCRATES' *house.*)

STREPSIADES

One rebuff shall not dishearten me. With the help of the gods I will enter the Thoughtery and learn myself. (*He hesitates.*) But at my age, memory has gone and the mind is slow to grasp things. How can all these fine distinctions, these subtleties be learned? (*Making up his mind*) Bah! why should I dally thus instead of rapping at the door? Slave, slave!
                                        (*He knocks and calls.*)

A DISCIPLE (*from within*)

A plague on you! Who are you?

STREPSIADES

Strepsiades, the son of Phido, of the deme of Cicynna.

DISCIPLE (*coming out of the door*)

You are nothing but an ignorant and illiterate fellow to let fly at the door with such kicks. You have brought on a miscarriage—of an idea!

STREPSIADES

Pardon me, please; for I live far away from here in the country. But tell me, what was the idea that miscarried?

DISCIPLE

I may not tell it to any but a disciple.

STREPSIADES

Then tell me without fear, for I have come to study among you.

DISCIPLE

Very well then, but reflect, that these are mysteries. Lately, a flea bit Chaerephon on the brow and then from there sprang on to the head of Socrates. Socrates asked Chaerephon, "How many times the length of its legs does a flea jump?"

STREPSIADES

And how ever did he go about measuring it?

DISCIPLE

Oh! it was most ingenious! He melted some wax, seized the flea and dipped its two feet in the wax, which, when cooled, left them shod with true Persian slippers. These he took off and with them measured the dis-tance.

STREPSIADES

Ah! great Zeus! what a brain! what subtlety!

DISCIPLE

I wonder what then would you say, if you knew another of Socrates' contrivances?

STREPSIADES

What is it? Pray tell me.

DISCIPLE

Chaerephon of the deme of Sphettia asked him whether he thought a gnat buzzed through its proboscis or through its anus.

STREPSIADES

And what did he say about the gnat?

DISCIPLE

He said that the gut of the gnat was narrow, and that, in passing through this tiny passage, the air is driven with force towards the breech; then after this slender channel, it encountered the rump, which was dis-tended like a trumpet, and there it resounded sonorously.

STREPSIADES

So the arse of a gnat is a trumpet. Oh! what a splendid arsevation! [3] Thrice happy Socrates! It would not be difficult to succeed in a law-suit, knowing so much about a gnat's guts!

DISCIPLE

Not long ago a lizard caused him the loss of a sublime thought.

STREPSIADES

In what way, please?

DISCIPLE

One night, when he was studying the course of the moon and its revolutions and was gazing open-mouthed at the heavens, a lizard crapped upon
him from the top of the roof.

STREPSIADES

A lizard crapping on Socrates! That's rich!

DISCIPLE

Last night we had nothing to eat.

STREPSIADES

Well, what did he contrive, to secure you some supper?

DISCIPLE

He spread over the table a light layer of cinders, bending an iron rod
the while; then he took up a pair of compasses and at the same moment
unhooked a piece of the victim which was hanging in the palaestra.

STREPSIADES

And we still dare to admire Thales! Open, open this home of knowledge
to me quickly! Haste, haste to show me Socrates; I long to become his
disciple. But do please open the door. (*The door opens, revealing the interior of the Thoughtery, in which the* DISCIPLES OF SOCRATES *are seen in
various postures of meditation and study; they are pale and emaciated
creatures.*) Ah! by Heracles! what country are those animals from?

DISCIPLE

Why, what are you astonished at? What do you think they resemble?

STREPSIADES

The captives of Pylos. But why do they look so fixedly on the ground?

DISCIPLE

They are seeking for what is below the ground.

STREPSIADES

Ah! they're looking for onions. Do not give yourselves so much trouble;
I know where there are some, fine big ones. But what are those fellows doing, bent all double?

DISCIPLE

They are sounding the abysses of Tartarus.

STREPSIADES

And what are their arses looking at in the heavens?

DISCIPLE

They are studying astronomy on their own account. But come in so that
the master may not find us here.

STREPSIADES

Not yet; not yet; let them not change their position. I want to tell
them my own little matter.

DISCIPLE

But they may not stay too long in the open air and away from school.

STREPSIADES (*pointing to a celestial globe*)

In the name of all the gods, what is that? Tell me.

DISCIPLE

That is astronomy.

STREPSIADES (*pointing to a map*)

And that?

DISCIPLE

Geometry.

STREPSIADES

What is that used for?

DISCIPLE

To measure the land.

STREPSIADES

But that is apportioned by lot.

DISCIPLE

No, no, I mean the entire earth.

STREPSIADES

Ah! what a funny thing! How generally useful indeed is this invention!

DISCIPLE

There is the whole surface of the earth. Look! Here is Athens.

STREPSIADES

Athens! you are mistaken; I see no courts in session.

DISCIPLE

Nevertheless it is really and truly the Attic territory.

STREPSIADES

And where are my neighbours of Cicynna?

DISCIPLE

They live here. This is Euboea; you see this island, that is so long and narrow.

STREPSIADES

I know. Because we and Pericles have stretched it by dint of squeezing it. And where is Lacedaemon?

DISCIPLE

Lacedaemon? Why, here it is, look.

STREPSIADES

How near it is to us! Think it well over, it must be removed to a greater distance.

DISCIPLE

But, by Zeus, that is not possible.

STREPSIADES

Then, woe to you! and who is this man suspended up in a basket?

DISCIPLE

That's *himself*.

STREPSIADES

Who's himself?

DISCIPLE

Socrates.

STREPSIADES

Socrates! Oh! I pray you, call him right loudly for me.

DISCIPLE

Call him yourself; I have no time to waste. (*He departs. The machine swings in* SOCRATES *in a basket.*)

STREPSIADES

Socrates! my little Socrates!

SOCRATES (*loftily*)
Mortal, what do you want with me?

STREPSIADES
First, what are you doing up there? Tell me, I beseech you.

SOCRATES (*pompously*)
I am traversing the air and contémplating the sun.

STREPSIADES
Thus it's not on the solid ground, but from the height of this basket, that you slight the gods, if indeed . . .

SOCRATES
I have to suspend my brain and mingle the subtle essence of my mind with this air, which is of the like nature, in order clearly to penetrate the things of heaven. I should have discovered nothing, had I remained on the ground to consider from below the things that are above; for the earth by its force attracts the sap of the mind to itself. It's just the same with the water-cress.

STREPSIADES
What? Does the mind attract the sap of the water-cress? Ah! my dear little Socrates, come down to me! I have come to ask you for lessons.

SOCRATES (*descending*)
And for what lessons?

STREPSIADES
I want to learn how to speak. I have borrowed money, and my merciless creditors do not leave me a moment's peace; all my goods are at stake.

SOCRATES
And how was it you did not see that you were getting so much into debt?

STREPSIADES
My ruin has been the madness for horses, a most rapacious evil; but teach me one of your two methods of reasoning, the one whose object is not to repay anything, and, may the gods bear witness, that I am ready to pay any fee you may name.

SOCRATES
By which gods will you swear? To begin with, the gods are not a coin current with us.

STREPSIADES
But what do you swear by then? By the iron money of Byzantium?

SOCRATES

Do you really wish to know the truth of celestial matters?

STREPSIADES

Why, yes, if it's possible.

SOCRATES

. . . and to converse with the clouds, who are our genii?

STREPSIADES

Without a doubt.

SOCRATES

Then be seated on this sacred couch.

STREPSIADES (*sitting down*)

I am seated.

SOCRATES

Now take this chaplet.

STREPSIADES

Why a chaplet? Alas! Socrates, would you sacrifice me, like Athamas?

SOCRATES

No, these are the rites of initiation.

STREPSIADES

And what is it I am to gain?

SOCRATES

You will become a thorough rattle-pate, a hardened old stager, the fine flour of the talkers. . . . But come, keep quiet.

STREPSIADES

By Zeus! That's no lie! Soon I shall be nothing but wheat-flour, if you powder me in that fashion.[4]

SOCRATES

Silence, old man, give heed to the prayers. (*In an hierophantic tone*) Oh! most mighty king, the boundless air, that keepest the earth suspended in space, thou bright Aether and ye venerable goddesses, the Clouds, who carry in your loins the thunder and the lightning, arise, ye sovereign powers and manifest yourselves in the celestial spheres to the eyes of your sage.

STREPSIADES

Not yet! Wait a bit, till I fold my mantle double, so as not to get wet. And to think that I did not even bring my travelling cap! What a misfortune!

SOCRATES (*ignoring this*)

Come, oh! Clouds, whom I adore, come and show yourselves to this man, whether you be resting on the sacred summits of Olympus, crowned with hoar-frost, or tarrying in the gardens of Ocean, your father, forming sacred choruses with the Nymphs; whether you be gathering the waves of the Nile in golden vases or dwelling in the Mæotic marsh or on the snowy rocks of Mimas, hearken to my prayer and accept my offering. May these sacrifices be pleasing to you.

(*Amidst rumblings of thunder the* CHORUS OF CLOUDS *appears.*)

CHORUS (*singing*)

Eternal Clouds, let us appear; let us arise from the roaring depths of Ocean, our father; let us fly towards the lofty mountains, spread our damp wings over their forest-laden summits, whence we will dominate the distant valleys, the harvest fed by the sacred earth, the murmur of the divine streams and the resounding waves of the sea, which the unwearying orb lights up with its glittering beams. But let us shake off the rainy fogs, which hide our immortal beauty and sweep the earth from afar with our gaze.

SOCRATES

Oh, venerated goddesses, yes, you are answering my call! (*To* STREPSIADES.) Did you hear their voices mingling with the awful growling of the thunder?

STREPSIADES

Oh! adorable Clouds, I revere you and I too am going to let off *my* thunder, so greatly has your own affrighted me. (*He farts.*) Faith! whether permitted or not, I must, I *must* crap!

SOCRATES

No scoffing; do not copy those damned comic poets. Come, silence! a numerous host of goddesses approaches with songs.

CHORUS (*singing*)

Virgins, who pour forth the rains, let us move toward Attica, the rich country of Pallas, the home of the brave; let us visit the dear land of Cecrops, where the secret rites are celebrated, where the mysterious sanctuary flies open to the initiate. . . . What victims are offered there to the deities of heaven! What glorious temples! What

statues! What holy prayers to the rulers of Olympus! At every season nothing but sacred festivals, garlanded victims, is to be seen.
Then Spring brings round again the joyous feasts of Dionysus, the
harmonious contests of the choruses and the serious melodies of the
flute.

STREPSIADES

By Zeus! Tell me, Socrates, I pray you, who are these women, whose
language is so solemn; can they be demi-goddesses?

SOCRATES

Not at all. They are the Clouds of heaven, great goddesses for the lazy;
to them we owe all, thoughts, speeches, trickery, roguery, boasting, lies,
sagacity.

STREPSIADES

Ah! that was why, as I listened to them, my mind spread out its wings;
it burns to babble about trifles, to maintain worthless arguments, to voice
its petty reasons, to contradict, to tease some opponent. But are they not
going to show themselves? I should like to see them, were it possible.

SOCRATES

Well, look this way in the direction of Parnes; I already see those who
are slowly descending.

STREPSIADES

But where, where? Show them to me.

SOCRATES

They are advancing in a throng, following an oblique path across the
dales and thickets.

STREPSIADES

Strange! I can see nothing.

SOCRATES

There, close to the entrance.

STREPSIADES

Hardly, if at all, can I distinguish them.

SOCRATES

You *must* see them clearly now, unless your eyes are filled with gum as
thick as pumpkins.

STREPSIADES

Aye, undoubtedly! Oh! the venerable goddesses! Why, they fill up the entire stage.

SOCRATES

And you did not know, you never suspected, that they were goddesses?

STREPSIADES

No, indeed; I thought the Clouds were only fog, dew and vapour.

SOCRATES

But what you certainly do not know is that they are the support of a crowd of quacks, the diviners, who were sent to Thurium, the notorious physicians, the well-combed fops, who load their fingers with rings down to the nails, and the braggarts, who write dithyrambic verses, all these are idlers whom the Clouds provide a living for, because they sing them in their verses.

STREPSIADES

It is then for this that they praise "the rapid flight of the moist clouds, which veil the brightness of day" and "the waving locks of the hundred-headed Typho" and "the impetuous tempests, which float through the heavens, like birds of prey with aerial wings loaded with mists" and "the rains, the dew, which the clouds outpour." As a reward for these fine phrases they bolt well-grown, tasty mullet and delicate thrushes.

SOCRATES

Yes, thanks to these. And is it not right and meet?

STREPSIADES

Tell me then why, if these really are the Clouds, they so very much resemble mortals. This is not their usual form.

SOCRATES

What are they like then?

STREPSIADES

I don't know exactly; well, they are like great packs of wool, but not like women—no, not in the least. . . . And these have noses.

SOCRATES

Answer my questions.

STREPSIADES

Willingly! Go on, I am listening.

SOCRATES

Have you not sometimes seen clouds in the sky like a centaur, a leopard, a wolf or a bull?

STREPSIADES

Why, certainly I have, but what of that?

SOCRATES

They take what metamorphosis they like. If they see a debauchee with long flowing locks and hairy as a beast, like the son of Xenophantes, they take the form of a Centaur in derision of his shameful passion.

STREPSIADES

And when they see Simon, that thiever of public money, what do they do then?

SOCRATES

To picture him to the life, they turn at once into wolves.

STREPSIADES

So that was why yesterday, when they saw Cleonymus, who cast away his buckler because he is the veriest poltroon amongst men, they changed into deer.

SOCRATES

And to-day they have seen Clisthenes; you see . . . they are women.

STREPSIADES

Hail, sovereign goddesses, and if ever you have let your celestial voice be heard by mortal ears, speak to me, oh! speak to me, ye all-powerful queens.

CHORUS-LEADER

Hail! veteran of the ancient times, you who burn to instruct yourself in fine language. And you, great high-priest of subtle nonsense, tell us your desire. To you and Prodicus alone of all the hollow orationers of to · day have we lent an ear—to Prodicus, because of his knowledge and his great wisdom, and to you, because you walk with head erect, a confident look, barefooted, resigned to everything and proud of our protection.

STREPSIADES

Oh! Earth! What august utterances! how sacred! how wondrous!

SOCRATES

That is because these are the only goddesses; all the rest are pure myth.

STREPSIADES

But by the Earth! is our father, Zeus, the Olympian, not a god?

SOCRATES

Zeus! what Zeus! Are you mad? There is no Zeus.

STREPSIADES

What are you saying now? Who causes the rain to fall? Answer me that!

SOCRATES

Why, these, and I will prove it. Have you ever seen it raining without clouds? Let Zeus then cause rain with a clear sky and without their presence!

STREPSIADES

By Apollo! that is powerfully argued! For my own part, I always thought it was Zeus pissing into a sieve. But tell me, who is it makes the thunder, which I so much dread?

SOCRATES

These, when they roll one over the other.

STREPSIADES

But how can that be? you most daring among men!

SOCRATES

Being full of water, and forced to move along, they are of necessity precipitated in rain, being fully distended with moisture from the regions where they have been floating; hence they bump each other heavily and burst with great noise.

STREPSIADES

But is it not Zeus who forces them to move?

SOCRATES

Not at all; it's the aerial Whirlwind.

STREPSIADES

The Whirlwind! ah! I did not know that. So Zeus, it seems, has no existence, and its the Whirlwind that reigns in his stead? But you have not yet told me what makes the roll of the thunder?

SOCRATES

Have you not understood me then? I tell you, that the Clouds, when full of rain, bump against one another, and that, being inordinately swollen out, they burst with a great noise.

STREPSIADES

How can you make me credit that?

SOCRATES

Take yourself as an example. When you have heartily gorged on stew at the Panathenæa, you get throes of stomach-ache and then suddenly your belly resounds with prolonged rumbling.

STREPSIADES

Yes, yes, by Apollo! I suffer, I get colic, then the stew sets to rumbling like thunder and finally bursts forth with a terrific noise. At first, it's but a little gurgling *pappax, pappax!* then it increases, *papapappax!* and when I take my crap, why, it's thunder indeed, *papapappax! pappax!! papapappax!!!* just like the clouds.

SOCRATES

Well then, reflect what a noise is produced by your belly, which is but small. Shall not the air, which is boundless, produce these mighty claps of thunder?

STREPSIADES

And this is why the names are so much alike: crap and clap. But tell me this. Whence comes the lightning, the dazzling flame, which at times consumes the man it strikes, at others hardly singes him. Is it not plain, that Zeus is hurling it at the perjurers?

SOCRATES

Out upon the fool! the driveller! he still savours of the golden age! If Zeus strikes at the perjurers, why has he not blasted Simon, Cleonymus and Theorus? Of a surety, greater perjurers cannot exist. No, he strikes his own temple, and Sunium, the promontory of Athens, and the towering oaks. Now, why should he do that? An oak is no perjurer.

STREPSIADES

I cannot tell, but it seems to me well argued. What is the lightning then?

SOCRATES

When a dry wind ascends to the Clouds and gets shut into them, it blows them out like a bladder; finally, being too confined, it bursts them, escapes with fierce violence and a roar to flash into flame by reason of its own impetuosity.

STREPSIADES

Ah, that's just what happened to me one day. It was at the feast of Zeus! I was cooking a sow's belly for my family and I had forgotten to slit it open. It swelled out and, suddenly bursting, discharged itself right into my eyes and burnt my face.

Leader of the Chorus

Oh, mortal, you who desire to instruct yourself in our great wisdom, the Athenians, the Greeks will envy you your good fortune. Only you must have the memory and ardour for study, you must know how to stand the tests, hold your own, go forward without feeling fatigue, caring but little for food, abstaining from wine, gymnastic exercises and other similar follies, in fact, you must believe as every man of intellect should, that the greatest of all blessings is to live and think more clearly than the vulgar herd, to shine in the contests of words.

Strepsiades

If it be a question of hardiness for labour, of spending whole nights at work, of living sparingly, of fighting my stomach and only eating chickpease, rest assured, I am as hard as an anvil.

Socrates

Henceforward, following our example, you will recognize no other gods but Chaos, the Clouds and the Tongue, these three alone.

Strepsiades

I would not speak to the others, even if I met them in the street; not a single sacrifice, not a libation, not a grain of incense for them!

Leader of the Chorus

Tell us boldly then what you want of us; you cannot fail to succeed, if you honour and revere us and if you are resolved to become a clever man.

Strepsiades

Oh, sovereign goddesses, it is only a very small favour that I ask of you; grant that I may outdistance all the Greeks by a hundred stadia in the art of speaking.

Leader of the Chorus

We grant you this, and henceforward no eloquence shall more often succeed with the people than your own.

Strepsiades

May the gods shield me from possessing great eloquence! That's not what I want. I want to be able to turn bad law-suits to my own advantage and to slip through the fingers of my creditors.

Leader of the Chorus

It shall be as you wish, for your ambitions are modest. Commit yourself fearlessly to our ministers, the sophists.

STREPSIADES

This I will do, for I trust in you. Moreover there is no drawing back, what with these cursed horses and this marriage, which has eaten up my vitals. (*More and more volubly from here to the end of speech*) So let them do with me as they will; I yield my body to them. Come blows, come hunger, thirst, heat or cold, little matters it to me; they may flay me, if I only escape my debts, if only I win the reputation of being a bold rascal, a fine speaker, impudent, shameless, a braggart, and adept at stringing lies, an old stager at quibbles, a complete table of laws, a thorough rattle, a fox to slip through any hole; supple as a leathern strap, slippery as an eel, an artful fellow, a blusterer, a villain; a knave with a hundred faces, cunning, intolerable, a gluttonous dog. With such epithets do I seek to be greeted; on these terms they can treat me as they choose, and, if they wish, by Demeter! they can turn me into sausages and serve me up to the philosophers.

CHORUS (*singing*)

Here have we a bold and well-disposed pupil indeed. When we have taught you, your glory among the mortals will reach even to the skies.

STREPSIADES (*singing*)

Wherein will that profit me?

CHORUS (*singing*)

You will pass your whole life among us and will be the most envied of men.

STREPSIADES (*singing*)

Shall I really ever see such happiness?

CHORUS (*singing*)

Clients will be everlastingly besieging your door in crowds, burning to get at you, to explain their business to you and to consult you about their suits, which, in return for your ability, will bring you in great sums.

LEADER OF THE CHORUS

But, Socrates, begin the lessons you want to teach this old man; rouse his mind, try the strength of his intelligence.

SOCRATES

Come, tell me the kind of mind you have; it's important that I know this, that I may order my batteries against you in the right fashion.

STREPSIADES

Eh, what! in the name of the gods, are you purposing to assault me then?

SOCRATES

No. I only wish to ask you some questions. Have you any memory?

STREPSIADES

That depends: if anything is owed me, my memory is excellent, but if I owe, alas! I have none whatever.

SOCRATES

Have you a natural gift for speaking?

STREPSIADES

For speaking, no; for cheating, yes.

SOCRATES

How will you be able to learn then?

STREPSIADES

Very easily, have no fear.

SOCRATES

Thus, when I throw forth some philosophical thought anent things celestial, you will seize it in its very flight?

STREPSIADES

Then I am to snap up wisdom much as a dog snaps up a morsel?

SOCRATES (*aside*)

Oh! the ignoramus! the barbarian! (*to* STREPSIADES) I greatly fear, old man, it will be necessary for me to have recourse to blows. Now, let me hear what you do when you are beaten.

STREPSIADES

I receive the blow, then wait a moment, take my witnesses and finally summon my assailant at law.

SOCRATES

Come, take off your cloak.

STREPSIADES

Have I robbed you of anything?

SOCRATES

No, but the usual thing is to enter the school without your cloak.

STREPSIADES

But I have not come here to look for stolen goods.

SOCRATES

Off with it, fool!

STREPSIADES (*He obeys.*)

Tell me, if I prove thoroughly attentive and learn with zeal, which ớ your disciples shall I resemble, do you think?

SOCRATES

You will be the image of Chaerephon.

STREPSIADES

Ah! unhappy me! Shall I then be only half alive?

SOCRATES

A truce to this chatter! follow me and no more of it.

STREPSIADES

First give me a honey-cake, for to descend down there sets me all a-tremble; it looks like the cave of Trophonius.

SOCRATES

But get in with you! What reason have you for thus dallying at the door?

(*They go into the Thoughtery.*)

LEADER OF THE CHORUS

Good luck! you have courage; may you succeed, you, who, though already so advanced in years, wish to instruct your mind with new studies and practise it in wisdom! (*The* CHORUS *turns and faces the Audience.*)

Spectators! By Bacchus, whose servant I am, I will frankly tell you the truth. May I secure both victory and renown as certainly as I hold you for adept critics and as I regard this comedy as my best. I wished to give you the first view of a work, which had cost me much trouble, but which I withdrew, unjustly beaten by unskilful rivals. It is you, oh, enlightened public, for whom I have prepared my piece, that I reproach with this. Nevertheless I shall never willingly cease to seek the approval of the discerning. I have not forgotten the day, when men, whom one is happy to have for an audience, received my Virtuous Young Man and my Pæderast with so much favour in this very place.[5] Then as yet virgin, my Muse had not attained the age for maternity; she had to expose her first-born for another to adopt, and it has since grown up under your generous patronage. Ever since you have as good as sworn me your faithful alliance. Thus, like the Electra of the poets, my comedy has come to seek you to-day, hoping again to encounter such enlightened spectators. As far away as she can discern her Orestes, she will be able to recognize him by his curly head. And note her modest demeanour! She has not sewn on a piece of hanging leather, thick and reddened at the end, to cause laughter among the children; she does not rail at the bald, neither does she dance the *cordax;* no old man is seen, who, while uttering his lines, batters his questioner with a stick to make his poor jests pass muster. She does not rush upon the scene carrying a torch and screaming, 'Iou! Iou!' No, she relies upon herself and her verses. . . . My value is so well known, that I take no further pride in it. I do not seek to deceive you, by reproducing the same subjects two or three times; I always invent fresh themes to present before you, themes that have no relation to each other and that are all clever. I attacked Cleon to his face and when he was all-powerful; but he has fallen, and now I have no desire to kick him when he is down. My rivals, on the contrary, now that this wretched Hyperbolus has given them the cue, have never ceased setting upon both him and his mother. First Eupolis presented his 'Maricas'; this was simply my 'Knights,' whom this plagiarist had clumsily furbished up again by adding to the piece an old drunken woman, so that she might dance the *cordax.* It was an old idea, taken from Phrynichus, who caused his old hag to be devoured by a monster of the deep. Then Hermippus fell foul of Hyperbolus and now all the others fall upon him and repeat my comparison of the eels. May those who find amusement in their pieces not be pleased with mine, but as for you, who love and applaud my inventions, why, posterity will praise your good taste.

FIRST SEMI-CHORUS (*singing*)

Oh, ruler of Olympus, all-powerful king of the gods, great Zeus, it is thou whom I first invoke; protect this chorus; and thou too, Posidon, whose dread trident upheaves at the will of thy anger both the bowels of the earth and the salty waves of the ocean. I invoke my illustrious father, the divine Aether, the universal sustainer of life, and Phoebus, who, from the summit of his chariot, sets the world aflame with his dazzling rays, Phoebus, a mighty deity amongst the gods and adored amongst mortals.

LEADER OF FIRST SEMI-CHORUS

Most wise spectators, lend us all your attention. Give heed to our just reproaches. There exist no gods to whom this city owes more than it does to us, whom alone you forget. Not a sacrifice, not a libation is there for those who protect you! Have you decreed some mad expedition? Well! we thunder or we fall down in rain. When you chose that enemy of heaven, the Paphlagonian tanner, for a general, we knitted our brow, we caused our wrath to break out; the lightning shot forth, the thunder pealed, the moon deserted her course and the sun at once veiled his beam threatening no longer to give you light, if Cleon became general. Nevertheless you elected him; it is said, Athens never resolves upon some fatal step but the gods turn these errors into her greatest gain. Do you wish that his election should even now be a success for you? It is a very simple thing to do; condemn this rapacious gull named Cleon for bribery and extortion, fit a wooden collar tight round his neck, and your error will be rectified and the commonweal will at once regain its old prosperity.

SECOND SEMI-CHORUS (*singing*)
Aid me also, Phoebus, god of Delos, who reignest on the cragged peaks of Cynthia; and thou, happy virgin, to whom the Lydian damsels offer pompous sacrifice in a temple of gold; and thou, goddess of our country, Athené, armed with the aegis, the protectress of Athens; and thou, who, surrounded by the bacchants of Delphi; roamest over the rocks of Parnassus shaking the flame of thy resinous torch, thou, Bacchus, the god of revel and joy.

LEADER OF SECOND SEMI-CHORUS
As we were preparing to come here, we were hailed by the Moon and were charged to wish joy and happiness both to the Athenians and to their allies; further, she said that she was enraged and that you treated her very shamefully, her, who does not pay you in words alone, but who renders you all real benefits. Firstly, thanks to her, you save at least a drachma each month for lights, for each, as he is leaving home at night, says, "Slave, buy no torches, for the moonlight is beautiful,"—not to name a thousand other benefits. Nevertheless you do not reckon the days correctly and your calendar is naught but confusion. Consequently the gods load her with threats each time they get home and are disappointed of their meal, because the festival has not been kept in the regular order of time. When you should be sacrificing, you are putting to the torture or administering justice. And often, we others, the gods, are fasting in token of mourning for the death of Memnon or Sarpedon, while you are devoting yourselves to joyous libations. It is for this, that last year, when the lot would have invested Hyperbolus with the duty of Amphictyon, we took his crown from him, to teach him that time must be divided according to the phases of the moon.

SOCRATES (*coming out*)
By Respiration, the Breath of Life! By Chaos! By the Air! I have never seen a man so gross, so inept, so stupid, so forgetful. All the little quibbles, which I teach him, he forgets even before he has learnt them. Yet I will not give it up, I will make him come out here into the open air. Where are you, Strepsiades? Come, bring your couch out here.

STREPSIADES (*from within*)

But the bugs will not allow me to bring it.

SOCRATES

Have done with such nonsense! place it there and pay attention.

STREPSIADES (*coming out, with the bed*)

Well, here I am.

SOCRATES

Good! Which science of all those you have never been taught, do you wish to learn first? The measures, the rhythms or the verses?

STREPSIADES

Why, the measures; the flour dealer cheated me out of two *choenixes* the other day.

SOCRATES

It's not about that I ask you, but which, according to you, is the best measure, the trimeter or the tetrameter?

STREPSIADES

The one I prefer is the semisextarius.[6]

SOCRATES

You talk nonsense, my good fellow.

STREPSIADES

I will wager your tetrameter is the semisextarius.

SOCRATES

Plague seize the dunce and the fool! Come, perchance you will learn the rhythms quicker.

STREPSIADES

Will the rhythms supply me with food?

SOCRATES

First they will help you to be pleasant in company, then to know what 's meant by enhoplian rhythm and what by the dactylic.

STREPSIADES

Of the dactyl? I know that quite well.

SOCRATES

What is it then, other than this finger here?[7]

STREPSIADES

Formerly, when a child, I used this one.

SOCRATES

You are as low-minded as you are stupid.

STREPSIADES

But, wretched man, I do not want to learn all this.

SOCRATES

Then what *do* you want to know?

STREPSIADES

Not that, not that, but the art of false reasoning.

SOCRATES

But you must first learn other things. Come, what are the male quadrupeds?

STREPSIADES

Oh! I know the males thoroughly. Do you take me for a fool then? The ram, the buck, the bull, the dog, the pigeon.

SOCRATES

Do you see what you are doing; is not the female pigeon called the same as the male?

STREPSIADES

How else? Come now!

SOCRATES

How else? With you then it's pigeon and pigeon!

STREPSIADES

That's right, by Posidon! but what names do you want me to give them?

SOCRATES

Term the female pigeonnette and the male pigeon.

STREPSIADES

Pigeonnette! hah! by the Air! That's splendid! for that lesson bring out your kneading-trough and I will fill him with flour to the brim.

SOCRATES

There you are wrong again; you make *trough* masculine and it should be feminine.

STREPSIADES

What? if I say, *him,* do I make the *trough* masculine?

SOCRATES

Assuredly! would you not say him for Cleonymus?

STREPSIADES

Well?

SOCRATES

Then trough is of the same gender as Cleonymus?

STREPSIADES

My good man! Cleonymus never had a kneading-trough; he used a round mortar for the purpose. But come, tell me what I *should* say!

SOCRATES

For trough you should say *her* as you would for Sostraté.

STREPSIADES

Her?

SOCRATES

In this manner you make it truly female.

STREPSIADES

That's it! *Her* for trough and *her* for Cleonymus.

SOCRATES

Now I must teach you to distinguish the masculine proper names from those that are feminine.

STREPSIADES

Ah! I know the female names well.

SOCRATES

Name some then.

STREPSIADES

Lysilla, Philinna, Clitagora, Demetria.

SOCRATES

And what are masculine names?

STREPSIADES

They are countless—Philoxenus, Melesias, Amynias.

SOCRATES

But, wretched man, the last two are not masculine.

STREPSIADES

You do not count them as masculine?

SOCRATES

Not at all. If you met Amynias, how would you hail him?

STREPSIADES

How? Why, I should shout, "Hi, there, Amynia!" [8]

SOCRATES

Do you see? it's a female name that you give him.

STREPSIADES

And is it not rightly done, since he refuses military service? But what use is there in learning what we all know?

SOCRATES

You know nothing about it. Come, lie down there.

STREPSIADES

What for?

SOCRATES

Ponder awhile over matters that interest you.

STREPSIADES

Oh! I pray you, not there! but, if I must lie down and ponder, let me lie on the ground.

SOCRATES

That's out of the question. Come! on the couch!

STREPSIADES (*as he lies down*)

What cruel fate! What a torture the bugs will this day put me to!

(*Socrates turns aside.*)

CHORUS (*singing*)

Ponder and examine closely, gather your thoughts together, let your mind turn to every side of things; if you meet with a difficulty, spring quickly to some other idea; above all, keep your eyes away from all gentle sleep.

STREPSIADES (*singing*)

Ow, Wow, Wow, Wow is me!

CHORUS (*singing*)
What ails you? why do you cry so?

STREPSIADES
Oh! I am a dead man! Here are these cursed Corinthians [9] advancing
upon me from all corners of the couch; they are biting me, they are
gnawing at my sides, they are drinking all my blood, they are yanking off
my balls, they are digging into my arse, they are killing me!

LEADER OF THE CHORUS
Not so much wailing and clamour, if you please.

STREPSIADES
How can I obey? I have lost my money and my complexion, my blood
and my slippers, and to cap my misery, I must keep awake on this couch,
when scarce a breath of life is left in me.

                                   (*A brief interval of silence ensues.*)

SOCRATES
Well now! what are you doing? are you reflecting?

STREPSIADES
Yes, by Posidon!

SOCRATES
What about?

STREPSIADES
Whether the bugs will entirely devour me.

SOCRATES
May death seize you, accursed man!

                                        (*He turns aside again.*)

STREPSIADES
Ah! it has already.

SOCRATES
Come, no giving way! Cover up your head; the thing to do is to find
an ingenious alternative.

STREPSIADES
An alternative! ah! I only wish one would come to me from within
these coverlets!

                                        (*Another interval of silence ensues.*)

SOCRATES

Wait! let us see what our fellow is doing! Ho! you, are you asleep?

STREPSIADES

No, by Apollo!

SOCRATES

Have you got hold of anything?

STREPSIADFS

No, nothing whatever.

SOCRATES

Nothing at all?

STREPSIADES

No, nothing except my tool, which I've got in my hand.

SOCRATES

Aren't you going to cover your head immediately and ponder?

STREPSIADES

On what? Come, Socrates, tell me.

SOCRATES

Think first what you want, and then tell me.

STREPSIADES

But I have told you a thousand times what I want. Not to pay any of my creditors.

SOCRATES

Come, wrap yourself up; concentrate your mind, which wanders too lightly; study every detail, scheme and examine thoroughly.

STREPSIADES

Alas! Alas!

SOCRATES

Keep still, and if any notion troubles you, put it quickly aside, then resume it and think over it again.

STREPSIADES

My *dear* little Socrates!

SOCRATES

What is it, old greybeard?

Strepsiades

I have a scheme for not paying my debts.

Socrates

Let us hear it.

Strepsiades

Tell me, if I purchased a Thessalian witch, I could make the moon descend during the night and shut it, like a mirror, into a round box and there keep it carefully. . . .

Socrates

How would you gain by that?

Strepsiades

How? why, if the moon did not rise, I would have no interest to pay.

Socrates

Why so?

Strepsiades

Because money is lent by the month.

Socrates

Good! but I am going to propose another trick to you. If you were condemned to pay five talents, how would you manage to quash that verdict? Tell me.

Strepsiades

How? how? I don't know, I must think.

Socrates

Do you always shut your thoughts within yourself? Let your ideas fly in the air, like a may-bug, tied by the foot with a thread.

Strepsiades

I have found a very clever way to annul that conviction; you will admit that much yourself.

Socrates

What is it?

Strepsiades

Have you ever seen a beautiful, transparent stone at the druggists' with which you may kindle fire?

Socrates

You mean a crystal lens.

STREPSIADES

That's right. Well, now if I placed myself with this stone in the sun and a long way off from the clerk, while he was writing out the conviction, I could make all the wax, upon which the words were written, melt.

SOCRATES

Well thought out, by the Graces!

STREPSIADES

Ah! I am delighted to have annulled the decree that was to cost me five talents.

SOCRATES

Come, take up this next question quickly.

STREPSIADES

Which?

SOCRATES

If, when summoned to court, you were in danger of losing your case for want of witnesses, how would you make the conviction fall upon your opponent?

STREPSIADES

That's very simple and easy.

SOCRATES

Let me hear.

STREPSIADES

This way. If another case had to be pleaded before mine was called, I should run and hang myself.

SOCRATES

You talk rubbish!

STREPSIADES

Not so, by the gods! if I were dead, no action could lie against me.

SOCRATES

You are merely beating the air. Get out! I will give you no more lessons.

STREPSIADES (*imploringly*)

Why not? Oh! Socrates! in the name of the gods!

SOCRATES

But you forget as fast as you learn. Come, what was the thing I taught you first? Tell me.

STREPSIADES

Ah! let me see. What was the first thing? What was it then? Ah! that thing in which we knead the bread, oh! my god! what do you call it?

SOCRATES

Plague take the most forgetful and silliest of old addlepates!

STREPSIADES

Alas! what a calamity! what will become of me? I am undone if I do not learn how to ply my tongue. Oh! Clouds! give me good advice.

CHORUS-LEADER

Old man, we counsel you, if you have brought up a son, to send him to learn in your stead.

STREPSIADES

Undoubtedly I have a son, as well endowed as the best, but he is un= willing to learn. What will become of me?

CHORUS-LEADER

And you don't make him obey you?

STREPSIADES

You see, he is big and strong; moreover, through his mother he is a descendant of those fine birds, the race of Coesyra. Nevertheless, I will go and find him, and if he refuses, I will turn him out of the house. Go in, Socrates, and wait for me awhile.

(SOCRATES *goes into the Thoughtery,* STREPSIADES *into his own house.*)

CHORUS (*singing*)

Do you understand, Socrates, that thanks to us you will be loaded with benefits? Here is a man, ready to obey you in all things. You see how he is carried away with admiration and enthusiasm. Profit by it to clip him as short as possible; fine chances are all too quickly gone.

STREPSIADES (*coming out of his house and pushing his son in front of him*)

No, by the Clouds! you stay here no longer; go and devour the ruins of your uncle Megacles' fortune.

PHIDIPPIDES

Oh! my poor father! what has happened to you? By the Olympian Zeus! you are no longer in your senses!

STREPSIADES

Look! "the Olympian Zeus." Oh! you fool! to believe in Zeus at your
age!

PHIDIPPIDES

What is there in that to make you laugh?

STREPSIADES

You are then a tiny little child, if you credit such antiquated rub
bish! But come here, that I may teach you; I will tell you something very
necessary to know to be a man; but do not repeat it to anybody.

PHIDIPPIDES

Tell me, what is it?

STREPSIADES

Just now you swore by Zeus.

PHIDIPPIDES

Sure I did.

STREPSIADES

Do you see how good it is to learn? Phidippides, there is no Zeus.

PHIDIPPIDES

What is there then?

STREPSIADES

The Whirlwind has driven out Zeus and is King now.

PHIDIPPIDES

What drivel!

STREPSIADES

You must realize that it is true.

PHIDIPPIDES

And who says so?

STREPSIADES

Socrates, the Melian, and Chaerephon, who knows how to measure
the jump of a flea.

PHIDIPPIDES

Have you reached such a pitch of madness that you believe those
bilious fellows?

STREPSIADES

Use better language, and do not insult men who are clever and full of wisdom, who, to economize, never shave, shun the gymnasia and never go to the baths, while you, you only await my death to eat up my wealth. But come, come as quickly as you can to learn in my stead.

PHIDIPPIDES

And what good can be learnt of them?

STREPSIADES

What good indeed? Why, all human knowledge. Firstly, you will know yourself grossly ignorant. But await me here awhile.

(*He goes back into his house.*)

PHIDIPPIDES

Alas! what is to be done? Father has lost his wits. Must I have him certificated for lunacy, or must I order his coffin?

STREPSIADES (*returning with a bird in each hand*)
Come! what kind of bird is this? Tell me.

PHIDIPPIDES

A pigeon.

STREPSIADES

Good! And this female?

PHIDIPPIDES

A pigeon.

STREPSIADES

The same for both? You make me laugh! In the future you must call this one a pigeonnette and the other a pigeon.

PHIDIPPIDES

A pigeonnette! These then are the fine things you have just learnt at the school of these sons of Earth! [10]

STREPSIADES

And many others; but what I learnt I forgot at once, because I am too old.

PHIDIPPIDES

So this is why you have lost your cloak?

STREPSIADES

I have not lost it, I have consecrated it to Philosophy.

PHIDIPPIDES

And what have you done with your sandals, you poor fool?

STREPSIADES

If I have lost them, it is for what was necessary, just as Pericles did.
But come, move yourself, let us go in; if necessary, do wrong to obey
your father. When you were six years old and still lisped, I was the one
who obeyed you. I remember at the feasts of Zeus you had a consuming
wish for a little chariot and I bought it for you with the first obolus which
I received as a juryman in the courts.

PHIDIPPIDES

You will soon repent of what you ask me to do.

STREPSIADES

Oh! now I am happy! He obeys. (*loudly*) Come, Socrates, come!
Come out quick! Here I am bringing you my son; he refused, but I have
persuaded him.

SOCRATES

Why, he is but a child yet. He is not used to these baskets, in which we
suspend our minds.

PHIDIPPIDES

To make you better used to them, I would you were hung.

STREPSIADES

A curse upon you! you insult your master!

SOCRATES

"I would you were hung!" What a stupid speech! and so emphatically
spoken! How can one ever get out of an accusation with such a tone,
summon witnesses or touch or convince? And yet when we think, Hyperbolus learnt all this for one talent!

STREPSIADES

Rest undisturbed and teach him. He has a most intelligent nature.
Even when quite little he amused himself at home with making houses,
carving boats, constructing little chariots of leather, and understood
wonderfully how to make frogs out of pomegranate rinds. Teach him
both methods of reasoning, the strong and also the weak, which by false
arguments triumphs over the strong; if not the two, at least the false,
and that in every possible way.

SOCRATES

The Just and Unjust Discourse themselves shall instruct him. I shall leave you.

STREPSIADES

But forget it not, he must always, always be able to confound the true. (*Socrates enters the Thoughtery; a moment later the* JUST *and the* UN-JUST DISCOURSE *come out; they are quarrelling violently.*)

JUST DISCOURSE

Come here! Shameless as you may be, will you dare to show your face to the spectators?

UNJUST DISCOURSE

Take me where you will. I seek a throng, so that I may the better annihilate you.

JUST DISCOURSE

Annihilate me! Do you forget who you are?

UNJUST DISCOURSE

I am Reasoning.

JUST DISCOURSE

Yes, the weaker Reasoning.[11]

UNJUST DISCOURSE

But I triumph over you, who claim to be the stronger.

JUST DISCOURSE

By what cunning shifts, pray?

UNJUST DISCOURSE

By the invention of new maxims.

JUST DISCOURSE

. . . which are received with favour by these fools.
(*He points to the audience.*)

UNJUST DISCOURSE

Say rather, by these wise men.

JUST DISCOURSE

I am going to destroy you mercilessly.

UNJUST DISCOURSE

How pray? Let us see you do it.

JUST DISCOURSE

By saying what is true.

UNJUST DISCOURSE

I shall retort and shall very soon have the better of you. First, I maintain that justice has no existence.

JUST DISCOURSE

Has no existence?

UNJUST DISCOURSE

No existence! Why, where is it?

JUST DISCOURSE

With the gods.

UNJUST DISCOURSE

How then, if justice exists, was Zeus not put to death for having put his father in chains?

JUST DISCOURSE

Bah! this is enough to turn my stomach! A basin, quick!

UNJUST DISCOURSE

You are an old driveller and stupid withal.

JUST DISCOURSE

And you a degenerate and shameless fellow.

UNJUST DISCOURSE

Hah! What sweet expressions!

JUST DISCOURSE

An impious buffoon.

UNJUST DISCOURSE

You crown me with roses and with lilies.

JUST DISCOURSE

A parricide.

UNJUST DISCOURSE

Why, you shower gold upon me.

JUST DISCOURSE

Formerly it was a hailstorm of blows.

UNJUST DISCOURSE

I deck myself with your abuse.

Just Discourse

What impudence!

Unjust Discourse

What tomfoolery!

Just Discourse

It is because of you that the youth no longer attends the schools. The Athenians will soon recognize what lessons you teach those who are fools enough to believe you.

Unjust Discourse

You are overwhelmed with wretchedness.

Just Discourse

And you, you prosper. Yet you were poor when you said, "I am the Mysian Telephus," and used to stuff your wallet with maxims of Pandeletus to nibble at.

Unjust Discourse

Oh! the beautiful wisdom, of which you are now boasting!

Just Discourse

Madman! But yet madder the city that keeps you, you, the corrupter of its youth!

Unjust Discourse

it is not you who will teach this young man; you are as old and out of date at Cronus.

Just Discourse

Nay, it will certainly be I, if he does not wish to be lost and to practise verbosity only.

Unjust Discourse (*to* Phidippides)

Come here and leave him to beat the air.

Just Discourse

You'll regret it, if you touch him.

Chorus-Leader (*stepping between them as they are about to come to blows*)

A truce to your quarrellings and abuse! But you expound what you taught us formerly, and you, your new doctrine. Thus, after hearing each of you argue, he will be able to choose betwixt the two schools.

JUST DISCOURSE

I am quite agreeable.

UNJUST DISCOURSE

And I too.

LEADER OF THE CHORUS

Who is to speak first?

UNJUST DISCOURSE

Let it be my opponent, he has my full consent; then I shall follow
upon the very ground he shall have chosen and shall shatter him with a
hail of new ideas and subtle fancies; if after that he dares to breathe another word, I shall sting him in the face and in the eyes with our maxims,
which are as keen as the sting of a wasp, and he will die.

CHORUS (*singing*)

Here are two rivals confident in their powers of oratory and in the
thoughts over which they have pondered so long. Let us see which
will come triumphant out of the contest. This wisdom, for which my
friends maintain such a persistent fight, is in great danger.

LEADER OF THE CHORUS

Come then, you, who crowned men of other days with so many virtues,
plead the cause dear to you, make yourself known to us.

JUST DISCOURSE

Very well, I will tell you what was the old education, when I used to
teach justice with so much success and when modesty was held in venera-
tion. Firstly, it was required of a child, that it should not utter a word.
In the street, when they went to the music-school, all the youths of the
same district marched lightly clad and ranged in good order, even when the
snow was falling in great flakes. At the master's house they had to stand
with their legs apart and they were taught to sing either, "Pallas, the Terrible, who overturneth cities," or "A noise resounded from afar" in the
solemn tones of the ancient harmony. If anyone indulged in buffoonery
or lent his voice any of the soft inflexions, like those which to-day the
disciples of Phrynis take so much pains to form, he was treated as an enemy of the Muses and belaboured with blows. In the wrestling school they
would sit with outstretched legs and without display of any indecency to
the curious. When they rose, they would smooth over the sand, so as to
leave no trace to excite obscene thoughts. Never was a child rubbed with
oil below the belt; the rest of their bodies thus retained its fresh bloom
and down, like a velvety peach. They were not to be seen approaching a
lover and themselves rousing his passion by soft modulation of the voice

and lustful gaze. At table, they would not have dared, before those older than themselves, to have taken a radish, an aniseed or a leaf of parsley, and much less eat fish or thrushes or cross their legs.

Unjust Discourse

What antiquated rubbish! Have we got back to the days of the festivals of Zeus Polieus, to the Buphonia, to the time of the poet Cecides and the golden cicadas?

Just Discourse

Nevertheless by suchlike teaching I built up the men of Marathon. But you, you teach the children of to-day to bundle themselves quickly into their clothes, and I am enraged when I see them at the Panathenæa forgetting Athené while they dance, and covering their tools with their bucklers. Hence, young man, dare to range yourself beside me, who follow justice and truth; you will then be able to shun the public place, to refrain from the baths, to blush at all that is shameful, to fire up if your virtue is mocked at, to give place to your elders, to honour your parents, in short, to avoid all that is evil. Be modesty itself, and do not run to applaud the dancing girls; if you delight in such scenes, some courtesan will cast you her apple and your reputation will be done for. Do not bandy words with your father, nor treat him as a dotard, nor reproach the old man, who has cherished you, with his age.

Unjust Discourse

If you listen to him, by Bacchus! you will be the image of the sons of Hippocrates and will be called *mother's big ninny*.

Just Discourse

No, but you will pass your days at the gymnasia, glowing with strength and health; you will not go to the public place to cackle and wrangle as is done nowadays; you will not live in fear that you may be dragged before the courts for some trifle exaggerated by quibbling. But you will go down to the Academy to run beneath the sacred olives with some virtuous friend of your own age, your head encircled with the white reed, enjoying your ease and breathing the perfume of the yew and of the fresh sprouts of the poplar, rejoicing in the return of springtide and gladly listening to the gentle rustle of the plane tree and the elm. (*With greater warmth from here on*) If you devote yourself to practising my precepts, your chest will be stout, your colour glowing, your shoulders broad, your tongue short, your hips muscular, but your tool small. But if you follow the fashions of the day, you will be pallid in hue, have narrow shoulders, a narrow chest, a long tongue, small hips and a big thing; you will know how to spin forth long-winded arguments on law. You will be persuaded also to regard as splendid everything that is shameful and as shameful everything that is honourable; in a word, you will wallow in degeneracy like Antimachus.

CHORUS (*singing*)

How beautiful, high-souled, brilliant is this wisdom that you practise! What a sweet odour of honesty is emitted by your discourse! Happy were those men of other days who lived when you were honoured! And you, seductive talker, come, find some fresh arguments, for your rival has done wonders.

LEADER OF THE CHORUS

You will have to bring out against him all the battery of your wit, if you desire to beat him and not to be laughed out of court.

UNJUST DISCOURSE

At last! I was choking with impatience, I was burning to upset his arguments! If I am called the Weaker Reasoning in the schools, it is just because I was the first to discover the means to confute the laws and the decrees of justice. To invoke solely the weaker arguments and yet triumph is an art worth more than a hundred thousand drachmae. But see how I shall batter down the sort of education of which he is so proud. Firstly, he forbids you to bathe in hot water. What grounds have you for condemning hot baths?

JUST DISCOURSE

Because they are baneful and enervate men.

UNJUST DISCOURSE

Enough said! Oh! you poor wrestler! From the very outset I have seized you and hold you round the middle; you cannot escape me. Tell me, of all the sons of Zeus, who had the stoutest heart, who performed the most doughty deeds?

JUST DISCOURSE

None, in my opinion, surpassed Heracles.

UNJUST DISCOURSE

Where have you ever seen cold baths called 'Bath of Heracles'? And yet who was braver than he?

JUST DISCOURSE

It is because of such quibbles, that the baths are seen crowded with young folk, who chatter there the livelong day while the gymnasia remain empty.

UNJUST DISCOURSE

Next you condemn the habit of frequenting the market-place, while I approve this. If it were wrong Homer would never have made Nestor speak in public as well as all his wise heroes. As for the art of speaking, he tells you, young men should not practise it; I hold the contrary. Furthermore he preaches chastity to them. Both precepts are equally harmful. Have you ever seen chastity of any use to anyone? Answer and try to confute me.

JUST DISCOURSE

To many; for instance, Peleus won a sword thereby.

UNJUST DISCOURSE

A sword! Ah! what a fine present to make him! Poor wretch! Hyperbolus, the lamp-seller, thanks to his villainy, has gained more than . . . I do not know how many talents, but certainly no sword.

JUST DISCOURSE

Peleus owed it to his chastity that he became the husband of Thetis.

UNJUST DISCOURSE

. . . who left him in the lurch, for he was not the most ardent; in those nocturnal sports between the sheets, which so please women, he possessed but little merit. Get you gone, you are but an old fool. But you, young man, just consider a little what this temperance means and the delights of which it deprives you—young fellows, women, play, dainty dishes, wine, boisterous laughter. And what is life worth without these? Then, if you happen to commit one of these faults inherent in human weakness, some seduction or adultery, and you are caught in the act, you are lost, if you cannot speak. But follow my teaching and you will be able to satisfy your passions, to dance, to laugh, to blush at nothing. Suppose you are caught in the act of adultery. Then up and tell the husband you are not guilty, and recall to him the example of Zeus, who allowed himself to be conquered by love and by women. Being but a mortal, can you be stronger than a god?

JUST DISCOURSE

Suppose your pupil, following your advice, gets the radish rammed up his arse and then is depilated with a hot coal;[12] how are you going to prove to him that he is not a broad-arse? [13]

UNJUST DISCOURSE

What's the matter with being a broad-arse?

JUST DISCOURSE

Is there anything worse than that?

UNJUST DISCOURSE

Now what will you say, if I beat you even on this point?

JUST DISCOURSE

I should certainly have to be silent then.

UNJUST DISCOURSE

Well then, reply! Our advocates, what are they?

JUST DISCOURSE

Sons of broad-arses.

UNJUST DISCOURSE

Nothing is more true. And our tragic poets?

JUST DISCOURSE

Sons of broad-arses.

UNJUST DISCOURSE

Well said again. And our demagogues?

JUST DISCOURSE

Sons of broad-arses.

UNJUST DISCOURSE

You admit that you have spoken nonsense. And the spectators, what are they for the most part? Look at them.

JUST DISCOURSE

I am looking at them.

UNJUST DISCOURSE

Well! What do you see?

JUST DISCOURSE

By the gods, they are nearly all broad-arses. (*pointing*) See, this one I know to be such and that one and that other with the long hair.

UNJUST DISCOURSE

What have you to say, then?

JUST DISCOURSE

I am beaten. Debauchees! in the name of the gods, receive my cloak; I pass over to your ranks.

(*He goes back into the Thoughtery.*)

UNJUST DISCOURSE
Well then! Are you going to take away your son or do you wish me to teach him how to speak?

STREPSIADES
Teach him, chastise him and do not fail to sharpen his tongue well, on one side for petty law-suits and on the other for important cases.

UNJUST DISCOURSE
Don't worry, I shall return him to you an accomplished sophist.

PHIDIPPIDES
Very pale then and thoroughly hang-dog-looking.

LEADER OF THE CHORUS
Take him with you. (*The* UNJUST DISCOURSE *and* PHIDIPPIDES *go into the* THOUGHTERY. *To* STREPSIADES, *who is just going into his own house.*) I think you will regret this. (*The* CHORUS *turns and faces the audience.*) Judges, we are all about to tell you what you will gain by awarding us the crown as equity requires of you. In spring, when you wish to give your fields the first dressing, we will rain upon you first; the others shall wait. Then we will watch over your corn and over your vine-stocks; they will have no excess to fear, neither of heat nor of wet. But if a mortal dares to insult the goddesses of the Clouds, let him think of the ills we shall pour upon him. For him neither wine nor any harvest at all! Our terrible slings will mow down his young olive plants and his vines. If he is making bricks, it will rain, and our round hailstones will break the tiles of his roof. If he himself marries or any of his relations or friends, we shall cause rain to fall the whole night long. Verily, he would prefer to live in Egypt than to have given this iniquitous verdict.

STREPSIADES (*coming out again*)
Another four, three, two days, then the eve, then the day, the fatal day of payment! I tremble, I quake, I shudder, for it's the day of the old moon and the new. Then all my creditors take the oath, pay their deposits,[14] swear my downfall and my ruin. As for me, I beseech them to be reasonable, to be just, "My friend, do not demand this sum, wait a little for this other and give me time for this third one." Then they will pretend that at this rate they will never be repaid, will accuse me of bad faith and will threaten me with the law. Well then, let them sue me! I care nothing for that, if only Phidippides has learnt to speak fluently. I am going to find out; I'll knock at the door of the school. (*He knocks.*) . . . Ho! slave, slave!

SOCRATES (*coming out*)
Welcome! Strepsiades!

STREPSIADES
Welcome! Socrates! But first take this sack (*offers him a sack of flour*);
it is right to reward the master with some present. And my son, whom you
took off lately, has he learnt this famous reasoning? Tell me.

SOCRATES
He has learnt it.

STREPSIADES
Wonderful! Oh! divine Knavery!

SOCRATES
You will win just as many causes as you choose.

STREPSIADES
Even if I have borrowed before witnesses?

SOCRATES
So much the better, even if there are a thousand of them!

STREPSIADES (*bursting into song*)
Then I am going to shout with all my might. "Woe to the usurers,
woe to their capital and their interest and their compound interest!
You shall play me no more bad turns. My son is being taught there,
his tongue is being sharpened into a double-edged weapon; he is my
defender, the saviour of my house, the ruin of my foes! His poor
father was crushed down with misfortune and he delivers him." Go
and call him to me quickly. Oh! my child! my dear little one! run
forward to your father's voice!

SOCRATES (*singing*)
Lo, the man himself!

STREPSIADES (*singing*)
Oh, my friend, my dearest friend!

SOCRATES (*singing*)
Take your son, and get you gone.

STREPSIADES (*as* PHIDIPPIDES *appears*)
Oh, my son! oh! oh! what a pleasure to see your pallor! You are ready
first to deny and then to contradict; it's as clear as noon. What a child of
your country you are! How your lips quiver with the famous, "What
have you to say now?" How well you know, I am certain, to put on the

look of a victim, when it is you who are making both victims and dupes! And what a truly Attic glance! Come, it's for you to save me, seeing it is you who have ruined me.

PHIDIPPIDES

What is it you fear then?

STREPSIADES

The day of the old and the new.

PHIDIPPIDES

Is there then a day of the old and the new?

STREPSIADES

The day on which they threaten to pay deposit against me.[14]

PHIDIPPIDES

Then so much the worse for those who have deposited! for it's not possible for one day to be two.

STREPSIADES

What?

PHIDIPPIDES

Why, undoubtedly, unless a woman can be both old and young at the same time.

STREPSIADES

But so runs the law.

PHIDIPPIDES

I think the meaning of the law is quite misunderstood.

STREPSIADES

What does it mean?

PHIDIPPIDES

Old Solon loved the people.

STREPSIADES

What has that to do with the old day and the new?

PHIDIPPIDES

He has fixed two days for the summons, the last day of the old moon and the first day of the new; but the deposits must only be paid on the first day of the new moon.

STREPSIADES

And why did he also name the last day of the old?

PHIDIPPIDES

So, my dear sir, that the debtors, being there the day before, might free themselves by mutual agreement, or that else, if not, the creditor might begin his action on the morning of the new moon.

STREPSIADES

Why then do the magistrates have the deposits paid on the last of the month and not the next day?

PHIDIPPIDES

I think they do as the gluttons do, who are the first to pounce upon the dishes. Being eager to carry off these deposits, they have them paid in a day too soon.

STREPSIADES

Splendid! (*to the audience*) Ah! you poor brutes, who serve for food to us clever folk! You are only down here to swell the number, true block-heads, sheep for shearing, heap of empty pots! Hence I will sing a song of victory for my son and myself. "Oh! happy, Strepsiades! what clever-ness is thine! and what a son thou hast here!" Thus my friends and my neighbours will say, jealous at seeing me gain all my suits. But come in, I wish to regale you first.

(*They both go in. A moment later a creditor arrives, with his witness.*)

PASIAS (*to the* WITNESS)

A man should never lend a single obolus. It would be better to put on a brazen face at the outset than to get entangled in such matters. I want to see my money again and I bring you here to-day to attest the loan. I am going to make a foe of a neighbour; but, as long as I live, I do not wish my country to have to blush for me. Come, I am going to summon Strepsi-ades. . . .

STREPSIADES (*coming out of his house*)

Who is this?

PASIAS

. . . . for the old day and the new.

STREPSIADES (*to the* WITNESS)

I call you to witness, that he has named two days. What do you want of me?

PASIAS

I claim of you the twelve minae, which you borrowed from me to buy
the dapple-grey horse.

STREPSIADES

A horse! do you hear him? I, who detest horses, as is well known.

PASIAS

I call Zeus to witness, that you swore by the gods to return them to me.

STREPSIADES

Because at that time, by Zeus! Phidippides did not yet know the irre-
futable argument.

PASIAS

Would you deny the debt on that account?

STREPSIADES

If not, what use is his science to me?

PASIAS

Will you dare to swear by the gods that you owe me nothing?

STREPSIADES

By which gods?

PASIAS

By Zeus, Hermes and Posidon!

STREPSIADES

Why, I would give three obols for the pleasure of swearing by them.

PASIAS

Woe upon you, impudent knave!

STREPSIADES

Oh! what a fine wine-skin you would make if flayed!

PASIAS

Heaven! he jeers at me!

STREPSIADES

It would hold six gallons easily.

PASIAS

By great Zeus! by all the gods! you shall not scoff at me with impunity.

STREPSIADES

Ah! how you amuse me with your gods! how ridiculous it seems to a sage to hear Zeus invoked.

PASIAS

Your blasphemies will one day meet their reward. But, come, will you repay me my money, yes or no? Answer me, that I may go.

STREPSIADES

Wait a moment, I am going to give you a distinct answer. (*He goes indoors and returns immediately with a kneading-trough.*)

PASIAS (*to the* WITNESS)

What do you think he will do? Do you think he will pay?

STREPSIADES

Where is the man who demands money? Tell me, what is this?

PASIAS

Him? Why, he is your kneading-trough.

STREPSIADES

And you dare to demand money of me, when you are so ignorant? I will not return an obolus to anyone who says *him* instead of *her* for a kneading-trough.

PASIAS

You will not repay?

STREPSIADES

Not if I know it. Come, an end to this, pack off as quick as you can.

PASIAS

I go, but, may I die, if it be not to pay my deposit for a summons.

(*Exit*)

STREPSIADES

Very well! It will be so much more loss to add to the twelve minæ. But truly it makes me sad, for I do pity a poor simpleton who says *him* for a kneading-trough

(*Another creditor arrives.*)

AMYNIAS

Woe! ah woe is me!

STREPSIADES

Wait! who is this whining fellow? Can it be one of the gods of Carcinus?

AMYNIAS

Do you want to know who I am? I am a man of misfortune!

STREPSIADES

Get on your way then.

AMYNIAS (*in tragic style*)

Oh! cruel god! Oh Fate, who hast broken the wheels of my chariot! Oh. Pallas, thou hast undone me!

STREPSIADES

What ill has Tlepolemus done you?

AMYNIAS

Instead of jeering me, friend, make your son return me the money he has had of me; I am already unfortunate enough.

STREPSIADES

What money?

AMYNIAS

The money he borrowed of me.

STREPSIADES

You have indeed had misfortune, it seems to me.

AMYNIAS

Yes, by the gods! I have been thrown from a chariot.

STREPSIADES

Why then drivel as if you had fallen off an ass? [15]

AMYNIAS

Am I drivelling because I demand my money?

STREPSIADES

No, no, you cannot be in your right senses.

AMYNIAS

Why?

STREPSIADES

No doubt your poor wits have had a shake.

AMYNIAS

But by Hermes! I will sue you at law, if you do not pay me.

STREPSIADES

Just tell me; do you think it is always fresh water that Zeus lets fall every time it rains, or is it always the same water that the sun pumps over the earth?

AMYNIAS

I neither know, nor care.

STREPSIADES

And actually you would claim the right to demand your money, when you know not an iota of these celestial phenomena?

AMYNIAS

If you are short, pay me the interest anyway.

STREPSIADES

What kind of animal is interest?

AMYNIAS

What? Does not the sum borrowed go on growing, growing every month, each day as the time slips by?

STREPSIADES

Well put. But do you believe there is more water in the sea now than there was formerly?

AMYNIAS

No, it's just the same quantity. It cannot increase.

STREPSIADES

Thus, poor fool, the sea, that receives the rivers, never grows, and yet you would have your money grow? Get you gone, away with you, quick! Slave! bring me the ox-goad!

AMYNIAS

I have witnesses to this.

STREPSIADES

Come, what are you waiting for? Will you not budge, old nag!

AMYNIAS

What an insult!

STREPSIADES

Unless you start trotting, I shall catch you and stick this in your arse, you sorry packhorse! (AMYNIAS *runs off*.) Ah! you start, do you? I was about to drive you pretty fast, I tell you—you and your wheels and your chariot!

(*He enters his house.*)

CHORUS (*singing*)

Whither does the passion of evil lead! here is a perverse old man,
who wants to cheat his creditors; but some mishap, which will speedily punish this rogue for his shameful schemings, cannot fail to overtake him from to-day. For a long time he has been burning to have
his son know how to fight against all justice and right and to gain
even the most iniquitous causes against his adversaries every one. I
think this wish is going to be fulfilled. But mayhap, mayhap, he will
soon wish his son were dumb rather!

STREPSIADES (*rushing out with* PHIDIPPIDES *after him*)

Oh! oh! neighbours, kinsmen, fellow-citizens, help! help! to the rescue,
I am being beaten! Oh! my head! oh! my jaw! Scoundrel! Do you beat
your own father?

PHIDIPPIDES (*calmly*)

Yes, father, I do.

STREPSIADES

See! he admits he is beating me.

PHIDIPPIDES

Of course I do.

STREPSIADES

You villain, you parricide, you gallows-bird!

PHIDIPPIDES

Go on, repeat your epithets, call me a thousand other names, if it
please you. The more you curse, the greater my amusement!

STREPSIADES

Oh! you ditch-arsed cynic!

PHIDIPPIDES

How fragrant the perfume breathed forth in your words.

STREPSIADES

Do you beat your own father?

PHIDIPPIDES

Yes, by Zeus! and I am going to show you that I do right in beating
you.

STREPSIADES

Oh, wretch! can it be right to beat a father?

PHIDIPPIDES

I will prove it to you, and you shall own yourself vanquished.

STREPSIADES

Own myself vanquished on a point like this?

PHIDIPPIDES

It's the easiest thing in the world. Choose whichever of the two reasonings you like.

STREPSIADES

Of which reasonings?

PHIDIPPIDES

The Stronger and the Weaker.

STREPSIADES

Miserable fellow! Why, I am the one who had you taught how to refute
what is right. and now you would persuade me it is right a son should beat
his father.

PHIDIPPIDES

I think I shall convince you so thoroughly that, when you have heard
me, you will not have a word to say.

STREPSIADES

Well, I am curious to hear what you have to say.

CHORUS (*singing*)

Consider well, old man, how you can best triumph over him. His
brazenness shows me that he thinks himself sure of his case; he has
some argument which gives him nerve. Note the confidence in his
look!

LEADER OF THE CHORUS

But how did the fight begin? tell the Chorus; you cannot help doing
that much.

STREPSIADES

I will tell you what was the start of the quarrel. At the end of the meal,
as you know, I bade him take his lyre and sing me the air of Simonides,
which tells of the fleece of the ram. He replied bluntly, that it was stupid,
while drinking, to play the lyre and sing, like a woman when she is grinding barley.

PHIDIPPIDES

Why, by rights I ought to have beaten and kicked you the very moment
you told me to sing!

STREPSIADES

That is just how he spoke to me in the house, furthermore he added, that Simonides was a detestable poet. However, I mastered myself and for a while said nothing. Then I said to him, 'At least, take a myrtle branch and recite a passage from Aeschylus to me.'—'For my own part,' he at once replied, 'I look upon Aeschylus as the first of poets, for his verses roll superbly; they're nothing but incoherence, bombast and turgidity.' Yet still I smothered my wrath and said, 'Then recite one of the famous pieces from the modern poets.' Then he commenced a piece in which Euripides shows, oh! horror! a brother, who violates his own uterine sister.[16] Then I could not longer restrain myself, and attacked him with the most injurious abuse; naturally he retorted; hard words were hurled on both sides, and finally he sprang at me, broke my bones, bore me to earth, strangled and started killing me!

PHIDIPPIDES

I was right. What! not praise Euripides, the greatest of our poets?

STREPSIADES

He the greatest of our poets? Ah! if I but dared to speak! but the blows would rain upon me harder than ever.

PHIDIPPIDES

Undoubtedly and rightly too.

STREPSIADES

Rightly! oh! what impudence! to me, who brought you up! when you could hardly lisp, I guessed what you wanted. If you said *broo, broo,* well, I brought you your milk; if you asked for *mam mam,* I gave you bread; and you had no sooner said, *caca,* than I took you outside and held you out. And just now, when you were strangling me, I shouted, I bellowed that I was about to crap; and you, you scoundrel, had not the heart to take me outside, so that, though almost choking, I was compelled to do my crapping right there.

CHORUS (*singing*)

Young men, your hearts must be panting with impatience. What is Phidippides going to say? If, after such conduct, he proves he has done well, I would not give an obolus for the hide of old men.

LEADER OF THE CHORUS

Come, you, who know how to brandish and hurl the keen shafts of the new science, find a way to convince us, give your language an appearance of truth.

PHIDIPPIDES

How pleasant it is to know these clever new inventions and to be able to defy the established laws! When I thought only about horses, I was not able to string three words together without a mistake, but now that the master has altered and improved me and that I live in this world of subtle thought, of reasoning and of meditation, I count on being able to prove satisfactorily that I have done well to thrash my father.

STREPSIADES

Mount your horse! By Zeus! I would rather defray the keep of a four-in-hand team than be battered with blows.

PHIDIPPIDES

I revert to what I was saying when you interrupted me. And first, answer me, did you beat me in my childhood?

STREPSIADES

Why, assuredly, for your good and in your own best interest.

PHIDIPPIDES

Tell me, is it not right, that in turn I should beat you for your good, since it is for a man's own best interest to be beaten? What! must your body be free of blows, and not mine? am I not free-born too? the children are to weep and the fathers go free? You will tell me, that according to the law, it is the lot of children to be beaten. But I reply that the old men are children twice over and that it is far more fitting to chastise them than the young, for there is less excuse for their faults.

STREPSIADES

But the law nowhere admits that fathers should be treated thus.

PHIDIPPIDES

Was not the legislator who carried this law a man like you and me? In those days he got men to believe him; then why should not I too have the right to establish for the future a new law, allowing children to beat their fathers in turn? We make you a present of all the blows which were received before his law, and admit that you thrashed us with impunity. But look how the cocks and other animals fight with their fathers; and yet what difference is there betwixt them and ourselves, unless it be that they do not propose decrees?

STREPSIADES

But if you imitate the cocks in all things, why don't you scratch up the dunghill, why don't you sleep on a perch?

PHIDIPPIDES

That has no bearing on the case, good sir; Socrates would find no connection, I assure you.

STREPSIADES

Then do not beat at all, for otherwise you have only yourself to blame afterwards.

PHIDIPPIDES

What for?

STREPSIADES

I have the right to chastise you, and you to chastise your son, if you have one.

PHIDIPPIDES

And if I have not, I shall have cried in vain, and you will die laughing in my face.

STREPSIADES

What say you, all here present? It seems to me that he is right, and I am of opinion that they should be accorded their right. If we think wrongly, it is but just we should be beaten.

PHIDIPPIDES

Again, consider this other point.

STREPSIADES

It will be the death of me.

PHIDIPPIDES

But you will certainly feel no more anger because of the blows I have given you.

STREPSIADES

Come, show me what profit I shall gain from it.

PHIDIPPIDES

I shall beat my mother just as I have you.

STREPSIADES

What do you say? what's that you say? Hah! this is far worse still.

PHIDIPPIDES

And what if I prove to you by our school reasoning, that one ought to beat one's mother?

STREPSIADES

Ah! if you do that, then you will only have to throw yourself, along with Socrates and his reasoning, into the Barathrum. Oh! Clouds! all our troubles emanate from you, from you, to whom I entrusted myself, body and soul.

LEADER OF THE CHORUS

No, you alone are the cause, because you have pursued the path of evil.

STREPSIADES

Why did you not say so then, instead of egging on a poor ignorant old man?

LEADER OF THE CHORUS

We always act thus, when we see a man conceive a passion for what is evil; we strike him with some terrible disgrace, so that he may learn to fear the gods.

STREPSIADES

Alas! oh Clouds! that's hard indeed, but it's just! I ought not to have cheated my creditors. . . . But come, my dear son, come with me to take vengeance on this wretched Chaerephon and on Socrates, who have deceived us both.

PHIDIPPIDES

I shall do nothing against our masters.

STREPSIADES

Oh! show some reverence for ancestral Zeus!

PHIDIPPIDES

Mark him and his ancestral Zeus! What a fool you are! Does any such being as Zeus exist?

STREPSIADES

Why, assuredly.

PHIDIPPIDES

No, a thousand times no! The ruler of the world is the Whirlwind, that has unseated Zeus.

STREPSIADES

He has not dethroned him. I believed it, because of this whirligig here. Unhappy wretch that I am! I have taken a piece of clay to be a god.

PHIDIPPIDES

Very well! Keep your stupid nonsense for your own consumption.

(*He goes back into* STREPSIADES' *house.*)

STREPSIADES

Oh! what madness! I had lost my reason when I threw over the gods through Socrates' seductive phrases. (*Addressing the statue of Hermes*) Oh! good Hermes, do not destroy me in your wrath. Forgive me; their babbling had driven me crazy. Be my counselor. Shall I pursue them at law or shall I . . . ? Order and I obey.—You are right, no law-suit; but up! let us burn down the home of those praters. Here, Xanthias, here! take a ladder, come forth and arm yourself with an axe; now mount upon the Thoughtery, demolish the roof, if you love your master, and may the house fall in upon them. Ho! bring me a blazing torch! There is more than one of them, arch-impostors as they are, on whom I am determined to have vengeance.

A DISCIPLE (*from within*)

Oh! oh!

STREPSIADES

Come, torch, do your duty! Burst into full flame!

DISCIPLE

What are you up to?

STREPSIADES

What am I up to? Why, I am entering upon a subtle argument with the beams of the house.

SECOND DISCIPLE (*from within*)

Hullo! hullo! who is burning down our house?

STREPSIADES

The man whose cloak you have appropriated.

SECOND DISCIPLE

You are killing us!

STREPSIADES

That is just exactly what I hope, unless my axe plays me false, or I fall and break my neck.

SOCRATES (*appearing at the window*)

Hi! you fellow on the roof, what are you doing up there?

STREPSIADES (*mocking* SOCRATES' *manner*)
I am traversing the air and contémplating the sun.

SOCRATES
Ah! ah! woe is upon me! I am suffocating!

SECOND DISCIPLE
And I, alas, shall be burnt up!

STREPSIADES
Ah! you insulted the gods! You studied the face of the moon! Chase them, strike and beat them down! Forward! they have richly deserved their fate—above all, by reason of their blasphemies.

LEADER OF THE CHORUS
So let the Chorus file off the stage. Its part is played.

1. City slaves were normally punished by being forced to leave the delights of urban life and to undergo the unwanted rigours of agricultural labour. The Peloponnesian War, with its almost annual invasions of Attica, rendered it impossible to till the fields of the country-side and thus difficult to punish the slaves of Athens.

2. The ending *-ippus* (Greek *hippos*, "horse") had honorific connotations suggesting wealth and status. The combining form *Phid-*, on the other hand (Greek *pheido*, "thrift") suggested precisely the opposite.

3. Aristophanes here coins the word *dientereuma*, meaning a "looking through intestines." A French translator renders, *"intestigation."*

4. A regular part of the ritual of sacrifice was the sprinkling of the head of the victim with flour.

5. These are characters from the lost *Banqueters*, which Aristophanes exhibited in 427, his first production.

6. Socrates here is speaking, of course, of poetical measures, whereas Strepsiades consistently misunderstands and takes them for measures of capacity. It is the same as if someone were to ask, "Do you like the hexameter?" and to receive the answer, "I prefer the kilometer."

7. The primary meaning of the Greek word *daktylos* was "finger."

8. The vocative case of Greek masculines in *-as* has the apparently feminine ending *-a*.

9. A pun on *koris*, the Greek word for "bug."

10. The sons of Earth were the Titans, who had fought against the gods. Hence the epithet here implies atheism or irreligion on the part of Socrates and his disciples.

11. The terminology of the sophists designated the Just Discourse as the stronger, the Unjust as the weaker, reasoning.

12. This was the punishment supposed to be meted out to adulterers.

13. The Greek word is *euryproktos;* its precise signification in ordinary usage is difficult to determine, and it has seemed better to give its etymologically literal translation in the text and then to explain in this note that it was probably only a general term of abuse.

14. By Athenian law, if anyone summoned another to appear in court,

he was obliged to deposit a sum sufficient to cover the costs of procedure.

15. A person who fell off an ass was one who got himself into trouble through no one's fault but his own, hence a stupid person. The expression also contains a pun, *ap' onou pesein,* "to fall off an ass" being very like *apo nou pesein,* "to lose one's wits."

16. Marriage with a half-sister was incestuous in the eyes of the Athenians only when the common parent was the mother.

IV
THE WASPS

CHARACTERS IN THE PLAY

PHILOCLEON
BDELYCLEON, *his Son*
SOSIAS, *Slave of Philocleon*
XANTHIAS, *Slave of Philocleon*
BOYS
DOGS
A GUEST
A BAKER'S WIFE
AN ACCUSER
CHORUS OF WASPS

INTRODUCTION

A LITTLE less than a year after the signal and merited failure of *The Clouds*, Aristophanes won the third victory of his career with *The Wasps*, which he produced at the Lenaean festival of 422 under the pseudonym of Philonides. The play is thoroughly political in its theme and genuinely comic in its treatment, and its construction testifies to a care and exhibits a skill that have not hitherto been observable in the poet's productions. It is evident that the disappointment of 423, so far from discouraging him, has challenged Aristophanes to greater achievement and taught him a number of fruitful lessons. What he has still to acquire is a sure and reliable sense of proportion, and the only significant defect of *The Wasps* lies in the fact that the first part is longer than the essential humour of its theme can justify, while the latter section is not developed to the full extent of its potentialities.

The play is customarily designated as a satire on an excessive passion for litigation and juridical proceedings which is supposed to have characterized the Athenian populace, but this pronouncement, apposite enough to *Les Plaideurs* of Racine, is both wide of the mark and far too general if applied to the *The Wasps* of Aristophanes. Nowhere in this comedy does the poet suggest that the Athenian judicial institutions themselves are anything but admirable, nor does he ever give us to understand that the litigious mania which he so amusingly lampoons was in any sense epidemic with his countrymen. A keener analysis and a sounder judgment disclose that the true targets of the poet's attack are the *abuses* of the Athenian judicial system, for which he obviously holds the demagogues solely or primarily culpable. Thus *The Wasps* is a sort of appendix to *The Knights*, a less direct and more specialized continuation of the fight against Cleon, begun as early as 426 with the lost *Babylonians*.

The first part of the play, as far as the parabasis, is taken up with the efforts of the antidemagogical Bdelycleon to prevent his father Philocleon, the tanner's friend, from indulging his insatiable craving for jury service. The old man has hitherto been completely successful in nullifying these attempts, and Bdelycleon in desperation has shut him up in the house and stretched a huge net around it. Two sleepy slaves strive manfully to keep watch on the front of the house, while Bdelycleon himself mounts guard on the roof.

The comedy opens with this tableau of varied vigilance, and as soon as the situation has been explained to the audience the action is initiated in a series of frantic and fantastic efforts on the part of Philocleon to escape his odious confinement and to get to court in time for the trials. First he is heard in the stove-chamber, "ferreting about like a rat in his hole," and a moment later he affects to be the smoke coming out of the chimney. Balked in this, he requests his son to let him go out to sell his ass, and when Bdelycleon, intending to deprive him of this excuse, fetches the ass himself, his father is discovered clinging to its belly like another Odysseus escaping from the Cyclops' cave. His son quickly shuts him up in the house again, but just as the slaves are piling stones against the door, a falling brick warns them that Philocleon has crept beneath the tiles of the roof and is about to fly away like a sparrow. As soon as this attempt has been foiled, the old man's fellow jurymen, costumed as wasps, arrive to take him to court. The sight of his worthy companions and contemporaries gives new zeal to his heart and fresh strength to his jaws, and even though he is toothless he gnaws a hole in the net and is letting himself down from his window, when his son awakes from a brief sleep and strives energetically to prevent his escape.

The Wasps come gallantly to the aid of their fellow creature and a lively combat ensues between the jurymen on the one hand and Bdelycleon and his slaves on the other. Eventually blows give place to words and a lengthy debate is held between the father and the son on the merits and the defects of the former's beloved profession. Bdelycleon finally convinces his father that he is really nothing but the tool of the demagogues and promises to let him amuse himself by holding trials in his own home if he will only refrain from judging in public. The old man agrees to this, and when all the paraphernalia of a typical court have been travestied and collected, the first plaintiff appears before the new domestic tribunal. The subsequent trial of the dog Labes for the theft of a Sicilian cheese is one of Aristophanes' most felicitous inspirations, particularly in its conclusion, when Philocleon is misled into voting for acquittal. This is the first time in his life that he has ever been so foolish, and he swoons quite away when he learns of the dreadful error that he has committed. Bdelycleon revives him and takes him into the house, attempting to console him with promises of the gay life that he is henceforth to lead.

The stage is now clear and the Chorus is at long last given an opportunity to deliver the parabasis. The anapæsts reproach the audience for their reception of *The Clouds* a year earlier and recite the services which the poet claims to have rendered his native city. The tender and nostalgic ode, together with the epirrheme and the antode, celebrates the glorious deeds of the old jurymen in their youth, at Marathon and under Cimon, and the antepirrheme explains why they are costumed as wasps. None of the comedies that have come down to us contains a parabasis so well integrated or so effective as this one.

At the conclusion of the parabasis Bdelycleon and his father emerge from the house on the way to a banquet; the new life of the old man is already beginning. Before he can embark on this, however, he must be taught how to act; the juryman must be made into a gentleman. The scene in which this takes place is one of Aristophanes' best, and the only adverse criticism that can be levelled against it is that it is not long enough; its quality is such that one is dissatisfied with its quantity. In all too short a time, we feel, the son becomes either satisfied with his father's behaviour or resigned to the impossibility of its improvement, and the pair depart for the dinner-party.

After a brief ode by the Chorus, Xanthias, the slave, returns with lurid reports of Philocleon's misbehaviour; he has drunk far too much, made a fool of himself, insulted all the guests, absconded with the flute-girl, and on the way home been guilty of assault and robbery. Immediately the miscreant enters in person, and a highly amusing scene follows in which he practises his newly acquired social and conversational graces on those whom he has recently maltreated. Finally his son contrives to get him into the house, but he can not keep him there, and soon the old man reappears, now dominated by Terpsichorean urges, and the comedy ends with a wild dance in which Philocleon matches his talents against those of the three little sons of Carcinus the tragedian.

Such is the hilarious and satisfying conclusion of the finest comedy that Aristophanes has so far produced. There have not been many who have justly appreciated its excellence, for it is of all the plays the hardest to learn to love. Its subject is alien to our sympathies and distant from our understanding, and only the candid light of intimate acquaintance can reveal the treasury of true wit and high art which it contains. *The Acharnians* was an excellent comedy in its own right, but it clearly promised even better ones to come. The fulfilment of these promises was prorogued or obstructed by the excessive courage of *The Knights* and the false direction of *The Clouds*. In *The Wasps* Aristophanes has ceased to disappoint us and has written a comedy which not only makes good most of the promises of *The Acharnians* but is itself filled with clearer and brighter auguries. The poet will not disappoint us again; from the work of the next ten years of his life there have been preserved four plays which represent for us the highest achievement of his art, and in them we shall see all the early promises fulfilled, not only those of *The Acharnians,* but the more difficult ones of *The Wasps* as well.

THE WASPS

(SCENE:—*In the background is the house of* PHILOCLEON, *surrounded by a huge net. Two slaves are on guard, one of them asleep. On the roof is* BDELYCLEON.)

SOSIAS (*waking* XANTHIAS *up*)

WHY, Xanthias! what are you doing, wretched man?

XANTHIAS

I am teaching myself how to rest; I have been awake and on watch the whole night.

SOSIAS

So you want to earn trouble for your ribs, eh? Don't you know what sort of animal we are guarding here?

XANTHIAS

Aye indeed! but I want to put my cares to sleep for a while.

(*He falls asleep again.*)

SOSIAS

Beware what you do. I too feel soft sleep spreading over my eyes.

XANTHIAS

Are you crazy, like a Corybant?

SOSIAS

No! It's Bacchus who lulls me off.

XANTHIAS

Then you serve the same god as myself. Just now a heavy slumber settled on my eyelids like a hostile Mede; I nodded and, faith! I had a wondrous dream.

SOSIAS

Indeed! and so had I. A dream such as I never had before. But first tell me yours.

609

XANTHIAS

I saw an eagle, a gigantic bird, descend upon the market-place; it seized a brazen buckler with its talons and bore it away into the highest heavens; then I saw it was Cleonymus had thrown it away.

SOSIAS

This Cleonymus is a riddle worth propounding among guests. How can one and the same animal have cast away his buckler both on land, in the sky and at sea?

XANTHIAS

Alas! what ill does such a dream portend for me?

SOSIAS

Rest undisturbed! Please the gods, no evil will befall you.

XANTHIAS

Nevertheless, it's a fatal omen when a man throws away his weapons. But what was your dream? Let me hear.

SOSIAS

Oh! it is a dream of high import. It has reference to the hull of the State; to nothing less.

XANTHIAS

Tell it to me quickly; show me its very keel.

SOSIAS

In my first slumber I thought I saw sheep, wearing cloaks and carrying staves, met in assembly on the Pnyx; a rapacious whale was haranguing them and screaming like a pig that is being grilled.

XANTHIAS

Faugh! faugh!

SOSIAS

What's the matter?

XANTHIAS

Enough, enough, spare me. Your dream stinks vilely of old leather.[1]

SOSIAS

Then this scoundrelly whale seized a balance and set to weighing ox-fat.[2]

XANTHIAS

Alas! it's our poor Athenian people, whom this accursed beast wishes to cut up and despoil of their fat.

SOSIAS

Seated on the ground close to it, I saw Theorus, who had the head of a crow. Then Alcibiades said to me in his lisping way, "Do you thee? Theoruth hath a crow'th head."

XANTHIAS

Ah! that's very well lisped indeed!

SOSIAS

Isn't this mighty strange? Theorus turning into a crow!

XANTHIAS

No, it is glorious.

SOSIAS

Why?

XANTHIAS

Why? He was a man and now he has suddenly become a crow; does it not foretoken that he will take his flight from here and go to the crows? [3]

SOSIAS

Interpreting dreams so aptly certainly is worth two obols.

XANTHIAS (*turning to the audience*)

Come, I must explain the matter to the spectators. But first a few words of preamble: expect nothing very high-flown from us, nor any jests stolen from Megara; we have no slaves, who throw baskets of nuts [4] to the spectators, nor any Heracles to be robbed of his dinner, nor does Euripides get loaded with contumely; and despite the happy chance that gave Cleon his fame we shall not go out of our way to belabour him again. Our little subject is not wanting in sense; it is well within your capacity [5] and at the same time cleverer than many vulgar comedies.—We have a master of great renown, who is now sleeping up there on the other story. He has bidden us keep guard over his father, whom he has locked in, so that he may not go out. This father has a curious complaint; not one of you could hit upon or guess it, if I did not tell you.—Well then, try! I hear Amynias, the son of Pronapus, over there, saying, "He is addicted to gambling." He's wrong! He is imputing his own malady to others. Yet love is indeed the principal part of his disease. Ah! here Sosias is telling Dercylus, "He loves drinking." Wrong again! the love of wine is a good man's failing. "Well then," says Nicostratus of the Scambonian deme, "he either loves sacrifices or else strangers." God no! he is not fond of strangers, Nicostratus, for he who says "Philoxenus" means a pederast. It's mere waste of time, you will not find it out. If you want to know it, keep silence! I will tell your our master's complaint; of all men, it is he who is fondest of the Heliaea. Thus, to be judging is his hobby, and he groans if he is not sitting on the first seat. He does not close an eye at night, and if he dozes off for an instant his mind flies instantly to the clepsydra. He is so accustomed to hold the balloting pebble, that he awakes with his three fingers pinched together as if he were offering incense to the new moon. If he sees scribbled on some doorway, "How charming is Demos, the son of Pyrilampes!" he will write beneath it, "How charming is Cemos!" His cock crowed one evening; said he, "He has had money from the accused to awaken me too late. As soon as he rises from supper he bawls for his shoes and away he rushes down there before dawn to sleep beforehand, glued fast to the column like an oyster. He is a merciless judge, never failing to draw the convicting line [6] and return home with his nails full of wax like a bumble-bee. Fearing he might run short of pebbles he keeps enough at home to cover a sea-beach, so that he may have the means of recording his sentence. Such is his madness, and all advice is useless; he only judges the more each day. So we keep him under lock and key, to prevent his going out; for his son is broken-hearted over this mania. At first he tried him with gentleness, wanted to persuade him to wear the cloak no longer, to go out no more; unable to convince him, he had him bathed and purified according to the ritual without any greater success, and then handed him over to the Corybantes; but the old man escaped them, and carrying off the kettledrum, rushed right into the midst of the Heliasts. As Cybelé could do nothing with her rites, his son took him to Aegina and forcibly made him lie one night in the temple of Asclepius, the God of Healing, but before daylight there he was to be seen at the gate of the tribunal. Since then we let him go out no more, but he escaped us by the drains or by the skylight, so we stuffed up every opening with old rags and made all secure; then he drove short sticks into the wall and sprang from rung to rung like a magpie. Now we have stretched nets all around the court and we keep watch and ward. The old man's name is Philocleon, it's the best name he could have, and the son is called Bdelycleon, for he is a man very fit to cure an insolent fellow of his boasting.

BDELYCLEON (*from the roof*)
Xanthias! Sosias! Are you asleep?

XANTHIAS
Alas!

SOSIAS
What is the matter?

XANTHIAS

Why, Bdelycleon is getting up.

BDELYCLEON

Will neither of you come here? My father has got into the stove-chamber and is ferreting about like a rat in his hole. Take care he does not escape through the bath drain. You there, put all your weight against the door.

XANTHIAS

Yes, master.

BDELYCLEON

By Zeus! what is that noise in the chimney? Hullo! who are you?

PHILOCLEON (*poking his head out of the chimney*)

I am the smoke going up.

BDELYCLEON

Smoke? smoke of what wood?

PHILOCLEON

Of fig-wood.[7]

BDELYCLEON

Ah! that's the most acrid of all. But you shall not get out. Where is the chimney cover? Come down again. Now, up with another cross-bar. Now look out for some fresh dodge. But am I not the most unfortunate of men? Henceforward I shall only be called the son of Capnius.

XANTHIAS

He is pushing the door.

BDELYCLEON

Throw your weight upon it, come, put heart into the work. I will come and help you. Watch both lock and bolt. Take care he does not gnaw through the peg.

PHILOCLEON (*from within*)

What are you doing, you wretches? Let me go out; it is imperative that I go and judge, or Dracontides will be acquitted.

XANTHIAS

Would you mind that?

PHILOCLEON

Once at Delphi, the god, whom I was consulting, foretold, that if an accused man escaped me, I should die of consumption.

XANTHIAS

Apollo the Saviour, what a prophecy!

PHILOCLEON

Ah! I beseech you, if you do not want my death, let me go.

XANTHIAS

No, Philocleon, no never, by Posidon!

PHILOCLEON

Well then, I shall gnaw through the net with my teeth.

XANTHIAS

But you have no teeth.

PHILOCLEON

Oh! you rascal, how can I kill you? How? Give me a sword, quick, or a conviction tablet.

BDELYCLEON

Our friend is planning some great crime.

PHILOCLEON

No, by Zeus! but I want to go and sell my ass and its panniers, for it's the first of the month.

BDELYCLEON

Could I not sell it just as well?

PHILOCLEON

Not as well as I could.

BDELYCLEON

No, but better.

PHILOCLEON

Bring out the ass anyway.

XANTHIAS

What a clever excuse he has found now! What cunning to get you to let him go out!

BDELYCLEON

Yes, but I have not swallowed the hook; I scented the trick. I will go in and fetch the ass, so that the old man may not point his weapons that way again. (*He goes in, returning immediately with the ass.*) Stupid old ass, are you weeping because you are going to be sold? Come, go a bit quicker. Why, what are you moaning and groaning for? You might be carrying another Odysseus.

XANTHIAS

Why, certainly, so he is! someone has crept beneath his belly.

BDELYCLEON

Who, who? Let's see. Why it's he! What does this mean? Who are you? Come, speak!

PHILOCLEON

I am Noman.

BDELYCLEON

Noman? Of what country?

PHILOCLEON

Of Ithaca, son of Apodrasippides.

BDELYCLEON

Ha! Mister Noman, you will not laugh presently. Pull him out quick. Ah! the wretch, where has he crept to? Does he not resemble a she-ass to the life?

PHILOCLEON

If you do not leave me in peace, I shall sue.

BDELYCLEON

And what will the suit be about?

PHILOCLEON

The shade of an ass.[8]

BDELYCLEON

You are a poor man of very little wit, but thoroughly brazen.

PHILOCLEON

A poor man! Ah! by Zeus! you know not now what I am worth; but you will know when you disembowel the old Heliast's money-bag.

BDELYCLEON

Come, get back indoors, both you and your ass.

PHILOCLEON

Oh! my brethren of the tribunal! oh! Cleon! to the rescue!

BDELYCLEON

Go and bawl in there under lock and key. And you there, pile plenty of stones against the door, thrust the bolt home into the staple, and to keep this beam in its place roll that great mortar against it. Quick's the word.

XANTHIAS

Oh! my god! whence did this brick fall on me?

BDELYCLEON

Perhaps a rat loosened it.

XANTHIAS

A rat? it's surely our gutter-judge, who has crept beneath the tiles of the roof.

BDELYCLEON

Ah! woe to us! there he is, he has turned into a sparrow; he will be flying off. Where is the net? where? Shoo! shoo! get back! Ah! by Zeus! I would rather have to guard Scioné than such a father.

XANTHIAS

And now that we have driven him in thoroughly and he can no longer escape without our knowledge, can we not have a few winks of sleep, no matter how few?

BDELYCLEON

Why, wretch! the other jurymen will be here almost directly to summon my father!

XANTHIAS

Why, it's scarcely dawn yet!

BDELYCLEON

Ah, they must have risen late to-day. Generally it is the middle of the night when they come to fetch him. They arrive here, carrying lanterns in their hands and singing the charming old verses of Phrynichus' *Sidonian Women;* it's their way of calling him.

XANTHIAS

Well, if need be, we will chase them off with stones.

BDELYCLEON

What! you dare to speak so? Why, this class of old men, if irritated, becomes as terrible as a swarm of wasps. They carry below their loins the sharpest of stings, with which to prick their foe; they shout and leap and their stings burn like so many sparks.

XANTHIAS

Have no fear! If I can find stones to throw into this nest of jurymen-wasps, I shall soon have them cleared off.
(*Enter the* CHORUS, *composed of old men costumed as wasps.*)

LEADER OF THE CHORUS

March on, advance boldly and bravely! Comias, your feet are dragging; once you were as tough as a dog-skin strap and now even Charinades walks better than you. Ha! Strymodorus of Conthylé, you best of mates, where is Euergides and where is Chabes of Phlya? Ha, ha, bravo! there you are, the last of the lads with whom we mounted guard together at Byzantium. Do you remember how, one night, prowling round, we noiselessly stole the kneading-trough of a baker's wife; we split it in two and cooked our green-stuff with it.—But let us hasten, for the case of Laches comes on to-day, and they all say he has embezzled a pot of money. Hence Cleon, our protector, advised us yesterday to come early and with a three days' stock of fiery rage so as to chastise him for his crimes. Let us hurry, comrades, before it is light; come, let us search every nook with our lanterns to see whether those who wish us ill have not set us some trap.

BOY

Father, father, watch out for the mud.

LEADER OF THE CHORUS

Pick up a blade of straw and trim your lamp.

BOY

No, I can trim it quite well with my finger.

LEADER OF THE CHORUS

Why do you pull out the wick, you little dolt? Oil is scarce, and it's not you who suffer when it has to be paid for. (*Strikes him.*)

BOY

If you teach us again with your fists, we shall put out the lamps and go home; then you will have no light and will squatter about in the mud like ducks in the dark.

LEADER OF THE CHORUS

I know how to punish offenders bigger than you. But I think I am treading in some mud. Oh! it's certain it will rain in torrents for four days at least; look at the snuff in our lamps; that is always a sign of heavy rain; but the rain and the north wind will be good for the crops that are still

standing. Why, what can have happened to our mate, who lives here?
Why does he not come to join our party? There used to be no need to haul
him in our wake, for he would march at our head singing the verses of
Phrynichus; he was a lover of singing. Should we not, friends, make a
halt here and sing to call him out? The charm of my voice will fetch him
out, if he hears it.

CHORUS (*singing*)

Why does the old man not show himself before the door? Why
does he not answer? Has he lost his shoes? has he stubbed his toe in
the dark and thus got a swollen ankle? Perhaps he has a tumour in
his groin. He was the hardest of us all; he alone *never* allowed himself to be moved. If anyone tried to move him, he would lower his
head, saying, "You might just as well try to boil a stone." But I bethink me, an accused man escaped us yesterday through his false pretence that he loved Athens and had been the first to unfold the Samian
plot. Perhaps his acquittal has so distressed Philocleon that he is
abed with fever—he is quite capable of such a thing.—Friend,
arise, do not thus vex your heart, but forget your wrath. To-day we
have to judge a man made wealthy by treason, one of those who set
Thrace free; we have to prepare him a funeral urn . . . so march
on, my boy, get going.

(*Here a duet begins between the* BOY *and the* CHORUS.)

BOY

Father, would you give me something if I asked for it?

CHORUS

Assuredly, my child, but tell me what nice thing do you want me
to buy you? A set of knuckle-bones, I suppose.

BOY

No, father, I prefer figs; they are better.

CHORUS

No, by Zeus! even if you were to hang yourself with vexation.

BOY

Well then, I will lead you no farther.

CHORUS

With my small pay, I am obliged to buy bread, wood, and stew;
and now you ask me for figs!

BOY

But, father, if the Archon should not form a court to-day, how are
we to buy our dinner? Have you some good hope to offer us or only
"Hellé's sacred waves"?

CHORUS

Alas! alas! I have not a notion how we shall dine.

BOY

Oh! my poor mother! why did you let me see this day?

CHORUS

So that you might give me troubles to feed on.

BOY

Little wallet, you seem like to be a mere useless ornament!

BOY AND CHORUS

It is our destiny to groan.

PHILOCLEON (*appearing at an upper window; singing*)

My friends, I have long been pining away while listening to you
from my window, but I absolutely know not what to do. I am detained
here, because I have long wanted to go with you to the law-court and
do all the harm I can. Oh! Zeus! cause the peals of thy thunder to
roll, change me quickly into smoke or make me into a Proxenides,
a tissue of falsehoods, like the son of Sellus. Oh, King of Heaven! hesitate not to grant me this favour, pity my misfortune or else may thy
dazzling lightning instantly reduce me to ashes; then carry me hence,
and may thy breath hurl me into some strong, hot marinade or
turn me into one of the stones on which the votes are counted.

CHORUS (*singing*)

Who is it detains you and shuts you in? Speak, for you are talking
to friends.

PHILOCLEON (*singing*)

My son. But no bawling, he is there in front asleep; lower your
voice.

CHORUS (*singing*)

But, poor fellow, what is his aim? what is his object?

PHILOCLEON (*singing*)

My friends, he will not have me judge nor do anyone any ill, but
he wants me to stay at home and enjoy myself, and I will not.

CHORUS (*singing*)
And does this wretch, this Demologocleon dare to say such odious things, just because you tell the truth about our navy? He would not have dared, had he not been a conspirator.

LEADER OF THE CHORUS
But meanwhile, you must devise some new dodge, so that you can come down here without his knowledge.

PHILOCLEON
But what? Try to find some way. For myself, I am ready for anything, so much do I burn to run along the tiers of the tribunal with my voting-pebble in my hand.

LEADER OF THE CHORUS
There is surely some hole through which you could manage to squeeze from within, and escape dressed in rags, like the crafty Odysseus.

PHILOCLEON
Everything is sealed fast; not so much as a gnat could get through. Think of some other plan; there is no possible hole of escape.

LEADER OF THE CHORUS
Do you recall how, when you were with the army at the taking of Naxos, you descended so readily from the top of the wall by means of the spits you had stolen?

PHILOCLEON
I remember that well enough, but what connection is there with present circumstances? I was young, clever at thieving, I had all my strength, none watched over me, and I could run off without fear. But to-day men-at-arms are placed at every outlet to watch me, and two of them are lying in wait for me at this very door armed with spits, just as folks lie in wait for a cat that has stolen a piece of meat.

CHORUS (*singing*)
Come, discover some way as quick as possible. Here is the dawn come, my dear little friend.

PHILOCLEON (*singing*)
The best way is to gnaw through the net. Oh! goddess who watchest over the nets,[9] forgive me for making a hole in this one.

CHORUS (*singing*)
It's acting like a man eager for his safety. Get your jaws to work.

PHILOCLEON (*singing*)

There! it's gnawed through! But no shouting! let Bdelycleon notice nothing!

CHORUS (*singing*)

Have no fear, have no fear! if he breathes a syllable, it will be to bruise his own knuckles; he will have to fight to defend his own head. We shall teach him not to insult the mysteries of the goddesses.

LEADER OF THE CHORUS

But fasten a rope to the window, tie it around your body and let yourself down to the ground, with your heart bursting with the fury of Diopithes.

PHILOCLEON

But if these notice it and want to fish me up and drag me back into the house, what will you do? Tell me that.

LEADER OF THE CHORUS

We shall call up the full strength of our oak-tough courage to your aid. That is what we will do.

PHILOCLEON

I trust myself to you and risk the danger. If misfortune overtakes me, take away my body, bathe it with your tears and bury it beneath the bar of the tribunal.

LEADER OF THE CHORUS

Nothing will happen to you, rest assured. Come, friend, have courage and let yourself slide down while you invoke your country's gods.

PHILOCLEON

Oh! mighty Lycus! noble hero and my neighbour, thou, like myself, takest pleasure in the tears and the groans of the accused. If thou art come to live near the tribunal, 'tis with the express design of hearing them incessantly; thou alone of all the heroes hast wished to remain among those who weep. Have pity on me and save him, who lives close to thee; I swear I will never make water, never, nor ever let a fart, against the railing of thy statue.

(*He slides down as quietly as possible; nevertheless* BDELYCLEON *wakes up.*)

BDELYCLEON (*to* XANTHIAS)

Ho, there! ho! get up!

XANTHIAS (*waking up*)
What's the matter?

BDELYCLEON
I thought I heard talking close to me. Is the old man at it again, escaping through some loophole?

XANTHIAS
No, by Zeus! no, but he is letting himself down by a rope.

BDELYCLEON
Ha, rascal! what are you doing there? You shall not descend. (*To* XANTHIAS) Mount quick to the other window, strike him with the boughs that hang over the entrance; perhaps he will turn back when he feels himself being thrashed.

PHILOCLEON (*to the audience*)
To the rescue! all you, who are going to have lawsuits this year— Smicythion, Tisiades, Chremon and Pheredipnus. It's now or never, before they force me to return, that you must help.

LEADER OF THE CHORUS
Why do we delay to let loose that fury, that is so terrible, when our nests are attacked?

CHORUS (*singing*)
I feel my angry sting is stiffening, that sharp sting, with which we punish our enemies. Come, children, cast your cloaks to the winds, run, shout, tell Cleon what is happening, that he may march against this foe of our city, who deserves death, since he proposes to prevent the trial of lawsuits.

(*The* BOYS *run off, taking the* CHORUS' *mantles with them.*)

BDELYCLEON (*rushing out of the house with the two slaves and seizing his father*)
Friends, listen to the truth, instead of bawling.

LEADER OF THE CHORUS
By Zeus! we will shout to heaven.

BDELYCLEON
And I shall not let him go.

LEADER OF THE CHORUS
Why, this is intolerable, 'tis manifest tyranny.

CHORUS (*singing*)
Oh! citizens, oh! Theorus, the enemy of the gods! and all you flatterers, who rule us! come to our aid.

XANTHIAS
By Heracles! they have stings. Do you see them, master?

BDELYCLEON
It was with these weapons that they killed Philippus the son of Gorgias when he was put on trial.

LEADER OF THE CHORUS
And you too shall die. Turn yourselves this way, all, with your stings out for attack and throw yourselves upon him in good and serried order, and swelled up with wrath and rage. Let him learn to know the sort of foes he has dared to irritate.

XANTHIAS
The fight will be fast and furious, by great Zeus! I tremble at the sight of their stings.

CHORUS (*singing*)
Let this man go, unless you want to envy the tortoise his hard shell.

PHILOCLEON
Come, my dear companions, wasps with relentless hearts, fly against him, animated with your fury. Sting him in the arse, eyes, and fingers.

BDELYCLEON
(*opening the door and trying to shove his struggling father in*)
Midas, Phryx, Masyntias, here! Come and help. Seize this man and hand him over to no one, otherwise you shall starve to death in chains. Fear nothing, I have often heard the crackling of fig-leaves in the fire. [10]

LEADER OF THE CHORUS
If you won't let him go, I shall bury this sting in your body.

PHILOCLEON
Oh, Cecrops, mighty hero with the tail of a dragon! Seest thou how these barbarians ill-use me—me, who have many a time made them weep a full bushel of tears?

LEADER OF THE CHORUS
Is not old age filled with cruel ills? What violence these two slaves offer to their old master! they have forgotten all bygones, the fur-coats and the jackets and the caps he bought for them; in winter he watched that their

feet should not get frozen. And only see them now; there is no gentleness in their look nor any recollection of the slippers of other days.

PHILOCLEON (*to* XANTHIAS)

Will you let me go, you accursed animal? Don't you remember the day when I surprised you stealing the grapes; I tied you to an olive-tree and I cut open your bottom with such vigorous lashes that folks thought you had been raped. Get away, you are ungrateful. But let go of me, and you too, before my son comes up.

LEADER OF THE CHORUS

You shall repay us for all this, and that soon. Tremble at our ferocious glance; you shall taste our just anger.

BDELYCLEON

Strike! strike! Xanthias! Drive these wasps away from the house.

XANTHIAS

That's just what I am doing.

BDELYCLEON

Blind them with smoke too!

XANTHIAS AND SOSIAS

You will not go? The plague seize you! Will you not clear off?

BDELYCLEON

Hit them with your stick Xanthias, and you Sosias, to smoke them out better, throw Aeschines, the son of Sellartius, on the fire.

XANTHIAS (*as the* CHORUS *retires from the unequal conquest*)
There, we were bound to drive you off sooner or later!

BDELYCLEON

Eh! by Zeus! you would not have put them to flight so easily if they had fed on the verses of Philocles.

CHORUS (*singing*)

It is clear to all the poor that tyranny has attacked us sorely. Proud emulator of Amynias, you, who only take pleasure in doing ill, see how you are preventing us from obeying the laws of the city; you do not even seek a pretext or any plausible excuse, but claim to rule alone.

BDELYCLEON

Hold! A truce to all blows and brawling! Had we not better confer together and come to some understanding?

LEADER OF THE CHORUS
Confer with you, the people's foe! with you, a royalist . . .

CHORUS (*singing*)
. . . and accomplice of Brasidas, you with your woollen-fringed coat and your long beard?

BDELYCLEON
Ah! it would be better to separate altogether from my father than to steer my boat daily through such stormy seas!

LEADER OF THE CHORUS
Oh! you have but reached the parsley and the rue, to use the common saying.[11] What you are suffering is nothing! but welcome the hour when the advocate shall adduce all these same arguments against you and shall summon your accomplices to give witness.

BDELYCLEON
In the name of the gods! withdraw or we shall fight you the whole day long.

CHORUS (*singing*)
No, not as long as I retain an atom of breath. Ha! your desire is to tyrannize over us!

BDELYCLEON
Everything is now tyranny with us, no matter what is concerned, whether it be large or small. Tyranny! I have not heard the word mentioned once in fifty years, and now it is more common than salt-fish, the word is even current on the market. If you are buying gurnards and don't want anchovies, the huckster next door, who is selling the latter, at once exclaims, "That is a man whose kitchen savours of tyranny!" If you ask for onions to season your fish, the green-stuff woman winks one eye and asks, "Ha, you ask for onions! are you seeking to tyrannize, or do you think that Athens must pay you your seasonings as a tribute?"

XANTHIAS
Yesterday I went to see a whore about noon and told her to get on top; she flew into a rage, pretending I wanted to restore the tyranny of Hippias.[12]

BDELYCLEON
That's the talk that pleases the people! As for myself, I want my father to lead a joyous life like Morychus instead of going away before dawn basely to calumniate and condemn; and for this I am accused of conspiracy and tyrannical practice!

PHILOCLEON

And quite right too, by Zeus! The most exquisite dishes do not make up to me for the life of which you deprive me. I scorn your red mullet and your eels, and would far rather eat a nice little lawsuitlet cooked in the pot.

BDELYCLEON

That's because you have got used to seeking your pleasure in it; but if you will agree to keep silence and hear me, I think I could persuade you that you deceive yourself altogether.

PHILOCLEON

I deceive myself, when I am judging?

BDELYCLEON

You do not see that you are the laughing-stock of these men, whom you are ready to worship. You are their slave and do not know it.

PHILOCLEON

I a slave, I, who lord it over all?

BDELYCLEON

Not at all, you think you are ruling when you are only obeying. Tell me, father, what do you get out of the tribute paid by so many Greek towns.

PHILOCLEON

Much, and I appoint my colleagues jurymen.

BDELYCLEON

And I also. (*To the slaves*) Release him.

PHILOCLEON

And bring me a sword; If I am worsted in this debate, I shall fall on the blade.

BDELYCLEON

Tell me whether you will accept the verdict of the Court.

PHILOCLEON

May I never drink my Heliast's pay in honour of the Good Genius, ii ı do not.

CHORUS (*singing*)

Now it is necessary for you, who are of our school, to say something novel, that you may not seem . . .

BDELYCLEON (*interrupting*)

And I must note down everything he says, so as to remember it; someone bring me a tablet, quick.

CHORUS (*singing*)

. . . to side with this youth in his opinions. You see how serious the question has become; if he should prevail, which the gods forfend, it will be all over for us.

PHILOCLEON

But what will you say of it, if he *should* triumph in the debate?

CHORUS (*singing*)

That old men are no longer good for anything; we shall be perpetually laughed at in the streets, shall be called thallophores, mere brief-bags.

LEADER OF THE CHORUS

You are to be the champion of all our rights and sovereignty. Come, take courage! Bring into action all the resources of your wit.

PHILOCLEON

At the outset I will prove to you that there exists no king whose might is greater than ours. Is there a pleasure, a blessing comparable with that of a juryman? Is there a being who lives more in the midst of delights, who is more feared, aged though he be? From the moment I leave my bed, men of power, the most illustrious in the city, await me at the bar of the tribunal; the moment I am seen from the greatest distance, they come forward to offer me a gentle hand,—that has pilfered the public funds; they entreat me, bowing right low and with a piteous voice, "Oh, father," they say, "pity me, I adjure you by the profit *you* were able to make in the public service or in the army, when dealing with the victuals." Why, the man who speaks thus would not know of my existence, had I not let him off on some former occasion.

BDELYCLEON

Let us note this first point, the supplicants.

PHILOCLEON

These entreaties have appeased my wrath, and I enter—firmly resolved to do nothing that I have promised. Nevertheless I listen to the accused. Oh! what tricks to secure acquittal! Ah! there is no form of flattery that is not addressed to the Heliast! Some groan over their poverty and exaggerate it. Others tell us anecdotes or some comic story from Aesop. Others, again, cut jokes; they fancy I shall be appeased if

I laugh. If we are not even then won over, why, then they drag forward
their young children by the hand, both boys and girls, who prostrate
themselves and whine with one accord, and then the father, trembling as
if before a god, beseeches me not to condemn him out of pity for them,
"If you love the voice of the lamb, have pity on my sons"; and because
I am fond of little sows,[13] I must yield to his daughter's prayers. Then
we relax the heat of our wrath a little for him. Is not this great power
indeed, which allows even wealth to be disdained?

BDELYCLEON

A second point to note, the disdain of wealth. And now recall to me
what are the advantages you enjoy, you, who pretend to rule over Greece?

PHILOCLEON

We are entrusted with the inspection of the young men, and thus we
have a right to examine their tools. If Oeagrus is accused, he is not acquitted before he has recited a passage from '*Niobé*' and he chooses the
finest. If a flute-player gains his case, he adjusts his mouth-strap in return and plays us the final air while we are leaving. A father on his death-
bed names some husband for his daughter, who is his sole heir; but we
care little for his will or for the shell so solemnly placed over the seal;
we give the young maiden to him who has best known how to secure our
favour. Name me another duty that is so important and so irresponsible.

BDELYCLEON

Aye, it's a fine privilege, and the only one on which I can congratulate
you; but surely to violate the will is to act badly towards the heiress.

PHILOCLEON

And if the Senate and the people have trouble in deciding some important case, it is decreed to send the culprits before the Heliasts; then
Euathlus and the illustrious Colaconymus, who cast away his shield,
swear not to betray us and to fight for the people. Did ever an orator
carry the day with his opinion if he had not first declared that the jury
should be dismissed for the day as soon as they had given their first
verdict? We are the only ones whom Cleon, the great bawler, does not
badger. On the contrary, he protects and caresses us; he keeps off the
flies, which is what you have never done for your father. Theorus, who
is a man not less illustrious than Euphemius, takes the sponge out of the
pot and blacks our shoes. See then what good things you deprive and
despoil me of. Pray, is this obeying or being a slave, as you pretended to
be able to prove?

BDELYCLEON

Talk away to your heart's content; you must come to a stop at last
and then you shall see that this grand power only resembles an anus; no
matter how much you wash it, you can never get it clean.

PHILOCLEON

But I am forgetting the most pleasing thing of all. When I return home
with my pay, everyone runs to greet me because of my money. First my
daughter bathes me, anoints my feet, stoops to kiss me and, while she
is calling me "her dearest father," fishes out my triobolus with her
tongue; [14] then my little wife comes to wheedle me and brings a nice
light cake; she sits beside me and entreats me in a thousand ways, "Do
take this now; do have some more." All this delights me hugely, and I
have no need to turn towards you or the steward to know when it shall
please him to serve my dinner, all the while cursing and grumbling. But
if he does not quickly knead my cake, I have something which is my
defence, my shield against all ills. If you do not pour me out drink, I have
brought this long-eared jar full of wine. How it brays, when I bend back
and bury its neck in my mouth! It farts like a whole army, and how I
laugh at your wine-skins. (*With increasing excitement*) As to power, am
I not equal to the king of the gods? If our assembly is noisy, all say as
they pass, "Great gods! the tribunal is rolling out its thunder!" If I let
loose the lightning, the richest, aye, the noblest are half dead with terror
and crap for fright. You yourself are afraid of me, yea, by Demeter!
you are afraid. But may I die if *you* frighten *me*.

CHORUS (*singing*)

Never have I heard speech so elegant or so sensible.

PHILOCLEON

Ah! he thought he had only to turn me round his finger; he should,
however have known the vigour of my eloquence.

CHORUS (*singing*)

He has said everything without omission. I felt myself grow taller
while I listened to him. Methought myself meting out justice in the
Islands of the Blest, so much was I taken with the charm of his words.

BDELYCLEON

How overjoyed they are! What extravagant delight! Ah! ah! you are
going to get a thrashing to-day.

CHORUS (*singing*)

Come, plot everything you can to beat him; 'tis not easy to soften
me if you do not talk on my side.

LEADER OF THE CHORUS

If you have nothing but nonsense to spout, it's time to buy a good mill-
stone, freshly cut withal, to crush my anger.

BDELYCLEON

The cure of a disease, so inveterate and so widespread in Athens, is a
difficult task and of too great importance for the scope of comedy. Nevertheless, my old father . . .

PHILOCLEON

Cease to call me by that name, for, if you do not prove me a slave and
that quickly too, you must die by my hand, even if I must be deprived
of my share in the sacred feasts.

BDELYCLEON

Listen to me, dear little father, unruffle that frowning brow and reckon,
you can do so without trouble, not with pebbles, but on your fingers, what
is the sum-total of the tribute paid by the allied towns; besides this we
have the direct imposts, a mass of percentage dues, the fees of the courts
of justice, the produce from the mines, the markets, the harbours, the
public lands and the confiscations. All these together amount to nearly
two thousand talents. Take from this sum the annual pay of the dicasts;
they number six thousand, and there have never been more in this town;
so therefore it is one hundred and fifty talents that come to you.

PHILOCLEON

What! our pay is not even a tithe of the state revenue?

BDELYCLEON

Why no, certainly not.

PHILOCLEON

And where does the rest go then?

BDELYCLEON

To those who say: "I shall never betray the interests of the masses;
I shall always fight for the people." And it is you, father, who let yourself
be caught with their fine talk, who give them all power over yourself.
They are the men who extort fifty talents at a time by threat and intimi-
dation from the allies. "Pay tribute to me," they say, "or I shall loose the
lightning on your town and destroy it." And you, you are content to gnaw
the crumbs of your own might. What do the allies do? They see that the
Athenian mob lives on the tribunal in niggard and miserable fashion,
and they count you for nothing, for not more than the vote of Connus;
it is on those wretches that they lavish everything, dishes of salt fish,

wine, tapestries, cheese, honey, sesamé-fruit, cushions, flagons, rich clothing, chaplets, necklets, drinking-cups, all that yields pleasure and health. And you, their master, to you as a reward for all your toil both on land and sea, nothing is given, not even a clove of garlic to eat with your little fish.

PHILOCLEON

No, undoubtedly not; I have had to send and buy some from Euchar-ides. But you told me I was a slave. Prove it then, for I am dying with impatience.

BDELYCLEON

Is it not the worst of all slaveries to see all these wretches and their flatterers, whom they gorge with gold, at the head of affairs? As for you, you are content with the three obols which they give you and which you have so painfully earned in the galleys, in battles and sieges. But what I stomach least is that you go to sit on the tribunal by order. Some young fairy, the son of Chaereas, to wit, enters your house wiggling his arse, foul with debauchery, on his straddling legs and charges you to come and judge at daybreak, and precisely to the minute. "He who presents himself after the opening of the Court," says he, "will not get the triobolus." But he himself, though he arrives late, will nevertheless get his drachma as a public advocate. If an accused man makes him some present, he shares it with a colleague and the pair agree to arrange the matter like two sawyers, one of whom pulls and the other pushes. As for you, you have only eyes for the public pay-clerk, and you see nothing.

PHILOCLEON

Can it be I am treated thus? Oh! what is it you are saying? You stir me to the bottom of my heart! I am all ears! I cannot express what I feel.

BDELYCLEON

Consider then; you might be rich, both you and all the others; I know not why you let yourself be fooled by these folk who call themselves the people's friends. A myriad of towns obey you, from the Euxine to Sardis. What do you gain thereby? Nothing but this miserable pay, and even that is like the oil with which the flock of wool is impregnated and is doled to you drop by drop, just enough to keep you from dying of hunger. They want you to be poor, and I will tell you why. It is so that you may know only those who nourish you, and so that, if it pleases them to loose you against one of their foes, you shall leap upon him with fury. If they wished to assure the well-being of the people, nothing would be easier for them. We have now a thousand towns that pay us tribute; let them command each of these to feed twenty Athenians; then twenty thousand of our citizens would be eating nothing but hare, would drink nothing but the purest of milk, and always crowned with garlands, would be enjoying the delights to which the great name of their country and the trophies of Marathon give them the right; whereas to-day you are like the hired labourers who gather the olives; you follow him who pays you.

PHILOCLEON

Alas! my hand is benumbed; I can no longer draw my sword. What has become of my strength?

BDELYCLEON

When they are afraid, they promise to divide Euboea among you and to give each fifty bushels of wheat, but what have they given you? Nothing excepting, quite recently, five bushels of barley, and even these you have only obtained with great difficulty, on proving you were not aliens, and then choenix by choenix. (*With increasing excitement*) *That* is why I always kept you shut in; I wanted you to be fed by me and no longer at the beck of these blustering braggarts. Even now I am ready to let you have all you want, provided you no longer let yourself be suckled by the pay-clerk.

LEADER OF THE CHORUS (*to* BDELYCLEON)

He was right who said, "Decide nothing till you have heard both sides," for now it seems to me that you are the one who gains the complete victory. My wrath is appeased and I throw away my sticks. (*To* PHILO-CLEON) But, you, our comrade and contemporary . . .

FIRST SEMI-CHORUS (*taking this up in song*)

. . . let yourself be won over by his words; come, be not too obstinate or too perverse. Would that *I* had a relative or kinsman to correct me thus! Clearly some god is at hand and is now protecting you and loading you with benefits. Accept them.

BDELYCLEON

I will feed him, I will give him everything that is suitable for an old man; oatmeal gruel, a cloak, soft furs, and a wench to rub his tool and his loins. But he keeps silent and will not utter a sound; that's a bad sign.

SECOND SEMI-CHORUS (*singing*)

He has thought the thing over and has recognized his folly; he is reproaching himself for not having followed your advice always. But there he is, converted by your words, and wiser now, so that he will no doubt alter his ways in the future and always believe in none but you.

PHILOCLEON

Alas! alas!

BDELYCLEON

Now why this lamentation?

PHILOCLEON (*in tragic style*)

A truce to your promises! What I love is down there, down there I want
to be, there, where the herald cries, "Who has not yet voted? Let him
rise!" I want to be the last of all to leave the urn. Oh, my soul, my soul!
where art thou? come! oh! dark shadows, make way for me! By
Heracles, may I reach the court in time to convict Cleon of theft.

BDELYCLEON

Come, father, in the name of the gods, believe me!

PHILOCLEON

Believe you! Ask me anything, anything, except one.

BDELYCLEON

What is it? Let us hear.

PHILOCLEON

Not to judge any more! Before I consent, I shall have appeared before
Pluto.

BDELYCLEON

Very well then, since you find so much pleasure in it, go down there
no more, but stay here and deal out justice to your slaves.

PHILOCLEON

But what is there to judge? Are you mad?

BDELYCLEON

Everything as in a tribunal. If a servant opens a door secretly, you
inflict upon him a simple fine; that's what you have repeatedly done
down there. Everything can be arranged to suit you. If it is warm in the
morning, you can judge in the sunlight; if it is snowing, then seated at
your fire; if it rains, you go indoors; and if you don't rise till noon, there
will be no Thesmothetes to exclude you from the precincts.

PHILOCLEON

The notion pleases me.

BDELYCLEON

Moreover, if a pleader is long-winded, you will not be hungering and
chafing and seeking vengeance on the accused.

PHILOCLEON

But could I judge as well with my mouth full?

BDELYCLEON

Much better. Is it not said, that the dicasts, when deceived by lying witnesses, have need to ruminate well in order to arrive at the truth?

PHILOCLEON

Well said, but you have not told me yet who will pay my salary.

BDELYCLEON

I will.

PHILOCLEON

So much the better; in this way I shall be paid by myself. Because that damned jester, Lysistratus, played me an infamous trick the other day. He received a drachma for the two of us and went on the fish-market to get it changed and then brought me back three mullet scales. I took them for obols and crammed them into my mouth; but the smell choked me and I quickly spat them out. So I dragged him before the court.

BDELYCLEON

And what did he say to that?

PHILOCLEON

Well, he pretended I had the stomach of a cock. "You have soon digested the money," he said with a laugh.

BDELYCLEON

You see, that is yet another advantage.

PHILOCLEON

And no small one either. Come, do as you will.

BDELYCLEON

Wait! I will bring everything here.

(*He goes into the house.*)

PHILOCLEON (*to himself*)

You see, the oracles are coming true; I have heard it foretold, that one day the Athenians would dispense justice in their own houses, that each citizen would have himself a little tribunal constructed in his porch similar to the altars of Hecaté, and that there would be such before every door.

BDELYCLEON (*returning with slaves who are carrying various objects*)

There, what do you think of that? I have brought you everything needful and much more into the bargain. See, here is a thunder-mug in case you have to pee; I shall hang it up beside you.

PHILOCLEON

Good idea! Right useful at my age. You have found the true alleviation of bladder troubles.

BDELYCLEON

Here is a fire, and near to it are lentils, should you want to have a bite to eat.

PHILOCLEON

That's admirably arranged. In this way, even when feverish, I shall nevertheless receive my pay; and besides, I could eat my lentils without quitting my seat. But why this cock?

BDELYCLEON

So that, should you doze during some pleading, he may awaken you by crowing up there.

PHILOCLEON

I want only for one thing more; all the rest is as good as can be.

BDELYCLEON

What is that?

PHILOCLEON

If only they could bring me an image of the hero Lycus.

BDELYCLEON

Here it is! Why, you might think it was the god himself!

PHILOCLEON

Oh! hero, my master! how repulsive you are to look at!

BDELYCLEON

He looks just like Cleonymus.

PHILOCLEON

That is why, hero though he be, he has no weapon.

BDELYCLEON

The sooner you take your seat, the sooner I shall call a case.

PHILOCLEON

Call it, for I have been seated ever so long.

BDELYCLEON

Let us see. What case shall we bring up first? Is there a slave who has done something wrong? Ah! you Thracian there, you burnt the stew-pot the other day.

PHILOCLEON

Wait, wait! This is a fine state of affairs! You almost made me judge without a bar, and that is the most sacred thing of all for us.

BDELYCLEON

There isn't any, by Zeus.

PHILOCLEON

I'll run indoors and get one myself. (*Exit*)

BDELYCLEON

What does it matter? Terrible thing, the force of habit.

XANTHIAS (*coming out of the house*)

Damn that animal! How can anyone keep such a dog?

BDELYCLEON

Hullo! what's the matter?

XANTHIAS

Oh, it's Labes, who has just rushed into the kitchen and seized a whole Sicilian cheese and gobbled it up.

BDELYCLEON

Good! this will be the first offence I shall make my father try. (*To* XANTHIAS) Come along and lay your accusation.

XANTHIAS

No, not I; the other dog vows he will be accuser, if the matter is brought up for trial.

BDELYCLEON

Well then, bring them both along.

XANTHIAS

That's what we'll have to do.
(*He goes back into the house. A moment later* PHILOCLEON *comes out.*)

BDELYCLEON

What is this?

PHILOCLEON

The pig-trough of the swine dedicated to Hestia.

BDELYCLEON

Did you steal it from a shrine?

PHILOCLEON

No, no, by addressing Hestia first, I might, thanks to her, crush an adversary. But put an end to delay by calling up the case. My verdict is already settled.

BDELYCLEON

Wait! I still have to bring out the tablets and the scrolls.

(*He goes into the house.*)

PHILOCLEON

Oh! I am boiling, I am dying with impatience at your delays. I could have traced the sentence in the dust.

BDELYCLEON (*coming out with tablets and scrolls*)

There you are.

PHILOCLEON

Then call the case.

BDELYCLEON

Right. Who is first on the docket?

PHILOCLEON

My god! This is unbearable! I have forgotten the urns.

BDELYCLEON

Now where are you going?

PHILOCLEON

To look for the urns.

BDELYCLEON

Don't bother, I have these pots.

PHILOCLEON

Very well, then we have all we need, except the clepsydra.

BDELYCLEON (*pointing to the thunder-mug*)

What is this if it is not a clepsydra?

PHILOCLEON

You know how to supply everything.

BDELYCLEON

Let fire be brought quickly from the house with myrtle boughs and in·
cense, and let us invoke the gods before opening the sitting.

LEADER OF THE CHORUS

Offer them libations and your vows and we will thank them that a
noble agreement has put an end to your bickerings and strife. And first
let there be a sacred silence.

CHORUS (*singing*)

Oh! god of Delphi! oh! Phoebus Apollo! convert into the greatest blessing for us all what is now happening before *t*his house, and
cure us of our error, oh, Paean, our helper!

BDELYCLEON (*solemnly*)

Oh! Powerful god, Apollo Aguieus, who watchest at the door of my
entrance hall, accept this fresh sacrifice; I offer it that you may deign to
soften my father's excessive severity; he is as hard as iron, his heart is
like sour wine; do thou pour into it a little honey. Let him become gentle
toward other men, let him take more interest in the accused than in the
accusers, may he allow himself to be softened by entreaties; calm his acrid
humour and deprive his irritable mind of all sting.

CHORUS (*singing*)

We unite our vows and chants to those of this new magistrate.
His words have won our favour and we are convinced that he loves
the people more than any of the young men of the present day.
(XANTHIAS *brings in two persons costumed as dogs, but with masks
that suggest Laches and Cleon.*)

BDELYCLEON

If there be any judge near at hand, let him enter; once the proceedings
have opened, we shall admit him no more.

PHILOCLEON

Who is the defendant?

BDELYCLEON

This one.

PHILOCLEON (*aside*)

He does not stand a chance.

BDELYCLEON

Listen to the indictment. A dog of Cydatheraea doth hereby charge
Labes of Aexonia with having devoured a Sicilian cheese by himself
without accomplices. Penalty demanded, a collar of fig-tree wood.

PHILOCLEON

Nay, a dog's death, if convicted.

BDELYCLEON

This is Labes, the defendant.

PHILOCLEON

Oh! what a wretched brute! how entirely he looks the rogue! He thinks to deceive me by keeping his jaws closed. Where is the plaintiff, the dog of Cydathenaea?

DOG

Bow wow! bow wow!

BDELYCLEON

Here he is.

PHILOCLEON

Why, he's another Labes, a great barker and a licker of dishes.

BDELYCLEON (*as Herald*)

Silence! Keep your seats! (*To the Cydathenaean dog.*) And you, up on your feet and accuse him.

PHILOCLEON

Go on, and I will help myself and eat these lentils.

DOG

Gentlemen of the jury, listen to this indictment I have drawn up. He has committed the blackest of crimes, against both me and the seamen. He sought refuge in a dark corner to glutton on a big Sicilian cheese, with which he sated his hunger.

PHILOCLEON

Why, the crime is clear; the filthy brute this very moment belched forth a horrible odour of cheese right under my nose.

DOG

And he refused to share with me. And yet can anyone style himself your benefactor, when he does not cast a morsel to your poor dog?

PHILOCLEON

He has not shared anything, not even with his comrade. His madness is as hot as my lentils.

BDELYCLEON

In the name of the gods, father! No hurried verdict without hearing the other side!

PHILOCLEON

But the evidence is plain; the fact speaks for itself.

DOG

Then beware of acquitting the most selfish of canine gluttons, who has devoured the whole cheese, rind and all, prowling round the platter.

PHILOCLEON

There is not even enough left for me to fill up the chinks in my pitcher.

DOG

Besides, you *must* punish him, because the same house cannot keep two thieves. Let me not have barked in vain, else I shall never bark again.

PHILOCLEON

Oh! the black deeds he has just denounced! What a shameless thief! Say, cock, is not that your opinion too? Ha, ha! He thinks as I do. Here, Thesmothetes! where are you? Hand me the thunder-mug.

BDELYCLEON

Get it yourself. I go to call the witnesses; these are a plate, a pestle, a cheese knife, a brazier, a stew-pot and other half-burnt utensils. (*To* PHILOCLEON) But you have not finished? you are piddling away still! Have done and be seated.

PHILOCLEON

Ha, ha! I reckon I know somebody who will crap for fright to-day.

BDELYCLEON

Will you never cease showing yourself hard and intractable, and especially to the accused? You tear them to pieces tooth and nail. (*To* LABES) Come forward and defend yourself. What means this silence? Answer.

PHILOCLEON

No doubt he has nothing to say.

BDELYCLEON

Not at all, I think he has got what happened once to Thucydides in court; his jaws suddenly set fast. Get away! I will undertake your defence.—Gentlemen of the jury, it is a difficult thing to speak for a dog who has been calumniated, but nevertheless I will try. He is a good dog, and he chases wolves finely.

PHILOCLEON

He is a thief and a conspirator.

BDELYCLEON

No, he is the best of all our dogs; he is capable of guarding a whole flock.

PHILOCLEON

And what good is that, if he eats the cheese?

BDELYCLEON

What? he fights for you, he guards your door; he is an excellent dog in every respect. Forgive him his larceny! he is wretchedly ignorant, he cannot play the lyre.

PHILOCLEON

I wish he did not know how to write either; then the rascal would not have drawn up his pleadings.

BDELYCLEON

Witnesses, I pray you, listen. Come forward, grating-knife, and speak up; answer me clearly. You were paymaster at the time. Did you grate out to the soldiers what was given you?—He says he did so.

PHILOCLEON

But, by Zeus! he lies.

BDELYCLEON

Oh! have patience. Take pity on the unfortunate. Labes feeds only on fish-bones and fishes' heads and has not an instant of peace. The other is good only to guard the house; he never moves from here, but demands his share of all that is brought in and bites those who refuse.

PHILOCLEON (*aside*)

Oh! Heaven! have I fallen ill? I feel my anger cooling! Woe to me! I am softening!

BDELYCLEON

Have pity, father, pity, I adjure you; you would not have him dead. Where are his puppies? (*A group of children costumed as puppies comes out.*) Come, poor little beasties, yap, up on your haunches, beg and whine!

PHILOCLEON

Descend, descend, descend, descend! [15]

BDELYCLEON

I will descend, although that word, "descend," has too often raised false hope. None the less, I will descend.

PHILOCLEON

Plague seize it! Have I then done wrong to eat! What! I, crying! Ah! I certainly should not be weeping, if I were not stuffed with lentils.

BDELYCLEON

Then he is acquitted?

PHILOCLEON

It is difficult to tell.

BDELYCLEON

Ah! my dear father, be good! be humane! Take this voting pebble and rush with your eyes closed to that second urn and, father, acquit him.

PHILOCLEON

No, I know no more how to acquit than to play the lyre.

BDELYCLEON

Come quickly, I will show you the way.
(*He takes his father by the hand and leads him to the second urn.*)

PHILOCLEON

Is this the first urn?

BDELYCLEON

Yes.

PHILOCLEON (*dropping in his vote*)

Then I have voted.

BDELYCLEON (*aside*)

I have fooled him and he has acquitted in spite of himself. (*To* PHILO-CLEON) Come, I will turn out the urns.

PHILOCLEON

What is the result?

BDELYCLEON

We shall see. (*He examines both urns.*) Labes, you stand acquitted. (PHILOCLEON *faints*) Eh! father, what's the matter, what is it? (*To slaves*) Water! water! (*To* PHILOCLEON) Pull yourself together, sir!

PHILOCLEON (*weakly*)
Tell me! Is he really acquitted?

BDELYCLEON
Yes, certainly.

PHILOCLEON (*falling back*)
Then it's all over with me!

BDELYCLEON
Courage, dear father, don't let this afflict you so terribly.

PHILOCLEON (*dolefully*)
And so I have charged my conscience with the acquittal of an accused
being! What will become of me? Sacred gods! forgive me. I did it despite myself; it is not in my character.

BDELYCLEON
Do not vex yourself, father; I will feed you well, will take you everywhere to eat and drink with me; you shall go to every feast; henceforth
your life shall be nothing but pleasure, and Hyperbolus shall no longer
have you for a tool. But come, let us go in.

PHILOCLEON (*resignedly*)
So be it; if you will, let us go in.

(*They all go into the house.*)

LEADER OF THE CHORUS
Go where it pleases you and may your happiness be great. (*The
CHORUS turns and faces the audience.*) You meanwhile, oh! countless
myriads, listen to the sound counsels I am going to give you and take
care they are not lost upon you. That would be the fate of vulgar spectators, not that of such an audience. Hence, people, lend me your ear, if
you love frank speaking.

The poet has a reproach to make against his audience; he says you
have ill-treated him in return for the many services he has rendered you.
At first he kept himself in the background and lent help secretly to other
poets, and like the prophetic Genius, who hid himself in the belly of
Eurycles, slipped within the spirit of another and whispered to him many
a comic hit. Later he ran the risks of the theatre on his own account, with
his face uncovered, and dared to guide his Muse unaided. Though over-
laden with success and honours more than any of your poets, indeed despite all his glory, he does not yet believe he has attained his goal; his
heart is not swollen with pride and he does not seek to seduce the young
folk in the wrestling school. If any lover runs up to him to complain be-

cause he is furious at seeing the object of his passion derided on the stage, he takes no heed of such reproaches, for he is inspired only with honest motives and his Muse is no pander. From the very outset of his dramatic career he has disdained to assail those who were men, but with a courage worthy of Heracles himself he attacked the most formidable monsters, and at the beginning went straight for that beast with the sharp teeth, with the terrible eyes that flashed lambent fire like those of Cynna, surrounded by a hundred lewd flatterers who spittle-licked him to his heart's content; he had a voice like a roaring torrent, the stench of a seal, the unwashed balls of a Lamia, and the arse of a camel. Our poet did not tremble at the sight of this horrible monster, nor did he dream of gaining him over; and again this very day he is fighting for your good. Last year besides, he attacked those pale, shivering and feverish beings who strangled your fathers in the dark, throttled your grandfathers, and who, lying in the beds of the most inoffensive, piled up against them lawsuits, summonses and witnesses to such an extent, that many of them flew in terror to the Polemarch for refuge. Such is the champion you have found to purify your country of all its evil, and last year you betrayed him, when he sowed the most novel ideas, which, however, did not strike root, because you did not understand their value; notwithstanding this, he swears by Bacchus, the while offering him libations, that none ever heard better comic verses. It is a disgrace to you not to have caught their drift at once; as for the poet, he is none the less appreciated by the *enlightened* judges. He shivered his oars in rushing boldly forward to board his foe. (*With increasing excitement*) But in future, my dear fellow-citizens, love and honour more those of your poets who seek to imagine and express some new thought. Make their ideas your own, keep them in your caskets like sweet-scented fruit. If you do, your clothing will emit an odour of wisdom the whole year through.

FIRST SEMI-CHORUS (*singing*)

Ah, once long ago we were brave in the dance, brave too in battle, and on this account alone the most courageous of men! That was formerly, was formerly; all that is gone now and these hairs of ours are whiter than the swan. But from what is left we must rekindle a youthful ardour; really we prefer our old age to the curly hair and the fine clothes and the effeminacy of many of the young.

LEADER OF THE FIRST SEMI-CHORUS

Should any among you spectators look upon me with wonder, because of this wasp waist, or not know the meaning of this sting, I will soon dispel his ignorance. We, who wear this appendage, are the true Attic men, who alone are noble and native to the soil, the bravest of all people. We are the ones who, weapon in hand, did so much for the country, when the barbarian shed torrents of fire and smoke over our city in his relentless desire to seize our nests by force. At once we ran up, armed with lance and buckler, and, drunk with the bitter wine of anger, we gave them battle, man standing to man and rage distorting our lips. A hail of arrows hid the sky. However, by the help of the gods, we drove off the foe towards evening. Before the battle an owl had flown over our army. Then we pursued them with our lance-point in their loins as one hunts the tunny-fish; they fled and we stung them in the jaw and in the eyes, so that even now the barbarians tell each other that there is nothing in the world more to be feared than the Attic wasp.

SECOND SEMI-CHORUS (*singing*)

Oh! at that time I was terrible, I feared nothing; forth on my galleys I went in search of my foe and subjected him. Then we never thought of rounding fine phrases, we never dreamt of calumny; it was who should prove the strongest rower. And thus we took many a town from the Medes, and 'tis to us that Athens owes the tributes that our young men thieve to-day.

LEADER OF THE SECOND SEMI-CHORUS

Look well at us, and you will see that we have all the character and habits of the wasp. Firstly, if roused, no beings are more irascible, more relentless than we are. In all other things, too, we act like wasps. We collect in swarms, in a kind of nests, and some go judging with the Archon, some with the Eleven, others at the Odeon; there are yet others, who hardly move at all, like the grubs in the cells, but remain glued to the walls, and bent double to the ground. We also pay full attention to the discovery of all sorts of means of existing and sting the first who comes, so as to live at his expense. Finally, we have among us drones, who have no sting and who, without giving themselves the least trouble, seize on our revenues as they flow past them and devour them. It's this that grieves us most of all, to see men who have never served or held either lance or oar in defence of their country, enriching themselves at our expense without ever raising a blister on their hands. In short, I give it as my deliberate opinion that in future every citizen not possessed of a sting shall not receive the triobolus.

(PHILOCLEON *comes out of the house, followed by his son and a slave. The* CHORUS *turns to face them.*)

PHILOCLEON

As long as I live, I will never give up this cloak; it's the one I wore in that battle when Boreas delivered us from such fierce attacks.

BDELYCLEON

You do not know what is good for you.

PHILOCLEON

Ah! I do not know how to use fine clothing! The other day, when cramming myself with fried fish, I dropped so many grease spots that I had to pay three obols to the cleaner.

BDELYCLEON

At least have a try, since you have once for all handed the care for your well-being over to me.

PHILOCLEON

Very well then! what must I do?

BDELYCLEON

Take off your cloak, and put on this tunic in its stead.

PHILOCLEON

Was it worth while to beget and bring up children, so that this one should now wish to choke me?

BDELYCLEON

Come, take this tunic and put it on without so much talk.

PHILOCLEON

Great gods! what sort of a cursed garment is this?

BDELYCLEON

Some call it a pelisse, others a Persian cloak.

PHILOCLEON

Ah! I thought it was a wraprascal like those made at Thymaetis.

BDELYCLEON

No wonder. It's only at Sardis you could have seen them, and you have never been there.

PHILOCLEON

Of course not, but it seems to me exactly like the mantle Morychus sports.

BDELYCLEON

Not at all; I tell you they are woven at Ecbatana.

PHILOCLEON

What! are there woollen ox-guts [16] then at Ecbatana?

BDELYCLEON

Whatever are you talking about? These are woven by the barbarians at great cost. I am certain this pelisse has consumed more than a talent of wool.

PHILOCLEON

It should be called wool-waster then instead of pelisse.

BDELYCLEON

Come, father, just hold still for a moment and put it on.

PHILOCLEON

Oh! horrors! what a waft of heat the hussy sends up my nose!

BDELYCLEON

Will you have done with this fooling?

PHILOCLEON

No by Zeus.

BDELYCLEON

But, good sir, . . .

PHILOCLEON

If need be, I prefer you should put me in the oven.

BDELYCLEON

Come, I will put it round you. There!

PHILOCLEON

At all events, bring out a crook.

BDELYCLEON

Why, whatever for?

PHILOCLEON

To drag me out of it before I am quite melted.

BDELYCLEON

Now take off those wretched clogs and put on these nice Laconian slippers.

PHILOCLEON

I put on odious slippers made by our foes! Never!

BDELYCLEON

Come! put your foot in and push hard. Quick!

PHILOCLEON

You're doing wrong here. You want me to put my foot on Laconian ground.

BDELYCLEON

Now the other.

PHILOCLEON

Ah! no, not that foot; one of its toes holds the Laconians in horror

BDELYCLEON

Positively you must.

PHILOCLEON

Alas! alas! Then I shall have no chilblains in my old age.

BDELYCLEON

Now, hurry up and get them on; and now imitate the easy effeminate gait of the rich. See, like this.

(He takes a few steps.)

PHILOCLEON *(trying to do likewise)*

There! . . . Look at my get-up and tell me which rich man I most resemble in my walk.

BDELYCLEON

Why, you look like a garlic plaster on a boil.

PHILOCLEON

Ah! I am longing to swagger and sway my arse about.

BDELYCLEON

Now, will you know how to talk gravely with well-informed men of good class?

PHILOCLEON

Undoubtedly.

BDELYCLEON

What will you say to them?

PHILOCLEON

Oh, lots of things. First of all I shall say, that Lamia, seeing herself caught, let flee a fart; then, that Cardopion and his mother . . .

BDELYCLEON

Come, no fabulous tales, pray! talk of realities, of domestic facts, as is usually done.

PHILOCLEON

Ah! I know something that is indeed most domestic. Once upon a time there was a rat and a cat . . .

BDELYCLEON

"Oh, you ignorant fool," as Theagenes said to the dung-gatherer in a rage. Are you going to talk of cats and rats among high-class people?

PHILOCLEON

Then what should I talk about?

BDELYCLEON

Tell some dignified story. Relate how you were sent on a solemn mission with Androcles and Clisthenes.

PHILOCLEON

On a mission! never in my life, except once to Paros, a job which brought me in two obols a day.[17]

BDELYCLEON

At least say, that you have just seen Ephudion doing well in the pancratium with Ascondas and, that despite his age and his white hair, he is still robust in loin and arm and flank and that his chest is a very breast-plate.

PHILOCLEON

Stop! stop! what nonsense! Who ever contested at the pancratium with a breast-plate on?

BDELYCLEON

That is how well-behaved folk like to talk. But another thing. When at wine, it would be fitting to relate some good story of your youthful days. What is your most brilliant feat?

PHILOCLEON

My best feat? Ah! when I stole Ergasion's vine-props.

BDELYCLEON

You and your vine-props! you'll be the death of me! Tell of one of your boar-hunts or of when you coursed the hare. Talk about some torch-race you were in; tell of some deed of daring.

PHILOCLEON

Ah! my most daring deed was when, quite a young man still, I prosecuted Phayllus, the runner, for defamation, and he was condemned by a majority of two votes.

BDELYCLEON

Enough of that! Now recline there, and practise the bearing that is fitting at table in society.

PHILOCLEON

How must I recline? Tell me quick!

BDELYCLEON

In an elegant style.

PHILOCLEON (*lying on the ground*)

Like this?

BDELYCLEON

Not at all.

PHILOCLEON

How then?

BDELYCLEON

Spread your knees on the tapestries and give your body the most easy curves, like those taught in the gymnasium. Then praise some bronze vase, survey the ceiling, admire the awning stretched over the court. Water is poured over our hands; the tables are spread; we sup and, after ablution, we now offer libations to the gods.

PHILOCLEON

But, by Zeus! this supper is but a dream, it appears!

BDELYCLEON

The flute-player has finished the prelude. The guests are Theorus, Aeschines, Phanus, Cleon, Acestor; and beside this last, I don't know who else. You are with them. Shall you know exactly how to take up the songs that are started?

PHILOCLEON

Quite well.

BDELYCLEON

Really?

PHILOCLEON

Better than any born mountaineer of Attica.

BDELYCLEON

That we shall see. Suppose me to be Cleon. I am the first to begin the song of Harmodius, and you take it up: "There never yet was seen in Athens . . ."

PHILOCLEON

. . . such a rogue or such a thief." [18]

BDELYCLEON

Why, you wretched man, it will be the end of you if you sing that. He will vow your ruin, your destruction, to chase you out of the country.

PHILOCLEON

Well! then I shall answer his threats with another song: "With your madness for supreme power, you will end by overthrowing the city, which even now totters towards ruin."

BDELYCLEON

And when Theorus, prone at Cleon's feet, takes his hand and sings, "Like Admetus, love those who are brave," what reply will you make him?

PHILOCLEON

I shall sing, "I know not how to play the fox, nor call myself the friend of both parties."

BDELYCLEON

Then comes the turn of Aeschines, the son of Sellus, and a well-trained and clever musician, who will sing, "Good things and riches for Clitagora and me and eke for the Thessalians!"

PHILOCLEON

"The two of us have squandered a great deal between us."

BDELYCLEON

At this game you seem at home. But come, we will go and dine with Philoctemon.—Slave! slave! place our dinner in a basket; we are going out for a good long drinking bout.

PHILOCLEON

By no means, it is too dangerous; for after drinking, one breaks in doors, one comes to blows, one batters everything. Anon, when the wine is slept off, one is forced to pay.

BDELYCLEON

Not if you are with decent people. Either they undertake to appease the offended person or, better still, you say something witty, you tell some comic story, perhaps one of those you have yourself heard at table, either in Aesop's style or in that of Sybaris; everyone laughs and the trouble is ended.

PHILOCLEON

Faith! it's worth while learning many stories then, if you are thus not punished for the ill you do. But come, no more delay!

(They go out.)

CHORUS *(singing)*

More than once have I given proof of cunning and never of stupidity, but how much more clever is Amynias, the son of Sellus and of the race of forelock-wearers; him we saw one day coming to dine with Leogaras, bringing as his share one apple and a pomegranate, and bear in mind he was as hungry as Antiphon. He went on an embassy to Pharsalus, and there he lived solely among the Thessalian mercenaries; indeed, is he not the vilest of mercenaries himself?

LEADER OF THE CHORUS

Oh! blessed, oh! fortunate Automenes, how enviable is your fortune! You have three sons, the most industrious in the world; one is the friend of all, a very able man, the first among the lyre-players, the favourite of the Graces. The second is an actor, and his talent is beyond all praise. As for Ariphrades, he is by far the most gifted; his father would swear to me, that without any master whatever and solely through the spontaneous effort of his happy nature, he taught himself to exercise his tongue in the whorehouses, where he spends the whole of his time.

Some have said that I and Cleon were reconciled. This is the truth of the matter: Cleon was harassing me, persecuting and belabouring me in every way; and, when I was being fleeced, the public laughed at seeing me uttering such loud cries; not that they cared about me, but simply curious to know whether, when trodden down by my enemy, I would not hurl at him some taunt. Noticing this, I have played the wheedler a bit; but now, look! the prop is deceiving the vine!

(XANTHIAS enters, weeping and wailing and rubbing his sides.)

XANTHIAS

Oh! tortoises! happy to have so hard a skin! Oh! creatures full of sense! what a happy thought to cover your bodies with this shell, which shields it from blows! As for me, I can no longer move; the stick has so belaboured my body.

LEADER OF THE CHORUS

Why, what's the matter, my child? for, old as he may be, one has the right to call anyone a child who has let himself be beaten.

XANTHIAS

Alas! my master is really the worst of all plagues. He was the most drunk of all the guests, and yet among them were Hippyllus, Antiphon, Lycon, Lysistratus, Theophrastus and Phrynichus. But he was a hundred times more insolent than any. As soon as he had stuffed himself with a host of good dishes, he began to leap and spring, to laugh and to fart like a little ass well stuffed with barley. Then he set to beating me with all his heart, shouting, "Slave! slave!" Lysistratus, as soon as he saw him, let fly this comparison at him. "Old fellow," said he, "you resemble one of the scum assuming the airs of a rich man or a stupid ass that has broken loose from its stable." "As for you," bawled the other at the top of his voice, "you are like a grasshopper, whose cloak is worn to the thread, or like Sthenelus after his clothes had been sold." All applauded excepting Theophrastus, who made a grimace as behoved a well-bred man like him. The old man called to him, "Hi! tell me then what you have to be proud of? Not so much mouthing, you, who so well know how to play the buffoon and to lick-spittle the rich!" In this way he insulted each in turn with the grossest of jests, and he reeled off a thousand of the most absurd and ridiculous speeches. At last, when he was thoroughly drunk, he started towards here, striking everyone he met. Wait, here he comes reeling along. I will be off for fear of his blows.

(PHILOCLEON *enters, inebriated and hilarious, carrying a torch; his other hand is occupied with a wholly nude flute-girl; he is followed by a group of angry victims of his exuberance.*)

PHILOCLEON (*singing*)

Halt! and let everyone begone, or I shall do an evil turn to some of those who insist on following me. Clear off, rascals, or I shall roast you with this torch!

GUEST

We shall all make you smart to-morrow for your youthful pranks. We shall come in a body to summon you to justice.

PHILOCLEON (*singing*)

Ho! ho! summon *me*? what old women's babble! Know that I can no longer bear to hear even the name of suits. Ha! ha! ha! *this* is what pleases *me*, "Down with the urns!" Get out of here! Down with the dicasts! away with them, away with them!

(*Dropping into speech; to the flute-girl*)

Mount up there, my little gilded cock-chafer; take hold of this rope's
end in your hand. Hold it tight, but have a care; the rope's a bit old and
worn. But even though it's worn, it still has its virtues. Do you see how
opportunely I got you away from the solicitations of those fellators, who
wanted you to make love to them in their own odd way? You therefore
owe me this return to gratify me. But will you pay the debt? Oh! I know
well you will not even try; you will play with me, you will laugh heartily
at me as you have done at many another man. And yet, if you would not
be a naughty girl, I would redeem you, when my son is dead, and you
should be my concubine, my little one. At present I am not my own master; I am very young and am watched very closely. My dear son never
lets me out of his sight; he's an unbearable creature, who would quarter
a thread and skin a flint; he is afraid I should get lost, for I am his only
father. But here he comes running towards us. But be quick, don't stir,
hold these torches. I am going to play him a young man's trick, the same
as he played me before I was initiated into the mysteries.

BDELYCLEON

Oh! oh! you debauched old dotard! you are amorous, it seems, of
pretty baggages; but, by Apollo, it shall not be with impunity!

PHILOCLEON

Ah! you would be very glad to eat a lawsuit in vinegar, you would.

BDELYCLEON

Only a rascal would steal the flute-girl away from the other guests.

PHILOCLEON

What flute-girl? Are you distraught, as if you had just returned from
Pluto?

BDELYCLEON

By Zeus! But here is the Dardanian wench in person.

PHILOCLEON

Nonsense. This is a torch that I have lit in the public square in honour
of the gods.

BDELYCLEON

Is this a torch?

PHILOCLEON

A torch? Certainly. Do you not see it is of several different colours?

BDELYCLEON

And what is that black part in the middle?

PHILOCLEON

That's the pitch running out while it burns.

BDELYCLEON

And there, on the other side, surely that is a girl's bottom?

PHILOCLEON

No. That's just a small bit of the torch, that projects.

BDELYCLEON

What do you mean? what bit? Hi! you woman! come here!

PHILOCLEON

Oh! What do you want to do?

BDELYCLEON

To take her away from you and lead her off. You are too much worn out and can do nothing.

(*He takes the girl into the house.*)

PHILOCLEON

Listen to me! One day, at Olympia, I saw Euphudion boxing bravely against Ascondas; he was already aged, and yet with a blow from his fist he knocked down his young opponent. So watch out that I don't blacken *your* eyes.

BDELYCLEON (*who has returned*)

By Zeus! you have Olympia at your finger-ends!
(*A* BAKER'S WIFE *enters with an empty basket; she brings* CHAEREPHON *with her as witness.*)

BAKER'S WIFE (*to* CHAEREPHON)

Come to my help, I beg you, in the name of the gods! This cursed man, when striking out right and left with his torch, knocked over ten loaves worth an obolus apiece, and then, to cap the deal, four others.

BDELYCLEON

Do you see what lawsuits you are drawing upon yourself with your drunkenness? You will have to plead.

PHILOCLEON

Oh, no, no! a little pretty talk and pleasant tales will soon settle the matter and reconcile her with me.

BAKER'S WIFE

Not so, by the goddesses twain! It shall not be said that you have with impunity spoilt the wares of Myrtia, the daughter of Ancylion and Sostraté.

PHILOCLEON

Listen, woman, I wish to tell you a lovely anecdote.

BAKER'S WIFE

By Zeus, no anecdotes for me, thank you.

PHILOCLEON

One night Aesop was going out to supper. A drunken bitch had the impudence to bark near him. Aesop said to her, "Oh, bitch, bitch! you would do well to sell your wicked tongue and buy some wheat."

BAKER'S WIFE

You make a mock of me! Very well! I don't care who you are, I shall summons you before the market inspectors for damage done to my business. Chaerephon here shall be my witness.

PHILOCLEON

But just listen, here's another will perhaps please you better. Lasus and Simonides were contesting against each other for the singing prize. Lasus said, "Damned if I care."

BAKER'S WIFE

Ah! really, did he now!

PHILOCLEON

As for you, Chaerephon, *can* you be witness to this woman, who looks as pale and tragic as Ino when she throws herself from her rock . . . at the feet of Euripides?

(*The* BAKER'S WIFE *and* CHAEREPHON *depart.*)

BDELYCLEON

Here, I suppose, comes another to summons you; *he* has his witness too. Ah! unhappy indeed we are!

(*A badly bruised man enters.*)

ACCUSER

I summons you, old man, for outrage.

BDELYCLEON

For outrage? Oh! in the name of the gods, do not summons him! I will be answerable for him; name the price and I will be more more grateful still.

PHILOCLEON

I ask for nothing better than to be reconciled with him; for I admit I struck him and threw stones at him. So, first come here. Will you leave it in my hands to name the indemnity I must pay, if I promise you my friendship as well, or will you fix it yourself?

ACCUSER

Fix it; I like neither lawsuits nor disputes.

PHILOCLEON

A man of Sybaris fell from his chariot and wounded his head most severely; he was a very poor driver. One of his friends came up to him and said, "Every man to his trade." Well then, go you to Pittalus to get mended.

BDELYCLEON

You are incorrigible.

ACCUSER (*to his witness*)

At all events, make a note of his reply. (*They start to leave.*)

PHILOCLEON

Listen, instead of going off so abruptly. A woman at Sybaris broke a box.

ACCUSER (*to his witness*)

I again ask you to witness this.

PHILOCLEON

The box therefore had the fact attested, but the woman said, "Never worry about witnessing the matter, but hurry off to buy a cord to tie it together with; that will be the more sensible course."

ACCUSER

Oh! go on with your ribaldry until the Archon calls the case.

(*He and his witness depart.*)

BDELYCLEON (*to* PHILOCLEON)

By Demeter! you'll stay here no longer! I am going to take you and carry you off.

PHILOCLEON

And what for?

BDELYCLEON

What for? I am going to carry you into the house, so that the accusers will not run out of witnesses.

PHILOCLEON

One day at Delphi, Aesop . . .

BDELYCLEON

I don't care a fig for that.

PHILOCLEON

. . . was accused of having stolen a sacred vase. But he replied, that the horn-beetle . . .

BDELYCLEON

Oh, dear, dear! You'll drive me crazy with your horn-beetle.
(PHILOCLEON *goes on with his fable while* BDELYCLEON *is carrying him off the scene by main force.*)

CHORUS (*singing*)

I envy you your happiness, old man. What a contrast to his former frugal habits and his very hard life! Taught now in quite another school, he will know nothing but the pleasures of ease. Perhaps he will jibe at it, for indeed it is difficult to renounce what has become one's second nature. However, many have done it, and adopting the ideas of others, have changed their use and wont. As for Philocleon's son, I, like all wise and judicious men, cannot sufficiently praise his filial tenderness and his tact. Never have I met a more amiable nature, and I have conceived the greatest fondness for him. How he triumphed on every point in his discussion with his father, when he wanted to bring him back to more worthy and honourable tastes!

XANTHIAS (*coming out of the house*)

By Bacchus! Some Evil Genius has brought this unbearable disorder into our house. The old man, full up with wine and excited by the sound of the flute, is so delighted, so enraptured, that he is spending the night executing the old dances that Thespis first produced on the stage, and just now he offered to prove to the modern tragedians, by disputing with them for the dancing prize, that they are nothing but a lot of old dotards.
(BDELYCLEON *comes out of the house with his father who is costumed as* POLYPHEMUS *in Euripides'* Cyclops.)

PHILOCLEON

"Who loiters at the door of the vestibule?"

XANTHIAS

Here comes our pest, our plague!

PHILOCLEON

Let down the barriers. The dance is now to begin.
(*He begins to dance in a manner grotesquely parodying that of Euripides.*)

XANTHIAS

Or rather the madness.

PHILOCLEON

Impetuous movement already twists and racks my sides. How my
nostrils wheeze! how my back cracks!

XANTHIAS

Go and fill yourself with hellebore.

PHILOCLEON

Phrynichus is as bold as a cock and terrifies his rivals.

XANTHIAS

He'll be stoned.

PHILOCLEON

His leg kicks out sky-high . . .

XANTHIAS

. . . and his arse gapes open.

PHILOCLEON

Mind your own business. Look how easily my leg-joints move. Isn't
that good?

XANTHIAS

God, no, it's merely insane!

PHILOCLEON

And now I summon and challenge my rivals. If there be a tragic poet
who pretends to be a skilful dancer, let him come and contest the matter
with me. Is there one? Is there *not* one?

XANTHIAS

Here comes one, and one only.
(*A very small dancer, costumed as a crab, enters.*)

PHILOCLEON

Who is the wretch?

XANTHIAS

The younger son of Carcinus.

PHILOCLEON

I will crush him to nothing; in point of keeping time, I will knock him out, for he knows nothing of rhythm.

XANTHIAS

Ah! ah! here comes his brother too, another tragedian, and another son of Carcinus.

(Another dancer, hardly larger than the first, and similarly costumed, enters.)

PHILOCLEON

Him I will devour for my dinner.

XANTHIAS

Oh! ye gods! I see nothing but crabs. Here is yet another son of Carcinus.

(A third dancer enters, likewise resembling a crab, but smaller than either of the others.)

PHILOCLEON

What's this? A shrimp or a spider?

XANTHIAS

It's a crab,—a hermit-crab, the smallest of its kind; it writes tragedies.

PHILOCLEON

Oh! Carcinus, how proud you should be of your brood! What a crowd of kinglets have come swooping down here! But we shall have to measure ourselves against them. Have marinade prepared for seasoning them, in case I prove the victor.

LEADER OF THE CHORUS

Let us stand out of the way a little, so that they may twirl at their ease.

CHORUS

(It divides in two and accompanies with its song the wild dancing of PHILOCLEON *and the sons of* CARCINUS *in the centre of the Orchestra.)*

Come, illustrious children of this inhabitant of the brine, brothers of the shrimps, skip on the sand and the shore of the barren sea; show us the lightning whirls and twirls of your nimble limbs. Glorious offspring of Phrynichus, let fly your kicks, so that the spectators may be overjoyed at seeing your legs so high in air. Twist, twirl, tap your bellies, kick your legs to the sky. Here comes your famous father, the ruler of the sea, delighted to see his three lecherous kinglets.[19] Go on with your dancing, if it pleases you, but as for us, we shall not join you. Lead us promptly off the stage, for never a comedy yet was seen where the Chorus finished off with a dance.

1. The reference is to Cleon; see the Glossary.

2. A pun on the Greek words *démos*, "people" and *demós*, "fat." Aristophanes has used this before; see note 13 on *The Knights*.

3. "Going to the crows" was the ancient way of "going to Hell."

4. The implication is that certain other poets had sought to gain the favour of the audience by incorporating in their comedies scenes in which such distributions were made.

5. The poet has consoled himself by ascribing the failure of *The Clouds* the year before to the stupidity of the spectators, and there is no reason to doubt that there was much in that comedy which baffled or eluded the vulgar comprehension; but the principal defects of the play cannot correctly be placed in this category, nor can its failure be plausibly deduced from this cause.

6. One of the methods by which a juryman signified the vote for condemnation was the tracing of a line horizontally across a waxed tablet; the other involved the use of a pebble, which was dropped in one or the other of two urns, that of conviction or that of acquittal.

7. The wood of the fig-tree, when burned, gives off the most acrid smoke, and thus is eminently suited to the proud sourness of Philocleon's temper.

8. "To quarrel over the shade of an ass" meant to dispute about next to nothing. The ancients explained the origin of this idiom by an aetiological tale of a traveller who had hired an ass and, being observed by the owner resting in the shade which the animal cast, was sued by that imaginative and avaricious individual on the ground that it had been the ass and not its shade that the traveller had hired.

9. The goddess here invoked is Artemis.

10. "The crackling of fig-leaves in the fire" meant much ado about nothing.

11. "The parsley and the rue" signified the mere beginnings of anything.

12. The name Hippias contains the stem of the Greek word for horse (*hippos*). This remark and those of Bdelycleon in the preceding speech suggest that the word tyranny was in Aristophanes' day used as frequently and as loosely as fascism and communism are today.

662

13. A pun on the Greek word *choiros,* which means both "sow" and "female genitalia." Aristophanes had made extensive use of this ambiguous word in one of the best scenes in *The Acharnians* (765–817).

14. Those in the ancient world who were too poor to afford a purse were wont to carry small coins in their mouths.

15. When the jurymen had been deeply moved by the pleading of the accused and had decided on acquittal, they commanded him to descend from the rostrum; apparently this was by no means an infallible indication of acquittal, and the accused had the right to finish his speech.

16. Philocleon is comparing the thick and shaggy cloth of the pelisse to the intestines of an ox, which have a crinkly appearance.

17. The mention of the salary gives away the fact that it was merely as a common soldier that Philocleon had been sent to Paros.

18. In all three cases where Philocleon finishes the line he adds something unpleasantly appropriate to the guest who is supposed to have led off the song.

19. A pun on the Greek words *triarchoi,* "three kings" and *triorchoi,* "having three testicles," i.e., endowed with 50% more sexuality than normal.

V
PEACE

Characters in the Play

TRYGAEUS
TWO SERVANTS OF TRYGAEUS
DAUGHTERS OF TRYGAEUS
HERMES
WAR
TUMULT
HIEROCLES, *a Soothsayer*
AN ARMOURER
A SICKLE-MAKER
A CREST-MAKER
SON OF LAMACHUS
SON OF CLEONYMUS
CHORUS OF HUSBANDMEN

INTRODUCTION

AT THE Great Dionysia of 421 Aristophanes ushered in the best period of his extant work with *Peace,* which won the second prize, the first going to *The Flatterers* of Eupolis. The verdict of the audience, if just, is to be construed entirely as testimony to the superlative excellence of the older dramatist's production, and in no sense as a slur on what is very nearly the most delightful of the eleven comedies of Aristophanes that have come down to us. The play exhibits signs of having been hastily composed, but the infectious gaiety and spontaneous warmth with which it is so liberally endowed are attributable less to an impromptu composition than to the sentiments which the events and the hopes of the time had inspired in the poet's heart.

The war of the Athenians with the Peloponnesians had begun as long ago as 431, and a decade of fighting had sorely afflicted the inhabitants of the rural districts of Attica. The frequent invasions of the Lacedæmonians had compelled them to relinquish their ancestral farms and their beloved rustic life and to find such habitation as they could in the congested city, from whose walls they might tearfully observe the destruction of their houses and the devastation of their fields. But a powerful Peace Party, which they and their urban sympathizers might have organized, was forestalled of its effectiveness by the chicanery of the demagogues and the success of the navy. The repeated proposals of Sparta for a cessation of hostilities were haughtily rejected, and it was only in 422, when Athens had experienced two years of military reverses and Cleon had been killed in battle, that a definitely pacifistic policy was actively adopted. Sparta likewise, in spite of her recent successes, was known to be just as weary of the war as her opponent, and there was thus, in the early months of 421, every reason to anticipate a favourable issue of the negotiations that had been opened in the latter part of the previous year.

The second of the three peace-comedies was thus composed in an atmosphere radically different from that which attended the production of *The Acharnians* four years earlier, and the two plays show little similarity in their emotional colouring. The later comedy has little of satire in it; its

667

author is too happy for that, and what he has written is at once a hymn of thanksgiving, a dance of joy, and a bright revery of future felicity.

The opening of the play presents us with two slaves of Trygaeus, who are breathlessly kneading cakes of excrement and feeding them to a dung-beetle which their master is keeping in his stable. Like Dicaeopolis in *The Acharnians,* he has despaired of obtaining peace through ordinary legislative channels and has resolved to do something about it himself, but his sentiments are more panhellenic and his project more fantastic than those of the earlier pacifist, for he has resolved to go to none other than Zeus himself in order to put an end to the war. A previous effort to climb to the divine residence on ladders has netted him nothing more than a broken head, and he now proposes to fly to heaven on the back of his malodorous and economical Pegasus.

The journey is negotiated with complete success, and at the door of the palace of Zeus he is rudely accosted by Hermes, from whom, after an easy propitiation, he learns of the disappointing state of affairs which the war has brought about in the celestial regions. The stupidities of the Greeks have utterly exhausted the patience of the gods, and they have moved away, as far away as possible, leaving their mortal subjects to the mercy of War and his slave Tumult. The first act of the new master of Hellenic affairs has been to cast Peace into a deep pit and then to heap numerous stones on her. He has then procured a huge mortar, in which he intends to grind up the cities of Greece into a wretched paste. No sooner has Hermes reported this than the villain himself appears and begins to realize his gruesome intentions; the cities, represented by their most noted products, are one by one tossed into the mortar, but the malignant god lacks a pestle and experiences difficulties in obtaining one. Both Sparta and Athens have lost theirs; Cleon and Brasidas are dead now. Thus the horrible fate of Greece is momentarily averted and War departs to make his own pestle.

Trygaeus, emerging from his hiding-place, realizes that he must liberate Peace immediately or else relinquish all hope of ever seeing her again, and he therefore summons to his aid a number of labourers and farmers from all parts of Greece. The Chorus now enters, highly and, under the circumstances, perilously elated at the prospect of putting an end to the war. When quiet has finally been restored and the objections of Hermes have melted away at the promise of future glory and sacrifices, the difficult task of extricating Peace is undertaken, with great enthusiasm and greater inefficiency. The difficulties are delightfully Hellenic; the Boeotians are only pretending; Lamachus is in the way; the Argives laugh at the others while they profit from their troubles; the Megarians are trying hard, but are too undernourished to be of much use; some of the Greeks are pulling one way and some another; the Laconians do their part, along with the Athenians, but even here it is only the farmers that are doing any real work. Through *their* exertions Peace is at last hauled out of the pit, along with Opora and Theoria, and Trygaeus starts on his return journey to the earth, taking Opora to his marriage-bed and Theoria to the Senate. The Chorus now delivers the parabasis.

The anapests recite Aristophanes' claims to distinction as a comic poet. The ode begs the Muse to bring peace and attacks Carcinus and his sons as tragic poets. The antode extends this attack to others. The parabasis is incomplete, lacking the epirrhemes. Nor are these the only evidences of hurried writing, for in the anapests four lines are used verbatim from the parabasis of *The Wasps,* and the material generally is not new. More significant is the fact that indications of hasty composition are found nowhere else in the play, which would suggest that the parabases of most of the comedies were written last, after all the rest had been finished, and were thus regarded by the poet as something separate and independent.

At the conclusion of the parabasis Trygaeus comes limping in with Opora and Theoria, and almost immediately sets about preparing to enjoy the peace which he has obtained. Opora is taken into his house to be bathed and dressed for the wedding, Theoria is presented to the Senate, and a gala feast is begun. While Trygaeus and his servant are roasting the meat a belligerent soothsayer appears, mouthing oracles about the impossibility of ending the war (these were sounder prophecies than Aristophanes then realized), and trying by persuasion and by fraud to get a share of the feast. He is followed by a man who has been economically hard pressed by the war, a sickle-maker, who gratefully presents Trygæus with a large number of his products. Right on his heels comes a large group of the least pitiable victims of the peace, those most detestable of war-time profiteers, the manufacturers of armaments, whose spokesman strives vainly to realize a little something out of the large and unmarketable stocks which the sudden cessation of hostilities has left on their hands. Trygaeus rejects their offers with no less alacrity than scorn, and after the sons of Lamachus and Cleonymus have sung snatches of songs suited to their fathers' characters, Opora is brought out, and the comedy ends with the singing of the *Hymen Hymenaeus.*

A bare and compendious outline of its plot inevitably and always preserves the frame and omits the picture of an Aristophanic comedy, but such a presentation does a greater injustice to *Peace* than to any of the other plays, for its charm and its excellence reside less in the plot and its incidents than in the quality of their treatment and the freshness of their atmosphere. From this point of view *Peace* is at once a development out of the youthful exuberance of *The Acharnians* and a prelude to the mature perfection of *The Birds*. When he composed it the poet was exulting in the fine first flush of a happiness that he was never again to experience, and, confidently anticipating a return to the pristine joys of rural life, he produced a comedy that is saturated with sunshine and redolent of the country-side. Trygaeus is not Dicaeopolis, and Aristophanes would not again so thoroughly speak his mind through the mouth of one of his characters; but neither *The Acharnians* nor any other play as a whole contains so full a measure of its author's heart as does *Peace*. Where Aristophanes is happiest, there is he most candid also, and it is thus particularly gratifying to observe the truth of the further proposition that where he is happiest, there is he bawdiest also. That the scholars of the nineteenth century should have been unable or unwilling to understand what *Peace* so plainly declares about the most delightful side of Aristophanes' nature is less surprising than revealing.

PEACE

(SCENE:—*Behind the Orchestra on the right the farmhouse of* TRY-
GAEUS, *in the centre the mouth of a cave closed up with huge boulders, on
the left the palace of* ZEUS. *In front of the farmhouse is a stable, the door
of which is closed. Two of* TRYGAEUS' *slaves are seen in front of the stable,
one of them kneading cakes of dung, the other taking the finished cakes
and throwing them into the stable.*)

FIRST SERVANT

QUICK, quick, bring the dung-beetle his cake.

SECOND SERVANT

There it is. Give it to him, and may it kill him! And may he never eat
a better.

FIRST SERVANT

Now give him this other one kneaded up with ass's dung.

SECOND SERVANT

There! I've done that too. And where's what you gave him just now?
Surely he can't have devoured it yet!

FIRST SERVANT

Indeed he has; he snatched it, rolled it between his feet and bolted it.
Come, hurry up, knead up a lot and knead them stiffly.

SECOND SERVANT

Oh, scavengers, help me in the name of the gods, if you do not wish to
see me fall down choked.

FIRST SERVANT

Come, come, another made from the stool of a fairy's favourite. That
will be to the beetle's taste; he likes it well ground.

671

SECOND SERVANT

There! I am free at least from suspicion; none will accuse me of tasting what I mix.

FIRST SERVANT

Faugh! come, now another! keep on mixing with all your might.

SECOND SERVANT

By god, no. I can stand this awful cesspool stench no longer.

FIRST SERVANT

I shall bring you the whole ill-smelling gear.

SECOND SERVANT

Pitch it down the sewer sooner, and yourself with it. (*To the* AUDI-ENCE) Maybe, one of you can tell me where I can buy a stopped-up nose, for there is no work more disgusting than to mix food for a dung-beetle and to carry it to him. A pig or a dog will at least pounce upon our excrement without more ado, but this foul wretch affects the disdainful, the spoilt mistress, and won't eat unless I offer him a cake that has been kneaded for an entire day. . . . But let us open the door a bit ajar without his seeing it. Has he done eating? Come, pluck up courage, cram yourself till you burst! The cursed creature! It wallows in its food! It grips it between its claws like a wrestler clutching his opponent, and with head and feet together rolls up its paste like a rope-maker twisting a hawser. What an indecent, stinking, gluttonous beast! I don't know what angry god let this monster loose upon us, but of a certainty it was neither Aphrodité nor the Graces.

FIRST SERVANT

Who was it then?

SECOND SERVANT

No doubt Zeus, the God of the Thundercrap.[1]

FIRST SERVANT

But perhaps some spectator, some beardless youth, who thinks himself a sage, will say, "What is this? What does the beetle mean?" And then an Ionian, sitting next him, will add, "I think it's an allusion to Cleon, who so shamelessly feeds on filth all by himself."—But now I'm going indoors to fetch the beetle a drink.

SECOND SERVANT

As for me, I will explain the matter to you all, children, youths, grown-ups and old men, aye, even to the decrepit dotards. My master is mad, not as you are, but with another sort of madness, quite a new kind. The livelong day he looks open-mouthed towards heaven and never stops addressing Zeus. "Ah! Zeus," he cries, "what are thy intentions? Lay aside thy besom; do not sweep Greece away!" Ah! Hush, hush! I think I hear his voice!

TRYGAEUS (*from within*)
Oh! Zeus, what art thou going to do for our people? Dost thou not see this, that our cities will soon be but empty husks?

SECOND SERVANT
As I told you, that is his form of madness. There you have a sample of his follies. When his trouble first began to seize him, he said to himself, "By what means could I go straight to Zeus?" Then he made himself very slender little ladders and so clambered up towards heaven; but he soon came hurtling down again and broke his head. Yesterday, to our misfortune, he went out and brought us back this thoroughbred, but from where I know not, this great beetle, whose groom he has forced me to become. He himself caresses it as though it were a horse, saying, "Oh! my little Pegasus, my noble aerial steed, may your wings soon bear me straight to Zeus!" But what is my master doing? I must stoop down to look through this hole. Oh! great gods! Here! neighbours, run here quick! here is my master flying off mounted on his beetle as if on horseback.
(*The Machine brings in* TRYGAEUS *astride an enormous figure of a dung beetle with wings spread.*)

TRYGAEUS (*intoning*)
Gently, gently, go easy, beetle; don't start off so proudly, or trust at first too greatly to your powers; wait till you have sweated, till the beating of your wings shall make your limb joints supple. Above all things, don't let off some foul smell. I adjure you; else I would rather have you stay right in the stable.

SECOND SERVANT (*intoning*)
Poor master! Is he crazy?

TRYGAEUS (*intoning*)
Silence! silence!

SECOND SERVANT (*intoning*)
But why start up into the air on chance?

TRYGAEUS (*intoning*)
'Tis for the weal of all the Greeks; I am attempting a daring and novel feat.

SECOND SERVANT (*intoning*)
But what is your purpose? What useless folly!

TRYGAEUS (*intoning*)
No words of ill omen! Give vent to joy and command all men to keep silence, to close down their drains and privies with new tiles and to cork up their own arses.

FIRST SERVANT (*speaking*)
No, I shall not be silent, unless you tell me where you are going.

TRYGAEUS
Why, where am I likely to be going across the sky, if it be not to visit Zeus?

FIRST SERVANT
For what purpose?

TRYGAEUS
I want to ask him what he reckons to do for all the Greeks.

SECOND SERVANT
And if he doesn't tell you?

TRYGAEUS
I shall pursue him at law as a traitor who sells Greece to the Medes.

SECOND SERVANT
Death seize me, if I let you go.

TRYGAEUS
It is absolutely necessary.

SECOND SERVANT (*loudly*)
Alas! alas! dear little girls, your father is deserting you secretly to go to heaven. Ah! poor orphans, entreat him, beseech him.
(*The little daughters of* TRYGAEUS *come out.*)

LITTLE DAUGHTER (*singing*)
Father! father! what is this I hear? Is it true? What! you would leave me, you would vanish into the sky, you would go to the crows? [2] Impossible! Answer, father, if you love me.

TRYGAEUS (*singing*)
Yes, I am going. You hurt me too sorely, my daughters, when you ask me for bread, calling me your daddy, and there is not the ghost

of an obolus in the house; if I succeed and come back, you will have
a barley loaf every morning—and a punch in the eye for sauce!

LITTLE DAUGHTER

But how will you make the journey? There's no ship that will take you
there.

TRYGAEUS

No, but this winged steed will.

LITTLE DAUGHTER

But what an idea, papa, to harness a beetle, to fly to the gods on.

TRYGAEUS

We see from Aesop's fables that they alone can fly to the abode of the
Immortals.[3]

LITTLE DAUGHTER

Father, father, that's a tale nobody can believe! that such a smelly
creature can have gone to the gods.

TRYGAEUS

It went to have vengeance on the eagle and break its eggs.

LITTLE DAUGHTER

Why not saddle Pegasus? you would have a more tragic appearance in
the eyes of the gods.

TRYGAEUS

Eh! don't you see, little fool, that then twice the food would be wanted?
Whereas my beetle devours again as filth what I have eaten myself.

LITTLE DAUGHTER

And if it fell into the watery depths of the sea, could it escape with its
wings?

TRYGAEUS (*exposing himself*)

I am fitted with a rudder in case of need, and my Naxos beetle will serve
me as a boat.

LITTLE DAUGHTER

And what harbour will you put in at?

TRYGAEUS

Why, is there not the harbour of Cantharus at the Piraeus?

LITTLE DAUGHTER

Take care not to knock against anything and so fall off into space; once a cripple, you would be a fit subject for Euripides, who would put you into a tragedy.[4]

TRYGAEUS (*as the Machine hoists him higher*)

I'll see to it. Good-bye! (*To the Athenians*) You, for love of whom I brave these dangers, do ye neither fart nor crap for the space of three days, for, if, while cleaving the air, my steed should scent anything, he would fling me head foremost from the summit of my hopes.

(*Intoning*)

Now come, my Pegasus, get a-going with up-pricked ears and make your golden bridle resound gaily. Eh! what are you doing? What are you up to? Do you turn your nose towards the cesspools? Come, pluck up a spirit; rush upwards from the earth, stretch out your speedy wings and make straight for the palace of Zeus; for once give up foraging in your daily food.—Hi! you down there, what are you after now? Oh! my god! it's a man taking a crap in the Piraeus, close to the whorehouses. But is it my death you seek then, my death? Will you not bury that right away and pile a great heap of earth upon it and plant wild thyme therein and pour perfumes on it? If I were to fall from up here and misfortune happened to me, the town of Chios would owe a fine of five talents for my death, all because of your damned arse.

(*Speaking*)

Alas! how frightened I am! oh! I have no heart for jests. Ah! machinist, take great care of me. There is already a wind whirling round my navel; take great care or, from sheer fright, I shall form food for my beetle. . . . But I think I am no longer far from the gods; aye, that is the dwelling of Zeus, I perceive. (*The beetle descends and comes to a halt in front of the house of* ZEUS. TRYGAEUS *dismounts and knocks at the door.*) Hullo! Hi! where is the doorkeeper? Will no one open?

HERMES (*from within*)

I think I can sniff a man. (*Opening the door*) Why, what plague is this?

TRYGAEUS

A horse-beetle.

HERMES

Oh! impudent, shameless rascal! oh! scoundrel! triple scoundrel! the greatest scoundrel in the world! how did you come here? Oh! scoundrel of all scoundrels! your name? Reply.

TRYGAEUS

Triple scoundrel.

HERMES

Your country?

TRYGAEUS

Triple scoundrel.

HERMES

Your father?

TRYGAEUS

My father? Triple scoundrel.

HERMES

By the Earth, you shall die, unless you tell me your name.

TRYGAEUS

I am Trygaeus of the Athmonian deme, a good vine-dresser, little ad
dicted to quibbling and not at all an informer.

HERMES

Why do you come?

TRYGAEUS

I come to bring you this meat.

HERMES (*changing his tone*)
Ah! my good friend, did you have a good journey?

TRYGAEUS

Glutton, be off! I no longer seem a triple scoundrel to you. Come, call
Zeus.

HERMES

Ah! ah! you are a long way yet from reaching the gods, for they moved
yesterday.

TRYGAEUS

To what part of the earth?

HERMES

Eh! of the earth, did you say?

TRYGAEUS

In short, where are they then?

HERMES

Very far, very far, right at the furthest end of the dome of heaven.

TRYGAEUS

But why have they left you all alone here?

HERMES

I am watching what remains of the furniture, the little pots and pans, the bits of chairs and tables, and odd wine-jars.

TRYGAEUS

And why have the gods moved away?

HERMES

Because of their wrath against the Greeks. They have located War in the house they occupied themselves and have given him full power to do with you exactly as he pleases; then they went as high up as ever they could, so as to see no more of your fights and to hear no more of your prayers.

TRYGAEUS

What reason have they for treating us so?

HERMES

Because they have afforded you an opportunity for peace more than once, but you have always preferred war. If the Laconians got the very slightest advantage, they would exclaim, "By the Twin Brethren! the Athenians shall smart for this." If, on the contrary, the latter triumphed and the Laconians came with peace proposals, you would say, "By Demeter, they want to deceive us. No, by Zeus, we will not hear a word; they will always be coming as long as we hold Pylos."

TRYGAEUS

Yes, that is quite the style our folk do talk in.

HERMES

So that I don't know whether you will ever see Peace again.

TRYGAEUS

Why, where has she gone to then?

HERMES

War has cast her into a deep pit.

TRYGAEUS

Where?

HERMES

Down there, at the very bottom. And you see what heaps of stones he has piled over the top, so that you should never pull her out again.

TRYGAEUS

Tell me, what is War preparing against us?

HERMES

All I know is that last evening he brought along a huge mortar.

TRYGAEUS

And what is he going to do with his mortar?

HERMES

He wants to pound up all the cities of Greece in it. . . . But I must say good-bye, for I think he is coming out; what an uproar he is making!

(*He departs in haste.*)

TRYGAEUS

Ah! great gods let us seek safety; I think I already hear the noise of this fearful war mortar. (*He hides.*)

WAR (*enters, carrying a huge mortar*)

Oh! mortals, mortals, wretched mortals, how your jaws will snap!

TRYGAEUS

Oh! divine Apollo! what a prodigious big mortar! Oh, what misery the very sight of War causes me! This then is the foe from whom I fly, who is so cruel, so formidable, so stalwart, so solid on his legs!

WAR

Oh! Prasiae! thrice wretched, five times, aye, a thousand times wretched! for thou shalt be destroyed this day.

(*He throws some leeks into the mortar.*)

TRYGAEUS (*to the audience*)

This, gentlemen, does not concern *us* over much; it's only so much the worse for the Laconians.

WAR

Oh! Megara! Megara! how utterly are you going to be ground up! what fine mincemeat are you to be made into!

(*He throws in some garlic.*)

TRYGAEUS (*aside*)

Alas! alas! what bitter tears there will be among the Megarians!

WAR (*throwing in some cheese*)

Oh, Sicily! you too must perish! Your wretched towns shall be grated like this cheese. Now let us pour some Attic honey into the mortar.

(*He does so.*)

TRYGAEUS (*aside*)

Oh! I beseech you! use some other honey; this kind is worth four obols; be careful, oh! be careful of our Attic honey.

WAR

Hi! Tumult, you slave there!

TUMULT

What do you want?

WAR

Out upon you! Standing there with folded arms! Take this cuff on the head for your pains.

TUMULT

Oh! how it stings! Master, have you got garlic in your fist, I wonder?

WAR

Run and fetch me a pestle.

TUMULT

But we haven't got one; it was only yesterday we moved.

WAR

Go and fetch me one from Athens, and hurry, hurry!

TUMULT

I'll hurry; if I return without one, I shall have no cause for laughing.

(*He runs off.*)

TRYGAEUS (*to the audience*)

Ah! what is to become of us, wretched mortals that we are? See the danger that threatens if he returns with the pestle, for War will quietly amuse himself with pounding all the towns of Hellas to pieces. Ah! Bac‑chus! cause this herald of evil to perish on his road!

WAR (*to the returning* TUMULT)

Well?

TUMULT

Well, what?

WAR

You have brought back nothing?

TUMULT

Alas! the Athenians have lost their pestle—the tanner, who ground
Greece to powder.

TRYGAEUS

Oh! Athené, venerable mistress! it is well for our city he is dead, and
before he could serve us with *this* hash.

WAR

Then go and seek one at Sparta and have done with it!

TUMULT

Aye, aye, master!

(*He runs off.*)

WAR (*shouting after him*)

Be back as quick as ever you can.

TRYGAEUS (*to the audience*)

What is going to happen, friends? This is the critical hour. Ah! if there
is some initiate of Samothrace among you, this is surely the moment to
wish this messenger some accident—some sprain or strain.

TUMULT (*returning*)

Alas! alas! thrice again, alas!

WAR

What is it? Again you come back without it?

TUMULT

The Spartans too have lost their pestle.⁵

WAR

How, varlet!

TUMULT

They had lent it to their allies in Thrace, who have lost it for them.

TRYGAEUS

Long life to you, Thracians! My hopes revive, pluck up courage, mortals!

WAR

Take all this stuff; I am going in to make a pestle for myself.

(He goes in, followed by TUMULT.*)*

TRYGAEUS *(coming out of his hiding-place)*

Now is the time to sing as Datis did, as he masturbated at high noon, "Oh pleasure! oh enjoyment! oh delights!" Now, oh Greeks! is the moment when freed of quarrels and fighting, we should rescue sweet Peace and draw her out of this pit, before some other pestle prevents us. Come, labourers, merchants, workmen, artisans, strangers, whether you be domiciled or not, islanders, come here, Greeks of all countries, come hurrying here with picks and levers and ropes! This is the moment to drain a cup in honour of the Good Genius.

(The CHORUS *enters; it consists of labourers and farmers from various Greek states.)*

LEADER OF THE CHORUS

Come hither all! quick, quick, hasten to the rescue! All peoples of Greece, now is the time or never, for you to help each other. You see yourselves freed from battles and all their horrors of bloodshed. The day hateful to Lamachus has come. *(To* TRYGAEUS*)* Come then, what must be done? Give your orders, direct us, for I swear to work this day without ceasing, until with the help of our levers and our engines we have drawn back into light the greatest of all goddesses, her to whom the olive is so dear.

TRYGAEUS

Silence! if War should hear your shouts of joy he would bound forth from his retreat in fury.

LEADER OF THE CHORUS

Such a decree overwhelms us with joy; how different to the edict, which bade us muster with provisions for three days.

TRYGAEUS

Let us beware lest the cursed Cerberus prevent us even from the nethermost hell from delivering the goddess by his furious howling, just as he did when on earth.

LEADER OF THE CHORUS

Once we have hold of her, none in the world will be able to take her from us. Huzza! huzza!

TRYGAEUS

You will work my death if you don't subdue your shouts. War will come running out and trample everything beneath his feet.

LEADER OF THE CHORUS

Well then! *Let* him confound, let him trample, let him overturn every-thing! We cannot help giving vent to our joy.

TRYGAEUS

Oh! cruel fate! My friends! in the name of the gods, what possesses you? Your dancing will wreck the success of a fine undertaking.

LEADER OF THE CHORUS

It's not I who want to dance; it's my legs that bound with delight.

TRYGAEUS

Enough, please, cease your gambols.

LEADER OF THE CHORUS

There! That's all.

TRYGAEUS

You say so, and nevertheless you go on.

LEADER OF THE CHORUS

Yet one more figure and it's done.

TRYGAEUS

Well, just this one; then you must dance no more.

LEADER OF THE CHORUS

No, no more dancing, if we can help you.

TRYGAEUS

But look, you are not stopping even now.

LEADER OF THE CHORUS

By Zeus, I am only throwing up my right leg, that's all.

TRYGAEUS

Come, I grant you that, but pray, annoy me no further.

LEADER OF THE CHORUS

Ah! the left leg too will have its fling; well, that's its right. I am so happy, so delighted at not having to carry my buckler any more. I fart for joy and I laugh more than if I had cast my old age, as a serpent does its skin.

TRYGAEUS

No, it's not time for joy yet, for you are not sure of success. But when you have got the goddess, then rejoice, shout and laugh; thenceforward you will be able to sail or stay at home, to make love or sleep, to attend festivals and processions, to play at cottabos, live like true Sybarites and to shout, Io, io!

CHORUS (*singing*)

Ah! God grant we may see the blessed day. I have suffered so much; have so oft slept with Phormio on hard beds. You will no longer find me a bitter and angry judge . . .

TRYGAEUS (*singing*)

Nor, naturally, hard in your ways, as heretofore.

CHORUS (*singing*)

. . . but turned indulgent and grown younger by twenty years through happiness. We have been killing ourselves long enough, tiring ourselves out with going to the Lyceum and returning laden with spear and buckler.—But what can we do to please you? Come, speak; for 'tis a good Fate that has named you our leader.

TRYGAEUS

How shall we set about removing these stones?

HERMES (*who has just returned*)

Rash reprobate, what do you propose doing?

TRYGAEUS

Nothing bad, as Cillicon said.

HERMES

You are undone, you wretch.

TRYGAEUS

Yes, if the lot had to decide my life, for Hermes would know how to turn the chance.

HERMES

You are lost, you are dead.

TRYGAEUS

On what day?

HERMES

This instant.

TRYGAEUS

But I have not provided myself with flour and cheese yet [6] to start for death.

HERMES

You *are* kneaded and ground already, I tell you.

TRYGAEUS

Hah! I have not yet tasted that gentle pleasure.

HERMES

Don't you know that Zeus has decreed death for him who is caught exhuming Peace?

TRYGAEUS

What! must I really and truly die?

HERMES

You must.

TRYGAEUS

Well then, lend me three drachmae to buy a young pig; I wish to have myself initiated before I die.[7]

HERMES

Oh! Zeus, the Thunderer!

TRYGAEUS

I adjure you in the name of the gods, master, don't report us!

HERMES

I may not, I cannot keep silent.

TRYGAEUS

In the name of the meats which I brought you so good-naturedly.

HERMES

Why, wretched man, Zeus will annihilate me, if I do not shout out at the top of my voice, to inform him what you are plotting.

TRYGAEUS

Oh, no! don't shout, I beg you, dear little Hermes. . . . And what are you doing, comrades? You stand there as though you were stocks and stones. Wretched men, speak, entreat him at once; otherwise he will be shouting.

CHORUS (*singing*)

Oh! mighty Hermes! do not do it; no, do not do it! If ever you have eaten some young pig, sacrificed by us on your altars, with pleasure, may this offering not be without value in your sight to-day.

TRYGAEUS (*singing*)

Do you not hear them wheedling you, mighty god?

CHORUS (*singing*)

Be not pitiless toward our prayers; permit us to deliver the goddess. Oh! the most human, the most generous of the gods, be favourable toward us, if it be true that you detest the haughty crests and proud brows of Pisander; we shall never cease, oh master, offering you sacred victims and solemn prayers.

TRYGAEUS

Have mercy, mercy, let yourself be touched by their words; never was your worship so dear to them as to-day. (*Aside*) Really they are the greatest thieves that ever were. (*To* HERMES) And I shall reveal to you a great and terrible plot that is being hatched against the gods.

HERMES

Hah! speak and perchance I shall let myself be softened.

TRYGAEUS

Know then, that the Moon and that infamous Sun are plotting against you, and want to deliver Greece into the hands of the barbarians.

HERMES

What for?

TRYGAEUS

Because it is to you that we sacrifice, whereas the barbarians worship them; hence they would like to see you destroyed, that they alone might receive the offerings.

HERMES

Is it then for this reason that these untrustworthy charioteers have for so long been defrauding us, one of them robbing us of daylight and the other nibbling away at the other's disk?

TRYGAEUS

Yes, certainly. So therefore, Hermes, my friend, help us with your whole heart to find and deliver the captive and we will celebrate the great Panathenaea in your honour as well as all the festivals of the other gods; for Hermes shall be the Mysteries, the Dipolia, the Adonia; everywhere

the towns, freed from their miseries, will sacrifice to Hermes the Libera-
tor; you will be loaded with benefits of every kind, and to start with, I
offer you this cup for libations as your first present.

HERMES

Ah! how golden cups do influence me! Come, friends, get to work. To
the pit quickly, pick in hand, and drag away the stones.

LEADER OF THE CHORUS

We go, but you, cleverest of all the gods, supervise our labours; tell
us, good workman as you are, what we must do; we shall obey your orders
with alacrity.

(*They begin to lift the stones.*)

TRYGAEUS

Quick, reach me your cup, and let us preface our work by addressing
prayers to the gods.

HERMES

Libation! Libation! Silence! Silence! Let us offer our libations and
our prayers, so that this day may begin an era of unalloyed happiness for
Greece and that he who has bravely pulled at the rope with us may never
resume his buckler.

TRYGAEUS

Aye, may we pass our lives in peace, caressing our mistresses and pok ·
ing the fire.

HERMES

May he who would prefer the war, oh Dionysus . . .

TRYGAEUS

Be ever drawing barbed arrows out of his elbows.

HERMES

If there be a citizen, greedy for military rank and honours, who refuses,
oh, divine Peace! to restore you to daylight . . .

TRYGAEUS

May he behave as cowardly as Cleonymus on the battlefield.

HERMES

If a lance-maker or a dealer in shields desires war for the sake of better
trade . . .

TRYGAEUS

May he be taken by pirates and eat nothing but barley.

HERMES

If some ambitious man does not help us, because he wants to become
a General, or if a slave is plotting to pass over to the enemy . . .

TRYGAEUS

Let his limbs be broken on the wheel, may he be beaten to death with
rods!

HERMES

As for us, may Fortune favour us! Io! Paean, Io!

TRYGAEUS

Don't say Paean, but simply, Io.

HERMES

Very well, then! Io! Io! I'll simply say, Io!

TRYGAEUS

To Hermes, the Graces, the Horae, Aphrodité, Eros!

HERMES

But not to Ares.

TRYGAEUS

No.

HERMES

Nor to Enyalius.

TRYGAEUS

No.

(*The stones have been removed and a rope attached to the cover of the
pit. The indented portions of the following scene are a sort of chanty.*)

HERMES

Come, all strain at the ropes to tear off the cover. Pull!

CHORUS

Heave away, heave, heave, oh!

HERMES

Come, pull harder, harder.

CHORUS

Heave away, heave, heave, oh!

HERMES

Still harder, harder still.

CHORUS

Heave away, heave! Heave away, heave, heave, oh!

TRYGAEUS

Come, come, there is no working together. Come! all pull at the
same instant! you Boeotians are only pretending. Beware!

HERMES

Come, heave away, heave!

TRYGAEUS

Heave away, heave oh!

CHORUS

Hi! you two pull as well.

TRYGAEUS

Why, I am pulling, I am hanging on to the rope and straining till
I am almost off my feet; I am working with all my might.

CHORUS

Why does not the work advance then?

TRYGAEUS

Lamachus, this is terrible! You are in the way, sitting there. We have
no use for your Medusa's head, friend. But wait, the Argives have not
pulled the least bit; they have done nothing but laugh at us for our pains
while they were getting gain with both hands.

HERMES

Ah! my dear sir, the Laconians at all events pull with vigour.

TRYGAEUS

But look! only those among them who generally hold the plough-tail
show any zeal, while the armourers impede them in their efforts.

HERMES

And the Megarians too are doing nothing, yet look how they are pulling and showing their teeth like famished curs.

TRYGAEUS

The poor wretches are dying of hunger I suppose.

HERMES

This won't do, friends. Come! all together! Everyone to the work and
with a good heart for the business.

CHORUS

Heave away, heave!

HERMES

Harder!

CHORUS

Heave away, heave!

HERMES

Come on then, by heaven.

CHORUS

We are moving it a little.

TRYGAEUS

Isn't it terrible and stupid! some pull one way and others another.
You Argives there, beware of a thrashing!

HERMES

Come, put your strength into it.

TRYGAEUS

Heave away, heave!

CHORUS

There are many ill-disposed folk among us.

TRYGAEUS

Do you at least, who long for peace, pull heartily.

CHORUS

But there are some who prevent us.

HERMES

Off to the Devil with you, Megarians! The goddess hates you. She
recollects that you were the first to rub her the wrong way. Athenians,
you are not well placed for pulling. There you are too busy with law-suits;
if you really want to free the goddess, get down a little towards the sea.[8]

LEADER OF THE CHORUS

Come, friends, none but husbandmen on the rope.

HERMES

Ah! that will do ever so much better.

LEADER OF THE CHORUS

He says the thing is going well. Come, all of you, together and with a will.

TRYGAEUS

It's the husbandmen who are doing all the work.

CHORUS

Come then, come, and all together!

HERMES

Hah! hah! at last there is some unanimity in the work.

CHORUS

Don't let us give up, let us redouble our efforts.

HERMES

There! now we have it!

CHORUS

Come then, all together! Heave away, heave! Heave away, heave! Heave away, heave! Heave away, heave! Heave away, heave! All together!

(PEACE *is drawn out of the pit. With her come* OPORA *and* THEORIA.)

TRYGAEUS

Oh! venerated goddess, who givest us our grapes, where am I to find the ten-thousand-gallon words wherewith to greet thee? I have none such at home. Oh! hail to thee, Opora, and thee, Theoria! How beautiful is thy face! How sweet thy breath! What gentle fragrance comes from thy bosom, gentle as freedom from military duty, as the most dainty perfumes!

HERMES

Is it then a smell like a soldier's knapsack?

TRYGAEUS

Oh! hateful soldier! your hideous satchel makes me sick! it stinks like the belching of onions, whereas this lovable deity has the odour of sweet fruits, of festivals, of the Dionysia, of the harmony of flutes, of the tragic poets, of the verses of Sophocles, of the phrases of Euripides . . .

HERMES

That's a foul calumny, you wretch! She detests that framer of subtleties and quibbles.

TRYGAEUS (*ignoring this*)

. . . of ivy, of straining-bags for wine, of bleating ewes, of provision-laden women hastening to the kitchen, of the tipsy servant wench, of the upturned wine-jar, and of a whole heap of other good things.

HERMES

Then look how the reconciled towns chat pleasantly together, how they laugh . . .

TRYGAEUS

And yet they are all cruelly mishandled; their wounds are bleeding still.

HERMES

But let us also scan the mien of the spectators; we shall thus find out the trade of each.

TRYGAEUS

Good god!

HERMES

Look at that poor crest-maker, tearing at his hair . . .

TRYGAEUS

. . . and at that pike-maker, who has just farted in yon sword-cutler's face.

HERMES

And do you see with what pleasure this sickle-maker . . .

TRYGAEUS

. . . is thumbing his nose at the spear-maker?

HERMES

Now tell the husbandmen to be off.

TRYGAEUS

Listen, good folk! Let the husbandmen take their farming tools and return to their fields as quickly as possible, but without either sword, spear or javelin. All is as quiet as if Peace had been reigning for a century. Come, let everyone go and till the earth, singing the Paean.

LEADER OF THE CHORUS (*to* PEACE)

Oh, thou, whom men of standing desired and who art good to husbandmen, I have gazed upon thee with delight; and now I go to greet my vines, to caress after so long an absence the fig trees I planted in my youth.

TRYGAEUS

Friends, let us first adore the goddess, who has delivered us from crests and Gorgons; then let us hurry to our farms, having first bought a nice little piece of salt fish to eat in the fields.

HERMES

By Posidon! what a fine crew they make and dense as the crust of a cake; they are as nimble as guests on their way to a feast.

TRYGAEUS

See, how their iron spades glitter and how beautifully their three-pronged mattocks glisten in the sun! How regularly they align the plants! I also burn to go into the country and to turn over the earth I have so long neglected.—Friends, do you remember the happy life that Peace afforded us formerly; can you recall the splendid baskets of figs, both fresh and dried, the myrtles, the sweet wine, the violets blooming near the spring, and the olives, for which we have wept so much? Worship, adore the goddess for restoring you so many blessings.

CHORUS (*singing*)

Hail! hail! thou beloved divinity! thy return overwhelms us with joy. When far from thee, my ardent wish to see my fields again made me pine with regret. From thee came all blessings. Oh! much desired Peace! thou art the sole support of those who spend their lives tilling the earth. Under thy rule we had a thousand delicious enjoyments at our beck; thou wert the husbandman's wheaten cake and his safeguard. So that our vineyards, our young fig-tree woods and all our plantations hail thee with delight and smile at thy coming.

LEADER OF THE CHORUS

But where was she then, I wonder, all the long time she spent away from us? Hermes, thou benevolent god, tell us!

HERMES

Wise husbandmen, hearken to my words, if you want to know why she was lost to you. The start of our misfortunes was the exile of Phidias; Pericles feared he might share his ill-luck, he mistrusted your peevish nature and, to prevent all danger to himself, he threw out that little spark, the Megarian decree, set the city aflame, and blew up the conflagration with a hurricane of war, so that the smoke drew tears from all Greeks both here and over there. At the very outset of this fire our vines were a-crackle, our casks knocked together; it was beyond the power of any man to stop the disaster, and Peace disappeared.

TRYGAEUS

That, by Apollo! is what no one ever told me; I could not think what connection there could be between Phidias and Peace.

LEADER OF THE CHORUS

Nor I, until now. This accounts for her beauty, if she is related to him. There are so many things that escape us.

HERMES

Then, when the towns subject to you saw that you were angered one against the other and were showing each other your teeth like dogs, they hatched a thousand plots to pay you no more dues and gained over the chief citizens of Sparta at the price of gold. They, being as shamelessly greedy as they were faithless in diplomacy, chased off Peace with ignominy to let loose War. Though this was profitable to *them*, it was the ruin of the husbandmen, who were innocent of all blame; for, in revenge, your galleys went out to devour their figs.

TRYGAEUS

And with justice too; did they not break down my black fig tree, which I had planted and dunged with my own hands?

LEADER OF THE CHORUS

Yes, by Zeus! yes, that was well done; the wretches broke a chest for me with stones, which held six medimni of corn.

HERMES

Then the rural labourers flocked into the city [9] and let themselves be bought over like the others. Not having even a grape-stone to munch and longing after their figs, they looked towards the demagogues. These well knew that the poor were driven to extremity and lacked even bread; but they nevertheless drove away the Goddess, each time she reappeared in answer to the wish of the country, with their loud shrieks that were as sharp as pitchforks; furthermore, they attacked the well-filled purses of the richest among our allies on the pretence that they belonged to Brasidas' party. And then you would tear the poor accused wretch to pieces with your teeth; for the city, all pale with hunger and cowed with terror, gladly snapped up any calumny that was thrown it to devour. So the strangers, seeing what terrible blows the informers dealt, sealed their lips with gold. They grew rich, while you, alas! you could only see that Greece was going to ruin. It was the tanner who was the author of all this woe.

TRYGAEUS

Enough said, Hermes leave that man in Hades, whither he has gone; he no longer belongs to us, but rather to you. That he was a cheat, a

braggart, a calumniator when alive, why, nothing could be truer; but anything you might say now would be an insult to one of your own folk.[10]
(*To* PEACE) Oh! venerated Goddess! why art thou silent?

HERMES

And how could she speak to the spectators? She is too angry at all that
they have made her suffer.

TRYGAEUS

At least let her speak a little to you, Hermes.

HERMES

Tell me, my dear, what are your feelings with regard to them? Come,
you relentless foe of all bucklers, speak; I am listening to you. (PEACE
whispers into HERMES' *ear.*) Is that your grievance against them? Yes,
yes, I understand. Hearken, you folk, this is her complaint. She says,
that after the affair of Pylos she came to you unbidden to bring you a
basket full of truces and that you thrice repulsed her by your votes in
the assembly.

TRYGAEUS

Yes, we did wrong, but forgive us, for our mind was then entirely ab-
sorbed in leather.

HERMES

Listen again to what she has just asked me. Who was her greatest foe
here? and furthermore, had she a friend who exerted himself to put an
end to the fighting?

TRYGAEUS

Her most devoted friend was Cleonymus; it is undisputed.

HERMES

How then did Cleonymus behave in fights?

TRYGAEUS

Oh! the bravest of warriors! Only he was not born of the father he
claims; he showed it quick enough in the army by throwing away his
weapons.

HERMES

There is yet another question she has just put to me. Who rules now i ᐧ
the rostrum?

TRYGAEUS

It's Hyperbolus who now holds empire on the Pnyx. (*To* PEACE)
What now? you turn away your head!

HERMES

She is vexed, that the people should give themselves a wretch of that
kind for their chief.

TRYGAEUS

Oh! we shall not employ him again; but the people, seeing themselves
without a leader, took him haphazard, just as a man, who is naked,
springs upon the first cloak he sees.

HERMES

She asks, what will be the result of such a choice by the city?

TRYGAEUS

We shall be more far-seeing in consequence.

HERMES

And why?

TRYGAEUS

Because he is a lamp-maker. Formerly we only directed our business
by groping in the dark; now we shall only deliberate by lamplight.

HERMES

Oh! oh! what questions she does order me to put to you!

TRYGAEUS

What are they?

HERMES

She wants to have news of a whole heap of old-fashioned things she
left here. First of all, how is Sophocles?

TRYGAEUS

Very well, but something very strange has happened to him.

HERMES

What then?

TRYGAEUS

He has turned from Sophocles into Simonides.

HERMES

Into Simonides? How so?

TRYGAEUS

Because, though old and broken-down as he is, he would put to sea
on a hurdle to gain an obolus.

HERMES

And wise Cratinus, is he still alive?

TRYGAEUS

He died about the time of the Laconian invasion.

HERMES

How?

TRYGAEUS

Of a swoon. He could not bear the shock of seeing one of his casks full
of wine broken. Ah! what a number of other misfortunes our city has
suffered! So, dearest mistress, nothing can now separate us from thee.

HERMES

If that be so, receive Opora here for a wife; take her to the country,
live with her, and grow fine grapes together.

TRYGAEUS (*to* OPORA)

Come, my dear one, come and accept my kisses. (*To* HERMES) Tell me,
Hermes, my master, do you think it would hurt me to love her a little,
after so long an abstinence?

HERMES

No, not if you swallow a potion of penny-royal afterwards.[11] But hasten to lead Theoria to the Senate; that was where she lodged before.

TRYGAEUS

Oh! fortunate Senate! Thanks to Theoria, what soups you will swallow for the space of three days! how you will devour meats and cooked
tripe! Come, farewell, friend Hermes!

HERMES

And to you also, my dear sir, may you have much happiness, and don't
forget me.

TRYGAEUS (*looking around for his dung-beetle*)

Come, beetle, home, home, and let us fly on a swift wing.

HERMES

Oh! he is no longer here.

TRYGAEUS

Where has he gone to then?

HERMES

He is 'harnessed to the chariot of Zeus and bears the thunderbolts.'

TRYGAEUS

But where will the poor wretch get his food?

HERMES

He will eat Ganymede's ambrosia.

TRYGAEUS

Very well then, but how am I going to descend?

HERMES

Oh! never fear, there is nothing simpler; place yourself beside the goddess.

TRYGAEUS

Come, my pretty maidens, follow me quickly; there are plenty of men
waiting for you with their tools ready.

(*He goes out, with* OPORA *and* THEORIA.)

LEADER OF THE CHORUS

Farewell and good luck be yours! Let us begin by handing over all this
gear to the care of our servants, for no place is less safe than a theatre;
there is always a crowd of thieves prowling around it, seeking to find some
mischief to do. Come, keep a good watch over all this. As for ourselves,
let us explain to the spectators what we have in our minds, the purpose of
our play.

(*The* CHORUS *turns and faces the audience.*)

Undoubtedly the comic poet who mounted the stage to praise himself
in the parabasis would deserve to be handed over to the sticks of the
beadles. Nevertheless, oh Muse, if it be right to esteem the most honest
and illustrious of our comic writers at his proper value, permit our poet
to say that he thinks he has deserved a glorious renown. First of all, he is
the one who has compelled his rivals no longer to scoff at rags or to war
with lice; and as for those Heracleses, always chewing and ever hungry,
he was the first to cover them with ridicule and to chase them from the
stage;[12] he has also dismissed that slave, whom one never failed to set
weeping before you, so that his comrade might have the chance of jeering
at his stripes and might ask, "Wretch, what has happened to your hide?
Has the lash rained an army of its thongs on you and laid your back
waste?" After having delivered us from all these wearisome ineptitudes

and these low buffooneries, he has built up for us a great art, like a palace with high towers, constructed of fine phrases, great thoughts and of jokes not common on the streets. Moreover it's not obscure private persons or women that he stages in his comedies; but, bold as Heracles, it's the very greatest whom he attacks, undeterred by the fetid stink of leather or the threats of hearts of mud. He has the right to say, "I am the first ever dared to go straight for that beast with the sharp teeth and the terrible eyes that flashed lambent fire like those of Cynna, surrounded by a hundred lewd flatterers, who spittle-licked him to his heart's content; it had a voice like a roaring torrent, the stench of a seal, the unwashed balls of a Lamia and the arse of a camel.[18] I did not recoil in horror at the sight of such a monster, but fought him relentlessly to win your deliverance and that of the islanders." Such are the services which should be graven in your recollection and entitle me to your thanks. Yet I have not been seen frequenting the wrestling school intoxicated with success and trying to seduce young boys; but I took all my theatrical gear and returned straight home. I pained folk but little and caused them much amusement; my conscience rebuked me for nothing. (*More and more rapidly from here on*) Hence both grown men and youths should be on my side and I likewise invite the bald to give me their votes; for, if I triumph, everyone will say, both at table and at festivals, "Carry this to the bald man, give these cakes to the bald one, do not grudge the poet whose talent shines as bright as his own bare skull the share he deserves."

FIRST SEMI-CHORUS (*singing*)

Oh, Muse! drive the war far from our city and come to preside over our dances, if you love me; come and celebrate the nuptials of the gods, the banquets of us mortals and the festivals of the fortunate; these are the themes that inspire thy most poetic songs. And should Carcinus come to beg thee for admission with his sons to thy chorus, refuse all traffic with them; remember they are but gelded birds, stork-necked dancers, mannikins about as tall as a goat's turd, in fact machine-made poets. Contrary to all expectation, the father has at last managed to finish a piece, but he admits that a cat strangled it one fine evening.

SECOND SEMI-CHORUS (*singing*)

Such are the songs with which the Muse with the glorious hair inspires the able poet and which enchant the assembled populace, when the spring swallow twitters beneath the foliage; but the god spare us from the chorus of Morsimus and that of Melanthius! Oh! what a bitter discordancy grated upon my ears that day when the tragic chorus was directed by this same Melanthius and his brother, these two Gorgons, these two Harpies, the plague of the seas, whose gluttonous bellies devour the entire race of fishes, these followers of old women, these goats with their stinking arm-pits. Oh! Muse, spit upon them abundantly and keep the feast gaily with me.

(TRYGAEUS *enters, limping painfully, accompanied by* OPORA *and* THEORIA.)

TRYGAEUS

Ah! it's a rough job getting to the gods! my legs are as good as broken through it. (*To the audience*) How small you were, to be sure, when seen from heaven! you had all the appearance too of being great rascals; but seen close, you look even worse.

SERVANT (*coming out of* TRYGAEUS' *house*)
Is that you, master?

TRYGAEUS

So I've been told.

SERVANT

What has happened to you?

TRYGAEUS

My legs pain me; it was such a damned long journey.

SERVANT

Oh! tell me . . .

TRYGAEUS

What?

SERVANT

Did you see any other man besides yourself strolling about in heaven?

TRYGAEUS

No, only the souls of two or three dithyrambic poets.

SERVANT

What were they doing up there?

TRYGAEUS

They were seeking to catch some lyric exordia as they flew by immersed in the billows of the air.

SERVANT

Is it true, what they tell us, that men are turned into stars after death?

TRYGAEUS

Quite true.

SERVANT

Then what star has Ion of Chios turned into?

TRYGAEUS

The Morning Star, the one he wrote a poem about; as soon as he got up there, everyone called him the Morning Star.

SERVANT

And those stars like sparks, that plough up the air as they dart across the sky.

TRYGAEUS

They are the rich leaving the feast with a lantern and a light inside it.— But hurry up, show this young girl into my house, (*pointing to* OPORA) clean out the bath, heat some water and prepare the nuptial couch for herself and me. When that's done, come back here; meanwhile I am off to present this other one to the Senate.

SERVANT

But where then did you get these girls?

TRYGAEUS

Where? why in heaven.

SERVANT

I would not give more than an obolus for gods who have got to keeping brothels like us mere mortals.

TRYGAEUS

They are not all like that, but there are some up there too who live by this trade.

SERVANT

Come, that's rich! But tell me, shall I give her something to eat?

TRYGAEUS

No, for she would touch neither bread nor cake; she is used to licking ambrosia at the table of the gods.

SERVANT

Well, we can give her something to lick down here too.

(*He takes* OPORA *into the house.*)

CHORUS (*singing*)
Here is a truly happy old man, as far as I can judge.

TRYGAEUS (*singing*)
Ah! but what shall I be, when you see me presently dressed for the
wedding?

CHORUS (*singing*)
Made young again by love and scented with perfumes, your lot
will be one we all shall envy.

TRYGAEUS (*singing*)
And when I lie beside her and fondle her breasts?

CHORUS (*singing*)
Oh! then you will be happier than those spinning-tops who call
Carcinus their father.

TRYGAEUS (*singing*)
And I well deserve it; have I not bestridden a beetle to save the
Greeks, who now, thanks to me, can make love at their ease and
sleep peacefully on their farms?

SERVANT (*returning from the house*)
The girl has quitted the bath; she is charming from head to foot, belly
and buttocks too; the cake is baked and they are kneading the sesamé-
biscuit; nothing is lacking but the bridegroom's tool.

TRYGAEUS
Let us first hasten to lodge Theoria in the hands of the Senate.

SERVANT
Tell me, who is this woman?

TRYGAEUS
Why, it's Theoria, with whom we used formerly to go to Brauron, to get
tipsy and frolic. I had the greatest trouble to get hold of her.

SERVANT
Ah! you charmer! what pleasure your pretty bottom will afford me
every four years!

TRYGAEUS (*to the audience*)
Let's see, which one of you is steady enough to be trusted by the Senate
with the care of this charming wench? (*to the* SERVANT) Hi! you, friend!
what are you drawing there?

SERVANT (*who has been making signs in the air*)
It's er . . . well, at the Isthmian Games I shall have a tent for my tour.

TRYGAEUS (*to the audience*)
Come, who wishes to take the charge of her? No one? Come, Theoria, I
am going to lead you into the midst of the spectators and confide you
to their care.

SERVANT
Ah! there is one who makes a sign to you.

TRYGAEUS
Who is it?

SERVANT
It's Ariphrades. He wishes to take her home at once.

TRYGAEUS
No, he must not. He would soon have her done for, absorbing all her
life-force. Come, Theoria, take off all these clothes. (THEORIA *undresses.
As soon as she is nude,* TRYGAEUS *conducts her to the front row of seats,
where the* SENATORS *sit.*) Senate, Prytanes, gaze upon Theoria and see
what precious blessings I place in your hands. Hasten to raise its limbs
and to immolate the victim. And look at this chimney.

SERVANT
God, what a beautiful one! It's black with smoke because the Senate
used to do its cooking there before the war.[14]

TRYGAEUS
Now that you have found Theoria again, you can start the most charming games from to-morrow, wrestling with her on the ground, on all fours,
or you can lay her on her side, or stand before her with bent knees, or,
well rubbed with oil, you can boldly enter the lists, as in the Pancratium,
belabouring your foe with blows from your fist or something else. The next
day you will celebrate equestrian games, in which the riders will ride side
by side, or else the chariot teams, thrown one on top of another, panting
and whinnying, will roll and knock against each other on the ground,
while other rivals, thrown out of their seats, will fall before reaching the
goal, utterly exhausted by their efforts.—Come, Prytanes, take Theoria.
Oh! look how graciously yonder fellow has received her; you would not
have been in such a hurry to introduce her to the Senate, if nothing were
coming to you through it;[15] you would not have failed to plead some
holiday as an excuse.

CHORUS (*singing*)
Such a man as you assures the happiness of all his fellow-citizens.

TRYGAEUS (*singing*)
When you are gathering your vintages you will prize me even better.

CHORUS (*singing*)
E'en from to-day we hail you as the deliverer of mankind.

TRYGAEUS (*singing*)
Wait until you have drunk a beaker of new wine, before you appraise my true merits.

CHORUS (*singing*)
Excepting the gods, there is none greater than yourself, and that will ever be our opinion.

TRYGAEUS (*singing*)
Yea, Trygaeus of Athmonia has deserved well of you, he has freed both husbandman and craftsman from the most cruel ills; he has vanquished Hyberbolus.

SERVANT
Well then, what must be done now?

TRYGAEUS
You must offer pots of green-stuff to the goddess to consecrate her altars.

SERVANT
Pots of green-stuff as we do to poor Hermes—and even he thinks the fare pretty mean?

TRYGAEUS
What will you offer then? A fatted bull?

SERVANT
Oh no! I don't want to start bellowing the battle-cry.[16]

TRYGAEUS
A great fat swine then?

SERVANT
No, no.

TRYGAEUS

Why not?

SERVANT

We don't want any of the swinishness of Theagenes.

TRYGAEUS

What other victim do you prefer then?

SERVANT

A sheep.

TRYGAEUS

A sheep?

SERVANT

Yes.

TRYGAEUS

But that's the Ionic form of the word.

SERVANT

Purposely. So that if anyone in the assembly says, "We must go to war,"
all may start bleating in alarm, "Oï, oï."

TRYGAEUS

A brilliant idea.

SERVANT

And we shall all be lambs one toward the other, yes, and milder still
toward the allies.

TRYGAEUS

Then go for the sheep and haste to bring it back with you; I will prepare the altar for the sacrifice.

(*They both leave.*)

CHORUS (*singing*)

How everything succeeds to our wish, when the gods are willing
and Fortune favours us! how opportunely everything falls out.

TRYGAEUS (*returning*)

Nothing could be truer, for look! here stands the altar all ready at my
door.

(*He enters his house.*)

CHORUS (*singing*)

Hurry, hurry, for the winds are fickle; make haste, while the divine will is set on stopping this cruel war and is showering on us the most striking benefits.

TRYGAEUS (*returning*)

Here is the basket of barley-seed mingled with salt, the chaplet and the sacred knife; and there is the fire; so we are only waiting for the sheep.

CHORUS (*singing*)

Hasten, hasten, for, if Chaeris sees you, he will come without bidding, he and his flute; and when you see him puffing and panting and out of breath, you will have to give him something.

TRYGAEUS (*to the* SERVANT *who has returned with a sheep and a vase of water*)

Come, seize the basket and take the lustral water and hurry to circle round the altar to the right.

SERVANT

There! that's done. What is your next bidding?

TRYGAEUS

Wait. I take this fire-brand first and plunge it into the water. Now quick, quick, you sprinkle the altar. Give me some barley-seed, purify yourself and hand me the basin; then scatter the rest of the barley among the audience.

SERVANT

Done.

TRYGAEUS

You have thrown it?

SERVANT

Yes, by Hermes! and all the spectators have had their share.

TRYGAEUS

At least the women got none.

SERVANT

Oh! their husbands will give them some this evening.

TRYGAEUS

Let us pray! Who is here? Are there any good men? [17]

SERVANT

Come, give me the water, so that I may sprinkle these people. Faith! they are indeed good, brave men.

(*He throws the lustral water on them.*)

TRYGAEUS

You believe so?

SERVANT

I am sure, and the proof of it is that we have flooded them with lustral water and they have not budged an inch.

TRYGAEUS

Let us pray, then, as soon as we can.

SERVANT

Yes, let us pray.

TRYGAEUS

Oh! Peace, mighty queen, venerated goddess, thou, who presidest over choruses and at nuptials, deign to accept the sacrifices we offer thee.

SERVANT

Receive it, greatly honoured mistress, and behave not like the courtesans, who half open the door to entice the gallants, draw back when they are stared at, to return once more if a man passes on. But do not thou act like this to us.

TRYGAEUS

No, but like an honest woman, show thyself to thy worshippers, who are worn with regretting thee all these thirteen years. Hush the noise of battle, be a true Lysimacha to us. Put an end to this tittle-tattle, to this idle babble, that set us defying one another. Cause the Greeks once more to taste the pleasant beverage of friendship and temper all hearts with the gentle feeling of forgiveness. Make excellent commodities flow to our markets, fine heads of garlic, early cucumbers, apples, pomegranates and nice little cloaks for the slaves; make them bring geese, ducks, pigeons and larks from Boeotia and baskets of eels from Lake Copais; we shall all rush to buy them, disputing their possession with Morychus, Teleas, Glaucetes and every other glutton. Melanthius will arrive on the market last of all; they'll say, "no more eels, all sold!" and then he'll start groaning and exclaiming as in his monologue of Medea, "I am dying, I am dying! Alas! I have let those hidden in the beet escape me!" And won't we laugh? These are the wishes, mighty goddess, which we pray thee to grant. (*To the* SERVANT) Take the knife and slaughter the sheep like a finished cook.

SERVANT

No, the goddess does not wish it.

TRYGAEUS

And why not?

SERVANT

Blood cannot please Peace, so let us spill none upon her altar.

TRYGAEUS

Then go and sacrifice the sheep in the house, cut off the legs and bring them here; thus the carcase will be saved for the Choregus.

(*The* SERVANT *goes into the house with the sheep.*)

CHORUS (*singing*)

You, who remain here, get chopped wood and everything needed for the sacrifice ready.

TRYGAEUS

Don't I look like a diviner preparing his mystic fire?

CHORUS (*singing*)

Undoubtedly. Will anything that a wise man ought to know escape you? Don't you know all that a man should know, who is distinguished for his wisdom and inventive daring?

TRYGAEUS

There! the wood catches. Its smoke blinds poor Stilbides. I am now going to bring the table and thus be my own slave.

(*He goes into the house.*)

CHORUS (*singing*)

You have braved a thousand dangers to save your sacred town. All honour to you! your glory will be ever envied.

TRYGAEUS (*returning with a table*)

Wait. Here are the legs, place them upon the altar. For myself, I mean to go back to the entrails and the cakes.

(*He is about to go into the house.*)

SERVANT (*going in ahead of him*)

I'll take care of them.

TRYGAEUS

But I want you here.

SERVANT (*returning*)
Well then, here I am. Do you think I have taken long?

TRYGAEUS
Just get this roasted. Ah! who is this man, crowned with laurel, who is coming to me?

SERVANT
He has a self-important look; is he some diviner?

TRYGAEUS
No, it's Hierocles, that oracle-monger from Oreus.

SERVANT
What is he going to tell us?

TRYGAEUS
Evidently he is coming to oppose the peace.

SERVANT
No, it's the odour of the fat that attracts him.

TRYGAEUS
Let us appear not to see him.

SERVANT
Very well.

HIEROCLES (*approaching*)
What sacrifice is this? to what god are you offering it?

TRYGAEUS (*to the* SERVANT)
Keep quiet.—(*Aloud*) Look after the roasting and keep your hands off the meat.

HIEROCLES
To whom are you sacrificing? Answer me.

TRYGAEUS
Ah! the tail is showing favourable omens.[18]

SERVANT
Aye, very favourable, oh, loved and mighty Peace!

HIEROCLES
Come, cut off the first offering [19] and make the oblation.

TRYGAEUS
It's not roasted enough.

HIEROCLES

Yea, truly, it's done to a turn.

TRYGAEUS

Mind your own business, friend! (*To the* SERVANT) Cut away.

HIEROCLES

Where is the table?

TRYGAEUS

Bring the libations.

(*The* SERVANT *departs.*)

HIEROCLES

The tongue is cut separately.

TRYGAEUS

We know all that. But just listen to one piece of advice.

HIEROCLES

And that is?

TRYGAEUS

Don't talk, for it is divine Peace to whom we are sacrificing.

HIEROCLES (*in an oracular tone*)

Oh! wretched mortals, oh, you idiots!

TRYGAEUS

Keep such ugly terms for yourself.

HIEROCLES (*as before*)

What! you are so ignorant you don't understand the will of the gods and you make a treaty, you, who are men, with apes, who are full of malice?

TRYGAEUS

Ha, ha, ha!

HIEROCLES

What are you laughing at?

TRYGAEUS

Ha, ha! your apes amuse me!

HIEROCLES (*resuming the oracular manner*)

You simple pigeons, you trust yourselves to foxes, who are all craft, both in mind and heart.

TRYGAEUS

Oh, you trouble-maker! may your lungs get as hot as this meat!

HIEROCLES

Nay, nay! if only the Nymphs had not fooled Bacis, and Bacis mortal men; and if the Nymphs had not tricked Bacis a second time . . .

TRYGAEUS (*mocking his manner*)

May the plague seize you, if you don't stop Bacizing!

HIEROCLES

. . . it would not have been written in the book of Fate that the bonds of Peace must be broken; but first . . .

TRYGAEUS

The meat must be dusted with salt.

HIEROCLES

. . . it does not please the blessed gods that we should stop the War until the wolf uniteth with the sheep.

(*A kind of oracle-match now ensues.*)

TRYGAEUS

How, you cursed animal, could the wolf ever unite with the sheep?

HIEROCLES

As long as the wood-bug gives off a fetid odour, when it flies; as long as the noisy bitch is forced by nature to litter blind pups, so long shall peace be forbidden.

TRYGAEUS

Then what should be done? Not to stop War would be to leave it to the decision of chance which of the two people should suffer the most, whereas by uniting under a treaty, we share the empire of Greece.

HIEROCLES

You will never make the crab walk straight.

TRYGAEUS

You shall no longer be fed at the Prytaneum; when the war is over, oracles are not wanted.

HIEROCLES

You will never smooth the rough spikes of the hedgehog.

TRYGAEUS

Will you never stop fooling the Athenians?

HIEROCLES

What oracle ordered you to burn these joints of mutton in honour of the gods?

TRYGAEUS

This grand oracle of Homer's: "Thus vanished the dark war-clouds and we offered a sacrifice to new-born Peace. When the flame had consumed the thighs of the victim and its inwards had appeased our hunger, we poured out the libations of wine." 'Twas I who arranged the sacred rites, but none offered the shining cup to the diviner.[20]

HIEROCLES

I care little for that. 'Tis not the Sibyl who spoke it.

TRYGAEUS

Wise Homer has also said: "He who delights in the horrors of civil war has neither country nor laws nor home." What noble words!

HIEROCLES

Beware lest the kite turn your brain and rob . . .

TRYGAEUS (*to the* SERVANT *who has returned with the libations*)

Look out, slave! This oracle threatens our meat. Quick, pour the libation, and give me some of the inwards.

HIEROCLES

I too will help myself to a bit, if you like.

TRYGAEUS

The libation! the libation!

HIEROCLES (*to the* SERVANT)

Pour out also for me and give me some of this meat.

TRYGAEUS

No, the blessed gods won't allow it yet; let us drink; and as for you, get you gone, for that's their will. Mighty Peace! stay ever in our midst.

HIEROCLES

Bring the tongue hither.

TRYGAEUS

Relieve us of your own.

HIEROCLES

The libation.

TRYGAEUS

Here! and this into the bargain. (*He strikes him.*)

HIEROCLES

You will not give me any meat?

TRYGAEUS

We cannot give you any until the wolf unites with the sheep.

HIEROCLES

I will embrace your knees.

TRYGAEUS

'Tis lost labour, good fellow; you will never smooth the rough spikes of the hedgehog. . . . Come, spectators, join us in our feast.

HIEROCLES

And what am I to do?

TRYGAEUS

You? go and eat the Sibyl.

HIEROCLES

No, by the Earth! no, you shall not eat without me; if you do not give, I shall take; it's common property.

TRYGAEUS (*to the* SERVANT)

Strike, strike this Bacis, this humbugging soothsayer.

HIEROCLES

I take to witness . . .

TRYGAEUS

And I also, that you are a glutton and an impostor. (*To the* SERVANT) Hold him tight and I'll beat the impostor with a stick.

SERVANT

You look to that; I will snatch the skin from him which he has stolen from us.

TRYGAEUS

Let go that skin, you priest from hell! do you hear! Oh! what a fine
crow has come from Oreus! Stretch your wings quickly for Elymnium.
(HIEROCLES *flees.* TRYGAEUS *and the* SERVANT *go into the house.*)

CHORUS (*singing*)

Oh! joy, joy! no more helmet, no more cheese nor onions! No, I
have no passion for battles; what I love is to drink with good comrades in the corner by the fire when good dry wood, cut in the height
of the summer, is crackling; it is to cook pease on the coals and beech-
nuts among the embers, it is to kiss our pretty Thracian while my
wife is at the bath.

LEADER OF THE CHORUS

Nothing is more pleasing, when the rain is sprouting our sowings, than
to chat with some friend, saying, "Tell me, Comarchides, what shall we
do? I would willingly drink myself, while the heavens are watering our
fields. Come, wife, cook three measures of beans, adding to them a little
wheat, and give us some figs. Syra! call Manes off the fields, it's impossible to prune the vine or to align the ridges, for the ground is too wet to-
day. Let someone bring me the thrush and those two chaffinches; there
were also some curds and four pieces of hare, unless the cat stole them last
evening, for I know not what the infernal noise was that I heard in the
house. Serve up three of the pieces for me, slave, and give the fourth to
my father. Go and ask Aeschinades for some myrtle branches with berries
on them, and then, for it's on the same road, invite Charinades to come
and drink with me to the honour of the gods who watch over our crops."

CHORUS (*singing*)

When the grasshopper sings his dulcet tune, I love to see the Lemnian vines beginning to ripen, the earliest plant of all. Likewise I love
to watch the fig filling out, and when it has reached maturity I eat it
with appreciation, exclaiming, "Oh! delightful season!" Then too I
bruise some thyme and infuse it in water. Indeed I grow a great deal
fatter passing the summer in this way . . .

LEADER OF THE CHORUS

. . . than in watching a damned lieutenant with three plumes and
military cloak of crimson, very livid indeed; he calls it the real Sardian
purple, but if he ever has to fight in this cloak he'll dye it another colour,
the real Cyzicene yellow, he the first to run away, shaking his plumes like
a buff hippalectryon, and I am left to do the real work. Once back again
in Athens, these brave fellows behave abominably; they write down these,
they scratch through others, and this backwards and forwards two or

three times at random. The departure is set for to-morrow, and some citizen has brought no provisions, because he didn't know he had to go; he stops in front of the statue of Pandion, reads his name, is dumbfounded and starts away at a run, weeping bitter tears. The townsfolk are less ill-used, but that is how the husbandmen are treated by these men of war, the hated of the gods and of men, who know nothing but how to throw away their shield. For this reason, if it please heaven, I propose to call these rascals to account, for they are lions in times of peace, but sneaking foxes when it comes to fighting.

TRYGAEUS (*coming out of his house, followed by the* SERVANT)
Oh! oh! what a crowd for the nuptial feast! Here! dust the tables with this crest, which is good for nothing else now. Halloa! produce the cakes, the thrushes, plenty of good jugged hare and the little loaves.
(*A* SICKLE-MAKER *enters with a comrade; one carries sickles, the other casks.*)

SICKLE-MAKER
Trygaeus, where is Trygaeus?

TRYGAEUS
I am cooking the thrushes.

SICKLE-MAKER
Trygaeus, my best of friends, what a fine stroke of business you have done for me by bringing back Peace! Formerly my sickles would not have sold at an obolus apiece, to-day I am being paid fifty drachmae for every one. And here is a neighbour who is selling his casks for the country at three drachmae each. So come, Trygaeus, take as many sickles and casks as you will for nothing. Accept them for nothing; it's because of our handsome profits on our sales that we offer you these wedding presents.

TRYGAEUS
Thanks. Put them all down inside there, and come along quick to the banquet. Ah! do you see that armourer yonder coming with a wry face?
(*Enter an armourer, followed by other personages who represent the various specialized trades which have profited by the war, a crest-maker, a manufacturer of breastplates, a trumpet-maker, a helmet-maker, a polisher of lances; each carries a sample of his products. The armourer is the only one who speaks.*)

ARMOURER
Alas! alas! Trygaeus, you have ruined me utterly.

TRYGAEUS

What! won't the crests go any more, friend?

ARMOURER

You have killed my business, my livelihood, and that of this poor lance maker too.

TRYGAEUS

Come, come, what are you asking for these two crests?

ARMOURER

What do you bid for them?

TRYGAEUS

What do I bid? Oh! I am ashamed to say. Still, as the clasp is of good workmanship, I would give two, even three measures of dried figs; I could use them for dusting the table.

ARMOURER

All right, tell them to bring me the dried figs. (*To the crest-maker*) That's better than nothing, my friend.

TRYGAEUS

Take them away, be off with your crests and get you gone; they are moulting, they are losing all their hair; I would not give a single fig for them.

ARMOURER

Good gods, what am I going to do with this fine ten-mina breastplate, which is so splendidly made?

TRYGAEUS

Oh, you will lose nothing over it. Sell it to me at cost price. It would be very useful as a thunder-mug . . .

ARMOURER

Cease your insults, both to me and my wares.

TRYGAEUS

. . . if propped on three stones. (*He sits on it.*) Look, it's admirable

ARMOURER

But how can you wipe yourself, idiot?

TRYGAEUS (*with appropriate gestures*)

I can put one hand through here, and the other there, and so . . .

ARMOURER

What! do you wipe yourself with both hands?

TRYGAEUS

Aye, so that I may not be accused of robbing the State, by blocking up an oar-hole in the galley.[21]

ARMOURER

Would you crap in a thunder-mug that cost ten minae?

TRYGAEUS

Undoubtedly, you rascal. Do you think I would sell my arse for a thousand drachmae?

ARMOURER

Come, have the money paid over to me.

TRYGAEUS

No, friend; I find it pinches my bottom. Take it away, I won't buy it.

ARMOURER

What is to be done with this trumpet, for which I gave sixty drachmæ the other day?

TRYGAEUS

Pour lead into the hollow and fit a good, long stick to the top; and you will have a balanced cottabus.

ARMOURER

Don't mock me.

TRYGAEUS

Well, here's another idea. Pour in lead as I said, add here a dish hung on strings, and you will have a balance for weighing the figs which you give your slaves in the fields.

ARMOURER

Cursed fate! I am ruined. Here are helmets, for which I gave a mina each. What am I to do with them? who will buy them?

TRYGAEUS

Go and sell them to the Egyptians; they will do for measuring laxatives.

ARMOURER

Ah! poor helmet-maker, things are indeed in a bad way.

TRYGAEUS

He has no cause for complaint.

ARMOURER

But helmets will be no more used.

TRYGAEUS

Let him learn to fit a handle to them and he can sell them for more
money.

ARMOURER

Let us be off, comrade.

TRYGAEUS

No, I want to buy these spears.

ARMOURER

What will you give?

TRYGAEUS

If they could be split in two, I would take them at a drachma per hundred to use as vine-props.

ARMOURER

The insolent dog! Let us go, friend.

(*The munitions-makers all depart.*)

TRYGAEUS (*as some young boys enter*)

Ah! here come the guests, young folks from the table to take a pee; I
fancy they also want to hum over what they will be singing presently. Hi!
child! what do you reckon to sing? Stand there and give me the opening
line.

BOY

"Glory to the young warriors. . . ." [22]

TRYGAEUS

Oh! leave off about your young warriors, you little wretch; we are at
peace and you are an idiot and a rascal.

BOY

"The skirmish begins, the hollow bucklers clash against each other."

TRYGAEUS

Bucklers! Leave me in peace with your bucklers.

BOY

"And then there came groanings and shouts of victory."

TRYGAEUS

Groanings! ah! by Bacchus! look out for yourself, you cursed squaller, if you start wearying us again with your groanings and hollow bucklers.

BOY

Then what should I sing? Tell me what pleases you.

TRYGAEUS

" 'Tis thus they feasted on the flesh of oxen," or something similar, as, for instance, "Everything that could tickle the palate was placed on the table."

BOY

" 'Tis thus they feasted on the flesh of oxen and, tired of warfare, un-harnessed their foaming steeds."

TRYGAEUS

That's splendid; tired of warfare, they seat themselves at table; sing sing to us how they still go on eating after they are satiated.

BOY

"The meal over, they girded themselves . . ."

TRYGAEUS

With good wine, no doubt?

BOY

". . . with armour and rushed forth from the towers, and a terrible shout arose." [23]

TRYGAEUS

Get you gone, you little scapegrace, you and your battles! You sing of nothing but warfare. Who is your father then?

BOY

My father?

TRYGAEUS

Why yes, your father.

BOY

I am Lamachus' son.

TRYGAEUS

Oh! oh! I could indeed have sworn, when I was listening to you, that you were the son of some warrior, who dreams of nothing but wounds and bruises, of some Bulomachus or Clausimachus; go and sing your plaguey songs to the spearmen. . . . Where is the son of Cleonymus? Sing me something before going back to the feast. I am at least certain he will not sing of battles, for his father is far too careful a man.

SON OF CLEONYMUS

"A Saian is parading with the spotless shield which I regret to say I have thrown into a thicket."

TRYGAEUS

Tell me, you little good-for-nothing, are you singing that for your father?

SON OF CLEONYMUS

"But I saved my life." [24]

TRYGAEUS

And dishonoured your family. But let us go in; I am very certain, that being the son of such a father, you will never forget this song of the buckler. (*To the* CHORUS) You, who remain to the feast, it's your duty to devour dish after dish and not to ply empty jaws. Come, put heart into the work and eat with your mouths full. For, believe me, poor friends, white teeth are useless furniture if they chew nothing.

LEADER OF THE CHORUS (*to* TRYGAEUS, *who is going into the house*)

Never fear; thanks all the same for your good advice. (*To the* CHORUS) And all of you, who yesterday were dying of hunger, come, stuff yourselves with this fine hare-stew; it's not every day that we find cakes lying neglected. Eat, eat, or I predict you will soon regret it.

TRYGAEUS (*coming out of the house*)

Silence! Keep silence! Here is the bride about to appear! Take nuptial torches and let all rejoice and join in our songs. Then, when we have danced, clinked our cups and thrown Hyperbolus through the doorway we will carry back all our farming tools to the fields and shall pray the gods to give wealth to the Greeks and to cause us all to gather in an abundant barley harvest, enjoy a noble vintage, to grant that we may choke with good figs, that our wives may prove fruitful, that in fact we may recover all our lost blessings, and that the sparkling fire may be restored to the hearth. (OPORA *comes out of the house, followed by torch-bearing slaves.*) Come, wife, to the fields and seek, my beauty, to brighten and enliven my nights. Oh! Hymen! oh! Hymenaeus!

LEADER OF THE CHORUS (*singing*)
Oh! thrice happy man, who so well deserve your good fortune! Oh!
Hymen! oh! Hymenaeus!

CHORUS (*singing*)
Oh! Hymen! oh! Hymenaeus!

TRYGAEUS (*singing*)
What shall we do to her?

CHORUS (*singing*)
What shall we do to her?

TRYGAEUS (*singing*)
We will gather her kisses.

CHORUS (*singing*)
We will gather her kisses.

LEADER OF THE CHORUS (*singing*)
But come, comrades, we who are in the first row, let us pick up the
bridegroom and carry him in triumph. Oh! Hymen! oh! Hymenaeus!
Oh! Hymen! oh! Hymenaeus!

TRYGAEUS (*singing*)
You shall have a fine house, no cares and the finest of figs. Oh! Hymen! oh! Hymenaeus! Oh! Hymen! oh! Hymenaeus!

LEADER OF THE CHORUS (*singing*)
The bridegroom's fig is great and thick; the bride's very soft and
tender.

TRYGAEUS (*singing*)
While eating and drinking deep draughts of wine, continue to re-
peat: Oh! Hymen! oh! Hymenaeus! Oh! Hymen! oh! Hymenaeus!
Hail, hail, my friends. All who come with me shall have cakes galore.

1. Zeus often bore the epithet *kataibatos*, "he who descends in thunder"; Aristophanes has added one letter and coined *skataibatos*, "he who descends in ordure." A French translator renders this as *Zeus Merdoyant*, *kataibatos* being *Foudroyant*.

2. "Going to the crows" was the ancient way of "going to Hell."

3. According to the fable the eagle and the beetle were at war; the eagle devoured the beetle's young and the latter retaliated by getting into its nest and tumbling out its eggs. The eagle then complained to Zeus and was advised to lay its eggs in his bosom; the beetle then flew up to the house of Zeus and began buzzing around his ears. When he rose to chase the insect away the eagle's eggs fell to the earth and were smashed to bits.

4. Euripides was often censured by the critics and laughed at by the comic poets because of the wretchedness of so many of his heroes. See *The Acharnians* (411 ff.).

5. The Spartan pestle was Brasidas; see the Glossary.

6. The usual fare of soldiers was bread, cheese, and onions.

7. See under Mysteries in the Glossary.

8. This is a reference to the fact that Athens' life depended on the maintenance of her naval supremacy.

9. This was a consequence of the Spartan invasions of Attica, which had taken place in almost every year of the war.

10. The tanner is, of course, Cleon. The following remarks of Trygaeus have always excited the sentimentalists, who readily forget the hostility of everything else that is said about Cleon in this play and eagerly foist upon Aristophanes a number of emotions utterly foreign to his age and repugnant to his personality. He was far too realistic to impute all the cardinal virtues to any dead scoundrel and what Trygaeus means is simply that the demagogue, now that he is dead and there is no longer any ulterior reason for attacking him, has ceased to have much value as a source of satirical humour. This does not, however, prevent him from making the familiar jest about leather, only a few lines below. How tightly the sentimentalists have to squint to see themselves mirrored in Aristophanes!

11. The ancients used infusions of penny-royal to alleviate the colic occasioned by excessive consumption of fruit.

12. The Heracles of comedy, traditionally a gluttonous buffoon, was a stock character that even Aristophanes, despite the disdain of the present remark, found useful on occasion; see *The Birds* (1574 ff.). The Heracles of Euripides' *Alcestis* is not far removed from his comic prototype.

13. These four lines are repeated verbatim from the parabasis of *The Wasps*.

14. This whole passage is one of the most brilliant examples of sustained and varied *double entendre* in ancient literature. The only point requiring comment is the Senate's cooking; this was the roasting, on a spit, of meats before the sacrifice; cf. a similar jest in *The Acharnians* (796).

15. One of the offices of the Prytanes was to introduce those who asked admission to the Senate, but it would seem that none could obtain this favour without payment. The refusal was most often made on the pretext of a festival, and such celebrations were extraordinarily numerous in the Athenian calendar. Thus the man who refused to be mulcted might have to wait a long time.

16. There is a pun here on the Greek words *bous,* "bull" and *boethein,* "to aid in battle."

17. Before sacrificing, the officiating person asked, "Who is here?" and those present answered, "Many good men."

18. At sacrifices the tail was cut off the victim and thrown into the fire. From the way it burnt one was supposed to be able to tell whether or not the sacrifice was agreeable to the deity.

19. The first offering was the part that belonged to the priest or diviner. Hierocles expects to receive this and is thus eager to see it cut off.

20. This "oracle" is not a real passage from Homer, but merely a sort of cento of epic formulae, improvised by Trygaeus to suit the occasion. The next one, however, is correctly quoted from the Iliad (IX, 63 f.).

21. The trierarchs, those officials whose duty it was to man the ships of the Athenian navy, were wont to supply an inadequate number of rowers and thus to save or to embezzle some of the wages which they or the state had to pay. In order to render the deficiency less obvious they would stop up the oar-holes at which rowers should have been and were not.

22. This is the opening line of *The Epigoni,* a post-Homeric epic which recounted the second and successful attack of the Argive army on the city of Thebes. The first attack, which was a failure, forms the subject of Aeschylus' *Seven Against Thebes.*

23. These lines are a sort of gentleman's quotation of *Iliad* IV, 446 ff.

24. This is a quotation from one of the most famous of the elegies of the Greek poet Archilochus of Paros; because of his unsoldierly conduct he is reported to have been forbidden to enter Spartan territory.

VI
THE BIRDS

CHARACTERS IN THE PLAY

EUELPIDES
PITHETAERUS
TROCHILUS, *Servant to Epops*
EPOPS (*the Hoopoe*)
A BIRD
A HERALD
A PRIEST
A POET
AN ORACLE-MONGER
METON, *a Geometrician*
AN INSPECTOR
A DEALER IN DECREES
IRIS
A PARRICIDE
CINESIAS, *a Dithyrambic Poet*
AN INFORMER
PROMETHEUS
POSIDON
TRIBALLUS
HERACLES
SLAVES OF PITHETAERUS
MESSENGERS
CHORUS OF BIRDS

INTRODUCTION

AFTER the production of *Peace* there intervene six years during which Aristophanes' literary activity is so lost to our view that we are by no means certain that he wrote for the theatre at all, and a copious list of titles preserved from plays that have not survived exhibits few that we may, and none that we must, assign to the years 420–415. In 414, however, the dramatist effected a twofold reappearance on the Athenian stage, and the Lenaean festival was graced with the lost *Amphiaraus*, while at the Great Dionysia the poet produced *The Birds*, which we have the great good fortune to possess. The play is the longest and the most lyrical of the eleven that have come down to us, and its general merits are such that the relatively small amount of bawdiness in it has led many to designate it as the finest, or at least the most delightful, of Aristophanes' compositions. This judgment, however, was not shared by the Athenian spectators, and the poet had to content himself with the second prize, but the inadequate award will surprise only those who have read the victorious *Knights* with insufficient candour or total absence of taste. *The Birds* is just such a comedy as the auguries evinced in the earlier creations of the poet's art have led us to expect, but it is also the first extant play which embodies the Utopian theme that is to dominate so much of Aristophanes' later work, and its central position as the sixth of the eleven thus acquires a more than chronological significance. Unfortunately it is no less fruitless than fascinating to speculate on the question of how much this is due to a desire on the poet's part to find in his comic Republics an escape from a world which he thought both misguided and incorrigible, and how much to his constant and enthusiastic effort fully to exploit every possibility offered by the traditional form of the Old Comedy. An important and primordial feature of this form was the *Gamos*, which had often been specialized into a motif of rejuvenation, and even in some of the earlier plays we may discern the beginnings of a generalization and extension whereby the rejuvenation is no longer effected in the individual alone, but in the society or the state as a whole. Such are the aims of Demos in *The Knights*, after Agoracritus has freshened him up on his stove, and the concluding scenes of *Peace* more closely approximate the realization of

727

similar dreams. But in these comedies the rejuvenation of society is subordinate and subsequent to the attainment of a particular political aim;
in *The Birds* it has attained its full maturity and becomes the central
motif of a comedy which is wholly political in its theme without taking a
stand or making an attack on any specific political issue.

The opening scene introduces us to a pair of typical Athenians, Euelpides and Pithetaerus, whose patience has been so thoroughly exhausted
by the stupidities and the annoyances of life in Athens that they have resolved to seek habitation elsewhere. Remembering the myth that Epops,
the hoopoe, had once, long ago, been a man, they trudge before us on their
long journey to consult, instead of the customary Pythian priestess, the
metamorphosed Tereus, and thus to derive double advantage from the
survivals of his human sympathies and the extent of his geographic
knowledge. Before leaving Athens they have purchased winged pets from
a bird-seller, to direct them on their adventure, and these hitherto disappointing guides now exhibit their true worth and indicate to their owners
that they have reached their destination. After duly knocking on a nearby
rock Euelpides attracts the attention of Trochilus, the slave of Epops,
who suddenly rushes forth from the thicket in which his master dwells,
and by his terrifying aspect chills the hearts and moves the bowels of the
eminently human Athenians. He is finally prevailed upon to summon
Epops, and Euelpides details the Sybaritic characteristics of the society
they are looking for. A number of places are suggested by Epops and rejected, for typically Athenian reasons, by Euelpides, and just as the latter
is rather diffidently enquiring what it is like to live with the birds, Pithetaerus, who has been silent for some time, suddenly bursts forth with a
grandiose and thoroughly Athenian scheme whereby the supreme power
of the universe may be put into the hands of the birds. The central position
of their habitat will enable them to dominate the gods by intercepting
their sacrificial supplies and they can terrorize mankind by the threat of
devastating the crops. Epops is quickly enchanted with the plan and
summons his aerial countrymen to a debate on the question, thus motivat-
ing the entrance of the Chorus.

A gaudy variety of winged creatures now assembles from all parts of
the world, but Pithetaerus' magnificent schemes seem for a while destined
to meet with premature frustration because of the inability of the birds
to control their anger at the presumptuousness which has prompted two
of their ancestral enemies to invade their domain. They are about to peck
out the eyes of the terrified Athenians, who hurriedly arm themselves
with kitchen utensils, but Epops finally succeeds in calming their wrath
and inducing them to listen to the splendid proposals of Pithetaerus. With
characteristic plausibility the Athenian demonstrates that the birds were
the lords of the universe long before the Olympians, and convinces his

astonished auditors that with their cooperation he and Euelpides will re-establish them in their pristine supremacy. The Chorus enthusiastically supports the plan and the two Athenians follow Epops into his thicket, to procure wings for themselves and to work out the details of the project.

The stage is now left to the Chorus, which delivers the parabasis. The anapests, introduced by a brief lyric passage on the charms of Procné, the nightingale mate of Epops, recount the origin and early history of the world as the birds conceive it, and add to this a list of the services which they render mankind and of the reasons why men should worship the birds as gods. The ode is a lovely lyric, interspersed with bird-calls, on the theme of the music produced by the birds. The epirrheme details the advantages of life with the birds. The antode is thematically similar to the ode, but surpasses it in poetic beauty. The antepirrheme catalogues the advantages of possessing wings. Nowhere in this comedy is its essentially general nature more clearly exhibited than here in the parabasis, where we expect a definite exposition of the dramatist's views or advice on some particular political question.

At the conclusion of the parabasis Pithetaerus and Euelpides, now equipped with wings, emerge from the thicket and set about the organization of the new city, which is forthwith named Nephelococcygia and placed under the protection of Athené Polias. Euelpides is dispatched on a complicated errand, and a priest is summoned to perform a sacrifice, but he never concludes the endless list of the birds to whom prayers are to be addressed, and Pithetaerus, in desperation, takes over the sacrifice himself. He is interrupted, however, by the arrival of a series of familiar and typically Athenian nuisances, who have learned of the new city and are now eager to ply their trades in fresh, and presumably more profitable, surroundings. Accordingly Pithetaerus is compelled to beat off, in increasingly rapid succession, a poet who would hymn the glories of Nephelococcygia, an oracle-monger bursting with sayings of Bacis, Meton, the great mathematician and calendar-reformer, who would exercise his geometry in the planning of the town, an inspector sent out by the ever alert and meddlesome Athens, and a seller of decrees, who arrives with a complete set of laws for the government of the city. Pithetaerus now perceives that he will never be given an opportunity to finish his sacrifice if he stays in the open; he accordingly goes into the thicket, and the stage is for the second time left to the Chorus, which delivers what is very nearly a second parabasis. There are no anapests, and hence the passage is not a parabasis in the strictest sense of the term, but we find an ode celebrating the new power of the birds, an epirrheme which puts a price on the head of Philocrates, the bird-seller, an antode extolling the happy life which the birds enjoy, and an antepirrheme advising the judges to award the victory to this comedy.

As soon as this has been delivered, Pithetaerus comes out of the thicket and announces that the sacrificial omens are propitious. A messenger arrives and reports that the walls have been completed, and subjoins an account of the ingenious methods by which the birds have solved the problems of construction. The general rejoicing evoked by this news is short-lived, for soon another messenger arrives, bearing the dreadful tidings that a god has eluded the sentries and slipped into the city; the militia has been called out and war seems imminent, when the god appears in person and turns out to be an astonished and unsuspecting Iris bearing a message from Zeus to the human race. She is rudely informed of the developments that have taken place, and the erotic threats of Pithetaerus send her tearfully on her way to report the news to the other immortals. Immediately after her departure a herald arrives from the earth and communicates to Pithetaerus the information that a bird-mania has become epidemic in Athens; Nephelococcygia has quite displaced Sparta in the affections of the discontented, and no less than ten thousand Athenians are on their way to settle in the new Utopia. Thus Pithetaerus is again forced to expel a number of irritating pests, and a parricide, who has heard that the mores of the birds approve of beating one's father, Cinesias, the dithyrambic poet, who longs to "gather fresh songs in the clouds, in the midst of the vapours and the fleecy snow," and an informer, who perceives the manifold advantages of wings in his profession, are rapidly and successively driven off with blows or threats. As soon as the last of this trio has departed, a furtive and masked figure slinks in, carrying an umbrella; its identity is finally revealed and Pithetaerus affectionately greets Prometheus, who, true to his traditional love of mankind and hatred of the gods, provides the founder of Nephelococcygia with preliminary information on the sad state of affairs which prevails amongst the Olympians, and with advice on how to handle the divine embassy which is on its way to conclude a treaty with the new and formidable city of the birds. The Chorus sings a brief ode and Pithetaerus commences the preparation of a splendid repast, when the Olympian delegation arrives, made up of Posidon, Heracles, and Triballus, a ridiculous and barbarous Thracian deity. "Oh! Democracy," exclaims the aristocratic Posidon, "whither, oh! whither are you leading us?" Pithetaerus demands that Zeus yield his sceptre to the birds and that Basileia, the personification of sovereignty, be given to him in marriage. Posidon gallantly refuses, but Heracles is immediately prejudiced in favour of Pithetaerus by the sight and the smell of the victuals he is preparing, and he easily forces or misinterprets Triballus into taking his side. The majority opinion thus enjoins complete capitulation to the requests of Pithetaerus, and the comedy ends with the *Hymenaeus* for his marriage to Basileia and Hosannas of praise in honour of the new lord of the universe.

Such is the plot of this beautiful and diversified comedy, a bright tissue of the purest and happiest fantasy, constructed with consummate skill, a song of unalloyed gaiety with never a false or bitter note. If its date had not been handed down to us, surely no one would suspect that it was written under the shadow of the impending Athenian debâcle in Sicily and only a year after the mutilation of the Hermae with its resultant psychoses of superstitious fear and savage vindictiveness. Only an isolated and ambiguous reference to the recall of Alcibiades suggests contemporary events; the rest of the play is written not for the year 414 but almost for the period of 459–404. This approach to timelessness is at once an explanation of why *The Birds* did not win the first prize, a foreshadowing of the New Comedy, and a testimony to the fact that forms of art develop in opposition, not in response, to the popular taste.

THE BIRDS

(SCENE:—*A wild and desolate region; only thickets, rocks, and a single tree are seen.* EUELPIDES *and* PITHETAERUS *enter, each with a bird in his hand.*)

EUELPIDES (*to his jay*)
Do YOU think I should walk straight for yon tree?

PITHETAERUS (*to his crow*)
Cursed beast, what are you croaking to me? . . . to retrace my steps?

EUELPIDES
Why, you wretch, we are wandering at random, we are exerting our-selves only to return to the same spot; we're wasting our time.

PITHETAERUS
To think that I should trust to this crow, which has made me cover more than a thousand furlongs!

EUELPIDES
And that I, in obedience to this jay, should have worn my toes down to the nails!

PITHETAERUS
If only I knew where we were. . . .

EUELPIDES
Could you find your country again from here?

PITHETAERUS
No, I feel quite sure I could not, any more than could Execestides find his.

EUELPIDES
Alas!

PITHETAERUS

Aye, aye, my friend, it's surely the road of "alases" we are following.

EUELPIDES

That Philocrates, the bird-seller, played us a scurvy trick, when he
pretended these two guides could help us to find Tereus, the Epops, who
is a bird, without being born of one. He has indeed sold us this jay, a true
son of Tharrhelides, for an obolus, and this crow for three, but what can
they do? Why, nothing whatever but bite and scratch! (*To his jay*)
What's the matter with you then, that you keep opening your beak? Do
you want us to fling ourselves headlong down these rocks? There is no
road that way.

PITHETAERUS

Not even the vestige of a trail in any direction

EUELPIDES

And what does the crow say about the road to follow?

PITHETAERUS

By Zeus, it no longer croaks the same thing it did.

EUELPIDES

And which way does it tell us to go now?

PITHETAERUS

It says that, by dint of gnawing, it will devour my fingers.

EUELPIDES

What misfortune is ours! we strain every nerve to get to the crows, do
everything we can to that end, and we cannot find our way! Yes, spectators, our madness is quite different from that of Sacas. He is not a citizen, and would fain be one at any cost; we, on the contrary, born of an
honourable tribe and family and living in the midst of our fellow-citizens,
we have fled from our country as hard as ever we could go. It's not that
we hate it; we recognize it to be great and rich, likewise that everyone
has the right to ruin himself paying taxes; but the crickets only chirrup
among the fig-trees for a month or two, whereas the Athenians spend their
whole lives in chanting forth judgments from their law-courts. That is
why we started off with a basket, a stew-pot and some myrtle boughs [1] and
have come to seek a quiet country in which to settle. We are going to
Tereus, the Epops, to learn from him, whether, in his aerial flights, he has
noticed some town of this kind.

PITHETAERUS

Here! look!

EUELPIDES

What's the matter?

PITHETAERUS

Why, the crow has been directing me to something up there for some
time now.

EUELPIDES

And the jay is also opening it beak and craning its neck to show me I
know not what. Clearly, there are some birds about here. We shall soon
know, if we kick up a noise to start them.

PITHETAERUS

Do you know what to do? Knock your leg against this rock.

EUELPIDES

And you your head to double the noise.

PITHETAERUS

Well then use a stone instead; take one and hammer with it.

EUELPIDES

Good idea! (*He does so.*) Ho there, within! Slave! slave!

PITHETAERUS

What's that, friend! You say, "slave," to summon Epops? It would be
much better to shout, "Epops, Epops!"

EUELPIDES

Well then, Epops! Must I knock again? Epops!

TROCHILUS (*rushing out of a thicket*)

Who's there? Who calls my master?

PITHETAERUS (*in terror*)

Apollo the Deliverer! what an enormous beak!
(*He defecates. In the confusion both the jay and the crow fly away.*)

TROCHILUS (*equally frightened*)

Good god! they are bird-catchers.

EUELPIDES (*reassuring himself*)

But is it so terrible? Wouldn't it be better to explain things?

TROCHILUS (*also reassuring himself*)

You're done for.

EUELPIDES

But we are not men.

TROCHILUS

What are you, then?

EUELPIDES (*defecating also*)

I am the Fearling, an African bird.

TROCHILUS

You talk nonsense.

EUELPIDES

Well, then, just ask it of my feet.

TROCHILUS

And this other one, what bird is it? (*To* PITHETAERUS) Speak up!

PITHETAERUS (*weakly*)

I? I am a Crapple, from the land of the pheasants.

EUELPIDES

But you yourself, in the name of the gods! what animal are you?

TROCHILUS

Why, I am a slave-bird.

EUELPIDES

Why, have you been conquered by a cock?

TROCHILUS

No, but when my master was turned into a hoopoe, he begged me to become a bird also, to follow and to serve him.

EUELPIDES

Does a bird need a servant, then?

TROCHILUS

That's no doubt because he was once a man. At times he wants to eat a dish of sardines from Phalerum; I seize my dish and fly to fetch him some. Again he wants some pea-soup; I seize a ladle and a pot and run to get it.

EUELPIDES

This is, then, truly a running-bird. Come, Trochilus, do us the kindness to call your master.

TROCHILUS

Why, he has just fallen asleep after a feed of myrtle-berries and a few grubs.

EUELPIDES

Never mind; wake him up.

TROCHILUS

I am certain he will be angry. However, I will wake him to please you.
(*He goes back into the thicket.*)

PITHETAERUS (*as soon as* TROCHILUS *is out of sight*)
You cursed brute! why, I am almost dead with terror!

EUELPIDES

Oh! my god! it was sheer fear that made me lose my jay.

PITHETAERUS

Ah! you big coward! were you so frightened that you let go your jay?

EUELPIDES

And did you not lose your crow, when you fell sprawling on the ground? Tell me that.

PITHETAERUS

Not at all.

EUELPIDES

Where is it, then?

PITHETAERUS

It flew away.

EUELPIDES

And you did not let it go? Oh! you brave fellow!

EPOPS (*from within*)
Open the thicket, that I may go out!
(*He comes out of the thicket.*)

EUELPIDES

By Heracles! what a creature! what plumage! What means this triple crest?

EPOPS

Who wants me?

EUELPIDES (*banteringly*)
The twelve great gods have used you ill, it seems.[2]

EPOPS
Are you twitting me about my feathers? I have been a man, strangers.

EUELPIDES
It's not you we are jeering at.

EPOPS
At what, then?

EUELPIDES
Why, it's your beak that looks so ridiculous to us.

EPOPS
This is how Sophocles outrages me in his tragedies. Know, I once was Tereus.

EUELPIDES
You were Tereus, and what are you now? a bird or a peacock?[3]

EPOPS
I am a bird.

EUELPIDES
Then where are your feathers? I don't see any.

EPOPS
They have fallen off.

EUELPIDES
Through illness?

EPOPS
No. All birds moult their feathers, you know, every winter, and others grow in their place. But tell me, who are you?

EUELPIDES
We? We are mortals.

EPOPS
From what country?

EUELPIDES
From the land of the beautiful galleys.[4]

EPOPS

Are you dicasts?

EUELPIDES

No, if anything, we are anti-dicasts.

EPOPS

Is that kind of seed sown among you?

EUELPIDES

You have to look hard to find even a little in our fields.

EPOPS

What brings you here?

EUELPIDES

We wish to pay you a visit.

EPOPS

What for?

EUELPIDES

Because you formerly were a man, like we are, formerly you had debts, as we have, formerly you did not want to pay them, like ourselves; furthermore, being turned into a bird, you have when flying seen all lands and seas. Thus you have all human knowledge as well as that of birds. And hence we have come to you to beg you to direct us to some cosy town, in which one can repose as if on thick coverlets.

EPOPS

And are you looking for a greater city than Athens?

EUELPIDES

No, not a greater, but one more pleasant to live in.

EPOPS

Then you are looking for an aristocratic country.

EUELPIDES

I? Not at all! I hold the son of Scellias in horror.

EPOPS

But, after all, what sort of city *would* please you best?

EUELPIDES

A place where the following would be the most important business transacted.—Some friend would come knocking at the door quite early in the morning saying, "By Olympian Zeus, be at my house early. as soon as you have bathed, and bring your children too. I am giving a nuptial feast, so don't fail, or else don't cross my threshold when I am in distress."

EPOPS

Ah! that's what may be called being fond of hardships! (*To* PITHETAERUS) And what say you?

PITHETAERUS

My tastes are similar.

EPOPS

And they are?

PITHETAERUS

I want a town where the father of a handsome lad will stop in the street and say to me reproachfully as if I had failed him, "Ah! Is this well done, Stilbonides? You met my son coming from the bath after the gymnasium and you neither spoke to him, nor kissed him, nor took him with you, nor ever once felt his balls. Would anyone call you an old friend of mine?"

EPOPS

Ah! wag, I see you are fond of suffering. But there is a city of delights such as you want. It's on the Red Sea.

EUELPIDES

Oh, no. Not a sea-port, where some fine morning the Salaminian galley can appear, bringing a process-server along. Have you no Greek town you can propose to us?

EPOPS

Why not choose Lepreum in Elis for your settlement?

EUELPIDES

By Zeus! I could not look at Lepreum without disgust, because of Melanthius.

EPOPS

Then, again, there is the Opuntian Locris, where you could live.

EUELPIDES

I would not be Opuntian for a talent. But come, what is it like to live with the birds? You should know pretty well.

EPOPS

Why, it's not a disagreeable life. In the first place, one has no purse.

EUELPIDES

That does away with a lot of roguery.

EPOPS

For food the gardens yield us white sesame, myrtle-berries, poppies and mint.

EUELPIDES

Why, 'tis the life of the newly-wed indeed.

PITHETAERUS

Ha! I am beginning to see a great plan, which will transfer the supreme power to the birds, if you will but take my advice.

EPOPS

Take your advice? In what way?

PITHETAERUS

In what way? Well, firstly, do not fly in all directions with open beak; it is not dignified. Among us, when we see a thoughtless man, we ask, "What sort of bird is this?" and Teleas answers, "It's a man who has no brain, a bird that has lost his head, a creature you cannot catch, for it never remains in any one place."

EPOPS

By Zeus himself! your jest hits the mark. What then is to be done?

PITHETAERUS

Found a city.

EPOPS

We birds? But what sort of city should we build?

PITHETAERUS

Oh, really, really! you talk like such a fool! Look down.

EPOPS

I am looking.

PITHETAERUS

Now look up.

EPOPS

I am looking.

PITHETAERUS

Turn your head round.

EPOPS

Ah! it will be pleasant for me if I end in twisting my neck off!

PITHETAERUS

What have you seen?

EPOPS

The clouds and the sky.

PITHETAERUS

Very well! is not this the pole of the birds then?

EPOPS

How their pole?

PITHETAERUS

Or, if you like it, their place. And since it turns and passes through the whole universe, it is called 'pole.' If you build and fortify it, you will turn your pole into a city.⁵ In this way you will reign over mankind as you do over the grasshoppers and you will cause the gods to die of rabid hunger.

EPOPS

How so?

PITHETAERUS

The air is between earth and heaven. When we want to go to Delphi, we ask the Boeotians for leave of passage; in the same way, when men sacrifice to the gods, unless the latter pay you tribute, you exercise the right of every nation towards strangers and don't allow the smoke of the sacrifices to pass through your city and territory.

EPOPS

By earth! by snares! by network! by cages! ⁶ I never heard of anything more cleverly conceived; and, if the other birds approve, I am going to build the city along with you.

PITHETAERUS

Who will explain the matter to them?

EPOPS

You must yourself. Before I came they were quite ignorant, but since I have lived with them I have taught them to speak.

PITHETAERUS

But how can they be gathered together?

EPOPS

Easily. I will hasten down to the thicket to waken my dear Procné and as soon as they hear our voices, they will come to us hot wing.

PITHETAERUS

My dear bird, lose no time, please! Fly at once into the thicket and awaken Procné.

(EPOPS *rushes into the thicket.*)

EPOPS (*from within; singing*)

Chase off drowsy sleep, dear companion. Let the sacred hymn gush from thy divine throat in melodious strains; roll forth in soft cadence your refreshing melodies to bewail the fate of Itys, which has been the cause of so many tears to us both. Your pure notes rise through the thick leaves of the yew-tree right up to the throne of Zeus, where Phoebus listens to you, Phoebus with his golden hair. And his ivory lyre responds to your plaintive accents; he gathers the choir of the gods and from their immortal lips pours forth a sacred chant of blessed voices.

(*The flute is played behind the scene, imitating the song of the nightingale.*)

PITHETAERUS

Oh! by Zeus! what a throat that little bird possesses. He has filled the whole thicket with honey-sweet melody!

EUELPIDES

Hush!

PITHETAERUS

What's the matter?

EUELPIDES

Be still!

PITHETAERUS

What for?

EUELPIDES

Epops is going to sing again.

EPOPS (*in the thicket, singing*)

Epopopoi popoi popopopoi popoi, here, here, quick, quick, quick, my comrades in the air; all you who pillage the fertile lands of the husbandmen, the numberless tribes who gather and devour the barley seeds, the swift flying race that sings so sweetly. And you whose gentle twitter resounds through the fields with the little cry of *tiotic-tiotiotiotiotiotiotio;* and you who hop about the branches of the ivy in the gardens; the mountain birds, who feed on the wild olive-berries or the arbutus, hurry to come at my call, *trioto, trioto, totobrix;* you also, who snap up the sharp-stinging gnats in the marshy vales, and you who dwell in the fine plain of Marathon, all damp with dew, and you, the francolin with speckled wings; you too, the halcyons, who flit over the swelling waves of the sea, come hither to hear the tidings; let all the tribes of long-necked birds assemble here; know that a clever old man has come to us, bringing an entirely new idea and proposing great reforms. Let all come to the debate here, here, here, here. *Torotorotorotorotix, kikkabau, kikkabau, torotorotoro-lililix.*

PITHETAERUS

Can you see any bird?

EUELPIDES

By Phoebus, no! and yet I am straining my eyesight to scan the sky.

PITHETAERUS

It was hardly worth Epops' while to go and bury himself in the thicket like a hatching plover.

A BIRD (*entering*)

Torotix, torotix.

PITHETAERUS

Wait, friend, there's a bird.

EUELPIDES

By Zeus, it *is* a bird, but what kind? Isn't it a peacock?

PITHETAERUS (*as* EPOPS *comes out of the thicket*)

Epops will tell us. What is this bird?

EPOPS

It's not one of those you are used to seeing; it's a bird from the marshes.

EUELPIDES

Oh! oh! but he is very handsome with his wings as crimson as flame.

EPOPS

Undoubtedly; indeed he is called flamingo.

EUELPIDES (*excitedly*)

Hi! I say! You!

PITHETAERUS

What are you shouting for?

EUELPIDES

Why, here's another bird.

PITHETAERUS

Aye, indeed; this one's a foreign bird too. (*To* EPOPS) What is this bird from beyond the mountains with a look as solemn as it is stupid?

EPOPS

He is called the Mede.[7]

EUELPIDES

The Mede! But, by Heracles, how, if a Mede, has he flown here without a camel?

PITHETAERUS

Here's another bird with a crest.
(*From here on, the numerous birds that make up the* CHORUS *keep rushing in.*)

EUELPIDES

Ah! that's curious. I say, Epops, you are not the only one of your kind then?

EPOPS

This bird is the son of Philocles, who is the son of Epops; so that, you see, I am his grandfather; just as one might say, Hipponicus, the son of Callias, who is the son of Hipponicus.

EUELPIDES

Then this bird is Callias! Why, what a lot of his feathers he has lost!

EPOPS

That's because he is honest; so the informers set upon him and the women too pluck out his feathers.

EUELPIDES

By Posidon, do you see that many-coloured bird? What is his name?

EPOPS

This one? That's the glutton.

EUELPIDES

Is there another glutton besides Cleonymus? But why, if he is Cleonymus, has he not thrown away his crest? But what is the meaning of all these crests? Have these birds come to contend for the double stadium prize? [8]

EPOPS

They are like the Carians, who cling to the crests of their mountains for greater safety.

PITHETAERUS

Oh, Posidon! look what awful swarms of birds are gathering here!

EUELPIDES

By Phoebus! what a cloud! The entrance to the stage is no longer visible so closely do they fly together.

PITHETAERUS

Here is the partridge.

EUELPIDES

Why, there is the francolin.

PITHETAERUS

There is the poachard.

EUELPIDES

Here is the kingfisher. (*To* EPOPS) What's that bird behind the king fisher?

EPOPS

That's the barber.

EUELPIDES

What? a bird a barber?

PITHETAERUS

Why, Sporgilus is one.

EPOPS

Here comes the owl.

EUELPIDES

And who is it brings an owl to Athens? [9]

EPOPS (*pointing to the various species*)

Here is the magpie, the turtle-dove, the swallow, the horned-owl, the buzzard, the pigeon, the falcon, the ring-dove, the cuckoo, the red-foot, the red-cap, the purple-cap, the kestrel, the diver, the ousel, the osprey, the woodpecker . . .

PITHETAERUS

Oh! what a lot of birds!

EUELPIDES

Oh! what a lot of blackbirds!

PITHETAERUS

How they scold, how they come rushing up! What a noise! what a noise!

EUELPIDES

Can they be bearing us ill-will?

PITHETAERUS

Oh! there! there! they are opening their beaks and staring at us.

EUELPIDES

Why, so they are.

LEADER OF THE CHORUS

Popopopopopo.[10] Where is he who called me? Where am I to find him?

EPOPS

I have been waiting for you a long while! I never fail in my word to my friends.

LEADER OF THE CHORUS

Tititititititi. What good news have you for me?

EPOPS

Something that concerns our common safety, and that is just as pleasant as it is to the point. Two men, who are subtle reasoners, have come here to seek me.

LEADER OF THE CHORUS

Where? How? What are you saying?

EPOPS

I say, two old men have come from the abode of humans to propose a vast and splendid scheme to us.

LEADER OF THE CHORUS

Oh! it's a horrible, unheard-of crime! What are you saying?

EPOPS

Never let my words scare you.

LEADER OF THE CHORUS

What have you done to me?

EPOPS

I have welcomed two men, who wish to live with us.

LEADER OF THE CHORUS

And you have dared to do that!

EPOPS

Yes, and I am delighted at having done so.

LEADER OF THE CHORUS

And are they already with us?

EPOPS

Just as much as I am.

CHORUS (*singing*)

Ah! ah! we are betrayed; 'tis sacrilege! Our friend, he who picked
up corn-seeds in the same plains as ourselves, has violated our ancient
laws; he has broken the oaths that bind all birds; he has laid a snare
for me, he has handed us over to the attacks of that impious race
which, throughout all time, has never ceased to war against us.

LEADER OF THE CHORUS

As for this traitorous bird, we will decide his case later, but the two
old men shall be punished forthwith; we are going to tear them to pieces.

PITHETAERUS

It's all over with us.

EUELPIDES

You are the sole cause of all our trouble. Why did you bring me from
down yonder?

PITHETAERUS

To have you with me.

EUELPIDES

Say rather to have me melt into tears.

PITHETAERUS

Go on! you are talking nonsense. How will you weep with your eyes
pecked out?

CHORUS (*singing*)

Io! io! forward to the attack, throw yourselves upon the foe,
spill his blood; take to your wings and surround them on all sides.
Woe to them! let us get to work with our beaks, let us devour them.
Nothing can save them from our wrath, neither the mountain forests,
nor the clouds that float in the sky, nor the foaming deep.

LEADER OF THE CHORUS

Come, peck, tear to ribbons. Where is the chief of the cohort? Let him
engage the right wing.

(*They rush at the two Athenians.*)

EUELPIDES

This is the fatal moment. Where shall I fly to, unfortunate wretch that
I am?

PITHETAERUS

Wait! Stay here!

EUELPIDES

That they may tear me to pieces?

PITHETAERUS

And how do you think to escape them?

EUELPIDES

I don't know at all.

PITHETAERUS

Come, I will tell you. We must stop and fight them. Let us arm ourselves with these stew-pots.

EUELPIDES

Why with the stew-pots?

PITHETAERUS

The owl will not attack us then.[11]

EUELPIDES

But do you see all those hooked claws?

PITHETAERUS

Take the spit and pierce the foe on your side.

EUELPIDES

And how about my eyes?

PITHETAERUS

Protect them with this dish or this vinegar-pot.

EUELPIDES

Oh! what cleverness! what inventive genius! You are a great general, even greater than Nicias, where stratagem is concerned.

LEADER OF THE CHORUS

Forward, forward, charge with your beaks! Come, no delay. Tear, pluck, strike, flay them, and first of all smash the stew-pot.

EPOPS (*stepping in front of the* CHORUS)

Oh, most cruel of all animals, why tear these two men to pieces, why kill them? What have they done to you? They belong to the same tribe, to the same family as my wife.

LEADER OF THE CHORUS

Are wolves to be spared? Are they not our most mortal foes? So let us punish them.

EPOPS

If they are your foes by nature, they are your friends in heart, and they come here to give you useful advice.

LEADER OF THE CHORUS

Advice or a useful word from their lips, from them, the enemies of my forebears?

EPOPS

The wise can often profit by the lessons of a foe, for caution is the mother of safety. It is just such a thing as one will not learn from a friend and which an enemy compels you to know. To begin with, it's the foe and not the friend that taught cities to build high walls, to equip long vessels of war; and it's this knowledge that protects our children, our slaves and our wealth.

LEADER OF THE CHORUS

Well then, I agree, let us first hear them, for that is best; one can even learn something in an enemy's school.

PITHETAERUS (*to* EUELPIDES)

Their wrath seems to cool. Draw back a little.

EPOPS

It's only justice, and you will thank me later.

LEADER OF THE CHORUS
Never have we opposed your advice up to now.

PITHETAERUS
They are in a more peaceful mood; put down your stew-pot and your two dishes; spit in hand, doing duty for a spear, let us mount guard inside the camp close to the pot and watch in our arsenal closely; for we must not fly.

EUELPIDES
You are right. But where shall we be buried, if we die?

PITHETAERUS
In the Ceramicus; for, to get a public funeral, we shall tell the Strategi that we fell at Orneae, fighting the country's foes.

LEADER OF THE CHORUS
Return to your ranks and lay down your courage beside your wrath as the hoplites do. Then let us ask these men who they are, whence they come, and with what intent. Here, Epops, answer me.

EPOPS
Are you calling me? What do you want of me?

LEADER OF THE CHORUS
Who are they? From what country?

EPOPS
Strangers, who have come from Greece, the land of the wise.

LEADER OF THE CHORUS
And what fate has led them hither to the land of the birds?

EPOPS
Their love for you and their wish to share your kind of life; to dwell and remain with you always.

LEADER OF THE CHORUS
Indeed, and what are their plans?

EPOPS
They are wonderful, incredible, unheard of.

LEADER OF THE CHORUS
Why, do they think to see some advantage that determines them to settle here? Are they hoping with our help to triumph over their foes or to be useful to their friends?

EPOPS

They speak of benefits so great it is impossible either to describe or conceive them; all shall be yours, all that we see here, there, above and below us; this they vouch for.

LEADER OF THE CHORUS

Are they mad?

EPOPS

They are the sanest people in the world.

LEADER OF THE CHORUS

Clever men?

EPOPS

The slyest of foxes, cleverness its very self, men of the world, cunning, the cream of knowing folk.

LEADER OF THE CHORUS

Tell them to speak and speak quickly; why, as I listen to you, I am beside myself with delight.

EPOPS (*to two attendants*)

Here, you there, take all these weapons and hang them up inside close to the fire, near the figure of the god who presides there and under his protection; (*to* PITHETAERUS) as for you, address the birds, tell them why I have gathered them together.

PITHETAERUS

Not I, by Apollo, unless they agree with me as the little ape of an armourer agreed with his wife, not to bite me, nor pull me by the balls, nor shove things into my . . .

EUELPIDES (*bending over and pointing his finger at his anus*)

Do you mean this?

PITHETAERUS

No, I mean my eyes.

LEADER OF THE CHORUS

Agreed.

PITHETAERUS

Swear it.

LEADER OF THE CHORUS

I swear it and, if I keep my promise, let judges and spectators give me
the victory unanimously.

PITHETAERUS

It is a bargain.

LEADER OF THE CHORUS

And if I break my word, may I succeed by one vote only.

EPOPS (*as* HERALD)

Hearken, ye people! Hoplites, pick up your weapons and return to your
firesides; do not fail to read the decrees of dismissal we have posted.

CHORUS (*singing*)

Man is a truly cunning creature, but nevertheless explain. Perhaps
you are going to show me some good way to extend my power, some
way that I have not had the wit to find out and which you have discovered. Speak! 'tis to your own interest as well as to mine, for if you
secure me some advantage, I will surely share it with you.

LEADER OF THE CHORUS

But what object can have induced you to come among us? Speak boldly,
for I shall not break the truce,—until you have told us all.

PITHETAERUS

I am bursting with desire to speak; I have already mixed the dough of
my address and nothing prevents me from kneading it. . . . Slave!
bring the chaplet and water, which you must pour over my hands. Be
quick![12]

EUELPIDES

Is it a question of feasting? What does it all mean?

PITHETAERUS

By Zeus, no! but I am hunting for fine, tasty words to break down the
hardness of their hearts. (*To the* CHORUS) I grieve so much for you,
who at one time were kings . . .

LEADER OF THE CHORUS

We kings? Over whom?

PITHETAERUS

. . . of all that exists, firstly of me and of this man, even of Zeus himself. Your race is older than Saturn, the Titans and the Earth.

LEADER OF THE CHORUS

What, older than the Earth!

PITHETAERUS

By Phoebus, yes.

LEADER OF THE CHORUS

By Zeus, but I never knew that before!

PITHETAERUS

That's because you are ignorant and heedless, and have never read your Aesop. He is the one who tells us that the lark was born before all other creatures, indeed before the Earth; his father died of sickness, but the Earth did not exist then; he remained unburied for five days, when the bird in its dilemma decided, for want of a better place, to entomb its father in its own head.

EUELPIDES

So that the lark's father is buried at Cephalae.

PITHETAERUS

Hence, if they existed before the Earth, before the gods, the kingship belongs to them by right of priority.

EUELPIDES

Undoubtedly, but sharpen your beak well; Zeus won't be in a hurry to hand over his sceptre to the woodpecker.

PITHETAERUS

It was not the gods, but the birds, who were formerly the masters and kings over men; of this I have a thousand proofs. First of all, I will point you to the cock, who governed the Persians before all other monarchs, before Darius and Megabazus. It's in memory of his reign that he is called the Persian bird.

EUELPIDES

For this reason also, even to-day, he alone of all the birds wears his tiara straight on his head, like the Great King.

PITHETAERUS

He was so strong, so great, so feared, that even now, on account of his ancient power, everyone jumps out of bed as soon as ever he crows at daybreak. Blacksmiths, potters, tanners, shoemakers, bathmen, corn-dealers, lyre-makers and armourers, all put on their shoes and go to work before it is daylight.

EUELPIDES

I can tell you something about that. It was the cock's fault that I lost a splendid tunic of Phrygian wool. I was at a feast in town, given to celebrate the birth of a child; I had drunk pretty freely and had just fallen asleep, when a cock, I suppose in a greater hurry than the rest, began to crow. I thought it was dawn and set out for Halimus. I had hardly got beyond the walls, when a footpad struck me in the back with his bludgeon; down I went and wanted to shout, but he had already made off with my mantle.

PITHETAERUS

Formerly also the kite was ruler and king over the Greeks.

LEADER OF THE CHORUS

The Greeks?

PITHETAERUS

And when he was king, he was the one who first taught them to fall on their knees before the kites.[13]

EUELPIDES

By Zeus! that's what I did myself one day on seeing a kite; but at the moment I was on my knees, and leaning backwards with mouth agape, I bolted an obolus and was forced to carry my meal-sack home empty.[14]

PITHETAERUS

The cuckoo was king of Egypt and of the whole of Phoenicia. When he called out "cuckoo," all the Phoenicians hurried to the fields to reap their wheat and their barley.

EUELPIDES

Hence no doubt the proverb, "Cuckoo! cuckoo! go to the fields, ye circumcised."[15]

PITHETAERUS

So powerful were the birds that the kings of Grecian cities, Agamemnon, Menelaus, for instance, carried a bird on the tip of their sceptres, who had his share of all presents.

EUELPIDES

That I didn't know and was much astonished when I saw Priam come upon the stage in the tragedies with a bird, which kept watching Lysicrates to see if he got any present.

PITHETAERUS

But the strongest proof of all is that Zeus, who now reigns, is represented as standing with an eagle on his head as a symbol of his royalty; his daughter has an owl, and Phoebus, as his servant, has a hawk.

EUELPIDES

By Demeter, the point is well taken. But what are all these birds doing in heaven?

PITHETAERUS

When anyone sacrifices and, according to the rite, offers the entrails to the gods, these birds take their share before Zeus. Formerly men always swore by the birds and never by the gods.

EUELPIDES

And even now Lampon swears by the goose whenever he wishes to deceive someone.

PITHETAERUS

Thus it is clear that you were once great and sacred, but now you are looked upon as slaves, as fools, as Maneses; stones are thrown at you as at raving madmen, even in holy places. A crowd of bird-catchers sets snares, traps, limed twigs and nets of all sorts for you; you are caught, you are sold in heaps and the buyers finger you over to be certain you are fat. Again, if they would but serve you up simply roasted; but they rasp cheese into a mixture of oil, vinegar and laserwort, to which another sweet and greasy sauce is added, and the whole is poured scalding hot over your back, for all the world as if you were diseased meat.

CHORUS (*singing*)

Man, your words have made my heart bleed; I have groaned over the treachery of our fathers, who knew not how to transmit to us the high rank they held from their forefathers. But 'tis a benevolent Genius, a happy Fate, that sends you to us; you shall be our deliverer and I place the destiny of my little ones and my own in your hands with every confidence.

LEADER OF THE CHORUS

But hasten to tell me what must be done; we should not be worthy to live, if we did not seek to regain our royalty by every possible means.

PITHETAERUS

First I advise that the birds gather together in one city and that they build a wall of great bricks, like that at Babylon, round the plains of the air and the whole region of space that divides earth from heaven.

EPOPS

Oh, Cebriones! oh, Porphyrion! what a terribly strong place!

PITHETAERUS

Then, when this has been well done and completed, you demand back the empire from Zeus; if he will not agree, if he refuses and does not at once confess himself beaten, you declare a sacred war against him and forbid the gods henceforward to pass through your country with their tools up, as hitherto, for the purpose of laying their Alcmenas, their Alopés, or their Semelés! if they try to pass through, you put rings on their tools so that they can't make love any longer. You send another messenger to mankind, who will proclaim to them that the birds are kings, that for the future they must first of all sacrifice to them, and only afterwards to the gods; that it is fitting to appoint to each deity the bird that has most in common with it. For instance, are they sacrificing to Aphrodité, let them at the same time offer barley to the coot; are they immolating a sheep to Posidon, let them consecrate wheat in honour of the duck; if a steer is being offered to Heracles, let honey-cakes be dedicated to the gull; if a goat is being slain for King Zeus, there is a King-Bird, the wren, to whom the sacrifice of a male gnat is due before Zeus himself even.[16]

EUELPIDES

This notion of an immolated gnat delights me! And now let the great Zeus thunder!

LEADER OF THE CHORUS

But how will mankind recognize us as gods and not as jays? Us, who have wings and fly?

PITHETAERUS

You talk rubbish! Hermes is a god and has wings and flies, and so do many other gods. First of all, Victory flies with golden wings, Eros is undoubtedly winged too, and Iris is compared by Homer to a timorous dove.[17]

EUELPIDES

But will not Zeus thunder and send his wingéd bolts against us?

LEADER OF THE CHORUS

If men in their blindness do not recognize us as gods and so continue to worship the dwellers in Olympus?

PITHETAERUS

Then a cloud of sparrows greedy for corn must descend upon their fields and eat up all their seeds; we shall see then if Demeter will mete them out any wheat.

EUELPIDES

By Zeus, she'll take good care she does not, and you will see her inventing a thousand excuses.

PITHETAERUS

The crows too will prove your divinity to them by pecking out the eyes
of their flocks and of their draught-oxen; and then let Apollo cure them,
since he is a physician and is paid for the purpose.

EUELPIDES

Oh! don't do that! Wait first until I have sold my two young bullocks.

PITHETAERUS

If on the other hand they recognize that you are God, the principle of
life, that you are Earth, Saturn, Posidon, they shall be loaded with
benefits.

LEADER OF THE CHORUS

Name me one of these then.

PITHETAERUS

Firstly, the locusts shall not eat up their vine-blossoms; a legion of
owls and kestrels will devour them. Moreover, the gnats and the gall-
bugs shall no longer ravage the figs; a flock of thrushes shall swallow the
whole host down to the very last.

LEADER OF THE CHORUS

And how shall we give wealth to mankind? This is their strongest passion.

PITHETAERUS

When they consult the omens, you will point them to the richest mines,
you will reveal the paying ventures to the diviner, and not another shipwreck will happen or sailor perish.

LEADER OF THE CHORUS

No more shall perish? How is that?

PITHETAERUS

When the auguries are examined before starting on a voyage, some bird
will not fail to say, "Don't start! there will be a storm," or else, "Go! you
will make a most profitable venture."

EUELPIDES

I shall buy a trading-vessel and go to sea. I will not stay with you.

PITHETAERUS

You will discover treasures to them, which were buried in former times, for you know them. Do not all men say, "None knows where my treasure lies, unless perchance it be some bird." [18]

EUELPIDES

I shall sell my boat and buy a spade to unearth the vessels.

LEADER OF THE CHORUS

And how are we to give them health, which belongs to the gods?

PITHETAERUS

If they are happy, is not that the chief thing towards health? The miserable man is never well.

LEADER OF THE CHORUS

Old Age also dwells in Olympus. How will they get at it? Must they die in early youth?

PITHETAERUS

Why, the birds, by Zeus, will add three hundred years to their life.

LEADER OF THE CHORUS

From whom will they take them?

PITHETAERUS

From whom? Why, from themselves. Don't you know the cawing crow lives five times as long as a man?

EUELPIDES

Ah! ah! these are far better kings for us than Zeus!

PITHETAERUS (*solemnly*)

Far better, are they not? And firstly, we shall not have to build them temples of hewn stone, closed with gates of gold; they will dwell amongst the bushes and in the thickets of green oak; the most venerated of birds will have no other temple than the foliage of the olive tree; we shall not go to Delphi or to Ammon to sacrifice; but standing erect in the midst of arbutus and wild olives and holding forth our hands filled with wheat and barley, we shall pray them to admit us to a share of the blessings they enjoy and shall at once obtain them for a few grains of wheat.

LEADER OF THE CHORUS

Old man, whom I detested, you are now to me the dearest of all; never shall I, if I can help it, fail to follow your advice.

CHORUS (*singing*)

Inspirited by your words, I threaten my rivals the gods, and I
swear that if you march in alliance with me against the gods and are
faithful to our just, loyal and sacred bond, we shall soon have shattered their sceptre.

LEADER OF THE CHORUS

We shall charge ourselves with the performance of everything that
requires force; that which demands thought and deliberation shall be
yours to supply.

EPOPS

By Zeus! it's no longer the time to delay and loiter like Nicias; let us
act as promptly as possible. . . . In the first place, come, enter my nest
built of brushwood and blades of straw, and tell me your names.

PITHETAERUS

That is soon done; my name is Pithetaerus, and his, Euelpides, of the
deme Crioa.

EPOPS

Good! and good luck to you.

PITHETAERUS

We accept the omen.

EPOPS

Come in here.

PITHETAERUS

Very well, you are the one who must lead us and introduce us.

EPOPS

Come then.

(*He starts to fly away.*)

PITHETAERUS (*stopping himself*)

Oh! my god! do come back here. Hi! tell us how we are to follow you.
You can fly, but we cannot.

EPOPS

Well, well.

PITHETAERUS

Remember Aesop's fables. It is told there that the fox fared very badly,
because he had made an alliance with the eagle.

EPOPS

Be at ease. You shall eat a certain root and wings will grow on your shoulders.

PITHETAERUS

Then let us enter. Xanthias and Manodorus, pick up our baggage.

LEADER OF THE CHORUS

Hi! Epops! do you hear me?

EPOPS

What's the matter?

LEADER OF THE CHORUS

Take them off to dine well and call your mate, the melodious Procné, whose songs are worthy of the Muses; she will delight our leisure moments.

PITHETAERUS

Oh! I conjure you, accede to their wish; for this delightful bird will leave her rushes at the sound of your voice; for the sake of the gods, let her come here, so that we may contemplate the nightingale.

EPOPS

Let is be as you desire. Come forth, Procné, show yourself to these strangers.

(PROCNÉ *appears; she resembles a young flute-girl.*)

PITHETAERUS

Oh! great Zeus! what a beautiful little bird! what a dainty form! what brilliant plumage! Do you know how dearly I should like to get between her thighs?

EUELPIDES

She is dazzling all over with gold, like a young girl.[19] Oh! how I should like to kiss her!

PITHETAERUS

Why, wretched man, she has two little sharp points on her beak!

EUELPIDES

I would treat her like an egg, the shell of which we remove before eating it; I would take off her mask and then kiss her pretty face.

EPOPS

Let us go in.

PITHETAERUS

Lead the way, and may success attend us.

[EPOPS *goes into the thicket, followed by* PITHETAERUS *and* EUELPIDES.)

CHORUS (*singing*)

Lovable golden bird, whom I cherish above all others, you, whom I associate with all my songs, nightingale, you have come, you have come, to show yourself to me and to charm me with your notes. Come, you, who play spring melodies upon the harmonious flute, lead off our anapests.

(*The* CHORUS *turns and faces the audience.*)

LEADER OF THE CHORUS

Weak mortals, chained to the earth, creatures of clay as frail as the foliage of the woods, you unfortunate race, whose life is but darkness, as unreal as a shadow, the illusion of a dream, hearken to us, who are immortal beings, ethereal, ever young and occupied with eternal thoughts, for we shall teach you about all celestial matters; you shall know thoroughly what is the nature of the birds, what the origin of the gods, of the rivers, of Erebus, and Chaos; thanks to us, even Prodicus will envy you your knowledge.

At the beginning there was only Chaos, Night, dark Erebus, and deep Tartarus. Earth, the air and heaven had no existence. Firstly, blackwinged Night laid a germless egg in the bosom of the infinite deeps of Erebus, and from this, after the revolution of long ages, sprang the graceful Eros with his glittering golden wings, swift as the whirlwinds of the tempest. He mated in deep Tartarus with dark Chaos, winged like himself, and thus hatched forth our race, which was the first to see the light. That of the Immortals did not exist until Eros had brought together all the ingredients of the world, and from their marriage Heaven, Ocean, Earth and the imperishable race of blessed gods sprang into being. Thus our origin is very much older than that of the dwellers in Olympus. We are the offspring of Eros; there are a thousand proofs to show it. We have wings and we lend assistance to lovers. How many handsome youths, who had sworn to remain insensible, have opened their thighs because of our power and have yielded themselves to their lovers when almost at the end of their youth, being led away by the gift of a quail, a waterfowl, a goose, or a cock.

And what important services do not the birds render to mortals! First of all, they mark the seasons for them, springtime, winter, and autumn. Does the screaming crane migrate to Libya,—it warns the husbandman to sow, the pilot to take his ease beside his tiller hung up in his dwelling, and Orestes to weave a tunic, so that the rigorous cold may not drive him any more to strip other folk. When the kite reappears, he tells of the return of spring and of the period when the fleece of the sheep must be clipped. Is the swallow in sight? All hasten to sell their warm tunic and to buy some light clothing. We are your Ammon, Delphi, Dodona, your Phoebus Apollo. Before undertaking anything, whether a business transaction, a marriage, or the purchase of food, you consult the birds by reading the omens, and you give this name of omen [20] to all signs that tell of the future. With you a word is an omen, you call a sneeze an omen, a meeting an omen, an unknown sound an omen, a slave or an ass an omen. Is it not clear that we are a prophetic Apollo to you? (*More and more rapidly from here on.*) If you recognize us as gods, we shall be your divining Muses, through us you will know the winds and the seasons, summer, winter, and the temperate months. We shall not withdraw ourselves to the highest clouds like Zeus, but shall be among you and shall give to you and to your children and the children of your children, health and wealth, long life, peace, youth, laughter, songs and feasts; in short, you will all be so well off, that you will be weary and cloyed with enjoyment.

First Semi-Chorus (*singing*)

Oh, rustic Muse of such varied note, *tiotiotiotiotiotinx,* I sing with you in the groves and on the mountain tops, *tiotiotiotinx.* I poured forth sacred strains from my golden throat in honour of the god Pan, *tiotiotiotinx,* from the top of the thickly leaved ash, and my voice mingles with the mighty choirs who extol Cybelé on the mountain tops, *totototototototototinx.* 'Tis to our concerts that Phrynichus comes to pillage like a bee the ambrosia of his songs, the sweetness of which so charms the ear, *tiotiotiotinx.*

Leader of First Semi-Chorus

If there is one of you spectators who wishes to spend the rest of his life quietly among the birds, let him come to us. All that is disgraceful and forbidden by law on earth is on the contrary honourable among us, the birds. For instance, among you it's a crime to beat your father, but with us it's an estimable deed; it's considered fine to run straight at your father and hit him, saying, "Come, lift your spur if you want to fight." The runaway slave, whom you brand, is only a spotted francolin with us. Are you Phrygian like Spintharus? Among us you would be the Phrygian bird, the goldfinch, of the race of Philemon. Are you a slave and a Carian like Execestides? Among us you can create yourself forefathers; [21] you can always find relations. Does the son of Pisias want to betray the gates of the city to the foe? Let him become a partridge, the fitting offspring of his father; among us there is no shame in escaping as cleverly as a partridge.

SECOND SEMI-CHORUS (*singing*)
So the swans on the banks of the Hebrus, *tiotiotiotiotiotinx,*
mingle their voices to serenade Apollo, *tiotiotiotinx,* flapping their
wings the while, *tiotiotiotinx;* their notes reach beyond the clouds
of heaven; they startle the various tribes of the beasts; a windless
sky calms the waves, *totototototototototinx;* all Olympus resounds,
and astonishment seizes its rulers; the Olympian graces and Muses
cry aloud the strain, *tiotiotiotinx.*

LEADER OF SECOND SEMI-CHORUS
There is nothing more useful nor more pleasant than to have wings.
To begin with, just let us suppose a spectator to be dying with hunger
and to be weary of the choruses of the tragic poets; if he were winged,
he would fly off, go home to dine and come back with his stomach filled.
Some Patroclides, needing to take a crap, would not have to spill it out
on his cloak, but could fly off, satisfy his requirements, let a few farts
and, having recovered his breath, return. If one of you, it matters not
who, had adulterous relations and saw the husband of his mistress in the
seats of the senators, he might stretch his wings, fly to her, and, having
laid her, resume his place. Is it not the most priceless gift of all, to be
winged? Look at Diitrephes! His wings were only wicker-work ones, and
yet he got himself chosen Phylarch and then Hipparch; from being
nobody, he has risen to be famous; he's now the finest gilded cock of
his tribe.

(PITHETAERUS *and* EUELPIDES *return; they now have wings.*)

PITHETAERUS
Halloa! What's this? By Zeus! I never saw anything so funny in all my
life.

EUELPIDES
What makes you laugh?

PITHETAERUS
Your little wings. D'you know what you look like? Like a goose painted
by some dauber.

EUELPIDES
And you look like a close-shaven blackbird.

PITHETAERUS
We ourselves asked for this transformation, and, as Aeschylus has it,
"These are no borrowed feathers, but truly our own."

EPOPS

Come now, what must be done?

PITHETAERUS

First give our city a great and famous name, then sacrifice to the gods.

EUELPIDES

I think so too.

LEADER OF THE CHORUS

Let's see. What shall our city be called?

PITHETAERUS

Will you have a high-sounding Laconian name? Shall we call it Sparta?

EUELPIDES

What! call my town Sparta? Why, I would not use *esparto* for my bed,[22] even though I had nothing but bands of rushes.

PITHETAERUS

Well then, what name can you suggest?

EUELPIDES

Some name borrowed from the clouds, from these lofty regions in which we dwell—in short, some well-known name.

PITHETAERUS

Do you like Nephelococcygia?

LEADER OF THE CHORUS

Oh! capital! truly that's a brilliant thought!

EUELPIDES

Is it in Nephelococcygia that all the wealth of Theogenes and most of Aeschines' is?

PITHETAERUS

No, it's rather the plain of Phlegra, where the gods withered the pride of the sons of the Earth with their shafts.

LEADER OF THE CHORUS

Oh! what a splendid city! But what god shall be its patron? for whom shall we weave the peplus?

EUELPIDES

Why not choose Athené Polias?

PITHETAERUS

Oh! what a well-ordered town it would be to have a female deity armed from head to foot, while Clisthenes was spinning!

LEADER OF THE CHORUS

Who then shall guard the Pelargicon?

PITHETAERUS

A bird.

LEADER OF THE CHORUS

One of us? What kind of bird?

PITHETAERUS

A bird of Persian strain, who is everywhere proclaimed to be the bravest of all, a true chick of Ares.

EUELPIDES

Oh! noble chick'

PITHETAERUS

Because he is a god well suited to live on the rocks. Come! into the air with you to help the workers who are building the wall; carry up rubble, strip yourself to mix the mortar, take up the hod, tumble down the ladder, if you like, post sentinels, keep the fire smouldering beneath the ashes, go round the walls, bell in hand, and go to sleep up there yourself; then despatch two heralds, one to the gods above, the other to mankind on earth and come back here.

EUELPIDES

As for yourself, remain here, and may the plague take you for a troublesome fellow!

(*He departs.*)

PITHETAERUS

Go, friend, go where I send you, for without you my orders cannot be obeyed. For myself, I want to sacrifice to the new god, and I am going to summon the priest who must preside at the ceremony. Slaves! slaves! bring forward the basket and the lustral water.

CHORUS (*singing*)

I do as you do, and I wish as you wish, and I implore you to address powerful and solemn prayers to the gods, and in addition to immolate a sheep as a token of our gratitude. Let us sing the Pythian chant in honour of the god, and let Chaeris accompany our voices.

PITHETAERUS (*to the flute-player*)

Enough! but, by Heracles! what is this? Great gods! I have seen many prodigious things, but I never saw a muzzled raven.[23] (*The* PRIEST *arrives.*) Priest! it's high time! Sacrifice to the new gods.

PRIEST

I begin, but where is the man with the basket? [24] Pray to the Hestia of the birds, to the kite, who presides over the hearth, and to all the god and goddess-birds who dwell in Olympus . . .

PITHETAERUS

Oh! Hawk, the sacred guardian of Sunium, oh, god of the storks!

PRIEST

. . . to the swan of Delos, to Leto the mother of the quails, and to Artemis, the goldfinch . . .

PITHETAERUS

It's no longer Artemis Colaenis, but Artemis the goldfinch.

PRIEST

. . . to Bacchus, the finch and Cybelé, the ostrich and mother of the gods and mankind . . .

PITHETAERUS

Oh! sovereign ostrich Cybelé, mother of Cleocritus!

PRIEST

. . . to grant health and safety to the Nephelococcygians as well as to the dwellers in Chios . . .

PITHETAERUS

The dwellers in Chios! Ah! I am delighted they should be thus mentioned on all occasions.

PRIEST

. . . to the heroes, the birds, to the sons of heroes, to the porphyrion, the pelican, the spoon-bill, the redbreast, the grouse, the peacock, the horned-owl, the teal, the bittern, the heron, the stormy petrel, the figpecker, the titmouse . . .

PITHETAERUS

Stop! stop! you drive me crazy with your endless list. Why, wretch, to what sacred feast are you inviting the vultures and the sea-eagles? Don't you see that a single kite could easily carry off the lot at once? Begone, you and your fillets and all; I shall know how to complete the sacrifice by myself.

(*The* PRIEST *departs.*)

CHORUS (*singing*)
It is imperative that I sing another sacred chant for the rite of the
lustral water, and that I invoke the immortals, or at least one of
them, provided always that you have some suitable food to offer
him; from what I see here, in the shape of gifts, there is naught whatever but horn and hair.

PITHETAERUS
Let us address our sacrifices and our prayers to the winged gods.

(*A* POET *enters.*)

POET
Oh, Muse! celebrate happy Nephelococcygia in your hymns.

PITHETAERUS
What have we here? Where did you come from, tell me? Who are you?

POET
I am he whose language is sweeter than honey, the zealous slave of the
Muses, as Homer has it.

PITHETAERUS
You a slave! and yet you wear your hair long?

POET
No, but the fact is all we poets are the assiduous slaves of the Muses,
according to Homer.

PITHETAERUS
In truth your little cloak is quite holy too through zeal! But, poet,
what ill wind drove you here?

POET
I have composed verses in honour of your Nephelococcygia, a host of
splendid dithyrambs and parthenia worthy of Simonides himself.

PITHETAERUS
And when did you compose them? How long since?

POET
Oh! 'tis long, aye, very long, that I have sung in honour of this city.

PITHETAERUS
But I am only celebrating its foundation with this sacrifice; I have
only just named it, as is done with little babies.

POET

"Just as the chargers fly with the speed of the wind, so does the voice
of the Muses take its flight. Oh! thou noble founder of the town of Aetna,
thou, whose name recalls the holy sacrifices, make us such gift as thy
generous heart shall suggest."

(*He puts out his hand.*)

PITHETAERUS

He will drive us silly if we do not get rid of him by some present. (*To
the* PRIEST's *acolyte*) Here! you, who have a fur as well as your tunic,
take it off and give it to this clever poet. Come, take this fur; you look to
me to be shivering with cold.

POET

My Muse will gladly accept this gift; but engrave these verses of
Pindar's on your mind.

PITHETAERUS

Oh! what a pest! It's impossible then to get rid of him!

POET

"Straton wanders among the Scythian nomads, but has no linen garment. He is sad at only wearing an animal's pelt and no tunic." Do you
get what I mean?

PITHETAERUS

I understand that you want me to offer you a tunic. Hi! you (*to the
acolyte*), take off yours; we must help the poet. . . . Come, you, take it
and get out.

POET

I am going, and these are the verses that I address to this city: "Phoebus
of the golden throne, celebrate this shivery, freezing city; I have travelled
through fruitful and snow-covered plains. Tralalá! Tralalá!"

(*He departs.*)

PITHETAERUS

What are you chanting us about frosts? Thanks to the tunic, you no
longer fear them. Ah! by Zeus! I could not have believed this cursed
fellow could so soon have learnt the way to our city. (*To a slave*) Come,
take the lustral water and circle the altar. Let all keep silence!

(*An* ORACLE-MONGER *enters.*)

ORACLE-MONGER

Let not the goat be sacrificed.

PITHETAERUS

Who are you?

ORACLE-MONGER

Who am I? An oracle-monger.

PITHETAERUS

Get out!

ORACLE-MONGER

Wretched man, insult not sacred things. For there is an oracle of Bacis, which exactly applies to Nephelococcygia.

PITHETAERUS

Why did you not reveal it to me before I founded my city?

ORACLE-MONGER

The divine spirit was against it.

PITHETAERUS

Well, I suppose there's nothing to do but hear the terms of the oracle.

ORACLE-MONGER

"But when the wolves and the white crows shall dwell together between Corinth and Sicyon . . ."

PITHETAERUS

But how do the Corinthians concern me?

ORACLE-MONGER

It is the regions of the air that Bacis indicates in this manner. "They must first sacrifice a white-fleeced goat to Pandora, and give the prophet who first reveals my words a good cloak and new sandals."

PITHETAERUS

Does it say sandals there?

ORACLE-MONGER

Look at the book. "And besides this a goblet of wine and a good share of the entrails of the victim."

PITHETAERUS

Of the entrails—does it say that?

ORACLE-MONGER

Look at the book. "If you do as I command, divine youth, you shall be an eagle among the clouds; if not, you shall be neither turtle-dove, nor eagle, nor woodpecker."

PITHETAERUS

Does it say all that?

ORACLE-MONGER

Look at the book.

PITHETAERUS

This oracle in no sort of way resembles the one Apollo dictated to me:
"If an impostor comes without invitation to annoy you during the sacrifice
and to demand a share of the victim, apply a stout stick to his ribs."

ORACLE-MONGER

You are drivelling.

PITHETAERUS

Look at the book. "And don't spare him, were he an eagle from out of
the clouds, were it Lampon himself or the great Diopithes."

ORACLE-MONGER

Does it say that?

PITHETAERUS

Look at the book and go and hang yourself.

ORACLE-MONGER

Oh! unfortunate wretch that I am.

(*He departs.*)

PITHETAERUS

Away with you, and take your prophecies elsewhere.

(*Enter* METON, *with surveying instruments.*)

METON

I have come to you . . .

PITHETAERUS (*interrupting*)

Yet another pest! What have you come to do? What's your plan?
What's the purpose of your journey? Why these splendid buskins? [25]

METON

I want to survey the plains of the air for you and to parcel them into
lots.

PITHETAERUS

In the name of the gods, who are you?

METON

Who am I? Meton, known throughout Greece and at Colonus.

PITHETAERUS

What are these things?

METON

Tools for measuring the air. In truth, the spaces in the air have precisely the form of a furnace. With this bent ruler I draw a line from top to
bottom; from one of its points I describe a circle with the compass. Do
you understand?

PITHETAERUS

Not in the least.

METON

With the straight ruler I set to work to inscribe a square within this
circle; in its centre will be the market-place, into which all the straight
streets will lead, converging to this centre like a star, which, although
only orbicular, sends forth its rays in a straight line from all sides.

PITHETAERUS

A regular Thales! Meton . . .

METON

What d'you want with me?

PITHETAERUS

I want to give you a proof of my friendship. Use your legs.

METON

Why, what have I to fear?

PITHETAERUS

It's the same here as in Sparta. Strangers are driven away, and blows
rain down as thick as hail.

METON

Is there sedition in your city?

PITHETAERUS

No, certainly not.

METON

What's wrong then?

PITHETAERUS

We are agreed to sweep all quacks and impostors far from our borders.

METON

Then I'll be going.

PITHETAERUS

I'm afraid it's too late. The thunder growls already.

(*He beats him.*)

METON

Oh, woe! oh, woe!

PITHETAERUS

I warned you. Now, be off, and do your surveying somewhere else.
(METON *takes to his heels. He is no sooner gone than an* INSPECTOR
arrives.)

INSPECTOR

Where are the Proxeni?

PITHETAERUS

Who is this Sardanapalus?

INSPECTOR

I have been appointed by lot to come to Nephelococcygia as inspector.

PITHETAERUS

An inspector! and who sends you here, you rascal?

INSPECTOR

A decree of Teleas.

PITHETAERUS

Will you just pocket your salary, do nothing, and get out?

INSPECTOR

Indeed I will; I am urgently needed to be at Athens to attend the
Assembly; for I am charged with the interests of Pharnaces.

PITHETAERUS

Take it then, and get on your way. This is your salary.

(*He beats him.*)

INSPECTOR

What does this mean?

PITHETAERUS

This is the assembly where you have to defend Pharnaces.

INSPECTOR

You shall testify that they dare to strike me, the inspector.

PITHETAERUS

Are you not going to get out with your urns? [26] It's not to be believed; they send us inspectors before we have so much as paid sacrifice to the gods.

(*The* INSPECTOR *goes into hiding. A* DEALER IN DECREES *arrives.*)

DEALER IN DECREES (*reading*)

"If the Nephelococcygian does wrong to the Athenian . . ."

PITHETAERUS

What trouble now? What book is that?

DEALER IN DECREES

I am a dealer in decrees, and I have come here to sell you the new laws.

PITHETAERUS

Which?

Which?

DEALER IN DECREES

"The Nephelococcygians shall adopt the same weights, measures and decrees as the Olophyxians."

PITHETAERUS

And you shall soon be imitating the Ototyxians.

(*He beats him.*)

DEALER IN DECREES

Ow! what are you doing?

PITHETAERUS

Now will you get out of here with your decrees? For I am going to let *you* see some severe ones.

(*The* DEALER IN DECREES *departs; the* INSPECTOR *comes out of hiding.*)

INSPECTOR (*returning*)

I summon Pithetaerus for outrage for the month of Munychion.

PITHETAERUS

Ha! my friend! are you still here?

(*The* DEALER IN DECREES *also returns.*)

DEALER IN DECREES

"Should anyone drive away the magistrates and not receive them, according to the decree duly posted . . ."

PITHETAERUS

What! rascal! you are back too?

(*He rushes at him.*)

INSPECTOR

Woe to you! I'll have you condemned to a fine of ten thousand drachmae.

PITHETAERUS

And I'll smash your urns.

INSPECTOR

Do you recall that evening when you crapped on the column where the
decrees are posted?

PITHETAERUS

Here! here! let him be seized. (*The* INSPECTOR *runs off.*) Why, don't
you want to stay any longer? But let us get indoors as quick as possible;
we will sacrifice the goat inside.

FIRST SEMI-CHORUS (*singing*)

Henceforth it is to me that mortals must address their sacrifices
and their prayers. Nothing escapes my sight nor my might. My
glance embraces the universe, I preserve the fruit in the flower by
destroying the thousand kinds of voracious insects the soil produces,
which attack the trees and feed on the germ when it has scarcely
formed in the calyx; I destroy those who ravage the balmy terrace
gardens like a deadly plague; all these gnawing crawling creatures
perish beneath the lash of my wing.

LEADER OF FIRST SEMI-CHORUS

I hear it proclaimed everywhere: "A talent for him who shall kill Diagoras of Melos, and a talent for him who destroys one of the dead tyrants." [27] We likewise wish to make our proclamation: "A talent to him
among you who shall kill Philocrates, the Struthian; four, if he brings
him to us alive. For this Philocrates skewers the finches together and sells
them at the rate of an obolus for seven. He tortures the thrushes by blowing them out, so that they may look bigger, sticks their own feathers into
the nostrils of blackbirds, and collects pigeons, which he shuts up and
forces them, fastened in a net, to decoy others." That is what we wish to
proclaim. And if anyone is keeping birds shut up in his yard, let him
hasten to let them loose; those who disobey shall be seized by the birds
and we shall put them in chains, so that in their turn they may decoy
other men.

Second Semi-Chorus (*singing*)

Happy indeed is the race of winged birds who need no cloak in winter! Neither do I fear the relentless rays of the fiery dog-days; when the divine grasshopper, intoxicated with the sunlight, as noon is burning the ground, is breaking out into shrill melody; my home is beneath the foliage in the flowery meadows. I winter in deep caverns, where I frolic with the mountain nymphs, while in spring I despoil the gardens of the Graces and gather the white, virgin berry on the myrtle bushes.

Leader of Second Semi-Chorus

I want now to speak to the judges about the prize they are going to award; if they are favourable to us, we will load them with benefits far greater than those Paris received. Firstly, the owls of Laurium, which every judge desires above all things, shall never be wanting to you; you shall see them homing with you, building their nests in your money-bags and laying coins. Besides, you shall be housed like the gods, for we shall erect gables [28] over your dwellings; if you hold some public post and want to do a little pilfering, we will give you the sharp claws of a hawk. Are you dining in town, we will provide you with stomachs as capacious as a bird's crop. But, if your award is against us, don't fail to have metal covers fashioned for yourselves, like those they place over statues; else, look out! for the day you wear a white tunic all the birds will soil it with their droppings.

Pithetaerus

Birds! the sacrifice is propitious. But I see no messenger coming from the wall to tell us what is happening. Ah! here comes one running himself out of breath as though he were in the Olympic stadium.

Messenger (*running back and forth*)

Where, where, where is he? Where, where, where is he? Where, where, where is he? Where is Pithetaerus, our leader?

Pithetaerus

Here am I.

Messenger

The wall is finished.

Pithetaerus

That's good news.

MESSENGER

It's a most beautiful, a most magnificent work of art. The wall is so broad that Proxenides, the Braggartian, and Theogenes could pass each other in their chariots, even if they were drawn by steeds as big as the Trojan horse.

PITHETAERUS

That's fine!

MESSENGER

Its length is one hundred stadia; I measured it myself.

PITHETAERUS

A decent length, by Posidon! And who built such a wall?

MESSENGER

Birds—birds only; they had neither Egyptian brickmaker, nor stone-mason, nor carpenter; the birds did it all themselves; I could hardly believe my eyes. Thirty thousand cranes came from Libya with a supply of stones, intended for the foundations. The water-rails chiselled them with their beaks. Ten thousand storks were busy making bricks; plovers and other water fowl carried water into the air.

PITHETAERUS

And who carried the mortar?

MESSENGER

Herons, in hods.

PITHETAERUS

But how could they put the mortar into the hods?

MESSENGER

Oh! it was a truly clever invention; the geese used their feet like spades; they buried them in the pile of mortar and then emptied them into the hods.

PITHETAERUS

Ah! to what use cannot feet be put? [29]

MESSENGER

You should have seen how eagerly the ducks carried bricks. To complete the tale, the swallows came flying to the work, their beaks full of mortar and their trowels on their backs, just the way little children are carried.

PITHETAERUS

Who would want paid servants after this? But tell me, who did the woodwork?

MESSENGER

Birds again, and clever carpenters too, the pelicans, for they squared up the gates with their beaks in such a fashion that one would have thought they were using axes; the noise was just like a dockyard. Now the whole wall is tight everywhere, securely bolted and well guarded; it is patrolled, bell in hand; the sentinels stand everywhere and beacons burn on the towers. But I must run off to clean myself; the rest is your business.

(*He departs.*)

LEADER OF THE CHORUS (*to* PITHETAERUS)

Well! what do you say to it? Are you not astonished at the wall being completed so quickly?

PITHETAERUS

By the gods, yes, and with good reason. It's really not to be believed. But here comes another messenger from the wall to bring us some further news! What a fighting look he has!

SECOND MESSENGER (*rushing in*)

Alas! alas! alas! alas! alas! alas!

PITHETAERUS

What's the matter?

SECOND MESSENGER

A horrible outrage has occurred; a god sent by Zeus has passed through our gates and has penetrated the realms of the air without the knowledge of the jays, who are on guard in the daytime.

PITHETAERUS

It's a terrible and criminal deed. What god was it?

SECOND MESSENGER

We don't know that. All we know is, that he has got wings.

PITHETAERUS

Why were not patrolmen sent against him at once?

SECOND MESSENGER

We have despatched thirty thousand hawks of the legion of Mounted Archers. All the hook-clawed birds are moving against him, the kestrel, the buzzard, the vulture, the great-horned owl; they cleave the air so that it resounds with the flapping of their wings; they are looking everywhere for the god, who cannot be far away; indeed, if I mistake not, he is coming from yonder side.

PITHETAERUS

To arms, all, with slings and bows! This way, all our soldiers; shoot and strike! Some one give me a sling!

CHORUS (*singing*)

War, a terrible war is breaking out between us and the gods! Come, let each one guard Air, the son of Erebus, in which the clouds float. Take care no immortal enters it without your knowledge.

LEADER OF THE CHORUS

Scan all sides with your glance. Hark! methinks I can hear the rustle of the swift wings of a god from heaven.

(*The Machine brings in* IRIS, *in the form of a young girl.*)

PITHETAERUS

Hi! you woman! where, where, where are you flying to? Halt, don't stir! keep motionless! not a beat of your wing! (*She pauses in her flight.*) Who are you and from what country? You must say whence you come.

IRIS

I come from the abode of the Olympian gods.

PITHETAERUS

What's your name, ship or head-dress? [30]

IRIS

I am swift Iris.

PITHETAERUS

Paralus or Salaminia?

IRIS

What do you mean?

PITHETAERUS

Let a buzzard rush at her and seize her.[31]

IRIS

Seize me? But what do all these insults mean?

PITHETAERUS

Woe to you!

IRIS

I do not understand it.

PITHETAERUS

By which gate did you pass through the wall, wretched woman?

IRIS

By which *gate*? Why, great gods, I don't know.

PITHETAERUS

You hear how she holds us in derision. Did you present yourself to the officers in command of the jays? You don't answer. Have you a permit, bearing the seal of the storks?

IRIS

Am I dreaming?

PITHETAERUS

Did you get one?

IRIS

Are you mad?

PITHETAERUS

No head-bird gave you a safe-conduct?

IRIS

A safe-conduct to *me*. You pocr fool!

PITHETAERUS

Ah! and so you slipped into this city on the sly and into these realms of air-land that don't belong to you.

IRIS

And what other roads can the gods travel?

PITHETAERUS

By Zeus! I know nothing about that, not I. But they won't pass this way. And you still dare to complain? Why, if you were treated according to your deserts, no Iris would ever have more justly suffered death.

IRIS

I am immortal.

PITHETAERUS

You would have died nevertheless.—Oh! that would be truly intoler-able! What! should the universe obey us and the gods alone continue their insolence and not understand that they must submit to the law of the strongest in their due turn? But tell me, where are you flying to?

IRIS

I? The messenger of Zeus to mankind, I am going to tell them to sacrifice sheep and oxen on the altars and to fill their streets with the rich smoke of burning fat.

PITHETAERUS

Of which gods are you speaking?

IRIS

Of which? Why, of ourselves, the gods of heaven.

PITHETAERUS

You, gods?

IRIS

Are there others then?

PITHETAERUS

Men now adore the birds as gods, and it's to them, by Zeus, that they must offer sacrifices, and not to Zeus at all!

IRIS (*in tragic style*)

Oh! fool! fool! Rouse not the wrath of the gods, for it is terrible indeed. Armed with the brand of Zeus, Justice would annihilate your race; the lightning would strike you as it did Licymnius and consume both your body and the porticos of your palace.

PITHETAERUS

Here! that's enough tall talk. Just you listen and keep quiet! Do you take me for a Lydian or a Phrygian and think to frighten me with your big words? Know, that if Zeus worries me again, I shall go at the head of my eagles, who are armed with lightning, and reduce his dwelling and that of Amphion to cinders. I shall send more than six hundred porphyrions clothed in leopards' skins up to heaven against him; and formerly a single Porphyrion gave him enough to do. As for you, his messenger, if you annoy me, I shall begin by getting between your thighs, and even though you are Iris, you will be surprised at the erection the old man can produce; it's three times as good as the ram on a ship's prow!

IRIS

May you perish, you wretch, you and your infamous words!

PITHETAERUS

Won't you get out of here quickly? Come, stretch your wings or look out for squalls!

IRIS

If my father does not punish you for your insults . . .

(*The Machine takes* IRIS *away.*)

PITHETAERUS

Ha! . . . but just you be off elsewhere to roast younger folk than us with your lightning.

CHORUS (*singing*)

We forbid the gods, the sons of Zeus, to pass through our city and the mortals to send them the smoke of their sacrifices by this road.

PITHETAERUS

It's odd that the messenger we sent to the mortals has never returned.

(*The* HERALD *enters, wearing a golden garland on his head.*)

HERALD

Oh! blessed Pithetaerus, very wise, very illustrious, very gracious, thrice happy, very . . . Come, prompt me, somebody, do

PITHETAERUS

Get to your story!

HERALD

All peoples are filled with admiration for your wisdom, and they award you this golden crown.

PITHETAERUS

I accept it. But tell me, why do the people admire me?

HERALD

Oh you, who have founded so illustrious a city in the air, you know not in what esteem men hold you and how many there are who burn with desire to dwell in it. Before your city was built, all men had a mania for Sparta; long hair and fasting were held in honour, men went dirty like Socrates and carried staves. Now all is changed. Firstly, as soon as it's dawn, they all spring out of bed together to go and seek their food, the same as you do; then they fly off towards the notices and finally devour the decrees. The bird-madness is so clear that many actually bear the names of birds. There is a halting victualler, who styles himself the partridge; Menippus calls himself the swallow; Opuntius the one-eyed crow;

Philocles the lark; Theogenes the fox-goose; Lycurgus the ibis; Chaerephon the bat; Syracosius the magpie; Midias the quail; indeed he looks
like a quail that has been hit hard on the head. Out of love for the birds
they repeat all the songs which concern the swallow, the teal, the goose
or the pigeon; in each verse you see wings, or at all events a few feathers.
This is what is happening down there. Finally, there are more than ten
thousand folk who are coming here from earth to ask you for feathers and
hooked claws; so, mind you supply yourself with wings for the immigrants.

PITHETAERUS

Ah! by Zeus, there's no time for idling. (*To some slaves*) Go as quick
as possible and fill every hamper, every basket you can find with wings.
Manes will bring them to me outside the walls, where I will welcome
those who present themselves.

CHORUS (*singing*)

This town will soon be inhabited by a crowd of men. Fortune
favours us alone and thus they have fallen in love with our city.

PITHETAERUS (*to the slave* MANES, *who brings in a basket full of wings*)
Come, hurry up and bring them along.

CHORUS (*singing*)

Will not man find here everything that can please him—wisdom,
love, the divine Graces, the sweet face of gentle peace?

PITHETAERUS (*as* MANES *comes in with another basket*)
Oh! you lazy servant! won't you hurry yourself?

CHORUS (*singing*)

Let a basket of wings be brought speedily. Come, beat him as I
do, and put some life into him; he is as lazy as an ass.

PITHETAERUS

Aye, Manes is a great craven.

CHORUS (*singing*)

Begin by putting this heap of wings in order; divide them in three
parts according to the birds from whom they came; the singing, the
prophetic and the aquatic birds; then you must take care to distribute them to the men according to their character.

PITHETAERUS (*to* MANES, *who is bringing in another basket*)
Oh! by the kestrels! I can keep my hands off you no longer; you are
too slow and lazy altogether.

(*He hits* MANES, *who runs away. A young* PARRICIDE *enters.*)

PARRICIDE (*singing*)

Oh! might I but become an eagle, who soars in the skies! Oh! might I fly above the azure waves of the barren sea!

PITHETAERUS

Ha! it would seem the news was true; I hear someone coming who talks of wings.

PARRICIDE

Nothing is more charming than to fly; I am bird-mad and fly towards you, for I want to live with you and to obey your laws.

PITHETAERUS

Which laws? The birds have many laws.

PARRICIDE

All of them; but the one that pleases me most is that among the birds it is considered a fine thing to peck and strangle one's father.

PITHETAERUS

Yes, by Zeus! according to us, he who dares to strike his father, while still a chick, is a brave fellow.

PARRICIDE

And therefore I want to dwell here, for I want to strangle my father and inherit his wealth.

PITHETAERUS

But we have also an ancient law written in the code of the storks, which runs thus, "When the stork father has reared his young and has taught them to fly, the young must in their turn support the father."

PARRICIDE (*petulantly*)

It's hardly worth while coming all this distance to be compelled to keep my father!

PITHETAERUS

No, no, young friend, since you have come to us with such willingness, I am going to give you these black wings, as though you were an orphan bird; furthermore, some good advice, that I received myself in infancy. Don't strike your father, but take these wings in one hand and these spurs in the other; imagine you have a cock's crest on your head and go and mount guard and fight; live on your pay and respect your father's life. You're a gallant fellow! Very well, then! Fly to Thrace and fight.

PARRICIDE

By Bacchus! You're right; I will follow your counsel.

PITHETAERUS

It's acting wisely, by Zeus..

(*The* PARRICIDE *departs, and the dithyrambic poet* CINESIAS *arrives.*)

CINESIAS (*singing*)

"On my light pinions I soar off to Olympus; in its capricious flight
my Muse flutters along the thousand paths of poetry in turn . . ."

PITHETAERUS

This is a fellow will need a whole shipload of wings.

CINESIAS (*singing*)

". . . and being fearless and vigorous, it is seeking fresh outlet."

PITHETAERUS

Welcome, Cinesias, you lime-wood man! Why have you come here
twisting your game leg in circles?

CINESIAS (*singing*)

"I want to become a bird, a tuneful nightingale."

PITHETAERUS

Enough of that sort of ditty. Tell me what you want.

CINESIAS

Give me wings and I will fly into the topmost airs to gather fresh songs
in the clouds, in the midst of the vapours and the fleecy snow.

PITHETAERUS

Gather songs in the clouds?

CINESIAS

'Tis on them the whole of our latter-day art depends. The most brilliant dithyrambs are those that flap their wings in empty space and are
clothed in mist and dense obscurity. To appreciate this, just listen.

PITHETAERUS

Oh! no, no, no!

CINESIAS

By Hermes! but indeed you shall. (*He sings.*) "I shall travel through
thine ethereal empire like a winged bird, who cleaveth space with his
long neck . . ."

PITHETAERUS

Stop! Way enough!

CINESIAS

". . . as I soar over the seas, carried by the breath of the winds . . ."

PITHETAERUS

By Zeus! I'll cut your breath short.
(*He picks up a pair of wings and begins trying to stop* CINESIAS' *mouth with them.*)

CINESIAS (*running away*)

". . . now rushing along the tracks of Notus, now nearing Boreas across the infinite wastes of the ether." Ah! old man, that's a pretty and clever idea truly!

PITHETAERUS

What! are you not delighted to be cleaving the air?

CINESIAS

To treat a dithyrambic poet, for whom the tribes dispute with each other, in this style! [32]

PITHETAERUS

Will you stay with us and form a chorus of winged birds as slender as Leotrophides for the Cecropid tribe?

CINESIAS

You are making game of me, that's clear; but know that I shall never leave you in peace if I do not have wings wherewith to traverse the air.
(CINESIAS *departs and an* INFORMER *arrives.*)

INFORMER

What are these birds with downy feathers, who look so pitiable to me? Tell me, oh swallow with the long dappled wings.

PITHETAERUS

Oh! it's a regular invasion that threatens us. Here comes another one, humming along.

INFORMER

Swallow with the long dappled wings, once more I summon you.

PITHETAERUS

It's his cloak I believe he's addressing; it stands in great need of the swallows' return.

INFORMER

Where is he who gives out wings to all comers?

PITHETAERUS

Here I am, but you must tell me for what purpose you want them.

INFORMER

Ask no questions. I want wings, and wings I must have.

PITHETAERUS

Do you want to fly straight to Pellené?

INFORMER

I? Why, I am an accuser of the islands, an informer . . .

PITHETAERUS

A fine trade, truly!

INFORMER

. . . a hatcher of lawsuits. Hence I have great need of wings to prowl round the cities and drag them before justice.

PITHETAERUS

Would you do this better if you had wings?

INFORMER

No, but I should no longer fear the pirates; I should return with the cranes, loaded with a supply of lawsuits by way of ballast.

PITHETAERUS

So it seems, despite all your youthful vigour, you make it your trade to denounce strangers?

INFORMER

Well, and why not? I don't know how to dig.

PITHETAERUS

But, by Zeus! there are honest ways of gaining a living at your age without all this infamous trickery.

INFORMER

My friend, I am asking you for wings, not for words.

PITHETAERUS

It's just my words that gives you wings.

INFORMER

And how can you give a man wings with your words?

PITHETAERUS

They all start this way.

INFORMER

How?

PITHETAERUS

Have you not often heard the father say to young men in the barbers'
shops, "It's astonishing how Diitrephes' advice has made my son fly to
horse-riding."—"Mine," says another, "has flown towards tragic poetry
on the wings of his imagination."

INFORMER

So that words give wings?

PITHETAERUS

Undoubtedly; words give wings to the mind and make a man soar to
heaven. Thus I hope that my wise words will give you wings to fly to
some less degrading trade.

INFORMER

But I do not want to.

PITHETAERUS

What do you reckon on doing then?

INFORMER

I won't belie my breeding; from generation to generation we have lived
by informing. Quick, therefore, give me quickly some light, swift hawk
or kestrel wings, so that I may summon the islanders, sustain the accusation here, and haste back there again on flying pinions.

PITHETAERUS

I see. In this way the stranger will be condemned even before he appears.

INFORMER

That's just it.

PITHETAERUS

And while he is on his way here by sea, you will be flying to the islands
to despoil him of his property.

INFORMER

You've hit it, precisely; I must whirl hither and thither like a perfect
humming-top.

PITHETAERUS

I catch the idea. Wait, I've got some fine Corcyraean wings. How do
you like them?

INFORMER

Oh! woe is me! Why, it's a whip!

PITHETAERUS

No, no; these are the wings, I tell you, that make the top spin.

INFORMER (*as* PITHETAERUS *lashes him*)

Oh! oh! oh!

PITHETAERUS

Take your flight, clear off, you miserable cur, or you will soon see what comes of quibbling and lying. (*The* INFORMER *flees. To his slaves*) Come, let us gather up our wings and withdraw.

(*The baskets are taken away.*)

CHORUS (*singing*)

In my ethereal flights I have seen many things new and strange and wondrous beyond belief. There is a tree called Cleonymus belonging to an unknown species; it has no heart, is good for nothing and is as tall as it is cowardly. In springtime it shoots forth calumnies instead of buds and in autumn it strews the ground with bucklers in place of leaves.

Far away in the regions of darkness, where no ray of light ever enters, there is a country, where men sit at the table of the heroes and dwell with them always—except in the evening. Should any mortal meet the hero Orestes at night, he would soon be stripped and covered with blows from head to foot.

(PROMETHEUS *enters, masked to conceal his identity.*)

PROMETHEUS

Ah! by the gods! if only Zeus does not espy me! Where is Pithetaerus?

PITHETAERUS

Ha! what is this? A masked man!

PROMETHEUS

Can you see any god behind me?

PITHETAERUS

No, none. But who are you, pray?

PROMETHEUS

What's the time, please?

PITHETAERUS

The time? Why, it's past noon. Who are you?

PROMETHEUS

Is it the fall of day? Is it no later than that?

PITHETAERUS

This is getting dull!

PROMETHEUS

What is Zeus doing? Is he dispersing the clouds or gathering them?

PITHETAERUS

Watch out for yourself!

PROMETHEUS

Come, I will raise my mask.

PITHETAERUS

Ah! my dear Prometheus!

PROMETHEUS

Sh! Sh! speak lower!

PITHETAERUS

Why, what's the matter, Prometheus?

PROMETHEUS

Sh! sh! Don't call me by my name; you will be my ruin, if Zeus should see me here. But, if you want me to tell you how things are going in heaven, take this umbrella and shield me, so that the gods don't see me.

PITHETAERUS

I can recognize Prometheus in this cunning trick. Come, quick then, and fear nothing; speak on.

PROMETHEUS

Then listen.

PITHETAERUS

I am listening, proceed!

PROMETHEUS

Zeus is done for.

PITHETAERUS

Ah! and since when, pray?

PROMETHEUS

Since you founded this city in the air. There is not a man who now sacrifices to the gods; the smoke of the victims no longer reaches us. Not

the smallest offering comes! We fast as though it were the festival of
Demeter. The barbarian gods, who are dying of hunger, are bawling like
Illyrians and threaten to make an armed descent upon Zeus, if he does
not open markets where joints of the victims are sold.

PITHETAERUS

What! there are other gods besides you, barbarian gods who dwell
above Olympus?

PROMETHEUS

If there were no barbarian gods, who would be the patron of Execestides?

PITHETAERUS

And what is the name of these gods?

PROMETHEUS

Their name? Why, the Triballi.

PITHETAERUS

Ah, indeed! 'tis from that no doubt that we derive the word 'tribulation.' [33]

PROMETHEUS

Most likely. But one thing I can tell you for certain, namely, that
Zeus and the celestial Triballi are going to send deputies here to sue for
peace. Now don't you treat with them, unless Zeus restores the sceptre
to the birds and gives you Basileia in marriage.

PITHETAERUS

Who is this Basileia?

PROMETHEUS

A very fine young damsel, who makes the lightning for Zeus; all
things come from her, wisdom, good laws, virtue, the fleet, calumnies, the
public paymaster and the triobolus.

PITHETAERUS

Ah! then she is a sort of general manageress to the god.

PROMETHEUS

Yes, precisely. If he gives you her for your wife, yours will be the almighty power. That is what I have come to tell you; for you know my
constant and habitual goodwill towards men.

PITHETAERUS

Oh, yes! it's thanks to you that we roast our meat.

PROMETHEUS

I hate the gods, as you know.

PITHETAERUS

Aye, by Zeus, you have always detested them.

PROMETHEUS

Towards them I am a veritable Timon; but I must return in all haste,
so give me the umbrella; if Zeus should see me from up there, he would
think I was escorting one of the Canephori.

PITHETAERUS

Wait, take this stool as well.
(PROMETHEUS *leaves.* PITHETAERUS *goes into the thicket.*)

CHORUS (*singing*)

Near by the land of the Sciapodes there is a marsh, from the borders
whereof the unwashed Socrates evokes the souls of men. Pisander
came one day to see his soul, which he had left there when still alive.
He offered a little victim, a camel, slit his throat and, following the
example of Odysseus, stepped one pace backwards. Then that bat of
a Chaerephon came up from hell to drink the camel's blood.
(POSIDON *enters, accompanied by* HERACLES *and* TRIBALLUS.)

POSIDON

This is the city of Nephelococcygia, to which we come as ambassadors.
(*To* TRIBALLUS) Hi! what are you up to? you are throwing your cloak
over the left shoulder. Come, fling it quick over the right! And why, pray,
does it draggle in this fashion? Have you ulcers to hide like Læspodias?
Oh! democracy! whither, oh! whither are you leading us? Is it possible
that the gods have chosen such an envoy? You are undisturbed? Ugh!
you cursed savage! you are by far the most barbarous of all the gods.—
Tell me, Heracles, what are we going to do?

HERACLES

I have already told you that I want to strangle the fellow who dared
to wall us out.

POSIDON

But, my friend, we are envoys of peace.

HERACLES

All the more reason why I wish to strangle him.
(PITHETAERUS *comes out of the thicket, followed by slaves, who are
carrying various kitchen utensils; one of them sets up a table on
which he places poultry dressed for roasting.*)

PITHETAERUS

Hand me the cheese-grater; bring me the silphium for sauce; pass me the cheese and watch the coals.

HERACLES

Mortal! we who greet you are three gods.

PITHETAERUS

Wait a bit till I have prepared my silphium pickle.

HERACLES

What are these meats?

PITHETAERUS

These are birds that have been punished with death for attacking the people's friends.

HERACLES

And you are going to season them before answering us?

PITHETAERUS (*looking up from his work for the first time*)

Ah! Heracles! welcome, welcome! What's the matter?

POSIDON

The gods have sent us here as ambassadors to treat for peace.

PITHETAERUS (*ignoring this*)

There's no more oil in the flask.

HERACLES

And yet the birds must be thoroughly basted with it.

POSIDON

We have no interest to serve in fighting you; as for you, be friends and we promise that you shall always have rain-water in your pools and the warmest of warm weather. So far as these points go we are plenipotentiaries.

PITHETAERUS

We have never been the aggressors, and even now we are as well disposed for peace as yourselves, provided you agree to one equitable condition, namely, that Zeus yield his sceptre to the birds. If only this is agreed to, I invite the ambassadors to dinner.

HERACLES

That's good enough for me. I vote for peace.

POSIDON

You wretch! you are nothing but a fool and a glutton. Do you want to dethrone your own father?

PITHETAERUS

What an error. Why, the gods will be much more powerful if the birds govern the earth. At present the mortals are hidden beneath the clouds, escape your observation, and commit perjury in your name; but if you had the birds for your allies, and a man, after having sworn by the crow and Zeus, should fail to keep his oath, the crow would dive down upon him unawares and pluck out his eye.

POSIDON

Well thought of, by Posidon!

HERACLES

My notion too.

PITHETAERUS (*to* TRIBALLUS)

And you, what's your opinion?

TRIBALLUS

Nabaisatreu.[34]

PITHETAERUS

D'you see? he also approves. But listen, here is another thing in which we can serve you. If a man vows to offer a sacrifice to some god, and then procrastinates, pretending that the gods can wait, and thus does not keep his word, we shall punish his stinginess.

POSIDON

Ah! and how?

PITHETAERUS

While he is counting his money or is in the bath, a kite will relieve him, before he knows it, either in coin or in clothes, of the value of a couple of sheep, and carry it to the god.

HERACLES

I vote for restoring them the sceptre.

POSIDON

Ask Triballus.

HERACLES

Hi! Triballus, do you want a thrashing?

TRIBALLUS

Sure, bashum head withum stick.[35]

HERACLES

He says, "Right willingly."

POSIDON

If that be the opinion of both of you, why, I consent too.

HERACLES

Very well! we accord you the sceptre.

PITHETAERUS

Ah! I was nearly forgetting another condition. I will leave Heré to Zeus, but only if the young Basileia is given me in marriage.

POSIDON

Then you don't want peace. Let us withdraw.

PITHETAERUS

It matters mighty little to me. Cook, look to the gravy.

HERACLES

What an odd fellow this Posidon is! Where are you off to? Are we going to war about a woman?

POSIDON

What else is there to do?

HERACLES

What else? Why, conclude peace.

POSIDON

Oh! you blockhead! do you always want to be fooled? Why, you are seeking your own downfall. If Zeus were to die, after having yielded them the sovereignty, you would be ruined, for you are the heir of all the wealth he will leave behind.

PITHETAERUS

Oh! by the gods! how he is cajoling you. Step aside, that I may have a word with you. Your uncle is getting the better of you, my poor friend. The law will not allow you an obolus of the paternal property, for you are a bastard and not a legitimate child.

HERACLES

I a bastard! What's that you tell me?

PITHETAERUS

Why, certainly; are you not born of a stranger woman? Besides, is not Athené recognized as Zeus' sole heiress? And no daughter would be that, if she had a legitimate brother.

HERACLES

But what if my father wished to give me his property on his death-bed, even though I be a bastard?

PITHETAERUS

The law forbids it, and this same Posidon would be the first to lay claim to his wealth, in virtue of being his legitimate brother. Listen; thus runs Solon's law: "A bastard shall not inherit, if there are legitimate children; and if there are no legitimate children, the property shall pass to the nearest kin."

HERACLES

And I get nothing whatever of the paternal property?

PITHETAERUS

Absolutely nothing. But tell me, has your father had you entered on the registers of his phratry?

HERACLES

No, and I have long been surprised at the omission.

PITHETAERUS

Why do you shake your fist at heaven? Do you want to fight? Why, be on my side, I will make you a king and will feed you on bird's milk and honey.

HERACLES

Your further condition seems fair to me. I cede you the young damsel.

POSIDON

But I, I vote against this opinion.

PITHETAERUS

Then it all depends on the Triballus. (*To the* TRIBALLUS) What do you say?

TRIBALLUS

Givum bird pretty gel bigum queen.

HERACLES

He says give her.

POSIDON

Why no, he does not say anything of the sort, or else, like the swallows he does not know how to walk.[36]

PITHETAERUS

Exactly so. Does he not say she must be given to the swallows?

POSIDON (*resignedly*)

All right, you two arrange the matter; make peace, since you wish it so; I'll hold my tongue.

HERACLES

We are of a mind to grant you all that you ask. But come up there with us to receive Basileia and the celestial bounty.

PITHETAERUS

Here are birds already dressed, and very suitable for a nuptial feast.

HERACLES

You go and, if you like, I will stay here to roast them.

PITHETAERUS

You to roast them? you are too much the glutton; come along with us.

HERACLES

Ah! how well I would have treated myself!

PITHETAERUS

Let some one bring me a beautiful and magnificent tunic for the wedding.

(*The tunic is brought.* PITHETAERUS *and the three gods depart.*)

CHORUS (*singing*)

At Phanæ, near the Clepsydra, there dwells a people who have neither faith nor law, the Englottogastors, who reap, sow, pluck the vines and the figs [37] with their tongues; they belong to a barbaric race, and among them the Philippi and the Gorgiases are to be found; 'tis these Englottogastorian Philippi who introduced the custom all over Attica of cutting out the tongue separately at sacrifices.

(A MESSENGER *enters.*)

MESSENGER (*in tragic style*)

Oh, you, whose unbounded happiness I cannot express in words, thrice happy race of airy birds, receive your king in your fortunate dwellings. More brilliant than the brightest star that illumes the earth, he is approaching his glittering golden palace; the sun itself does not shine with more dazzling glory. He is entering with his bride at his side, whose

beauty no human tongue can express; in his hand he brandishes the lightning, the winged shaft of Zeus; perfumes of unspeakable sweetness per-
vade the ethereal realms. 'Tis a glorious spectacle to see the clouds of
incense wafting in light whirlwinds before the breath of the zephyr! But
here he is himself. Divine Muse! let thy sacred lips begin with songs of
happy omen.

(PITHETAERUS *enters, with a crown on his head; he is accompanied by*
BASILEIA.)

CHORUS (*singing*)
Fall back! to the right! to the left! advance! Fly around this
happy mortal, whom Fortune loads with her blessings. Oh! oh! what
grace! what beauty! Oh, marriage so auspicious for our city! All
honour to this man! 'tis through him that the birds are called to such
glorious destinies. Let your nuptial hymns, your nuptial songs, greet
him and his Basileia! 'Twas in the midst of such festivities that the
Fates formerly united Olympian Heré to the King who governs the
gods from the summit of his inaccessible throne. Oh! Hymen! oh!
Hymenaeus! Rosy Eros with the golden wings held the reins and
guided the chariot; 'twas he, who presided over the union of Zeus
and the fortunate Heré. Oh! Hymen! oh! Hymenaeus!

PITHETAERUS
I am delighted with your songs, I applaud your verses. Now celebrate
the thunder that shakes the earth, the flaming lightning of Zeus and the
terrible flashing thunderbolt.

CHORUS (*singing*)
Oh, thou golden flash of the lightning! oh, ye divine shafts of
flame, that Zeus has hitherto shot forth! Oh, ye rolling thunders,
that bring down the rain! 'Tis by the order of *our* king that ye shall
now stagger the earth! Oh, Hymen! 'tis through thee that he commands the universe and that he makes Basileia, whom he has robbed
from Zeus, take her seat at his side. Oh! Hymen! oh! Hymenæus!

PITHETAERUS (*singing*)
Let all the winged tribes of our fellow-citizens follow the bridal
couple to the palace of Zeus and to the nuptial couch! Stretch forth
your hands, my dear wife! Take hold of me by my wings and let us
dance; I am going to lift you up and carry you through the air.

(PITHETAERUS *and* BASILEIA *leave dancing; the* CHORUS *follows*
them.)

CHORUS (*singing*)
Alalaí! Ië Paión! Tenélla kállinike! Loftiest art thou of gods!

1. Myrtle boughs were part of the necessary paraphernalia of sacrifice, and this rite was an indispensable feature of the ceremonial founding of a city.

2. An extraordinarily felicitous or unfortunate experience was ascribed to the benevolence or the malignity of no less than a dozen divinities.

3. One naturally expects Euelpides to say, "a bird or a man?" Aristophanes makes frequent use of this humorous figure, for which the Greeks had the technical term *para prosdokian*, "contrary to expectation."

4. A reference to Athens' naval supremacy.

5. There is a pun here on the Greek words *polos*, "pole" and *polis*, "city."

6. Epops swears by all that he holds most terrible.

7. This scene, in which various birds appear and are identified, is an excellent example of the artistic restraint which characterizes Aristophanes' maturity. It is highly amusing to have the birds represent human beings and thus afford opportunities for personal jibes, but this device is much more amusing for not being carried out completely. No less than twenty-eight species are introduced, and although it would doubtless have been possible to connect all of these with human individuals or races, the resulting scene would have been too long for the essential humour of its theme.

8. In this event the competitors wore full armour and had to run the length of the track, round a mark at the end of it, and run back to the starting line.

9. The Athenian Acropolis was infested with owls. To bring owls to Athens was thus carrying coals to Newcastle.

10. In the Greek the *popopopopopo* runs right into the word *pou*, "where?" and the *titititititi* into *tina*, "what?" The effect is thus not merely birdlike, but also suggestive of a high pitch of excitement which causes the Leader of the Chorus to stutter. The second case could be rendered "t-t-t-t-t-t-tell me, etc." but the first seems quite untranslatable; there is nothing birdlike in "wh-wh-wh-wh-wh-wh-where's the man who called me?"

11. A reference to the Feast of Pots, celebrated at Athens in honour of

Athené. The owl, an Athenian bird, will spare Pithetaerus and Euelpides when he recognizes their provenance by the stew-pots.

12. Since banqueters washed their hands before eating and wore chaplets at feasts, the suggestion is that the speech of Pithetaerus is to be something of a treat.

13. The appearance of the kite was a sign of Spring and was greeted with reverential actions.

14. Those in the ancient world who were too poor to afford a purse were wont to carry small coins in their mouths.

15. The origin and the meaning of this proverb are far from certain, but there is probably a play on two meanings of *psolos*, "circumcised" and "with erected penis." If the proverb was really current in Greece in this form it probably meant, "The cuckoo is here; time to stop making love and get to work." Euelpides then adapts it to the circumcised Egyptians and Phoenicians, in whose countries the cuckoo arrived at harvest time.

16. The connexions of these birds with the gods are various. The Greek word for coot is *phaleris*, which suggests the phallus. The duck lives in Posidon's realm. The gull is as voracious as Heracles. The wren was called *basiliskos*, "little king" because of Aesop's fable, according to which the birds had agreed to choose as their king the one who could fly the highest; the eagle naturally was victorious in this competition, but when he had ascended as far as he could, the wren, who had concealed himself in his plumage, took off from his back and flew a bit higher.

17. This comparison is made of Iris and Ilithyia in the *Hymn to Apollo* (114) and of Hera and Athené in the *Iliad* (V, 778).

18. The usual form of this proverb is reported to have been, "No one can see me, except some bird."

19. Golden ornaments seem not to have been worn by matrons in the ancient world; the restriction to young girls probably went back to Homeric times.

20. The antiquity and the importance of divination by the actions of birds had made the Greek word *ornis*, "bird" the regular term for "omen."

21. A pun of the Greek word *pappas*, which normally means "grandfather," but is also the name of some kind of bird, we do not know just what kind.

22. The Greek word for esparto is *spartos*. The pun on Sparta is thus one of the few that can be translated.

23. The flute-player was costumed as a raven, but also wore the *phorbeia*, "a sort of leathern muzzle fitting closely round the piper's mouth on each side of the pipe. It was intended to make the breath flow more evenly through the instrument."

24. A regular feature of the sacrificial rite was a basket of cane containing the sacred paraphernalia.

25. Buskins were a standard part of the tragic costume; here they are mentioned as symbolic of Meton's pompous manner. It does not follow that he was wearing them.

26. These were the ancient ballot-boxes; the Inspector has brought them along in order immediately to set democracy going in Nephelococcygia.

27. A jibe at the groundless tyrannophobia of the Athenians. See note 12 on *The Wasps*.

28. There is a pun here on the two meanings of the Greek word *aetos*, "eagle" and "gable."

29. An adaptation of the proverb, "To what use cannot hands be put?"

30. Iris must be visualized as speeding rapidly through the air with her robes flying like a ship's sails or the ribbons of a bonnet.

31. The buzzard is chosen with an eye to its name, *triorchos*, which also means "having three testicles."

32. A reference to the third of the Athenian choral competitions, in which dithyrambs were performed. Apparently each tribe supplied a chorus to compete in its name. Cinesias thus means that his talents are such that each tribe is eager to have him compose for and direct its chorus.

33. The pun here is hardly better in the Greek than in the translation; the word rendered "tribulation" is *epitribé*.

34. The word *nabaisatreu* is probably not designed to mean anything, but the first two letters suggest the Greek affirmative particles *ne* and *nai*, and this is all that Pithetaerus needs.

35. The broken Greek of Triballus seems here to be a threat in answer to that of Heracles, but its interpretation is very uncertain.

36. The meaning of Triballus' remark is wholly clear; the point of Posidon's, however, is undiscoverable.

37. A pun on the word *sykon*, "fig" and *sykophantes*, "informer." The etymology of the latter word is very obscure. The connexion with *sykon* seems obvious enough, but this does not help much.

VII
LYSISTRATA

CHARACTERS IN THE PLAY

LYSISTRATA
CLEONICÉ
MYRRHINÉ
LAMPITO
MAGISTRATES
CINESIAS
CHILD OF CINESIAS
HERALD OF THE LACEDAEMONIANS
ENVOYS OF THE LACEDAEMONIANS
AN ATHENIAN CITIZEN
CHORUS OF OLD MEN
CHORUS OF WOMEN

INTRODUCTION

THREE years after the production of *The Birds,* Aristophanes brought out *Lysistrata* at the Lenaean festival of 411. We have no information on the award of the prizes, and although it is difficult to imagine how a better comedy can have been produced on that occasion, we know enough of the unpredictable whims of Athenian popular taste to realize that Aristophanes may very well have been disappointed in the reception accorded one of his most excellent productions. Although the theme of the play classes it with *The Acharnians* and *Peace,* its atmosphere and treatment are radically different from those of its predecessors. The two earlier peace-plays are fantastic in detail but realistic in essence. In 425, Athens might have concluded a wise and profitable truce with Sparta, and in 421, it must have seemed that the trials and the tribulations of the war would soon be things of the past. In 411, however, Athens had her back against the wall and was fighting for her life; peace could have been obtained only by a surrender at once complete and disastrous. The pacific fantasy of *Lysistrata* is thus far more thoroughly divorced from contemporary realities than that of either *Peace* or *The Acharnians,* and in keeping with this the idealistic revery which it presents is panhellenic and Utopian to an extent which renders the play spiritually much more closely akin to *The Birds* and *The Ecclesiazusae* than to any of the earlier comedies. At the same time it looks to the future more clearly than any other play of Aristophanes that has come down to us, for its timelessness is almost equal to that of the New Comedy and far in excess of anything that we find in the Old. This should have made it in modern times the most popular of the poet's compositions, and the fact that it has not been so is a sad tribute to the omnipotence of Christian prudery, but the success of a not too emasculated adaptation produced in New York in 1930 might induce the true son of the twentieth century, who is also a philhellenist, to hope that his grandchildren may dwell in a clearer and healthier atmosphere.

As the play opens we see Lysistrata pacing up and down in front of her house, in a state of great excitement and annoyance. Her plans have been carefully laid and the moment for action is at hand; the women of Athens have been sent to seize the Acropolis and female representatives of various other states in Greece have agreed to meet her here at this time; and they are not here. Finally they do arrive, and when all have assembled Lysistrata unfolds her plan. It is a magnificent and well-conceived scheme, whereby the women of Greece are to force their husbands to put an end to the war, by the simple expedient of refusing to lie with them. But its authoress has not adequately estimated the reluctance of the women to deprive themselves of corporeal delights. Like all revolutionary leaders, she is herself undersexed, and only the loyal support of the athletic Lampito, the delegate from hardy Sparta, prevents the cause from dying an ignoble and infant death. The other women ultimately steel their hearts and still their qualms, and an awful oath of celibacy is tearfully sworn over a bowl of wine.

A great commotion heard offstage testifies to the occupation of the Acropolis, and the revolution is now in full swing. Lysistrata and the other Athenians go to join their active countrywomen, while the delegates from abroad set out to incite similar insurrections in their respective cities. The scene shifts to the entrance of the Acropolis, and a group of old men, who constitute one of the two Choruses in the play, come slowly and painfully up the steep path, carrying faggots and logs and pots of fire. They intend to smoke the women out of the citadel, but meet with unexpected and effective resistance from a group of women who make up the other Chorus. Armed with pots of water and inspired by revolutionary zeal, they drench the old men and extinguish their fire. The first attempt at suppression has thus been successfully repulsed, but another difficulty now appears in the person of a magistrate accompanied by Scythian policemen. He orders his officers to force the gates and arrest Lysistrata, but the heroine forestalls this by coming out of the Acropolis voluntarily. The magistrate immediately orders his Scythians to seize her, but Lysistrata's cohorts rush at them so fiercely that they retire in trepidation and defecation. The cowardice of his officers thus compels the disappointed magistrate to shift from deeds to words, and Lysistrata eloquently expounds her plan and explains her actions. Her words are fruitless, of course, and the women turn to deeds, sousing the official with water and dressing him up like a corpse on the bier. He departs in towering and helpless wrath, to show his fellow magistrates the treatment he has received, and the victorious women retire into the Acropolis.

The stage is thus left to the two Choruses, and we expect them to cooperate in delivering a parabasis. The interlude which follows, however, is in substance merely an argument between the sexes, although it exhibits the formal features of ode and epirrheme. There are no anapests, and the passage is thus formally reminiscent of the second parabasis in

The Birds, with the difference that in the present instance each of the parts is found twice, because of the presence of two choruses.

Several days must be supposed to have elapsed during this interlude. At its conclusion Lysistrata steps forth from the Acropolis in deep anxiety and disillusionment, and we learn that she is experiencing the characistic difficulties of a revolutionary leader. Initial enthusiasm has cooled, with the result that attempted defections are growing more and more numerous. Feminine frailty is becoming increasingly inadequate to the strain of living on the Acropolis with the owls and without the men. A series of instances of intended desertion now ensues; there is wool at home to be spread, and flax to be stripped, and the hooting of the owls is unbearable. The most ingenious of the women has slipped the sacred helmet of Pallas under her robe and asks Lysistrata's permission to go to the midwife, immediately. The revolution seems destined to fail in a very short time, but just at the moment when things look blackest the enemy shows signs of weakness, and Cinesias, the husband of one of Lysistrata's high command, named Myrrhiné, enters. The condition of his household is deplorable, but his own is patently worse, and Lysistrata instructs his wife to make the wretched man the fulcrum of the revolution's success. The obedient subordinate carries out her orders with fiendish thoroughness, tantalizing her husband beyond all human endurance, and finally leaving him much more tortured than he was before. The tide has now turned and the agonized enemy will soon capitulate. A herald arrives from Sparta, and his figure leaves no doubt that Lampito has been as effective as Lysistrata; "Are you a man or a Priapus?" asks the Athenian official who meets him, "or is that a lance you're hiding under your clothes?" Soon the envoys arrive and Lysistrata wisely reconciles the opposing parties; peace is made and the comedy ends in general rejoicing.

So far as the extant material enables us to judge, *Lysistrata* is the first comedy of Aristophanes in which women form the chorus or play any important rôle. Evidently the poet found this type of play enjoyable to write, for there are two others amongst the eleven in which the chorus or the principal characters are female. The feminine triad consistently exhibits Aristophanes' wit at its most brilliant best, but this is only what would be expected by anyone candid enough to recognize that the sexual phenomena of human life are the most copious sources of the finest humour. It is regrettable and thoroughly human that those persons to whom this fact needs to be pointed out are invariably unwilling or unable to accept it when it is pointed out; *Lysistrata* is not for them.

LYSISTRATA

(SCENE:—*At the base of the Orchestra are two buildings, the house of* LYSISTRATA *and the entrance to the Acropolis; a winding and narrow path leads up to the latter. Between the two buildings is the opening of the Cave of Pan.* LYSISTRATA *is pacing up and down in front of her house.*)

LYSISTRATA

AH! if only they had been invited to a Bacchic revelling, or a feast of Pan or Aphrodité or Genetyllis, why! the streets would have been impassable for the thronging tambourines! Now there's never a woman here—ah! except my neighbour Cleonicé, whom I see approaching yonder. . . . Good day, Cleonicé.

CLEONICÉ

Good day, Lysistrata; but pray, why this dark, forbidding face, my dear? Believe me, you don't look a bit pretty with those black lowering brows.

LYSISTRATA

Oh, Cleonicé, my heart is on fire; I blush for our sex. Men *will* have it we are tricky and sly. . . .

CLEONICÉ

And they are quite right, upon my word!

LYSISTRATA

Yet, look you, when the women are summoned to meet for a matter of the greatest importance, they lie in bed instead of coming.

CLEONICÉ

Oh! they will come, my dear; but it's not easy, you know, for women to leave the house. One is busy pottering about her husband; another is getting the servant up; a third is putting her child asleep or washing the brat or feeding it.

809

LYSISTRATA

But I tell you, the business that calls them here is far and away more urgent.

CLEONICÉ

And why *do* you summon us, dear Lysistrata? What is it all about?

LYSISTRATA

About a big thing.

CLEONICÉ (*taking this in a different sense; with great interest*)
And is it thick too?

LYSISTRATA

Yes, very thick.

CLEONICÉ

And we are not all on the spot! Imagine!

LYSISTRATA (*wearily*)
Oh! if it were what you suppose, there would be never an absentee. No, no, it concerns a thing I have turned about and about this way and that *so* many sleepless nights.

CLEONICÉ (*still unable to be serious*)
It must be something mighty fine and subtle for you to have turned it about so!

LYSISTRATA

So fine, it means just this, Greece saved by the women!

CLEONICÉ

By the women! Why, its salvation hangs on a poor thread then!

LYSISTRATA

Our country's fortunes depend on us—it is with us to undo utterly the Peloponnesians.

CLEONICÉ

That would be a noble deed truly!

LYSISTRATA

To exterminate the Boeotians to a man!

CLEONICÉ

But surely you would spare the eels.

LYSISTRATA

For Athens' sake I will never threaten so fell a doom; trust me for that. However, if the Boeotian and Peloponnesian women join us, Greece is saved.

CLEONICÉ

But how should women perform so wise and glorious an achievement, we women who dwell in the retirement of the household, clad in diaphanous garments of yellow silk and long flowing gowns, decked out with flowers and shod with dainty little slippers?

LYSISTRATA

Ah, but those are the very sheet-anchors of our salvation—those yellow tunics, those scents and slippers, those cosmetics and transparent robes.

CLEONICÉ

How so, pray?

LYSISTRATA

There is not a man will wield a lance against another . . .

CLEONICÉ

Quick, I will get me a yellow tunic from the dyer's.

LYSISTRATA

. . . or want a shield.

CLEONICÉ

I'll run and put on a flowing gown.

LYSISTRATA

. . . or draw a sword.

CLEONICÉ

I'll haste and buy a pair of slippers this instant.

LYSISTRATA

Now tell me, would not the women have done best to come?

CLEONICÉ

Why, they should have *flown* here!

LYSISTRATA

Ah! my dear, you'll see that like true Athenians, they will do everything too late.[1] . . . Why, there's not a woman come from the shore, not one from Salamis.

CLEONICÉ

But I know for certain they embarked at daybreak.

LYSISTRATA

And the dames from Acharnae! why, I thought they would have been the very first to arrive.

CLEONICÉ

Theagenes' wife at any rate is sure to come; she has actually been to consult Hecaté. . . . But look! here are some arrivals—and there are more behind. Ah! ha! now what countrywomen may they be?

LYSISTRATA

They are from Anagyra.

CLEONICÉ

Yes! upon my word, 'tis a levy *en masse* of all the female population of Anagyra!

(MYRRHINÉ *enters, followed by other women.*)

MYRRHINÉ

Are we late, Lysistrata? Tell us, pray; what, not a word?

LYSISTRATA

I cannot say much for you, Myrrhiné! you have not bestirred yourself overmuch for an affair of such urgency.

MYRRHINÉ

I could not find my girdle in the dark. However, if the matter is so pressing, here we are; so speak.

CLEONICÉ

No, let's wait a moment more, till the women of Boeotia arrive and those from the Peloponnese.

LYSISTRATA

Yes, that is best. . . . Ah! here comes Lampito. (LAMPITO, *a husky Spartan damsel, enters with three others, two from Boeotia and one from Corinth.*) Good day, Lampito, dear friend from Lacedaemon. How well and handsome you look! what a rosy complexion! and how strong you seem; why, you could strangle a bull surely!

LAMPITO

Yes, indeed, I really think I could. It's because I do gymnastics and practise the bottom-kicking dance.

CLEONICÉ (*opening* LAMPITO's *robe and baring her bosom*)
And what superb breasts!

LAMPITO
La! you are feeling me as if I were a beast for sacrifice.

LYSISTRATA
And this young woman, where is she from?

LAMPITO
She is a noble lady from Boeotia.

LYSISTRATA
Ah! my pretty Boeotian friend, you are as blooming as a garden.

CLEONICÉ (*making another inspection*)
Yes, on my word! and her "garden" is so thoroughly weeded too!

LYSISTRATA (*pointing to the Corinthian*)
And who is this?

LAMPITO
'Tis an honest woman, by my faith! she comes from Corinth.

CLEONICÉ
Oh! honest, no doubt then—as honesty goes at Corinth.

LAMPITO
But who has called together this council of women, pray?

LYSISTRATA
I have.

LAMPITO
Well then, tell us what you want of us.

CLEONICÉ
Yes, please tell us! What *is* this very important business you wish to inform us about?

LYSISTRATA
I will tell you. But first answer me one question.

CLEONICÉ
Anything you wish.

LYSISTRATA

Don't you feel sad and sorry because the fathers of your children are far away from you with the army? For I'll wager there is not one of you whose husband is not abroad at this moment.

CLEONICÉ

Mine has been the last five months in Thrace—looking after Eucrates.

MYRRHINÉ

It's seven long months since mine left for Pylos.

LAMPITO

As for mine, if he ever does return from service, he's no sooner home than he takes down his shield again and flies back to the wars.

LYSISTRATA

And not so much as the shadow of a lover! Since the day the Milesians betrayed us, I have never once seen an eight-inch gadget even, to be a leathern consolation to us poor widows. . . . Now tell me, if I have discovered a means of ending the war, will you all second me?

CLEONICÉ

Yes verily, by all the goddesses, I swear I will, though I have to put my gown in pawn, and drink the money the same day.[2]

MYRRHINÉ

And so will I, though I must be split in two like a flat-fish, and have half myself removed.

LAMPITO

And I too; why to secure peace, I would climb to the top of Mount Taygetus.

LYSISTRATA

Then I will out with it at last, my mighty secret! Oh! sister women, if we would compel our husbands to make peace. we must refrain . . .

CLEONICÉ

Refrain from what? tell us, tell us!

LYSISTRATA

But will you do it?

MYRRHINÉ

We will, we will, though we should die of it.

LYSISTRATA

We must refrain from the male altogether. . . . Nay, why do you turn your backs on me? Where are you going? So, you bite your lips, and shake your heads, eh? Why these pale, sad looks? why these tears? Come, will you do it—yes or no? Do you hesitate?

CLEONICÉ

I will not do it, let the war go on.

MYRRHINÉ

Nor will I; let the war go on.

LYSISTRATA (*to* MYRRHINÉ)

And you say this, my pretty flat-fish, who declared just now they might split you in two?

CLEONICÉ

Anything, anything but that! Bid me go through the fire, if you will; but to rob us of the sweetest thing in all the world, Lysistrata darling!

LYSISTRATA (*to* MYRRHINÉ)

And you?

MYRRHINÉ

Yes, I agree with the others; I too would sooner go through the fire.

LYSISTRATA

Oh, wanton, vicious sex! the poets have done well to make tragedies upon us; we are good for nothing then but love and lewdness! But you, my dear, you from hardy Sparta, if *you* join me, all may yet be well; help me, second me, I beg you.

LAMPITO

'Tis a hard thing, by the two goddesses it is! for a woman to sleep alone without ever a strong male in her bed. But there, peace must come first.

LYSISTRATA

Oh, my darling, my dearest, best friend, you are the only one deserving the name of woman!

CLEONICÉ

But if—which the gods forbid—we do refrain altogether from what you say, should we get peace any sooner?

LYSISTRATA

Of course we should, by the goddesses twain! We need only sit indoors with painted cheeks, and meet our mates lightly clad in transparent gowns of Amorgos silk, and perfectly depilated; they will get their tools up and be wild to lie with us. That will be the time to refuse, and they will hasten to make peace, I am convinced of that!

LAMPITO

Yes, just as Menelaus, when he saw Helen's naked bosom, threw away his sword, they say.

CLEONICÉ

But, oh dear, suppose our husbands go away and leave us.

LYSISTRATA

Then, as Pherecrates says, we must "flay a skinned dog," that's all.

CLEONICÉ

Fiddlesticks! these proverbs are all idle talk. . . . But if our husbands drag us by main force into the bedchamber?

LYSISTRATA

Hold on to the door posts.

CLEONICÉ

But if they beat us?

LYSISTRATA

Then yield to their wishes, but with a bad grace; there is no pleasure in it for them, when they do it by force. Besides, there are a thousand ways of tormenting them. Never fear, they'll soon tire of the game; there's no satisfaction for a man, unless the woman shares it.

CLEONICÉ

Very well, if you *must* have it so, we agree.

LAMPITO

For ourselves, no doubt we shall persuade our husbands to conclude a fair and honest peace; but there is the Athenian populace, how are we to cure these folk of their warlike frenzy?

LYSISTRATA

Have no fear; we undertake to make our own people listen to reason.

LAMPITO

That's impossible, so long as they have their trusty ships and the vast treasures stored in the temple of Athené.

LYSISTRATA

Ah! but we have seen to that; this very day the Acropolis will be in our hands. That is the task assigned to the older women; while we are here in council, they are going, under pretence of offering sacrifice, to seize the citadel.

LAMPITO

Well said indeed! everything is going for the best.

LYSISTRATA

Come, quick, Lampito, and let us bind ourselves by an inviolable oath.

LAMPITO

Recite the terms; we will swear to them.

LYSISTRATA

With pleasure. Where is our Scythian policewoman? Now, what are *you* staring at, pray? Lay this shield on the earth before us, its hollow upwards, and someone bring me the victim's inwards.

CLEONICÉ

Lysistrata, say, what oath are we to swear?

LYSISTRATA

What oath? Why, in Aeschylus, they sacrifice a sheep, and swear over a buckler; ³ we will do the same.

CLEONICÉ

No, Lysistrata, one cannot swear peace over a *buckler*, surely.

LYSISTRATA

What other oath do you prefer?

CLEONICÉ

Let's take a white horse, and sacrifice it, and swear on its entrails.

LYSISTRATA

But where shall we *get* a white horse?

CLEONICÉ

Well, what oath shall we take then?

LYSISTRATA

Listen to me. Let's set a great black bowl on the ground; let's sacrifice a skin of Thasian wine into it, and take oath not to add one single drop of water.

LAMPITO
Ah! that's an oath pleases me more than I can say.

LYSISTRATA
Let them bring me a bowl and a skin of wine.

CLEONICÉ
Ah! my dears, what a noble big bowl! what fun it will be to empty it!

LYSISTRATA
Set the bowl down on the ground, and lay your hands on the victim.
. . . Almighty goddess, Persuasion, and thou, bowl, boon comrade of
joy and merriment, receive this our sacrifice, and be propitious to us poor
women!

CLEONICÉ (*as* LYSISTRATA *pours the wine into the bowl*)
Oh! the fine red blood! how well it flows!

LAMPITO
And what a delicious bouquet, by Castor!

CLEONICÉ
Now, my dears, let me swear first, if you please.

LYSISTRATA
No, by Aphrodité, unless it's decided by lot. But come, then, Lampito,
and all of you, put your hands to the bowl; and do you, Cleonicé, repeat
for all the rest the solemn terms I am going to recite. Then you must all
swear, and pledge yourselves by the same promises,—*I will have naught
to do whether with lover or husband* . . .

CLEONICÉ (*faintly*)
I will have naught to do whether with lover or husband . . .

LYSISTRATA
Albeit he come to me with an erection . . .

CLEONICÉ (*her voice quavering*)
Albeit he come to me with an erection . . . (*in despair*) Oh! Lysistrata, I cannot *bear* it!

LYSISTRATA (*ignoring this outburst*)
I will live at home unbulled . . .

CLEONICÉ
I will live at home unbulled . . .

LYSISTRATA
Beautifully dressed and wearing a saffron-coloured gown . . .

CLEONICÉ
Beautifully dressed and wearing a saffron-coloured gown . . .

LYSISTRATA
To the end I may inspire my husband with the most ardent longings.

CLEONICÉ
To the end I may inspire my husband with the most ardent longings.

LYSISTRATA
Never will I give myself voluntarily . . .

CLEONICÉ
Never will I give myself voluntarily . . .

LYSISTRATA
And if he has me by force . . .

CLEONICÉ
And if he has me by force . . .

LYSISTRATA
I will be cold as ice, and never stir a limb . . .

CLEONICÉ
I will be cold as ice, and never stir a limb . . .

LYSISTRATA
I will neither extend my Persian slippers toward the ceiling . . .

CLEONICÉ
I will neither extend my Persian slippers toward the ceiling . . .

LYSISTRATA
Nor will I crouch like the carven lions on a knife-handle.

CLEONICÉ
Nor will I crouch like the carven lions on a knife-handle.

LYSISTRATA
And if I keep my oath, may I be suffered to drink of this wine.

CLEONICÉ (*more courageously*)
And if I keep my oath, may I be suffered to drink of this wine.

LYSISTRATA

But if I break it, let my bowl be filled with water.

CLEONICÉ

But if I break it, let my bowl be filled with water.

LYSISTRATA

Will you all take this oath?

ALL

We do.

LYSISTRATA

Then I'll now consume this remnant.

(*She drinks.*)

CLEONICÉ (*reaching for the cup*)

Enough, enough, my dear; now let us all drink in turn to cement our friendship.

(*They pass the cup around and all drink. A great commotion is heard off stage.*)

LAMPITO

Listen! what do those cries mean?

LYSISTRATA

It's what I was telling you; the women have just occupied the Acropolis. So now, Lampito, you return to Sparta to organize the plot, while your comrades here remain as hostages. For ourselves, let us go and join the rest in the citadel, and let us push the bolts well home.

CLEONICÉ

But don't you think the men will march up against us?

LYSISTRATA

I laugh at them. Neither threats nor flames shall force our doors; they shall open only on the conditions I have named.

CLEONICÉ

Yes, yes, by Aphrodité; otherwise we should be called cowardly and wretched women.

(*She follows* LYSISTRATA *out.*)

(*The scene shifts to the entrance of the Acropolis. The* CHORUS OF OLD MEN *slowly enters, carrying faggots and pots of fire.*)

LEADER OF CHORUS OF OLD MEN

Go easy, Draces, go easy; why, your shoulder is all chafed by these damned heavy olive stocks. But forward still, forward, man, as needs 'nust.

FIRST SEMI-CHORUS OF OLD MEN (*singing*)

What unlooked-for things do happen, to be sure, in a long life! Ah! Strymodorus, who would ever have thought it? Here we have the women, who used, for our misfortune, to eat our bread and live in our houses, daring nowadays to lay hands on the holy image of the goddess, to seize the Acropolis and draw bars and bolts to keep any from entering!

LEADER OF CHORUS OF OLD MEN

Come, Philurgus, man, let's hurry there; let's lay our faggots all about the citadel, and on the blazing pile burn with our hands these vile con-spiratresses, one and all—and Lycon's wife first and foremost!

SECOND SEMI-CHORUS OF OLD MEN (*singing*)

Nay, by Demeter, never will I let them laugh at me, whiles I have a breath left in my body. Cleomenes himself, the first who ever seized our citadel, had to quit it to his sore dishonour; spite his Lacedaemo-nian pride, he had to deliver me up his arms and slink off with a single garment to his back. My word! but he was filthy and ragged! and what an unkempt beard, to be sure! He had not had a bath for six long years!

LEADER OF CHORUS OF OLD MEN

Oh! but that was a mighty siege! Our men were ranged seventeen deep before the gate, and never left their posts, even to sleep. These women, these enemies of Euripides and all the gods, shall I do nothing to hinder their inordinate insolence? else let them tear down my trophies of Mara-thon.

FIRST SEMI-CHORUS OF OLD MEN (*singing*)

But look, to finish this toilsome climb only this last steep bit is left to mount. Truly, it's no easy job without beasts of burden, and how these logs do bruise my shoulder! Still let us carry on, and blow up our fire and see it does not go out just as we reach our destina-tion. Phew! phew! (*Blowing the fire*) Oh! dear! what a dreadful smoke!

SECOND SEMI-CHORUS OF OLD MEN (*singing*)

It bites my eyes like a mad dog. It is Lemnian fire for sure, or it would never devour my eyelids like this. Come on, Laches, let's hurry, let's bring succour to the goddess; it's now or never! Phew! phew! (*Blowing the fire*) Oh dear! what a confounded smoke!

LEADER OF CHORUS OF OLD MEN

There now, there's our fire all bright and burning, thank the gods! Now, why not first put down our loads here, then take a vine-branch, light it at the brazier and hurl it at the gate by way of battering-ram? If they don't answer our summons by pulling back the bolts, then we set fire to the woodwork, and the smoke will choke them. Ye gods! what a smoke! Pfaugh! Is there never a Samian general will help me unload my burden? —Ah! it shall not gall my shoulder any more. (*Setting down the wood*) Come, brazier, do your duty, make the embers flare, that I may kindle a brand; I want to be the first to hurl one. Aid me, heavenly Victory; let us punish for their insolent audacity the women who have seized our citadel, and may we raise a trophy of triumph for success!

(*They begin to build a fire. The* CHORUS OF WOMEN *now enters, carrying pots of water.*)

LEADER OF CHORUS OF WOMEN

Oh! my dears, methinks I see fire and smoke; can it be a conflagration? Let us hurry all we can.

FIRST SEMI-CHORUS OF WOMEN (*singing*)

Fly, fly, Nicodicé, ere Calycé and Crityllé perish in the fire, or are stifled in the smoke raised by these accursed old men and their pitiless laws. But, great gods, can it be I come too late? Rising at dawn, I had the utmost trouble to fill this vessel at the fountain. Oh! what a crowd there was, and what a din! What a rattling of water-pots! Servants and slave-girls pushed and thronged me! However, here I have it full at last; and I am running to carry the water to my fellow-townswomen, whom our foes are plotting to burn alive.

SECOND SEMI-CHORUS OF WOMEN (*singing*)

News has been brought us that a company of old, doddering greybeards, loaded with enormous faggots, as if they wanted to heat a furnace, have taken the field, vomiting dreadful threats, crying that they must reduce to ashes these horrible women. Suffer them not, oh! goddess, but, of thy grace, may I see Athens and Greece cured of their warlike folly. 'Tis to this end, oh! thou guardian deity of our city, goddess of the golden crest, that they have seized thy sanctuary. Be their friend and ally, Athené, and if any man hurl against them lighted firebrands, aid us to carry water to extinguish them.

LEADER OF CHORUS OF WOMEN

What is this I see, ye wretched old men? Honest and pious folk ye cannot be who act so vilely.

LEADER OF CHORUS OF OLD MEN

Ah, ha! here's something new! a swarm of women stand posted outside to defend the gates!

LEADER OF CHORUS OF WOMEN

Fart at us, would you? we seem a mighty host, yet you do not see the ten-thousandth part of our sex.

LEADER OF CHORUS OF OLD MEN

Ho, Phaedrias! shall we stop their cackle? Suppose one of us were to break a stick across their backs, eh?

LEADER OF CHORUS OF WOMEN

Let us set down our water-pots on the ground, to be out of the way, if they should dare to offer us violence.

LEADER OF CHORUS OF OLD MEN

Let someone knock out two or three teeth for them, as they did to Bupalus; they won't talk so loud then.

LEADER OF CHORUS OF WOMEN

Come on then; I wait you with unflinching foot, and no other bitch will ever grab your balls.

LEADER OF CHORUS OF OLD MEN

Silence! or my stick will cut short your days.

LEADER OF CHORUS OF WOMEN

Now, just you dare to touch Stratyllis with the tip of your finger!

LEADER OF CHORUS OF OLD MEN

And if I batter you to pieces with my fists, what will you do?

LEADER OF CHORUS OF WOMEN

I will tear out your lungs and entrails with my teeth.

LEADER OF CHORUS OF OLD MEN

Oh! what a clever poet is Euripides! how well he says that woman is the most shameless of animals.

LEADER OF CHORUS OF WOMEN

Let's pick up our water-jars again, Rhodippé.

LEADER OF CHORUS OF OLD MEN
You damned women, what do you mean to do here with your water?

LEADER OF CHORUS OF WOMEN
And you, old death-in-life, with your fire? Is it to cremate yourself?

LEADER OF CHORUS OF OLD MEN
I am going to build you a pyre to roast your female friends upon.

LEADER OF CHORUS OF WOMEN
And I,—I am going to put out your fire.

LEADER OF CHORUS OF OLD MEN
You put out my fire—*you?*

LEADER OF CHORUS OF WOMEN
Yes, you shall soon see.

LEADER OF CHORUS OF OLD MEN
I don't know what prevents me from roasting you with this torch.

LEADER OF CHORUS OF WOMEN
I am getting you a bath ready to clean off the filth.

LEADER OF CHORUS OF OLD MEN
A bath for *me*, you dirty slut?

LEADER OF CHORUS OF WOMEN
Yes, indeed, a nuptial bath—tee hee!

LEADER OF CHORUS OF OLD MEN (*turning to his followers*)
Do you hear that? What insolence!

LEADER OF CHORUS OF WOMEN
I am a free woman, I tell you.

LEADER OF CHORUS OF OLD MEN
I will make you hold your tongue, never fear!

LEADER OF CHORUS OF WOMEN
Ah ha! you shall never sit any more amongst the Heliasts.

LEADER OF CHORUS OF OLD MEN (*to his torch*)
Burn off her hair for her!

LEADER OF CHORUS OF WOMEN (*to her pot*)
Achelous, do your duty!
(*The women pitch the water in their water-pots over the old men.*)

LEADER OF CHORUS OF OLD MEN
Oh, dear! oh, dear! oh, dear!

LEADER OF CHORUS OF WOMEN
Was it hot?

LEADER OF CHORUS OF OLD MEN
Hot, great gods! Enough, enough!

LEADER OF CHORUS OF WOMEN
I'm watering you, to make you bloom afresh.

LEADER OF CHORUS OF OLD MEN
Alas! I am too dry! Ah, me how! how I am trembling with cold!
(*A* MAGISTRATE *enters, with a few Scythian policemen.*)

MAGISTRATE
These women, have they made din enough, I wonder, with their tambourines? bewept Adonis enough upon their terraces? I was listening to the speeches last assembly day, and Demostratus, whom heaven confound! was saying we must all go over to Sicily—and lo! his wife was dancing round repeating: "Alas! alas! Adonis, woe is me for Adonis!" Demostratus was saying we must levy hoplites at Zacynthus—and there was his wife, more than half drunk, screaming on the house-roof: "Weep, weep for Adonis!"—while that infamous *Mad Ox* was bellowing away on his side.—Do you not blush, you women, for your wild and uproarious doings?

LEADER OF CHORUS OF OLD MEN
But you don't know all their effrontery yet! They abused and insulted us; then soused us with the water in their water-pots, and have set us wringing out our clothes, for all the world as if we had bepissed ourselves.

MAGISTRATE
And well done too, by Posidon! We men must share the blame of their ill conduct; it is we who teach them to love riot and dissoluteness and sow the seeds of wickedness in their hearts. You see a husband go into a shop: "Look you, jeweller," says he, "you remember the necklace you made for my wife. Well, the other evening, when she was dancing, the catch came open. Now, I am bound to start for Salamis; will you make it convenient to go up to-night to make her fastening secure?" Another will go to the cobbler, a great, strong fellow, with a great, long tool, and tell him: "The strap of one of my wife's sandals presses her little toe, which is extremely sensitive; come in about midday to supple the thing and stretch it." Now see the results. Take my own case—as a Magistrate

I have enlisted rowers; I want money to pay them, and the women slam the door in my face. But why do we stand here with arms crossed? Bring me a crowbar; *I'll* chastise their insolence!—Ho! there, my fine fellow! (*to one of the Scythians*) what are you gaping at the crows for? looking for a tavern, I suppose, eh? Come on, bring crowbars here, and force open the gates. I will put a hand to the work myself.

LYSISTRATA (*opening the gate and walking out*)
No need to force the gates; I am coming out—here I am. And why bolts and bars? What we want here is not bolts and bars and locks, but common sense.

MAGISTRATE (*jumping nervously, then striving manfully to regain his dignity*)
Really, my fine lady! Where is my officer? I want him to tie that woman's hands behind her back.

LYSISTRATA
By Artemis, the virgin goddess! if he touches me with the tip of his finger, officer of the public peace though he be, let him look out for himself!
(*The first Scythian defecates in terror.*)

MAGISTRATE (*to another officer*)
How now, are you afraid? Seize her, I tell you, round the body. Two of you at her, and have done with it!

CLEONICÉ
By Pandrosos! if you lay a hand on her, I'll trample you underfoot till the crap comes out of you!
(*The second Scythian defecates in terror.*)

MAGISTRATE
Look at the mess you've made! Where is there another officer? (*To the third Scythian*) Bind *that* minx first, the one who speaks so prettily!

MYRRHINÉ
By Phoebé, if you touch her with one finger, you'd better call quick for a surgeon!
(*The third Scythian defecates in terror.*)

MAGISTRATE
What's that? Where's the officer? (*To the fourth Scythian*) Lay hold of her. Oh! but I'm going to stop your foolishness for you all!

CLEONICÉ

By the Tauric Artemis, if you go near her, I'll pull out your hair, scream as you like.

(The fourth Scythian defecates in terror.)

MAGISTRATE

Ah! miserable man that I am! My own officers desert me. What ho! are we to let ourselves be bested by a mob of women? Ho! Scythians mine, close up your ranks, and forward!

LYSISTRATA

By the holy goddesses! you'll have to make acquaintance with four companies of women, ready for the fray and well armed to boot.

MAGISTRATE

Forward, Scythians, and bind them!

(The Scythians advance reluctantly.)

LYSISTRATA

Forward, my gallant companions; march forth, ye vendors of grain and eggs, garlic and vegetables, keepers of taverns and bakeries, wrench and strike and tear; come, a torrent of invective and insult! *(They beat the Scythians who retire in haste.)* Enough, enough! now retire, never rob the vanquished!

(The women withdraw.)

MAGISTRATE

How unfortunate for my officers!

LYSISTRATA

Ah, ha! so you thought you had only to do with a set of slave-women! you did not know the ardour that fills the bosom of free-born dames.

MAGISTRATE

Ardour! yes, by Apollo, ardour enough—especially for the wine-cup!

LEADER OF CHORUS OF OLD MEN

Sir, sir! what good are words? they are of no avail with wild beasts of this sort. Don't you know how they have just washed us down—and with no very fragrant soap!

LEADER OF CHORUS OF WOMEN

What would you have? You should never have laid rash hands on us. If you start afresh, I'll knock your eyes out. My delight is to stay at home as coy as a young maid, without hurting anybody or moving any more than a milestone; but 'ware the wasps, if you go stirring up the wasps' nest!

CHORUS OF OLD MEN (*singing*)
Ah! great gods! how get the better of these ferocious creatures?
'tis past all bearing! But come, let us try to find out the reason of the
dreadful scourge. With what end in view have they seized the citadel
of Cranaus, the sacred shrine that is raised upon the inaccessible rock
of the Acropolis?

LEADER OF CHORUS OF OLD MEN (*to the* MAGISTRATE)
Question them; be cautious and not too credulous. It would be culpable
negligence not to pierce the mystery, if we may.

MAGISTRATE (*addressing the women*)
I would ask you first why you have barred our gates.

LYSISTRATA
To seize the treasury; no more money, no more war.

MAGISTRATE
Then money is the cause of the war?

LYSISTRATA
And of all our troubles. It was to find occasion to steal that Pisander
and all the other agitators were forever raising revolutions. Well and
good! but they'll never get another drachma here.

MAGISTRATE
What do you propose to do then, pray?

LYSISTRATA
You ask me that! Why, we propose to administer the treasury ourselves.

MAGISTRATE
You do?

LYSISTRATA
What is there in that to surprise you? Do we not administer the budget
of household expenses?

MAGISTRATE
But that is not the same thing.

LYSISTRATA
How so—not the same thing?

MAGISTRATE
It is the treasury supplies the expenses of the war.

LYSISTRATA

That's our first principle—no war!

MAGISTRATE

What! and the safety of the city?

LYSISTRATA

We will provide for that.

MAGISTRATE

You?

LYSISTRATA

Yes, *we!*

MAGISTRATE

What a sorry business!

LYSISTRATA

Yes, we're going to save you, whether you like it or not.

MAGISTRATE

Oh! the impudence of the creatures!

LYSISTRATA

You seem annoyed! but it has to be done, nevertheless.

MAGISTRATE

But it's the very height of iniquity!

LYSISTRATA (*testily*)

We're going to *save* you, my good man.

MAGISTRATE

But if I don't *want* to be saved?

LYSISTRATA

Why, all the more reason!

MAGISTRATE

But what a notion, to concern yourselves with questions of peace and war!

LYSISTRATA

We will explain our idea.

MAGISTRATE

Out with it then; quick, or . . . (*threatening her*).

LYSISTRATA (*sternly*)
Listen, and never a movement, please!

MAGISTRATE (*in impotent rage*)
Oh! it is too much for me! I cannot keep my temper!

LEADER OF CHORUS OF WOMEN
Then look out for yourself; you have more to fear than we have.

MAGISTRATE
Stop your croaking, you old crow! (*To* LYSISTRATA) Now you, say
what you have to say.

LYSISTRATA
Willingly. All the long time the war has lasted, we have endured in
modest silence all you men did; you never allowed us to open our lips.
We were far from satisfied, for we knew how things were going; often in
our homes we would hear you discussing, upside down and inside out,
some important turn of affairs. Then with sad hearts, but smiling lips,
we would ask you: Well, in today's Assembly did they vote peace?—But,
"Mind your own business!" the husband would growl, "Hold your
tongue, please!" And we would say no more.

CLEONICÉ
I would not have held *my* tongue though, not I!

MAGISTRATE
You would have been reduced to silence by blows then.

LYSISTRATA
Well, for my part, I would say no more. But presently I would come to
know you had arrived at some fresh decision more fatally foolish than
ever. "Ah! my dear man," I would say, "what madness next!" But he
would only look at me askance and say: "Just weave your web, please;
else your cheeks will smart for hours. War is men's business!"

MAGISTRATE
Bravo! well said indeed!

LYSISTRATA
How now, wretched man? not to let us contend against your follies was
bad enough! But presently we heard you asking out loud in the open
street: "Is there never a man left in Athens?" and, "No, not one, not one,"
you were assured in reply. Then, then we made up our minds without
more delay to make common cause to save Greece. Open your ears to
our wise counsels and hold your tongues, and we may yet put things on
a better footing.

MAGISTRATE

You put things indeed! Oh! this is too much! The *insolence* of the creatures!

LYSISTRATA

Be still!

MAGISTRATE

May I die a thousand deaths ere I obey one who wears a veil!

LYSISTRATA

If that's all that troubles you, here, take my veil, wrap it round your head, and hold your tongue.

CLEONICÉ

Then take this basket; put on a girdle, card wool, munch beans. The war shall be women's business.

LEADER OF CHORUS OF WOMEN

Lay aside your water-pots, we will guard them, we will help our friends and companions.

CHORUS OF WOMEN (*singing*)

For myself, I will never weary of the dance; my knees will never grow stiff with fatigue. I will brave everything with my dear allies, on whom Nature has lavished virtue, grace, boldness, cleverness, and whose wisely directed energy is going to save the State.

LEADER OF CHORUS OF WOMEN

Oh! my good, gallant Lysistrata, and all my friends, be ever like a bundle of nettles; never let your anger slacken; the winds of fortune blow our way.

LYSISTRATA

May gentle Love and the sweet Cyprian Queen shower seductive charms on our breasts and our thighs. If only we may stir so amorous a feeling among the men that they stand as firm as sticks, we shall indeed deserve the name of peace-makers among the Greeks.

MAGISTRATE

How will that be, pray?

LYSISTRATA

To begin with, we shall not see you any more running like mad fellows to the Market holding lance in fist.

CLEONICÉ

That will be something gained, anyway, by the Paphian goddess, it will!

LYSISTRATA

Now we see them, mixed up with saucepans and kitchen stuff, armed to the teeth, looking like wild Corybantes!

MAGISTRATE

Why, of course; that's what brave men should do.

LYSISTRATA

Oh! but what a funny sight, to behold a man wearing a Gorgon's-head buckler coming along to buy fish!

CLEONICÉ

The other day in the Market I saw a phylarch with flowing ringlets; he was on horseback, and was pouring into his helmet the broth he had just bought at an old dame's still. There was a Thracian warrior too, who was brandishing his lance like Tereus in the play; he had scared a good woman selling figs into a perfect panic, and was gobbling up all her ripest fruit.

MAGISTRATE

And how, pray, would you propose to restore peace and order in all the countries of Greece?

LYSISTRATA

It's the easiest thing in the world!

MAGISTRATE

Come, tell us how; I am curious to know.

LYSISTRATA

When we are winding thread, and it is tangled, we pass the spool across and through the skein, now this way, now that way; even so, to finish off the war, we shall send embassies hither and thither and everywhere, to disentangle matters.

MAGISTRATE

And is it with your yarn, and your skeins, and your spools, you think to appease so many bitter enmities, you silly women?

LYSISTRATA

If only you had common sense, you would always do in politics the same as we do with our yarn.

MAGISTRATE

Come, how is that, eh?

LYSISTRATA

First we wash the yarn to separate the grease and filth; do the same with all bad citizens, sort them out and drive them forth with rods— they're the refuse of the city. Then for all such as come crowding up in search of employments and offices, we must card them thoroughly; then, to bring them all to the same standard, pitch them pell-mell into the same basket, resident aliens or no, allies, debtors to the State, all mixed up together. Then as for our Colonies, you must think of them as so many isolated hanks; find the ends of the separate threads, draw them to a centre here, wind them into one, make one great hank of the lot, out of which the public can weave itself a good, stout tunic.

MAGISTRATE

Is it not a sin and a shame to see them carding and winding the State, these women who have neither art nor part in the burdens of the war?

LYSISTRATA

What! wretched man! why, it's a far heavier burden to us than to you. In the first place, we bear sons who go off to fight far away from Athens.

MAGISTRATE

Enough said! do not recall sad and sorry memories!

LYSISTRATA

Then secondly, instead of enjoying the pleasures of love and making the best of our youth and beauty, we are left to languish far from our husbands, who are all with the army. But say no more of ourselves; what afflicts me is to see our girls growing old in lonely grief.

MAGISTRATE

Don't the men grow old too?

LYSISTRATA

That is not the same thing. When the soldier returns from the wars, even though he has white hair, he very soon finds a young wife. But a woman has only one summer; if she does not make hay while the sun shines, no one will afterwards have anything to say to her, and she spends her days consulting oracles that never send her a husband.

MAGISTRATE

But the old man who can still get an erection . . .

LYSISTRATA

But you, why don't you get done with it and die? You are rich; go buy yourself a bier, and I will knead you a honey-cake for Cerberus. Here, take this garland.

(*Drenching him with water.*)

CLEONICÉ

And this one too.

(*Drenching him with water.*)

MYRRHINÉ

And these fillets.

(*Drenching him with water.*)

LYSISTRATA

What else do you need? Step aboard the boat; Charon is waiting for you, you're keeping him from pushing off.

MAGISTRATE

To treat me so scurvily! What an insult! I will go show myself to my fellow-magistrates just as I am.

LYSISTRATA

What! are you blaming us for not having exposed you according to custom? Nay, console yourself; we will not fail to offer up the third-day sacrifice for you, first thing in the morning.[4]

(*She goes into the Acropolis, with* CLEONICÉ *and* MYRRHINÉ.)

LEADER OF CHORUS OF OLD MEN

Awake, friends of freedom; let us hold ourselves aye ready to act.

CHORUS OF OLD MEN (*singing*)

I suspect a mighty peril; I foresee another tyranny like Hippias'.
I am sore afraid the Laconians assembled here with Clisthenes have,
by a stratagem of war, stirred up these women, enemies of the gods,
to seize upon our treasury and the funds whereby I lived.

LEADER OF CHORUS OF OLD MEN

Is it not a sin and a shame for them to interfere in advising the citizens, to prate of shields and lances, and to ally themselves with Laconians, fellows I trust no more than I would so many famished wolves? The whole thing, my friends, is nothing else but an attempt to re-establish tyranny. But I will never submit; I will be on my guard for the future; I will always carry a blade hidden under myrtle boughs; I will post myself in the public square under arms, shoulder to shoulder with Aristogiton; and now, to make a start, I must just break a few of that cursed old jade's teeth yonder.

LEADER OF CHORUS OF WOMEN

Nay, never play the brave man, else when you go back home, your own mother won't know you. But, dear friends and allies, first let us lay our burdens down.

CHORUS OF WOMEN (*singing*)

Then, citizens all, hear what I have to say. I have useful counsel to give our city, which deserves it well at my hands for the brilliant distinctions it has lavished on my girlhood. At seven years of age, I carried the sacred vessels; at ten, I pounded barley for the altar of Athené; next, clad in a robe of yellow silk, I played the bear to Artemis at the Brauronia; presently, when I was grown up, a tall, handsome maiden, they put a necklace of dried figs about my neck, and I was one of the Canephori.

LEADER OF CHORUS OF WOMEN

So surely I am bound to give my best advice to Athens. What matters that I was born a woman, if I can cure your misfortunes? I pay my share of tolls and taxes, by giving men to the State. But you, you miserable greybeards, you contribute nothing to the public charges; on the contrary, you have wasted the treasure of our forefathers, as it was called, the treasure amassed in the days of the Persian Wars. You pay nothing at all in return; and into the bargain you endanger our lives and liberties by your mistakes. Have you one word to say for yourselves? . . . Ah! don't irritate me, you there, or I'll lay my slipper across your jaws; and it's pretty heavy.

CHORUS OF OLD MEN (*singing*)

Outrage upon outrage! things are going from bad to worse. Let us punish the minxes, every one of us that has balls to boast of. Come, off with our tunics, for a man must savour of manhood; come, my friends, let us strip naked from head to foot. Courage, I say, we who in our day garrisoned Lipsydrion; let us be young again, and shake off eld.

LEADER OF CHORUS OF OLD MEN

If we give them the least hold over us, that's the end! their audacity will know no bounds! We shall see them building ships, and fighting sea-fights, like Artemisia; and, if they want to mount and ride as cavalry, we had best cashier the knights, for indeed women excel in riding, and have a fine, firm seat for the gallop. Just think of all those squadrons of Amazons

Micon has painted for us engaged in hand-to-hand combat with men.
Come then, we must now fit collars to all these willing necks.

CHORUS OF WOMEN (*singing*)
By the blessed goddesses, if you anger me, I will let loose the
beast of my evil passions, and a very hailstorm of blows will set you
yelling for help. Come, dames, off with your tunics, and quick's the
word; women must smell the smell of women in the throes of passion. . . . Now just you dare to measure strength with me, old greybeard, and I warrant you you'll never eat garlic or black beans any
more. No, not a word! my anger is at boiling point, and I'll do with
you what the beetle did with the eagle's eggs.[5]

LEADER OF CHORUS OF WOMEN
I laugh at your threats, so long as I have on my side Lampito here,
and the noble Theban, my dear Ismenia. . . . Pass decree on decree,
you can do us no hurt, you wretch abhorred of all your fellows. Why, only
yesterday, on occasion of the feast of Hecaté, I asked my neighbours of
Boeotia for one of their daughters for whom my girls have a lively liking
—a fine, fat eel to wit; and if they did not refuse, all along of your silly
decrees! We shall never cease to suffer the like, till some one gives you a
neat trip-up and breaks your neck for you! (*To* LYSISTRATA *as she comes
out from the Acropolis*) You, Lysistrata, you who are leader of our glorious enterprise, why do I see you coming towards me with so gloomy an air?

LYSISTRATA
It's the behaviour of these naughty women, it's the female heart and
female weakness that so discourage me.

LEADER OF CHORUS OF WOMEN
Tell us, tell us, what is it?

LYSISTRATA
I only tell the simple truth.

LEADER OF CHORUS OF WOMEN
What has happened so disconcerting? Come, tell your friends.

LYSISTRATA
Oh! the thing is so hard to tell—yet so impossible to conceal.

LEADER OF CHORUS OF WOMEN
Never seek to hide any ill that has befallen our cause.

LYSISTRATA
To blurt it out in a word—we want laying!

Leader of Chorus of Women

Oh! Zeus, oh! Zeus!

Lysistrata

What use calling upon Zeus? The thing is even as I say. I cannot stop them any longer from lusting after the men. They are all for deserting. The first I caught was slipping out by the postern gate near the cave of Pan; another was letting herself down by a rope and pulley; a third was busy preparing her escape; while a fourth, perched on a bird's back, was just taking wing for Orsilochus' house, when I seized her by the hair. One and all, they are inventing excuses to be off home. (*Pointing to the gate*) Look! there goes one, trying to get out! Halloa there! whither away so fast?

First Woman

I want to go home; I have some Milesian wool in the house, which is getting all eaten up by the worms.

Lysistrata

Bah! you and your worms! go back, I say!

First Woman

I will return immediately, I swear I will by the two goddesses! I only have just to spread it out on the bed.

Lysistrata

You shall not do anything of the kind! I say, you shall not go.

First Woman

Must I leave my wool to spoil then?

Lysistrata

Yes, if need be.

Second Woman

Unhappy woman that I am! Alas for my flax! I've left it at home unstript!

Lysistrata

So, here's another trying to escape to go home and strip her flax!

Second Woman

Oh! I swear by the goddess of light, the instant I have put it in condition I will come straight back.

LYSISTRATA

You shall do nothing of the kind! If once you began, others would want to follow suit.

THIRD WOMAN

Oh! goddess divine, Ilithyia, patroness of women in labour, stay, stay the birth, till I have reached a spot less hallowed than Athené's mount! [6]

LYSISTRATA

What mean you by these silly tales?

THIRD WOMAN

I am going to have a child—now, this *minute!*

LYSISTRATA

But you were not pregnant yesterday!

THIRD WOMAN

Well, I am to-day. Oh! let me go in search of the midwife, Lysistrata, quick, quick!

LYSISTRATA

What is this fable you are telling me? (*Feeling her stomach*) Ah! what have you got there so hard?

THIRD WOMAN

A male child.

LYSISTRATA

No, no, by Aphrodité! nothing of the sort! Why, it feels like something hollow—a pot or a kettle. (*Opening her robe*) Oh! you silly creature, if you have not got the sacred helmet of Pallas—and you said you were with child!

THIRD WOMAN

And so I am, by Zeus, I am!

LYSISTRATA

Then why this helmet, pray?

THIRD WOMAN

For fear my pains should seize me in the Acropolis; I mean to lay my eggs in this helmet, as the doves do.

LYSISTRATA

Excuses and pretences every word! the thing's as clear as daylight. Anyway, you must stay here now till the fifth day, your day of purification.

THIRD WOMAN

I cannot sleep any more in the Acropolis, now I have seen the snake that guards the temple.

FOURTH WOMAN

Ah! and those awful owls with their dismal hooting! I cannot get a wink of rest, and I'm just dying of fatigue.

LYSISTRATA

You wicked women, have done with your falsehoods! You want your husbands, that's plain enough. But don't you think they want you just as badly? They are spending dreadful nights, oh! I know that well enough. But hold out, my dears, hold out! A little more patience, and the victory will be ours. An oracle promises us success, if only we remain united. Shall I repeat the words?

THIRD WOMAN

Yes, tell us what the oracle declares.

LYSISTRATA

Silence then! Now—"Whenas the swallows, fleeing before the hoopoes, shall have all flocked together in one place, and shall refrain them from all amorous commerce, then will be the end of all the ills of life; yea, and Zeus, who doth thunder in the skies, shall set above what was erst below. . . ."

THIRD WOMAN

What! shall the men be underneath?

LYSISTRATA

"But if dissension do arise among the swallows, and they take wing from the holy temple, it will be said there is never a more wanton bird in all the world."

THIRD WOMAN

Ye gods! the prophecy is clear.

LYSISTRATA

Nay, never let us be cast down by calamity! let us be brave to bear, and go back to our posts. It would be shameful indeed not to trust the promises of the oracle.

(*They all go back into the Acropolis.*)

CHORUS OF OLD MEN (*singing*)

I want to tell you a fable they used to relate to me when I was a little boy. This is it: Once upon a time there was a young man called

Melanion, who hated the thought of marriage so sorely that he fled away to the wilds. So he dwelt in the mountains, wove himself nets, and caught hares. He never, never came back, he had such a horror of women. As chaste as Melanion, we loathe the jades just as much as he did.

AN OLD MAN (*beginning a brief duet with one of the women*)
You dear old woman, I would fain kiss you.

WOMAN
I will set you crying without onions.

OLD MAN
And give you a sound kicking.

WOMAN (*pointing*)
Ah, ha! what a dense forest you have there!

OLD MAN
So was Myronides one of the bushiest of men of this side; his backside was all black, and he terrified his enemies as much as Phormio.

CHORUS OF WOMEN (*singing*)
I want to tell you a fable too, to match yours about Melanion. Once there was a certain man called Timon, a tough customer, and a whimsical, a true son of the Furies, with a face that seemed to glare out of a thorn-bush. He withdrew from the world because he couldn't abide bad men, after vomiting a thousand curses at them. He had a holy horror of ill-conditioned fellows, but he was mighty tender towards women.

WOMAN (*beginning another duet*)
Suppose I up and broke your jaw for you!

OLD MAN
I am not a bit afraid of you.

WOMAN
Suppose I let fly a good kick at you?

OLD MAN
I should see your thing then.

WOMAN
You would see that, for all my age, it is very well plucked.

LYSISTRATA (*rushing out of the Acropolis*)
Ho there! come quick, come quick!

ONE OF THE WOMEN
What is it? Why these cries?

LYSISTRATA
A man! a man! I see him approaching all afire with the flames of love.
Oh! divine Queen of Cyprus, Paphos and Cythera, I pray you still be
propitious to our enterprise.

WOMAN
Where is he, this unknown foe?

LYSISTRATA
Over there—beside the Temple of Demeter.

WOMAN
Yes, indeed, I see him; but who is he?

LYSISTRATA
Look, look! do any of you recognize him?

MYRRHINÉ (*joyfully*)
I do, I do! it's my husband Cinesias.

LYSISTRATA
To work then! Be it your task to inflame and torture and torment him.
Seductions, caresses, provocations, refusals, try every means! Grant every
favour,—always excepting what is forbidden by our oath on the wine-
bowl.

MYRRHINÉ
Have no fear, I'll do it.

LYSISTRATA
Well, I shall stay here to help you cajole the man and set his passions
aflame. The rest of you withdraw.
(CINESIAS *enters, in obvious and extreme sexual excitement. A slave
follows him carrying an infant.*)

CINESIAS
Alas! alas! how I am tortured by spasm and rigid convulsion! Oh! I
am racked on the wheel!

LYSISTRATA
Who is this that dares to pass our lines?

CINESIAS

It is I.

LYSISTRATA

What, a man?

CINESIAS

Very much so!

LYSISTRATA

Get out.

CINESIAS

But who are you that thus repulses me?

LYSISTRATA

The sentinel of the day.

CINESIAS

For the gods' sake, call Myrrhiné.

LYSISTRATA

Call Myrrhiné, you say? And who are you?

CINESIAS

I am her husband, Cinesias, son of Paeon.

LYSISTRATA

Ah! good day, my dear friend. Your name is not unknown amongst
us. Your wife has it forever on her lips; and she never touches an egg or
an apple without saying: "This is for Cinesias."

CINESIAS

Really and truly?

LYSISTRATA

Yes, indeed, by Aphrodité! And if we fall to talking of men, quick your
wife declares: "Oh! all the rest, they're good for nothing compared with
Cinesias."

CINESIAS

Oh! please, please go and call her to me!

LYSISTRATA

And what will you give me for my trouble?

CINESIAS

Anything I've got, if you like. (*Pointing to the evidence of his condition*) I will give you what I have here!

LYSISTRATA

Well, well, I will tell her to come.

(*She enters the Acropolis.*)

CINESIAS

Quíck, oh! be quick! Life has no more charms for me since she left my house. I am sad, sad, when I go indoors; it all seems so empty; my victuals have lost their savour. And all because of this erection that I can't get rid of!

MYRRHINÉ (*to* LYSISTRATA, *over her shoulder*)

I love him, oh! I love him; but he won't let himself be loved. No! I shall not come.

CINESIAS

Myrrhiné, my little darling Myrrhiné, what are you saying? Come down to me quick.

MYRRHINÉ

No indeed, not I.

CINESIAS

I call you, Myrrhiné, Myrrhiné; won't you *please* come?

MYRRHINÉ

Why should you call me? You do not want me.

CINESIAS

Not want you! Why, here I stand, stiff with desire!

MYRRHINÉ

Good-bye.

(*She turns, as if to go.*)

CINESIAS

Oh! Myrrhiné, Myrrhiné, in our child's name, hear me; at any rate hear the child! Little lad, call your mother.

CHILD

Mamma, mamma, mamma!

CINESIAS

There, listen! Don't you pity the poor child? It's six days now you've never washed and never fed the child.

MYRRHINÉ

Poor darling, your father takes mighty little care of you!

CINESIAS

Come down, dearest, come down for the child's sake.

MYRRHINÉ

Ah! what a thing it is to be a mother! Well, well, we must come down, I suppose.

CINESIAS (*as* MYRRHINÉ *approaches*)

Why, how much younger and prettier she looks! And how she looks at me so lovingly! Her cruelty and scorn only redouble my passion.

MYRRHINÉ (*ignoring him; to the child*)

You are as sweet as your father is provoking! Let me kiss you, my treasure, mother's darling!

CINESIAS

Ah! what a bad thing it is to let yourself be led away by other women! Why give me such pain and suffering, and yourself into the bargain?

MYRRHINÉ (*as he is about to embrace her*)

Hands off, sir!

CINESIAS

Everything is going to rack and ruin in the house.

MYRRHINÉ

I don't care.

CINESIAS

But your web that's all being pecked to pieces by the cocks and hens, don't you care for that?

MYRRHINÉ

Precious little.

CINESIAS

And Aphrodité, whose mysteries you have not celebrated for so long? Oh! won't you please come back home?

MYRRHINÉ

No, at least, not till a sound treaty puts an end to the war.

CINESIAS

Well, if you wish it so much, why, we'll make it, your treaty.

MYRRHINÉ

Well and good! When that's done, I will come home. Till then, I am bound by an oath.

CINESIAS

At any rate, lie with me for a little while.

MYRRHINÉ

No, no, no! (*she hesitates*) but just the same I can't say I don't love you.

CINESIAS

You love me? Then why refuse to lie with me, my little girl, my sweet Myrrhiné?

MYRRHINÉ (*pretending to be shocked*)

You must be joking! What, before the child!

CINESIAS (*to the slave*)

Manes, carry the lad home. There, you see, the child is gone; there's nothing to hinder us; won't you lie down now?

MYRRHINÉ

But, miserable man, where, where?

CINESIAS

In the cave of Pan; nothing could be better.

MYRRHINÉ

But how shall I purify myself before going back into the citadel?

CINESIAS

Nothing easier! you can wash at the Clepsydra.

MYRRHINÉ

But my oath? Do you want me to perjure myself?

CINESIAS

I'll take all responsibility; don't worry.

MYRRHINÉ

Well, I'll be off, then, and find a bed for us.

CINESIAS

There's no point in that; surely we can lie on the ground.

MYRRHINÉ

No, no! even though you are bad, I don't like your lying on the bare earth.

(*She goes back into the Acropolis.*)

CINESIAS (*enraptured*)

Ah! how the dear girl loves me!

MYRRHINÉ (*coming back with a cot*)

Come, get to bed quick; I am going to undress. But, oh dear, we must get a mattress.

CINESIAS

A mattress? Oh! no, never mind about that!

MYRRHINÉ

No, by Artemis! lie on the bare sacking? never! That would be squalid.

CINESIAS

Kiss me!

MYRRHINÉ

Wait a minute!

(*She leaves him again.*)

CINESIAS

Good god, hurry up!

MYRRHINÉ (*coming back with a mattress*)

Here is a mattress. Lie down, I am just going to undress. But you've got no pillow.

CINESIAS

I don't want one either!

MYRRHINÉ

But *I* do.

(*She leaves him again.*)

CINESIAS

Oh god, oh god, she treats my tool just like Heracles!

MYRRHINÉ (*coming back with a pillow*)

There, lift your head, dear! (*Wondering what else to tantalize him with; to herself*) Is that all, I wonder?

CINESIAS (*misunderstanding*)

Surely, there's nothing else. Come, my treasure.

MYRRHINÉ

I am just unfastening my girdle. But remember what you promised me
about making peace; mind you keep your word.

CINESIAS

Yes, yes, upon my life I will.

MYRRHINÉ

Why, you have no blanket!

CINESIAS

My god, what difference does *that* make? What I want is to make love!

MYRRHINÉ (*going out again*)

Never fear—directly, directly! I'll be back in no time.

CINESIAS

The woman will kill me with her blankets!

MYRRHINÉ (*coming back with a blanket*)

Now, get yourself up.

CINESIAS (*pointing*)

I've got *this* up!

MYRRHINÉ

Wouldn't you like me to scent you?

CINESIAS

No, by Apollo, no, please don't!

MYRRHINÉ

Yes, by Aphrodité, but I will, whether you like it or not.

(*She goes out again.*)

CINESIAS

God, I wish she'd hurry up and get through with all this!

MYRRHINÉ (*coming back with a flask of perfume*)

Hold out your hand; now rub it in.

CINESIAS

Oh! in Apollo's name, I don't much like the smell of it; but perhaps
it will improve when it's well rubbed in. It does not somehow smack of
the marriage bed!

MYRRHINÉ

Oh dear! what a scatterbrain I am; if I haven't gone and brought Rhodian perfumes!

CINESIAS

Never mind, dearest, let it go now.

MYRRHINÉ

You don't really *mean* that.

(*She goes.*)

CINESIAS

Damn the man who invented perfumes!

MYRRHINÉ (*coming back with another flask*)

Here, take this bottle.

CINESIAS

I have a better one all ready for you, darling. Come, you provoking creature, to bed with you, and don't bring another thing.

MYRRHINÉ

Coming, coming; I'm just slipping off my shoes. Dear boy, will you vote for peace?

CINESIAS

I'll think about it. (*MYRRHINÉ runs away.*) I'm a dead man, she ıs killing me! She has gone, and left me in torment! (*in tragic style*) I must have someone to lay, I must! Ah me! the loveliest of women has choused and cheated me. Poor little lad, how am I to give you what you want so badly? Where is Cynalopex? quick, man, get him a nurse, do!

LEADER OF CHORUS OF OLD MEN

Poor, miserable wretch, baulked in your amorousness! what tortures are yours! Ah! you fill me with pity. Could any man's back and loins stand such a strain. He stands stiff and rigid, and there's never a wench to help him!

CINESIAS

Ye gods in heaven, what pains I suffer!

LEADER OF CHORUS OF OLD MEN

Well, there it is; it's her doing, that abandoned hussy!

CINESIAS

No, no! rather say that sweetest, dearest darling.

(*He departs.*)

LEADER OF CHORUS OF OLD MEN

That dearest darling? no, no, that hussy, say I! Zeus, thou god of the skies, canst not let loose a hurricane, to sweep them all up into the air, and whirl them round, then drop them down crash! and impale them on the point of this man's tool!

(*A Spartan* HERALD *enters; he shows signs of being in the same condition as* CINESIAS.)

HERALD

Say, where shall I find the Senate and the Prytanes? I am bearer of despatches.

(*An Athenian* MAGISTRATE *enters.*)

MAGISTRATE

Are you a man or a Priapus?

HERALD (*with an effort at officiousness*)

Don't be stupid! I am a herald, of course, I swear I am, and I come from Sparta about making peace.

MAGISTRATE (*pointing*)

But look, you are hiding a lance under your clothes, surely.

HERALD (*embarrassed*)

No, nothing of the sort.

MAGISTRATE

Then why do you turn away like that, and hold your cloak out from your body? Have you got swellings in the groin from your journey?

HERALD

By the twin brethren! the man's an old maniac.

MAGISTRATE

But you've got an erection! You lewd fellow!

HERALD

I tell you no! but enough of this foolery.

MAGISTRATE (*pointing*)

Well, what is it you have *there* then?

HERALD

A Lacedaemonian 'skytalé.'

MAGISTRATE

Oh, indeed, a 'skytalé,' is it? Well, well, speak out frankly; I know all about these matters. How are things going at Sparta now?

HERALD

Why, everything is turned upside down at Sparta; and all the allies have erections. We simply must have Pellené.

MAGISTRATE

What is the reason of it all? Is it the god Pan's doing?

HERALD

No, it's all the work of Lampito and the women who are acting at her instigation; they have kicked the men out from between their thighs.

MAGISTRATE

But what are you doing about it?

HERALD

We are at our wits' end; we walk bent double, just as if we were carrying lanterns in a wind. The jades have sworn we shall not so much as touch them till we have all agreed to conclude peace.

MAGISTRATE

Ah! I see now, it's a *general* conspiracy embracing all Greece. Go back to Sparta and bid them send envoys plenipotentiary to treat for peace. I will urge our Senators myself to name plenipotentiaries from us; and to persuade them, why, I will show them my own tool.

HERALD

What could be better? I fly at your command.

(*They go out in opposite directions.*)

LEADER OF CHORUS OF OLD MEN

No wild beast is there, no flame of fire, more fierce and untamable than woman; the leopard is less savage and shameless.

LEADER OF CHORUS OF WOMEN

And yet you dare to make war upon me, wretch, when you might have me for your most faithful friend and ally.

LEADER OF CHORUS OF OLD MEN

Never, never can my hatred cease towards women.

LEADER OF CHORUS OF WOMEN

Well, suit yourself. Still I cannot bear to leave you all naked as you are; folks would laugh at you. Come, I am going to put this tunic on you.

LEADER OF CHORUS OF OLD MEN

You are right, upon my word! it was only in my confounded fit of rage that I took it off.

LEADER OF CHORUS OF WOMEN

Now at any rate you look like a man, and they won't make fun of you. Ah! if you had not offended me so badly, I would take out that nasty insect you have in your eye for you.

LEADER OF CHORUS OF OLD MEN

Ah! so that's what was annoying me so! Look, here's a ring, just remove the insect, and show it to me. By Zeus! it has been hurting my eye for a long time now.

LEADER OF CHORUS OF WOMEN

Well, I agree, though your manners are not over and above pleasant. Oh! what a huge great gnat! just look! It's from Tricorythus, for sure.

LEADER OF CHORUS OF OLD MEN

A thousand thanks! the creature was digging a regular well in my eye; now that it's gone, my tears can flow freely.

LEADER OF CHORUS OF WOMEN

I will wipe them for you—bad, naughty man though you are. Now, just one kiss.

LEADER OF CHORUS OF OLD MEN

A kiss? certainly not!

LEADER OF CHORUS OF WOMEN

Just one, whether you like it or not.

LEADER OF CHORUS OF OLD MEN

Oh! those confounded women! how they do cajole us! How true the saying: " 'Tis impossible to live with the baggages, impossible to live without 'em!" Come, let us agree for the future not to regard each other any more as enemies; and to clinch the bargain, let us sing a choric song.

COMBINED CHORUS OF WOMEN AND OLD MEN (*singing*)

We desire, Athenians, to speak ill of no man; but on the contrary to say much good of everyone, and to do the like. We have had enough of misfortunes and calamities. If there is any man or woman who wants a bit of money—two or three minas or so; well, our purse is full. If only peace is concluded, the borrower will not have to pay back. Also I'm inviting to supper a few Carystian friends, who are excellently well qualified. I have still a drop of good soup left, and a young porker I'm going to kill, and the flesh will be sweet and tender. I shall expect you at my house to-day; but first away to the baths with you, you and your children; then come all of you, ask no one's leave, but walk straight up, as if you were at home; never fear, the door will be . . . shut in your faces!

LEADER OF CHORUS OF OLD MEN

Ah! here come the envoys from Sparta with their long flowing beards; why, you would think they wore pigstyes between their thighs. (*Enter the* LACONIAN ENVOYS *afflicted like their herald.*) Hail to you, first of all, Laconians; then tell us how you fare.

LACONIAN ENVOY

No need for many words; you can see what a state we are in.

LEADER OF CHORUS OF OLD MEN

Alas! the situation grows more and more strained! the intensity of the thing is simply frightful.

LACONIAN ENVOY

It's beyond belief. But to work! summon your Commissioners, and let us patch up the best peace we may.

LEADER OF CHORUS OF OLD MEN

Ah! our men too, like wrestlers in the arena, cannot endure a rag over their bellies; it's an athlete's malady, which only exercise can remedy. (*The* MAGISTRATE *returns; he too now has an evident reason to desire peace.*)

MAGISTRATE

Can anybody tell us where Lysistrata is? Surely she will have some compassion on our condition.

LEADER OF CHORUS OF OLD MEN (*pointing*)

Look! now he has the very same complaint. (*To the* MAGISTRATE) Don't you feel a strong nervous tension in the morning?

MAGISTRATE

Yes, and a dreadful, dreadful torture it is! Unless peace is made very soon, we shall find no recourse but to make love to Clisthenes.

LEADER OF CHORUS OF OLD MEN

Take my advice, and arrange your clothes as best you can; one of the fellows who mutilated the Hermae might see you.

MAGISTRATE

Right, by Zeus.
(*He endeavours, not too successfully, to conceal his condition.*)

LACONIAN ENVOY

Quite right, by the Dioscuri. There, I will put on my tunic.

MAGISTRATE

Oh! what a terrible state we are in! Greeting to you, Laconian fellow-sufferers.

LACONIAN ENVOY (*addressing one of his countrymen*)

Ah! my boy, what a terrible thing it would have been if these fellows had seen us just now when we were on full stand!

MAGISTRATE

Speak out, Laconians, what is it brings you here?

LACONIAN ENVOY

We have come to treat for peace.

MAGISTRATE

Well said; we are of the same mind. Better call Lysistrata, then; she is the only person who will bring us to terms.

LACONIAN ENVOY

Yes, yes— and Lysistratus into the bargain, if you will.

MAGISTRATE

Needless to call her; she has heard your voices, and here she comes.
(*She comes out of the Acropolis.*)

LEADER OF CHORUS OF OLD MEN

Hail, boldest and bravest of womankind! The time is come to show yourself in turn uncompromising and conciliatory, exacting and yielding, haughty and condescending. Call up all your skill and artfulness. Lo! the foremost men in Hellas, seduced by your fascinations, are agreed to entrust you with the task of ending their quarrels.

LYSISTRATA

It will be an easy task—if only they refrain from mutual indulgence in masculine love; if they do, I shall know the fact at once. Now, where is the gentle goddess Peace? (*The goddess, in the form of a beautiful nude girl is brought in by the Machine.*) Lead hither the Laconian envoys. But, look you, no roughness or violence; our husbands always behaved so boorishly. Bring them to me with smiles, as women should. If any refuse to give you his hand, then take hold of his tool. Bring up the Athenians too; you may lead them either way. Laconians, approach; and you, Athenians, on my other side. Now hearken all! I am but a woman; but I have good common sense; Nature has endowed me with discriminating judgment, which I have yet further developed, thanks to the wise teachings of my father and the elders of the city. First I must bring a reproach against you that applies equally to both sides. At Olympia, and Thermopylae, and Delphi, and a score of other places too numerous to mention, you celebrate before the same altars ceremonies common to all Hellenes; yet you go cutting each other's throats, and sacking Hellenic cities, when all the while the barbarian yonder is threatening you! That is my first point.

MAGISTRATE (*devouring the goddess with his eyes*)
Good god, this erection is killing me!

LYSISTRATA
Now it is to you I address myself, Laconians. Have you forgotten how Periclidas, your own countryman, sat a suppliant before our altars? How pale he was in his purple robes! He had come to crave an army of us; it was the time when Messenia was pressing you sore, and the Sea-god was shaking the earth. Cimon marched to your aid at the head of four thousand hoplites, and saved Lacedaemon. And, after such a service as that, you ravage the soil of your benefactors!

MAGISTRATE
They do wrong, very wrong, Lysistrata.

LACONIAN ENVOY
We do wrong, very wrong. (*Looking at the goddess*) Ah! great gods! what a lovely bottom Peace has!

LYSISTRATA
And now a word to the Athenians. Have you no memory left of how, in the days when you wore the tunic of slaves, the Laconians came, spear in hand, and slew a host of Thessalians and partisans of Hippias the tyrant? They, and they only, fought on your side on that eventful day; they delivered you from despotism, and thanks to them our nation could change the short tunic of the slave for the long cloak of the free man.

LACONIAN ENVOY (*looking at* LYSISTRATA)
I have never seen a woman of more gracious dignity.

MAGISTRATE (*looking at* PEACE)
I have never seen a woman with a finer body!

LYSISTRATA

Bound by such ties of mutual kindness, how can you bear to be at war?
Stop, stay the hateful strife, be reconciled; what hinders you?

LACONIAN ENVOY

We are quite ready, if they will give us back our rampart.

LYSISTRATA

What rampart, my dear man?

LACONIAN ENVOY

Pylos, which we have been asking for and craving for ever so long.

MAGISTRATE

In the Sea-god's name, you shall never have it!

LYSISTRATA

Agree, my friends, agree.

MAGISTRATE

But then what city shall we be able to stir up trouble in?

LYSISTRATA

Ask for another place in exchange.

MAGISTRATE

Ah! that's the ticket! Well, to begin with, give us Echinus, the Maliac
gulf adjoining, and the two legs of Megara.

LACONIAN ENVOY

No, by the Dioscuri, surely not all that, my dear sir.

LYSISTRATA

Come to terms; never make a difficulty of two legs more or less!

MAGISTRATE (*his eye on* PEACE)

Well, I'm ready to strip down and get to work right now.

(*He takes off his mantle.*)

LACONIAN ENVOY (*following out this idea*)

And I also, to dung it to start with.

LYSISTRATA

That's just what you shall do, once peace is signed. So, if you really
want to make it, go consult your allies about the matter.

MAGISTRATE

What allies, I should like to know? Why, we are *all* erected; there's no one who is not mad to be mating. What we all want is to be in bed with our wives; how should our allies fail to second our project?

LACONIAN ENVOY

And ours too, for certain sure!

MAGISTRATE

The Carystians first and foremost, by the gods!

LYSISTRATA

Well said, indeed! Now go and purify yourselves for entering the Acropolis, where the women invite you to supper; we will empty our provision baskets to do you honour. At table, you will exchange oaths and pledges; then each man will go home with his wife.

MAGISTRATE

Come along then, and as quick as may be.

LACONIAN ENVOY

Lead on; I'm your man.

MAGISTRATE

Quick, quick's the word, say I.

(*They follow* LYSISTRATA *into the Acropolis.*)

CHORUS OF WOMEN (*singing*)

Embroidered stuffs, and dainty tunics, and flowing gowns, and golden ornaments, everything I have, I offer them to you with all my heart; take them all for your children, for your girls, in case they are chosen Canephori. I invite you every one to enter, come in and choose whatever you will; there is nothing so well fastened, you cannot break the seals, and carry away the contents. Look about you everywhere . . . you won't find a blessed thing, unless you have sharper eyes than mine. And if any of you lacks corn to feed his slaves and his young and numerous family, why, I have a few grains of wheat at home; let him take what I have to give, a big twelve-pound loaf included. So let my poorer neighbours all come with bags and wallets; my man, Manes, shall give them corn; but I warn them not to come near my door, but—beware the dog!

(*Another* MAGISTRATE *enters, and begins knocking at the gate.*)

SECOND MAGISTRATE

I say, you, open the door! (*To the* WOMEN) Go your way, I tell you. (*As the women sit down in front of the gate*) Why, bless me, they're sitting down now; I shall have to singe 'em with my torch to make 'em stir! What impudence! I won't take this. Oh, well, if it's absolutely neces-, sary, just to please you, we'll have to take the trouble.

AN ATHENIAN
And I'll share it with you.
(*He brandishes the torch he is carrying and the* CHORUS OF WOMEN *departs. The* CHORUS OF OLD MEN *follows shortly after.*)

SECOND MAGISTRATE
No, no, you must be off—or I'll tear your hair out, I will; be off, I say, and don't annoy the Laconian envoys; they're just coming out from the banquet-hall.

ATHENIAN
Such a merry banquet I've never seen before! The Laconians were simply charming. After the drink is in, why, we're all wise men, every one of us.

MAGISTRATE
It's only natural, to be sure, for sober, we're all fools. Take my advice, my fellow-countrymen, our envoys should always be drunk. We go to Sparta; we enter the city sober; why, we must be picking a quarrel directly. We don't understand what they say to us, we imagine a lot they don't say at all, and we report home all wrong, all topsy-turvy. But, look you, to-day it's quite different; we're enchanted whatever happens; instead of Clitagora, they might sing us Telamon, and we should clap our hands just the same. A perjury or two into the bargain, why! What does that matter to merry companions in their cups?
(*The two* CHORUSES *return.*) But here they are back again! Will you be-gone, you loafing scoundrels.

                    (*The* CHORUSES *retire again.*)

ATHENIAN
Ah ha! here's the company coming out already.
(*Two choruses, one Laconian and one Athenian, enter, dancing to the music of flutes; they are followed by the women under the leadership of* LYSISTRATA.)

A LACONIAN
My dear, sweet friend, come, take your flute in hand; I would fain dance and sing my best in honour of the Athenians and our noble selves.

ATHENIAN
Yes, take your flute, in the gods' name. What a delight to see him dance!

LACONIAN (*dancing and singing*)

Oh! Mnemosyné! inspire these men, inspire my muse who knows our exploits and those of the Athenians. With what a god-like ardour did they swoop down at Artemisium on the ships of the Medes! What a glorious victory was that! For the soldiers of Leonidas, they were like fierce boars whetting their tusks. The sweat ran down their faces, and drenched all their limbs, for verily the Persians were as many as the sands of the seashore. Oh! Artemis, huntress queen, whose arrows pierce the denizens of the woods, virgin goddess, be thou favourable to the peace we here conclude; through thee may our hearts be long united! May this treaty draw close for ever the bonds of a happy friendship! No more wiles and stratagems! Aid us, oh! aid us, maiden huntress!

MAGISTRATE

All is for the best; and now, Laconians, take your wives away home with you, and you, Athenians, yours. May husband live happily with wife, and wife with husband. Dance, dance, to celebrate our bliss, and let us be heedful to avoid like mistakes for the future.

CHORUS OF ATHENIANS (*singing*)

Appear, appear, dancers, and the Graces with you! Let us invoke, one and all, Artemis, and her heavenly brother, gracious Apollo, patron of the dance, and Dionysus, whose eye darts flame, as he steps forward surrounded by the Maenad maids, and Zeus, who wields the flashing lightning, and his august, thrice-blessed spouse, the Queen of Heaven! These let us invoke, and all the other gods, calling all the inhabitants of the skies to witness the noble Peace now concluded under the fond auspices of Aphrodité. Io Paean! Io Paean! dance, leap, as in honour of a victory won. *Euoí! Euoí! Euaí! Euaí!*

MAGISTRATE

And you, our Laconian guests, sing us a new and inspiring strain!

LACONIAN (*singing*)

Leave once more, oh! leave once more the noble height of Taygetus, oh! Muse of Lacedaemon, and join us in singing the praises of Apollo of Amyclae, and Athené of the Brazen House, and the gallant twin sons of Tyndareus, who practise arms on the banks of the Eurotas river. Haste, haste hither with nimble-footed pace, let us sing Sparta, the city that delights in choruses divinely sweet and graceful dances, when our maidens bound lightly by the river side, like frolicsome fillies, beating the ground with rapid steps and shaking their long locks in the wind, as Bacchantes wave their wands in

the wild revels of the Wine-god. At their head, oh! chaste and beauteous goddess, daughter of Leto, Artemis, do thou lead the song and
dance. With a fillet binding thy waving tresses, appear in thy loveliness; leap like a fawn, strike thy divine hands together to animate
the dance, and aid us to renown the valiant goddess of battles, great
Athené of the Brazen House!

(All depart, singing and dancing.)

1. This was a constant weakness of Athenian democracy; lacking any sort of centralization it was fatally inefficient in crises.

2. Aristophanes frequently jests on the actual or supposed bibulousness of the Athenian women.

3. The reference is to *The Seven Against Thebes,* 42 ff.

4. This sacrifice was offered to the spirit of the departed on the third day after the funeral.

5. According to the fable the eagle and the beetle were at war; the eagle devoured the beetle's young and the latter retaliated by getting into its nest and tumbling out its eggs. The eagle then complained to Zeus and was advised to lay its eggs in his bosom; the beetle then flew up to the house of Zeus and began buzzing around his ears. When he rose to chase the insect away the eagle's eggs fell to the earth and were smashed to bits.

6. The Acropolis was sacred to Athené, a virgin goddess.

VIII
THE THESMOPHORIAZUSAE

CHARACTERS IN THE PLAY

EURIPIDES
MNESILOCHUS, *Father-in-law of Euripides*
AGATHON
SERVANT OF AGATHON
HERALD
WOMEN
CLISTHENES
A MAGISTRATE
A SCYTHIAN POLICEMAN
CHORUS OF THESMOPHORIAZUSAE—*women
    celebrating the* THESMOPHORIA

INTRODUCTION

THE otherwise unfortunate year 411 witnessed the production of two of Aristophanes' comedies, and the exhibition of *Lysistrata* at the Lenaea was supplemented by *The Thesmophoriazusae* at the Great Dionysia two months later. No notice of the prizes awarded at this festival has been preserved, but it is tempting to conjecture and not impossible to believe that the composition of *The Frogs* in 405 was suggested or motivated by a victory of *The Thesmophoriazusae* six years earlier. The detachment from contemporary realities so noteworthy in *The Birds* and clearly recognizable in *Lysistrata* despite a pacifistic theme, is equally characteristic of *The Thesmophoriazusae*, for the subject of the play is essentially literary and has nothing whatever to do with any political or social issues. The ridicule of Euripides, which is the general theme of the comedy, is foreshadowed in *The Acharnians*, but there the target of Aristophanes' gibes is the wretchedness of so many of the dramatist's heroes, and only a part of the play is devoted to it, whereas here it is the tragedian's notorious misogyny that creates the humorous situation, and the whole of the comedy is occupied with this.

When the play opens we find Euripides and his father-in-law Mnesilochus arriving in front of the house of the dramatist Agathon, to seek his assistance in a matter of great importance. The women of Athens have resolved to punish Euripides for the insults to their sex which are so numerous in his tragedies, and his case is to be discussed and decided in their Assembly at the Thesmophoria this very day. Convinced that they will condemn him to death unless there is someone present at the meeting to defend him, he has decided to ask the effeminate Agathon to undertake this office. The latter is soon displayed by the eccyclema, ensconced in his boudoir, but he politely and firmly refuses Euripides' request. Mnesilochus accordingly volunteers to lend whatever assistance he can, and Euripides immediately sets about removing all possible evidences of his relative's masculinity. His face is shaved and his loins singed, and he is then fitted out with a complete set of feminine garments generously loaned by Agathon from his well-stocked wardrobe. Mnesilochus departs for the meeting, making every effort to speak and to act in as womanly a fashion as possible.

The scene shifts to the Thesmophorion, where the debate on Euripides is opened and a speaker recommends that he be put to death. Mnesilochus makes an eloquent and misguided defense of the dramatist, in the course of which he repeatedly insults the fair sex by pointing out how many of their sins have never even been mentioned by his son-in-law. The infuriated Assembly is about to chastise him immediately and violently, when, to make matters worse, the notorious pederast Clisthenes, who has somehow got wind of Euripides' scheme, rushes in and informs the horrified women that there is a man in their midst. An investigation is forthwith made, and Mnesilochus is eventually discovered. Clisthenes departs to report the matter to the magistrates, and the Chorus, or rather its leader, delivers something resembling a parabasis, in which the virtues of men and women are compared, greatly to the advantage of the latter. Formally the passage is highly incomplete, for it contains only the anapests and one epirrheme. Remembering the parabasis in *Peace* we may perhaps conjecture that *The Thesmophoriazusae* was also somewhat hastily composed.

Even before the delivery of the parabasis, Mnesilochus has been energetically racking his brain to discover an effective means of escape, and he has been able to think of nothing better than the device of Oeax in the tragedy *Palamedes*. He accordingly has sent to his son-in-law messages written on wooden statues, in lieu of oars, and flung about in all directions. The ingenious adaptation of the dramatist's artifice is eminently unsuccessful, and as soon as the Chorus leader has completed his delivery of the epirrheme, Mnesilochus adopts another tactic and begins reciting lines from the part of Helen in the recent tragedy of that name. The same curious prank of fortune which had brought her husband to Egypt now summons Euripides to the Thesmophorion, costumed as Menelaus and reciting many of the lines of that fortunate hero. So far all is well, but the more difficult problem of effecting the escape of Mnesilochus remains unsolved, and the arrival of the magistrate to whom Clisthenes has reported the women's plight frustrates the purposes and necessitates the retirement of the wily tragedian. The customary Scythian policeman, whom the magistrate has brought with him, arrests Mnesilochus and binds him to a post, to be, in his feminine attire, a wretched and ridiculous spectacle to the world at large. But Euripides has promised never to abandon him, "so long as one of his numberless artifices remains untried," and Mnesilochus accordingly makes another effort, using the poet's *Andromeda* as the source of his inspiration. He quotes a long and lugubrious lament made by the heroine of that play, and his son-in-law promptly replies from the wings in the rôle of Echo. A ludicrous scene ensues in which Euripides repeats the final word or phrase of everything that is said by his father-in-law or by the Scythian, but this is far from setting the poor man free, and eventually the dramatist appears as Perseus and seeks to rescue the maiden Mnesilochus; "Each man has his own particular weakness," he says, "as for me I am aflame with love for this virgin." The old man's back is turned and there is no need to untie him; the policeman therefore has no objections to anything that Euripides may wish to do, but the intimation that Mnesilochus is actually to be released elicits prompt and uncompromising opposition. Euripides is now convinced that the refinements of his dramaturgical ingenuity are lost on the torpid barbarian, and he resolves to invent some artifice better adapted to the brutish nature of his opponent. Making his peace with the Chorus by promising never to malign them in the future, he departs to change his costume and almost immediately returns, rather transparently disguised as an old bawd, and bringing with him two girls, a flute-player and a dancer. The Chorus penetrates his disguise without difficulty, but the Scythian is so captivated by the dancing girl that he suspects nothing and is readily induced to go offstage for a while. Euripides quickly releases his father-in-law and takes him home, and the Chorus is obliging enough to start the distressed policeman off in the opposite direction from that in which the pair have departed.

Such is the ending of what is perhaps the best comedy that its author produced. Nowhere else do we find so perfect a blend of animal and intellectual ingredients, embodied in a play so skillfully constructed and so artistically unified; nor is Aristophanes' wit ever so brilliant as it is in *The Thesmophoriazusae.* With it the best decade of the poet's career is brought to a close, and in the three comedies that have survived from the later years we shall never meet quite the same Aristophanes again.

THE THESMOPHORIAZUSAE

(SCENE:—*Behind the orchestra are two buildings, one the house of the poet* AGATHON, *the other the Thesmophorion.* EURIPIDES *enters from the right, at a rapid pace, with an air of searching for something; his father-in-law* MNESILOCHUS, *who is extremely aged, follows him as best he can, with an obviously painful expenditure of effort.*)

MNESILOCHUS

GREAT ZEUS! will the swallow never appear to end the winter of my discontent? Why the fellow has kept me on the run ever since early this morning; he wants to kill me, that's certain. Before I lose my spleen entirely, Euripides, can you at least tell me where you are leading me?

EURIPIDES

What need for you to hear what you are going to see?

MNESILOCHUS

How is that? Repeat it. No need for me to hear . . .

EURIPIDES

What you are going to see.

MNESILOCHUS

Nor consequently to see . . .

EURIPIDES

What you have to hear.

MNESILOCHUS

What is this wiseacre stuff you are telling me? I must neither see nor hear?

EURIPIDES

Ah! but you have two things there that are essentially distinct.

MNESILOCHUS

Seeing and hearing?

EURIPIDES

Undoubtedly.

MNESILOCHUS

In what way distinct?

EURIPIDES

In this way. Formerly, when Aether separated the elements and bore the animals that were moving in her bosom, she wished to endow them with sight, and so made the eye round like the sun's disc and bored ears in the form of a funnel.

MNESILOCHUS

And because of this funnel I neither see nor hear. Ah! great gods! I am delighted to know it. What a fine thing it is to talk with wise men!

EURIPIDES

I will teach you many another thing of the sort.

MNESILOCHUS

That's well to know; but first of all I should like to find out how to grow lame, so that I need not have to follow you all about.

EURIPIDES

Come, hear and give heed!

MNESILOCHUS

I'm here and waiting.

EURIPIDES

Do you see that little door?

MNESILOCHUS

Yes, certainly.

EURIPIDES

Silence!

MNESILOCHUS

Silence about what? About the door?

EURIPIDES

Pay attention!

MNESILOCHUS
Pay attention and be silent about the door? Very well.

EURIPIDES
That is where Agathon, the celebrated tragic poet, dwells.

MNESILOCHUS
Who is this Agathon?

EURIPIDES
He's a certain Agathon . . .

MNESILOCHUS
Swarthy, robust of build?

EURIPIDES
No, another.

MNESILOCHUS
I have never seen him. He has a big beard?

EURIPIDES
Have you never *seen* him?

MNESILOCHUS
Never, so far as I know.

EURIPIDES
And yet you have made love to him. Well, it must have been without knowing who he was. (*The door of* AGATHON'S *house opens.*)Ah! let us step aside; here is one of his slaves bringing a brazier and some myrtle branches; no doubt he is going to offer a sacrifice and pray for a happy poetical inspiration for Agathon.

SERVANT OF AGATHON (*standing on the threshold; solemnly*)
Silence! oh, people! keep your mouths sedately shut! The chorus of the Muses is moulding songs at my master's hearth. Let the winds hold their breath in the silent Aether! Let the azure waves cease murmuring on the shore! . . .

MNESILOCHUS
Bombax.[1]

EURIPIDES
Be still! I want to hear what he is saying.

SERVANT

. . . Take your rest, ye winged races, and you, ye savage inhabitants
of the woods, cease from your erratic wandering . . .

MNESILOCHUS (*more loudly*)

Bombalobombax.

SERVANT

. . . for Agathon, our master, the sweet-voiced poet, is going . . .

MNESILOCHUS

. . . to be made love to?

SERVANT

Whose voice is that?

MNESILOCHUS

It's the silent Aether.

SERVANT

. . . is going to construct the framework of a drama. He is rounding
fresh poetical forms, he is polishing them in the lathe and is welding them;
he is hammering out sentences and metaphors; he is working up his subject like soft wax. First he models it and then he casts it in bronze . . .

MNESILOCHUS

. . . and sways his buttocks amorously.

SERVANT

Who is the rustic that approaches this sacred enclosure?

MNESILOCHUS

Take care of yourself and of your sweet-voiced poet! I have a strong
tool here both well rounded and well polished, which will pierce your
enclosure and penetrate you.

SERVANT

Old man, you must have been a *very* insolent fellow in your youth!

EURIPIDES (*to the* SERVANT)

Let him be, friend, and, quick, go and call Agathon to me.

SERVANT

It's not worth the trouble, for he will soon be here himself. He has
started to compose, and in winter it is never possible to round off strophes
without coming to the sun to excite the imagination.

EURIPIDES

And what am I to do?

SERVANT

Wait till he gets here.

(He goes into the house.)

EURIPIDES

Oh, Zeus! what hast thou in store for me to-day?

MNESILOCHUS

Great gods, what is the matter now? What are you grumbling and groaning for? Tell me; you must not conceal anything from your father-in-law.

EURIPIDES

Some great misfortune is brewing against me.

MNESILOCHUS

What is it?

EURIPIDES

This day will decide whether it is all over with Euripides or not.

MNESILOCHUS

But how? Neither the tribunals nor the Senate are sitting, for it is the third day of the Thesmophoria.

EURIPIDES

That is precisely what makes me tremble; the women have plotted my ruin, and to-day they are to gather in the Temple of Demeter to execute their decision.

MNESILOCHUS

What have they against you?

EURIPIDES

Because I mishandle them in my tragedies.

MNESILOCHUS

By Posidon, you would seem to have thoroughly deserved your fate. But how are you going to get out of the mess?

EURIPIDES

I am going to beg Agathon, the tragic poet, to go to the Thesmophoria.

MNESILOCHUS

And what is he to do there?

EURIPIDES

He would mingle with the women, and stand up for me, if needful.

MNESILOCHUS

Would he be openly present or secretly?

EURIPIDES

Secretly, dressed in woman's clothes.

MNESILOCHUS

That's a clever notion, thoroughly worthy of you. The prize for trickery is ours.

(The door of AGATHON'S *house opens.)*

EURIPIDES

Silence!

MNESILOCHUS

What's the matter?

EURIPIDES

Here comes Agathon.

MNESILOCHUS

Where, where?

EURIPIDES

That's the man they are bringing out yonder on the eccyclema.

*(*AGATHON *appears on the eccyclema, softly reposing on a bed, clothed in a saffron tunic, and surrounded with feminine toilet articles.)*

MNESILOCHUS

I am blind then! I see no man here, I only see Cyrené.

EURIPIDES

Be still! He is getting ready to sing.

MNESILOCHUS

What subtle trill, I wonder, is he going to warble to us?

AGATHON

(He now sings a selection from one of his tragedies, taking first the part of the leader of the chorus and then that of the whole chorus.)

(As LEADER OF THE CHORUS)

Damsels, with the sacred torch in hand, unite your dance to shouts of joy in honour of the nether goddesses; celebrate the freedom of your country.

(As CHORUS)

To what divinity is your homage addressed? I wish to mingle mine with it.

(As LEADER OF THE CHORUS)

Oh! Muse! glorify Phoebus with his golden bow, who erected the walls of the city of the Simois.

(As CHORUS)

To thee, oh Phoebus, I dedicate my most beauteous songs; to thee, the sacred victor in the poetical contests.

(As LEADER OF THE CHORUS)

And praise Artemis too, the maiden huntress, who wanders on the mountains and through the woods . . .

(As CHORUS)

I, in my turn, celebrate the everlasting happiness of the chaste Artemis, the mighty daughter of Leto!

(As LEADER OF THE CHORUS)

. . . and Leto and the tones of the Asiatic lyre, which wed so well with the dances of the Phrygian Graces.

(As CHORUS)

I do honour to the divine Leto and to the lyre, the mother of songs of male and noble strains. The eyes of the goddess sparkle while listening to our enthusiastic chants. Honour to the powerful Phoebus! Hail! thou blessed son of Leto.

MNESILOCHUS

Oh! ye venerable Genetyllides, what tender and voluptuous songs! They surpass the most lascivious kisses in sweetness; I feel a thrill of delight pass up me as I listen to them. (*To* EURIPIDES) Young man, if you are one, answer my questions, which I am borrowing from Aeschylus' "Lycurgeia." Whence comes this androgyne? What is his country? his dress? What contradictions his life shows! A lyre and a hair-net! A wrestling school oil flask and a girdle! What could be more contradictory? What relation has a mirror to a sword? (*To* AGATHON) And you yourself, who are you? Do you pretend to be a man? Where is your tool, pray? Where is the cloak, the footgear that belong to that sex? Are you a

woman? Then where are your breasts? Answer me. But you keep silent.
Oh! just as you choose; your songs display your character quite sufficiently.

AGATHON

Old man, old man, I hear the shafts of jealousy whistling by my ears,
but they do not hit me. My dress is in harmony with my thoughts. A
poet must adopt the nature of his characters. Thus, if he is placing women
on the stage, he must contract all their habits in his own person.

MNESILOCHUS (*aside*)

Then you make love horse-fashion when you are composing a Phaedra.

AGATHON

If the heroes are men, everything in him will be manly. What we don't
possess by nature, we must acquire by imitation.

MNESILOCHUS (*aside*)

When you are staging Satyrs, call me; I will do my best to help you
from behind, if I can get my tool up.

AGATHON

Besides, it is bad taste for a poet to be coarse and hairy. Look at the
famous Ibycus, at Anacreon of Teos, and at Alcaeus, who handled music
so well; they wore head-bands and found pleasure in the lascivious dances
of Ionia. And have you not heard what a dandy Phrynichus was and how
careful in his dress? For this reason his pieces were also beautiful, for the
works of a poet are copied from himself.

MNESILOCHUS

Ah! so it is for this reason that Philocles, who is so hideous, writes
hideous pieces; Xenocles, who is malicious, malicious ones, and Theognis,
who is cold, such cold ones?

AGATHON

Yes, necessarily and unavoidably; and it is because I knew this that I
have so well cared for my person.

MNESILOCHUS

How, in the gods' name?

EURIPIDES

Come, leave off badgering him; I was just the same at his age, when
I began to write.

MNESILOCHUS

Ah! then, by Zeus! I don't envy you your fine manners.

EURIPIDES (*to* AGATHON)

But listen to the cause that brings me here.

AGATHON

Say on.

EURIPIDES

Agathon, wise is he who can compress many thoughts into few words. Struck by a most cruel misfortune, I come to you as a suppliant.

AGATHON

What are you asking?

EURIPIDES

The women purpose killing me to-day during the Thesmophoria, because I have dared to speak ill of them.

AGATHON

And what can I do for you in the matter?

EURIPIDES

Everything. Mingle secretly with the women by making yourself pass as one of themselves; then do you plead my cause with your own lips, and I am saved. You, and you alone, are capable of speaking of me worthily.

AGATHON

But why not go and defend yourself?

EURIPIDES

Impossible. First of all, I am known; further, I have white hair and a long beard; whereas you, you are good-looking, charming, and are close-shaven; you are fair, delicate, and have a woman's voice.

AGATHON

Euripides!

EURIPIDES

Well?

AGATHON

Have you not said in one of your pieces, "You love to see the light, and don't you believe your father loves it too?" [2]

EURIPIDES

Yes.

AGATHON

Then never you think I am going to expose myself in your stead; it would be madness. It's up to you to submit to the fate that overtakes you; one must not try to trick misfortune, but resign oneself to it with good grace.

MNESILOCHUS

You fairy! That's why your arse is so accessible to lovers.

EURIPIDES

But what prevents your going there?

AGATHON

I should run more risk than you would.

EURIPIDES

Why?

AGATHON

Why? I should look as if I were wanting to trespass on secret nightly pleasures of the women and to rape their Aphrodité.

MNESILOCHUS (*aside*)

Wanting to rape indeed! you mean wanting to be raped. Ah! great gods! a fine excuse truly!

EURIPIDES

Well then, do you agree?

AGATHON

Don't count upon it.

EURIPIDES

Oh! I am unfortunate indeed! I am undone!

MNESILOCHUS

Euripides, my friend, my son-in-law, never despair.

EURIPIDES

What can be done?

MNESILOCHUS

Send him to the devil and do with me as you like.

EURIPIDES

Very well then, since you devote yourself to my safety, take off your cloak first.

MNESILOCHUS

There, it lies on the ground. But what do you want to do with me?

EURIPIDES

To shave off this beard of yours, and to remove all your other hair as well.

MNESILOCHUS

Do what you think fit; I yield myself entirely to you.

EURIPIDES

Agathon, you always have razors about you; lend me one.

AGATHON

Take it yourself, there, out of that case.

EURIPIDES

Thanks. (*To* MNESILOCHUS) Now sit down and puff out your right cheek.

MNESILOCHUS (*as he is being shaved*)

Ow! Ow! Ow!

EURIPIDES

What are you shouting for? I'll cram a spit down your gullet, if you're not quiet.

MNESILOCHUS

Ow! Ow! Ow! Ow! Ow! Ow! (*He jumps up and starts running away.*)

EURIPIDES

Where are you running to now?

MNESILOCHUS

To the temple of the Eumenides. No, by Demeter! I won't let myself be gashed like that.

EURIPIDES

But you will get laughed at, with your face half-shaven like that.

MNESILOCHUS

Little care I.

EURIPIDES

In the gods' names, don't leave me in the lurch. Come here.

MNESILOCHUS

Oh! by the gods! (*He returns reluctantly and resumes his seat.*)

EURIPIDES

Keep still and hold up your head. Why do you want to fidget about like this?

MNESILOCHUS

Mm, mm.

EURIPIDES

Well! why mm, mm? There! it's done and well done too!

MNESILOCHUS

Alas, I shall fight without armour.

EURIPIDES

Don't worry; you look charming. Do you want to see yourself?

MNESILOCHUS

Yes, I do; hand the mirror here.

EURIPIDES

Do you see yourself?

MNESILOCHUS

But this is not I, it is Clisthenes!

EURIPIDES

Stand up; I am now going to remove your hair. Bend down.

MNESILOCHUS

Alas! alas! they are going to grill me like a pig.

EURIPIDES

Come now, a torch or a lamp! Bend down and watch out for the tender end of your tool!

MNESILOCHUS

Aye, aye! but I'm afire! oh! oh! Water, water, neighbour, or my perineum will be alight!

EURIPIDES

Keep up your courage!

MNESILOCHUS

Keep my courage, when I'm being burnt up?

EURIPIDES

Come, cease your whining, the worst is over.

MNESILOCHUS

Oh! it's quite black, all burnt down there!

EURIPIDES

Don't worry! Satyrus will wash it.

MNESILOCHUS

Woe to him who dares to wash me!

EURIPIDES

Agathon, you refuse to devote yourself to helping me; but at any rate lend me a tunic and a belt. You cannot say you have not got them.

AGATHON

Take them and use them as you like; I consent.

MNESILOCHUS

What shall I take?

EURIPIDES

First put on this long saffron-coloured robe.

MNESILOCHUS

By Aphrodité! what a sweet odour! how it smells of young male tools! Hand it to me quickly. And the belt?

EURIPIDES

Here it is.

MNESILOCHUS

Now some rings for my legs.

EURIPIDES

You still want a hair-net and a head-dress.

AGATHON

Here is my night cap.

EURIPIDES

Ah! that's fine.

MNESILOCHUS

Does it suit me?

AGATHON

It could not be better.

EURIPIDES

And a short mantle?

AGATHON

There's one on the couch; take it.

EURIPIDES

He needs slippers.

AGATHON

Here are mine.

MNESILOCHUS

Will they fit me? (*To* AGATHON) You don't like a loose fit.

AGATHON

Try them on. Now that you have all you need, let me be taken inside.
(*The eccyclema turns and* AGATHON *disappears.*)

EURIPIDES

You look for all the world like a woman. But when you talk, take good
care to give your voice a woman's tone.

MNESILOCHUS (*falsetto*)

I'll try my best.

EURIPIDES

Come, get yourself to the temple.

MNESILOCHUS

No, by Apollo, not unless you swear to me . . .

EURIPIDES

What?

MNESILOCHUS

. . . that, if anything untoward happen to me, you will leave nothing
undone to save me.

EURIPIDES

Very well! I swear it by the Aether, the dwelling-place of the king of
the gods.

MNESILOCHUS

Why not rather swear it by the sons of Hippocrates?

EURIPIDES

Come, I swear it by all the gods, both great and small.

MNESILOCHUS

Remember, it's the heart, and not the tongue, that has sworn; [3] for the oaths of the tongue concern me but little.

EURIPIDES

Hurry up! The signal for the meeting has just been raised on the Temple of Demeter. Farewell.

(They both depart. The scene changes to the interior of the Thesmophorion, where the women who form the chorus are assembled. Mnesilochus enters, in his feminine attire, striving to act as womanly as possible, and giving his voice as female a pitch and lilt as he can; he pretends to be addressing his slave-girl.)

MNESILOCHUS

Here, Thratta, follow me. Look, Thratta, at the cloud of smoke that arises from all these lighted torches. Ah! beautiful Thesmophorae! grant me your favours, protect me, both within the temple and on my way back! Come, Thratta, put down the basket and take out the cake, which I wish to offer to the two goddesses. Mighty divinity, oh, Demeter, and thou, Persephoné, grant that I may be able to offer you many sacrifices; above all things, grant that I may not be recognized. Would that my well-holed daughter might marry a man as rich as he is foolish and silly, so that she may have nothing to do but amuse herself. But where can a place be found for hearing well? Be off, Thratta, be off; slaves have no right to be present at this gathering.

(He sits down amongst the women.)

WOMAN HERALD

Silence! Silence! Pray to the Thesmophorae, Demeter and Cora; pray to Plutus, Calligenia, Curotrophus, the Earth, Hermes and the Graces, that all may happen for the best at this gathering, both for the greatest advantage of Athens and for our own personal happiness! May the award be given her who, by both deeds and words, has most deserved it from the Athenian people and from the women! Address these prayers to heaven and demand happiness for yourselves. Io Paean! Io Paean! Let us rejoice!

CHORUS *(singing)*

May the gods deign to accept our vows and our prayers! Oh! almighty Zeus, and thou, god with the golden lyre, who reignest on sacred Delos, and thou, oh, invincible virgin, Pallas, with the eyes of azure and the spear of gold, who protectest our illustrious city, and thou, the daughter of the beautiful Leto, queen of the forests, who art adored under many names, hasten hither at my call. Come, thou mighty Posidon, king of the Ocean, leave thy stormy whirlpools of Nereus; come, goddesses of the seas, come, ye nymphs, who wander on the mountains. Let us unite our voices to the sounds of the golden lyre, and may wisdom preside at the gathering of the noble matrons of Athens.

WOMAN HERALD

Address your prayers to the gods and goddesses of Olympus, of Delphi, Delos and all other places; if there be a man who is plotting against the womenfolk or who, to injure them, is proposing peace to Euripides and the Medes, or who aspires to usurping the tyranny, plots the return of a tyrant, or unmasks a supposititious child; or if there be a slave who, a confidential party to a wife's intrigues, reveals them secretly to her husband, or who, entrusted with a message, does not deliver the same faithfully; if there be a lover who fulfils naught of what he has promised a woman, whom he has abused on the strength of his lies; if there be an old woman who seduces the lover of a maiden by dint of her presents and treacherously receives him in her house; if there be a host or hostess who sells false measure, pray the gods that they will overwhelm them with their wrath, both them and their families, and that they may reserve all their favours for you.

CHORUS (*singing*)

Let us ask the fulfilment of these wishes both for the city and for the people, and may the wisest of us cause her opinion to be accepted. But woe to those women who break their oaths, who speculate on the public misfortune, who seek to alter the laws and the decrees, who reveal our secrets to the foe and admit the Medes into our territory so that they may devastate it! I declare them both impious and criminal. Oh! almighty Zeus! see to it that the gods protect us, albeit we are but women!

WOMAN HERALD

Hearken, all of you! this is the decree passed by the Senate of the Women under the presidency of Timoclea and at the suggestion of Sostraté; it is signed by Lysilla, the secretary: "There will be a gathering of the people on the morning of the third day of the Thesmophoria, which is a day of rest for us; the principal business there shall be the punishment that it is meet to inflict upon Euripides for the insults with whicn he has loaded us." Now who asks to speak?

FIRST WOMAN

I do.

WOMAN HERALD

First put on this garland, and then speak.

LEADER OF THE CHORUS

Silence! let all be quiet! Pay attention! for here she is spitting as orators generally do before they begin; no doubt she has much to say.

FIRST WOMAN

If I have asked to speak, may the goddesses bear me witness, it was not for sake of ostentation. But I have long been pained to see us women insulted by this Euripides, this son of the green-stuff woman,[4] who loads us with every kind of indignity. Has he not hit us enough, calumniated us sufficiently, wherever there are spectators, tragedians, and a chorus? Does he not style us adulterous, lecherous, bibulous, treacherous, and garrulous? Does he not repeat that we are all vice, that we are the curse of our husbands? So that, directly they come back from the theatre, they look at us doubtfully and go searching every nook, fearing there may be some hidden lover. We can do nothing as we used to, so many are the false ideas which he has instilled into our husbands. Is a woman weaving a garland for herself? It's because she is in love. Does she let some vase drop while going or returning to the house? her husband asks her in whose honour she has broken it: "It can only be for that Corinthian stranger." Is a maiden unwell? Straightway her brother says, "That is a colour that does not please me." [5] And if a childless woman wishes to substitute one, the deceit can no longer be a secret, for the neighbours will insist on being present at her delivery. Formerly the old men married young girls, but they have been so calumniated that none think of them now, thanks to that line of his: "A woman is the tyrant of the old man who marries her." Again, it is because of Euripides that we are incessantly watched, that we are shut up behind bolts and bars, and that dogs are kept to frighten off the adulterers. Let that pass; but formerly it was we who had the care of the food, who fetched the flour from the storeroom, the oil and the wine; we can do it no more. Our husbands now carry little Spartan keys on their persons, made with three notches and full of malice and spite. Formerly it sufficed to purchase a ring marked with the same sign for three obols, to open the most securely sealed-up door; but now this pestilent Euripides has taught men to hang seals of worm-eaten wood about their necks.[6] My opinion, therefore, is that we should rid ourselves of our enemy by poison or by any other means, provided he dies. That is what I announce publicly; as to certain points, which I wish to keep secret, I propose to record them on the secretary's minutes.

CHORUS (*singing*)

Never have I listened to a cleverer or more eloquent woman.
Everything she says is true; she has examined the matter from all
sides and has weighed up every detail. Her arguments are close,
varied, and happily chosen. I believe that Xenocles himself, the son
of Carcinus, would seem to talk mere nonsense, if placed beside her.

SECOND WOMAN

I have only a very few words to add, for the last speaker has covered
the various points of the indictment; allow me only to tell you what happened to me. My husband died at Cyprus, leaving me five children, whom
I had great trouble to bring up by weaving chaplets on the myrtle market.
Anyhow, I lived as well as I could until this wretch had persuaded the
spectators by his tragedies that there were no gods; since then I have not
sold as many chaplets by half. I charge you therefore and exhort you all
to punish him, for does he not deserve it in a thousand respects, he who
loads you with troubles, who is as coarse toward you as the vegetables
upon which his mother reared him? But I must back to the market to
weave my chaplets; I have twenty to deliver yet.

CHORUS (*singing*)

This is even more animated and more trenchant than the first
speech; all she has just said is full of good sense and to the point;
it is clever, clear and well calculated to convince. Yes! we must have
striking vengeance on the insults of Euripides.

MNESILOCHUS

Oh, women! I am not astonished at these outbursts of fiery rage; how
could your bile not get inflamed against Euripides, who has spoken so
ill of you? As for myself, I hate the man, I swear it by my children; it
would be madness not to hate him! Yet, let us reflect a little; we are
alone and our words will not be repeated outside. Why be so bent on his
ruin? Because he has known and shown up two or three of our faults,
when we have a thousand? As for myself, not to speak of other women, I
have more than one great sin upon my conscience, but this is the blackest
of them. I had been married three days and my husband was asleep by
my side; I had a lover, who had seduced me when I was seven years old;
impelled by his passion, he came scratching at the door; I understood at
once he was there and was going down noiselessly. "Where are you going?" asked my husband. "I am suffering terribly with colic," I told him,
"and am going to the can." "Go ahead," he replied, and started pounding
together juniper berries, aniseed, and sage. As for myself, I moistened
the door-hinge and went to find my lover, who laid me, half-reclining
upon Apollo's altar and holding on to the sacred laurel with one hand.

Well now! Consider! that is a thing of which Euripides has never spoken. And when we bestow our favours on slaves and muleteers for want of better, does he mention this? And when we eat garlic early in the morning after a night of wantonness, so that our husband, who has been keeping guard upon the city wall, may be reassured by the smell and suspect nothing, has Euripides ever breathed a word of this? Tell me. Neither has he spoken of the woman who spreads open a large cloak before her husband's eyes to make him admire it in full daylight to conceal her lover by so doing and afford him the means of making his escape. I know another, who for ten whole days pretended to be suffering the pains of labour until she had secured a child; the husband hurried in all directions to buy drugs to hasten her deliverance, and meanwhile an old woman brought the infant in a stew-pot; to prevent its crying she had stopped up its mouth with honey. With a sign she told the wife that she was bringing a child for her, who at once began exclaiming, "Go away, friend, go away, I think I am going to be delivered; I can feel him kicking his heels in the belly . . . of the stew-pot." The husband goes off full of joy, and the old wretch quickly takes the honey out of the child's mouth, which starts crying; then she seizes the baby, runs to the father and tells him with a smile on her face, "It's a lion, a lion, that is born to you; it's your very image. Everything about it is like you, even his little tool, curved like the sky." Are these not our everyday tricks? Why certainly, by Artemis, and we are angry with Euripides, who assuredly treats us no worse than we deserve!

CHORUS (*singing*)

Great gods! where has she unearthed all that? What country gave birth to such an audacious woman? Oh! you wretch! I should not have thought ever a one of us could have spoken in public with such impudence. 'Tis clear, however, that we must expect everything and, as the old proverb says, must look beneath every stone, lest it conceal some orator ready to sting us.

LEADER OF THE CHORUS

There is but one thing in the world worse than a shameless woman, and that's another woman.

FIRST WOMAN

By Aglaurus! you have lost your wits, friends! You must be bewitched to suffer this plague to belch forth insults against us all. Is there no one has any spirit at all? If not, we and our maid-servants will punish her. Run and fetch coals and let's depilate her in proper style, to teach her not to speak ill of her sex.

MNESILOCHUS

Oh! no! not that part of me, my friends. Have we not the right to speak frankly at this gathering? And because I have uttered what I thought right in favour of Euripides, do you want to depilate me for my trouble?

FIRST WOMAN

What! we ought not to punish you, who alone have dared to defend the man who has done so much harm, whom it pleases to put all the vile women that ever were upon the stage, who only shows us Melanippés and Phaedras? But of Penelopé he has never said a word, because she was reputed chaste and good.

MNESILOCHUS

I know the reason. It's because not a single Penelopé exists among the women of to-day, but all without exception are Phaedras.

FIRST WOMAN

Women, you hear how this creature still dares to speak of us all.

MNESILOCHUS

And, Heaven knows, I have not said all that I know. Do you want any more?

FIRST WOMAN

You cannot tell us any more; you have crapped out all you know.

MNESILOCHUS

Why, I have not told the thousandth part of what we women do. Have I said how we use the hollow handles of our brooms to draw up wine unbeknown to our husbands?

FIRST WOMAN

The cursed jade!

MNESILOCHUS

And how we give meats to our pimps at the feast of the Apaturia and then accuse the cat . . .

FIRST WOMAN

You're crazy!

MNESILOCHUS

. . . Have I mentioned the woman who killed her husband with a hatchet? Of another, who caused hers to lose his reason with her potions? And of the Acharnian woman . . .

FIRST WOMAN

Die, you bitch!

MNESILOCHUS

. . . who buried her father beneath the bath?

FIRST WOMAN

And yet we listen to such things!

MNESILOCHUS

Have I told how you attributed to yourself the male child your slave had just borne and gave her your little daughter?

FIRST WOMAN

This insult calls for vengeance. Look out for your hair!

MNESILOCHUS

By Zeus! don't touch me.

FIRST WOMAN (*slapping him*)

There!

MNESILOCHUS (*hitting back*)

There! tit for tat!

FIRST WOMAN

Hold my cloak, Philista!

MNESILOCHUS

Come on then, and by Demeter . . .

FIRST WOMAN

Well! what?

MNESILOCHUS

. . . I'll make you crap forth the sesame-cake you have eaten.

LEADER OF THE CHORUS

Stop wrangling! I see a woman running here in hot haste. Keep silent, so that we may hear the better what she has to say.

(*Enter* CLISTHENES, *dressed as a woman.*)

CLISTHENES

Friends, whom I copy in all things, my hairless chin sufficiently evidences how dear you are to me; I am women-mad and make myself their champion wherever I am. Just now on the market-place I heard mention of a thing that is of the greatest importance to you; I come to tell it to you, to let you know it, so that you may watch carefully and be on your guard against the danger which threatens you.

LEADER OF THE CHORUS

What is it, my child? I can well call you child, for you have so smooth a skin.

CLISTHENES

They say that Euripides has sent an old man here to-day, one of his relations . . .

LEADER OF THE CHORUS

With what object? What is his idea?

CLISTHENES

. . . so that he may hear your speeches and inform him of your deliberations and intentions.

LEADER OF THE CHORUS

But how would a man fail to be recognized amongst women?

CLISTHENES

Euripides singed and depilated him and disguised him as a woman.

MNESILOCHUS

This is pure invention! What man is fool enough to let himself be depilated? As for myself, I don't believe a word of it.

CLISTHENES

Nonsense! I should not have come here to tell you, if I did not know it on indisputable authority.

LEADER OF THE CHORUS

Great gods! what is it you tell us! Come, women, let us not lose a moment; let us search and rummage everywhere! Where can this man have hidden himself to escape our notice? Help us to look, Clisthenes; we shall thus owe you double thanks, dear friend.

CLISTHENES

Well then! let us see. To begin with you; who are you?

MNESILOCHUS *(aside)*

Wherever am I to stow myself?

CLISTHENES

Each and every one must pass the scrutiny.

MNESILOCHUS (*aside*)

Oh! great gods!

FIRST WOMAN

You ask me who I am? I am the wife of Cleonymus.

CLISTHENES (*to the* LEADER OF THE CHORUS)

Do you know this woman?

LEADER OF THE CHORUS

Yes, yes, pass on to the rest.

CLISTHENES

And she who carries the child?

FIRST WOMAN

Surely; she's my nurse.

MNESILOCHUS (*aside*)

This is the end.

(*He runs off.*)

CLISTHENES

Hi! you there! where are you going? Stop. What are you running
away for?

MNESILOCHUS (*dancing on one leg*)

I want to take a pee, you brazen thing.

CLISTHENES

Well, be quick about it; I shall wait for you here.

LEADER OF THE CHORUS

Wait for her and examine her closely; she's the only one we do not
know.

CLISTHENES

That's a long leak you're taking.

MNESILOCHUS

God, yes; I am constricted; I ate some cress yesterday.

CLISTHENES

What are you chattering about cress? Come here and be quick.
(*He starts to pull* MNESILOCHUS *back.*)

MNESILOCHUS

Oh! don't pull a poor sick woman about like that.

CLISTHENES (*looking* MNESILOCHUS *square in the eye*)
Tell me, who is your husband?

MNESILOCHUS (*embarrassed*)
My husband? Do you know a certain individual at Cothocidae . . . ?

CLISTHENES
Whom do you mean? Give his name.

MNESILOCHUS
He's an individual to whom the son of a certain individual one day . . .

CLISTHENES
You are drivelling! Let's see, have you ever been here before?

MNESILOCHUS
Why certainly, every year.

CLISTHENES
Who is your tent companion?

MNESILOCHUS
A certain . . . Oh! my god!

CLISTHENES
That's not an answer!

FIRST WOMAN
Withdraw, all of you; I am going to examine her thoroughly about last year's mysteries. But move away, Clisthenes, for no man may hear what is going to be said. Now answer my questions! What was done first?

MNESILOCHUS
Let's see now. What was done first? Oh! we drank.

FIRST WOMAN
And then?

MNESILOCHUS
We drank to our healths.

FIRST WOMAN
You will have heard that from someone. And then?

MNESILOCHUS
Xenylla asked for a cup; there wasn't any thunder-mug.

FIRST WOMAN

You're talking nonsense. Here, Clisthenes, here! This is the man you were telling us about.

CLISTHENES

What shall we do with him?

FIRST WOMAN

Take off his clothes, I can get nothing out of him.

MNESILOCHUS

What! are you going to strip a mother of nine children naked?

CLISTHENES

Come, undo your girdle, you shameless thing.

FIRST WOMAN

Ah! what a sturdy frame! but she has no breasts like we have.

MNESILOCHUS

That's because I'm barren. I never had any children.

FIRST WOMAN

Oh! indeed! just now you were the mother of nine.

CLISTHENES

Stand up straight. What do you keep pushing that thing down for?

FIRST WOMAN (*peering from behind*)

There's no mistaking it.

CLISTHENES (*also peering from behind*)

Where has it gone to now?

FIRST WOMAN

To the front.

CLISTHENES (*from in front*)

No.

FIRST WOMAN (*from behind*)

Ah! it's behind now.

CLISTHENES

Why, friend, it's just like the Isthmus; you keep pulling your stick backwards and forwards more often than the Corinthians do their ships.

FIRST WOMAN

Ah! the wretch! this is why he insulted us and defended Euripides.

MNESILOCHUS

Aye, wretch indeed, what troubles have I not got into now!

FIRST WOMAN

What shall we do?

CLISTHENES

Watch him closely, so that he does not escape. As for me, I'll go to report the matter to the magistrates.

LEADER OF THE CHORUS

Let us kindle our lamps; let us go firmly to work and with courage, let us take off our cloaks and search whether some other man has not come here too; let us pass round the whole Pnyx,[7] examine the tents and the passages. Come, be quick, let us start off on a light toe and rummage all round in silence. Let us hasten, let us finish our round as soon as possible.

CHORUS (*singing*)

Look quickly for the traces that might show you a man hidden here, let your glance fall on every side; look well to the right and to the left. If we seize some impious fellow, woe to him! He will know how we punish the outrage, the crime, the sacrilege. The criminal will then acknowledge at last that gods exist; his fate will teach all men that the deities must be revered, that justice must be observed and that they must submit to the sacred laws. If not, then woe to them! Heaven itself will punish sacrilege; being aflame with fury and mad with frenzy, all their deeds will prove to mortals, both men and women, that the deity punishes injustice and impiety, and that she is not slow to strike.

LEADER OF THE CHORUS

But I think I have now searched everywhere and that no other man is hidden among us.

FIRST WOMAN

Where are you flying to? Stop! stop! Ah! miserable woman that I am, he has torn my child from my breast and has disappeared with it.

MNESILOCHUS

Scream as loud as you will, but you'll never feed him again. If you do not let me go this very instant, I am going to cut open the veins of his thighs with this cutlass and his blood shall flow over the altar.

FIRST WOMAN

Oh! great gods! oh! friends, help me! terrify him with your shrieks, triumph over this monster, permit him not to rob me of my only child.

LEADER OF THE CHORUS

Oh! oh! venerable Moirai, what fresh attack is this? It's the crowning act of audacity and shamelessness! What has he done now, friends, what has he done?

MNESILOCHUS

Ah! your insolence passes all bounds, but I know how to curb it!

LEADER OF THE CHORUS

What a shameful deed! the measure of his iniquities is full!

FIRST WOMAN

Aye, it's shameful that he should have robbed me of my child.

CHORUS (*singing*)

It's past belief to be so criminal and so impudent!

MNESILOCHUS (*singing*)

Ah! you're not near the end of it yet.

CHORUS (*singing*)

Little I care whence you come; you shall not return to boast of having acted so odiously with impunity, for you shall be punished.

MNESILOCHUS (*speaking*)

You won't do it, by the gods!

CHORUS (*singing*)

And what immortal would protect you for your crime?

MNESILOCHUS (*speaking*)

You talk in vain! I shall not let go the child.

CHORUS (*singing*)

By the goddesses, you will not laugh presently over your crime and your impious speech. For with impiety, as 'tis meet, shall we reply to your impiety. Soon fortune will turn round and overwhelm you.

LEADER OF THE CHORUS

Come there, bring some firewood. Let's roast the wretch as quickly as we can.

FIRST WOMAN

Bring faggots, Mania! (*To* MNESILOCHUS) You will be nothing but charcoal soon.

MNESILOCHUS

Grill away, roast me, but you, my child, take off this Cretan robe and blame no one but your mother for your death. But what does this mean? The little girl is nothing but a skin filled with wine and shod with Persian slippers. Oh! you wanton, you tippling women, who think of nothing but wine; you are a fortune to the drinking-shops and are our ruin; for the sake of drink, you neglect both your household and your shuttle!

FIRST WOMAN

Faggots, Mania, plenty of them.

MNESILOCHUS

Bring as many as you like. But answer me; are you the mother of this brat?

FIRST WOMAN

I carried it ten months.

MNESILOCHUS

You carried it?

FIRST WOMAN

I swear it by Artemis.

MNESILOCHUS

How much does it hold? Three cotylae? Tell me.

FIRST WOMAN

Oh! what have you done? You have stripped the poor child quite naked, and it is so small, so small.

MNESILOCHUS

So small?

FIRST WOMAN

Yes, quite small, to be sure.

MNESILOCHUS

How old is it? Has it seen the feast of cups thrice or four times?

FIRST WOMAN

It was born about the time of the last Dionysia. But give it back to me.

MNESILOCHUS

No, may Apollo bear me witness.

FIRST WOMAN

Well, then we are going to burn him.

MNESILOCHUS

Burn me, but then I shall rip this open instantly.

FIRST WOMAN

No, no, I adjure you, don't; do anything you like to me rather than that.

MNESILOCHUS

What a tender mother you are; but nevertheless I shall rip it open.
(*He tears open the wine-skin.*)

FIRST WOMAN

Oh, my beloved daughter! Mania, hand me the sacred cup, that I may at least catch the blood of my child.

MNESILOCHUS

Hold it below; that's the only favour I grant you.
(*He pours the wine into the cup.*)

FIRST WOMAN

Out upon you, you pitiless monster!

MNESILOCHUS

This robe belongs to the priestess.

SECOND WOMAN

What belongs to the priestess?

MNESILOCHUS

Here, take it.
(*He throws her the Cretan robe.*)

SECOND WOMAN

Ah! unfortunate Mica! Who has robbed you of your daughter, your beloved child?

FIRST WOMAN

That wretch. But as you are here, watch him well, while I go with Clisthenes to the Magistrates and denounce him for his crimes.

MNESILOCHUS

Ah! how can I secure safety? what device can I hit on? what can I
think of? He whose fault it is, he who hurried me into this trouble, will
not come to my rescue. Let me see, whom could I best send to him? Ha! I
know a means taken from *Palamedes;* like him, I will write my misfortune on some oars, which I will cast into the sea. Where might I find some
oars? Hah! what if I took these statues instead of oars, wrote upon them
and then threw them towards this side and that. That's the best thing to
do. Besides, like oars they are of wood.

(*singing*)

Oh! my hands, keep up your courage, for my safety is at stake.
Come, my beautiful tablets, receive the traces of my stylus and be
the messengers of my sorry fate. Oh! oh! this R looks miserable
enough! Where is it running to then? Come, off with you in all directions, to the right and to the left; and hurry yourselves, for there's
much need indeed!

(*He sits down to wait for Euripides. The Chorus turns and faces the
audience.*)

LEADER OF THE CHORUS

Let us address ourselves to the spectators to sing our praises, despite
the fact that each one says much ill of women. If the men are to be believed, we are a plague to them; through us come all their troubles,
quarrels, disputes, sedition, griefs and wars. But if we are truly such a
pest, why marry us? Why forbid us to go out or show ourselves at the
window? You want to keep this pest, and take a thousand cares to do it.
If your wife goes out and you meet her away from the house, you fly
into a fury. Ought you not rather to rejoice and give thanks to the gods?
for if the pest has disappeared, you will no longer find it at home. If we
fall asleep at friends' houses from the fatigue of playing and sporting,
each of you comes prowling round the bed to contemplate the features of
this pest. If we seat ourselves at the window, each one wants to see the
pest, and if we withdraw through modesty, each wants all the more to see
the pest perch herself there again. It is thus clear that we are better than
you, and the proof of this is easy. Let us find out which is the worse of the
two sexes. We say, "It's you," while you aver, "it's we." Come, let us compare them in detail, each individual man with a woman. Charminus is not
equal to Nausimaché, that's certain. Cleophon is in every respect inferior
to Salabaccho. It's a long time now since any of you has dared to contest
the prize with Aristomaché, the heroine of Marathon, or with Stratonicé.
Among the last year's Senators, who have just yielded their office to
other citizens, is there one who equals Eubulé? Not even Anytus would

say that. Therefore we maintain that men are greatly our inferiors. You see no woman who has robbed the state of fifty talents rushing about the city in a magnificent chariot; our greatest peculations are a measure of corn, which we steal from our husbands, and even then we return it to them the very same day. But we could name many amongst you who do quite as much, and who are, even more than ourselves, gluttons, parasites, cheats and kidnappers of slaves. We know how to keep our property better than you. We still have our cylinders, our beams, our baskets and our sunshades; whereas many among you have lost the wood of your spears as well as the iron, and many others have cast away their bucklers on the battlefield.

There are many reproaches we have the right to bring against men. The most serious is this, that the woman, who has given birth to a useful citizen, whether taxiarch or strategus should receive some distinction; a place of honour should be reserved for her at the Stenia, the Scirophoria, and the other festivals that we keep. On the other hand, she of whom a coward was born or a worthless man, a bad trierarch or an unskilful pilot, should sit with shaven head, behind her sister who had borne a brave man. Oh! citizens! is it just that the mother of Hyperbolus should sit dressed in white and with loosened tresses beside that of Lamachus and lend out money on usury? He, who may have made a deal of this nature with her, so far from paying her interest, should not even repay the capital, saying, "What, pay you interest? after you have given us this delightful son?"

MNESILOCHUS

I have contracted quite a squint by looking round for him, and yet Euripides does not come. Who is keeping him? No doubt he is ashamed of his cold Palamedes. What will attract him? Let us see! By which of his pieces does he set most store? Ah! I'll imitate his Helen, his last-born. I just happen to have a complete woman's outfit.

SECOND WOMAN

What are you ruminating about now? Why are you rolling up your eyes? You'll have no reason to be proud of your Helen, if you don't keep quiet until one of the Magistrates arrives.

MNESILOCHUS (*as Helen*)

"These shores are those of the Nile with the beautiful nymphs, these waters take the place of heaven's rain and fertilize the white earth, that produces the black syrmea."

SECOND WOMAN

By bright Hecaté, you're a cunning varlet.

MNESILOCHUS
"Glorious Sparta is my country and Tyndareus is my father."

SECOND WOMAN
He your father, you rascal! Why, it's Phrynondas.

MNESILOCHUS
"I was given the name of Helen."

SECOND WOMAN
What! you are again becoming a woman, before we have punished you for having pretended it the first time!

MNESILOCHUS
"A thousand warriors have died on my account on the banks of the Scamander."

SECOND WOMAN
Would that you had done the same!

MNESILOCHUS
"And here I am upon these shores; Menelaus, my unhappy husband, does not yet come. Ah! Why do I still live?"

SECOND WOMAN
Because of the criminal negligence of the crows!

MNESILOCHUS
"But what sweet hope is this that sets my heart a-throb? Oh, Zeus! grant it may not prove a lying one!"

(EURIPIDES *enters.*)

EURIPIDES (*as Menelaus*)
"To what master does this splendid palace belong? Will he welcome strangers who have been tried on the billows of the sea by storm and shipwreck?"

MNESILOCHUS
"This is the palace of Proteus."

SECOND WOMAN
Of what Proteus? you thrice cursed rascal! how he lies! By the goddesses, it's ten years since Proteas died.

EURIPIDES
"What is this shore whither the wind has driven our boat?"

MNESILOCHUS

" 'Tis Egypt."

EURIPIDES

"Alas! how far we are from own country!"

SECOND WOMAN

Don't believe that cursed fool. This is Demeter's Temple.

EURIPIDES

"Is Proteus in these parts?"

SECOND WOMAN

Ah, now, stranger, it must be sea-sickness that makes you so distraught! You have been told that Proteas is dead, and yet you ask if he
is in these parts.

EURIPIDES

"He is no more! Oh! woe! where lie his ashes?"

MNESILOCHUS

" 'Tis on his tomb you see me sitting."

SECOND WOMAN

You call an altar a tomb! Beware of the rope!

EURIPIDES

"And why remain sitting on this tomb, wrapped in this long veil, oh,
stranger lady?"

MNESILOCHUS

"They want to force me to marry a son of Proteus."

SECOND WOMAN

Ah! wretch, why tell such shameful lies? Stranger, this is a rascal who
has slipped in amongst us women to rob us of our trinkets.

MNESILOCHUS (*to* SECOND WOMAN)

"Shout! load me with your insults, for little care I."

EURIPIDES

"Who is the old woman who reviles you, stranger lady?"

MNESILOCHUS

" 'Tis Theonoé, the daughter of Proteus."

SECOND WOMAN

I! Why, my name's Crityllé, the daughter of Antitheus, of the deme of Gargettus; as for you, you are a rogue.

MNESILOCHUS

"Your entreaties are vain. Never shall I wed your brother; never shall I betray the faith I owe my husband, Menelaus, who is fighting before Troy."

EURIPIDES

"What are you saying? Turn your face towards me."

MNESILOCHUS

"I dare not; my cheeks show the marks of the insults I have been forced to suffer."

EURIPIDES

"Oh! great gods! I cannot speak, for very emotion. . . . Ah! what do I see? Who are you?"

MNESILOCHUS

"And you, what is your name? for my surprise is as great as yours."

EURIPIDES

"Are you Grecian or born in this country?"

MNESILOCHUS

"I am Grecian. But now your name, what is it?"

EURIPIDES

"Oh! how you resemble Helen!"

MNESILOCHUS

"And you Menelaus, if I can judge by these pot-herbs." [4]

EURIPIDES

"You are not mistaken, 'tis none other than that unfortunate mortal who stands before you."

MNESILOCHUS

"Ah! how you have delayed coming to your wife's arms! Press me to your heart, throw your arms about me, for I wish to cover you with kisses. Carry me away, carry me away, quick, quick, far, very far from here."

SECOND WOMAN

By the goddesses, woe to him who would carry you away! I should thrash him with my torch.

EURIPIDES

"Do you propose to prevent me from taking my wife, the daughter of Tyndareus, to Sparta?"

SECOND WOMAN

You seem to me to be a cunning rascal too; you are in collusion with this man, and it wasn't for nothing that you kept babbling about Egypt. But the hour for punishment has come; here is the Magistrate with his Scythian.

EURIPIDES

This is getting awkward. Let me hide myself.

MNESILOCHUS

And what is to become of me, poor unfortunate man that I am?

EURIPIDES

Don't worry. I shall never abandon you, as long as I draw breath and one of my numberless artifices remains untried.

MNESILOCHUS

The fish has not bitten this time.

(*A* MAGISTRATE *enters, accompanied by a Scythian policeman.*)

MAGISTRATE

Is this the rascal Clisthenes told us about? Why are you trying to make yourself so small? Officer, arrest him, fasten him to the post, then take up your position there and keep guard over him. Let none approach him. A sound lash with your whip for him who attempts to break the order.

SECOND WOMAN

Excellent, for just now a rogue almost took him from me.

MNESILOCHUS

Magistrate, in the name of that hand which you know so well how to bend when money is placed in it, grant me a slight favour before I die.

MAGISTRATE

What favour?

MNESILOCHUS

Order the archer to strip me before lashing me to the post; the crows, when they make their meal on the poor old man, would laugh too much at this robe and head-dress.

MAGISTRATE

It is in that gear that you must be exposed by order of the Senate, so that your crime may be patent to the passers-by.

(*He departs.*)

MNESILOCHUS (*as the* SCYTHIAN *seizes him*)

Oh! cursed robe, the cause of all my misfortune! My last hope is thus destroyed!

LEADER OF THE CHORUS

Let us now devote ourselves to the sports which the women are accustomed to celebrate here, when time has again brought round the mighty Mysteries of the great goddesses, the sacred days which Pauson himself honours by fasting and would wish feast to succeed feast, that he might keep them all holy. Spring forward with a light step, whirling in mazy circles; let your hands interlace, let the eager and rapid dancers sway to the music and glance on every side as they move.

CHORUS (*singing*)

Let the chorus sing likewise and praise the Olympian gods in their pious transport. It's wrong to suppose that, because I am a woman and in this temple, I am going to speak ill of men; but since we want something fresh, we are going through the rhythmic steps of the round dance for the first time.

Start off while you sing to the god of the lyre and to the chaste goddess armed with the bow. Hail! thou god who flingest thy darts so far, grant us the victory! The homage of our song is also due to Heré, the goddess of marriage, who interests herself in every chorus and guards the approach to the nuptial couch. I also pray Hermes, the god of the shepherds, and Pan and the beloved Graces to bestow a benevolent smile upon our songs.

Let us lead off anew, let us double our zeal during our solemn days, and especially let us observe a close fast; let us form fresh measures that keep good time, and may our songs resound to the very heavens. Do thou, oh divine Bacchus, who art crowned with ivy, direct our chorus; 'tis to thee that both my hymns and my dances are dedicated; oh, Evius, oh, Bromius, oh, thou son of Semelé, oh, Bacchus, who delightest to mingle with the dear choruses of the nymphs upon the mountains, and who repeatest, while dancing with them, the sacred hymn, *Euios, Euios, Euoi!* Echo, the nymph of Cithaeron, returns thy words, which resound beneath the dark vaults of the thick foliage and in the midst of the rocks of the forest; the ivy enlaces thy brow with its tendrils charged with flowers.

SCYTHIAN (*he speaks with a heavy foreign accent*)
You shall stay here in the open air to wail.

MNESILOCHUS
Archer, I adjure you.

SCYTHIAN
You're wasting your breath.

MNESILOCHUS
Loosen the wedge a little.

SCYTHIAN
Aye, certainly.

MNESILOCHUS
Oh! by the gods! why, you are driving it in tighter.

SCYTHIAN
Is that enough?

MNESILOCHUS
Oh! Oh! Ow! Ow! May the plague take you!

SCYTHIAN
Silence! you cursed old wretch! I am going to get a mat to lie upon, so as to watch you close at hand at my ease.

MNESILOCHUS
Ah! what exquisite pleasures Euripides is securing for me! But, oh, ye gods! oh, Zeus the Deliverer, all is not yet lost! I don't believe him the man to break his word; I just caught sight of him appearing in the form of Perseus, and he told me with a mysterious sign to turn myself into Andromeda. And in truth am I not really bound? It's certain, then, that he is coming to my rescue; for otherwise he would not have steered his flight this way.

(*As Andromeda, singing*)
Oh Nymphs, ye virgins who are so dear to me, how am I to approach him? how can I escape the sight of this Scythian? And Echo, thou who reignest in the inmost recesses of the caves, oh! favour my cause and permit me to approach my spouse. A pitiless ruffian has chained up the most unfortunate of mortal maids. Alas! I had barely escaped the filthy claws of an old fury, when another mischance overtook me! This Scythian does not take his eye off me and he has exposed me as food for the crows. Alas! what is to become of me, alone here and without friends! I am not seen mingling in the dances nor in

the games of my companions, but heavily loaded with fetters I am
given over to the voracity of a Glaucetes. Sing no bridal hymn for
me, oh women, but rather the hymn of captivity, and in tears. Ah!
how I suffer! great gods! how I suffer! Alas! alas! and through my
own relatives too! My misery would make Tartarus dissolve into
tears! Alas! in my terrible distress, I implore the mortal who first
shaved me and depilated me, then dressed me in this long robe, and
then sent me to this Temple into the midst of the women, to save me.
Oh! thou pitiless Fate! I am then accursed, great gods! Ah! who
would not be moved at the sight of the appalling tortures under which
I succumb? Would that the blazing shaft of the lightning would
wither . . . this barbarian for me! The immortal light has no
further charm for my eyes since I have been descending the shortest
path to the dead, tied up, strangled, and maddened with pain.
(*In the following scene* EURIPIDES, *from off stage, impersonates*
Echo.)

EURIPIDES

Hail! beloved girl. As for your father, Cepheus, who has exposed you
in this guise, may the gods annihilate him.

MNESILOCHUS

And who are you whom my misfortunes have moved to pity?

EURIPIDES

I am Echo, the nymph who repeats all she hears. It was I, who last
year lent my help to Euripides in this very place. But, my child, give
yourself up to the sad laments that belong to your pitiful condition.

MNESILOCHUS

And you will repeat them?

EURIPIDES

I will not fail you. Begin.

MNESILOCHUS (*singing*)

"Oh! thou divine Night! how slowly thy chariot threads its way
through the starry vault, across the sacred realms of the Air and
mighty Olympus."

EURIPIDES (*singing*)

Mighty Olympus.

MNESILOCHUS (*singing*)

"Why is it necessary that Andromeda should have all the woes
for her share?"

EURIPIDES (*singing*)

For her share.

MNESILOCHUS (*speaking*)

"Sad death!"

EURIPIDES

Sad death!

MNESILOCHUS

You weary me, old babbler.

EURIPIDES

Old babbler.

MNESILOCHUS

Oh! you are too unbearable.

EURIPIDES

Unbearable.

MNESILOCHUS

Friend, let me talk by myself. Do please let me. Come, that's enough.

EURIPIDES

That's enough.

MNESILOCHUS

Go and hang yourself!

EURIPIDES

Go and hang yourself!

MNESILOCHUS

What a plague!

EURIPIDES

What a plague!

MNESILOCHUS

Cursed brute!

EURIPIDES

Cursed brute!

MNESILOCHUS

Beware of blows!

EURIPIDES

Beware of blows!

SCYTHIAN

Hullo! what are you jabbering about?

EURIPIDES

What are you jabbering about?

SCYTHIAN

I shall go and call the Magistrates.

EURIPIDES

I shall go and call the Magistrates.

SCYTHIAN

This is odd!

EURIPIDES

This is odd!

SCYTHIAN

Whence comes this voice?

EURIPIDES

Whence comes this voice?

SCYTHIAN

You are mad.

EURIPIDES

You are mad.

SCYTHIAN

Ah! beware!

EURIPIDES

Ah! beware!

SCYTHIAN (*to* MNESILOCHUS)

Are you mocking me?

EURIPIDES

Are you mocking me?

MNESILOCHUS

No, it's this woman, who stands near you.

EURIPIDES

Who stands near you.

SCYTHIAN

Where is the hussy!

MNESILOCHUS

She's running away.

SCYTHIAN

Where are you running to?

EURIPIDES

Where are you running to?

SCYTHIAN

You shall not get away.

EURIPIDES

You shall not get away.

SCYTHIAN

You are chattering still?

EURIPIDES

You are chattering still?

SCYTHIAN

Stop the hussy.

EURIPIDES

Stop the hussy.

SCYTHIAN

What a babbling, cursed woman!

(EURIPIDES *now enters, costumed as Perseus.*)

EURIPIDES

"Oh! ye gods! to what barbarian land has my swift flight taken me? I am Perseus; I cleave the plains of the air with my winged feet, and I am carrying the Gorgon's head to Argos."

SCYTHIAN

What, are you talking about the head of Gorgos, the scribe?

EURIPIDES

No, I am speaking of the head of the Gorgon.

SCYTHIAN

Why, yes! of Gorgos!

EURIPIDES

"But what do I behold? A young maiden, beautiful as the immortals, chained to this rock like a vessel in port?"

MNESILOCHUS

"Take pity on me, oh stranger! I am so unhappy and distraught! Free me from these bonds."

SCYTHIAN

You keep still! a curse upon your impudence! you are going to die, and yet you will be chattering!

EURIPIDES

"Oh! virgin! I take pity on your chains."

SCYTHIAN

But this is no virgin; he's an old rogue, a cheat and a thief.

EURIPIDES

You have lost your wits, Scythian. This is Andromeda, the daughter of Cepheus.

SCYTHIAN (*lifting up* MNESILOCHUS' *robe*)
But look at his tool; it's pretty big.

EURIPIDES

Give me your hand, that I may descend near this young maiden. Each man has his own particular weakness; as for me I am aflame with love for this virgin.

SCYTHIAN

Oh! I'm not jealous; and as he has his arse turned this way, why, I don't care if you make love to him.

EURIPIDES

"Ah! let me release her, and hasten to join her on the bridal couch."

SCYTHIAN

If you are so eager to make the old man, you can bore through the plank, and so get at him.

EURIPIDES

No, I will break his bonds.

SCYTHIAN

Beware of my lash!

EURIPIDES

No matter.

SCYTHIAN

This blade shall cut off your head.

EURIPIDES

"Ah! what can be done? what arguments can I use? This savage will understand nothing! The newest and most cunning fancies are a dead letter to the ignorant. Let us invent some artifice to fit in with his coarse nature."

(*He departs.*)

SCYTHIAN

I can see the rascal is trying to outwit me.

MNESILOCHUS

Ah! Perseus! remember in what condition you are leaving me.

SCYTHIAN

Are you wanting to feel my lash again!

CHORUS (*singing*)

Oh! Pallas, who art fond of dances, hasten hither at my call. Oh! thou chaste virgin, the protectress of Athens, I call thee in accordance with the sacred rites, thee, whose evident protection we adore and who keepest the keys of our city in thy hands. Do thou appear, thou whose just hatred has overturned our tyrants. The womenfolk are calling thee; hasten hither at their bidding along with Peace, who shall restore the festivals. And ye, august goddesses, display a smiling and propitious countenance to our gaze; come into your sacred grove, the entry to which is forbidden to men; 'tis there in the midst of the sacred orgies that we contemplate your divine features. Come, appear, we pray it of you, oh, venerable Thesmophorae! If you have ever answered our appeal, oh! come into our midst.

(*During this ode the* SCYTHIAN *falls asleep. At the end of it* EURIPIDES *returns, thinly disguised as an old procuress; the* CHORUS *recognizes him, the* SCYTHIAN *does not; he carries a harp, and is followed by a dancing girl and a young flute-girl.*)

EURIPIDES

Women, if you will be reconciled with me, I am willing, and I undertake never to say anything ill of you in future. Those are my proposals for peace.

LEADER OF THE CHORUS
And what impels you to make these overtures?

EURIPIDES (*to the* CHORUS)
This unfortunate man, who is chained to the post, is my father-in-law; if you will restore him to me, you will have no more cause to complain of me; but if not, I shall reveal your pranks to your husbands when they return from the war.

LEADER OF THE CHORUS
We accept peace, but there is this barbarian whom you must buy over.

EURIPIDES
I'll take care of that. Come, my little wench, bear in mind what I told you on the road and do it well. Come, go past him and gird up your robe. And you, you little dear, play us the air of a Persian dance.

SCYTHIAN (*waking*)
What is this music that makes me so blithe?

EURIPIDES
Scythian, this young girl is going to practise some dances, which she has to perform at a feast presently.

SCYTHIAN
Very well! let her dance and practise; I won't hinder her. How nimbly she bounds! just like a flea on a fleece.

EURIPIDES
Come, my dear, off with your robe and seat yourself on the Scythian's knee; stretch forth your feet to me, that I may take off your slippers.

SCYTHIAN
Ah! yes, seat yourself, my little girl, ah ' yes, to be sure. What a firm little titty! it's just like a turnip.

EURIPIDES (*to the flute-girl*)
An air on the flute, quick! Are you afraid of the Scythian?

SCYTHIAN
What a nice arse! Hold still, won't you? A nice twat, too.

EURIPIDES
That's so! (*To the dancing girl*) Resume your dress, it is time to be going.

SCYTHIAN

Give me a kiss.

EURIPIDES

Come, give him a kiss.

SCYTHIAN

Oh! oh! oh! my god, what soft lips! like Attic honey. But might she not stay with me?

EURIPIDES

Impossible, officer; good evening.

SCYTHIAN

Oh! oh! old woman, do me this pleasure.

EURIPIDES

Will you give a drachma?

SCYTHIAN

Aye, that I will.

EURIPIDES

Hand over the money.

SCYTHIAN

I have not got it, but take my quiver in pledge. I'll bring her back. (*To the dancing girl*) Follow me, my fine young wench. Old woman, you keep an eye on this man. But what's your name?

EURIPIDES

Artemisia.

SCYTHIAN

I'll remember it. Artemuxia.

(*He takes the dancing girl away.*)

EURIPIDES (*aside*)

Hermes, god of cunning, receive my thanks! everything is turning out for the best. (*To the flute-girl*) As for you, friend, go along with them. Now let me loose his bonds. (*To* MNESILOCHUS) And you, directly I have released you, take to your legs and run off full tilt to your home to find your wife and children.

MNESILOCHUS

I shall not fail in that as soon as I am free.

EURIPIDES (*releasing* MNESILOCHUS)

There! It's done. Come, fly, before the Scythian lays his hand on you again.

MNESILOCHUS

That's just what I am doing.

(*Both depart in haste.*)

SCYTHIAN (*returning*)

Ah! old woman! what a charming little girl! Not at all a prude, and so obliging! Eh! where is the old woman? Ah! I am undone! And the old man, where is he? Hi, old woman, old woman! Ah! but this is a dirty trick! Artemuxia! she has tricked me, that's what the little old woman has done! Get clean out of my sight, you cursed quiver! (*Picks it up and throws it across the stage.*) Ha! you are well named quiver, for you have made me quiver indeed. Oh! what's to be done? Where is the old woman then? Artemuxia!

LEADER OF THE CHORUS

Are you asking for the old woman who carried the lyre?

SCYTHIAN

Yes, yes; have you seen her?

LEADER OF THE CHORUS

She has gone that way along with the old man.

SCYTHIAN

Dressed in a long robe?

LEADER OF THE CHORUS

Yes; run quick, and you will overtake them.

SCYTHIAN

Ah! rascally old woman! Which way has she fled? Artemuxia!

LEADER OF THE CHORUS

Straight on; follow your nose. But, hi! where are you running to now? Come back, you are going exactly the wrong way.

SCYTHIAN

Ye gods! ye gods! and all this while Artemuxia is escaping.

(*He runs off.*)

LEADER OF THE CHORUS

Go your way! and a pleasant journey to you! But our sports have lasted long enough; it is time for each of us to be off home; and may the two goddesses reward us for our labours!

1. This ejaculation and its exaggerated form two lines below are probably meant to convey Mnesilochus' mock wonder at the magnificent sounds of Agathon's verses.

2. A quotation from Euripides' *Alcestis* (691).

3. The wretched tragedian was never allowed to forget this infamous line from *Hippolytus* (612).

4. Aristophanes never tires of twitting Euripides with the fact or fancy that his mother had sold vegetables.

5. The implication is that her brother thinks her to be with child.

6. The women would break the seals that their husbands had placed on the doors and then duplicate them on their return; the worm-eaten wood was far more difficult to copy.

7. The women are now speaking as if they were holding a regular popular Assembly, on the Pnyx.

IX
THE FROGS

Characters in the Play

The God Dionysus
Xanthias, *his slave*
Aeschylus
Euripides
Heracles
Pluto
Charon
Aeacus
A Servant of Pluto
A Corpse
A Maidservant of Persephonē
A Landlady *in Hades*
Plathané, *her servant*
Chorus of Frogs
Chorus of Initiated Persons

INTRODUCTION

At the Lenaean festival of 405, six years after the performance of *The Thesmophoriazusae*, Aristophanes produced *The Frogs,* which was awarded the highest prize. The subject of the play is almost wholly literary and its treatment contains astonishingly few passages that can arouse the antipathy of the puritan. It has consequently enjoyed a modern popularity entirely out of proportion to its rather slender merits. Poorly constructed and deficient in wit, it exhibits a solemnity of manner and a thinness of spirit hardly to be expected from the author of *The Birds* and *The Thesmophoriazusae.*

Dionysus, the patron god of tragedy, has deeply mourned the recent death of Euripides, and his nostalgic yearning for the "clever rogue" has finally grown so intense that he has resolved to go down to Hades and bring him back to earth again; the play opens at the commencement of this arduous journey. Since no one but Heracles has ever accomplished such a feat before, Dionysus has acquired a club and slipped a lion's skin over his saffron robe, and in this ludicrous costume he knocks at the house of the very hero he plans to emulate, and obtains advice and directions. With his slave Xanthias accompanying him he soon reaches the Acherusian lake and is ferried across by Charon while the Chorus of Frogs sings lyrics of the rain and the marshes. Xanthias has had to walk around the lake, but he meets his master on the other side, and shortly the real Chorus of the play, composed of initiates into the Mysteries, appears. From them Dionysus learns that he has already reached the house of Pluto, and he knocks at the door. A series of foolish and not overly amusing incidents ensues, in which the costume of Heracles alternately arouses the wrath and elicits the blandishments of the enemies and the friends acquired by that hero on his previous visit to the underworld. The former sort of reception induces Dionysus to place the lion's skin on the shoulders of Xanthias, while the latter causes him quickly to abrogate this arrangement. Eventually they enter the house and the stage is left to the Chorus, which delivers the parabasis.

The ode praises the Athenians and makes a gibe at the demagogue Cleophon. The epirrheme gives the spectators the sound and bold advice

917

that they should restore the oligarchical revolutionaries of 411 to the rights of citizenship. The antode attacks a little known person by the name of Cligenes, and the antepirrheme compliments the advice of the epirrheme. There are no anapests. The tone of the parabasis is fervently patriotic, and this will doubtless have been the reason for the unique repetition of the play, a few days after its regular performance, in response to popular demand.

At the conclusion of the parabasis Aeacus, the slave of Pluto, and Xanthias emerge from the house and are engaging in friendly conversation, when a great commotion is heard offstage. In this way the poet introduces the famous and lengthy contest between Aeschylus and Euripides which occupies the whole of the latter portion of the comedy. The connection of this with what precedes is so loose that some scholars have been led into the assumption that it was originally composed for an entirely different play and was hurriedly tacked on to the unfinished *Frogs* at the news of the death of Euripides. Dionysus now abandons or forgets the original purpose for which he has come to Hades and announces that the winner of the contest will be the poet whom he will take back to Athens. With their patron god sitting as judge, the two tragedians compare their talents in every department of dramatic art. The fundamental notion of the scene is a happy one, but it is longer than its essential humour allows, and the parodies of Aeschylus are inept and misdirected. The contest is extremely close, and Dionysus experiences great difficulty in arriving at a decision; "My choice shall fall on him my soul desires," he finally says, and we remember that it was his ardent and insatiable craving for Euripides that brought him to the underworld. Thus we are greatly surprised when it turns out to be Aeschylus that he wishes to restore to the light of day. Is this the poet's intent, or is it merely another example of the carelessness with which the play is constructed?

The person and the poetry of Euripides bulk large in the plays of Aristophanes, and the comic poet's attitude toward him has been the subject of much discussion and the cause of many misstatements. It is wholly wide of the mark to speak of him as having *attacked* Euripides; the experiments and the innovations of the restless tragedian provided good material for harmless satire, and his excessive pathos and ingenious intellectualism were obvious targets for gibes, but he is never accused of pederasty or of cowardice, of venality or of sycophancy, nor is it ever suggested that any of the other tragic poets of the time is even remotely to be compared with him. If we will assume Aristophanes to be speaking through the mask of Dionysus in the final scene of *The Frogs*, we must also remember that the god has no easy time choosing Aeschylus, and that it is his deepest and most nostalgic emotions that are ultimately decisive.

THE FROGS

(SCENE:—*In the background are two houses, that of* HERACLES *and that of* PLUTO. *Enter* DIONYSUS, *disguised as* HERACLES, *with lion-skin and club, but with the high boots of tragedy and a tunic of saffron silk. He is followed by* XANTHIAS, *seated on a donkey and carrying an immense bale of luggage on a porter's pole. They advance for a while in silence.*)

XANTHIAS (*looking round at his burden with a groan*)
SIR, shall I say one of the regular things
That people in a theatre always laugh at?

DIONYSUS
Say what you like, except "I'm overloaded."
But mind, not that. That's simply wormwood to me.

XANTHIAS (*disappointed*)
Not anything funny?

DIONYSUS
Not "Oh, my poor blisters!"

XANTHIAS
Suppose I made the great joke?

DIONYSUS
Why, by all means.
Don't be afraid. Only, for mercy's sake,
Don't . . .

XANTHIAS
Don't do what?

DIONYSUS
Don't shift your luggage pole
Across, and say, "I want to blow my nose." [1]

919

XANTHIAS (*greatly disappointed*)
Nor that I've got such a weight upon my back
That unless some one helps me quickly I shall sneeze?

DIONYSUS
Oh, please, no. Keep it till I need emetics.

XANTHIAS
Then what's the good of carrying all this lumber
If I mayn't make one single good old wheeze
Like Phrynichus, Amipsias, and Lycis?

DIONYSUS
Ah no; don't make them.—When I sit down there
                    (*Pointing to the auditorium*)
And hear some of those choice products, I go home
A twelvemonth older.

XANTHIAS (*to himself*)
            Oh, my poor old neck:
Blistered all round, and mustn't say it's blistered,
Because that's funny!

DIONYSUS
            Airs and insolence!
When I, Dionysus, child of the Great Jug,
Must work and walk myself, and have him riding
Lest he should tire himself or carry things!

XANTHIAS
Am I not carrying things?

DIONYSUS
            They're carrying you.

XANTHIAS (*showing the baggage*)
I'm carrying this.

DIONYSUS
    How?

XANTHIAS
            With my back half broken.

DIONYSUS
That bag is clearly carried by a donkey.

XANTHIAS

No donkey carries bags that *I* am carrying.

DIONYSUS

I suppose you know the donkey's carrying *you*.

XANTHIAS (*turning cross*)

I don't. I only know my shoulder's sore!

DIONYSUS

Well, if it does no good to ride the donkey,
Go turns, and let the poor beast ride on you.

XANTHIAS (*aside*)

Just like my luck.—Why wasn't I on board
At Arginusae? [2] Then I'd let you have it.

DIONYSUS

Dismount, you rascal.—Here's the door close by
Where I must turn in first—and I on foot! (*Knocking.*)
Porter! Hi, porter! Hi!

HERACLES (*entering from the house*)

Who's knocking there?
More like a mad bull butting at the door,
Whoever he is . . . (*seeing* DIONYSUS). God bless us, what's all this?
(*He examines* DIONYSUS *minutely, then chokes with silent emotion.*)

DIONYSUS (*aside to* XANTHIAS)

Boy!

XANTHIAS

What, sir?

DIONYSUS

Did you notice?

XANTHIAS

Notice what?

DIONYSUS

The man's afraid.

XANTHIAS

Yes, sir; (*aside*) afraid you're cracked!

HERACLES (*struggling with laughter*)
I wouldn't if I possibly could help it:
I'm trying to bite my lips, but all the same . . . (*Roars with laughter.*)

DIONYSUS
Don't be absurd! Come here. I want something.

HERACLES
I would, but I can't yet shake this laughter off:
The lion-skin on a robe of saffron silk!
How comes my club to sort with high-heeled boots?
What's the idea? Where have you come from now?

DIONYSUS
I've been at sea, serving with Clisthenes.[3]

HERACLES
You fought a battle?

DIONYSUS
Yes: sank several ships,
Some twelve or thirteen.

HERACLES
Just you two?

DIONYSUS
Of course.

XANTHIAS (*aside*)
And then I woke, and it was all a dream!

DIONYSUS
Well, one day I was sitting there on deck
Reading the *Andromeda,* when all at once
A great desire came knocking at my heart,
You'd hardly think . . .

HERACLES
A great desire? How big?

DIONYSUS
Oh, not so big. Perhaps as large as Molon.

HERACLES
Who was the lady?

DIONYSUS

Lady?

HERACLES

Well, the girl?

DIONYSUS

Great Heaven, there wasn't one!

HERACLES

Well, I have always
Considered Clisthenes a perfect lady!

DIONYSUS

Don't mock me, brother! It's a serious thing,
A passion that has worn me to a shadow.

HERACLES

Well, tell us all about it.

DIONYSUS (*with the despair of an artist explaining himself to a common athlete*)

No; I can't.
You never . . . But I'll think of an analogy.
You never felt a sudden inward craving
For . . . pease-broth?

HERACLES

Pease-broth? Bless me, crowds of times.

DIONYSUS

See'st then the sudden truth? Or shall I put it
Another way?

HERACLES

Oh, not about pease-broth.
I see it quite.

DIONYSUS

Well, I am now consumed
By just that sort of restless craving for
Euripides.

HERACLES

Lord save us, the man's dead!

DIONYSUS

He is; and no one in this world shall stop me
From going to see him!

HERACLES

Down to the place of shades?

DIONYSUS

The place of shades or any shadier still.

HERACLES

What do you want to get?

DIONYSUS

I want a poet,
For most be dead; only the false live on.

HERACLES

Iophon's still alive.

DIONYSUS

Well, there you have it;
The one good thing still left us, if it is one.
For even as to that I have my doubts.

HERACLES

But say, why don't you bring up Sophocles
By preference, if you must have some one back?

DIONYSUS

No, not till I've had Iophon quite alone
And seen what note he gives without his father.
Besides, Euripides, being full of tricks,
Would give the slip to his master, if need were,
And try to escape with me; while Sophocles,
Content with us, will be content in Hell.

HERACLES

And Agathon, where is he?

DIONYSUS

Gone far away,
A poet true, whom many friends regret.

HERACLES

Beshrew him! Where?

DIONYSUS
To feast with peaceful kings!

HERACLES
And Xenocles?

DIONYSUS
Oh, plague take Xenocles!

HERACLES
Pythangelus, then?
(DIONYSUS *shrugs his shoulders in expressive silence.*)

XANTHIAS (*to himself*)
And no one thinks of me,
When all my shoulder's skinning, simply skinning.

HERACLES
But aren't there other pretty fellows there
All writing tragedies by tens of thousands,
And miles verboser than Euripides?

DIONYSUS
Leaves without fruit; trills in the empty air,
And starling chatter, mutilating art!
Give them one chance and that's the end of them,
One weak assault on an unprotected Muse.
Search as you will, you'll find no poet now
With grit in him, to wake a word of power.[4]

HERACLES
How "grit"?

DIONYSUS
The grit that gives them heart to risk
Bold things—vast Ether, residence of God,
Or Time's long foot, or souls that won't take oaths
While tongues go swearing falsely by themselves.

HERACLES
You like that stuff?

DIONYSUS
Like it? I rave about it.

HERACLES (*reflecting*)
Why, yes; it's devilish tricky, as you say.

DIONYSUS

"Ride not upon my soul!" Use your own donkey.

HERACLES (*apologising*)
I only meant it was obviously humbug!

DIONYSUS
If ever I need advice about a *dinner,*
I'll come to you!

XANTHIAS (*to himself*)
And no one thinks of me.

DIONYSUS
But why I came in these especial trappings—
Disguised as you, in fact—was this. I want you
To tell me all the hosts with whom you stayed
That time you went to fetch up Cerberus:
Tell me your hosts, your harbours, bakers' shops,
Inns, taverns—reputable and otherwise—
Springs, roads, towns, posts, and landladies that keep
The fewest fleas.

XANTHIAS (*as before*)
And no one thinks of me!

HERACLES (*impressively*)
Bold man, and will you dare . . .

DIONYSUS
Now, don't begin
That sort of thing; but tell the two of us
What road will take us quickest down to Hades.—
And, please, no great extremes of heat or cold.

HERACLES
Well, which one had *I* better tell you first?—
Which now?—Ah, yes; suppose you got a boatman
To tug you, with a hawser—round your neck . . .

DIONYSUS
A chokey sort of journey, that.

HERACLES
Well, then,
There *is* a short road, quick and smooth, the surface
Well pounded—in a mortar.

DIONYSUS
The hemlock way?

HERACLES
Exactly.

DIONYSUS
Cold and bitter! Why, it freezes
All your shins numb.

HERACLES
Do you mind one short and steep?

DIONYSUS
Not in the least . . . You know I'm no great walker.

HERACLES
Then just stroll down to Ceramicus . . .

DIONYSUS
Well?

HERACLES
Climb up the big tower . . .

DIONYSUS
Good; and then?

HERACLES
Then watch
And see them start the torch-race down below;
Lean over till you hear the men say "Go,"
And then, go.

DIONYSUS
Where?

HERACLES
Why, over.

DIONYSUS
Not for me.
It'd cost me two whole sausage bags of brains.
I won't go that way.

HERACLES
Well, how *will* you go?

DIONYSUS

The way *you* went that time.

HERACLES (*impressively*)
The voyage is long.
You first come to a great mere, fathomless
And very wide.

DIONYSUS (*unimpressed*)
How do I get across?

HERACLES (*with a gesture*)
In a little boat, like that; an aged man
Will row you across the ferry . . . for two obols.[5]

DIONYSUS

Those two old obols, everywhere at work!
I wonder how they found their way down there?

HERACLES

Oh, Theseus took them!—After that you'll see
Snakes and queer monsters, crowds and crowds.

DIONYSUS
Now don't:
Don't play at bogies! You can never move me!

HERACLES

Then deep, deep mire and everlasting filth,
And, wallowing there, such as have wronged a guest,
Or picked a wench's pocket while they kissed her,[6]
Beaten their mothers, smacked their father's jaws,
Or sworn perjurious oaths before high heaven.

DIONYSUS

And with them, I should hope, such as have learned
Cinesias's latest Battle Dance,
Or copied out a speech of Morsimus!

HERACLES

Then you will find a breath about your ears
Of music, and a light before your eyes
Most beautiful—like this—and myrtle groves,
And joyous throngs of women and of men,
And clapping of glad hands.

DIONYSUS
And who will *they* be?

HERACLES
The Initiated.[7]

XANTHIAS (*aside*)
Yes; and I'm the donkey
Holiday-making at the Mysteries!
But I won't stand this weight one moment longer.
                    (*He begins to put down his bundle.*)

HERACLES
And they will forthwith tell you all you seek.
They have their dwelling just beside the road,
At Pluto's very door.—So now good-bye;
And a pleasant journey, brother.

DIONYSUS
                    Thanks; good-bye.
Take care of yourself. (*To* XANTHIAS, *while* HERACLES *returns
into the house*) Take up the bags again.

XANTHIAS
Before I've put them down?

DIONYSUS
                    Yes, and be quick.

XANTHIAS
No, really, sir; we ought to hire a porter.

DIONYSUS
And what if I can't find one?

XANTHIAS
                    Then I'll go.

DIONYSUS
All right.—Why, here's a funeral, just in time.
                    (*Enter a* FUNERAL *on the right.*)
Here, sir—it's you I'm addressing—the defunct;
Do you care to carry a few traps to Hades?

THE CORPSE (*sitting up*)
How heavy?

DIONYSUS

What you see.

CORPSE

You'll pay two drachmas?

DIONYSUS

Oh, come, that's rather much.

CORPSE

Bearers, move on!

DIONYSUS

My good man, wait! See if we can't arrange.

CORPSE

Two drachmas down, or else don't talk to me.

DIONYSUS

Nine obols?

CORPSE (*lying down again*)

Strike me living if I will!

(*Exit the* FUNERAL.)

XANTHIAS

That dog's too proud! He'll come to a bad end.—
Well, I'll be porter.

DIONYSUS

That's a good brave fellow.
(*They walk across the stage.* DIONYSUS *peers into the distance.*)

DIONYSUS

What *is* that?

XANTHIAS

That? A lake.

DIONYSUS

By Zeus, it is!
The mere he spoke of.

XANTHIAS

Yes; I see a boat.

DIONYSUS

Yes; by the powers!

XANTHIAS
And yonder must be Charon.

DIONYSUS
Charon, ahoy!

BOTH
Ahoy! Charon, ahoy!
(CHARON *enters. He is an old, grim, and squalid Ferryman,*
wearing a slave's felt cap and a sleeveless tunic.)

CHARON
Who is for rest from sufferings and cares?
Who's for the Carrion Crows, and the Dead Donkeys;
Lethé and Sparta and the rest of Hell?

DIONYSUS
I!

CHARON
Get in.

DIONYSUS
Where do you touch? The Carrion Crows,
You said?

CHARON (*gruffly*)
The Dogs will be the place for you.
Get in.

DIONYSUS
Come, Xanthias.

CHARON
I don't take slaves:
Unless he has won his freedom? Did he fight
The battle of the Cold Meat Unpreserved?

XANTHIAS
Well, no; my eyes were very sore just then [8] . . .

CHARON
Then trot round on your legs!

XANTHIAS
Where shall I meet you?

CHARON

At the Cold Seat beside the Blasting Stone.

DIONYSUS (*to* XANTHIAS, *who hesitates*)

You understand?

XANTHIAS

Oh, quite. (*Aside*) Just like my luck.
What can have crossed me when I started out?

(*Exit* XANTHIAS.)

CHARON

Sit to your oar. (DIONYSUS *does his best to obey*) Any more passengers?
If so, make haste. (*To* DIONYSUS) What are you doing there?

DIONYSUS

Why, what you told me; sitting on my oar.

CHARON

Oh, are you? Well, get up again and sit

(*Pushing him down*)

Down there—fatty!

DIONYSUS (*doing everything wrong*)

Like that?

CHARON

Put out your arms

And stretch . . .

DIONYSUS

Like that?

CHARON

None of your nonsense here!
Put both your feet against the stretcher.—Now,
In good time, row!

DIONYSUS (*fluently, putting down his oars*)

And how do you expect
A man like me, with no experience,
No seamanship, no Salamis,—to row?

CHARON

You'll row all right; as soon as you fall to,
You'll hear a first-rate tune that *makes* you row.

DIONYSUS

Who sings it?

CHARON
Certain cycnoranidae.

That's music!

DIONYSUS
Give the word then, and we'll see.
(CHARON *gives the word for rowing and marks the time. A* CHORUS OF
FROGS *is heard off stage.*)

FROGS
O brood of the mere and the spring,
Gather together and sing
   From the depths of your throat
   By the side of the boat,
Co-äx, as we move in a ring;

As in Limnae we sang the divine
Nyseïan Giver of Wine,
   When the people in lots
   With their sanctified Pots
Came reeling around my shrine.

     Co-äx, co-äx, co-äx,
     Brekekekex co-äx.

     DIONYSUS
     Don't sing any more;
     I begin to be sore!

     FROGS
     Brekekekex co-äx.

     Co-äx, co-äx, co-äx,
     Brekekekex co-äx!

     DIONYSUS
     Is it nothing to you
     If I'm black and I'm blue?

     FROGS
     Brekekekex co-äx!

DIONYSUS
A plague on all of your swarming packs.
There's nothing in you except co-äx!

FROGS
Well, and what more do you need?
Though it's none of your business indeed,
  When the Muse thereanent
  Is entirely content,
And horny-hoof Pan with his reed:

When Apollo is fain to admire
My voice, on account of his lyre
  Which he frames with the rushes
  And watery bushes—
Co-äx!—which I grow in the mire.

        Co-äx, co-äx, co-äx,
        Brekekekex co-äx!

            DIONYSUS
        Peace, musical sisters!
        I'm covered with blisters.[9]

            FROGS
        Brekekekex co-äx.

        Co-äx, co-äx, co-äx,
        Brekekekex co-äx!
          Our song we can double
          Without the least trouble:
        Brekekekex co-äx.

Sing we now, if ever hopping
  Through the sedge and flowering rushes;
In and out the sunshine flopping,
We have sported, rising, dropping,
  With our song that nothing hushes.

Sing, if e'er in days of storm
  Safe our native oozes bore us,
Staved the rain off, kept us warm,
Till we set our dance in form,
  Raised our hubble-bubbling chorus:

Brekekekex co-äx, co-äx!

DIONYSUS
Brekekekex co-äx, co-äx!
    I can sing it as loud as you.

FROGS
    Sisters, that he never must do!

DIONYSUS
Would you have me row till my shoulder cracks?

FROGS
Brekekekex co-äx, co-äx!

DIONYSUS
Brekekekex co-äx, co-äx!
Groan away till you burst your backs.
    It's nothing to me.

FROGS
    Just wait till you see.

DIONYSUS
I don't care how you scold.

FROGS
    Then all day long
    We will croak you a song
As loud as our throat can hold.

Brekekekex co-äx, co-äx!!

DIONYSUS
Brekekekex co-äx, co-äx!!
I'll see you don't outdo me in that.

FROGS
Well, *you* shall never beat *us*—that's flat!

DIONYSUS
I'll make you cease your song
If I shout for it all day long;
    My lungs I'll tax
    With co-äx, co-äx
—I assure you they're thoroughly strong—
Until your efforts at last relax:
Brekekekex co-äx, co-äx!!

(*No answer from the* FROGS.)
Brekekekex co-äx, co-äx!!!
I knew in the end I should stop your quacks!

CHARON
Easy there! Stop her! Lay her alongside.—
Now pay your fare and go.

DIONYSUS (*peering about him*)
There are the obols.
Ho, Xanthias! . . . Where's Xanthias?—Is that you?

XANTHIAS (*from off stage*)
Hullo!

DIONYSUS
Come this way.

XANTHIAS (*entering*)
Oh, I'm glad to see you!

DIONYSUS (*looking round*)
Well, and what have we here?

XANTHIAS
Darkness—and mud.

DIONYSUS
Did you see any of the perjurers here,
And father-beaters, as he said we should?

XANTHIAS
Why, didn't you?

DIONYSUS
I? Lots.
(*Looking full at the audience.*)
I see them now.
Well, what are we to do?

XANTHIAS
Move further on.
This is the place he said was all aswarm
With horrid beasts.

DIONYSUS

A plague on what he said!
Exaggerating just to frighten me,
Because he knew my courage and was jealous.
Naught lives so flown with pride as Heracles!
Why, my best wish would be to meet with something,
Some real adventure, worthy of our travels!

XANTHIAS (*listening*)

Stay!—Yes, upon my word. I hear a noise.

DIONYSUS (*nervously*)

God bless me, where?

XANTHIAS

Behind.

DIONYSUS

Go to the rear.

XANTHIAS

No; it's in front somewhere.

DIONYSUS

Then get in front.

XANTHIAS

Why, there I see it.—Save us!—A great beast. . . .

DIONYSUS (*cowering behind* XANTHIAS)

What like?

XANTHIAS

Horrid! . . . At least it keeps on changing!
It was a bull; now it's a mule; and now
A fair young girl.

DIONYSUS

Where is it? Let me at it!

XANTHIAS

Stay, sir; it's not a girl now, it's a dog.

DIONYSUS

It must be Empusa!

XANTHIAS
Yes. At least its head
Is all on fire.

DIONYSUS
Has it a leg of brass?

XANTHIAS
Yes, that it has. And the other leg of cow-dung.
It's she!

DIONYSUS
Where shall I go?

XANTHIAS
Well, where shall I?

DIONYSUS (*running forward and addressing the Priest of* DIONYSUS *in
his seat of state in the centre of the front row of the audience*)
My Priest, protect me and we'll sup together!

XANTHIAS
We're done for, O Lord Heracles.

DIONYSUS (*cowering again*)
Oh, don't!
Don't shout like that, man, and don't breathe that name.

XANTHIAS
Dionysus, then!

DIONYSUS
No, no. That's worse than the other. . . .
Keep on the way you're going.

XANTHIAS (*after searching about*)
Come along, sir.

DIONYSUS
What is it?

XANTHIAS
Don't be afraid, sir. All goes well.
And we can say as said Hegelochus,
"Beyond these storms I catch a *piece* of *tail!*" [10]
Empusa's gone.

DIONYSUS

Swear it.

XANTHIAS

By Zeus, she's gone!

DIONYSUS

Again.

XANTHIAS

By Zeus, she's gone!

DIONYSUS
Your solemn oath.

XANTHIAS

By Zeus!!

DIONYSUS (*raising himself*)
Dear me, that made me feel quite pale.

XANTHIAS (*pointing to the Priest*)
And this kind gentleman turned red for sympathy.

DIONYSUS
How can I have sinned to bring all this upon me?
What power above is bent on my destruction?

XANTHIAS
The residence of God, or Time's long foot?

DIONYSUS (*listening as flute-playing is heard outside*)
I say!

XANTHIAS

What is it?

DIONYSUS
Don't you hear it?

XANTHIAS
What?

DIONYSUS

Flutes blowing.

XANTHIAS

Yes. And such a smell of torches
Floating towards us, all most Mystery-like!

DIONYSUS

Crouch quietly down and let us hear the music.
(*They crouch down at the left. Music is heard far off.* XANTHIAS *puts down the bundle.*)

CHORUS (*unseen*)
Iacchus, O Iacchus!
Iacchus, O Iacchus!

XANTHIAS

That's it, sir. These are the Initiated
Rejoicing somewhere here, just as he told us.
Why, it's the old Iacchus hymn that used
To warm the cockles of Diagoras!

DIONYSUS

Yes, it must be. However, we'd best sit
Quite still and listen, till we're sure of it.
(*There enters gradually the* CHORUS, *consisting of Men Initiated in the Eleusinian Mysteries. They are led by a hierophant or Initiating Priest, and accompanied by a throng of Worshipping Women. They have white robes, wreaths upon their brows, and torches in their hands.*)

CHORUS (*singing, off stage*)
Thou that dwellest in the shadow
Of great glory here beside us,
Spirit, Spirit, we have hied us
To thy dancing in the meadow!
Come, Iacchus; let thy brow
Toss its fruited myrtle bough;
We are thine, O happy dancer; O our comrade, come and guide us!
Let the mystic measure beat:
Come in riot fiery fleet;
Free and holy all before thee,
While the Charites adore thee,
And thy Mystae wait the music of thy feet!

XANTHIAS

O Virgin of Demeter, highly blest,
What an entrancing smell of roasted pig! [11]

DIONYSUS

Hush! hold your tongue! Perhaps they'll give you some.

CHORUS (*singing, as they enter*)
Spirit, Spirit, lift the shaken
    Splendour of thy tossing torches!
    All the meadow flashes, scorches:
Up, Iacchus, and awaken!
Come, thou star that bringest light
To the darkness of our rite,
Till thine old men leap as young men, leap with every thought forsaken
    Of the dulness and the fear
    Left by many a circling year:
    Let thy red light guide the dances
    Where thy banded youth advances
To be merry by the blossoms of the mere!

LEADER OF THE CHORUS

Hush, oh hush! for our song begins. Let every one stand aside
Who owns an intellect muddled with sins, or in arts like these untried:
If the mystic rites of the Muses true he has never seen nor sung:
If he never the magical music knew of Cratinus the Bull-eater's tongue:
If he likes in a comedy nothing but riot and meaningless harlequinade:
Or in matters of politics cannot keep quiet and see that cabals be allayed,
But blows up spite and keeps it alight to serve his personal ends:
Or being in power at a critical hour, accepts little gifts from his friends:
Or goes selling a ship, or betraying a fort, or takes to the trade of a
    smuggler,
Attempting again, in Thorycion's sort,—that pestilent revenue-juggler,—
From Aegina before us to stock Epidaurus with tar and canvas and hide,
Or tries to persuade some friend in the trade for the enemy's ships to
    provide:
Or a teacher of choirs who forgets his position and damages Hecaté's
    shrines: [12]
Or the robber of poets, the mere politician, who spites us with pitiful
    fines [13]
Because we have suitably made him absurd in the God's traditional
    rhyme:
Behold, I give word: and again give word: and give word for the third,
    last time:
Make room, all such, for our dance and song.—Up, you, and give us a
    lay
That is meet for our mirth-making all night long and for this great festival
    day.

CHORUS (*singing*)
Forth fare all;
This mead's bowers
Bear fresh flowers;
Forth, I call.
Leap, mock, dance, play;
Enough and to spare we have feasted to-day!

March: raise high
Her whose hands
Save these lands;
Raise due cry:
Maid, Maid, save these,
Tho' it may not exactly Thorycion please!

LEADER OF THE CHORUS
One hymn to the Maiden; now raise ye another
To the Queen of the Fruits of the Earth.
To Demeter the Corn-giver, Goddess and Mother,
Make worship in musical mirth.

CHORUS (*singing*)
Approach, O Queen of orgies pure,
And us, thy faithful band, ensure
From morn to eve to ply secure
Our mocking and our clowning:
To grace thy feast with many a hit
Of merry jest or serious wit,
And laugh, and earn the prize, and flit
Triumphant to the crowning.

LEADER OF THE CHORUS (*speaking*)
Now call the God of blooming mien; [14]
Raise the mystic chorus:
Our comrade he and guide unseen,
With us and before us.

CHORUS (*singing*)
Iacchus high in glory, thou whose day
Of all is merriest, hither, help our play;
Show, as we throne thee at thy Maiden's side,
How light to thee are our long leagues of way.
Iacchus, happy dancer, be our guide.

Thyself, that poorest men thy joy should share,
Didst rend thy robe, thy royal sandal tear,
    That feet unshod might dance, and robes rent wide
Wave in thy revel with no after care.
    Iacchus, happy dancer, be our guide.

Lo there! but now across the dance apace
A maiden tripped, a maiden fair of face,
    Whose tattered smock and kerchief scarce could hide
The merry bosom peering from its place.
    Iacchus, happy dancer, be our guide.

XANTHIAS (*singing*)
I always liked to follow some one else:
Suppose we join and dance?

DIONYSUS (*singing*)
Why, so say I.

(*They join the dance.*)

LEADER OF THE CHORUS (*singing*)
Perhaps 'twill best beseem us
To deal with Archedemus,
Who is toothless still and rootless, at seven years from birth:

Yet he leads the public preachers
Of those poor dead upper creatures,
And is prince of all the shadiness on earth!

And Clisthenes, says rumour,
In a wild despairing humour
Sits huddled up and tearing out his hair among the graves.

To believe he would incline us
That a person named Sebinus
Is tossing yet unburied on the waves!

While Callias, says tattle,
Has attended a sea-battle,
And lionesses' scalps were the uniform he wore! [15]

DIONYSUS (*singing*)
You'd oblige us much by telling
Me the way to Pluto's dwelling.
We are strangers newly lighted on your shore.

LEADER OF THE CHORUS (*singing*)
No need of distant travel
That problem to unravel;
For know that while you ask me, you are standing at the door.

DIONYSUS (*singing*)
Then up, my lad, be packing!

XANTHIAS (*singing*)
There's the Devil in the sacking:
It can't stay still a second on the floor!

LEADER OF THE CHORUS (*speaking*)
Now onward through Demeter's ring
Through the leaves and flowers,
All who love her junketing,
All who know her powers!
Fare forward you, while I go here
With matron and with maiden,
To make their night-long roaming clear
With tossing torches laden.

CHORUS (*singing*)
Then on 'mid the meadows deep,
Where thickest the rosebuds creep
And the dewdrops are pearliest:
A jubilant step advance
In our own, our eternal dance,
Till its joy the Glad Fates entrance
Who threaded it earliest.

For ours is the sunshine bright,
Yea, ours is the joy of light
All pure, without danger:
For we thine Elect have been,
Thy secrets our eyes have seen,
And our hearts we have guarded clean
Toward kinsman and stranger!
(*The* CHORUS *lines up on one side of the Orchestra.*)

DIONYSUS (*approaching the door of Pluto's house*)
I ought by rights to knock; but how, I wonder.
I don't know how they do knock in this country.

XANTHIAS

Oh, don't waste time. Go in and do your best,
Like Heracles in heart as well as garb.

DIONYSUS (*knocking*)

Ho there!
(*The door opens and a Porter appears, whose dress shows him to be*
AEACUS, *the Judge of the Dead.*)

AEACUS

Who summons?

DIONYSUS
Heracles the Brave.

AEACUS

Thou rash, impure, and most abandoned man,
Foul, inly foul, yea foulest upon earth,
Who harried our dog, Cerberus, choked him dumb,
Fled, vanished, and left me to bear the blame,
Who kept him!—Now I have thee on the hip!
So close the black encaverned rocks of Styx
And Acheronian crags a-drip with blood
Surround thee, and Cocytus' circling hounds,
And the hundred-headed serpent, that shall rend
Thy bowels asunder; to thy lungs shall cleave
The lamprey of Tartessus, and thy reins
And inmost entrails in one paste of gore
Tithrasian Gorgons gorge for evermore!
—To whom, even now, I speed my indignant course!
(*The Porter retires.*)

DIONYSUS (*who has fallen prostrate*)

Please! [16]

XANTHIAS
What's the matter? Quick, get up again
Before they come and see you.

DIONYSUS
But I feel
Faint.—Put a cold wet sponge against my heart.

XANTHIAS (*producing a sponge*)
There; you apply it.

DIONYSUS
Thanks. Where is it?

XANTHIAS
There.
(DIONYSUS *takes and applies it.*)
Ye golden gods, is it there you keep your heart?

DIONYSUS
The nervous shock made it go down and down!

XANTHIAS
You *are* the greatest coward I ever saw,
Of gods or humans!

DIONYSUS
I a coward?—I had
The presence of mind to ask you for a sponge.
Few had done more!

XANTHIAS
Could any one do less?

DIONYSUS
A coward would still be flat there, sniffing salts;
I rose, called for a sponge, and used the sponge.

XANTHIAS
That *was* brave, by Posidon!

DIONYSUS
I should think so.—
And weren't *you* frightened at his awful threats
And language?

XANTHIAS
I? I never cared a rap.

DIONYSUS
Oh, you're a hero, aren't you?—and want glory.
Well, you be *me!* Put on this lion's hide
And take the club—if you're so dauntless-hearted.
I'll take my turn, and be your luggage-boy.

XANTHIAS
Over with both of them! Of course I will.
(*He proceeds to put on the lion-skin.*)

Now watch if Xanthias-Heracles turns faint,
Or shows the same "presence of mind," as you.

DIONYSUS

The true Melitean jail-bird, on my life! . . .
Well, I suppose I'd better take the luggage.
(*The exchange is just effected when the door again opens
and there enters a* MAID OF PERSEPHONÉ.)

MAID

Dear Heracles, and is it you once more?
Come in! No sooner did my mistress learn
Your coming, than she set her bread to bake,
Set pots of split-pea porridge, two or three,
A-boiling, a whole ox upon the coals,
Cakes in the oven, and big buns.—Oh, come in.

XANTHIAS (*as* HERACLES)

She is very kind; perhaps some other time.

MAID

Oh, really; but I mustn't let you go!
She's doing everything herself! Braised game,
Spices and fruits and stoups of the sweetest wine—
Come in with me.

XANTHIAS

Most kind, but . . .

MAID

No excuses.

I won't let go.—A flute-player, very pretty,
Is waiting for you, and two or three such sweet
Young dancing girls.

XANTHIAS (*wavering*)

Did you say dancing girls?

MAID

Yes. Do come in.—They just were going to serve
The fish, and have the table lifted in.

XANTHIAS

I will! I'll chance it!—Go straight in and tell
Those dancing girls that Heracles is coming!
(*The* MAID *retires again.*)
Here, boy, take up the bags and follow me.

DIONYSUS

Stop, please!—You didn't take it seriously
When I just dressed you as Heracles for fun?
You can't be so ridiculous, Xanthias.
Take up the bags at once and bring them in.

XANTHIAS

What? Surely you don't mean to take away
Your own gift?

DIONYSUS

Mean it? No; I'm doing it!
Off with that lion-skin, quick.

(*Begins to strip off the lion-skin by force.*)

XANTHIAS

Help! I'm assaulted . . .

(*Giving way.*)

I leave it with the Gods!

DIONYSUS (*proceeding to dress himself again*)
The Gods, indeed!
What senseless vanity to expect to be
Alcmena's son, a mortal and a slave!

XANTHIAS

Well, take it. I don't care.—The time may be,
God willing, when you'll feel the need of me!

CHORUS (*singing*)
That's the way such points to settle,
Like a chief of tested mettle,
    Weather-worn on many seas,
Not in one fixed pattern stopping,
Like a painted thing, but dropping
    Always towards the side of ease.
'Tis this instinct for soft places,
    To keep warm while others freeze,
Marks a man of gifts and graces,
    Like our own Theramenes!

DIONYSUS (*singing*)
Surely 'twould the matter worsen,
If I saw this low-bred person
    On his cushions sprawling, so,

Served him drinking, watched him winking: [17]—
If he knew what I was thinking—
    And he would, for certain, know,
Being a mighty shrewd deviser
Of such fancies—with a blow
P'raps he'd loosen an incisor
    From the forefront of my row!

(*During this song there has entered along the street a* LANDLADY, *who is soon followed by her servant,* PLATHANÉ.)

LANDLADY

Ho, Plathané, here, I want you, Plathané! . . .
Here is that scamp who came to the inn before,
Ate sixteen loaves of bread. . . .

PLATHANÉ
            Why, so it is:

The very man!

XANTHIAS (*aside*)
Here's fun for somebody.

LANDLADY

And twenty plates of boiled meat, half an obol
At every gulp!

XANTHIAS (*aside*)
Some one'll catch it now!

LANDLADY

And all that garlic.

DIONYSUS
        Nonsense, my good woman,
You don't know what you're saying.

PLATHANÉ
                Did you think
I wouldn't know you in those high-heeled boots?

LANDLADY

And all the salt-fish I've not mentioned yet. . . .

PLATHANÉ (*to* LANDLADY)
No, you poor thing; and all the good fresh cheese
The man kept swallowing, and the baskets with it!

LANDLADY (*to* XANTHIAS)
And when he saw me coming for the money
Glared like a wild bull! Yes, and roared at me!

XANTHIAS
Just what he does! His manners everywhere.

LANDLADY
Tugged at his sword! Pretended to be mad!

PLATHANÉ
Yes, you poor thing; I don't know how you bore it!

LANDLADY
And we got all of a tremble, both of us,
And ran up the ladder to the loft! And he,
He tore the matting up—and off he went!

XANTHIAS
Like him, again.

PLATHANÉ
But something must be done!

LANDLADY (*to* PLATHANÉ)
Run, you, and fetch me my protector, Cleon.

PLATHANÉ (*to the* LANDLADY, *as they run excitedly to go off in different
directions*)
And you fetch me Hyperbolus, if you meet him. . . .
Then we shall crush him!

LANDLADY (*returning*)
Oh, that ugly jaw!
If I could throw a stone, I'd like to break
Those wicked teeth that ground my larder dry!

PLATHANÉ (*returning on the other side*)
And I should like to fling you in the pit!

LANDLADY (*turning again as she goes off*)
And I should like to get a scythe, and cut
That throat that swallowed all my sausages.

PLATHANÉ (*the same*)
Well, I'll go straight to Cleon, and this same day
We'll worm them out in a law-court, come what may!
(*The* LANDLADY *and* PLATHANÉ *go off in different directions.*)

DIONYSUS

Plague take me! No friend left me in the world. . . .
Except old Xanthias!

XANTHIAS

I know, I know!
We all see what you want. But that's enough!
I won't be Heracles.

DIONYSUS

Now don't say that,
Xanthias—old boy!

XANTHIAS

And how am I to be
Alcmena's son—a mortal and a slave?

DIONYSUS

I know you're angry, and quite justly so.
Hit me if you like; I won't say one word back.
But, mark, if ever again in this wide world
I rob you of these clothes, destruction fall
On me myself, my wife, my little ones,—
And, if you like, on the old bat Archedemus!

XANTHIAS

That oath will do. I take it on those terms.

CHORUS (*singing*)
Now 'tis yours to make repayment
For the honour of this raiment;
    Wear it well, as erst you wore;
If it needs some renovating,
Think of whom you're personating,
    Glare like Heracles and roar.
Else, if any fear you show, sir,
    Any weakness at the core,
Any jesting, back you go, sir,
    To the baggage as before!

XANTHIAS (*singing*)
Thank you for your kind intention,
But I had some comprehension
    Of the task I undertook.
Should the lion-skin make for profit,

He'll attempt to make me doff it—
That I know—by hook or crook.
Still I'll make my acting real,
Peppery gait and fiery look.
Ha! Here comes the great ordeal:
See the door. I'm sure it shook!
(*The central door opens and the Porter,* AEACUS, *comes
out with two other slaves.*)

AEACUS

Here, seize this dog-stealer and lead him forth
To justice, quick.

DIONYSUS (*imitating* XANTHIAS)
Here's fun for somebody.

XANTHIAS (*in a Heraclean attitude*)
Stop, zounds! Not one step more!

AEACUS
You want to fight?
Ho, Ditylas, Sceblyas, and Pardocas,
Forward! Oblige this person with some fighting!

DIONYSUS (*while the Scythians gradually overpower* XANTHIAS)
How shocking to assault the constables—
And stealing other people's things!

AEACUS
Unnatural,
That's what I call it.

DIONYSUS
Quite a pain to see.

XANTHIAS (*now overpowered and disarmed*)
Now, by Lord Zeus, if ever I've been here
Or stol'n from you the value of one hair,
You may take and hang me on the nearest tree! . . .
Now, listen: and I'll act quite fairly by you;
(*Suddenly indicating* DIONYSUS)
Take this poor boy, and put him to the question! [18]
And if you find me guilty, hang me straight.

AEACUS
What tortures do you allow?

XANTHIAS
Use all you like.
Tie him in the ladder, hang him by the feet,
Whip off his skin with bristle-whips and rack him;
You might well try some vinegar up his nose,
And bricks upon his chest, and so on. Only
No scourges made of . . . leek or young shalott.[19]

AEACUS
A most frank offer, most frank.—If my treatment
Disables him, the value shall be paid.

XANTHIAS
Don't mention it. Remove him and begin.

AEACUS
Thank you, we'll do it here, that you may witness
Exactly what he says. (*To* DIONYSUS) Put down your bundle,
And mind you tell the truth.

DIONYSUS (*who has hitherto been speechless with horror, now bursting out*)
I warn all present,
To torture me is an illegal act,
Being immortal! And whoever does so
Must take the consequences.

AEACUS
Why, who *are* you?

DIONYSUS
The immortal Dionysus, son of Zeus;
And this my slave.

AEACUS (*to* XANTHIAS)
You hear his protest?

XANTHIAS
Yes;
All the more reason, that, for whipping him;
If he's a real immortal he won't feel it.

DIONYSUS
Well, but you claim to be immortal too;
They ought to give you just the same as me.

XANTHIAS

That's fair enough. All right; whichever of us
You first find crying, or the least bit minding
Your whip, you're free to say he's no true god.

AEACUS

Sir, you behave like a true gentleman;
You come to justice of yourself!—Now then,
Strip, both.

XANTHIAS

How will you test us?

AEACUS
Easily:
You'll each take whack and whack about.

XANTHIAS

All right.

AEACUS (*striking* XANTHIAS)

There.

XANTHIAS (*controlling himself with an effort*)
Watch now, if you see me even wince.

AEACUS

But I've already hit you!

XANTHIAS
I think not.

AEACUS

Upon my word, it looks as if I hadn't.
Well, now I'll go and whack the other.

(*Strikes* DIONYSUS.)

DIONYSUS (*also controlling himself*)
When?

AEACUS

I've done it.

DIONYSUS (*with an air of indifference*)
Odd, it didn't make me sneeze!

AEACUS

It *is* odd!—Well, I'll try the first again.

(*He crosses to* XANTHIAS.)

XANTHIAS

All right. Be quick. (*The blow falls*) Whe-ew

AEACUS

Ah, why "whe-ew"?

It didn't hurt you?

XANTHIAS (*recovering himself*)
No; I just was thinking
When my Diomean Feast would next be due.

AEACUS

A holy thought!—I'll step across again.

(*Strikes* DIONYSUS, *who howls.*)

DIONYSUS

Ow-ow!

AEACUS

What's that?

DIONYSUS (*recovering himself*)
I saw some cavalry.

AEACUS

What makes your eyes run?

DIONYSUS
There's a smell of onions!

AEACUS

You're sure it didn't hurt you?

DIONYSUS
Hurt? Not it.

AEACUS

I'll step across again then to the first one.

(*Strikes* XANTHIAS, *who also howls.*)

XANTHIAS

Hi-i!

AEACUS

What is it now?

XANTHIAS

Take out that thorn.

(*Pointing to his foot.*)

AEACUS

What does it mean?—Over we go again.

(*Strikes* DIONYSUS.)

DIONYSUS

O Lord! (*hurriedly turning his wail into a line of poetry*) "of Delos or of
Pytho's rock."

XANTHIAS (*triumphantly*)

It hurts. You heard?

DIONYSUS

It doesn't! I was saying
A verse of old Hipponax to myself.

XANTHIAS

You're making nothing of it. Hit him hard
Across the soft parts underneath the ribs.

AEACUS (*to* XANTHIAS)

A good idea! Turn over on your back!

(*Strikes him.*)

XANTHIAS (*as before*)

O Lord!

DIONYSUS

It hurts!

XANTHIAS (*as though continuing*)
"Posidon ruler free
Of cliffs Aegean and the grey salt sea."

AEACUS

Now, by Demeter, it's beyond my powers
To tell which one of you's a god!—Come in;
We'll ask my master. He and Persephassa
Will easily know you, being gods themselves.

DIONYSUS

Most wisely said. Indeed I could have wished
You'd thought of that before you had me swished.
(*They all go into the house. The* CHORUS, *left alone on the stage, turns
    towards the audience.*)

CHORUS (*singing*)
Draw near, O Muse, to the spell of my song,
    Set foot in the sanctified place,
And see thy faithful Athenians throng,
To whom the myriad arts belong,
    The myriad marks of grace,

Greater than Cleophon's own,
On whose lips, with bilingual moan,
    A swallow from Thrace
    Has taken his place
And chirps in blood-curdling tone
On the gibberish-tree's thick branches high
    As he utters a nightingale note,
        A tumultuous cry
        That he's certain to die
Even with an equal vote!

LEADER OF THE CHORUS

It behoves this sacred Chorus, in its wisdom and its bliss,
To assist the state with counsel. Now our first advice is this:
Let Athenians all stand equal; penal laws be swept away.
Some of us have been misguided, following Phrynichus astray;
Now for all of these, we urge you, let full freedom be decreed
To confess the cause that tripped them and blot out that old misdeed.
Next, no man should live in Athens outcast, robbed of every right.
Shame it is that low-born aliens, just for sharing one sea-fight,
Should forthwith become 'Plataeans' and instead of slaves be masters—
(Not that in the least I blame you for thus meeting our disasters;
No; I pay respectful homage to the one wise thing you've done):
But remember these men also, your own kinsmen, sire and son,
Who have ofttimes fought beside you, spilt their blood on many seas:
Grant for that one fault the pardon which they crave you on their knees.
You whom Nature made for wisdom, let your vengeance fall to sleep;
Greet as kinsmen and Athenians, burghers true to win and keep,
Whosoe'er will brave the storms and fight for Athens at your side!
But be sure, if still we spurn them, if we wrap us in our pride,

Stand alone, with Athens tossing in the long arm of the waves,
Men in days to come shall wonder, and not praise you in your graves.

CHORUS (*singing*)
An' I the make of a man may trow,
    And the ways that lead to a fall,
Not long will the ape that troubles us now,
Not long little Cligenes—champion, I vow,
    Of rascally washermen all,

Who hold over soap their sway
And lye and Cimolian clay
    (Which they thriftily mix
    With the scrapings of bricks)—
Not long will our little one stay!
Oh, 'tis well he is warlike and ready to kick
    For if once home from supper he trotted,
        Talking genially thick
        And without his big stick,
    We should probably find him garotted.

LEADER OF THE CHORUS
It has often struck our notice that the course our city runs
Is the same towards men and money.—She has true and worthy sons:
She has good and ancient silver, she has good and recent gold.
These are coins untouched with alloys; everywhere their fame is told;
Not all Hellas holds their equal, not all Barbary far and near,
Gold or silver, each well minted, tested each and ringing clear.
Yet, we never use them! Others always pass from hand to hand,
Sorry brass just struck last week and branded with a wretched brand.
So with men we know for upright, blameless lives and noble names,
Trained in music and palaestra, freemen's choirs and freemen's games,
These we spurn for men of brass, for red-haired things of unknown breed,
Rascal cubs of mongrel fathers—them we use at every need!
Creatures just arrived in Athens, whom our city, years ago,
Scarcely would have used as scapegoats [20] to be slaughtered for a show!
Even now, O race demented, there is time to change your ways;
Use once more what's worth the using. If we 'scape, the more the praise
That we fought our fight with wisdom; or, if all is lost for good,
Let the tree on which they hang us be, at least, of decent wood!
(*The door opens, and the two slaves,* AEACUS *and* XANTHIAS, *return.*)

AEACUS

By Zeus, that's what I call a gentleman!
That master of yours!

XANTHIAS
Gentleman? That he is!
There's nothing in his head but wine and wenches!

AEACUS

But not to whip you when you were clean convicted,
A slave caught masquerading as his master!

XANTHIAS *(significantly)*
I'd like to see him try it!

AEACUS
There you go!
The old slave trick, that I'm so fond of too.

XANTHIAS

You like it, eh?

AEACUS
Like it? Why, when I get
Behind my master's back and quietly curse him,
I feel just like the Blessed in the Mysteries!

XANTHIAS

What about muttering as you go outside
After a whacking?

AEACUS
Yes; I like that too.

XANTHIAS *(with increasing excitement)*
And prying into people's secrets, eh?

AEACUS *(the same)*
By Zeus, there's nothing like it in the world!

XANTHIAS

Oh! Zeus makes brethren meet!—And what of list'ning
To what the masters say?

AEACUS
It makes me mad!

XANTHIAS

And telling every word of it to strangers?

AEACUS

Madder than mad, stark staring crimson madder!

XANTHIAS

O Lord Apollo, clap your right hand there,
Give me your cheek to kiss, and you kiss me!
(*They embrace; a loud noise is heard inside the house.*)
But Zeus!—our own Zeus of the Friendly Jailbirds—
What is that noise . . . those shouts and quarrelling . . .
Inside?

AEACUS

That? Aeschylus and Euripides!

XANTHIAS

Eh?

AEACUS

Yes; there's a big business just astir,
And hot dissension among all the dead.

XANTHIAS

About what?

AEACUS

There's a law established here
Concerning all the large and liberal arts,
Which grants the foremost master in each art
Free entertainment at the Central Hearth,
And also a special throne in Pluto's row . . .

XANTHIAS

Oh, now I understand!

AEACUS

To hold until
There comes one greater; then he must make way.

XANTHIAS

But how has this affected Aeschylus?

AEACUS

Aeschylus held the throne of tragedy,
As greatest . . .

XANTHIAS
Held it? Why, who holds it now?

AEACUS
Well, when Euripides came down, he gave
Free exhibitions to our choicest thieves,
Footpads, cut-purses, burglars, father-beaters,
—Of whom we have numbers here; and when they heard
The neat retorts, the fencing, and the twists,
They all went mad and thought him something splendid.
And he, growing proud, laid hands upon the throne
Where Aeschylus sat.

XANTHIAS
And wasn't pelted off?

AEACUS
Not he. The whole folk clamoured for a trial
To see which most was master of his craft.

XANTHIAS
The whole jail-folk?

AEACUS
Exactly;—loud as trumpets.

XANTHIAS
And were there none to fight for Aeschylus?

AEACUS
Goodness is scarce, you know. (*Indicating the audience*) The same as
here!

XANTHIAS
And what does Pluto mean to do about it?

AEACUS
Why, hold a trial and contest on the spot
To test their skill for certain.

XANTHIAS (*reflecting*)
But, I say,
Sophocles surely must have claimed the throne?

AEACUS

Not he; as soon as ever he came down,
He kissed old Aeschylus, and wrung his hand,
And Aeschylus made room on half his seat.
And now he means to wait—or so, at least,
Clidemides informs us—in reserve.
If Aeschylus wins the day, he'll rest content:
If not, why then, he says, for poor Art's sake,
He must show fight against Euripides!

XANTHIAS

It is to be, then?

AEACUS

Certainly, quite soon.
Just where you stand we'll have the shock of war.
They'll weigh the poetry line by line . . .

XANTHIAS

Poor thing,
A lamb set in the meat-scale and found wanting!

AEACUS

They'll bring straight-edges out, and cubit-rules,
And folded cube-frames . . .

XANTHIAS

Is it bricks they want?

AEACUS

And mitre-squares and wedges! Line by line
Euripides will test all tragedies!

XANTHIAS

That must make Aeschylus angry, I should think?

AEACUS

Well, he did stoop and glower like a mad bull.

XANTHIAS

Who'll be the judge?

AEACUS

That was a difficulty.
Both found an utter dearth of proper critics;
For Aeschylus objected to the Athenians. . . .

XANTHIAS

Perhaps he thought the jail-folk rather many?

AEACUS

And all the world beside, he thought mere dirt
At seeing what kind of thing a poet was.
So, in the end, they fixed upon your master
As having much experience in the business.
But come in; when the master's face looks grave
There's mostly trouble coming for the slave.

CHORUS (*singing*)

Eftsoons shall dire anger interne be the Thunderer's portion
  When his foe's glib tusk fresh whetted for blood he descries;
Then fell shall his heart be, and mad; and a pallid distortion
    Descend as a cloud on his eyes.

Yea, words with plumes wild on the wind and with helmets a-glancing,
  With axles a-splinter and marble a-shiver, eftsoons
Shall bleed, as a man meets the shock of a Thought-builder's prancing
    Stanzas of dusky dragoons.

The deep crest of his mane shall uprise as he slowly unlimbers
  The long-drawn wrath of his brow, and lets loose with a roar
Epithets welded and screwed, like new torrent-swept timbers
    Blown loose by a giant at war.

Then rises the man of the Mouth; then battleward flashes
  A tester of verses, a smooth and serpentine tongue,
To dissect each phrase into mincemeat, and argue to ashes
    That high-towered labour of lung!

(*The door opens again. Enter* EURIPIDES, DIONYSUS, *and* AESCHYLUS.)

EURIPIDES

Pray, no advice to me! I won't give way;
I claim that I'm more master of my art.

DIONYSUS

You hear him, Aeschylus. Why don't you speak?

EURIPIDES

He wants to open with an awful silence—
The blood-curdling reserve of his first scenes.

DIONYSUS

My dear sir, I must beg! Control your language!

EURIPIDES

I know him; I've seen through him years ago;
Bard of the "noble savage," wooden-mouthed,
No door, no bolt, no bridle to his tongue,
A torrent of pure bombast—tied in bundles!

AESCHYLUS (*breaking out*)

How say'st thou, Son o' the Goddess of the Greens? [21]—
You dare speak thus of me, you phrase-collector,
Blind-beggar-bard and scum of rifled rag-bags!
Oh, you shall rue it!

DIONYSUS

Stop! Stop, Aeschylus;
Strike not thine heart to fire on rancour old.

AESCHYLUS

No; I'll expose this crutch-and-cripple playwright,
And what he's worth for all his insolence.

DIONYSUS (*to attendants*)

A lamb, a black lamb, quick, boys! Bring it out
To sacrifice; a hurricane's let loose! [22]

AESCHYLUS (*to* EURIPIDES)

You and your Cretan dancing-solos! You
And the ugly amours that you set to verse!

DIONYSUS (*interposing*)

One moment, please, most noble Aeschylus!
And you, poor wretch, if you have any prudence,
Get out of the hailstones quick, or else, by Zeus,
Some word as big as your head will catch you crash
Behind the ear, and knock out all the . . . Telephus!
Nay, Aeschylus, pray, pray control your anger;
Examine and submit to be examined
With a cool head. Two poets should not meet
In fishwife style; but here are you, straight off,
Ablaze and roaring like an oak on fire.

EURIPIDES

For my part I'm quite ready, with no shrinking,
To bite first or be bitten, as he pleases.

Here are my dialogue, music, and construction;
Here's Peleus at your service, Meleager,
And Aeolus, and . . . yes, Telephus, by all means!

DIONYSUS

Do you consent to the trial, Aeschylus? Speak.

AESCHYLUS

I well might take objection to the place;
It's no fair field for him and me.

DIONYSUS
Why not?

AESCHYLUS

Because my writings haven't died with me,
As his have; so he'll have them all to hand. . . .
However, I waive the point, if you think fit.

DIONYSUS

Go, some one, bring me frankincense and fire
That I may pray for guidance, to decide
This contest in the Muses' strictest ways;
To whom, meantime, uplift your hymn of praise!

CHORUS (*singing*)
All hail, ye nine heaven-born virginal Muses,
Whiche'er of ye watch o'er the manners and uses
    Of the founts of quotation, when, meeting in fray—
All hearts drawn tense for who wins and who loses—
With wrestling lithe each the other confuses,
Look on the pair that do battle to-day!
These be the men to take poems apart
        By chopping, riving, sawing;
    Here is the ultimate trial of Art
        To due completion drawing!

DIONYSUS

Won't you two pray before you show your lines?

AESCHYLUS (*going up to the altar*)
Demeter, thou who feedest all my thought,
Grant me but worthiness to worship thee!

DIONYSUS (*to* EURIPIDES)
Won't you put on some frankincense?

EURIPIDES (*staying where he is*)
                    Oh, thank you;
The gods I pray to are of other metal!

DIONYSUS
Your own stamp, eh? New struck?

EURIPIDES
                    Exactly so.

DIONYSUS
Well, pray away then to your own peculiar.

EURIPIDES (*esoterically*)
Ether, whereon I batten! Vocal cords!
Reason, and nostrils swift to scent and sneer,
Grant that I duly probe each word I hear.

CHORUS (*singing*)
All of us to hear are yearning
Further from these twins of learning,
What dread road they walk, what burning
        Heights they climb of speech and song.
Tongues alert for battle savage,
Tempers keen for war and ravage,
        Angered hearts to both belong.
He will fight with passes witty
Smooth and smacking of the city,
        Gleaming blades unflecked with rust;
He will seize—to end the matter—
Tree-trunks torn and clubbed, to batter
Brains to bits, and plunge and scatter
        Whole arena-fulls of dust!

LEADER OF THE CHORUS
Now, quick to work. Be sure you both do justice to your cases,
Clear sense, no loose analogies, and no long commonplaces.

EURIPIDES
A little later I will treat my own artistic mettle,
This person's claims I should prefer immediately to settle.
I'll show you how he posed and prosed; with what audacious fooling
He tricked an audience fresh and green from Phrynichus's schooling.
Those sole veiled figures on the stage were first among his graces,
Achilles, say, or Niobé, who never showed their faces,
But stood like so much scene-painting, and never a grunt they uttered!

DIONYSUS
Why, no, by Zeus, no more they did!

EURIPIDES
                        And on the Chorus spluttered
Through long song-systems, four on end, the actors mute as fishes!

DIONYSUS
I somehow loved that silence, though; and felt it met my wishes
As no one's talk does nowadays!

EURIPIDES
                        You hadn't yet seen through it!
That's all.

DIONYSUS
            I really think you're right! But still, what made him do it?

EURIPIDES
The instinct of a charlatan, to keep the audience guessing
If Niobé ever meant to speak—the play meantime progressing!

DIONYSUS
Of course it was! The sly old dog, to think of how he tricked us!—
Don't (*to* AESCHYLUS) ramp and fume!

EURIPIDES
                        We're apt to do so when the facts convict us!
—Then after this tomfoolery, the heroine, feeling calmer,
Would utter some twelve wild-bull words, on mid-way in the drama,
Long ones. with crests and beetling brows, and gorgons round the border,
That no man ever heard on earth.

AESCHYLUS
            The red plague . . . !

DIONYSUS
                                    Order, order!

EURIPIDES
Intelligible—not one line!

DIONYSUS (*to* AESCHYLUS)
            Please! Won't your teeth stop gnashing?

EURIPIDES

All fosses and Scamander-beds, and bloody targes flashing,
With gryphon-eagles bronze-embossed, and crags, and riders reeling,
Which somehow never quite joined on.

DIONYSUS

By Zeus, sir, quite my feeling!
A question comes in Night's long hours, that haunts me like a spectre,
What kind of fish or fowl you'd call a "russet hippalector."

AESCHYLUS (*breaking in*)

It was a ship's sign, idiot, such as every joiner fixes!

DIONYSUS

Indeed! I thought perhaps it meant that music-man Eryxis!

[EURIPIDES

You like then, in a tragic play, a cock? You think it mixes?]

AESCHYLUS (*to* EURIPIDES)

And what did you yourself produce, O fool with pride deluded?

EURIPIDES

Not "hippalectors," thank the Lord, nor "tragelaphs," as you did—
The sort of ornament they use to fill a Persian curtain!
—I had the Drama straight from you, all bloated and uncertain,
Weighed down with rich and heavy words, puffed out past comprehension.
I took the case in hand; applied treatment for such distension—
Beetroot, light phrases, little walks, hot book-juice, and cold reasoning;
Then fed her up on solos. . . .

DIONYSUS (*aside*)

With Cephisophon for seasoning!

EURIPIDES

I didn't rave at random, or plunge in and make confusions.
My first appearing character explained, with due allusions,
The whole play's pedigree.

DIONYSUS (*aside*)

Your own you left in wise obscurity!

EURIPIDES

Then no one from the start with me could idle with security.
They had to work. The men, the slaves, the women, all made speeches,
The kings, the little girls, the hags . . .

AESCHYLUS

Just see the things he teaches!
And shouldn't you be hanged for that?

EURIPIDES

No, by the lord Apollo!
It's democratic!

DIONYSUS (*to* EURIPIDES)
That's no road for you, my friend, to follow;
You'll find the "little walk" too steep; I recommend you quit it.[23]

EURIPIDES
Next, I taught all the town to talk with freedom.

AESCHYLUS

I admit it.
'Twere better, ere you taught them, you had died amid their curses!

EURIPIDES
I gave them canons to apply and squares for marking verses;
Taught them to see, think, understand, to scheme for what they wanted,
To fall in love, think evil, question all things. . . .

AESCHYLUS

Granted, granted!

EURIPIDES
I put things on the stage that came from daily life and business,
Where men could catch me if I tripped; could listen without dizziness
To things they knew, and judge my art. I never crashed and lightened
And bullied people's senses out; nor tried to keep them frightened
With Magic Swans and Aethiop knights, loud barb and clanging vizor!
Then look at my disciples, too, and mark what creatures his are!
Phormisius is his product and the looby lump Megaenetus,
All trumpet, lance, moustache, and glare, who twist their clubs of pine at
     us;
While Clitophon is mine, sirs, and Theramenes the Matchless!

DIONYSUS
Theramenes! Ah, that's the man! All danger leaves him scratchless.
His friends may come to grief, and he be found in awkward fixes,
But always tumbles right end up, not aces—no: all sixes!

EURIPIDES (*more rapidly*)
This was the kind of lore I brought
To school my town in ways of thought;
I mingled reasoning with my art
And shrewdness, till I fired their heart
To brood, to think things through and through;
And rule their houses better, too.

DIONYSUS (*still more rapidly*)
Yes, by the powers, that's very true!
No burgher now, who comes indoors,
But straight looks round the house and roars:
"Where is the saucepan gone? And who
    Has bitten that sprat's head away?
And, out, alas! The earthen pot
I bought last year is not, is not!
    Where are the leeks of yesterday?
    And who has gnawed this olive, pray?"
Whereas, before they took his school,
Each sat at home, a simple, cool,
Religious, unsuspecting fool,
    And happy in his sheep-like way!

CHORUS (*singing*)
Great Achilles, gaze around thee!
'Twill astound thee and confound thee.
Answer now: but keep in bound the
    Words that off the course would tear,
Bit in teeth, in turmoil flocking.
Yes: it's monstrous—shameful—shocking—
    Brave old warrior. But beware!

Don't retort with haste or passion;
Meet the squalls in sailor fashion,
    Mainsail reefed and mast nigh bare;
Then, when safe beyond disaster
You may press him fiercer, faster,
Close and show yourself his master,
    Once the wind is smooth and fair!

LEADER OF THE CHORUS
O thou who first of the Greeks did build great words to heaven-high towers,
And the essence of tragedy-padding distilled, give vent to thy pent-up
    showers.

AESCHYLUS

I freely admit that I take it amiss, and I think my anger is just,
At having to answer a man like this. Still, lest I should seem nonplussed,
Pray, tell me on what particular ground a poet should claim admiration?

EURIPIDES

If his art is true, and his counsel sound; and if he brings help to the nation,
By making men better in some respect.

AESCHYLUS

              And suppose you have done the reverse,
And have had upon good strong men the effect of making them weaker
   and worse,
What, do you say, should your recompense be?

DIONYSUS

              The gallows! You needn't ask him.

AESCHYLUS

Well, think what they were when he had them from me! Good six-footers,
   solid of limb,
Well-born, well-bred, not ready to fly from obeying their country's call,
Nor in latter-day fashion to loiter and lie, and keep their consciences
   small;
Their life was in shafts of ash and of elm, in bright plumes fluttering wide,
In lance and greaves and corslet and helm, and hearts of sevenfold hide!

EURIPIDES (*aside*)

Oh, now he's begun and will probably run a whole armourer's shop on
   my head!
(*To* AESCHYLUS) Stop! How was it due in especial to you, if they were
   so very—well-bred?

DIONYSUS

Come, answer him, Aeschylus! Don't be so hot, or smoulder in silent
   disdain.

AESCHYLUS (*crushingly*)

By a tragedy 'brimming with Ares!'

DIONYSUS
            A what?

AESCHYLUS
              The "Seven against Thebes."

DIONYSUS

Pray explain.

AESCHYLUS

There wasn't a man could see that play but he hungered for havoc and gore.

DIONYSUS

I'm afraid that tells in the opposite way. For the Thebans profited more,
It urged them to fight without flinching or fear, and they did so; and long may you rue it!

AESCHYLUS

The same thing was open to all of you here, but it didn't amuse you to do it!
Then next I taught you for glory to long, and against all odds stand fast;
That was "The Persians," which bodied in song the noblest deed of the past.

DIONYSUS

Yes, yes! When Darius arose from the grave it gave me genuine joy,
And the Chorus stood with its arms a-wave, and observed, "Yow—oy, Yow—oy!" ²⁴

AESCHYLUS

Yes, that's the effect for a play to produce! For observe, from the world's first start
Those poets have all been of practical use who have been supreme in their art.
First, Orpheus withheld us from bloodshed impure, and vouchsafed us the great revelation;
Musaeus was next, with wisdom to cure diseases and teach divination.
Then Hesiod showed us the season to plough, to sow, and to reap. And the laurels
That shine upon Homer's celestial brow are equally due to his morals!
He taught men to stand, to march, and to arm. . . .

DIONYSUS

So that was old Homer's profession?
Then I wish he could keep his successors from harm, like Pantacles in the procession,
Who first got his helmet well strapped on his head, and then tried to put in the plume!

AESCHYLUS

There be many brave men that he fashioned and bred, like Lamachus,
   now in his tomb.

And in his great spirit my plays had a part, with their heroes many and
   brave—

Teucers, Patrocluses, lions at heart; who made my citizens crave

To dash like them at the face of the foe, and leap at the call of a
   trumpet!—

But no Stheneboea I've given you, no; no Phaedra, no heroine-strumpet!

If I've once put a woman in love in one act of one play, may my teaching
   be scouted!

EURIPIDES

No, you hadn't exactly the style to attract Aphrodité!

AESCHYLUS

                                        I'm better without it.

A deal too much of that style she found in some of your friends and you,

And once, at least, left you flat on the ground!

DIONYSUS

                                 By Zeus, that's perfectly true.

If he dealt his neighbours such rattling blows, we must think how he suffered in person.

EURIPIDES

And what are the public defects you suppose my poor Stheneboea to
   worsen?

AESCHYLUS (*evading the question with a jest*)

She makes good women, and good men's wives, when their hearts are
   weary and want ease,

Drink jorums of hemlock and finish their lives, to gratify Bellerophontes!

EURIPIDES

But did I invent the story I told of—Phaedra, say? Wasn't it history?

AESCHYLUS

It was true, right enough; but the poet should hold such a truth en-
   veloped in mystery,

And not represent it or make it a play. It's his duty to teach, and you know
   it.

As a child learns from all who may come in his way, so the grown world
   learns from the poet.

Oh, words of good counsel should flow from his voice—

EURIPIDES

And words like Mount Lycabettus
Or Parnes, such as you give us for choice, must needs be good counsel?—
Oh, let us,
Oh, let us at least use the language of men!

AESCHYLUS

Flat cavil, sir! cavil absurd!
When the subject is great and the sentiment, then, of necessity, great
grows the word;
When heroes give range to their hearts, is it strange if the speech of them
over us towers?
Nay, the garb of them too must be gorgeous to view, and majestical,
nothing like ours.
All this I saw, and established as law, till you came and spoilt it.

EURIPIDES

How so?

AESCHYLUS

You wrapped them in rags from old beggarmen's bags, to express their
heroical woe,
And reduce the spectator to tears of compassion!

EURIPIDES

Well, what was the harm if I did?

AESCHYLUS (*evading the question as before*)

Bah, your modern rich man has adopted the fashion, for remission of
taxes to bid;
"He couldn't provide a trireme if he tried;" he implores us his state to
behold.

DIONYSUS

Though rags outside may very well hide good woollens beneath, if it's
cold!
And when once he's exempted, he gaily departs and pops up at the fish-
mongers' stalls.

AESCHYLUS (*continuing*)

Then, next, you have trained in the speechmaking arts nigh every infant
that crawls.
Oh, this is the thing that such havoc has wrought in the wrestling-school,
narrowed the hips
Of the poor pale chattering children, and taught the crews of the pick of
the ships

To answer back pat to their officer's nose! How unlike my old sailor of
yore,
With no thought in his head but to guzzle his brose and sing as he bent
at the oar!

DIONYSUS

And spit on the heads of the rowers below,[25] and garott stray lubbers on
shore!
But our new man just sails where it happens to blow, and argues, and
rows no more!

AESCHYLUS (*more rapidly*)

What hasn't he done that is under the sun,
And the love-dealing dames that with him have begun?
    One's her own brother's wife;
    One says Life is not Life;
And one goes into shrines to give birth to a son!
Our city through him is filled to the brim
With monkeys who chatter to every one's whim;
    Little scriveners' clerks
    With their winks and their larks,
But for wrestle or race not a muscle in trim!

DIONYSUS (*still more rapidly*)

Not a doubt of it! Why, I laughted fit to cry
At the Panathenaea, a man to espy,
    Pale, flabby, and fat,
    And bent double at that,
Puffing feebly behind, with a tear in his eye;

Till there in their place, with cord and with brace,
Were the Potters assembled to quicken his pace;
    And down they came, whack!
    On sides, belly, and back,
Till he blew out his torch and just fled from the race! [26]

CHORUS (*singing*)

Never were such warriors, never
    Prize so rich and feud so keen:
    Dangerous, too, such knots to sever:
He drives on with stern endeavour,
He falls back, but rallies ever,
    Marks his spot and stabs it clean!

Change your step, though! Do not tarry;
Other ways there be to harry
  Old antagonists in art.
Show whatever sparks you carry,
Question, answer, thrust and parry—
Be they new or ancient, marry,
  Let them fly, well-winged and smart!

If you fear, from former cases,
  That the audience p'raps may fail
To appreciate your paces,
Your allusions and your graces,
Look a moment in their faces!
  They will tell another tale.

Oft from long campaigns returning
Thro' the devious roads of learning
  These have wandered, books in hand:
Nature gave them keen discerning
Eyes; and you have set them burning!
Sharpest thought or deepest yearning—
  Speak, and these will understand.

                    EURIPIDES
Quite so; I'll turn then to his prologues straight,
And make in that first part of tragedy
My first review in detail of this Genius!
His exposition always was obscure.

                    DIONYSUS
Which one will you examine!

                    EURIPIDES
              Which? Oh, lots!
First quote me that from the Oresteia, please.

                    DIONYSUS
Ho, silence in the court! Speak, Aeschylus.

    AESCHYLUS (*quoting the first lines of The Choëphori*)
"Guide of the Dead, warding a father's way,
Be thou my light and saviour, where I pray,
In this my fatherland, returned, restored."

DIONYSUS (*to* EURIPIDES)
You find some false lines there?

EURIPIDES
About a dozen!

DIONYSUS
Why, altogether there are only three!

EURIPIDES
But every one has twenty faults in drawing!
(AESCHYLUS *begins to interrupt*.)

DIONYSUS
No, stop, stop, Aeschylus; or perhaps you'll find
Your debts run up to more than three iambics.

AESCHYLUS (*raging*)
Stop to let *him* speak?

DIONYSUS
Well, that's my advice.

EURIPIDES
He's gone straight off some thousand miles astray.

AESCHYLUS
Of course it's foolery—but what do *I* care?
Point out the faults.

EURIPIDES
Repeat the lines again.

AESCHYLUS
"Guide of the Dead, warding a father's way, . . ."

EURIPIDES
Orestes speaks those words, I take it, standing
On his dead father's tomb?

AESCHYLUS
I don't deny it.

EURIPIDES
Then what's the father's way that Hermes wards?
Is it the way Orestes' father went,
To darkness by a woman's dark intent?

AESCHYLUS

No, no! He calls on Eriunian Hermes,
Guide of the Dead, and adds a word to say
That office is derived from Hermes' father.

EURIPIDES

That's worse than I supposed! For if your Hermes
Derives his care of dead men from his father, . . .

DIONYSUS (*interrupting*)

Why, resurrectioning's the family trade!

AESCHYLUS

Dionysus, dull of fragrance is thy wine!

DIONYSUS

Well, say the next; and (*to* EURIPIDES) you look out for slips.

AESCHYLUS

"Be thou my light and saviour where I pray
In this my fatherland returned, restored."

EURIPIDES

Our noble Aeschylus repeats himself.

DIONYSUS

How so?

EURIPIDES

Observe his phrasing, and you'll see.
First to this land "returned" and then "restored";
'Returned' is just the same thing as 'restored.'

DIONYSUS

Why, yes! It's just as if you asked your neighbour,
'Lend me a pail, or, if not that, a bucket.'

AESCHYLUS

Oh, too much talking has bemuzzed your brain!
The words are not the same; the line is perfect.

DIONYSUS

Now, is it really? Tell me how you mean.

AESCHYLUS

Returning home is the act of any person
Who has a home; he comes back, nothing more;
An exile both returns and is restored!

DIONYSUS

True, by Apollo! (*To* EURIPIDES) What do you say to that?

EURIPIDES

I don't admit Orestes was restored.
He came in secret with no legal permit.

DIONYSUS

By Hermes, yes! (*aside*) I wonder what they mean!

EURIPIDES

Go on then to the next.

(AESCHYLUS *is silent*.)

DIONYSUS

Come, Aeschylus,
Do as he says; (*to* EURIPIDES) and you look out for faults.

AESCHYLUS

"Yea, on this bank of death, I call my lord
To hear and list. . . ."

EURIPIDES

Another repetition!
"To hear and list"—the same thing palpably!

DIONYSUS

The man was talking to the dead, you dog,
Who are always called three times—and then don't hear.

AESCHYLUS

Come, how did *you* write prologues?

EURIPIDES

Oh, I'll show you.
And if you find there any repetitions
Or any irrelevant padding,—spit upon me!

DIONYSUS

Oh, do begin. I mustn't miss those prologues
In all their exquisite exactitude!

EURIPIDES

"At first was Oedipus in happy state."

AESCHYLUS

He wasn't! He was born and bred in misery.
Did not Apollo doom him still unborn
To slay his father? . . .

DIONYSUS (*aside*)
His poor unborn father?

AESCHYLUS
"A happy state at first," you call it, do you?

EURIPIDES (*contemptuously resuming*)
"At first was Oedipus in happy state,
Then changed he, and became most desolate."

AESCHYLUS

He didn't. He was never anything else!
Why, he was scarcely born when they exposed him
In winter, in a pot, that he might never
Grow up and be his father's murderer.
Then off he crawled to Polybus with sore feet,
Then married an old woman, twice his age,
Who further chanced to be his mother, then
Tore out his eyes: the lucky dog he was!

DIONYSUS

At least he fought no sea-fight with a colleague
Called Erasinides!

EURIPIDES
That's no criticism.
I write my prologues singularly well!

AESCHYLUS

By Zeus, I won't go pecking word by word
At every phrase; I'll take one little oil-can,[27]
God helping me, and send your prologues pop!

EURIPIDES
My prologues pop . . . with oil-cans?

AESCHYLUS
Just one oil-can!
You write them so that nothing comes amiss,
The bed-quilt, or the oil-can, or the clothes-bag,
All suit your tragic verse! Wait and I'll prove it.

EURIPIDES

You'll prove it? Really?

AESCHYLUS
Yes.

DIONYSUS
Begin to quote.

EURIPIDES

"Aegyptus, so the tale is spread afar,
With fifty youths fled in a sea-borne car,
But, reaching Argos . . ."

AESCHYLUS
Found his oil-can gone!

DIONYSUS

What's that about the oil-can! Drat the thing!
Quote him another prologue, and let's see.

EURIPIDES

"Dionysus, who with wand and fawn-skin dight
On great Parnassus races in the light
Of lamps far-flashing, . . ."

AESCHYLUS
Found his oil-can gone!

DIONYSUS

Alas! again the oil-can finds our heart!

EURIPIDES (*beginning to reflect anxiously*)
Oh, it won't come to much, though! Here's another,
With not a crack to stick the oil-can in!
"No man hath bliss in full and flawless health;
Lo, this one hath high race, but little wealth;
That, base in blood, hath . . ."

AESCHYLUS
Found his oil-can gone!

DIONYSUS

Euripides!

EURIPIDES

Well?

DIONYSUS
Better furl your sails;
This oil-can seems inclined to raise the wind!

EURIPIDES
Bah, I disdain to give a thought to it!
I'll dash it from his hands in half a minute.
                    (*He racks his memory.*)

DIONYSUS
Well, quote another;—and beware of oil-cans.

EURIPIDES
"Great Cadmus long ago, Agenor's son,
From Sidon racing, . . ."

AESCHYLUS
Found his oil-can gone!

DIONYSUS
Oh, this is awful! Buy the thing outright,
Before it messes every blessed prologue!

EURIPIDES
I buy him off?

DIONYSUS
I strongly recommend it.

EURIPIDES
No; I have many prologues yet to cite
Where he can't find a chink to pour his oil.
"As rapid wheels to Pisa bore him on,
Tantalian Pelops . . ."

AESCHYLUS
Found his oil-can gone!

DIONYSUS
What did I tell you? There it sticks again!
You might let Pelops have a new one, though—
You get quite good ones very cheap just now.

EURIPIDES
By Zeus, not yet! I still have plenty left.
"From earth King Oeneus, . . ."

AESCHYLUS
          Found his oil can gone!

EURIPIDES
You *must* first let me quote one line entire!
"From earth King Oeneus goodly harvest won,
But, while he worshipped, . . ."

AESCHYLUS
          Found his oil-can gone!

DIONYSUS
During the prayers! Who can have been the thief!

EURIPIDES (*desperately*)
Oh, let him be! I defy him answer this—
"Great Zeus in heaven, the word of truth has flown, . . ."

DIONYSUS
O mercy! *His* is certain to be gone!
They bristle with long oil-cans, hedgehog-wise,
Your prologues; they're as bunged up as your eyes!
For God's sake change the subject.—Take his songs!

EURIPIDES
Songs? Yes, I have materials to show
How bad his are, and always all alike.

CHORUS (*singing*)
          What in the world shall we look for next?
          Aeschylus' music! I feel perplexed
               How he can want it mended.
          I have always held that never a man
          Had written or sung since the world began
               Melodies half so splendid!
          (Can he really find a mistake
               In the master of inspiration?
               I feel some consternation
          For our Bacchic prince's sake!)

EURIPIDES
Wonderful songs they are! You'll see directly;
I'll run them all together into one.

DIONYSUS
I'll take some pebbles, then, and count for you.

EURIPIDES (*singing*)
"O Phthian Achilles, canst hark to the battle's man-slaying shock,
    Yea, shock, and not to succour come?
Lo, we of the mere give worship to Hermes, the fount of our stock,
    Yea, shock, and not to succour come!"

DIONYSUS
Two shocks to you, Aeschylus, there!

EURIPIDES (*singing*)
"Thou choice of Achaea, wide-ruling Atrides, give heed to my
    schooling!
    Yea, shock, and not to succour come."

DIONYSUS
A third shock that, I declare!

EURIPIDES (*singing*)
"Ah, peace, and give ear! For the Bee-Maids be near to ope wide
    Artemis' portals.
    Yea, shock-a-nock a-succour come!
Behold it is mine to sing of the sign of the way fate-laden to mortals;
    Yah, shocker-knocker succucum!" 28

DIONYSUS
O Zeus Almighty, what a chain of shocks!
I think I'll go away and take a bath;
The shocks are too much for my nerves and kidneys!

EURIPIDES
Not till you've heard another little set
Compounded from his various cithara-songs.

DIONYSUS
Well then, proceed; but don't put any shocks in!

EURIPIDES (*singing*)
"How the might twin-throned of Achaea for Hellene chivalry bringeth
    Flattothrat toflattothrat!
The prince of the powers of storm, the Sphinx thereover he wingeth
    Flattothrat toflattothrat!
With deedful hand and lance the furious fowl of the air
    Flattothrat toflattothrat!
That the wild wind-walking hounds unhindered tear
    Flattothrat toflattothrat!

And War toward Ajax leaned his weight,
  Flattothrat toflattothrait!"

DIONYSUS
What's Flattothrat? Was it from Marathon
You gathered this wool-gatherer's stuff, or where?

AESCHYLUS
Clean was the place I found them, clean the place
I brought them, loath to glean with Phrynichus
The same enchanted meadow of the Muse.
But any place will do for *him* to poach,
Drink-ditties of Meletus, Carian pipings,
And wakes, and dancing songs.—Here, let me show you!
Ho, some one bring my lyre! But no; what need
Of lyres for this stuff? Where's the wench that plays
The bones?—Approach, Euripidean Muse,
These songs are meet for your accompaniment!

DIONYSUS
This Muse was once . . . no Lesbian; not at all!

AESCHYLUS (*to* EURIPIDES)
"Ye halcyons by the dancing sea
 Who babble everlastingly,
  While on your bathing pinions fall
 The dewy foam-sprays, fresh and free;
  And, oh, ye spiders deft to crawl
  In many a chink of roof and wall,
 While left and right, before, behind,
 Your fingers wi-i-i-i-ind [29]
  The treasures of the labouring loom,
 Fruit of the shuttle's minstrel mind,
 Where many a songful dolphin trips
 To lead the dark-blue-beakèd ships,
  And tosses with aerial touch
  Temples and race-courses and such.
 O bright grape tendril's essence pure,
 Wine to sweep care from human lips;
 Grant me, O child, one arm-pressúre!"
      (*Breaking off*.)
That foot, you see?

DIONYSUS
I do.

AESCHYLUS

And he?

EURIPIDES

Of course I see the foot!

AESCHYLUS

And this is the stuff to trial you bring
And face my songs with the kind of thing
That a man might sing when he dances a fling
    To mad Cyrené's flute!

There, that's your choral stuff! But I've not finished,
I want to show the spirit of his solos!

                        (*Sings again; mysteriously.*)

            "What vision of dreaming,
                Thou fire-hearted Night,
            Death's minion dark-gleaming,
                Hast thou sent in thy might?
And his soul was no soul, and the Murk was his mother, a horror to sight!

        Black dead was his robe, and his eyes
            All blood, and the claws of him great;
        Ye maidens, strike fire and arise;
            Take pails to the well by the gate,
Yea, bring me a cruse of hot water, to wash off this vision of fate.

            Thou Sprite of the Sea,
                It is e'en as I feared!
            Fellow-lodgers of me,
                What dread thing hath appeared?
Lo, Glycé hath stolen my cock, and away from the neighbourhood cleared!
                                    (*Wildly.*)

        (Ye Nymphs of the Mountain give aid!
        And what's come to the scullery-maid?)
                                    (*Tearfully.*)
            And I—ah, would I were dead!—
                To my work had given my mind;
            A spindle heavy with thread
                My hands did wi-i-i-ind,
And I meant to go early to market, a suitable buyer to find!

(*Almost weeping.*)
—But he rose, rose, in the air
On quivering blades of flight;
He left me care, care;
And tears, tears of despair,
Fell, fell, and dimmed my sight!

(*Recovering himself; in florid, tragic style.*)
Children of Ida's snows,
Cretans, take up your bows,
And ring the house with many a leaping limb!
And thou, fair maid of bliss,
Dictynna, Artemis,
Range with thy bandogs through each corner dim;
Yea, Thou of twofold Fires,
Grant me my deep desires,
Thou Zeus-born Hecaté; in all men's eyes
Let the detective sheen
Flashed from thy torches keen,
Light me to Glycé's house, and that lost fowl surprise!"

DIONYSUS
Come, stop the singing!

AESCHYLUS
I've had quite enough!
What I want is to bring him to the balance;
The one sure test of what art is worth!

DIONYSUS
So that's my business next? Come forward, please;
I'll weigh out poetry like so much cheese!
(*A large pair of scales is brought forward.*)

CHORUS (*singing*)
Oh, the workings of genius are keen and laborious!
Here's a new wonder, incredible, glorious!
Who but this twain have the boldness of brain
To so quaint an invention to run?
Such a marvellous thing, if another had said it had
Happened to him, I should never have credited;
I should have just thought that he must
Simply be talking for fun!

DIONYSUS
Come, take your places by the balance.

AESCHYLUS *and* EURIPIDES
There!

DIONYSUS
Now, each take hold of it, and speak your verse,
And don't let go until I say "Cuckoo."

AESCHYLUS *and* EURIPIDES
(*taking their stand at either side of the balance*)
We have it.

DIONYSUS
Now, each a verse into the scale!

EURIPIDES
"Would God no Argo e'er had winged the brine."

AESCHYLUS
"Sperchius, and ye haunts of grazing kine!"

DIONYSUS
Cuckoo! Let go.—Ah, down comes Aeschylus
Far lower.

EURIPIDES
Why, what can be the explanation?

DIONYSUS
That river he put in, to wet his wares
The way wool-dealers do, and make them heavier!
Besides, you know, the verse you gave had wings!

AESCHYLUS
Well, let him speak another and we'll see.

DIONYSUS
Take hold again then.

AESCHYLUS *and* EURIPIDES
There you are.

DIONYSUS
Now speak.

EURIPIDES
"Persuasion, save in speech, no temple hath."

AESCHYLUS
"Lo, one god craves no offering, even Death."

DIONYSUS
Let go, let go!

EURIPIDES
Why, his goes down again!

DIONYSUS
He put in Death, a monstrous heavy thing!

EURIPIDES
But my Persuasion made a lovely line!

DIONYSUS
Persuasion has no bulk and not much weight.
Do look about you for some ponderous line
To force the scale down, something large and strong.

EURIPIDES
Where have I such a thing, now? Where?

DIONYSUS (*mischievously*)
I'll tell you:
"Achilles has two aces and a four!"—
Come, speak your lines; this is the final bout.

EURIPIDES
"A mace of weighted iron his right hand sped."

AESCHYLUS
"Chariot on chariot lay, dead piled on dead."

DIONYSUS
He beats you this time too!

EURIPIDES
How does he do it?

DIONYSUS
Two chariots and two corpses in the scale—
Why, ten Egyptians couldn't lift so much!

AESCHYLUS

Come, no more line-for-lines! Let him jump in
And sit in the scale himself, with all his books,
His wife, his children, his Cephisophon!
I'll back two lines of mine against the lot!

(*The central door opens and* PLUTO *comes forth.*)

PLUTO (*to* DIONYSUS)
                    Well, is the strife decided?

DIONYSUS

I won't decide! The men are both my friends;
Why should I make an enemy of either?
The one's so good, and I so love the other!

PLUTO

In that case you must give up all you came for!

DIONYSUS

And if I do decide?

PLUTO
                    Why, not to make
Your trouble fruitless, you may take away
Whichever you decide for.

DIONYSUS
                    Hearty thanks!
Now, both, approach, and I'll explain.—I came
Down here to fetch a poet: "Why a poet?"
That his advice may guide the city true
And so keep up my worship! Consequently,
I'll take whichever seems the best adviser.
Advise me first of Alcibiades,
Whose birth gives travail still to mother Athens.

PLUTO

What is her disposition towards him?

DIONYSUS
                    Well,
She loves and hates, and longs still to possess.
I want the views of both upon that question!

EURIPIDES

Out on the burgher, who to serve his state
Is slow, but swift to do her deadly hate,
With much wit for himself, and none for her.

DIONYSUS

Good, by Posidon, that!—And what say you?
                    (*To* AESCHYLUS.)

AESCHYLUS

No lion's whelp within thy precincts raise;
But, if it *be* there, bend thee to its ways!

DIONYSUS

By Zeus the Saviour, still I can't decide!
The one so fine, and the other so convincing!
Well, I must ask you both for one more judgment;
What steps do you advise to save our country?

EURIPIDES

I know and am prepared to say!

DIONYSUS
Say on.

EURIPIDES

Where Mistrust now has sway, put Trust to dwell,
And where Trust is, Mistrust; and all is well.

DIONYSUS

I don't quite follow. Please say that again,
Not quite so cleverly and rather plainer.

EURIPIDES

If we count all the men whom now we trust,
Suspect; and call on those whom now we spurn
To serve us, we may find deliverance yet.

DIONYSUS

And what say you?

AESCHYLUS
First tell me about the city;
What servants does she choose? The good?

DIONYSUS

Great Heavens,

She loathes them!

AESCHYLUS

And takes pleasure in the vile?

DIONYSUS

Not she, but has perforce to let them serve her!

AESCHYLUS

What hope of comfort is there for a city
That quarrels with her silk and hates her hodden?

DIONYSUS

That's just what *you* must answer, if you want
To rise again!

AESCHYLUS

I'll answer there, not here.

DIONYSUS

No; better send up blessing from below.

AESCHYLUS

Her safety is to count her enemy's land
Her own, yea, and her own her enemy's;
Her ships her treasures, and her treasure dross!

DIONYSUS

Good;—though it all goes down the juror's throat!

PLUTO

Come, give your judgment!

DIONYSUS

Well, I'll judge like this;
My choice shall fall on him my soul desires!

EURIPIDES

Remember all the gods by whom you swore
To take me home with you, and choose your friend!

DIONYSUS

My tongue hath sworn;—but I'll choose Aeschylus!

EURIPIDES

What have you done, you traitor?

DIONYSUS
I? I've judged
That Aeschylus gets the prize. Why shouldn't I?

EURIPIDES
Canst meet mine eyes, fresh from thy deed of shame?

DIONYSUS
What is shame, that the . . . Theatre deems no shame?

EURIPIDES
Hard heart! You mean to leave your old friend dead?

DIONYSUS
Who knoweth if to live is but to die? . . .
If breath is bread and sleep a woolly lie?

PLUTO
Come in, then, both.

DIONYSUS
Again?

PLUTO
To feast with me
Before you sail.

DIONYSUS
With pleasure! That's the way
Duly to crown a well-contented day!

CHORUS (*singing*)
O blessed are they who possess
An extra share of brains!
'Tis a fact that more or less
All fortunes of men express;
As now, by showing
An intellect glowing,
This man his home regains;
Brings benefit far and near
To all who may hold him dear,
And staunches his country's tear,—
All because of his brains!

Then never with Socrates
Make one of the row of fools

Who gabble away at ease,
Letting art and music freeze,
And freely neglect
In every respect
The drama's principal rules!
Oh, to sit in a gloomy herd
A-scraping of word on word,
All idle and all absurd,—
That is the fate of fools!

PLUTO

Then farewell, Aeschylus! Go your ways,
And save your town for happier days
By counsel wise; and a school prepare
For all the fools—there are plenty there!
And take me some parcels, I pray; this sword
Is for Cleophon; these pretty ropes for the board
Of providers. But ask them one halter to spare
For Nicomachus; one, too, is Myrmex's share.
    And, along with this venomous
    Draught for Archenomus,
        Take them my confident prayer,
That they all will come here for a visit, and stay.
And bid them be quick; for, should they delay,
Or meet my request with ingratitude, say
    I will fetch them myself, by Apollo!
And hurry the gang of them down with a run
All branded and chained—with Leucolophus' son
    The sublime Adimantus to follow!

AESCHYLUS

I will do as you wish.—And as for my throne,
I beg you let Sophocles sit there alone,
On guard, till perchance I return some day;
For he—all present may mark what I say—
    Is my second in art and in wit.
And see, above all, that this devil-may-care
Child of deceit with his mountebank air
Shall never on that imperial chair
    By the wildest of accidents sit!

PLUTO (*to the* CHORUS)

With holy torches in high display
    Light ye the Marchers' triumphal advance;

Let Aeschylus' music on Aeschylus' way
  Echo in song and in dance!

LEADER OF THE CHORUS

Peace go with him and joy in his journeying! Guide ye our poet
Forth to the light, ye powers that reign in the Earth and below it;
Send good thoughts with him, too, for the aid of a travailing nation,
So shall we rest at the last, and forget our long desolation,
War and the clashing of wrong.—And for Cleophon, why, if he'd rather,
Let him fight all alone with his friends, in the far-off fields of his father.

1. What the Greek literally says is as follows:

> DIONYSUS
>   Don't shift your luggage pole
> Across, and say, "I want to take a crap."

> XANTHIAS
> Nor that I've got such a weight upon my back
> That unless some one helps me quickly I shall fart?

2. Any slave that had fought in this battle was set free.

3. What the Greek literally says is as follows:

> DIONYSUS
> I went aboard Clisthenes.

> HERACLES
> Did you fight?

> DIONYSUS
> We sank twelve or thirteen enemy ships.

> HERACLES
> You two?

> DIONYSUS
> Yes, by Apollo!

> XANTHIAS (*aside*)
> And then I woke up!

> DIONYSUS
> As I was reading the *Andromeda* on the ship, I suddenly felt
> my heart afire with a wish so *very* violent!

> HERACLES
> A wish? How big a one?

996

DIONYSUS

Not so big; about as large as Molon.

HERACLES

For a woman?

DIONYSUS

No.

HERACLES

For a boy, then?

DIONYSUS

Not at all.

HERACLES

For a man, then?

DIONYSUS

Faugh!

HERACLES

Were you making love to Clisthenes?

4. What Dionysus is really saying is that the inferior poets can do no more than piddle; there is none with any seminal fluid in him.

5. The diobolus had for a long time been the standard salary of Athenian public officials, but during the Peloponnesian War the demagogues had effected an increase to three obols.

6. Literally, "or made love to a boy and cheated him out of his pay."

7. One of the chief promises which the Mysteries held out to their devotees was a blissful afterlife.

8. Ophthalmia was a very common complaint in the ancient world, but it would also seem to have been used as an excuse to escape military service.

9. What the Greek literally says is as follows:

DIONYSUS

My hands are full of blisters and my arse is covered with sweat; what with all this bending over it will soon be saying . . .

FROGS

Brekekekex koäx koäx.

10. For the details of what actually was said by this actor, see Hegelochus in the Glossary.

11. Pigs were sacrificed before the Mysteries.

12. Literally, "Defecates on Hecaté's shrines."

13. The reference is to those who had put through laws designed to reduce the costs and restrict the freedom of comedy.

14. Dionysus.

15. In the Greek Sebinus is called an Anaphlystian, for which see the Glossary, and, a little below, the name of the father of Callias is comically altered from Hipponicus to Hippocinus, "he who makes love to a mare."

16. What the Greek literally says is as follows:

XANTHIAS (*as soon as* AEACUS *has gone*)
What are you doing?

DIONYSUS (*squatting*)
I have crapped. Invoke the god.

This is sufficient to make the true sense of what follows quite clear. The phrase, "Invoke the god" was the usual utterance at libations.

17. What the Greek really says is: "Would it not be ridiculous if Xanthias, a slave, were stretched out on the Milesian cushions, kissing the dancing girl and asking for a thunder-mug, and I, watching all this, would be playing with my tool, etc."

18. The word of a slave was valid in Athenian courts only if given under torture. Since a man's personal servants would naturally know a great deal about his actions, it was a gesture of confident innocence to give one's slaves up to be examined under torture.

19. Whips of leek or shalott were used in certain religious rites in which ceremonial scourging took place.

20. These scapegoats were individuals whom the community chose to be the bearers of all their sins and then exiled or killed. This exceedingly primitive religious survival is reported to have been practised in various parts of Greece.

21. A parody of a verse, perhaps from the *Telephus,* of Euripides. Originally the word "Sea" stood in place of "Greens." Aristophanes never tires of twitting Euripides with the fact or fancy that his mother had sold vegetables.

22. Such animals were sacrificed to Typhon, the god of storms.

23. Euripides had at various times uttered in his plays highly anti-democratic sentiments. See, e.g., *Orestes* 902–930.

24. This exclamation is not found in *The Persians,* but various ungreek ones are, e.g., *oi, oá, ioá.*

25. Literally, "to fart in the face of the rower below and to crap on his mate, etc."

26. Literally, "they beat his belly, sides, flanks, and arse; these blows knocked such a fart out of him that it blew out his torch and he ran away."

27. "An ancient Athenian carried a cruse of olive oil about with him, both to anoint himself with after washing and to eat like butter with his

food. Naturally he was apt to lose it, especially when travelling. In my first edition I could find no object which both ancient Greeks and modern Englishmen would habitually use and lose except an umbrella. But since then motors have come in.

"The point of this famous bit of fooling is, I think, first, that Euripides' tragic style is so little elevated that oil-cans and clothes-bags are quite at home in it; secondly, that there is a certain monotony of grammatical structure in Euripides' prologues, so that you can constantly finish a sentence by a half-line with a verb in it.

"The first point, though burlesquely exaggerated, is true and important. Euripides' style, indeed, is not prosaic. It is strange that competent students of Greek tragic diction should ever have thought it so. But it is wide in its range, and uses colloquial words by the side of very romantic or archaic ones—a dangerous and difficult process, which only a great master of language can successfully carry through. Cf. the 'light weight' of his lines, below, 1365 ff.

"As to the second point, it is amusing to make out the statistics. Of the extant Greek tragedies, the following can have *lekythion apólese,* 'found his oil-can gone,' stuck on to one of the first ten lines of the prologue: Aesch. *Prom.* 8, *Sept.* 6, *Eum.* 3, and several other lines; Soph. *O. T.* 4, *El.* 5, *Trach.* 3 and 6, *Antig.* 2 and 7; Euripides, *Tro.* 10, *Hec.* 2, *Phoen.* 7, *Hclid.* 2 and 4, *Her.* 9, *Hel.* 4, *El.* 10, *I. A.* 54 (=6), and *I. T.* 2, quoted here. Thus all three tragedians have such passages in the opening of about half their extant plays, and the 'monotony,' if such it be, belongs rather to the style of the tragic prologue than to Euripides."—Gilbert Murray.

28. It should be noted that in the Greek this refrain does not change, but becomes increasingly meaningless in each new context.

29. The singing of more than one note for a single syllable seems to have been very late in making its appearance in Greek music, and this passage testifies to the fact that in Aristophanes' time it must have been regarded as something very new and daring.

X

THE ECCLESIAZUSAE

Characters in the Play

PRAXAGORA
BLEPYRUS, *husband of Praxagora*
WOMEN
A MAN
CHREMES
A CITIZEN
HERALD
A GIRL
A YOUNG MAN
THREE OLD WOMEN
A SERVANT MAID *to* PRAXAGORA
CHORUS OF WOMEN

INTRODUCTION

BETWEEN *The Frogs* (405) and *The Ecclesiazusae* (392) there is a gap of thirteen years during which we know next to nothing of Aristophanes' literary productions; it is abundantly clear that he did a great deal of writing in these years, but none of it has come down to us, and we are quite unable to form any notion of the nature or the quality of the work that he did at this time. Now it happens that the period 405–392 witnessed a number of events in the history of Athens which were either decisive or significant for her future development. The disaster of Aegospotami was followed in rapid succession by the siege and surrender of the city, the destruction of the walls, the second oligarchical revolution, the reign of terror under the Thirty, and the final triumph of Thrasybulus with the resultant restoration of the democracy and the proclamation of a generous amnesty. A few years later came the trial and the execution of Socrates, and the epoch designated, not without invidious overtones, as the fourth century had evidently begun long before 392. The cultural differences, really qualitative, but often perversely conceived in quantitative terms, between this century and its immediate predecessor inevitably prejudice the reader of the two latest of the plays of Aristophanes, and the mere fact that they were written after 400 condemns them beforehand in the eyes of the excusably partisan or culpably myopic lover of fifth-century Athenian civilization. Even a casual reading of *The Ecclesiazusae* discovers the absence of the parabasis and the reduced importance of the Chorus, but a more intimate acquaintance with the play reveals that within a changed form the poet is still Aristophanes; his best years are behind him, but his dotage, if he ever had any, lies in the far distant future.

There is much in the play that is reminiscent of *Lysistrata*, and if *The Frogs* suggests a successful production of *The Thesmophoriazusae*, *The Ecclesiazusae* may furnish similar, if less cogent, evidence of an earlier victory in 411. In *Lysistrata* we witness the women of Athens effecting a successful revolution to put an end to the war; *The Ecclesiazusae* we find their seizure of power establishing community of property as a

1003

panacea for all the social and economic ills which beset Athens in the first two decades of the fourth century. Thus an Utopian subject and a feminine insurrection permit us to deduce a twofold legacy from both *The Birds* and *Lysistrata,* but the similarities to the latter are more numerous and more specific.

The initial scene is the most remarkable of these, for when the play opens we are presented with the revolutionary leader Praxagora anxiously awaiting the arrival of her fellow conspirators, who have promised to meet her here, in front of her house, at this time. One by one they put in an appearance, and when their number is finally complete, Praxagora instructs and exercises them in the proper and masculine mode of behaviour in the Assembly. As soon as they have satisfied her that they will not betray their sex and thwart her purposes, they don the clothes they have filched from their husbands, attach the false beards they have secretly procured, and Praxagora leads them off to the Assembly, where they hope to seize the helm of state and establish the new order of society.

Immediately after their departure a distressed and ludicrous figure emerges from the house; it is Blepyrus, the husband of Praxagora, whom an urgent need to defecate has driven outdoors wearing his wife's clothes, the only garments which the confused and harassed man has been able to find in the dark. Soon a friend of his, with the prophetic name of Chremes, appears, newly returned from the Assembly, and reports the extraordinary enactments that have just been adopted. The session was unusually well attended, and a great multitude of pale-faced persons, looking like shoemakers, had arrived early and preëmpted the front seats. One of their number, a very beautiful young man, made an eloquent and persuasive speech, in which he proposed that the direction of public affairs be entrusted to the women of the state, and the motion was carried amidst the enthusiastic plaudits of the shoemakers. "It's the one and only innovation that has *not* yet been tried at Athens," remarks Aristophanes, under the mask of Chremes, and we remember that the poet has lived through a lot of history. Blepyrus is delighted with the vision of the luxurious and indolent life he is henceforth to lead, and the two friends part just before Praxagora and the women who form the Chorus return from their legislative adventure. They fortunately have sufficient time to discard their masculine disguises before the reappearance of Blepyrus, who gratuitously informs his wife of the developments in the Assembly. She soon takes the lead in the conversation, and proceeds to explain the operation and to demonstrate the perfection of the new organization of society. The ductile Blepyrus is easily converted, and, entranced by the prospect of being pointed out as the husband of the dictator, he follows his wife to the market-place, where she is to supervise the redistribution of property. We might expect a parabasis at this point, but the manuscripts of the play merely indicate that the Chorus performed a dance, and we are forcibly reminded that we are in the Fourth Century.

In the scene which follows, we find a highly witty dialogue between Chremes, who has arranged his property in a travesty of a sacred procession and intends to devote it to the common store, and a nameless citizen who adopts a thoroughly sceptical attitude toward the new order, preferring to wait and see how the others act. The arrival, however, of a female herald to announce a sumptuous feast provided by the state puts a new complexion on things, and the wily citizen, proposing to share the benefits without assuming any of the burdens of the new economy, follows Chremes to the public banquet.

The community of property established by the revolutionaries is to apply not only to material things but also to the relationships between the sexes. The women are not, however, unaware that the economy of free love cannot be allowed to operate on the principle of *laissez-faire,* and have consequently decreed that the old and the unattractive are to have prior rights over the young and the beautiful. The final scene of the comedy exhibits a specimen case of the practical workings of this arrangement. The two houses of the stage-setting are now those of two prostitutes, the one youthful and alluring, the other all too liberally endowed with years and cosmetics. A young man who finds himself strongly attracted to the girl is horrified to discover that he must satisfy the demands of the old woman first, but his arguments and his resistance are entirely fruitless; the law must be obeyed and he resigns himself to the inevitable. Just as he is about to enter the old woman's house he is rescued by the girl, but his joy is not destined to endure, and the unfortunate fellow is almost immediately set upon by a woman far older and much more hideous than the first. His youthful rescuer retires from the unequal contest, but just as the second old woman is taking him home with her, a voice from behind demands where she is going. The young man invokes blessings on his unknown saviour's head, only to discover that it is a third old woman, frightful beyond belief; and he is now dragged off by two harridans, one on each arm. Their contesting claims are left unsettled, and the play ends with an appeal to the judges and the departure of the Chorus for the feast.

The Utopia established by Praxagora bears so remarkable a resemblance to the ideal state described in Plato's *Republic* that the precise nature of the obvious connection between the comedy and the Dialogue has been the subject of much discussion. The chronological difficulty arising from the fact that *The Republic* cannot have been published until about twenty years after *The Ecclesiazusae* leaves us a choice of two explanations, since no one wishes to assume that the philosopher's theories were derived from the dramatist's caricatures. It may be that community of property had already been suggested as a social and economic panacea, but it seems more reasonable to suppose that the ideas presented in *The Republic* were known for some time before their final publication.

The Ecclesiazusae is far from being one of the best of Aristophanes' comedies, and its form is more suggestive of the Middle than of the Old Comedy, but it presents an amusing subject treated with great wit in a play that is very well constructed, and its faults are those of its time rather than of its author. Much of the adverse criticism which has been levelled against it has been motivated by prudery, and a puritanical hostility has sought and unfortunately been able to find a number of minor flaws which give a specious validity to an unreasoning prejudice. When we approach it rationally and candidly we are pleasantly surprised to discover that it is a far better play than we had been led to expect.

THE ECCLESIAZUSAE

(SCENE:—*The Orchestra represents a public square in Athens; in the background are two houses with an alley between them.*)

PRAXAGORA

(*swinging the lantern, which is to be a signal for the other women; in high tragic style*)

OH! THOU shining light of my earthenware lamp, from this high spot shalt thou look abroad. Oh! lamp, I will tell thee thine origin and thy future; 'tis the rapid whirl of the potter's wheel that has lent thee thy shape, and thy wick counterfeits the glory of the sun; mayst thou send the agreed signal flashing afar! In thee alone do we confide, and thou art worthy, for thou art near us when we practise the various postures in which Aphrodité delights upon our couches, and none dreams even in the midst of her sports of seeking to avoid thine eye that watches us. Thou alone shinest into the secret recesses of our thighs and dost singe the hair that groweth there, and with thy flame dost light the actions of our loves. If we open some cellar stored with fruits and wine, thou art our companion, and never dost thou betray or reveal to a neighbour the secrets thou hast learned about us. Therefore thou shalt know likewise the whole of the plot that I have planned with my friends, the women, at the festival of the Scirophoria.

(*She pauses and looks about her.*)

I see none of those I was expecting, though dawn approaches; the Assembly is about to gather and we must take our seats in spite of Phyromachus, who forsooth would say, "It is meet the women sit apart and hidden from the eyes of the men." Why, have they not been able then to procure the false beards that they must wear, or to steal their husbands' cloaks? Ah! I see a light approaching; let us draw somewhat aside, for fear it should be a man.

(*She hides in the alley. From the right a woman enters, followed almost immediately by others. All are carrying staffs, men's sandals, and cloaks over their arms.*)

FIRST WOMAN

Let us start, it is high time; as we left our dwellings, the cock was crowing for the second time.

PRAXAGORA (*to herself*)

And I have spent the whole night waiting for you. (*She emerges from the alley.*) But come, let us call our neighbour by scratching at her door; and gently too, so that her husband may hear nothing.

SECOND WOMAN

(*coming out of her house; she is dressed like a man, with a staff in her hand*)

I was putting on my shoes, when I heard you scratching, for I was not asleep, so there! Oh! my dear, my husband (he is a Salaminian) never left me an instant's peace, but was at me, for ever at me, all night long, so that it was only just now that I was able to filch his cloak.

PRAXAGORA

I see Clinareté coming too, along with Sostraté and their next-door neighbour Philaeneté. (*To the women that are just arriving; in a loud voice*) Hurry yourselves then, for Glycé has sworn that the last comer shall forfeit three measures of wine and a *choenix* of pease.

SECOND WOMAN

Don't you see Melisticé, the wife of Smicythion, hurrying hither in her big shoes? I think she is the only one of us all who has had no trouble in getting rid of her husband.

FIRST WOMAN

And can't you see Geusistraté, the tavern-keeper's wife, with a lamp in her hand?

PRAXAGORA

And the wives of Philodoretus and Chaeretades, and a great many others; all the useful people in the city, in fact.

THIRD WOMAN

Oh! my dear, I have had such trouble in getting away! My husband ate such a surfeit of sprats last evening that he was coughing and choking the whole night long.

PRAXAGORA

Take your seats, and, since you are all gathered here at last, let us see if what we decided on at the feast of the Scirophoria has been duly done.

FIRST WOMAN

Yes. Firstly, as agreed, I have let the hair under my armpits grow thicker than a bush; furthermore, whilst my husband was at the Assembly, I rubbed myself from head to foot with oil and then stood the whole day long in the sun.

SECOND WOMAN

So did I. I began by throwing away my razor, so that I might get quite hairy, and no longer resemble a woman.

PRAXAGORA

Have you the beards that we had all to get ourselves for the Assembly?

FIRST WOMAN

Yea, by Hecaté! Is this not a fine one?

SECOND WOMAN

Aye, much finer even than the one Epicrates has.

PRAXAGORA (*to the other women*)

And you?

FIRST WOMAN

Yes, yes; look, they all nod assent.

PRAXAGORA

I see that you have got all the rest too, Spartan shoes, staffs and men's cloaks, as it was arranged.

FIRST WOMAN

I have brought Lamias' club, which I stole from him while he slept.

PRAXAGORA

What, the club that makes him fart with its weight?

SECOND WOMAN

By Zeus the Deliverer, if he had the skin of Argus, he would know better than any other how to shepherd the popular herd.

PRAXAGORA

But come, let us finish what has yet to be done, while the stars are still shining; the Assembly, at which we mean to be present, will open at dawn.

FIRST WOMAN

Good; you must take up your place at the foot of the platform and facing the Prytanes.

SECOND WOMAN

I have brought this with me to card during the Assembly.

(*She shows some wool.*)

PRAXAGORA

During the Assembly, wretched woman?

SECOND WOMAN

Surely, by Artemis! shall I hear any less well if I am doing a bit of carding? My little ones are all but naked.

PRAXAGORA

Think of her wanting to card! whereas we must not let anyone see the smallest part of our bodies.[1] 'Twould be a fine thing if one of us, in the midst of the discussion, rushed on to the speaker's platform and, flinging her cloak aside, showed her Phormisius. If, on the other hand, we are the first to take our seats closely muffled in our cloaks, none will know us. Let us fix these beards on our chins, so that they spread all over our bosoms. How can we fail then to be mistaken for men? Agyrrhius has deceived everyone, thanks to the beard of Pronomus; yet he was no better than a woman, and you see how he now holds the first position in the city. Thus, I adjure you by this day that is about to dawn, let us dare to copy him and let us be clever enough to possess ourselves of the management of affairs. Let us save the ship of state, which just at present none seems able either to sail or row.

FIRST WOMAN (*in a tragic style*)

But where shall we find orators in an Assembly of women?

PRAXAGORA

Nothing simpler. Is it not said that the cleverest speakers are those who get made love to most often? Well, thanks to the gods, we are that by nature.

FIRST WOMAN

There's no doubt of that; but the worst of it is our inexperience.

PRAXAGORA

That's the very reason we are gathered here, in order to prepare the speech we must make in the Assembly. Hasten, therefore, all you who know aught of speaking, to fix on your beards.

SECOND WOMAN

Oh! you stupid thing! is there ever a one among us cannot use her tongue?

PRAXAGORA

Come, look sharp, on with your beard and become a man. As for me,
I will do the same in case I should have a fancy for getting on to the platform. Here are the chaplets.

(*They all put on their beards.*)

SECOND WOMAN

Oh! great gods! my dear Praxagora, do look here! Is it not laughable?

PRAXAGORA

How laughable?

SECOND WOMAN

Our beards look like broiled cuttle-fishes.

PRAXAGORA (*pretending to be the herald*)

Priest, bring in the cat.² Step forward, please! Silence, Ariphrades! Go
and take your seat. Now, who wishes to speak?

SECOND WOMAN

I do.

PRAXAGORA

Then put on this chaplet and success be with you.

SECOND WOMAN

There!

PRAXAGORA

Well then! begin.

SECOND WOMAN

Before drinking?

PRAXAGORA

Hah! she wants to drink!

SECOND WOMAN

Why, what else is the meaning of this chaplet?

PRAXAGORA

Get you hence! you would probably have played us this trick also before the people.

SECOND WOMAN

Well! don't the men drink then in the Assembly? ³

PRAXAGORA

Now she's telling us the men drink!

SECOND WOMAN

Yes, by Artemis, and neat wine too. That's why their decrees breathe of drunkenness and madness. And why libations, why so many cere-monies, if wine plays no part in them? Besides, they abuse each other like drunken men, and you can see the archers dragging more than one uproarious drunkard out of the market-place.

PRAXAGORA

Go back to your seat, you are wandering.

SECOND WOMAN (*returning to her seat*)

Ah! I should have done better not to have muffled myself in this beard; my throat's afire and I feel I shall die of thirst.

PRAXAGORA

Who else wishes to speak?

FIRST WOMAN (*rising*)

I do.

PRAXAGORA

Quick then, take the chaplet; the time's running short. Try to speak worthily, let your language be truly manly, and lean on your staff with dignity.

FIRST WOMAN

I had rather have seen one of your regular orators giving you wise advice; but, as that is not to be, it behoves me to break silence; I cannot, for my part indeed, allow the tavern-keepers to fill up their wine-pits with water. No, by the two goddesses . . .

PRAXAGORA

What? by the two goddesses! [4] Wretched woman, where are your senses?

FIRST WOMAN

Eh! what? . . . I have not asked you for a drink.

PRAXAGORA

No, but you want to pass for a man, and you swear by the two god-desses. Otherwise you did very well.

FIRST WOMAN

Well then. By Apollo . . .

PRAXAGORA

Stop! All these details of language must be adjusted; else it is quite useless to go to the Assembly.

FIRST WOMAN

Give me back the chaplet; I wish to speak again, for I think I have got hold of something good. You women who are listening to me . . .

PRAXAGORA

Women again; why, you wretched creature, it's men that you are addressing.

FIRST WOMAN

That's the fault of Epigonus; I caught sight of him way over there, and I thought I was speaking to women.

PRAXAGORA

Come, withdraw and remain seated in the future. I am going to take this chaplet myself and speak in your name. May the gods grant success to my plans!

My country is as dear to me as it is to you, and I groan, I am grieved at all that is happening in it. Scarcely one in ten of those who rule it is honest, and all the others are bad. If you appoint fresh chiefs, they will do still worse. It is hard to correct your peevish humour; you fear those who love you and throw yourselves at the feet of those who betray you. There was a time when we had no assemblies, and then we all thought Agyrrhius a dishonest man; now they are established, he who gets money thinks everything is as it should be, and he who does not, declares all who sell their votes to be worthy of death.

SECOND WOMAN

By Aphrodité, that is well spoken.

PRAXAGORA

Why, wretched woman, you have actually called upon Aphrodité. Oh! what a fine thing it would have been if you had said that in the Assembly!

SECOND WOMAN

But I would not have done it then.

PRAXAGORA

Well, mind you don't fall into the habit. (*Resuming the oratorical manner*) When we were discussing the alliance,[5] it seemed as though it were all over with Athens if it fell through. No sooner was it made than we were vexed and angry, and the orator who had caused its adoption was compelled to seek safety in flight. Is there talk of equipping a fleet?

The poor man says, yes, but the rich citizen and the countryman say, no. You were angered against the Corinthians and they with you; now they are well disposed towards you, be so towards them. As a rule the Argives are dull, but the Argive Hieronymus is a distinguished chief. Herein lies a spark of hope; but Thrasybulus is far from Athens and you do not recall him.

SECOND WOMAN

Oh! what a brilliant man!

PRAXAGORA (*to her*)

That's better! that's fitting applause. (*Continuing her speech*) Citizens, you are the ones who are the cause of all this trouble. You vote yourselves salaries out of the public funds and care only for your own personal interests; hence the state limps along like Aesimus. But if you hearken to me, you will be saved. I assert that the direction of affairs must be handed over to the women, for they are the ones who have charge and look after our households.

ALL THE WOMEN

Very good, very good, that's perfect! Go on, go on.

PRAXAGORA (*ignoring this interruption*)

They are worth more than you are, as I shall prove. First of all they wash all their wool in warm water, according to the ancient practice; you will never see them changing their method. Ah! if Athens only acted thus, if it did not take delight in ceaseless innovations, would not its happiness be assured? Then the women sit down to cook, just as they always did; they carry things on their head just as they always did; they keep the Thesmophoria, just as they always did; they knead their cakes just as they always did; they make their husbands angry just as they always did; they receive their lovers in their houses just as they always did; they buy dainties just as they always did; they love unmixed wine just as they always did; they delight in being loved just as they always did. Let us therefore hand Athens over to them without endless discussions, without bothering ourselves about what they will do; let us simply hand them over the power, remembering that they are mothers and will therefore spare the blood of our soldiers; besides, who will know better than a mother how to forward provisions to the front? Woman is adept at getting money for herself and will not easily let herself be deceived; she understands deceit too well herself. I omit a thousand other advantages. Take my advice and you will live in perfect happiness.

FIRST WOMAN

How beautiful this is, my dearest Praxagora, how clever! But where, pray, did you learn all these pretty things?

PRAXAGORA

When the countryfolk were seeking refuge in the city,[6] I lived on the Pnyx with my husband, and there I learnt to speak through listening to the orators.

FIRST WOMAN

Then, dear, it's not astonishing that you are so eloquent and clever; henceforward you shall be our leader, so put your great ideas into execution. But if Cephalus belches forth insults against you, what answer will you give him in the Assembly?

PRAXAGORA

I shall say that he is drivelling.

FIRST WOMAN

But all the world knows that.

PRAXAGORA

I shall furthermore say that he is a raving madman.

FIRST WOMAN

There's nobody who does not know that.

PRAXAGORA

That he, as excellent a statesman as he is, is a clumsy potter.

FIRST WOMAN

And if the blear-eyed Neoclides comes to insult you?

PRAXAGORA

To him I shall say, "Go and look at a dog's arse."

FIRST WOMAN

And if they fly at you?

PRAXAGORA

Oh! I shall shake them off as best I can; never fear, I know how to use this tool.[7]

FIRST WOMAN

But there is one thing we don't think of. If the Scythians drag you away, what will you do?

PRAXAGORA

With my arms akimbo like this, I will never, never let myself be taken round the middle.

FIRST WOMAN

If they seize you, we will bid them let you go.

SECOND WOMAN

That's the best way. But how are we going to remember to lift our arms in the Assembly when it's our legs we are used to lifting?

PRAXAGORA

It's difficult; yet it must be done, and the arm shown naked to the shoulder in order to vote. Quick now, put on these tunics and these Laconian shoes, as you see the men do each time they go to the Assembly or for a walk. When this is done, fix on your beards, and when they are arranged in the best way possible, dress yourselves in the cloaks you have stolen from your husbands; finally start off, leaning on your staffs and singing some old man's song as the villagers do.

FIRST WOMAN

Well spoken; and let us hurry to get to the Pnyx before the women from the country, for they will no doubt not fail to come there.

PRAXAGORA

Quick, quick, for it's the custom that those who are not at the Pnyx early in the morning return home empty-handed.

(PRAXAGORA *and the* FIRST *and* SECOND WOMEN *depart; those who are left behind form the* CHORUS.)

LEADER OF THE CHORUS

Move forward, citizens, move forward; let us not forget to give ourselves this name and may that of *woman* never slip out of our mouths; woe to us, if it were discovered that we had laid such a plot in the darkness of night.

CHORUS (*singing*)

Let us go to the Assembly then, fellow-citizens; for the Thesmothetes have declared that only those who arrive at daybreak with haggard eye and covered with dust, without having snatched time to eat anything but a snack of garlic-pickle, shall alone receive the triobolus. Walk up smartly, Charitimides, Smicythus and Draces, and do not fail in any point of your part; let us first demand our fee and then vote for all that may perchance be useful for our partisans. . . . Ah! what am I saying? I meant to say, for our fellow-citizens. Let us drive away these men of the city who used to stay at home and chatter round the table in the days when only an obolus was paid, whereas now one is stifled by the crowds at the Pnyx. No! during the archonship of generous Myronides, none would have dared to let himself be paid for the trouble he spent over public business; each one brought his own meal of bread, a couple of onions, three olives and some wine in a little wine-skin. But nowadays we run here to earn the three obols, for the citizen has become as mercenary as the stonemason.

(*The* CHORUS *marches away.* BLEPYRUS *appears in the doorway of his house, wearing* PRAXAGORA'S *Persian sandals and saffron robe.*)

BLEPYRUS

What does this mean? My wife has vanished! it is nearly daybreak and she does not return! I had to take a crap! I woke up and hunted in the darkness for my shoes and my cloak; but grope where I would, I couldn't find them. Meanwhile Mr. O'Shit [8] was already knocking on the door and I had only just time to seize my wife's little mantle and her Persian slippers. But where shall I find a place where I *can* take a crap? Bah! One place is as good as another at night-time; no one will see me. Ah! what a damned fool I was to take a wife at my age, and how I could thrash myself for having acted so stupidly! It's certainty she's not gone out for any honest purpose. But the thing to do now is to take a crap.

(*He squats.*)

A MAN (*looking out of the window of the house next door*)

Who's that? Is that not my neighbour Blepyrus? Why, yes, it's no other. Tell me, what's all that yellow about you? Can it be Cinesias who has befouled you so?

BLEPYRUS

No, no, I only slipped on my wife's tunic to come out in.

MAN

And where is your cloak?

BLEPYRUS

I cannot tell you; I hunted for it vainly on the bed.

MAN

And why did you not ask your wife for it?

BLEPYRUS

Ah! why indeed! because she is not in the house; she has run away, and I greatly fear that she may be doing me an ill turn.

MAN

But, by Posidon, it's the same with myself. My wife has disappeared with my cloak, and what is still worse, with my shoes as well; I cannot find them anywhere.

BLEPYRUS

Nor can I my Laconian ones; but as I urgently needed to crap, I popped my feet into these slippers, so as not to soil my blanket, which is brand new.

MAN

What does it mean? Can some friend have invited her to a feast?

BLEPYRUS

I expect so, for she does not generally misconduct herself, as far as I know.

MAN

What are you doing, making well-ropes? Are you never going to be done? As for myself, I would like to go to the Assembly, and it is time to start, but I've got to find my cloak; I have only one.

BLEPYRUS

I am going to have a look too, when I have finished crapping; but I really think there must be a wild pear obstructing my rectum.

MAN

Is it the one which Thrasybulus spoke about to the Lacedaemonians?

BLEPYRUS

Oh! oh! oh! how stopped up I am! Whatever am I to do? It's not merely for the present that I am frightened; but when I have eaten, where is my crap to find an outlet now? This damned McPear [9] fellow has bolted the door. Call a doctor; but who is the cleverest in this branch o the science? Amynon? Perhaps he would not come. Ah! Antisthenes! Let him be brought to me, cost what it will. To judge by his noisy sighs, that man knows what an arse wants, when it needs to crap. Oh! venerated Ilithyia! I shall burst unless the door gives way. Have pity! pity! Let me not become a thunder-mug for the comic poets.

(*Enter* CHREMES, *returning from the Assembly.*)

CHREMES

Hi! friend, what are you doing there? You're not crapping, are you?

BLEPYRUS (*finding relief at last*)

Oh! there! it is over and I can get up again.

CHREMES

What's this? You have your wife's tunic on.

BLEPYRUS

It was the first thing that came to my hand in the darkness. But where are you coming from?

CHREMES

From the Assembly.

BLEPYRUS

Is it already over then?

CHREMES

Certainly.

BLEPYRUS

Why, it is scarcely daylight.

CHREMES

I did laugh, ye gods, at the vermilion rope-marks that were to be seen all about the Assembly.[10]

BLEPYRUS

Did you get the triobolus?

CHREMES

Would it had so pleased the gods! but I arrived just too late, and am quite ashamed of it; I bring back nothing but this empty wallet.

BLEPYRUS

But why is that?

CHREMES

There was a crowd, such as has never been seen at the Pnyx, and the folk looked pale and wan, like so many shoemakers, so white were they in hue; both I and many another had to go without the triobolus.

BLEPYRUS

Then if I went now, I should get nothing.

CHREMES

No, certainly not, nor even had you gone at the second cock-crow.

BLEPYRUS

Oh! what a misfortune! "Oh, Antilochus! no triobolus! Even death would be better! I am undone!" But what can have attracted such a crowd at that early hour?

CHREMES

The Prytanes started the discussion of measures closely concerning the safety of the state; immediately, that blear-eyed fellow, the son of Neoclides, was the first to mount the platform. Then the folk shouted with their loudest voice, "What! he dares to speak, and that, too, when the safety of the state is concerned, and he a man who has not known how to save even his own eyebrows!" He, however, shouted louder than all of them, and looking at them asked, "Why, what ought I to have done?"

BLEPYRUS

Pound together garlic and laserpitium juice, add to this mixture some Laconian spurge, and rub it well into the eyelids at night. That's what I should have answered, had I been there.

CHREMES

After him that clever rascal Evaeon began to speak; he was naked, so far as we all could see, but he declared he had a cloak; he propounded the most popular, the most democratic, doctrines. "You see," he said, "I have the greatest need of sixteen drachmae, the cost of a new cloak, my health demands it; nevertheless I wish first to care for that of my fellow-citizens and of my country. If the fullers were to supply tunics to the indigent at the approach of winter, none would be exposed to pleurisy. Let him who has neither beds nor coverlets go to sleep at the tanners' after taking a bath; and if they shut the door in winter, let them be condemned to give him three goat-skins."

BLEPYRUS

By Dionysus, a fine, a very fine notion! Not a soul will vote against his proposal, especially if he adds that the flour-sellers must supply the poor with three measures of corn, or else suffer the severest penalties of the law; this is the only way Nausicydes can be of any use to us.

CHREMES

Then we saw a handsome young man rush into the tribune, he was all pink and white like young Nicias, and he began to say that the direction of matters should be entrusted to the women; this the crowd of shoe-makers began applauding with all their might, while the country-folk assailed him with groans.

BLEPYRUS

And, indeed, they did well.

CHREMES

But they were outnumbered, and the orator shouted louder than they, saying much good of the women and much ill of you.

BLEPYRUS (*eagerly*)
And what did he say?

CHREMES
First he said you were a rogue . . .

BLEPYRUS
And you?

CHREMES
Wait a minute! . . . and a thief . . .

BLEPYRUS
I alone?

CHREMES
And an informer.

BLEPYRUS
I alone?

CHREMES
Why, no, by the gods! this whole crowd here.

> (*He points to the audience.*)

BLEPYRUS
And who avers the contrary?

CHREMES
He maintained that women were both clever and thrifty, that they never divulged the Mysteries of Demeter, while you and I go about babbling incessantly about whatever happens at the Senate.

BLEPYRUS
By Hermes, he was not lying!

CHREMES
Then he added that the women lend each other clothes, trinkets of gold and silver, drinking-cups, and not before witnesses too, but all by themselves, and that they return everything with exactitude without ever cheating each other; whereas, according to him, *we* are ever ready to deny the loans we have effected.

BLEPYRUS
Yes, by Posidon, and in spite of witnesses.

CHREMES

Again, he said that women were not informers, nor did they bring lawsuits, nor hatch conspiracies; in short, he praised the women in every possible manner.

BLEPYRUS

And what was decided?

CHREMES

To confide the direction of affairs to them; it's the one and only innovation that has *not* yet been tried at Athens.

BLEPYRUS

And *it* was voted?

CHREMES

Yes.

BLEPYRUS

And everything that used to be the men's concern has been given over to the women?

CHREMES

You express it exactly.

BLEPYRUS

Thus it will be my wife who will go to the courts now in my stead?

CHREMES

And it will be she who will keep your children in your place.

BLEPYRUS

I shall no longer have to tire myself out with work from daybreak onwards?

CHREMES

No, 'twill be the women's business, and you can stay at home and amuse yourself with farting the whole day through.

BLEPYRUS

Well, what I fear for us fellows now is, that, holding the reins of government, they will forcibly compel us . . .

CHREMES

To do what?

BLEPYRUS

. . . to lay them.

CHREMES

And if we are not able?

BLEPYRUS

They will give us no dinner.

CHREMES

Well then, do your duty; dinner and love-making form a double enjoyment.

BLEPYRUS

Ah! but I hate compulsion.

CHREMES

But if it is for the public good, let us resign ourselves. It's an old saying that our absurdest and maddest decrees always somehow turn out for our good. May it be so in this case, oh gods, oh venerable Pallas! But I must be off; so, good-bye to you!
(*Exit.*)

BLEPYRUS

Good-bye, Chremes.

(*He goes back into his house.*)

CHORUS (*returning from the Assembly, still dressed like men; singing*)
March along, go forward. Is there some man following us? Turn round, examine everywhere and keep a good look-out; be on your guard against every trick, for they might spy on us from behind. Let us make as much noise as possible as we tramp. It would be a disgrace for all of us if we allowed ourselves to be caught in this deed by the men. Come, wrap yourselves up well, and search both right and left, so that no mischance may happen to us. Let us hasten our steps; here we are close to the meeting-place whence we started for the Assembly, and here is the house of our leader, the author of this bold scheme, which is now decreed by all the citizens. Let us not lose a moment in taking off our false beards, for we might be recognized and denounced. Let us stand under the shadow of this wall; let us glance round sharply with our eye to beware of surprises, while we quickly resume our ordinary dress. Ah! here is our leader, returning from the Assembly. Hasten to relieve your chins of these flowing manes. Look at your comrades yonder; they have already made themselves women again some while ago.
(*They remove the beards as* PRAXAGORA *and the other women enter from the right through the Orchestra.*)

PRAXAGORA

Friends, success has crowned our plans. But off with these cloaks and these boots quick, before any man sees you; unbuckle the Laconian straps and get rid of your staffs; (*to the* LEADER) and you help them with their toilet. As for myself, I am going to slip quietly into the house and replace my husband's cloak and other gear where I took them from, before he can suspect anything.

LEADER OF THE CHORUS

There! it's done according to your bidding. Now tell us how we can be of service to you, so that we may show you our obedience, for we have never seen a cleverer woman than you.

PRAXAGORA

Wait! I only wish to use the power given me in accordance with your wishes; for, in the market-place, in the midst of the shouts and danger, I appreciated your indomitable courage.
(*Just as she is about to enter the house* BLEPYRUS *appears in the doorway.*)

BLEPYRUS

Eh, Praxagora! where are you coming from?

PRAXAGORA

How does that concern you, dear?

BLEPYRUS

Why, greatly! what a silly question!

PRAXAGORA

You don't think I have come from a lover's?

BLEPYRUS

No, perhaps not from only one.

PRAXAGORA

You can make yourself sure of that.

BLEPYRUS

And how?

PRAXAGORA

You can see whether my hair smells of perfume.

BLEPYRUS

What? cannot a woman possibly be laid without perfume, eh!

PRAXAGORA

The gods forfend, as far as I am concerned.

BLEPYRUS

Why did you go off at early dawn with my cloak?

PRAXAGORA

A companion, a friend who was in labour, had sent to fetch me.

BLEPYRUS

Could you not have told me?

PRAXAGORA

Oh, my dear, would you have me caring nothing for a poor woman in that plight?

BLEPYRUS

A word would have been enough. There's something behind all this.

PRAXAGORA

No, I call the goddesses to witness! I went running off; the poor woman who summoned me begged me to come, whatever might betide.

BLEPYRUS

And why did you not take *your* mantle? Instead of that, you carry off mine, you throw your dress upon the bed and you leave me as the dead are left, bar the chaplets and perfumes.

PRAXAGORA

It was cold, and I am frail and delicate; I took your cloak for greater warmth, leaving you thoroughly warm yourself beneath your coverlets.

BLEPYRUS

And my shoes and staff, those too went off with you?

PRAXAGORA

I was afraid they might rob me of the cloak, and so, to look like a man, I put on your shoes and walked with a heavy tread and struck the stones with your staff.

BLEPYRUS

D'you know you have made us lose a *sextary* of wheat, which I should have bought with the triobolus of the Assembly?

PRAXAGORA

Be comforted, for she had a boy.

BLEPYRUS

Who? the Assembly?

PRAXAGORA

No, no, the woman I helped. But has the Assembly taken place then?

BLEPYRUS

Did I not tell you of it yesterday?

PRAXAGORA

True; I remember now.

BLEPYRUS

And don't you know the decrees that have been voted?

PRAXAGORA

No indeed.

BLEPYRUS

Go to! you can live on lobster from now on, for they say the government is handed over to you.

PRAXAGORA

To do what—to spin?

BLEPYRUS

No, that you may rule . . .

PRAXAGORA

What?

BLEPYRUS

. . . over all public business.

PRAXAGORA (*as she exclaims this* CHREMES *reappears*)
Oh! by Aphrodité! how happy Athens will be!

BLEPYRUS

Why so?

PRAXAGORA

For a thousand reasons. None will dare now to do shameless deeds, to give false testimony or lay informations.

BLEPYRUS

Stop! in the name of the gods! Do you want me to die of hunger?

CHREMES

Good sir, let your wife speak.

PRAXAGORA

There will be no more thieves, nor envious people, no more rags nor misery, no more abuse and no more prosecutions and law-suits.

CHREMES

By Posidon! that's grand, if it's true!

PRAXAGORA

I shall prove it and you shall be my witness and even he (*pointing to Blepyrus*) will have no objections to raise.

CHORUS (*singing*)

You have served your friends, but now it behoves you to apply your ability and your care to the welfare of the people. Devote the fecundity of your mind to the public weal; adorn the citizens' lives with a thousand enjoyments and teach them to seize every favourable opportunity. Devise some ingenious method to secure the much-needed salvation of Athens; but let neither your acts nor your words recall anything of the past, for 'tis only innovations that please.

LEADER OF THE CHORUS

But do not fail to put your plans into execution immediately; it's quick action that pleases the audience.

PRAXAGORA

I believe my ideas are good, but what I fear is that the public will cling to the old customs and refuse to accept my reforms.

CHREMES

Have no fear about that. Love of novelty and disdain for traditions, these are the dominating principles among us.

PRAXAGORA (*to the audience*)

Let none contradict nor interrupt me until I have explained my plan. I want all to have a share of everything and all property to be in common; there will no longer be either rich or poor; no longer shall we see one man harvesting vast tracts of land, while another has not ground enough to be buried in, nor one man surround himself with a whole army of slaves, while another has not a single attendant; I intend that there shall only be one and the same condition of life for all.

BLEPYRUS

But how do you mean for all?

PRAXAGORA (*impatiently*)
You'll eat dung before I do! [11]

BLEPYRUS
Won't the dung be common too?

PRAXAGORA
No, no, but you interrupted me too soon. This is what I was going to
say: shall begin by making land, money, everything that is private property, common to all. Then we shall live on this common wealth, which
we shall take care to administer with wise thrift.

BLEPYRUS
And how about the man who has no land, but only gold and silver coins,
that cannot be seen?

PRAXAGORA
He must bring them to the common stock, and if he fails he will be a
perjured man.

BLEPYRUS
That won't worry him much, for has he not gained them by perjury?

PRAXAGORA
But his riches will no longer be of any use to him.

BLEPYRUS
Why?

PRAXAGORA
The poor will no longer be obliged to work; each will have all that he
needs, bread, salt fish, cakes, tunics, wine, chaplets and chick-pease; of
what advantage will it be to him not to contribute his share to the common wealth? What do you think of it?

BLEPYRUS
But is it not the biggest robbers that have all these things?

CHREMES
Yes, formerly, under the old order of things; but now that all goods are
in common, what will he gain by not bringing his wealth into the general
stock?

BLEPYRUS
If someone saw a pretty wench and wished to lay her, he would take
some of his reserve store to make her a present and stay the night with
her; this would not prevent him claiming his share of the common property.

PRAXAGORA

But he can sleep with her for nothing; I intend that women shall belong to all men in common, and each shall beget children by any man that wishes to have her.

BLEPYRUS

But all will go to the prettiest woman and try to lay her.

PRAXAGORA

The ugliest and the most flat-nosed will be side by side with the most charming, and to win the latter's favours, a man will first have to get into the former.

BLEPYRUS

But what about us oldsters? If we have to lay the old women first, how can we keep our tools from failing before we get into the Promised Land?

PRAXAGORA

They will make no resistance. Never fear; they will make no resistance.

BLEPYRUS

Resistance to what?

PRAXAGORA

To the pleasure of the thing. This is the way that matters will be ordered for you.

BLEPYRUS

It's very well conceived for you women, for every wench's hole will be filled; but what about the men? The women will run away from the ugly ones and chase the good-looking.

PRAXAGORA

The ugly will follow the handsomest into the public places after supper and see to it that the law, which forbids the women to sleep with the big, handsome men before having satisfied the ugly shrimps, is complied with.

BLEPYRUS

Thus ugly Lysicrates' nose will be as proud as the handsomest face?

PRAXAGORA

Yes, by Apollo! this is a truly popular decree, and what a set-back it will be for one of those elegants with their fingers loaded with rings, when a man with heavy shoes says to him, "Give way to me and wait till I have done; you will pass in after me."

BLEPYRUS

But if we live in this fashion, how will each one know his children?

PRAXAGORA

The youngest will look upon the oldest as their fathers.

BLEPYRUS

Ah! how heartily they will strangle all the old men, since even now, when each one knows his father, they make no bones about strangling him! then, my word! won't they just scorn and crap upon the old folks!

PRAXAGORA

But those around will prevent it. Hitherto, when anyone saw an old man beaten, he would not meddle, because it did not concern him; but now each will fear the sufferer may be his own father and such violence will be stopped.

BLEPYRUS

What you say is not so silly after all; but it would be highly unpleasant were Epicurus and Leucolophas to come up and call me father.

CHREMES

But it would be far worse, were . . .

BLEPYRUS

Were what?

CHREMES

. . . Aristyllus to embrace you and style you his father.

BLEPYRUS

He'll regret it if he does!

CHREMES

For you would smell vilely of mint if he kissed you. But he was born before the decree was carried, so that you have not to fear his kiss.

BLEPYRUS

It would be awful. But who will till the soil?

PRAXAGORA

The slaves. Your only cares will be to scent yourself, and to go and dine, when the shadow of the gnomon is ten feet long on the dial.

BLEPYRUS

But how shall we obtain clothing? Tell me that!

PRAXAGORA

You will first wear out those you have, and then we women will weave you others.

BLEPYRUS

Now another point: if the magistrates condemn a citizen to the payment of a fine, how is he going to do it? Out of the public funds? That would not be right surely.

PRAXAGORA

But there will be no more lawsuits.

BLEPYRUS

This rule will ruin you.

CHREMES

I think so too.

PRAXAGORA

Besides, my dear, why should there be lawsuits?

BLEPYRUS

Oh! for a thousand reasons, on my faith! Firstly, because a debtor denies his obligation.

PRAXAGORA

But where will the lender get the money to lend, if all is in common? unless he steals it out of the treasury? and he could not hide that!

CHREMES

Well thought out, by Demeter!

BLEPYRUS

But tell me this: here are some men who are returning from a feast and are drunk and they strike some passer-by; how are they going to pay the fine? Ah! you are puzzled now!

PRAXAGORA

They will have to take it out of their pittance; and being thus punished through their belly, they will not care to begin again.

BLEPYRUS

There will be no more thieves then, eh?

PRAXAGORA

Why steal, if you have a share of everything?

BLEPYRUS

People will not be robbed any more at night?

CHREMES

Not if you sleep at home.

PRAXAGORA

Even if you sleep outdoors there will be no more danger, for all will have the means of living. Besides, if anyone wanted to steal your cloak, you would give it to him yourself. Why not? You will only have to go to the common store and be given a better one.

BLEPYRUS

There will be no more playing at dice?

PRAXAGORA

What object will there be in playing?

BLEPYRUS

But what kind of life is it you propose to set up?

PRAXAGORA

The life in common. Athens will become nothing more than a single house, in which everything will belong to everyone; so that everybody will be able to go from one house to the other at pleasure.

BLEPYRUS

And where will the meals be served?

PRAXAGORA

The law-courts and the porticoes will be turned into dining-halls.

BLEPYRUS

And what will the speaker's platform be used for?

PRAXAGORA

I shall place the bowls and the ewers there; and young children will sing the glory of the brave from there, also the infamy of cowards, who out of very shame will no longer dare to come to the public meals.

BLEPYRUS

Well thought out, by Apollo! And what will you do with the urns?

PRAXAGORA

I shall have them taken to the market-place, and standing close to the statue of Harmodius, I shall draw a lot for each citizen, which by its letter will show the place where he must go to dine. Thus, those for whom I have drawn an R will go to the royal portico; if it's a T, they will go to the portico of Theseus; if it's an F, to that of the flour-market.

BLEPYRUS

To cram himself there like a capon? [12]

PRAXAGORA

No, to dine there.

BLEPYRUS

And the citizen whom the lot has not given a letter showing where he is to dine will be driven off by everyone?

PRAXAGORA (*with great solemnity*)

But that will not occur. Each man will have plenty; he will not leave the feast until he is well drunk, and then with a chaplet on his head and a torch in his hand; and then the women running to meet you in the cross-roads will say, "This way, come to our house, you will find a beautiful young girl there."—"And I," another will call from her balcony, "have one so pretty and as white as milk; but before touching her, you must sleep with me." And the ugly men, watching closely after the handsome fellows, will say, "Hi! friend, where are you running to? Go in, but you must do nothing; it's the ugly and the flat-nosed to whom the law gives the right to make love first; amuse yourself on the porch while you wait, in handling your fig-leaves and playing with yourself." Well, tell me, does that picture suit you?

BLEPYRUS AND CHREMES

Marvellously well.

PRAXAGORA

I must now go to the market-place to receive the property that is go-ing to be placed in common and to choose a woman with a loud voice as my herald. I have all the cares of state on my shoulders, since the power has been entrusted to me. I must likewise go to busy myself about estab-lishing the common meals, and you will attend your first banquet to-day.

BLEPYRUS

Are we going to banquet?

PRAXAGORA

Why, undoubtedly! Furthermore, I propose abolishing the whores.

BLEPYRUS

And what for?

PRAXAGORA

It's clear enough why; so that, instead of them, *we* may have the first-fruits of the young men. It is not meet that tricked-out slaves should rob free-born women of their pleasures. Let the courtesans be free to sleep with the slaves.

BLEPYRUS

I will march at your side, so that I may be seen and that everyone may say, "Look at the Dictator's husband!"

(*He follows* PRAXAGORA *into their house.*)

CHREMES

As for me, I shall arrange my belongings and take inventory of them, in order that I may take them to the market-place.

(*He departs.*)
(*There is an interlude of dancing by the* CHORUS, *after which* CHREMES *returns with his belongings and arranges them in a long line.*)

CHREMES

Come hither, my beautiful sieve, I have nothing more precious than you, come, all clotted with the flour of which I have poured so many sacks through you; you shall act the part of Canephorus in the procession of my chattels. Where is the sunshade carrier? Ah! this stew-pot shall take his place. Great gods, how black it is! it could not be more so if Lysicrates had boiled the drugs in it with which he dyes his hair. Hither, my beautiful mirror. And you, my tripod, bear this urn for me; you shall be the water-bearer; and you, cock, whose morning song has so often roused me in the middle of the night to send me hurrying to the Assembly, you shall be my flute-girl. Scaphephorus, do you take the large basin, place in it the honeycombs and twine the olive-branches over them, bring the tripods and the phial of perfume; as for the humble crowd of little pots, I will just leave them behind.

CITIZEN (*watching* CHREMES *from a distance*)

What folly to carry one's goods to the common store; I have a little more sense than that. No, no, by Posidon, I want first to ponder and calculate over the thing at leisure. I shall not be fool enough to strip myself of the fruits of my toil and thrift, if it is not for a very good reason; let us see first which way things turn. (*He walks over to* CHREMES) Hi! friend, what means this display of goods? Are you moving or are you going to pawn your stuff?

CHREMES

Neither.

CITIZEN

Why then are you setting all these things out in line? Is it a procession that you are starting off to Hiero, the public crier?

CHREMES

No, but in accordance with the new law that has been decreed, I am going to carry all these things to the market-place to make a gift of them to the state.

CITIZEN

Oh! bah! you don't mean that.

CHREMES

Certainly.

CITIZEN

Oh! Zeus the Deliverer! you unfortunate man!

CHREMES

Why?

CITIZEN

Why? It's as clear as noonday.

CHREMES

Must the laws not be obeyed then?

CITIZEN

What laws, you poor fellow?

CHREMES

Those that have been decreed.

CITIZEN

Decreed! Are you mad, I ask you?

CHREMES

Am I mad?

CITIZEN

Oh! this is the height of folly!

CHREMES

Because I obey the law?

CITIZEN

Is that the duty of a smart man?

CHREMES

Absolutely.

CITIZEN

Say rather of a ninny.

CHREMES

Don't you propose taking what belongs to you to the common stock?

CITIZEN

I'll take good care I don't until I see what the majority are doing.

CHREMES

There's but one opinion, namely, to contribute every single thing one has.

CITIZEN

I am waiting to see it, before I believe that.

CHREMES

At least, so they say in every street.

CITIZEN (*sardonically*)

And they will go on saying so.

CHREMES

Everyone talks of contributing all he has.

CITIZEN (*in the same tone*)

And will go on talking of it.

CHREMES

You weary me with your doubts and dubitations.

CITIZEN (*in the same tone*)

Everybody else will doubt it.

CHREMES

The pest seize you!

CITIZEN (*in the same tone*)

It *will* take you. (*Then seriously*) What? give up your goods! Is there a man of sense who will do such a thing? Giving is not one of our customs. Receiving is another matter; it's the way of the gods themselves. Look at the position of their hands on their statues; when we ask a favour, they present their hands turned palm up so as not to give, but to receive.

CHREMES

Wretch, let me do what is right. Come, I'll make a bundle of all these things. Where is my strap?

CITIZEN

Are you really going to carry them in?

CHREMES

Undoubtedly, and there are my two tripods strung together already.

CITIZEN

What folly! Not to wait to see what the others do, and then . . .

CHREMES

Well, and then what?

CITIZEN

. . . wait and put it off again.

CHREMES

What for?

CITIZEN

That an earthquake may come or an ill-omened flash of lightning, that a black cat may run across the street and no one carry in anything more, you fool!

CHREMES

It would be a fine thing if I were to find no room left for placing all this.

CITIZEN

You are much more likely to lose your stuff. As for placing it, you can be at ease, for there will be room enough as long as a month hence.

CHREMES

Why?

CITIZEN

I know these people; a decree is readily passed, but it is not so easily attended to.

CHREMES

All will contribute their property, my friend.

CITIZEN

But what if they don't?

CHREMES

But there is no doubt that they will.

CITIZEN (*insistently*)

But *anyhow,* what if they don't?

CHREMES

Do not worry; they will.

CITIZEN

And what if they oppose it?

CHREMES

We shall compel them to do so.

CITIZEN

And what if they prove the stronger?

CHREMES

I snail leave my goods and go off.

CITIZEN

And what if they sell them for you?

CHREMES

The plague take you!

CITIZEN

And if it does?

CHREMES

It will be a gocd riddance.

CITIZEN (*in an incredulous tone*)

You are really *bent* on contributing, then?

CHREMES

'Pon my soul, yes! Look, there are all my neighbours carrying in all they have.

CITIZEN (*sarcastically*)

Oh yes, it's Antisthenes; he's the type that *would* contribute! He would just as soon spend the next month sitting on the can.

CHREMES

The pest seize you!

CITIZEN

Will Callimachus, the chorus-master, contribute anything?

CHREMES

Why, more than Callias!

CITIZEN

The man must want to spend *all* his money!

CHREMES

How you weary me!

CITIZEN

Ah! I weary you? But, wretch, see what comes of decrees of this kind. Don't you remember the one reducing the price of salt?

CHREMES

Why, certainly I do.

CITIZEN

And do you remember that about the copper coinage?

CHREMES

Ah! that cursed money did me enough harm. I had sold my grapes and had my mouth stuffed with pieces of copper; indeed I was going to the market to buy flour, and was in the act of holding out my bag wide open, when the herald started shouting, "Let none in future accept pieces of copper; those of silver are alone current."

CITIZEN

And quite lately, were we not all swearing that the impost of one-fortieth, which Euripides had conceived, would bring five hundred talents to the state, and everyone was vaunting Euripides to the skies? But when the thing was looked at closely, it was seen that this fine decree was mere moonshine and would produce nothing, and you would have willingly burnt this very same Euripides alive.

CHREMES

The cases are quite different, my good fellow. We were the rulers then, but now it's the women.

CITIZEN

Whom, by Posidon, I will never allow to piss on my nose.

CHREMES

I don't know what the devil you're chattering about. Slave, pick up that bundle.

HERALD (*a woman*)

Let all citizens come, let them hasten at our leader's bidding! It is the new law. The lot will teach each citizen where he is to dine; the tables are already laid and loaded with the most exquisite dishes; the couches are covered with the softest of cushions; the wine and water are already being mixed in the ewers; the slaves are standing in a row and waiting to pour scent over the guests; the fish is being grilled, the hares are on the spit and the cakes are being kneaded, chaplets are being plaited and the fritters are frying; the youngest women are watching the pea-soup in the saucepans, and in the midst of them all stands Smoeus, dressed as a knight, washing the crockery. And Geron has come, dressed in a grand tunic and finely shod; he is joking with another young fellow and has already divested himself of his heavy shoes and his cloak. The pantry man is waiting, so come and use your jaws.

(*Exit*)

CITIZEN

All right, I'll go. Why should I delay, since the state commands me?

CHREMES

And where are you going to, since you have not deposited your belongings?

CITIZEN

To the feast.

CHREMES

If the women have any wits, they will first insist on your depositing your goods.

CITIZEN

But I am going to deposit them.

CHREMES

When?

CITIZEN

I am not the man to make delays.

CHREMES

How do you mean?

CITIZEN

There will be many less eager than I.

CHREMES

In the meantime you are going to dine.

CITIZEN

What else should I do? Every sensible man must give his help to the state.

CHREMES

But if admission is forbidden you?

CITIZEN

I shall duck my head and slip in.

CHREMES

And if the women have you beaten?

CITIZEN

I shall summon them.

CHREMES

And if they laugh in your face?

CITIZEN

I shall stand near the door . . .

CHREMES

And then?

CITIZEN

. . . and seize upon the dishes as they pass.

CHREMES

Then go there, but after me. Sicon and Parmeno, pick up all this baggage.

CITIZEN

Come, I will help you carry it.

CHREMES (*pushing him away*)

No, no, I should be afraid of your pretending to the leader that what I am depositing belonged to you.

(*Exit with his belongings.*)

CITIZEN

Let me see! let me think of some good trick by which I can keep my goods and yet take my share of the common feast. (*He reflects for a moment.*) Ha! that's a fine idea! Quick! I'll go and dine, ha! ha!

(*Exit laughing.*)

(*Interlude of dancing by the* CHORUS.)

(*The scene shifts to a different section of Athens and the two houses are now to be thought of as those of two prostitutes.*)

FIRST OLD WOMAN (*leaning out of the window of one house*)

How is this? no men are coming? And yet it must be fully time! Then it is for naught that I have painted myself with white lead, dressed myself in my beautiful yellow robe, and that I am here, frolicking and humming between my teeth to attract some passer-by! Oh, Muses, alight upon my lips, inspire me with some soft Ionian love-song!

YOUNG GIRL (*in the window of the other house*)

You putrid old thing, you have placed yourself at the window before me. You were expecting to strip my vines during my absence and to trap some man in your snares with your songs. If you sing, I shall follow suit; all this singing will weary the spectators, but is nevertheless very pleasant and very diverting.

FIRST OLD WOMAN (*thumbing her nose at the* YOUNG GIRL)

Ha! here is an old man; take him and lead him away. (*To the flute-player*) As for you, you young flute-player, let us hear some airs that are worthy of you and me.

(*She sings*)

Let him who wishes to taste pleasure come to my side. These young things know nothing about it; it's only the women of ripe age who understand the art of love, and no one could know how to fondle the lover who possessed me so well as myself; the young girls are all flightiness.

YOUNG GIRL (*singing in her turn*)

Don't be jealous of the young girls; voluptuousness resides in the pure outline of their beautiful limbs and blossoms on their rounded breasts; but you, old woman, you who are tricked out and perfumed as if for your own funeral, are an object of love only for grim Death himself.

FIRST OLD WOMAN (*singing again*)

May your tongue be stopped; may you be unable to find your couch when you want to be loved. And on your couch, when your lips seek a lover, may you embrace only a viper!

YOUNG GIRL (*singing again*)

Alas! alas! what is to become of me? There is no lover! I am left here alone; my mother has gone out. (*Interrupting her song*) There's no need to mention the rest. (*Then singing again*) Oh! my dear nurse, I adjure you to call Orthagoras, and may heaven bless you. Ah! poor child, desire is consuming you like an Ionian woman; (*interrupting again*) and yet you are no stranger to the wanton arts of the Lesbian women. (*Resuming her song*) But you shall not rob me

of my pleasures; you will not be able to reduce or filch the time that
first belongs to me.

FIRST OLD WOMAN

Sing as much as you please, peep out like a cat lying in wait, but none
shall pass through your door without first having been to see me.

YOUNG GIRL

If anyone enter your house, it will be to carry out your corpse. And that
will be something new for you, you rotten old thing!

FIRST OLD WOMAN

Can anything be new to an old woman? My old age will not harm you.

YOUNG GIRL

Ah! shame on your painted cheeks!

FIRST OLD WOMAN

Why do you speak to me at all?

YOUNG GIRL

And why do you place yourself at the window?

FIRST OLD WOMAN

I am singing to myself about my lover, Epigenes.

YOUNG GIRL

Can you have any other lover than that old fop Geres?

FIRST OLD WOMAN

Epigenes will show you that himself, for he is coming to me. See, here
he is.

YOUNG GIRL

He's not thinking of you in the least.

FIRST OLD WOMAN

Aye, but he is.

YOUNG GIRL

Old starveling! Let's see what he will do. I will leave my window.

FIRST OLD WOMAN

And I likewise. You will see I am much wiser than you.

A YOUNG MAN (*sings*)

Ah! could I but sleep with the young girl without first making
love to the old fiat-nose! It is intolerable for a free-born man.

FIRST OLD WOMAN (*singing to the same tune*)

Willy nilly, you must first gratify my desire. There shall be no
nonsense about that, for my authority is the law and the law must be
obeyed in a democracy.

(*Speaking*) But come, let me hide, to see what he's going to do. (*She
retires.*)

YOUNG MAN

Ah! ye gods, if I were to find the sweet child alone! the wine has fired
my lust.

YOUNG GIRL (*reappearing in her window*)

I have tricked that cursed old wretch; she has left her window, thinking
I would stay at home. Ah! here is the lover we were talking of.

(*She sings*)

This way, my love, this way, come here and haste to rest the
whole night in my arms. I worship your lovely curly hair; I am consumed with ardent desire. Oh! Eros, in thy mercy, compel him to my
bed.

YOUNG MAN (*standing beneath the* YOUNG GIRL'S *window and singing*)

Come down and haste to open the door unless you want to see me
fall dead with desire. Dearest treasure, I am burning to yield myself
to voluptuous sport, lying on your bosom, to let my hands play with
your bottom. Aphrodité, why dost thou fire me with such delight in
her? Oh! Eros, I beseech thee, have mercy and make her share my
couch. Words cannot express the tortures I am suffering. Oh! my
adored one, I adjure you, open your door for me and press me to your
heart; 'tis for you that I am suffering. Oh! my jewel, my idol, you
child of Aphrodité, the confidante of the Muses, the sister of the
Graces, you living picture of voluptuousness, oh! open for me, press
me to your heart, 'tis for you that I am suffering.

(*He knocks.*)

FIRST OLD WOMAN (*reappearing suddenly*)

What are you knocking for? Are you looking for me?

YOUNG MAN

What an idea!

FIRST OLD WOMAN

But you were tapping at the door.

YOUNG MAN

Death would be sweeter.

FIRST OLD WOMAN

Why do you come with that torch in your hand?

YOUNG MAN

I am looking for a man from Anaphlystia.

FIRST OLD WOMAN

What's his name?

YOUNG MAN

Oh! it's not Sebinus, whom no doubt you are expecting.

FIRST OLD WOMAN (*taking him by the arm*)

By Aphrodité, you *must*, whether you like it or not.

YOUNG MAN (*shaking her off*)

We are not now concerned with cases dated sixty years back; they are remanded for a later day; we are dealing only with those of less than twenty.

FIRST OLD WOMAN

That was under the old order of things, sweetheart, but now you must first busy yourself with us.

YOUNG MAN

Aye, *if I want to,* according to the rules of draughts, where we may either take or leave.

FIRST OLD WOMAN

But it's not according to the rules of draughts that you take your seat at the banquet.

YOUNG MAN

I don't know what you mean; it's at *this* door I want to knock.

FIRST OLD WOMAN (*standing in his way*)

Not before knocking at mine first.

YOUNG MAN (*haughtily*)

For the moment I really have no need for old leather.

FIRST OLD WOMAN

I know that you love me; perhaps you are surprised to find me at the door. But come, let me kiss you.

YOUNG MAN (*pulling back; sarcastically*)

No, no, my dear, I am afraid of your lover.

FIRST OLD WOMAN

Of whom?

YOUNG MAN

The most gifted of painters.

FIRST OLD WOMAN

And who is he?

YOUNG MAN

The artist who paints the little bottles on coffins. But get you indoors, lest he should find you at the door.

FIRST OLD WOMAN

I know what you want.

YOUNG MAN

I can say as much of you.

FIRST OLD WOMAN (*hanging on to him*)

By Aphrodité, who has granted me this good chance, I won't let you go.

YOUNG MAN

You are drivelling, you little old hag.

FIRST OLD WOMAN

Rubbish! I am going to lead you to my couch.

YOUNG MAN

What need for buying hooks? I will let her down to the bottom of the well and pull up the buckets with her old carcase, for she's crooked enough for that.

FIRST OLD WOMAN

A truce to your jeering, poor boy, and follow me.

YOUNG MAN

Nothing compels me to do so, unless you have paid the levy of five hundredths for me.[13]

FIRST OLD WOMAN

Look, by Aphrodité, there is nothing that delights me as much as sleeping with a lad of your years.

YOUNG MAN

And I abhor such as you, and I will never, never consent.

FIRST OLD WOMAN

But, by Zeus, here is something will force you to it.

(*She shows him a document.*)

YOUNG MAN

What's that?

FIRST OLD WOMAN

A decree, which orders you to enter my house.

YOUNG MAN

Read it out then, and let's hear.

FIRST OLD WOMAN

Listen. "The women have decreed that if a young man desires a young girl, he can only lay her after having satisfied an old woman; and if he refuses and goes to seek the maiden, the old women are authorized to seize him and drag him in."

YOUNG MAN

Alas! I shall become a Procrustes.

FIRST OLD WOMAN

Obey the law.

YOUNG MAN

But if a fellow-citizen, a friend, came to pay my ransom?

FIRST OLD WOMAN

No man may dispose of anything above a medimnus.

YOUNG MAN

But may I not enter an excuse?

FIRST OLD WOMAN

There's no evasion.

YOUNG MAN

I shall declare myself a merchant and so escape service.

FIRST OLD WOMAN

Beware what you do!

YOUNG MAN

Well! what is to be done?

FIRST OLD WOMAN

Follow me.

YOUNG MAN

Is it absolutely necessary?

FIRST OLD WOMAN

Yes, as surely as if Diomedes had commanded it.

YOUNG MAN

Well then, first spread out a layer of origanum upon four pieces of
wood; bind fillets round your head, bring phials of scent and place a
bowl filled with lustral water before your door.[14]

FIRST OLD WOMAN

Will you buy a chaplet for me too?

YOUNG MAN

Yes, if you outlast the tapers; for I expect to see you fall down dead
as you go in.

YOUNG GIRL (*running out of her house*)

Where are you dragging this unfortunate man to?

FIRST OLD WOMAN

To my own bed.

YOUNG GIRL

That's not right. A young fellow like him is not of the age to suit you.
You ought to be his mother rather than his wife. With these laws in
force, the earth will be filled with Oedipuses.

(*She takes him away with her.*)

FIRST OLD WOMAN

Oh! you cursed pest! it's envy that makes you say this; but I will be
revenged.

(*She goes back into her house.*)

YOUNG MAN

By Zeus the Deliverer, what a service you have done me, by freeing
me of this old wretch! with what ardour I will show you my gratitude
in a substantial form!

(*Just as he begins to go in with the* YOUNG GIRL *an even older and uglier
woman enters.*)

SECOND OLD WOMAN

Hi! you there! where are you taking that young man to, in defiance
of the law? The decree ordains that he must first sleep with me.

YOUNG MAN

Oh! what a misfortune! Where does *this* hag come from? She's a more frightful monster than the other even.

SECOND OLD WOMAN

Come here.

(*She takes him by the arm.*)

YOUNG MAN (*to the* YOUNG GIRL)

Oh! I beg you, don't let me be led off by her!

SECOND OLD WOMAN

It's not I but the law that leads you off.

YOUNG MAN

No, it's not the law, but an Empusa with a body covered with blemishes and blotches.

SECOND OLD WOMAN

Follow me, my handsome little friend, come along quickly without any more ado.

YOUNG MAN

Oh! let me go to the can first, so that I may gather my wits somewhat. Else I should be so terrified that you would see me letting out something yellow.

SECOND OLD WOMAN

Never mind! you can crap, if you want, in my house.

YOUNG MAN

More than I want to, I'm afraid; but I offer you two good securities.

SECOND OLD WOMAN

I don't require them.

(*A* THIRD OLD WOMAN, *the ugliest yet, now appears.*)

THIRD OLD WOMAN

Hi! friend, where are you off to with that woman?

YOUNG MAN

I am not going with her, but am being dragged by force. Oh! whoever you are, may heaven bless you for having had pity on me in my dire misfortune. (*Turns round and sees the* THIRD OLD WOMAN.) Oh Heracles! oh Pan! oh Corybantes! oh Dioscuri! Why, she is still more awful! Oh! what a monster! great gods! Are you an ape plastered with white lead, or the ghost of some old hag returned from the dark borderlands of death?

THIRD OLD WOMAN (*taking his other arm*)

No jesting! Follow me.

SECOND OLD WOMAN

No, come this way.

THIRD OLD WOMAN

I will never let you go.

SECOND OLD WOMAN

Nor will I.

YOUNG MAN

But you will rend me asunder, you cursed wretches.

SECOND OLD WOMAN

I'm the one he must go with according to the law.

THIRD OLD WOMAN

Not if an uglier old woman than yourself appears.

YOUNG MAN

But if you kill me at the outset, how shall I afterwards go to find this beautiful girl of mine?

THIRD OLD WOMAN

That's your problem. But begin by obeying.

YOUNG MAN

Of which one must I rid myself first?

THIRD OLD WOMAN

Don't you know? Come here.

YOUNG MAN

Then let the other one release me.

SECOND OLD WOMAN

Come to *my* house.

YOUNG MAN

If this dame will let me go.

THIRD OLD WOMAN

No, by all the gods, I'll not let you go.

SECOND OLD WOMAN

Nor will I.

YOUNG MAN

You would make very bad boatwomen.

SECOND OLD WOMAN

Why?

YOUNG MAN

Because you would tear your passengers to pieces in dragging them on board.

THIRD OLD WOMAN

Then come along, do, and hold your tongue.

SECOND OLD WOMAN

No, by Zeus, come with me.

YOUNG MAN

It's clearly a case for the decree of Cannonus; I must cut myself in two in order to lay you both. But how am I to work two oars at once?

THIRD OLD WOMAN

Easily enough; you have only to eat a full pot of onions.[15]

YOUNG MAN

Oh! great gods! here I am close to the door and being dragged in!

SECOND OLD WOMAN (*to* THIRD OLD WOMAN)

You will gain nothing by this, for I shall rush into your house with you.

YOUNG MAN

Oh, no! no! better to suffer a single misfortune than two.

THIRD OLD WOMAN

Ah! by Hecaté, whether you wish it or not . . .

YOUNG MAN

What a fate is mine, that I must make love to such a stinking harridan the whole night through and all day; then, when I am rid of her, I have still to tackle a brick-coloured hag! Am I not truly unfortunate? Ah! by Zeus the Deliverer; under what fatal star must I have been born, that I must sail in company with such monsters! But if my bark sinks in the sewer of these strumpets, may I be buried at the very threshold of the door; let this hag be stood upright on my grave, let her be coated alive with pitch and her legs covered with molten lead up to the ankles, and let her be set alight as a funeral lamp.

(*The* YOUNG MAN *is dragged off by the two* OLD WOMEN, *one on each arm.*)

(*Interlude of dancing by the* CHORUS.)

A SERVANT-MAID TO PRAXAGORA (*she comes from the banquet*)

What happiness is the people's! what joy is mine, and above all that of my mistress! Happy are ye, who form choruses before our house! Happy are ye, both neighbours and fellow-citizens! Happy am I myself! I am but a servant, and yet I have poured on my hair the most exquisite essences. Let thanks be rendered to thee, Oh, Zeus! But a still more delicious aroma is that of the wine of Thasos; its sweet bouquet delights the drinker for a long time, whereas the others lose their bloom and vanish quickly. Therefore, long life to the wine-jars of Thasos! Pour yourselves out unmixed wine, it will cheer you the whole night through, if you choose the liquor that possesses most fragrance. (*To the* CHORUS) But tell me, friends, where is my mistress's husband?

LEADER OF THE CHORUS

Wait for him here; he will no doubt pass this way.

MAID-SERVANT

Ah! there he is just going to dinner. Oh! master! what joy! what blessedness is yours!

BLEPYRUS

Mine?

MAID-SERVANT

None can compare his happiness to yours; you have reached its utmost height, you who, alone out of thirty thousand citizens have not yet dined.

LEADER OF THE CHORUS

Aye, here is undoubtedly a truly happy man.

MAID-SERVANT

Where are you off to?

BLEPYRUS

I am going to dine.

MAID-SERVANT

By Aphrodité, you will be the last of all, far and away the last. Yet my mistress has bidden me take you and take with you these young girls. Some Chian wine is left and lots of other good things. Therefore hurry, and invite likewise all the spectators whom we have pleased, and such of the judges as are not against us, to follow us; we will offer them everything they can desire.

BLEPYRUS

Generously invite everyone and omit no one, old or young. Dinner is ready for all; they need only go home. As for me, I shall go to the banquet with the customary torch in my hand.

MAID-SERVANT

But why do you tarry, Blepyrus? Take these young girls with you and, while you are away a while, I will whet my appetite with some dining-song.

LEADER OF THE CHORUS

I have but a few words to say: let the wise judge me because of whatever is wise in this piece, and those who like a laugh by whatever has made them laugh. In this way I address pretty well everyone. If the lot has assigned my comedy to be played first of all, don't let that be a disadvantage to me; engrave in your memory all that shall have pleased you in it and judge the competitors equitably as you have bound yourselves by oath to do. Don't act like vile courtesans, who never remember any but their last lover.

MAID-SERVANT

It is time, friends, high time to go to the banquet, if we want to have our share of it. Open your ranks and let the Cretan rhythms regulate your dances.

BLEPYRUS

That's what I am doing.

MAID-SERVANT

And you others, let your light steps too keep time. Very soon we'll be eating *lépadotémachosélachogáleokrániolei psanodrímypotrímmatosílphi-otyromélitokátakechýmenokíchlepikóssyphophátto peristeraléktryonópto-kepháliokinklopeleíolagoíosiraíobaphétragalópterygón.*[16] Come, quickly, seize hold of a plate, snatch up a cup, and let's run to secure a place at table. The rest will have their jaws at work by this time.

CHORUS (*as they depart, dancing, with* BLEPYRUS *leading them*)
Dance gaily! *Iai! Iai!* We shall dine! *Euoi! Euai! Euai!* As for a triumph! *Euoi! Euoi! Euai! Euai!*

1. The operation of carding would expose the arms, and their soft and telltale contours would disastrously evince the sex of the carder.

2. It is not easy to see why Praxagora here substitutes the cat for the usual young pig. Rogers seems on the right track when he says that the word for the young pig, *choiridion,* meaning also "young female genitalia," was avoided by Praxagora in an "assembly of ladies," but the implication that this was motivated by considerations of delicacy is misguided and Victorian. The real point is, perhaps, that this word would have provoked a number of irrelevant and feminine remarks, and the revolutionary leader has for some time been energetically striving to bring her followers down to the serious business that lies before them.

3. This is the usual gibe at the bibulousness of the Athenian women.

4. An oath used by women only.

5. A reference to the alliance with Thebes that Athens had concluded in 395. It was quickly joined by other states and for a while there were high hopes, but like most such developments in fourth-century history, it came to little.

6. A reference to the Spartan invasions of Attica in the early years of the Peloponnesian War; the inhabitants of the rural districts sought refuge in the city, where they were very inadequately housed.

7. There is a pun here on the two senses of *hypokrouein,* "to interrupt" and "to make love to."

8. Blepyrus personifies his intestinal urges under the name *Kopreios,* which is formed, in the usual manner of personal names, from *kopros,* "excrement."

9. The Greek is *Achradousios,* formed from *achras,* "wild pear" and at the same time suggesting the deme Acherdus.

10. These were signs of lateness; see note 2 on *The Acharnians.*

11. Praxagora's remark is merely an idiomatic phrase of abuse; Blepyrus understands, or affects to understand, it literally.

12. There is a pun here on the two Greek words *kaptein,* "to stuff" and *kappa,* the name of the letter *K.*

13. We do not know what the tax here referred to was, and the point

of the Young Man's remark is thus obscure; only one thing is clear, and this is that the rights of citizenship are involved. It may be that the Young Man may not rate as a slave unless a tax has been paid on his assessed value, but it is equally possible that the Old Woman may not derive the benefits of the new law until she has paid a capital levy of some sort.

14. These are the customary formalities connected with the laying-out of the dead.

15. The Greek word here translated as "onions" is *bolboi;* we do not know just what plant it signifies, but the ancient commentators know of its aphrodisiac effects, and these are sufficient to explain its use here.

16. This magnificent word, the longest that has ever been constructed in an Indo-Germanic language, is here merely transliterated from the Greek, and the accents indicate how it should be read. The precise signification of some of the components is not entirely certain, but so far as we can tell the ingredients of the dish are: limpets, slices of salt fish, thornbacks, whistle-fishes, cornel-berries, a remoulade of leftover brains seasoned with silphium and cheese, thrushes basted with honey, blackbirds, ringdoves, squabs, chickens, fried mullets, wagtails, rock-pigeons, hare, and wings ground up in new wine that has been boiled down.

XI
PLUTUS

CHARACTERS IN THE PLAY

CHREMYLUS
CARIO, *Servant of Chremylus*
PLUTUS, *God of Riches*
BLEPSIDEMUS, *friend of Chremylus*
POVERTY
WIFE OF CHREMYLUS
A JUST MAN
AN INFORMER
AN OLD WOMAN
A YOUTH
HERMES
A PRIEST OF ZEUS
CHORUS OF RUSTICS

INTRODUCTION

PRODUCED in 388, four years after *The Ecclesiazusae, Plutus* is the latest comedy of Aristophanes which we possess, although we know that he wrote at least two more, which were produced in the name of his son Ararus. We have no information regarding the festival at which the play was brought out, nor are we told what prize it won. It is the least amusing of the extant comedies, and its chief interest for the modern reader lies in the fact that it is the nearest thing to a representative of the Middle Comedy that has come down to us. The later centuries of the ancient world and the schoolmasters of the Byzantine Empire, however, were inordinately fond of it, the former because of what they regarded as its refinement, the latter because it only infrequently offended their moral tastes.

The subject of the play is the Utopian situation produced by the restoration to Plutus, the God of Wealth, of the sight of his eyes. Chremylus, the human hero of the play, has consulted the oracle of Apollo on the question of how his son may succeed in life without becoming a scoundrel, and the god has directed him to follow the first man he meets on leaving the temple. The object of the divine reference has turned out to be a dirty and disreputable blind man, and Chremylus has been dutifully dogging his heels ever since he first laid eyes on him. By the time the play begins Cario, the slave of Chremylus and a character much more of the New than of the Old Comedy, has quite lost patience with his master's latest foolishness and demands in no uncertain terms to know the reasons and the purposes of it. Chremylus explains, but Cario is far from convinced and insists on finding out who the blind man is. Plutus discloses his identity with the greatest reluctance, for ever since the malignity of Zeus had deprived him of his vision, he has experienced nothing but the worst of treatment at the hands of mankind every time he has revealed his name. At this point Chremylus is suddenly inspired with the magnificent idea that if the blindness of Plutus is healed, all the ills of human life will be rectified, and we remember *The Birds* and the birth of Pithetaerus' projects.

Plutus is sceptical at first, but Chremylus convinces him without too much difficulty, and after dispatching his slave to fetch the husbandmen who are his boon companions, he takes the god into his house. The entrance of the Chorus has thus been motivated, and soon Cario comes in at the head of the rustic band, which plays a very unimportant rôle in the comedy. Chremylus comes out and greets his country neighbours, but their mutual felicitations are interrupted by the arrival of Blepsidemus, a friend of Chremylus, who finds much that is suspicious in the sudden affluence of the household. Once it has been made quite clear to him that he too stands to profit by the situation, his hostile attitude loses its principal or solitary *raison d'être* and he enthusiastically supports the proposals of Chremylus. At this point both friends are frightened out of their wits by the entrance of a woman of superhuman stature and terrifying aspect, looking for all the world like some Fury detached from a tragic chorus. She turns out to be Poverty, and Chremylus engages her in a long debate on the question of whether it is she or Plutus who most benefits mankind; the scene is the descendant and the souvenir of the Agon in the Old Comedy. Beaten in the argument, Poverty leaves the stage with laments and threats, but Chremylus laughs at these and summons Cario, with whom he takes Plutus to the temple of Asclepius to be healed of his blindness.

The stage is now left to the Chorus, and if we have not read *The Ecclesiazusae* we expect the delivery of the parabasis; all that we have is the indication that there was an interlude of dancing by the Chorus. We must, however, assume the lapse of a considerable amount of time during this, for the scene which follows consists mainly of Cario's amusing report of the miraculous cure that has been performed on Plutus, and in a little while the god himself returns, rejoicing in the light that he can see again and in the Utopia which he is about to materialize. The scenes which follow the return of Plutus are more reminiscent of the Old Comedy than anything else in the play, for they represent the familiar series of anonymous and typical characters who illustrate the various social effects of the revolution which has been effected in the first part of the comedy. Thus the poet brings in first the happy Just Man, for whom the world has only now become tolerable, and after him the Informer, who fails to arouse the pity which seems his only means of livelihood at present, the Old Woman, whose gigolo will now have no reason to consort with her, Hermes, who is unable to find any use for his rascally talents in the Utopian society that a seeing Plutus has established, and finally a priest of Zeus, whom the hunger induced by a sacrificeless profession has driven to transfer his services to the new lord of the universe. The comedy ends rather lamely with the assurance of Chremylus to the old woman that her young man will be with her this evening and the beginning of a sacred procession to install Plutus on the Acropolis.

If we make *Plutus* the first, rather than the last, comedy of Aristophanes that we read, we find it a sufficiently amusing play, but if we come to it fresh from *Peace* or *The Thesmophoriazusae* it is a singularly disappointing performance. One may suspect, however, that if we knew the history of Athens as intimately from 410 to 388 as we know it from 431 to 411 we should be astonished at the resistance to change exhibited by the Old Comedy. The thirty-seven years between *The Acharnians* and *Plutus* brought with them an amount of alteration of the form and the spirit of comedy that is impressive and depressing enough, but the changes in the social and economic life of Athens during this period were incomparably greater.

PLUTUS

(SCENE:—*The Orchestra represents a public square in Athens. In the background is the house of* CHREMYLUS. *A ragged old blind man enters, followed by* CHREMYLUS *and his slave* CARIO.)

CARIO

WHAT an unhappy fate, great gods, to be the slave of a fool! A servant may give the best of advice, but if his master does not follow it, the pooɪ slave must inevitably have his share in the disaster; for fortune does not allow him to dispose of his own body, it belongs to his master who has bought it. Alas! 'tis the way of the world. But the god, Apollo (*in tragic style*), whose oracles the Pythian priestess on her golden tripod makes known to us, deserves my censure, for surely he is a physician and a cunning diviner; and yet my master is leaving his temple infected with mere madness and insists on following a blind man. Is this not opposed to all good sense? It is for us, who see clearly, to guide those who don't; whereas he clings to the trail of a blind fellow and compels me to do the same without answering my questions with ever a word. (*To* CHREMYLUS) Aye, master, unless you tell me why we are following this unknown fellow, I will not be silent, but I will worry and torment you, for you cannot beat me because of my sacred chaplet of laurel.

CHREMYLUS

No, but if you worry me I will take off your chaplets, and then you will only get a sounder thrashing.

CARIO

That's an old song! I am going to leave you no peace till you have told me who this man is; and if I ask it, it's entirely because of my interest in you.

CHREMYLUS

Well, be it so. I will reveal it to you as being the most faithful and the most rascally of all my servants. I honoured the gods and did what was right, and yet I was none the less poor and unfortunate.

1063

CARIO

I know it but too well.

CHREMYLUS

Others amassed wealth—the sacrilegious, the demagogues, the informers, indeed every sort of rascal.

CARIO

I believe you.

CHREMYLUS

Therefore I came to consult the oracle of the god, not on my own account, for my unfortunate life is nearing its end, but for my only son; I wanted to ask Apollo if it was necessary for him to become a thorough knave and renounce his virtuous principles, since that seemed to me to be the only way to succeed in life.

CARIO (*with ironic gravity*)

And with what responding tones did the sacred tripod resound?

CHREMYLUS

You shall know. The god ordered me in plain terms to follow the first man I should meet upon leaving the temple and to persuade him to accompany me home.

CARIO

And who was the first one you met?

CHREMYLUS

This blind man.

CARIO

And you are stupid enough not to understand the meaning of such an answer? Why, the god was advising you thereby, and that in the clearest possible way, to bring up your son according to the fashion of your country.

CHREMYLUS

What makes you think that?

CARIO

Is it not evident to the blind, that nowadays to do nothing that is right is the best way to get on?

CHREMYLUS

No, that is not the meaning of the oracle; there must be another that is nobler. If this blind man would tell us who he is and why and with what object he has led us here, we should no doubt understand what our oracle really does mean.

CARIO (*to* PLUTUS)

Come, tell us at once who you are, or I shall give effect to my threat. (*He menaces him.*) And quick too, be quick, I say.

PLUTUS

I'll thrash you.

CARIO (*to* CHREMYLUS)

Do you understand who he says he is?

CHREMYLUS

It's to you and not to me that he replies thus: your mode of questioning him was ill-advised. (*To* PLUTUS) Come, friend, if you care to oblige an honest man, answer me.

PLUTUS

I'll knock you down.

CARIO (*sarcastically*)

Ah! what a pleasant fellow and what a delightful prophecy the god has given you!

CHREMYLUS (*to* PLUTUS)

By Demeter, you'll have no reason to laugh presently.

CARIO

If you don't speak, you wretch, I will surely do you an ill turn.

PLUTUS

Friends, take yourselves off and leave me.

CHREMYLUS

That we very certainly shan't.

CARIO

This, master, is the best thing to do. I'll undertake to secure him the most frightful death; I will lead him to the verge of a precipice and then leave him there, so that he'll break his neck when he pitches over.

CHREMYLUS

Well then, seize him right away.

(CARIO *does so.*)

PLUTUS

Oh, no! Have mercy!

CHREMYLUS

Will thou speak then?

PLUTUS

But if you learn who I am, I know well that you will ill-use me and will not let me go again.

CHREMYLUS

I call the gods to witness that you have naught to fear if you will only speak.

PLUTUS

Well then, first unhand me.

CHREMYLUS

There! we set you free.

PLUTUS

Listen then, since I must reveal what I had intended to keep a secret. I am Plutus.

CARIO

Oh! you wretched rascal! You Plutus all the while, and you never said so!

CHREMYLUS

You, Plutus, and in this piteous guise! Oh, Phoebus Apollo! oh, ye gods of heaven and hell! Oh, Zeus! is it really and truly as you say?

PLUTUS

Yes.

CHREMYLUS

Plutus' very own self?

PLUTUS

His own very self and none other.

CHREMYLUS

But tell me, how come you're so squalid?

PLUTUS

I have just left Patrocles' house, who has not had a bath since his birth.

CHREMYLUS

But your infirmity; how did that happen? Tell me.

PLUTUS

Zeus inflicted it on me, because of his jealousy of mankind. When I was young, I threatened him that I would only go to the just, the wise, the men of ordered life; to prevent my distinguishing these, he struck me with blindness! so much does he envy the good!

CHREMYLUS

And yet, it's only the upright and just who honour him.

PLUTUS

Quite true.

CHREMYLUS

Therefore, if ever you recovered your sight, you would shun the wicked?

PLUTUS

Undoubtedly.

CHREMYLUS

You would visit the good?

PLUTUS

Assuredly. It is a very long time since I saw them.

CARIO (*to the audience*)

That's not astonishing. I, who see clearly, don't see a single one.

PLUTUS

Now let me leave you, for I have told you everything.

CHREMYLUS

No, certainly not! we shall fasten ourselves on to you faster than ever.

PLUTUS

Did I not tell you, you were going to plague me?

CHREMYLUS

Oh! I adjure you, believe what I say and don't leave me; for you will seek in vain for a more honest man than myself.

CARIO

There is only one man more worthy; and that is I.

PLUTUS

All talk like this, but as soon as they secure my favours and grow rich, their wickedness knows no bounds.

CHREMYLUS

And yet all men are not wicked.

PLUTUS

All. There's no exception.

CARIO

You shall pay for that opinion.

CHREMYLUS

Listen to what happiness there is in store for you, if you but stay with us. I have hope; aye, I have good hope with the god's help to deliver you from that blindness, in fact to restore your sight.

PLUTUS

Oh! do nothing of the kind, for I don't wish to recover it.

CHREMYLUS

What's that you say?

CARIO

This fellow hugs his own misery.

PLUTUS

If you were mad enough to cure me, and Zeus heard of it, he would overwhelm me with his anger.

CHREMYLUS

And is he not doing this now by leaving you to grope your wandering way?

PLUTUS

I don't know; but I'm horribly afraid of him.

CHREMYLUS

Indeed? Ah! you are the biggest poltroon of all the gods! Why, Zeus with his throne and his lightnings would not be worth an obolus if you recovered your sight, were it but for a few moments.

PLUTUS

Impious man, don't talk like that.

CHREMYLUS

Fear nothing! I will prove to you that you are far more powerful and mightier than he.

PLUTUS

I mightier than he?

CHREMYLUS

Aye, by heaven! (*To* CARIO) For instance, what is the basis of the power that Zeus wields over the other gods?

CARIO

Money; he has so much of it.

CHREMYLUS

And who gives it to him?

CARIO (*pointing to Plutus*)

This fellow.

CHREMYLUS

If sacrifices are offered to him, is not Plutus their cause?

CARIO

Undoubtedly, for it's wealth that all demand and clamour most loudly for.

CHREMYLUS

Thus it's Plutus who is the fount of all the honours rendered to Zeus, whose worship he can wither up at the root, if it so pleases him.

PLUTUS

And how so?

CHREMYLUS

Not an ox, nor a cake, nor indeed anything at all could be offered, if you did not wish it.

PLUTUS

Why?

CHREMYLUS

Why? but what means are there to buy anything if you are not there to give the money? Hence if Zeus should cause you any trouble, you will destroy his power without other help.

PLUTUS

So it's because of me that sacrifices are offered to him?

CHREMYLUS

Most assuredly. Whatever is dazzling, beautiful or charming in the eyes of mankind, comes from you. Does not everything depend on wealth?

CARIO

I myself was bought for a few coins; if I'm a slave, it's only because I was not rich.

CHREMYLUS

And what of the Corinthian whores? If a poor man offers them proposals, they do not listen; but if it be a rich one, instantly they turn their arses to him.

CARIO

It's the same with the lads; they care not for love, to them money means everything.

CHREMYLUS

You speak of male whores; yet some of them are honest, and it's not money they ask of their patrons.

CARIO

What then?

CHREMYLUS

A fine horse, a pack of hounds.

CARIO

Yes, they would blush to ask for money and cleverly disguise their shame.

CHREMYLUS

It is in you that every art, all human inventions, have had their origin; it is through you that one man sits cutting leather in his shop.

CARIO

That another fashions iron or wood.

CHREMYLUS

That yet another chases the gold he has received from you.

CARIO

That one is a fuller.

CHREMYLUS

That the other washes wool.

CARIO

That this one is a tanner.

CHREMYLUS

And that other sells onions.

CARIO

And if the adulterer, caught red-handed, is depilated, it's on account of you.

PLUTUS

Oh! great gods! I knew naught of all this!

CARIO (*to* CHREMYLUS)

Is it not he who lends the Great King all his pride? Is it not he who draws the citizens to the Assembly?

CHREMYLUS

And tell me, is it not you who equip the triremes?

CARIO

And who feed our mercenaries at Corinth? Are not you the cause of Pamphilus' sufferings?

CHREMYLUS

And of the needle-seller's with Pamphilus?

CARIO

It is not because of you that Agyrrhius farts so loudly?

CHREMYLUS

And that Philepsius rolls off his fables? That troops are sent to succour the Egyptians? And that Lais is kept by Philonides?

CARIO

That the tower of Timotheus . . .

CHREMYLUS

. . . (*To* CARIO) May it fall upon your head! (*To* PLUTUS) In short, Plutus, it is through you that everything is done; you must realize that you are the sole cause both of good and evil.

CARIO

In war, it's the flag under which you serve that victory favours.

PLUTUS

What! I can do so many things by myself and unaided?

CHREMYLUS

And many others besides; wherefore men are never tired of your gifts. They get weary of all else,—of love . . .

CARIO

Bread.

CHREMYLUS

Music.

CARIO

Sweetmeats.

CHREMYLUS

Honours.

CARIO

Cakes.

CHREMYLUS

Battles.

CARIO

Figs.

CHREMYLUS

Ambition.

CARIO

Gruel.

CHREMYLUS

Military advancement.

CARIO

Lentil soup.

CHREMYLUS

But of you they never tire. If a man has thirteen talents, he has all the greater ardour to possess sixteen; if that wish is achieved, he will want forty or will complain that he knows not how to make both ends meet.

PLUTUS

All this, I suppose, is very true; there is but one point that makes me feel a bit uneasy.

CHREMYLUS

And that is?

PLUTUS

How could I use this power, which you say I have?

CHREMYLUS

Ah! they were quite right who said there's nothing more timorous than Plutus

PLUTUS

No, no; it was a thief who calumniated me. Having broken into a house, he found everything locked up and could take nothing, so he dubbed my prudence fear.

CHREMYLUS

Don't be disturbed; if you support me zealously, I'll make you more sharp-sighted than Lynceus.

PLUTUS

And how should you be able to do that, you. who are but a mortal?

CHREMYLUS

I have great hope, after the answer Apollo gave me, shaking his sacred laurels the while.

PLUTUS

Is *he* in the plot then?

CHREMYLUS

Surely.

PLUTUS

Take care what you say.

CHREMYLUS

Never fear, friend; for, be well assured, that if it has to cost me my life, I will carry out what I have in my head.

CARIO

And I will help you, if you permit it.

CHREMYLUS

We shall have many other helpers as well—all the worthy folk who are wanting for bread.

PLUTUS

Ah! they'll prove sorry helpers.

CHREMYLUS

No, not so, once they've grown rich. But you, Cario, run quick . . .

CARIO

Where?

CHREMYLUS

. . . to call my comrades, the other husbandmen (you'll probably find the poor fellows toiling away in the fields), that each of them may come here to take his share of the gifts of Plutus.

CARIO

I'm off. But let someone come from the house to take this morsel of meat.[1]

CHREMYLUS

I'll see to that; you run your hardest. As for you, Plutus, the most excellent of all the gods, come in here with me; this is the house you must fill with riches to-day, by fair means or foul.

PLUTUS

I don't at all like going into other folks' houses in this manner; I have never got any good from it. If I got inside a miser's house, straightway he would bury me deep underground; if some honest fellow among his friends came to ask him for the smallest coin, he would deny ever having seen me. Then if I went to a fool's house, he would sacrifice in dicing and wenching, and very soon I should be completely stripped and pitched out of doors.

CHREMYLUS

That's because you have never met a man who knew how to avoid the two extremes; moderation is the strong point in my character. I love saving as much as anybody, and I know how to spend, when it's needed. But let us go in; I want to make you known to my wife and to my only son, whom I love most of all after yourself.

PLUTUS

I'm quite sure of that.

CHREMYLUS

Why should I hide the truth from you?

(*They enter* CHREMYLUS' *house.*)

CARIO (*to the* CHORUS, *which has followed him in*)

Come, you active workers, who, like my master, eat nothing but garlic and the poorest food, you who are his friends and his neighbours, hasten your steps, hurry yourselves; there's not a moment to lose; this is the critical hour, when your presence and your support are needed by him.

LEADER OF THE CHORUS

Why, don't you see we are speeding as fast as men can, who are already enfeebled by age? But do you deem it fitting to make us run like this before ever telling us why your master has called us?

CARIO

I've grown hoarse with the telling, but you won't listen. My master is going to drag you all out of the stupid, sapless life you are leading and ensure you one full of all delights.

LEADER OF THE CHORUS

And how is he going to manage that?

CARIO

My poor friends, he has brought with him a disgusting old fellow, all bent and wrinkled, with a most pitiful appearance, bald and toothless; upon my word, I even believe he is circumcised like some vile barbarian.

LEADER OF THE CHORUS

This news is worth its weight in gold! What are you saying? Repeat it to me; no doubt it means he is bringing back a heap of wealth.

CARIO

No, but a heap of all the infirmities attendant on old age.

LEADER OF THE CHORUS

If you are tricking us, you shall pay us for it. Beware of our sticks!

CARIO

Do you deem me so brazen as all that, and my words mere lies?

LEADER OF THE CHORUS

What serious airs the rascal puts on! Look! his legs are already shriek-ing, "oh! oh!" They are asking for the shackles and wedges.

CARIO

It's in the tomb that it's your lot to judge. Why don't you go there? Charon has given you your ticket.

LEADER OF THE CHORUS

Plague take you! you cursed rascal, who rail at us and have not even the heart to tell us why your master has made us come. We were pressed for time and tired out, yet we came with all haste, and in our hurry we have passed by lots of wild onions without even gathering them.

CARIO

I will no longer conceal the truth from you. Friends, it's Plutus whom my master brings, Plutus, who will give you riches.

LEADER OF THE CHORUS

What! we shall really all become rich?

CARIO
Aye, certainly; you will then be Midases, provided you grow ass's ears

LEADER OF THE CHORUS
What joy, what happiness! If what you tell me is true, I long to dance with delight.

CARIO (*singing, with appropriate gestures*)
And I too, *threttanelo!* [2] I want to imitate the Cyclops and lead your troop by stamping like this. Do you, my dear little ones, cry, aye, cry again and bleat forth the plaintive song of the sheep and of the stinking goats; follow me like lascivious goats with their tools out.

LEADER OF THE CHORUS
(*Singing, to the same tune and with similar mimicry*)
As for us, *threttanelo!* we will seek you, dear Cyclops, bleating, and if we find you with your wallet full of fresh herbs, all disgusting in your filth, sodden with wine and sleeping in the midst of your sheep, we will seize a great flaming stake and burn out your eye.

CARIO
I will copy that Circé of Corinth, whose potent philtres compelled the companions of Philonides like swine to swallow balls of dung, which she herself had kneaded with her hands; and do you too grunt with joy and follow your mother, my little pigs.

LEADER OF THE CHORUS
Oh! Circé with the potent philtres, who besmear your companions so filthily, what pleasure I shall have in imitating the son of Laertes! I will hang you up by your balls, I will rub your nose with dung like a goat, and like Aristyllus you shall say through your half-opened lips, "Follow your mother, my little pigs."

CARIO
Enough of tomfoolery, assume a grave demeanour; unknown to my master I am going to take bread and meat; and when I have fed well, I shall resume my work.
(*Interlude of dancing by the* CHORUS.)

CHREMYLUS (*coming out of his house*)
To say, "Hail! my dear neighbours!" is an old form of greeting and well worn with use; so therefore I embrace you, because you have not crept like tortoises, but have come rushing here in all haste. Now help me to watch carefully and closely over the god.

LEADER OF THE CHORUS

Be at ease. You shall see with what martial zeal I will guard him. What! we jostle each other at the Assembly for three obols, and am I going to let Plutus in person be stolen from me?

CHREMYLUS

But I see Blepsidemus; by his bearing and his haste I can readily see he knows or suspects something.

BLEPSIDEMUS

What has happened then? Whence, how has Chremylus suddenly grown rich? I don't believe a word of it. Nevertheless, nothing but his sudden fortune was being talked about in the barber-shops. But I am above all surprised that his good fortune has not made him forget his friends; that is not the usual way!

CHREMYLUS

By the gods, Blepsidemus, I will hide nothing from you. To-day things are better than yesterday; let us share, for are you not my friend?

BLEPSIDEMUS

Have you really grown rich as they say?

CHREMYLUS

I shall be soon, if the god agrees to it. But there is still some risk to run.

BLEPSIDEMUS

What risk?

CHREMYLUS

Well . . .

BLEPSIDEMUS

Tell me, quick!

CHREMYLUS

If we succeed, we are happy for ever, but if we fail, it is all over with us.

BLEPSIDEMUS

It's a bad business, and one that doesn't please me! To grow rich all at once and yet to be fearful! ah! I suspect something that's little good.

CHREMYLUS

What do you mean?

BLEPSIDEMUS

No doubt you have just stolen some gold and silver from some temple and are repenting.

CHREMYLUS

Nay! heaven preserve me from that!

BLEPSIDEMUS

A truce to idle phrases! the thing is only too apparent, my friend.

CHREMYLUS

Don't suspect such a thing of me.

BLEPSIDEMUS

Alas! then there is no honest man! not one, that can resist the attraction of gold!

CHREMYLUS

By Demeter, you have no common sense.

BLEPSIDEMUS (*aside*)

How he has changed!

CHREMYLUS

But, good gods, you are mad, my dear fellow!

BLEPSIDEMUS (*aside*)

His very look is distraught; he has done some crime!

CHREMYLUS

Ah! I know the tune you are playing now; you think I have stolen, and want your share.

BLEPSIDEMUS

My share of what, pray?

CHREMYLUS

You are beside the mark; the thing is quite otherwise.

BLEPSIDEMUS

Perhaps it's not a theft, but some piece of knavery!

CHREMYLUS

You are insane!

BLEPSIDEMUS

What? You have done no man an injury?

CHREMYLUS

No! assuredly not!

BLEPSIDEMUS

But, great gods, what am I to think? You won't tell me the truth.

CHREMYLUS

You accuse me without really knowing anything.

BLEPSIDEMUS

Listen, friend, no doubt the matter can yet be hushed up, before it gets noised abroad, at trifling expense; I will buy the orators' silence.

CHREMYLUS

Aye, you will lay out three minae and, as my friend, you will reckon twelve against me.

BLEPSIDEMUS

I know someone who will come and seat himself at the foot of the tribunal, holding a supplicant's bough in his hand and surrounded by his wife and children, for all the world like the *Heraclidae* of Pamphilus.

CHREMYLUS

Not at all, poor fool! But, thanks to me, worthy folk alone shall be rich henceforth.

BLEPSIDEMUS

What are you saying? Have you then stolen so much as all that?

CHREMYLUS

Oh! your insults will be the death of me.

BLEPSIDEMUS

You're the one who is courting death.

CHREMYLUS

Not so, you wretch, since I have Plutus.

BLEPSIDEMUS

You have Plutus? Which one?

CHREMYLUS

The god himself.

BLEPSIDEMUS

And where is he?

CHREMYLUS

There.

BLEPSIDEMUS

Where?

CHREMYLUS

Indoors.

BLEPSIDEMUS

Indoors?

CHREMYLUS

Aye, certainly.

BLEPSIDEMUS

Get you gone! Plutus in your house?

CHREMYLUS

Yes, by the gods!

BLEPSIDEMUS

Are you telling the truth?

CHREMYLUS

I am.

BLEPSIDEMUS

Swear it by Hestia.

CHREMYLUS

I swear it by Posidon.

BLEPSIDEMUS

The god of the sea?

CHREMYLUS

Yes, and by all the other Posidons, if such there be.

BLEPSIDEMUS

And you don't send him to us, to your friends?

CHREMYLUS

We've not got to that point yet.

BLEPSIDEMUS

What do you say? Is there no chance of sharing?

CHREMYLUS

Why, no. We must first . . .

BLEPSIDEMUS

Do what?

CHREMYLUS

. . . restore him his sight.

BLEPSIDEMUS

Restore whom his sight? Speak!

CHREMYLUS

Plutus. It must be done, no matter how.

BLEPSIDEMUS

Is he then really blind?

CHREMYLUS

Yes, undoubtedly.

BLEPSIDEMUS

I am no longer surprised he never came to me.

CHREMYLUS

If it please the gods, he'll come there now.

BLEPSIDEMUS

Must we not go and seek a physician?

CHREMYLUS

Seek physicians at *Athens?* Nay! there's no art where there's no fee.[2]

BLEPSIDEMUS (*running his eyes over the audience*)

Let's look carefully.

CHREMYLUS (*after a thorough survey*)

There is not one.

BLEPSIDEMUS

It's a positive fact; I don't know of one.

CHREMYLUS

But I have thought the matter well over, and the best thing is to make Plutus lie in the Temple of Asclepius.

BLEPSIDEMUS

Unquestionably that's the very best thing. Hurry and lead him away to the temple.

CHREMYLUS

I am going there.

BLEPSIDEMUS

Then hurry up.

CHREMYLUS

That's just what I am doing.

(*They are just leaving when* POVERTY *comes running in; she is a picture of squalor and the two men recoil in horror.*)

POVERTY

Unwise, perverse, unholy men! What are you daring to do, you pitiful, wretched mortals? Whither are you flying? Stop! I command it!

BLEPSIDEMUS

Oh! great gods!

POVERTY

My arm shall destroy you, you infamous beings! Such an attempt is not to be borne; neither man nor god has ever dared the like. You shall die!

CHREMYLUS

And who are you? Oh! what a ghastly pallor!

BLEPSIDEMUS

Perhaps it's some Erinys, some Fury, from the theatre; there's a kind of wild tragic look in her eyes.

CHREMYLUS

But she has no torch.

BLEPSIDEMUS

Let's knock her down!

POVERTY

Who do you think I am?

CHREMYLUS

Some wine-shop keeper or egg-woman. Otherwise you would not have shrieked so loud at us, who have done nothing to you.

POVERTY

Indeed? And have you not done me the most deadly injury by seeking to banish me from every country?

CHREMYLUS

Why, have you not got the Barathrum left? But who are you? Answer me quickly!

POVERTY

I am one that will punish you this very day for having wanted to make me disappear from here.

BLEPSIDEMUS

Might it be the tavern-keeper in my neighbourhood, who is always cheating me in measure?

POVERTY

I am Poverty, who have lived with you for so many years.

BLEPSIDEMUS

Oh! great Apollo! oh, ye gods! whither shall I fly?

(*He starts to run away.*)

CHREMYLUS

Here! what are you doing! You coward! Are going to leave me here?

BLEPSIDEMUS (*still running*)

Not I.

CHREMYLUS

Stop then! Are two men to run away from one woman?

BLEPSIDEMUS

But, you wretch, it's Poverty, the most fearful monster that ever drew breath.

CHREMYLUS

Stay where you are, I beg of you.

BLEPSIDEMUS

No! no! a thousand times, no!

CHREMYLUS

Could we do anything worse than leave the god in the lurch and fly before this woman without so much as ever offering to fight?

BLEPSIDEMUS

But what weapons have we? Are we in a condition to show fight? Where is the breastplate, the buckler, that this wretch has not pawned?

CHREMYLUS

Be at ease. Plutus will readily triumph over her threats unaided.

POVERTY

Dare you reply, you scoundrels, you who are caught red-handed at the most horrible crime?

CHREMYLUS

As for you, you cursed jade, you pursue me with your abuse, though I have never done you the slightest harm.

POVERTY

Do you think it is doing me no harm to restore Plutus to the use of his eyes?

CHREMYLUS

Is this doing you harm, that we shower blessings on all men?

POVERTY

And what do you think will ensure their happiness?

CHREMYLUS

Ah! first of all we shall drive you out of Greece.

POVERTY

Drive me out? Could you do mankind a greater harm?

CHREMYLUS

Yes—if I gave up my intention to deliver them from you.

POVERTY

Well, let us discuss this point first. I propose to show that I am the sole cause of all your blessings, and that your safety depends on me alone. If I don't succeed, then do what you like to me.

CHREMYLUS

How dare you talk like this, you impudent hussy?

POVERTY

Agree to hear me and I think it will be very easy for me to prove that you are entirely on the wrong road, when you want to make the just men wealthy.

BLEPSIDEMUS

Oh! cudgel and rope's end, come to my help!

POVERTY

Why such wrath and these shouts, before you hear my arguments?

BLEPSIDEMUS

But who could listen to such words without exclaiming?

POVERTY

Any man of sense.

CHREMYLUS

But if you lose your case, what punishment will you submit to?

POVERTY

Choose what you will.

CHREMYLUS

That's all right.

POVERTY

You shall suffer the same if you are beaten!

CHREMYLUS

Do you think twenty deaths a sufficiently large stake?

BLEPSIDEMUS

Good enough for her, but for us two would suffice.

POVERTY

You won't escape, for is there indeed a single valid argument to oppose me with?

LEADER OF THE CHORUS

To beat her in this debate, you must call upon all your wits. Make no allowances and show no weakness!

CHREMYLUS

It is right that the good should be happy, that the wicked and the impious, on the other hand, should be miserable; that is a truth, I believe, which no one will gainsay. To realize this condition of things is a proposal as great as it is noble and useful in every respect, and we have found a means of attaining the object of our wishes. If Plutus recovers his sight and ceases from wandering about unseeing and at random, he will go to seek the just men and never leave them again; he will shun the perverse and ungodly; so, thanks to him, all men will become honest, rich and pious. Can anything better be conceived for the public weal?

BLEPSIDEMUS

Of a certainty, no! I bear witness to that. It is not even necessary she should reply.

CHREMYLUS

Does it not seem that everything is extravagance in the world, or rather madness, when you watch the way things go? A crowd of rogues enjoy blessings they have won by sheer injustice, while more honest folks are miserable, die of hunger, and spend their whole lives with you. Now, if Plutus became clear-sighted again and drove out Poverty, it would be the greatest blessing possible for the human race.

POVERTY

Here are two old men, whose brains are easy to confuse, who assist each other to talk rubbish and drivel to their hearts' content. But if your wishes were realized, your profit would be great! Let Plutus recover his sight and divide his favours out equally to all, and none will ply either trade or art any longer; all toil would be done away with. Who would wish to hammer iron, build ships, sew, turn, cut up leather, bake bricks, bleach linen, tan hides, or break up the soil of the earth with the plough and garner the gifts of Demeter, if he could live in idleness and free from all this work?

CHREMYLUS

What nonsense all this is! All these trades which you just mention will be plied by our slaves.

POVERTY

Your slaves! And by what means will these slaves be got?

CHREMYLUS

We will buy them.

POVERTY

But first say, who will sell them, if everyone is rich?

CHREMYLUS

Some greedy dealer from Thessaly—the land which supplies so many.

POVERTY

But if your system is applied, there won't be a single slave-dealer left. What rich man would risk his life to devote himself to this traffic? You will have to toil, to dig and submit yourself to all kinds of hard labour; so that your life would be more wretched even than it is now.

CHREMYLUS

May this prediction fall upon yourself!

POVERTY

You will not be able to sleep in a bed, for no more will ever be manufactured; nor on carpets, for who would weave them, if he had gold? When you bring a young bride to your dwelling, you will have no essences wherewith to perfume her, nor rich embroidered cloaks dyed with dazzling colours in which to clothe her. And yet what is the use of being rich, if you are to be deprived of all these enjoyments? On the other hand, you have all that you need in abundance, thanks to me; to the artisan I am like a severe mistress, who forces him by need and poverty to seek the means of earning his livelihood.

CHREMYLUS

And what good thing can you give us, unless it be burns in the bath,⸴ and swarms of brats and old women who cry with hunger, and clouds uncountable of lice, gnats and flies, which hover about the wretch's head, trouble him, awake him and say, "You will be hungry, but get up!" Besides, to possess a rag in place of a mantle, a pallet of rushes swarming with bugs, that do not let you close your eyes, for a bed; a rotten piece of matting for a coverlet; a big stone for a pillow, on which to lay your head; to eat mallow roots instead of bread, and leaves of withered radish instead of cake; to have nothing but the cover of a broken jug for a stool, the stave of a cask, and broken at that, for a kneading-trough, that is the life you make for us! Are these the mighty benefits with which you pretend to load mankind?

POVERTY

It's not my life that you describe; you are attacking the existence beggars lead.

CHREMYLUS

Is Beggary not Poverty's sister?

POVERTY

Thrasybulus and Dionysius are one and the same according to you. No, my life is not like that and never will be. The beggar, whom you have depicted to us, never possesses anything. The poor man lives thriftily and attentive to his work; he has not got too much, but he does not lack what he really needs.

CHREMYLUS

Oh! what a happy life, by Demeter! to live sparingly, to toil incessantly and not to leave enough to pay for a tomb!

POVERTY

That's it! Jest, jeer, and never talk seriously! But what you don't know is this, that men with me are worth more, both in mind and body, than with Plutus. With him they are gouty, big-bellied, heavy of limb and scandalously stout; with me they are thin, wasp-waisted, and terrible to the foe.

CHREMYLUS

No doubt it's by starving them that you give them that waspish waist.

POVERTY

As for behaviour, I will prove to you that modesty dwells with me and insolence with Plutus.

CHREMYLUS

Oh! the sweet modesty of stealing and burglary.

POVERTY

Look at the orators in our republics; as long as they are poor, both state and people can only praise their uprightness; but once they are fattened on the public funds, they conceive a hatred for justice, plan intrigues against the people and attack the democracy.

CHREMYLUS

That is absolutely true, although your tongue is very vile. But it matters not, so don't put on those triumphant airs; you shall not be punished any the less for having tried to persuade me that poverty is worth more than wealth.

POVERTY

Not being able to refute my arguments, you chatter at random and exert yourself to no purpose.

CHREMYLUS

Then tell me this, why does all mankind flee from you?

POVERTY

Because I make them better. Children do the very same; they flee from the wise counsels of their fathers. So difficult is it to see one's true interest.

CHREMYLUS

Will you say that Zeus cannot discern what is best? Well, he takes Plutus to himself . . .

BLEPSIDEMUS

. . . and banishes Poverty to the earth.

POVERTY

Ah me! how purblind you are, you old fellows of the days of Cronus! Why, Zeus is poor, and I will clearly prove it to you. In the Olympic games, which he founded, and to which he convokes the whole of Greece every four years, why does he only crown the victorious athletes with wild olive? If he were rich he would give them gold.

CHREMYLUS

That's the way he shows that he clings to his wealth; he is sparing with it, won't part with any portion of it, only bestows baubles on the victors and keeps his money for himself.

POVERTY

But wealth coupled to such sordid greed is yet more shameful than poverty.

CHREMYLUS

May Zeus destroy you, both you and your chaplet of wild olive!

POVERTY

Thus you dare to maintain that Poverty is not the fount of all blessings!

CHREMYLUS

Ask Hecaté whether it is better to be rich or starving; she will tell you that the rich send her a meal every month and that the poor make it disappear before it is even served. But go and hang yourself and don't breathe another syllable. I will not be convinced against my will.

POVERTY

"Oh! citizens of Argos! do you hear what he says?" [5]

CHREMYLUS

Invoke Pauson, your boon companion, rather.

POVERTY

Alas! what is to become of me?

CHREMYLUS

Get you gone, be off quick and a pleasant journey to you.

POVERTY

But where shall I go?

CHREMYLUS

To gaol; but hurry up, let us put an end to this.

POVERTY (*as she departs*)

One day you will recall me.

CHREMYLUS

Then you can return; but disappear for the present. I prefer to be rich; you are free to knock your head against the walls in your rage.

BLEPSIDEMUS

And I too welcome wealth. I want, when I leave the bath all perfumed
with essences, to feast bravely with my wife and children and to fart in
the faces of toilers and Poverty.

CHREMYLUS

So that hussy has gone at last! But let us make haste to put Plutus to
bed in the Temple of Asclepius.

BLEPSIDEMUS

Let us make haste; else some bothering fellow may again come to
interrupt us.

CHREMYLUS (*loudly*)

Cario, bring the coverlets and all that I have got ready from the house;
let us conduct the god to the temple, taking care to observe all the proper
rites.
(CARIO *comes out of the house with a bundle under one arm and leading*
PLUTUS *with the other.* CHREMYLUS *and* BLEPSIDEMUS *join him and
all four of them depart.*)
(*Interlude of dancing by the* CHORUS.)

CARIO

Oh! you old fellows, who used to dip out the broth served to the poor
at the festival of Theseus with little pieces of bread hollowed like a spoon,
how worthy of envy is your fate! How happy you are, both you and all
just men!

LEADER OF THE CHORUS

My good fellow, what has happened to your friends? You seem the
bearer of good tidings.

CARIO

What joy for my master and even more for Plutus! The god has regained his sight; his eyes sparkle with the greatest brilliancy, thanks to
the benevolent care of Asclepius.

LEADER OF THE CHORUS

Oh! what transports of joy! oh! what shouts of gladness!

CARIO

Aye! one is compelled to rejoice, whether one will or not.

LEADER OF THE CHORUS

I will sing to the honour of Asclepius, the son of illustrious Zeus, with
a resounding voice; he is the beneficent star which men adore.

CHREMYLUS' WIFE (*coming out of the house*)
What mean these shouts? Is there good news? With what impatience
have I been waiting in the house, and for so long too!

CARIO
Quick! quick, some wine, mistress. And drink some yourself, (*aside*)
it's much to your taste. I bring you all blessings in a lump.

WIFE
Where are they?

CARIO
In my words, as you are going to see.

WIFE
Have done with trifling! come, speak.

CARIO
Listen, I am going to tell you everything from the feet to the head.

WIFE
Oh! don't throw anything at my head.

CARIO
Not even the happiness that has come to you?

WIFE
No, no, nothing . . . to annoy me.

CARIO
Having arrived near to the temple with our patient, then so unfortunate,
but now at the apex of happiness, of blessedness, we first led him down to
the sea to purify him.

WIFE
Ah! what a singular pleasure for an old man to bathe in the cold sea-
water!

CARIO (*in the manner of the tragic messenger*)
Then we repaired to the temple of the god. Once the wafers and the
various offerings had been consecrated upon the altar, and the cake of
wheaten-meal had been handed over to the devouring Hephaestus, we
made Plutus lie on a couch according to the rite, and each of us prepared
himself a bed of leaves.

WIFE
Had any other folk come to beseech the deity?

CARIO

Yes. Firstly, Neoclides, who is blind, but steals much better than those who see clearly; then many others attacked by complaints of all kinds. The lights were put out and the priest enjoined us to sleep, especially recommending us to keep silent should we hear any noise. There we were all lying down quite quietly. I could not sleep; I was thinking of a certain stew-pan full of pap placed close to an old woman and just behind her head. I had a furious longing to slip towards that side. But just as I was lifting my head, I noticed the priest, who was sweeping off both the cakes and the figs on the sacred table; then he made the round of the altars and sanctified the cakes that remained, by stowing them away in a bag. I therefore resolved to follow such a pious example and made straight for the pap.

WIFE

You rogue! and had you no fear of the god?

CARIO

Aye, indeed! I feared that the god with his crown on his head might have been near the stew-pan before me. I said to myself, "Like priest, like god." On hearing the noise I made, the old woman put out her hand, but I hissed and bit it, just as a sacred serpent might have done.[6] Quick she drew back her hand, slipped down into the bed with her head beneath the coverlets and never moved again; only she let flee a fart in her fear which stank worse than a weasel. As for myself, I swallowed a goodly portion of the pap and, having made a good feed, went back to bed.

WIFE

And did not the god come?

CARIO

He did not tarry; and when he was near us, oh! dear! such a good joke happened. My belly was quite blown up, and I let a *thunderous* fart!

WIFE

Doubtless the god pulled a wry face?

CARIO

No, but Iaso blushed a little and Panacea turned her head away, holding her nose; my farts are not perfume.

WIFE

And what did the god do?

CARIO

He paid not the slightest heed.

WIFE

He must then be a pretty coarse kind of god?

CARIO

I don't say that, but he's used to tasting stools.

WIFE

Impudent knave, go on with you!

CARIO

Then I hid myself in my bed all a-tremble. Asclepius did the round of the patients and examined them all with great attention; then a slave placed beside him a stone mortar, a pestle and a little box.

WIFE

Of stone?

CARIO

No, not of stone.

WIFE

But how could you see all this, you arch-rascal, when you say you were hiding all the time?

CARIO

Why, great gods, through my cloak, for it's not without holes! He first prepared an ointment for Neoclides; he threw three heads of Tenian garlic into the mortar, pounded them with an admixture of fig-tree sap and lentisk, moistened the whole with Sphettian vinegar, and, turning back the patient's eyelids, applied his salve to the interior of the eyes, so that the pain might be more excruciating. Neoclides shrieked, howled, sprang towards the foot of his bed and wanted to bolt, but the god laughed and said to him, "Keep where you are with your salve; by doing this you will not go and perjure yourself before the Assembly."

WIFE

What a wise god and what a friend to our city!

CARIO

Thereupon he came and seated himself at the head of Plutus' bed, took a perfectly clean rag and wiped his eyelids; Panacea covered his head and face with a purple cloth, while the god whistled, and two enormous snakes came rushing from the sanctuary.

WIFE

Great gods!

CARIO

They slipped gently beneath the purple cloth and, as far as I could judge, licked the patient's eyelids; for, in less time than even you need, mistress, to drain down ten beakers of wine, Plutus rose up; he could see. I clapped my hands with joy and awoke my master, and the god immediately disappeared with the serpents into the sanctuary. As for those who were lying near Plutus, you can imagine that they embraced him tenderly. Dawn broke and not one of them had closed an eye. As for myself, I did not cease thanking the god who had so quickly restored to Plutus his sight and had made Neoclides blinder than ever.

WIFE

Oh! thou great Asclepius! How mighty is thy power! (*To* CARIO) But tell me, where is Plutus now?

CARIO

He is approaching, escorted by an immense crowd. The rich, whose wealth is ill-gotten, are knitting their brows and shooting at him looks of fierce hate, while the just folk, who led a wretched existence, embrace him and grasp his hand in the transport of their joy; they follow in his wake, their heads wreathed with garlands, laughing and blessing their deliverer; the old men make the earth resound as they walk together keeping time. Come, all of you, all, down to the very least, dance, leap and form yourselves into a chorus; no longer do you risk being told, when you go home, "There is no meal in the bag."

WIFE

And I, by Hecaté! I will string you a garland of cakes for the good tidings you have brought me.

CARIO

Hurry, make haste then; our friends are close at hand.

WIFE

I will go indoors to fetch some gifts of welcome, to celebrate these eyes that have just been opened.

(*She goes back into the house.*)

CARIO

Meantime I am going forth to meet them.

(*Exit*)

(*Interlude of dancing by the* CHORUS.)

PLUTUS

I adore thee, oh! thou divine sun, and thee I greet, thou city, the beloved of Pallas; be welcome, thou land of Cecrops, which hast received

me. Alas! what manner of men I associated with! I blush to think of it.
While, on the other hand, I shunned those who deserved my friendship;
I knew neither the vices of the ones nor the virtues of the others. A twofold mistake, and in both cases equally fatal! Ah! what a misfortune was
mine! But I want to change everything; and in the future I mean to prove
to mankind that, if I gave to the wicked, it was against my will.

CHREMYLUS (*to the wings*)
Get you gone! Oh! what a lot of friends spring into being when you are
fortunate! They dig me with their elbows and bruise my shins to prove
their affection. Each one wants to greet me. What a crowd of old fellows
thronged round me on the market-place!

WIFE
Oh! thou, who art dearest of all to me, and thou too, be welcome! Allow me, Plutus, to shower these gifts of welcome over you in due accord
with custom.

PLUTUS
No. This is the first house I enter after having regained my sight; I
shall take nothing from it, for it is my place rather to give.

WIFE
Do you refuse these gifts?

PLUTUS
I will accept them at your fireside, as custom requires. Besides, we shall
thus avoid a ridiculous scene; it is not meet that the poet should throw
dried figs and dainties to the spectators; it is a vulgar trick to make them
laugh.[7]

WIFE
You are right. Look! yonder's Dexinicus, who was already getting to
his feet to catch the figs as they flew past him.
(*Interlude of dancing by the* CHORUS.)

CARIO
How pleasant it is, friends, to live well, especially when it costs nothing!
What a deluge of blessings flood our household, and that too without our
having wronged a single soul! Ah! what a delightful thing is wealth! The
bin is full of white flour and the wine-jars run over with fragrant liquor;
all the chests are crammed with gold and silver, it is a sight to see; the
tank is full of oil, the phials with perfumes, and the garret with dried figs.
Vinegar flasks, plates, stew-pots and all the platters are of brass; our
rotten old wooden trenchers for the fish have to-day become dishes of

silver; even the thunder-mug is of ivory. We others, the slaves, we play at odd and even with gold pieces, and carry luxury so far that we no longer wipe our arses with stones, but use garlic stalks instead. My master, at this moment, is crowned with flowers and sacrificing a pig, a goat and a ram; it's the smoke that has driven me out, for I could no longer endure it, it hurt my eyes so.

(*A* JUST MAN *enters, followed by a small slave-lad who carries a thread-bare cloak and a pair of badly worn sandals.*)

JUST MAN

Come, my child, come with me. Let us go and find the god.

CARIO

Who's this?

JUST MAN

A man who was once wretched, but now is happy.

CARIO

A just man then?

JUST MAN

That's right.

CARIO

Well! what do you want?

JUST MAN

I come to thank the god for all the blessings he has showered on me. My father had left me a fairly decent fortune, and I helped those of my friends who were in want; it was, to my thinking, the most useful thing I could do with my fortune.

CARIO

And you were quickly ruined?

JUST MAN

Quite.

CARIO

And since then you have been living in misery?

JUST MAN

Quite; I thought I could count, in case of need, upon the friends whose property I had helped, but they turned their backs upon me and pre-tended not to see me.

CARIO

They laughed at you, that's obvious.

JUST MAN

Quite. With my empty coffers, I had no more friends. But my lot has changed, and so I come to the god to make him the acts of gratitude that are his due.

CARIO

But why are you bringing this old cloak, which your slave is carrying? Tell me.

JUST MAN

I wish to dedicate it to the god.

CARIO

Were you initiated into the Great Mysteries in that cloak? [8]

JUST MAN

No, but I shivered in it for thirteen years.

CARIO

And this footwear?

JUST MAN

These also are my winter companions.

CARIO

And you wish to dedicate them too?

JUST MAN

Certainly.

CARIO

Fine presents to offer to the god!
                    (*An* INFORMER *enters, followed by a witness.*)

INFORMER (*before he sees* CARIO)

Alas! alas! I am a lost man. Ah! thrice, four, five, twelve times, or rather ten thousand times unhappy fate! Why, why must fortune deal me such rough blows?

CARIO

Oh, Apollo, my tutelary! oh! ye favourable gods! what has overtaken this man?

INFORMER (*to* CARIO)

Ah! am I not deserving of pity? I have lost everything; this cursed god has stripped me bare. Ah! if there be justice in heaven, he shall be struck blind again.

JUST MAN

I think I know what's the matter. If this man is unfortunate, it's because he's of little account and small honesty; and indeed he looks it too.

CARIO

Then, by Zeus! his plight is but just.

INFORMER

He promised that if he recovered his sight, he would enrich us all unaided; whereas he has ruined more than one.

CARIO

But whom has he thus ill-used?

INFORMER

Me.

CARIO

You were doubtless a villainous thief then.

INFORMER

No, it is rather you yourselves who were such wretches; I am certain you have got my money.

CARIO

Ha! by Demeter! an informer! What impudence! He's ravenously hungry, that's certain.

INFORMER

You shall follow me this very instant to the market-place, where the torture of the wheel shall force the confession of your misdeeds from you.

CARIO (*with a threatening gesture*)

Watch out, now!

JUST MAN

By Zeus the Deliverer, what gratitude all Greeks owe to Plutus, if he destroys these vile informers!

INFORMER

You are laughing at me. Well, then I denounce you as their accomplice. Where did you steal that new cloak from? Yesterday I saw you with one utterly worn out.

JUST MAN

I fear you not, thanks to this ring, for which I paid Eudemus a drachma.

CARIO

Ah! there's no ring to preserve you from the informer's bite.

INFORMER

The insolent wretches! But, my fine jokers, you have not told me what you are up to here. Nothing good, I'm sure of that.

CARIO

Nothing of any good for you, be sure of *that*.

INFORMER

By Zeus! it's at my expense that you are about to dine.

CARIO

You and your witness, I hope you both burst . . .

JUST MAN

With an empty belly.

INFORMER

You deny it? I reckon, you villains, that there is much salt fish and roast meat in this house. (*He sniffs elaborately.*)

CARIO

Can you smell anything, rascal?

JUST MAN

The cold, perhaps.

INFORMER

Can such outrages be borne, oh, Zeus! Ye gods! how cruel it is to see me treated thus, when I am such an honest fellow and such a good citizen!

JUST MAN

You an honest man! you a good citizen!

INFORMER

A better one than any.

JUST MAN

Ah! well then, answer my questions.

INFORMER

Concerning what?

JUST MAN
Are you a husbandman?

INFORMER
D'ye take me for a fool?

JUST MAN
A merchant?

INFORMER
I assume the title, when it serves me.[9]

JUST MAN
Do you ply any trade?

INFORMER
No, most assuredly not!

JUST MAN
Then how do you live, if you do nothing?

INFORMER
I superintend public and private business.

JUST MAN
You do? And by what right, pray?

INFORMER
Because it pleases me to do so.

JUST MAN
Like a thief you sneak yourself in where you have no business. You are
hated by all and you claim to be an honest man.

INFORMER
What, you fool? I have not the right to dedicate myself entirely to my
country's service?

JUST MAN
Is the country served by vile intrigue?

INFORMER
It is served by watching that the established law is observed—by allowing no one to violate it.

JUST MAN
That's the duty of the tribunals; they are established to that end.

INFORMER

And who is the prosecutor before the dicasts?

JUST MAN

Whoever wishes to be.

INFORMER

Well then, it is I who choose to be prosecutor; and thus all public affairs fall within my province.

JUST MAN

I pity Athens for being in such vile clutches. But would you not prefer to live quietly and free from all care and anxiety?

INFORMER

To do nothing is to live an animal's life.

JUST MAN

Thus you will not change your mode of life?

INFORMER

No, though they gave me Plutus himself and the silphium of Battus.

CARIO (*to the* INFORMER)

Come, quick, off with your cloak.

(*The* INFORMER *does not move.*)

JUST MAN

Hi! friend! it's you they are speaking to.

CARIO

Off with your shoes.

(*The* INFORMER *still remains motionless.*)

JUST MAN

I say, all this is addressed to you.

INFORMER (*defiantly*)

Very well! let one of you come near me, if he dares.

CARIO

I dare.

(*He strips the* INFORMER *of his cloak and shoes. The witness runs away.*)

INFORMER

Alas! I am robbed of my clothes in full daylight.

CARIO

That's what comes of meddling with other folk's business and living at their expense.

INFORMER (*over his shoulder to the departing witness*)

You see what is happening; I call you to witness.

CARIO (*laughing*)

Look how the witness whom you brought is taking to his heels.

INFORMER

Great gods! I am all alone and they assault me.

CARIO

Shout away!

INFORMER

Oh! woe, woe is me!

CARIO

Give me that old ragged cloak, that I may dress out the informer.

JUST MAN

No, no; I have dedicated it to Plutus.

CARIO

And where would your offering be better bestowed than on the shoulders of a rascal and a thief? To Plutus fine, rich cloaks should be given.

JUST MAN

And what then shall be done with these shoes? Tell me.

CARIO

I will nail them to his brow as gifts are nailed to the trunks of the wild olive.

INFORMER

I'm off, for you are the strongest, I own. But if I find someone to join me, let him be as weak as he will, I will summon this god, who thinks himself so strong, before the court this very day, and denounce him as manifestly guilty of overturning the democracy by his will alone and without the consent of the Senate or the Assembly.

JUST MAN

Now that you are rigged out from head to foot with my old clothes, hasten to the bath and stand there in the front row to warm yourself better; that's the place I formerly had.

CARIO

Ah! the bath-man would grab you by the balls and fling you through the door; he would only need to see you to appraise you at your true value. . . . But let us go in, friend, that you may address your thanksgivings to the god.

(*Interlude of dancing by the* CHORUS.)

(*An* OLD WOMAN *enters, dressed as a young girl and trying to walk in a youthful and alluring manner. She carries a plate of food.*)

OLD WOMAN (*coyly*)

My *dear* old men, am I near the house where the new god lives, or have I missed the road?

LEADER OF THE CHORUS

You are at his door, my pretty little maid, who question us so sweetly.

OLD WOMAN

Then I will summon someone in the house.

CHREMYLUS

No need. I am here myself. But what brings you here?

OLD WOMAN

Ah! a cruel, unjust fate! My dear friend, this god has made life unbearable to me through ceasing to be blind.

CHREMYLUS

What does this mean? Can you be a female informer?

OLD WOMAN

Most certainly not.

CHREMYLUS

Have you *drunk* up your money then?

OLD WOMAN

You are mocking me! No! I am being devoured with a consuming fire.

CHREMYLUS

Then tell me what is consuming you so fiercely.

OLD WOMAN

Listen! I loved a young man, who was poor, but so handsome, so well-built, so honest! He readily gave way to all I desired and acquitted himself so well! I, for my part, refused him nothing.

CHREMYLUS

And what did he generally ask of you?

OLD WOMAN

Very little; he bore himself towards me with astonishing discretion! perchance twenty drachmae for a cloak or eight for footwear; sometimes he begged me to buy tunics for his sisters or a little mantle for his mother; at times he needed four bushels of corn.

CHREMYLUS

That's very little, in truth; I admire his modesty.

OLD WOMAN

And it wasn't as a reward for his complacency that he ever asked me for anything, but as a matter of pure friendship; a cloak I had given would remind him from whom he had got it.

CHREMYLUS

It was a fellow who loved you madly.

OLD WOMAN

But it's no longer so, for the faithless wretch has sadly altered! I had sent him this cake with the sweetmeats you see here on this dish and let him know that I would visit him in the evening . . .

CHREMYLUS

Well?

OLD WOMAN

He sent me back my presents and added this tart to them, on condition that I never set foot in his house again. Besides, he sent me this message, "Once upon a time the Milesians were brave."

CHREMYLUS

An honest lad, indeed! What do you expect? When poor, he would devour anything; now he is rich, he no longer cares for lentils.

OLD WOMAN

Formerly he came to me every day.

CHREMYLUS

To see if you were being buried?

OLD WOMAN

No! he longed to hear the sound of my voice.

CHREMYLUS (*aside*)

And to carry off some present.

OLD WOMAN

If I was downcast, he would call me his little duck or his little dove in a most tender manner . . .

CHREMYLUS (*aside*)

And then would ask for the money to buy a pair of sandals.

OLD WOMAN

When I was at the Mysteries of Eleusis in a carriage, someone made eyes at me; he was so jealous that he beat me the whole of that day.

CHREMYLUS (*aside*)

That was because he liked to feed alone.

OLD WOMAN

He told me I had very beautiful hands.

CHREMYLUS (*aside*)

Aye, no doubt, when they handed him twenty drachmae.

OLD WOMAN

That my whole body breathed a sweet perfume.

CHREMYLUS (*aside*)

Yes, like enough, if you poured him out Thasian wine.

OLD WOMAN

That my glance was gentle and charming.

CHREMYLUS (*aside*)

He was no fool. He knew how to drag drachmae from a sex-starved old woman.

OLD WOMAN

Ah! the god has done very, very wrong, saying he would support the victims of injustice.

CHREMYLUS

Well, what should he do? Speak, and it shall be done.

OLD WOMAN

Compel him, whom I have loaded with benefits, to repay them in his turn; if not, he does not merit the least of the god's favours.

CHREMYLUS
And did he not do this every night?

OLD WOMAN
He swore he would never leave me, as long as I lived.

CHREMYLUS
Aye, rightly; but he thinks you are no longer alive.

OLD WOMAN
Ah! friend, I am pining away with grief.

CHREMYLUS (*aside*)
You are *rotting* away, it seems to me.

OLD WOMAN
I have grown so thin, I could slip through a ring.

CHREMYLUS
Yes, if it were as large as the hoop of a sieve.
(*A young man enters, wearing a garland on his head and carrying a torch in his hand.*)

OLD WOMAN
But here is the youth, the cause of my complaint; he looks as though he were going to a festival.

CHREMYLUS
Yes, if his chaplet and his torch are any guides.

YOUTH (*to the* OLD WOMAN, *with cool politeness*)
Greeting to you.

OLD WOMAN (*in a puzzled tone*)
What was that he said?

YOUTH
My ancient old dear, you have grown white very quickly, by heaven!

OLD WOMAN
Oh! what an insult!

CHREMYLUS
It is a long time, then, since he saw you?

OLD WOMAN
A long time? My god! he was with me yesterday.

CHREMYLUS

It must be, then, that, unlike other people, he sees more clearly when he's drunk.

OLD WOMAN

No, but I have always known him for an insolent fellow.

YOUTH

Oh! divine Posidon! Oh, ye gods of old age! what wrinkles she has on her face!
(*He holds his torch close to her, in order to inspect her more closely.*)

OLD WOMAN

Oh! oh! keep your distance with that torch.

CHREMYLUS (*aside*)

It's just as well; if a single spark were to reach her, she would catch fire like an old olive branch.

YOUTH

I propose to have a game with you.

OLD WOMAN (*eagerly*)

Where, naughty boy?

YOUTH

Here. Take some nuts in your hand.

OLD WOMAN

What game is this?

YOUTH

Let's play at guessing how many . . . teeth you have.

CHREMYLUS

Ah! I'll tell you; she's got three, or perhaps four.

YOUTH

Pay up; you've lost! she has only one single grinder.

OLD WOMAN

You wretch! you're not in your right senses. Do you insult me thus before this crowd?

YOUTH

I am washing you thoroughly; that's doing you a service.

CHREMYLUS

No, no! as she is there, she can still deceive; but if this white-lead is washed off, her wrinkles will come out plainly.

OLD WOMAN

You are only an old fool!

YOUTH

Ah! he is playing the gallant, he is playing with your tits, and thinks I do not see it.

OLD WOMAN (*to* CHREMYLUS)

Oh! no, by Aphrodité, don't do that, you naughty jealous fellow.

CHREMYLUS

Oh! most certainly not, by Hecaté! Verily and indeed I would need to be mad! But, young man, I cannot forgive you, if you cast off this beautiful child.

YOUTH

Why, I adore her.

CHREMYLUS

But nevertheless she accuses you . . .

YOUTH

Accuses me of what?

CHREMYLUS

. . . of having told her insolently, "Once upon a time the Milesians were brave."

YOUTH

Oh! I shall not dispute with you about her.

CHREMYLUS

Why not?

YOUTH

Out of respect for your age; with anyone but you I should not be so easy; come, take the girl and be happy.

CHREMYLUS

I see, I see; you don't want her any more.

OLD WOMAN

Nay! this is a thing that cannot be allowed.

YOUTH

I cannot argue with a woman who has been laid by every one of these thirteen thousand men.

(*He points to the audience.*)

CHREMYLUS

Yet, since you liked the wine, you should now consume the lees.

YOUTH

But these lees are quite rancid and fusty.

CHREMYLUS

Pass them through a straining-cloth; they'll clarify.

YOUTH

But I want to go in with you to offer these chaplets to the god.

OLD WOMAN

And I too have something to tell him.

YOUTH

Then I won't enter.

CHREMYLUS

Come, have no fear; she won't harm you.

YOUTH

That's true; I've been managing the old bark so long.

OLD WOMAN

Go in; I'll follow after you.

(*They enter the house.*)

CHREMYLUS

Good gods! that old hag has fastened herself to her youth like a limpet to its rock.

(*He follows them in.*)
(*Interlude of dancing by the* CHORUS.)
(HERMES *enters and begins knocking on the door.*)

CARIO (*opening the door*)

Who is knocking at the door? Halloa! I see no one; it was then by chance it gave forth that plaintive tone.

HERMES (*to* CARIO, *who is about to close the door*)

Cario! stop!

CARIO

Eh! friend, was it you who knocked so loudly? Tell me.

HERMES

No, I was going to knock and you forestalled me by opening. Come, call your master quick, then his wife and his children, then his slave and his dog, then yourself and his pig.

CARIO

And what's it all about?

HERMES

It's about this, rascal! Zeus wants to serve you all with the same sauce and hurl the lot of you into the Barathrum.

CARIO (*aside*)

Have a care for your tongue, you bearer of ill tidings! (*To* HERMES) But why does he want to treat us in that scurvy fashion?

HERMES

Because you have committed the most dreadful crime. Since Plutus has recovered his sight, there is nothing for us other gods, neither incense, nor laurels, nor cakes, nor victims, nor anything in the world.

CARIO

And you will never be offered anything more; you governed us too ill

HERMES

I care nothing at all about the other gods, but it's myself. I tell you I am dying of hunger.

CARIO

That's reasoning like a wise fellow.

HERMES

Formerly, from earliest dawn, I was offered all sorts of good things in the wine-shops,—wine-cakes, honey, dried figs, in short, dishes worthy of Hermes. Now, I lie the livelong day on my back, with my legs in the air, famishing.

CARIO

And quite right too, for you often had them punished who treated you so well.

HERMES

Ah! the lovely cake they used to knead for me on the fourth of the month!

CARIO

You recall it vainly; your regrets are useless!

HERMES

Ah! the ham I was wont to devour!

CARIO

Well then! make use of your legs and hop on one leg upon the wine-skin,[10] to while away the time.

HERMES

Oh! the grilled entrails I used to swallow down!

CARIO

Your own have got the colic, I think

HERMES

Oh! the delicious tipple, half-wine, half-water!

CARIO

Here, take this and be off. (*He farts.*)

HERMES (*in tragic style*)

Would you render service to the friend that loves you?

CARIO

Willingly, if I can.

HERMES

Give me some well-baked bread and a big hunk of the victims they are sacrificing in your house.

CARIO

That would be stealing.

HERMES

Do you forget, then, how I used to take care he knew nothing about it when you were stealing something from your master?

CARIO

Because I used to share it with you, you rogue; some cake or other always came your way.

HERMES

Which afterwards you ate up all by yourself.[11]

CARIO

But then you did not share the blows when I was caught.

HERMES

Forget past injuries, now you have taken Phylé. Ah! how I should like to live with you! Take pity and receive me.

CARIO

You would leave the gods to stop here?

HERMES

One is much better off among you.

CARIO

What! you would desert! Do you think that is honest?

HERMES

"Where I live well, there is my country."

CARIO

But how could we employ you here?

HERMES

Place me near the door; I am the watchman god and would shift off the robbers.

CARIO

Shift off! Ah! but we have no love for shifts.

HERMES

Entrust me with business dealings.

CARIO

But we are rich; why should we keep a haggling Hermes?

HERMES

Let me intrigue for you.

CARIO

No, no, intrigues are forbidden; we believe in good faith.

HERMES

I will work for you as a guide.

CARIO

But the god sees clearly now, so we no longer want a guide.

HERMES

Well then, I will preside over the games. Ah! what can you object to in that? Nothing is fitter for Plutus than to give scenic and gymnastic games.[12]

CARIO

How useful it is to have so many names! Here you have found the means of earning your bread. I don't wonder the jurymen so eagerly try to get entered for many tribunals.

HERMES

So then, you admit me on these terms?

CARIO

Go and wash the entrails of the victims at the well, so that you may show yourself serviceable at once.

(*They both enter the house. A* PRIEST *of* ZEUS *comes hurrying in.*)

PRIEST

Can anyone tell me where Chremylus is?

CHREMYLUS (*emerging from the house*)

What would you with him, friend?

PRIEST

Much ill. Since Plutus has recovered his sight, I am perishing of starvation; I, the priest of Zeus the Deliverer, have nothing to eat!

CHREMYLUS

And what is the cause of that, pray?

PRIEST

No one dreams of offering sacrifices.

CHREMYLUS

Why not?

PRIEST

Because all men are rich. Ah! when they had nothing, the merchant who escaped from shipwreck, the accused who was acquitted, all immolated victims; another would sacrifice for the success of some wish and the priest joined in at the feast; but now there is not the smallest victim, not one of the faithful in the temple, but thousands who come there to take a crap.

CHREMYLUS

Why don't you take your share of *those* offerings?

PRIEST (*ignoring this*)

Hence I think I too am going to say good-bye to Zeus the Deliverer and stop here myself.

CHREMYLUS

Be at ease, all will go well, if it so please the god. Zeus the Deliverer is here; he came of his own accord.

PRIEST

Ha! that's good news.

(*He moves toward the door.*)

CHREMYLUS

Wait a little; we are going to install Plutus presently in the place he formerly occupied behind the Temple of Athené; there he will watch over our treasures for ever. (*Calling out*) Let lighted torches be brought to the priest. Take these and walk in solemn procession in front of the god.

PRIEST

That's magnificent!

CHREMYLUS

Let Plutus be summoned.

(PLUTUS *comes out of the house, followed by the* OLD WOMAN.)

OLD WOMAN

And I, what am I to do?

CHREMYLUS

Take the pots of vegetables which we are going to offer to the god in honour of his installation and carry them on your head; you just happen luckily to be wearing a beautiful embroidered robe.

OLD WOMAN

And what about the object of my coming?

CHREMYLUS

Everything shall be according to your wish. The young man will be with you this evening.

OLD WOMAN

Oh! if you promise me his visit, I will right willingly carry the pots.

(*She puts them on her head.*)

CHREMYLUS

Those are strange pots indeed! Generally the scum rises to the top of the pots, but here the pots are raised to the top of the old woman.[13]

(PLUTUS *begins to march solemnly off the stage; the* OLD WOMAN *follows him.*)

LEADER OF THE CHORUS

Let us withdraw without more tarrying, and follow the others, singing as we go

(*They do so.*)

1. A sacrifice had naturally preceded the consultation of the oracle, and Cario has brought home the remnants, which were customarily given to the other members of the household.

2. An imitation of the sound of plucked strings on a lyre.

3. This comedy exhibits numerous indications of the deplorable economic conditions prevalent at Athens in the early decades of the fourth century.

4. The baths were the refuge of the poor in the winter, and these unfortunates would seem to have sometimes got too close to the furnaces which heated the water.

5. A line from the lost *Telephus* of Euripides; Aristophanes had already quoted this in *The Knights* (813).

6. The temple of Asclepius naturally contained several of the snakes which were sacred to that deity.

7. This seems to have become a fairly common practice, and Aristophanes has already disclaimed it, in *The Wasps* (58).

8. The point of Cario's question is not entirely clear and has been variously explained; it seems probable that the clothes worn for initiation were the oldest ones possessed.

9. Merchants were exempt from military service and it was thus occasionally useful to be such a person.

10. At feasts of Dionysus a game was played in which the competitors hopped one-legged on a full and greased wine-skin.

11. Hermes, as god of thefts, normally received offerings of cakes from Cario, but even these did not advantage him, for the slave would eat them soon after placing them on the altar. Such offerings were regularly consumed either by the priest of the god involved or by the person who had made the sacrifice.

12. Such spectacles were normally provided by the wealthy.

13. A pun on the two meanings of the Greek word *graus*, "old woman" and "scum."

THE PLAYS OF
MENANDER

I
THE GIRL FROM SAMOS

CHARACTERS IN THE PLAY

DEMEAS, *an Athenian citizen*
PARMENO, *his domestic slave*
A COOK
CHRYSIS, *a Samian girl*
NICERATUS, *neighbour of* DEMEAS
MOSCHION, DEMEAS' *adopted son*

INTRODUCTION

by L. A. Post

THE *Samia* or *Girl from Samos* is Menander's Comedy of Errors. The chief interest lies in plot and situation. At the same time the characters are well defined and sufficiently individual for the purposes of the play. There are two middle-aged men whose features stand out in vivid contrast. Demeas is well-to-do, good-humoured and peaceable. He likes to be comfortable himself and to have every one about him comfortable. There is a certain timidity about him that makes him scrupulous in his dealings with others. He would be very uncomfortable if he had actually wronged anyone, or if he were accused of injustice, whether rightly or wrongly. There is a genuine humanity in his willingness to befriend the unfortunate, but his judgment is sound and he would not willingly suffer impositions beyond certain limits. His own good-will is such that he has a genuine horror of real meanness or ingratitude. In fact his very tenderness might turn to fury if his comfortable confidence in the reciprocal affection and honesty of those about him were actually invaded by a brutal affront.

His neighbour, Niceratus, is on the other hand a very uncomfortable man. He is poor and honest, and his pride is inordinate. He is always on his guard against slights and strikes out at the slightest suspicion, and, since he is a very suspicious man, he is always striking out at those around him. He flaunts his poverty and his honesty, and his manners are intolerable. There is nothing in his position to induce respect; he must therefore compel respect by his irascibility. He has a wife and a daughter, Plangon. Naturally they are afraid of him. He has no dowry to give with his daughter, so that she can hardly hope to escape by marrying. It is not surprising that she should secretly have become attached to her wealthy neighbour's son, Moschion. This callow youth is in turn sincerely attached to her and shows the seriousness of his intentions by accepting all responsibility for the baby that is born to her. Like most young men in Greek comedy, however, he is rather a heedless fellow. He has a nice sense of his own importance and is the hero of numerous romances which have no existence beyond his own imagination. As a matter of fact he is not really Demeas' son, but an adopted foundling. Of this he has no suspicion.

The little romance of Moschion and Plangon had been able to flourish undetected, largely because both Demeas and Niceratus were absent from Athens. It is their return that provides the complications of the plot. Naturally the lovers could hope for no sympathy from the stern Niceratus. It was essential that he should know nothing of the existence of his grandson, whom Plangon had been nursing for some time with the connivance of her mother. From Demeas on the other hand the young people had everything to hope. He was rich and generous, he might well be moved by entreaties to acquiesce in the marriage of the two lovers. The matter, however, required delicate handling. Above all it was necessary to gain time.

The other members of Demeas' household have not yet been mentioned. Demeas had no wife, but he had a mistress whose position in the household was practically that of a wife. She is Chrysis, the girl from Samos, whose fortunes provide the main interest of the play. She had been expelled from Samos, along with the other Athenian inhabitants, in the year 322, after the Macedonian victory over Athens. Arriving in Athens as a refugee, destitute even of the means of proving her identity, she had by her plight moved Demeas to compassion. He had taken her in and had made her his wife in all but name. Legally he could not marry her until she could prove her citizenship. Any children born of the union must be illegitimate. Under such circumstances it was the woman's duty to prevent the birth of children. Certainly it rested entirely with Demeas to decide whether children, if born, should be permitted to live. Now it so happened that Chrysis did bear a child in the absence of Demeas. Either she followed his orders and exposed it to die, or more probably (the plot is not certain) her baby died a natural death shortly before the father's return. There is no great improbability in the coincidence that both Chrysis and Plangon had babies. They were not necessarily born on the same date. We must merely suppose that, when the imminent arrival of Demeas and Niceratus made it necessary to conceal Plangon's baby, Chrysis was able and willing to act as temporary mother. She knew better than anyone the good humour and generosity of Demeas' nature. She was sure of his yielding in the end to Moschion's entreaties. In the meantime she could protect the child and say nothing of Moschion's interest in it. The servants of course had to be admitted to the secret. It probably did not seem a very dangerous secret to Demeas' steward Parmeno, so that he let Moschion and Chrysis arrange matters in their own way without any misgivings. In any case he took no responsibility upon himself.

It should be noted that the baby in *The Girl from Samos* is not a mute hero whose success story is the theme of the play, as in *The Arbitration,* but a symbol of the lasting union and serious intentions of the lovers. Menander could not use the device of a clandestine marriage that makes Romeo and Juliet one in spite of parents. The clandestine babe will do as well. He need not make his own way, for his father stands sponsor for him. It is accordingly about Moschion that the plot is spun. He gains as his allies in succession Chrysis, Demeas, and Niceratus. To the Greeks a baby without a wedding was a better guarantee of love and union than a wedding without a baby.

So Demeas and Niceratus came home. Niceratus did not find an unexpected infant, but Demeas did. What was Chrysis doing with a baby? It was certainly taking a liberty to bring up an infant without his permission, but after all he was fond of her. She would always have a home with him. It wasn't really the thing to do, but he hesitated, she entreated, and in the end he found her irresistible. Naturally it hadn't entered his head that he was not the child's father. In fact he was a little flattered that Chrysis should be so eager to make herself still further dependent on him. In the meantime he had news for Moschion. Moschion must marry Plangon. Demeas had incurred a great obligation to Niceratus (Niceratus may have saved his life at sea) and in order to repay it Moschion should take his daughter without a dowry. Moschion consented with alacrity. There was no need to mention the baby until Plangon was safely in his possession, when there could not possibly be any difficulty. So all was bustle and confusion. Parmeno was sent to the market for a cook and provisions. Niceratus gave orders to his wife and daughter and then departed to do his own catering in person. This was the situation at the end of the first act of the play.

But of course there really couldn't be a wedding until the end of the fifth act. The lovers' luck was too good to last. Misunderstandings soon come thick and fast until it looks as if there would be no wedding at all; and it is hard to get the misunderstandings explained because the truth itself involves some difficulties and because the misunderstandings are so terrible that they quite deprive the victims of the ability to listen to reason. One character after another loses his balance and contributes to the confusion. The discovery that calms one sets another going until the dance is ended. Chrysis and the baby come flying first from one house, then from the other. Comic irony is everywhere. It is always just the attempt to clear things up, to make the best of them, that introduces new complications. The general result is a rollicking farce, full of verve and wit, but not without a generous measure of sympathetic character-study and fine feeling for the decencies of life. It was probably explained in the prologue that Chrysis and Moschion were brother and sister, so that the spectators could look forward to seeing Chrysis in the end restored to citizenship and united in lawful marriage to Demeas.

At the beginning of the part that has come down to us Demeas appears on the stage and relates an incident that has aroused his suspicion, not of the truth, that Chrysis is passing off Plangon's baby as her own, but of a far worse crime, that she has so far forgotten what was due to him as to form a connection with his son Moschion. If Moschion is the child's father and Chrysis its mother, her interest in the infant and her entreaties appear in a new and terrible light. This soliloquy does not interrupt the action of the play. It depicts with great skill the train of feeling that has been set going in the mind of Demeas and that turns him before our eyes from a genial, cautious, indulgent friend into a maniac, blind with jealousy and indignation.

THE GIRL FROM SAMOS

DEMEAS

*(He comes stealthily from his own house, evidently in great excitement
about some problem that puzzles him. At last he communicates his
situation to the spectators.)*

As soon as I was in the house, since I was all intent on getting ready for
the wedding, I merely mentioned the situation to the household, and gave
orders to get ready whatever would be needed, clean up, bake cakes, have
the rites in order. It was all promptly under way, you may be sure, but
the fact that they were hurrying operations produced some confusion,
naturally. There was the baby screaming on a couch, where they had
tossed it out of the way, and at the same time they kept shouting: "Give
me some flour, water, olive oil, charcoal." Now I was handing out one
thing and another myself and lending a hand, so, as it happened, I had
gone into the pantry and was sorting out a number of things and investi-
gating, so that I didn't come straight out again at once.

In the meantime, however, down from the floor above comes a woman
into the room in front of the pantry. For there happens to be a weaving-
room, which you must pass through either to get upstairs or into the
pantry. Moschion's nurse the woman was, she's an old woman, who has
been a slave of mine, but has her freedom now. So when she saw the baby
screaming unattended to, since she had no idea that I was in there, she
thought it was quite safe to speak freely and went to it. Then after she had
made the usual remarks: "Darling baby! Precious blessing! But where's
its mamma," she kissed it and walked up and down with it until it
stopped crying. Then she exclaimed: "Oh my goodness, only day before
yesterday Moschion himself was like that and I used to nurse and fondle
him; and now here's a babe of his for someone else to nurse [and see grow
up to be a father. . . ." *Here the text is faulty.*] Just then a slave girl
ran in from outside and the old woman said to her: "Give the baby his
bath, for goodness' sake. What does it mean? Don't you look after the
baby when his father's getting married?" Then the girl says quickly:
"Confound you, how loud you're talking! The master's in there." "Indeed he isn't? Where?" "In the pantry." Then raising her voice: "The

1125

mistress wants you, nurse. Move and be quick about it. He hasn't heard you. That's very lucky." And the old woman exclaiming: "Heaven help me how I chatter!" took herself off somewhere or other.

I meanwhile sauntered out very quietly, just the way you saw me come from the house, as if I had heard nothing and hadn't noticed a thing. As I came along, however, I took note that it was the girl from Samos herself who had it and was suckling it, so one thing's certain, it's her baby, but who the father is, whether it's mine or . . . But I refuse to pronounce the words to you, gentlemen, or to think them either. I simply state the case and report what I heard myself without upbraiding anyone for the present. I can bear witness, before God I can, that the boy has always behaved himself up to now, and has recognized his duty to me perfectly. On the other hand, though, when I realize that the words were spoken, in the first place, by his old nurse, and, in the second place, that she didn't mean me to hear; and then when I call to mind how the woman fondled it and insisted on keeping it in spite of me, I'm absolutely furious. (*As* DEMEAS *reaches the point where he can stand the strain no longer, the steward* PARMENO *arrives from the market accompanied by a cook and slaves with provisions for the wedding. At sight of* PAR-MENO, DEMEAS *resolves to extract the truth from him.*)

But see, here's Parmeno back from the market just in the nick of time. I'd better let him and the men get by.

(*He steps aside. Meanwhile* PARMENO *addresses the cook.*)

PARMENO

Cook, I'm damned if I know why you carry knives with you. Your chatter would reduce anything to mincemeat.

COOK

Are you trying to be funny with me, you ignoramus?

PARMENO

I?

COOK

It looks so to me, by heaven. If I inquire how many tables you are going to set, how many women there are, what time you want dinner served, whether I need to engage a butler, whether you've enough crockery in the house, whether the bakehouse has a roof, whether everything else is available . . .

PARMENO

You are reducing me to mincemeat, my dear fellow, in case you didn't know it, and your technique is perfect.

COOK

Go to the devil.

PARMENO

The same to you by all means. Just get in with you.
(*As the* COOK *and the servants disappear,* DEMEAS *steps out and calls.*)

DEMEAS

Parmeno!

PARMENO

Is someone calling *me?*

DEMEAS

Yes indeed, *you.*

PARMENO

God save you, master.

DEMEAS

Put away your basket and come to me here.

PARMENO (*entering with the basket*)
No bad luck, I hope.

DEMEAS (*alone*)
I imagine that fellow doesn't miss anything that goes on among the
servants. He's a Paul Pry if anyone ever was. But he's at the door.

PARMENO (*as he emerges, to some one inside*)
Give the cook anything he wants, Chrysis, and keep the old woman
away from the wine jars.

DEMEAS (*impatient*)
By the gods, will you . . .
(DEMEAS' *demeanour so frightens* PARMENO *that he becomes incapable
of telling a straight story and increases* DEMEAS' *suspicion by his
attempts at evasion.*)

PARMENO

What's to be done, master?

DEMEAS

What's to be done? Just step over here away from the door. A little
further.

PARMENO

There.

DEMEAS

Now just you listen, Parmeno. I don't want to flog you, by the twelve gods, for a good many reasons.

PARMENO

Flog me? What have I done?

DEMEAS

You are helping to keep something a secret from me; so I have ob-served.

PARMENO

No, by Dionysus, no, by Apollo, not I! By Zeus, Saviour, by Asclepius!

DEMEAS

Stop! No more oaths.

PARMENO

Well, you're wrong, or may I never . . .

DEMEAS

Here you, look here.

PARMENO

Well?

DEMEAS

Speak. Whose baby is it?

PARMENO

Uh?

DEMEAS

I ask you whose baby it is.

PARMENO

Chrysis'.

DEMEAS

Who is the father?

PARMENO

You, master.

DEMEAS

That finishes you. You are trying to fool me.

PARMENO

I?

DEMEAS

Yes, I know all the details; I've been told. Moschion's the father;
you're a party to it; and it's his doing that she is nursing it now herself.

PARMENO

Who says so?

DEMEAS

I saw her. Now just answer me this. Is this so?

PARMENO

It is, master; but the secret . . .

DEMEAS

What secret? Hey, men, give me a whip for this miscreant.

PARMENO

Don't, in heaven's name.

DEMEAS

I'll brand you.

PARMENO

You'll brand me?

DEMEAS

Yes, now.

PARMENO (*taking flight*)

I'm lost.

DEMEAS

Where are you off to, you carrion? Catch him.

(PARMENO *escapes and* DEMEAS' *worst suspicions are confirmed.*)

DEMEAS

O citadel of Cecrops' land! O far-flung sky! O . . . Why the outcry,
Demeas? Why the outcry, fool! Restrain yourself. Endure. For Moschion
is innocent of any fault. (*To the audience*) That's a strange thing to say
perhaps, gentlemen, but it's the truth. For if he had done this thing
wilfully, wrought upon by passion, or hating me, he would be guided by
the same purpose now as then and would be up in arms against me. The
truth is he has proved his innocence to me by his joyful reception of the
proposed marriage. His eagerness wasn't due to love, as I guessed at the
time, but to his desire to escape at last from my Helen there within. For
she it is who is to blame for this. Evidently she caught him somewhere
when he was fired with wine, when he wasn't master of himself. Strong

drink and youth often do such deeds, when they overcome a man—who may well have had no intention of injuring his neighbours. However I look at it, it's unreasonable that a boy who behaved with such propriety and restraint where others not connected with him were concerned, should have treated *me* like this, let him be adopted and not my son by birth ten times over. I'm not considering that, but his character.

But a vile, vile harlot, a consuming plague . . . But what's the use? That won't do any good, Demeas, you've got to play the man now. Forget your fondness, cease to love, and conceal to the utmost the unfortunate facts for your son's sake; as for the base Samian, thrust her out of doors head first to perdition. You've a pretext—because she kept the baby. Give her no other explanation, but grit your teeth and be firm. Show your breeding and stick to it.

(*As* DEMEAS *makes this resolve, the door of his house opens and the* COOK *emerges to see what can be keeping* PARMENO *so long.*)

COOK

Well, then, is he out here in front? Boy! Parmeno! (*Disgusted*) The fellow's given me the slip, why, before he'd lent a hand at all.

(DEMEAS *at once charges through the open door and proceeds to carry out his purpose. As he goes by he shouts at the* COOK.)

DEMEAS

Clear the way, you.

COOK (*peering breathlessly after him*)

Heracles, what's up? Boy! Some old lunatic has just burst into the house, or whatever is the matter? What do I see? Boy! By Posidon, the man's crazy, I believe; at any rate he's shrieking at the top of his voice. It would be very nice, wouldn't it, if my dishes lying right there in his way were to be smashed to flinders one and all. He's coming out. May you perish root and branch, Parmeno, for bringing me here! I'll step aside a bit.

(*At this minute the door opens and there come flying out* CHRYSIS, *nurse, and baby, pursued by the irate* DEMEAS, *who berates them.*)

DEMEAS

Don't you hear? Be off.

CHRYSIS (*bewildered*)

Where on earth am I to go, for pity's sake?

DEMEAS

To the devil, off with you!

CHRYSIS

O unkind fate!

(*She bursts into tears.*)

DEMEAS (*with bitter irony*)

Oh, yes, unkind fate! Very moving, tears, to be sure. I'll put an end. I fancy, to your . . .

(*He suddenly checks himself.*)

CHRYSIS

To my doing what?

DEMEAS

Nothing. You've got the baby and the old woman. Clear out at once.

CHRYSIS

Because I kept the baby and because . . . ?

DEMEAS

No "ands" at all. Because you kept the baby.

CHRYSIS

Is that all that's wrong? I don't understand.

DEMEAS

You didn't know how to live in luxury.

CHRYSIS

I didn't know how? What do you mean?

DEMEAS

Yet you came to me with nothing but the dress you had on, mind you, Chrysis, and a very plain one too.

CHRYSIS

What of it?

DEMEAS

It was I you thought the world of in those days, when you weren't doing so well.

CHRYSIS

And who is it now?

DEMEAS

No more of this. You have everything of yours. I'm giving you servants besides, see? Leave the house, Chrysis.

COOK

It's a fit of temper. I must go to him. Oh, sir, reflect.

DEMEAS

What have you to say?

COOK

Don't bite me!

(*He retires.*)

DEMEAS

Well, some other woman will put up with what I have to offer, Chrysis, from now on, and thank the gods too.

CHRYSIS

What's the matter?

DEMEAS

Why, you've got a son, that's all.

COOK

He's not biting yet. (*To* DEMEAS.) Even so . . .

DEMEAS (*to the* COOK)

I'll smash your head, you fellow, if you give me any more of your talk.

COOK

Well, you've the right; but look, I'm going in now.

(*Exit.*)

DEMEAS (*resorting to sarcasm*)

The great lady! Now you'll discover in the city just who you are. Lady-loves like you, Chrysis, make a bare ten shillings, running about to dinners and drinking strong drink until they die—or until they go hungry, if they don't die promptly and speedily. Nobody will know what it is like any better than you will, I fancy, and you'll find out just what you amounted to when you made your mistake. (CHRYSIS *approaches.*) Stay where you are.

(*He slams the door in her face.*)

CHRYSIS

Oh, what an unlucky girl I am!

(*She weeps bitterly.*)
(*At this point* NICERATUS *appears on the scene escorting from the market a skinny old sheep as his contribution to his daughter's wedding.*)

NICERATUS

When this sheep is sacrificed, the gods and goddesses will get their due. It has blood, bile enough, fine bones, a big spleen, just what the Olympians require. And I'll make hash of the fleece and send it to my friends for a taste, since that's all that's left for me. (*The sheep is taken into* NICERATUS' *house and he spies* CHRYSIS.) But, Heracles, what's this? Here's Chrysis standing in front of the house in tears. Verily it's no other. Whatever has happened?

CHRYSIS

I've been shown the door by your good-natured friend. Just that.

NICERATUS

O Heracles! Who? Demeas?

CHRYSIS

Yes.

NICERATUS

What for?

CHRYSIS

On account of the baby.

NICERATUS

The women told me that you had gone crazy and were keeping a baby that you had let live. But he's mild as mild.

CHRYSIS

He wasn't angry at once, only afterward, just now. And he had told me to get everything in the house ready for the wedding, and then in the midst of it in he rushed from outside like a madman and now he's shut the door in my face.

NICERATUS

Demeas? Is he mad?

At this point there is a considerable gap in our text

Niceratus evidently offers Chrysis a refuge in his house. His wife and daughter would be glad to welcome the baby, who, it will be remembered, was really Plangon's son by Moschion. We can only guess how Demeas learned that Plangon, not Chrysis, was the babe's mother. Probably he met Moschion, who, having heard of the expulsion of Chrysis, would betray anxiety for the infant's fate and

by trying to calm his father would further provoke him. Demeas
would at length, in spite of his resolutions, give vent to his indignation in such a storm of fury that Moschion, alarmed, would be glad
to acquaint him with the true story and make his escape. Demeas,
overcome with joy at finding his suspicions groundless, so that he
may make friends once more with his mistress, is inclined to take a
cheerful view of life and plans to celebrate the wedding of Plangon
and Moschion with more zest than ever. In this hilarious mood he
accosts Niceratus and makes the mistake of appealing to that irascible man's non-existent sense of humour. Niceratus learns that Chrysis
is forgiven because the baby she was cherishing was really Plangon's
and that the joke is now on him, since it is his daughter who is responsible for the superfluous infant. Imagine the feelings of the proud
and impecunious Niceratus at the prospect of having permanently on
his hands not only an unwed daughter but a fatherless grandson to
boot. Naturally violent as he is, his fury is on this occasion unre-
strained. When Demeas proceeds to hint at Moschion's connection
with the affair, Niceratus misunderstands his embarrassment and
assumes that he intends to break off the match. He rushes off.

DEMEAS

But come back and . . . What shall I say? Wait a bit, sir.

NICERATUS

I'm off. It's all over. All the arrangements are upset.

(*He tears into his house in a rage.*)

DEMEAS

By Zeus, my friend here will be angry at what he has heard. He'll roar.
The fellow's rough and brutal; he doesn't care anything for anyone. But
that I should suspect such things! Beast that I am, I ought . . . By
Hephaestus, I don't deserve to live. (*Angry words are heard from within.*)
Heracles, how loud he shouts! That's it, he is calling for fire. He says
he'll burn the baby. What now! I shall see my grandson burnt alive before my eyes! There, he's coming out. He's a tornado or a thunderbolt,
not a man.

NICERATUS (*rushing out*)

Demeas, Chrysis is taking sides against me and behaving most out-
rageously.

DEMEAS

How's that?

NICERATUS

She's persuaded my wife to admit nothing at all, nor the girl either. She's keeping the baby in spite of me and refuses to give it up. So don't be surprised if I murder the woman herself.

DEMEAS

Murder?

NICERATUS

Yes, since she's a party to it all.

DEMEAS

Oh, never do that, Niceratus.

NICERATUS

I wanted to warn you.

(*He rushes in again.*)

DEMEAS (*left cowering*)

He's a raving maniac. There he goes flying in. How am I to deal with this terrible situation? I know I never ran into such a row before. It's certainly much the best to make a plain statement of the facts. Why, heavens! The door's banging again.

(*This time* CHRYSIS *comes flying out, still holding the infant, the murderous* NICERATUS *in hot pursuit with upraised stick.*)

CHRYSIS

Heaven help me! What shall I do? Where shall I go for refuge? He'll get the baby from me.

DEMEAS (*at his own doorway*)

Chrysis, here!

CHRYSIS

Who's there?

DEMEAS

Run inside.

(CHRYSIS *gets behind him.*)

NICERATUS

Where are you going? Where are you off to?

DEMEAS

Jove, I've a prize-fight on my hands to-day, it seems. (*He intercepts* NICERATUS.) What do you want? What person are you after?

NICERATUS

Demeas, get out of my way. Let me get possession of the child and then hear what the women have to say about the matter.

DEMEAS

He's mad. What, are you going to strike me?

NICERATUS

Indeed I am.

DEMEAS (*to* CHRYSIS)

Scoot in, you. (*To* NICERATUS.) But I swear I'll strike too. (*They struggle.*) Run, Chrysis, he's too much for me.

(CHRYSIS *gets safely in with the child. As* NICERATUS *follows in hot pursuit,* DEMEAS *seizes him.*)

NICERATUS

You're the assailant now. I protest.

DEMEAS

But you have a stick to beat a free-woman and are in pursuit of her.

NICERATUS

That's a quibble.

DEMEAS

So was your protest too.

NICERATUS

She refused to give me the baby.

DEMEAS (*incriminating himself to get an opening for explanations*)

What an idea, my own offspring!

NICERATUS (*incredulous and threatening*)

But it's not yours!

DEMEAS (*alarmed*)

Wait a bit. Help, help!

NICERATUS (*turning towards* DEMEAS' *house*)

Go on shouting. I'll go in and murder the woman.

DEMEAS

What's to be done? Here's more trouble. I won't let him. (*Returns to the battle.*) Where are you going? Do wait.

NICERATUS

Don't you lay a hand on me.

DEMEAS

Do control yourself.

NICERATUS

You've wronged me somehow, Demeas. You show it, and you know all about the affair.

DEMEAS

Then ask *me* about it and don't bother the women.

NICERATUS

Has your son made a fool of me?

DEMEAS

Nonsense. He'll marry the girl. But that isn't it. Just take a stroll with me here—just for a little.

NICERATUS

Stroll?

DEMEAS

And recover your self-possession. (*They stroll.*) Didn't you ever hear them tell at the play how Zeus turned to gold and leaked through a roof and seduced a girl imprisoned there in days gone by?

NICERATUS

Pray tell me what has that to do with it?

DEMEAS

Possibly one must be prepared for anything. Take a look and see whether your roof leaks anywhere.

NICERATUS

It's mostly leaks. But what has that got to do with it?

DEMEAS

Sometimes Zeus turns to gold, sometimes to water. You see? It's his doing. How quick we were to discover it!

NICERATUS

And you are taking me for a booby.

DEMEAS

By Apollo, no, I'm not. Why, surely you're not a whit less noble than Acrisius. If Zeus condescended in his case, your daughter surely . . .

NICERATUS

Alas! alas! Moschion has played me this trick.

DEMEAS

He'll marry her, never fear. But this thing, I'm quite certain, is an act of God. I can name you thousands walking about in our midst who are of divine parentage, but you think something terrible has occurred. In the first place there's Chaerephon, the fellow that gets his dinners gratis; doesn't he look like a god to you?

NICERATUS

He does look like one. What's the use? I won't fight you when it can't do any good.

DEMEAS

That's a sensible man, Niceratus. Androcles lives all these years, runs, jumps, makes a lot of money, walks about with a swarthy face. He couldn't die a paleface, even if you were to cut his throat. Isn't he a god? Just pray for a blessing on it. Burn some incense. My son will come for your daughter directly. *Must* we make a long story of it—for you're a man of sense. Suppose he *was* caught speeding then; won't *you* be speedy now?

NICERATUS

I'll get things ready in the house.

DEMEAS

We've a lead that you must overtake. You're worldly wise. (*He means that the baby has got ahead of the wedding, which must now be speeded up to catch it. Then to himself*) I'm very grateful to all the gods to find that there's no truth in what I believed just now.

(*Here the act ends. Between the acts the spectators are entertained by the usual troupe of revellers. At the beginning of the next act* MOS-CHION *comes on the scene. He has been brooding on the enormity of his father's suspicions and feels very ill-used.*)

MOSCHION

Just now when with great difficulty I got clear of the charge that was brought against me, I was content with that and asked for nothing better. As I get more self-possessed, however, and analyse the situation, I'm perfectly furious now. I'm exceedingly provoked to think what my father supposed me capable of doing. If it were all in order with the girl and there weren't so many obstacles—my oath, my fondness, the lapse of time, our intimacy—enforcing me to servitude, I'd certainly not be here when next he brings any such charge against me. Instead I'd relieve the city of my presence and dash off for some place in Bactria or Caria to pass the time a-soldiering there. As a matter of fact, however, my beloved Plangon, I shall because of you do no deed of valour. 'Tis not permitted; love forbids, who rules just now as sovereign o'er my will. Still I mustn't let it pass altogether abjectly or mean-spiritedly. Rather I'll simply pretend, if nothing else, and frighten him by saying that I'm going to cut the cable. That will make him more careful hereafter not to be rude to me again, when he sees that I don't take it as a matter of course this time. (PAR-MENO *at this moment arrives on the scene, having gradually recovered his wits.*) But see, here's just the man I wanted most, turned up in the very nick of time.

PARMENO (*failing to notice* MOSCHION)

By Zeus most high, a stupid, miserable piece of work I've done! When I was quite innocent of any fault, I took fright and ran away from my master. What had I done to deserve that? Let's examine the charges plainly one by one like this. (*He counts on his fingers.*) The young master misdemeaned himself with a girl of free status. No fault of Parmeno's there surely. Pregnancy on her part. Parmeno not responsible. The baby came under our roof. He brought it, not I. Somebody in the house has admitted the fact. What of it? Where's any fault on Parmeno's part in that? There isn't any. Why then did you take to your heels like that, you numskull, you chicken-heart? Nonsense, a man threatens to brand me. He's mistaken, to be sure, but it doesn't make a difference of one iota whether you are branded justly or unjustly; any way it isn't nice.

MOSCHION (*accosting him*)

Here you.

PARMENO

Hello, sir.

MOSCHION

Leave that nonsense you're talking and go in at once.

PARMENO

What am I to do?

MOSCHION

Bring me a cloak and a sword of some sort.

PARMENO

Bring you a sword?

MOSCHION

Yes, and hurry.

PARMENO

What for?

MOSCHION

Get a move on, stop talking, and do what I tell you.

PARMENO

But what's up?

MOSCHION

If I take a strap . . .

PARMENO

No, no, no, I'm going all right.

MOSCHION

Why the delay then? (PARMENO *goes*.) My father will come to me now. Of course he'll entreat me to stay at home. And he'll entreat in vain for a while; that's required. Then, when I think the time has come, I'll yield. Only I must be plausible and that, by Dionysus, is just what I can't achieve. He's at the door, coming out.

(*It is, however, not* DEMEAS, *but* PARMENO *who appears.*)

PARMENO (*persuasively*)

You seem to be a long way behind the march of events here. What you know, what you've heard of the situation isn't at all exact, so you're all worked up about nothing. Give up your plans and come in now.

MOSCHION (*sternly*)

Haven't you got it?

PARMENO

No, they're celebrating your wedding. They're mixing the wine, while incense rises, and burnt offering ascends upon Hephaestus' flame.

MOSCHION

Here you, haven't you got it?

PARMENO

No! I tell you they've been waiting for you ever so long. Aren't you in a hurry to fetch the bride? Happiness is yours. You've no troubles. Cheer up. What do you want?

MOSCHION (*with all the wounded dignity of adolescence*)

Will you give me advice, say, you polluted thief of a slave?

(*Beats him.*)

PARMENO

What are you doing, Moschion?

MOSCHION

Will you run in at once and get what I tell you?

PARMENO (*plaintively*)

My lip's split.

MOSCHION

Still chattering, you?

PARMENO

I'm going. Zeus knows I am. But I've struck a peck of trouble.

MOSCHION

Won't you hurry?

PARMENO (*at the door*)

They're holding the wedding really.

MOSCHION

Go. Hurry. Bring me some news. (PARMENO *goes in.*) Now he'll come
to me. However, gentlemen, if he doesn't beg me to stay at home, but
loses his temper instead and lets me go—which didn't occur to me just
now—what shall I do? Probably he won't do that, but if? For nothing
is impossible. I *shall* look a fool, by Zeus, if I face about now.

(*Here the text ends. The stages seems to be set for* NICERATUS *and others
to misunderstand* MOSCHION'S *delay in coming for the bride. How
the final solution is brought about we can only guess. Very likely*
CHRYSIS *is found to be* MOSCHION'S *sister and a citizen, so that she
can be legally married to* DEMEAS. MOSCHION *must of course be
united to* PLANGON.)

11
THE ARBITRATION

Characters in the Play

Syriscus, *a charcoal-burner*
Davus, *a goat-herd*
Smicrines, *an Athenian business man*
Onesimus, *slave of* Charisius
Habrotonon, *harp-girl of* Charisius
Pamphila, *daughter of* Smicrines *and wife of* Charisius
Charisius, *a young Athenian, son-in-law of* Smicrines
Sophrona, *the old nurse of* Pamphila
Chaerestratus, *neighbour of* Charisius
Simias, *a friend of* Charisius
Cario, *a cook*

INTRODUCTION

by L. A. Post

THE *Epitrepontes* or *Arbitration* is more fully preserved than the other plays of Menander. We have more than half of it in good condition and can follow the plot almost throughout. Furthermore, the parts that are best preserved are of the greatest interest; they are not the sort of clowning of which we have so much in the extant parts of the *Shearing of Glycera*. Menander's interest in the theme of love is well illustrated in the *Arbitration*. In fact it is almost a problem play; and, though it begins and ends with a note of comedy, the crisis of the play is thoroughly tragic. Since we have the merest scraps of the first act, we do not know whether the situation was explained in a prologue or not. The probabilities are that it was.

The principal characters of the play are Pamphila and Charisius. The latter is a young man who is devoted to philosophy and strict in his morals. In a modern drama he would be a rather priggish clergyman. In the play we see how love operates to broaden his sympathies, to teach him humility and to make a new man of him.

Charisius has a servant Onesimus, who apes his master's philosophy, but is only a slave after all. The master has generous impulses, but the slave is concerned only for his own hide. He has a great deal of curiosity and gets into trouble by his well-meant interference.

Pamphila was a young girl, brought up in seclusion, like all Athenian girls of means. About six months before our play opens she had been married to the man of her father's choice. She had come to love the upright Charisius and her patience wins for her in the end her husband's friendship and respect.

Smicrines, the father of Pamphila, is a shrewd man of business. He is crude and excitable. He has the practical man's contempt for sentiment. He had married his daughter to Charisius because he approved of the frugal habits of the latter. His alarm when Charisius suddenly becomes a spendthrift is excellent material for comedy.

Sophrona, Pamphila's old nurse, appears only in the final scene of the play. Chaerestratus and Simias are young men, friends of Charisius, who laugh at his serious ways and help him to drown his sorrows. CARIO, the cook, is the usual comic figure. Habrotonon is the harp-girl, a slave, whom Charisius hires as a companion.

The event that produces the complications of the drama had happened ten months before. Pamphila had been assaulted by a drunken youth at the all-night festival of the Tauropolia, in which women took part. Five months after her marriage to Charisius, she bore in his absence a son. Her nurse, Sophrona, helped her to conceal the fact and saw to it that the baby was exposed in the fields, either to die or to be rescued by some chance passer. The discovery that Charisius is himself the baby's father will of course provide a conventional solution of the problem of the play.

Charisius meanwhile would have known nothing of his wife's predicament except for the officious interference of Onesimus, who informed him of the fact. Charisius might have repudiated his wife, but chose instead to give her the opportunity to repudiate him. Her secret might thus be kept from her father and from the outside world. He embarked on a life of extravagant self-indulgence. He stayed away from home and spent money at a rate that was sure to lead Smicrines to take action. When the play opens, Charisius is staying at the house of Chaerestratus. The scene shows the two houses, that of Chaerestratus, where Charisius is entertaining his companions and the harp-girl, Habrotonon, and that of Charisius, where his wife, Pamphila, lives deserted.

To understand the plot, it should be noted that we have here a favourite theme of folklore, the outcast babe who, by fortune's favor, gains or regains a lofty status. Euripides treats it in his *Ion* and with a difference in his *Andromache*. There Molossus, whose story is the theme, has nevertheless no part in the action. So here the mute and helpless babe gains through Davus his life, through Syriscus his hope of freedom, through Habrotonon his status as Charisius' son, though a bastard, then through Pamphila his rightful place as symbol of a reunited family and cherished scion of a cultured citizen. When Smicrines capitulates, the babe's success can go no further. His story supplies the framework of the action and every scene is relevant to his advancement.

THE ARBITRATION

ACT I

OF THE first act of the play we possess very little. We can, however, guess at the general course of the action. There was probably a prologue which explained the facts that have already been mentioned. There was a good deal of jesting on the part of the cook. He is a loud-mouthed drunken railer. He knows all the back-stairs gossip of Athens and retails it boisterously with the embroidery of a crude imagination. He insists on knowing why Charisius, who has recently married, is away from home with the harp-girl Habrotonon, and Onesimus finds his companion's free and easy ways rather trying. He is too discreet to tell all he knows. Finally Chaerestratus comes from his house and orders the cook to go inside and prepare lunch. Onesimus also departs, but Chaerestratus remains to observe a new arrival. This is Smicrines, the father of Pamphila. He is as unattractive as she is charming. He is the strict old man, who has no patience with weakness or extravagance, and insists always on the letter of the bond. On the present occasion he is in a state of great excitement, because he has heard in the city of Charisius' extravagant expenditures on cooks and harp-girls. "Twelve drachmas a day to a slave dealer for a girl! Why, a man could live on that for a month and six days besides!" "Yes," says Chaerestratus in a sarcastic aside, "it would keep him alive on poor-house soup." Smicrines finally goes into Charisius' house to see what Pamphila has to say about her husband's conduct. Thereupon Chaerestratus retires into his own house to inform Charisius that his father-in-law has arrived and is likely to make trouble.

ACT II

At the beginning of the second act Smicrines reappears. Knowing nothing of Pamphila's baby, he is indignant at Charisius' behaviour and sees no justification for it. He is not quite sure what to do, but is determined to do something. He is about to set out for the city to ask

1147

advice, when he is confronted with a strange situation. Two slaves, rudely clad in skins, are involved in a dispute. They come on the stage arguing. Syriscus, the charcoal-burner, is accompanied by his wife, who carries a baby. He is eloquently expostulating with the sullen Davus, a goat-herd, who maintains his case with equal heat.

SYRISCUS
You're afraid of a fair trial.

DAVUS
It's a put-up game of yours, curse you.

SYRISCUS
You've no right to keep what's not yours. We must get someone to arbitrate.

DAVUS
I'm willing; let's argue it out.

SYRISCUS
Who's to decide it?

DAVUS
Anyone will do for me. It serves me right though. Why did I give you anything?

SYRISCUS (*indicating* SMICRINES)
How about that man? Does he suit you as a judge?

DAVUS
Yes, good luck to it.

SYRISCUS (*to* SMICRINES)
If you please, sir, could you spare us a minute?

SMICRINES (*testily*)
You? What for?

SYRISCUS
We have a disagreement about something.

SMICRINES
Well, what's that to me?

SYRISCUS
We are looking for someone to decide it impartially. So if nothing prevents, do settle our dispute.

SMICRINES

Confound the rascals. Do you mean to say that you go about arguing cases, you fellows in goatskins?

SYRISCUS

Suppose we do. It won't take long and it's no trouble to understand the case. Grant the favour, sir. Don't be contemptuous, please. Justice should rule at every moment, everywhere. Whoever happens to come along should make this cause his own concern, for it's a common interest that touches all men's lives.

DAVUS (*alarmed at this burst of eloquence*)

I've got quite an orator on my hands. Why did I give him anything?

SMICRINES

Well, tell me. Will you abide by my decision?

SYRISCUS

Absolutely.

SMICRINES

I'll hear the case. Why shouldn't I? (*Turning to the sullen* DAVUS) You speak first, you that aren't saying anything.

DAVUS (*sure of his case but not very sure of his words, which come slowly enough to leave room for frequent pauses*)

I'll go back a bit first—not just my dealings with this fellow—so you'll understand the transaction. In the scrubland not far from here I was watching my flocks, sir, perhaps a month ago to-day, all by myself, when I found a baby left deserted there with a necklace and some such trinkets as these.

(*He shows some trinkets.*)

SYRISCUS

The dispute is about them.

DAVUS

He won't let me speak.

SMICRINES (*to* SYRISCUS)

If you interrupt, I'll take my stick to you.

DAVUS

And serve him right too.

SMICRINES

Go on.

DAVUS

I will. I picked it up and went back home with it and was going to raise it. That's what I intended then. In the night, though, like every one else, I thought it over to myself and argued it out: "Why should I bring up a baby and have all that trouble? Where am I to get all that money to spend? What do I want with all that worry?" That's the state I was in. Early next morning I was tending my flock again, when along came this fellow, he's a charcoal-burner, to this same spot to get out stumps there. He had made friends with me before that. So we got talking together and he saw that I was gloomy and said: "Why so thoughtful, Davus?" "Why indeed," said I, "I meddle with what doesn't concern me." So I tell him what had happened, how I found the baby and how I picked it up. And he broke in at once, before I had finished my story, and began entreating me: "As you hope for luck, Davus," he kept saying every other thing, "do give me the baby, as you hope for fortune, as you hope for freedom. I've a wife, you see," says he, "and she had a baby, but it died." Meaning this woman who is here now with the child. Did you entreat me, Syriscus?

SYRISCUS

I admit it.

DAVUS

He spent the whole day at it. Finally I yielded to his coaxing and teasing and promised him the child and he went off wishing me a million blessings. When he took it too, he kissed my hands. Didn't you?

SYRISCUS

Yes, I did.

DAVUS

He took himself off. Just now he and his wife happened on me and all of a sudden he claims the objects that I found with the child—it was some small matters, tomfoolery, nothing really—and says he's cheated because I don't consent and lay claim to them myself. I say, though, that he ought to be thankful for the share he did get by his entreaties. Though I don't give him all of it, that's no reason why I should have to stand examination. Even if he had found it while we were going about together and it had been a case of share-your-luck, why he would have got part and I the rest. But I was alone when I found it and you weren't even there and yet you think you ought to have all and I nothing.

To conclude, I have given you something of mine. If you are satisfied with it, you may still keep it; but if you aren't satisfied and have changed your mind, then give it back again to me and take neither more nor less than your due. But for you to have the whole business, part with my consent, the rest forced from me, is not fair. That's all I have to say.

SYRISCUS (*keeping a respectful eye on the stick*)
It that all?

SMICRINES
Didn't you hear what he said? He has finished.

SYRISCUS
(*His words come fast enough but his flights of eloquence have a tendency
to sink unexpectedly. However, his quick turns and lively gestures supply
any deficiencies and* DAVUS *is left stranded just where he thought himself
most secure*)
Good. Then I'll take my turn. He was alone when he found the baby.
He is right about everything that he has mentioned. The facts are as
stated, sir. I dispute nothing. I got the child from him by entreating and
imploring him. For his story is true.

Information came to me from a certain shepherd that he had been talking to, one of his fellow-workmen, to the effect that he had also found at
the same time some trinkets. (*With a dramatic gesture toward the infant.*)
To claim these has come, sir, in person, my client here. Give me the child,
wife. (*Taking the baby from his wife's arms.*) This infant claims from
you his necklace and his tokens, Davus. He says that they were placed
with him for his adornment, not for your bread and butter. I too support
his claim, since I have been made his guardian. You made me so yourself,
when you gave him to me. (*Appealing to* SMICRINES.) It is now your part,
sir, it seems to me, to decide whether the trinkets, gold or whatever they
are, are to be kept for the child as his mother, whoever she was, intended
them, until he grows up, or whether the very man who robbed him is to
keep another's property, just because he found it first. But why then
didn't I claim them when I got the baby? Because I wasn't entitled yet
to speak for him. Nor have I come now to claim anything for myself. Share
your luck indeed! Never call it finding where there's a party wronged.
Here is no find appropriated, but a fund misappropriated.

Think of this too, sir. Perhaps this babe is better born than we. He may,
though brought up among labourers, look down on our condition, seek his
own native level, have pluck to ply some noble occupation, hunt lions,
bear arms, take part in races at the games. You have seen actors, I am
sure, and all these things are familiar to you. A certain Neleus and Pelias,
the famous ones, were found by an aged goat-herd clad in a goatskin just
like mine. When he saw that they were nobler born than he, he told them
all, how he found and picked them up, and he gave them a wallet full of
tokens and from that they found out everything about themselves for certain and now became kings, who once were goat-herds. Yes, but if some
Davus had stolen and sold these tokens to get twelve shillings for himself,
they would have passed their lives in ignorance of their great and noble

birth. Surely, sir, it is not right for me to sustain his body, while Davus seizes and destroys his hope of preserving his identity. Men have been kept by means of tokens from marrying their sisters, have found and rescued a mother, have saved a brother's life. Life is full of pitfalls for us all, sir. We must use foresight to avoid them, must look a long way ahead to find the means.

But give him back, says he, if you're not satisfied. There he thinks he has something solid to fall back on. He's wrong. It's not right for you, when you are required to restore something that belongs to the child, to claim him as well to boot—so that you can do your thieving more undisturbed another time, now that chance has preserved something that belongs to him. I have finished. Give your decision, whatever you believe to be right.

SMICRINES

Why, it's easily decided. Everything that was left with the child belongs to him. That's my verdict.

DAVUS (*expectantly*)

Good. But the child?

SMICRINES

By Zeus, I'll not assign him to you, who have been trying to wrong him, but rather to the one who came to his aid and prosecuted you when you would have defrauded him.

SYRISCUS

Heaven bless you, sir.

DAVUS (*disappointed and furious*)

The verdict's scandalous, so help me Zeus. I alone found all of it and I've been stripped of all of it, and the man that didn't find anything has it. Am I to hand it over?

SMICRINES

Yes.

DAVUS

The verdict's scandalous, curse me if it isn't!

SYRISCUS

Hurry up with it.

DAVUS

Heracles, what treatment!

SYRISCUS

Undo your wallet, and let me see. That's where you carry it. (*Appealing to* SMICRINES *who is leaving*.) Wait a minute, please, to see that he hands it over.

DAVUS

Why did I ever let him judge the case?

SYRISCUS

Hand it over, you scum.

DAVUS

Disgraceful, the way I've been treated!

SMICRINES (*to* SYRISCUS)

Have you everything?

SYRISCUS

I really think so. Unless he swallowed something while I was pleading, when it was going against him.

DAVUS

I wouldn't have believed it.

(SMICRINES *departs*.)

SYRISCUS

Good-bye, sir. It's high time all judges were like that.

DAVUS

Heracles, what a skin game! There never was a more scandalous verdict.

SYRISCUS

You were a thief.

DAVUS

Thief yourself, see to it now that you keep them for him safe and sound. Don't you fear, I'll have my eye on you the whole time.

SYRISCUS

Clear out and be hanged. (DAVUS *goes*.) Now wife, take these things and carry them inside to the master. We'll wait here for Chaerestratus just now and set off for our work to-morrow when we have paid the rent. But first we must check these things off one at a time. Have you a box? Well, put them in your dress fold.

(*As* SYRISCUS *tells over the objects and tosses them to his wife,* ONESIMUS *comes from the house and squints at the sun to note the time. He is*

responsible for the entertainment provided by his master CHARISIUS
in the house of CHAERESTRATUS.)

ONESIMUS

A slower cook was never seen. By this time yesterday they had been at
the wine for a long while.

SYRISCUS (*examining the trinkets*)

This looks like a fowl or something and a very plump one too. Here is
something set with stones. Here is a toy axe.

ONESIMUS (*true to his ruling passion*)

What's this?

SYRISCUS

Here is an iron ring with gold trimmings. The seal is a bull or a goat.
I can't tell which, done by Cleostratus, it says.

ONESIMUS (*recognizing the ring*)

Here, let me see it.

SYRISCUS (*handing him the ring*)

There. But who are *you?*

ONESIMUS

The very same.

SYRISCUS

Who's the same?

ONESIMUS

The ring.

SYRISCUS

What ring? I don't understand.

ONESIMUS

My master Charisius'.

SYRISCUS

You're crazy.

ONESIMUS

He lost it.

SYRISCUS

Put down the ring, plague take you.

ONESIMUS

Put down our ring for you? How came it to be in your possession?

SYRISCUS

O Apollo and the gods, what a frightful plague! What a job it is to
protect an orphan's property! Every one who comes up is suddenly all
agog for plunder. Put down the ring, I say.

ONESIMUS

Are you trying to be funny with me? It belongs to the master, by
Apollo and the gods.

SYRISCUS

Without a doubt I'd sooner have my throat cut than sacrifice anything
to him. It's settled. I'll go to law with them all one after another. They're
the babe's, not mine. Here is a necklace or something. Take it, wife. And
a bit of red cloth. Go on in. (*To* ONESIMUS.) Now what have you to say?

ONESIMUS

I? This belongs to Charisius. He lost it once when he had been drinking,
so he said.

SYRISCUS

Well, Chaerestratus is my master. Either keep it safe or give it back to
me, so that I may produce it intact for you.

ONESIMUS

I prefer to look after it myself.

SYRISCUS

It makes no difference to me either way, for I believe we both turn in
here at the same house. (*Both turn to enter* CHAERESTRATUS' *house where*
CHARISIUS *is temporarily established with his party.*)

ONESIMUS

Just now, though, the party is under way, and it isn't perhaps a good
time to tell him about it. But to-morrow I will.

SYRISCUS

I'll wait for you and to-morrow I'll be ready to leave the decision to
anyone you please. I've not come off badly this time either, but apparently
I've got to neglect everything else and devote my time to lawsuits. That's
the only way to keep things nowadays.
(*They go in and a chorus of revellers enter and entertain the audience.*)

ACT III

(ONESIMUS *comes from the house in great perplexity and soliloquizes.*)

ONESIMUS

AT LEAST half a dozen times I've started to go to the master and show him the ring. I get up close to him, right by his side, and then duck. In fact I'm sorry for what I told him the last time. (*Thoughtfully.*) You see he keeps saying pretty frequently: 'Perdition take the rascal that told me of this.' Really I'm afraid he'll come to terms with his wife, then take me and put me out of the way, because I told him her secret and because I have knowledge of it. It's just as well that I refrained from adding another complication. This too might get me into pretty hot water.

(*Here he is interrupted by sounds of a struggle.* CHARISIUS' *harp-girl,* HABROTONON, *is trying to escape from the importunities of his guests, who have noticed how little attention she gets from their host. She finally breaks away.*)

HABROTONON

Let me go, please, and don't bother me. Apparently I've been unintentionally making a fool of my unfortunate self. I thought I had a lover, but the fellow's hatred for me is something diabolical. He has got so now that he won't even let me, mercy on us, have a place at the same table with him, but puts me at a distance.

ONESIMUS (*to himself*)

Then shall I give it back to the man I just had it of? Nonsense.

HABROTONON (*puzzled as she reflects on* CHARISIUS' *strange conduct*)
My goodness, what ails the man to throw away all that money? As far as he is concerned I'm qualified to carry the basket for the goddess, for pity's sake. Holy and pure from marriage rites, as they say, I've sat since day before yesterday.

ONESIMUS (*wondering what excuse he is to make to* SYRISCUS)
But then how, ye gods, how, I entreat you . . .

(*At this moment* SYRISCUS *comes from the house in search of* ONESIMUS, *whom he suspects of appropriating the ring under false pretences.*)

SYRISCUS

Where can he be? I've looked for him everywhere inside. Here you. Give me back the ring, my friend, or show it to the man you're finally going to. Let's get the case settled. I've to go somewhere.

ONESIMUS (*embarrassed, but superior*)
This is the way it is, fellow. This ring really does belong to my master Charisius, I'm absolutely certain of that, but I'm afraid to bring it to his attention. It just about means making him father of the child it was found with, if I deliver it to him.

SYRISCUS
How's that, you simpleton?

ONESIMUS
He lost it one time at the Tauropolia when there was a night celebration with women taking part. The natural inference is that he assaulted a girl; she had a baby and of course abandoned it, the one in question. Now if the girl could be found first, then one might produce the ring and it would be definite evidence of something. Otherwise it means suspicion and disturbance.

SYRISCUS (*still suspicious*)
Just look to that yourself. But if you're trying to frighten me off, meaning me to take back the ring and give you a little present, you're out of your head. I'm not the man to compromise.

ONESIMUS
I don't ask you to either.

SYRISCUS
I'll be back when I have done an errand, for I'm going to town just now. I'll see then what's to be done about it.
(*As* SYRISCUS *leaves,* HABROTONON *approaches* ONESIMUS. *It has occurred to her that she may still win* CHARISIUS' *favour by a new method.*)

HABROTONON
Is it the baby that the woman is nursing now inside that this charcoal-burner found?

ONESIMUS
So he says.

HABROTONON
Isn't that great! For pity's sake!

ONESIMUS
And with it was this ring of my master's.

HABROTONON (*impressively indignant*)
Oh! you wretch! If he really is your young master, and you look on and see him brought up as a slave, wouldn't you deserve to be put to death?

ONESIMUS (*surrounded by pitfalls*)
But there's this to be said, no one knows who his mother is.

HABROTONON
But he lost it, you say, at the Tauropolia?

ONESIMUS
Yes, when he was carousing, so the boy that attended him said.

HABROTONON
Evidently he attacked the women who were celebrating the revels by themselves. In fact I was there when just such a thing occurred.

ONESIMUS
You were there?

HABROTONON
Yes, last year at the Tauropolia. I was playing the lute for some young ladies and she was with them. I wasn't a performer myself, for at that time I hadn't—I mean I didn't yet know what a man is. (ONESIMUS *smiles knowingly*.) Indeed I didn't, by Aphrodite.

ONESIMUS
Yes, but do you know who the girl was?

HABROTONON
I could ask. She was a friend of the women that I was with.

ONESIMUS
Did you hear who her father was?

HABROTONON
I don't know anything about her except that I should recognize her if I saw her. A good-looking girl, goodness, yes, and rich too, they said.

ONESIMUS
Perhaps it's the same one.

HABROTONON
I don't know about that. Well, while she was with us there, she strayed off and then suddenly comes running up alone, crying and tearing her hair. She had utterly ruined a very fine Tarantine shawl, and delicate, my goodness. Why, it was all in tatters.

ONESIMUS

And she had this ring?

HABROTONON

Perhaps she did, but she didn't show it to me. I'm going to stick to the truth, you see.

ONESIMUS

What am I to do now?

HABROTONON

You look to that. But, if you're sensible and take my advice, you'll let your master know of this. If the child's mother is free born, why shouldn't he know of what's occurred?

ONESIMUS

Let's find out first who she is, Habrotonon. Will you help me to do that now?

HABROTONON

I really can't until I am sure who the man in question is. I'm afraid I might give information to the ladies I spoke of with no result. For all anyone knows someone else may have lost it after receiving the ring from him as a pledge. Perhaps he was dicing and gave it as security for an agreement, or he bound himself to something, found himself in a tight place and handed over the ring. Any number of other things of the sort regularly happen at drinking-bouts. Until I know the man responsible I'll neither look for her nor report anything of the sort.

ONESIMUS

Indeed you're quite right. What is to be done, though?

HABROTONON

See here, Onesimus. See if you approve of my idea. I'll pretend it all happened to me. I'll take this ring and go in to him.

ONESIMUS

Go on and explain, I see it at once.

HABROTONON

When he notices that I have the ring he'll ask me where I got it. I'll say: "At the Tauropolia when I was still a maid," taking on myself all that happened to her. Most of it I know.

ONESIMUS

Magnificent!

HABROTONON

If the escapade comes home to him, he'll immediately dash straight into the trap. He's been drinking and he'll tell everything first without stopping to think. Whatever he says I'll agree to, for safety's sake mentioning nothing before he does.

ONESIMUS

Superfine, by Helius!

HABROTONON

I'll be cunning and use vague language, to keep from going wrong, like: "How reckless you were, what a savage!"

ONESIMUS

Fine!

HABROTONON

"How roughly you handled me and the clothes you ruined, alas!" I'll say. But first I want to go inside and get the baby, cry over and hug him and ask the woman where she got him.

ONESIMUS

Lord save us! (*His fears are aroused by a certain touch of genius in* HABROTONON's *technique.*)

HABROTONON

And to cap it all I'll say: "So now, take note, you've a baby born," and I'll produce our foundling here.

ONESIMUS

There's brass and trickiness, Habrotonon!

HABROTONON

And if this test works and he proves to be the child's father, we'll look for the girl at our leisure.

ONESIMUS

You don't mention the fact that you'll get your freedom. For as soon as he supposes you to be the child's mother, he'll obviously buy your liberty at once.

HABROTONON

I don't know. I hope so.

ONESIMUS

So you don't know? But, Habrotonon, do I get any thanks for my part?

HABROTONON

Goodness, yes! I shall consider you responsible for everything I get.

ONESIMUS

But if after that you purposely forget to look for the mother and play me false, how about that?

HABROTONON

For pity's sake, why do you think I want children? Liberty is all I pray for. (*Fervently.*) Ye gods, may that be my reward for what I'm doing.

ONESIMUS

I hope it will be.

HABROTONON

So you approve?

ONESIMUS

I approve most heartily, for if you play any tricks, I'll attack you then. There'll be a way. For the present, though, let's see if it's so.

HABROTONON (*looking pointedly at the ring*)

So you agree?

ONESIMUS (*loath to relinquish the ring*)

By all means.

HABROTONON

Go ahead and give me my ring.

ONESIMUS

Go ahead and take it.

HABROTONON (*as she receives the ring*)

Dear Lady *Eloquence,* be with me to help and give the words I speak success.

(*She goes in to play her part while* ONESIMUS *soliloquizes.*)

ONESIMUS

Intuitional, the female. When she sees that love won't lead her to liberty, and that she's not getting anywhere that way, she takes the other route. As for me, though, I shall be a slave all my days, moonstruck driveller that I am with no foresight at all about such things. But perhaps I shall get something from her if she has any luck. In fact I deserve to . . . How I waste my time counting on anything! I think I'm possessed, expecting gratitude from a woman! I only hope I shan't be worse off than I am. My mistress' case is pretty shaky now, for it only needs the discovery of a girl of citizen birth as mother of this baby to make him take her. Citizen or not, this one's bound to separate in any case and this time I think I've rather neatly avoided the charge that I have a finger in the pie. I've sworn off being too helpful. If anyone discovers that I haven't minded my own business or haven't held my tongue about anything another time, he may take my teeth and pull them. [*Clenched teeth are a symbol of obstinate silence in Greek.*] (*He sees* SMICRINES *approaching from the city.*) But who's this coming? Smicrines, coming back from town all excited again. Perhaps he has learned the truth from someone. I'll take myself off out of his way to avoid trouble.

Onesimus retires to the house as Smicrines appears and delivers a tirade of which we can guess the drift. Just enough of the manuscript is preserved to indicate the development of the plot. Here and there a brief phrase can be reconstructed. Smicrines has accumulated in town further evidence of his son-in-law's extravagance. As he puts it, "The whole city buzzes with the scandal." He knows for how many days Charisius has been living with the harp-girl, how much he spends on cooks, guesses that he gambles, and is so thoroughly alarmed for his ducats and his daughter that he is resolved to rescue them both from Charisius' hands without delay. He soon has new evidence of Charisius' misdeeds.

For Habrotonon has been playing her part within so successfully that Charisius has acknowledged as his the baby with which she confronted him. The resulting confusion completely breaks up the party. The cook emerges with his slaves and outfit, leaving the house in high dudgeon because of the interruption which has spoiled the feast that he was providing. He is violently berating the household as he leaves. "A high time they're having with their lunch," comments Smicrines, and the cook continues: "Bad luck for me, bad luck and plenty of it. This time I've been caught somehow off my guard, but if ever again you happen to want a cook, you may go to the devil." Smicrines questions the cook and gets a good deal more than the truth. He hears not only that Charisius has a son by Habrotonon, but that he intends to purchase her freedom at a ruinous cost and keep her in violation of the terms of his marriage contract, which no doubt forbade him to raise children except Pamphila's or to establish another woman as her rival. The cook departs hastily, as Simias and other guests come from the house. They comment freely on Charisius' predicament. The comrade who had been so high and mighty about self-indulgence was now involved in a public scandal. Smicrines accosts them and gets confirmation of what the cook had

told him. "But perhaps," he says, "I'm being indiscreet and meddling where I'm not concerned, since apparently I have grounds for
taking my daughter and leaving. I'll do just that. I've practically
made up my mind. I call you to witness that my daughter's rights
have been infringed." Simias and Chaerestratus fail to mollify the
old man. When someone asserts that Charisius hates the so-called
life of pleasure, Smicrines retorts with a list of his recent outings,
and expresses indignation at his treatment of his connections by marriage, to whom doubtless he had originally been recommended by
his frugality. "This Sir Touch-me-not won't have everything his own
way. He *will* waste his substance in a tavern, will he, live with the
beauty that he's adopting into the household, while he completely
cuts the acquaintance of his legal wife and her father?" No, no,
Smicrines will see to that. Here the act ends.

ACT IV

AT THE beginning of the fourth act Smicrines is talking to Pamphila,
whom he has summoned from the house in order to take her away.
He is astounded to find that she does not at once agree to leave her
husband when she hears how he is behaving. We have two or three
scraps of the long argument that ensued between them. Pamphila
remonstrates in ladylike tones: "Necessary for my own good perhaps, but that's what you must make me see. Otherwise you'd be, not
a father dealing with his daughter, but a master with his slave." Smicrines retorts: "Is there room here for argument and demonstration?
Isn't it as plain as day? The case cries to heaven, Pamphila. If, however, you insist on my explaining, I'm prepared. I will put before
you three possibilities. He'd be ruined for evermore and so would
you." He then points out how impossible she would find the situation, if she were to attempt to live in the house with Charisius,
supposing him to bring home a mistress and her child. "It's hard,"
he said, "Pamphila, for a free woman to hold her own against a
bought mistress, who schemes more, knows more, has no shame,
humours the man better." Neither can Charisius afford to keep up
two households. "Look at the expense. Double for Thesmophoria
and Scirophoria. Realize how ruinous it will be for his capital.
Mustn't we agree that his case is desperate? Consider your position
again. He says he has to go off to the Piraeus. He'll go there and stay
a while. You'll be miserable about it, I'm sure. You'll wait a long
while without your dinner, while he of course is drinking with his
mistress." The third possibility, that Charisius might spend all his

time with the harp-girl and desert Pamphila altogether, must have been presented by Smicrines in even darker colours.

Pamphila, however, held her own against her father's eloquence and even against the despair in her own heart. When he pointed out her distress she agreed: "Indeed my eyes are all swollen with weeping." But marriage was for her a life-partnership. No matter how much she might suffer, no matter to what straits she might be brought, she would not of her own accord leave her husband. Charisius meanwhile was listening to this conversation. His feelings are described later. The effect on Smicrines of his daughter's determination to face ruin and misery rather than forsake her husband can be imagined. He goes off in a towering rage resolved to return with assistance and remove his daughter by force. Pamphila is left alone. She is desperately unhappy and sees no hope for herself, now that she has a rival, who has presented Charisius with a son. As she stands dejected by her door, the supposed rival, Habrotonon, comes out with the baby, still playing the part of anxious mother. Pamphila naturally desires at first to avoid the woman, not guessing with what dramatic suddenness her sorrow is to be turned to joy.

HABROTONON (*coming out*)
I am going out with him. He's been wailing, my goodness, ever so long. There's something wrong with my baby.

PAMPHILA (*seeing her rival*)
Will no god take pity on me in my misery?

HABROTONON
Darling baby, when will you see your mother? (*Noticing* PAMPHILA.) But who is this next door?

PAMPHILA
I will go.

HABROTONON (*recognizing her*)
Wait a minute, ma'am.

PAMPHILA
Are you speaking to me?

HABROTONON
Yes. Look and see if you recognize me. (*As* PAMPHILA *turns,* HABROTONON *scans her face.*) She's the very one I saw. How do you do, my dear?

PAMPHILA
But who are you?

HABROTONON

Just give me your hand. Tell me, my dear, didn't you attend a celebration for girls at last year's Tauropolia?

(*But* PAMPHILA'*s eye is caught by the trinkets that the babe is wearing. She exclaims at the sight.*)

PAMPHILA

Woman, where, tell me, did you get that child?

HABROTONON

Do you see something you recognize that he's wearing? Have no fear of me, ma'am.

PAMPHILA

Isn't he your own?

HABROTONON

I pretended he was, not to wrong his real mother, but to find her when I had time. And now I have found her, for you are the one I saw that other time.

PAMPHILA

But who is his father?

HABROTONON

Charisius.

PAMPHILA

Are you certain, my dear?

HABROTONON

Indeed I am. But aren't you the young wife that lives here?

PAMPHILA

Yes indeed.

HABROTONON

Happy woman, some god has taken pity on you. But someone is coming out next door. I heard a noise. Take me in with you, so that I can go on and tell you all the rest of the story just as it happened.

(*While* HABROTONON *is giving the overjoyed* PAMPHILA *a full account of the adventures of the baby that had brought sorrow but was now bringing greater joy, we learn of the crisis* CHARISIUS *has passed through. He had by chance overheard* PAMPHILA'*s conversation with her father. As she steadfastly refused to let anything induce her to desert her husband, not even his disloyalty to her,* CHARISIUS, *long*

torn between love and pride, had been completely humbled. ONESI-
MUS, *eavesdropping as usual, grew more and more alarmed as he
saw* CHARISIUS *become furious with rage, rage against himself and
against anyone who might seem to have injured the gentle* PAMPHILA.
Not feeling safe in the same house with his master, ONESIMUS *slips
out and gives vent to his feelings.*)

ONESIMUS

He's not quite sane. By Apollo, he's mad. He's really gone mad. By the
gods he *is* mad. My master I mean, Charisius. He's had an atrabilious
stroke or some such thing. How else can you explain it? He spent a long
time by the door inside just now craning his neck and listening. His wife's
father was having a talk with her about the business, I suppose. The way
he kept changing colour, gentlemen, I don't care even to mention. Then
he cried out: 'Oh darling! what a wonderful thing to say!' and beat his
head violently. Then again after a while: 'What a wife I had and now
have lost, alas!' And to cap it all, when he had heard them to the end and
had gone in at last, inside there was groaning, tearing of hair, continual
frenzy. Over and over again he'd repeat: 'Criminal that I am, when I had
myself done a thing like that, when I had myself got an illegitimate child,
to be so unfeeling, so utterly unforgiving to her in the same unhappy situation. No humanity; no mercy.' He calls himself names as hard as he can,
his eyes are bloodshot with fury. I'm shaking in my shoes; I'm all wilted
with terror. If he catches sight of me, who told on her, anywhere, while
he's in this state, he'll maybe kill me. That's why I've quietly slipped out
here. Where am I to turn though? What can I think of? It's all over. I'm
done for. He's at the door coming out. O Zeus Saviour, help me if you can.
(*As* ONESIMUS *hides,* CHARISIUS *comes out in a state of complete abase-
ment and soliloquizes.*)

CHARISIUS

Oh, wasn't I a paragon, thinking always of my reputation, trying to
discover what honour and dishonour really are, without spot or flaw in
my own life! Heaven has used me well, just as I deserve. Precisely there
I showed that I was only human. You poor, poor fool, swollen with con-
ceit and loud in your preaching, intolerant of your wife's misfortune that
she couldn't help, I will exhibit the same fault in you yourself, and then
she will treat you gently, though you are bringing shame on her. You
shall be revealed as having neither luck, nor skill, nor heart. How different from your intentions at that minute were her words to her father:
'She had come to her husband to share his life, she had no right to run
away from the misfortune that had come.' But you with your mighty
superiority are behaving like a savage. Where is your wisdom now? What
will happen to her if you go on? Her father is going to show no considera-

tion for her. What care I for her father? I'll tell him plainly: 'You stop making trouble, Smicrines. My wife is not going to leave me. What do you mean by upsetting and brow-beating Pamphila?'

(*No sooner has* CHARISIUS *made up his mind to make his wife's cause his own than he reaps his just reward, for* HABROTONON *comes to bring him the good news about the baby. Naturally she is not a welcome sight to* CHARISIUS, *who almost at the same moment espies the unlucky* ONESIMUS. *In vain* ONESIMUS *affirms his innocence of eavesdropping.* HABROTONON *confesses that she is not after all the mother of* CHARISIUS' *child. Still more furious at the thought of the fraud that has been practised on him,* CHARISIUS *drives the abject* ONESIMUS *to throw all the blame on* HABROTONON, *who at last makes* CHARISIUS *listen.*)

HABROTONON

Stop attacking us, you foolish man. The child is your own lawful wife's, no other.

CHARISIUS

Would he were!

HABROTONON

By Demeter I swear it.

CHARISIUS

What sort of a story is that?

HABROTONON

Absolutely true.

CHARISIUS

Is the child really Pamphila's? It was mine before.

HABROTONON

And yours as well, to be sure.

CHARISIUS

Pamphila's! Habrotonon, I beg you, you mustn't excite me!

(*The fourth act ends when* CHARISIUS *is finally convinced and goes to* PAMPHILA. *Husband and wife are reunited.*)

ACT V

THE fifth act rounds out the story. Unfortunately we cannot be certain what happened to Habrotonon. Of course she gets her free-

dom. So in all probability does Onesimus. Simias and Chaerestratus
are involved in the explanations, but we do not know just how their
relations with Charisius and Habrotonon had been complicated by
her temporary appearance in the rôle of mother of his son. At any
rate all is set right. Habrotonon is complimented on her wit and
courage and is perhaps placed in charge of Simias, who remarks, as
the stage is cleared: "A girl like this couldn't have escaped his atten-
tions (*i.e.* 'Chaerestratus'), but I will treat her with respect."

Smicrines remains to be dealt with. At this moment he reappears,
equipped to abduct Pamphila and dragging Sophrona with him. She
is Pamphila's old nurse, who had assisted her with the baby. She had
been sent to meet him and to mollify him, but he is too headstrong
to listen. The only result is to provoke him further. Since his excitement has been rendered meaningless by the course of events, he is an
excellent subject for ridicule.

SMICRINES (*berating and shaking* SOPHRONA)

If I don't smash your head, Sophrona, I hope to be hanged. You'll
admonish me too, will you? I'm too hasty about carrying off my daughter,
you cursed hag? Am I to wait for her good husband to consume my
dowry; and then make speeches about my own property? You too urge
that, do you? Isn't it better to take the bull by the horns? You'll be good
and sorry if you say another word. My dispute is with Pamphila. Just
you urge her to change her mind when you see her. For, Sophrona, as I
hope for salvation, when I'm on the way home—did you see the pond as
you passed? That's where I'm going to spend the night ducking the life
out of you and I'll force you to agree with me instead of taking sides
against me. (*He approaches* CHARISIUS' *house where he expects to find*
PAMPHILA *alone and unprotected.*) The door is shut, so I must knock.
Boys! Boys! Open the door, someone. Boys! Don't you hear me?

ONESIMUS

(*Opening the door but not admitting* SMICRINES, *for his newly-gained
freedom has made him suddenly bold*)

Who's that knocking? Ha, Smicrines, that strict accountant, come for
his dowry and his daughter.

SMICRINES (*surprised*)

Himself, curse you.

ONESIMUS

And sure, he's right. His haste befits a man of calculation and great
wisdom. (*He notices* SOPHRONA, *helpless in the grip of* SMICRINES *and is
struck by her humorous resemblance to Persephoné or to any other beauty
in the hands of a ravisher.*) And his prize, Lord save us, what a stunner!

SMICRINES

By all the gods and spirits . . .

ONESIMUS

Do you believe, Smicrines, that the gods can spare the time to mete out daily to every individual his share of good or evil?

SMICRINES

What's that?

ONESIMUS

I'll make it quite plain. The total number of cities in the world is approximately a thousand. Each has thirty thousand inhabitants. Are the gods busy damning or saving each of them one by one? Surely not, for so you make them lead a life of toil. Then are they not at all concerned for us, you'll say. In each man they have placed his character as commander. This ever present guardian it is that ruins one man, if he fails to use it aright, and saves another. (*Indicating himself.*) This is our god, this the cause of each man's good or evil fortune. Propitiate this by doing nothing absurd or foolish, that good fortune may attend you.

SMICRINES

So my character, you scurvy knave, is doing something foolish now, is it?

ONESIMUS

It's wrecking you.

SMICRINES

What impudence!

ONESIMUS

But do you really think it right, Smicrines, to separate a daughter from her husband?

SMICRINES

Who says it is right? In this case though it's necessary.

ONESIMUS

You see? Wrong is necessary by his reasoning. It's not his character but something else that is ruining him. (*He taps his forehead significantly.*) Now this once, when you were bent on evil action, pure luck has delivered you. You arrive to find what was amiss all settled and atonement made. But another time, Smicrines, I warn you, don't let me catch you getting headstrong. But now I release you from these charges. Go find inside your grandson and salute him.

SMICRINES

My grandson, you carrion!

ONESIMUS

So you too were a blockhead for all you thought you were so wise. Is this the way you kept your eye on a young girl ripe for marriage? That's the reason we have these miraculous five-month infants to bring up.

SMICRINES

I don't know what you mean.

ONESIMUS

Yes, but the old woman knows, I fancy. That time at the Tauropolia it was my master, Sophrona, who found her separated from the dancers. Do you see?

SOPHRONA

Yes.

ONESIMUS

And now they've recognized each other and all's well.

SMICRINES (*to* SOPHRONA)

What's this he's saying, you cursed hag?

SOPHRONA (*quoting Euripides*)

'Twas Nature's will who recketh naught of laws,
And Nature made her woman for this very cause.

SMICRINES

What, have you lost your senses?

SOPHRONA

I'll quote you a whole passage from the *Auge* of Euripides, complete, if you won't see at last.

SMICRINES

Your tragic airs drive me wild. Are you fully aware of what he is saying?

SOPHRONA

I'm well aware.

ONESIMUS

You may be sure that the nurse knew before.

SMICRINES

But it's a frightful thing.

SOPHRONA

There never was anything more fortunate. If what you say is true, the child belongs to both, and all is well.

(*The rest is missing.* SMICRINES, ONESIMUS, *and* SOPHRONA *will be ready to go in after a few more lines, and with their disappearance the play will end.*)

III
THE SHEARING OF GLYCERA

CHARACTERS IN THE PLAY

SOSIA, POLEMON'S *sergeant*
DORIS, *slave of* GLYCERA
MOSCHION, *a wealthy young man*
DAVUS, *his slave*
PATAECUS, *an elderly friend of* POLEMON
POLEMON, *a Corinthian soldier*
GLYCERA, *a foundling, mistress of* POLEMON

INTRODUCTION

by L. A. Post

IN THE *Perikeiromené* or *Shearing of Glycera*, Menander treats again the theme of love and the improvement effected in a man by enforced prostration at the feet of a mistress. In this play the hero is of a very different type from Charisius of *The Arbitration*. He is a Corinthian, Polemon by name, who has seen service in Macedonian armies at a time when such service brought comparative wealth to the soldier. Polemon is a notable representative of the military type. He evidently is perfectly at home in camps and thoroughly at a loss to deal with situations that do not yield to the sword. He is an overgrown boy, petulant, simple-minded, rash in action, difficult to live with, but always forgivable.

The heroine may also be contrasted with Pamphila in *The Arbitration*. Glycera has in her life no background of wealth. Originally one of those forlorn abandoned infants of whom we hear so often in Greek comedy, she had been picked up and reared by a woman of modest income, who had, however, because of those same Macedonian wars that enriched the soldier, been reduced to the very depths of poverty. It was out of the question that Glycera should marry; rather it was matter of congratulation that she could be joined in an irregular union to the prosperous soldier Polemon, who at least loved his mistress and treated her with lavish generosity.

Another character is Moschion, the Bob Acres of the play. He is the spoiled darling of a wealthy lady, Myrrhiné, whom he supposes to be his mother. He cuts a dash in the town and is chock-full of that inordinate self-esteem which is the favourite target of comedy. In reality he is twin brother to Glycera and in origin like her a foundling. This fact, known to her, but not to him, is important for the motivation of the play. His supposed mother, Myrrhiné, does not appear in the parts of the play that have come down to us. She is not only Moschion's adopted mother but a good friend of Glycera.

There are four other characters: Moschion's slave Davus; Glycera's maid Doris, who is Polemon's slave, bought for Glycera's service; Sosia, Polemon's sergeant, who is boisterous at all times and often drunk to boot; and Pataecus, an elderly friend of Polemon, who turns out at the end of the play to be the long-lost father of the once more united twins.

Of the play we have less than half, but still enough to give us a good deal of the plot, since our material comprises sections from near the beginning, the middle, and the end of the play. Unfortunately one long scene is concerned chiefly with humorous by-play which, in the condition of the text, is not very intelligible. I shall accordingly omit some of it in my translation. The text is badly mutilated and uncertain in many places. There are two houses in the scene, that occupied by Myrrhiné and Moschion, and the house which Polemon provides for Glycera. The play probably began with the scene which gives it its title. There is an altercation between Glycera and Polemon. The latter had the evening before returned from the war and had surprised Glycera in the embrace of her fashionable neighbour, Moschion. He naturally leapt to the conclusion that Glycera was unfaithful to him and now in a fit of frenzy draws his sword and leaves her reft of her locks, an object of derision and aversion.

After this brief scene the stage is cleared and the personified figure of Misapprehension appears. Most of her speech remains. She tells how the twins were exposed and how they were found by a woman who took them up. The rest can be given in her own words.

MISAPPREHENSION

The woman gladly took the girl herself, and gave the boy to a rich lady who wanted a baby; she lives in the house that you see here on your right. Now several years passed, and the war and the misfortunes of Corinth went from bad to worse. The old lady was in dire need; the girl was now grown up—you saw her on the stage a moment ago—and this impetuous youth that you also saw, a Corinthian by birth, had fallen in love with her; so she gave the girl into his keeping, ostensibly as her own daughter. Later though, when she had become quite feeble and foresaw her life approaching harbour, as it were, she did not let the secret die, but told the young woman how she had picked her up, and gave her at the same time the baby clothes that she had been wrapped in. She also told her of her brother by birth, of whom she had known nothing, thus providing for certain possibilities. The girl might for instance be some day in need of assistance, and she knew that he was her only kinsman. The disclosure was also a safeguard to prevent any accidental developments between the young people because of me, Misapprehension. Anything might have happened, for he was rich and constantly fired with wine, she knew, while the girl was young and pretty, and there was no stability in her present protector.

Well, the woman died and the soldier not long ago bought the house here on your left. But though the girl lives next door to her brother, she has disclosed nothing. She does not want to bring about any alteration in his position, for he seems to be brilliantly placed; she wants him to profit by the gifts of fortune. He did get sight of her, however, by accident. He has plenty of self-confidence, as I said, and so has been purposely visiting the house. Last evening she happened to be sending her maid on some errand, and, as soon as he saw her at the door up he rushed and fell a-kissing and a-hugging her. She, though, knowing beforehand that he was her brother, didn't run away. But Polemon arrives and sees them. The rest he has told himself, how he left her with a warning that he would see her again when he had time, while she stood weeping and lamenting that she could not freely do as she had. Now all this blaze was kindled for the sake of what is coming. It has made Polemon fall into a rage. That was my doing; he's not that kind of person naturally. And it is the first step towards bringing the rest of the story to light, so that the twins may find their friends at last.

So if anyone is offended at what he has seen (*Polemon cutting off Glycera's hair*) and has supposed that the girl was disgraced, he will have to alter his views; for a god may overrule the evil that is done and turn it into good. Farewell, our audience, be gracious and support us in the rest of our play. (*The first act ends as* MISAPPREHENSION *leaves the stage.*)

THE SHEARING OF GLYCERA

ACT II

(SOSIA *comes from* POLEMON'S *house, carrying a cloak. He has been sent for it from the country where* POLEMON *is at present staying.*)

SOSIA

OUR blustering warrior of a while ago, who sets his ban on women having hair, lies flat on his back a-sobbing. When I left just now, lunch was being got for them, and his comrades were met to console him. And since he has no way of learning what is happening here, he has dispatched me for the special purpose of fetching a cloak—not that he needs anything, he wants me to have the walk.

(*Meanwhile* GLYCERA, *frightened out of her wits at the soldier's violence, has decided that she must at any cost gain assistance. She resolves to appeal to her neighbour, Myrrhiné, and to enlist her support. She will say nothing to* MOSCHION, *if she can avoid it. She orders* DORIS *first to make sure that* SOSIA *has gone, for he will not be so ready as* DORIS *to risk* POLEMON'S *vengeance by helping* GLYCERA. DORIS *will then get in touch with Myrrhiné, as a preliminary to* GLYCERA'S *flight.* SOSIA *lingers only a moment after* DORIS *appears.*)

DORIS

I'll go out and see, mistress.

SOSIA (*aside*)

There's Doris! What a girl she's got to be, how she is flourishing! They do live somehow, I can see that with half an eye, so they do. But I'll be off.
                                              (*He goes to report to* POLEMON.)

DORIS (*at the door of Myrrhiné's house*)

I'll knock, since none of them are out of doors. Unhappy the woman whose husband is a soldier! A violent lot they are, one and all, you never can trust them. O mistress mine, how unfairly he treats you! (*Calling*) Boys! It will cheer him up to hear that she's crying now, for that's what

1179

master wanted. (*Someone comes to Myrrhiné's door.*) Boy, please ask . . .

(*Here our text breaks off and a page or two are missing, in which Myr-rhiné probably appeared and, on hearing of* GLYCERA'S *plight, con-sented to take her in and hear her story. The transfer is soon made.* GLYCERA *leaves behind her wardrobe and her maid, which belong to* POLEMON, *and is welcomed by Myrrhiné.* MOSCHION *was not at home. Perhaps he was keeping out of the way of his belligerent neighbour. But* MOSCHION'S *servant* DAVUS *was in the house and drew his own conclusions from what he had seen. He comes from the house as the revellers who are to amuse the spectators between acts come in sight. He speaks to those inside.*)

DAVUS

But, fellows, here come a crowd of young men carousing. Mistress is in a class by herself, I'll say. She is taking the girl right into the house. There's a mother for you! Now to find my young master, for apparently the moment has come when he can't arrive on the scene too soon, so it looks to me. (DAVUS *goes to the city and the band of revellers occupy the stage and amuse the audience between acts.*)

ACT III

(DAVUS *returns with* MOSCHION, *who naturally finds it hard to believe that his mother has really taken* GLYCERA *into the house by way of facilitating his amours.*)

MOSCHION (*protesting*)

DAVUS, you've often enough before now brought me stories that hadn't a word of truth in them. In fact, you're a fraud and a good-for-nothing. So if you're leading me on a wild-goose chase this time too. . . .

DAVUS (*confident*)

String me up for a beating at once, if I am.

MOSCHION

That's drawing it mild.

DAVUS

Then treat me to all the horrors of war. But if I *am* right and you find her here in the house, what then? I've managed it all for you, Moschion, I wasted tons of arguments persuading the girl to come to this house, and your mother to take her in and carry out your wishes in everything; what am I offered by way of promotion?

(*There is an exchange of pleasantries between* Moschion *and* Davus, *and the latter is finally promised as a reward the opportunity to start in business on a small scale. He then continues.*)

Davus

Amen to that, as they say in meeting. Now then, this way, master, the portals wait thy entrance.

Moschion (*approaching the door*)

Audacity's my cue now; console the poor girl and cheer her up; snap my fingers at that miserable major, ostrich plumes and all.

Davus

Absolutely.

Moschion (*discreetly*)

Just you run in, please, Davus, and spy out the general situation. Find out where my mother is, whether they're expecting me or not. I needn't mention every little thing in a case of this sort, you know the ropes.

Davus

I'll go.

Moschion

I'll be waiting for you, Davus, pacing the street in front. (Davus *goes in.*) Well, she did betray some such feeling when I accosted her last evening. When I rushed up, instead of running off, she threw her arms about me and hugged me. I'm not unattractive, it would seem, to look at or to have to do with either. I really think so, by Athena, the hussies like me. But I really must knock wood.

Davus (*returning*)

Moschion, she's made her toilet and is sitting there.

Moschion

O you darling!

Davus

Your mother is going about arranging something or other, but lunch is ready and, as far as I can judge by what they are doing, they're waiting for you—and have been for some time, for that matter.

Moschion

Is there anything unattractive about me? Did you tell them that I was here?

DAVUS

No indeed.

MOSCHION

Then go and tell them now.

DAVUS

As you see, I'm there and back. (*Exit.*)

MOSCHION (*to himself*)

She'll be bashful when I enter, that's of course; and she'll hide her face, that's the way they do. But as I go in, I must kiss mother the first thing, make her my staunch ally, dance attendance on her, follow her wishes implicitly, for it might be her affair, the way she treats it. But someone is coming out. (DAVUS *comes from the house quite crestfallen.*) What does this mean, fellow? How you hesitate about approaching me, Davus!

DAVUS

Yes, by Zeus, for I don't understand it. When I went and told your mother that you were here, 'No more of that,' says she, 'how has he heard? Did you go blabbing to him that this girl was frightened and sought refuge here?' 'Certainly I did.' 'May you never see the year out,' says she. 'Now just you clear out, boy, and march off out of the way.' It's really so. All our hopes are dashed to the ground. She was anything but glad to hear that you had come.

MOSCHION

You scoundrel, you've played me a fine trick.

DAVUS

Nonsense! It's your mother . . .

MOSCHION

What's that? Isn't she taking the girl in freely? Or what is the matter? Didn't you say you persuaded the girl to come to the house for my sake?

DAVUS

I told you that I persuaded her to come? By Apollo, I never did. Do you think, master, that I'm not telling the truth?

MOSCHION

So you didn't say either just now that you helped persuade my mother yourself to take her into the house on my account?

DAVUS

Yes, that, as you see, I did say. Oh yes, I recall it.

MOSCHION

And that you thought she was doing it for my sake.

DAVUS

That I can't say, but I certainly urged her.

MOSCHION

Very well. Just step this way.

DAVUS

Where?

MOSCHION

Not far. You'll find out.

DAVUS

What was I going to say, Moschion? . . . At that time I . . . Wait just a bit.

MOSCHION

A cock-and-bull story to me, eh?

DAVUS

No, no, by Asclepius, no indeed, if you'll only listen. Most likely she doesn't want, don't you see, to surrender to the first assault with no formalities. She wants to know first all about you, to hear what you have to say. Yes indeed. You see she hasn't come like a flute-girl or like some moth-eaten street-walker either.

MOSCHION

That sounds to me like talking sense again, Davus.

DAVUS

Think it over. It's not absurd. She's left home. That's no cock-and-bull story. If you'll just disappear for three or four days, you'll find someone will get attached to you. I was given to understand that. You must listen now.

MOSCHION

Where am I to tie you up and leave you? You're arranging for me to cool my heels a longish while. You lied a moment ago and now here you are rattling on again.

DAVUS

I can't think with you interrupting. Ship oars, as it were, and go in-doors quietly.

MOSCHION
While you take to your heels!

DAVUS
Of course! Don't you see that I have provisions?

MOSCHION (*pretending to yield, but retaining* DAVUS)
To be sure. Well, you lead the way, Davus. By going in with me, you can help me get something straightened out here. I yield the point to you.

DAVUS (*to himself*)
A close shave, by Heracles. Even now I'm wilted with terror. The situation isn't so easily diagnosed as I once supposed.

(MOSCHION *departs into the house, preceded by* DAVUS. *Meanwhile* POLEMON *has been somewhat consoled by* SOSIA'S *report that he had seen* GLYCERA. *Though he knows nothing as yet of* GLYCERA'S *leaving his house, his anxiety leads him to dispatch* SOSIA *on another scouting expedition.* SOSIA *is talking to himself as he approaches* POLEMON'S *house.*)

SOSIA
Again I'm sent with his sword and cloak to see what she's doing and report on my return. I'm within an ace of telling him I found his rival in the house, just to make him jump up and come running. I would, too, if I weren't heartily sorry for him. To see my master so unfortunate! It's no dream either. Seeing is believing. What a bitter home-coming! (*As he enters* POLEMON'S *house,* DORIS *slips out and waits for his reappearance with some concern.*)

DORIS (*alone*)
The sergeant has come. It's a bad situation in every way, so it is, by Apollo. And at that there's the biggest item still to be accounted for, my master, once he gets back from the country—what a row he'll make when he appears on the scene.

(*As* SOSIA *comes out,* DORIS *retires to avoid his truculence. He has discovered* GLYCERA'S *absence and intends to find her. He is speaking to the servants within as he appears.*)

SOSIA
But you've let her go, you ungodly swine, you've let her leave the house!

DORIS (*to herself*)
The fellow's coming out again showing signs of temper. I'll retire a bit.

SOSIA (*to himself*)

She's gone straight off next door, that's plain, to her lover; as for us, we can curse our luck good and plenty, that's her attitude.

DORIS (*to herself*)

The captain got a fortune-teller when he got you. You're pretty warm.

SOSIA

I'll knock at their door. (SOSIA *is just about to knock boldly at Myrrhiné's door when* DAVUS *appears at some point of vantage and speaks.*)

DAVUS

What do you want, you unfortunate specimen of humanity? Where are you going in such a hurry?

SOSIA

Do you live here?

DAVUS

Perhaps. But what's keeping you from your work?

SOSIA

For heaven's sake, have you people lost your wits? Have you the audacity to keep a free woman under lock and key, in violation of the rights of her lawful master?

DAVUS

How vile, how unscrupulous a man must be to descend to such scurrilous charges!

SOSIA

Do you think we're chicken-hearted, that we're not men?

DAVUS

Oh yes, heaven knows you're men, shilling-a-day men. When you've got a few guinea-a-day men on your side, then we'll be ready to fight you.

SOSIA

Heracles, what a shameless exhibition! So you admit you have her; speak out.

DAVUS

Fellow, begone.

Sosia (*pretending to call to a comrade*)

Hilarion! He's gone. He happens to be an eye-witness and says you have her.

DAVUS

Before long I hope to see some of you tied up and howling.

SOSIA

Who do you think you're playing with? What are you drivelling about? We'll storm this wretched shanty double quick. Get the lady-killer into his armour.

DAVUS

Hard luck, you poor thing. Have you been hanging around all this time, because you thought she was here?

SOSIA

To arms, fellows! (*Turning to* DAVUS.) They'll ransack the whole place quick as a wink, call 'em shilling-a-day men or not.

DAVUS

I wasn't serious when I said that. The truth is you're a sewer-rat.

SOSIA

You call yourselves civilized . . .

DAVUS

But we haven't got her.

SOSIA

Faugh! I'll take a pike to you.

DAVUS

Clear out and be damned. I'm going, since you've apparently lost your wits.

(DAVUS *disappears and* DORIS *comes from her hiding-place.*)

DORIS

Sosia!

SOSIA

If you'll just step this way, Doris, I'll give you a very bad time. You're at the bottom of this.

DORIS

Bless you, tell me why. Because she was frightened and took refuge somewhere with a woman?

SOSIA

Frightened and took refuge somewhere with a woman?

DORIS

As a matter of fact she's gone to Myrrhiné's next door. If that isn't so, may I never get what I want.

SOSIA

You see where she's off to—where the object of her affection is, that's where.

(*Here the text breaks off entirely. Perhaps seventy lines are missing. When the next fragment takes up the story,* POLEMON *is present, accompanied by* SOSIA *and his army, a motley crew, and at least one light-'o-love,* HABROTONON, *who has her flute with her.* SOSIA *is drunk and boisterous.* POLEMON *is ready for any violence in order to regain* GLYCERA. *The restraining influence is provided by* PATAE-CUS, *an elderly friend of* POLEMON. POLEMON *had appealed to him to aid in the recovery of* GLYCERA. PATAECUS *had agreed to act in* POLEMON'S *interest, but insisted on the dismissal of the army, before negotiations should be undertaken.* POLEMON *is inclined to listen, but* SOSIA *is all for action.*)

SOSIA

He's come from them with his pockets lined. Trust me. He's a traitor to you and the army.

PATAECUS (*to* SOSIA)

Go off and have a nap, my dear fellow. Forget these battles. You're not well. (*Turning to* POLEMON) I'll talk to you. You're not so tipsy.

SOSIA (*indignant*)

Not so tipsy! When I've drunk perhaps half a pint, because I knew what would happen, worse luck, and was keeping myself fit for the emergency.

PATAECUS

Quite right. Just do as I say.

(SOSIA *subsides for a moment.*)

POLEMON (*to* PATAECUS)

What advice have you for me?

PATAECUS

That's a proper question. Now then, it's my turn to talk to you.

SOSIA (*to a light-o'-love in the company*)

Sound the alarm, Habrotonon.

(*There is a new outbreak on the part of the army.*)

PATAECUS (*to* POLEMON)

First send this fellow inside with his followers.

SOSIA (*protesting*)

That's poor strategy. Are you going to dismiss the army when you should carry the place by assault? This Pataecus here is ruining me.

PATAECUS (*impatiently*)

Is there no one in command?

POLEMON (*to* SOSIA)

For heaven's sake, fellow, be off.

SOSIA

I'm off. I thought you would *do* something.

(*He departs with* HABROTONON *and the army amid scurrilous jests. All go inside but* SOSIA, *who collapses at the door and goes to sleep.*)

PATAECUS

If your statement is correct about what took place, Polemon, and the girl is your lawful wife——

POLEMON

The very idea! Of course she is.

PATAECUS

But it's of some importance.

POLEMON

I have always looked on her as my wife.

PATAECUS

Don't shout. Who put her into your hands?

POLEMON

Who? Why, she herself.

PATAECUS

Very fine. Very likely you suited her then. Now, though, you don't, and she's gone off because you didn't use her properly.

POLEMON

What! Not use her properly! That hurts me more than anything you have said yet.

PATAECUS

I know perfectly well that you'll say in the end that at the present moment you're behaving like a lunatic. What's the idea? Whom are you going to abduct? She is her own mistress. When a man's at a disadvantage and loves a woman, no course is open but to win her by fair words.

POLEMON

But haven't I a case against the man who seduced her in my absence?

PATAECUS

A case to justify lodging a complaint, if you finally resort to argument. But if you take the law into your own hands, you lose your case. You see the offence doesn't justify retaliation, but only the lodging of a complaint.

POLEMON

Not even now?

(*Now that she has gone to* MOSCHION, *as he supposes.*)

PATAECUS

Not even now.

POLEMON

I don't know what I'm to say, by Demeter, except that I shall hang myself. Glycera has gone and left me—gone and left me, Glycera—Pataecus. Well, if you really think that's the best we can do—since you used to be a friend of hers and have often talked with her before—you go and speak with her; plead my case with her, I entreat you.

PATAECUS

You see, I think that's the best you can do.

POLEMON

Of course you can speak effectively, Pataecus?

PATAECUS

Oh, passably.

POLEMON

But, Pataecus, really you must. Our only hope is in that. If ever I have done her the least wrong—if it doesn't remain through all the one object of my ambition—I wish you could see her fine clothes.

PATAECUS

Don't worry.

POLEMON

Do please look at them, Pataecus. You'll feel for me more strongly.

PATAECUS

O Lord!

POLEMON

Come this way. What clothes! and what a marvellous sight she is, when she puts any of them on! Maybe you hadn't seen her?

PATAECUS

Oh yes, I have.

POLEMON

For that matter, she was handsome enough, no doubt of that, to be worth looking at. But what's the good of dragging in the fact that she's handsome now, addlepate that I am, rambling on about what makes no difference.

PATAECUS

Not at all, not at all.

POLEMON

Really? But indeed you must take a look. Do step this way. Come along.

PATAECUS (*yielding to the inevitable*)

I'm coming.

(*As they disappear into* POLEMAN'S *house to inspect* GLYCERA'S *wardrobe,* MOSCHION *comes from Myrrhiné's house armed for combat. He shouts at the retreating enemy, who can no longer hear him.*)

MOSCHION

Make yourselves scarce this minute, you; get in. Armed with spears have they leapt forth upon me! But they couldn't storm a swallow's nest, the sort of sneaking villains that are here. (*Looking round and seeing no one but the drunken* SOSIA.) "But," says he, "they had trained soldiers," and your far-famed soldiers amount to this one Sosia here. (*Reflectively*) There have been a good many made miserable in recent times, for, whatever the reason may be, misery's a crop that doesn't fail anywhere in Greece nowadays, but I don't believe among them all there's a living human being as miserable as I am; no, I don't. As soon as I entered, instead of doing as I always have, going to my mother in her room, or summoning someone from the inner rooms to me, I went into a little room out of the way and there I lay down most composedly. Meanwhile I send Davus in to make my presence known, no other message, to my mother. He, however, with mighty little concern for me, finding them in the midst of lunch, proceeded to stow away all he could, while I in the meantime was lying on my couch and saying to myself: 'My mother will be here directly with a message from my sweetheart, letting me know on what terms she consents to join me.' I was practising a speech myself——

(*Here there is a long gap of about one hundred and sixty verses.* Mos- chion *probably went on to relate how he was finally undeceived in regard to* Glycera's *intentions by overhearing a conversation be- tween her and his mother, which also roused his curiosity in regard to his own identity and in regard to* Glycera's *antecedents. At the point where we are able to take up the story again, these difficulties are in process of solution.* Glycera *has come out and is talking to* Pataecus, *who, it will be remembered, had agreed to act as* Pole- mon's *ambassador and to induce her, if possible, to return to the soldier.* Glycera *is emphatically pointing out to* Pataecus *that he has made a great mistake in accepting* Polemon's *view that she had left him for* Moschion, *and that she had formed a liaison with the latter during the soldier's absence.*)

GLYCERA (*excited and emphatic*)
You're not considering what possible *aim* I could have had in that case in coming to his *mother's* house and in taking refuge *here*. Could I have hoped that he would *marry* me? Oh yes, he's quite on a level with *me* in birth. If not that, then maybe I hoped to become his *mistress*. Well, in that case wouldn't I and he too do our best, for pity's sake, to keep it a *secret* from his parents? Should I, instead, have planted myself recklessly in his *father's* way? Should I have been foolish enough to choose a course that would make me hated *here* and implant in *your* minds a suspicion that could never again be effaced? Should I feel no *shame* even, Pataecus? Did you too come to me convinced of *that;* did you suppose that I had come to be *that sort?*

PATAECUS
I hope not indeed, by Zeus on high. I hope, moreover, that you'll prove our suspicions really false, as I for my part am convinced they were. But go back to Polemon nevertheless.

GLYCERA
Let him insult other girls hereafter.

PATAECUS

The outrage wasn't a deliberate act.

GLYCERA

It was a wicked act, and even a slave girl, for pity's sake, isn't treated like that.

(*A few lines are missing in which* GLYCERA *offers to produce evidence of her free status and describes the tokens that were her only heritage. She begs* PATAECUS *to take her part and help her assert her independence. He begins to suspect that she may be his long-lost daughter. She is speaking of the tokens.*)

GLYCERA

From her I received some keepsakes of my father and mother, which she bade me keep in my possession at all times and not lose.

PATAECUS

Well, what do you want?

GLYCERA

I want them brought to me.

PATAECUS

You're still determined to break with the man for good? What's your wish, my dear girl?

GLYCERA

I want you to arrange it for me. Will you do it?

PATAECUS

It shall be done. It's but a trifle; but you ought to take everything into consideration.

GLYCERA

I know my own affairs best.

PATAECUS

So that's that. Which of the maids knows where you keep these things?

GLYCERA

Doris does.

PATAECUS (*going to the door of* POLEMON'S *house*)

Tell Doris to come outside, some one. (*To* GLYCERA) All the same, Glycera, I entreat you, do yield and forgive him on the terms I propose.

DORIS (*coming out*)

Oh, mistress, what is it? What trouble we are in!

GLYCERA

Fetch me out the casket that has the embroidered things in it, Doris.
Do you know it?

DORIS

Yes, indeed.

GLYCERA

The one I gave you to keep. Why are you crying, poor girl?

PATAECUS

By God Almighty I have a very strange feeling.

(*Here a few verses are missing. We next find* PATAECUS *and* GLYCERA
examining the contents of the casket together. PATAECUS *is attempting to identify the embroidery with some that he remembered from
long ago.*)

PATAECUS

The same as I saw then. Isn't this next one a goat or a bull or some
such beast.

GLYCERA

It's a stag, my friend, not a goat.

PATAECUS

It has horns, I know that. And the third one here is a winged horse.
These things belonged to my wife, poor, poor woman.

(*He weeps as he studies the tokens. From this point the metre more and
more suggests operatic music. During this conversation* MOSCHION
has been listening unseen. He soliloquizes.)

MOSCHION

It's an impossibility, that's the only conclusion I can arrive at, any
way I look at it, that my mother should have had a child and should
secretly have abandoned a daughter born to her. But if it did happen and
Glycera is my sister, then my disaster is complete, curse the luck.

PATAECUS (*to* GLYCERA)

Well I knew some of them—the relics of my past.

GLYCERA

Examine me on any point you please.

PATAECUS
Where did you get these things that you have? Tell me.

GLYCERA
They are the clothes I had once as a foundling.

MOSCHION (*to himself*)
Launch out into the deep! Borne helpless on the waves I reach the crisis of my own fortune.

PATAECUS
Was there no other? Make that clear to me.

GLYCERA
There was indeed. With me a brother was abandoned.

MOSCHION (*to himself*)
That answers one of my questions.

PATAECUS
What then caused your separation?

GLYCERA
I could explain it all, for I have heard the tale. But question me about myself, since that is mine to tell. The rest I've given her my oath I'll not disclose.

MOSCHION (*to himself*)
That statement gives me a plain clue, for she gave my mother an oath. Where in the world am I?

PATAECUS
Who took you in and kept you, pray?

GLYCERA
A woman kept me, she who found me lying there.

PATAECUS
Some indication of the place had you from her?

GLYCERA
A spring she mentioned and a shady nook.

PATAECUS
The same that he who left the babes described to me.

GLYCERA
And who was he? If naught prevents, let me know too.

PATAECUS

A servant left you there, 'twas I who feared to rear you.
              (*He embraces* GLYCERA *as his long-lost daughter.*)

GLYCERA

You abandoned your own children? What induced you?

PATAECUS

Many are the sudden freaks, my child, of fortune. Your mother died in
bearing you, and just the day before, my daughter—

GLYCERA

What happened, pray? God's mercy, how I tremble!

PATAECUS

I was reduced to poverty, though used to wealth.

GLYCERA

What! In one day? A frightful blow, ye gods!

PATAECUS

News reached me that the ship which was our sole support was lost
beneath the wild Aegean's briny waves.

GLYCERA

O pity! what a fate was mine!

PATAECUS

And so I chose to think that, facing beggary with clinging babes like
boats in tow, 'twould class a man as utter fool to try to keep them. I sacrificed the best of all things, daughter. What is the rest like?

GLYCERA

It shall all be listed. There was a necklace with a few engraved gems
that were put with the babes as marks of recognition.

PATAECUS

Shall we inspect them.

GLYCERA

We can't now.

PATAECUS

Why so?

GLYCERA

My brother got the rest as his share, of course.

MOSCHION (*to himself*)
Then this man, so it seems, is my father.

PATAECUS
Can you tell me what there was?

GLYCERA
There was a silver girdle.

PATAECUS
So there was.

GLYCERA
And the pattern on it girls in a dance. You recall it then? And a transparent wrap and a gold head-band. That completes the list.

(*Here another gap intervenes with some indication that* MOSCHION *at this point declares himself and embraces his father and his sister.* GLYCERA'S *fortune is made and* POLEMON *has now no hope of winning her back. It is, however, just her new-found security that gives her confidence to face him and accept him once more as a lover. The final scene is preserved.* POLEMON *is talking to* DORIS.)

POLEMON
I intended to hang myself.

DORIS
Oh, don't do that.

POLEMON
But what am I to do, Doris? How am I to live, God have mercy on me, apart from her?

DORIS
She'll come back to you—

POLEMON
Gracious heaven, what news!

DORIS
If you'll do your best to be kind hereafter.

POLEMON
I'd never fall short in anything, I assure you, for you are more than right. Go at once. I'll set you free to-morrow, Doris. (*Exit* DORIS.) But let me tell you what you are to say. She's gone in. Oh, my angry, angry passions, how you took me by storm! It was a brother, not a lover to

whom she gave that kiss. And I, fiend that I was, utterly blind with jealousy, at once ran amuck. As a result I was going to hang myself and for good reason. (DORIS *returns*.) What news, my dear Doris?

DORIS

Good news; she will come to you.

POLEMON

Are you mocking me?

DORIS

No, by Aphrodité. But she was dressing up and parading for her father. Now you ought at once to celebrate her good fortune with a feast—it came in time of need—now that her ship has come in at last.

POLEMON

By Zeus I will, for you're quite right. The cook from the market is in the house; let him slaughter the sow.

DORIS

But where's the basket, and the other requirements?

POLEMON

The basket can wait, only let him get the sow slaughtered. Better than that, I'll rob some altar of a wreath myself and put it on.

(*Does so.*)

DORIS

Yes, you'll look a lot more convincing so.

POLEMON

Now bring Glycera at once.

DORIS

Really she was just about to come out—with her father.

POLEMON

What, he? What will become of me?

(POLEMON *retreats into his house.*)

DORIS

Goodness, what are you doing? He's run away. Is it so terrible when a door rattles? I'll go in myself to do what I can to help.

(DORIS *also retires as* PATAECUS *leads* GLYCERA, *now handsomely arrayed, on to the stage.*)

PATAECUS (*to* GLYCERA)

I'm quite delighted to hear you say you'll do your part to be friends again. When prosperity arrives, to accept satisfaction then, that's a mark of the true Greek spirit. But let some one run and fetch him.

POLEMON (*emboldened, from his retreat*)

No, I'll come out myself. I was preparing a Thanksgiving feast, to ~elebrate the news that Glycera had discovered those that she wanted to.

PATAECUS

You are quite right. Now, though, attend to what I'm going to say. I bestow this woman on you as your lawful wife.

POLEMON

As such I take her.

PATAECUS

With a dowry of three talents.

POLEMON

That's very good too.

PATAECUS

From now on forget that you are a soldier and spare your friends any inconsiderate acts.

POLEMON

Heaven help me! When I've come within an ace of ruin this time, is it likely I shall ever be inconsiderate again? I won't even find fault with Glycera. Only be friends, dearest.

GLYCERA

I will, for this time your losing your head led to good fortune.

POLEMON

So it did, my dear.

GLYCERA

Consequently I've consented to forgive you.

POLEMON (*as they go in together*)

Do join our celebration, Pataecus.

PATAECUS

I must set about arranging another wedding, since I'm marrying my son to Philinus' daughter.

MOSCHION (*appearing suddenly and protesting*)

O powers above——

(*This is all we have of the play, which is evidently drawing to a close.*)

GLOSSARY

In order not to swell unreasonably an already bulky volume, the following classes of proper names have been omitted from this Glossary: 1. Geographical names of purely ornamental or entirely obvious significance; 2. Personal names introduced for merely genealogical reasons; 3. The names of a large number of Persian generals; 4. Names of persons in Comedy about whom nothing is known beyond what can be deduced from the contexts in which they are mentioned. Not all the omissions are covered by these categories, but it is hoped that nothing really important has failed of treatment. The utmost brevity has been everywhere necessary, but inequalities have been unavoidable. The names in comedy generally require more extensive comment, but many are included simply because their meaning is significant; in these cases the translation is given in quotation marks.

Orthographical variants have not been separately entered. There is a regrettable amount of caprice in the transliteration of Greek names, and it has seemed best to give here a special compendium of variations.

VARIANT	NORMAL FORM	VARIANT	NORMAL FORM
a (final)	é or as	k	c
ai	ae	oi	oe
ede or ed (final)	edes	os (final)	us
i or e	ei	ou	u
id (final)	ides	u	y

It will be observed that in the Glossary the forms above styled "normal" are by no means exclusively or consistently employed.

Until the latter half of the nineteenth century it was customary to designate Greek deities and heroes by the names of their Roman "equivalents," and some of the translations used in this book exhibit this practice. These Roman names have not been separately entered; the following list will direct the reader to the relevant articles in the Glossary.

ROMAN	GREEK	ROMAN	GREEK
Aesculapius	Asclepius	Minerva	Athene
Ceres	Demeter	Neptune	Poseidon
Diana	Artemis	Pollux	Polydeuces
Hercules	Heracles	Proserpina	Persephone
Juno	Hera	Saturn	Cronus
Jupiter, Jove	Zeus	Ulysses	Odysseus
Mars	Ares	Venus	Aphrodite
Mercury	Hermes	Vulcan	Hephaestus

GLOSSARY

ABAE. An old town in Phocis, noted for its temple and oracle of Apollo.

ACADEMY. A public garden in the suburbs of Athens; later the site of Plato's school.

ACASTUS. Brother of Alcestis and son of Pelias, King of Iolcus. He drove Jason and Medea into exile after the latter had contrived the death of Pelias. He likewise exiled Peleus who had fallen in love with his wife Hippolyte.

ACESTOR. An alien *nouveau-riche* tragic poet, also called Sacas, father of Cleon's secretary Tisamenus.

ACHAEA. In Homer this is practically the equivalent of Hellas, and Achaeans, Argives, and Danaans indifferently denote what a later age called Hellenes. The tragic dramatists are wont to imitate the epic poet in this usage.

ACHAEUS. Son of Xuthus and Creusa, who was regarded in the legends as the founder of the race of the Achaeans.

ACHARNIAN. Of or from Acharnae, an Attic deme some seven miles north of Athens. It was the largest of the rural towns in Attica. Mount Parnes, located just behind it, was so closely timbered that the chief occupation of the Acharnians was the manufacture of charcoal. Their military valour had long been famous, and the Spartan invasions which occurred so frequently during the Peloponnesian War could not but render them actively hostile to the Periclean policy of exhausting the enemy by refusing to meet him in a large and potentially decisive conflict.

ACHELOUS. The largest and most celebrated river in Greece, rising on Mount Pindus, flowing through Acarnania, and emptying into the Ionian Sea. Also the god of this river, who was one of the most important of the numerous river-gods.

ACHERON. A river in the Underworld.

ACHILLES. Son of Peleus and Thetis, father of Neoptolemus, the greatest of the Greek warriors before Troy, finally slain by Paris.

ACRISIUS. See DANAE.

ACROPOLIS. The citadel of Athens, a plateau of rock about 200 feet high on which numerous temples were located. In early times the residence of the kings of the city. The public treasury was also situated here.

ACTAEON. A grandson of Cadmus, who saw Artemis and her nymphs bathing. In anger the goddess changed him into a stag, and he was torn to pieces by his own hunting hounds.

ADIMANTUS. An Athenian general suspected of treachery at the battle of Aegospotami; he was also a friend of Alcibiades.

ADMETUS. King of Pherae in Thessaly, husband of Alcestis, son of Pheres.

ADONIA. The festival in honor of Adonis.

ADONIS. A fair youth whom Aphrodite loved so much that after his death, from a hunting wound or by the arrow of Artemis, she was allowed to have him on earth for half of each year. He is thus a symbol of the vegetation cycle. At Athens there were festivals in his honour in which only women took part.

ADRASTEIA. A goddess identified with Nemesis, a requiter of the sin of Pride. A district north of the Troad is called by her name.

ADRASTUS. King of Argos, and father-in-law to Polyneices.

ADRIA. A town between the mouths of the Po and the Adige from which the Adriatic takes its name.

AEACUS. Father of Peleus, Telamon, and Psamathe; so famous for his justice that he became one of the judges in the Underworld.

AEGEUS. An early king of Athens, the father of Theseus.

AEGIALEUS. Son of Adrastus, the only Argive hero to fall in the attack upon Thebes made ten years after Polyneices' abortive attempt to take the city.

AEGICORES. The name of a legendary Attic tribe, so called after a son of Ion.

AEGINA. 1. A daughter of the river-god Asopus, wife of Aeacus. 2. An island in the Saronic Gulf.

AEGIPLANCTUS. A mountain in Megaris.

AEGIS. The shield of Zeus, from which lightning and thunder were thought to come; it was also carried by his daughter Athene. It is pictured as blazing brightly and fringed with golden tassels; in its centre is the awful head of a Gorgon.

AEGISTHUS. Son of Thyestes, and cousin of Agamemnon. See Introduction to Aeschylus' *Oresteia*.

AEGYPTUS. A king of Egypt whose fifty sons sought to marry the fifty daughters of Danaus, the twin brother of Aegyptus. See the Introduction to Aeschylus' *The Suppliants*.

AENEAS. Trojan hero in the *Iliad*. After the fall of Troy, according to the legend, he led a band of Trojan survivors to Italy, where his descendants founded Rome.

AENIAN. The Aenianes were a tribe of southern Thessaly.

AEOLUS. Ruler of Thessaly, father of Xuthus, ancestor of the Aeolians.

AESCHINES. A great boaster, who was particularly fond of talking about his wealth, although wherein this consisted was uncertain.

AETHER. Anglicized Ether, the upper air of the bright sky, thought somehow purer and more rarefied than the lower air. Aristophanes regularly ascribed to Euripides a deification of Aether.

AETHIOP KNIGHTS. The reference is to Memnon, son of Tithonus. He was king of Aethiopia and aided the Trojans. Achilles finally slew him. He was a leading character in at least two lost plays of Aeschylus.

AETNA. 1. A volcanic mountain in the northeast of Sicily. One of the Titans was believed to have been buried under it by the victorious Zeus. 2. A town in Sicily, founded by the Syracusan tyrant Hiero.

AETOLIA. A wild and mountainous region in western Greece. In mythology it is the scene of many hunting legends.

AEXONIA. A deme of Attica, more correctly Aexoneis. The inhabitants were reputed to be very slanderous. Laches was a demesman of Aexoneis.

AGAMEMNON. Son of Atreus, brother of Menelaus, king of Mycenae, leader of the Greek forces against Troy.

AGATHON. A fifth-century Athenian tragic dramatist whose personal delicacy and precious style are frequently satirized by Aristophanes.

AGENOR. Son of Poseidon, king of Phoenicia, father of Cadmus.

AGLAURUS. Daughter of Cecrops, an Athenian heroine who gave her life to save her city.

AGORACRITUS. "Market-place judge."

AGUIEUS. A title of Apollo, as guardian of streets and highways. Statues of him stood in front of the houses, and to these sacrifices were made.

AGYRRHIUS. An Athenian statesman who had indulged in paederasty in his earlier years. He had been involved in a trial for embezzlement, but had won the people's favor by introducing pay for attendance at the Assembly. The comic poets hated him because he had reduced the financial benefits which they had received from the state. He had become quite wealthy himself, and it would seem that he either ate too much or had a defective digestive tract.

AIDONEUS. The equivalent of Hades, the god of the Underworld.

AJAX. Name of two Greek heroes in the Trojan War. One was the son of Telamon and was a perfect soldier, tall, strong, tireless, reliable. The other was the son of Oileus, small but swift; he often acted in conjunction with his bulkier namesake.

ALAE. The equivalent of Halae, a deme or village in Attica to which the statue of Artemis was supposed to have been brought from the Taurians.

ALCATHOUS. A king of Megara.

ALCESTIS. Daughter of Pelias, and wife of Admetus, King of Thessaly. See Euripides' *Alcestis*.

ALCIBIADES. An Athenian, son of Clinias, born around 450. Of a noble and wealthy family, gifted with beauty of person and an irresistible charm of manner, he might have become one of the greatest statesmen in Athens' history if he had possessed more self-control and stability. But the wildness of his life and the insecurity of his policy prevented the populace from ever quite placing complete confidence in him, and his magnificent ambitions experienced a series of frustrations.

ALCIDES. Heracles, grandson of Alcaeus.

ALCMENA. Wife of Amphitryon and mother, by Zeus, of Heracles.

ALEXANDER. See PARIS.

ALOPE. A mortal woman, who bore to Poseidon a son named Hippothoön.

ALPHEUS. A river in the Peloponnesus, flowing through Arcadia and Elis, near Olympia.

ALTHAEA. Wife of Oeneus, a king of Calydon. Dionysus had been her lover.

AMAZONS. A race of belligerent women who lived without contact with men, according to mythology, in the Caucasian regions, from which they were reputed to have made a number of invasions of Asia Minor and other countries. In the reign of Theseus they attacked Attica, and in the Trojan War they played a late and ineffective part. An attack on them was one of the exploits of Heracles.

AMIPSIAS. A successful fifth-century Athenian comic poet.

AMORGOS. An island in the Aegean, noted for the manufacture of very fine textiles; these were not silk, of course, but extremely soft linen, and the designation "transparent" must be taken to mean "clinging" or "revealing."

AMPHANAE. A town in Thessaly.

AMPHIARAUS. An Argive seer and hero, one of the ill-fated Seven even though he foresaw the gloomy outcome of the expedition. His wife had tricked him into going, and the prophet bade his sons avenge him. When the attack on the city of Thebes was repulsed, Amphiaraus is reported to have been pursued by Periclymenus, but just as the Theban was about to catch him, the earth opened up and swallowed the seer. The spot where this miracle occurred was in latter days oracular, its interpretations of dreams being especially sought after.

AMPHICTYON. A delegate to the Amphictyonic Council, which carried on the affairs of the religious associations of Greek states which were called Amphictyonic Leagues. The derivation of the term is uncertain.

AMPHION. Son of Zeus by Antiope, whom Lycus of Thebes had ill-treated. Amphion and his brother Zethus accordingly attacked and captured the city, eventually putting to death Lycus and his wife Dirce. The city was then fortified with a wall. Later Amphion married Niobe and became by her the father of numerous progeny, but Apollo killed them all and Amphion ended his own life because of his grief.

AMPHITHEUS. The name contains the

Greek word *theos,* "god"; it is found in connection with the legend of Demeter's search for Persephone, but the genealogy which Aristophanes makes his character expound is, of course, fictitious.

AMPHITRITE. A daughter of Nereus, wife of Poseidon. Goddess of the sea, and mother of Triton.

AMYNIAS. A cowardly brother of Aeschines.

AMYNON. A notorious homosexual.

ANAPHLYSTIA. An Attic seaport whose name suggests the Greek word *anaphlan,* "masturbate."

ANACREON. An Ionian lyric poet, born at Teos on the coast of Asia Minor. His compositions were famous for the frequency with which they celebrated the pleasures of wine and women.

ANAURUS. A stream near Amphanae in Thessaly.

ANDROMACHE. See prologue to Euripides' *Andromache.*

ANDROMEDA. Daughter of Cepheus, king of Aethiopia, and Cassiopia. Her boastful mother vaunted her daughter's beauty to excess and Poseidon dispatched a sea-monster to lay waste her country, which was to be preserved only if Andromeda were given up to the awful creature. She was chained to a rock, but Perseus found her and rescued her. She was the heroine of a tragedy by Euripides, one of his most popular, in which the famous echo scene, parodied in *The Thesmophoriazusae,* was incorporated. Originally it seems to have consisted of a solo lyric by Andromeda with responses by Echo.

ANDROS. A large island in the Aegean, southeast of Euboea.

ANTHRACYLLUS. Imaginary name of an Acharnian. It contains the Greek word *anthrax,* "charcoal."

ANTIGONE. See Introduction to Sophocles' *Oedipus the King* and *Oedipus at Colonus.*

ANTILOCHUS. A Greek hero in the *Iliad,* the son of Nestor.

ANTIPHON. An Athenian, famous for his poverty and his ravenous appetite; the orator of this name cannot be the person to whom Aristophanes refers.

ANTISTHENES. One of the most constipated men in Athens in the early fourth century; he was also a miser.

AORIA. An old name for Boeotia.

APATURIA. An Athenian festival concerned mainly with matters pertaining to the tribal survivals in the organization of the state. The name suggests the Greek word *apate,* "fraud."

APHRODITE. The Greek goddess of love. Her cult was practised chiefly in Cyprus; hence she is called Cypris. Other seats of her worship were Cythera and Paphos.

APIAN. An older equivalent of Argive.

APIDANUS. A river in Thessaly.

APODRASIPPIDES. A comic name, formed from the Greek words *apodranai,* "to run away" and *hippos,* "horse."

APOLLO. Often called Phoebus. In tragedy he is usually the god of healing, of prophecy, and of music. Notable points in connection with him are: his building of the Trojan walls with Poseidon; his consistent support of Troy in the Trojan War; his unusual gift of prophecy to Cassandra.

ARACHNE. A mountain in Argolis.

ARCADIA. Anglicized into Arcady. The mountainous central region of the Peloponnesus, suited only to stock-raising. The god Pan was extensively worshipped there. A later and romantic age idealized the pastoral life of Arcadia into what has ever since been connoted by the name.

ARCHEDEMUS. A demagogue, who initiated the prosecution of the Generals, after Arginusae.

ARCHEPTOLEMUS. An Athenian politician of conservative sentiments who had endeavoured to effect peace in 425, but was defeated by the vehement oratory of Cleon. In later years he became definitely anti-democratic in his views, and we find him supporting the counter-revolution of 411. The restoration of the democracy brought a trial for treason, a condemnation, and the death penalty.

ARCHON. The title of nine Athenian magistrates. The word means "ruler." The functions of the archons were mainly judicial and religious in the fifth and fourth centuries, but in earlier times they had held the supreme power in the state.

ARCTURUS. A star, whose morning rising in September indicated the vintage season, and the time when the cattle came down from their upland pastures.

ARES. The Greek god of war. The Areopagus at Athens was often called, by a doubtful etymology, the Hill of Ares.

ARGADES. The name of a legendary Attic tribe, so called after a son of Ion.

ARGINUSAE. Three islands off the Asia Minor coast, opposite Mitylene. The greatest naval battle of the Peloponnesian War took place here in 406 and the Athenian fleet won a brilliant victory, but the commanding officers, either because of a storm or in a moment of negligence, failed to pick up the men who were left on the disabled ships or were in the sea, and when they returned to Athens they were condemned to death. The incident is full of strange and unexplained factors, and we can never hope to understand it fully.

ARGIVES. Inhabitants of Argos, or Greeks generally.

ARGO. The name of the ship in which Jason and his heroic crew set out to fetch the Golden Fleece.

ARGOLIS. Often Anglicized into The Argolid. The later and more restricted name for the region of the Peloponnesus in which the town of Argos was situated, roughly the northeast corner.

ARGOS. A city in the northeast corner of the Peloponnesus; also the region in which this city was situated, The Argolid. This region was one of the centers of the Achaean or Mycenaean civilization and plays a large rôle in Greek mythological history. In later historical times Argos was often at war with Sparta, and in the Peloponnesian War she played a clever and generally neutral game, profiting immensely from the conflict between the chief states of Greece. On occasion she sided definitely with Athens, but was never of any great or permanent use to her.

ARGUS. 1. The name of an early king of Argos. 2. The name of the builder of the ship Argo. 3. Most frequently a son of Earth, endowed with a hundred eyes and thus proverbial for vigilance. It was he whom Hera set to watch over Io, and he was finally slain by Hermes at the command of Zeus; his eyes were then transferred to the tail of the peacock.

ARIADNE. Daughter of Minos and Pasiphae. She fell in love with Theseus, was deserted by him on the island of Naxos, where Dionysus found her.

ARIGNOTUS. A popular and talented harpplayer, son of Automenes and brother of the pervert Ariphrades.

ARIMASPI. A people who supposedly dwelt in the north of Scythia.

ARIPHRADES. A sexual pervert, the black sheep in the family of Automenes.

ARISTIDES. An Athenian, surnamed The Just. He is typical of the men of old whom Aristophanes so greatly admires; he had fought at Marathon in 490 and was one of the commanders of the fleet of the Delian Confederacy in 477; he played a great part in the organization of the Confederacy in its early years.

ARISTOGITON. One of the Tyrant-slayers; see Harmodius.

ARISTOMACHE. "Best in the fight."

ARISTYLLUS. A sexual pervert in the manner of Ariphrades. In *Plutus* (314) there is the usual pun on the two meanings of *choiros*, "sow" and "female genitalia."

ARTEMIS. Daughter of Zeus and Leto, twin sister of Apollo, born at Delos, the virgin goddess of the hunt, also identified with the Moon; protectress of animals and especially of their young, she was also thought to preside over human childbirth. At Tauris human sacrifices were made to a goddess whom the Greeks called Artemis; see also BRAURON.

ARTEMISIA. The queen of Halicarnassus under Xerxes, who aided him in his expedition against Greece in 480 and fought bravely and not too intelligently at Salamis.

ARTEMISIUM. A promontory at the northern end of the island of Euboea; in 480 the Greek fleet had won a naval battle against the Persians there.

ARTEMO. Anacreon had written satirically about a man of this name calling him *periphoretos,* "carried around," perhaps because he was wont to ride in a litter and *poneros,* "a scoundrel." Aristophanes has combined the two epithets and dubs Cratinus a *periponeros Artemon,* "an especially knavish Artemo," meaning, presumably, to impute to him all of the vices which characterized the Anacreontic original.

ASCLEPIUS. A son of Apollo who learned to heal the sick and revive the dead; slain by Zeus; he was later deified and became the god of medicine.

ASOPUS. A river in Boeotia.

ASPASIA. A Milesian woman of great charm and intelligence, who was the mistress of Pericles.

ASTYANAX. Son of Hector and Andromache.

ATALANTA. An Arcadian maiden, the mother of Parthenopaeus. She selected her husband, usually said to be Melanion, because he vanquished her in a foot-race.

ATE. Daughter of Eris and Zeus, an ancient goddess, who led men into rash actions.

ATHAMAS. In a tragedy by Sophocles called *Athamas* this king of Orchomenus was brought in with a chaplet on his head, about to be sacrificed.

ATHENE. Also called Pallas, a virgin goddess, daughter of Zeus, special protectress of Athens. Although regularly thought of as a warrior goddess, she was also the patroness of peaceful arts and of wisdom. Her epithet Polias means "guardian of cities."

ATHMONIAN DEME. Noted for its vineyards.

ATHOS. A mountain on a peninsula which projects from Chalcidice in Macedonia.

ATLAS. A Titan who was condemned to hold the heavens on his shoulders. The name is also given to the mountain range of northwestern Africa.

ATREIDAE. A patronymic referring to Agamemnon and Menelaus, the sons of Atreus.

ATREUS. See Introduction to Aeschylus' *Oresteia.*

AULIS. A harbour in Boeotia from which the Greek expedition sailed against Troy.

AURORA. The goddess of the dawn.

AUTOMENES. Father of three sons, one of whom was a talented actor; his name is not known. The other two were Arignotus and Ariphrades.

AUTONOE. Daughter of Cadmus, sister of Agave, and mother of Actaeon.

AXIOS. A river in Thrace.

AZANIA. A part of Arcadia.

BACCHIOS. A name for Dionysus.

BACCHUS. Dionysus.

BACIS. A famous Boeotian seer.

BACTRIA. A far-eastern province of the Empires of the Persians and of Alexander.

BARATHRUM. A deep pit at Athens into which criminals were thrown.

BARCAEAN. A name derived from a region in northern Africa.

BASILEIA. "Sovereignty."

BATTUS. The founder of Cyrene, and the first ruler of that city. Many of his successors bore this same name. Their wealth, derived from the exportation of silphium, was proverbially enormous.

BDELYCLEON. "Hater of Cleon."

BELLEROPHON. The rider of the winged steed Pegasus, by whose aid he slew the Chimaera. See STHENOBOEA.

BELUS. See Introduction to Aeschylus' *The Suppliants.*

BISTONES. A people of Thrace.

BLEPSIDEMUS. "People-watcher," *i.e.,* Suspicious.

BOEBIAN. Referring to a lake in Thessaly.

BOEOTIA. A fertile region in Greece, northwest of Attica, allied with Sparta in the Peloponnesian War.

BOREAS. The North Wind.

BOSPHORUS. The channel between the Black Sea and the Sea of Marmora.

BRAGGARTIAN. The Greek is *Kompaseus,* formed as if it were a local adjective from the name of some deme.

BRASIDAS. The best general produced by Sparta in the earlier years of the Peloponnesian War. In 422 he lost his life at Amphipolis, just after winning a brilliant victory.

BRAURON. An Attic deme, site of the worship of the Tauric Artemis, introduced by Iphigenia. Here took place the *Brauronia,* a festival at which selected young girls acted as bears.

BROMIUS. Dionysus.

BULOMACHUS. "Desiring battle."

BUPALUS. See HIPPONAX.

BUPHONIA. The ritual slaughter of a bull at the Dipolia.

BYBLINE. Mythical mountains in Africa.

BYBLOS. A wine district in Thrace.

BYRSINA. Comic name for Myrsina, mother of Hippias, with a pun on *byrsa,* "leather."

BYZANTIUM. Captured by Cimon in 471.

CADMUS. The legendary founder of Thebes. Hence the Thebans are often called Cadmeans.

CALCHAS. Agamemnon's seer.

CALLIAS. Wealthy scion of an illustrious family, who squandered all his riches in extravagant living.

CALLICHORUS. A fountain near Eleusis.

CALLIGENIA. Originally a name of Persephone; later that of one of her attendants; also that of the fourth day of the Thesmophoria.

CALLIMACHUS. A choregus who was very poor.

CALLISTO. An Arcadian nymph, beloved by Zeus, whom Hera in her jealousy caused to have slain.

CALYPSO. A nymph living on the island of Ogygia, with whom Odysseus remained for seven years on his journey home from Troy.

CAMARINA. A city in Sicily.

CANEPHORUS. A basket-bearer. At the festivals of various divinities the sacred objects were carried in baskets, sometimes gilded, which young maidens from the best families bore on their heads.

CANNONUS. The author of a law whereby a man accused of a crime against the state had to plead his case in chains before the people, but had the right to a separate trial.

CANOBUS or CANOPUS. A city on the coast of lower Egypt, in the Nile delta.

CANTHARUS. Greek *kantharos.* 1. The name of one of the harbours in the Piraeus. 2. Also the word for dung-beetle and the name of a kind of boat used at Naxos.

CAPANEUS. One of the seven Argive champions who attacked Thebes. Because of his boastful defiance, Zeus struck him with lightning as he was scaling the walls of Thebes.

CAPHAREUS. A rocky promontory on the southeast of Euboea.

CAPNIUS. "Smoky."

CARCINUS. A tragic poet, who had three sons of very diminutive stature. One was named Xenocles; the names of the others are uncertain. All three wrote tragedies and introduced an inordinate amount of new-fangled dancing into their productions. The Greek *karkinos* also means "crab."

CARIA. A country in the southwest of Asia Minor; the inhabitants seem to have been exceptionally stupid and coarse.

CARTHAGE. A wealthy and powerful city on the northern coast of Africa, originally a Phoenician colony. The demagogue Hyperbolus had proposed an expedition against Carthage in 425 or earlier, and Alcibiades dreamed of attacking this city as soon as Sicily had been conquered.

CARYSTUS. A town in Euboea famous for its loose morals.

CASSANDRA. Daughter of Priam and Hecuba. She possessed the gift of prophecy from Apollo who ordained subsequently that no one should believe her. Cf. Aeschylus' *Agamemnon*.

CASTALIA. A fountain on Mt. Parnassus.

CASTOR. See DIOSCURI.

CATAGELA. A comic name, formed from *Gela,* a town in Sicily, and the common prefix *kata-,* but the result is also a pun, for it suggests *katagelan,* "to laugh at."

CAUCASUS. A range of mountains between the Black Sea and the Caspian.

CAŸSTER. A river in Lydia.

CEBRIONES. One of the Titans.

CECIDES. One of the earliest dithyrambic poets known to the ancients.

CECROPS. The legendary first king of Attica. The citadel of Athens was called Cecropia after him.

CELEUS. Name of the son, and perhaps also of the father, of Triptolemus. He had treated Demeter kindly when she was searching for Persephone.

CEMOS. A comic name; the Greek *kemos* means "the funnel-shaped top of a voting-urn."

CENAEUM. The northwest promontory of Euboea, where there was a temple of Zeus.

CENCHREAE. A town in the Argolid.

CENTAURS. A mythical race, half man and half horse, who supposedly dwelt in Thessaly.

CENTRAL HEARTH. The Underworld Prytaneum.

CEPHALAE. An Attic deme; the Greek *kephale* also means "head."

CEPHALLENIA. A large island in the Ionian Sea, near Ithaca.

CEPHEUS. The father of Andromeda.

CEPHISOPHON. A domestic slave of Euripides, whom Aristophanes accuses of composing parts of the dramatist's works.

CEPHISUS or CEPHISSUS. A stream in Attica. The god of the stream called

Cephisus was an ancestor of Creusa.

CERAMICUS. The name of two sections of Athens. The one referred to in *The Frogs* (129) and *The Birds* (395) was an attractive suburb in which those who had given their lives for the state were buried. The one referred to in *The Knights* (772) was inside the city and famous for the number of prostitutes found there.

CERBERUS. A dog stationed at the entrance to Hades, to keep the living from getting in and the dead from getting out. He was proverbially fierce and difficult to handle. In *Peace* (313) the reference is to Cleon.

CEŸX. A king of Trachis who gave Heracles and Deianeira a home there.

CHAEREPHON. 1. A disciple of Socrates, who was very pale and unhealthy-looking. 2. A parasite in the late fourth century.

CHAERIS. A flute-player of little talent, who had the further habit of turning up uninvited. This latter characteristic is the point of the mention of him in *The Birds* (858).

CHALCIS. A Euboean city, on the Euripus. So many colonies were sent out from Chalcis to the three-fingered Macedonian peninsula in the northern Aegean that that region was called Chalcidice. The colonies there were mostly subject to Athens in the fifth century, but they frequently revolted.

CHALYBES. A people who dwelt on the south shore of the Black Sea.

CHAONIANS. A people living in Epirus, northwest of Greece. In *The Knights* (78) there is a pun on the Greek word *chanein,* "to gape."

CHAOS. In the cosmogony of Hesiod the yawning and infinite abyss out of which all things developed. The word is related to the Greek word *chanein,* "to gape."

CHARITES. The Graces.

CHARMINUS. An unsuccessful admiral, unequal to Nausimache, "Sea-fight."

CHARON. The ferryman of the Styx.

CHARYBDIS. A monster who swallowed

down the waters of the sea thrice daily and thrice daily spewed them forth again. Opposite SCYLLA.

CHEIRON. The wisest of the Centaurs, son of Cronus and Philyra. He was the teacher of gods and heroes, most notably Achilles. He was slain by one of the poisoned arrows of Heracles.

CHERSONESE. The modern Gallipoli Peninsula.

CHIOS. A large island in the Aegean, conquered by the Persians in 494, later one of the most powerful and loyal of Athens' allies.

CHOENIX. A Greek measure of capacity, about the same as a quart dry measure.

CHOLARGIAN DEME. Location unknown. Pericles had belonged to it.

CHOLLIDAN DEME. One of the rural demes of Attica.

CHOREGUS. The wealthy person whose duty it was to meet the expenses of the chorus in the dramatic and lyric spectacles of a given year. He was expected to entertain the poet and the members of the chorus after the performance.

CHREMES. Character in *The Ecclesiazusae*. The name is very frequent in the Middle and the New Comedy, where it is always applied to a secondary character; it is thus one of the points in *The Ecclesiazusae* which reflect the fourth century.

CHRYSA. 1. Town in the Troad. 2. Cf. Introduction to Sophocles' *Philoctetes*.

CHRYSEIS. Agamemnon's favourite concubine at Troy.

CICYNNA. A rural deme in Attica.

CILICIA. A district in the southeast of Asia Minor.

CILLICON. A man who had betrayed his native city to its enemy; the names are variously reported. When he was asked what he had had in mind, he replied, "Nothing bad," and the remark became proverbial.

CIMMERII. A people who lived near the Caspian Sea.

CIMOLIAN CLAY. A sort of fuller's-earth, from Cimolus, a tiny island north of Melos.

CIMON. A great Athenian statesman and general in the period immediately following the Persian Wars. He was the leader of the conservative group, which had as one of its chief objectives the maintenance of friendship with Sparta.

CINESIAS. A popular dithyrambic poet, famous for his thinness and misbehaviour. He was reported to have smeared excrement on the statues of Hecate. The point of the jest in *The Frogs* (1437) is somewhat obscure.

CIRCE. The daughter of the Sun, one of the sea-nymphs, who lived on an island and was highly skilled in magic. When Odysseus landed there she turned his companions into swine. The reference in *Plutus* (302ff.) is to the famous fourth-century courtesan Laïs of Corinth.

CISSEUS. A king in Thrace, the father of Hecuba.

CISSIA. A region near Persia whose people were famed for their skill as professional mourners.

CITHAERON. A range of mountains separating Boeotia from Megaris and Attica.

CLAUSIMACHUS. A comic name, formed from *klausai*, "to weep," and *mache*, "battle."

CLEAENETUS. The father of Cleon, but the point of the reference in *The Knights* (574) has never been satisfactorily explained.

CLEOMENES. A king of Sparta, who in the sixth century twice invaded Attica. On the second occasion he was finally besieged in the Acropolis.

CLEON. The most renowned of the Athenian demagogues. A tanner by trade, he soon turned to politics, and from the death of Pericles in 429 to his own in 422 he was the most powerful man in Athens. Aristophanes constantly attacks his rapacity, sham patriotism, vulgarity, and jingoism; his status as a citizen is also questioned. For a defense of the man, see Grote's *History of Greece*.

CLEONICE. "Glorious victory."

CLEONYMUS. A large and gluttonous coward, who had once in battle thrown away his shield and fled. Aristophanes never let him forget it.

CLEOPHON. A demagogue who violently opposed peace in the last years of the Peloponnesian War.

CLEPSYDRA. 1. The water-clock which measured the time allowed for speeches in the law-courts. 2. A spring on the Acropolis.

CLIGENES. A little known politician of demagogical aspirations.

CLINIAS. The father of Alcibiades.

CLISTHENES. Athens' most noted homosexual, at whom Aristophanes never tires of poking fun.

CLITOPHON. A dilettante in philosophy.

CLOPIDIANS. A comic name, formed after the analogy of Cropidians, from the deme Cropidae, with a pun on *klope*, "theft."

CNOSSUS. The leading city of Crete, famed for the dances held in honour of Zeus and Apollo.

COCYTUS. A river in the Underworld.

COESYRA. A name frequently borne by the female children of the wealthy and noble family of the Alcmeonidae.

COLACONYMUS. A comic name, formed from Cleonymus, and *kolax*, "flatterer."

COLAENIS. Name under which Artemis was worshipped in the Attic deme Myrrhinous. It is reported that this name was derived from Colaenus, an early king of Athens, who had built a temple to the goddess.

COLCHIS. A country at the extreme east of the Black Sea.

COLONUS. An Attic deme about a mile northwest from Athens. It was the birthplace of Sophocles and the legendary tomb of Oedipus.

CONNAS. A flute-player. He is reported to have won many victories in the musical contests at the Olympic games, and later to have taken to drink, with

the result that in his old age his trophies were his only possessions.

CONTHYLE. A deme in Attica.

COPAÏC EELS. These Boeotian delicacies came from Lake Copaïs.

CORA or CORE. See PERSEPHONE.

CORCYRAEAN WINGS. By these are meant whips, an article for which the island of Corcyra, the modern Corfu, was especially famous.

CORDAX. A dance, the precise nature of which is not known. It seems to have been performed only in comedy.

CORINTH. A city on the Isthmus, famous for its prostitutes.

CORYBANTES. Priests of Cybele, who worshipped her in orgiastic dances; they were supposed to be able to cure insanity.

CORYCIA. A nymph, from whom a cave on Mt. Parnassus was named. It was near the fountain of Castalia.

COTTABUS. The name of a convivial game which was very popular in Greece. There would seem to have been numerous varieties, but in all of them the fundamental point was to test one's skill in throwing wine from a cup into some other vessel at an agreed distance.

COTYLA. A liquid measure, about half a pint. The word means "cup."

CRANAUS. The mythical founder of Athens.

CRAPPLE. The Greek is *epikechodos*, literally "one who has just defecated"; a lexicon usually quite staid astonishes us with "Shitterling."

CRATES. A comic poet earlier than Aristophanes.

CRATHIS. A river in southern Italy, which made golden the hair of men and the fleece of sheep.

CRATINUS. An older comic poet; in 423 he won the first prize and neatly turned the tables on Aristophanes, who had cast slurs on his senility the year before (*Knights* 526ff.)

CREON. 1. Brother of Jocasta. 2. A legendary king of Corinth.

CRETE. A large island south of the Aegean, in the fifth century famous for looseness of morals, but in the Heroic Age more highly respected.

CRISA. A town in Phocis.

CRONUS. Father of Hera, Poseidon, and Zeus. He was deprived of his throne by Zeus.

CUROTROPHUS. An epithet of various divinities; it means "nourishing the young."

CYANEAN. See SYMPLEGADES.

CYBELE. An Asiatic goddess identified with Rhea. Her worship was wild and orgiastic in character, and hence it became closely connected with that of Dionysus.

CYCHREA. An old name for Salamis.

CYCLOPES. One-eyed giants, assistants of Hephaestus, who were supposed to dwell likewise as shepherds in Sicily.

CYCNORANIDAE. "Swan-frogs."

CYCNUS. A famous robber slain by Heracles.

CYDATHENAEA. An Attic deme, birthplace of Cleon and of Aristophanes.

CYLLENE. A mountain in the Peloponnesus, sacred to Hermes.

CYNALOPEX. Nickname of the brothelkeeper Philostratus; it means "dogfox." The mention of the dog-fox in the oracle in *The Knights* (1067ff.) immediately suggests Philostratus, and this passage may serve as an index to his character.

CYNNA. One of the best known courtesans in Athens.

CYNTHUS. A mountain in Delos, the birthplace of Apollo and Artemis.

CYPRIS. Aphrodite.

CYPRUS. A large island in the Mediterranean, south of Cilicia.

CYRENE. 1. A city in northern Africa, west of Egypt. 2. In Aristophanes, the name of a famous courtesan, perhaps of Corinthian origin, nicknamed *dodekamechanos* to indicate her mastery of no less than a dozen methods of making love.

CYRUS. Founder of the Persian Empire.

CYTHERA. An island off the southern tip of the Peloponnesus, famous for its worship of Aphrodite.

CYZICENE YELLOW. No such dye is known to have existed, but the inhabitants of Cyzicus had a reputation for cowardice and effeminacy and the name suggests the Greek word *chezein*, "to defecate." It may be that we should correct the text in such a way as to get the comic name "Chezicene."

DAEDALUS. A mythical person who was supposed to have made the first advances in the arts of sculpture and architecture.

DANAAN. Equivalent of Greek.

DANAE. Daughter of Acrisius, king of Argos, who confined her in a brazen tower, since an oracle had told him that she would bear a child who would kill him. Zeus visited her in a shower of gold, and she gave birth to Perseus. Acrisius shut mother and child in a chest, cast it into the sea, but both were rescued.

DANAI. Descendants of Danaus. Used frequently for the Greeks in general.

DANAUS. See Introduction to Aeschylus' *The Suppliants*.

DARDANUS. Mythical ancestor of the Trojans. Hence Dardanian is the equivalent of Trojan.

DARIUS. King of Persia, father of Xerxes.

DATIS. A Persian name. The man referred to in *Peace* (289ff.) is otherwise unknown; he cannot be the famous commander at Marathon. His remark contains a mistake in Greek, but this can hardly be the whole point of its citation.

DAULIS or DAULIA. An ancient town in Phocis.

DEIANEIRA. See Sophocles' *The Trachiniae.*

DELOS. A small island in the Aegean, birthplace of Apollo and Artemis.

DELPHI. A town in Phocis, site of a famous oracular shrine of Apollo and of the Pythian Games.

DEME. The term applied to the smallest divisions of Attica, corresponding to wards or townships in modern states.

DEMETER. Goddess of agriculture, mother of Persephone.

DEMOLOGOCLEON. A comic name meaning "mob-orator Cleon" and applied, or misapplied, to Bdelycleon in *The Wasps* (343).

DEMOS. 1. The Greek word for "people" and the name of a character in *The Knights* who is designed to personify the Athenian populace. 2. The name of a young man of great beauty, the son of Pyrilampes and stepbrother of Plato.

DEMOSTHENES. A distinguished Athenian general. It was he who first attacked Pylos, but Cleon stole his victory from under his nose.

DEMOSTRATUS. The man who had first proposed the ill-fated Sicilian expedition; he was nicknamed "mad ox."

DEO. Another name for Demeter.

DEXITHEUS. A talented performer on the lyre.

DIAGORAS. The Melian, an Ionian philosopher, the earliest known atheist. Because of his doctrines a price was put on his head. This is the man to whom reference is made in *The Birds* (1073) and *The Clouds* (830); the poet mentioned in *The Frogs* (320) was a different person.

DICAEOPOLIS. "Honest citizen."

DICASTS. Athenian jurymen.

DICTYNNA. Another name for Artemis.

DIITREPHES. A man who had become wealthy through the manufacture of wicker flasks; the handles of these were called *ptera*, "wings."

DIOCLES. A Megarian hero.

DIOMEAN FEAST. A festival held in honour of Heracles in the Attic deme of Diomea.

DIOMEDES. Son of Tydeus. A Greek hero in the Trojan War.

DIOMIALAZON. "Diomean boaster."

DIONYSIA. Festivals of Dionysus.

DIONYSIUS. The great tyrant of Syracuse in the fourth century.

DIONYSUS. Son of Zeus and Semele, god of wine and of the productive power of nature, patron of drama at Athens. His worship was orgiastic and when first introduced into Greece was strongly opposed by the staid. He had an oracular shrine in Thrace.

DIOPITHES. A soothsayer given to prophetic seizures of such violence that even the ancients doubted his sanity.

DIOSCURI. Castor and Pollux, sons of Leda and Tyndareus, or, according to another tradition, of Leda and Zeus. They were hence brothers of Helen. Castor was famed for his skill in dealing with horses, and Pollux for his skill in boxing. Both were regarded as protectors of sailors.

DIPOLIA. An ancient festival of Zeus Polieus.

DIRCE. Wife of Lycus, an ancient king of Thebes. A famous fountain there took its name from her.

DIRPHYS. A town in Euboea.

DITHYRAMB. A form of choral lyric poetry, the early history and precise nature of which are highly uncertain. By the end of the fifth century, the dithyramb was remarkable chiefly for its bombastic and far-fetched phraseology.

DITYLAS. A Scythian name, like the Sceblyas and Pardocas which immediately follow it.

DODONA. An ancient oracle of Zeus in Epirus. The sounds made by the wind in the sacred oaks were interpreted by the priests.

DORO. "Bribery."

DORUS. Son of Xuthus and Creusa. In the legends he was regarded as the founder of the race of the Dorians.

DRYAS. Father of the Thracian king Lycurgus.

DUNGTOWNITE. The Greek is *Kopreios*, which is formed like the name of some deme, but from *kopros*, "ordure."

ECBATANA. A great city in Persia.

ECHIDNA. A monster, half woman and half serpent, the mother of Cerberus.

ECHINUS. 1. A town in Thessaly. 2. In *Lysistrata* (1169f.) there seems to be a series of plays on geographical names with reference to the sexual parts of the heroine; the word *echi-*

nos had various meanings, amongst which one may note the following: "Hedgehog," "sea-urchin," "vase," "the prickly husk of a chestnut."

ECHION. Father of Pentheus.

ELECTRA. Daughter of Agamemnon and Clytemnestra.

ELECTRYON. Father of Alcmena. Amphitryon was exiled from Mycenae for killing him.

ELEUSIS. A town near Athens, where the mysteries in honour of Demeter and Persephone were celebrated.

ELEUTHERAE. A town in Attica near the borders of Boeotia.

ELEVEN. A group of Athenian officials who had the function of a modern Chief of Police; they were also the executioners in cases of capital punishment.

ELYMNIUM. A small place in the neighbourhood of Oreus.

EMPUSA. A terrible spectre haunting lonely places at night and associated with Hecate. The Empusa had the power of taking on any shape or likeness.

ENCELADUS. One of the giants who made war on gods. Zeus killed him and buried him under Mt. Aetna.

ENGLOTTOGASTORS. A comic name, containing the words *glotta,* "tongue" and *gaster,* "belly," and denoting men who live by their tongues, *i.e.,* the grafting politicians of Athens.

ENYALIUS. Ares.

EPAPHUS. See Introduction to Aeschylus' *The Suppliants.*

EPEIOS. The builder of the wooden horse at Troy.

EPICRATES. An Athenian who had grown so imposing a beard that he was nicknamed *sakesphoros,* "shield-bearer."

EPIDAURUS. A town in Argolis on the Saronic gulf.

EPIGONUS. A notorious and extraordinarily effeminate homosexual.

EPOPS. The Greek means "hoopoe," but in translating it is more convenient to take *epops* as a proper name acquired by Tereus after his transformation.

ERASINIDES. One of the Arginusae generals who were put to death.

ERASINUS. A river in the Peloponnesus.

EREBUS. The darkness surrounding the Underworld.

ERECHTHEUS. A legendary king of Athens. The Athenians were often called Erechtheidae after him.

ERICHTHONIUS. Another name for Erechtheus.

ERIDANUS. A river in Italy, later supposed to be the Po.

ERINYES. The Furies. See Introduction to Aeschylus' *Oresteia.*

EROS. The god of love.

ERYMANTHUS. A mountain in Arcadia, the haunt of the savage boar slain by Heracles.

ERYTHEIA. A small island on which Gades was built. Here dwelt the monster Geryon.

ERYTHRAE. A town near Cithaeron.

ETEOCLES. Son of Oedipus and Jocasta. Cf. Sophocles' *Oedipus at Colonus,* note 2.

ETEOCLUS. One of the seven Argive champions who attacked Thebes.

ETRURIA. A country in central Italy.

EUATHLUS. A glib and scoundrelly orator.

EUBOEA. A long and narrow island northeast of the Attic and Boeotian coasts, subject to Athens.

EUBULE. "Good councillor."

EUCRATES. One of the earliest demagogues, a dealer in oakum. The man mentioned in *Lysistrata* (103) was a brother of Nicias.

EUDEMUS. A dealer in magic charms and rings.

EUELPIDES. "Hopeful."

EUERGIDES. "Benefactor."

EUMELUS. Son of Admetus and Alcestis.

EUMENIDES. "Benevolent," a euphemism for the Erinyes. In tragedy they are usually called simply "The Goddesses."

EUMOLPUS. The mythical founder of the Eleusinian mysteries. His family, the Eumolpidae, were the hereditary priests of the mysteries.

EUPHEMIUS. An extremely abject flatterer.

EUPHORIDES. "Good Carrier" (of charcoal?).

EUPOLIS. A comic poet, one of the greatest; he seems to have been but a little older than Aristophanes.

EURIPIDES. The man referred to in *Ecclesiazusae* (825ff.) is probably the son of the dramatist.

EURIPUS. The channel between Euboea and Boeotia.

EUROTAS. The chief river in Laconia, on whose banks Sparta was situated.

EURYCLES. A soothsayer who had the knack of making his voice seem to come out of his belly.

EURYSACES. Son of Ajax and Tecmessa. The name comes from an adjective which means "with a broad shield."

EURYSTHEUS. King of Argos, enemy and master of Heracles to whom he assigned the twelve labours.

EURYTUS. 1. King of Oechalia and father of Iole. See Sophocles' *The Trachiniae.* 2. A chief of the Epeians.

EUTHYMENES. The archon in 437.

EUXINE. The Black Sea.

EVAEON. A pauper whose clothes were so worn that he might as well not have had any on.

EVENUS. A river in Aetolia.

EVIUS. A name for Dionysus, derived like the Evivus and Evoe which follow it, from the cries of the Bacchantes.

EXECESTIDES. A Carian who had palmed himself off as an Athenian citizen; this necessitated the invention of imaginary ancestors. He is also reported to have been a skilled lyre-player, who had won prizes at various games.

FEARLING. The Greek is *hypodedios,* "one who has got frightened."

FEAST OF CUPS. A part of the Dionysia, in which there was held a great public banquet to which each citizen brought his own provisions.

FEAST OF POTS. A part of the Dionysia, taking place on the same day as the Feast of Cups; it involved a drinking competition. In later times the two feasts were celebrated on successive days.

FLATTOTHRATT. An onomatopoeic word designed to imitate the twanging of strings on a lyre.

GANYMEDES. A handsome Trojan youth whom Zeus made cup-bearer to the gods.

GARGETTUS. An Attic deme northeast of Athens. The body of Eurystheus was supposed to be buried there, and in later times this deme was the birthplace of the great philosopher Epicurus.

GELA. A city in Sicily.

GELEON. The eldest son of Ion, after whom a legendary Attic tribe was named.

GENERAL. See STRATEGUS.

GENETYLLIS. One of a number of minor deities, the Genetyllides, pictured as companions of Aphrodite; they presided over the act of generation.

GERAESTUS. A town on the southwest tip of Euboea.

GERETOTHEODORUS. A comic name, compounded from two regular names, Geres and Theodorus.

GERYON. A triple-bodied monster whose cattle Heracles carried off.

GLANIS. A soothsayer, quite fictitious, the elder brother of Bacis.

GLAUCETES. A glutton, particularly fond of fish. He was nicknamed *Psetta,* "turbot."

GLAUCUS. A sea god.

GLYCE. "Sweet."

GNIDUS. A city in Asia Minor.

GNOMON. A primitive form of sundial, in which the length rather than the direction of the shadow told the time; a ten-foot shadow means shortly before sunset.

GOOD GENIUS. The divine and special comrade and protector of individuals and communities.

GORGIAS. A brilliant sophist and rhetorician from Leontini in Sicily; he may have had non-Greek ancestry.

GORGONS. Three horrible sisters, of whom Medusa was the most renowned in mythology. They had serpents on their heads instead of hair, and were endowed with wings, claws, and enormous teeth. Anyone who looked at Medusa's head was turned to stone.

GORGOPIS. A bay near Corinth.

GRAEAE. Three old women, who possessed but one eye and one tooth, which they could loan to one another.

HADES. The god of the Underworld. It is also used as a name for the Underworld.

HAEMON. A Theban, the son of Creon.

HALIMUS. An Attic deme, on the shore, not far from the Piraeus, famous as the birthplace of the historian Thucydides.

HALIRROTHIUS. Son of Poseidon, who was slain by Ares. Ares was tried for the murder on a hill in Athens, which hence was called the Areopagus.

HALYS. A great river in Asia Minor which empties into the Black Sea.

HARMODIUS. A youth in sixth-century Athens, whose remarkable beauty attracted the notice and elicited the advances of Hipparchus, the younger brother of the reigning tyrant Hippias. The natural jealousy of Aristogiton, the lover of Harmodius, was intensified and embittered by the arrogance of his rival's approaches, and the two friends eventually decided that with a single action they should free their city of tyranny and avenge their private insults. They laid their plans with great care, but the necessity of secrecy and their own impatience of delay prevented them from enlisting an adequate number of supporters, and a misunderstood intimacy of one of their associates with Hippias prematurely precipitated the coup. The liberators succeeded in killing only Hipparchus, but the incident had the effect of making Hippias so suspicious and so vindictive that popular sentiment finally turned against him, and he was expelled, not without a number of initial difficulties and the ultimate intervention of Sparta. Harmodius and Aristogiton immediately became and forever remained the dear heroes of all Athenians of anti-tyrannical opinion, and the scolium, or drinking-song, which celebrated their inspiring exploit was one of the most frequently rendered of such compositions.

HARMONIA. Daughter of Ares and Aphrodite, who became the wife of Cadmus.

HARPIES. Monstrous birds with heads of maidens.

HEBE. The goddess of youth, who married Heracles after he was received among the gods.

HEBRUS. The principal river in Thrace.

HECATE. A confusing divinity, identified with the Moon, Artemis, and Persephone, and invoked by sorcerers. She is the great sender of visions, of madness, and of sudden terror. Sometimes she is called one of the Titans, sometimes, as Artemis, the daughter of Leto.

HECTOR. Son of Priam and Hecuba, the leading hero of the Trojans.

HECUBA. Queen of Troy, the wife of Priam.

HEGELOCHUS. An Athenian actor who, in a performance of Euripides' *Orestes* had made a slight and fatal slip in diction; he had pronounced *galen' horo* (*galena* with the final *a* elided) so that it sounded like *galen horo* (*galen* without any *a* to elide). This created a ridiculous line, for instead of saying, "After the storm I perceive the calm," he tragically declaimed, "After the storm I perceive the cat."

HELEN. Daughter of Zeus and Leda, sister of the Dioscuri. Paris stole her from her husband Menelaus and thus precipitated the Trojan War. See Introduction to Euripides' *Helen,* and the close of his *Orestes.*

HELENUS. Son of Priam and Hecuba, noted for his powers of prophecy.

HELIAEA. The democratic courts of Athens. The jurors were chosen by lot from all classes, and were paid three obols a day for their services.

HELIASTS. Jurymen in the Heliaea.

HELICON. A celebrated range of mountains in Boeotia, sacred to Apollo and the Muses.

HELIOS. The god of the Sun.

HELLE. A heroine of mythology who fell into the straits which were thereafter named the Hellespont.

HELLEBORE. The ancient cure for insanity.

HELLESPONT. The straits of the Dardanelles.

HEPHAESTUS. God of fire and metallurgy, associated with all volcanic places, particularly Lemnos and Aetna.

HERA. Sister and wife of Zeus. A goddess associated with Argos, who is portrayed as jealous and hostile to all the women loved by Zeus, and to his irregular offspring.

HERACLES. A Greek hero, later deified, son of Zeus and Alcmena. Through the trickery of the jealous Hera Eurystheus was given power over Heracles and the hero was forced to exert his great strength in the performance of labours for his master (See Sophocles, *The Trachiniae,* 1090ff. and Euripides, *Heracles,* 349ff.)

HERMAE. Busts of Hermes with the phallus in front. One night, just before the sailing of the Sicilian Expedition, the Hermae were all mutilated, and the populace was filled with superstitious dread.

HERMAEAN (mount). Probably the northeast promontory of Lemnos.

HERMES. Son of Zeus and Maia, a god of various attributes. Messenger of the Olympians, he was also the guide of the souls of the dead. Trickery and thievery were his innate talents. As bringer of good luck he was called Eriunian.

HERMIONE. Daughter of Menelaus and Helen.

HESIOD. A famous early Greek poet, born at Ascra in Boeotia, probably toward the end of the ninth century; he is the author of *Works and Days,* a didactic poem which gives a great deal of sound and practical advice on agriculture.

HESIONE. 1. Daughter of Oceanus and wife of Prometheus. 2. Daughter of Laomedon, who was captured by Heracles and given to Telamon, by whom she became the mother of Teucer.

HESPERUS. The evening star.

HESTIA. The goddess of the hearth, to whom the first prayers or libations were offered.

HIERO. A crier at public auctions.

HIERONYMUS. A poet with long hair, the son of Xenophantes. The Hieronymus referred to in *The Acharnians* (389) may be the same poet, and the mention of the helmet of Hades may be a jibe at his hair, but it seems farfetched. The man of this name that we find in *The Ecclesiazusae* (201) was not a poet at all, but merely a very stupid person whom the Athenian populace was, or is alleged to have been, misguided enough to regard as wise.

HIPPALECTRYON. Anglicized hippalector, a fabulous monster mentioned in the lost *Myrmidons* of Aeschylus. Literally the word means "horse-rooster."

HIPPARCH. A cavalry officer.

HIPPIAS. A tyrant of Athens, see HARMODIUS. In *The Wasps* (502) there is a pun on *hippiazein,* "to make love horse-fashion."

HIPPOCRATES. An Athenian whose three sons were proverbially stupid; the family appears to have lived in a frightful hovel.

HIPPODAMIA. Daughter of Oenomaus and wife of Pelops.

HIPPODAMUS. The father of Archeptolemus.

HIPPOLYTUS. See Introduction to Euripides' *Hippolytus.*

HIPPOMEDON. One of the seven Argive champions who attacked Thebes.

HIPPONAX. An iambic poet of the sixth century, born at Ephesus, but banished about 540. He took up residence at Clazomenae, and here was insulted or caricatured by the sculptor Bupalus, about whom he then wrote such scurrilous verses that the wretched man is reported to have found life no longer endurable and accordingly to have committed suicide.

HOMOLE. A haunt of the Centaurs in Thessaly.

HOPLETES. The name of a legendary Attic tribe, so called after a son of Ion.

HOPLITES. The heavy-armed soldiers in Greek armies.

HORAE. The Seasons.

HYACINTHUS. A Spartan youth, loved and accidentally killed by Apollo.

HYADES. A contellation. The name literally means "The Rainers."

HYDRA. A monster slain by Heracles whose blood he used to poison his arrows.

HYLLUS. Son of Heracles and Deianeira.

HYMEN. The god of marriage. The *Hymen Hymenaeus* was the song sung at weddings.

HYPERBOLUS. An Athenian demagogue, whom Aristophanes constantly attacks. He had been a seller of lamps. It was he that proposed an expedition against Carthage. In general he seems to have been, in the eyes of the comic poet, a sort of poor imitation of Cleon and there is little that is cast up at him which is not also found in the attacks on Cleon.

HYSIAE. A town near Cithaeron.

IACCHUS. A son of Zeus and Demeter, partly identified with Dionysus.

IASO. Goddess of healing.

IBYCUS. A choral lyric poet of the sixth century, born at Rhegium in Italy. Erotic motifs seem to have played a large rôle in his works, which have not come down to us.

ICARIAN. The sea around the island of Icaria in the Aegean.

IDA. A mountain in the Troad, the scene of the judgment of Paris.

ILION. An alternate name for Troy.

ILITHYIA. Goddess of childbirth.

ILLYRIANS. A savage and rude people,

who inhabited what is now Albania.

INACHUS. Son of Oceanus and Tethys, the father of Io. He was the first king of Argos, and gave his name to the river Inachus there.

INFORMERS. Political blackmailers.

INO. Daughter of Cadmus, with whom Athamas had illicit relations. Hera drove him mad and he slew one of his and Ino's children. Ino took the other and threw herself into the sea; both were changed into marine deities, Ino becoming Leucothea, or Leucothoe, and the son, Melicertes, Palaemon.

IO. Daughter of Inachus. See Introduction to Aeschylus' *The Suppliants.*

IOLAS. Boeotian dialect form of Iolaus.

IOLCUS. A town in Thessaly where Pelias and Jason lived.

IOLE. Daughter of Eurytus. See Sophocles' *The Trachiniae.*

ION. 1. Son of Apollo and Creusa, legendary ancestor of the Ionians. 2. A fifth-century tragic poet, from Chios.

IONIA. The fringe of Greek settlements on the coast of Asia Minor, from Miletus to Phocaea. The Ionic dialect was also spoken in the northern islands and in Euboea. The Ionians were regarded as cowardly and lascivious by the other Greeks.

IOPHON. Son of Sophocles; it was suspected that the father was partly responsible for the virtues of the son's compositions.

IPHIANASSA. See Sophocles' *Electra,* note 1.

IPHIGENIA. Daughter of Agamemnon and Clytemnestra, sacrificed by her father at Aulis, that the Greek expedition might sail for Troy.

IPHITUS. See Sophocles' *The Trachiniae,* (248ff.).

IRIS. The messenger goddess.

ISMENE. Daughter of Oedipus and Jocasta.

ISMENIAS. A noble Theban name.

ISMENUS. A river near Thebes, by whose side was a temple of Apollo.

ISTER. The Danube.

ISTHMIAN GAMES. A great national

festival, held every other year, respectively one and three years after the Olympics.

ISTHMUS. The narrow neck of land connecting the Peloponnesus with northern Greece. The chief city on the Isthmus was Corinth and the ability to send ships westward to Sicily and Italy and eastward to Asia Minor was mainly responsible for the commercial supremacy of Corinth in the early ages of Greek history. The jest in *The Thesmophoriazusae* (648) refers to the Corinthian habit of hauling their ships over the short stretch of land that lay between the two seas.

ITHACA. An island in the Ionian Sea, the home of Odysseus.

ITYLUS. See ITYS.

ITYS. Son of Tereus and Procne, slain by his mother. In a parallel myth his name is Itylus.

IXION. A king of the Lapithae, whom Zeus befriended. Ixion treacherously attempted to win the love of Hera, and was punished by being chained forever to a wheel in the Underworld which never ceased revolving.

JASON. A Greek hero, the leader of the Argonauts, and husband of Medea.

JOCASTA. Wife of Laius, and mother of Oedipus.

KING. The ruler of the Persian Empire was *The* King for the Greeks; he is usually called The Great King. He was the only Persian who might wear his tiara straight. His wealth was proverbially enormous and he became a symbol of incredible magnificence. The term "King's Eye" was applied to a number of officials who constituted a sort of royal intelligence service and kept the monarch informed of what was going on throughout his vast realm.

KNIGHTS. In early Attic history, the second highest income bracket; later the cavalry arm, 1000 in number, 100 from each tribe. These men were chosen from the two highest income

brackets; they were traditionally conservative, and they had actively opposed Cleon.

KORE. See PERSEPHONE.

LABDACUS. A king of Thebes, the father of Laius. The name Labdacidae is often given to his descendants.

LABES. The Aexonian dog, accused of theft in *The Wasps* of Aristophanes. The name suggests both the Greek *labein*, "to take" and Laches.

LACEDAEMON. See SPARTA.

LACHES. An Athenian general accused by Cleon of embezzlements on an expedition to Sicily in 427. The old man of this name in *Lysistrata* cannot be the same person.

LACONIA. A region in the southeastern Peloponnesus, chief town Sparta.

LACRATIDES. An Acharnian; a man of this name is reported to have been one of the accusers of Pericles.

LAERTES. Father of Odysseus.

LAESPODIAS. An Athenian general who had also served as an ambassador.

LAÏS. A famous Corinthian courtesan.

LAIUS. A king of Thebes, the husband of Jocasta, and father of Oedipus by whom he was killed.

LAMACHUS. An Athenian general, one of the most dependable soldiers that the city possessed.

LAMIA. One of a species of fabulous and formidable monsters, endowed by ancient superstition with a variety of forms, but not often with testicles. Usually pictured as female, they had the blood-thirsty manners of a vampire. An aetiological myth related that there had once been a queen of Libya named Lamia, beloved of Zeus, hated of Hera, and by her robbed of her children, in return for which injury the queen took to stealing the offspring of others and to murdering them. She had become a favourite subject of bawdy folktales.

LAMIAS. The keeper of the public prison. His name suggests Lamia. Compare also *Wasps* (1177).

LAMPON. An eminent diviner.

LAOMEDON. King of Troy, father of Priam. Apollo and Poseidon built the walls of Troy, but Laomedon refused to pay them his promised reward. Poseidon therefore sent a sea-monster against the city to which the Trojans from time to time were compelled to sacrifice a maiden. Heracles killed the monster, but Laomedon again treacherously failed to pay a promised reward. Heracles therefore took an expedition against Troy, killed Laomedon, and gave his daughter Hesione to Telamon.

LAPITHAE. A mythical people of Thessaly. At the wedding of Peirithous, a bloody battle arose between the Lapithae and the Centaurs, a subject found frequently in Greek art.

LARISSA. A town in eastern Thessaly.

LASUS. A famous lyric poet, contemporary of Simonides.

LAURIUM. The Attic deme in which the silver-mines were located. The "owls of Laurium" are coins made from Laurian metal and stamped with the Athenian emblem, the owl.

LEDA. Wife of Tyndareus, King of Sparta, by whom or by Zeus she became the mother of the Dioscuri, Clytemnestra, and Helen. The legends record that Zeus visited her in the form of a swan.

LEITUS. The commander of the Boeotians in the Trojan War.

LEMNOS. A large volcanic island in the Aegean. A myth told that the Lemnian women had murdered all their husbands.

LENAEA. One of the festivals of Dionysus. The name means "Feast of Vats."

LEOGORAS. One of Athens' greatest gourmets.

LEONIDAS. The Spartan commander at Thermopylae.

LEOTROPHIDES. A poet of such slender and delicate physique that in later ages he became proverbial for these qualities.

LEPREUM. A town in Elis. It is dragged in by the heels in *The Birds* (149)

merely to build up a gibe at Melanthius, who was a leper.

LERNA. A district in Argolis where Heracles slew the Hydra.

LESBOS. A large island off the Asia Minor coast. The word Lesbian had in ancient times sometimes the same connotations that it does today.

LETHE. A river in Hades, from which the souls of the departed drank and were rendered quite oblivious of their past experiences.

LETO. Mother of Apollo and Artemis, hence, occasionally, also of the Moon and of Hecate.

LEUCADIA. An island in the Ionian Sea.

LEUCE. A strip of sand off the mouth of the Borysthenes (the Dnieper).

LEUCIPPUS. His daughters were priestesses of Athene and Artemis.

LEUCOLOPHUS. In *The Frogs* of Aristophanes (1513) the father of Adimantus. In *The Ecclesiazusae* (645) an unknown man, who cannot be the same as the father of Adimantus.

LEUCOTHOE. A sea goddess. See INO.

LIBYA. Equivalent of Africa.

LICYMNIUS. The half-brother of Alcmena, who was killed by Tlepolemus, the son of Heracles. In *The Birds* (1242) the reference is to a tragedy of this name by Euripides, in which some person or thing was consumed by lightning.

LIMNA. A sea-coast town in Troezen.

LINUS. The personification of a dirge or lamentation.

LIPSYDRION. A locality, not a deme, in Attica, above Parnes, which was fortified by the exiled nobles of the family of the Alcmeonidae, but in vain, for the partisans of Hippias successfully besieged the place. Aristophanes is very fond of having his old warriors reminisce about events which took place long before they were born, and the reference to Lipsydrion (*Lysistrata*, 665) is one of the most remarkable examples of this, for the date of the siege is somewhere between 514 and 510.

LOCRIS. 1. A district in Greece just north

of Boeotia. 2. A district just north of the Gulf of Corinth.

LOXIAS. Alternate name for Apollo.

LYCABETTUS. A mountain in Attica.

LYCAON. Son of Ares with whom Heracles fought.

LYCEAN. "Light-bringing," an epithet of Apollo. The Lyceum in Athens was a gymnasium in the vicinity of the temple of Lycean Apollo.

LYCIA. A small district in southern Asia Minor.

LYCOMEDE. Achilles' father-in-law.

LYCON. An indigent politician, in 399 one of the accusers of Socrates. His wife, Rhodia, was a woman of notorious infidelity.

LYCURGUS. 1. A mythical king in Thrace who persecuted Dionysus. For this act he was driven mad by the gods. 2. Probably the grandfather of the fourth-century orator, Lycurgus.

LYCUS. A mythical tyrant of Thebes, who sought to kill the children of Heracles. Also the patron hero of the Athenian law-courts.

LYDIA. A country in southwestern Asia Minor. Many Athenian slaves were Lydians.

LYNCEUS. A mythological hero, noted for his extraordinary keenness of vision.

LYSICLES. A demagogue before Cleon; he had been a sheep-dealer. After Pericles' death he married Aspasia, but shortly thereafter lost his life in battle.

LYSICRATES. An Athenian general, reported to have been a thief and a rogue (*Birds* 513). The man mentioned in *The Ecclesiazusae* (630 and 736) as possessing an ugly nose (the Athenian Bardolph?) and dyeing his hair raven black may or may not be the same person.

LYSIMACHA. "Dissolver of conflict."

LYSISTRATA. "Disbander of armies."

MACARIA. Daughter of Heracles.

MACISTUS. An unknown mountain in Euboea.

MAENADS. A name given to the frenzied worshippers of Dionysus.

MAENALUS. A mountain in Arcadia.

MAEOTIS. The Sea of Azov. The Amazons lived in this area.

MAGNES. An early comic poet; flourished around 460, died shortly before 424.

MAGNESIA. District in Thessaly.

MAIA. The mother of Hermes.

MALEA. A promontory of southeastern Laconia.

MALIS. A district in southern Thessaly.

MANES. A common slave-name.

MANIA. Feminine form of Manes.

MARATHON. A village in a plain on the east shore of Attica, site of the Athenian defeat of the Persians in 490.

MARILADES. Name of an Acharnian, derived from *marile*, "charcoal-embers."

MARON. A priest of Apollo whom Odysseus spared when he took the city of Ismarus.

MARPSIAS. A contentious orator.

MEDEA. A Colchian princess, who, after aiding the Argonauts, returned with Jason to Greece as his wife.

MEDES. Really a separate Iranian people, they were regularly confused with the Persians by the Greeks.

MEDUSA. One of the Gorgons.

MEGABAZUS. A Persian name. No such person ever sat on the throne of Persia, but the appellation was a familiar one and it would further suggest to the Greek the words in his own tongue *mega bazon*, "talking big."

MEGACLES. A name frequently borne by the Alcmeonidae.

MEGARA. 1. A Greek state west of Attica and south of Boeotia, ruined by Pericles' boycott. Comedy was reputed to have originated thence. 2. The name of a wife of Heracles, the daughter of Creon, king of Thebes.

MEGAREUS. See Sophocles, *Antigone*, note 3.

MELANION. The hero who won the foot-race with Atalanta; he is not usually called a woman-hater.

MELANIPPE. A mythological heroine who was seduced by Aeolus.

MELANTHIUS. A tragic poet, brother of Morsimus. His dramas seem to have been almost as unpleasant as his personality; a glutton and a leper, he was noted for his flattery and his pederasty, and his voice is reputed to have been exceptionally harsh.

MELETUS. A writer of drinking-songs and bad tragedies, but much better known as one of the accusers of Socrates.

MELOS. An island in the Aegean, birthplace of Diagoras the atheist.

MEMNON. A son of Zeus, slain by Achilles.

MEMPHIS. A famous city in Egypt.

MENELAUS. King of Sparta, son of Atreus, brother of Agamemnon, husband of Helen, father of Hermione and Megapenthes.

MENIPPUS. An Athenian horse-trader, nicknamed *chelidon*, which means both "tender hollow of a hoof" and "swallow."

MENOECEUS. Father of Jocasta and Creon. See also Sophocles' *Antigone*, note 3.

MERIONES. A Cretan, one of the Greek warriors at Troy.

MEROPE. Wife of the Corinthian king, Polybus. The foster-mother of Oedipus.

MESSAPIUS. A mountain in Boeotia, near Euboea.

MESSENIA. The southwestern section of the Peloponnesus, subject to Sparta in historical times, but so oppressed that revolts were not unknown. The incident referred to in *Lysistrata* (1141) took place in 464.

METON. A great mathematician, astronomer, and calendar reformer; he seems to have been interested in town-planning also.

MICON. An Athenian fresco-painter.

MIDAS. A slave-name, like the Phryx and Masyntias which follow it.

MIDIAS. An Athenian who bred quails.

MILESIANS. The inhabitants of Miletus, a Greek city on the coast of Asia Minor. After the Persian Wars they became subjects of Athens. It would appear that the demagogue Cleon had attempted to have their tribute raised. The proverb that they had once been

brave is reported to have originated as an oracular response to Polycrates, the sixth-century tyrant of Samos, when he was considering making them his allies. The city was famous for its gay life and easy morals, and the artificial penises there manufactured were considered superior to any others. Miletus revolted from Athens in 412.

MILTIADES. Athenian hero at the battle of Marathon in 490. He was credited with the victory, but this is probably unjust to Callimachus, the polemarch.

MIMAS. One of the giants who fought against the gods.

MINOS. King of Crete, husband of Pasiphae, and father of Phaedra and Ariadne.

MINOTAUR. A Cretan monster, half man and half bull, born of a union between Pasiphae and a bull. The Minotaur, to whom the Athenians had to make annual human sacrifice, was finally slain by Theseus.

MINYAE. An ancient Greek race, originally located in Thessaly.

MITYLENE. (Also spelled Mytilene.) The chief city on the island of Lesbos. In 428 Mitylene, followed by all the other towns on the island except Methymna, had revolted. After the revolt had been suppressed and Lesbos recovered in the following year, a debate was held at Athens as to suitable punishment. Led on by Cleon's oratory the Assembly voted a wholesale massacre, but rescinded the decree the next day. A ship was sent out to overtake the previous one bearing the fateful command, and an exciting race across the Aegean was narrowly won by the pursuers. The bribe which Cleon is accused of having taken from the Mitylenaeans must have been connected with some later incident.

MNEMOSYNE. Goddess of memory and mother of the Muses.

MNESILOCHUS. It is by no means certain that he actually was the father-in-law of Euripides, but this term is more convenient to the translator than any vaguer one such as "kinsman."

MOIRAI. The Fates, the Roman Parcae.

MOLON. An otherwise unknown man, reported to have been of gigantic stature.

MOLOSSI. A people who inhabited Epirus.

MORSIMUS. A writer of very bad tragedies, brother of Melanthius.

MORYCHUS. An Athenian dandy and gourmet.

MOSCHUS. A bad lyre-player.

MOTHON. A crude kind of dance, of which sailors are reported to have been fond.

MUSAEUS. A very ancient poet of Thrace.

MYCENAE. An ancient city in Argolis, Agamemnon's kingdom.

MYCONUS. An island in the Aegean.

MYRMIDONS. The people of whom Achilles was the leader.

MYRONIDES. A successful Athenian general in the period immediately after the Persian Wars.

MYRTILUS. The treacherous charioteer of Oenomaus, who betrayed his master and was killed by Pelops.

MYSIA. A district in northwestern Asia Minor.

MYSTAE. Initiates into the Mysteries.

MYSTERIES. Symbolic rituals in honour of various gods, witnessed only by initiates. The formulae were supposed to be secret. The most famous of the Mysteries were those of Demeter, Persephone, and Iacchus at Eleusis in Attica.

NAUPACTUS. A town on the northern shore of the Gulf of Corinth.

NAUPHANTE. Name of a trireme, formed from *naus*, "ship," as is Nauson, the name of her mother.

NAUPLIA. A town on the coast of Argolis, near the city of Argos.

NAUPLIUS. King of Euboea, and father of Palamedes. Odysseus foully slew Palamedes, hence to gain revenge Nauplius lighted a false beacon on Euboea and lured the Greek fleet to destruction as it sailed home from Troy.

NAUSICYDES. A grain-profiteer.

NAXOS. An island in the Aegean, laid waste by the Persians in 490, conquered by Cimon in 471.

NELEUS. Father of Nestor, and grandfather of Antilochus.

NEMEA. A valley in Argolis where Heracles slew the Nemean lion.

NEMESIS. A Greek goddess, who punished those guilty of *hybris*, "overweening pride."

NEOCLIDES. An orator afflicted with ophthalmia.

NEOPTOLEMUS. The son of Achilles

NEPHELOCOCCYGIA. The name finally chosen for the city of the birds in Aristophanes' comedy of that name. Formed from *nephele*, "cloud" and *kokkyx*, "cuckoo," it has been variously rendered with various success. The German *Wolkenkukelheim* and the French *Coucou-les-Nuées* are both good, but the English efforts have been less felicitous; we here suggest "Cuckoo-on-Cloud."

NEREUS. A sea god, father of the Nereids.

NESSUS. See the Introduction to Sophocles' *The Trachiniae*.

NESTOR. King of Pylos, son of Neleus, father of Antilochus, and the oldest and wisest of the Greek chiefs in the Trojan War.

NICIAS. A wealthy aristocrat, leader of the conservative party at Athens. He frequently and ineffectively served the state as military commander, and he was in charge of the Sicilian expedition after the recall of Alcibiades and the death of Lamachus. After the debacle he was executed by the Syracusans. Superstitious and pusillanimous, he was the worst sort of person to command an army, and it is regrettable that the lives of so many others should have depended on the judgment of such an individual. The effeminate of the same name mentioned in *The Ecclesiazusae* (428) was probably his grandson.

NICODICE. A woman's name, formed from *nike*, "victory" and *dike*, "justice."

NICOMACHUS. A corrupt under-secretary in the public service.

NICOSTRATUS. A man who was inordinately fond of sacrifices and of foreigners.

NIOBE. Daughter of Tantalus, wife of Amphion of Thebes, mother of fourteen children, because of which she thought herself superior to Leto. All her offspring were slain by Apollo and Artemis and Niobe herself was turned by Zeus into a stone on Mt. Sipylus in Lydia, which shed tears in the summer.

NISUS. King of Megara, and father of Scylla.

NOMAN. When Odysseus was asked by the Cyclops to give his name, he answered "Noman." After the monster's eye had been burned out and he had called on his fellow Cyclopes for assistance, they asked who was harming him and he said "Noman." They naturally left him to his fate, and Odysseus made good his escape.

NOTUS. The South Wind.

NYSA. The legendary scene of the nurture of Dionysus. There are several places which are given this name.

OCEANUS. The god of the water which was believed to surround the whole earth. He was the husband of Tethys.

ODEON. The name of one of the buildings in which trials were held; it had formerly been used for musical contests.

ODYSSEUS. King of Ithaca, son of Laertes, husband of Penelope, father of Telemachus. Famous for his craftiness and adroitness, he is usually the villain of the tragic plots in which he appears.

OEA. An unidentified crag in Attica.

OEAGRUS. A popular actor.

OEAX. Brother of Palamedes.

OECHALIA. A town in Euboea.

OECLEUS. Father of Amphiaraus.

OEDIPUS. King of Thebes, son of Laius and Jocasta, father of Eteocles, Polyneices, Antigone, and Ismene. It was his sad fate unwittingly to kill his father and to marry his mother.

OENEUS. King of Pleuron and Calydon in Aetolia, father of Tydeus, Meleager, Althaea, and Deianeira.

OENIADAE. A town in Acarnania, a district near Aetolia.

OENOE. A town in the central Peloponnesus.

OENOMAUS. King of Pisa in Elis. Pelops contested with him in a famous chariot race.

OETA. A mountain in southern Thessaly on which Heracles' funeral pyre was placed.

OLOPHYXIANS. The inhabitants of Olophyxus, a small town on the Chalcidian peninsula of Acte. The only point of their introduction is to build up to the pun in the name Ototyxians, from *ototyzein*, "to wail."

OLYMPIA. A place in Elis, in the Peloponnesus, where the Olympic games were celebrated every four years; citizens of every state in Greece took part. A famous temple of Zeus was located there.

OLYMPUS. A mountain between Macedonia and Thessaly. In Greek mythology it is regarded as the home of the gods.

OMPHALE. A Lydian queen under whom Heracles served in bondage.

ONESIMUS. "Profitable."

OPORA. Goddess of the harvest.

OPUNTIAN LOCRIS. A state in central Greece, north of Phocis. An inhabitant of this state was called *Opountios*, which was also the name of an informer who had only one eye.

ORESTES. 1. Son of Agamemnon and Clytemnestra, brother of Electra. 2. The name of a notorious brigand.

OREUS. A town in Euboea.

ORION. In mythology a hunter. After his death he was placed as a constellation among the stars.

ORNEAE. A town in the Argolid, the scene of some Athenian military operations in 415. The name of the town suggests the Greek word *ornis*, "bird."

ORPHEUS. A mythical character, regarded as a great poet. A mystery religion developed out of the stories of his life and death.

ORTHIAN MODE. This was one of the most high-pitched of the many modes in Greek music.

ORTYGIA. An ancient name of Delos.

OSSA. A mountain in Thessaly.

PACTOLUS. A river in Lydia, whose golden sands became proverbial.

PAEAN. Originally an independent god of healing. Later this divinity was fused into that of Apollo, and Paean became simply another name for him. It was then transferred to designate a hymn of thanksgiving addressed to Apollo. Aristophanes uses it in both senses, and occasionally with a pun on the Greek word *paiein,* "to strike."

PAEON. The fictitious name of the father of Cinesias. The Greek *paion* means "striking," but has a secondary sense of "making love to."

PAEONIA. A district in Macedonia.

PALAEMON. A sea god. See INO.

PALAMEDES. See NAUPLIUS.

PALLAS. Athene.

PALLENE. Probably an Attic deme between Athens and Marathon.

PAMPHILA. "Dear to all."

PAMPHILUS. A demagogue, caught embezzling state funds and deprived of his property. The needle-seller's name was Aristoxerus, and he was hand in glove with Pamphilus, sharing the profits of his peculations and the sorrows of his indigence (*Plutus* 174f.). In *Plutus* 385 we find a reference to the painting of the Heracleidae by another Pamphilus.

PAMPHYLIA. A district in Asia Minor between Lycia and Cilicia.

PAN. An originally Arcadian god of flocks and shepherds. Sudden terror (panic) was caused by him.

PANATHENAEA. A festival of Athene, celebrated in Athens every five years. It was accompanied by feasting and a number of ceremonial performances, choral poetry, dancing, etc.

PANCRATIUM. A kind of fighting event in Greek games in which both boxing and wrestling were allowed.

PANDELETUS. A notorious informer.

PANDION. King of Athens and father of Aegeus.

PANDORA. In Greek mythology, the first woman on earth and the cause of numberless evils to mankind. In *The Birds* her name is mentioned because of its meaning, "giver of all."

PANDROSOS. Daughter of Cecrops and first priestess of Athene.

PANGAEUS. A mountain in Macedonia.

PANTHOOS. Father of the Trojan heroes, Euphorbus and Polydamas.

PANURGIPPARCHIDES. "Rogue-Hipparch."

PAPHLAGONIA. A country in northern Asia Minor; its inhabitants were coarse and backward. The Greeks knew them only as slaves.

PAPHOS. A town on the west coast of Cyprus, celebrated as the chief centre of Aphrodite's worship.

PARALUS. Name of one of the two especially swift galleys which were reserved for the delivery of official messages, the serving of summonses, the recall of persons to trial, etc. The other one was called Salaminia.

PARIS. Son of Hecuba and Priam, who carried off Helen, the wife of Menelaus. Aphrodite promised Helen to him, if he gave her the award for beauty in her contest with Hera and Athene.

PARNASSUS. A mountain near Delphi, the haunt of Apollo and the Muses.

PARNES. A well-wooded mountain in Attica.

PAROS. An island in the Aegean Sea.

PARRHASIA. A range of mountains in Arcadia.

PARTHENICA. Choral lyric poems designed to be sung by groups of virgins.

PARTHENOPAEUS. Son of Atalanta, one of the seven champions who attacked Thebes.

PASIPHAE. See MINOS and MINOTAUR.

PATROCLIDES. An Athenian who had the misfortune to defecate while sitting in the theatre.

PATROCLUS. A Greek hero in the Trojan War. He was Achilles' closest friend and was slain by Hector.

PAUSON. A painter who was also a scoundrel.

PEGASUS. See BELLEROPHON.

PEIRITHOUS. King of the Lapithae in Thessaly. He became a warm friend of Theseus.

PELARGICON. The wall around the plateau of the Acropolis at Athens.

PELASGUS. A mythical king of Argos. Sometimes the Greeks as a whole are called Pelasgians because of a tradition which said that a Pelasgus, not the Argive king, was the ancestor of the earliest inhabitants of Greece.

PELEIADES. The priestesses who interpret the oracle at Dodona.

PELEUS. Son of Aeacus and King of Phthia. Husband of Thetis and father of Achilles.

PELIAS. King of Iolcus, father of Alcestis and Acastus. He sent Jason on the quest for the Golden Fleece. On Jason's return, Medea deceitfully persuaded Pelias' daughters that they could restore their father's youth by cutting him to pieces and boiling him.

PELION. A mountain in Thessaly.

PELLENE. A city in Achaea, allied with Sparta. Heavy cloaks were made there.

PELOPS. He came to Greece as an exile from Phrygia. He married Hippodamia, daughter of Oenomaus, and was the ancestor of the house of Atreus, whose members are called Pelopidae. The Peloponnesus takes its name from him.

PENEUS. The chief river in Thessaly.

PENTHEUS. King of Thebes, son of Agave and grandson of Cadmus.

PEPLUS. A woman's outer garment in the form of a large rectangular piece of cloth, usually richly embroidered or at least decorated around its borders, and worn thrown around the shoulders and gathered up with the arms so that it fell in heavy folds; for ordinary uses the peplus was fairly short, but there were very long and impractical ones for display purposes. In Aristophanes the word (in the present translation) always signifies the Sacred Peplus, a huge piece of cloth woven by the maidens of Athens, embroidered with pictures of mythological events in which Athene took part, and presented to that goddess at the Panathenaea.

PERGASAE. A rural Attic deme.

PERICLES. The leading Athenian statesman in the period after the Persian Wars. He had been a prominent member of the democratic faction as early as 469, and the ostracism of the conservative Cimon in 461 brought this group to power; the murder of Ephialtes shortly thereafter left Pericles in a position of undisputed control. From then until his death in 429 he was, with one exception, annually re-elected General, and he ruled Athens almost as a tyrant but quite within the constitutional framework of the democracy. His policy was aggressive and imperialistic, in contrast to the pro-Spartan line of his conservative predecessors, and he recognized that this made a war sooner or later inevitable. In 432 it was obvious that the outbreak of hostilities was imminent and Pericles struck the first blow with the famous Megarian Decree. This is the butt of several of Aristophanes' gibes, as are the great power which the statesman wielded and the alliance which he had contracted with Aspasia. The reference in *The Clouds* (859) is to a remark which Pericles made in the course of the annual examination which all Athenian magistrates had to undergo at the close of their terms and in which they had to render an account of their conduct of office. Any expenditures of public funds naturally had to be explained on such occasions, and on one of them Pericles accounted for a rather large sum only by saying that he had spent it "for what was necessary." The vagueness of this answer aroused Spartan suspicions, and dissatisfaction with the manner in which their kings were conducting the war in Attica suggested that what Pericles had really done was to bribe the monarchs to withhold their attacks. These unfortunates were forthwith recalled; one of them was exiled and the other fined for treachery.

PERRHAEBIA. A district in Thessaly.

PERSEPHASSA. Persephone.

PERSEPHONE. The daughter of Zeus and Demeter, who became the wife of Hades and the queen of the Underworld.

PERSEUS. A mythical hero, son of Zeus and Danae. He was the slayer of Medusa.

PHAEAX. A politician of some importance and an orator of great plausibility in Athens in the early years of the Peloponnesian War.

PHAEDRA. Daughter of Minos and wife of Theseus.

PHAETHON. Son of Helios, who was allowed to drive the chariot of the Sun. The youth could not control the horses, and was killed by Zeus to prevent the earth from catching fire.

PHALERUM. A port near the Piraeus; Phaleric anchovies were a favourite Athenian delicacy.

PHALES. The god of the phallus.

PHALLUS. The male sexual organ in a state of tumescence. Festivals of Dionysus, in which rites of fertility played a large part, always included a phallic procession in which was carried a huge figure of this symbol of fruitfulness and generation.

PHANAE. A town on the island of Chios, mentioned in *The Birds* (1694) with a pun on the word *phainein*, "to inform against."

PHANOTEUS. A Phocian ally of Clytemnestra and Aegisthus.

PHARNACES. A Persian satrap.

PHAROS. An island off the coast of Egypt.

PHARSALUS. A town in Thessaly.

PHASIS. A river in Colchis, flowing into the east end of the Euxine. In *Acharnians* (726) there is a pun on *phainein*, "to inform against."

PHAŸLLUS. A celebrated runner.

PHELLEUS. A mountain in Attica.

PHERAE. An ancient town in Thessaly.

PHERECRATES. A successful comic poet.

PHERES. Father of Admetus.

PHIDIAS. A great Greek sculptor, friend of Pericles, attacked by the enemies of that statesman.

PHILIPPUS. 1. The father of Aristophanes. 2. An orator.

PHILISTA. "Dearest."

PHILOCLEON. "Lover of Cleon."

PHILOCLES. A bad tragic poet, father of Morsimus and Melanthius. The point of the jibe in *Birds* (281ff.) is as follows: Sophocles had written a play called *Tereus;* Philocles had written one with the same title and had plagiarized Sophocles liberally; Epops considers himself the Tereus of Sophocles and is thus the father of Philocles and the grandfather of the sad bird who has just entered and is also named Epops, following the Greek practice of naming children after their grandfathers.

PHILOCTETES. Son of Poeas, a great archer, dear friend of Heracles, whose pyre he lighted.

PHILOMEL. Daughter of Pandion and sister of Procne.

PHILONIDES. The man who maintained the courtesan Laïs.

PHILOSTRATUS. See CYNALOPEX.

PHILOXENUS. "Fond of aliens," the name of a notorious pederast.

PHINEUS. King of Salmydessus in Thrace. He blinded his sons because of a false accusation by their stepmother against them. The gods then blinded him and sent the Harpies to torment him. He was delivered from these monsters by two of the Argonauts.

PHLEGRA. Battleground of gods and Titans.

PHLYA. An Attic deme.

PHOCIS. A country in northern Greece in which the Delphic oracle was situated.

PHOCUS. A half-brother of Peleus and Telamon, who slew him out of jealousy.

PHOEBE. Another name for Artemis. Also a sister of Clytemnestra.

PHOENICIA. A country on the extreme eastern shore of the Mediterranean.

PHOENIX. The old guardian of Achilles.

PHOLOE. A mountain in Arcadia where Heracles fought the Centaurs.

PHORCYS. A sea deity, father of the Graeae and the Gorgons.

PHORMIO. A successful Athenian admiral in the early years of the Peloponnesian War, something of a martinet and of austere and frugal personal habits. His hirsuteness was notorious.

PHORMISIUS. A very hairy man who was rather important politically in the years following the Sicilian expedition.

PHRATRY. A subdivision of a tribe, in the survivals of the old tribal organization of Attica. Enrollment in a phratry was the token of legitimacy.

PHRYGIAN. Trojan; Phrygia was a country in northwestern Asia Minor.

PHRYNICHUS. 1. A tragic dramatist, the most important before Aeschylus, noted for the preponderance of lyric and dancing in his plays. 2. The name of a comic poet, a contemporary and rival of Aristophanes. 3. The name of a prominent member of the oligarchical revolutionary group in 411.

PHRYNIS. A composer of "modernistic" music for the lyre, and a talented performer on that instrument.

PHRYX. "Phrygian," a slave-name.

PHTHIA. A district in southeastern Thessaly, the realm of Achilles.

PHYLARCH. The commander of a division of cavalry. Each of the ten tribes contributed 100 horsemen, and a member of the knightly class was chosen from each tribe to be phylarch (tribe-commander) of his tribe's contingent.

PHYLE. An Attic deme on the Boeotian border. In 404 Thrasybulus, at the head of an army of exiled democrats, captured Phyle and thus provided the entering wedge for the expulsion of the Thirty. After the restoration of the democracy in 403 an almost complete amnesty was declared.

PIERIA. A district on the southeast coast of Macedonia, an early haunt of the Muses.

PINDUS. A mountain between Thessaly and Epirus.

PIRAEUS. The port of Athens. Themistocles had brought about the construction of the Long Walls connecting it with the metropolis and making it, in a very real sense, part thereof.

PIRENE. A famous fountain at Corinth, where Bellerophon caught Pegasus.

PISA. A district in Elis in the Peloponnesus.

PISANDER. An oligarch who loved to wear splendid uniforms, but was really a coward. In 411 he was one of the leaders of the reactionary revolution.

PITHETAERUS. "Persuader of friends."

PITTALUS. A noted physician at Athens.

PITTHEUS. King of Troezen, the son of Pelops, father of Aethra, and grandfather of Theseus.

PLATAEA. A Boeotian town near the Attic border. The sympathies of the inhabitants had always been with Athens, and they aided the Athenians at Marathon. In 479 the final defeat of the Persians on land took place near Plataea, and her territory was proclaimed inviolable thereafter.

PLATHANE. "Bread-pan."

PLEIADES. A constellation.

PLEISTHENES. One tradition makes him the father of Agamemnon and Menelaus.

PLEISTUS. A river in Phocis.

PLEURON. An ancient city in Aetolia.

PLUTO. The supreme god of the Underworld.

PLUTUS. The god of wealth.

PNYX. The place where sessions of the Athenian popular assembly were held.

POEAS. The father of Philoctetes.

POLEMARCH. Originally the supreme commander of the Athenian military, one of the nine archons, in Aristophanes' time merely a judicial official whose special province was the supervision of suits involving foreigners.

POLEMON. "Belligerent."

POLIAS or POLIEUS. "Guardian of Cities."

POLYBUS. King of Corinth, the foster-father of Oedipus.

POLYDEUCES. An alternate name for Pollux. See DIOSCURI.

POLYDORUS. 1. Father of Labdacus. 2. Son of Hecuba and Priam.

POLYMESTOR. A Thracian king, a treacherous ally of Priam.

POLYNEICES. Son of Oedipus and Jocasta. His name means literally "much-wrangling."

POLYPHEMUS. One of the Cyclopes.

POLYXENA. Daughter of Priam and Hecuba, who was sacrificed to appease the shade of Achilles.

PONTUS. The Black Sea.

PORPHYRION. 1. One of the Titans. 2. The name of a bird, probably a kind of coot.

POSEIDON. God of the sea; also the causer of earthquakes. He was a brother of Zeus and the father of Cyclopes. Horse-racing was under his patronage.

POTIDAEA. A town on the Chalcidian peninsula of Pallene, subject to Athens.

POTNIAE. A place in Boeotia.

PRAMNIUM. A mountain on the island of Icaria, west of Samos.

PRASIAE. A town in Laconia.

PRAXAGORA. "Active in the market-place."

PREPIS. A notorious Athenian homosexual.

PRIAM. King of Troy during the Trojan War.

PRIAPUS. A god of fertility, usually represented with erected penis.

PRINIDES. The name of an Acharnian; it is formed from *prinos,* "ilex," the wood of which seems to have been used to make charcoal.

PROCNE. A daughter of Pandion, who slew her son Itys in order to avenge herself on Tereus, her husband, who had sought to put her out of the way and to marry Philomela, her sister. Procne was changed into a nightingale, Tereus into a hoopoe.

PROCRUSTES. A famous brigand of myth-ology, who forced people to lie in beds which did not fit them; those who were too large had their limbs sawed off, while those who were too small were stretched on the rack. The name is derived from the word *prokrouein,* which means both "to stretch" and "to lay a woman before someone else."

PRODICUS. A sophist, famous for the breadth of his knowledge, contemporary with Socrates.

PROMETHEUS. One of the Titans, a great benefactor of mankind. He stole fire from heaven and brought it to earth, thereafter teaching men all the useful arts. Zeus punished him by chaining him to a rock in the Caucasus and sending an eagle to eat his liver. He was finally freed by Heracles.

PRONOMUS. A flute-player who had grown an immense beard.

PROPONTIS. The Sea of Marmora.

PROTESILAUS. The first Greek to be slain in the war at Troy.

PROTEUS. A mythical king of Egypt.

PROXENI. Citizens of Greek states appointed, because of family connections or other ties, to be representatives and protectors of the citizens of some other state who were temporarily or permanently residing in the native state of the Proxenus. Thus some Spartan might be chosen Proxenus of Athens at Sparta, and his duty would be to take care of any Athenians there resident. The position of the Proxeni is closely paralleled in those consuls in modern times who are chosen from out of the citizen body of the state in which they serve and are not citizens of the state which they represent.

PROXENIDES. A famous boaster.

PRYTANES. The Athenian Council of 500 did not customarily operate as a whole, but in tenths, each group of fifty representatives of a single tribe having control of affairs for one tenth of the fiscal year of 360 days. These fifty Councillors, when in power, were called Prytanes.

PRYTANEUM. The building in which the

Prytanes conducted their business, ate their meals, and entertained foreign ambassadors.

PSACAS. "Sputterer."

PSEUDARTABAS. "Fake Artabas." Many Persian names contained the form Arta-.

PYANEPSIA. A festival of Apollo.

PYLADES. The devoted friend of Orestes. His father was Strophius, King of Phocis.

PYLOS. The name of three towns on the west coast of the Peloponnesus; it is uncertain which was the home of Nestor. One was on the Bay of Navarino, and was the site of the Athenian victory under Cleon in 425.

PYRRHANDRUS. A comic name, meaning "yellow man." The reference is to the colour of ordure as usually designated by the Greeks.

PYRRHUS. Alternate name for Neoptolemus.

PYTHIAN. Pertaining to the Delphian Apollo.

RHADAMANTHUS. One of the judges in the Underworld.

RHEA. Wife of Cronus and mother of Demeter, Hera, Hades, Poseidon, and Zeus. Later she was identified with Cybele.

RHESUS. A king of Thrace during the Trojan War; an ally of the Trojans.

RHIUM. A promontory at the entrance of the Gulf of Corinth.

RHODES. A large island in the southeastern Aegean.

SAÏAN. Thracian.

SALABACCHO. A famous courtesan.

SALAMINIA. See PARALUS.

SALAMIS. An island off the coasts of Attica and Megara, scene of the decisive defeat of the Persian navy in 480. From the sixth century Salamis had been subject to Athens.

SALMYDESSUS. A town in Thrace on the shores of the Black Sea.

SAMOS. An island off the Ionian coast.

SAMOTHRACE. An island off the coast of Thrace. The mysteries of the Cabiri were celebrated here, but in this case we have to do with genuine mysteries, for no trustworthy information has been preserved regarding them. It would seem that the initiates were popularly credited with the power of making their each wish come true.

SAMPHORAS. A horse with the brand Sampi, an obsolete Greek letter.

SARDANAPALUS. The last king of the Assyrian Empire, famous for his luxurious manner of life.

SARDIS. The capital of Lydia, fabulously wealthy.

SARONIC GULF. A bay of the Aegean Sea between Attica and Argolis.

SARPEDON. Son of Zeus, a prince of Lycia, and an ally of the Trojans during the war.

SATYRS. A mythological race of beings, with many goatish characteristics, who formed part of the retinue of Dionysus, and symbolized the animal elements of human nature. On vases they are frequently painted with penis erect, "attacking" nymphs from behind.

SATYRUS. An Athenian homosexual.

SCAMANDER. A famous river in the Troad.

SCAPHEPHORUS. The bearer of an urn containing honey and cakes in religious processions. This office was customarily filled by the daughters of the resident aliens.

SCELLIAS. The father of one Aristocrates.

SCIAPODES. A fabulous race of beings thought to inhabit the tropical borders of the Atlantic. They were believed to walk on all fours and to possess enormous feet, which served on occasion as umbrellas, shielding them from the hot rays of the sun.

SCIONE. A town on the Chalcidian isthmus of Pallene, which withstood for two years the siege begun by the Athenians in 423.

SCIRONIAN. Referring to some rocks between Attica and Megaris, where Theseus slew the robber Sciron.

SCIROPHORIA. A festival of Athene in which the women took part.

SCYLLA. A sea monster, living in a cave on the Italian side of the straits between Italy and Sicily.

SCYROS. An island off Euboea.

SCYTHIANS. A rude nomadic people dwelling northeast of Thrace; the Athenians employed Scythian archers as policemen.

SEBINUS. An Athenian, whose name suggests *binein,* "to make love to."

SELLI. A prehistoric tribe, dwelling near Dodona.

SELLUS. Father of Aeschines; the name is also given as Sellartius.

SEMELE. Daughter of Cadmus and mother of Dionysus.

SENATE. The usual, but not too precise, translation of the Greek *boule.* In Athens this body had 500 members chosen by lot, ten from each tribe. They held office for one year, and functioned through the rotating committees called Prytanes. The *Boule* had the normal executive, deliberative, and initiative functions of any ancient derivative of the prehistoric and Homeric Council of Elders.

SEPIAN. Referring to a promontory in southeastern Thessaly, not far from Mt. Pelion.

SERIPHUS. A tiny Aegean island.

SIBYL. A name given to several inspired prophetesses of the gods.

SICINNIS. A dance of the Satyrs.

SICYON. A town on the Corinthian Gulf, west of Corinth.

SIDON. A city in Phoenicia.

SIGEUM. The northwestern promontory of the Troad, the site of the Greek camp in the Trojan War.

SILENIAE. A part of the shore of Salamis.

SILENUS. A Satyr who is said to have brought up and instructed Dionysus.

SILPHIUM. A plant which grew in Cyrene and adjacent countries; its juice was highly valued as a flavouring element in food and as a medicine. Its effects seem to have been rather like those now popularly ascribed to certain kinds of beans.

SIMOIS. A river in the Troad.

SIMONIDES. One of the finest of the early Greek poets composing choral lyric. He seems to have been the first to write for money, and he thus became the hireling poet *par excellence* in the minds of the ancients.

SINIS. A robber slain by Theseus. See SCIRONIAN.

SIPYLIAN. Referring to a mountain in Phrygia.

SIRENS. Sea-nymphs, who had the power of charming and luring to destruction all who heard their songs.

SIRIUS. The dog star.

SISYPHUS. Son of Aeolus, King of Corinth, and founder of the royal house there. For his wickedness in life he was severely punished in the Underworld. One tradition makes him the father of Odysseus.

SITALCES. A king of Thrace, who had built up a very large and powerful empire in the latter half of the fifth century.

SKYTALE. A Spartan method of sending messages in cipher. The papyrus or other writing material was wound around a staff and then written on lengthwise. Once unwound it was very difficult to read unless one could wind it around a staff of the same size; this, of course, only the recipient of the message was supposed to be able to do.

SMICRINES. "Testy."

SMICYTHES. An Athenian pederast so extremely effeminate that Aristophanes (*Knights* 969) after mentioning his name, adds "and *her* husband." In the Greek this had a clearer point than it can possibly be given in English, for the name is in the accusative case, *Smikythen,* and the case ending *-en* for masculines whose nominative ends in *-es* is also the accusative ending of feminines whose nominative ends in *-e.* Thus *Smikythen* could also be the accusative of the woman's name *Smikythe.*

SOCRATES. The famous philosopher. See the remarks in the Introduction to

The Clouds. To this we may add that we have no evidence of his not having been clean in his habits. He was, on the other hand, very fond of conversation, and no one could be with him for long without getting drawn into a philosophic discussion of some sort.

SOLON. A famous Athenian statesman and law-giver in the sixth century.

SOPHRONA. "Wise."

SPARTA. The chief town in Laconia, head of the Peloponnesian Confederacy.

SPERCHEIUS. A river in southern Thessaly.

SPHETTIA. More correctly Sphettus, a deme in Attica. The name suggests the word *sphex*, "wasp."

SPHINX. A monster who proposed a riddle to the Thebans and killed all who could not solve it. Oedipus gave her the correct answer, whereupon she slew herself.

STADIA. Greek measures of length, each about 600 feet.

STENIA. A festival which served as a prelude to the Thesmophoria.

STHENELUS. 1. The father of Eurystheus. 2. The son of Capaneus and squire of Diomedes. 3. A tragic actor.

STHENOBOEA. The Potiphar's wife of Greek mythology. She fell in love with Bellerophon, and when that chaste hero would have nothing to do with her, she compassed his death by slandering him to her husband.

STILBIDES. A celebrated Athenian diviner.

STRATEGUS. The title, usually translated "General," of ten Athenian officials who were annually elected by popular vote, one from each tribe, and had charge of the military. It was a position in which a man of judgment and eloquence could exercise an enormous influence on the foreign policies of the city; the most remarkable instance is Pericles.

STRATON. An Athenian homosexual of especial effeminacy.

STRATONICE. "Army victory."

STREPSIADES. "Twister."

STROPHIUS. King of Phocis and father of Pylades.

STRUTHIAN. "Sparrovian."

STRYMON. An important river in Macedonia.

STYX. The principal river of the Underworld which the souls of the dead had to cross.

SUNIUM. A promontory, the southern tip of Attica, with a famous temple of Athene.

SUSA. The winter residence of the Persian king.

SYBARIS. A Greek city in southern Italy. In the latter half of the sixth century it had been very wealthy and its inhabitants had acquired a reputation of maximum luxury and voluptuousness. The Sybaritic fable seems to have been much like those of Aesop, but to have dealt with human rather than animal characters.

SYMPLEGADES. In mythology two islands at the entrance of the Black Sea. The Argo was the first ship to sail between them.

SYRA. Female slave-name, meaning "Syrian."

SYRACOSIUS. A strident orator.

SYRISCUS. "Little Syrian."

TAENARUS. A town in Laconia near which was an entrance to the Underworld, according to tradition.

TALAOS. Father of Hippomedon.

TALTHYBIUS. The herald of Agamemnon at Troy.

TANTALUS. The father of Pelops. He was a king either of Lydia or Argos or Corinth. For divulging secrets entrusted to him he was punished horribly in the Underworld.

TAPHIANS. People who dwelt in islands in the Ionian Sea. They slew Alcmena's brothers and Amphitryon exacted vengeance from them.

TARTARUS. The Underworld.

TARTESSUS. A town in Spain; the lampreys caught there were a great delicacy in the ancient world. The name, however, suggests Tartarus and thus has a terrifying sound.

TAURIANS. A people who lived north of the Black Sea. See Introduction to Euripides' *Iphigenia in Tauris.*

TAUROPOLIA. An Athenian festival in which the women took part.

TAXIARCH. An officer in the Athenian army, in command of a relatively small number of men; we do not know precisely how many.

TAŸGETUS. A lofty mountain range to the west of Sparta.

TECMESSA. The concubine of Ajax, son of Telamon.

TEIRESIAS. A blind Theban seer.

TELAMON. Son of Aeacus, brother of Peleus, and father of Ajax. He was one of the Argonauts. See Euripides' *The Trojan Women,* note 9.

TELEAS. An Athenian gourmet.

TELEMACHUS. Son of Odysseus and Penelope.

TELEPHUS. A son of Heracles, who became king of Mysia. He attempted to keep the Greek expedition against Troy from landing on the coast of Asia Minor, but Dionysus made him trip over a vine and he was wounded by Achilles. An oracle informed him that the wound could be healed only by the man who had inflicted it and the Greeks were simultaneously informed that Telephus was indispensable to them. Achilles healed the wound and Telephus gave valuable directions for reaching Troy. Euripides had made Telephus the hero of a tragedy by that name, and had brought him on the stage in the beggarly disguise in which he effected entrance into the Greek camp.

TELEUTAS. A Phrygian king, the father of Tecmessa.

TENOS. An island in the Aegean.

TEREUS. See PROCNE.

TETHYS. The wife of Oceanus.

TEUCER. Son of Telamon and half-brother of Ajax. He was known as the best archer among the Greeks at Troy.

TEUMESSUS. A Boeotian town near Thebes.

TEUTHRAS. An ancient king of Mysia.

THALES. The earliest Greek philosopher, famous in later times for his practical as well as his scientific wisdom.

THALLOPHORES. Old men who carried olive-shoots in the Panathenaic procession. This office was assigned only to those who were too feeble or too doting to be of any other use.

THAMYRIS. A Thracian bard who had blasphemed the Muses by challenging them to a contest in song, for which act they blinded him.

THANATOS. The god of death.

THASOS. An island in the northern Aegean, famous for its fragrant wine.

THEAGENES. A very squalid Athenian.

THEBES. The chief city in Boeotia, allied with Sparta. Also the name of a city in Egypt and of one in Cilicia.

THEMIS. A goddess, the personification of law, custom, and equity.

THEMISCYRA. A region near the Sea of Azov, where the Amazons lived.

THEMISTOCLES. One of the most distinguished statesmen that Athens produced. To him the city owed the Greek victory at Salamis and her naval supremacy. Likewise it was through his astuteness that the walls were constructed without Spartan hindrance right after the departure of the Persians. He is reported to have ended his life by drinking poison, but the motivation of this action is unknown.

THEOGENES. A great boaster.

THEOGNIS. A tragic poet whose pieces exhibited a distressing coldness.

THEOPHANES. A satellite of Cleon.

THEORIA. A divine personification of festivals or spectacles.

THEORUS. A satellite of Cleon.

THERAMENES. Leader of the moderately anti-democratic group in Athens after the Sicilian expedition. He strove always to avoid extremes and was thus forced to transfer his allegiance repeatedly. This earned him the nickname *kothornos,* "buskin."

THERMODON. A river on whose banks

the Amazons were supposed to have dwelt.

THERMOPYLAE. The pass from Thessaly into southern Greece; it was here that Leonidas and his Spartans made their famous and futile stand. A meeting of an Amphictyonic Council was held in the neighbourhood of Thermopylae every year.

THERSITES. The ugliest of the Greeks before Troy, who is presented in the *Iliad* as a backbiter.

THESEUS. King of Attica, son of Aegeus and Aethra, father of Hippolytus, Demophoön, Acamas, and Melanippus. He was the most famous and most active of the legendary heroes of Athens.

THESMOPHORIA. A festival of the Thesmophorae, Demeter and Persephone, held by the matrons of Athens each year; the celebrants were called Thesmophoriazusae.

THESMOTHETES. The title of six of the nine archons at Athens; their special functions were in the field of judicial administration.

THESPROTIA. A district in Epirus.

THESSALY. A large region in northern Greece, noted for its horses and its witchcraft.

THESTOR. The father of Calchas, the Greek seer.

THETIS. A sea goddess, the wife of Peleus and mother of Achilles.

THORICUS. A town in Attica.

THRACE. An extensive country northeast of Greece, in mythology famous for its prophetic minstrels, in historical times for its warlike inhabitants and rigorous climate.

THRASYBULUS. The leader of the democratic exiles in the expulsion of The Thirty in 403, and an important figure in Athens' political life right down to his death in 388. On one occasion he had announced that he would speak in opposition to a proposed alliance of Athens with Thebes against Sparta, but had changed his mind at the last moment and let the measure go through. To the disap-

pointed Lacedaemonians he offered the explanation that just as he was about to speak he was seized with an attack of indigestion from eating wild pears.

THRATTA. "Thracian."

THUCYDIDES. Son of Milesias, conservative, chief opponent of Pericles down to 443, no relation to the historian of that name.

THURIUM. An Athenian colony in southern Italy, founded in 443.

THYESTES. Brother of Atreus. See Introduction to Aeschylus' *Oresteia*.

THYIAD. A Bacchant.

THYMAETIS. An Attic deme on the shore, not far from the Piraeus.

TIMON. A celebrated misanthrope.

TIMOTHEUS. The wealthy son of the Athenian admiral Conon.

TIRYNS. An ancient town in Argolis.

TISAMENOPHAENIPPUS. A comic name, formed from two proper names, Tisamenus and Phaenippus. The former was a son of Acestor and secretary to Cleon. The latter is quite unknown.

TITANS. Giants, born of Earth and Heaven, who warred against the gods.

TITHONUS. A mythological character who was married to Eos, the dawn. She requested eternal life for him, but neglected to add that this should be also eternal youth, and the wretched man grew ever older but was unable to die.

TITHRASIAN. From the Attic deme Tithras.

TMOLUS. A mountain range in Lydia.

TRACHIS. A town in Thessaly.

TRAGELAPH. "Goat-stag."

TRIBALLUS. The Triballi were a rude and distant people living north of the Thracians and often at war with them.

TRICORYTHUS. A marshy deme near Marathon.

TRIERARCH. The title of the wealthy persons in Athens upon whom, once or twice in a lifetime, fell the onerous public duty of underwriting the equipment and manpower of a trireme.

TRIOBOLUS. A three-obol coin, the pay of all public servants in the Athenian democracy. The practice had begun under Pericles.

TRIPTOLEMUS. One of the heroes in the Demeter legends. In return for his kind treatment of her when she was searching for her daughter, the goddess granted to Triptolemus the knowledge of agriculture; this he taught to mankind, thus becoming the originator of civilization.

TRITON. 1. A sea divinity, son of Poseidon and Amphitrite. When he blew his trumpet he calmed the sea. 2. A river and lake in Libya.

TRIVIA. Daughter of Demeter, sometimes called Hecate, and sometimes identified with Persephone.

TROCHILUS. "Wren."

TROEZEN. A town in southeastern Argolis.

TROPHONIUS. Builder of the temple at Delphi.

TRYGAEUS. "Vineman."

TYDEUS. One of the seven champions who attacked Thebes. The father of Diomedes.

TYNDAREUS. King of Sparta, husband of Leda, and the putative or actual father of Castor, Polydeuces, Helen, and Clytemnestra.

TYPHO. A many-headed monster.

TYRE. A city of Phoenicia.

TYRRHENIA. An alternate name for Etruria.

URANUS. Father of Cronus.

VORACIANS. The Greek is *Tragasaia,* from the little town of Tragasae in the Troad, but with a pun on the word *tragein,* "to devour."

XANTHIAS. A frequent slave-name, from Xanthus, a river in Lydia.

XENOCLES. See CARCINUS.

XENOPHANTES. Father of Hieronymus.

XUTHUS. See Euripides' *Ion.*

ZACYNTHUS. An island off the northwest corner of the Peloponnesus; part of the Athenian Empire at the time of the Peloponnesian War.

ZETHUS. A Theban, the brother of Amphion.

ZEUXIS. A great painter.